B 7
D1583523

FOR REFERENCE ONLY

ST/ESA/STAT/SER.G/62 (Vol. II)

Department of Economic and Social Affairs
Statistics Division

2013
International Trade
Statistics Yearbook

Volume II
Trade by Product

United Nations
New York, 2014

STAFFS UNIVERSITY LIBRARY

DEPARTMENT OF ECONOMIC AND SOCIAL AFFAIRS

The Department of Economic and Social Affairs of the United Nations Secretariat is a vital interface between global policies in the economic, social and environmental spheres and national action. The Department works in three main interlinked areas: (i) it compiles, generates and analyses a wide range of economic, social and environmental data and information on which Member States of the United Nations draw to review common problems and to take stock of policy options; (ii) it facilitates the negotiations of Member States in many intergovernmental bodies on joint courses of action to address ongoing or emerging global challenges; and (iii) it advises interested Governments on the ways and means of translating policy frameworks developed in United Nations conferences and summits into programmes at the country level and, through technical assistance, helps build national capacities.

NOTE

Symbols of United Nations documents are composed of capital letters combined with figures.

The designations employed and the presentation of material in this publication do not imply the expression of any opinion whatsoever on the part of the Secretariat of the United Nations concerning the legal status of any country, territory, city or area, or of its authorities, or concerning the delimitation of its frontiers or boundaries.

Where the designation "country or area" appears in this publication, it covers countries, territories, cities or areas. In previous issues of this publication, where the designation "country" appears in the headings of tables, it should be interpreted to cover countries, territories, cities or areas.

In some tables, the designation "developed" economies is intended for statistical convenience and does not necessarily express a judgement about the stage reached by a particular country or area in the development process.

ST/ESA/STAT/SER.G/62 Vol. II

UNITED NATIONS PUBLICATION

Sales No E.15.XVII.3 H

ISBN 978-92-1-161590-6
e-ISBN 978-92-1-057134-0
ISSN 1010-447X

Enquiries should be directed to
Sales and Marketing Section
Outreach Division
Department of Public Information
United Nations
New York 10017
USA

E-mail: publications@un.org
Internet: http://unp.un.org

Copyright © United Nations, 2014
All rights reserved

STAFFORDSHIRE
UNIVERSITY
LIBRARY

- 8 MAY 2015

SITE: Thompson

CLASS NO. S 380

PREFACE

The *2013 International Trade Statistics Yearbook* (2013 ITSY) is the sixty-second edition of this yearbook. Its objective is to inform about the detailed merchandise and services imports and exports of individual countries (areas) by commodity and service category and by partner country (volume I), the world trade in individual products (3-digit SITC groups and 11 main EBOPS categories) (volume II) and total world merchandise trade - up to the year 2013. The two volumes are prepared at different points in time during 2014: *Volume I - Trade by Country* is made electronically available in June, and *Volume II - Trade by Product,* in December, as the preparation of the tables in Volume II requires additional country data which, normally, become available later in the year.

Beginning with the 2013 edition, trade in services data was introduced to the *International Trade Statistics Yearbook: Volume I - Trade by Country and Volume II – Trade by Product*. Therefore, the content and format of the yearbook were redesigned to take into account new additions of graphs/tables and analytical text. The data used in the tables and graphs in both volumes of the yearbook are taken at a specific time (June/December 2014) from the publicly available UN Comtrade (http://comtrade.un.org) and UN Service Trade (http://unstats.un.org/unsd/servicetrade) databases. Users are advised to visit these databases for additional and more current information as they are continuously updated.

The *International Trade Statistics Yearbook* is prepared by the Trade Statistics Branch of the Statistics Division, Department of Economic and Social Affairs of the United Nations Secretariat. Under the general supervision of the Chief of Branch, Ronald Jansen, the programme manager is Markie Muryawan and the chief editor is Kenneth Iversen, assisted by Marjorie Imperial-Damaso. Bekuretsion Amdemariam has the leading role in the processing of the data for UN Comtrade and Htu Aung for UN Service Trade. Habibur Rahman Khan, Kenneth Iversen, Nancy Snyder, Karoly Kovacs, Michael Behrman, Salomon Cameo and Markie Muryawan provided valuable contribution to the inclusion of trade in services data and the improvement of production processes. However, all staff of the branch are involved in the generation of the data and the review/validation of the yearbook. Markie Muryawan, Salomon Cameo and Luis Gonzalez Morales developed the original software which is maintained by Michael Behrman and Daniel Eshetie. Matthias Reister and Nelnan Koumtingue made very substantial contributions to earlier redesigned yearbook as its first programme manager and first chief editor of 2008 edition, respectively.

Comments and feedback on the yearbook are welcome. They may be sent to comtrade@un.org / tradeserv@un.org or to United Nations Statistics Division, Trade Statistics Branch, New York, New York 10017, USA.

05923477

TABLE OF CONTENTS

TABLE OF CONTENTS (continued)

Part 2 COMMODITY TRADE PROFILES
Full list of included 3-digit SITC groups (SITC, Rev.3)

Manufactured goods classified chiefly by material (SITC Section 6)

Machinery and transport equipment (SITC Section 7)

Miscellaneous manufactured articles (SITC Section 8)

Commodities and transactions not classified elsewhere in the SITC (SITC Section 9)

Part 3 SERVICE TRADE PROFILES
Main sub-categories of the Extended Balance of Payments Services Classifications (EBOPS 2002)

INTRODUCTION

1.   The *International Trade Statistics Yearbook: Volume II - Trade by Product*, provides an overview of the latest trends of trade in goods and services showing international trade for 257 individual commodities (3-digit SITC groups) and for the 11 main Extended Balance of Payments Services (EBOPS) categories. The publication is aimed at both specialist trade data users and common audience at large. The presented data, charts and analyses will benefit policy makers, government agencies, non-government organizations, civil society organizations, journalists, academics, researchers, students, businesses and anyone who is interested in trade issues.

2.   The main content of the yearbook is divided into three parts. Part 1 consists of 11 detailed world data tables on merchandise trade. Part 2 contains the commodity trade profiles for 257 individual commodities. Part 3 contains profiles of service trade for the 11 main EBOPS categories. The profiles offer an insight into the trends in individual commodities and service categories by means of brief descriptive text, concise data tables and charts using latest available data. For further information on data availability, please see the sources section of this Introduction.

3.   The yearbook is also made available online at the publications repository of the UN Statistics Division (http://unstats.un.org/unsd/pubs). For more detailed and latest available data, please consult UN Comtrade (http://comtrade.un.org) and UN ServiceTrade (http://unstats.un.org/unsd/servicetrade), which are the sources of the information presented in the yearbook, and which are continuously updated.

Concepts and definitions of International Merchandise Trade Statistics

4.   The merchandise trade data in this Yearbook have been compiled by national statistical authorities largely complying with the United Nations recommended *International Merchandise Trade Statistics, Concepts and Definitions 2010* (IMTS 2010).[1] The main elements of the concepts and definitions are:

>   i.   Coverage: As a general guideline, it is recommended that international merchandise trade statistics record all goods which add to or subtract from the stock of material resources of a country by entering (imports) or leaving (exports) its economic territory. The general guideline is subject to the clarifications provided in IMTS 2010, in particular, to the specific guidelines in chapter 1 concerning the inclusion or exclusion of certain categories of goods.

>   ii.   Time of recording: As a general guideline, it is recommended that goods be recorded at the time when they enter or leave the economic territory of a country.

>   iii.   Statistical territory: The statistical territory of a country is the territory with respect to which trade data are being compiled. The definition of the statistical territory may or may not coincide with the economic territory of a country or its customs territory, depending on the availability of data sources and other considerations. It follows that when the statistical territory of a country and its economic territory differ, international merchandise trade statistics do not provide a complete record of inward and outward flows of goods.

>   iv.   Trade systems: Depending on what parts of the economic territory are included in the statistical territory, the trade data-compilation system adopted by a country (its trade system) may be referred to as general or special.

a) The general trade system is in use when the statistical territory coincides with the economic territory. Consequently, it is recommended that the statistical territory of a country applying the general trade system comprises all applicable territorial elements. In this case, imports include goods entering the free circulation area, premises for inward processing, industrial free zones, premises for customs warehousing or commercial free zones and exports include goods leaving those territorial elements;

b) The special trade system is in use when the statistical territory comprises only a particular part of the economic territory, so that certain flows of goods which are in the scope of IMTS 2010 are not included in either import or export statistics of the compiling country. The strict definition of the special trade system is in use when the statistical territory comprises only the free circulation area, that is, the part within which goods "may be

---

[1] At its forty-first session, held from 23 to 26 February 2010, the Statistical Commission adopted the revised recommendations "International merchandise trade statistics: concepts and definitions 2010" (IMTS 2010) which provide very important amendments while retaining the existing conceptual framework contained in the previous recommendations. The publication is available under Statistical Papers, Series M No. 52, Rev.3 (United Nations publication, Sales No. E.10.XVII.13) and electronically at: http://unstats.un.org/unsd/pubs/gesgrid.asp?id=449.

disposed of without customs restriction". Consequently, in such a case, imports include only goods entering the free circulation area of a compiling country and exports include only goods leaving the free circulation area of a compiling country.

c) The relaxed definition of the special trade system is in use when (a) goods that enter a country for, or leave it after, inward processing, as well as (b) goods that enter or leave an industrial free zone, are also recorded and included in international merchandise trade statistics

v.   Classification: It is recommended that countries use the *Harmonized Commodity Description and Coding System* (HS) for the collection, compilation and dissemination of international merchandise trade statistics as suggested by the Statistical Commission at its twenty-seventh session (22 February to 3 March 1993).[2] The Harmonized System was adopted by the Customs Co-operation Council in June 1983, and the International Convention on the Harmonized System (HS Convention) entered into force on 1 January 1988 (HS 1988).[3] In accordance with the preamble to the HS Convention, which recognized the importance of ensuring that the HS be kept up to date in the light of changes in technology or in patterns of international trade, the HS is regularly reviewed and revised. The fifth edition, HS 2012, came into effect 1 January 2012.[4] The *Standard International Trade Classification (SITC)*[5] which was in the past used by countries in data compilation and reporting has been recognized for its continued use in analysis.[6]

vi.   Valuation: At its fifteenth session, in 1953, the Economic and Social Council, taking the view that trade statistics must reflect economic realities, recommended that the Governments of Member States of the United Nations, wherever possible, use transaction values in the compilation of their national statistics of external trade or, when national practices are based on other values, endeavour to provide supplementary statistical data based on transaction values (Economic and Social Council resolution 469 B (XV)). To promote the comparability of international merchandise trade statistics and taking into account the commercial and data reporting practices of the majority of countries, it is recommended that: (a) The statistical value of imported goods be a CIF-type value; (b) The statistical value of exported goods be an FOB-type value; however, countries are encouraged to compile FOB-type value of imported goods as supplementary information. FOB-type values include the transaction value of the goods and the value of services performed to deliver goods to the border of the exporting country. CIF-type values include the transaction value of the goods, the value of services performed to deliver goods to the border of the exporting country and the value of the

---

[2] See Official Records of the Economic and Social Council, 1993, Supplement No. 6 (E/1993/26), para. 162 (d).
[3] See Customs Co-operation Council, The Harmonized Commodity Description and Coding System, Brussels, 1989.
[4] See World Customs Organization, Harmonized Commodity Description and Coding System, Fifth Edition (2012), Brussels 2010.
[5] Standard International Trade Classification, Original, Statistical Papers, Series M No.10, Second Edition, 1951 (United Nations publication, Sales No. E.51.XVII.1); subsequent editions are published as United Nations publications under Series M No.34.
[6] See Official Records of the Economic and Social Council, 1999, Supplement No. 4 (E/1993/24), para. 24 (c).

services performed to deliver the goods from the border of the exporting country to the border of the importing country.

vii.   <u>Partner country:</u> It is recommended that in the case of imports, the country of origin be recorded; and that in the case of exports, the country of last known destination be recorded. The country of origin of a good (for imports) is determined by rules of origin established by each country. The country of last known destination is the last country - as far as it is known at the time of exportation - to which goods are to be delivered, irrespective of where they have been initially dispatched to and whether or not, on their way to that last country, they are subject to any commercial transactions or other operations which change their legal status. Further, it is recommended that country of consignment be recorded for imports as the second partner country attribution, alongside country of origin; the compilation of export statistics on the country of consignment basis is only encouraged, depending on a country's needs and circumstances.

5.   The commodity trade profiles (part 2 of this publication) are based on the detailed trade data as reported by countries (or areas) and published on UN Comtrade without any adjustments for conceptual differences such as differences in the trade system, valuation and partner attribution. The explanatory notes on UN Comtrade inform about the trade system, valuation and partner attribution of individual reporter countries (or areas). For more detailed information on national practices in the compilation and dissemination of international merchandise trade data please go to http://unstats.un.org/unsd/tradereport/introduction_MM.asp.

Concepts and definitions of Statistics of International Trade in Services

6.   The trade in services data in this Yearbook have been compiled by national statistical authorities or central banks largely complying with the *Manual on Statistics of International Trade in Services 2010* (MSITS 2010).[7]

7.   The main elements of the concepts and definitions of MSITS 2010 are:

i.   <u>Definitions:</u> In general, MSITS 2010 respects the 2008 SNA use of the term services, which is defined as follows (2008 SNA, para. 6.17):

a) Services are the result of a production activity that changes the conditions of the consuming units, or facilitates the exchange of products or financial assets. These types of service may be described as change-effecting services and margin services, respectively. Change-effecting services are outputs produced to order and typically consist of changes in the conditions of the consuming units realized by the activities of producers at the demand of the consumers. They can also be referred to as

---

[7] At its forty-first session, held from 23 to 26 February 2010, the Statistical Commission adopted the revised "Manual on Statistics of International Trade in Services" (MSITS 2010) , which sets out an internationally agreed framework for the compilation and reporting of statistics of international trade in services and align with the revisions of well-established revised international statistical standards. The publication is available under Statistical Papers, Series M No. 86, Rev.1 (United Nations publication, Sales No.E.10.XVII.14) and electronically at http://unstats.un.org/unsd/tradeserv/TFSITS/msits2010.htm.

"transformation services". Change-effecting services are not separate entities over which ownership rights can be established. They cannot be traded separately from their production. By the time their production is completed, they must have been provided to the consumers.

b) MSITS 2010 defines "international trade in services" as trade in services between residents and non-residents of an economy, as well as the supply of services through foreign affiliates established abroad and the supply of services through the presence of foreign individuals, either as foreign service suppliers themselves or as employees of a foreign service supplier.

Importantly, the services data included in this Yearbook only reflect trade in services between residents and non-residents.

    ii.   <u>Concept and definition of residence</u>: The residence of an institutional unit is the economic territory with which it has the strongest connection, constituting its centre of predominant economic interest. Each institutional unit is a resident of one and only one economic territory, as determined by its centre of predominant economic interest. An institutional unit is resident in an economic territory when there exists, within the economic territory, some location, dwelling, place of production, or other premises on which or from which the unit engages and intends to continue engaging, either indefinitely or over a finite but long period of time, in economic activities and transactions on a significant scale. The location need not be fixed as long as it remains within the economic territory. Actual or intended location for one year or more is used as an operational criterion. While the choice of one year as a specific period is somewhat arbitrary, it is adopted to eliminate uncertainty and facilitate international consistency. More specific criteria for determining residence are given in the MSITS 2010.

    iii.   <u>Valuation</u>: The market price is used as the basis for valuation of transactions in international trade in services. Market prices for transactions are defined as amounts of money that willing buyers pay to acquire something from willing sellers. The exchanges are made between independent parties and based on commercial considerations only and are sometimes called "at arm's length" transactions. These transactions will generally be valued at the actual price agreed between the supplier and the consumer.

    iv.   <u>Time of recording of transactions</u>: The appropriate time for recording transactions in services is when they are delivered or received (the "accruals basis"). Some services, such as certain transport or hotel services are provided within a discrete period, in which case there is no problem in determining the time of recording. Other services are supplied or take place on a continuous basis, for example, construction, operating leasing and insurance services. When construction takes place with a prior contract of sale, the ownership of the structure is effectively transferred progressively as the work proceeds. When services are provided over a period of time (such as freight, insurance and construction), there may be advance payments or settlements at later dates for such services. The provision of services should be recorded on an accrual basis in each accounting period, that is to say it should be recorded when the service is rendered and not when the payment occurs.

     v.   <u>Framework and scope</u>: MSITS 2010 recommends that the Sixth Edition of the Balance of Payments and International Investment Position Manual (BPM6)[8] recommendations on the principles of recording (regarding residence, valuation, time of recording, currency of recording and conversion) should be followed. The Extended Balance of Payments Services Classification (EBOPS) is a more detailed classification than that of BPM5 for international trade in services between residents and non-residents, by breaking down a number of the BPM5 service items. The main components of the EBOPS classification are presented in paragraph 7.vii below.

     vi.   <u>Partner country</u>: It is recommended that the breakdown by partner economy for services transactions between residents and non-residents be recorded, the aim being to report partner detail, first, at the level of services trade as a whole and, second, for each of the main types of services in EBOPS and (as a longer-term goal) for the more detailed EBOPS items. Partner country data for trade in services are not included in this publication, as most countries do not currently compile these data by partner country.

     vii.   <u>Classification</u>: In 1996, OECD and Eurostat, in consultation with IMF, developed for use by their members a more detailed classification than that presented in the IMF's Balance of Payments Manual (BPM5) for international trade in services between residents and non-residents, by breaking down a number of the BPM5 service items. This more detailed classification is termed the Extended Balance of Payments Services Classification (EBOPS). The EBOPS classification was published in 2002 in the MSITS 2002 and was subsequently revised to the EBOPS 2010 classification, as published in the MSITS 2010. The services data in this Yearbook follow the EBOPS 2002 classification (which corresponds to the BPM5 recommendations) due to the fact that most countries have not yet transitioned to the EBOPS 2010 classification (which corresponds to the BPM6 recommendations).

The 11 main EBOPS 2002 standard services components (as presented in the MSITS 2002) are:[9]

a) Transportation: covers all transportation services that are performed by residents of one economy for those of another and that involve the carriage of passengers, the movement of goods (freight), rentals (charters) of carriers with crew, and related supporting and auxiliary services. Some related items that are excluded from transportation services are freight insurance (included in insurance services); goods procured in ports by non-resident carriers and repairs of transportation equipment (both are treated as goods, not

---

[8] International Monetary Fund. *Sixth Edition of the Balance of Payments Manual (BPM6)*. 2009. http://www.imf.org/external/pubs/ft/bop/2007/pdf/bpm6.pdf. The previous edition of this manual was the *Fifth Edition of the Balance of Payments Manual (BPM5)*, which was published in 1992. https://www.imf.org/external/pubs/ft/bopman/bopman.pdf.

[9] The full detailed EBOPS 2002 classification is available as an on-line annex to the MSITS 2002. http://unstats.un.org/unsd/tradekb/Attachment358.aspx.

services); repairs of railway facilities, harbours and airfield facilities (included in construction services); and rentals or charters of carriers without crew (included in operational leasing services).

b) Travel: covers primarily the goods and services acquired from an economy by travelers during visits of less than one year to that economy. Includes business and personal travel, which includes health-related expenditure (total expenditure by those travelling for medical reasons), education-related expenditure (i.e., total expenditure by students), and all other personal travel expenditure.

c) Communications services: covers postal and courier services (which cover the pick-up, transport and delivery of letters, newspapers, periodicals, brochures, other printed matter, parcels and packages, including post office counter and mailbox rental services) and telecommunications services (which cover the transmission of sound, images or other information by telephone, telex, telegram, radio and television cable and broadcasting, satellite, electronic mail, facsimile services etc., including business network services, teleconferencing and support services). It does not include the value of the information transported. Also included are cellular telephone services, Internet backbone services and on-line access services, including provision of access to the Internet.

d) Construction services: covers work performed on construction projects and installation by employees of an enterprise in locations outside the territory of an enterprise.

e) Insurance services: covers the provision of various types of insurance to non-residents by resident insurance enterprises, and vice versa. These services are estimated or valued by the service charges included in total premiums rather than by the total value of the premiums.

f) Financial services: covers financial intermediation and auxiliary services, except those of life insurance enterprises and pension funds (which are included in life insurance and pension funding) and other insurance services that are conducted between residents and non-residents. Such services may be provided by banks, stock exchanges, factoring enterprises, credit card enterprises and other enterprises.

g) Computer and information services: covers hardware and software-related services and data-processing services; news agency services include the provision of news, photographs, and feature articles to the media; and database services and web search portals (search engine services that find internet addresses for clients who input keyword queries).

h) Royalties and license fees: covers international payments and receipts of franchising fees and the royalties paid for the use of registered trademarks and international payments and receipts for the authorised use of intangible, non-produced, non-financial assets and proprietary rights (such as patents, copyrights and industrial processes and designs) and with the use, through licensing agreements, of produced originals or prototypes (such as manuscripts, computer programs, and cinematographic works and sound recordings).

i) Other business services: covers merchanting, other trade-related services, operational leasing services, legal services, accounting, auditing, bookkeeping and tax consulting services, business and management consulting and public relations services, advertising, market research and public opinion polling, research and development, architectural, engineering and other technical services, waste treatment and de-pollution, agricultural, mining, and other on-site processing services, other business services, and services between related enterprises, not included elsewhere (n.i.e.).

j) Personal, cultural, and recreational services: covers services and associated fees related to the production of motion pictures (on film or videotape), radio and television programmes (live or on tape) and musical recordings services, as well as those services associated with museums, libraries, archives and other cultural, sporting and recreational activities.

k) Government services, not included elsewhere (n.i.e.): covers government transactions (including those of international organizations) not contained in the other components of EBOPS as defined above. Included are all transactions (in both goods and services) by embassies, consulates, military units and defence agencies with residents of economies in which the embassies, consulates, military units and defence agencies are located and all transactions with other economies. Excluded are transactions with residents of the home economies represented by the embassies, consulates, military units and defence agencies, and transactions in the commissaries, post exchanges and these embassies and consulates.

Description of world trade tables of part 1 (Tables A to K)

8.   Table A: Total merchandise trade by regions and countries or areas in U.S. dollars: It provides a breakdown of merchandise imports, exports and trade balance for world, regional groupings, selected economic and/or trade groupings and individual countries or areas.

9.   Total imports and exports by countries or areas in national currency (Table B): This table contains totals of imports and exports and the trade balance of individual countries (or areas) in national currency.

10.   External trade conversion factors (Table C): The conversion factors for imports and exports shown in table C are used to convert trade data expressed in terms of national currency to U.S. dollars (see paragraph 13 for details).

11.   World exports by provenance and destination in U.S. dollars (Table D: This table provides a breakdown of the world exports by regions and countries (or areas) according to their provenance (origin) and destination, both for total of trade and detailed by individual SITC sections and aggregations of sections, groups, subgroups and basic headings of SITC (see below in this paragraph for details).

Aggregations of SITC, Rev. 3 codes	Description
0-9	Total trade
0 and 1	Food, beverages and tobacco
041-045	Cereals
2 and 4	Crude materials (excluding fuels), oils, fats
22	Oil seeds and, oleaginous fruit
26	Textile fibers
27	Crude fertilizers and minerals
28	Metalliferous ores and metal scrap
4	Animal and vegetable oils, fats and waxes
3	Mineral fuels and related materials
5	Chemicals
7	Machinery and transport equipment
781.2, 784.1, 785.1, 785.2 and 785.31	Passenger road vehicles and their parts
6 and 8	Other manufactured goods
65	Textile yarn and fabrics
67	Iron and steel
68	Non-ferrous metals
691-695, 699 and 812	Other manufactured metal products
84	Clothing

12.   Growth of world exports by provenance and destination (Table E): This table shows the growth of world exports in recent years up to the year 2013 by provenance (origin) and destination, for total exports and for a limited set of commodity classes. The annual average rates of change in percentage terms given in this table have been uniformly calculated by the use of the compound interest formula.

13.   Structure of world exports by provenance and destination (Table F): This table shows the distribution (in percent) of exports by provenance (origin) and destination for total exports and a limited set of commodity classes as well as the commodity composition (in percent) of total exports by provenance (origin) and destination.

14.   Indices of total exports and imports by countries or areas: Quantum and unit value indices and terms of trade in U.S. dollars (2000 = 100) (Table G): This table shows the volume and unit value (or price) indices for total exports and imports as well as the terms of trade and purchasing power of exports for individual countries or areas in U.S. dollars and with the year 2000 as base year.

15.   Indices of total exports and imports by regions: Quantum and unit value indices and terms of trade in U.S. dollars (2000 = 100) (Table H): This table shows the volume and unit value indices for total exports and imports as well as the terms of trade by regions in U.S. dollars and with the year 2000 as base year.

16.   Indices and values of manufactured goods exports: Unit value and volume indices (2000 = 100) and value in thousand million U.S. dollars (Table I): This table presents the unit value and the volume indices and the value of exports of manufactured goods for most developed economies and some developing economies. Manufactured goods are defined here to comprise

sections 5 through 8 of the SITC. Unit value indices are presented both in U.S. dollars and in national currency.

17. <u>Indices and values of fuel imports – Developed economies: Unit value and volume indices (2000 = 100) and value in thousand million U.S. dollars (Table J):</u> This table presents the unit value and the volume indices and the value of fuels imports for most developed economies. Fuel comprises section 3 of the SITC. Unit value indices are presented both in U.S. dollars and in national currency.

18. <u>Some indicators on fuel imports - Developed economies (Table K):</u> This table shows fuel imports as a percentage of total imports and exports, and the ratio of unit value indices of manufactured goods exports and fuel imports.

19. For the general note and footnotes, see the end of the tables. The most recent data for tables B, C, G, I, J and K are published on a monthly or quarterly basis in the *United Nations Monthly Bulletin of Statistics* (MBS).[10] Slightly different versions of Table A containing quarterly and monthly data and table H containing quarterly data are published on a monthly or quarterly basis as table 34 and table 38 in the MBS.[11] Updated, although different versions of Table D, are published as table 40, 41 and 42 in the July, September and November editions of the MBS.

Description of tables and graphs of commodity profiles in part 2 and service trade profiles in part 3

20. Part 2 contains detailed data (commodity trade profiles) for 3-digits groups of the *Standard International Trade Classification, Revision 3* (SITC).[12] All SITC groups are covered except the following groups as these were poorly reported and contain many estimates which are not sufficiently explainable: SITC group 286, Ores and concentrates of uranium and thorium; SITC group 345, Coal, water or other producer gases; SITC group 911, Postal packages not classified according to kind; and SITC group 931, Special transactions and commodities not classified according to kind. At the global level, special transactions and commodities not classified according to kind accounted for 3.0 percent of total world exports of commodities and 3.9 percent of total world imports of commodities in 2013.

21. Part 3 contains detailed data (service trade profiles) for 11 main EBOPS sub-categories. Not all countries reported data for every service category for every year. While such data may reflect the fact that certain countries may not have trade in a particular service category in a given year, it also partially reflects the fact that not all reporters always have sufficient information to allocate all international service transactions to their appropriate service

---

[10] The MBS is available as printed publication and its database can be accessed online at: http://unstats.un.org/unsd/mbs/app/DataSearchTable.aspx. In addition the tables are also available online at http://unstats.un.org/unsd/trade/data/tables.asp.

[11] The difference between table A in this publication and table 34 in the MBS relates to the calculation of regional aggregations (see paragraph 19). The volume indices in table H are calculated using the values of table A as input. The volume indices for some regions are therefore slightly different than the ones published in table 39 of the MBS.

[12] Standard International Trade Classification, Revision 3, Statistical Papers, Series M No.34/Rev.3, (United Nations publication, Sales No. E.86.XVII.12).

categories. However, world total service trade figures in this Yearbook are not affected by this phenomenon, because they are based on the separately reported Total EBOPS Services category (EBOPS code 200), and are therefore not based on an aggregation of the 11 main EBOPS sub-categories. At the global level, the effect of unallocated services (reported total services minus aggregated main EBOPS sub-categories) is relatively minor (as the reporters that are unable to allocate service transactions generally account for a relatively small share of total world trade); for example, unallocated services in 2012 represented 4.3 percent of total world exports of services and 3.0 percent of total world imports of services.

22.   For certain commodities or service categories users will find spikes in growth rates and significant asymmetries between the total values of imports and exports. Reasons for these spikes can often be relatively easy identified (as caused i.e. by changes in the prices or classification changes) but the reasons for the asymmetries between the reported imports and exports are often less apparent.[13] However, it was decided to retain the information on these commodities and service categories as the results shown are a reflection of the data provided by countries (the influence of any estimates contained in the data is not significant) and to leave it to the users to assess the usefulness of this information for their specific purposes.

23.   The following tables and graphs appear for each SITC commodity group and EBOPS category:

24.   <u>Imports and exports in current US$ (Table 1)</u>: In part 2, this table shows the values of imports and exports from 1999 to 2013 for the commodity group, and the share of the commodity group on the SITC section to which it belongs and its share on world trade. In part 3, this table shows the values of imports and exports from 2000 to 2012 for the EBOPS category and its share of world service trade, which is based on the reported Total EBOPS Services category (EBOPS code 200).

25.   <u>Top exporting and importing countries or areas in the latest year available (Tables 2 and 3)</u>: These tables present the top 15 exporting and importing countries or areas in the order of magnitude based on exports or imports values for the latest available year. For each country (or area), the tables show the value of exports or imports in current U.S. dollars, the average growth rate over the last five years (calculated using the compound interest formula), the annual growth rate for the latest available year, the share of world trade, and the cumulative share of world trade. In part 2, in preparing these tables estimates were made for countries whose data were not yet available; the estimated values of exports and imports are shown in italic. In part 3, no estimations to reported data were made.

26.   <u>Annual growth rates of exports (Graph 1)</u>: In part 2, this graph presents the annual growth rate of exports of the commodity group, the annual growth rate of exports of the SITC section to which the commodity group belongs and the annual growth rate of total exports over the last fifteen years. The annual growth rate of total exports comprises all SITC sections. In part 3, this graph presents the annual growth rate of exports of the EBOPS category, and the annual growth

---

[13] In merchandise trade, it should be noted that most countries report their imports valued CIF and their exports valued FOB. Therefore, world trade measured in terms of exports is expected to be lower than world trade measured in terms of imports. This applies to the total of trade as well as all commodities and SITC groups.

rate of total service exports since 2000. The annual growth rate of total exports comprises reported Total EBOPS Services category (EBOPS code 200).

27.   Trade balance by MDG Regions (Graph 2): This graph presents, for the latest year available, exports, imports and the trade balance by regions according to the regions used in the Millennium Development Goal (MDG) Indicator Database (for further information on country grouping by MDG regions, see Country Nomenclature and Country Grouping).

Sources

28.   Figures on the total imports and exports of countries (or areas) presented in world tables A and B are mainly taken from *International Financial Statistics* (IFS) published monthly by the International Monetary Fund (IMF) but also from other sources such as national publications and websites and the *United Nations Monthly Bulletin of Statistics Questionnaire* (see the general note of table B for details).

29.   The external trade conversion figures in world table C are derived from *International Financial Statistics* (IFS) published monthly by the International Monetary Fund (IMF).

30.   The data presented in world tables D, E and F are derived from UN Comtrade data, supplemented by estimated data for non-available countries and areas.

31.   The data presented in world tables G and H on the volume and unit value indices, and terms of trade for total exports and imports by countries (or areas) and regions are mostly derived from *International Financial Statistics* (IFS) published monthly by the International Monetary Fund (IMF), but also from other sources such as national publications and websites and the *United Nations Monthly Bulletin of Statistics Questionnaire*.

32.   The data presented in world tables I, J and K on unit value and volume indices and value for manufactured goods exports and fuel imports are obtained from sources such as national publications and websites and the *United Nations Monthly Bulletin of Statistics Questionnaire*.

33.   The data in the commodity profiles in part 2 (commodity trade profiles) and the service trade profiles in part 3 of the publication are obtained from data directly submitted by countries to the United Nations Statistics Division (UNSD). All data published in the country profiles is available in UN Comtrade (http://comtrade.un.org) and UN ServiceTrade (http://unstats.un.org/unsd/servicetrade).

34.   In some cases, original countries data are received via international and regional partner organizations, such as the Organization for Economic Co-operation and Development (OECD), the Food and Agriculture Organization of the United Nations (FAO), the International Monetary Fund (IMF), the International Trade Centre (ITC), the Caribbean Community (CARICOM) Secretariat, the Common Market of Eastern and Southern Africa (COMESA), the Economic Community of West African States (ECOWAS) and the UN regional commissions such as the Economic Commission for Latin America and the Caribbean (ECLAC) and the Economic and Social Commission for Western Asia (ESCWA). Data for the European Union (EU-28) is

received from the Statistical Office of the European Union (Eurostat).

35.   Tables A to K show data as available by end of November 2014. Part 2 and 3 contain data available in UN Comtrade and UN ServiceTrade by the beginning of December 2014.

Method of Estimation

36.   For table A (part 1) estimates for missing data are made in order to arrive to regional totals but are otherwise not shown. The estimation process is automated using quarterly year-on-year growth rates for the extrapolation of missing quarterly data (unless quarterly data can be estimated using available monthly data within the quarter). Regional totals containing estimated data are printed in bold. For world tables D, E and F (part 1) and the commodity tables and graphs in commodity trade profile (part 2) data for missing reporters are estimated either through the extrapolation of the data of the two adjacent years, or, if this is not possible, through the use of the data reported by the trading partners (so called mirror data). Mirror statistics is also used in case the partner distribution or confidential data make it necessary to adjust the reported data. In addition, modifications to the received data are made in cases where the provided data are obviously incomplete, in particular in the case of unreported petroleum oils exports in merchandise data. For tables H, I and J (part 1) the missing data required for the calculation of regional totals are estimated using a variety of methods and additional data sources. All estimates are reviewed and adjusted where necessary.

37.   For part 3 (the service trade profiles), only received data are shown and no estimation is undertaken for missing reporters.

Conversion of classification

38.   <u>Conversion of classification for merchandise data</u>: All countries follow recommendation to report their detailed merchandise trade data according to the Harmonized Commodity Description and Coding System (HS) (see paragraph 4.C.v). In order to provide comparable time series data in UN Comtrade for all countries, the data reported in the latest HS classification is converted into earlier versions of the HS, and to corresponding or earlier versions of the Standard International Trade Classification (SITC).[14] The latest edition of the HS classification was its fifth and was released in 2012. The commodities in this publication are mostly presented according to the three-digit sections of SITC, Rev.3 as the SITC sections provide a limited set of economically meaningful main categories.[15] In addition, data according to SITC, Rev.3 is available for long time series.

39.   <u>Conversion of classification for trade in services data</u>: For services data, most countries

---

[14] Detailed information on the data conversions used for UN Comtrade can be found on the website of the United Nations Statistics Division at:
http://unstats.un.org/unsd/trade/conversions/HS%20Correlation%20and%20Conversion%20tables.htm.
[15] Standard International Trade Classification, Revision 3, Statistical Papers, Series M No.34/Rev.3, (United Nations publication, Sales No. E.86.XVII.12). SITC, Revision 4 was accepted by the United Nations Statistical Commission at its thirty-seventh session in March 2006 (see Official Records of the Economic and Social Council, 2006, Supplement No. 4, (E/CN.3/2006/32), chapter III, para. 26 (b)). Yet, it will require several years until a time series of data according to SITC, Revision 4 will be sufficiently long for publication.

are still compiling data according to the EBOPS 2002 classification and, therefore, all services data presented in this Yearbook are presented according to this classification. For the cases in which a country has transitioned to the EBOPS 2010 classification (as presented in MSTIS 2010) and did not provide UNSD with data based on EBOPS 2002, and for those countries for which the IMF is the only data source,[16] the data were converted to the EBOPS 2002 classification in order to maintain consistency across countries. The conversion was based on the IMF's BPM5-to-BPM6 Conversion Matrix (available at http://www.imf.org/external/pubs/ft/bop/2008/08-10b.pdf). The World Trade Organization (WTO) performed several of the conversions and shared them with UNSD. The countries for which such conversions were made include: Angola; Armenia; Australia; Azerbaijan; Belarus; Canada; China, Hong Kong; China, Macao; El Salvador; Fiji; Gambia; Guinea; Guyana; India; Kazakhstan; Liberia; Nepal; Philippines; Russian Federation; Samoa; Saudi Arabia; Singapore; and Yemen.

Currency conversion and Period

40.   Currency conversion: For both merchandise and trade in services data in this publication, conversion of values from national currencies into United States dollars is done by means of currency conversion factors based on official exchange rates. Values in currencies subject to fluctuation are converted into United States dollars using weighted average exchange rates specially calculated for this purpose. The weighted average exchange rate for a given currency for a given year is the component monthly factors, furnished by the International Monetary Fund in its IFS publication, weighted by the value of the relevant trade in each month; a monthly factor is the exchange rate (or the simple average rate) in effect during that month. These factors are applied to total imports and exports and to the trade in individual commodities with individual countries. The conversion factors applied to the data presented in table A are published quarterly in the *UN Monthly Bulletin of Statistics* (http://unstats.un.org/unsd/mbs/default.aspx) and are also available at: http://unstats.un.org/unsd/trade/data/tables.asp. For data published on UN Comtrade the applied conversion factors are available in a country's metadata on UN Comtrade.

41.   Period: Generally, data refer to calendar years; however, for those countries which report according to some other reference year, the data are presented in the calendar year which covers the majority of the reference year used by the country.

Country Nomenclature and Country Grouping

42.   Country nomenclature: The naming of countries (or areas) in this publication follows in general the *United Nations Standard Country or Area Codes for Statistical Use*.[17] The names and composition of countries as reporter are changing over time. Also, countries rarely follow the identical nomenclature in the recording of partner information. For example when former geographical entities commonly referred to in national statistics have changed, countries may introduce the corresponding changes in their statistics at different times. In this publication,

---

[16] The IMF is only presenting data on a BPM6 basis (which corresponds to the EBOPS 2010 classification) for data from 2009 onwards.
[17] Standard Country or Area Codes for Statistical Use, Series M No. 49, Rev.4, (United Nations publication, Sales No. M.98.XVII.9). The latest information is available online at: http://unstats.un.org/unsd/methods/m49/m49.htm.

wherever possible, areas of the world have been designated the names they currently bear.

It should be noted that, in this publication:

i.   Data published for China exclude those for Taiwan Province of China. Data representing the trade with Taiwan Province, which may have been reported by any reporting country or area, are included in the grouping Asia, nes. For statistical purposes, data for China also do not include those for Hong Kong Special Administrative Region and Macao Special Administrative Region.

ii.   Beginning 1 January 2000, Botswana, Lesotho, Namibia, South Africa and Swaziland provide their international trade statistics separately.

iii.   On 4 February 2003, the official name of the Federal Republic of Yugoslavia has been changed to Serbia and Montenegro.

iv.   On 3 June 2006, Serbia and Montenegro formally dissolved into two independent countries: Montenegro and Serbia.

v.   On 10 October 2010 the federation of the Netherlands Antilles was formally dissolved. The former Dutch Caribbean dependency ceased to exist with a change of the five islands' constitutional status. Under the new political structure, Curaçao and Sint Maarten (Dutch part) have become autonomous countries within the Kingdom of the Netherlands, joining Aruba, which gained the status in 1986. The islands of the remaining territorial grouping, alternately known as Bonaire, Sint Eustatius and Saba or the BES islands, are special municipalities and part of the country of the Netherlands and overseas territories of the European Union. For statistical purposes, the data for the Netherlands do not include the BES islands. Data referring to Netherlands Antilles (as a partner) prior to 2011 refer to the former territory which included Curaçao, Sint Maarten (Dutch part), Bonaire, Sint Eustatius and Saba.

vi.   On 9 July 2011, Sudan formally dissolved into two independent countries: Sudan and South Sudan. Data provided for Sudan prior to 1 January 2012 refer to the former Sudan (including South Sudan). Data referring to Sudan (as a partner) for 2012 are attributed to Sudan excluding South Sudan.

43.   Regional groupings: This publication uses the regional groupings of the Millennium Development Goal (MDG) Indicator Database which are shown below (for their composition, see table A and http://unstats.un.org/unsd/mdg/default.aspx). The category 'Other' applies only to the presentation of data by trading partner and consists of Antarctica, Bunkers, Free Zones, 'Special Categories' (confidential partner) and Areas nes.:

World
Developed Countries
  - Asia-Pacific
  - Europe
  - North America
South-eastern Europe
Commonwealth of Independent States
  - CIS Europe
  - CIS Asia
Northern Africa
Sub-Saharan Africa
Latin America & the Caribbean
  - Caribbean
  - Latin America
Eastern Asia
Southern Asia
South-eastern Asia
Western Asia
Oceania
Other

44.   Aggregations: All regional aggregations are calculated as the sum of their components. This also includes the regional and world totals presented in table A (in bold) which, up to the 2007 edition of this yearbook and in the tables currently published in the *United Nations Monthly Bulletin of Statistics,* are calculated by subtracting re-exports from the imports and exports.

45.   Additional country groupings: The composition of the additional country groupings which are used in world table A is as follows:

ANCOM-Andean Common Market
Bolivia (Plurinational State of), Colombia, Ecuador and Peru

APEC-Asian-Pacific Economic Co-operation
Australia, Brunei Darussalam, Canada, Chile, China, Hong Kong Special Administrative Region of China, Indonesia, Japan, Malaysia, Mexico, New Zealand, Papua New Guinea, Peru, Philippines, Republic of Korea, Russian Federation, Singapore, Taiwan Province of China, Thailand, United States of America and Viet Nam

ASEAN-Association of South-East Asian Nations
Brunei Darussalam, Cambodia, Indonesia, Lao People's Democratic Republic, Malaysia, Myanmar, Philippines, Singapore, Thailand and Viet Nam

CACM-Central American Common Market
Costa Rica, El Salvador, Guatemala, Honduras and Nicaragua

CARICOM-Caribbean Community and Common Market
Antigua and Barbuda, Bahamas (member of the Community only), Barbados, Belize, Dominica, Grenada, Guyana, Haiti, Jamaica, Montserrat, Saint Kitts and Nevis, Saint Lucia, Saint Vincent and the Grenadines, Suriname, Trinidad and Tobago

COMESA-Common Market for Eastern and Southern Africa
Burundi, Comoros, Democratic Republic of the Congo, Djibouti, Egypt, Eritrea, Ethiopia, Kenya, Libya, Madagascar, Malawi, Mauritius, Rwanda, Seychelles, Sudan, Swaziland, Uganda, Zambia and Zimbabwe

ECOWAS - Economic Community of West African States
Benin, Burkina Faso, Cabo Verde, Cote d'Ivoire, Gambia, Ghana, Guinea, Guinea-Bissau, Liberia, Mali, Niger, Nigeria, Senegal, Sierra Leone and Togo

EFTA - European Free Trade Association
Iceland, Liechtenstein, Norway and Switzerland

EMCCA – Economic and Monetary Community of Central Africa
Cameroon, Central African Republic, Chad, Congo, Equatorial Guinea and Gabon

EU-28 - European Union 28
Austria, Belgium, Bulgaria, Croatia, Cyprus, Czech Republic, Denmark, Estonia, Finland, France, Germany, Greece, Hungary, Ireland, Italy, Latvia, Lithuania, Luxembourg, Malta, Netherlands, Poland, Portugal, Romania, Slovakia, Slovenia, Spain, Sweden and United Kingdom.

EU-27 - European Union 27
Austria, Belgium, Bulgaria, Cyprus, Czech Republic, Denmark, Estonia, Finland, France, Germany, Greece, Hungary, Ireland, Italy, Latvia, Lithuania, Luxembourg, Malta, Netherlands, Poland, Portugal, Romania, Slovakia, Slovenia, Spain, Sweden and United Kingdom.

EU-25 - European Union 25
Austria, Belgium, Denmark, Finland, France, Germany, Greece, Ireland, Italy, Luxembourg, Netherlands, Portugal, Spain, Sweden and United Kingdom (EU15) plus Czech Republic, Estonia, Hungary, Latvia, Lithuania, Malta, Poland, Slovakia, Slovenia, and Cyprus

EU-15 – European Union 15
Austria, Belgium, Denmark, Finland, France, Germany, Greece, Ireland, Italy, Luxembourg, Netherlands, Portugal, Spain, Sweden, United Kingdom.

LAIA - Latin American Integration Association (formerly Latin American Free Trade Association)
Argentina, Bolivia (Plurinational State of), Brazil, Chile, Colombia, Cuba, Ecuador, Mexico, Paraguay, Panama, Peru, Uruguay and Venezuela (Bolivarian Republic of)

LDC - Least developed countries
Afghanistan, Angola, Bangladesh, Benin, Bhutan, Burkina Faso, Burundi, Cambodia, Central African Republic, Chad, Comoros, Democratic Republic of the Congo, Djibouti, Equatorial Guinea, Eritrea, Ethiopia, Gambia, Guinea, Guinea-Bissau, Haiti, Kiribati, Lao People's Democratic Republic, Lesotho, Liberia, Madagascar, Malawi, Mali, Mauritania, Mozambique, Myanmar, Nepal, Niger, Rwanda, Sao Tome and Principe, Senegal, Sierra Leone, Solomon Islands, Somalia, South Sudan, Sudan, Timor-Leste, Togo, Tuvalu, Uganda, United Republic of Tanzania, Vanuatu, Yemen and Zambia

MERCOSUR-Mercado Comun Sud-Americano
Argentina, Brazil, Paraguay, Uruguay and Venezuela

NAFTA-Northern American Free Trade Area
Canada, Mexico and United States of America

OECD-Organization for Economic Cooperation and Development
Australia, Austria, Belgium, Canada, Chile, Czech Republic, Denmark, Estonia, Finland, France, Germany, Greece, Hungary, Iceland, Ireland, Israel, Italy, Japan, Luxembourg, Mexico, Netherlands, New Zealand, Norway, Poland, Portugal, Republic of Korea, Slovakia, Slovenia, Spain, Sweden, Switzerland, Turkey, United Kingdom and United States of America

OPEC-Organization of Petroleum Exporting Countries
Algeria, Angola, Ecuador, Iran (Islamic Republic of), Iraq, Kuwait, Libya, Nigeria, Qatar, Saudi Arabia, United Arab Emirates and Venezuela (Bolivarian Republic of).

Abbreviations and Explanation of symbols

Names of some countries (or areas) or groups of countries (or areas) and of some commodities or groups of commodities have been abbreviated. Exact titles of countries or commodities can be found in various editions of the following publications:

(i)   Standard Country or Area Codes for Statistical Use
(ii)   Standard International Trade Classification (SITC)
(iii)   Harmonized Commodity Description and Coding System (HS)
(iv)   Extended Balance of Payments Classification (EBOPS)

In addition, the following abbreviations and symbols are used in this publication:

Not available	(na)
Not available	blank
Not available	...
Not applicable	–
Not applicable	.
Magnitude of less than half the unit used	0 or 0.0
More than 100,000 percent	>
Thousand	thsd
Million	mln
Billion	bln
Average	Avg.
Not elsewhere specified	nes
U.S. dollar	US$
Cumulated	Cum.
Imports	Imp
Exports	Exp
Balance	Bal
General trade system	G
Special trade system	S
Cost, insurance and freight	CIF
Free on board	FOB
Not included elsewhere	n.i.e.

Disclaimer

The tables, graphs and text contained in Part 2 and 3 of this publication are provided only for illustration and despite all efforts might contain errors. When using this data users are advised to verify the latest information on UN Comtrade and UN ServiceTrade which is the source of this data.

Contact

This yearbook has been produced by the Trade Statistics Branch of the United Nations Statistics Division/ Department of Economic and Social Affairs. For questions or comments please contact us at:

Trade Statistics Branch
United Nations Statistics Division
2 United Nations Plaza, DC2-1540
New York, New York 10017
e-mail (merchandise): comtrade@un.org
e-mail (services): tradeserv@un.org

http://unstats.un.org/unsd/trade

2013
International Trade
Statistics Yearbook

Volume II
Trade by Product

Part 1 – World Trade Tables

- Total imports and exports by regions and countries or areas in U.S. dollars (Table A)
- Total imports and exports by countries or areas in national currency (Table B)
- External trade conversion factors (Table C)
- World exports by provenance and destination in U.S. dollars (Table D)
- Growth of world exports by provenance and destination (Table E)
- Structure of world exports by provenance and destination (Table F)
- Indices of total exports and imports by countries or areas (Table G)
- Indices of total exports and imports by regions (Table H)
- Indices and values of manufactured goods exports (Table I)
- Indices and values of fuel imports - Developed economies (Table J)
- Some indicators on fuel imports - Developed economies (Table K)

Total imports and exports by regions and countries or areas (Table A)
Imports CIF, exports FOB and balance: million U.S. dollars
Importations et exportations totales par régions et pays ou zones (Tableau A)
Importations CIF, exportations FOB, et balance : en millions de dollars E.-U.

Country or Area - Pays ou Zone	IMP EXP BAL	G/ S	2000	2005	2006	2007	2008	2009	2010	2011	2012	2013
World	IMP		6521536	10608676	12200208	14039129	16229371	12493498	15166963	18081742	18127986	18401453
Monde	EXP		6356563	10355384	11972964	13792073	16008961	12402221	15098934	18029362	18068177	18459279
	BAL		-164972	-253292	-227244	-247056	-220410	-91277	-68029	-52379	-59809	57825
Developed Countries[1,2]	IMP		4497925	6901821	7834602	8813309	9846832	7410761	8635733	10103721	9864994	9871054
Pays Developpés[1,2]	EXP		4131930	6154635	6951155	7952636	8872607	6879465	7995847	9292606	9070521	9201229
	BAL		-365995	-747187	-883447	-860674	-974225	-531297	-639886	-811115	-794473	-669825
Asia-Pacific	IMP		465262	667124	745551	816489	996936	741279	925893	1135144	1184367	1114910
Asie-Pacifique	EXP		557030	722700	792942	883435	999919	759462	1014420	1131745	1092667	1008739
	BAL		91768	55576	47390	66946	2983	18182	88527	-3399	-91699	-106171
Australia	IMP	G	71537	125283	139279	165364	200273	165470	201639	243700	260939	242133
Australie	EXP	G	63878	105833	123316	141122	186965	153884	212362	271697	256664	253052
	BAL		-7659	-19449	-15963	-24241	-13308	-11587	10724	27997	-4275	10920
Japan	IMP	G	379490	514987	579603	619662	762626	550550	692435	854098	885610	832424
Japon	EXP	G	479274	594940	646755	714211	782049	580719	769772	822564	798621	714613
	BAL		99783	79953	67151	94549	19422	30169	77337	-31534	-86989	-117811
New Zealand	IMP	G	14235	26854	26669	31463	34036	25259	31819	37346	37818	40354
Nouvelle-Zélande	EXP	G	13879	21926	22871	28102	30905	24859	32285	37484	37383	41074
	BAL		-356	-4928	-3798	-3362	-3131	-401	466	138	-435	720
Europe	IMP		2533386	4183278	4818709	5593484	6269024	4740528	5345998	6248664	5878748	5961888
Europe	EXP		2515996	4169697	4743462	5500188	6128234	4749467	5314924	6227769	5976581	6154222
	BAL		-17390	-13580	-75247	-93296	-140790	8939	-31074	-20895	97833	192333
Andorra	IMP	S	1021	1796	1780	1917	1931	1589	1518	1596	1396	1455
Andorre	EXP	S	45	142	150	127	96	63	54	77	68	99
	BAL		-975	-1654	-1630	-1790	-1835	-1526	-1464	-1519	-1327	-1356
Austria	IMP	S	68986	119950	130945	156760	176172	136081	150601	182340	169657	172596
Autriche	EXP	S	64167	117722	130376	157317	173397	130791	144889	169519	158821	166546
	BAL		-4819	-2228	-570	557	-2775	-5290	-5712	-12821	-10836	-6050
Belgium	IMP	S	176992	319101	352968	413074	466437	354666	391333	466833	439492	452163
Belgique	EXP	S	187876	335738	366758	431850	471932	371397	407055	475981	446637	469921
	BAL		10884	16638	13790	18776	5494	16731	15721	9148	7145	17757
Croatia	IMP	G	7887	18560	21488	25830	30728	21203	20051	22708	20762	20961
Croatie	EXP	G	4432	8773	10376	12364	14112	10474	11806	13375	12347	11928
	BAL		-3455	-9788	-11112	-13465	-16617	-10729	-8244	-9333	-8415	-9033
Czech Republic	IMP	S	33934	76343	93453	118467	142172	105256	126600	152122	141515	143957
République tchèque	EXP	S	29057	77988	95165	122760	146406	113175	133020	162897	157167	161902
	BAL		-4877	1645	1712	4293	4234	7920	6420	10775	15652	17945
Denmark	IMP	S	44364	72505	84220	97366	109158	80372	83170	96431	92300	98374
Danemark	EXP	S	50390	81912	90660	101599	115929	91817	95758	111900	106127	111350
	BAL		6025	9407	6440	4233	6772	11445	12589	15469	13827	12976
Estonia	IMP	S	4236	10188	11882	15064	16058	10151	12282	17757	17796	18142
Estonie	EXP	S	3166	7676	8759	10960	12468	9058	11607	16724	16083	16291
	BAL		-1070	-2513	-3123	-4105	-3590	-1094	-675	-1033	-1713	-1851
Faeroe Islands	IMP	G	532	743	790	1016	988	783	780	986	1144	1110
Iles Féroé	EXP	G	472	599	651	746	852	762	839	1007	945	1080
	BAL		-60	-144	-139	-270	-136	-22	59	20	-199	-29
Finland	IMP	G	33900	58474	69448	81756	92160	60866	68773	84235	76558	77579
Finlande	EXP	G	45482	65238	77287	90092	96890	62872	69492	79126	73114	74433
	BAL		11582	6764	7839	8336	4730	2005	719	-5108	-3444	-3146

Total imports and exports by regions and countries or areas (Table A)
Imports CIF, exports FOB and balance: million U.S. dollars *[cont.]*

Importations et exportations totales par régions et pays ou zones (Tableau A)
Importations CIF, exportations FOB et balance : en millions de dollars E.-U. *[suite]*

Country or Area - Pays ou Zone	IMP EXP BAL	G/S	2000	2005	2006	2007	2008	2009	2010	2011	2012	2013
France	IMP	S	310831	490611	546505	631447	715783	560484	608652	712726	666275	670521
France	EXP	S	298765	443619	490702	550458	608942	476098	516955	585191	558081	567591
	BAL		-12066	-46992	-55803	-80989	-106840	-84386	-91697	-127535	-108194	-102930
Germany	IMP	S	495450	780514	922381	1055997	1186681	926154	1056170	1256168	1164626	1190098
Allemagne	EXP	S	550223	977970	1122112	1323818	1451390	1120666	1261577	1476955	1408370	1452574
	BAL		54773	197456	199731	267822	264709	194512	205408	220787	243744	262476
Gibraltar	IMP		480	502	639	796	769	679	627	703	605	748
Gibraltar	EXP		126	199	242	304	281	266	259	246	253	279
	BAL		-354	-302	-397	-492	-488	-413	-368	-457	-353	-469
Greece	IMP	S	28323	57816	66376	82521	95740	72636	67328	67468	63380	62084
Grèce	EXP	S	10965	18489	21733	26660	31431	24657	27991	33836	35485	36269
	BAL		-17359	-39327	-44643	-55861	-64309	-47979	-39337	-33633	-27895	-25815
Hungary	IMP	S	31955	65783	77206	94397	106380	78034	87612	100989	94282	99091
Hongrie	EXP	S	28016	62179	74217	93985	107465	84586	94759	110897	103047	108426
	BAL		-3939	-3604	-2989	-412	1085	6552	7147	9908	8765	9335
Iceland	IMP	G	2591	4554	5078	6097	5614	3604	3920	4833	4772	4787
Islande	EXP	G	1891	2944	3242	4342	5191	4057	4604	5344	5064	4990
	BAL		-700	-1610	-1836	-1755	-423	453	685	510	292	204
Ireland	IMP	G	51444	71507	76432	87049	84932	62595	60686	67167	63228	65998
Irlande	EXP	G	77097	107923	109005	122252	127050	119264	118951	127012	117770	115335
	BAL		25653	36416	32573	35203	42118	56669	58265	59845	54542	49337
Italy	IMP	S	238021	384837	442599	511870	563436	414725	486968	558813	489096	477298
Italie	EXP	S	239902	372962	417219	500239	544962	406685	446852	523283	501534	517636
	BAL		1881	-11875	-25379	-11631	-18474	-8040	-40116	-35530	12438	40338
Latvia	IMP	S	3187	8592	11430	15182	15775	9346	11143	15442	16078	16781
Lettonie	EXP	S	1867	5108	5893	7892	9278	7174	8850	11995	12683	13317
	BAL		-1320	-3483	-5538	-7290	-6497	-2173	-2292	-3446	-3395	-3464
Lithuania	IMP	G	5219	15510	19413	24445	31295	18341	23385	31547	31992	35211
Lituanie	EXP	G	3548	11782	14153	17162	23770	16496	20726	28104	29625	32616
	BAL		-1671	-3729	-5259	-7283	-7525	-1845	-2658	-3443	-2367	-2595
Luxembourg	IMP	S	10707	17908	19737	22572	25828	19246	21738	26312	24180	23912
Luxembourg	EXP	S	7833	12672	13993	16359	17734	12905	14293	16798	13989	14086
	BAL		-2875	-5236	-5744	-6213	-8094	-6342	-7444	-9515	-10190	-9826
Malta	IMP	G	3400	3807	4073	4508	5757	4840	5735	7411	7923	7479
Malte	EXP	G	2443	2376	2705	2985	3610	2917	3721	5284	5697	5182
	BAL		-957	-1432	-1368	-1523	-2147	-1923	-2014	-2127	-2226	-2297
Netherlands	IMP	S	198926	310600	358510	421092	495056	382278	440024	507759	501163	507478
Pays-Bas	EXP	S	213425	349844	399635	472660	545897	431695	492742	569513	554699	567674
	BAL		14499	39244	41125	51568	50840	49418	52718	61754	53536	60196
Norway	IMP	G	34395	55473	64272	80378	90293	68970	77326	90787	87316	89988
Norvège	EXP	G	60064	103737	122112	136371	171764	116778	130669	160305	161026	153188
	BAL		25669	48265	57840	55992	81471	47808	53344	69518	73710	63201
Poland	IMP	S	48970	100759	127260	162437	204873	149723	178149	206844	196198	205174
Pologne	EXP	S	31684	89214	110941	138756	168674	136786	159829	187151	183523	202107
	BAL		-17285	-11545	-16319	-23680	-36200	-12938	-18320	-19693	-12675	-3067
Portugal	IMP	S	38196	53398	65639	76376	94726	71742	75576	82481	72306	75066
Portugal	EXP	S	23280	32129	42906	50246	57558	44350	48738	59608	58255	62841
	BAL		-14916	-21269	-22734	-26129	-37168	-27393	-26838	-22872	-14051	-12225

Total imports and exports by regions and countries or areas (Table A)

Imports CIF, exports FOB and balance: million U.S. dollars *[cont.]*

Importations et exportations totales par régions et pays ou zones (Tableau A)

Importations CIF, exportations FOB et balance : en millions de dollars E.-U. *[suite]*

Country or Area - Pays ou Zone	IMP EXP BAL	G/S	2000	2005	2006	2007	2008	2009	2010	2011	2012	2013
Slovakia	IMP	S	13413	36168	47310	62102	74034	56898	66110	81505	79077	83637
Slovaquie	EXP	S	11889	31997	41939	57765	70982	55541	64012	79011	79882	85244
	BAL		-1524	-4171	-5371	-4337	-3052	-1357	-2098	-2494	805	1607
Slovenia	IMP	S	10116	19626	23032	29499	33991	24085	26305	31405	28392	29380
Slovénie	EXP	S	8732	17896	21293	26857	29600	22646	24717	29242	27080	28629
	BAL		-1384	-1730	-1739	-2642	-4391	-1439	-1588	-2163	-1312	-751
Spain	IMP	S	152901	287644	326046	384956	417049	290744	315548	362835	325836	333932
Espagne	EXP	S	113348	191000	213350	248917	277695	220848	246274	298458	286219	310996
	BAL		-39553	-96644	-112697	-136038	-139353	-69897	-69274	-64377	-39618	-22936
Sweden	IMP	G	73328	111580	127648	153463	168993	120262	148474	174730	164114	159667
Suède	EXP	G	87737	130885	147899	168979	183907	131042	158090	187243	172725	167620
	BAL		14409	19305	20251	15516	14914	10780	9616	12513	8611	7953
Switzerland	IMP	S	76104	119784	132030	153181	173686	147894	166924	196790	188618	191705
Suisse	EXP	S	74867	126099	141679	164809	191813	166847	185790	223225	213982	217079
	BAL		-1237	6314	9649	11627	18127	18953	18866	26435	25364	25374
United Kingdom	IMP	G	333579	508644	588118	621869	642529	486279	562493	638940	648671	645516
Royaume-Uni	EXP	G	283206	382887	446312	440556	467157	356758	410006	478460	476284	476991
	BAL		-50373	-125757	-141806	-181312	-175372	-129521	-152487	-160480	-172387	-168525
North America	IMP		**1499277**	**2051420**	**2270342**	**2403337**	**2580873**	**1928954**	**2363843**	**2719913**	**2801878**	**2794256**
Amérique du Nord	EXP		**1058904**	**1262237**	**1414752**	**1569013**	**1744455**	**1370536**	**1666503**	**1933092**	**2001272**	**2038269**
	BAL		**-440373**	**-789183**	**-855590**	**-834324**	**-836418**	**-558418**	**-697339**	**-786820**	**-800606**	**-755987**
Bermuda	IMP	G	720	985	1094	1167	1159	1064	988	916	910	980
Bermudes	EXP	G	...	49	27	27	24	29	15	13	11	11
	BAL		...	-936	-1067	-1140	-1135	-1035	-973	-903	-899	-969
Canada[3]	IMP	G	238811	314566	350259	380701	408827	321247	392119	451246	462423	461925
Canada[3]	EXP	G	276641	360673	388315	420293	456419	314002	387481	452132	454833	458397
	BAL		37830	46107	38056	39593	47593	-7245	-4638	886	-7590	-3528
Greenland	IMP	G	363	593	618	678	895	742	808	915	850	780
Groenland	EXP	G	272	402	396	431	487	360	380	475	480	490
	BAL		-92	-190	-222	-247	-407	-382	-428	-441	-370	-290
United States[4]	IMP	G	1259300	1735060	1918080	2020400	2169490	1605300	1969180	2265890	2336520	2329060
Etats-Unis[4]	EXP	G	781918	901082	1025970	1148200	1287440	1056040	1278490	1480290	1545710	1579050
	BAL		-477382	-833978	-892110	-872200	-882050	-549260	-690690	-785600	-790810	-750010
South-Eastern Europe	IMP		29538	**82986**	103572	140131	170970	116966	125313	154685	145618	**152522**
Europe du Sud-est	EXP		19549	**49008**	60952	76659	93953	76969	89828	115549	107523	**122874**
	BAL		-9989	**-33979**	-42620	-63471	-77016	-39996	-35486	-39136	-38095	**-29648**
Albania	IMP	G	1091	2618	3058	4188	5251	4550	4406	5396	4882	4902
Albanie	EXP	G	261	658	798	1078	1355	1091	1545	1951	1968	2332
	BAL		-829	-1960	-2261	-3110	-3896	-3459	-2861	-3445	-2914	-2570
Bosnia and Herzegovina	IMP	S	3083	7072	7345	9772	12282	8794	9204	11047	10018	10303
Bosnie-Herzégovine	EXP	S	1067	2400	3323	4166	5066	3939	4802	5850	5160	5688
	BAL		-2017	-4672	-4023	-5606	-7217	-4856	-4402	-5196	-4858	-4615
Bulgaria	IMP	S	6505	18162	23270	30086	37018	23552	25473	32579	32712	34350
Bulgarie	EXP	S	4809	11739	15101	18575	22485	16378	20571	28222	26670	29492
	BAL		-1696	-6423	-8168	-11511	-14532	-7175	-4902	-4357	-6042	-4858
Montenegro	IMP	S	.	.	1842	2867	3731	2313	2186	2544	2309	2354
Monténégro	EXP	S	.	.	556	626	617	388	437	632	471	498
	BAL		.	.	-1285	-2241	-3115	-1926	-1749	-1912	-1838	-1856

Total imports and exports by regions and countries or areas (Table A)

Imports CIF, exports FOB and balance: million U.S. dollars *[cont.]*

Importations et exportations totales par régions et pays ou zones (Tableau A)

Importations CIF, exportations FOB et balance : en millions de dollars E.-U. *[suite]*

Country or Area - Pays ou Zone	IMP EXP BAL	G/S	2000	2005	2006	2007	2008	2009	2010	2011	2012	2013
Romania	IMP	S	13055	40463	51106	69602	82965	54256	61885	76251	70260	73452
Roumanie	EXP	S	10367	27730	32336	40042	49539	40621	49357	62659	57904	65881
	BAL		-2688	-12733	-18770	-29560	-33426	-13635	-12528	-13592	-12355	-7571
Serbia	IMP	S	.	.	13188	18400	22880	18462	16686	19862	18927	...
Serbie	EXP	S	.	.	6437	8817	10971	11862	9766	11779	11348	...
	BAL		.	.	-6752	-9584	-11908	-6599	-6920	-8082	-7579	...
Serbia and Montenegro[5]	IMP	S	3711	...	.	.	.	.	.	.	.	.
Serbie et Monténégro[5]	EXP	S	1723	...	.	.	.	.	.	.	.	.
	BAL		-1988	...	.	.	.	.	.	.	.	.
TFYR Macedonia	IMP	S	2094	3228	3763	5216	6843	5038	5474	7007	6511	6600
L'ex-Ry de Macédoine	EXP	S	1323	2041	2401	3356	3920	2692	3351	4455	4002	4267
	BAL		-771	-1187	-1362	-1860	-2923	-2346	-2123	-2552	-2509	-2333
CIS	IMP		**70777**	**188718**	**253434**	**352604**	**470011**	**304021**	**385468**	**510023**	**530402**	**535890**
CEI	EXP		**143257**	**336580**	**418466**	**497669**	**707830**	**440357**	**575065**	**761791**	**777515**	**762067**
	BAL		**72480**	**147862**	**165033**	**145065**	**237818**	**136337**	**189597**	**251767**	**247114**	**226177**
Asia	IMP		**13519**	**34874**	**45544**	**59849**	**73095**	**59330**	**56331**	**70848**	**79917**	**95445**
Asie	EXP		**17794**	**43808**	**58070**	**70828**	**139120**	**76419**	**99167**	**133280**	**135080**	**131848**
	BAL		**4275**	**8935**	**12527**	**10978**	**66025**	**17089**	**42836**	**62431**	**55163**	**36403**
Armenia	IMP	S	882	1768	2194	3282	4427	3303	3783	4196	4267	4386
Arménie	EXP	S	294	950	1004	1219	1057	698	1011	1316	1428	1479
	BAL		-588	-818	-1190	-2063	-3370	-2605	-2771	-2881	-2839	-2907
Azerbaijan	IMP	G	1172	4211	5267	5714	7170	6123	6601	9756	9653	10713
Azerbaïdjan	EXP	G	1745	4347	6372	6058	47756	14701	21360	26571	23908	23975
	BAL		573	136	1105	345	40586	8578	14760	16815	14255	13263
Georgia	IMP	G	710	2488	3675	5212	6302	4500	5257	7058	7842	7874
Géorgie	EXP	G	324	865	936	1232	1495	1134	1677	2189	2377	2909
	BAL		-386	-1622	-2738	-3980	-4806	-3367	-3580	-4869	-5465	-4965
Kazakhstan	IMP	G	5040	17979	24120	33260	38452	28409	24024	30000	35307	45966
Kazakhstan	EXP	G	8812	28301	38762	48351	71971	43196	57244	83316	88575	81912
	BAL		3772	10322	14642	15091	33519	14787	33220	53316	53268	35945
Kyrgyzstan	IMP	S	558	1189	1931	2789	4072	3040	3223	4261	5374	6070
Kirghizistan	EXP	S	511	674	891	1321	1856	1673	1756	1979	1683	1791
	BAL		-47	-515	-1040	-1468	-2217	-1367	-1467	-2282	-3691	-4279
Tajikistan	IMP	G	675	1354	1723	2455	3270	2569	2658	3186	3779	4121
Tadjikistan	EXP	G	784	891	1399	1468	1406	1010	1196	1256	1358	1163
	BAL		109	-464	-324	-987	-1864	-1559	-1462	-1931	-2421	-2958
Uzbekistan	IMP	G	2697	3666	4380	4848	7076	9023	8386	9953	...	13799
Ouzbékistan	EXP	G	2817	4749	5617	8029	10369	10735	11587	13254	...	15087
	BAL		120	1083	1237	3181	3293	1712	3201	3301	...	1288
Europe	IMP		57259	153844	207890	292755	396916	244691	329137	439175	450485	440445
Europe	EXP		125463	292772	360396	426842	568710	363939	475898	628511	642435	630219
	BAL		68205	138928	152506	134087	171794	119248	146761	189336	191950	189773
Belarus	IMP	G	8646	16708	22351	28693	39381	28569	34884	45771	46404	42999
Bélarus	EXP	G	7326	15979	19734	24275	32571	21304	25284	41419	46060	37232
	BAL		-1320	-729	-2618	-4418	-6811	-7265	-9601	-4352	-345	-5766
Republic of Moldova	IMP	G	776	2292	2693	3690	4899	3278	3855	5191	5213	5493
République de Moldova	EXP	G	472	1091	1050	1340	1591	1283	1542	2217	2162	2399
	BAL		-305	-1201	-1643	-2350	-3308	-1995	-2314	-2975	-3051	-3094

Total imports and exports by regions and countries or areas (Table A)

Imports CIF, exports FOB and balance: million U.S. dollars *[cont.]*

Importations et exportations totales par régions et pays ou zones (Tableau A)

Importations CIF, exportations FOB et balance : en millions de dollars E.-U. *[suite]*

Country or Area - Pays ou Zone	IMP EXP BAL	G/ S	2000	2005	2006	2007	2008	2009	2010	2011	2012	2013
Russian Federation	IMP	G	33880	98708	137807	199754	267101	167411	229655	305605	314150	314967
Fédération de Russie	EXP	G	103093	241473	301244	351930	467581	301656	397668	516481	525383	527266
	BAL		69213	142766	163437	152176	200480	134245	168013	210877	211233	212299
Ukraine	IMP	G	13956	36136	45039	60618	85535	45433	60742	82608	84718	76987
Ukraine	EXP	G	14573	34228	38368	49296	66967	39696	51405	68394	68830	63321
	BAL		617	-1908	-6671	-11322	-18568	-5737	-9337	-14214	-15887	-13666
Northern Africa	IMP		**46956**	**80241**	**86800**	**112469**	**164473**	**146452**	**161273**	**182446**	**206871**	**210902**
Afrique du nord	EXP		**49865**	**110314**	**131233**	**153521**	**207537**	**134078**	**164438**	**161581**	**199525**	**176950**
	BAL		**2909**	**30074**	**44433**	**41051**	**43064**	**-12374**	**3165**	**-20864**	**-7346**	**-33952**
Algeria	IMP	S	9172	20383	20985	27525	39578	39333	40228	47279	50352	54965
Algérie	EXP	S	22019	46693	52760	59761	79587	45240	57786	73661	72857	65555
	BAL		12848	26310	31775	32236	40010	5907	17558	26383	22505	10590
Egypt[6,7]	IMP	G	13963	19816	20722	27063	48775	44946	52923	58903	65774	59662
Egypte[6,7]	EXP	G	4675	10652	13694	16200	26246	23062	26438	30528	29409	28493
	BAL		-9288	-9163	-7028	-10863	-22528	-21884	-26485	-28376	-36365	-31169
Libya	IMP	G	3703	6058	6053	6753	9116	10037	10506	7999	22996	27012
Libye	EXP	G	10137	31278	40333	47048	62031	37265	46016	18015	58954	43989
	BAL		6434	25220	34280	40295	52915	27228	35510	10016	35959	16977
Morocco	IMP	S	11534	20790	23980	32010	42366	32881	35385	44294	43290	44934
Maroc	EXP	S	7175	11190	12744	15340	20345	14054	17765	21524	21291	21847
	BAL		-4359	-9601	-11236	-16670	-22021	-18827	-17620	-22770	-21999	-23088
Tunisia	IMP	G	8567	13177	15043	19101	24622	19241	22218	23958	24447	24317
Tunisie	EXP	G	5850	10494	11694	15163	19319	14449	16427	17847	17008	17061
	BAL		-2717	-2683	-3349	-3938	-5303	-4791	-5791	-6111	-7439	-7256
Sub-Saharan Africa	IMP		**78799**	**166090**	**200393**	**240121**	**294286**	**251946**	**289945**	**360550**	**355036**	**372770**
Afrique subsaharienne	EXP		**93497**	**203351**	**232159**	**277126**	**362434**	**258311**	**337132**	**428742**	**417361**	**420968**
	BAL		**14698**	**37262**	**31766**	**37005**	**68148**	**6365**	**47187**	**68192**	**62325**	**48198**
Angola[3]	IMP	S	3040	8353	11600	9617	14544	22548	16574	17330	22340	22670
Angola[3]	EXP	S	7703	23670	31084	43452	72179	40080	46437	65801	70088	67144
	BAL		4663	15317	19484	33835	57634	17533	29864	48471	47748	44474
Benin	IMP	S	567	1018	1228	2037	2290	1553	1494	2701	2202	2148
Bénin	EXP	S	392	574	741	1052	1285	423	437	1397	1402	1154
	BAL		-174	-445	-487	-984	-1005	-1130	-1057	-1304	-800	-995
Botswana	IMP	G	2079	3172	3076	4077	5232	4771	5666	7300	8114	7007
Botswana	EXP	G	2661	4455	4509	5170	5077	3514	4692	5893	5971	7765
	BAL		581	1283	1434	1093	-155	-1257	-975	-1407	-2143	758
Burkina Faso	IMP	G	608	1255	1323	1685	2009	2084	2157	2574	3420	3499
Burkina Faso	EXP	G	213	467	588	623	693	868	1319	2353	2183	2161
	BAL		-395	-788	-735	-1062	-1315	-1216	-837	-221	-1237	-1338
Burundi	IMP	S	148	267	431	319	402	402	509	752	751	811
Burundi	EXP	S	50	95	58	62	54	62	100	122	132	99
	BAL		-98	-172	-372	-257	-348	-340	-409	-630	-619	-712
Cabo Verde	IMP	G	237	438	543	753	819	709	743	947	766	727
Cabo Verde	EXP	G	11	18	21	19	32	35	45	69	53	69
	BAL		-227	-420	-522	-734	-788	-674	-698	-878	-713	-658
Cameroon	IMP	S	1483	2725	3161	4218	5376	4322	4847	6498	7101	7006
Cameroun	EXP	S	1823	2849	3587	3622	4279	3391	3896	4597	4500	4204
	BAL		341	123	427	-596	-1097	-931	-952	-1901	-2602	-2802

Total imports and exports by regions and countries or areas (Table A)
Imports CIF, exports FOB and balance: million U.S. dollars *[cont.]*

Importations et exportations totales par régions et pays ou zones (Tableau A)
Importations CIF, exportations FOB et balance : en millions de dollars E.-U. *[suite]*

Country or Area - Pays ou Zone	IMP EXP BAL	G/S	2000	2005	2006	2007	2008	2009	2010	2011	2012	2013
Cent. Afr. Rep.	IMP	S	118	173	203	251	298	273	244	276	276	250
Rép. centrafricaine	EXP	S	163	129	158	181	150	81	91	116	112	140
	BAL		45	-44	-44	-70	-149	-192	-153	-161	-163	-111
Chad	IMP	S	483	954	1346	1794	1906	2289	2507	2700	2600	2997
Tchad	EXP	S	236	3095	3342	3653	4345	2636	3411	4599	3901	4496
	BAL		-248	2141	1995	1859	2439	347	903	1899	1301	1498
Comoros	IMP	S	43	98	116	139	174	171	190	277	300	285
Comores	EXP	S	14	12	10	14	9	16	18	25	25	25
	BAL		-29	-86	-106	-125	-165	-155	-172	-251	-275	-260
Congo	IMP	S	479	1343	2073	2606	3142	2987	2987	5200	5200	5500
Congo	EXP	S	2489	4745	6078	5635	8300	6100	8200	11500	11000	9800
	BAL		2010	3402	4004	3029	5159	3113	5213	6300	5800	4300
Cote d'Ivoire	IMP	S	2485	5860	5825	6694	7863	7023	7863	6714	9774	12898
Côte d'Ivoire	EXP	S	3611	7693	8477	8692	10301	10326	10285	10928	10861	13748
	BAL		1127	1834	2652	1998	2438	3303	2423	4214	1087	849
Dem. Rep. of the Congo	IMP	S	697	2270	2740	2950	4300	3900	4500	5500	6100	6300
Rép. dém. du Congo	EXP	S	824	2190	2320	2600	4400	3500	5300	6600	6300	6300
	BAL		126	-80	-420	-350	100	-400	800	1100	200	0
Djibouti	IMP	G	207	277	336	473	574	451	420	511	580	560
Djibouti	EXP	G	32	40	55	58	69	77	100	93	95	120
	BAL		-175	-238	-281	-415	-505	-373	-320	-418	-485	-440
Equatorial Guinea	IMP	G	451	1310	2023	2369	3934	5205	5680	6014	5987	6990
Guinée équatoriale	EXP	G	1097	7062	8218	10205	15996	9108	9964	13532	15467	13981
	BAL		646	5753	6195	7836	12062	3903	4285	7518	9480	6990
Ethiopia	IMP	G	1261	4095	5207	5805	8268	7644	8527	8886	11980	...
Ethiopie	EXP	G	486	903	1043	1279	1606	1635	2311	2872	2995	...
	BAL		-775	-3191	-4164	-4526	-6663	-6009	-6216	-6014	-8985	...
Gabon	IMP	S	996	1472	1726	2155	2607	2514	2984	3666	3630	3886
Gabon	EXP	S	2605	5068	5454	6302	9566	5451	8691	9768	7704	9514
	BAL		1610	3596	3728	4147	6959	2937	5706	6102	4075	5628
Gambia	IMP	G	187	260	259	323	324	304	301	344	380	351
Gambie	EXP	G	15	8	11	13	14	15	15	...	...	...
	BAL		-172	-252	-248	-310	-310	-289	-286	...	...	...
Ghana	IMP	G	2974	5344	6748	8057	10243	8038	11038	15967	17965	17759
Ghana	EXP	G	1317	2801	3725	4322	5625	5840	7960	12784	11976	13691
	BAL		-1657	-2543	-3023	-3735	-4618	-2199	-3077	-3183	-5989	-4067
Guinea	IMP	S	612	820	900	1218	1366	1060	1405	2106	2300	2150
Guinée	EXP	S	666	890	900	1203	1342	1050	1471	1433	1400	1300
	BAL		54	70	0	-15	-24	-10	66	-673	-900	-850
Guinea-Bissau	IMP	G	60	120	110	110	199	202	197	260	250	240
Guinée-Bissau	EXP	G	62	89	74	107	128	120	120	230	130	210
	BAL		3	-31	-36	-3	-71	-82	-77	-30	-120	-30
Kenya	IMP	G	3105	6149	7311	8989	11080	10207	12074	14783	16288	16358
Kenya	EXP	G	1734	3293	3437	4080	4975	4463	5149	5756	6127	5856
	BAL		-1372	-2856	-3874	-4910	-6105	-5743	-6925	-9027	-10162	-10503
Lesotho	IMP	G	809	1410	1496	1741	1995	1973	2206	2591	2587	2284
Lesotho	EXP	G	221	650	689	770	883	723	801	1168	1099	934
	BAL		-589	-760	-807	-971	-1113	-1250	-1404	-1422	-1489	-1350

Total imports and exports by regions and countries or areas (Table A)

Imports CIF, exports FOB and balance: million U.S. dollars *[cont.]*

Importations et exportations totales par régions et pays ou zones (Tableau A)

Importations CIF, exportations FOB et balance : en millions de dollars E.-U. *[suite]*

Country or Area - Pays ou Zone	IMP EXP BAL	G/ S	2000	2005	2006	2007	2008	2009	2010	2011	2012	2013
Liberia	IMP	S	...	310	467	499	813	551	710	814	1076	1210
Libéria	EXP	S	...	131	158	200	242	149	222	367	459	540
	BAL		...	-179	-309	-299	-571	-402	-488	-447	-617	-670
Madagascar	IMP	S	999	1680	1744	2449	3843	3160	2546	2628	2486	3198
Madagascar	EXP	S	828	831	994	1371	1670	1095	1082	1249	1236	1947
	BAL		-171	-849	-750	-1078	-2173	-2065	-1464	-1379	-1250	-1250
Malawi	IMP	G	533	1163	1206	1380	1700	2096	2173	2428	2372	2831
Malawi	EXP	G	379	508	541	709	860	1080	1130	1400	1260	1196
	BAL		-153	-655	-665	-671	-840	-1015	-1044	-1028	-1112	-1636
Mali	IMP	S	807	1544	1819	2183	3343	2487	3430	3391	2940	3699
Mali	EXP	S	552	1092	1559	1567	2082	1783	1996	2392	2163	2601
	BAL		-255	-453	-260	-616	-1261	-704	-1434	-999	-776	-1098
Mauritania	IMP	S	354	1344	1089	1428	1669	1337	1708	2453	2971	2686
Mauritanie	EXP	S	343	556	1268	1356	1651	1407	1799	2458	2624	...
	BAL		-11	-787	180	-72	-18	70	91	6	-347	...
Mauritius	IMP	G	2206	3157	3627	3894	4655	3734	4387	5149	5355	5399
Maurice	EXP	G	1803	2138	2329	2238	2386	1939	2262	2565	2649	2872
	BAL		-403	-1018	-1298	-1656	-2269	-1795	-2125	-2584	-2706	-2527
Mozambique	IMP	S	1158	2408	2869	3210	4008	3764	4600	6306	6800	8600
Mozambique	EXP	S	364	1783	2381	2650	2653	2147	3000	3604	4100	4300
	BAL		-794	-625	-488	-560	-1355	-1617	-1600	-2702	-2700	-4300
Namibia	IMP	G	1539	2567	2868	3528	4314	5066	5372	6336	6733	7498
Namibie	EXP	G	1317	2067	2638	2924	3113	3379	4096	4391	4090	3480
	BAL		-222	-500	-230	-604	-1201	-1687	-1276	-1945	-2643	-4018
Niger	IMP	S	390	934	955	1163	1659	1502	2179	1814	1799	1909
Niger	EXP	S	284	490	507	664	902	593	642	903	1503	1613
	BAL		-107	-444	-448	-499	-757	-909	-1537	-910	-296	-295
Nigeria	IMP	G	8721	21314	26760	37576	42378	33906	44235	64105	35703	44598
Nigéria	EXP	G	20975	55145	57444	65133	80615	56742	84000	114500	114000	...
	BAL		12254	33831	30684	27557	38237	22836	39765	50395	78297	...
Rwanda	IMP	G	211	432	547	736	1131	1227	1401	1775	1999	2480
Rwanda	EXP	G	52	125	147	176	267	193	255	464	470	689
	BAL		-159	-307	-400	-559	-865	-1035	-1146	-1311	-1529	-1792
Saint Helena[8]	IMP	G	10	12	15	16	16	16	...	...	...	...
Sainte-Hélèna[8]	EXP	G	0	1	0	0	0	1	...	...	...	...
	BAL		-10	-12	-15	-15	-16	-16	...	...	...	...
Sao Tome and Principe	IMP	S	30	50	71	79	114	103	112	132	140	140
Sao Tomé-et-Principe	EXP	S	3	7	8	7	11	8	11	11	11	12
	BAL		-27	-43	-63	-72	-103	-95	-101	-121	-129	-128
Senegal	IMP	G	1513	3190	3444	4271	5706	4549	4442	5390	5883	6067
Sénégal	EXP	G	921	1576	1556	1652	2007	1906	2059	2432	2382	2440
	BAL		-592	-1614	-1888	-2618	-3699	-2643	-2383	-2958	-3501	-3627
Seychelles	IMP	G	343	675	758	861	1106	821	649	750	800	930
Seychelles	EXP	G	193	340	380	356	437	402	400	483	496	577
	BAL		-150	-335	-378	-506	-668	-419	-249	-267	-303	-353
Sierra Leone	IMP	S	149	345	389	445	534	521	771	1715	1604	1780
Sierra Leone	EXP	S	13	159	231	245	216	233	319	317	1081	1893
	BAL		-136	-186	-158	-199	-319	-287	-452	-1398	-523	113

Total imports and exports by regions and countries or areas (Table A)

Imports CIF, exports FOB and balance: million U.S. dollars *[cont.]*

Importations et exportations totales par régions et pays ou zones (Tableau A)

Importations CIF, exportations FOB et balance : en millions de dollars E.-U. *[suite]*

Country or Area - Pays ou Zone	IMP EXP BAL	G/ S	2000	2005	2006	2007	2008	2009	2010	2011	2012	2013
South Africa[3,9]	IMP	G	26795	54848	67644	79873	94901	64439	80131	99726	101413	101264
Afrique du Sud[3,9]	EXP	G	29987	51640	58197	69787	84488	62627	81822	96922	87367	83531
	BAL		3192	-3208	-9447	-10086	-10413	-1812	1691	-2804	-14047	-17733
Sudan[10]	IMP	G	1553	6757	8074	8450	9352	9691	10045	9236	9230	9918
Soudan[10]	EXP	G	1807	4824	5657	8866	11671	8257	11404	9689	4067	7086
	BAL		254	-1933	-2417	416	2319	-1434	1360	453	-5164	-2832
Swaziland	IMP	G	1039	1897	1918	1853	1665	1617	1710	1940	1946	...
Swaziland	EXP	G	903	1761	1779	1885	1681	1479	1557	1901	1897	...
	BAL		-137	-136	-139	33	16	-138	-153	-39	-49	...
Togo	IMP	S	562	1054	1091	1243	1499	1951	996	1800	1793	2108
Togo	EXP	S	362	659	634	700	901	811	641	1100	997	1048
	BAL		-200	-396	-457	-543	-598	-1140	-356	-700	-796	-1059
Uganda	IMP	G	1511	2049	2555	3497	4559	4265	4709	4565	5230	4927
Ouganda	EXP	G	469	1017	1188	2003	2717	3004	3115	2399	2861	2847
	BAL		-1043	-1033	-1367	-1494	-1841	-1261	-1594	-2166	-2369	-2080
United Rep. of Tanzania	IMP	G	1523	3292	4246	5337	7081	6296	7708	10702	11266	12235
Rép.-Unie de Tanzanie	EXP	G	663	1676	1736	2022	2674	2367	3522	4392	5075	5043
	BAL		-860	-1616	-2510	-3315	-4407	-3929	-4186	-6310	-6191	-7191
Zambia	IMP	S	997	2564	3086	4033	5017	3827	5319	7173	8000	10165
Zambie	EXP	S	681	1791	3828	4641	5187	4389	7207	9009	8550	10596
	BAL		-316	-773	742	608	170	562	1888	1837	550	431
Zimbabwe	IMP	G	1861	2350	2300	2550	2950	2900	3800	4400	4400	4300
Zimbabwe	EXP	G	1923	1850	2000	2400	2200	2269	3199	3512	3800	3552
	BAL		62	-500	-300	-150	-750	-631	-601	-888	-600	-748
Latin America & The Caribbean	IMP		376134	515014	614285	733270	896727	673642	863947	1048258	1077119	1117487
Amérique latine et les Caraïbes	EXP		355954	560598	670245	759828	888668	680162	865537	1074384	1086531	1091259
	BAL		-20181	45583	55961	26557	-8059	6520	1590	26126	9412	-26228
The Caribbean	IMP		26914	37591	44074	50404	61394	48543	50664	57049	56360	53457
Les Caraïbes	EXP		11431	17520	23738	24777	30405	19530	22021	29618	29994	31613
	BAL		-15483	-20071	-20336	-25628	-30990	-29013	-28643	-27431	-26366	-21844
Anguilla	IMP	S	99	133	143	248	272	169	157	153	150	145
Anguilla	EXP	S	4	7	13	9	11	23	12	16	8	4
	BAL		-95	-126	-130	-239	-260	-146	-145	-137	-142	-141
Antigua and Barbuda	IMP	G	338	526	671	727	806	699	501	471	535	515
Antigua-et-Barbuda	EXP	G	42	121	164	174	92	206	35	29	29	32
	BAL		-296	-405	-507	-553	-713	-493	-466	-442	-506	-483
Aruba	IMP	S	835	1028	1041	1114	1134	1149	1069	1283	1258	1303
Aruba	EXP	S	173	102	109	98	100	136	125	151	173	167
	BAL		-662	-927	-932	-1016	-1034	-1013	-945	-1132	-1085	-1136
Bahamas[11]	IMP	G	2074	2230	2401	2449	2354	2699	2863	3411	3658	3276
Bahamas[11]	EXP	G	576	562	674	485	560	585	621	727	829	715
	BAL		-1498	-1668	-1726	-1965	-1794	-2114	-2241	-2684	-2829	-2561
Barbados	IMP	G	1156	1604	1586	1709	1879	1471	1562	1805	1806	1759
Barbade	EXP	G	272	359	385	419	445	369	429	465	570	463
	BAL		-884	-1245	-1201	-1291	-1433	-1102	-1133	-1340	-1236	-1296
Cayman Islands	IMP	G	693	1191	1048	1029	1078	893	828	911	910	929
Îles Caïmanes	EXP	G	4	52	17	21	15	19	13	22	20	30
	BAL		-689	-1138	-1032	-1008	-1064	-874	-815	-890	-890	-899

Total imports and exports by regions and countries or areas (Table A)
Imports CIF, exports FOB and balance: million U.S. dollars *[cont.]*
Importations et exportations totales par régions et pays ou zones (Tableau A)
Importations CIF, exportations FOB et balance : en millions de dollars E.-U. *[suite]*

Country or Area - Pays ou Zone	IMP EXP BAL	G/S	2000	2005	2006	2007	2008	2009	2010	2011	2012	2013
Cuba	IMP	S	3363	8130	10174	10889	14249	...	...	...	...	...
Cuba	EXP	S	1219	2159	2980	3998	3680	...	...	...	...	...
	BAL		-2144	-5972	-7194	-6892	-10570	...	...	...	...	...
Dominica	IMP	S	148	165	167	196	247	225	224	226	208	203
Dominique	EXP	S	54	41	42	38	40	34	37	29	36	38
	BAL		-95	-124	-124	-158	-207	-191	-187	-197	-173	-165
Dominican Republic[3,12]	IMP	G	6416	7207	8745	11289	14020	10057	12885	14522	14939	13876
République dominicaine[3,12]	EXP	G	966	1395	1931	2635	2394	1690	2536	3728	4129	4622
	BAL		-5450	-5811	-6814	-8654	-11626	-8367	-10349	-10795	-10810	-9254
Grenada	IMP	S	246	334	331	365	377	293	317	329	336	368
Grenade	EXP	S	78	28	25	33	30	29	24	28	35	33
	BAL		-168	-306	-305	-332	-347	-264	-293	-302	-301	-336
Haiti	IMP	G	1040	1449	1879	1681	2310	2121	3147	3018	3170	3397
Haïti	EXP	G	313	470	480	522	475	576	579	767	814	899
	BAL		-727	-979	-1399	-1159	-1835	-1546	-2568	-2251	-2356	-2498
Jamaica	IMP	G	3302	4458	5314	6394	7734	4860	5201	6489	6485	6200
Jamaïque	EXP	G	1295	1499	1874	2070	2542	1319	1331	1603	1709	1574
	BAL		-2007	-2959	-3440	-4324	-5192	-3540	-3870	-4886	-4776	-4626
Montserrat	IMP	S	...	30	30	30	38	30	29	33	35	40
Montserrat	EXP	S	...	1	1	3	4	3	1	2	2	2
	BAL		...	-28	-29	-27	-34	-26	-28	-31	-34	-38
Neth. Antilles[13]	IMP	S	2862	1950	2209	2549	3079	2607	2687	...	...	...
Antilles néer.[13]	EXP	S	2009	608	695	676	1088	810	811	...	...	...
	BAL		-853	-1342	-1515	-1872	-1991	-1797	-1876	...	...	...
Saint Kitts-Nevis	IMP	S	196	210	250	272	325	302	228	248	226	249
Saint-Kitts-et-Nevis	EXP	S	29	30	35	32	43	43	45	34	50	50
	BAL		-167	-180	-214	-241	-282	-260	-183	-214	-176	-199
Saint Lucia	IMP	S	355	479	592	635	657	539	601	670	683	598
Sainte-Lucie	EXP	S	47	89	98	107	145	163	228	256	156	171
	BAL		-308	-390	-494	-528	-512	-376	-373	-414	-527	-427
Saint Vincent-Grenadines	IMP	S	148	241	269	327	373	334	345	332	357	378
St.Vincent-Grenadines	EXP	S	50	40	38	48	52	50	44	39	44	48
	BAL		-97	-201	-231	-279	-321	-284	-301	-293	-314	-330
Trinidad and Tobago	IMP	S	3308	5694	6484	7662	9596	6953	6483	9976	9400	8799
Trinité-et-Tobago	EXP	S	4274	9941	14159	13393	18663	9140	10188	14842	13100	12700
	BAL		966	4247	7675	5731	9067	2187	3705	4866	3700	3902
Turks and Caicos Islands	IMP	G	149	304	498	581	591	375	302	...	...	...
Îles Turques et Caïques	EXP	G	9	15	18	16	25	21	16	...	...	...
	BAL		-140	-289	-480	-564	-566	-355	-286	...	...	...
Latin America	IMP		**349220**	**477423**	**570211**	**682866**	**835333**	**625098**	**813283**	**991209**	**1020759**	**1064030**
Amérique latine	EXP		**344523**	**543078**	**646507**	**735051**	**858264**	**660632**	**843516**	**1044765**	**1056537**	**1059646**
	BAL		**-4698**	**65655**	**76296**	**52185**	**22931**	**35533**	**30234**	**53556**	**35778**	**-4384**
Argentina	IMP	S	25154	28693	34158	44707	57413	39105	56443	74319	68507	74002
Argentine	EXP	S	26341	40351	46568	55779	70588	56065	68500	84269	75219	83026
	BAL		1187	11658	12410	11072	13175	16961	12057	9950	6711	9024
Belize	IMP	G	524	593	676	684	837	669	709	831	882	930
Belize	EXP	G	218	208	266	254	290	224	280	340	340	315
	BAL		-306	-385	-410	-430	-547	-445	-430	-491	-541	-616

Total imports and exports by regions and countries or areas (Table A)

Imports CIF, exports FOB and balance: million U.S. dollars *[cont.]*

Importations et exportations totales par régions et pays ou zones (Tableau A)

Importations CIF, exportations FOB et balance : en millions de dollars E.-U. *[suite]*

Country or Area - Pays ou Zone	IMP EXP BAL	G/S	2000	2005	2006	2007	2008	2009	2010	2011	2012	2013
Bolivia (Plurinational State of)	IMP	G	1830	2341	2814	3457	5081	4434	5182	7551	8109	9221
Bolivie (État plurinational de)	EXP	G	1230	2791	3875	4458	7058	4918	6179	8107	10312	11189
	BAL		-600	450	1060	1001	1977	483	998	555	2203	1967
Brazil	IMP	G	58643	77628	95838	126645	182377	133673	191537	236946	228377	244677
Brésil	EXP	G	55119	118529	137807	160649	197942	152995	201915	256040	242580	242179
	BAL		-3524	40901	41969	34004	15565	19322	10378	19094	14203	-2498
Chile	IMP	S	18507	32735	38406	47164	61903	41364	57928	73545	79080	80443
Chili	EXP	S	19210	41267	58680	67666	66456	51963	68996	80027	79712	77877
	BAL		703	8532	20274	20502	4553	10599	11068	6482	632	-2566
Colombia	IMP	G	11539	21204	26046	33164	39320	32898	40683	54675	58633	59397
Colombie	EXP	G	13043	21146	24388	29786	38265	32784	39710	56507	59573	58657
	BAL		1505	-59	-1658	-3378	-1055	-114	-973	1832	941	-740
Costa Rica	IMP	S	6389	9812	11520	12957	15366	11460	13557	16218	17513	17923
Costa Rica	EXP	S	5850	7026	8216	9376	9575	8711	9343	10238	11151	11542
	BAL		-539	-2786	-3305	-3582	-5791	-2750	-4214	-5980	-6362	-6381
Ecuador	IMP	G	3721	10287	12114	13565	18852	15090	20591	24286	25304	27065
Equateur	EXP	G	4927	10100	12728	13852	18818	13863	17415	22345	23765	24958
	BAL		1206	-187	615	287	-34	-1227	-3176	-1941	-1539	-2107
El Salvador	IMP	S	4948	6834	7628	8677	9754	7255	8548	10118	10270	10772
El Salvador	EXP	S	2941	3387	3513	3977	4579	3797	4472	4979	5340	5491
	BAL		-2006	-3448	-4115	-4700	-5175	-3457	-4077	-5139	-4929	-5281
Guatemala	IMP	S	5171	8810	10157	11861	12835	10066	12051	14518	14873	14368
Guatemala	EXP	S	2711	3477	3665	4489	5412	3835	5907	7201	7139	6975
	BAL		-2460	-5333	-6492	-7371	-7423	-6232	-6145	-7317	-7734	-7392
Guyana	IMP	S	582	788	889	1059	1312	1161	1397	1763	1997	1750
Guyana	EXP	S	502	553	588	679	795	763	880	1116	1415	1380
	BAL		-80	-235	-301	-381	-518	-398	-517	-647	-581	-370
Honduras	IMP	S	2980	4853	5695	6762	8831	6133	7079	8953	9464	9169
Honduras	EXP	S	1297	1892	2054	2120	2883	2304	2712	3892	4427	3923
	BAL		-1682	-2960	-3641	-4642	-5948	-3829	-4367	-5060	-5037	-5246
Mexico[3,14]	IMP	G	174500	221414	256130	283264	310561	234385	301482	350856	370746	381202
Mexique[3,14]	EXP	G	166368	213891	250441	272055	291827	229683	298138	349569	370889	380107
	BAL		-8132	-7523	-5689	-11209	-18734	-4702	-3344	-1287	143	-1095
Nicaragua	IMP	G	1805	2595	3000	3579	4300	3438	4229	5180	5847	5647
Nicaragua	EXP	G	643	858	1027	1194	1473	1393	1845	2294	2644	2408
	BAL		-1163	-1737	-1973	-2385	-2827	-2045	-2384	-2886	-3204	-3239
Panama	IMP	S	3379	4180	4831	6872	9050	7801	9145	11342	12633	...
Panama	EXP	S	859	1018	1093	1164	1247	948	832	785	...	...
	BAL		-2519	-3162	-3738	-5709	-7803	-6853	-8313	-10556	...	...
Paraguay	IMP	S	2193	3790	6090	5859	9033	6940	10040	12317	11502	12142
Paraguay	EXP	S	2200	3153	3472	4724	6407	5080	6517	7776	7282	9432
	BAL		7	-637	-2618	-1136	-2626	-1860	-3524	-4540	-4220	-2710
Peru[3]	IMP	S	7407	12084	14897	19580	28373	21006	28818	37112	41089	42199
Pérou[3]	EXP	S	6955	17368	23830	27882	31529	26885	35565	46118	45600	41484
	BAL		-452	5284	8933	8301	3157	5879	6747	9005	4510	-715
Suriname	IMP	G	243	829	894	1111	1518	1356	1380	1667	1755	2300
Suriname	EXP	G	395	789	1123	1287	1668	1393	1851	2345	2525	2550
	BAL		152	-40	229	177	149	37	471	677	769	250

Total imports and exports by regions and countries or areas (Table A)

Imports CIF, exports FOB and balance: million U.S. dollars [cont.]

Importations et exportations totales par régions et pays ou zones (Tableau A)

Importations CIF, exportations FOB et balance : en millions de dollars E.-U. [suite]

Country or Area - Pays ou Zone	IMP EXP BAL	G/S	2000	2005	2006	2007	2008	2009	2010	2011	2012	2013
Uruguay	IMP	G	3466	3879	4757	5726	8943	6209	8619	10623	10642	10990
Uruguay	EXP	G	2295	3405	3953	4485	6421	5417	6707	7997	8601	8844
	BAL		-1171	-474	-804	-1241	-2523	-792	-1912	-2626	-2041	-2146
Venezuela (Bolivarian Rep.	IMP	G	16213	24027	33616	46097	49602	40597	33815	38346	43501	46363
Venezuela (Rép. bolivarienne	EXP	G	31413	51859	59208	69165	95021	57603	65745	92811	97340	86700
	BAL		15200	27832	25592	23068	45419	17006	31930	54465	53840	40337
Eastern Asia	IMP		**742209**	**1416437**	**1646399**	**1909513**	**2206817**	**1857749**	**2516769**	**3048707**	**3130269**	**3278260**
Asie Orientale	EXP		**774892**	**1537821**	**1840231**	**2185425**	**2473784**	**2091251**	**2714089**	**3197937**	**3346975**	**3540657**
	BAL		**32683**	**121383**	**193831**	**275912**	**266968**	**233502**	**197320**	**149231**	**216705**	**262396**
China	IMP	S	225024	660206	791797	956233	1131620	1004170	1396200	1742850	1817780	1950380
Chine	EXP	S	249203	761953	969380	1217790	1428660	1201790	1578270	1899180	2048940	2210250
	BAL		24179	101747	177583	261557	297040	197620	182070	156330	231160	259870
China, Hong Kong SAR	IMP	G	212805	299533	334681	367647	388505	347311	433111	483633	504405	523558
Chine, Hong Kong RAS	EXP	G	201860	289337	316816	344509	362675	318510	390143	428732	442799	458959
	BAL		-10945	-10196	-17865	-23138	-25830	-28801	-42968	-54901	-61606	-64599
China, Macao SAR	IMP	G	2255	3913	4565	5366	5365	4622	5513	7769	8877	10141
Chine, Macao RAS	EXP	G	2539	2476	2557	2543	1997	961	870	869	1021	1138
	BAL		284	-1438	-2008	-2823	-3368	-3661	-4643	-6899	-7856	-9002
Korea, Republic of	IMP	G	160479	267559	309350	356852	435275	323085	425212	524418	519569	515561
Corée, République de	EXP	G	172272	284422	325468	371492	422007	363534	466384	555216	547879	559649
	BAL		11793	16863	16118	14640	-13268	40449	41172	30798	28310	44088
Mongolia	IMP	G	615	1184	1486	2117	3616	2131	3278	6527	6739	6355
Mongolie	EXP	G	536	1065	1543	1889	2539	1903	2899	4780	4385	4273
	BAL		-79	-119	57	-228	-1077	-229	-379	-1747	-2354	-2082
Southern Asia	IMP		94740	235858	280721	343079	465685	379522	505562	639137	657587	625785
Asie Méridionale	EXP		91012	187109	233539	271120	350844	282591	373616	491233	452037	461321
	BAL		-3728	-48750	-47181	-71959	-114841	-96931	-131946	-147904	-205551	-164464
Afghanistan	IMP	G	1176	2471	2582	2819	3020	3336	5154	6390	6200	5400
Afghanistan	EXP	G	137	384	408	497	540	403	388	376	350	500
	BAL		-1039	-2087	-2174	-2322	-2480	-2933	-4766	-6014	-5850	-4900
Bangladesh	IMP	G	8358	12881	14964	17263	22473	20631	26071	33978	34133	33576
Bangladesh	EXP	G	4787	7233	9103	10233	11777	12443	14195	19807	25113	27033
	BAL		-3572	-5648	-5861	-7030	-10695	-8188	-11877	-14171	-9020	-6543
Bhutan	IMP	G	235	387	419	526	543	529	854	1052	990	1038
Bhoutan	EXP	G	127	258	414	675	520	495	641	678	535	528
	BAL		-108	-129	-5	148	-23	-34	-213	-374	-455	-510
India[15]	IMP	G	51563	142865	178485	229349	321025	257200	350192	464507	489689	466033
Inde[15]	EXP	G	42378	99618	121812	150160	194816	164912	226334	302892	296827	314656
	BAL		-9185	-43247	-56674	-79189	-126210	-92288	-123858	-161615	-192863	-151377
Iran (Islamic Rep. of)[16,17]	IMP	S	14347	40041	40772	45000	57401	50768	65404	61760	56500	49000
Iran (Rép. islamique d')[16,17]	EXP	S	28345	56252	77012	83000	113668	78830	101316	130500	95500	82000
	BAL		13998	16211	36240	38000	56267	28062	35912	68740	39000	33000
Maldives	IMP	G	389	742	923	1092	1382	963	1091	1465	1554	1733
Maldives	EXP	G	76	104	135	108	126	76	74	127	162	167
	BAL		-313	-638	-788	-984	-1256	-886	-1017	-1338	-1393	-1567
Nepal	IMP	G	1526	2282	2488	3139	3562	4398	5501	5762	6499	6385
Népal	EXP	G	700	863	838	870	937	823	951	917	960	920
	BAL		-826	-1419	-1650	-2269	-2625	-3574	-4550	-4845	-5539	-5465

Total imports and exports by regions and countries or areas (Table A)

Imports CIF, exports FOB and balance: million U.S. dollars *[cont.]*

Importations et exportations totales par régions et pays ou zones (Tableau A)

Importations CIF, exportations FOB et balance : en millions de dollars E.-U. *[suite]*

Country or Area - Pays ou Zone	IMP EXP BAL	G/S	2000	2005	2006	2007	2008	2009	2010	2011	2012	2013
Pakistan	IMP	G	10864	25356	29828	32590	42327	31648	37783	43955	42920	44647
Pakistan	EXP	G	9028	16050	16932	17838	20323	17523	21410	25383	22807	25121
	BAL		-1836	-9306	-12896	-14752	-22003	-14125	-16373	-18572	-20114	-19526
Sri Lanka	IMP	G	6281	8833	10259	11301	13953	10049	13512	20268	19102	17973
Sri Lanka	EXP	G	5433	6347	6886	7740	8137	7085	8307	10553	9784	10397
	BAL		-848	-2487	-3373	-3560	-5816	-2965	-5205	-9715	-9318	-7576
South-eastern Asia	IMP		379470	599981	687700	774039	939039	728238	955444	**1150886**	1225406	**1242370**
Asie du Sud-est	EXP		429596	654491	770652	865146	988287	813295	1051891	**1238302**	1252687	**1271080**
	BAL		50126	54510	82952	91106	49248	85057	96447	**87416**	27281	**28709**
Brunei Darussalam	IMP	S	1107	1447	1679	2101	2572	2449	3365	...	3563	...
Brunéi Darussalam	EXP	S	3907	6242	7634	7693	10322	7200	9172	...	12982	...
	BAL		2801	4794	5956	5592	7750	4751	5808	...	9418	...
Cambodia	IMP	S	1424	3927	4749	5300	6508	5830	6791	9300	11000	13000
Cambodge	EXP	S	1123	3200	3800	4400	4708	4196	5143	6950	8200	9100
	BAL		-302	-727	-949	-900	-1800	-1634	-1648	-2350	-2800	-3900
Indonesia	IMP	S	43075	75725	80650	93101	127538	93786	135323	176881	190992	186351
Indonésie	EXP	S	65404	86995	103528	118014	139606	119646	158074	200587	188516	182659
	BAL		22329	11270	22878	24913	12068	25860	22751	23706	-2476	-3692
Lao P.Dem.R.	IMP	S	535	882	1060	1067	1405	1461	2060	2398	2700	2900
Rép. dém. populaire lao	EXP	S	330	553	882	842	1085	1053	1746	2216	2400	2600
	BAL		-205	-329	-177	-225	-320	-408	-314	-182	-300	-300
Malaysia	IMP	G	81963	114410	131085	146171	156348	123757	164622	187473	196393	206015
Malaisie	EXP	G	98229	140870	160571	175966	199414	157244	198612	228086	227538	228277
	BAL		16266	26459	29486	29795	43066	33487	33990	40613	31145	22262
Myanmar	IMP	G	2371	1908	2538	3247	4256	4348	4760	9019	9181	11600
Myanmar	EXP	G	1620	3776	4539	6253	6882	6662	8661	9238	8877	10300
	BAL		-751	1868	2001	3006	2626	2314	3901	219	-304	-1300
Philippines	IMP	G	36887	46963	54077	57708	60491	45856	58533	64097	65845	65048
Philippines	EXP	G	37767	41255	47427	50518	49462	38421	51541	48316	52071	53882
	BAL		880	-5708	-6651	-7190	-11030	-7436	-6992	-15781	-13773	-11166
Singapore	IMP	G	134546	200050	238711	263155	319781	245785	310791	365770	379723	373016
Singapour	EXP	G	137806	229652	271809	299270	338176	269832	351867	409503	408393	410250
	BAL		3259	29602	33098	36115	18396	24048	41076	43733	28670	37234
Thailand	IMP	S	61923	118158	128654	141294	179168	134734	185121	228845	250238	248748
Thaïlande	EXP	S	68963	110178	130795	153858	175897	151910	195373	226412	228175	225087
	BAL		7039	-7980	2142	12563	-3270	17176	10252	-2433	-22062	-23661
Timor-Leste	IMP	S		102	88	199	258	283	298	337	670	844
Timor-Leste	EXP	S		43	61	19	49	35	42	53	77	51
	BAL		.	-58	-27	-180	-209	-248	-256	-283	-593	-793
Viet Nam	IMP	G	15638	36408	44410	60697	80714	69949	83779	104041	115101	131260
Viet Nam	EXP	G	14447	31726	39606	48313	62685	57096	71658	94518	115458	132478
	BAL		-1191	-4682	-4804	-12384	-18029	-12853	-12121	-9523	357	1218
Western Asia	IMP		**198063**	**410471**	**479796**	**606001**	757727	609815	710884	864243	915190	972638
Asie Occidentale	EXP		**261901**	**554227**	**655780**	**742941**	1052398	737247	921030	1254949	1345894	1399901
	BAL		**63838**	**143756**	**175984**	**136939**	294670	127431	210146	390706	430704	427263
Bahrain	IMP	G	4633	9393	10515	11488	10800	7300	9800	12730	14900	13000
Bahreïn	EXP	G	6194	10242	12200	13634	17316	11874	15400	19650	20500	17500
	BAL		1561	849	1685	2146	6516	4574	5600	6920	5600	4500

Total imports and exports by regions and countries or areas (Table A)

Imports CIF, exports FOB and balance: million U.S. dollars *[cont.]*

Importations et exportations totales par régions et pays ou zones (Tableau A)

Importations CIF, exportations FOB et balance : en millions de dollars E.-U. *[suite]*

Country or Area - Pays ou Zone	IMP EXP BAL	G/ S	2000	2005	2006	2007	2008	2009	2010	2011	2012	2013
Cyprus	IMP	G	3846	6282	6951	8687	10873	7882	8646	8723	7381	6388
Chypre	EXP	G	951	1303	1153	1254	1755	1342	1507	1960	1829	2075
	BAL		-2895	-4979	-5798	-7433	-9118	-6540	-7139	-6763	-5552	-4313
Iraq	IMP		...	...	...	...	33000	37000	43915	49000	57000	61000
Iraq	EXP		...	...	...	...	61273	41929	52483	83300	94400	89550
	BAL		...	...	...	...	28273	4929	8567	34300	37400	28550
Israel[18]	IMP	S	31404	47142	50334	59039	67656	49278	61209	75830	75392	74868
Israël[18]	EXP	S	31404	42770	46789	54065	60825	47934	58392	67648	63191	66607
	BAL		0	-4371	-3544	-4973	-6831	-1344	-2817	-8182	-12201	-8260
Jordan	IMP	G	4597	10506	11447	13511	16764	14534	15085	18463	20691	21701
Jordanie	EXP	G	1899	4302	5175	5725	7788	6531	7023	7964	7926	7896
	BAL		-2698	-6204	-6272	-7786	-8976	-8002	-8062	-10499	-12765	-13804
Kuwait	IMP	S	7157	15801	17243	21353	24840	19891	22691	25144	27259	29644
Koweït	EXP	S	19434	44869	55081	61483	85741	50321	61701	101769	113260	112849
	BAL		12278	29068	37838	40130	60901	30430	39009	76625	86001	83204
Lebanon	IMP	G	6230	9633	9647	12251	16754	16574	18460	20165	21287	21236
Liban	EXP	G	715	2337	2814	3574	4454	4187	5021	4267	4485	4059
	BAL		-5515	-7296	-6833	-8677	-12300	-12387	-13439	-15898	-16802	-17176
Oman	IMP	G	5040	8827	10915	15978	22925	17865	19775	23620	29447	34333
Oman	EXP	G	11319	18692	21585	24136	37719	28053	36601	47092	53174	56429
	BAL		6279	9865	10670	8158	14795	10188	16827	23472	23727	22096
Qatar	IMP	S	3252	10061	16441	23430	27900	24922	23240	22333	25223	27038
Qatar	EXP	S	11594	25763	34052	44456	67307	48007	74800	114448	132985	136855
	BAL		8342	15702	17611	21027	39407	23085	51560	92115	107761	109817
Saudi Arabia	IMP	S	30197	59458	69800	90215	115133	95544	106864	131587	155592	163902
Arabie saoudite	EXP	S	77480	180736	211306	233300	313427	192296	251147	364699	388400	375934
	BAL		47283	121278	141506	143086	198294	96752	144283	233112	232808	212032
State of Palestine	IMP	S	2383	2668	2759	3284	3466	3601	3959	4374	4697	4580
État de Palestine	EXP	S	401	335	367	513	558	518	576	746	782	839
	BAL		-1982	-2332	-2392	-2771	-2908	-3082	-3383	-3628	-3915	-3740
Syrian Arab Rep.	IMP	S	4055	10862	11488	14655	18105	15291	16950	16400	7800	5800
République arabe syrienne	EXP	S	4674	8708	10919	11546	15410	10855	14000	10700	4000	3000
	BAL		620	-2154	-569	-3109	-2695	-4436	-2950	-5700	-3800	-2800
Turkey	IMP	S	54503	116774	139576	170063	201964	140928	185544	240842	236545	251650
Turquie	EXP	S	27775	73476	85535	107272	132027	102143	113883	134907	152462	151807
	BAL		-26728	-43298	-54041	-62791	-69937	-38785	-71661	-105935	-84083	-99843
United Arab Emirates	IMP	G	35009	84654	100057	132500	177000	150000	165000	205000	220000	245000
Emirats arabes unis	EXP	G	49835	117287	142505	154000	239213	185000	220000	285000	300000	365000
	BAL		14827	32633	42448	21500	62213	35000	55000	80000	80000	120000
Yemen	IMP	S	2327	5401	6081	8513	10548	9206	9746	10034	11975	12500
Yémen	EXP	S	3795	5604	6653	6299	7584	6256	8497	10801	8500	9500
	BAL		1469	204	572	-2215	-2964	-2949	-1249	766	-3475	-3000
Oceania	IMP		**6924**	**11059**	**12507**	**14592**	**16803**	**14386**	**16625**	**19084**	**19494**	**21775**
Océanie	EXP		**5111**	**7252**	**8551**	**10002**	**10619**	**8495**	**10461**	**12289**	**11609**	**10974**
	BAL		**-1813**	**-3807**	**-3956**	**-4589**	**-6184**	**-5891**	**-6164**	**-6796**	**-7885**	**-10801**
American Samoa[19]	IMP	S	506	520	579	650	680	600	550	700	690	...
Samoa américaines[19]	EXP	S	346	374	439	450	570	470	300	280	300	...
	BAL		-160	-146	-141	-200	-110	-130	-250	-420	-390	...

Total imports and exports by regions and countries or areas (Table A)
Imports CIF, exports FOB and balance: million U.S. dollars *[cont.]*

Importations et exportations totales par régions et pays ou zones (Tableau A)
Importations CIF, exportations FOB et balance : en millions de dollars E.-U. *[suite]*

Country or Area - Pays ou Zone	IMP EXP BAL	G/S	2000	2005	2006	2007	2008	2009	2010	2011	2012	2013
Cook Islands	IMP	G	50	81	100	107	111	72	81	84	90	150
Iles Cook	EXP	G	9	5	3	5	4	3	5	3	5	6
	BAL		-41	-76	-96	-102	-107	-69	-76	-81	-85	-145
Fiji	IMP	G	857	1607	1804	1801	2265	1441	1817	2182	2254	2822
Fidji	EXP	G	539	705	693	755	922	631	842	1070	1224	1107
	BAL		-318	-903	-1111	-1046	-1343	-811	-975	-1112	-1030	-1715
French Polynesia	IMP	S	905	1723	1656	1863	2187	1732	1740	1796	1706	1801
Polynésie française	EXP	S	200	217	235	197	195	148	153	168	139	152
	BAL		-705	-1506	-1420	-1667	-1991	-1584	-1587	-1628	-1567	-1649
Guam	IMP	G	...	...	501	688	649	635	698	708	693	687
Guam	EXP	G	...	52	53	91	105	51	46	55	46	45
	BAL		...	...	-448	-596	-544	-584	-652	-653	-647	-642
Kiribati	IMP	G	39	74	62	70	75	67	73	92	100	112
Kiribati	EXP	G	4	4	6	10	8	6	4	9	6	8
	BAL		-36	-70	-56	-60	-68	-61	-69	-83	-94	-105
Marshall Islands	IMP	G	55	68	...	...	...	...	...	...	...	...
Iles Marshall	EXP	G	9	...	...	...	...	...	...	...	...	...
	BAL		-46	...	...	...	...	...	...	...	...	...
New Caledonia	IMP	S	922	1774	2117	2809	3233	2574	3312	3698	3245	3240
Nouvelle-Calédonie	EXP	S	606	1090	1349	2104	1300	993	1493	1661	1321	1196
	BAL		-317	-684	-768	-705	-1933	-1581	-1820	-2037	-1923	-2044
Niue	IMP	G	2	...	4	7	8	6	...	...	...	...
Nioué	EXP	G	0	0	1	3	0	...	...	...	...	...
	BAL		-2	...	-2	-4	-8	...	...	...	...	...
Palau	IMP	S	123	...	...	108	130	94	103	125	136	145
Palaos	EXP	S	...	...	...	...	...	...	...	...	...	...
	BAL		...	...	...	...	...	...	...	...	...	...
Papua New Guinea	IMP	G	1151	1728	2287	2945	3547	3198	3950	4887	5500	...
Papouasie-Nouvelle-Guinée	EXP	G	2068	3276	4167	4684	5714	4404	5742	6908	6328	5951
	BAL		917	1548	1880	1738	2167	1206	1792	2021	828	...
Samoa	IMP	S	90	187	219	227	249	204	278	319	308	326
Samoa	EXP	S	14	12	11	15	11	12	13	17	34	24
	BAL		-76	-175	-208	-212	-238	-193	-264	-302	-274	-302
Solomon Islands	IMP	S	92	185	217	287	329	270	300	474	500	530
Iles Salomon	EXP	S	69	103	121	165	210	163	221	411	470	440
	BAL		-23	-82	-95	-123	-119	-107	-79	-64	-30	-90
Tonga	IMP	G	69	120	116	143	168	145	159	193	199	210
Tonga	EXP	G	9	10	10	9	9	8	8	14	14	15
	BAL		-60	-110	-107	-134	-158	-137	-151	-179	-185	-195
Tuvalu	IMP	G	5	13	13	16	...	...	...	...	...	...
Tuvalu	EXP	G	0	0	0	0	...	...	...	...	...	...
	BAL		-5	-13	-13	-16	...	...	...	...	...	...
Vanuatu	IMP	G	87	149	217	231	314	294	284	305	290	311
Vanuatu	EXP	G	26	38	49	50	57	58	48	67	55	39
	BAL		-61	-111	-168	-180	-257	-236	-236	-238	-236	-273
Non Petrol. Export[20]	IMP		...	...	...	...	...	...	...	...	...	...
Pétrole N. Compris[20]	EXP		**102397**	**73931**	**68523**	**63510**	**58864**	**54558**	**50567**	**46868**	**43440**	**40262**
	BAL		...	...	...	...	...	...	...	...	...	...

Total imports and exports by regions and countries or areas (Table A)

Imports CIF, exports FOB and balance: million U.S. dollars *[cont.]*

Importations et exportations totales par régions et pays ou zones (Tableau A)

Importations CIF, exportations FOB et balance : en millions de dollars E.-U. *[suite]*

Country or Area - Pays ou Zone	IMP EXP BAL	G/S	2000	2005	2006	2007	2008	2009	2010	2011	2012	2013
Additional Country Groupings												
ANCOM[21]	IMP		24496	45917	55871	69767	91626	73428	95273	123624	133135	137882
ANCOM[21]	EXP		26154	51405	64821	75978	95671	78449	98869	133077	139249	136287
	BAL		1658	5488	8950	6212	4045	5021	3596	9452	6114	-1595
APEC	IMP		3312192	5086450	5781474	6434905	7369438	5700654	7356580	**8786456**	9108189	**9204848**
CEAP	EXP		3110918	4682138	5442282	6209945	7050851	5632969	7232236	**8474500**	8694901	**8862202**
	BAL		-201274	-404312	-339192	-224960	-318587	-67685	-124344	**-311956**	-413288	**-342646**
ASEAN	IMP		379470	599879	687612	773840	938780	727955	955146	**1150549**	1224736	**1241526**
ANASE	EXP		429596	654447	770591	865127	988238	813260	1051849	**1238249**	1252610	**1271028**
	BAL		50126	54568	82979	91287	49457	85305	96704	**87700**	27874	**29502**
CACM	IMP		21293	32904	37999	43836	51085	38353	45464	54987	57967	57879
MCAC	EXP		13442	16640	18475	21156	23921	20040	24279	28604	30701	30340
	BAL		-7850	-16264	-19524	-22680	-27164	-18313	-21186	-26383	-27266	-27539
CARICOM	IMP		**13681**	19630	22432	25302	30362	23710	24987	31270	31532	30762
CARICOM	EXP		**8146**	14732	19953	19543	25844	14895	16573	22622	21652	20970
	BAL		**-5535**	-4899	-2479	-5759	-4518	-8815	-8414	-8648	-9880	-9792
COMESA	IMP		**34753**	**62257**	**69328**	**82905**	**119508**	**112095**	**127574**	**139065**	**168263**	**166749**
COMESA	EXP		**27005**	**63659**	**79804**	**95999**	**128477**	**94201**	**117055**	**96696**	**131338**	**121452**
	BAL		**-7749**	**1402**	**10476**	**13094**	**8969**	**-17894**	**-10519**	**-42369**	**-36925**	**-45297**
ECOWAS	IMP		**20021**	43804	51861	68256	81045	66441	81958	110640	87856	101142
CEDEA	EXP		**29437**	71790	76625	86193	106386	80893	111531	**151221**	150609	**153922**
	BAL		**9416**	27986	24764	17937	25341	14452	29573	**40581**	62753	**52779**
EMCCA	IMP		4010	7976	10531	13392	17263	17589	19249	24354	24794	26630
CEMAC	EXP		8414	22948	26836	29598	42636	26767	34252	44112	42684	42135
	BAL		4404	14972	16305	16206	25373	9177	15002	19758	17890	15504
LAIA	IMP		329913	450393	539871	646990	794758	**595975**	775203	**941479**	966493	**1008468**
ALAI	EXP		331178	527036	629024	715662	835258	**642519**	821164	**1018486**	1029157	**1034492**
	BAL		1265	76643	89153	68672	40500	**46544**	45961	**77007**	62664	**26024**
LDCs[21]	IMP		**41663**	**84879**	**101396**	**116779**	**151556**	**151663**	**166492**	**199223**	**217246**	**227763**
PMA[21]	EXP		**33176**	**80020**	**99459**	**125393**	**174190**	**123522**	**151996**	**195461**	**201225**	**211492**
	BAL		**-8487**	**-4859**	**-1937**	**8614**	**22634**	**-28141**	**-14496**	**-3762**	**-16021**	**-16271**
MERCOSUR	IMP		105669	138017	174459	229034	307369	226523	300454	372551	362529	388173
MERCOSUR	EXP		117368	217296	251009	294802	376379	277160	349383	448894	431021	430181
	BAL		11699	79279	76550	65768	69010	50637	48929	76343	68493	42008
NAFTA	IMP		1672611	2271040	2524469	2684365	2888878	2160932	2662781	3067992	3169689	3172187
ALENA	EXP		1224927	1475646	1664726	1840548	2035686	1599725	1964109	2281991	2371432	2417554
	BAL		-447684	-795394	-859743	-843816	-853191	-561207	-698672	-786001	-798257	-754633
OECD[21]	IMP		4914427	7536141	8566782	9653761	10834392	8140613	9601326	11286042	11063490	11087763
OCDE[21]	EXP		4535681	6781000	7683431	8783085	9793154	7636075	8954852	10419215	10222307	10371953
	BAL		-378746	-755140	-883350	-870677	-1041238	-504538	-646474	-866828	-841183	-715810
OPEC[21]	IMP		**137962**	**313446**	**371983**	**474666**	609344	539635	593064	694168	741771	798257
OPEP[21]	EXP		**298292**	**661452**	**793159**	**896334**	1288881	847176	1078846	1466850	1561550	**1561969**
	BAL		**160330**	**348005**	**421176**	**421669**	679536	307541	485782	772681	819780	**763711**
EU28	IMP		2441670	4065333	4695447	5458473	6126598	4602699	5190906	6070520	5705249	5786286
UE28	EXP		2394656	3976749	4523977	5253360	5832015	4519035	5064144	5930405	5681646	5874954
	BAL		-47013	-88584	-171470	-205113	-294583	-83664	-126763	-140115	-23603	88668

Total imports and exports by regions and countries or areas (Table A)
Imports CIF, exports FOB and balance: million U.S. dollars *[cont.]*

Importations et exportations totales par régions et pays ou zones (Tableau A)
Importations CIF, exportations FOB et balance : en millions de dollars E.-U. *[suite]*

Country or Area - Pays ou Zone	IMP EXP BAL	G/S	2000	2005	2006	2007	2008	2009	2010	2011	2012	2013
Extra-EU28[22,23]	IMP		913310	1470442	1714282	1985545	2336609	1721874	2029009	2405295	2311903	2234492
Extra-UE28[22,23]	EXP		781270	1303309	1448509	1694259	1928718	1527320	1791433	2161865	2162563	2305992
	BAL		-132040	-167132	-265774	-291287	-407891	-194554	-237576	-243430	-149340	71500
Memorandum Items												
World excluding intra-EU28 trade	IMP		4993176	8013784	9219044	10566201	12439382	9612673	12005066	14416517	14734640	14849659
Monde excl. le intra-UE28 com.	EXP		4743177	7681944	8897495	10232971	12105664	9410506	11826223	14260823	14549094	14890317
	BAL		-249999	-331841	-321548	-333230	-333718	-202167	-178843	-155694	-185546	40658
World excluding intra-EU28 trade as percent of World	IMP		77	76	76	75	77	77	79	80	81	81
Monde excl. le intra-UE28 com.comme pour cent du Monde	EXP		75	74	74	74	76	76	78	79	81	81

Total imports and exports by regions and countries or areas (Table A)
Imports CIF, exports FOB and balance: million U.S. dollars *[cont.]*

Importations et exportations totales par régions et pays ou zones (Tableau A)
Importations CIF, exportations FOB, et balance: en millions de dollars E.-U. *[suite]*

General note:

Table A is based on data as available at the end of November 2014. An earlier version of this table has been published in Volume I of the 2013 ITSY which has been produced earlier this year. The totals of imports and exports presented in world trade table A and D are not necessarily identical as table A is mainly based on data of the IMF's International Financial Statistics (IFS) which is a different data collection system with different aims, procedures, timetable and sources for update and maintenance than UN Comtrade on which table D is based (see the introduction for details). Nevertheless, discrepancies between both tables are in general minor and usually do not affect the overall information provided. A systematic comparison of the figures from both sources (which includes the description of known and relevant conceptual differences) is available at http://unstats.un.org/unsd/trade/imts/annual%20totals.htm. Overall, the discrepancies in the world total or world aggregate of exports in table A and table D is around 1.0 percent for all years shown, which is minor, given the differences between the two sources.

Column "G/S" indicates the trade system: G = General Trade System; S = Special Trade System. For further information on sources and presentation of table A as well as for a brief table description please see the introduction.

Remarque générale:

Tableau A est basé sur les données telles que disponible fin novembre 2014. Une version antérieure de ce tableau est publiée dans le volume I de l'annuaire 2013 ITSY qui a été produit plus tôt cette année. Les importations et exportations totales présentées dans les tableaux A et D ne sont pas nécessairement identiques du fait que le tableau A est basé principalement sur les données des Statistiques Financières Internationales (IFS) du FMI qui est un différent système de collecte des données avec des objectifs, des procédures, un calendrier et des sources de mise à jour et de maintenance différents de ceux de UN Comtrade sur lequel le tableau D est basé (voir l'introduction pour les détails). Toutefois, les écarts entre les deux tableaux sont en général mineurs et n'affectent pas substantiellement l'information fournie. Une comparaison systématique des données de ces deux sources (incluant une description des différences conceptuelles pertinentes connues) est disponible à http://unstats.un.org/unsd/trade/imts/annual%20totals.htm. En général, la différence entre les totaux des exportations mondiales présentés dans les tableaux A et D est d'environ 1,0 pour cent pour chacune des années publiées, ce qui est mineur étant donné les différences entre les deux sources.

La colonne "G/S" indique le système commercial : G=Système du Commerce Général ; S= Système du Commerce Spécial. Pour plus d'information sur les sources et la présentation du tableau A ainsi qu'une brève description, se il vous plaît se référer à l'introduction.

1	This classification is intended for statistical convenience and does not, necessarily, express a judgement about the stage reached by a particular country in the development process.
2	Developed Economies of America, Europe, and the Asia-Pacific region.
3	Imports FOB.
4	Including the trade of the U.S. Virgin Islands and Puerto Rico but excluding shipments of merchandise between the United States and its other possessions (Guam and American Samoa). Data include imports and exports of non-monetary gold.
5	Beginning 2006, data for Serbia and Montenegro is reported separately.
6	Prior to 2008, special trade.
7	Imports exclude petroleum imported without stated value. Exports cover domestic exports.
8	Year ending 31 March of the following year.
9	Exports include gold.
10	Including South Sudan.
11	Trade statistics exclude certain oil and chemical products.
12	Export and import values exclude trade in the processing zone.

1 Cette classification est utilisée pour plus de commodité dans la présentation des statistiques et n'implique pas nécessairement un jugement quant au stade de développement auquel est parvenu un pays donné.
2 Économies développées de l'Amérique, de l'Europe, et de la région Asie-Pacifique.
3 Importations FOB.
4 Y compris le commerce des Iles Vierges américaines et de Porto Rico mais non compris les échanges de marchandise, entre les Etats-Unis et leurs autres possessions (Guam et Samoa américaines). Les données comprennent les importations et exportations d'or non-monétaire.
5 Depuis début 2006, les données relatives à la Serbie et au Monténégro sont déclarées séparément.
6 Avant 2008, commerce special.
7 Non compris le pétrole brute dont la valeur des importations ne sont pas stipulée. Les exportations sont les exportations d'intérieur.
8 Année finissant le 31 mars de l'année suivante.
9 Les exportations comprennent l'or.
10 Y compris Soudan du Sud.
11 Les statistiques commerciales font exclusion de certains produits pétroliers et chimiques.
12 Les valeurs à l'exportation et à l'importation excluent le commerce de la zone de transformation.

Total imports and exports by regions and countries or areas (Table A)

Imports CIF, exports FOB and balance: million U.S. dollars *[cont.]*

Importations et exportations totales par régions et pays ou zones (Tableau A)

Importations CIF, exportations FOB, et balance: en millions de dollars E.-U. *[suite]*

13 The Netherlands Antilles was dissolved on October 10, 2010. Beginning 2011, data are reported separately for Curaçao, Sint Maarten (Dutch part), Bonaire, Saint Eustatius and Saba.

14 Trade data include maquiladoras and exclude goods from customs-bonded warehouses. Total exports include revaluation and exports of silver.

15 Excluding military goods, fissionable materials, bunkers, ships, and aircraft.

16 Data include oil and gas.The value of oil exports and total exports are rough estimates based on information published in various petroleum industry journals.

17 Year ending 20 March of the year stated.

18 Imports and exports net of returned goods. The figures also exclude Judea and Samaria and the Gaza area.

19 Year ending 30 September of the years stated.

20 Data refer to total exports less petroleum exports of Asia Middle East countries where petroleum, in this case, is the sum of SITC groups 333, 334 and 335.

21 The figures for the country groupings aim to always reflect the membership of the grouping of the latest year published.

22 Excluding intra-EU trade.

23 In the year 2000, the trade values refer to extra-EU27.

13 Les Antilles néerlandaises ont été dissoutes le 10 Octobre 2010. A partir de 2011, les données sont présentées séparément pour Curaçao, Saint-Martin (partie néerlandaise), Bonaire, Saint-Eustache et Saba.

14 Les statistiques du commerce extérieur comprennent maquiladoras et ne comprennent pas les marchandises provenant des entrepôts en douane. Les exportations comprennent la réévaluation et les données sur les exportations d'argent.

15 À l'exclusion des marchandises militaires, des matières fissibles, des soutes, des bateaux, et de l'avion.

16 Les données comprennent le pétrole et le gaz. La valeur des exportations de pétrole et des exportations totales sont des évaluations grossières basées sur l'information publiée à divers journaux d'industrie de pétrole.

17 Année finissant le 20 mars de l'année indiquée.

18 Importations et exportations nets, ne comprenant pas les marchandises retournées. Sont également exclues les données de la Judée et de Samaria et ainsi que la zone de Gaza.

19 Année finissant le 30 septembre de l'année indiquée.

20 Les données se rapportent aux exportations totales moins les exportations pétrolières de Moyen-Orient d'Asie. Dans ce cas, le pétrole est la somme des groupes CTCI 333, 334 et 335.

21 Les figures pour les regroupements de pays visent à toujours refléter la composition des regroupements de la dernière année publiée.

22 Non compris le commerce d'intra-UE.

23 En l'année 2000, les valeurs du commerce se réfèrent à extra-UE27.

Total imports and exports by countries and areas (Table B)

Imports CIF, exports FOB and balance: million of national currency

Importations et exportations totales par pays ou zone (Tableau B)

Importations CIF, exportations FOB et balance : en millions de monnaie nationale

Country or Area - Pays ou Zone	IMP EXP BAL	G/ S	2000	2005	2006	2007	2008	2009	2010	2011	2012	2013
Albania	IMP	G	157218	262080	299134	376194	439894	431107	458430	544004	528492	517311
Albanie	EXP	G	37547	65766	78122	97171	112572	103244	160961	196896	213030	246389
leks	BAL		-119671	-196314	-221012	-279023	-327322	-327863	-297469	-347108	-315462	-270922
Algeria	IMP	S	690426	1493640	1525940	1903390	2549100	2857890	2991940	3446050	3906680	4358250
Algérie	EXP	S	1657220	3421550	3837340	4128640	5108650	3286510	4297730	5371280	5631780	5198500
dinars	BAL		966794	1927910	2311400	2225250	2559550	428620	1305790	1925230	1725100	840250
Andorra	IMP	S	1111	1442	1417	1396	1314	1138	1143	1149	1086	1094
Andorre	EXP	S	49	114	120	93	65	46	41	55	53	74
euros	BAL		-1062	-1328	-1297	-1304	-1248	-1093	-1102	-1094	-1032	-1019
Anguilla[1]	IMP	S	269	360	386	669	734	456	425	414	405	391
Anguilla[1]	EXP	S	12	20	36	25	31	62	34	44	22	10
EC dollars	BAL		-257	-340	-350	-645	-703	-394	-391	-370	-382	-381
Australia	IMP	G	123461	164137	184750	196756	236528	208834	219177	236109	251966	251101
Australie	EXP	G	110464	138716	163551	168067	222364	196091	230820	263000	248002	262308
dollars	BAL		-12997	-25421	-21199	-28689	-14164	-12743	11643	26891	-3964	11207
Austria	IMP	S	74935	96499	104201	114255	119567	97573	113652	131008	131982	129962
Autriche	EXP	S	69692	94705	103742	114680	117527	93739	109373	121774	123544	125412
euros	BAL		-5243	-1794	-459	425	-2040	-3834	-4279	-9234	-8438	-4550
Bahamas[2]	IMP	G	2074	2230	2401	2449	2354	2699	2863	3411	3658	3276
Bahamas[2]	EXP	G	576	562	674	485	560	585	621	727	829	715
dollars	BAL		-1498	-1668	-1726	-1965	-1794	-2114	-2241	-2684	-2829	-2561
Bangladesh	IMP	G	436450	828667	1032510	1188830	1541410	1424360	1817430	2519300	2794049	2622244
Bangladesh	EXP	G	249860	465466	627999	704728	807824	859045	989345	1468340	2055570	2110807
taka	BAL		-186590	-363201	-404511	-484102	-733586	-565315	-828085	-1050960	-738479	-511438
Barbados	IMP	G	2312	3209	3172	3419	3757	2941	3124	3610	3611	3518
Barbade	EXP	G	545	719	770	837	891	737	858	929	1140	926
dollars	BAL		-1767	-2490	-2402	-2582	-2866	-2204	-2266	-2680	-2472	-2592
Belgium	IMP	S	192180	256440	281170	301120	316330	254370	295080	335460	341760	340570
Belgique	EXP	S	203940	269740	292090	315000	319750	266240	306990	341940	347330	353920
euros	BAL		11760	13300	10920	13880	3420	11870	11910	6480	5570	13350
Benin[3]	IMP	S	400640	536963	642109	976266	1025190	729900	739000	1274186	1123022	1061854
Bénin[3]	EXP	S	279400	305000	384847	501725	574200	199300	216900	661661	716846	567969
CFA francs	BAL		-121240	-231963	-257262	-474541	-450990	-530600	-522100	-612525	-406176	-493885
Bhutan	IMP	G	10556	17035	19012	21745	23495	25650	39084	48698	52978	60681
Bhoutan	EXP	G	5720	11386	18772	27859	22591	23974	29324	31486	28600	30924
ngultrum	BAL		-4835	-5649	-240	6114	-905	-1676	-9760	-17212	-24377	-29757
Bosnia and Herzegovina	IMP	S	6583	11181	11389	13898	16287	12324	13611	15514	15253	15170
Bosnie-Herzégovine	EXP	S	2265	3783	5164	5937	6714	5510	7097	8218	7858	8380
marka	BAL		-4318	-7398	-6225	-7962	-9573	-6815	-6514	-7296	-7395	-6790
Botswana	IMP	G	10617	16154	18011	24965	35575	33830	38430	49819	61968	58761
Botswana	EXP	G	13647	22615	26434	31765	33799	24726	31884	39981	45599	65251
pula	BAL		3031	6461	8424	6800	-1777	-9104	-6546	-9838	-16369	6489
Brunei Darussalam	IMP	S	1908	2410	2663	3166	3647	3570	4582	...	4455	...
Brunéi Darussalam	EXP	S	6734	10397	12133	11556	14593	10477	12477	...	16221	...
dollars	BAL		4826	7987	9470	8390	10945	6908	7896	...	11766	...
Bulgaria	IMP	S	13857	28688	36142	42757	49079	33006	37640	45779	49794	50594
Bulgarie	EXP	S	10247	18515	23493	26427	29736	22882	30435	39634	40623	43447
leva	BAL		-3610	-10173	-12649	-16330	-19343	-10124	-7205	-6145	-9171	-7147

Total imports and exports by countries and areas (Table B)

Imports CIF, exports FOB and balance: million of national currency *[cont.]*

Importations et exportations totales par pays ou zone (Tableau B)

Importations CIF, exportations FOB et balance : en millions de monnaie nationale *[suite]*

Country or Area - Pays ou Zone	IMP EXP BAL	G/S	2000	2005	2006	2007	2008	2009	2010	2011	2012	2013
Burkina Faso[3]	IMP	G	435018	664610	689692	804264	903555	977000	1067200	1214100	1747100	1728600
Burkina Faso[3]	EXP	G	148803	246855	307459	298583	310400	411500	650200	1110400	1111500	1066793
CFA francs	BAL		-286215	-417755	-382233	-505681	-593155	-565500	-417000	-103700	-635600	-661807
Burundi	IMP	S	106059	286959	442512	346099	477345	494828	626742	952852	1084050	1261190
Burundi	EXP	S	35223	104300	60536	67364	64301	76330	123698	154405	192156	153896
francs	BAL		-70836	-182659	-381976	-278735	-413044	-418498	-503044	-798447	-891894	-1107294
Cabo Verde	IMP	G	27517	38856	47654	60416	62128	56296	61810	75184	66145	60252
Cabo Verde	EXP	G	1271	1562	1815	1548	2408	2796	3708	5453	4573	5720
escudos	BAL		-26245	-37294	-45839	-58867	-59720	-53499	-58102	-69731	-61572	-54531
Cameroon[3]	IMP	S	1060100	1442630	1647350	2012920	2418150	2030400	2402090	3066038	3624298	3457200
Cameroun[3]	EXP	S	1305100	1509220	1868450	1727470	1925560	1591270	1931580	2168788	2297090	2074320
CFA francs	BAL		245000	66590	221100	-285450	-492590	-439130	-470510	-897249	-1327208	-1382880
Canada[4]	IMP	G	354728	380858	397044	407301	433999	365359	403701	446442	462026	475686
Canada[4]	EXP	G	410994	436351	440365	450321	483488	357373	398857	447502	454416	472025
dollars	BAL		56266	55493	43321	43020	49489	-7986	-4844	1060	-7610	-3661
Cayman Islands	IMP	G	575	976	874	858	899	745	690	760	759	775
Îles Caïmanes	EXP	G	3	43	14	18	12	16	11	18	17	25
dollars	BAL		-572	-934	-860	-840	-886	-729	-679	-741	-742	-749
Cent. Afr. Rep.[3]	IMP	S	83301	92307	105900	119817	134342	128100	120800	130500	140800	123471
Rép. centrafricaine[3]	EXP	S	114628	67516	82400	86268	67171	38100	45000	54600	57300	69144
CFA francs	BAL		31327	-24791	-23500	-33549	-67171	-90000	-75800	-75900	-83500	-54327
Chad[3]	IMP	S	342260	501095	705902	862680	850830	1086030	1238190	1274186	1325178	1481657
Tchad[3]	EXP	S	166725	1625100	1752700	1757100	1939000	1251290	1683940	2170835	1987768	2222486
CFA francs	BAL		-175535	1124005	1046798	894420	1088170	165260	445750	896649	662589	740829
Comoros	IMP	S	22961	39041	45189	49716	58775	60204	70577	98027	114855	105568
Comores	EXP	S	7476	4757	3893	4965	3023	5666	6686	8913	9575	9260
francs	BAL		-15485	-34284	-41296	-44751	-55752	-54538	-63891	-89114	-105280	-96308
Cote d'Ivoire[3]	IMP	S	1770500	3093580	3043440	3203000	3530350	3279800	3881200	3174000	4987000	6366187
Côte d'Ivoire[3]	EXP	S	2573000	4060100	4432540	4154700	4652700	4846700	5063200	5146700	5538300	6785989
CFA francs	BAL		802500	966520	1389100	951700	1122350	1566900	1182000	1972700	551300	419803
Cuba	IMP	S	3363	7528	9420	10083	13194	...	...	...	...	...
Cuba	EXP	S	1219	1999	2759	3701	3407	...	...	...	...	...
pesos	BAL		-2144	-5529	-6661	-6381	-9787	...	...	...	...	...
Cyprus[5]	IMP	G	2402	2920	3185	3688	7367	5654	6517	6261	5743	4807
Chypre[5]	EXP	G	590	606	530	535	1190	963	1137	1406	1423	1565
euros	BAL		-1812	-2314	-2655	-3154	-6176	-4691	-5381	-4855	-4321	-3243
Czech Republic	IMP	S	1309570	1829960	2104810	2391320	2406490	1989040	2411560	2687560	2766890	2816390
République tchèque	EXP	S	1121100	1868590	2144570	2479230	2473740	2138620	2532800	2878690	3072600	3166870
koruny	BAL		-188470	38630	39760	87910	67250	149580	121240	191130	305710	350480
Denmark	IMP	S	358871	435127	499949	528959	553294	429697	467473	517249	534301	552269
Danemark	EXP	S	408239	491479	538296	551637	586893	490066	538321	600069	614674	625217
kroner	BAL		49368	56352	38347	22678	33599	60369	70848	82820	80373	72948
Djibouti	IMP	G	36699	49285	59664	84103	101940	80101	74643	90741	103078	99524
Djibouti	EXP	G	5616	7020	9805	10320	12219	13750	17772	16475	16883	21327
francs	BAL		-31083	-42265	-49859	-73783	-89722	-66351	-56871	-74266	-86195	-78197
Dominica	IMP	S	401	446	451	528	667	608	604	610	562	548
Dominique	EXP	S	145	112	115	102	108	92	99	78	97	103
EC dollars	BAL		-256	-335	-336	-426	-559	-516	-505	-532	-466	-445

Total imports and exports by countries and areas (Table B)

Imports CIF, exports FOB and balance: million of national currency *[cont.]*

Importations et exportations totales par pays ou zone (Tableau B)

Importations CIF, exportations FOB et balance : en millions de monnaie nationale *[suite]*

Country or Area - Pays ou Zone	IMP EXP BAL	G/ S	2000	2005	2006	2007	2008	2009	2010	2011	2012	2013
Equatorial Guinea[3]	IMP	G	321101	690983	1056240	1135860	1750920	2455370	2823080	2828600	3061470	3457200
Guinée équatoriale[3]	EXP	G	781038	3726030	4291360	4893310	7120100	4296900	4952770	6364350	7908810	6914400
CFA francs	BAL		459937	3035047	3235120	3757450	5369180	1841530	2129690	3535750	4847340	3457200
Estonia[6]	IMP	S	72214	128435	147770	171846	170488	113780	144994	12727	13848	13665
Estonie[6]	EXP	S	53900	96747	108946	124990	132483	101412	136915	12004	12518	12269
euros	BAL		-18314	-31688	-38824	-46856	-38005	-12368	-8079	-723	-1330	-1395
Ethiopia	IMP	G	10369	35487	45297	52080	79453	90310	123153	150260	212288	...
Ethiopie	EXP	G	3991	7826	9072	11451	15377	19058	32842	48459	52902	...
birr	BAL		-6378	-27661	-36224	-40629	-64076	-71252	-90311	-101801	-159386	...
Extra-EU28[7,8]	IMP		992695	1183933	1364607	1446811	1585231	1235636	1532089	1728314	1798553	1682566
Extra-UE28[7,8]	EXP		849740	1049491	1152361	1234321	1309147	1093962	1353195	1554252	1683051	1737052
euros	BAL		-142956	-134442	-212246	-212490	-276084	-141675	-178894	-174062	-115502	54485
Fiji	IMP	G	1822	2723	3124	2890	3601	2808	3465	3911	4034	5206
Fidji	EXP	G	1155	1193	1202	1210	1471	1230	1605	1916	2191	2045
dollars	BAL		-667	-1530	-1923	-1680	-2130	-1578	-1859	-1995	-1843	-3161
Finland	IMP	G	36837	47028	55253	59615	62402	43654	51899	60537	59519	58399
Finlande	EXP	G	49485	52453	61489	65688	65581	45064	52439	56854	56878	56037
euros	BAL		12647	5425	6237	6073	3179	1410	540	-3683	-2641	-2362
France	IMP	S	337489	394287	435307	460263	485613	402066	459203	512214	518109	504916
France	EXP	S	324256	356543	390910	401458	412968	341585	390002	420592	434026	427463
euros	BAL		-13233	-37744	-44397	-58805	-72645	-60481	-69201	-91622	-84083	-77453
Gabon[3]	IMP	S	708000	775920	901909	1033780	1160260	1179200	1475500	1730900	1850500	1916070
Gabon[3]	EXP	S	1852560	2671630	2849750	3023690	4256840	2532700	4262000	4605000	3936600	4703770
CFA francs	BAL		1144560	1895710	1947841	1989910	3096580	1353500	2786500	2874100	2086100	2787700
Gambia	IMP	G	2391	7418	7277	7984	7151	8098	8404	10117	12167	12557
Gambie	EXP	G	192	229	322	311	303	400	420	...	...	...
dalasis	BAL		-2199	-7189	-6955	-7672	-6847	-7699	-7983	...	...	...
Germany	IMP	S	538311	628087	733994	769887	805842	664615	797098	902524	905926	896158
Allemagne	EXP	S	597441	786265	893041	965236	984139	803312	951959	1061230	1095770	1093810
euros	BAL		59130	158178	159047	195349	178297	138697	154861	158706	189844	197652
Ghana	IMP	G	1617	4846	6189	7539	10863	11336	15799	24151	32311	34742
Ghana	EXP	G	732	2540	3415	4041	5947	8224	11390	19325	21501	26740
cedis	BAL		-885	-2307	-2774	-3498	-4916	-3112	-4409	-4826	-10810	-8002
Gibraltar	IMP		318	276	347	398	420	434	406	439	382	478
Gibraltar	EXP		84	110	131	152	154	170	167	154	159	178
pounds	BAL		-234	-166	-216	-246	-266	-264	-239	-285	-223	-300
Grenada[1]	IMP	S	664	902	893	986	1019	790	855	889	907	995
Grenade[1]	EXP	S	211	75	69	90	82	79	65	74	93	89
EC dollars	BAL		-453	-827	-825	-896	-937	-712	-790	-815	-813	-906
Guyana	IMP	S	106113	157564	178065	214469	267225	236700	284494	359765	408065	359423
Guyana	EXP	S	91521	110536	117710	137419	161819	155511	179122	227778	289278	283431
dollars	BAL		-14593	-47028	-60355	-77050	-105406	-81189	-105372	-131987	-118787	-75992
Haiti	IMP	G	21936	58802	75779	61983	90553	87498	125207	122361	132961	147759
Haïti	EXP	G	6725	19017	19226	19232	18626	23741	23045	31077	34197	39113
gourdes	BAL		-15211	-39785	-56553	-42750	-71927	-63756	-102162	-91285	-98764	-108646
Hungary	IMP	S	9064050	13145500	16224700	17285300	18102100	15634900	18205700	20283900	21211900	22154000
Hongrie	EXP	S	7942790	12425500	15591100	17207800	18301700	16946100	19688600	22262900	23183300	24244000
forint	BAL		-1121260	-720000	-633600	-77500	199600	1311200	1482900	1979000	1971400	2090000

Total imports and exports by countries and areas (Table B)

Imports CIF, exports FOB and balance: million of national currency *[cont.]*

Importations et exportations totales par pays ou zone (Tableau B)

Importations CIF, exportations FOB et balance : en millions de monnaie nationale *[suite]*

Country or Area - Pays ou Zone	IMP EXP BAL	G/S	2000	2005	2006	2007	2008	2009	2010	2011	2012	2013
Iceland	IMP	G	203847	287257	357965	389234	468598	446128	477222	560692	597262	584224
Islande	EXP	G	148516	185286	227785	277420	452428	500855	561032	619682	633029	609788
kronur	BAL		-55331	-101971	-130180	-111814	-16170	54727	83810	58990	35767	25564
India[9]	IMP	G	2316550	6300170	8091050	9435340	13939400	12398400	16002000	21698200	26149700	27173600
Inde[9]	EXP	G	1906530	4393450	5521660	6190170	8412350	7967180	10341000	14121400	15840400	18438500
rupees	BAL		-410020	-1906720	-2569390	-3245170	-5527050	-4431220	-5661000	-7576800	-10309300	-8735100
Ireland	IMP	G	55909	57465	60857	63486	57585	45061	45764	48302	49151	49672
Irlande	EXP	G	83889	86732	86772	89226	86395	85804	89703	91227	91688	86886
euros	BAL		27980	29268	25915	25740	28810	40743	43940	42925	42538	37214
Italy	IMP	S	258506	309292	352465	373341	382049	297608	367390	401428	380293	359455
Italie	EXP	S	260415	299923	332013	364743	369015	291732	337344	375904	390182	389858
euros	BAL		1909	-9369	-20452	-8598	-13034	-5876	-30046	-25524	9889	30403
Jamaica	IMP	G	141987	277869	349303	442859	559908	426608	452907	557482	575761	620963
Jamaïque	EXP	G	55621	93441	123220	142858	183976	115838	116061	137660	151648	157132
dollars	BAL		-86366	-184428	-226083	-300001	-375932	-310770	-336846	-419822	-424113	-463831
Japan	IMP	G	40915000	56852400	67407600	72854000	78959000	51365900	60622700	68037500	70655000	81249300
Japon	EXP	G	51654200	65656500	75246200	83931400	81018100	54170600	67399600	65546500	63747600	69774200
yen	BAL		10739200	8804100	7838600	11077400	2059100	2804700	6776900	-2491000	-6907400	-11475100
Jordan	IMP	G	3259	7449	8116	9579	11897	10319	10710	13109	14691	15407
Jordanie	EXP	G	1347	3050	3669	4059	5527	4637	4986	5654	5627	5606
dinars	BAL		-1913	-4399	-4447	-5520	-6370	-5682	-5724	-7454	-9063	-9801
Kenya	IMP	G	236613	464495	526870	605121	766743	788097	957949	1315670	1376680	1408810
Kenya	EXP	G	132183	248929	247900	274596	342954	344949	408103	511036	517804	504300
shillings	BAL		-104430	-215566	-278970	-330525	-423789	-443148	-549846	-804634	-858876	-904510
Kuwait	IMP	S	2195	4614	5001	6061	6679	5723	6499	6938	7632	8407
Koweït	EXP	S	5963	13102	15981	17424	22999	14468	17674	28074	31699	32003
dinars	BAL		3767	8488	10981	11363	16321	8746	11175	21136	24067	23597
Latvia	IMP	S	1934	4867	6378	7780	7528	4710	5912	7719	8794	8880
Lettonie	EXP	S	1131	2888	3293	4040	4429	3602	4695	5999	6937	7043
lati	BAL		-803	-1979	-3085	-3740	-3099	-1108	-1217	-1721	-1856	-1837
Lesotho	IMP	G	5614	8967	10157	12245	16564	16524	16107	18866	21303	22140
Lesotho	EXP	G	1527	4137	4697	5421	7289	6066	5857	8487	9035	9048
maloti	BAL		-4088	-4830	-5460	-6824	-9274	-10458	-10250	-10378	-12268	-13091
Libya	IMP	G	1911	7954	7935	8501	11195	12535	13301	9792	29016	34330
Libye	EXP	G	5222	41028	52885	59306	75959	46583	58336	22031	74433	55946
dinars	BAL		3310	33075	44950	50805	64764	34048	45034	12240	45417	21615
Lithuania	IMP	G	20877	43152	53275	61504	73006	45311	60953	78160	85914	91521
Lituanie	EXP	G	14193	32767	38888	43192	55511	40732	54039	69643	79579	84779
litai	BAL		-6684	-10385	-14386	-18311	-17495	-4579	-6914	-8517	-6336	-6742
Luxembourg	IMP	S	11633	14399	15715	16471	17516	13799	16422	18901	18796	18013
Luxembourg	EXP	S	8498	10178	11144	11946	11988	9250	10785	12065	10880	10604
euros	BAL		-3135	-4222	-4571	-4525	-5528	-4549	-5637	-6836	-7916	-7409
Madagascar	IMP	S	1349440	3408100	3723950	4528410	6532110	6188990	5305220	5303830	5438550	7061508
Madagascar	EXP	S	1115280	1703630	2112390	2518410	2865560	2146110	2245580	2534440	2713360	4303130
ariary	BAL		-234160	-1704470	-1611560	-2010000	-3666550	-4042880	-3059640	-2769390	-2725190	-2758378
Malawi	IMP	G	32283	137982	164463	193141	238898	295947	327166	380171	594760	1029800
Malawi	EXP	G	23625	60251	73800	99259	120850	152460	170050	220446	308495	435222
kwacha	BAL		-8658	-77731	-90663	-93882	-118048	-143487	-157116	-159725	-286265	-594578

Total imports and exports by countries and areas (Table B)
Imports CIF, exports FOB and balance: million of national currency *[cont.]*
Importations et exportations totales par pays ou zone (Tableau B)
Importations CIF, exportations FOB et balance : en millions de monnaie nationale *[suite]*

Country or Area - Pays ou Zone	IMP EXP BAL	G/S	2000	2005	2006	2007	2008	2009	2010	2011	2012	2013
Malaysia	IMP	G	311459	433196	480506	502045	519804	434670	528828	573626	606677	649068
Malaisie	EXP	G	373270	533372	588588	604300	663014	552518	638822	697862	702641	719815
ringgit	BAL		61811	100176	108082	102255	143210	117848	109994	124236	95964	70747
Mali[3]	IMP	S	573900	814199	951536	1047120	1495190	1174000	1693100	1597000	1500000	1827380
Mali[3]	EXP	S	392300	580700	810480	745860	939101	841300	989200	1128300	1104600	1284100
CFA francs	BAL		-181600	-233499	-141056	-301260	-556089	-332700	-703900	-468700	-395400	-543280
Malta[10]	IMP	G	1492	1318	1387	1400	3897	3475	4330	5337	6187	5641
Malte[10]	EXP	G	1072	822	920	928	2456	2087	2809	3819	4439	3904
euros	BAL		-420	-496	-467	-472	-1441	-1388	-1521	-1518	-1749	-1737
Mauritania	IMP	S	84529	356730	292385	369792	395103	350662	474099	689657	881753	808917
Mauritanie	EXP	S	81881	147717	340634	349865	392204	368978	498120	691133	777808	...
ouguiyas	BAL		-2647	-209013	48249	-19927	-2899	18317	24020	1475	-103945	...
Mauritius	IMP	G	57940	93282	115502	121037	132165	118444	134882	147815	160996	165661
Maurice	EXP	G	47511	63219	74037	69708	67970	61681	69550	73586	79658	88148
rupees	BAL		-10429	-30063	-41465	-51329	-64195	-56763	-65332	-74229	-81338	-77513
Montenegro	IMP	S	.	.	1457	2073	2530	1654	1657	1823	1800	1773
Monténégro	EXP	S	.	.	441	455	416	277	330	454	367	376
euros	BAL		.	.	-1016	-1618	-2114	-1377	-1327	-1369	-1433	-1398
Morocco	IMP	S	122527	184380	210554	261287	326042	263982	297963	357987	373201	377777
Maroc	EXP	S	76242	99264	111979	125517	155740	113020	149583	173977	183562	183687
dirhams	BAL		-46286	-85116	-98575	-135770	-170302	-150962	-148380	-184010	-189639	-194090
Namibia	IMP	G	10755	16391	19530	24800	35854	42199	39242	46102	55511	72772
Namibie	EXP	G	9164	13164	17922	20584	25745	28373	29944	31912	33637	33691
dollars	BAL		-1591	-3227	-1608	-4216	-10109	-13826	-9298	-14191	-21874	-39081
Nepal	IMP	G	108505	162951	181293	207316	250448	339990	402351	427616	555841	601983
Népal	EXP	G	49823	61608	60959	57675	65490	63788	69497	67960	81723	86000
rupees	BAL		-58682	-101343	-120334	-149641	-184958	-276202	-332854	-359656	-474118	-515983
Netherlands	IMP	S	216056	249845	285370	306827	335929	274026	331914	364921	389855	382066
Pays-Bas	EXP	S	231854	281300	318094	344310	370488	309369	371552	409358	431403	427447
euros	BAL		15798	31455	32724	37483	34559	35343	39638	44437	41548	45381
New Zealand	IMP	G	31463	38160	41082	42653	48037	39719	44024	47201	46681	49230
Nouvelle-Zélande	EXP	G	30536	31098	35303	38126	43353	39556	44764	47468	46160	50028
dollars	BAL		-927	-7062	-5779	-4527	-4684	-163	740	267	-521	798
Niger[3]	IMP	S	281400	497402	496223	550541	759672	704900	1081200	854400	918442	938383
Niger[3]	EXP	S	201500	257932	265600	317891	407503	278900	318700	428000	765369	790217
CFA francs	BAL		-79900	-239470	-230623	-232650	-352169	-426000	-762500	-426400	-153073	-148166
Niue	IMP	G	4	...	6	9	11	9	...	...	...	...
Nioué	EXP	G	1	0	2	4	0	...	...	...	...	...
NZ dollars	BAL		-4	...	-4	-5	-11	...	...	...	...	...
Norway	IMP	G	302840	357658	411756	468919	504480	430362	467285	508628	507649	528783
Norvège	EXP	G	529812	668759	782943	795365	953153	731306	788120	898593	935720	899351
kroner	BAL		226972	311101	371187	326446	448673	300944	320835	389965	428071	370568
Oman	IMP	G	1938	3394	4197	6143	8815	6869	7603	9082	11323	13201
Oman	EXP	G	4352	7187	8300	9280	14503	10787	14073	18107	20445	21697
rials Omani	BAL		2414	3793	4103	3137	5689	3917	6470	9025	9123	8496
Pakistan	IMP	G	582681	1509810	1797830	1979320	2949020	2587860	3218900	3797900	4009090	4531900
Pakistan	EXP	G	484476	955464	1020480	1083400	1423450	1433550	1824380	2188530	2129180	2553390
rupees	BAL		-98205	-554346	-777350	-895920	-1525570	-1154310	-1394520	-1609370	-1879910	-1978510

Total imports and exports by countries and areas (Table B)
Imports CIF, exports FOB and balance: million of national currency *[cont.]*

Importations et exportations totales par pays ou zone (Tableau B)
Importations CIF, exportations FOB et balance : en millions de monnaie nationale *[suite]*

Country or Area - Pays ou Zone	IMP EXP BAL	G/S	2000	2005	2006	2007	2008	2009	2010	2011	2012	2013
Panama	IMP	S	3379	4180	4831	6872	9050	7801	9145	11342	12633	...
Panama	EXP	S	859	1018	1093	1164	1247	948	832	785	...	...
balboas	BAL		-2519	-3162	-3738	-5709	-7803	-6853	-8313	-10556	...	...
Papua New Guinea	IMP	G	3196	5363	6997	8748	9611	8816	10741	11618	11465	...
Papouasie-Nouvelle-Guinée	EXP	G	5742	10154	12734	13881	15426	12107	15602	16376	13181	13337
kina	BAL		2546	4792	5737	5134	5815	3290	4861	4758	1716	...
Philippines	IMP	G	1636810	2587380	2773800	2652970	2668510	2185440	2637540	2776230	2780230	2764680
Philippines	EXP	G	1682810	2272550	2432760	2328880	2182680	1830980	2322990	2092230	2200090	2291110
pesos	BAL		46000	-314830	-341040	-324090	-485830	-354460	-314550	-684000	-580140	-473570
Poland	IMP	S	213072	326120	394030	446895	485833	463383	536221	611004	638288	648195
Pologne	EXP	S	137909	288682	343779	382199	399353	423241	481058	553430	597096	638600
zlotys	BAL		-75163	-37438	-50251	-64696	-86480	-40142	-55163	-57574	-41192	-9595
Portugal	IMP	S	41425	42939	52232	55627	64194	51368	57053	59229	56234	56523
Portugal	EXP	S	25241	25874	34137	36655	38950	31768	36762	42828	45324	47337
euros	BAL		-16184	-17066	-18095	-18972	-25244	-19600	-20291	-16401	-10910	-9186
Qatar	IMP	S	11838	36621	59846	85284	101556	90716	84593	81293	91813	98418
Qatar	EXP	S	42203	93774	123948	161821	244998	174746	272271	416592	484065	498153
riyals	BAL		30365	57153	64102	76537	143442	84030	187678	335300	392252	399735
Rwanda	IMP	G	82586	240070	302370	403210	621619	697270	816383	1068472	1232286	1593550
Rwanda	EXP	G	20521	69516	81267	96685	146375	109491	148698	279326	290123	443368
francs	BAL		-62065	-170554	-221103	-306525	-475244	-587779	-667685	-789146	-942162	-1150182
Saint Helena[11]	IMP	G	7	7	8	8	9	10	...	...	...	...
Sainte-Hélèna[11]	EXP	G	0	0	0	0	0	0	...	...	...	...
pounds	BAL		-7	-6	-8	-8	-9	-10	...	...	...	...
Saint Kitts-Nevis[1]	IMP	S	529	568	674	735	877	816	616	669	609	672
Saint-Kitts-et-Nevis[1]	EXP	S	79	81	96	86	116	115	122	92	134	136
EC dollars	BAL		-450	-487	-578	-649	-761	-701	-494	-577	-475	-536
Saint Lucia[1]	IMP	S	959	1293	1598	1715	1775	1454	1623	1809	1844	1614
Sainte-Lucie[1]	EXP	S	127	239	265	288	392	439	616	691	421	461
EC dollars	BAL		-832	-1054	-1334	-1427	-1383	-1015	-1007	-1118	-1422	-1153
Saint Vincent-Grenadines[1]	IMP	S	399	649	727	882	1007	901	933	896	964	1021
St.Vincent-Grenadines[1]	EXP	S	136	108	103	129	141	135	119	105	117	130
EC dollars	BAL		-263	-542	-624	-754	-866	-766	-814	-791	-847	-891
Samoa	IMP	S	298	508	608	594	659	550	690	739	707	753
Samoa	EXP	S	47	32	30	40	30	31	34	39	78	55
talas	BAL		-251	-475	-578	-553	-630	-519	-657	-700	-628	-697
Saudi Arabia	IMP	S	113240	222790	261400	338090	431750	358290	400740	493450	583470	614630
Arabie saoudite	EXP	S	290550	677140	791340	874400	1175350	721110	941800	1367620	1456500	1409750
riyals	BAL		177310	454350	529940	536310	743600	362820	541060	874170	873030	795120
Senegal[3]	IMP	G	1081500	1686340	1795600	2036880	2534380	2141970	2202040	2544280	3005460	2994550
Sénégal[3]	EXP	G	655000	832400	813600	790790	895210	895780	1020270	1146420	1216270	1207150
CFA francs	BAL		-426500	-853940	-982000	-1246090	-1639170	-1246190	-1181770	-1397860	-1789190	-1787400
Serbia	IMP	S	.	.	878227	1069410	1260290	1243650	1301240	1455390	1663980	...
Serbie	EXP	S	.	.	428051	513222	603512	796525	762974	861352	1000870	...
dinars	BAL				-450176	-556188	-656778	-447125	-538266	-594038	-663110	...
Seychelles	IMP	G	1955	3712	4181	5757	9959	10979	7844	9280	10942	11206
Seychelles	EXP	G	1106	1868	2097	2413	4070	5381	4828	5983	6792	6966
rupees	BAL		-849	-1843	-2084	-3344	-5890	-5598	-3016	-3296	-4150	-4239

Total imports and exports by countries and areas (Table B)

Imports CIF, exports FOB and balance: million of national currency *[cont.]*

Importations et exportations totales par pays ou zone (Tableau B)

Imports CIF, exportations FOB et balance : en millions de monnaie nationale *[suite]*

Country or Area - Pays ou Zone	IMP EXP BAL	G/S	2000	2005	2006	2007	2008	2009	2010	2011	2012	2013
Sierra Leone	IMP	S	314639	996003	1152180	1327420	1592540	1761570	3061130	7464310	6965750	7711540
Sierra Leone	EXP	S	26771	457994	684311	732081	643014	780941	1263280	1376320	4697590	8198430
leones	BAL		-287868	-538009	-467869	-595339	-949526	-980629	-1797850	-6087990	-2268160	486890
Singapore	IMP	G	232176	333191	378924	395980	450893	356299	423222	459655	474554	466762
Singapour	EXP	G	237826	382532	431559	450587	476762	391118	478841	514741	510329	513391
dollars	BAL		5650	49341	52635	54607	25869	34819	55619	55086	35775	46629
Slovakia[12]	IMP	S	619789	1124440	1397540	1525560	1573010	40714	49868	58556	61518	62937
Slovaquie[12]	EXP	S	548527	994571	1239360	1419850	1509110	39721	48272	56783	62144	64172
euros	BAL		-71262	-129869	-158180	-105710	-63900	-993	-1596	-1773	626	1235
Solomon Islands	IMP	S	468	1393	1650	2197	2549	2175	2419	3607	3677	3870
Iles Salomon	EXP	S	351	779	924	1259	1631	1316	1786	3115	3456	3213
dollars	BAL		-117	-614	-725	-938	-918	-859	-633	-492	-221	-657
South Africa[4,13]	IMP	G	186382	349181	461042	561678	777808	541038	585573	724631	832538	977097
Afrique du Sud[4,13]	EXP	G	208476	328760	396584	490643	692359	523013	596879	703669	717014	807054
rands	BAL		22094	-20421	-64458	-71035	-85449	-18025	11306	-20962	-115524	-170043
Spain	IMP	S	166138	231372	259559	280431	282251	208437	238082	260823	253401	251354
Espagne	EXP	S	123100	153559	169872	181479	188184	158254	185799	214486	222644	234240
euros	BAL		-43038	-77813	-89687	-98952	-94067	-50183	-52283	-46337	-30757	-17114
Sri Lanka	IMP	G	485084	888358	1066620	1251140	1510730	1154390	1526600	2241490	2441880	2322680
Sri Lanka	EXP	G	420114	638275	716579	856806	881320	813911	937737	1167590	1245530	1342970
rupees	BAL		-64970	-250083	-350041	-394334	-629410	-340479	-588863	-1073900	-1196350	-979710
Suriname	IMP	G	324	2266	2453	3049	4167	3723	3788	5457	5792	7590
Suriname	EXP	G	533	2156	3082	3534	4578	3823	5082	7703	8331	8415
dollars	BAL		209	-110	629	485	410	101	1293	2247	2539	825
Swaziland	IMP	G	7261	12083	13001	12999	14044	13558	12446	14261	16072	...
Swaziland	EXP	G	6312	11256	12121	13245	14044	12287	11348	13906	15669	...
emalangeni	BAL		-949	-827	-880	247	0	-1271	-1098	-355	-403	...
Sweden	IMP	G	672400	833800	939500	1034700	1097900	912900	1067100	1133500	1111400	1039900
Suède	EXP	G	804200	977300	1089400	1139600	1194400	996700	1136000	1214500	1170200	1091600
kronor	BAL		131800	143500	149900	104900	96500	83800	68900	81000	58800	51700
Switzerland	IMP	S	128615	149094	165410	183578	186883	160187	173685	174388	176781	177642
Suisse	EXP	S	126549	156977	177475	197533	206330	180534	193253	197907	200612	201213
francs	BAL		-2066	7883	12065	13955	19447	20347	19568	23519	23831	23571
Syrian Arab Rep.	IMP	S	45515	121928	128956	164504	203226	171644	190264	184090	87555	65105
République arabe syrienne	EXP	S	52471	97747	122570	129601	172977	121849	157150	120108	44900	33675
pounds	BAL		6956	-24181	-6386	-34903	-30249	-49795	-33114	-63983	-42655	-31430
Thailand	IMP	S	2494140	4754640	4871630	4870190	5962480	4601980	5856590	6973650	7776160	7630840
Thaïlande	EXP	S	2773830	4439310	4946450	5302120	5851370	5194600	6176300	6896540	7091640	6916440
baht	BAL		279690	-315330	74820	431930	-111110	592620	319710	-77110	-684520	-714400
Togo[3]	IMP	S	400131	559229	567154	592909	675911	919400	492900	851064	918367	1037160
Togo[3]	EXP	S	258447	348200	329600	335487	403025	382200	318800	516674	510204	518580
CFA francs	BAL		-141684	-211029	-237554	-257422	-272886	-537200	-174100	-334389	-408163	-518580
Tonga	IMP	G	123	235	236	281	324	292	302	332	343	372
Tonga	EXP	G	16	20	20	18	18	16	16	25	24	27
pa'anga	BAL		-107	-215	-216	-263	-306	-276	-286	-308	-319	-346
Trinidad and Tobago	IMP	S	20840	35869	40932	48491	60325	43993	41329	63949	60458	56695
Trinité-et-Tobago	EXP	S	26925	62628	89349	84772	117301	57721	64955	95097	84254	81821
dollars	BAL		6086	26759	48417	36281	56977	13728	23626	31148	23795	25126

Country or Area - Pays ou Zone	IMP EXP BAL	G/ S	2000	2005	2006	2007	2008	2009	2010	2011	2012	2013
Tunisia	IMP	G	11738	17102	20004	24437	30241	25878	31817	33702	38183	39509
Tunisie	EXP	G	8005	13608	15558	19410	23637	19469	23519	25092	26548	27701
dinars	BAL		-3733	-3494	-4446	-5028	-6604	-6408	-8298	-8610	-11635	-11808
Tuvalu	IMP	G	9	17	17	18	...	...	...	...	...	...
Tuvalu	EXP	G	0	0	0	0	...	...	...	...	...	...
Aust. dollars	BAL		-9	-17	-17	-18	...	...	...	...	...	...
Uganda	IMP	G	2486280	3657730	4683590	6020770	7786490	8624240	10256300	11567100	13087500	12738600
Ouganda	EXP	G	759273	1810950	2175110	3445310	4651150	6066440	6750430	6082240	7167850	7372070
shillings	BAL		-1727007	-1846780	-2508480	-2575460	-3135340	-2557800	-3505870	-5484860	-5919650	-5366530
United Kingdom	IMP	G	220397	279853	319741	310516	345826	310660	363828	398513	409157	412752
Royaume-Uni	EXP	G	187133	210704	242899	219981	251565	227727	265243	298421	300457	304977
pounds	BAL		-33264	-69149	-76842	-90535	-94261	-82933	-98585	-100092	-108700	-107775
United Rep. of Tanzania	IMP	G	1219380	3726100	5335330	6621420	8470080	8309960	10877900	16904700	17832200	19601900
Rép.-Unie de Tanzanie	EXP	G	531058	1896770	2176990	2510570	3201860	3124060	4988840	6915020	8033240	8080800
shillings	BAL		-688322	-1829330	-3158340	-4110850	-5268220	-5185900	-5889060	-9989680	-9798960	-11521100
United States[14]	IMP	G	1259300	1735060	1918080	2020400	2169490	1605300	1969180	2265890	2336520	2329060
Etats-Unis[14]	EXP	G	781918	901082	1025970	1148200	1287440	1056040	1278490	1480290	1545710	1579050
dollars	BAL		-477382	-833978	-892110	-872200	-882050	-549260	-690690	-785600	-790810	-750010
Vanuatu	IMP	G	11975	16295	24039	23503	31667	31086	27390	27256	26907	29446
Vanuatu	EXP	G	3579	4124	5397	5106	5721	6150	4681	6012	5072	3653
vatu	BAL		-8396	-12171	-18643	-18398	-25946	-24936	-22709	-21244	-21835	-25793
Yemen	IMP	S	375833	1029880	1196810	1693230	2106740	1863120	2130020	2145305	2565747	2686130
Yémen	EXP	S	613937	1073920	1311180	1253200	1514970	1269610	1866510	2309173	1822079	2041460
rials	BAL		238104	44040	114370	-440030	-591770	-593510	-263510	163868	-743668	-644670
Zambia	IMP	S	3089	11418	11077	16038	18480	19124	25508	34952	41136	54893
Zambie	EXP	S	2072	8078	13585	18482	19098	21759	34541	43832	44012	57187
kwacha	BAL		-1017	-3340	2508	2444	618	2635	9033	8880	2877	2293

Total imports and exports by countries or areas (Table B)

Imports CIF, exports FOB and balance: millions of national currency [cont.]

Importations et exportations totales par pays ou zone (Tableau B)

Importations CIF, exportations FOB, et balance : en millions de monnaie nationale [suite]

General note:

This table contains totals of imports and exports of countries or areas which report data in national currency. Countries that are not included in this table may report their trade in US dollars and are shown in Table A. Export and import values are as compiled by the International Monetary Fund (IMF) except for Andorra, Bermuda, Cayman Is., Cuba, Gibraltar, Montenegro, Niue, Palau, Russian Federation (beginning 1994), Serbia and Montenegro, State of Palestine, Turkmenistan, Turks and Caicos, Tuvalu and Uzbekistan.

Column "G/S" indicates the trade system: G = General Trade System; S = Special Trade System. For further information on sources and presentation as well as for a brief table description please see the introduction.

Remarque générale:

Cette table contient des totaux d'd'importations et d'd'exportations les pays ou les secteurs qui rapportent des données dans la monnaie nationale.Les pays qui ne sont pas inclus dans cette table peuvent rapporter leurs échanges des dollars d'USA et sont montrés dans le Tableau A. Export et les valeurs d'importation sont comme compilé par le Fonds monétaire international (FMI) excepté Andorre, État de Palestine, les Bermudes, Iles Caïmanes, le Cuba, la Fédération Russe (commençant 1994), Gibraltar, Montenegro, Nioué, Palaos, Serbie et Monténégro, Turkmenistan, Iles Turque Caicos, Tuvalu et Ouzbékistan.

La colonne "G/S" indique le système commercial : G=Système du Commerce Général ; S= Système du Commerce Spécial. Pour plus d'information sur les sources et la présentation ainsi qu'une brève description du tableau, se il vous plaît se référer à l'introduction.

1	East Caribbean dollar.
2	Trade statistics exclude certain oil and chemical products.
3	Comptoirs Francais du Afrique franc pegged to the euro at CFAF 655.957 per euro.
4	Imports FOB.
5	Prior to January 2008, data for Cyprus are in pounds.
6	Prior to January 2011, data for Estonia are in krooni.
7	Excluding intra-EU trade.
8	In the year 2000, the trade values refer to extra-EU27.
9	Excluding military goods, fissionable materials, bunkers, ships, and aircraft.
10	Prior to January 2008, data for Malta are in liri.
11	Year ending 31 March of the following year.
12	Prior to January 2009, data for Slovakia are in koruny.
13	Exports include gold.
14	Including the trade of the U.S. Virgin Islands and Puerto Rico but excluding shipments of merchandise between the United States and its other possessions (Guam and American Samoa). Data include imports and exports of non-monetary gold.

1	Dollar des caraïbes orientales.
2	Les statistiques commerciales font exclusion de certains produits pétroliers et chimiques.
3	Comptoirs Français du Afrique franc est chevillé à l'euro à CFAF 655,957 par euro.
4	Importations FOB.
5	Avant janvier 2008, les données de Chypre étaient en livres.
6	Avant janvier 2011, les données de l'Estonie étaient en krooni.
7	Non compris le commerce d'intra-UE.
8	En l'année 2000, les valeurs du commerce se réfèrent à extra-UE27.
9	À l'exclusion des marchandises militaires, des matières fissibles, des soutes, des bateaux, et de l'avion.
10	Avant janvier 2008, les données de Malte étaient en lire.
11	Année finissant le 31 mars de l'année suivante.
12	Avant janvier 2009, les données de Slovaquie étaient en couronnes.
13	Les exportations comprennent l'or.
14	Y compris le commerce des Iles Vierges américaines et de Porto Rico mais non compris les échanges de marchandise, entre les Etats-Unis et leurs autres possessions (Guam et Samoa américaines). Les données comprennent les importations et exportations d'or non-monétaire.

External trade conversion factors (Table C)
Imports, exports: US dollars per national currency
Facteurs de conversion pour le commerce extérieur (Tableau C)
Importations, exportations : monnaie nationale en dollars É.-U.

Country or Area	Unit	2000	2005	2006	2007	2008	2009	2010	2011	2012	2013
						Imports - Importations					
Albania	lek	0.00694	0.00999	0.01022	0.01113	0.01194	0.01055	0.00961	0.00992	0.00924	0.00948
Algeria	dinar	0.01328	0.01365	0.01375	0.01446	0.01553	0.01376	0.01345	0.01372	0.01289	0.01261
Andorra	euro	0.91856	1.24575	1.25635	1.37289	1.46993	1.39638	1.32850	1.38935	1.28572	1.32989
Anguilla	EC dollar	0.37037	0.37037	0.37037	0.37037	0.37037	0.37037	0.37037	0.37037	0.37037	0.37037
Australia	dollar	0.57943	0.76328	0.75388	0.84045	0.84672	0.79235	0.91998	1.03215	1.03561	0.96428
Austria	euro[1]	0.92061	1.24302	1.25666	1.37202	1.47342	1.39466	1.32511	1.39182	1.28546	1.32805
Bahamas	dollar	1.00000	1.00000	1.00000	1.00000	1.00000	1.00000	1.00000	1.00000	1.00000	1.00000
Bangladesh	taka	0.01915	0.01554	0.01449	0.01452	0.01458	0.01448	0.01435	0.01349	0.01222	0.01280
Barbados	dollar	0.50000	0.50000	0.50000	0.50000	0.50000	0.50000	0.50000	0.50000	0.50000	0.50000
Belgium	euro	0.92097	1.24435	1.25536	1.37179	1.47453	1.39429	1.32619	1.39162	1.28597	1.32767
Benin	CFA franc[2,3]	0.00142	0.00190	0.00191	0.00209	0.00223	0.00213	0.00202	0.00212	0.00196	0.00202
Bhutan	ngultrum	0.02228	0.02272	0.02203	0.02420	0.02311	0.02064	0.02185	0.02160	0.01868	0.01710
Bosnia and Herzegovina	marka	0.46840	0.63248	0.64496	0.70309	0.75413	0.71357	0.67617	0.71203	0.65677	0.67918
Botswana	pula	0.19586	0.19636	0.17078	0.16330	0.14708	0.14102	0.14744	0.14653	0.13094	0.11925
Brunei Darussalam	dollar	0.58002	0.60052	0.63034	0.66365	0.70507	0.68607	0.73436	...	0.79981	...
Bulgaria	lev	0.46942	0.63311	0.64383	0.70366	0.75425	0.71358	0.67675	0.71166	0.65695	0.67893
Burkina Faso	CFA franc[3]	0.00140	0.00189	0.00192	0.00209	0.00222	0.00213	0.00202	0.00212	0.00196	0.00202
Burundi	franc	0.00139	0.00093	0.00097	0.00092	0.00084	0.00081	0.00081	0.00079	0.00069	0.00064
Cabo Verde	escudo	0.00863	0.01127	0.01139	0.01247	0.01319	0.01259	0.01201	0.01260	0.01158	0.01206
Cameroon	CFA franc[3]	0.00140	0.00189	0.00192	0.00210	0.00222	0.00213	0.00202	0.00212	0.00196	0.00203
Canada	dollar	0.67322	0.82594	0.88217	0.93469	0.94200	0.87926	0.97131	1.01076	1.00086	0.97107
Cent. Afr. Rep.	CFA franc[2,3]	0.00142	0.00187	0.00191	0.00209	0.00222	0.00213	0.00202	0.00212	0.00196	0.00203
Chad	CFA franc[2,3]	0.00141	0.00190	0.00191	0.00208	0.00224	0.00211	0.00202	0.00212	0.00196	0.00202
Comoros	franc	0.00187	0.00252	0.00256	0.00279	0.00296	0.00284	0.00270	0.00282	0.00261	0.00270
Cote d'Ivoire	CFA franc[3]	0.00140	0.00189	0.00191	0.00209	0.00223	0.00214	0.00203	0.00212	0.00196	0.00203
Cyprus	euro[4]	1.60134	2.15118	2.18248	2.35531	1.47595	1.39396	1.32657	1.39312	1.28507	1.32883
Czech Republic	koruna	0.02591	0.04172	0.04440	0.04954	0.05908	0.05292	0.05250	0.05660	0.05115	0.05111
Denmark	krone	0.12362	0.16663	0.16846	0.18407	0.19729	0.18704	0.17791	0.18643	0.17275	0.17813
Djibouti	franc	0.00563	0.00563	0.00563	0.00563	0.00563	0.00563	0.00563	0.00563	0.00563	0.00563
Dominica	EC dollar[5]	0.37037	0.37037	0.37037	0.37037	0.37037	0.37037	0.37037	0.37037	0.37037	0.37037
Equatorial Guinea	CFA franc[3]	0.00140	0.00190	0.00191	0.00209	0.00225	0.00212	0.00201	0.00213	0.00196	0.00202
Estonia	euro[6]	0.05866	0.07933	0.08041	0.08766	0.09419	0.08922	0.08471	1.39528	1.28515	1.32768
Ethiopia	birr	0.12160	0.11538	0.11495	0.11147	0.10406	0.08464	0.06924	0.05914	0.05643	...
Extra-EU28	euro	0.92003	1.24200	1.25625	1.37236	1.47399	1.39351	1.32434	1.39170	1.28542	1.32803
Fiji	dollar	0.47029	0.59029	0.57749	0.62303	0.62885	0.51330	0.52434	0.55797	0.55877	0.54209
Finland	euro[1]	0.92026	1.24339	1.25692	1.37140	1.47688	1.39429	1.32514	1.39146	1.28629	1.32843
France	euro[1]	0.92101	1.24430	1.25545	1.37193	1.47398	1.39401	1.32545	1.39146	1.28597	1.32799
Gabon	CFA franc[2,3]	0.00141	0.00190	0.00191	0.00208	0.00225	0.00213	0.00202	0.00212	0.00196	0.00203
Gambia	dalasi	0.07831	0.03500	0.03563	0.04040	0.04531	0.03755	0.03577	0.03397	0.03126	0.02792
Germany	euro[1]	0.92038	1.24269	1.25666	1.37163	1.47260	1.39352	1.32502	1.39184	1.28556	1.32800
Ghana	cedi	1.83930	1.10265	1.09025	1.06865	0.94292	0.70912	0.69865	0.66114	0.55600	0.51115
Gibraltar	pound	1.51023	1.81623	1.84441	2.00293	1.83115	1.56517	1.54366	1.60367	1.58595	1.56431
Grenada	EC dollar[5]	0.37037	0.37037	0.37037	0.37037	0.37037	0.37037	0.37037	0.37037	0.37037	0.37037
Guyana	dollar	0.00548	0.00500	0.00499	0.00494	0.00491	0.00490	0.00491	0.00490	0.00489	0.00487
Haiti	gourde	0.04740	0.02464	0.02479	0.02712	0.02550	0.02424	0.02514	0.02466	0.02384	0.02299
Hungary	forint	0.00353	0.00500	0.00476	0.00546	0.00588	0.00499	0.00481	0.00498	0.00444	0.00447
Iceland	krona	0.01271	0.01585	0.01419	0.01566	0.01198	0.00808	0.00821	0.00862	0.00799	0.00819
India	rupee	0.02226	0.02268	0.02206	0.02431	0.02303	0.02074	0.02188	0.02141	0.01873	0.01715
Ireland	euro[1]	0.92013	1.24436	1.25593	1.37116	1.47490	1.38911	1.32607	1.39056	1.28641	1.32868
Italy	euro[1]	0.92076	1.24425	1.25572	1.37105	1.47477	1.39353	1.32548	1.39206	1.28610	1.32784

2000	2005	2006	2007	2008	2009	2010	2011	2012	2013	Unité	Pays ou Zone
				Exports - Exportations							
0.00696	0.01001	0.01021	0.01109	0.01204	0.01056	0.00960	0.00991	0.00924	0.00946	lek	Albanie
0.01329	0.01365	0.01375	0.01447	0.01558	0.01377	0.01345	0.01371	0.01294	0.01261	dinar	Algérie
0.91870	1.24575	1.24932	1.37288	1.47712	1.39441	1.32073	1.39424	1.28550	1.32866	euro	Andorre
0.37037	0.37037	0.37037	0.37037	0.37037	0.37037	0.37037	0.37037	0.37037	0.37037	dollar C.O.	Anguilla
0.57827	0.76295	0.75399	0.83968	0.84081	0.78476	0.92004	1.03307	1.03493	0.96471	dollar	Australie
0.92072	1.24303	1.25673	1.37179	1.47538	1.39527	1.32473	1.39208	1.28554	1.32799	euro[1]	Autriche
1.00000	1.00000	1.00000	1.00000	1.00000	1.00000	1.00000	1.00000	1.00000	1.00000	dollar	Bahamas
0.01916	0.01554	0.01449	0.01452	0.01458	0.01448	0.01435	0.01349	0.01222	0.01281	taka	Bangladesh
0.50000	0.50000	0.50000	0.50000	0.50000	0.50000	0.50000	0.50000	0.50000	0.50000	dollar	Barbade
0.92123	1.24467	1.25563	1.37095	1.47594	1.39497	1.32595	1.39200	1.28592	1.32776	euro	Belgique
0.00140	0.00188	0.00192	0.00210	0.00224	0.00212	0.00202	0.00211	0.00196	0.00203	franc CFA[2,3]	Bénin
0.02225	0.02269	0.02205	0.02421	0.02301	0.02066	0.02186	0.02152	0.01869	0.01707	ngultrum	Bhoutan
0.47100	0.63434	0.64339	0.70175	0.75446	0.71484	0.67656	0.71189	0.65663	0.67873	marka	Bosnie-Herzégovine
0.19495	0.19700	0.17059	0.16276	0.15022	0.14212	0.14714	0.14739	0.13095	0.11900	pula	Botswana
0.58029	0.60031	0.62922	0.66572	0.70734	0.68722	0.73513	...	0.80031	...	dollar	Brunéi Darussalam
0.46931	0.63406	0.64280	0.70289	0.75617	0.71575	0.67589	0.71206	0.65652	0.67881	lev	Bulgarie
0.00143	0.00189	0.00191	0.00209	0.00223	0.00211	0.00203	0.00212	0.00196	0.00203	franc CFA[3]	Burkina Faso
0.00142	0.00091	0.00096	0.00092	0.00084	0.00081	0.00081	0.00079	0.00069	0.00064	franc	Burundi
0.00859	0.01122	0.01135	0.01242	0.01321	0.01252	0.01206	0.01258	0.01161	0.01206	escudo	Cabo Verde
0.00140	0.00189	0.00192	0.00210	0.00222	0.00213	0.00202	0.00212	0.00196	0.00203	franc CFA[3]	Cameroun
0.67310	0.82657	0.88180	0.93332	0.94401	0.87864	0.97148	1.01035	1.00092	0.97113	dollar	Canada
0.00142	0.00191	0.00192	0.00210	0.00223	0.00212	0.00202	0.00212	0.00196	0.00202	franc CFA[2,3]	Rép. centrafricaine
0.00141	0.00190	0.00191	0.00208	0.00224	0.00211	0.00203	0.00212	0.00196	0.00202	franc CFA[2,3]	Tchad
0.00187	0.00252	0.00256	0.00279	0.00296	0.00284	0.00269	0.00282	0.00261	0.00270	franc	Comores
0.00140	0.00189	0.00191	0.00209	0.00221	0.00213	0.00203	0.00212	0.00196	0.00203	franc CFA[3]	Côte d'Ivoire
1.61099	2.15054	2.17544	2.34513	1.47432	1.39317	1.32577	1.39342	1.28543	1.32632	euro[4]	Chypre
0.02592	0.04174	0.04437	0.04952	0.05918	0.05292	0.05252	0.05659	0.05115	0.05112	couronne	République tchèque
0.12343	0.16666	0.16842	0.18418	0.19753	0.18736	0.17788	0.18648	0.17265	0.17810	couronne	Danemark
0.00563	0.00563	0.00563	0.00563	0.00563	0.00563	0.00563	0.00563	0.00563	0.00563	franc	Djibouti
0.37037	0.37037	0.37037	0.37037	0.37037	0.37037	0.37037	0.37037	0.37037	0.37037	dollar C.O.[5]	Dominique
0.00140	0.00190	0.00191	0.00209	0.00225	0.00212	0.00201	0.00213	0.00196	0.00202	franc CFA[3]	Guinée équatoriale
0.05874	0.07934	0.08040	0.08769	0.09411	0.08932	0.08477	1.39329	1.28480	1.32778	euro[6]	Estonie
0.12182	0.11539	0.11498	0.11170	0.10442	0.08581	0.07035	0.05927	0.05662	...	birr	Ethiopie
0.91942	1.24185	1.25699	1.37262	1.47326	1.39614	1.32385	1.39094	1.28491	1.32753	euro	Extra-UE28
0.46700	0.59080	0.57690	0.62377	0.62687	0.51264	0.52454	0.55841	0.55861	0.54154	dollar	Fidji
0.91911	1.24375	1.25693	1.37151	1.47741	1.39517	1.32520	1.39175	1.28546	1.32828	euro[1]	Finlande
0.92139	1.24422	1.25528	1.37115	1.47455	1.39379	1.32552	1.39135	1.28582	1.32781	euro[1]	France
0.00141	0.00190	0.00191	0.00208	0.00225	0.00215	0.00204	0.00212	0.00196	0.00202	franc CFA[2,3]	Gabon
0.07833	0.03531	0.03563	0.04016	0.04548	0.03756	0.03578	...	...	...	dalasi	Gambie
0.92097	1.24382	1.25651	1.37150	1.47478	1.39506	1.32524	1.39174	1.28528	1.32799	euro[1]	Allemagne
1.79936	1.10275	1.09065	1.06940	0.94582	0.71012	0.69889	0.66155	0.55701	0.51202	cedi	Ghana
1.50704	1.81242	1.84738	2.00487	1.82327	1.56954	1.54645	1.60246	1.58625	1.56579	livre	Gibraltar
0.37037	0.37037	0.37037	0.37037	0.37037	0.37037	0.37037	0.37037	0.37037	0.37037	dollar C.O.[5]	Grenade
0.00548	0.00500	0.00499	0.00494	0.00491	0.00490	0.00491	0.00490	0.00489	0.00487	dollar	Guyana
0.04649	0.02470	0.02495	0.02715	0.02548	0.02424	0.02513	0.02468	0.02381	0.02299	gourde	Haïti
0.00353	0.00500	0.00476	0.00546	0.00587	0.00499	0.00481	0.00498	0.00444	0.00447	forint	Hongrie
0.01273	0.01589	0.01423	0.01565	0.01147	0.00810	0.00821	0.00862	0.00800	0.00818	couronne	Islande
0.02223	0.02267	0.02206	0.02426	0.02316	0.02070	0.02189	0.02145	0.01874	0.01707	roupie	Inde
0.91904	1.24432	1.25623	1.37013	1.47058	1.38997	1.32605	1.39226	1.28446	1.32743	euro[1]	Irlande
0.92123	1.24353	1.25664	1.37148	1.47680	1.39403	1.32462	1.39206	1.28538	1.32775	euro[1]	Italie

External trade conversion factors (Table C)

Imports, exports: US dollars per national currency [cont.]

Facteurs de conversion pour le commerce extérieur (Tableau C)

Importations, exportations : monnaie nationale en dollars É.-U. [suite]

Country or Area	Unit	2000	2005	2006	2007	2008	2009	2010	2011	2012	2013
						Imports - Importations [cont.]					
Jamaica	dollar	0.02325	0.01604	0.01521	0.01444	0.01381	0.01139	0.01148	0.01164	0.01126	0.00998
Japan	yen	0.00928	0.00906	0.00860	0.00851	0.00966	0.01072	0.01142	0.01255	0.01253	0.01025
Jordan	dinar	1.41044	1.41044	1.41044	1.41044	1.40908	1.40845	1.40845	1.40845	1.40845	1.40845
Kenya	shilling	0.01312	0.01324	0.01388	0.01486	0.01445	0.01295	0.01260	0.01124	0.01183	0.01161
Kuwait	dinar	3.25974	3.42469	3.44816	3.52271	3.71925	3.47591	3.49173	3.62404	3.57183	3.52635
Latvia	lat	1.64778	1.76533	1.79203	1.95139	2.09557	1.98447	1.88479	2.00044	1.82835	1.88976
Lesotho	loti	0.14414	0.15726	0.14728	0.14216	0.12047	0.11943	0.13694	0.13731	0.12145	0.10315
Libya	dinar	1.93754	0.76161	0.76288	0.79436	0.81428	0.80068	0.78987	0.81692	0.79251	0.78684
Lithuania	lita	0.25000	0.35944	0.36439	0.39746	0.42866	0.40478	0.38365	0.40363	0.37237	0.38473
Luxembourg	euro[1]	0.92046	1.24367	1.25595	1.37045	1.47456	1.39473	1.32369	1.39215	1.28647	1.32746
Madagascar	ariary	0.00074	0.00049	0.00047	0.00054	0.00059	0.00051	0.00048	0.00050	0.00046	0.00045
Malawi	kwacha	0.01650	0.00843	0.00733	0.00714	0.00712	0.00708	0.00664	0.00639	0.00399	0.00275
Malaysia	ringgit	0.26316	0.26411	0.27281	0.29115	0.30078	0.28471	0.31130	0.32682	0.32372	0.31740
Mali	CFA franc[2,3]	0.00141	0.00190	0.00191	0.00209	0.00224	0.00212	0.00203	0.00212	0.00196	0.00202
Malta	euro[7]	2.27827	2.88838	2.93558	3.21953	1.47727	1.39269	1.32442	1.38875	1.28058	1.32580
Mauritania	ouguiya	0.00419	0.00377	0.00372	0.00386	0.00422	0.00381	0.00360	0.00356	0.00337	...
Mauritius	rupee	0.03807	0.03384	0.03140	0.03217	0.03522	0.03152	0.03252	0.03484	0.03326	0.03259
Montenegro	euro	.	1.24575	1.26362	1.38311	1.47495	1.39837	1.31872	1.39522	1.28304	1.32759
Morocco	dirham	0.09413	0.11276	0.11389	0.12251	0.12994	0.12456	0.11875	0.12373	0.11600	0.11894
Namibia	dollar	0.14310	0.15662	0.14687	0.14226	0.12032	0.12004	0.13690	0.13744	0.12130	0.10303
Nepal	rupee	0.01407	0.01400	0.01373	0.01514	0.01422	0.01293	0.01367	0.01347	0.01169	0.01061
Netherlands	euro[1]	0.92071	1.24317	1.25630	1.37241	1.47369	1.39504	1.32572	1.39142	1.28551	1.32825
New Zealand	dollar	0.45242	0.70372	0.64916	0.73766	0.70854	0.63595	0.72277	0.79122	0.81014	0.81970
Niger	CFA franc[3]	0.00139	0.00188	0.00192	0.00211	0.00218	0.00213	0.00202	0.00212	0.00196	0.00203
Niue	NZ dollar	0.45360	...	0.65005	0.73592	0.70944	0.65079	...	...	...	...
Norway	krone	0.11357	0.15510	0.15609	0.17141	0.17898	0.16026	0.16548	0.17849	0.17200	0.17018
Oman	rial Omani	2.60078	2.60078	2.60078	2.60078	2.60078	2.60078	2.60078	2.60078	2.60078	2.60078
Pakistan	rupee	0.01865	0.01679	0.01659	0.01647	0.01435	0.01223	0.01174	0.01157	0.01071	0.00985
Panama	balboa	1.00000	1.00000	1.00000	1.00000	1.00000	1.00000	1.00000	1.00000	1.00000	...
Papua New Guinea	kina	0.36017	0.32221	0.32685	0.33668	0.36908	0.36271	0.36772	0.42064	0.47970	...
Philippines	peso	0.02254	0.01815	0.01950	0.02175	0.02267	0.02098	0.02219	0.02309	0.02368	0.02353
Poland	zloty	0.22983	0.30896	0.32297	0.36348	0.42169	0.32311	0.33223	0.33853	0.30738	0.31653
Portugal	euro[1]	0.92205	1.24357	1.25669	1.37301	1.47562	1.39664	1.32466	1.39256	1.28580	1.32806
Qatar	riyal	0.27473	0.27473	0.27473	0.27473	0.27473	0.27473	0.27473	0.27473	0.27473	0.27473
Rwanda	franc	0.00255	0.00180	0.00181	0.00182	0.00182	0.00176	0.00172	0.00166	0.00162	0.00156
Saint Helena	pound	1.51611	1.82040	1.84263	2.00168	1.85324	1.56448	...	...	...	...
Saint Kitts-Nevis	EC dollar[5]	0.37037	0.37037	0.37037	0.37037	0.37037	0.37037	0.37037	0.37037	0.37037	0.37037
Saint Lucia	EC dollar[5]	0.37037	0.37037	0.37037	0.37037	0.37037	0.37037	0.37037	0.37037	0.37037	0.37037
Saint Vincent-Grenadines	EC dollar[5]	0.37037	0.37037	0.37037	0.37037	0.37037	0.37037	0.37037	0.37037	0.37037	0.37037
Samoa	tala	0.30374	0.36869	0.35986	0.38259	0.37763	0.37144	0.40273	0.43132	0.43616	0.43270
Saudi Arabia	riyal	0.26667	0.26688	0.26702	0.26684	0.26667	0.26667	0.26667	0.26667	0.26667	0.26667
Senegal	CFA franc[3]	0.00140	0.00189	0.00192	0.00210	0.00225	0.00212	0.00202	0.00212	0.00196	0.00203
Serbia	dinar	.	0.01468	0.01502	0.01721	0.01815	0.01484	0.01282	0.01365	0.01137	...
Seychelles	rupee	0.17549	0.18180	0.18120	0.14962	0.11101	0.07475	0.08270	0.08082	0.07309	0.08299
Sierra Leone	leone	0.00047	0.00035	0.00034	0.00033	0.00034	0.00030	0.00025	0.00023	0.00023	0.00023
Singapore	dollar	0.57950	0.60041	0.62997	0.66457	0.70922	0.68983	0.73435	0.79575	0.80017	0.79916
Slovakia	euro[8]	0.02164	0.03217	0.03385	0.04071	0.04707	1.39751	1.32569	1.39191	1.28544	1.32891
Solomon Islands	dollar	0.19652	0.13276	0.13144	0.13068	0.12919	0.12416	0.12400	0.13152	0.13596	0.13698
South Africa	rand	0.14376	0.15708	0.14672	0.14220	0.12201	0.11910	0.13684	0.13762	0.12181	0.10364
Spain	euro[1]	0.92032	1.24321	1.25615	1.37273	1.47758	1.39488	1.32537	1.39111	1.28585	1.32853

2000	2005	2006	2007	2008	2009	2010	2011	2012	2013	Unité	Pays ou Zone
				Exports - Exportations *[suite]*							
0.02328	0.01604	0.01521	0.01449	0.01382	0.01139	0.01147	0.01164	0.01127	0.01002	dollar	Jamaïque
0.00928	0.00906	0.00860	0.00851	0.00965	0.01072	0.01142	0.01255	0.01253	0.01024	yen	Japon
1.41044	1.41044	1.41044	1.41044	1.40903	1.40845	1.40845	1.40845	1.40845	1.40845	dinar	Jordanie
0.01312	0.01323	0.01386	0.01486	0.01451	0.01294	0.01262	0.01126	0.01183	0.01161	shilling	Kenya
3.25932	3.42469	3.44654	3.52858	3.72796	3.47802	3.49114	3.62497	3.57302	3.52615	dinar	Koweït
1.65011	1.76872	1.78931	1.95344	2.09490	1.99146	1.88513	1.99970	1.82816	1.89083	lat	Lettonie
0.14443	0.15722	0.14671	0.14201	0.12109	0.11918	0.13680	0.13763	0.12160	0.10323	loti	Lesotho
1.94149	0.76235	0.76266	0.79331	0.81664	0.79997	0.78882	0.81772	0.79205	0.78629	dinar	Libye
0.25000	0.35956	0.36395	0.39735	0.42820	0.40500	0.38355	0.40354	0.37227	0.38472	lita	Lituanie
0.92175	1.24507	1.25565	1.36941	1.47938	1.39507	1.32523	1.39232	1.28586	1.32830	euro[1]	Luxembourg
0.00074	0.00049	0.00047	0.00054	0.00058	0.00051	0.00048	0.00049	0.00046	0.00045	ariary	Madagascar
0.01605	0.00843	0.00733	0.00714	0.00712	0.00708	0.00664	0.00635	0.00409	0.00275	kwacha	Malawi
0.26316	0.26411	0.27281	0.29119	0.30077	0.28460	0.31090	0.32684	0.32383	0.31713	ringgit	Malaisie
0.00141	0.00188	0.00192	0.00210	0.00222	0.00212	0.00202	0.00212	0.00196	0.00203	franc CFA[2,3]	Mali
2.27775	2.89004	2.93896	3.21645	1.47020	1.39730	1.32456	1.38361	1.28351	1.32724	euro[7]	Malte
0.00419	0.00377	0.00372	0.00388	0.00421	0.00381	0.00361	0.00356	0.00337	...	ouguiya	Mauritanie
0.03794	0.03383	0.03146	0.03211	0.03510	0.03144	0.03253	0.03486	0.03326	0.03258	rupee	Maurice
.	1.24575	1.26143	1.37725	1.48166	1.39902	1.32172	1.39043	1.28472	1.32688	euro	Monténégro
0.09411	0.11273	0.11380	0.12222	0.13063	0.12435	0.11876	0.12372	0.11599	0.11893	dirham	Maroc
0.14370	0.15702	0.14720	0.14205	0.12093	0.11909	0.13679	0.13761	0.12159	0.10328	dollar	Namibie
0.01405	0.01401	0.01375	0.01508	0.01431	0.01291	0.01368	0.01350	0.01174	0.01069	rupee	Népal
0.92051	1.24367	1.25634	1.37277	1.47345	1.39541	1.32617	1.39124	1.28580	1.32806	euro[1]	Pays-Bas
0.45450	0.70508	0.64784	0.73707	0.71287	0.62844	0.72123	0.78967	0.80985	0.82102	dollar	Nouvelle-Zélande
0.00141	0.00190	0.00191	0.00209	0.00221	0.00213	0.00201	0.00211	0.00196	0.00204	franc CFA[3]	Niger
0.45625	0.70409	0.64899	0.73408	0.71697	...	...	...	...	...	dollar NZ	Nioué
0.11337	0.15512	0.15596	0.17146	0.18021	0.15968	0.16580	0.17840	0.17209	0.17033	couronne	Norvège
2.60078	2.60078	2.60078	2.60078	2.60078	2.60078	2.60078	2.60078	2.60078	2.60078	rial omani	Oman
0.01864	0.01680	0.01659	0.01646	0.01428	0.01222	0.01174	0.01160	0.01071	0.00984	rupee	Pakistan
1.00000	1.00000	1.00000	1.00000	1.00000	1.00000	1.00000	1.00000	...	...	balboa	Panama
0.36016	0.32260	0.32721	0.33740	0.37042	0.36377	0.36801	0.42186	0.48004	0.44619	kina	Papouasie-Nouvelle-Guinée
0.02244	0.01815	0.01950	0.02169	0.02266	0.02098	0.02219	0.02309	0.02367	0.02352	peso	Philippines
0.22975	0.30904	0.32271	0.36305	0.42237	0.32319	0.33224	0.33817	0.30736	0.31649	zloty	Pologne
0.92232	1.24175	1.25688	1.37079	1.47773	1.39603	1.32576	1.39181	1.28530	1.32753	euro[1]	Portugal
0.27473	0.27473	0.27473	0.27473	0.27473	0.27473	0.27473	0.27473	0.27473	0.27473	riyal	Qatar
0.00255	0.00180	0.00181	0.00182	0.00182	0.00176	0.00171	0.00166	0.00162	0.00155	franc	Rwanda
1.51611	1.82040	1.84263	2.00168	1.85324	1.56448	...	...	...	...	livre	Sainte-Hélèna
0.37037	0.37037	0.37037	0.37037	0.37037	0.37037	0.37037	0.37037	0.37037	0.37037	dollar C.O.[5]	Saint-Kitts-et-Nevis
0.37037	0.37037	0.37037	0.37037	0.37037	0.37037	0.37037	0.37037	0.37037	0.37037	dollar C.O.[5]	Sainte-Lucie
0.37037	0.37037	0.37037	0.37037	0.37037	0.37037	0.37037	0.37037	0.37037	0.37037	dollar C.O.[5]	St.Vincent-Grenadines
0.30446	0.36885	0.35979	0.38398	0.37987	0.37169	0.40204	0.43183	0.43625	0.43228	tala	Samoa
0.26667	0.26691	0.26702	0.26681	0.26667	0.26667	0.26667	0.26667	0.26667	0.26667	riyal	Arabie saoudite
0.00141	0.00189	0.00191	0.00209	0.00224	0.00213	0.00202	0.00212	0.00196	0.00202	franc CFA.[3]	Sénégal
.	0.01473	0.01504	0.01718	0.01818	0.01489	0.01280	0.01368	0.01134	...	dinar	Serbie
0.17468	0.18180	0.18108	0.14746	0.10742	0.07472	0.08289	0.08074	0.07309	0.08287	rupee	Seychelles
0.00049	0.00035	0.00034	0.00033	0.00034	0.00030	0.00025	0.00023	0.00023	0.00023	leone	Sierra Leone
0.57944	0.60035	0.62983	0.66418	0.70932	0.68990	0.73483	0.79555	0.80025	0.79910	dollar	Singapour
0.02167	0.03217	0.03384	0.04068	0.04704	1.39826	1.32606	1.39145	1.28543	1.32836	euro[8]	Slovaquie
0.19654	0.13276	0.13143	0.13067	0.12903	0.12415	0.12400	0.13151	0.13595	0.13697	dollar	Iles Salomon
0.14384	0.15707	0.14675	0.14224	0.12203	0.11974	0.13708	0.13774	0.12185	0.10350	rand	Afrique du Sud
0.92078	1.24382	1.25594	1.37160	1.47566	1.39553	1.32548	1.39150	1.28554	1.32768	euro[1]	Espagne

External trade conversion factors (Table C)
Imports, exports: US dollars per national currency *[cont.]*

Facteurs de conversion pour le commerce extérieur (Tableau C)
Importations, exportations : monnaie nationale en dollars É.-U. *[suite]*

Country or Area	Unit	2000	2005	2006	2007	2008	2009	2010	2011	2012	2013
						Imports - Importations *[cont.]*					
Sri Lanka	rupee	0.01295	0.00994	0.00962	0.00903	0.00924	0.00871	0.00885	0.00904	0.00782	0.00774
Suriname	dollar	0.75087	0.36591	0.36446	0.36430	0.36430	0.36430	0.36424	0.30557	0.30303	0.30303
Swaziland	lilangeni	0.14311	0.15699	0.14749	0.14252	0.11858	0.11926	0.13741	0.13605	0.12111	...
Sweden	krona	0.10905	0.13382	0.13587	0.14832	0.15392	0.13174	0.13914	0.15415	0.14766	0.15354
Switzerland	franc	0.59172	0.80342	0.79820	0.83442	0.92938	0.92326	0.96108	1.12846	1.06696	1.07917
Syrian Arab Rep.	pound	0.08909	0.08909	0.08909	0.08909	0.08909	0.08909	0.08909	0.08909	0.08909	0.08909
Thailand	baht	0.02483	0.02485	0.02641	0.02901	0.03005	0.02928	0.03161	0.03282	0.03218	0.03260
Togo	CFA franc[2,3]	0.00141	0.00189	0.00192	0.00210	0.00222	0.00212	0.00202	0.00211	0.00195	0.00203
Tonga	pa'anga	0.56409	0.51366	0.49387	0.50805	0.51709	0.49573	0.52617	0.58081	0.58111	0.56303
Trinidad and Tobago	dollar	0.15874	0.15874	0.15841	0.15801	0.15907	0.15805	0.15685	0.15601	0.15548	0.15519
Tunisia	dinar	0.72984	0.77051	0.75204	0.78163	0.81420	0.74352	0.69829	0.71089	0.64026	0.61547
Tuvalu	Aust. dollar	0.58059	0.76341	0.76129	0.85025	...	...	...	...	...	...
Uganda	shilling	0.00061	0.00056	0.00055	0.00058	0.00059	0.00049	0.00046	0.00039	0.00040	0.00039
United Kingdom	pound	1.51354	1.81754	1.83936	2.00269	1.85795	1.56531	1.54604	1.60331	1.58538	1.56393
United Rep. of Tanzania	shilling	0.00125	0.00088	0.00080	0.00081	0.00084	0.00076	0.00071	0.00063	0.00063	0.00062
Vanuatu	vatu	0.00725	0.00914	0.00902	0.00981	0.00991	0.00945	0.01038	0.01118	0.01079	0.01057
Yemen	rial	0.00619	0.00524	0.00508	0.00503	0.00501	0.00494	0.00458	0.00468	0.00467	0.00465
Zambia	kwacha	0.32281	0.22458	0.27859	0.25148	0.27149	0.20012	0.20852	0.20522	0.19448	0.18518

2000	2005	2006	2007	2008	2009	2010	2011	2012	2013	Unité	Pays ou Zone
					Exports - Exportations *[suite]*						
0.01293	0.00994	0.00961	0.00903	0.00923	0.00870	0.00886	0.00904	0.00786	0.00774	rupee	Sri Lanka
0.74176	0.36602	0.36444	0.36430	0.36430	0.36430	0.36426	0.30437	0.30303	0.30303	dollar	Suriname
0.14300	0.15648	0.14673	0.14234	0.11969	0.12040	0.13721	0.13672	0.12107	...	lilangeni	Swaziland
0.10910	0.13392	0.13576	0.14828	0.15397	0.13148	0.13916	0.15417	0.14760	0.15355	couronne	Suède
0.59161	0.80329	0.79830	0.83433	0.92964	0.92418	0.96138	1.12793	1.06665	1.07885	franc	Suisse
0.08909	0.08909	0.08909	0.08909	0.08909	0.08909	0.08909	0.08909	0.08909	0.08909	livre	République arabe syrienne
0.02486	0.02482	0.02644	0.02902	0.03006	0.02924	0.03163	0.03283	0.03218	0.03254	baht	Thaïlande
0.00140	0.00189	0.00192	0.00209	0.00224	0.00212	0.00201	0.00213	0.00195	0.00202	franc CFA[2,3]	Togo
0.55465	0.50972	0.49525	0.50918	0.51314	0.50336	0.52832	0.58369	0.58245	0.56340	pa'anga	Tonga
0.15873	0.15874	0.15847	0.15799	0.15910	0.15834	0.15685	0.15607	0.15548	0.15522	dollar	Trinité-et-Tobago
0.73083	0.77115	0.75167	0.78120	0.81733	0.74217	0.69844	0.71126	0.64064	0.61588	dinar	Tunisie
0.57480	0.76222	0.75492	0.84252	...	...	...	...	...	...	dollar aust.	Tuvalu
0.00062	0.00056	0.00055	0.00058	0.00058	0.00050	0.00046	0.00039	0.00040	0.00039	shilling	Ouganda
1.51340	1.81718	1.83744	2.00270	1.85700	1.56660	1.54578	1.60331	1.58520	1.56402	livre	Royaume-Uni
0.00125	0.00088	0.00080	0.00081	0.00084	0.00076	0.00071	0.00064	0.00063	0.00062	shilling	Rép.-Unie de Tanzanie
0.00726	0.00915	0.00900	0.00984	0.00992	0.00936	0.01033	0.01119	0.01078	0.01055	vatu	Vanuatu
0.00618	0.00522	0.00507	0.00503	0.00501	0.00493	0.00455	0.00468	0.00466	0.00465	rial	Yémen
0.32860	0.22177	0.28175	0.25113	0.27162	0.20172	0.20865	0.20555	0.19426	0.18529	kwacha	Zambie

External trade conversion factors (Table C)
Imports, exports: US dollars per national currency *[cont.]*

Facteurs de conversion pour le commerce extérieur (Tableau C)
Importations, exportations : monnaie nationale en dollars É.-U. *[suite]*

General note:

Trade conversion factors are weighted averages of monthly or quarterly exchange rates, the weights being the corresponding monthly or quarterly values of imports and exports. The exchange rates are as compiled by the IMF or provided by the country concerned. The conversion factors shown in this table are used to obtain trade data in terms of US dollars.

For further information on sources and presentation, as well as for a brief table description, please see the introduction.

1   The conversion factors are calculated for each country of euro zone separately and may vary due to differences in relative weights of monthly or quarterly values of imports and exports.

2   The conversion factors are not trade weighted.
3   Comptoirs Francais du Afrique franc pegged to the euro at CFAF 655.957 per euro.
4   Prior to January 2008, data for Cyprus are in pounds.
5   East Caribbean dollar.
6   Prior to January 2011, data for Estonia are in krooni.
7   Prior to January 2008, data for Malta are in liri.
8   Prior to January 2009, data for Slovakia are in koruny.

Note generale :

Les facteurs de conversion pour le commerce extérieur sont les moyennes pondérées des taux de change mensuelles ou trimestrielles. Les coefficients de pondération sont les valeurs mensuelles ou trimestrielles correspondantes des importations ou des exportations. Les taux de change sont les taux calculés par le secretariat du FMI ou fournis par le pays. Les facteurs de conversion montrés dans cette table sont employés pour obtenir les données commerciales en termes de dollars de E.U..

Pour plus d'information sur les sources et la présentation ainsi qu'une brève description du tableau, se il vous plaît se référer à l'introduction.

1   Les facteurs de conversion sont calculés pour chaque pays d'euro zone séparément et peuvent varier en raison des différences dans les ponderation relatifs de valeurs mensuelles ou trimestrielles des importations et des exportations.

2   Les facteurs de conversion ne sont pas pondérés.
3   Comptoirs Français du Afrique franc est chevillé à l'euro à CFAF 655,957 par euro.
4   Avant janvier 2008, les données de Chypre étaient en livres.
5   Dollar des caraïbes orientales.
6   Avant janvier 2011, les données de l'Estonie étaient en krooni.
7   Avant janvier 2008, les données de Malte étaient en lire.
8   Avant janvier 2009, les données de Slovaquie étaient en couronnes.

World exports by provenance and destination (Table D)

In million U.S. dollars f.o.b.

Exports from	Year	World 1/ Monde 1/	Developed economies 2/ Economies développées 2/						Commonwealth of Independent States Communauté d'Etats Indépendants	
			Asia-Pacific Asie-Pacifique		Europe		North America Amérique du Nord			
			Total	Japan Japon	Total	Germany Allemagne	Total	U.S.A. É.-U.	Total	Europe

Total trade (SITC, Rev. 3, 0-9) 3/

Exports from	Year	World 1/	Total	Total	Japan	Total	Germany	Total	U.S.A.	Total	Europe
World 1/	2000	6352781	4389795	413809	337448	2563432	476836	1412554	1176790	77192	65057
	2010	15080032	8406923	759500	557432	5429555	990564	2217867	1785380	389056	314401
	2011	18085459	9862797	926152	681572	6384483	1142579	2552161	2041852	542223	447958
	2012	18172037	9668090	962770	705224	6064100	1088446	2641219	2110483	562128	456705
	2013	18658648	9769986	896111	648100	6211246	1122466	2662629	2117922	574234	457823
Developed Economies - Asia-Pacific 2/	2000	556339	283778	30765	14422	93424	21063	159589	150831	1004	824
	2010	1007411	331697	73639	41538	115968	22128	142089	131244	10412	9621
	2011	1130240	373487	91009	54805	130828	26071	151650	140669	15265	13870
	2012	1092115	364268	88353	52281	108416	23073	167498	154984	15871	14306
	2013	1006696	328647	80521	47093	91820	21052	156306	146044	14214	12577
Japan	2000	479276	243818	9835	.	83786	19997	150197	142480	793	624
	2010	769774	243061	17798	.	95563	20290	129700	120338	9161	8543
	2011	823184	262233	19739	.	105874	23503	136621	127675	13754	12530
	2012	798568	259286	20383	.	86576	20797	152327	142040	14585	13201
	2013	715097	238107	19161	.	75694	18959	143252	134540	13036	11583
Developed Economies - Europe 2/	2000	2526891	2122774	63491	46070	1802299	345325	256985	232387	31181	28101
	2010	5338267	4128089	107805	65978	3623709	707241	396575	352732	164092	148639
	2011	6240309	4762361	128461	77533	4182931	815862	450969	401547	214872	195192
	2012	5993957	4499093	130635	79972	3907016	785265	461442	415020	223512	203163
	2013	6290828	4711609	130116	79470	4108710	818285	472784	422475	231115	208041
France	2000	295345	239365	6445	4983	204528	44461	28392	25937	2392	1952
	2010	511651	371697	12364	7793	326578	82989	32755	29231	10476	9481
	2011	581542	422207	14954	9065	370762	96160	36490	32468	12971	11898
	2012	556576	396235	13788	9492	344535	91548	37913	34114	14725	13365
	2013	566879	405196	13308	9038	352154	93187	39735	35790	13680	11809
Germany	2000	549607	458641	15684	12137	382583	.	60374	56393	8923	8069
	2010	1271096	946837	28739	17374	821272	.	96826	86847	48260	43828
	2011	1482202	1085941	34224	21400	938202	.	113515	103075	66060	60460
	2012	1416184	1019921	35520	22186	860790	.	123611	112086	66735	61246
	2013	1458647	1051362	35870	22938	884132	.	131360	117840	66630	60596
Developed Economies - North America 2/	2000	1057790	699131	86693	71335	193929	31336	418509	241624	3504	2715
	2010	1664232	937712	96113	69476	303197	51718	538403	289464	10696	8796
	2011	1930847	1068633	110248	76937	345170	52639	613215	331764	14739	12250
	2012	1999674	1089644	117146	80403	342186	51756	630313	337836	17381	14551
	2013	2035229	1088285	106784	75526	334815	50215	646686	345749	18000	14812
United States	2000	780332	436300	79685	65252	179776	29242	176839	.	3325	2563
	2010	1277109	599501	85165	60543	265503	48041	248832	.	9164	7484
	2011	1479730	678910	97169	66160	300433	48779	281308	.	12823	10583
	2012	1545565	696763	104354	70043	300096	48355	292313	.	15318	12745
	2013	1578001	693652	94396	65143	298526	46945	300731	.	16135	13229
South-Eastern Europe	2000	19514	13492	50	37	12585	2634	857	764	813	674
	2010	89957	59420	259	213	57848	13649	1313	1137	4969	4273
	2011	115518	76671	354	276	74345	18610	1972	1627	6855	5886
	2012	107446	69938	405	314	67472	16854	2062	1761	6668	5617
	2013	122785	80838	451	359	78034	20166	2353	2072	8106	7069
Commonwealth of Independent States	2000	143026	80581	2953	2937	70362	11064	7266	5777	28980	24076
	2010	574046	285348	13703	13475	251872	20034	19774	15952	96921	70645
	2011	762950	403234	18890	18730	360627	28930	23718	20192	162832	128402
	2012	777878	415196	21856	21549	373123	30621	20217	16448	158831	118704
	2013	760959	412780	25801	25287	369820	28376	17158	13793	151012	107064
Russian Federation	2000	103093	65496	2771	2764	57875	9232	4850	4648	13824	10807
	2010	397068	212878	12625	12494	187499	15862	12754	11933	49000	31999
	2011	512935	297617	17484	17413	264274	22766	15859	15288	89460	67139
	2012	522258	310599	19906	19790	277505	24039	13188	12843	85370	60035
	2013	525660	318694	24311	23907	282811	22886	11572	11101	82596	53266

For general note and footnotes see end of table

Exportations mondiales par provenance et destination (Tableau D)

En millions de dollars E.-U. f.o.b.

⟵ Exportations vers

South-Eastern Europe Europe du Sud-est	Northern Africa Afrique du Nord	Sub-Saharan Africa Afrique subsaharienne	Latin America and the Caribbean Amérique latine et Caraïbes	Eastern Asia Asie orientale	Southern Asia Asie méridionale	South-eastern Asia Asie du Sud-est	Western Asia Asie occidentale	Oceania Océanie	Others 4/ Autre 4/	Année	Exportations en provence de
Commerce total (CTCI, Rev. 3, 0-9) 3/											
27383	54343	74585	363617	700308	81715	355980	191734	6354	29776	2000	Monde 1/
115556	179731	303408	886175	2569489	450313	913025	652250	26031	188075	2010	
146479	199977	380488	1110775	3138304	561588	1097136	784869	33902	226919	2011	
140375	217113	399587	1144041	3271841	553005	1177101	819423	31524	187832	2012	
143768	222466	418588	1126033	3406928	536170	1218489	880254	31918	329814	2013	
153	1694	4909	22054	140231	6988	78409	13637	2260	1223	2000	Economies Développées -
422	4118	12141	46359	393669	31535	135540	32799	6490	2228	2010	Asie-Pacifique 2/
613	3728	14673	47317	440408	35367	154294	34944	7312	2832	2011	
631	4358	13621	45166	408987	30354	159531	38984	7788	2555	2012	
546	3663	12176	37487	401191	23109	138227	37746	6144	3545	2013	
108	1196	3721	20779	124536	4751	68494	10619	460	0	2000	Japon
384	3160	8849	42346	306983	14261	112867	25991	2710	0	2010	
565	2365	10811	42231	322669	16698	123072	26196	2589	...	2011	
470	3013	9883	40999	293426	14532	129438	30311	2624	...	2012	
411	2418	8968	34412	265544	11749	110974	27839	1638	...	2013	
19337	29952	31466	57255	78360	22285	40579	83737	1260	8706	2000	Economies Développées -
76561	83910	85992	127969	265306	74618	88567	218201	3210	21751	2010	Europe 2/
94295	83858	108077	155306	328669	86966	104541	261190	3324	36850	2011	
90367	92080	105091	164775	325649	73639	113694	259136	3364	43558	2012	
97645	98283	109930	166482	348091	69615	118042	288908	3797	47311	2013	
1282	9180	7741	7237	9366	2416	4752	10136	822	658	2000	France
4676	20396	15016	13984	26338	7000	13568	25906	1610	983	2010	
5537	21799	17517	15314	33476	7288	14872	27591	1841	1129	2011	
5355	20944	15593	16084	34444	6239	18082	25898	1617	1358	2012	
5958	20758	16252	17505	34023	5164	19034	26448	2086	774	2013	
4185	4001	5607	13858	21330	4087	9799	17506	132	1537	2000	Allemagne
16420	11127	15445	35536	100250	19628	23476	53170	532	415	2010	
19915	10320	18784	40939	124083	22059	27631	63769	309	2393	2011	
19443	10630	17759	42389	118615	19107	29208	63993	450	7936	2012	
20650	11480	18279	43497	124689	17147	29548	69817	362	5187	2013	
562	5660	6348	174598	88921	5584	48918	23864	393	308	2000	Economies Développées -
1408	12627	18988	312632	203227	27974	74607	63140	834	386	2010	Amérique du Nord 2/
1799	12935	23295	378973	237370	32734	81431	77732	976	231	2011	
1688	11775	24926	412407	242836	30062	80518	87297	1128	12	2012	
1647	12488	26469	421440	261845	30164	84304	89787	772	28	2013	
509	5028	5928	170376	83248	4635	47368	22928	378	307	2000	Etats-Unis
1137	11215	17076	300493	183656	24298	70437	59046	709	376	2010	
1437	11509	21102	364814	210382	28320	76434	72895	880	225	2011	
1334	10247	22610	398448	215745	26403	75521	82143	1034	...	2012	
1407	10977	24052	408196	232281	26335	78980	85296	690	...	2013	
2212	358	156	160	218	139	76	1700	1	188	2000	Europe du Sud-est
12072	1289	879	488	1453	802	565	7662	16	343	2010	
14752	1709	1155	664	1936	1101	354	9962	21	338	2011	
13023	2271	1207	839	2451	891	392	9253	87	425	2012	
13251	3102	1182	1319	2791	865	921	10087	46	277	2013	
2633	1375	555	5983	9128	2991	1714	9063	4	19	2000	Communauté d'Etats
9800	6900	1928	6963	51449	18149	10453	35670	4	50462	2010	Indépendants
16856	8904	3213	11173	78062	18107	11488	40176	13	8892	2011	
17621	12784	3239	9781	83681	19203	11650	44410	100	1385	2012	
12753	9815	3308	10212	87167	16343	15435	41026	19	1089	2013	
1822	746	344	4307	6980	1896	1120	6556	2	0	2000	Fédération de Russie
5722	4195	695	4089	33789	9686	6514	20350	2	50147	2010	
10387	6144	1764	7508	53245	8904	7664	22148	10	8085	2011	
11225	7874	1612	6844	56993	10681	7130	23654	90	184	2012	
7789	5406	1668	8168	59971	9343	8415	23542	16	50	2013	

Voir la fin du tableau pour la remarque générale et les notes.

World exports by provenance and destination (Table D)

In million U.S. dollars f.o.b.

Exports from	Year	World 1/ Monde 1/	Developed economies 2/ Economies développées 2/		Asia-Pacific Asie-Pacifique		Europe		North America Amérique du Nord		Commonwealth of Independent States Communauté d'Etats Indépendants	
			Total	Total	Japan Japon	Total	Germany Allemagne	Total	U.S.A. É.-U.	Total	Europe

Total trade (SITC, Rev. 3, 0-9) 3/ [cont.]

Exports from	Year	World 1/ Monde 1/	Total	Total	Japan Japon	Total	Germany Allemagne	Total	U.S.A. É.-U.	Total	Europe
Northern Africa	2000	50201	41077	490	424	35543	3933	5043	4216	101	81
	2010	154015	111132	695	520	89673	3835	20764	17349	609	524
	2011	162531	114679	1086	858	90230	3986	23363	18660	874	816
	2012	198662	145341	2337	2157	121784	4435	21220	15532	840	656
	2013	177793	127395	3188	2255	109915	9104	14292	10525	847	697
Sub-Saharan Africa	2000	94703	59378	2643	2070	34100	3117	22634	21660	240	191
	2010	336116	160390	10544	8478	81832	8434	68014	61900	870	787
	2011	455954	212909	16989	10647	120717	10923	75202	67550	1087	930
	2012	458460	205597	18140	12621	129508	9273	57949	51516	1165	973
	2013	402820	172710	17233	12198	118518	8919	36959	32324	1218	1064
South Africa	2000	26298	15863	1873	1362	10979	1902	3011	2790	79	33
	2010	82626	36256	7457	6428	21078	5497	7721	7184	383	351
	2011	108002	41842	8565	7625	24449	5739	8828	8205	379	357
	2012	99207	35095	6721	5736	20018	4069	8356	7833	508	460
	2013	95225	33834	6526	5612	20040	3842	7268	6898	527	460
Latin America and the Caribbean	2000	353078	265627	8570	7727	43901	6927	213157	206833	1330	1280
	2010	880692	503120	23987	21312	118568	18042	360566	327221	8123	7745
	2011	1093504	618631	30122	26154	153137	22369	435372	392153	9199	8495
	2012	1096801	623767	28850	24686	143355	19828	451562	407432	8944	8249
	2013	1094363	627007	27411	23532	135919	17633	463677	409925	9251	8305
Brazil	2000	55119	33697	2852	2481	16230	2520	14614	14048	522	487
	2010	197356	74437	7750	7123	45134	8080	21553	19240	4747	4510
	2011	256039	98147	10378	9488	57591	9331	30177	27032	5181	4670
	2012	242580	93484	8557	7991	53017	7662	31910	28827	4283	3851
	2013	242178	88595	8496	7973	50980	6908	29119	26412	4119	3504
Eastern Asia	2000	776206	410957	101770	90091	125356	27229	183831	173168	4994	3848
	2010	2723194	1118778	230253	183712	447063	95697	441463	408128	68074	47618
	2011	3222721	1275588	280429	223552	496705	104412	498454	460408	85963	62088
	2012	3396494	1280548	290196	227960	462087	92424	528266	487973	96059	69061
	2013	3613890	1296679	283874	221402	464465	90394	548340	506633	104292	74913
China	2000	249203	142806	45499	41654	41976	9278	55331	52156	3183	2411
	2010	1577764	771088	151029	121044	313723	68047	306336	283780	53821	36052
	2011	1898388	896344	185915	148269	359795	76400	350633	325011	67227	46853
	2012	2048782	911389	193226	151627	337391	69213	380772	352438	75653	52425
	2013	2209007	931031	191818	150133	340740	67343	398473	369064	83517	58425
Southern Asia	2000	91623	55027	8440	7705	29131	3854	17456	16377	1848	1204
	2010	354892	125413	8554	6015	79534	10703	37325	34909	5092	3272
	2011	493516	163166	10217	7130	105564	14307	47385	44090	6004	3799
	2012	446157	155743	11489	7798	91940	12866	52314	48838	5731	3805
	2013	482843	170905	12306	8724	99511	14339	59089	55236	5986	4081
South-Eastern Asia	2000	426829	218844	69522	57853	65445	12034	83878	80866	606	556
	2010	1051658	376088	145061	103173	124398	23042	106629	100320	5074	4585
	2011	1244399	428344	175187	128240	140217	25283	112940	105933	6742	6128
	2012	1245273	429699	179121	127967	134542	24428	116233	109322	6969	6325
	2013	1261736	426862	173105	122738	130465	25806	123293	115678	7646	6790
Western Asia	2000	251583	136105	36650	35897	56362	8137	43094	42034	2575	1496
	2010	895697	264050	45239	42788	134156	15673	84655	44730	14113	7885
	2011	1222466	359159	59324	55872	182242	18833	117593	56939	17780	10093
	2012	1349709	384338	71193	66917	181343	17300	131802	63492	20150	11290
	2013	1397994	320478	31662	28546	167489	17753	121328	57109	22536	12402
Oceania	2000	4996	3023	1772	879	995	184	255	252	14	10
	2010	9855	5686	3649	753	1738	368	299	293	11	10
	2011	10505	5935	3837	838	1771	353	327	320	11	10
	2012	9411	4919	3052	869	1525	322	342	329	8	6
	2013	10713	5789	3659	970	1766	424	364	359	10	8

For general note and footnotes see end of table

Exportations mondiales par provenance et destination (Tableau D)

En millions de dollars E.-U. f.o.b.

← Exportations vers

South-Eastern Europe Europe du Sud-est	Northern Africa Afrique septentrio-nale	Sub-Saharan Africa Afrique du Nord	Latin America and the Caribbean Amérique latine et Caraïbes	Eastern Asia Asie orientale	Southern Asia Asie méridionale	South-eastern Asia Asie du Sud-est	Western Asia Asie occidentale	Oceania Océanie	Others 4/ Autre 4/	Année	Exportations en provence de ↓
Commerce total (CTCI, Rev. 3, 0-9) 3/ *[suite]*											
92	1179	336	2058	315	793	277	3122	1	849	2000	Afrique du Nord
390	6254	3390	4392	7934	5632	1498	11189	11	1584	2010	
432	6111	4268	6381	6009	7523	1666	12436	43	2110	2011	
515	8241	4074	6649	10405	6170	1929	12312	4	2182	2012	
651	8826	3910	5321	7403	5564	2085	13845	3	1942	2013	
65	421	12333	2545	9492	5265	1955	2156	40	813	2000	Afrique subsaharienne
189	2121	64728	12134	57086	20311	6970	8904	194	2221	2010	
212	5835	77986	25106	77665	31669	8602	11387	1557	1939	2011	
709	2896	83348	21511	79460	35863	11096	13354	546	2916	2012	
479	1308	83502	13820	74173	29273	11738	12581	727	1289	2013	
30	91	4123	576	2662	531	739	1013	6	587	2000	Afrique du sud
53	443	22880	1560	12100	3643	2225	2647	41	394	2010	
87	531	26110	2194	19544	9206	3511	4018	22	555	2011	
93	558	27458	2051	17629	7279	4056	3550	58	871	2012	
84	535	26851	1698	19077	5049	3582	3455	32	500	2013	
324	1359	1679	61878	8864	2275	2795	2808	18	4122	2000	Amérique latine et Caraïbes
1629	7688	8465	188014	99696	13665	18491	14697	57	17049	2010	
2329	10675	12090	246756	131443	14692	24568	19809	75	3236	2011	
2059	9973	12263	231264	139004	19521	26959	19288	61	3699	2012	
2154	9872	9680	218796	151603	18949	24226	19866	41	2917	2013	
129	506	888	13886	2603	621	926	1338	4	...	2000	Brésil
603	4182	5053	47682	37983	6603	6597	9440	28	...	2010	
840	5407	7205	57715	53526	6718	9829	11439	32	1	2011	
817	5556	7060	51030	50333	8799	10592	10599	24	4	2012	
766	5020	6477	54642	56920	6079	9216	10317	19	9	2013	
688	3065	8358	25191	220193	13062	68294	18703	1258	1511	2000	Asie orientale
5648	22699	57311	137838	838547	104785	258845	98289	9323	3057	2010	
6811	21573	74970	173822	990127	129148	323549	125212	11639	4321	2011	
6059	27012	78182	183989	1082598	121927	371267	136402	8710	3741	2012	
6244	27541	86814	182687	1198772	127286	419756	147851	11886	4081	2013	
356	1410	3602	7125	62121	4510	17341	6683	65	2	2000	Chine
4371	15588	44235	91249	322611	68699	138203	64868	3032	...	2010	
5360	16636	56302	121082	394265	86063	170146	81714	3248	1	2011	
4890	20558	64612	134484	456791	82048	204337	90746	3275	...	2012	
4937	21765	70897	133232	525547	89284	244087	101780	2929	...	2013	
48	2664	2171	1904	13211	3396	3786	7528	32	8	2000	Asie méridionale
616	6288	16325	11282	78576	23207	25859	60786	181	1268	2010	
658	8273	21866	14441	109388	27929	39572	73393	203	28623	2011	
623	8333	24618	16478	88485	26943	36419	74654	174	7956	2012	
737	8251	31293	16983	85366	32160	41293	77615	165	12089	2013	
156	1009	4131	6782	75803	11386	98150	8580	996	386	2000	Asie Sud-est
687	5972	18594	27407	265046	53667	263635	29653	4777	1059	2010	
901	11096	21187	36669	317655	66604	310995	35115	7114	1977	2011	
757	5883	24970	35993	312542	59436	321161	38168	7720	1974	2012	
808	6004	25548	36927	321456	59627	325836	41874	7345	1802	2013	
1112	5607	2105	2934	55141	7535	10745	16833	9	10881	2000	Asie occidentale
6135	19862	14624	10555	306301	75866	27097	71254	680	85160	2010	
6820	25277	17652	14033	418248	109644	35140	83508	1229	133977	2011	
6323	31504	23979	15046	494461	128756	41785	86160	1437	115769	2012	
6851	33310	24689	14393	465670	122904	35782	99059	558	251764	2013	
2	0	38	276	499	14	283	2	82	764	2000	Océanie
1	4	43	141	1199	103	899	5	255	1508	2010	
1	5	56	135	1324	106	937	5	396	1594	2011	
1	3	69	142	1258	239	701	5	405	1660	2012	
1	2	88	164	1401	310	843	9	414	1681	2013	

Voir la fin du tableau pour la remarque générale et les notes.

World exports by provenance and destination (Table D)

In million U.S. dollars f.o.b.

Exports from	Year	World 1/ Monde 1/	Developed economies 2/ Economies développées 2/							Commonwealth of Independent States Communauté d'Etats Indépendants	
			Total	Asia-Pacific Asie-Pacifique		Europe		North America Amérique du Nord			
				Total	Japan Japon	Total	Germany Allemagne	Total	U.S.A. É.-U.	Total	Europe

Food, beverages and tobacco (SITC, Rev. 3, 0 and 1)

Exports from	Year	World 1/ Monde 1/	Total	Total	Japan Japon	Total	Germany Allemagne	Total	U.S.A. É.-U.	Total	Europe
World 1/	2000	387158	271669	40607	36935	175575	32544	55488	44008	9830	8629
	2010	966282	587614	60079	48643	415698	70441	111837	84321	43699	37380
	2011	1164162	691215	74051	59818	486898	83648	130265	98912	51511	43183
	2012	1174696	680182	75008	60134	470972	80451	134201	101351	54797	44444
	2013	1254569	724758	73054	56970	510636	86894	141069	106994	59104	47506
Developed Economies - Asia-Pacific 2/	2000	19827	9698	4288	3292	2443	277	2966	2615	52	44
	2010	41755	16123	7639	4514	3937	434	4547	3953	698	597
	2011	51717	19094	9316	5678	4640	565	5138	4435	758	642
	2012	52653	18479	8972	5281	3981	473	5526	4821	697	558
	2013	54669	17947	8455	4667	4121	505	5371	4695	744	613
Japan	2000	2088	612	72	.	107	14	432	395	9	9
	2010	4615	957	81	.	193	34	683	640	81	80
	2011	4487	1028	95	.	205	32	728	682	38	38
	2012	4432	1035	106	.	185	35	744	695	31	31
	2013	4447	1025	104	.	199	42	722	671	37	36
Developed Economies - Europe 2/	2000	178436	151893	5172	4319	136289	26443	10433	8969	3784	3519
	2010	423670	351081	8284	5929	323732	56795	19064	15801	15700	14821
	2011	500255	409275	10256	7196	377163	67086	21856	18127	18470	17376
	2012	489786	396898	10285	6964	364042	64949	22571	18753	19188	17950
	2013	536304	434470	10771	7117	399589	71581	24110	20082	21083	19701
France	2000	31410	26548	981	902	23387	4572	2180	1853	351	335
	2010	58758	45877	1426	1190	41011	6755	3441	2776	902	852
	2011	69712	52464	1612	1338	46933	7838	3920	3156	985	915
	2012	66663	50570	1752	1423	44726	7230	4091	3318	1056	971
	2013	71556	53883	1799	1405	47770	7632	4314	3501	1129	1032
Germany	2000	21712	18446	290	250	17384	.	772	696	643	595
	2010	62920	53953	774	524	51373	.	1806	1554	2757	2530
	2011	75568	63905	1165	813	60427	.	2313	1984	3271	2972
	2012	72829	60754	945	555	57581	.	2228	1881	3114	2811
	2013	79208	66229	906	514	62980	.	2342	1970	2940	2656
Developed Economies - North America 2/	2000	63390	38861	13367	12830	6717	914	18777	10624	986	886
	2010	118039	61099	14841	13323	10048	1288	36210	17298	1879	1675
	2011	141576	69809	17949	16066	11623	1468	40237	18987	2255	1994
	2012	141946	71736	17551	15460	11054	1426	43131	20388	2898	2518
	2013	151887	75114	16171	14056	12839	1716	46104	22137	2234	1886
United States	2000	47084	25762	11994	11534	5619	835	8149	.	955	858
	2010	88113	39643	12717	11457	8054	1158	18872	.	1475	1306
	2011	107718	45934	15502	13890	9217	1312	21214	.	1614	1396
	2012	106859	46511	14993	13165	8880	1292	22638	.	2150	1817
	2013	114158	48162	13742	11873	10596	1589	23824	.	1693	1408
South-Eastern Europe	2000	1232	651	17	12	588	125	45	39	75	57
	2010	8623	4395	20	6	4258	445	117	94	332	301
	2011	10359	5494	54	35	5300	624	139	115	451	403
	2012	10843	5568	89	66	5343	595	136	113	470	443
	2013	12941	6190	69	44	5943	639	177	147	575	532
Commonwealth of Independent States	2000	3263	709	150	145	524	90	35	32	2117	1721
	2010	21157	2059	256	249	1687	260	116	104	10972	7488
	2011	27366	3788	260	252	3412	313	116	98	13182	8407
	2012	37029	5701	501	486	5068	361	132	113	16043	9535
	2013	37329	5654	575	547	4938	449	142	122	18208	10831
Russian Federation	2000	1016	394	140	137	231	34	23	21	379	91
	2010	6835	895	215	211	614	97	65	59	1638	657
	2011	10082	1461	226	221	1183	109	53	44	2127	810
	2012	14132	1872	268	265	1550	141	54	45	4053	1353
	2013	13709	1774	224	218	1485	138	65	52	4732	1656

For general note and footnotes see end of table

Exportations mondiales par provenance et destination (Tableau D)

En millions de dollars E.-U. f.o.b.

⟵ Exportations vers

South-Eastern Europe Europe du Sud-est	Northern Africa Afrique septentrionale	Sub-Saharan Africa Afrique du Nord	Latin America and the Caribbean Amérique latine et Caraïbes	Eastern Asia Asie orientale	Southern Asia Asie méridionale	South-eastern Asia Asie du Sud-est	Western Asia Asie occidentale	Oceania Océanie	Others 4/ Autre 4/	Année	Exportations en provenance de
				**Produits alimentaires, boisson et tabac (CTCI, Rev. 3, 0 et 1)**							
2492	7291	8285	22269	23732	5192	16029	17811	795	1762	2000	Monde 1/
11569	21665	33702	56294	69605	22921	55092	58830	2044	3246	2010	
13224	28391	43981	69734	89083	25265	71737	74694	2421	2907	2011	
13180	29428	46299	73942	97036	25756	75367	72201	2612	3897	2012	
13953	29063	48738	74891	106761	27727	82984	80532	2573	3483	2013	
5	394	394	490	3380	855	3012	993	455	98	2000	Economies Développées -
14	827	870	988	9450	1561	7012	2969	844	399	2010	Asie-Pacifique 2/
13	1179	1189	1254	11630	1745	9153	4483	1102	117	2011	
7	1158	1253	1111	12433	2083	9444	4159	1211	619	2012	
6	990	1504	1080	14982	1551	9379	4511	1172	804	2013	
0	0	18	23	1135	6	205	26	56	0	2000	Japon
0	39	29	37	2728	14	593	103	33	...	2010	
0	7	40	35	2483	11	737	71	36	...	2011	
0	7	56	23	2359	20	787	72	41	...	2012	
0	31	45	24	2338	14	825	76	33	...	2013	
1688	2963	3064	3113	2851	484	2053	5467	136	941	2000	Economies Développées -
7115	7026	8771	5146	8854	1369	4980	12853	316	459	2010	Europe 2/
8328	8880	10761	6265	13060	1589	6500	16174	380	573	2011	
8202	8015	11024	6551	13389	2179	7009	16294	368	670	2012	
9175	8856	12139	7020	14827	1924	7790	17747	390	883	2013	
79	984	883	429	542	106	406	968	112	2	2000	France
243	3103	2206	611	2247	131	1345	1825	255	14	2010	
349	4625	2591	768	3331	215	1717	2341	301	25	2011	
392	3122	2648	774	3311	209	1880	2374	279	49	2012	
389	3541	2923	879	3462	156	2039	2798	297	59	2013	
193	367	112	203	255	126	188	974	1	204	2000	Allemagne
1026	507	746	333	733	300	426	2110	2	25	2010	
1264	520	884	416	1362	290	609	3008	3	37	2011	
1252	613	713	386	1660	610	724	2913	3	87	2012	
1445	739	935	465	1774	478	803	3253	4	143	2013	
73	1936	805	9298	5475	785	2248	2770	78	74	2000	Economies Développées -
121	2936	2592	21626	14594	2072	5670	5047	231	171	2010	Amérique du Nord 2/
119	3369	3357	26721	19557	2385	7266	6470	159	108	2011	
162	2355	3053	27673	19589	2224	7074	5018	162	1	2012	
166	2733	3199	29829	22073	2619	8154	5591	166	9	2013	
71	1499	658	8266	4943	268	1952	2558	77	74	2000	Etats-Unis
94	2355	2081	19367	12760	828	4981	4145	214	171	2010	
90	2856	2749	24284	17006	989	6381	5564	146	104	2011	
144	1575	2451	25250	17343	1082	6142	4063	149	...	2012	
133	1987	2434	27052	19595	1215	7019	4713	155	...	2013	
284	44	6	3	4	34	5	114	1	13	2000	Europe du Sud-est
2549	124	52	7	182	91	122	754	0	14	2010	
2810	249	48	20	84	32	23	1125	0	23	2011	
2874	455	58	18	129	115	34	1100	0	23	2012	
2662	1176	66	16	360	109	100	1671	0	16	2013	
27	17	15	7	160	30	2	163	...	14	2000	Communauté d'Etats
112	1863	297	91	2046	835	155	2658	0	69	2010	Indépendants
181	2532	615	115	2223	843	72	3639	0	176	2011	
217	4241	695	142	2648	1595	115	5534	0	97	2012	
210	2452	1018	234	3004	1475	423	4558	0	93	2013	
6	6	0	1	155	7	1	67	...	0	2000	Fédération de Russie
62	985	132	39	1913	124	51	985	...	11	2010	
107	1482	576	64	2089	137	19	1923	0	97	2011	
127	1920	327	105	2212	631	26	2840	0	18	2012	
105	877	621	197	2514	472	141	2262	0	14	2013	

Voir la fin du tableau pour la remarque générale et les notes.

World exports by provenance and destination (Table D)

In million U.S. dollars f.o.b.

| Exports from | Year | World 1/ Monde 1/ | Developed economies 2/ Economies développées 2/ | | | | | | | Commonwealth of Independent States Communauté d'Etats Indépendants | |
| | | | Total | Asia-Pacific Asie-Pacifique | | Europe | | North America Amérique du Nord | | | |
				Total	Japan Japon	Total	Germany Allemagne	Total	U.S.A. É.-U.	Total	Europe
Food, beverages and tobacco (SITC, Rev. 3, 0 and 1) [cont.]											
Northern Africa	2000	2277	1661	281	279	1299	71	81	58	63	63
	2010	8474	3635	128	120	3278	222	229	171	459	451
	2011	9184	4196	139	130	3819	212	237	180	669	649
	2012	8527	3816	158	149	3433	254	225	174	487	476
	2013	9723	4258	174	162	3813	214	271	209	584	574
Sub-Saharan Africa	2000	10517	6453	512	439	5327	618	613	538	105	104
	2010	30429	14499	767	537	12043	1211	1689	1443	370	322
	2011	36350	16446	803	595	13531	1470	2112	1837	451	393
	2012	40378	18185	952	780	14348	1340	2885	2614	481	402
	2013	36985	16433	991	785	13739	1205	1703	1422	517	449
South Africa	2000	2168	1261	176	144	923	69	161	110	8	7
	2010	7886	2879	296	199	2257	247	326	200	185	180
	2011	8620	2854	289	182	2254	244	311	191	191	185
	2012	8321	2701	274	169	2086	216	341	214	182	176
	2013	9006	3247	481	349	2412	248	353	216	209	205
Latin America and the Caribbean	2000	47177	31343	2605	2313	13659	2245	15080	14395	1096	1082
	2010	136566	69878	5709	5103	33203	5068	30966	28685	6632	6392
	2011	168534	85839	7723	6774	39948	6594	38168	35395	7294	6967
	2012	169860	82150	7738	6786	37187	5871	37225	34638	6919	6520
	2013	175131	85004	8008	7007	37225	5156	39771	37426	6873	6352
Brazil	2000	10142	6609	710	514	4599	667	1300	1179	471	460
	2010	48051	18169	1823	1701	13047	2210	3299	2678	4258	4052
	2011	58415	23427	2890	2668	15964	2900	4573	3792	4410	4166
	2012	57354	21630	2886	2748	14964	2486	3780	3044	3537	3246
	2013	57396	21110	2822	2693	14609	2106	3679	3036	3402	3038
Eastern Asia	2000	21062	11178	7892	7697	1446	308	1841	1605	297	254
	2010	56783	24737	11703	10685	5903	1345	7131	6206	2221	1842
	2011	69229	28872	14052	12758	6706	1454	8115	7091	2710	2258
	2012	71866	29943	15052	13750	6329	1468	8562	7454	2786	2298
	2013	75455	29137	13895	12564	6743	1458	8499	7441	2977	2435
China	2000	13027	7217	4960	4877	1214	296	1044	910	189	162
	2010	43054	20634	9041	8313	5554	1309	6039	5282	1923	1585
	2011	52771	24192	10901	9947	6369	1425	6921	6077	2406	2010
	2012	54667	25005	11801	10847	5938	1416	7267	6357	2449	2011
	2013	58335	24830	11208	10172	6351	1423	7272	6393	2657	2171
Southern Asia	2000	8344	3486	828	754	1715	288	944	857	581	432
	2010	28393	6301	1084	864	3783	520	1434	1232	1531	1019
	2011	37474	8383	1478	1202	4753	664	2152	1892	1850	1250
	2012	39155	8189	1247	950	4694	542	2247	1983	1592	1099
	2013	46701	9715	1311	1000	5446	615	2958	2619	1661	1131
South-Eastern Asia	2000	23691	12540	5244	4705	3056	465	4240	3874	168	159
	2010	64363	26363	9073	7032	7986	1318	9304	8444	985	885
	2011	80882	31850	11350	8801	9637	1538	10863	9802	1196	1060
	2012	81051	31430	11808	9101	9316	1700	10306	9248	1094	962
	2013	82019	32268	11992	8686	9605	1719	10671	9586	1155	1031
Western Asia	2000	7475	2824	147	100	2321	624	356	328	508	307
	2010	26723	6586	311	159	5456	1292	819	680	1908	1575
	2011	29798	7244	373	194	5948	1428	923	747	2214	1776
	2012	30216	7226	397	226	5791	1303	1038	844	2135	1677
	2013	34011	7670	402	225	6199	1415	1068	888	2484	1963
Oceania	2000	467	372	105	50	191	76	76	75	0	0
	2010	1306	859	263	122	384	243	212	210	10	10
	2011	1437	926	298	137	418	233	210	207	9	9
	2012	1388	862	258	135	386	169	217	206	7	6
	2013	1412	896	239	110	434	222	222	219	10	8

For general note and footnotes see end of table

Exportations mondiales par provenance et destination (Tableau D)

En millions de dollars E.-U. f.o.b.

← Exportations vers

South-Eastern Europe Europe du Sud-est	Northern Africa Afrique septentrio-nale	Sub-Saharan Africa Afrique du Nord	Latin America and the Caribbean Amérique latine et Caraïbes	Eastern Asia Asie orientale	Southern Asia Asie méridionale	South-eastern Asia Asie du Sud-est	Western Asia Asie occidentale	Oceania Océanie	Others 4/ Autre 4/	Année	Exportations en provence de

Produits alimentaires, boisson et tabac (CTCI, Rev. 3, 0 et 1) *[suite]*

10	169	84	5	11	2	10	238	1	24	2000	Afrique du Nord
44	873	983	54	32	114	76	2121	2	82	2010	
61	913	900	42	38	112	81	2045	2	126	2011	
36	887	904	56	48	94	106	2006	1	86	2012	
50	1014	1048	56	77	82	116	2325	2	110	2013	
22	203	2013	79	234	458	186	717	6	43	2000	Afrique subsaharienne
69	643	8763	621	828	1196	1055	1735	104	546	2010	
50	558	10628	1377	1151	1978	1413	2138	55	105	2011	
149	639	11510	2151	929	2139	1735	2382	12	65	2012	
119	570	12077	342	1029	1915	1578	2344	18	44	2013	
4	8	536	11	103	65	36	130	0	7	2000	Afrique du sud
5	43	3569	38	390	60	199	481	13	23	2010	
3	14	3826	432	593	76	195	428	6	3	2011	
3	27	3894	357	392	63	236	442	7	16	2012	
2	24	4081	137	479	56	280	476	5	11	2013	
167	811	566	8780	1541	396	736	1499	12	230	2000	Amérique latine et Caraïbes
623	4588	3901	24797	7473	4917	5673	7794	19	270	2010	
745	7113	5793	30636	10397	3681	7068	9668	24	277	2011	
729	7679	5844	32653	12130	3847	7883	9719	23	283	2012	
735	7010	4773	32400	14304	3477	9360	10807	20	367	2013	
85	185	264	1061	372	139	250	705	0	...	2000	Brésil
371	2837	2732	4412	3258	3737	2703	5569	5	...	2010	
526	4019	3803	5425	4744	2833	2913	6305	10	...	2011	
419	4421	3547	5564	5803	3180	3131	6110	8	4	2012	
436	3603	3180	5851	6935	2751	3667	6455	7	0	2013	
26	145	346	185	6265	195	2052	310	34	28	2000	Asie orientale
87	545	1181	1527	14001	1043	9489	1778	160	12	2010	
113	634	1750	1858	17141	1186	12884	1863	206	11	2011	
102	634	1826	1922	18150	1108	13276	1825	281	13	2012	
97	687	2083	2192	19506	1046	15642	1820	256	11	2013	
26	142	295	145	3365	152	1242	247	5	...	2000	Chine
84	512	1108	1415	8372	937	6700	1298	72	...	2010	
108	596	1603	1742	10657	985	8977	1419	87	...	2011	
97	571	1653	1775	11645	907	9113	1350	101	...	2012	
93	645	1880	2076	12956	954	10712	1428	104	...	2013	
11	216	182	102	413	819	622	1907	2	1	2000	Asie méridionale
42	627	1408	220	1786	4671	3196	8574	7	30	2010	
53	822	2739	298	1663	6106	5351	10177	20	12	2011	
60	1026	4184	325	1986	6199	6215	9355	9	15	2012	
66	1078	4466	340	1947	8858	8095	10431	13	31	2013	
36	127	651	150	3275	655	4999	976	46	70	2000	Asie Sud-est
145	741	3701	1022	8512	2636	16846	2833	249	329	2010	
151	1008	4576	977	11742	3396	20997	3731	325	933	2011	
132	1164	4163	1159	13554	1741	21567	3649	368	1030	2012	
157	1023	4079	1181	14247	1788	21419	3623	377	703	2013	
143	266	151	58	102	478	71	2659	0	217	2000	Asie occidentale
647	867	1176	187	1782	2414	581	9713	3	857	2010	
599	1131	1620	165	323	2211	671	13182	3	434	2011	
509	1173	1783	178	1974	2430	666	11158	4	980	2012	
510	1474	2285	200	330	2879	670	15102	5	402	2013	
0	...	7	0	22	0	32	0	24	10	2000	Océanie
1	3	7	7	64	2	237	1	111	5	2010	
1	3	4	5	72	1	258	1	145	10	2011	
1	0	2	4	77	3	244	1	171	16	2012	
1	0	2	2	76	3	257	1	154	10	2013	

Voir la fin du tableau pour la remarque générale et les notes.

World exports by provenance and destination (Table D)

In million U.S. dollars f.o.b.

| Exports from | Year | World 1/ Monde 1/ | Developed economies 2/ Economies développées 2/ | Asia-Pacific Asie-Pacifique | | Europe | | North America Amérique du Nord | | Commonwealth of Independent States Communauté d'Etats Indépendants | |
			Total	Total	Japan Japon	Total	Germany Allemagne	Total	U.S.A. É.-U.	Total	Europe
						Cereals (SITC, Rev. 3, 041-045)					
World 1/	2000	33057	11128	3011	2929	6972	796	1146	848	618	517
	2010	83637	24717	5957	5675	16190	2278	2570	1895	1167	393
	2011	116181	34376	8225	7836	23070	3234	3081	2375	1651	704
	2012	119731	34626	7612	7263	23244	3185	3770	3087	1923	716
	2013	122192	35760	7191	6789	23693	3335	4876	4166	2365	1050
Developed Economies - Asia-Pacific 2/	2000	2868	502	432	394	69	0	1	0	0	0
	2010	4635	558	507	422	49	0	1	1	0	0
	2011	8094	1137	1023	829	112	18	2	1	0	0
	2012	8661	837	744	582	92	1	1	1	0	0
	2013	8089	871	749	574	107	12	15	14	0	0
Japan	2000	14	0	0	.	0	...	0	0	0	0
	2010	28	2	0	.	1	0	0	0	0	0
	2011	21	2	1	.	1	0	0	0	0	0
	2012	35	1	0	.	1	0	0	0	0	0
	2013	18	2	1	.	1	0	0	0	0	0
Developed Economies - Europe 2/	2000	8358	5731	32	30	5632	749	67	63	229	210
	2010	18436	12520	37	30	12434	2085	49	45	159	148
	2011	24072	16842	23	15	16734	2958	85	80	340	325
	2012	22662	16546	30	22	16418	2897	98	91	285	274
	2013	25344	16882	58	48	16709	3054	115	98	377	369
France	2000	3913	2939	2	2	2928	409	9	9	11	10
	2010	7678	4389	7	6	4378	628	4	4	22	20
	2011	10843	6136	8	7	6120	874	8	7	44	44
	2012	8944	5732	13	12	5710	708	9	9	68	66
	2013	10865	6581	38	36	6526	811	17	16	71	70
Germany	2000	1594	700	28	28	672	.	0	0	45	37
	2010	2673	1602	10	10	1590	.	2	2	8	8
	2011	3150	2190	6	6	2183	.	0	0	12	12
	2012	3176	2246	8	8	2231	.	7	7	14	14
	2013	4157	2373	11	11	2337	.	25	25	25	25
Developed Economies - North America 2/	2000	12694	3716	2350	2343	603	26	763	508	130	109
	2010	25661	7143	4568	4538	988	39	1587	1047	12	12
	2011	35369	9678	6226	6209	1557	57	1895	1337	19	17
	2012	28161	8278	5062	5043	979	23	2238	1708	18	18
	2013	28458	7560	3775	3755	1131	23	2654	2136	22	22
United States	2000	9733	2775	2096	2094	424	26	255	.	130	109
	2010	20084	5245	4224	4196	481	36	540	.	10	9
	2011	28323	6936	5618	5601	761	37	557	.	15	13
	2012	20638	5339	4383	4364	427	15	529	.	18	18
	2013	20325	4171	3111	3092	542	16	517	.	21	21
South-Eastern Europe	2000	149	20	...	...	20	3	0	0	24	18
	2010	2343	973	0	0	973	52	0	0	47	35
	2011	2899	1348	25	25	1323	76	0	0	86	80
	2012	3421	1457	49	49	1407	82	1	1	104	103
	2013	4686	1467	29	29	1432	48	7	5	149	147
Commonwealth of Independent States	2000	281	34	...	.	31	0	3	3	118	81
	2010	5985	341	45	45	292	17	3	3	764	57
	2011	8960	1540	37	36	1501	17	2	2	1008	129
	2012	15022	2906	235	225	2671	71	0	0	1326	187
	2013	12631	2417	357	338	2059	77	1	0	1573	377
Russian Federation	2000	96	5	...	...	5	0	0	0	35	5
	2010	2396	33	8	8	25	0	0	0	171	6
	2011	4439	394	5	5	389	2	0	0	276	15
	2012	6251	561	6	6	555	26	0	0	411	28
	2013	4752	259	10	10	248	13	0	0	449	15

For general note and footnotes see end of table

Exportations mondiales par provenance et destination (Tableau D)

En millions de dollars E.-U. f.o.b.

⟵ Exportations vers

South-Eastern Europe Europe du Sud-est	Northern Africa Afrique septentrio-nale	Sub-Saharan Africa Afrique du Nord	Latin America and the Caribbean Amérique latine et Caraïbes	Eastern Asia Asie orientale	Southern Asia Asie méridionale	South-eastern Asia Asie du Sud-est	Western Asia Asie occidentale	Oceania Océanie	Others 4/ Autre 4/	Année	Exportations en provence de ↓
				Céréales (CTCI, Rev. 3, 041-045)							
176	3109	1999	5108	2820	1776	2530	3580	115	97	2000	Monde 1/
992	8052	8016	11623	6144	3998	7288	10823	329	487	2010	
1184	11646	11099	16449	8983	5184	10440	14411	345	413	2011	
1468	11218	12035	16823	10417	6293	9557	14249	421	700	2012	
1206	10183	11718	16070	11381	7457	8755	15947	381	969	2013	
...	115	226	7	429	491	684	303	100	11	2000	Economies Développées - Asie-Pacifique 2/
...	165	274	5	669	319	1605	641	129	269	2010	
...	252	388	10	1373	264	2849	1567	223	31	2011	
...	176	475	...	1649	359	3122	1201	313	528	2012	
...	151	754	11	1207	236	2194	1648	307	710	2013	
...	...	7	...	4	0	0	2	0	...	2000	Japon
...	0	9	0	10	6	2	0	0	...	2010	
...	0	13	0	4	0	3	0	0	...	2011	
...	...	12	...	13	6	3	0	0	...	2012	
...	0	8	0	5	0	3	0	0	...	2013	
91	822	224	136	108	172	8	830	0	6	2000	Economies Développées - Europe 2/
420	2641	1017	168	133	47	94	1236	0	1	2010	
529	3839	1082	207	81	18	20	1109	0	4	2011	
572	2318	870	188	64	814	10	994	0	1	2012	
511	3009	1211	284	168	764	9	2126	0	2	2013	
11	463	171	84	54	70	0	110	0	...	2000	France
31	2150	595	109	71	1	14	295	0	0	2010	
71	3388	679	201	75	2	9	236	0	3	2011	
62	1847	696	173	48	30	3	286	0	0	2012	
82	2274	742	207	161	19	3	726	0	0	2013	
1	193	14	0	26	85	1	529	...	0	2000	Allemagne
5	184	332	23	16	39	0	463	...	0	2010	
7	67	355	1	4	14	0	500	...	0	2011	
3	117	138	1	4	397	2	254	...	0	2012	
5	309	349	1	4	320	2	766	0	2	2013	
15	1603	528	3224	1224	502	734	940	4	74	2000	Economies Développées - Amérique du Nord 2/
4	1902	1701	7391	3488	602	1162	1990	96	171	2010	
2	2179	2222	10202	5299	751	2092	2811	10	104	2011	
6	1117	1846	9135	4009	662	1674	1406	10	...	2012	
5	1237	1910	9786	4356	588	1819	1168	9	...	2013	
15	1231	411	2641	1042	95	501	816	4	74	2000	Etats-Unis
3	1487	1362	6197	3106	65	819	1528	92	171	2010	
2	1850	1785	8792	4696	156	1599	2377	10	104	2011	
5	432	1400	7750	3595	188	1161	740	10	...	2012	
2	671	1309	8100	3887	228	1176	752	9	...	2013	
28	14	2	0	0	22	0	41	...	0	2000	Europe du Sud-est
501	91	43	0	161	75	98	354	0	0	2010	
573	200	36	0	58	12	0	585	...	2	2011	
798	315	45	0	91	101	0	508	...	2	2012	
608	992	54	0	287	93	43	992	...	...	2013	
2	8	...	3	2	12	...	102	...	0	2000	Communauté d'Etats Indépendants
43	1783	280	38	106	409	114	2106	0	...	2010	
62	2374	592	59	57	489	22	2758	0	0	2011	
77	4106	641	91	327	1155	52	4340	0	0	2012	
55	2257	951	191	425	1089	369	3304	0	0	2013	
0	4	...	...	1	7	...	45	...	...	2000	Fédération de Russie
26	974	130	36	39	104	39	844	...	...	2010	
45	1406	570	55	18	88	1	1586	...	0	2011	
71	1871	304	89	13	485	1	2444	0	0	2012	
45	783	591	181	86	412	118	1828	...	0	2013	

Voir la fin du tableau pour la remarque générale et les notes.

World exports by provenance and destination (Table D)

In million U.S. dollars f.o.b.

Exports from	Year	World 1/ Monde 1/	Developed economies 2/ Economies développées 2/ Total	Asia-Pacific Asie-Pacifique Total	Japan Japon	Europe Total	Germany Allemagne	North America Amérique du Nord Total	U.S.A. É.-U.	Commonwealth of Independent States Communauté d'Etats Indépendants Total	Europe

Cereals (SITC, Rev. 3, 041-045) *[cont.]*

Exports from	Year	World 1/ Monde 1/	Total	Total	Japan Japon	Total	Germany Allemagne	Total	U.S.A. É.-U.	Total	Europe
Northern Africa	2000	111	2	0	0	1	0	0	0	0	0
	2010	398	27	0	0	27	1	0	0	3	3
	2011	72	19	0	0	19	0	0	...	0	0
	2012	95	32	...	...	32	0	0	0	0	0
	2013	217	39	0	0	39	0	1	0	2	0
Sub-Saharan Africa	2000	152	31	26	26	5	0	0	0	...	...
	2010	938	48	23	23	25	0	0	0	0	0
	2011	1674	96	16	16	78	0	1	1	0	0
	2012	1642	20	0	0	19	0	1	0	...	...
	2013	1592	270	197	196	72	0	2	2	0	0
South Africa	2000	92	25	25	25	1	...	0	0	...	...
	2010	570	42	23	23	19	0	0	0	...	...
	2011	1103	74	16	16	58	0	0	0	0	0
	2012	761	3	0	0	2	0	0	0	...	...
	2013	941	249	196	196	52	0	0	0	0	0
Latin America and the Caribbean	2000	2917	436	48	46	288	3	100	100	2	0
	2010	9281	1312	360	358	678	35	273	265	6	6
	2011	14725	1597	472	468	807	44	318	311	19	19
	2012	19259	2570	1135	1129	741	59	695	684	52	52
	2013	18582	3884	1659	1644	1012	61	1214	1192	4	3
Brazil	2000	17	1	1	0	0	0	0	0	...	...
	2010	2601	501	116	116	333	0	52	52	0	0
	2011	4033	593	226	226	344	7	22	22	2	2
	2012	6530	1286	816	816	249	5	222	221	3	3
	2013	7068	1923	902	902	698	35	322	322	0	0
Eastern Asia	2000	1666	63	56	56	5	1	2	1	63	59
	2010	560	117	101	97	13	1	4	3	24	13
	2011	634	94	71	67	19	1	3	3	26	18
	2012	470	92	81	78	7	1	4	3	8	6
	2013	542	65	52	50	7	1	5	4	9	7
China	2000	1643	61	56	55	5	0	1	1	63	59
	2010	539	109	97	97	12	1	1	0	24	13
	2011	609	86	67	67	18	1	1	1	23	15
	2012	443	85	77	77	6	1	1	1	6	3
	2013	514	58	50	50	6	1	2	2	6	4
Southern Asia	2000	1181	174	7	1	120	6	46	36	8	8
	2010	5355	370	35	2	250	14	86	57	58	38
	2011	8207	659	49	4	448	32	163	122	65	39
	2012	10783	726	57	3	475	25	193	145	92	49
	2013	13062	936	74	5	601	25	261	207	143	48
South-Eastern Asia	2000	2358	370	60	33	149	6	161	135	20	19
	2010	9041	1223	281	159	396	25	546	455	91	79
	2011	10768	1331	282	168	448	27	601	509	82	73
	2012	8686	1113	219	132	372	27	523	437	33	25
	2013	7972	1276	241	149	448	30	587	492	81	75
Western Asia	2000	322	50	0	0	49	3	1	1	23	13
	2010	1002	85	1	0	65	9	19	19	2	1
	2011	706	34	0	0	23	4	10	10	6	4
	2012	868	48	0	0	31	1	16	16	4	1
	2013	1017	92	0	0	76	3	16	15	4	1
Oceania	2000	0	0	0	...	...	...	0	0	...	...
	2010	2	0	0	...	0	...	0	0	...	...
	2011	2	0	0	...	...	...	0	0	...	...
	2012	1	0	0	...	...	...	...	...	...	...
	2013	1	0	0	...	...	...	...	...	...	...

For general note and footnotes see end of table

Exportations mondiales par provenance et destination (Tableau D)

En millions de dollars E.-U. f.o.b.

←—— Exportations vers

South-Eastern Europe Europe du Sud-est	Northern Africa Afrique septentrionale	Sub-Saharan Africa Afrique du Nord	Latin America and the Caribbean Amérique latine et Caraïbes	Eastern Asia Asie orientale	Southern Asia Asie méridionale	South-eastern Asia Asie du Sud-est	Western Asia Asie occidentale	Oceania Océanie	Others 4/ Autre 4/	Année	Exportations en provenance de ↓

Céréales (CTCI, Rev. 3, 041-045) [suite]

South-Eastern Europe	Northern Africa	Sub-Saharan Africa	Latin America and the Caribbean	Eastern Asia	Southern Asia	South-eastern Asia	Western Asia	Oceania	Others 4/	Année	Exportations en provenance de
9	30	12	...	...	0	...	57	...	0	2000	Afrique du Nord
7	182	29	...	1	0	...	143	0	5	2010	
0	44	3	...	0	0	0	4	...	1	2011	
2	39	3	...	0	0	...	18	...	0	2012	
5	75	5	...	2	0	0	89	...	...	2013	
0	2	95	0	4	7	1	12	0	0	2000	Afrique subsaharienne
0	1	722	3	87	15	44	17	0	1	2010	
0	2	845	390	239	20	19	62	0	1	2011	
1	0	1218	324	13	26	30	9	0	1	2012	
1	0	874	101	122	25	179	19	0	0	2013	
...	0	49	0	4	6	0	7	0	0	2000	Afrique du sud
0	0	383	1	85	9	38	11	0	1	2010	
0	1	368	387	238	13	13	10	0	0	2011	
0	0	408	318	8	0	22	2	0	1	2012	
...	0	454	97	115	1	18	5	...	0	2013	
0	313	118	1662	5	137	31	207	...	5	2000	Amérique latine et Caraïbes
6	1178	367	3755	410	740	903	603	0	1	2010	
3	2597	1193	5547	494	904	1043	1326	0	0	2011	
3	2915	1426	7041	1839	890	762	1739	0	21	2012	
13	2343	439	5602	2344	618	1255	1952	0	128	2013	
...	...	1	14	...	...	...	0	...	...	2000	Brésil
...	379	176	369	280	288	382	225	...	...	2010	
...	888	527	500	375	571	249	328	...	...	2011	
0	1014	545	887	1239	842	248	462	...	3	2012	
0	853	228	826	1447	515	768	509	0	...	2013	
12	21	184	41	685	43	504	51	0	0	2000	Asie orientale
1	2	63	2	271	24	37	5	13	0	2010	
0	1	51	2	370	25	60	5	0	...	2011	
0	0	9	2	275	31	51	1	0	...	2012	
...	0	2	3	391	23	48	1	0	0	2013	
12	21	166	41	682	42	504	51	0	...	2000	Chine
1	2	62	1	263	24	36	5	13	...	2010	
0	1	51	1	360	25	58	5	...	...	2011	
0	0	9	1	262	31	48	1	...	...	2012	
...	0	2	3	375	23	46	1	...	...	2013	
0	72	96	0	2	154	36	639	0	0	2000	Asie méridionale
2	15	711	1	21	1001	493	2669	0	13	2010	
3	48	1381	3	142	1572	1054	3276	2	1	2011	
2	143	2700	9	648	1773	1695	2993	1	0	2012	
2	51	2912	24	496	3404	1378	3713	2	0	2013	
3	18	505	34	362	163	533	338	11	0	2000	Asie Sud-est
7	42	2792	259	787	259	2694	785	88	14	2010	
11	70	3292	29	865	740	3275	712	108	252	2011	
6	40	2783	28	1496	17	2155	791	95	129	2012	
4	48	2587	61	1569	64	1447	643	62	128	2013	
15	90	10	0	0	75	0	58	...	1	2000	Asie occidentale
3	50	17	0	10	505	45	273	0	12	2010	
2	41	13	0	6	388	6	195	0	16	2011	
1	48	19	4	8	465	8	249	...	15	2012	
1	21	18	6	14	554	14	291	...	1	2013	
...	...	...	...	...	...	...	...	0	0	2000	Océanie
...	...	0	...	0	...	0	0	2	...	2010	
...	...	...	...	0	...	0	...	2	...	2011	
...	...	...	...	0	...	0	...	1	...	2012	
...	...	...	...	...	...	0	...	1	...	2013	

Voir la fin du tableau pour la remarque générale et les notes.

World exports by provenance and destination (Table D)

In million U.S. dollars f.o.b.

Exports from	Year	World 1/ Monde 1/	Developed economies 2/ Economies développées 2/ Total	Asia-Pacific Asie-Pacifique Total	Japan Japon	Europe Total	Germany Allemagne	North America Amérique du Nord Total	U.S.A. É.-U.	Commonwealth of Independent States Communauté d'Etats Indépendants Total	Europe
Crude materials (excluding fuels), oils, fats (SITC, Rev. 3, 2 and 4)											
World 1/	2000	213040	135132	21274	19728	83987	15219	29871	23137	3273	2923
	2010	693334	298816	50494	47293	203307	38027	45015	33449	12139	10434
	2011	893777	374234	61498	57330	255110	47097	57626	43417	16318	14079
	2012	843871	342746	54669	50845	230172	44167	57905	44400	16996	13628
	2013	840070	331870	53315	49876	224397	43331	54158	41455	17276	14112
Developed Economies - Asia-Pacific 2/	2000	17277	6994	3049	2577	2422	328	1523	1155	175	174
	2010	81493	15588	11183	10548	2871	637	1534	1134	570	537
	2011	113893	22324	15921	15142	4414	928	1989	1296	727	697
	2012	105355	19801	13293	12645	4427	1003	2081	1409	566	549
	2013	114849	18043	12588	11980	3656	775	1799	1367	403	375
Japan	2000	3369	747	30	.	437	96	280	268	5	4
	2010	10992	1554	44	.	824	162	686	667	57	49
	2011	12369	1816	42	.	1077	227	698	676	77	67
	2012	13457	1950	35	.	1050	308	865	847	87	80
	2013	12528	1635	34	.	898	238	703	686	76	67
Developed Economies - Europe 2/	2000	61147	51554	1528	1332	47664	9918	2362	2044	810	782
	2010	158072	120176	2353	1861	113739	23584	4083	3443	2789	2634
	2011	199068	150867	2753	2243	143494	30404	4619	3896	3865	3670
	2012	186520	139001	2379	1921	131800	28784	4822	4090	4118	3872
	2013	186639	139577	2629	2144	131714	29231	5233	4351	4252	3972
France	2000	6036	5195	62	54	4960	957	173	159	43	39
	2010	13471	11107	66	50	10818	2019	223	201	157	150
	2011	17316	14428	91	72	14039	2945	298	274	211	204
	2012	15199	12425	92	70	11943	2667	390	353	221	212
	2013	14516	11761	84	64	11321	2311	355	324	272	257
Germany	2000	9272	7481	98	75	7114	.	269	236	175	169
	2010	25909	20697	205	138	19539	.	953	860	637	610
	2011	33158	26710	236	170	25373	.	1101	992	815	778
	2012	29946	23596	185	119	22362	.	1049	947	821	780
	2013	28680	22610	215	153	21328	.	1067	978	728	692
Developed Economies - North America 2/	2000	53039	35036	6987	6666	10335	1651	17714	12780	60	49
	2010	121258	49485	7877	7392	21809	2972	19799	12177	332	298
	2011	141887	53670	9241	8670	21228	2971	23201	14330	279	245
	2012	140869	49272	8794	8244	18004	3407	22474	14154	418	331
	2013	134141	49110	9147	8627	17388	3044	22576	14779	570	514
United States	2000	30471	15489	4053	3903	6505	965	4931	.	55	43
	2010	85505	26687	4215	3947	14854	1878	7618	.	296	264
	2011	97215	26529	4554	4247	13106	2209	8869	.	258	227
	2012	96233	23533	4095	3776	11121	2591	8318	.	390	304
	2013	90239	23204	4343	4042	11067	2343	7795	.	548	494
South-Eastern Europe	2000	1742	850	9	8	826	121	15	5	105	105
	2010	7052	3361	163	162	3183	463	15	14	51	43
	2011	9754	4972	185	185	4701	588	85	15	71	64
	2012	7939	3754	183	182	3463	415	109	21	74	71
	2013	8901	4559	227	227	4235	520	97	30	66	62
Commonwealth of Independent States	2000	9234	4892	597	597	4206	457	88	79	1628	1361
	2010	28542	9398	385	383	8754	641	259	247	4501	3331
	2011	39442	11674	528	524	10928	825	217	204	7285	5724
	2012	40656	11420	451	433	10783	686	186	180	7864	5251
	2013	38719	11401	658	643	10531	739	212	196	7772	5418
Russian Federation	2000	4752	2850	588	587	2214	173	48	40	338	229
	2010	13044	5245	365	364	4677	351	202	191	1053	381
	2011	18054	6510	475	475	5856	437	179	168	1345	424
	2012	18783	6072	404	404	5512	405	156	151	2858	1052
	2013	18172	6158	552	551	5411	348	194	180	2973	1208

For general note and footnotes see end of table

Exportations mondiales par provenance et destination (Tableau D)

En millions de dollars E.-U. f.o.b.

← Exportations vers

South-Eastern Europe Europe du Sud-est	Northern Africa Afrique septentrio-nale	Sub-Saharan Africa Afrique du Nord	Latin America and the Caribbean Amérique latine et Caraïbes	Eastern Asia Asie orientale	Southern Asia Asie méridionale	South-eastern Asia Asie du Sud-est	Western Asia Asie occidentale	Oceania Océanie	Others 4/ Autre 4/	Année	Exportations en provence de ↓

Matières brutes (sauf combustibles), huiles et graisses (CTCI, Rev. 3, 2 et 4)

South-Eastern Europe	Northern Africa	Sub-Saharan Africa	Latin America and the Caribbean	Eastern Asia	Southern Asia	South-eastern Asia	Western Asia	Oceania	Others 4/	Année	Exportations en provence de
1139	2698	3043	10288	32726	6974	9134	6392	84	2156	2000	Monde 1/
5648	11147	11181	26805	230453	36044	31376	28403	218	1105	2010	
8205	14026	14783	34553	305249	44660	42008	38344	279	1118	2011	
7637	12826	14010	33331	291776	45288	40838	36836	290	1298	2012	
7985	11953	13883	31079	307820	41095	38753	36255	273	1828	2013	
56	116	351	117	6159	678	1505	377	29	721	2000	Economies Développées -
11	47	724	251	56595	2566	3330	1655	92	63	2010	Asie-Pacifique 2/
16	27	931	389	80028	3042	4173	2014	106	116	2011	
124	57	675	312	73810	3313	4475	1984	111	127	2012	
110	72	787	268	85001	2750	4840	2350	99	125	2013	
1	3	41	33	1879	111	525	22	1	...	2000	Japon
6	11	170	53	7490	230	1329	90	2	...	2010	
8	14	183	79	8333	249	1523	85	1	...	2011	
11	8	199	97	9123	245	1642	89	4	...	2012	
19	7	210	111	8509	222	1635	101	2	...	2013	
397	1141	627	612	2813	636	651	1534	11	360	2000	Economies Développées -
2236	3673	1451	1540	14344	3316	1901	6382	24	240	2010	Europe 2/
3687	3818	1820	1852	18526	4290	2426	7668	24	226	2011	
3412	4428	1939	2012	16840	4163	2478	7910	23	196	2012	
3729	4140	1888	2101	17540	3243	2371	7533	29	236	2013	
16	118	62	61	280	115	29	109	7	0	2000	France
72	300	102	107	1032	171	129	281	10	3	2010	
104	376	117	112	1207	204	211	331	14	1	2011	
93	354	123	126	1047	174	217	397	16	6	2012	
109	318	117	179	1085	133	203	315	13	11	2013	
95	91	101	110	601	125	140	206	1	146	2000	Allemagne
270	247	297	287	1980	421	330	735	7	0	2010	
311	334	407	343	2397	605	382	851	0	1	2011	
363	532	386	352	2097	601	384	814	0	1	2012	
356	457	290	347	2232	462	410	785	0	1	2013	
26	190	314	5427	8312	522	1923	975	21	232	2000	Economies Développées -
138	1848	656	11511	43868	2792	5546	4843	35	205	2010	Amérique du Nord 2/
220	2246	782	14630	52978	3572	6668	6673	48	122	2011	
223	2278	743	14385	57753	2997	6544	6226	30	0	2012	
97	1762	661	13634	54104	2614	6702	4846	40	...	2013	
21	165	250	5057	6440	360	1472	911	19	232	2000	Etats-Unis
35	1519	481	10328	35122	2024	4717	4070	20	205	2010	
40	1851	575	12963	41047	2648	5731	5406	45	122	2011	
46	1984	560	12605	43798	2316	5756	5225	19	...	2012	
36	1502	530	12241	39934	2093	5816	4302	33	...	2013	
231	122	2	8	102	6	3	310	0	3	2000	Europe du Sud-est
1233	176	141	12	382	81	6	1600	0	8	2010	
1537	180	223	11	495	150	7	2087	0	20	2011	
1224	187	274	17	538	46	12	1782	0	31	2012	
1175	186	252	14	702	110	32	1769	0	36	2013	
127	270	6	47	1256	178	63	768	0	0	2000	Communauté d'Etats
642	1012	71	84	8366	1833	154	2480	1	0	2010	Indépendants
807	1385	181	268	12181	2242	146	3262	1	12	2011	
673	1854	123	275	11853	2772	259	3561	0	0	2012	
808	1371	72	190	11036	2423	360	3286	0	0	2013	
23	190	1	12	973	45	21	300	0	0	2000	Fédération de Russie
65	501	27	54	4576	456	91	975	1	...	2010	
100	843	62	161	6912	540	106	1464	1	12	2011	
197	945	71	160	5827	598	184	1872	0	0	2012	
213	748	21	117	5671	497	183	1591	0	0	2013	

Voir la fin du tableau pour la remarque générale et les notes.

World exports by provenance and destination (Table D)

In million U.S. dollars f.o.b.

Exports from	Year	World 1/ Monde 1/	Developed economies 2/ Economies développées 2/	Asia-Pacific Asie-Pacifique		Europe		North America Amérique du Nord		Commonwealth of Independent States Communauté d'Etats Indépendants	
			Total	Total	Japan Japon	Total	Germany Allemagne	Total	U.S.A. É.-U.	Total	Europe
	**Crude materials (excluding fuels), oils, fats (SITC, Rev. 3, 2 and 4) [cont.]**										
Northern Africa	2000	1414	946	61	24	773	42	111	102	12	12
	2010	4402	2067	132	25	1493	89	442	423	21	20
	2011	5701	2608	156	39	1846	149	606	594	67	65
	2012	5322	2357	116	22	1619	122	622	599	75	70
	2013	4654	2342	92	26	1682	116	568	537	33	29
Sub-Saharan Africa	2000	7519	4538	521	506	3485	555	532	471	15	15
	2010	31574	11785	1617	1533	8417	1381	1751	1282	355	350
	2011	45205	18974	2165	2091	14071	1467	2738	2145	424	378
	2012	47503	18273	2004	1868	14200	1600	2069	1551	385	306
	2013	42380	14504	1709	1628	10667	1244	2128	1626	403	378
South Africa	2000	2693	1932	411	400	1205	338	315	306	8	8
	2010	13434	4594	1216	1152	2975	837	404	385	94	94
	2011	18776	5734	1573	1527	3666	542	496	452	67	67
	2012	16942	5134	1338	1292	3034	308	762	735	84	74
	2013	17510	4980	1237	1198	3046	284	697	678	86	78
Latin America and the Caribbean	2000	25161	15222	2677	2602	7717	1255	4828	4006	149	149
	2010	120145	45348	12524	12135	23743	5065	9082	7443	907	853
	2011	155444	56055	14884	14106	29914	5758	11258	9062	931	825
	2012	142733	49617	13438	12817	25499	4870	10679	8514	921	845
	2013	147792	47906	12466	12000	25178	4479	10262	8080	1213	1077
Brazil	2000	9140	6169	900	881	4222	771	1047	980	12	12
	2010	54257	19555	3922	3790	13083	2666	2550	1810	321	295
	2011	75880	24734	5210	5003	16701	2443	2822	1961	347	269
	2012	65790	20170	3666	3627	13786	1796	2718	1945	206	181
	2013	71528	20962	3813	3778	14234	2146	2915	2195	127	100
Eastern Asia	2000	11347	4318	1979	1894	1470	229	869	814	91	88
	2010	25936	9487	3317	3121	3924	790	2246	1932	349	320
	2011	34374	12132	4345	4024	4910	1075	2877	2511	492	457
	2012	32176	10862	3840	3549	3996	893	3025	2660	450	412
	2013	31570	10448	3538	3257	4021	955	2889	2588	411	367
China	2000	4575	2767	1241	1205	1051	169	475	454	56	53
	2010	11994	6162	1885	1773	2767	590	1510	1316	203	177
	2011	15546	7613	2285	2083	3381	795	1947	1737	323	296
	2012	14925	7173	2226	2061	2792	681	2155	1927	288	256
	2013	15192	6975	2102	1931	2811	695	2062	1891	244	213
Southern Asia	2000	2589	1252	296	277	664	105	292	279	92	72
	2010	19928	2788	472	416	1623	309	693	657	582	498
	2011	21494	5299	548	465	2594	449	2157	2089	188	117
	2012	23738	8933	704	547	2212	444	6016	5853	236	182
	2013	20474	5528	710	615	1915	385	2903	2784	217	156
South-Eastern Asia	2000	18168	7767	3106	2833	3213	376	1448	1324	71	69
	2010	81689	25678	9790	9190	10931	1737	4956	4561	1397	1340
	2011	109923	31416	10063	9287	13661	2081	7692	7103	1604	1542
	2012	92518	25306	8736	8043	10992	1575	5579	5156	1553	1480
	2013	89211	23703	8666	8002	9905	1401	5132	4788	1575	1505
Western Asia	2000	2650	1083	115	110	885	111	83	73	61	47
	2010	10427	2134	110	93	1878	238	147	128	282	210
	2011	14700	2707	126	109	2404	288	177	162	384	294
	2012	15802	2705	152	121	2324	244	229	199	336	259
	2013	17407	3054	200	176	2514	282	340	310	359	259
Oceania	2000	1753	680	348	304	325	70	6	6	3	0
	2010	2817	1519	571	433	941	120	8	8	2	0
	2011	2891	1536	582	444	945	115	9	8	2	...
	2012	2740	1445	580	452	852	122	13	13	0	...
	2013	3333	1696	686	552	990	161	20	19	0	0

For general note and footnotes see end of table

Exportations mondiales par provenance et destination (Tableau D)

En millions de dollars E.-U. f.o.b.

←—— Exportations vers

South-Eastern Europe Europe du Sud-est	Northern Africa Afrique septentrio-nale	Sub-Saharan Africa Afrique du Nord	Latin America and the Caribbean Amérique latine et Caraïbes	Eastern Asia Asie orientale	Southern Asia Asie méridionale	South-eastern Asia Asie du Sud-est	Western Asia Asie occidentale	Oceania Océanie	Others 4/ Autre 4/	Année	Exportations en provenance de ↓

Matières brutes (sauf combustibles), huiles et graisses (CTCI, Rev. 3, 2 et 4) [suite]

South-Eastern Europe	Northern Africa	Sub-Saharan Africa	Latin America and the Caribbean	Eastern Asia	Southern Asia	South-eastern Asia	Western Asia	Oceania	Others 4/	Année	Exportations en provenance de
35	45	13	89	63	63	32	106	0	9	2000	Afrique du Nord
38	320	225	259	366	440	125	513	0	28	2010	
78	466	229	350	442	586	163	671	0	42	2011	
97	346	204	309	414	665	186	592	0	77	2012	
61	224	197	209	359	430	215	565	0	19	2013	
18	113	1004	116	755	328	374	229	1	28	2000	Afrique subsaharienne
72	156	3929	617	10451	1323	1547	1164	6	169	2010	
74	214	4857	666	14812	1789	2128	1150	30	88	2011	
356	145	4814	1803	14646	2664	2635	1434	3	345	2012	
156	117	4925	268	15878	1778	2740	1595	10	6	2013	
10	6	112	23	358	62	154	29	0	0	2000	Afrique du sud
13	15	584	84	6596	573	762	114	2	1	2010	
21	18	732	132	10185	713	953	217	2	0	2011	
15	16	739	112	8504	1230	901	202	1	5	2012	
8	28	680	89	9687	832	886	228	1	3	2013	
145	361	222	3381	3244	1370	669	389	1	7	2000	Amérique latine et Caraïbes
833	1842	764	9727	49182	4952	3234	3111	2	243	2010	
1143	2797	952	12532	66033	5643	4381	4732	2	245	2011	
1008	1517	806	11244	62941	6373	4196	3838	3	270	2012	
1234	2121	555	11492	68725	5648	4148	3564	3	1183	2013	
41	196	50	682	1211	328	210	241	1	...	2000	Brésil
143	859	182	2229	26216	824	1628	2297	1	...	2010	
243	994	261	3148	38540	1283	2594	3733	0	...	2011	
235	781	220	2307	34428	1407	3068	2967	1	...	2012	
274	956	184	2458	40350	941	2692	2584	1	...	2013	
7	33	46	98	5248	440	948	116	1	1	2000	Asie orientale
82	144	308	628	9290	1694	3159	788	4	0	2010	
123	216	396	938	11787	2254	4761	1271	4	0	2011	
94	221	400	840	11349	1978	4926	1049	5	0	2012	
119	224	407	825	11357	1966	4779	1029	5	0	2013	
6	18	23	42	1000	251	360	52	0	...	2000	Chine
74	109	150	346	2324	851	1277	496	2	...	2010	
113	176	194	591	2740	1180	1800	814	2	...	2011	
84	179	192	478	2962	990	1891	686	2	...	2012	
106	189	200	486	3394	984	1950	664	1	...	2013	
6	31	39	56	495	215	223	179	0	0	2000	Asie méridionale
23	83	154	139	11581	2208	1165	1172	3	30	2010	
26	136	189	244	10293	2186	1871	1052	1	9	2011	
29	120	190	229	8766	2274	1807	1150	2	4	2012	
27	145	217	220	8231	2517	1708	1644	3	18	2013	
41	202	375	281	4015	2228	2373	794	15	4	2000	Asie Sud-est
143	1685	2618	1831	22810	12969	10430	2068	48	12	2010	
239	2269	3990	2425	34099	16414	14353	3034	53	27	2011	
171	1424	3594	1626	28458	15165	12532	2581	83	26	2012	
144	1338	3672	1590	29825	14663	10023	2577	73	27	2013	
49	73	35	55	159	300	142	617	0	75	2000	Asie occidentale
196	159	140	93	2587	1783	320	2625	0	107	2010	
254	270	233	144	2903	2405	457	4729	1	212	2011	
227	244	249	163	3780	2667	470	4728	10	222	2012	
324	252	249	117	4241	2682	452	5498	0	177	2013	
1	...	8	1	106	9	228	...	4	714	2000	Océanie
0	0	0	112	631	88	459	0	4	0	2010	
0	1	1	106	673	88	474	1	10	0	2011	
0	3	0	117	627	210	319	0	19	0	2012	
0	2	0	149	821	270	384	0	11	0	2013	

Voir la fin du tableau pour la remarque générale et les notes.

World exports by provenance and destination (Table D)

In million U.S. dollars f.o.b.

Exports from	Year	World 1/ Monde 1/	Developed economies 2/ Economies développées 2/					North America Amérique du Nord		Commonwealth of Independent States Communauté d'Etats Indépendants	
			Total	Asia-Pacific Asie-Pacifique Total	Japan Japon	Europe Total	Germany Allemagne	Total	U.S.A. É.-U.	Total	Europe

Oil seeds and, oleaginous fruit (SITC, Rev. 3, 22)

Exports from	Year	World 1/	Total	Total	Japan	Total	Germany	Total	U.S.A.	Total	Europe
World 1/	2000	14373	7300	1662	1637	5059	977	579	313	95	80
	2010	56392	17513	3059	3018	13315	3224	1139	772	838	790
	2011	68204	22251	3388	3339	17397	4380	1467	1014	973	905
	2012	78812	24910	3768	3698	19528	6024	1613	1085	961	857
	2013	84265	25646	3783	3698	19784	5887	2079	1593	1454	1337
Developed Economies - Asia-Pacific 2/	2000	419	154	110	106	7	1	38	36	...	...
	2010	536	282	119	114	158	2	5	3	0	0
	2011	1358	1156	69	64	1067	184	20	17	0	0
	2012	1863	1304	95	89	1159	122	50	48	0	0
	2013	2471	1298	142	135	1097	174	59	55	0	0
Japan	2000	1	0	...	.	0	0	0	0	...	...
	2010	2	2	0	.	1	0	1	1	0	0
	2011	2	1	0	.	0	0	0	0	0	0
	2012	5	2	0	.	1	0	1	1	0	0
	2013	3	2	0	.	1	0	0	0	0	0
Developed Economies - Europe 2/	2000	1531	1331	2	1	1317	564	12	11	13	13
	2010	5310	4921	2	1	4906	1958	12	10	138	134
	2011	6958	6488	4	2	6468	2662	16	14	223	218
	2012	8660	8126	7	3	8099	3829	20	13	237	230
	2013	8037	7327	6	3	7290	3803	31	19	363	348
France	2000	558	429	0	0	428	178	1	1	5	5
	2010	1034	941	0	0	939	366	1	1	45	45
	2011	1526	1389	1	1	1384	728	3	3	73	73
	2012	1410	1267	4	1	1260	732	3	3	74	73
	2013	1322	1069	1	1	1063	598	4	4	127	126
Germany	2000	159	125	0	0	125	.	0	0	0	0
	2010	347	304	0	0	303	.	1	1	25	23
	2011	423	365	0	0	363	.	2	1	43	42
	2012	345	285	1	0	283	.	2	1	41	40
	2013	361	283	1	0	281	.	2	1	60	57
Developed Economies - North America 2/	2000	6985	3005	1250	1239	1411	146	345	141	2	1
	2010	24909	5533	2423	2420	2220	609	891	575	74	74
	2011	25277	5778	2712	2709	1922	356	1144	767	51	51
	2012	34822	6784	2959	2954	2703	1044	1122	701	82	81
	2013	30794	6903	2815	2794	2857	909	1232	863	232	231
United States	2000	5818	2338	823	813	1311	137	204	.	2	1
	2010	19752	2849	1220	1220	1312	538	316	.	51	51
	2011	18777	2404	1063	1063	964	315	377	.	49	49
	2012	26950	3285	1187	1185	1678	906	421	.	81	80
	2013	24078	3565	1095	1076	2102	781	368	.	230	228
South-Eastern Europe	2000	60	34	...	...	34	6	0	0	0	0
	2010	1374	894	0	0	892	106	1	1	18	18
	2011	2194	1500	0	0	1495	169	4	4	25	24
	2012	1290	937	0	0	930	84	6	6	33	32
	2013	2092	1537	0	0	1512	124	24	11	28	27
Commonwealth of Independent States	2000	413	231	0	...	228	18	3	3	49	34
	2010	1281	831	0	0	816	60	16	16	110	83
	2011	1877	1170	4	...	1151	107	15	15	136	95
	2012	2480	1622	18	1	1604	49	1	0	161	73
	2013	2703	1675	15	1	1659	118	1	0	228	145
Russian Federation	2000	191	105	...	...	105	14	0	0	6	1
	2010	82	66	...	...	66	13	0	0	2	0
	2011	202	126	...	...	120	11	6	6	6	0
	2012	390	182	1	1	181	14	0	0	35	10
	2013	325	188	...	...	188	10	0	0	26	11

For general note and footnotes see end of table

Exportations mondiales par provenance et destination (Tableau D)

En millions de dollars E.-U. f.o.b.

← Exportations vers

South-Eastern Europe Europe du Sud-est	Northern Africa Afrique septentrio-nale	Sub-Saharan Africa Afrique du Nord	Latin America and the Caribbean Amérique latine et Caraïbes	Eastern Asia Asie orientale	Southern Asia Asie méridionale	South-eastern Asia Asie du Sud-est	Western Asia Asie occidentale	Oceania Océanie	Others 4/ Autre 4/	Année	Exportations en provence de ↓
Graines et fruits oléagineux (CTCI, Rev. 3, 22)											
33	167	107	1676	3233	263	793	464	4	240	2000	Monde 1/
487	1152	209	3461	25658	1167	2813	2818	9	268	2010	
506	1388	219	3962	30284	1294	4052	3082	17	175	2011	
453	1762	219	4892	36270	1096	5113	3076	9	49	2012	
444	1365	345	4616	40164	1145	4980	3221	17	868	2013	
...	0	1	13	193	41	8	7	1	...	2000	Economies Développées -
0	...	0	1	25	205	4	15	2	...	2010	Asie-Pacifique 2/
...	...	3	1	146	23	3	22	3	...	2011	
...	0	2	1	154	345	4	53	1	0	2012	
...	0	1	1	696	153	37	283	2	...	2013	
...	...	0	0	0	...	0	0	...	...	2000	Japon
...	...	0	0	0	...	0	0	...	...	2010	
...	...	0	0	0	0	1	0	...	...	2011	
...	0	0	0	2	0	0	0	...	...	2012	
...	...	0	0	1	...	0	0	0	...	2013	
9	12	2	7	47	90	0	19	0	0	2000	Economies Développées -
183	9	21	4	4	1	1	28	0	1	2010	Europe 2/
185	8	6	5	6	1	1	33	0	1	2011	
220	14	8	8	4	2	1	35	0	6	2012	
183	15	9	67	6	4	3	51	0	9	2013	
2	10	0	5	31	73	0	3	0	...	2000	France
35	2	1	1	2	0	0	6	0	0	2010	
57	2	1	1	1	0	0	3	0	1	2011	
53	2	0	1	0	0	0	5	0	6	2012	
65	2	1	39	0	1	0	8	0	9	2013	
0	0	0	1	15	17	0	0	...	0	2000	Allemagne
15	0	0	1	0	0	0	1	...	0	2010	
11	0	0	1	1	0	0	1	...	0	2011	
12	0	1	2	1	0	0	2	0	0	2012	
10	0	1	2	1	0	1	2	0	0	2013	
3	51	3	1098	1927	32	457	173	2	232	2000	Economies Développées -
17	630	9	2828	12698	486	1452	970	7	205	2010	Amérique du Nord 2/
20	517	8	3181	12482	588	1621	903	6	122	2011	
50	1146	12	3978	18709	258	2644	1152	7	...	2012	
24	510	23	3259	16627	115	2559	529	13	...	2013	
3	43	3	923	1674	0	428	171	2	232	2000	Etats-Unis
17	594	6	2148	11854	79	1363	580	6	205	2010	
20	441	6	2317	11523	2	1479	407	6	122	2011	
29	1039	9	3000	16191	9	2506	795	7	...	2012	
18	442	19	2505	14319	88	2427	453	13	...	2013	
4	...	0	5	6	0	0	10	...	0	2000	Europe du Sud-est
219	3	24	3	0	33	0	180	...	0	2010	
228	9	1	3	1	103	0	326	...	0	2011	
117	0	1	3	1	0	0	198	...	...	2012	
112	11	39	4	2	75	3	283	...	0	2013	
10	11	...	1	9	5	...	98	...	0	2000	Communauté d'Etats
14	16	1	1	2	26	2	279	0	...	2010	Indépendants
37	67	0	8	4	110	5	340	...	0	2011	
40	111	0	0	24	25	30	466	0	0	2012	
50	126	0	1	23	138	90	373	0	0	2013	
...	1	...	...	9	3	...	68	...	...	2000	Fédération de Russie
...	...	...	...	0	2	...	11	...	...	2010	
0	4	...	...	2	5	0	60	...	0	2011	
0	1	...	...	23	9	1	139	...	0	2012	
1	4	...	1	17	8	6	75	...	...	2013	

Voir la fin du tableau pour la remarque générale et les notes.

World exports by provenance and destination (Table D)

In million U.S. dollars f.o.b.

Exports from	Year	World 1/ Monde 1/	Developed economies 2/ Economies développées 2/						Commonwealth of Independent States Communauté d'Etats Indépendants	
			Total	Asia-Pacific Asie-Pacifique		Europe		North America Amérique du Nord		
				Total	Japan Japon	Total	Germany Allemagne	Total	U.S.A. É.-U.	Total	Europe

Oil seeds and, oleaginous fruit (SITC, Rev. 3, 22) [cont.]

Exports from	Year	World 1/ Monde 1/	Total	Total	Japan Japon	Total	Germany Allemagne	Total	U.S.A. É.-U.	Total	Europe
Northern Africa	2000	12	4	0	...	4	1	0	0	0	0
	2010	94	24	1	0	23	1	1	1	0	0
	2011	87	30	0	0	30	3	0	0	0	0
	2012	73	33	1	1	32	3	0	0	0	0
	2013	86	43	2	2	40	5	1	0	0	0
Sub-Saharan Africa	2000	328	103	38	37	57	2	9	8	1	0
	2010	1603	295	120	115	140	8	35	31	1	1
	2011	1404	246	117	115	111	8	18	14	0	0
	2012	1767	344	193	187	117	9	33	32	3	3
	2013	2292	593	215	215	341	140	37	34	1	1
South Africa	2000	26	17	7	6	9	1	1	1	0	...
	2010	119	26	9	8	17	1	0	0	...	...
	2011	82	24	10	9	13	1	1	1	...	...
	2012	117	22	10	9	12	0	0	0	0	...
	2013	44	13	6	5	8	0	0	0	...	...
Latin America and the Caribbean	2000	3743	2029	120	116	1786	218	123	70	0	0
	2010	19066	4171	272	266	3803	421	96	75	414	404
	2011	25883	5192	345	334	4712	818	135	94	416	402
	2012	24668	5020	379	366	4449	821	192	138	332	331
	2013	32700	5427	432	417	4533	539	461	421	466	466
Brazil	2000	2190	1612	103	103	1508	201	1	1	...	...
	2010	11096	2667	193	193	2474	135	0	0	175	164
	2011	16424	3195	257	255	2935	189	2	1	171	158
	2012	17361	3445	299	298	3142	285	4	3	89	89
	2013	22923	3436	331	329	2931	168	175	175	15	15
Eastern Asia	2000	428	251	119	113	128	11	5	2	20	20
	2010	719	254	77	72	152	29	25	15	21	17
	2011	845	301	82	76	188	34	31	19	28	25
	2012	1087	386	93	87	186	27	107	83	8	7
	2013	1044	339	83	75	163	26	93	79	10	7
China	2000	417	251	118	113	128	11	5	2	20	20
	2010	707	253	77	72	152	29	24	15	21	17
	2011	827	300	82	76	188	34	30	18	28	25
	2012	1067	384	93	86	186	27	105	82	8	7
	2013	1018	335	82	74	163	26	91	78	10	7
Southern Asia	2000	244	85	8	8	47	7	30	29	7	7
	2010	979	177	12	3	113	20	52	42	23	23
	2011	1688	250	14	5	154	28	81	66	43	42
	2012	1599	238	15	5	144	22	78	59	53	51
	2013	1518	391	60	44	200	35	131	102	55	50
South-Eastern Asia	2000	130	26	13	12	2	1	11	11	0	0
	2010	224	39	21	21	17	1	1	1	3	3
	2011	292	53	27	26	24	1	2	2	3	3
	2012	143	12	3	2	8	0	1	1	1	1
	2013	132	16	4	4	10	1	1	1	0	0
Western Asia	2000	65	39	2	2	36	4	1	1	3	3
	2010	259	85	6	6	76	9	3	3	36	33
	2011	285	83	8	7	73	12	2	2	48	44
	2012	300	105	6	6	95	13	4	3	53	48
	2013	347	97	8	7	81	15	9	8	71	62
Oceania	2000	15	6	1	1	5	0	0	0	...	...
	2010	39	6	6	...	...	...	0	0	...	...
	2011	56	6	6	...	0	...	0	0	...	...
	2012	61	0	0	...	0	...	0	0	...	...
	2013	49	0	0	...	0	...	0	0	...	...

For general note and footnotes see end of table

Exportations mondiales par provenance et destination (Tableau D)

En millions de dollars E.-U. f.o.b.

← Exportations vers

Graines et fruits oléagineux (CTCI, Rev. 3, 22) [suite]

South-Eastern Europe / Europe du Sud-est	Northern Africa / Afrique septentrionale	Sub-Saharan Africa / Afrique du Nord	Latin America and the Caribbean / Amérique latine et Caraïbes	Eastern Asia / Asie orientale	Southern Asia / Asie méridionale	South-eastern Asia / Asie du Sud-est	Western Asia / Asie occidentale	Oceania / Océanie	Others 4/ Autre 4/	Année	Exportations en provence de
0	6	0	...	...	...	...	1	...	0	2000	Afrique du Nord
0	10	1	0	0	1	0	58	...	0	2010	
0	14	0	0	0	0	0	40	...	...	2011	
0	11	0	0	0	0	0	28	...	0	2012	
2	8	0	0	0	0	0	32	...	0	2013	
1	35	81	7	22	0	1	71	...	6	2000	Afrique subsaharienne
0	42	141	40	344	30	142	514	0	54	2010	
1	87	172	46	377	16	82	321	7	50	2011	
2	51	161	34	448	62	233	390	0	41	2012	
0	13	247	8	490	110	218	612	0	0	2013	
0	...	8	1	0	0	0	0	...	0	2000	Afrique du sud
0	0	36	1	1	0	54	0	...	0	2010	
...	0	34	1	1	0	22	0	...	0	2011	
...	0	17	0	2	0	75	0	...	0	2012	
...	0	18	1	1	1	9	0	...	0	2013	
0	24	15	528	920	62	142	24	...	0	2000	Amérique latine et Caraïbes
31	360	3	546	12198	188	604	552	0	0	2010	
10	536	8	653	16799	234	1179	856	...	0	2011	
3	279	11	809	16455	181	1036	543	...	0	2012	
45	519	6	1253	21839	262	1228	802	0	855	2013	
...	19	0	87	379	62	20	10	...	...	2000	Brésil
24	16	2	33	7548	40	447	145	...	...	2010	
8	12	4	40	11655	113	844	382	...	...	2011	
...	43	5	49	12654	34	903	138	...	...	2012	
40	26	1	172	17865	94	964	312	...	...	2013	
3	11	2	4	73	1	43	20	0	0	2000	Asie orientale
15	42	2	14	174	26	85	86	0	...	2010	
13	78	5	9	234	18	92	67	0	...	2011	
12	103	7	8	309	32	144	77	0	...	2012	
13	106	1	3	270	31	155	116	0	...	2013	
3	11	2	4	65	1	41	20	0	...	2000	Chine
15	42	2	14	166	26	82	86	0	...	2010	
13	78	5	9	221	18	87	67	0	...	2011	
12	103	7	8	296	31	139	77	0	...	2012	
13	106	1	3	255	31	150	114	0	...	2013	
0	15	2	12	12	14	67	27	0	0	2000	Asie méridionale
3	14	3	15	152	76	409	102	0	3	2010	
4	39	6	46	168	97	908	127	0	...	2011	
3	32	8	48	147	94	875	100	0	0	2012	
8	38	9	19	189	134	555	119	1	0	2013	
0	0	1	1	22	5	74	0	0	...	2000	Asie Sud-est
0	12	3	5	59	7	83	12	0	0	2010	
0	21	7	6	65	9	110	18	0	1	2011	
...	7	8	0	14	11	84	7	0	0	2012	
...	1	6	0	18	5	79	4	0	0	2013	
2	1	0	0	0	6	1	13	...	0	2000	Asie occidentale
4	14	1	3	1	87	1	22	...	5	2010	
8	13	2	4	4	93	3	27	...	1	2011	
6	8	2	1	5	88	3	26	...	2	2012	
7	16	3	1	5	118	5	19	...	3	2013	
...	...	...	0	...	7	0	...	1	0	2000	Océanie
...	...	...	0	1	0	0	32	0	0	2010	
...	...	...	0	1	0	0	50	...	0	2011	
...	...	...	0	0	0	0	59	1	0	2012	
...	...	...	0	1	0	0	48	...	0	2013	

Voir la fin du tableau pour la remarque générale et les notes.

World exports by provenance and destination (Table D)

In million U.S. dollars f.o.b.

Exports from	Year	World 1/ Monde 1/	Developed economies 2/ Economies développées 2/ Total	Asia-Pacific Asie-Pacifique Total	Japan Japon	Europe Total	Germany Allemagne	North America Amérique du Nord Total	U.S.A. É.-U.	Commonwealth of Independent States Communauté d'Etats Indépendants Total	Europe
						Textile fibres (SITC, Rev. 3, 26)					
World 1/	2000	21757	8969	930	833	7003	937	1035	663	623	610
	2010	39435	8496	645	501	6566	1102	1284	1019	1037	985
	2011	51923	11404	970	794	8877	1617	1557	1235	1335	1267
	2012	49267	9788	809	625	7386	1372	1593	1249	1204	1128
	2013	48455	10038	764	625	7754	1460	1520	1186	1191	1120
Developed Economies - Asia-Pacific 2/	2000	4239	1397	272	234	1018	140	108	100	6	4
	2010	4855	704	92	64	482	59	130	123	53	46
	2011	7908	1004	150	126	709	101	144	139	67	57
	2012	7612	858	103	89	607	95	148	144	73	66
	2013	7362	735	75	61	540	82	120	117	68	57
Japan	2000	1008	169	9	.	117	27	43	40	2	1
	2010	1417	274	10	.	153	33	111	107	51	44
	2011	1658	323	7	.	195	60	120	117	67	56
	2012	1617	289	4	.	156	47	129	127	73	65
	2013	1663	237	3	.	133	42	101	100	67	57
Developed Economies - Europe 2/	2000	4640	3218	66	49	3046	387	106	95	94	90
	2010	6213	3243	44	28	3047	484	151	130	337	314
	2011	7461	4208	59	40	3941	685	207	178	391	358
	2012	7268	3661	62	50	3415	606	184	153	449	417
	2013	7876	3909	49	40	3647	668	213	188	443	414
France	2000	594	455	16	16	427	40	11	10	5	4
	2010	475	224	5	5	210	34	9	9	1	0
	2011	536	281	8	8	260	43	14	12	1	0
	2012	500	239	9	9	213	34	17	14	1	1
	2013	583	274	6	6	254	40	13	12	1	1
Germany	2000	1394	967	12	6	915	.	40	37	42	40
	2010	1420	750	5	2	694	.	51	45	81	71
	2011	1793	1032	8	5	956	.	68	59	98	85
	2012	1672	868	4	2	811	.	53	45	116	103
	2013	1785	906	4	3	816	.	85	78	125	113
Developed Economies - North America 2/	2000	3431	954	201	192	383	76	370	44	8	7
	2010	8214	634	131	117	285	31	218	30	98	98
	2011	11214	840	197	188	389	71	254	30	89	88
	2012	8973	678	106	101	298	40	273	32	86	85
	2013	8486	714	127	123	315	38	272	31	106	104
United States	2000	3248	902	199	192	378	76	325	.	6	5
	2010	8006	596	129	116	279	30	188	.	98	97
	2011	10988	799	196	187	379	70	224	.	89	88
	2012	8739	636	105	100	290	39	241	.	85	84
	2013	8260	673	126	121	307	37	240	.	104	103
South-Eastern Europe	2000	43	18	0	0	17	5	1	0	1	1
	2010	156	113	0	0	112	39	0	0	5	4
	2011	227	172	0	0	172	56	0	0	11	10
	2012	219	159	0	0	158	48	0	0	8	7
	2013	215	155	0	0	155	39	0	0	7	6
Commonwealth of Independent States	2000	1721	749	7	7	735	70	7	7	489	484
	2010	3050	185	1	1	181	39	3	2	407	395
	2011	2566	202	0	0	198	39	4	4	534	526
	2012	2915	132	0	0	129	19	2	2	389	368
	2013	2671	158	1	1	155	20	2	2	367	351
Russian Federation	2000	37	9	0	0	9	4	0	0	3	1
	2010	33	11	1	...	11	5	...	...	5	2
	2011	37	13	...	...	13	4	...	...	7	6
	2012	38	5	...	...	5	1	...	...	25	18
	2013	52	8	...	...	8	1	...	...	31	22

For general note and footnotes see end of table

Exportations mondiales par provenance et destination (Tableau D)

En millions de dollars E.-U. f.o.b.

← Exportations vers

South-Eastern Europe Europe du Sud-est	Northern Africa Afrique septentrionale	Sub-Saharan Africa Afrique du Nord	Latin America and the Caribbean Amérique latine et Caraïbes	Eastern Asia Asie orientale	Southern Asia Asie méridionale	South-eastern Asia Asie du Sud-est	Western Asia Asie occidentale	Oceania Océanie	Others 4/ Autre 4/	Année	Exportations en provence de
					Fibres textiles (CTCI, Rev. 3, 26)						
171	287	753	1632	4588	1366	2138	1178	11	41	2000	Monde 1/
368	691	1676	2646	12536	4335	4402	3192	19	35	2010	
487	746	2133	3304	17453	4977	6300	3683	34	66	2011	
476	642	2147	2237	19079	4853	5931	2833	27	51	2012	
546	751	2155	2318	17014	5032	6094	3250	34	31	2013	
3	8	49	41	1595	348	718	63	10	2	2000	Economies Développées -
0	17	177	14	2707	379	716	70	17	0	2010	Asie-Pacifique 2/
0	23	191	14	4874	577	1053	81	24	0	2011	
3	41	207	17	4965	456	906	62	25	...	2012	
1	42	221	22	4808	449	925	65	25	0	2013	
1	1	35	9	498	51	227	13	0	...	2000	Japon
0	9	158	6	498	74	305	40	0	...	2010	
0	13	169	5	650	66	340	25	0	...	2011	
0	6	186	13	625	62	335	27	0	...	2012	
0	5	197	17	696	55	361	28	0	...	2013	
116	147	280	87	233	77	36	350	0	2	2000	Economies Développées -
292	304	598	95	497	166	95	585	0	0	2010	Europe 2/
361	270	716	105	687	195	91	435	0	2	2011	
349	276	763	101	648	299	173	547	0	0	2012	
399	344	858	102	711	278	125	705	0	0	2013	
2	10	22	2	74	8	1	15	0	...	2000	France
1	20	27	2	171	8	0	21	0	...	2010	
1	24	33	2	159	12	0	22	0	...	2011	
0	27	37	2	161	14	0	19	0	0	2012	
2	27	39	2	201	14	0	22	0	0	2013	
59	36	59	41	33	28	23	105	0	2	2000	Allemagne
62	54	122	29	137	44	38	104	...	0	2010	
81	54	151	26	132	60	35	124	0	0	2011	
80	59	144	30	125	67	48	135	0	0	2012	
82	71	157	36	134	71	57	147	0	0	2013	
3	16	108	993	600	133	359	257	0	...	2000	Economies Développées -
2	99	266	1538	3132	502	1007	935	0	...	2010	Amérique du Nord 2/
4	163	317	2258	3873	805	1584	1280	0	...	2011	
4	123	333	1310	4423	433	879	704	0	...	2012	
4	161	306	1404	3166	545	1167	912	1	...	2013	
3	16	83	987	520	129	347	256	0	...	2000	Etats-Unis
1	94	154	1523	3130	479	1003	928	0	...	2010	
2	156	190	2248	3870	783	1579	1272	0	...	2011	
2	116	206	1300	4422	405	873	693	0	...	2012	
3	154	191	1392	3164	518	1162	900	1	...	2013	
9	1	0	0	0	1	0	11	...	1	2000	Europe du Sud-est
7	1	9	0	2	2	0	17	...	0	2010	
11	0	10	0	2	2	0	18	0	0	2011	
10	1	10	0	4	3	3	20	...	0	2012	
14	1	11	0	3	3	0	22	0	0	2013	
27	4	4	28	149	89	34	147	...	0	2000	Communauté d'Etats
6	50	0	3	1328	667	47	356	0	...	2010	Indépendants
6	33	0	3	1046	548	17	176	0	0	2011	
5	9	0	0	1706	517	12	145	0	...	2012	
8	12	0	0	1371	484	8	265	...	...	2013	
1	0	0	0	2	2	0	20	...	...	2000	Fédération de Russie
1	0	0	0	7	7	0	3	0	...	2010	
0	0	0	0	3	6	2	6	...	0	2011	
1	0	...	0	2	3	0	3	...	...	2012	
2	0	...	0	3	6	0	1	...	...	2013	

Voir la fin du tableau pour la remarque générale et les notes.

World exports by provenance and destination (Table D)

In million U.S. dollars f.o.b.

| Exports from | Year | World 1/ Monde 1/ | Developed economies 2/ Economies développées 2/ | | | | | | | Commonwealth of Independent States Communauté d'Etats Indépendants | |
| | | | Asia-Pacific Asie-Pacifique | | Europe | | North America Amérique du Nord | | | |
			Total	Total	Japan Japon	Total	Germany Allemagne	Total	U.S.A. É.-U.	Total	Europe

Textile fibres (SITC, Rev. 3, 26) [cont.]

Exports from	Year	World 1/ Monde 1/	Total	Total	Japan Japon	Total	Germany Allemagne	Total	U.S.A. É.-U.	Total	Europe
Northern Africa	2000	223	117	10	10	91	6	16	15	0	0
	2010	397	57	3	3	50	8	3	1	1	0
	2011	432	83	4	4	69	11	9	8	1	1
	2012	360	86	2	2	75	7	8	7	2	2
	2013	312	97	3	3	87	5	7	6	2	2
Sub-Saharan Africa	2000	1453	602	22	21	562	78	18	13	0	0
	2010	2260	513	17	9	489	27	7	7	0	0
	2011	2746	665	23	8	622	54	20	18	0	0
	2012	2983	569	57	6	482	43	30	28	0	0
	2013	2909	466	8	7	444	77	14	14	0	0
South Africa	2000	190	119	10	10	100	13	9	4	0	0
	2010	296	123	6	4	115	9	2	2	...	...
	2011	420	163	4	4	155	13	3	3	0	...
	2012	415	121	4	4	114	14	2	2	0	0
	2013	420	131	5	5	124	11	2	2	0	...
Latin America and the Caribbean	2000	1003	428	21	20	241	58	167	165	1	1
	2010	2022	441	41	40	285	92	115	113	0	0
	2011	3166	569	71	70	391	113	107	105	0	0
	2012	3447	474	52	51	286	86	136	135	0	0
	2013	2359	448	47	41	315	87	86	84	0	0
Brazil	2000	92	35	0	0	32	15	2	2	...	...
	2010	1025	109	29	29	63	10	16	16	0	0
	2011	1770	114	41	41	67	14	6	6	0	0
	2012	2275	98	36	36	48	7	14	14	...	...
	2013	1307	104	27	26	76	9	1	1	0	0
Eastern Asia	2000	3414	1010	263	244	550	60	197	182	5	5
	2010	5216	1699	212	154	1017	211	470	435	113	109
	2011	7396	2321	295	213	1467	313	559	513	183	176
	2012	6643	2069	289	219	1202	276	579	534	153	146
	2013	6630	2170	279	212	1327	307	564	522	151	143
China	2000	1085	495	159	158	320	27	16	16	2	1
	2010	2368	901	96	83	573	118	232	219	47	44
	2011	3775	1298	138	112	832	184	327	305	97	94
	2012	3220	1103	144	126	638	158	321	300	75	71
	2013	3158	1203	155	135	751	172	297	280	73	68
Southern Asia	2000	462	148	19	16	111	17	18	16	16	16
	2010	4529	338	23	17	250	48	66	61	9	7
	2011	5344	522	33	25	392	83	97	89	15	11
	2012	5606	439	32	23	307	75	100	91	16	13
	2013	6558	536	39	28	364	76	134	125	20	16
South-Eastern Asia	2000	589	91	38	28	34	7	19	17	0	0
	2010	1909	352	74	61	174	25	104	102	4	4
	2011	2650	501	128	111	245	34	127	125	5	5
	2012	2583	388	100	80	187	25	101	98	6	5
	2013	2349	385	132	110	177	26	76	72	9	9
Western Asia	2000	540	238	12	12	216	33	10	9	3	2
	2010	614	217	8	7	194	38	16	15	10	8
	2011	814	318	8	7	282	57	28	27	37	35
	2012	657	275	6	3	239	52	31	26	20	19
	2013	726	264	3	1	228	36	33	25	19	17
Oceania	2000	1	0	0	...	0	...	0	0	...	...
	2010	0	0	0	0	0	...	0	0	0	0
	2011	0	0	0	...	0	...	...	...	...	...
	2012	0	0	0	0	0	...	0	0	0	...
	2013	0	0	0	...	0	...	0	0	...	...

For general note and footnotes see end of table

Exportations mondiales par provenance et destination (Tableau D)

En millions de dollars E.-U. f.o.b.

← Exportations vers

South-Eastern Europe Europe du Sud-est	Northern Africa Afrique septentrio-nale	Sub-Saharan Africa Afrique du Nord	Latin America and the Caribbean Amérique latine et Caraïbes	Eastern Asia Asie orientale	Southern Asia Asie méridionale	South-eastern Asia Asie du Sud-est	Western Asia Asie occidentale	Oceania Océanie	Others 4/ Autre 4/	Année	Exportations en provence de
\multicolumn{12}{c}{Fibres textiles (CTCI, Rev. 3, 26) [suite]}

South-Eastern Europe	Northern Africa	Sub-Saharan Africa	Latin America and the Caribbean	Eastern Asia	Southern Asia	South-eastern Asia	Western Asia	Oceania	Others 4/	Année	Exportations en provence de
1	1	5	6	29	29	13	23	0	0	2000	Afrique du Nord
2	7	21	6	82	168	11	42	...	0	2010	
3	8	24	10	78	141	18	66	...	0	2011	
2	8	15	3	46	142	7	48	...	1	2012	
2	6	15	4	33	97	13	44	...	0	2013	
0	40	263	63	117	151	175	24	0	16	2000	Afrique subsaharienne
3	33	312	315	389	199	457	36	0	2	2010	
5	26	516	26	677	140	633	49	8	0	2011	
12	36	436	18	1010	248	620	31	0	4	2012	
5	54	305	2	955	276	798	42	6	0	2013	
0	4	19	1	33	7	2	4	0	0	2000	Afrique du sud
2	1	21	0	108	33	5	2	0	0	2010	
4	2	25	1	178	34	8	4	0	0	2011	
4	7	23	1	204	37	15	3	0	0	2012	
4	10	25	1	219	25	2	2	...	0	2013	
0	2	1	345	156	22	17	30	0	0	2000	Amérique latine et
6	20	5	356	614	129	321	131	...	0	2010	Caraïbes
10	46	15	433	1205	137	534	215	0	0	2011	
10	19	9	351	1485	190	716	193	0	0	2012	
10	10	7	343	863	112	485	81	0	0	2013	
0	0	1	39	2	3	3	9	...	...	2000	Brésil
0	8	1	105	346	100	277	80	...	...	2010	
0	29	12	110	862	95	407	140	...	...	2011	
...	11	7	118	1111	149	640	142	...	...	2012	
...	5	4	108	532	75	433	47	...	...	2013	
1	16	15	50	1452	310	493	60	0	1	2000	Asie orientale
35	62	160	255	980	761	781	370	0	0	2010	
66	81	216	373	1309	949	1222	676	0	0	2011	
54	61	228	352	1076	856	1258	535	0	...	2012	
79	70	257	357	1113	807	1193	434	0	0	2013	
0	1	2	12	224	171	163	15	0	...	2000	Chine
28	33	30	121	266	484	226	232	0	...	2010	
59	50	51	205	415	663	459	479	0	...	2011	
47	31	57	190	319	535	467	395	0	...	2012	
69	44	79	193	293	500	426	278	0	...	2013	
2	8	19	8	62	67	86	46	0	0	2000	Asie méridionale
5	29	87	38	2366	978	438	223	0	18	2010	
5	40	92	43	2923	1014	451	236	0	3	2011	
5	37	90	44	3139	1176	468	189	0	2	2012	
4	32	115	59	3395	1546	620	227	0	4	2013	
0	4	5	8	183	88	179	31	0	...	2000	Asie Sud-est
2	19	18	23	355	323	518	295	1	0	2010	
3	13	21	34	661	409	683	320	1	0	2011	
5	9	37	34	488	473	875	267	1	0	2012	
3	6	40	20	497	359	746	282	1	0	2013	
8	39	3	4	12	51	28	135	0	18	2000	Asie occidentale
6	50	22	3	84	61	13	132	0	14	2010	
13	43	16	5	116	61	14	131	0	60	2011	
16	24	18	6	89	60	15	91	0	42	2012	
18	14	20	4	99	76	15	170	0	27	2013	
0	...	1	...	...	0	0	...	0	0	2000	Océanie
...	...	...	0	0	0	0	...	0	...	2010	
...	...	0	0	0	0	0	0	0	...	2011	
...	...	0	0	0	0	0	0	0	0	2012	
...	...	0	...	0	0	0	0	0	0	2013	

Voir la fin du tableau pour la remarque générale et les notes.

World exports by provenance and destination (Table D)

In million U.S. dollars f.o.b.

| Exports from | Year | World 1/ Monde 1/ | Developed economies 2/ Economies développées 2/ | Asia-Pacific Asie-Pacifique | | Europe | | North America Amérique du Nord | | Commonwealth of Independent States Communauté d'Etats Indépendants | |
			Total	Total	Japan Japon	Total	Germany Allemagne	Total	U.S.A. É.-U.	Total	Europe

Crude fertilizers and minerals (SITC, Rev. 3, 27)

Exports from	Year	World 1/ Monde 1/	Total	Total	Japan Japon	Total	Germany Allemagne	Total	U.S.A. É.-U.	Total	Europe
World 1/	2000	13356	8892	1119	967	6085	845	1688	1247	269	234
	2010	30081	16008	1601	1267	11314	1582	3092	2430	1109	956
	2011	36719	18564	1939	1497	13146	2066	3479	2739	1551	1381
	2012	37101	17391	1829	1408	11669	1817	3893	3095	1912	1675
	2013	36049	17140	1569	1208	11701	1855	3870	2991	1778	1554
Developed Economies - Asia-Pacific 2/	2000	463	201	110	93	48	6	42	40	1	1
	2010	813	240	85	51	102	30	54	52	1	0
	2011	1011	295	85	51	141	22	70	68	2	1
	2012	1003	259	93	54	105	22	62	61	5	5
	2013	808	168	41	10	66	17	61	60	0	0
Japan	2000	184	46	6	.	19	4	21	21	1	1
	2010	466	57	13	.	23	9	22	21	0	0
	2011	554	64	10	.	23	9	31	30	0	0
	2012	527	57	13	.	19	7	25	24	5	5
	2013	460	57	13	.	18	8	26	25	0	0
Developed Economies - Europe 2/	2000	5217	4320	76	64	4028	726	217	192	61	59
	2010	10142	7587	79	62	7272	1267	236	197	210	201
	2011	11885	8805	97	74	8460	1618	248	211	276	267
	2012	10699	7703	69	51	7404	1437	230	197	251	240
	2013	11158	8087	71	48	7787	1531	229	198	259	251
France	2000	508	445	6	6	426	99	12	11	5	4
	2010	865	691	5	4	660	132	26	17	13	13
	2011	898	697	5	4	670	127	22	15	13	12
	2012	787	613	6	5	583	113	25	18	16	16
	2013	820	652	7	5	619	126	26	22	16	16
Germany	2000	836	730	9	7	712	.	9	8	6	5
	2010	1829	1551	11	8	1523	.	18	16	26	25
	2011	2205	1810	12	9	1778	.	19	17	31	29
	2012	1865	1529	10	7	1488	.	30	26	33	31
	2013	1863	1551	13	9	1504	.	34	32	28	26
Developed Economies - North America 2/	2000	2525	1652	375	324	508	64	768	397	4	3
	2010	3639	2150	346	245	584	121	1220	689	11	10
	2011	4108	2370	431	256	610	127	1329	731	13	12
	2012	3922	2296	383	233	528	117	1385	726	11	10
	2013	3725	2372	341	216	528	117	1503	765	11	9
United States	2000	1790	1187	330	297	487	60	371	.	4	3
	2010	2459	1325	265	240	530	104	530	.	11	9
	2011	2720	1439	298	250	543	108	597	.	13	12
	2012	2706	1394	264	228	471	89	659	.	11	10
	2013	2642	1453	241	212	475	86	738	.	11	9
South-Eastern Europe	2000	61	33	0	0	32	3	1	1	4	4
	2010	185	103	0	0	103	5	0	0	3	2
	2011	226	111	0	0	111	8	0	0	6	5
	2012	182	85	0	0	85	6	0	0	4	4
	2013	205	102	0	0	101	6	0	0	7	6
Commonwealth of Independent States	2000	461	219	2	2	210	2	7	0	122	98
	2010	1700	508	4	4	477	16	27	27	600	499
	2011	2983	717	3	3	676	35	38	38	911	794
	2012	3311	624	1	1	600	23	22	22	1296	1115
	2013	2772	688	1	1	677	20	10	10	1182	1014
Russian Federation	2000	298	155	2	2	146	1	7	0	46	35
	2010	808	336	4	4	310	10	22	22	90	64
	2011	1467	486	3	3	447	21	37	37	99	71
	2012	1689	453	1	1	430	18	22	22	314	262
	2013	1373	512	1	1	501	14	10	10	278	219

For general note and footnotes see end of table

Exportations mondiales par provenance et destination (Tableau D)

En millions de dollars E.-U. f.o.b.

⟵ Exportations vers

South-Eastern Europe / Europe du Sud-est	Northern Africa / Afrique septentrionale	Sub-Saharan Africa / Afrique du Nord	Latin America and the Caribbean / Amérique latine et Caraïbes	Eastern Asia / Asie orientale	Southern Asia / Asie méridionale	South-eastern Asia / Asie du Sud-est	Western Asia / Asie occidentale	Oceania / Océanie	Others 4/ / Autre 4/	Année	Exportations en provence de ↓
					Engrais et minéraux bruts (CTCI, Rev. 3, 27)						
107	212	226	688	1244	334	683	588	9	106	2000	Monde 1/
253	588	754	1621	4736	1520	1655	1639	34	164	2010	
356	1066	982	2023	5930	2107	1967	2001	48	124	2011	
331	1006	960	2339	6163	2219	2223	2371	70	115	2012	
344	749	855	1881	6269	2086	2392	2320	45	190	2013	
0	0	2	2	170	8	72	3	3	0	2000	Economies Développées -
0	1	20	5	413	19	91	10	10	2	2010	Asie-Pacifique 2/
0	0	23	7	545	15	101	12	12	0	2011	
0	0	11	8	557	20	108	16	18	0	2012	
0	0	5	7	432	19	133	29	8	5	2013	
...	0	1	0	100	7	28	1	0	...	2000	Japon
...	1	2	2	315	17	66	4	1	...	2010	
...	0	1	3	398	10	73	3	1	...	2011	
...	0	2	2	366	11	78	3	3	...	2012	
...	0	3	4	291	16	76	12	1	...	2013	
40	114	45	81	197	38	87	140	2	93	2000	Economies Développées -
94	302	156	197	691	226	236	332	2	108	2010	Europe 2/
107	386	146	259	872	244	281	443	3	63	2011	
103	396	128	279	818	228	280	458	2	52	2012	
104	339	118	254	943	222	284	450	3	96	2013	
2	15	12	7	6	2	5	9	1	...	2000	France
5	59	21	15	28	4	11	15	1	1	2010	
5	83	21	14	34	5	11	14	2	...	2011	
4	58	16	17	32	4	11	15	2	0	2012	
3	42	19	19	35	5	12	15	2	0	2013	
6	11	6	10	7	5	32	13	1	10	2000	Allemagne
13	13	12	32	59	21	65	37	0	0	2010	
20	27	24	58	78	21	79	57	0	0	2011	
19	32	10	53	46	16	74	53	0	0	2012	
17	16	11	50	64	14	66	47	0	0	2013	
0	19	37	328	296	38	118	34	0	0	2000	Economies Développées -
1	15	42	568	572	82	117	71	10	...	2010	Amérique du Nord 2/
1	26	96	708	591	62	124	101	16	...	2011	
2	62	65	787	479	41	98	70	11	...	2012	
2	28	48	631	396	44	104	81	8	...	2013	
0	8	14	233	227	11	80	26	0	...	2000	Etats-Unis
1	14	18	537	384	32	90	45	0	...	2010	
1	12	35	629	404	38	83	51	16	...	2011	
2	50	34	707	337	39	88	42	2	...	2012	
2	27	44	573	341	42	97	48	4	...	2013	
21	0	0	0	0	0	0	2	0	0	2000	Europe du Sud-est
50	5	0	0	2	1	0	17	...	4	2010	
71	12	0	0	3	2	0	21	0	0	2011	
50	9	1	0	3	2	1	18	0	8	2012	
52	10	0	0	4	2	2	19	...	9	2013	
11	52	0	3	14	12	15	14	...	0	2000	Communauté d'Etats
23	110	4	37	166	144	36	71	0	0	2010	Indépendants
24	494	41	115	375	114	45	146	0	0	2011	
20	357	35	177	379	205	79	141	0	0	2012	
31	223	19	85	251	157	66	71	0	0	2013	
8	50	0	3	13	8	12	5	...	...	2000	Fédération de Russie
7	82	1	21	85	115	35	35	...	...	2010	
6	383	29	65	181	87	44	87	...	0	2011	
7	288	27	107	178	153	77	84	...	0	2012	
20	182	4	49	129	119	62	20	...	0	2013	

Voir la fin du tableau pour la remarque générale et les notes.

World exports by provenance and destination (Table D)

In million U.S. dollars f.o.b.

Exports from	Year	World 1/ Monde 1/	Developed economies 2/ Economies développées 2/							Commonwealth of Independent States Communauté d'Etats Indépendants	
			Total	Asia-Pacific Asie-Pacifique		Europe		North America Amérique du Nord			
				Total	Japan Japon	Total	Germany Allemagne	Total	U.S.A. É.-U.	Total	Europe

Crude fertilizers and minerals (SITC, Rev. 3, 27) [cont.]

Exports from	Year	World 1/ Monde 1/	Total	Total	Japan Japon	Total	Germany Allemagne	Total	U.S.A. É.-U.	Total	Europe
Northern Africa	2000	540	331	43	6	218	4	70	64	5	5
	2010	1779	947	113	8	549	4	284	276	10	10
	2011	2476	1287	136	21	757	60	394	393	53	51
	2012	2499	1162	99	7	627	36	437	424	59	54
	2013	2024	968	70	7	526	3	371	355	16	16
Sub-Saharan Africa	2000	506	245	23	21	185	5	37	34	0	0
	2010	1670	812	21	17	498	22	292	290	2	2
	2011	1394	566	38	34	485	27	43	31	2	2
	2012	2246	931	39	35	636	28	256	252	2	2
	2013	1512	671	26	23	369	18	276	275	1	1
South Africa	2000	208	154	13	12	111	1	30	28	0	...
	2010	481	311	20	16	253	3	37	35	2	2
	2011	657	353	27	22	288	12	39	27	2	2
	2012	943	599	38	35	308	11	253	249	1	1
	2013	791	477	25	23	182	5	269	268	0	0
Latin America and the Caribbean	2000	730	540	49	48	194	6	297	285	0	0
	2010	1772	1043	143	137	398	37	501	450	5	5
	2011	2126	1236	138	127	440	43	658	601	6	6
	2012	2456	1377	163	134	435	46	779	724	8	8
	2013	2431	1230	130	109	378	35	722	666	9	9
Brazil	2000	281	212	31	31	148	1	33	33	0	0
	2010	709	405	21	21	270	23	114	75	...	...
	2011	772	438	18	18	294	32	126	88	1	1
	2012	769	406	18	17	268	41	120	89	0	0
	2013	796	393	10	9	245	27	137	101	0	0
Eastern Asia	2000	1379	819	361	338	255	12	204	192	47	47
	2010	3115	1665	663	632	619	19	383	365	117	109
	2011	3727	1970	819	785	614	40	537	513	110	103
	2012	3599	1748	769	728	484	37	495	476	116	106
	2013	3596	1536	677	636	441	35	419	399	113	98
China	2000	1103	704	296	275	215	11	192	180	27	27
	2010	2606	1484	546	515	576	15	362	345	57	49
	2011	3047	1743	657	624	569	35	516	493	58	52
	2012	2942	1566	632	592	461	31	473	455	72	63
	2013	2966	1371	560	521	407	29	404	386	62	55
Southern Asia	2000	400	188	26	22	133	6	29	27	9	7
	2010	1579	349	54	41	245	17	50	43	15	9
	2011	2054	475	69	51	299	24	107	99	17	8
	2012	2198	491	69	51	271	20	151	139	18	11
	2013	2538	548	69	49	322	24	156	142	20	14
South-Eastern Asia	2000	492	83	40	37	39	2	4	3	0	0
	2010	1013	109	83	60	8	3	17	16	2	2
	2011	1262	128	101	76	6	3	21	21	1	1
	2012	1154	115	90	77	7	2	19	18	1	0
	2013	1470	172	106	83	14	3	53	53	1	1
Western Asia	2000	582	260	14	11	234	9	12	11	15	10
	2010	2640	493	10	9	456	40	27	25	132	107
	2011	3431	601	22	19	545	59	35	33	154	131
	2012	3680	597	53	36	487	42	58	56	142	120
	2013	3620	593	31	25	492	45	70	68	158	135
Oceania	2000	2	0	0	0	0	...	0	0	...	...
	2010	32	2	0	...	2	2	0	0	...	...
	2011	36	2	0	...	2	2	0	0	...	...
	2012	152	2	2	0	0	...	0	0	...	...
	2013	189	6	6	.	0	...	0	0	...	...

For general note and footnotes see end of table

Exportations mondiales par provenance et destination (Tableau D)

En millions de dollars E.-U. f.o.b.

← Exportations vers

South-Eastern Europe Europe du Sud-est	Northern Africa Afrique septentrio-nale	Sub-Saharan Africa Afrique du Nord	Latin America and the Caribbean Amérique latine et Caraïbes	Eastern Asia Asie orientale	Southern Asia Asie méridionale	South-eastern Asia Asie du Sud-est	Western Asia Asie occidentale	Oceania Océanie	Others 4/ Autre 4/	Année	Exportations en provence de ↓
			Engrais et minéraux bruts (CTCI, Rev. 3, 27) *[suite]*								
19	5	7	79	24	26	18	26	0	0	2000	Afrique du Nord
31	79	60	233	72	161	102	76	...	8	2010	
61	42	44	293	111	327	139	115	0	4	2011	
65	43	48	297	99	408	174	138	0	4	2012	
35	52	80	192	94	237	191	155	0	3	2013	
2	1	102	21	20	47	33	35	0	2	2000	Afrique subsaharienne
0	4	357	66	119	46	19	241	3	1	2010	
1	11	441	13	87	65	12	183	2	10	2011	
1	11	476	10	169	73	29	543	1	1	2012	
1	4	424	4	124	28	42	212	1	0	2013	
0	0	24	2	18	3	4	2	0	0	2000	Afrique du sud
0	4	102	3	33	9	8	7	2	0	2010	
1	2	183	5	57	28	10	15	1	0	2011	
1	7	185	2	47	54	28	18	1	0	2012	
1	3	161	1	53	17	40	38	1	0	2013	
0	1	9	130	26	12	11	2	0	1	2000	Amérique latine et Caraïbes
0	5	23	368	229	50	42	6	1	1	2010	
0	10	18	463	255	88	40	5	0	2	2011	
0	8	15	600	255	123	63	6	0	1	2012	
1	12	19	570	367	145	65	11	1	2	2013	
...	...	7	19	23	10	8	2	...	...	2000	Brésil
0	1	21	50	165	38	26	4	0	...	2010	
0	0	17	58	190	40	27	2	0	...	2011	
0	0	12	78	189	50	31	3	0	...	2012	
0	0	16	73	235	39	36	4	0	...	2013	
3	5	10	14	313	72	83	13	1	0	2000	Asie orientale
3	13	46	63	744	125	265	73	1	0	2010	
3	10	61	64	910	179	322	94	2	0	2011	
3	14	50	59	948	164	370	123	3	0	2012	
3	9	40	76	1021	207	461	126	3	0	2013	
2	5	9	14	201	65	64	11	0	...	2000	Chine
3	13	39	62	532	111	234	70	1	...	2010	
3	10	54	62	593	160	278	85	1	...	2011	
3	14	42	58	635	136	306	109	1	...	2012	
3	9	35	76	758	148	384	120	1	...	2013	
0	3	4	2	96	27	26	44	0	0	2000	Asie méridionale
0	14	21	31	667	157	90	229	2	4	2010	
2	10	27	24	921	198	133	240	1	3	2011	
1	10	36	28	991	226	138	257	1	0	2012	
2	15	45	26	1165	209	167	336	1	3	2013	
0	0	2	0	56	13	179	157	2	0	2000	Asie Sud-est
0	0	5	0	225	107	513	47	4	0	2010	
0	0	9	1	315	124	608	69	6	1	2011	
0	0	11	2	242	88	616	70	8	0	2012	
0	0	11	1	248	299	595	130	14	0	2013	
11	12	7	28	34	43	43	117	...	11	2000	Asie occidentale
49	41	20	54	827	402	122	466	0	35	2010	
84	64	75	76	936	688	141	572	...	40	2011	
85	94	84	93	1222	641	132	531	9	48	2012	
113	57	47	33	1224	518	105	699	0	73	2013	
...	...	0	...	...	...	...	...	1	0	2000	Océanie
...	...	0	0	8	0	21	...	0	0	2010	
...	...	0	0	8	0	20	...	6	0	2011	
...	...	0	0	1	...	135	0	14	...	2012	
...	...	0	0	0	...	177	...	6	0	2013	

Voir la fin du tableau pour la remarque générale et les notes.

World exports by provenance and destination (Table D)

In million U.S. dollars f.o.b.

Exports from	Year	World 1/ Monde 1/	Developed economies 2/ Economies développées 2/ Asia-Pacific Asie-Pacifique Total	Asia-Pacific Total	Japan Japon	Europe Total	Germany Allemagne	North America Amérique du Nord Total	U.S.A. É.-U.	Commonwealth of Independent States Communauté d'Etats Indépendants Total	Europe

Exports to ———→

Metalliferous ores and metal scrap (SITC, Rev. 3, 28)

Exports from	Year	World 1/ Monde 1/	Total	Total	Japan Japon	Total	Germany Allemagne	Total	U.S.A. É.-U.	Total	Europe
World 1/	2000	49054	31497	6542	6262	18942	3743	6013	3508	1215	1078
	2010	297680	121163	31205	30372	76327	15577	13631	7944	3465	3191
	2011	383425	145780	37720	36386	90247	17777	17813	10204	5445	5084
	2012	343919	126039	32663	31700	77412	15513	15963	9258	5444	4325
	2013	345373	117746	31955	31185	71610	14232	14181	8122	5293	4572
Developed Economies - Asia-Pacific 2/	2000	8135	3562	1686	1556	968	111	908	567	163	163
	2010	65656	11872	9516	9309	1525	436	830	460	485	460
	2011	92178	17259	14271	13940	1785	506	1203	545	592	575
	2012	83617	14801	11786	11564	1816	644	1199	556	442	433
	2013	92187	13364	11293	11112	1154	377	917	518	288	271
Japan	2000	879	105	1	.	78	10	26	24	...	...
	2010	4974	541	1	.	286	31	254	254	3	3
	2011	5348	630	3	.	417	59	210	209	3	3
	2012	6468	745	1	.	417	155	327	325	4	4
	2013	5718	526	1	.	304	88	220	219	3	3
Developed Economies - Europe 2/	2000	10941	9207	185	182	8557	1823	465	357	90	89
	2010	51962	37131	484	452	35336	7717	1311	1076	101	90
	2011	66784	46805	718	673	44629	9802	1457	1170	353	350
	2012	59980	41870	423	400	39860	8549	1587	1303	425	410
	2013	53840	38210	354	328	36152	7849	1703	1419	534	503
France	2000	1300	1258	7	6	1203	262	48	46	1	0
	2010	5265	4547	17	16	4467	672	63	58	3	3
	2011	6381	5540	26	25	5422	884	92	86	3	3
	2012	5673	4895	22	21	4764	867	109	106	3	3
	2013	5217	4557	20	19	4451	708	86	81	10	6
Germany	2000	2336	2053	12	12	1948	.	93	72	2	2
	2010	10895	9042	41	38	8442	.	559	516	16	15
	2011	13656	11462	60	58	10790	.	612	547	26	25
	2012	12148	10128	26	24	9536	.	567	505	37	34
	2013	10423	8876	26	25	8277	.	572	519	33	33
Developed Economies - North America 2/	2000	7430	5402	638	600	2356	334	2408	1141	8	6
	2010	40535	21473	1987	1858	13560	1470	5926	2716	68	43
	2011	50530	22784	2636	2530	12465	1585	7683	3591	27	3
	2012	43376	18105	2173	2057	9143	1397	6789	3436	113	37
	2013	40418	17059	2483	2381	8600	1206	5977	2991	117	69
United States	2000	4357	2588	382	368	940	197	1266	.	8	6
	2010	28621	13032	1106	991	8716	567	3210	.	68	43
	2011	34005	12077	1320	1217	6664	1036	4092	.	26	3
	2012	28254	8592	902	793	4336	881	3353	.	112	37
	2013	26137	8181	1162	1076	4034	809	2985	.	116	69
South-Eastern Europe	2000	589	252	7	7	235	45	9	1	87	87
	2010	3147	1015	0	0	1011	193	4	4	12	8
	2011	4127	1467	4	4	1390	164	73	3	5	4
	2012	3495	1036	1	1	944	132	90	3	9	9
	2013	3189	890	0	0	837	187	53	1	2	2
Commonwealth of Independent States	2000	2714	1223	29	29	1161	203	33	33	686	558
	2010	9806	3142	26	26	3015	168	100	98	1775	1628
	2011	16230	3719	64	64	3633	196	22	20	3813	3588
	2012	14798	3255	61	61	3172	192	22	22	3810	2935
	2013	13737	3090	204	204	2875	186	10	9	3704	3230
Russian Federation	2000	985	495	27	27	457	46	11	11	170	155
	2010	3228	1361	8	8	1279	45	74	72	155	152
	2011	5350	1441	16	16	1422	62	3	2	171	141
	2012	5253	1253	33	33	1217	68	3	3	810	292
	2013	4934	1105	117	117	980	50	8	7	856	559

For general note and footnotes see end of table

Exportations mondiales par provenance et destination (Tableau D)

En millions de dollars E.-U. f.o.b.

←—— Exportations vers

South-Eastern Europe Europe du Sud-est	Northern Africa Afrique septentrionale	Sub-Saharan Africa Afrique du Nord	Latin America and the Caribbean Amérique latine et Caraïbes	Eastern Asia Asie orientale	Southern Asia Asie méridionale	South-eastern Asia Asie du Sud-est	Western Asia Asie occidentale	Oceania Océanie	Others 4/ Autre 4/	Année	Exportations en provence de

Minerais métallifères et dechets de metaux (CTCI, Rev. 3, 28)

South-Eastern Europe	Northern Africa	Sub-Saharan Africa	Latin America and Caribbean	Eastern Asia	Southern Asia	South-eastern Asia	Western Asia	Oceania	Others 4/	Année	Exportations en provence de
463	344	589	1397	8568	1145	1400	1318	1	1116	2000	Monde 1/
2825	2230	3011	6080	129555	10492	6353	12353	33	119	2010	
4594	2342	3540	8552	174672	12724	7892	17643	37	201	2011	
3929	1943	3229	7224	157822	13623	7392	17062	20	191	2012	
4409	2220	3640	7816	169160	11447	7530	15910	30	172	2013	
51	100	271	14	2906	177	266	248	1	375	2000	Economies Développées -
2	22	470	151	48318	1616	1192	1446	21	61	2010	Asie-Pacifique 2/
3	0	660	250	68133	1999	1364	1782	22	115	2011	
101	6	390	168	61960	2130	1794	1683	15	127	2012	
85	5	488	117	72227	1749	1923	1814	8	120	2013	
...	0	1	0	723	8	42	1	...	...	2000	Japon
0	0	1	1	4322	7	97	2	...	...	2010	
0	0	0	1	4600	6	101	7	...	...	2011	
...	0	...	1	5512	11	191	4	0	...	2012	
...	0	0	1	4941	15	226	5	0	...	2013	
50	65	30	62	743	243	176	258	0	18	2000	Economies Développées -
635	891	38	148	6819	2141	575	3475	7	1	2010	Europe 2/
1748	983	70	197	8551	2892	856	4328	1	0	2011	
1465	934	145	275	7021	2644	699	4501	1	0	2012	
1751	803	65	190	6076	1756	580	3868	7	0	2013	
2	1	1	4	15	10	1	7	0	...	2000	France
2	51	4	8	411	104	10	124	0	1	2010	
2	86	1	10	441	128	15	154	0	...	2011	
4	67	2	11	350	109	20	213	0	0	2012	
0	50	2	17	352	69	16	143	0	0	2013	
1	0	8	5	160	40	20	33	0	13	2000	Allemagne
42	2	16	26	1150	249	64	282	6	...	2010	
14	13	12	21	1321	383	104	299	...	...	2011	
36	35	13	23	1148	372	70	286	0	...	2012	
17	29	9	23	948	241	30	218	0	...	2013	
4	1	18	351	1442	71	109	23	0	0	2000	Economies Développées -
104	481	48	1280	13476	699	1160	1741	5	...	2010	Amérique du Nord 2/
173	665	70	2364	18962	1039	1349	3085	13	...	2011	
152	347	52	2555	16720	1196	1084	3050	3	...	2012	
51	640	33	2973	15547	930	889	2174	3	...	2013	
0	1	18	345	1249	57	75	16	0	...	2000	Etats-Unis
6	229	44	1048	11071	600	956	1563	5	...	2010	
0	403	67	1999	14794	898	1194	2534	12	...	2011	
0	189	49	2141	12595	1004	966	2604	2	...	2012	
0	466	31	2696	11296	661	754	1934	3	...	2013	
75	0	0	2	52	4	3	112	0	1	2000	Europe du Sud-est
640	9	107	7	313	33	1	1010	...	...	2010	
824	0	211	7	369	27	2	1215	...	...	2011	
670	0	258	6	434	22	3	1057	...	0	2012	
633	0	180	9	535	13	19	908	...	...	2013	
56	38	0	5	340	31	8	328	0	0	2000	Communauté d'Etats
464	3	0	9	3475	57	13	868	...	...	2010	Indépendants
553	18	1	54	6755	97	18	1201	...	0	2011	
381	8	0	28	6247	75	29	964	0	...	2012	
496	0	0	11	5387	36	7	1005	...	0	2013	
1	7	0	2	211	3	4	92	...	...	2000	Fédération de Russie
22	3	0	0	1158	27	9	493	...	...	2010	
30	18	...	19	2884	40	11	736	...	...	2011	
86	8	...	6	2312	34	19	723	0	...	2012	
76	...	0	1	2159	15	4	717	...	0	2013	

Voir la fin du tableau pour la remarque générale et les notes.

World exports by provenance and destination (Table D)

In million U.S. dollars f.o.b.

Exports to → → Exports from	Year	World 1/ Monde 1/	Developed economies 2/ Economies développées 2/							Commonwealth of Independent States Communauté d'Etats Indépendants	
				Asia-Pacific Asie-Pacifique		Europe		North America Amérique du Nord			
			Total	Total	Japan Japon	Total	Germany Allemagne	Total	U.S.A. É.-U.	Total	Europe

Metalliferous ores and metal scrap (SITC, Rev. 3, 28) [cont.]

Exports from	Year	World	Total	Total	Japan	Total	Germany	Total	U.S.A.	Total	Europe
Northern Africa	2000	174	136	0	0	132	13	3	1	6	6
	2010	641	289	1	1	288	25	0	0	0	0
	2011	845	430	0	0	427	30	3	3	0	0
	2012	684	297	1	1	286	40	10	10	1	0
	2013	680	345	0	0	333	59	12	12	4	1
Sub-Saharan Africa	2000	2503	2007	223	217	1444	333	340	291	13	13
	2010	18724	6716	1194	1151	4413	987	1109	668	321	316
	2011	23743	7779	1693	1660	4795	798	1291	748	350	340
	2012	23585	7872	1476	1436	5162	738	1233	763	337	260
	2013	25813	7714	1236	1189	5212	563	1266	806	219	196
South Africa	2000	1383	1094	194	188	702	264	199	196	8	8
	2010	10908	3584	950	911	2313	771	321	306	91	91
	2011	15637	4604	1280	1253	2919	485	405	374	65	65
	2012	13793	3894	1100	1066	2342	268	452	431	82	72
	2013	14578	3869	1032	1001	2469	237	368	352	85	77
Latin America and the Caribbean	2000	10211	6699	1794	1760	3155	739	1751	1046	92	92
	2010	72757	29110	11103	10857	13810	4091	4196	2793	170	142
	2011	94266	36841	13148	12558	17934	4262	5758	3836	162	90
	2012	83457	31034	11596	11212	14660	3491	4778	2943	177	120
	2013	82057	29263	10671	10450	14644	3446	3947	2083	318	211
Brazil	2000	3536	2135	465	461	1396	435	273	221	12	12
	2010	33014	11815	3407	3294	7433	2316	975	300	67	52
	2011	47064	15990	4590	4408	10263	2026	1137	334	103	40
	2012	35917	11575	2989	2982	7555	1329	1030	315	39	19
	2013	37437	12438	3118	3118	8347	1819	972	314	52	30
Eastern Asia	2000	897	269	170	157	72	8	28	24	11	10
	2010	4881	1345	709	693	545	70	91	70	2	2
	2011	6170	1596	977	899	493	99	127	98	28	28
	2012	4974	850	522	492	244	26	85	65	8	8
	2013	4621	819	552	532	181	39	85	77	2	2
China	2000	114	61	32	30	23	2	7	6	2	1
	2010	836	374	160	155	181	18	34	30	2	2
	2011	657	277	136	80	111	14	30	24	28	27
	2012	474	151	52	49	45	11	54	45	8	8
	2013	402	99	46	44	24	5	29	29	2	1
Southern Asia	2000	556	217	157	153	37	1	22	21	30	27
	2010	10034	594	257	255	328	54	10	9	456	430
	2011	6957	937	231	226	695	28	11	11	7	4
	2012	4961	776	309	308	445	33	22	21	3	1
	2013	4021	455	346	344	102	19	8	7	12	0
South-Eastern Asia	2000	2772	1837	1277	1257	533	67	28	12	0	0
	2010	13269	6929	5373	5331	1518	276	38	38	48	48
	2011	13277	4447	3402	3367	890	208	155	155	61	61
	2012	11971	4469	3727	3684	619	129	123	122	78	73
	2013	14469	4724	4047	3990	499	115	177	177	78	78
Western Asia	2000	672	223	74	74	135	12	14	11	26	26
	2010	4862	744	49	42	678	77	17	11	26	25
	2011	6921	884	57	49	800	88	27	23	46	41
	2012	7705	865	53	52	786	71	26	14	40	38
	2013	8738	900	114	114	760	94	26	21	15	10
Oceania	2000	1459	462	301	269	157	54	3	3	3	...
	2010	1407	804	504	398	299	13	0	0	2	0
	2011	1397	832	521	416	312	13	0	.	2	...
	2012	1317	810	536	432	273	71	0	0	...	...
	2013	1604	913	653	542	260	93	0	0	...	...

For general note and footnotes see end of table

Exportations mondiales par provenance et destination (Tableau D)

En millions de dollars E.-U. f.o.b.

⟵ Exportations vers

South-Eastern Europe Europe du Sud-est	Northern Africa Afrique septentrio-nale	Sub-Saharan Africa Afrique du Nord	Latin America and the Caribbean Amérique latine et Caraïbes	Eastern Asia Asie orientale	Southern Asia Asie méridionale	South-eastern Asia Asie du Sud-est	Western Asia Asie occidentale	Oceania Océanie	Others 4/ Autre 4/	Année	Exportations en provence de ↓

Minerais métallifères et dechets de metaux (CTCI, Rev. 3, 28) [suite]

16	0	0	...	9	2	0	6	...	0	2000	Afrique du Nord
2	0	4	15	201	49	4	71	...	5	2010	
9	0	4	41	243	66	1	44	...	7	2011	
21	1	8	3	252	49	1	47	...	6	2012	
17	1	10	3	209	56	5	27	...	3	2013	
13	4	146	13	235	24	36	10	...	1	2000	Afrique subsaharienne
61	10	2017	72	8388	624	359	115	0	41	2010	
42	13	2105	121	11750	836	521	207	0	19	2011	
55	7	2090	106	10993	1389	539	197	0	0	2012	
40	26	2634	88	13148	1045	684	212	2	0	2013	
9	0	6	13	206	13	29	4	...	0	2000	Afrique du sud
10	9	83	66	6201	471	302	91	0	0	2010	
7	13	46	96	9648	566	419	173	...	0	2011	
0	0	47	87	8002	1074	443	164	0	0	2012	
0	13	94	73	9068	687	557	131	0	0	2013	
144	125	83	917	1416	262	238	233	...	0	2000	Amérique latine et Caraïbes
788	805	302	4371	31323	2291	1602	1995	...	0	2010	
1109	626	401	5458	42049	2665	1874	3080	0	0	2011	
984	607	273	4005	38671	3197	1730	2779	...	0	2012	
1171	669	214	4298	39409	2574	1801	2340	...	0	2013	
41	111	30	335	556	34	78	205	...	...	2000	Brésil
115	722	82	1520	15593	438	712	1950	...	...	2010	
227	550	110	2242	23113	584	1077	3069	...	...	2011	
231	534	104	1433	17649	512	1284	2557	...	...	2012	
232	650	94	1584	18852	290	1120	2125	...	...	2013	
0	0	10	1	576	7	24	1	0	0	2000	Asie orientale
0	0	17	16	3075	132	292	2	0	...	2010	
0	0	5	46	4007	147	337	3	0	...	2011	
1	0	9	10	3716	104	273	4	0	...	2012	
0	1	7	32	3332	118	277	34	0	...	2013	
0	0	5	0	36	2	7	0	0	...	2000	Chine
0	0	12	2	355	37	53	0	0	...	2010	
0	0	1	9	236	51	53	2	0	...	2011	
1	0	4	3	222	37	46	3	...	...	2012	
0	1	1	6	176	49	35	34	0	...	2013	
2	0	2	18	238	28	4	18	...	0	2000	Asie méridionale
7	1	6	1	7949	576	44	399	...	0	2010	
0	11	6	2	5515	272	54	151	...	1	2011	
0	10	2	2	3547	212	66	341	...	0	2012	
0	20	5	7	2591	179	96	647	0	7	2013	
28	0	19	16	457	151	262	1	0	0	2000	Asie Sud-est
...	0	1	2	4343	1188	751	7	0	...	2010	
3	4	1	1	6294	1335	1067	63	1	0	2011	
4	0	0	4	5700	839	862	14	0	0	2012	
0	0	1	8	7544	1146	923	35	10	0	2013	
24	10	4	0	92	146	59	80	...	8	2000	Asie occidentale
122	5	2	9	1567	1017	135	1224	0	11	2010	
128	21	7	12	1765	1283	233	2483	0	59	2011	
97	21	3	16	2329	1598	253	2425	0	57	2012	
164	55	4	17	2834	1625	238	2844	0	41	2013	
1	...	5	...	61	...	215	...	0	713	2000	Océanie
...	...	...	...	309	70	224	...	0	0	2010	
...	...	0	...	279	67	217	...	0	...	2011	
...	...	0	47	233	167	60	...	0	...	2012	
...	...	0	62	321	220	87	...	0	...	2013	

Voir la fin du tableau pour la remarque générale et les notes.

World exports by provenance and destination (Table D)

In million U.S. dollars f.o.b.

Exports from	Year	World 1/ Monde 1/	Developed economies 2/ Economies développées 2/	Asia-Pacific Asie-Pacifique		Europe		North America Amérique du Nord		Commonwealth of Independent States Communauté d'Etats Indépendants	
			Total	Total	Japan Japon	Total	Germany Allemagne	Total	U.S.A. É.-U.	Total	Europe

Animal and vegetable oils, fats and waxes (SITC, Rev. 3, 4)

Exports from	Year	World 1/	Total	Total	Japan	Total	Germany	Total	U.S.A.	Total	Europe
World 1/	2000	19172	9127	727	528	6718	801	1682	1403	539	455
	2010	80070	31500	1961	1356	24181	3468	5358	4425	2684	2226
	2011	109384	43362	2544	1812	33409	4682	7410	6464	3120	2520
	2012	106420	41799	2389	1687	32468	4319	6942	5929	3009	2334
	2013	98798	41822	2136	1468	32842	4532	6844	5911	2879	2227
Developed Economies - Asia-Pacific 2/	2000	326	115	59	48	26	3	30	29	0	0
	2010	736	155	61	24	43	6	50	45	0	0
	2011	987	179	80	34	44	9	55	51	0	0
	2012	889	177	76	33	41	10	60	54	0	0
	2013	927	212	70	17	63	14	80	73	0	0
Japan	2000	81	37	1	.	11	2	25	24	0	0
	2010	137	64	1	.	22	5	40	36	0	0
	2011	155	68	1	.	24	7	43	39	0	0
	2012	156	72	2	.	25	8	45	42	0	0
	2013	167	81	4	.	27	12	50	45	0	0
Developed Economies - Europe 2/	2000	6475	5137	188	105	4456	624	493	438	268	257
	2010	18741	16092	400	228	14653	2666	1039	908	594	570
	2011	25844	22147	405	242	20614	3625	1128	991	849	813
	2012	25736	21531	429	264	19943	3454	1159	1028	874	828
	2013	26874	22402	478	304	20715	3647	1209	1071	773	736
France	2000	436	332	3	3	324	34	6	5	10	10
	2010	1421	1317	8	7	1294	149	15	13	27	26
	2011	2485	2327	14	13	2294	329	19	15	40	40
	2012	1912	1740	13	10	1702	204	25	22	43	43
	2013	1676	1489	12	10	1443	140	34	30	44	43
Germany	2000	1012	827	8	3	811	.	8	8	58	57
	2010	2443	2005	24	16	1959	.	22	20	189	187
	2011	3600	2935	23	17	2878	.	34	32	234	229
	2012	3822	3029	17	13	2970	.	42	40	238	233
	2013	3829	3067	17	13	3018	.	32	31	160	155
Developed Economies - North America 2/	2000	1871	754	79	74	159	10	515	314	26	19
	2010	6981	2446	157	139	376	31	1913	1214	6	5
	2011	8505	3806	193	171	711	105	2903	2216	14	9
	2012	8365	3566	187	166	542	89	2837	2115	19	15
	2013	6846	3069	151	135	438	86	2480	1860	5	5
United States	2000	1439	404	59	55	143	9	202	.	26	18
	2010	4459	1096	74	62	324	16	698	.	2	1
	2011	4760	1207	67	54	453	43	686	.	5	1
	2012	4443	1285	75	61	487	81	722	.	4	1
	2013	3572	1099	66	54	413	82	620	.	1	1
South-Eastern Europe	2000	50	18	...	...	17	2	1	0	5	5
	2010	518	345	0	...	345	16	0	0	0	0
	2011	772	533	0	...	532	40	0	0	1	1
	2012	668	438	0	0	438	14	0	0	1	1
	2013	809	543	0	...	543	23	1	1	1	1
Commonwealth of Independent States	2000	337	102	0	0	98	3	3	3	126	80
	2010	3449	955	0	0	953	14	1	1	822	491
	2011	4563	1112	0	0	1110	23	2	1	869	419
	2012	6640	1593	0	0	1591	38	3	2	781	255
	2013	5900	1349	2	1	1340	18	6	6	706	191
Russian Federation	2000	79	3	0	0	3	0	0	0	29	1
	2010	589	264	0	0	264	8	0	0	122	4
	2011	958	378	0	0	377	10	1	1	194	7
	2012	2084	599	0	0	599	26	0	0	432	76
	2013	2011	665	1	0	663	11	1	1	428	53

For general note and footnotes see end of table

Exportations mondiales par provenance et destination (Tableau D)

En millions de dollars E.-U. f.o.b.

← Exportations vers

South-Eastern Europe Europe du Sud-est	Northern Africa Afrique septentrio-nale	Sub-Saharan Africa Afrique du Nord	Latin America and the Caribbean Amérique latine et Caraïbes	Eastern Asia Asie orientale	Southern Asia Asie méridionale	South-eastern Asia Asie du Sud-est	Western Asia Asie occidentale	Oceania Océanie	Others 4/ Autre 4/	Année	Exportations en provence de ↓
\multicolumn{12}{c}{Hulies et graisses d'origine animale ou vegetale (CTCI, Rev. 3, 4)}

South-Eastern Europe Europe du Sud-est	Northern Africa Afrique septentrio-nale	Sub-Saharan Africa Afrique du Nord	Latin America and the Caribbean Amérique latine et Caraïbes	Eastern Asia Asie orientale	Southern Asia Asie méridionale	South-eastern Asia Asie du Sud-est	Western Asia Asie occidentale	Oceania Océanie	Others 4/ Autre 4/	Année	Exportations en provence de
118	758	746	1496	1622	2773	873	1046	20	54	2000	Monde 1/
607	3357	4045	5237	10997	12691	5696	3073	47	136	2010	
761	5508	6051	7118	13607	16007	8371	5245	66	166	2011	
743	4319	5624	6760	14449	16623	7463	5354	90	188	2012	
654	3840	5267	6309	12200	14995	5549	5055	69	157	2013	
...	0	14	0	126	36	32	0	2	0	2000	Economies Développées -
0	0	20	4	425	59	59	5	7	0	2010	Asie-Pacifique 2/
0	0	11	11	495	49	228	5	9	0	2011	
0	0	18	9	403	35	220	16	10	...	2012	
0	0	2	4	239	19	430	13	8	0	2013	
...	0	0	0	27	1	16	0	0	...	2000	Japon
0	...	...	1	57	1	15	0	0	...	2010	
0	...	...	1	64	1	20	0	0	...	2011	
0	...	0	1	62	1	18	1	0	...	2012	
0	0	0	2	60	1	21	1	0	...	2013	
80	279	165	147	92	55	27	189	6	31	2000	Economies Développées -
359	145	375	412	261	62	102	247	11	83	2010	Europe 2/
429	266	593	500	390	73	130	347	15	105	2011	
401	724	605	526	418	98	144	331	12	71	2012	
346	613	493	589	845	150	218	351	15	79	2013	
3	34	12	2	2	6	2	28	5	...	2000	France
2	8	11	7	19	2	6	16	6	0	2010	
3	18	19	7	22	4	13	23	8	...	2011	
3	20	29	11	15	3	16	24	7	...	2012	
4	16	12	14	39	4	25	21	8	0	2013	
13	26	10	5	33	19	4	16	0	1	2000	Allemagne
31	64	85	15	14	7	12	19	...	0	2010	
42	136	159	18	22	6	16	30	0	1	2011	
42	259	154	19	21	11	19	29	...	1	2012	
41	216	40	18	178	7	60	42	0	1	2013	
9	41	78	534	200	42	25	161	0	0	2000	Economies Développées -
1	391	183	1630	1632	221	98	372	1	0	2010	Amérique du Nord 2/
2	658	176	2037	1176	105	93	436	0	0	2011	
1	375	146	1794	1811	146	119	387	0	0	2012	
2	171	146	1558	1409	59	103	322	1	...	2013	
9	40	77	526	139	38	20	161	0	...	2000	Etats-Unis
1	391	168	1579	574	219	76	354	1	...	2010	
2	646	167	1866	284	104	48	431	0	...	2011	
1	375	131	1669	416	126	54	381	0	...	2012	
2	171	141	1423	291	56	70	316	1	...	2013	
16	1	0	0	0	0	0	10	...	0	2000	Europe du Sud-est
165	0	...	...	0	0	0	7	...	0	2010	
230	0	...	...	0	...	...	7	...	1	2011	
219	0	0	0	0	...	0	6	...	3	2012	
204	10	17	...	1	...	0	33	...	2	2013	
5	69	...	3	1	10	0	21	...	0	2000	Communauté d'Etats
56	465	56	1	45	663	6	381	1	0	2010	Indépendants
66	474	119	13	109	975	8	815	1	2	2011	
56	1022	71	18	91	1605	19	1383	0	0	2012	
50	753	38	26	469	1298	66	1144	0	0	2013	
2	36	...	0	1	0	0	8	...	...	2000	Fédération de Russie
5	52	16	1	13	40	...	76	1	...	2010	
6	145	13	4	14	15	0	185	1	2	2011	
5	304	27	...	18	65	0	632	0	0	2012	
23	310	3	0	26	59	0	495	0	0	2013	

Voir la fin du tableau pour la remarque générale et les notes.

World exports by provenance and destination (Table D)

In million U.S. dollars f.o.b.

| Exports from | Year | World 1/ Monde 1/ | Developed economies 2/ Economies développées 2/ | | | | | | | Commonwealth of Independent States Communauté d'Etats Indépendants | |
| | | | | Asia-Pacific Asie-Pacifique | | Europe | | North America Amérique du Nord | | | |
			Total	Total	Japan Japon	Total	Germany Allemagne	Total	U.S.A. É.-U.	Total	Europe

Animal and vegetable oils, fats and waxes (SITC, Rev. 3, 4) [cont.]

Exports from	Year	World 1/ Monde 1/	Total	Total	Japan Japon	Total	Germany Allemagne	Total	U.S.A. É.-U.	Total	Europe
Northern Africa	2000	245	188	0	0	178	0	10	10	...	...
	2010	725	418	1	0	304	3	113	107	3	3
	2011	1127	435	0	0	287	4	147	140	4	4
	2012	1040	481	1	1	351	4	128	123	5	4
	2013	992	575	1	1	448	4	126	116	3	3
Sub-Saharan Africa	2000	226	105	2	2	101	6	2	2	0	0
	2010	818	155	10	10	137	49	8	7	0	0
	2011	1208	188	7	7	176	42	5	4	0	0
	2012	1266	230	7	6	219	20	4	4	0	0
	2013	1147	289	6	5	277	12	6	5	0	0
South Africa	2000	38	5	0	...	5	0	1	0	...	...
	2010	225	8	1	1	5	1	2	2	0	0
	2011	309	11	2	2	9	1	0	0	0	0
	2012	332	14	2	2	12	2	0	0	0	0
	2013	247	16	0	0	15	2	1	1	0	0
Latin America and the Caribbean	2000	2612	341	44	32	206	25	90	84	40	40
	2010	8707	1272	134	65	869	68	268	226	9	3
	2011	12369	2132	157	86	1594	160	381	329	12	2
	2012	11622	1902	207	112	1280	104	415	333	8	6
	2013	10125	1611	161	79	1045	90	405	332	6	6
Brazil	2000	476	83	24	20	41	5	18	18	1	1
	2010	1630	241	45	35	149	21	47	46	0	0
	2011	2550	477	50	39	367	29	60	60	0	0
	2012	2520	357	54	39	240	20	63	62	0	0
	2013	1788	307	46	33	210	27	51	51	0	0
Eastern Asia	2000	304	54	21	17	19	4	14	12	2	2
	2010	592	201	56	45	56	17	89	77	10	8
	2011	818	290	79	62	91	22	120	100	15	12
	2012	856	354	96	73	123	19	135	114	12	9
	2013	878	391	110	87	133	35	148	128	9	7
China	2000	116	33	12	10	15	3	7	6	0	0
	2010	391	157	36	28	52	16	69	60	5	3
	2011	570	229	45	33	84	21	100	83	8	6
	2012	584	280	59	43	110	17	111	93	8	6
	2013	630	320	78	60	116	33	126	109	6	4
Southern Asia	2000	284	164	21	20	107	5	36	36	25	12
	2010	978	390	43	39	274	9	72	71	34	6
	2011	1491	611	74	68	419	28	117	116	37	12
	2012	1355	449	53	48	292	20	103	101	26	8
	2013	1365	519	44	37	339	19	136	131	23	7
South-Eastern Asia	2000	6010	1948	307	229	1173	103	468	459	38	36
	2010	35921	8305	1065	788	5469	479	1772	1742	1193	1137
	2011	48754	10918	1515	1126	6877	520	2526	2495	1305	1245
	2012	45052	10041	1300	971	6684	486	2057	2021	1269	1205
	2013	39500	9406	1076	783	6206	507	2124	2075	1334	1266
Western Asia	2000	272	41	1	0	21	2	18	16	9	3
	2010	1017	124	23	18	69	6	32	26	11	3
	2011	2061	375	19	16	329	7	26	20	13	2
	2012	2261	454	20	13	393	11	41	34	13	2
	2013	2605	729	30	19	576	11	123	113	19	5
Oceania	2000	160	160	3	...	157	14	0	0	...	...
	2010	888	642	10	0	632	102	1	1	...	...
	2011	883	636	13	0	623	98	0	0	...	...
	2012	670	582	11	0	571	50	0	0	...	...
	2013	830	729	9	0	720	66	0	0	...	...

For general note and footnotes see end of table

Exportations mondiales par provenance et destination (Tableau D)

En millions de dollars E.-U. f.o.b.

← Exportations vers

South-Eastern Europe Europe du Sud-est	Northern Africa Afrique septentrio-nale	Sub-Saharan Africa Afrique du Nord	Latin America and the Caribbean Amérique latine et Caraïbes	Eastern Asia Asie orientale	Southern Asia Asie méridionale	South-eastern Asia Asie du Sud-est	Western Asia Asie occidentale	Oceania Océanie	Others 4/ Autre 4/	Année	Exportations en provence de ↓
	Hulies et graisses d'origine animale ou vegetale (CTCI, Rev. 3, 4) [suite]

South-Eastern Europe Europe du Sud-est	Northern Africa Afrique septentrio-nale	Sub-Saharan Africa Afrique du Nord	Latin America and the Caribbean Amérique latine et Caraïbes	Eastern Asia Asie orientale	Southern Asia Asie méridionale	South-eastern Asia Asie du Sud-est	Western Asia Asie occidentale	Oceania Océanie	Others 4/ Autre 4/	Année	Exportations en provence de
...	15	1	3	0	0	...	30	...	7	2000	Afrique du Nord
1	140	47	1	2	3	0	97	...	12	2010	
4	332	70	0	3	0	1	250	0	28	2011	
7	205	59	1	5	2	1	209	0	65	2012	
3	94	68	2	8	1	2	223	...	13	2013	
0	0	112	0	5	0	2	1	0	0	2000	Afrique subsaharienne
...	1	595	0	11	3	5	41	0	7	2010	
0	2	929	4	4	4	19	58	0	0	2011	
20	7	945	1	23	3	28	5	0	4	2012	
19	5	774	1	16	3	33	5	0	4	2013	
0	0	26	0	5	0	1	0	...	0	2000	Afrique du sud
...	0	210	0	4	0	1	0	0	0	2010	
...	...	294	0	2	1	0	2	0	0	2011	
...	0	310	1	3	1	1	1	0	2	2012	
...	...	227	0	1	0	2	0	0	1	2013	
0	175	89	733	114	995	78	43	1	4	2000	Amérique latine et Caraïbes
0	635	333	2393	1406	2188	266	191	1	12	2010	
0	1555	399	3510	1739	2343	349	322	0	7	2011	
3	592	387	3649	2287	2488	247	52	1	5	2012	
0	887	218	3319	1520	2325	162	38	1	38	2013	
...	48	7	47	47	213	24	5	1	...	2000	Brésil
...	104	39	185	815	190	16	39	0	...	2010	
0	389	67	257	819	403	85	53	...	...	2011	
0	186	37	240	1009	614	49	28	0	...	2012	
0	262	18	206	585	391	16	2	0	...	2013	
0	0	0	1	215	2	28	1	0	0	2000	Asie orientale
1	2	5	8	242	12	97	13	0	...	2010	
1	16	13	22	252	16	129	63	1	...	2011	
1	3	11	15	296	16	135	13	0	...	2012	
2	3	8	29	282	13	128	12	1	...	2013	
0	0	0	1	74	1	7	0	0	...	2000	Chine
1	1	4	8	138	9	59	10	0	...	2010	
1	16	10	21	133	11	81	61	0	...	2011	
1	2	8	13	163	10	87	12	0	...	2012	
2	2	7	27	171	9	76	10	0	...	2013	
0	1	3	1	29	34	19	7	0	0	2000	Asie méridionale
1	2	8	17	275	144	50	54	0	2	2010	
2	5	12	21	356	262	106	79	0	0	2011	
1	3	11	34	424	275	69	63	0	0	2012	
1	5	12	33	406	210	80	76	0	0	2013	
5	175	270	68	839	1569	663	421	10	4	2000	Asie Sud-est
21	1544	2369	661	6663	9237	4853	1040	26	11	2010	
24	2079	3651	897	9054	12048	7151	1568	39	19	2011	
28	1303	3295	648	8626	11839	6437	1486	64	17	2012	
25	1223	3398	649	6973	10790	4276	1364	43	20	2013	
1	2	13	5	1	30	1	161	0	8	2000	Asie occidentale
3	34	53	7	35	98	18	625	0	9	2010	
4	118	77	6	24	131	17	1295	0	3	2011	
4	82	76	5	61	117	23	1403	1	22	2012	
4	75	96	21	28	125	33	1474	0	2	2013	
0	...	...	...	...	0	0	...	0	0	2000	Océanie
...	0	...	102	1	0	141	0	1	...	2010	
...	1	0	98	6	0	141	0	1	...	2011	
...	3	0	60	3	0	21	...	1	...	2012	
...	2	0	79	2	0	17	0	0	...	2013	

Voir la fin du tableau pour la remarque générale et les notes.

World exports by provenance and destination (Table D)

In million U.S. dollars f.o.b.

Exports from	Year	World 1/ Monde 1/	Developed economies 2/ Economies développées 2/ Total	Asia-Pacific Asie-Pacifique Total	Japan Japon	Europe Total	Germany Allemagne	North America Amérique du Nord Total	U.S.A. É.-U.	Commonwealth of Independent States Communauté d'Etats Indépendants Total	Europe
Mineral fuels and related materials (SITC, Rev. 3, 3)											
World 1/	2000	656575	442314	71801	66628	222528	29297	147985	137275	11138	9697
	2010	2265497	1201063	133021	110690	711678	63748	356364	278046	37690	33417
	2011	3155832	1628706	189639	155953	976255	90488	462812	348303	57124	52107
	2012	3321556	1687604	217670	181997	1027433	94730	442501	322456	69087	58864
	2013	3269373	1659094	214032	178176	1029843	117262	415219	283768	61491	50181
Developed Economies - Asia-Pacific 2/	2000	15224	7843	5798	5119	901	85	1144	1143	7	7
	2010	74265	30483	25202	22064	4180	237	1102	1030	55	53
	2011	94060	40094	33937	29532	5132	325	1025	987	69	68
	2012	88120	38159	34042	30389	3255	158	862	853	68	65
	2013	83321	36401	32428	27684	3174	108	799	750	70	65
Japan	2000	1520	518	83	.	40	4	395	394	7	7
	2010	13048	2884	1467	.	568	3	849	778	54	53
	2011	16293	3330	2267	.	332	5	731	692	69	68
	2012	13457	2436	1709	.	113	9	614	606	68	65
	2013	16682	4809	3385	.	660	10	764	715	67	64
Developed Economies - Europe 2/	2000	131104	119054	136	102	101978	20559	16940	13150	384	367
	2010	372417	315103	519	469	284608	45008	29976	25227	2313	2024
	2011	507834	425777	758	683	385663	61579	39356	32684	3552	3024
	2012	531890	432557	1212	1067	396534	65615	34811	31578	4195	3685
	2013	556486	453807	1120	1003	420058	84501	32629	28373	5084	4512
France	2000	8183	7258	28	13	6660	1009	570	561	16	15
	2010	18717	14723	42	39	13341	1826	1340	1227	10	10
	2011	26539	20190	26	22	18545	2288	1619	1405	17	15
	2012	24946	18734	77	73	16944	1724	1712	1582	86	84
	2013	22207	17631	107	71	16074	1406	1449	1392	30	26
Germany	2000	7757	5384	13	9	4961	.	410	406	35	33
	2010	23907	22556	37	24	22295	.	225	213	320	279
	2011	33312	31630	52	34	31254	.	323	281	475	408
	2012	38362	36369	45	25	36100	.	224	174	573	503
	2013	41244	39072	45	23	38849	.	177	141	915	837
Developed Economies - North America 2/	2000	49685	41512	1485	1328	2019	97	38009	35232	8	8
	2010	172781	118229	3964	3677	16628	1188	97637	85146	492	446
	2011	245253	160154	5274	4787	31512	1594	123367	105397	1113	1045
	2012	253238	161684	4985	4533	32426	1175	124273	105879	601	568
	2013	267992	172985	4555	4121	31795	946	136636	111940	507	495
United States	2000	13340	5570	1001	845	1793	80	2776	.	8	7
	2010	80728	29744	2097	1815	15156	931	12491	.	483	439
	2011	129233	49609	2988	2517	28653	1347	17968	.	1088	1021
	2012	137340	50888	3074	2627	29420	1054	18393	.	569	537
	2013	148278	57271	3031	2602	29548	862	24692	.	457	446
South-Eastern Europe	2000	1442	243	...	...	231	6	12	12	225	152
	2010	7164	2501	0	0	2430	120	71	71	1042	716
	2011	9305	3328	0	0	3256	213	72	71	1595	1098
	2012	9230	3141	0	0	3021	145	121	121	1598	1018
	2013	10104	3297	0	0	3264	242	33	33	2031	1482
Commonwealth of Independent States	2000	62917	41875	302	302	40039	3736	1534	215	10329	9053
	2010	337275	238777	11814	11708	215778	12202	11185	8119	32881	29549
	2011	461767	319358	15078	15078	289216	19675	15064	12245	49561	46016
	2012	480060	318928	16982	16938	291315	20952	10631	7720	61396	52743
	2013	478366	327790	21717	21388	298417	19995	7656	5162	52609	42943
Russian Federation	2000	52166	36681	302	302	36076	3554	303	189	6979	6287
	2010	260668	190116	11783	11708	171758	11096	6575	5989	25310	23797
	2011	346530	246261	15078	15078	221443	17461	9740	9395	33869	32190
	2012	368853	249616	16950	16938	226596	18304	6070	6052	49421	42772
	2013	372036	261607	21585	21257	235831	17369	4191	4135	42693	34830

For general note and footnotes see end of table

Exportations mondiales par provenance et destination (Tableau D)

En millions de dollars E.-U. f.o.b.

← Exportations vers

South-Eastern Europe Europe du Sud-est	Northern Africa Afrique septentrionale	Sub-Saharan Africa Afrique du Nord	Latin America and the Caribbean Amérique latine et Caraïbes	Eastern Asia Asie orientale	Southern Asia Asie méridionale	South-eastern Asia Asie du Sud-est	Western Asia Asie occidentale	Oceania Océanie	Others 4/ Autre 4/	Année	Exportations en provenance de ↓

Combustibles minéraux et produits assimiles (CTCI, Rev. 3, 3)

South-Eastern Europe Europe du Sud-est	Northern Africa Afrique septentrionale	Sub-Saharan Africa Afrique du Nord	Latin America and the Caribbean Amérique latine et Caraïbes	Eastern Asia Asie orientale	Southern Asia Asie méridionale	South-eastern Asia Asie du Sud-est	Western Asia Asie occidentale	Oceania Océanie	Others 4/ Autre 4/	Année	Exportations en provenance de
3229	7442	5750	33958	88961	11884	25845	12504	1115	12436	2000	Monde 1/
16003	24327	41759	120881	497549	76104	138340	55186	3360	53235	2010	
21052	36652	54259	194054	692643	117696	186863	67800	6523	92459	2011	
22750	43958	63688	191813	770923	125527	205168	78216	6189	56633	2012	
17109	43261	64552	167366	780282	119694	210435	77760	4965	63366	2013	
0	8	65	320	3610	499	1633	112	421	706	2000	Economies Développées -
0	11	352	2427	23613	7196	8697	289	542	601	2010	Asie-Pacifique 2/
0	1	456	2398	29282	8389	11774	362	712	524	2011	
0	1	265	1917	28120	6408	10064	326	842	1950	2012	
1	1	245	872	28438	5072	9282	160	706	2073	2013	
...	0	2	42	701	27	220	4	0	...	2000	Japon
0	1	14	1068	4577	186	4232	32	0	...	2010	
0	1	84	668	6443	213	5369	79	38	...	2011	
0	1	23	622	6047	429	3766	28	37	...	2012	
0	1	84	103	7351	231	3961	62	13	...	2013	
784	1350	1171	767	506	436	286	1985	6	4375	2000	Economies Développées -
3428	7894	11705	6740	1714	441	2101	8712	88	12178	2010	Europe 2/
5221	7851	17323	7743	3435	1072	3095	15182	75	17507	2011	
6143	14140	17024	9599	9700	1037	4827	17110	77	15482	2012	
5679	13753	17629	10021	7862	533	4642	16333	18	21126	2013	
8	212	257	130	23	21	19	204	3	34	2000	France
21	716	1329	260	49	93	157	875	4	478	2010	
48	829	2030	462	113	193	127	1841	4	684	2011	
29	1573	1464	366	86	293	66	1741	4	505	2012	
32	744	1399	265	153	27	121	1629	5	173	2013	
22	10	35	117	35	12	13	38	0	2056	2000	Allemagne
73	58	203	109	179	44	94	217	0	54	2010	
102	31	290	124	198	63	72	277	0	50	2011	
80	33	212	252	225	59	75	351	60	73	2012	
92	45	201	124	264	51	77	290	0	113	2013	
73	105	134	6228	821	95	419	287	2	0	2000	Economies Développées -
159	1135	1425	38875	5495	1125	4057	1789	2	0	2010	Amérique du Nord 2/
268	1759	1844	60587	8290	1992	5121	4123	2	0	2011	
315	1466	1980	69194	8076	1904	5030	2923	63	1	2012	
178	2134	3464	69917	8367	1492	5200	3720	28	...	2013	
61	96	125	6142	582	85	418	251	2	...	2000	Etats-Unis
159	1133	1411	38100	3025	1101	3965	1606	2	...	2010	
268	1707	1838	59152	4726	1883	5114	3848	2	...	2011	
273	1389	1977	68014	4642	1731	5025	2769	63	...	2012	
155	2132	3461	69213	5520	1270	5133	3638	28	...	2013	
661	13	65	17	0	1	12	186	...	19	2000	Europe du Sud-est
2213	45	165	12	3	69	234	840	5	35	2010	
2494	188	139	7	4	72	36	1399	2	39	2011	
2019	324	325	5	1	60	71	1657	1	27	2012	
1864	326	343	2	2	40	431	1722	1	45	2013	
1626	28	22	4633	697	251	464	2989	1	2	2000	Communauté d'Etats
9947	1130	74	1897	27882	3626	6022	15012	0	27	2010	Indépendants
12712	2137	320	2624	48545	3853	6682	15612	0	362	2011	
14054	2483	185	1426	53205	3583	6704	17533	80	483	2012	
9167	2282	211	2290	56378	2455	9596	15367	0	222	2013	
1407	24	15	3416	590	15	428	2611	0	0	2000	Fédération de Russie
7905	756	24	1188	20193	886	3753	10515	0	21	2010	
9124	1834	251	2048	36271	1114	4950	10684	0	124	2011	
9780	1997	175	831	40254	837	3943	11771	80	149	2012	
6371	1669	189	1748	41728	621	4665	10726	...	19	2013	

Voir la fin du tableau pour la remarque générale et les notes.

World exports by provenance and destination (Table D)

In million U.S. dollars f.o.b.

Exports from	Year	World 1/ Monde 1/	Developed economies 2/ Économies développées 2/ Total	Asia-Pacific Asie-Pacifique Total	Japan Japon	Europe Total	Germany Allemagne	North America Amérique du Nord Total	U.S.A. É.-U.	Commonwealth of Independent States Communauté d'États Indépendants Total	Europe

Mineral fuels and related materials (SITC, Rev. 3, 3) [cont.]

Exports from	Year	World 1/ Monde 1/	Total	Total	Japan Japon	Total	Germany Allemagne	Total	U.S.A. É.-U.	Total	Europe
Northern Africa	2000	34262	28468	95	95	24088	2706	4285	3508	10	0
	2010	102163	81369	318	291	62648	1362	18402	15207	52	0
	2011	102592	80021	547	547	58995	1095	20479	15912	9	1
	2012	141277	112958	1906	1873	92629	1772	18423	12979	127	1
	2013	119022	93963	2807	1981	79917	6398	11239	8114	115	1
Sub-Saharan Africa	2000	45316	27722	229	193	9449	279	18044	17389	3	3
	2010	170944	86912	1938	1118	30082	1228	54892	50096	3	3
	2011	243980	120637	7163	1916	53463	2759	60010	53980	1	1
	2012	243713	118633	9925	5592	65062	2449	43647	38549	1	1
	2013	199802	93624	9415	5468	59336	2692	24872	21362	1	1
South Africa	2000	2664	1005	72	36	902	32	31	29	0	0
	2010	8842	1471	46	36	1364	123	61	60	2	2
	2011	11333	1815	109	81	1633	168	73	73	0	0
	2012	11602	1466	72	58	1270	59	124	124	1	1
	2013	10222	1493	63	54	1305	53	126	123	0	0
Latin America and the Caribbean	2000	62260	43938	434	371	3985	406	39519	38681	2	1
	2010	179704	92572	416	406	13583	336	78573	66414	9	0
	2011	249439	133217	507	507	22621	123	110089	90800	37	8
	2012	256046	129405	1155	1155	24293	185	103957	82761	16	5
	2013	236357	126078	1160	1150	24362	612	100556	69067	9	9
Brazil	2000	908	600	0	0	66	6	533	529	...	...
	2010	19843	7330	72	72	2788	247	4470	4136	...	...
	2011	26791	10437	0	0	3918	31	6518	5866	...	...
	2012	26469	11098	31	31	4601	66	6466	5736	0	0
	2013	17822	7720	11	1	3425	111	4284	3704	0	0
Eastern Asia	2000	19504	7958	5952	5704	452	46	1553	1477	97	78
	2010	75645	17405	7748	5784	4588	276	5069	4852	441	356
	2011	105879	24310	14516	11932	5592	592	4202	4002	654	539
	2012	113194	25724	15885	11514	5122	551	4716	4517	568	460
	2013	113921	26580	16067	10621	5454	426	5059	4853	615	433
China	2000	7855	3226	2080	1973	436	46	711	689	70	51
	2010	26673	4607	2240	2032	1317	273	1050	868	294	222
	2011	32274	6642	3438	3087	1988	497	1216	1067	447	352
	2012	31013	6185	2823	2472	1915	549	1447	1308	382	295
	2013	33786	5479	2105	1829	1879	423	1496	1307	443	286
Southern Asia	2000	26842	16072	5330	5318	10595	184	147	147	11	3
	2010	98874	26752	2468	2358	23644	6	640	639	70	8
	2011	150234	38783	2596	2446	34637	368	1550	1474	104	11
	2012	122369	30429	3423	3164	25783	10	1224	1222	75	11
	2013	128257	32445	3595	3504	25040	39	3810	3747	67	12
South-Eastern Asia	2000	45412	18800	16753	13540	405	19	1643	1637	2	2
	2010	165632	46862	41508	26438	2777	35	2578	2432	37	35
	2011	231234	67149	60289	40805	4109	48	2751	2659	34	29
	2012	225751	66891	61133	40562	3384	63	2374	2146	49	44
	2013	217325	59265	53719	35160	2296	39	3250	3069	67	64
Western Asia	2000	161909	88235	34693	34556	28386	1172	25155	24686	58	22
	2010	508185	144096	37125	36377	50731	1748	56240	18814	298	227
	2011	753726	215876	48972	47719	82058	2117	84846	28093	393	267
	2012	856188	249050	66977	65167	84611	1656	97462	34132	392	262
	2013	857907	232801	67393	66039	76729	1266	88680	27297	316	165
Oceania	2000	699	595	595	0	0	...	0	0	...	...
	2010	447	3	1	0	1	...	0	0	...	...
	2011	530	1	1	...	0	0	0	0	0	0
	2012	481	44	44	42	0	0	0	0	...	...
	2013	512	57	57	55	0	0	0	0	...	...

For general note and footnotes see end of table

Exportations mondiales par provenance et destination (Tableau D)

En millions de dollars E.-U. f.o.b.

⟵ Exportations vers

South-Eastern Europe Europe du Sud-est	Northern Africa Afrique septentrio-nale	Sub-Saharan Africa Afrique du Nord	Latin America and the Caribbean Amérique latine et Caraïbes	Eastern Asia Asie orientale	Southern Asia Asie méridionale	South-eastern Asia Asie du Sud-est	Western Asia Asie occidentale	Oceania Océanie	Others 4/ Autre 4/	Année	Exportations en provence de ↓

Combustibles minéraux et produits assimiles (CTCI, Rev. 3, 3) [suite]

35	472	59	1830	167	173	173	2219	...	656	2000	Afrique du Nord
79	1916	138	3109	6993	3005	736	3798	0	968	2010	
6	2315	224	4642	5119	4432	842	3546	40	1395	2011	
5	3254	425	4778	9420	3603	1123	4030	...	1554	2012	
95	4160	297	3492	6629	3620	1361	3960	0	1330	2013	
9	37	3589	1793	6329	4023	787	293	28	702	2000	Afrique subsaharienne
12	799	16354	9142	37315	15296	3098	1245	24	744	2010	
21	4418	20501	21403	49727	20519	2911	1365	1417	1060	2011	
31	949	23043	15950	51588	25893	4183	1547	460	1434	2012	
34	48	20068	11858	45267	21678	4804	1471	228	720	2013	
2	35	580	45	129	83	42	168	1	573	2000	Afrique du sud
12	74	2629	383	964	1945	407	616	4	334	2010	
20	9	3165	373	2144	1934	528	812	2	533	2011	
23	37	3529	256	1674	2032	846	1004	17	717	2012	
27	23	3443	300	1482	1808	503	718	2	422	2013	
3	1	92	15543	438	209	176	105	0	1751	2000	Amérique latine et Caraïbes
18	289	771	45266	17226	2226	5770	613	6	14937	2010	
116	43	903	75707	26654	3850	6994	1453	10	453	2011	
0	83	1036	70030	36962	7603	8835	1512	6	559	2012	
0	21	147	53148	41340	7755	5860	1056	0	943	2013	
...	...	25	238	36	1	8	0	...	...	2000	Brésil
...	0	55	6590	4054	1255	530	29	...	...	2010	
...	0	73	8840	4884	1705	804	48	...	...	2011	
0	...	67	5625	4848	3432	1261	137	1	0	2012	
...	0	54	3638	4051	1587	736	35	0	...	2013	
10	7	77	363	6606	489	2581	66	133	1116	2000	Asie orientale
0	294	791	4636	22255	1910	23467	1272	651	2523	2010	
45	28	1821	5971	32919	2329	31917	1375	819	3688	2011	
6	21	1681	5943	33146	1925	38581	1554	948	3096	2012	
0	145	2387	4020	31419	2080	40869	1712	971	3123	2013	
10	6	59	209	2528	334	1360	53	0	...	2000	Chine
0	10	507	2761	8912	645	8081	735	122	...	2010	
45	27	772	4078	10898	812	7706	622	223	...	2011	
6	18	713	4251	10539	409	7461	797	252	...	2012	
0	11	763	3230	11246	1000	10465	856	293	...	2013	
0	2008	8	679	7173	177	502	212	0	0	2000	Asie méridionale
7	2895	3874	3654	40451	2783	7982	9868	0	539	2010	
21	4417	5245	5143	53798	3821	14050	12650	35	12168	2011	
16	3450	6089	5433	38463	2653	12057	16519	1	7184	2012	
14	3194	9451	3846	33461	2532	12638	19659	5	10944	2013	
3	9	28	78	13054	1725	11077	110	523	3	2000	Asie Sud-est
7	176	1654	463	45338	10124	57795	757	1873	545	2010	
9	135	1570	483	61296	15083	81245	875	2772	582	2011	
13	43	2147	244	56411	12216	83058	1188	2877	615	2012	
0	223	2867	533	52176	12800	84516	1637	2525	717	2013	
25	3405	439	1706	49457	3807	7735	3937	...	3106	2000	Asie occidentale
133	7742	4455	4646	269078	28303	18351	10992	133	19958	2010	
137	13359	3912	7331	373397	52283	22168	9858	550	54462	2011	
149	17744	9485	7277	445770	58644	30608	12318	740	24013	2012	
77	16975	7443	7366	468860	59635	31199	10964	367	21905	2013	
0	...	0	...	101	...	2	...	1	0	2000	Océanie
0	...	1	14	186	1	28	...	34	179	2010	
...	...	0	15	178	0	27	...	88	220	2011	
...	...	2	17	61	0	28	...	94	235	2012	
...	...	0	3	82	1	37	0	115	218	2013	

Voir la fin du tableau pour la remarque générale et les notes.

World exports by provenance and destination (Table D)

In million U.S. dollars f.o.b.

| Exports from | Year | World 1/ Monde 1/ | Developed economies 2/ Economies développées 2/ | Asia-Pacific Asie-Pacifique | | Europe | | North America Amérique du Nord | | Commonwealth of Independent States Communauté d'Etats Indépendants | |
			Total	Total	Japan Japon	Total	Germany Allemagne	Total	U.S.A. É.-U.	Total	Europe
							Chemicals (SITC, Rev. 3, 5)				
World 1/	2000	565810	375573	29175	21233	260843	42853	85555	66203	7294	6109
	2010	1657426	997834	74052	52080	718756	126626	205027	163670	44114	38382
	2011	1933602	1141031	88941	62968	819889	142662	232201	186398	54774	47828
	2012	1899611	1099829	87821	61613	781171	137087	230837	184149	59403	50331
	2013	1954341	1128557	83480	58147	812925	142757	232152	184765	63986	53849
Developed Economies - Asia-Pacific 2/	2000	39061	14664	1393	353	6096	976	7176	6972	23	19
	2010	86979	21370	2502	524	9026	1715	9841	9586	159	151
	2011	94250	22554	2711	568	9883	2074	9959	9679	187	179
	2012	89481	21630	2579	584	9065	1848	9986	9702	191	179
	2013	85259	20662	2354	549	8202	1748	10107	9764	200	192
Japan	2000	35160	12405	386	.	5500	899	6520	6354	22	18
	2010	78419	17469	559	.	8145	1570	8765	8594	153	147
	2011	84507	18269	572	.	8893	1860	8804	8625	179	172
	2012	78957	17199	490	.	7950	1573	8760	8588	179	169
	2013	75823	16498	424	.	7236	1522	8838	8610	180	173
Developed Economies - Europe 2/	2000	317227	260770	11709	8571	212386	36774	36675	33940	4360	4031
	2010	884208	704932	27919	18934	581126	105098	95888	86922	29614	27341
	2011	1001340	792184	31308	21436	657386	121858	103490	94359	35540	32872
	2012	966929	755656	31354	21630	620418	117569	103884	94386	36203	33168
	2013	1023391	795803	30964	21061	660270	122918	104568	93781	39552	36004
France	2000	40440	32870	1270	908	27982	5990	3618	3362	530	469
	2010	91304	67228	3399	2446	56267	11793	7562	6703	3168	2931
	2011	99606	72746	3832	2965	62151	13518	6763	5930	3309	3056
	2012	97450	70638	3480	2677	60411	13082	6747	5950	3219	2936
	2013	101395	72316	3215	2405	62631	13863	6469	5637	3700	3352
Germany	2000	69666	53574	3003	2398	43606	.	6964	6328	1211	1124
	2010	187400	144104	5597	4143	124276	.	14232	12961	7641	7099
	2011	213341	162725	6429	4752	139701	.	16595	15080	9365	8728
	2012	204297	153160	6456	4763	127328	.	19376	17890	9740	9021
	2013	216625	161825	6590	4838	134201	.	21034	19355	10416	9638
Developed Economies - North America 2/	2000	94865	61283	8502	6582	24815	2845	27966	12116	312	267
	2010	221883	129967	15938	12064	60943	11032	53087	24580	1208	1123
	2011	246465	139608	16720	12707	61601	8168	61287	29122	1363	1271
	2012	243805	137339	17201	13157	60709	7939	59430	27213	1431	1310
	2013	246438	137408	15382	11407	61168	7627	60858	27953	1549	1387
United States	2000	80057	48161	8179	6371	24133	2719	15849	.	302	260
	2010	188730	101947	15415	11738	58031	10638	28500	.	1158	1077
	2011	207030	106512	16109	12386	58245	7790	32158	.	1297	1211
	2012	206944	106380	16637	12842	57532	7545	32211	.	1374	1257
	2013	208624	105564	14883	11151	57781	7204	32899	.	1473	1317
South-Eastern Europe	2000	1338	541	2	2	513	46	26	26	148	138
	2010	5966	2754	14	13	2601	668	138	136	818	742
	2011	8162	4111	19	13	3800	1144	293	291	1042	956
	2012	7825	3917	20	13	3625	1174	272	263	1081	981
	2013	8401	4391	25	15	4189	1420	177	173	1217	1096
Commonwealth of Independent States	2000	8542	4566	35	33	3214	282	1318	1286	1361	839
	2010	27874	9743	126	66	7879	570	1737	1299	5114	4012
	2011	39351	14176	171	101	11938	854	2068	1746	7346	5944
	2012	43743	16115	186	60	13919	725	2010	1636	10556	7656
	2013	37199	12093	158	70	10061	842	1874	1513	10737	7650
Russian Federation	2000	6181	3740	23	21	2535	218	1183	1165	607	189
	2010	16068	6517	84	55	5583	362	850	749	2171	1689
	2011	21792	8467	112	71	7076	553	1279	1168	3457	2896
	2012	24610	8517	103	34	7272	486	1142	1054	5858	3958
	2013	23533	8703	75	27	7508	569	1120	1004	6383	4272

For general note and footnotes see end of table

Exportations mondiales par provenance et destination (Tableau D)

En millions de dollars E.-U. f.o.b.

← Exportations vers

South-Eastern Europe Europe du Sud-est	Northern Africa Afrique septentrio-nale	Sub-Saharan Africa Afrique du Nord	Latin America and the Caribbean Amérique latine et Caraïbes	Eastern Asia Asie orientale	Southern Asia Asie méridionale	South-eastern Asia Asie du Sud-est	Western Asia Asie occidentale	Oceania Océanie	Others 4/ Autre 4/	Année	Exportations en provence de
						Produits chimiques (CTCI, Rev. 3, 5)					
2698	4509	7656	39045	68014	8935	27490	16979	324	7295	2000	Monde 1/
14566	16669	28595	112684	237768	50847	84387	61085	1291	7586	2010	
17821	18406	35252	138440	278152	61067	102631	73741	1529	10758	2011	
17494	20163	35739	144297	273136	58384	106345	72789	1629	10404	2012	
19135	22169	40406	147350	269164	59560	115754	83162	1126	3971	2013	
2	52	161	1390	16114	491	5662	301	95	107	2000	Economies Développées -
36	73	560	1272	50079	1513	10795	868	226	29	2010	Asie-Pacifique 2/
36	93	508	1442	54410	1714	12028	982	268	27	2011	
33	82	385	1483	51428	1626	11289	1035	278	22	2012	
31	81	310	1352	49480	1403	10571	885	273	11	2013	
2	45	105	1298	15458	446	5143	230	6	...	2000	Japon
29	65	249	1038	48084	1155	9441	730	5	...	2010	
32	84	289	1128	52026	1254	10426	813	6	...	2011	
26	69	229	1150	48458	1174	9652	813	8	...	2012	
26	67	220	1029	46953	1084	9041	719	6	...	2013	
2196	3327	3858	9210	8697	2803	4844	10664	146	6351	2000	Economies Développées -
11462	10232	10482	25684	33792	9625	13356	32741	372	1916	2010	Europe 2/
13852	10862	12370	29869	39642	10786	15387	38006	387	2456	2011	
13607	11848	12321	32086	39360	9812	15755	37382	381	2518	2012	
14965	13031	13246	34153	42631	9976	16628	40482	386	2539	2013	
193	1065	1052	1207	1065	286	690	1358	122	2	2000	France
871	2945	2928	2988	3331	941	2292	4306	301	5	2010	
976	2966	3121	3560	4088	1049	2863	4587	330	11	2011	
906	3113	3167	3778	4076	966	2761	4484	298	43	2012	
1057	3370	3533	4282	4437	992	2690	4679	313	27	2013	
423	372	617	2378	2718	681	1316	2344	6	4026	2000	Allemagne
2113	1328	1894	6547	10814	2770	3257	6813	6	111	2010	
2400	1431	2245	7588	12564	3054	3776	8007	8	178	2011	
2465	1481	2026	8092	12732	2794	3786	7845	7	169	2012	
2712	1594	2110	8418	13756	2812	3923	8879	11	169	2013	
19	215	666	17202	9182	676	3844	1453	13	0	2000	Economies Développées -
94	851	1591	42784	27389	4646	8856	4441	56	0	2010	Amérique du Nord 2/
73	849	1994	51215	30630	5216	10705	4788	25	0	2011	
69	920	2130	53519	28855	4110	10238	5157	36	0	2012	
93	957	2107	55327	29124	3845	10612	5382	35	0	2013	
17	207	648	16767	8305	619	3605	1413	12	...	2000	Etats-Unis
58	792	1500	41074	25789	4206	7927	4230	50	...	2010	
67	830	1823	49312	28557	4729	9280	4602	21	...	2011	
65	902	1947	51540	27078	3765	8895	4977	23	...	2012	
89	938	1967	53412	27079	3435	9446	5193	29	...	2013	
223	21	21	18	9	19	19	262	0	57	2000	Europe du Sud-est
1395	73	57	61	88	87	49	578	0	6	2010	
1686	79	80	137	75	159	67	722	1	5	2011	
1584	126	63	148	90	85	40	685	1	4	2012	
1712	119	70	55	93	81	42	616	0	5	2013	
65	78	40	548	1031	245	118	488	1	1	2000	Communauté d'Etats
256	121	450	2986	4795	2133	864	1390	0	22	2010	Indépendants
452	255	541	5199	5660	2400	1366	1879	2	75	2011	
426	223	824	4347	5556	2460	1306	1881	0	49	2012	
446	277	785	3462	4925	1329	986	2107	0	51	2013	
38	48	16	378	889	159	62	243	1	0	2000	Fédération de Russie
132	45	199	1713	2414	1526	531	819	0	1	2010	
198	74	194	3049	3009	1309	816	1195	0	26	2011	
267	76	468	2887	3021	1580	784	1145	0	6	2012	
335	111	449	2595	2280	682	577	1410	...	8	2013	

Voir la fin du tableau pour la remarque générale et les notes.

World exports by provenance and destination (Table D)

In million U.S. dollars f.o.b.

| Exports from | Year | World 1/ Monde 1/ | Developed economies 2/ Economies développées 2/ | | | | | | | Commonwealth of Independent States Communauté d'Etats Indépendants | |
| | | | Asia-Pacific Asie-Pacifique | | | Europe | | North America Amérique du Nord | | | |
			Total	Total	Japan Japon	Total	Germany Allemagne	Total	U.S.A. É.-U.	Total	Europe
						Chemicals (SITC, Rev. 3, 5) [cont.]					
Northern Africa	2000	2350	1095	25	2	1015	49	55	54	3	3
	2010	9661	3635	26	10	3347	158	263	249	24	10
	2011	11302	4369	102	22	3792	84	475	464	40	30
	2012	11695	4395	28	6	3910	138	458	430	47	35
	2013	10656	3936	18	10	3635	42	284	274	25	18
Sub-Saharan Africa	2000	2848	947	141	79	446	64	361	330	38	38
	2010	9791	2205	221	117	982	130	1002	983	4	3
	2011	11659	2961	339	233	1434	151	1188	1164	52	52
	2012	12041	2972	597	473	1382	109	993	961	41	40
	2013	11640	2554	285	103	1401	152	868	819	46	45
South Africa	2000	2055	874	137	79	382	57	355	324	1	0
	2010	6113	1802	218	115	841	118	743	725	3	3
	2011	7229	2264	333	232	951	133	980	967	12	12
	2012	7349	2312	590	467	933	78	788	772	5	5
	2013	6870	1765	281	103	795	87	689	668	7	6
Latin America and the Caribbean	2000	16624	7477	325	259	2088	315	5064	4945	12	11
	2010	47841	20185	907	729	7363	746	11915	11447	73	69
	2011	59569	26835	1295	1073	9161	884	16379	15678	75	69
	2012	56239	23877	923	682	8270	704	14684	14041	73	63
	2013	55142	22775	860	564	7130	742	14784	14117	79	73
Brazil	2000	3565	1471	157	141	649	152	665	641	3	3
	2010	12235	5080	417	358	2849	377	1814	1744	21	21
	2011	15055	6626	582	509	3458	476	2586	2491	19	18
	2012	15004	6816	434	373	2980	323	3401	3315	23	21
	2013	14268	6148	328	281	2835	313	2984	2898	26	24
Eastern Asia	2000	45641	11728	4104	3441	4184	868	3439	3221	444	368
	2010	190461	51039	16865	13308	18984	4199	15191	14163	3970	3072
	2011	236095	66146	23263	18346	23583	4735	19300	17995	5145	4032
	2012	232343	63041	21103	16074	22041	4119	19897	18565	5364	4162
	2013	243654	62881	19570	15133	23236	4201	20075	18696	5794	4414
China	2000	12098	6060	1714	1493	2570	645	1775	1661	131	93
	2010	87519	35343	9397	7605	14940	3352	11006	10218	2698	2094
	2011	114723	46294	13765	11024	18423	3731	14107	13140	3539	2772
	2012	113522	43570	12106	8894	17083	3251	14381	13432	3836	2942
	2013	119566	43841	11424	8422	17573	3319	14844	13836	4278	3238
Southern Asia	2000	5011	1852	170	101	1149	223	533	481	233	152
	2010	31877	10679	735	436	5831	966	4113	3877	998	605
	2011	41838	13585	945	547	7160	1232	5480	5132	1369	900
	2012	42506	14909	1063	636	7132	1312	6714	6261	1312	916
	2013	46696	16982	1172	711	8408	1541	7401	6943	1414	1018
South-Eastern Asia	2000	21083	6188	2395	1681	2423	199	1369	1309	43	41
	2010	81117	22707	8045	5696	10176	591	4487	4064	216	198
	2011	106001	31687	10944	7703	15815	587	4928	4659	353	298
	2012	108646	31940	11345	7865	15656	557	4939	4673	333	283
	2013	106893	26845	11029	7771	10729	560	5087	4893	334	292
Western Asia	2000	11203	4458	374	128	2513	213	1571	1522	315	201
	2010	59685	18596	744	184	10490	748	7363	6363	1916	1056
	2011	77341	22664	984	218	14326	887	7354	6108	2262	1223
	2012	83999	23863	1280	351	15015	869	7568	6018	2770	1538
	2013	78518	21978	1460	639	14452	931	6065	5836	3039	1659
Oceania	2000	16	2	1	0	1	0	0	0	...	...
	2010	84	22	12	0	9	4	1	1	0	0
	2011	229	151	140	0	10	4	1	1	0	0
	2012	360	174	142	82	30	24	2	2	0	0
	2013	454	249	203	113	43	32	2	2	0	0

For general note and footnotes see end of table

Exportations mondiales par provenance et destination (Tableau D)

En millions de dollars E.-U. f.o.b.

←—— Exportations vers

South-Eastern Europe Europe du Sud-est	Northern Africa Afrique septentrio-nale	Sub-Saharan Africa Afrique du Nord	Latin America and the Caribbean Amérique latine et Caraïbes	Eastern Asia Asie orientale	Southern Asia Asie méridionale	South-eastern Asia Asie du Sud-est	Western Asia Asie occidentale	Oceania Océanie	Others 4/ Autre 4/	Année	Exportations en provenance de
						Produits chimiques (CTCI, Rev. 3, 5) *[suite]*					
9	172	44	118	32	545	42	255	0	34	2000	Afrique du Nord
116	740	475	862	190	1887	160	1381	0	190	2010	
132	671	634	1183	126	2242	184	1583	0	139	2011	
206	968	768	1384	210	1654	147	1802	0	112	2012	
237	813	760	1414	87	1274	69	1931	0	109	2013	
5	9	1245	105	116	233	72	69	0	6	2000	Afrique subsaharienne
5	36	5339	280	462	936	252	249	5	19	2010	
5	73	6229	397	434	834	323	310	5	34	2011	
20	66	6352	426	547	667	511	405	4	30	2012	
18	49	6875	390	428	564	382	311	2	22	2013	
5	9	658	101	114	160	70	62	0	1	2000	Afrique du sud
4	30	2840	232	408	353	207	222	2	8	2010	
5	42	3256	337	380	395	273	258	3	6	2011	
1	31	3316	365	399	240	352	303	3	21	2012	
1	22	3492	367	352	289	316	247	1	11	2013	
2	19	147	8269	362	66	162	83	0	24	2000	Amérique latine et Caraïbes
13	91	459	23839	1746	417	438	380	3	196	2010	
27	123	576	28258	2121	337	526	469	1	220	2011	
30	129	545	27737	2146	342	589	480	1	290	2012	
27	114	492	27718	2056	402	610	617	0	251	2013	
1	10	88	1693	156	21	80	40	0	...	2000	Brésil
2	38	309	5570	657	206	186	164	3	...	2010	
2	53	404	6499	855	147	219	229	1	...	2011	
2	59	334	6345	868	115	196	246	1	0	2012	
3	46	310	6202	821	176	261	270	0	5	2013	
42	205	628	1318	23683	1634	5179	760	17	3	2000	Asie orientale
276	1504	3784	9115	77451	15851	21375	6002	88	5	2010	
407	1751	5219	12327	90192	19824	26842	8143	95	5	2011	
431	1883	5469	13262	86325	19563	28809	8064	125	5	2012	
451	1985	6277	14764	90164	20253	31636	9306	137	5	2013	
23	91	219	511	2632	779	1356	290	6	...	2000	Chine
191	841	2557	6309	14455	10910	10730	3429	55	...	2010	
289	1018	3709	8529	18225	14198	14061	4800	59	...	2011	
304	1113	3965	9461	17086	13636	15511	4959	82	...	2012	
295	1200	4625	10708	17610	14005	17493	5424	87	...	2013	
8	65	352	280	647	492	517	560	4	0	2000	Asie méridionale
102	444	2520	1753	4925	3295	3031	4060	17	54	2010	
102	534	3377	2454	6759	4572	3846	5003	24	213	2011	
137	617	3532	2818	5864	4126	4296	4817	23	56	2012	
205	702	4475	2794	5920	4604	4541	4854	28	178	2013	
14	55	275	232	6051	1229	6582	369	43	1	2000	Asie Sud-est
37	257	1184	2538	22390	6299	23489	1834	151	14	2010	
44	300	1500	4325	28952	7155	29014	2414	223	34	2011	
39	285	1605	4720	30026	6943	30379	2094	243	39	2012	
41	294	1655	4051	31609	7475	32237	2088	232	32	2013	
113	291	211	354	2089	501	445	1714	0	711	2000	Asie occidentale
775	2248	1690	1510	14462	4156	1688	7158	351	5135	2010	
1006	2816	2213	1633	19151	5826	2311	9441	469	7550	2011	
912	3017	1731	2367	22615	6995	2954	8985	512	7278	2012	
911	3748	3339	1869	12528	8354	7397	14583	6	767	2013	
0	0	7	0	0	0	3	...	4	0	2000	Océanie
0	0	4	1	1	1	34	1	20	0	2010	
...	...	12	3	1	1	32	1	28	0	2011	
0	...	13	0	113	1	33	0	25	0	2012	
0	...	15	0	119	1	43	0	27	0	2013	

Voir la fin du tableau pour la remarque générale et les notes.

World exports by provenance and destination (Table D)

In million U.S. dollars f.o.b.

Exports from	Year	World 1/ Monde 1/	Developed economies 2/ Economies développées 2/ Total	Asia-Pacific Asie-Pacifique Total	Japan Japon	Europe Total	Germany Allemagne	North America Amérique du Nord Total	U.S.A. É.-U.	Commonwealth of Independent States Communauté d'Etats Indépendants Total	Europe
Machinery and transport equipment (SITC, Rev. 3, 7)											
World 1/	2000	2618088	1798566	136989	102459	985348	188643	676230	554454	19720	15828
	2010	5128903	2744113	227184	145649	1650128	353854	866802	711404	131062	111055
	2011	5804580	3079054	256895	161782	1862979	405171	959180	787414	184888	159077
	2012	5830723	3005385	276160	172527	1694768	375410	1034457	854054	207100	173809
	2013	6033879	3081320	269333	174058	1751679	383275	1060308	879006	204095	167924
Developed Economies - Asia-Pacific 2/	2000	338298	189906	9501	291	63126	14800	117279	110881	536	422
	2010	471514	170048	15894	217	59112	13145	95042	87425	7623	7150
	2011	496280	181817	16665	233	64416	15284	100735	93415	11792	10793
	2012	492700	188907	18494	225	54589	13524	115824	107295	12421	11276
	2013	430090	172130	15489	204	47968	12058	108673	101536	10662	9553
Japan	2000	329680	185109	7675	.	61931	14533	115503	109214	526	414
	2010	458036	163744	12958	.	57669	12865	93117	85702	7565	7106
	2011	480313	174181	13209	.	62868	14982	98104	91039	11715	10728
	2012	476118	181219	15208	.	53106	13250	112905	104692	12351	11225
	2013	414378	164643	12381	.	46456	11812	105806	98909	10583	9501
Developed Economies - Europe 2/	2000	1018009	834930	24242	16806	696779	127486	113908	104620	11239	9766
	2010	1868337	1330804	38526	19282	1148392	234020	143886	128352	69457	62165
	2011	2181257	1537596	48598	23926	1321237	277110	167761	150945	98246	89133
	2012	2055144	1418766	51057	25885	1190189	256876	177520	160510	103940	94813
	2013	2146230	1482868	51574	27044	1243785	267614	187508	168434	102184	91833
France	2000	132952	103387	1699	1089	86545	19223	15143	14101	962	653
	2010	199558	131919	4132	1539	115433	39671	12354	11472	4181	3746
	2011	218936	146087	5730	1828	125490	44985	14867	13808	6004	5541
	2012	213311	136858	4646	2308	116564	44972	15649	14624	7753	7056
	2013	216300	141809	4766	2590	120089	45751	16954	15760	6255	5117
Germany	2000	272345	223326	8768	6855	175308	.	39250	37072	4105	3664
	2010	584810	396711	15509	8546	322673	.	58529	51928	23995	21368
	2011	696182	464166	18923	11084	377556	.	67687	61417	35744	32466
	2012	664782	436362	20861	12202	340055	.	75445	67989	36790	33734
	2013	683228	448406	21003	12917	346806	.	80596	71404	36056	32583
Developed Economies - North America 2/	2000	523666	335332	36795	28250	99404	18363	199133	101693	1535	1086
	2010	550261	283609	24424	13069	72711	17573	186475	80784	4813	3714
	2011	610726	315698	29292	14372	79347	19916	207060	88537	6866	5488
	2012	651446	335682	34152	15700	78543	19932	222987	97861	8068	6652
	2013	648373	325306	28691	14747	76640	18368	219975	95333	8160	6617
United States	2000	412200	227821	35994	27866	94397	17580	97431	.	1458	1018
	2010	449130	193263	22926	12499	64670	16374	105667	.	3945	2992
	2011	500949	217981	27776	13815	71746	18410	118459	.	5926	4706
	2012	532008	228823	32611	15150	71108	18597	125104	.	7114	5865
	2013	532729	221997	27335	14246	70040	17245	124622	.	7254	5882
South-Eastern Europe	2000	2785	2115	3	0	2009	521	103	93	83	72
	2010	26562	20294	31	17	19851	6454	412	374	1711	1516
	2011	33408	25247	55	22	24615	8567	576	529	2122	1864
	2012	31144	23552	55	20	22900	8188	596	550	1846	1604
	2013	38264	29053	60	29	28002	9704	991	944	2278	2086
Commonwealth of Independent States	2000	10405	3201	38	34	2870	479	293	271	4444	3311
	2010	27163	5432	250	228	4660	998	522	445	15149	12049
	2011	33975	5899	271	249	5092	987	536	479	21393	17584
	2012	43327	6844	354	313	5828	1229	663	606	28619	20127
	2013	42655	7039	268	248	6108	1279	663	618	27079	18138
Russian Federation	2000	6422	2634	35	34	2410	387	189	179	1573	749
	2010	11538	3068	236	227	2467	564	366	295	3680	2368
	2011	12537	3185	255	247	2538	466	392	362	4332	2991
	2012	18528	3359	324	308	2581	551	455	415	9535	4581
	2013	21398	4149	251	247	3364	754	534	498	11077	5185

For general note and footnotes see end of table

Exportations mondiales par provenance et destination (Tableau D)

En millions de dollars E.-U. f.o.b.

⟵ Exportations vers

South-Eastern Europe Europe du Sud-est	Northern Africa Afrique septentrio-nale	Sub-Saharan Africa Afrique du Nord	Latin America and the Caribbean Amérique latine et Caraïbes	Eastern Asia Asie orientale	Southern Asia Asie méridionale	South-eastern Asia Asie du Sud-est	Western Asia Asie occidentale	Oceania Océanie	Others 4/ Autre 4/	Année	Exportations en provenance de ↓
	**Machines et matériel de transport (CTCI, Rev. 3, 7)**

South-Eastern Europe	Northern Africa	Sub-Saharan Africa	Latin America and the Caribbean	Eastern Asia	Southern Asia	South-eastern Asia	Western Asia	Oceania	Others 4/	Année	Exportations en provenance de
7387	17501	28869	158646	287439	22724	198711	71331	2013	5181	2000	Monde 1/
32423	56318	102634	348063	981086	120378	369011	223512	14494	5808	2010	
40218	49687	127452	404437	1086700	137409	413818	254890	16862	9165	2011	
37592	57134	122357	414793	1121045	122569	450581	271373	13704	7091	2012	
41503	59564	132452	427669	1200661	118421	453708	292650	16211	5626	2013	
76	919	3093	17123	67403	2899	46357	8977	622	389	2000	Economies Développées - Asie-Pacifique 2/
269	2588	7615	34989	150972	8665	62994	21921	3778	51	2010	
395	1830	9416	34276	155454	10238	66281	20897	3843	43	2011	
348	2499	8697	32848	135972	8373	73952	24660	3999	26	2012	
319	1710	7391	27500	118546	6092	59601	23283	2822	36	2013	
74	909	2942	16949	66606	2790	45359	8114	304	0	2000	Japon
264	2566	7166	34611	149507	8405	61397	20237	2574	...	2010	
379	1801	8832	33833	153533	9983	64252	19432	2372	...	2011	
321	2457	7983	32324	134206	8140	71893	22833	2391	...	2012	
293	1667	6830	27085	116889	5913	57656	21356	1462	...	2013	
6111	11738	15230	29051	38462	8120	22918	36043	553	3614	2000	Economies Développées - Europe 2/
24484	31850	34242	59130	140228	32139	44866	96824	1764	2549	2010	
30819	28887	42578	71158	169960	35004	50660	111797	1674	2877	2011	
29441	30016	39971	73131	161836	27346	56276	109174	1793	3454	2012	
32801	33368	41835	76918	170300	24776	56477	119772	2241	2691	2013	
536	4200	4160	4149	5250	1384	2817	5172	337	600	2000	France
2141	8564	5485	7480	13680	4041	7781	13296	603	388	2010	
2488	8103	6532	7513	17164	3670	7657	12741	692	287	2011	
2520	8201	5239	8127	18303	2936	10984	11380	558	449	2012	
2813	8181	5432	8804	16889	2530	11580	10883	984	141	2013	
1738	1857	3307	7626	12322	1917	5981	9509	102	555	2000	Allemagne
6638	6061	8708	19992	67556	10367	13717	30565	476	26	2010	
8799	5310	10730	23138	83991	12258	15855	35918	239	34	2011	
8648	5395	10459	24017	78602	9650	17559	36890	338	72	2012	
9121	6003	10881	24398	81754	8948	17180	39968	305	209	2013	
266	2440	3056	84864	48817	2259	32401	12523	171	1	2000	Economies Développées - Amérique du Nord 2/
581	2795	8106	120593	64712	7204	31984	25589	266	10	2010	
685	2319	9684	137661	68399	8363	31968	28597	484	0	2011	
573	3202	10769	150654	67173	6554	31756	36494	514	8	2012	
699	3467	10697	153819	74086	6980	29832	35090	236	1	2013	
244	2348	2934	83422	47397	2166	32085	12159	164	1	2000	Etats-Unis
520	2537	7211	116778	62627	6723	30927	24399	198	...	2010	
590	2046	8798	133654	65557	7724	30857	27385	431	...	2011	
492	2937	9685	146768	64593	5961	30361	34797	478	...	2012	
614	3126	9822	149884	71153	6556	28481	33642	199	...	2013	
193	70	20	25	35	42	17	154	0	30	2000	Europe du Sud-est
1176	479	375	273	410	275	95	1465	8	1	2010	
1599	568	529	360	590	417	143	1816	15	1	2011	
1346	797	403	430	651	409	136	1490	83	2	2012	
1649	823	321	983	709	352	187	1864	42	3	2013	
197	155	103	138	841	677	146	496	1	6	2000	Communauté d'Etats Indépendants
549	489	176	681	1922	1626	410	725	1	2	2010	
613	513	267	841	1505	1740	616	519	4	65	2011	
831	581	268	998	1753	2265	571	588	7	2	2012	
765	475	219	1011	2183	1914	1335	623	11	1	2013	
165	100	84	117	765	568	115	294	1	6	2000	Fédération de Russie
302	366	87	431	1646	1120	297	540	1	0	2010	
279	444	207	648	1255	1241	571	309	3	63	2011	
415	474	151	683	1519	1675	484	230	2	1	2012	
359	367	89	776	1613	1492	1160	306	10	0	2013	

Voir la fin du tableau pour la remarque générale et les notes.

World exports by provenance and destination (Table D)

In million U.S. dollars f.o.b.

Exports from	Year	World 1/ Monde 1/	Developed economies 2/ Economies développées 2/							Commonwealth of Independent States Communauté d'Etats Indépendants	
			Total	Asia-Pacific Asie-Pacifique		Europe		North America Amérique du Nord			
				Total	Japan Japon	Total	Germany Allemagne	Total	U.S.A. É.-U.	Total	Europe
Machinery and transport equipment (SITC, Rev. 3, 7) [cont.]											
Northern Africa	2000	1754	1566	1	1	1559	277	6	5	1	1
	2010	9202	6879	52	51	6651	952	175	173	9	5
	2011	11184	8653	95	92	8327	1077	230	228	17	7
	2012	11121	8608	86	79	8292	1014	230	224	23	6
	2013	12558	9746	52	49	9441	1183	253	251	33	28
Sub-Saharan Africa	2000	5308	3385	403	155	2340	969	642	609	15	14
	2010	23862	9769	1045	502	5791	2445	2933	2702	67	42
	2011	28808	11229	959	503	6767	2673	3502	3237	98	68
	2012	28886	10633	928	413	6364	2183	3341	3132	201	171
	2013	31054	9260	991	553	5534	2069	2735	2625	173	142
South Africa	2000	4570	3150	390	143	2156	950	604	577	14	14
	2010	16296	8495	1018	484	4854	2409	2624	2410	63	40
	2011	18984	9583	923	475	5483	2633	3177	2929	76	64
	2012	19089	8360	892	395	4473	2106	2995	2823	188	160
	2013	17880	7692	940	539	4364	1999	2388	2311	159	129
Latin America and the Caribbean	2000	122150	108687	764	615	6608	1776	101316	98437	19	18
	2010	221033	167570	1740	1022	13051	5151	152779	144778	324	311
	2011	249219	184244	1980	988	15857	6108	166406	159005	613	488
	2012	264485	201234	2176	1203	16726	5781	182332	175284	782	645
	2013	281712	213925	2284	1085	16821	4520	194820	188026	819	585
Brazil	2000	15416	8675	358	290	3065	497	5252	5157	3	3
	2010	33109	9903	436	230	5688	1797	3779	3561	76	74
	2011	38812	11059	434	169	5744	1662	4881	4576	251	141
	2012	38251	12475	319	135	6599	1514	5557	5289	435	327
	2013	44217	14272	435	249	8053	1173	5784	5527	441	226
Eastern Asia	2000	347614	188125	37112	32788	64658	14462	86355	82182	1052	698
	2010	1414802	565713	99435	78971	237560	54823	228718	213396	25974	20492
	2011	1607371	618728	111119	86838	249702	53281	257907	240608	35689	28306
	2012	1671127	615849	118498	93313	226121	46842	271230	252965	42156	32627
	2013	1784527	623865	118253	94235	223738	45126	281874	262763	42454	32497
China	2000	82600	46255	10601	9716	16464	3921	19191	18323	325	217
	2010	781074	376271	63827	50927	161483	37055	150961	142241	16412	12828
	2011	902599	419563	73635	57896	174515	36998	171412	161871	22789	17893
	2012	965288	426072	79268	62662	159779	33007	187026	176118	27721	20981
	2013	1039527	431488	81346	65041	155907	30957	194236	183018	27873	21045
Southern Asia	2000	3620	1639	150	103	956	203	532	511	71	33
	2010	34729	12713	741	256	8053	1557	3919	3781	598	511
	2011	44613	15282	892	466	9195	1814	5194	4987	908	741
	2012	42021	14328	988	481	8653	1604	4687	4492	973	728
	2013	48153	15402	1122	614	9292	1685	4988	4769	881	704
South-Eastern Asia	2000	225568	118401	27610	23208	38165	7455	52626	51240	145	131
	2010	403713	139133	44268	31720	49064	12064	45801	43686	1395	1280
	2011	422482	138457	46003	33712	50390	12685	42064	39716	2170	1999
	2012	449558	144965	48240	34473	49889	12607	46835	44775	2677	2421
	2013	470247	154509	49398	34808	55431	13731	49680	46965	3081	2620
Western Asia	2000	18758	11174	341	203	6813	1825	4020	3894	570	265
	2010	77380	31951	663	311	25161	4671	6128	5497	3942	1819
	2011	84887	36020	865	378	27967	5669	7188	5711	4975	2607
	2012	89462	35830	1003	422	26649	5629	8178	6327	5394	2738
	2013	99657	38006	999	439	28893	5937	8115	6711	6291	3121
Oceania	2000	153	105	29	4	59	28	18	17	10	10
	2010	345	197	114	3	70	1	12	9	0	0
	2011	370	186	100	3	65	0	21	18	0	0
	2012	302	187	128	1	26	0	34	33	0	0
	2013	358	211	153	1	26	1	33	32	0	0

For general note and footnotes see end of table

Exportations mondiales par provenance et destination (Tableau D)

En millions de dollars E.-U. f.o.b.

← Exportations vers

South-Eastern Europe Europe du Sud-est	Northern Africa Afrique septentrionale	Sub-Saharan Africa Afrique du Nord	Latin America and the Caribbean Amérique latine et Caraïbes	Eastern Asia Asie orientale	Southern Asia Asie méridionale	South-eastern Asia Asie du Sud-est	Western Asia Asie occidentale	Oceania Océanie	Others 4/ Autre 4/	Année	Exportations en provence de ↓
			**Machines et matériel de transport (CTCI, Rev. 3, 7) [suite]**								
0	62	28	0	1	3	1	66	0	26	2000	Afrique du Nord
86	697	351	12	37	14	346	621	9	142	2010	
118	423	375	49	42	12	359	915	0	222	2011	
126	694	332	20	41	15	296	777	1	187	2012	
160	710	356	23	24	27	294	997	1	186	2013	
4	25	1370	92	140	40	118	107	3	8	2000	Afrique subsaharienne
16	320	11289	492	408	264	323	485	18	412	2010	
25	448	13945	536	1087	298	330	593	18	201	2011	
47	954	14673	512	522	290	342	579	37	97	2012	
42	426	18190	499	639	232	432	643	442	76	2013	
4	21	967	88	136	25	96	65	2	2	2000	Afrique du sud
16	220	6361	257	327	167	124	238	13	15	2010	
22	410	7557	358	278	228	209	252	5	6	2011	
27	417	8452	445	400	211	247	261	5	78	2012	
21	408	7814	417	523	164	277	376	3	25	2013	
3	47	290	11643	631	99	526	174	1	30	2000	Amérique latine et Caraïbes
106	388	1586	44863	3189	521	1240	1183	20	43	2010	
198	306	2178	53242	3978	623	2561	1192	26	58	2011	
236	230	2184	49597	5242	692	2619	1608	14	46	2012	
76	220	1877	55306	5596	612	1888	1333	10	51	2013	
1	41	254	6013	131	70	97	130	1	...	2000	Brésil
62	313	1166	19351	829	232	360	803	16	...	2010	
38	214	1448	22049	1242	396	1526	573	15	0	2011	
137	148	1544	19694	1510	372	1283	646	8	0	2012	
22	182	1477	25658	988	233	588	346	6	3	2013	
234	1157	3449	11502	92408	4160	37352	7457	528	188	2000	Asie orientale
3233	10903	28494	73327	490467	44730	118779	45411	7743	27	2010	
3597	9119	36082	89281	553500	53486	142135	56047	9687	19	2011	
2795	11765	31071	89738	604302	49228	158080	59765	6360	16	2012	
2948	11300	35157	91470	682507	48023	174525	62675	9567	35	2013	
39	283	1034	2120	21483	1303	7934	1814	10	...	2000	Chine
2372	6061	19157	42795	196975	30524	62648	25503	2355	...	2010	
2659	6035	22558	54113	230539	37663	73523	30779	2378	0	2011	
2097	7307	22619	58353	266916	34676	84396	32947	2185	...	2012	
2155	7574	25174	59245	317400	34170	96227	36382	1838	...	2013	
3	69	318	125	154	336	455	448	1	1	2000	Asie méridionale
196	1122	4000	1542	1307	2529	5451	5131	17	124	2010	
225	1032	4502	2195	1727	3132	7883	6968	67	693	2011	
144	1660	4741	2600	1585	3039	5934	6893	23	101	2012	
131	1563	5394	3332	2032	4309	6324	8499	28	257	2013	
31	254	1346	3706	37735	3155	57988	2659	114	32	2000	Asie Sud-est
246	1921	3216	9416	122274	13754	100232	11337	716	73	2010	
278	1833	4015	12119	126763	14933	108395	12443	813	262	2011	
285	1694	4787	11567	134560	14332	117570	16260	737	124	2012	
326	1938	5458	13426	139848	13433	118718	18748	641	121	2013	
268	563	567	375	809	934	418	2227	7	846	2000	Asie occidentale
1480	2767	3183	2742	5152	8657	2183	12819	127	2375	2010	
1666	2408	3875	2715	3688	9160	2376	13106	174	4723	2011	
1421	3044	4448	2694	7395	10025	2992	13084	107	3029	2012	
1587	3563	5545	3376	4170	11670	4022	19121	138	2167	2013	
0	...	1	0	2	...	13	0	13	10	2000	Océanie
0	0	1	3	7	1	109	1	26	0	2010	
0	0	5	4	7	2	109	0	56	0	2011	
0	0	12	4	12	1	57	1	28	0	2012	
0	0	11	7	20	1	73	2	32	1	2013	

Voir la fin du tableau pour la remarque générale et les notes.

World exports by provenance and destination (Table D)

In million U.S. dollars f.o.b.

| Exports from | Year | World 1/ Monde 1/ | Developed economies 2/ Economies développées 2/ | | | | | North America Amérique du Nord | | Commonwealth of Independent States Communauté d'Etats Indépendants | |
| | | | Asia-Pacific Asie-Pacifique | | Europe | | | | | | |
			Total	Total	Japan Japon	Total	Germany Allemagne	Total	U.S.A. É.-U.	Total	Europe

Passenger road vehicles and their parts (SITC, Rev. 3, 781.2, 784.1, 785.1, 785.2 and 785.31)

Exports from	Year	World	Dev Total	AP Total	Japan	Eur Total	Germany	NA Total	USA	CIS Total	Europe
World 1/	2000	318983	280540	12905	6829	143922	24206	123712	108466	1650	1442
	2010	583175	413212	25490	7918	244679	40987	143044	121388	19342	17595
	2011	668613	460074	28807	10782	280558	51052	150709	127947	31678	28884
	2012	677513	455821	32952	12492	246935	48766	175934	150981	34946	31086
	2013	705946	473781	33028	12392	255584	48049	185169	159748	33294	28113
Developed Economies - Asia-Pacific 2/	2000	63560	52590	3693	30	12486	2479	36412	33920	154	148
	2010	95933	58677	7739	5	13965	2017	36972	33189	5401	5095
	2011	92997	56151	7523	6	13810	2136	34818	31620	8093	7679
	2012	103794	62251	9031	5	10765	1872	42456	38654	8592	7878
	2013	97646	59703	7819	4	9648	1665	42236	38998	7023	6189
Japan	2000	62192	52147	3482	.	12472	2478	36193	33701	154	148
	2010	94231	58370	7474	.	13936	2015	36961	33178	5401	5094
	2011	91501	55767	7238	.	13778	2130	34751	31553	8091	7676
	2012	101954	61852	8749	.	10735	1870	42368	38567	8589	7875
	2013	95667	59101	7515	.	9588	1661	41999	38761	7023	6189
Developed Economies - Europe 2/	2000	162532	149044	6302	5066	122455	18702	20287	19464	1177	1103
	2010	297971	242435	9477	5219	203718	28804	29240	25901	8226	7692
	2011	355605	277926	12566	7431	233625	36282	31736	28163	14498	13651
	2012	334708	254699	13804	8410	203858	33841	37037	33070	15238	14503
	2013	353479	268498	14769	8717	212116	34610	41613	37729	13737	12776
France	2000	19406	17382	163	131	17193	2757	26	15	28	28
	2010	21614	19076	378	222	18655	3273	44	19	220	219
	2011	23680	20300	352	221	19893	3696	55	37	238	236
	2012	20661	17296	338	221	16909	3424	49	25	361	356
	2013	19141	16584	299	182	16120	3078	165	94	217	206
Germany	2000	61492	55191	4192	3688	37221	.	13778	13357	786	726
	2010	130646	99157	6311	3709	72233	.	20613	18066	3400	3116
	2011	156535	114662	8260	5387	83782	.	22621	19820	6045	5637
	2012	148435	107035	8786	5971	71105	.	27145	24040	6390	6020
	2013	150972	109348	8995	6106	71004	.	29320	26417	5665	5229
Developed Economies - North America 2/	2000	53034	48252	1254	948	2618	1281	44381	34581	21	17
	2010	77288	56878	1340	523	7454	4119	48084	36168	461	237
	2011	89223	63974	1971	774	10348	5680	51654	38831	986	600
	2012	102550	72349	2677	1138	10361	6271	59311	45837	1216	916
	2013	103495	70067	2718	932	9255	5057	58094	43917	1830	1440
United States	2000	18078	13450	1150	845	2503	1265	9798	.	18	15
	2010	40379	20577	1318	510	7346	4099	11913	.	456	233
	2011	49439	24978	1954	768	10204	5653	12821	.	956	573
	2012	55545	26335	2651	1123	10210	6229	13473	.	1197	900
	2013	58246	26012	2694	918	9142	5031	14176	.	1812	1425
South-Eastern Europe	2000	62	19	...	...	19	0	0	0	1	1
	2010	2985	2439	0	0	2437	489	1	1	68	66
	2011	3720	2947	0	0	2945	655	1	1	85	78
	2012	4004	2951	0	0	2949	627	1	1	107	93
	2013	6627	5256	0	0	4901	884	354	354	129	112
Commonwealth of Independent States	2000	478	135	0	0	134	7	1	1	247	135
	2010	1583	77	1	0	72	3	4	4	1464	1130
	2011	2667	71	1	1	63	3	8	7	2550	1915
	2012	3571	103	1	1	88	0	13	13	3401	2159
	2013	3932	93	0	0	84	3	8	8	3724	1866
Russian Federation	2000	360	132	0	0	131	6	1	1	142	34
	2010	262	53	1	0	49	2	3	3	193	113
	2011	491	49	1	1	44	2	4	4	426	316
	2012	1012	35	1	1	28	0	6	5	963	427
	2013	1518	34	0	0	27	1	7	6	1455	441

For general note and footnotes see end of table

Exportations mondiales par provenance et destination (Tableau D)

En millions de dollars E.-U. f.o.b.

← Exportations vers

South-Eastern Europe Europe du Sud-est	Northern Africa Afrique septentrio-nale	Sub-Saharan Africa Afrique du Nord	Latin America and the Caribbean Amérique latine et Caraïbes	Eastern Asia Asie orientale	Southern Asia Asie méridionale	South-eastern Asia Asie du Sud-est	Western Asia Asie occidentale	Oceania Océanie	Others 4/ Autre 4/	Année	Exportations en provenance de ↓

Véhicules routiers et pièces detachées pour transports passagères (CTCI, Rev. 3, 781.2, 784.1, 785.1, 785.2 et 785.31)

650	1379	2307	11647	3869	859	4280	11464	194	146	2000	Monde 1/
2763	6526	10905	34644	37810	4041	11943	40982	383	625	2010	
3471	6190	13581	41984	49996	4536	13960	42239	388	517	2011	
3057	9918	13521	39824	50162	3069	17030	49365	363	439	2012	
3276	9248	15235	43072	56239	2954	15121	53295	348	83	2013	
21	95	453	2729	1350	381	1826	3888	73	...	2000	Economies Développées -
46	459	1786	4868	8322	1189	2871	12148	167	...	2010	Asie-Pacifique 2/
57	306	1611	4656	8180	1374	3234	9211	124	0	2011	
50	353	1587	4511	7498	840	5137	12835	139	0	2012	
50	317	1581	4632	7462	789	3721	12236	132	0	2013	
21	94	451	2696	1346	380	1712	3123	67	...	2000	Japon
46	459	1780	4859	8315	1188	2840	10834	139	...	2010	
56	306	1601	4638	8172	1370	3197	8196	107	...	2011	
49	353	1580	4508	7492	836	5107	11469	119	...	2012	
50	316	1574	4630	7455	785	3703	10915	114	...	2013	
496	953	1338	1614	1198	180	793	5576	101	61	2000	Economies Développées -
2395	2625	3204	4122	20909	644	2043	11263	102	3	2010	Europe 2/
3001	3182	4194	5541	30183	651	3023	13294	109	2	2011	
2667	5136	4343	4950	30972	467	3067	13065	105	1	2012	
2832	4750	4980	6146	33541	340	2871	15688	95	2	2013	
52	490	275	347	30	101	44	591	67	0	2000	France
134	660	189	255	148	159	46	682	43	1	2010	
165	918	183	427	325	10	94	972	49	1	2011	
126	1150	183	351	342	3	125	676	48	0	2012	
127	768	181	349	277	3	111	481	41	2	2013	
224	175	520	601	871	53	425	2578	17	51	2000	Allemagne
829	1009	1494	2361	15591	213	867	5686	39	0	2010	
1072	1003	1891	2779	21152	285	1170	6446	29	0	2011	
929	1415	1821	2606	20278	193	1077	6663	30	0	2012	
882	1255	2062	3375	19453	180	1236	7522	23	0	2013	
13	22	76	3539	299	2	86	721	4	0	2000	Economies Développées -
24	245	1664	5295	4602	138	496	7476	8	...	2010	Amérique du Nord 2/
29	94	2166	6051	6893	142	548	8331	10	...	2011	
26	393	2375	6764	7428	74	549	11364	11	...	2012	
28	302	2450	6774	10084	59	521	11374	8	...	2013	
12	22	73	3448	278	2	85	685	4	...	2000	Etats-Unis
21	212	1586	4974	4582	120	492	7351	8	...	2010	
26	77	2048	5677	6822	130	542	8171	10	...	2011	
24	292	2244	6335	7377	72	541	11117	11	...	2012	
26	224	2306	6347	9923	58	516	11014	8	...	2013	
9	4	0	3	17	0	0	8	...	0	2000	Europe du Sud-est
99	140	16	0	0	0	0	215	7	0	2010	
130	206	34	0	0	1	0	306	11	0	2011	
103	423	39	0	0	0	0	371	8	0	2012	
151	404	43	3	2	0	0	630	9	0	2013	
9	3	1	15	14	1	9	45	...	0	2000	Communauté d'Etats
1	5	0	2	9	0	1	24	...	...	2010	Indépendants
1	0	2	10	8	1	1	20	...	2	2011	
1	1	1	19	9	2	1	34	...	...	2012	
2	15	1	12	8	5	1	71	...	...	2013	
8	2	1	15	14	1	1	44	...	...	2000	Fédération de Russie
0	5	0	0	8	0	1	2	...	...	2010	
1	0	2	2	7	0	1	0	...	2	2011	
0	1	1	7	4	0	1	1	...	...	2012	
2	14	0	9	2	0	1	2	...	...	2013	

Voir la fin du tableau pour la remarque générale et les notes.

World exports by provenance and destination (Table D)

In million U.S. dollars f.o.b.

| Exports from | Year | World 1/ Monde 1/ | Developed economies 2/ Economies développées 2/ | Asia-Pacific Asie-Pacifique | | Europe | | North America Amérique du Nord | | Commonwealth of Independent States Communauté d'Etats Indépendants | |
			Total	Total	Japan Japon	Total	Germany Allemagne	Total	U.S.A. É.-U.	Total	Europe

Passenger road vehicles and their parts (SITC, Rev. 3, 781.2, 784.1, 785.1, 785.2 and 785.31) *[cont.]*

Exports from	Year	World 1/ Monde 1/	Total	Asia-Pacific Total	Japan Japon	Europe Total	Germany Allemagne	North America Total	U.S.A. É.-U.	CIS Total	Europe
Northern Africa	2000	6	4	0	0	4	0	0	0	...	...
	2010	146	73	0	0	73	40	1	0	0	0
	2011	322	266	0	0	264	6	1	1	1	1
	2012	884	745	0	0	743	82	1	1	0	0
	2013	1596	1125	2	0	1123	109	0	0	17	16
Sub-Saharan Africa	2000	1106	889	269	136	527	395	93	93	0	0
	2010	4983	3778	768	422	1158	1000	1852	1822	0	0
	2011	5065	3909	586	410	1108	943	2215	2121	0	0
	2012	4383	3188	567	337	642	542	1979	1979	0	0
	2013	4046	2921	740	498	630	545	1552	1551	0	0
South Africa	2000	1048	874	262	130	520	394	92	92	0	0
	2010	4621	3760	765	419	1144	999	1850	1820	0	...
	2011	4751	3889	583	406	1093	941	2213	2118	...	...
	2012	4066	3161	563	334	624	540	1973	1973	0	...
	2013	3701	2873	738	496	587	537	1549	1549	0	0
Latin America and the Caribbean	2000	19792	16933	185	165	947	715	15801	14262	0	0
	2010	32971	19701	317	142	2855	2749	16530	15605	196	196
	2011	37649	21132	268	137	3559	2933	17305	16218	282	281
	2012	38585	23180	386	224	3584	2953	19210	18116	234	234
	2013	43907	26475	326	164	2522	2076	23626	22249	196	195
Brazil	2000	2025	526	1	0	224	7	302	301	...	...
	2010	5197	615	68	1	538	526	9	7	0	0
	2011	5332	143	21	2	105	93	18	14	0	...
	2012	4601	45	20	2	5	1	20	14	0	0
	2013	6429	47	20	4	4	1	23	20	...	...
Eastern Asia	2000	16143	11584	1081	456	3790	407	6713	6129	25	23
	2010	45296	19255	3548	1028	5803	958	9904	8329	2870	2549
	2011	57989	24492	3959	1310	8284	1585	12248	10369	4311	3832
	2012	60771	26746	4080	1342	7796	1729	14871	12415	5382	4579
	2013	62630	28477	3836	1244	7935	2269	16706	14067	5902	4852
China	2000	1855	772	232	197	62	6	478	467	3	3
	2010	9390	3422	929	758	1201	259	1292	1214	435	417
	2011	12616	3575	1162	966	1180	294	1232	1123	868	825
	2012	13519	3951	1228	996	1174	288	1549	1341	1162	1091
	2013	13656	3662	1164	944	962	200	1535	1205	1380	1274
Southern Asia	2000	265	104	3	1	99	5	2	2	3	0
	2010	6039	2077	168	3	1899	148	9	7	89	86
	2011	5513	1481	132	6	1338	136	10	7	48	38
	2012	6159	1469	193	8	1270	145	6	4	77	43
	2013	7793	1850	243	14	1550	112	56	54	38	25
South-Eastern Asia	2000	839	374	118	25	235	40	20	11	0	0
	2010	9985	2927	2118	572	681	83	127	89	120	117
	2011	9903	2578	1771	702	628	95	179	139	272	267
	2012	10810	3316	2190	1023	791	123	335	282	228	223
	2013	12257	4226	2534	797	1235	210	457	369	112	109
Western Asia	2000	1165	612	1	1	608	176	3	3	21	15
	2010	7994	4894	13	5	4562	576	320	272	447	428
	2011	7955	5145	29	5	4585	598	531	469	551	541
	2012	7289	4820	22	3	4086	580	712	609	470	458
	2013	8534	5090	41	21	4583	508	467	452	585	532
Oceania	2000	1	1	0	0	0	...	0	0	...	...
	2010	3	1	0	0	1	0	0	0	...	...
	2011	5	3	0	0	2	...	0	0	0	0
	2012	5	3	1	0	2	0	0	0	...	...
	2013	4	2	1	0	1	...	0	0	...	...

For general note and footnotes see end of table

Exportations mondiales par provenance et destination (Tableau D)

En millions de dollars E.-U. f.o.b.

← Exportations vers

South-Eastern Europe Europe du Sud-est	Northern Africa Afrique septentrio-nale	Sub-Saharan Africa Afrique du Nord	Latin America and the Caribbean Amérique latine et Caraïbes	Eastern Asia Asie orientale	Southern Asia Asie méridionale	South-eastern Asia Asie du Sud-est	Western Asia Asie occidentale	Oceania Océanie	Others 4/ Autre 4/	Année	Exportations en provence de ↓

Véhicules routiers et pièces detachées pour transports passagères (CTCI, Rev. 3, 781.2, 784.1, 785.1, 785.2 et 785.31) *[suite]*

South-Eastern Europe	Northern Africa	Sub-Saharan Africa	Latin America and the Caribbean	Eastern Asia	Southern Asia	South-eastern Asia	Western Asia	Oceania	Others 4/	Année	Exportations en provence de
...	1	0	...	...	...	0	0	...	0	2000	Afrique du Nord
0	59	5	...	2	0	0	7	...	0	2010	
0	46	4	0	0	0	0	6	...	0	2011	
27	91	5	0	0	0	0	15	1	1	2012	
49	164	7	0	0	0	...	229	0	5	2013	
0	1	126	0	57	0	31	3	0	0	2000	Afrique subsaharienne
6	29	994	1	131	2	38	4	0	0	2010	
5	18	966	1	112	1	35	16	0	0	2011	
3	21	908	0	166	15	31	2	0	47	2012	
1	19	871	2	188	1	37	2	...	4	2013	
0	0	86	0	56	0	30	0	0	0	2000	Afrique du sud
6	28	657	0	131	2	37	1	0	0	2010	
5	17	692	1	110	0	35	1	...	0	2011	
2	20	643	0	162	0	30	0	0	47	2012	
0	18	580	1	187	0	37	0	...	4	2013	
0	10	52	2758	10	19	5	5	0	0	2000	Amérique latine et Caraïbes
0	76	67	11998	595	16	139	182	0	2	2010	
0	68	63	14831	928	40	123	179	0	4	2011	
0	32	85	13762	1002	5	133	148	0	2	2012	
1	28	84	15463	1507	0	97	54	0	2	2013	
...	10	51	1409	2	19	3	4	0	...	2000	Brésil
0	63	60	4343	0	9	102	4	0	...	2010	
...	55	52	4950	2	40	86	6	...	...	2011	
...	19	55	4410	2	5	61	5	...	...	2012	
...	25	58	6271	1	0	27	1	...	...	2013	
61	211	220	915	884	182	1183	811	14	54	2000	Asie orientale
47	1674	2079	6821	2856	1141	2281	6196	57	19	2010	
78	1345	3042	9273	3363	1195	2899	7906	80	6	2011	
60	2342	2547	8240	2630	831	2688	9221	79	4	2012	
59	1811	2690	7764	3001	781	2688	9367	79	11	2013	
4	12	62	80	180	31	651	60	1	...	2000	Chine
13	358	1151	1817	324	587	746	529	8	...	2010	
21	456	1661	3198	354	764	980	729	9	...	2011	
20	644	1392	3011	364	736	1090	1136	12	...	2012	
32	588	1592	3296	326	684	1235	852	11	...	2013	
0	8	22	21	0	80	11	15	0	0	2000	Asie méridionale
9	556	797	592	27	665	524	682	2	19	2010	
4	432	1146	787	9	845	296	444	17	3	2011	
1	647	1264	1056	14	600	279	748	2	1	2012	
8	661	1834	1555	23	674	354	794	3	0	2013	
0	6	7	52	25	7	329	37	2	1	2000	Asie Sud-est
1	118	236	904	143	166	3545	1777	37	11	2010	
1	73	301	774	155	248	3790	1667	34	9	2011	
2	57	335	414	134	193	5132	978	15	8	2012	
1	75	434	576	146	223	4814	1620	18	12	2013	
41	66	12	1	13	7	7	356	0	29	2000	Asie occidentale
137	540	56	42	214	80	6	1009	0	570	2010	
166	420	51	59	163	37	11	859	0	492	2011	
116	421	32	109	307	43	12	584	1	374	2012	
94	703	262	146	278	81	17	1230	1	47	2013	
...	...	0	...	...	...	...	...	0	0	2000	Océanie
...	0	0	...	...	...	0	...	1	...	2010	
...	...	0	0	1	...	0	...	1	...	2011	
...	...	0	0	1	0	0	0	1	...	2012	
...	...	0	0	0	...	0	0	2	...	2013	

Voir la fin du tableau pour la remarque générale et les notes.

World exports by provenance and destination (Table D)

In million U.S. dollars f.o.b.

Exports from	Year	World 1/ Monde 1/	Developed economies 2/ Economies développées 2/ Total	Asia-Pacific Asie-Pacifique Total	Japan Japon	Europe Total	Germany Allemagne	North America Amérique du Nord Total	U.S.A. É.-U.	Commonwealth of Independent States Communauté d'Etats Indépendants Total	Europe

Other manufactured goods (SITC, Rev. 3, 6 and 8)

Exports from	Year	World 1/ Monde 1/	Total	Total	Japan Japon	Total	Germany Allemagne	Total	U.S.A. É.-U.	Total	Europe
World 1/	2000	1641266	1159258	104784	84829	682377	138235	372098	313624	20345	16876
	2010	3582193	2141304	186090	134958	1401176	266547	554038	460267	103327	77876
	2011	4238026	2510185	225418	164500	1655880	328673	628887	524491	130360	100485
	2012	4197838	2397046	228477	164794	1514562	295565	654007	544950	144833	108332
	2013	4341742	2459624	224125	158826	1562859	304821	672640	564490	156890	116660
Developed Economies - Asia-Pacific 2/	2000	102599	42208	5325	1930	13668	3644	23215	22048	218	166
	2010	180417	48864	8658	2578	18325	4602	21880	20362	1193	1073
	2011	202382	55526	9783	2709	21359	5461	24384	22862	1596	1409
	2012	193567	52417	8681	2262	18856	4631	24880	23275	1791	1576
	2013	173628	47225	7925	1912	16830	4196	22470	21191	1958	1691
Japan	2000	89968	35395	1375	.	12381	3478	21639	20559	215	164
	2010	158209	37908	2275	.	16136	4341	19497	18145	1170	1053
	2011	175765	42915	2857	.	18436	5102	21622	20288	1570	1388
	2012	169612	40877	2419	.	16047	4291	22411	20965	1758	1548
	2013	150188	36108	2206	.	13763	3882	20139	19011	1917	1655
Developed Economies - Europe 2/	2000	677388	570924	17788	13204	486970	100870	66166	60944	9402	8645
	2010	1332253	1049595	26146	17135	939207	183541	84242	75992	39924	35789
	2011	1582377	1239881	31268	20048	1110057	225048	98556	88990	50596	45452
	2012	1469570	1131632	31159	20356	1000080	201265	100392	91185	50827	45733
	2013	1532853	1172484	30765	19644	1038739	210429	102980	94060	53307	48129
France	2000	69667	58683	2212	1860	50245	11675	6226	5461	431	384
	2010	115937	89980	2840	2158	79945	18313	7194	6270	1865	1616
	2011	132032	102415	3133	2414	91096	21417	8186	7156	2184	1927
	2012	122238	93794	3239	2516	82103	18912	8453	7501	2090	1822
	2013	125318	95725	3011	2256	83404	19290	9310	8385	2034	1777
Germany	2000	127887	107652	3018	2157	93679	.	10955	10095	2264	2096
	2010	294261	233565	5534	3540	209229	.	18802	17236	10230	9440
	2011	350521	275161	6258	3977	246130	.	22773	20866	13956	12938
	2012	320428	247237	6263	3992	218314	.	22661	20817	13363	12337
	2013	329832	253443	6392	3998	223660	.	23391	21468	13164	12045
Developed Economies - North America 2/	2000	222921	151023	16851	14088	39474	6253	94699	51858	395	318
	2010	322578	197787	18905	13682	62716	10024	116167	54495	1205	1020
	2011	359125	216257	21115	14834	67752	10945	127390	59900	1589	1345
	2012	365432	217214	21700	14977	67770	10615	127744	57121	1770	1475
	2013	372360	216787	21110	14739	68972	10593	126705	57140	1983	1689
United States	2000	165174	95373	15874	13228	36670	5947	42829	.	349	279
	2010	253278	135531	17789	12912	56103	9621	61640	.	1050	896
	2011	282720	147894	19825	13963	60606	10437	67464	.	1376	1170
	2012	293130	152491	20515	14278	61378	10174	70599	.	1535	1276
	2013	301013	152796	20019	14021	63242	10152	69535	.	1721	1464
South-Eastern Europe	2000	10591	8971	17	13	8305	1808	648	582	177	149
	2010	32726	24899	30	15	24335	5269	534	423	1004	948
	2011	41958	31879	41	21	31072	7157	766	565	1535	1465
	2012	37877	28158	56	31	27311	6019	792	659	1580	1484
	2013	40750	30622	67	42	29743	7075	811	681	1912	1791
Commonwealth of Independent States	2000	31237	16352	1249	1245	12213	2077	2890	2792	5106	3958
	2010	85822	37944	1773	1741	31862	4771	4309	4212	16790	13059
	2011	104271	44851	2492	2437	37647	6154	4713	4593	23212	18333
	2012	113302	46611	3093	3029	38201	6463	5317	5150	32069	22017
	2013	105178	41180	2184	2150	33922	4856	5074	4851	32612	21058
Russian Federation	2000	20412	12932	1181	1179	9588	1460	2163	2115	1350	486
	2010	46785	27025	1139	1125	22607	2859	3280	3222	4384	2607
	2011	52746	30518	1337	1321	25771	3652	3410	3344	5416	3217
	2012	62069	33585	1816	1802	27549	3993	4219	4104	12759	6202
	2013	59661	30260	1623	1608	24529	3517	4108	3933	13818	6067

For general note and footnotes see end of table

Exportations mondiales par provenance et destination (Tableau D)

En millions de dollars E.-U. f.o.b.

← Exportations vers

South-Eastern Europe Europe du Sud-est	Northern Africa Afrique septentrio- nale	Sub-Saharan Africa Afrique du Nord	Latin America and the Caribbean Amérique latine et Caraïbes	Eastern Asia Asie orientale	Southern Asia Asie méridionale	South-eastern Asia Asie du Sud-est	Western Asia Asie occidentale	Oceania Océanie	Others 4/ Autre 4/	Année	Exportations en provenance de ↓

Articles manufacturés divers (CTCI, Rev. 3, 6 et 8)

South-Eastern Europe	Northern Africa	Sub-Saharan Africa	Latin America	Eastern Asia	Southern Asia	South-eastern Asia	Western Asia	Oceania	Others 4/	Année	Exportations en provenance de
9845	13595	17979	87015	180668	22572	66774	56703	1638	4874	2000	Monde 1/
33811	44646	70033	188214	483270	118152	194266	193738	2834	8597	2010	
41486	44147	86664	225594	566002	143599	234471	240736	3636	11148	2011	
37970	49315	93871	235224	581347	135745	260360	249356	3876	8896	2012	
40504	52160	100066	232727	594399	148122	284454	260726	3352	8718	2013	
20	205	719	2343	37315	1498	15120	2101	435	418	2000	Economies Développées -
60	537	1409	5395	80658	4370	32242	4812	789	86	2010	Asie-Pacifique 2/
131	553	1598	6527	87891	5021	36854	5638	972	74	2011	
101	515	1613	6608	79752	4662	38722	6333	986	66	2012	
58	505	1720	5794	71537	4131	34392	5311	934	63	2013	
18	201	563	2211	34439	1304	13567	1972	83	...	2000	Japon
56	447	1070	5100	75492	3867	28614	4402	84	...	2010	
127	432	1222	5962	81699	4458	32089	5174	119	...	2011	
94	444	1219	6270	74958	4178	33679	6009	125	...	2012	
53	458	1427	5536	65841	3675	30103	4968	103	...	2013	
7697	8470	6123	12081	19788	7926	7751	23530	367	3329	2000	Economies Développées -
23657	21452	16457	25426	58260	23441	17082	52694	608	3659	2010	Europe 2/
28615	21765	18561	30036	74677	29772	20850	63059	681	3882	2011	
26241	22225	19309	31233	74950	25172	21570	62717	667	3026	2012	
28285	23435	19993	32113	80359	25731	23749	69275	632	3489	2013	
431	2476	1193	1051	1971	424	652	2111	235	8	2000	France
1256	4412	2727	2157	5337	1410	1585	4723	427	59	2010	
1485	4573	2769	2475	6750	1725	1950	5177	459	71	2011	
1327	4296	2611	2475	6849	1430	1831	5000	429	106	2012	
1457	4304	2529	2677	7290	1121	2049	5541	438	151	2013	
1524	1044	1070	2787	3817	904	1667	3434	15	1709	2000	Allemagne
4677	2296	2844	6843	15304	4146	4275	10048	26	7	2010	
5805	2228	3309	7917	19607	4585	5044	12349	47	514	2011	
5227	2177	3169	7964	19372	4249	5132	12105	35	397	2012	
5598	2116	3258	8323	20710	3512	5658	13445	36	569	2013	
60	697	1043	43277	13811	979	6732	4841	63	0	2000	Economies Développées -
193	1332	2433	57873	32238	6795	9143	13464	113	0	2010	Amérique du Nord 2/
274	1119	2811	65930	35746	8490	9934	16863	112	1	2011	
230	939	2868	70987	36442	7138	10319	17387	137	0	2012	
273	914	3218	73048	37926	8477	10891	18720	123	0	2013	
53	641	1002	42513	13143	880	6514	4643	61	...	2000	Etats-Unis
155	1162	2248	55711	29736	6200	8681	12699	104	...	2010	
225	958	2534	63442	33108	7668	9475	15940	100	...	2011	
201	855	2650	68471	34203	6462	9857	16281	123	...	2012	
241	788	2767	70753	35852	7729	10381	17874	112	...	2013	
587	85	31	84	67	31	17	523	0	19	2000	Europe du Sud-est
3295	385	71	116	388	155	50	2356	1	5	2010	
4182	443	113	123	688	224	69	2693	1	8	2011	
3801	378	72	217	1041	167	82	2374	1	7	2012	
3919	464	101	242	925	136	119	2285	1	26	2013	
568	688	262	560	3651	1049	876	2122	1	1	2000	Communauté d'Etats
1437	1245	641	1296	6474	6023	2487	11470	2	12	2010	Indépendants
2085	1145	994	1260	7666	6441	2380	14130	6	101	2011	
1378	1550	881	1218	8285	4407	2069	14805	11	18	2012	
1314	1897	892	1251	7160	3373	1680	13795	7	17	2013	
171	319	145	381	2710	817	484	1103	0	0	2000	Fédération de Russie
405	539	142	752	3113	3980	1477	4960	1	6	2010	
575	542	295	677	3452	4431	1111	5632	5	92	2011	
401	620	206	820	3807	3263	1177	5412	8	10	2012	
364	578	251	974	3694	2459	1028	6220	6	9	2013	

Voir la fin du tableau pour la remarque générale et les notes.

World exports by provenance and destination (Table D)

In million U.S. dollars f.o.b.

Exports from	Year	World 1/ Monde 1/	Developed economies 2/ Economies développées 2/ Total	Asia-Pacific Asie-Pacifique Total	Japan Japon	Europe Total	Germany Allemagne	North America Amérique du Nord Total	U.S.A. É.-U.	Commonwealth of Independent States Communauté d'Etats Indépendants Total	Europe
Other manufactured goods (SITC, Rev. 3, 6 and 8) [cont.]											
Northern Africa	2000	8011	7227	27	23	6791	787	409	394	9	1
	2010	18797	13010	39	23	11805	1050	1166	1125	43	37
	2011	20748	14554	47	29	13172	1368	1335	1283	72	64
	2012	19247	12712	43	27	11494	1132	1175	1125	79	68
	2013	19135	12527	44	28	11304	1148	1178	1134	56	48
Sub-Saharan Africa	2000	17928	12653	827	689	9791	618	2035	1919	8	8
	2010	58283	31555	4931	4648	21091	1965	5533	5233	44	40
	2011	63865	35701	5477	5234	24872	1949	5352	5077	60	37
	2012	58591	30301	3669	3443	21888	1548	4743	4619	53	49
	2013	60330	30633	3795	3617	22336	1512	4501	4385	57	48
South Africa	2000	8588	5284	678	552	3444	452	1162	1062	2	2
	2010	29664	16909	4663	4443	8684	1758	3562	3401	35	32
	2011	32144	18397	5332	5128	9437	1737	3628	3548	32	29
	2012	26761	13811	3507	3314	7064	1273	3241	3148	48	45
	2013	26688	13642	3479	3327	7211	1154	2952	2895	46	41
Latin America and the Caribbean	2000	73163	54744	1743	1546	7992	869	45009	44202	21	18
	2010	147634	81772	2675	1901	17664	1589	61434	59478	162	106
	2011	170161	95845	3701	2676	20836	2557	71308	69187	168	130
	2012	161004	96537	3280	1909	16933	1958	76324	74043	230	169
	2013	158370	96943	2535	1633	14929	1539	79480	77233	247	198
Brazil	2000	14499	8863	718	645	3358	408	4787	4533	8	8
	2010	28042	12730	1080	972	6271	783	5379	5094	71	69
	2011	33680	16075	1245	1123	7568	1520	7262	6967	78	75
	2012	31396	14816	1147	1004	6138	1082	7532	7240	81	76
	2013	29425	13887	1075	959	5460	688	7352	7132	123	115
Eastern Asia	2000	327649	186360	44289	38458	52386	11301	89685	83791	3013	2361
	2010	940184	444611	89711	70579	172557	34162	182343	167050	35100	21524
	2011	1132164	521670	111623	88227	204689	43046	205358	187688	41240	26472
	2012	1216845	532585	115174	89383	197109	38493	220302	201449	44722	29094
	2013	1279477	540772	111528	84861	200264	38111	228981	209512	51991	34731
China	2000	128535	77216	24867	22355	20229	4200	32120	30105	2412	1835
	2010	625981	327004	63780	49539	127609	25454	135615	123705	32280	19139
	2011	778133	390775	80877	63216	155043	32934	154855	140951	37699	23515
	2012	867950	403342	84995	64685	149864	30304	168483	153282	40976	25940
	2013	940873	418387	83632	62737	156205	30521	178549	162603	48012	31473
Southern Asia	2000	44120	30005	1628	1130	13744	2800	14634	13743	844	507
	2010	132931	63617	2887	1607	35398	7021	25332	23535	1191	525
	2011	168660	81383	3734	1990	46881	9744	30768	28439	1569	769
	2012	162313	77414	4022	1988	42589	8853	30804	28411	1539	866
	2013	175364	88213	4288	2177	48439	9839	35486	32848	1744	1058
South-Eastern Asia	2000	84399	51745	13529	11297	16406	3163	21810	20787	149	129
	2010	201399	96528	26775	20431	32449	5676	37304	35266	993	801
	2011	239089	110643	32242	25407	35778	6899	42624	40273	1327	1158
	2012	240231	114217	34586	26661	34269	7259	45363	42790	1206	1104
	2013	253606	120873	36295	27239	36032	7690	48546	45812	1350	1220
Western Asia	2000	39467	25848	855	695	14221	4036	10772	10440	1005	615
	2010	124757	48170	1002	426	33437	6877	13730	13035	5677	2952
	2011	148704	59067	1374	636	41441	8344	16252	15556	7396	3849
	2012	156289	55274	1318	575	37854	7328	16102	15053	8967	4696
	2013	166692	58934	1445	647	41133	7833	16356	15575	9670	4999
Oceania	2000	1794	1197	656	510	417	10	125	124	0	0
	2010	4412	2951	2559	193	329	1	63	62	0	0
	2011	4524	2928	2523	253	324	1	81	81	0	0
	2012	3571	1973	1696	154	209	0	69	69	0	0
	2013	3998	2430	2145	136	214	1	70	70	0	0

For general note and footnotes see end of table

Exportations mondiales par provenance et destination (Tableau D)

En millions de dollars E.-U. f.o.b.

← Exportations vers

South-Eastern Europe / Europe du Sud-est	Northern Africa / Afrique septentrio-nale	Sub-Saharan Africa / Afrique du Nord	Latin America and the Caribbean / Amérique latine et Caraïbes	Eastern Asia / Asie orientale	Southern Asia / Asie méridionale	South-eastern Asia / Asie du Sud-est	Western Asia / Asie occidentale	Oceania / Océanie	Others 4/ / Autre 4/	Année	Exportations en provence de ↓

Articles manufacturés divers (CTCI, Rev. 3, 6 et 8) [suite]

South-Eastern Europe	Northern Africa	Sub-Saharan Africa	Latin America and the Caribbean	Eastern Asia	Southern Asia	South-eastern Asia	Western Asia	Oceania	Others 4/	Année	Exportations en provence de
3	260	107	17	41	7	19	220	0	101	2000	Afrique du Nord
27	1686	856	69	314	167	54	2398	0	174	2010	
36	1314	961	116	242	138	37	3093	0	185	2011	
46	2052	959	101	269	135	71	2658	1	164	2012	
47	1871	963	127	225	105	28	3000	0	186	2013	
4	27	2568	356	1038	165	407	678	2	21	2000	Afrique subsaharienne
13	160	13831	962	7154	1261	677	2264	32	331	2010	
25	116	15311	716	7236	895	739	2585	31	450	2011	
105	139	14740	664	7666	890	795	2919	29	290	2012	
108	92	15349	460	7569	989	1090	3647	23	313	2013	
3	13	1049	305	958	119	333	516	2	3	2000	Afrique du sud
3	60	6893	565	3136	544	524	976	6	13	2010	
15	34	7571	561	3399	539	598	984	5	8	2011	
25	30	7523	517	2760	371	588	1031	25	33	2012	
25	29	7337	389	3236	292	626	1019	20	28	2013	
3	120	282	14131	2642	131	503	509	3	73	2000	Amérique latine et Caraïbes
35	490	975	39401	20866	631	2106	1077	7	113	2010	
95	293	1265	45687	22196	496	2444	1494	10	168	2011	
50	217	1241	39175	19183	480	2386	1353	9	145	2012	
77	225	1187	37350	18164	448	2048	1563	6	111	2013	
2	74	154	4157	696	61	275	209	1	...	2000	Brésil
25	135	610	9528	2969	349	1190	430	4	...	2010	
26	128	812	11234	3254	294	1287	487	5	0	2011	
21	83	811	10933	2683	260	1276	427	4	0	2012	
28	94	729	9891	2964	169	1044	493	4	0	2013	
368	1508	3791	11711	84941	5973	19780	9557	543	104	2000	Asie orientale
1956	9304	22721	48547	214838	39075	80463	42881	675	11	2010	
2521	9818	29648	63372	255387	49624	101920	56130	823	12	2011	
2626	12481	37712	72223	278744	46967	123913	63866	986	20	2012	
2611	13172	40454	69124	289864	53424	146252	70856	939	19	2013	
252	860	1960	4095	31066	1530	5081	4019	44	...	2000	Chine
1649	8052	20740	37600	91341	24777	48711	33401	426	...	2010	
2146	8783	27432	52006	120597	31158	63766	43271	498	1	2011	
2302	11369	35470	60165	146825	31429	85415	50004	653	...	2012	
2289	12145	38256	57486	161532	38170	106964	57025	605	...	2013	
19	274	1257	647	4309	1173	1428	4134	24	4	2000	Asie méridionale
162	1116	4248	3095	18450	7214	4828	28477	40	491	2010	
231	1330	5786	4076	20390	7996	6237	37035	54	2574	2011	
233	1450	5711	4539	21011	8235	5917	35695	63	507	2012	
277	1480	6913	5069	24399	8902	7776	29961	67	562	2013	
27	349	1149	1281	10611	2213	13341	3351	176	8	2000	Asie Sud-est
100	1101	3013	4713	34049	7380	43194	9836	451	40	2010	
165	1094	4671	5805	43920	8978	50356	11136	855	137	2011	
115	1222	3440	6038	41604	8493	51972	10920	865	140	2012	
136	1115	3449	6019	45488	8812	53992	11650	521	200	2013	
488	911	631	252	2185	1423	796	5134	0	793	2000	Asie occidentale
2877	5838	3348	1317	9272	21629	1912	22006	60	2651	2010	
3126	5157	4911	1945	9572	25511	2619	26877	25	2498	2011	
3046	6146	5285	2220	12044	28976	2524	28327	56	3425	2012	
3397	6991	5768	2128	10528	33562	2413	30657	32	2612	2013	
1	...	15	275	268	4	5	2	24	2	2000	Océanie
0	0	30	3	308	10	27	2	56	1026	2010	
0	...	34	2	391	13	32	1	66	1057	2011	
0	0	40	2	358	23	20	3	64	1089	2012	
0	0	59	3	256	34	24	5	67	1121	2013	

Voir la fin du tableau pour la remarque générale et les notes.

World exports by provenance and destination (Table D)

In million U.S. dollars f.o.b.

Exports from	Year	World 1/ Monde 1/	Developed economies 2/ Economies développées 2/	Asia-Pacific Asie-Pacifique Total	Japan Japon	Europe Total	Germany Allemagne	North America Amérique du Nord Total	U.S.A. É.-U.	Commonwealth of Independent States Communauté d'Etats Indépendants Total	Europe
World 1/	2000	165829	81475	6531	4737	55465	10709	19479	15311	2410	2073
	2010	259786	109263	9703	7008	72642	14289	26918	22527	9713	6796
	2011	302047	125668	12004	8855	84059	16948	29605	24813	12017	8490
	2012	290799	116421	11691	8541	74314	14839	30416	25580	13157	9445
	2013	313815	124453	12013	8579	80110	15935	32330	27426	14078	10342
Developed Economies - Asia-Pacific 2/	2000	7516	1628	247	9	697	153	685	637	10	10
	2010	7590	1506	313	5	629	132	563	533	15	14
	2011	8606	1694	331	5	753	166	609	576	23	22
	2012	8345	1575	303	4	664	143	607	575	22	22
	2013	7326	1465	291	5	632	150	542	510	25	25
Japan	2000	7023	1334	56	.	656	151	621	582	10	10
	2010	7086	1137	32	.	601	127	504	480	15	14
	2011	8035	1280	26	.	722	160	532	506	23	22
	2012	7820	1210	27	.	641	141	543	518	22	22
	2013	6843	1124	23	.	613	148	488	463	25	25
Developed Economies - Europe 2/	2000	57057	45239	1016	712	41014	7949	3209	2886	930	910
	2010	65944	48536	939	587	44914	8979	2682	2323	2048	1976
	2011	75520	55286	1070	681	51286	10345	2931	2529	2465	2368
	2012	67703	48826	1054	696	44836	9061	2936	2585	2497	2398
	2013	71963	52146	1096	691	47972	9617	3078	2723	2751	2629
France	2000	6607	4840	95	69	4436	911	309	284	43	42
	2010	5684	3649	61	39	3382	645	206	188	77	70
	2011	6092	3890	72	45	3610	692	208	188	105	98
	2012	5360	3408	68	44	3121	611	219	200	79	71
	2013	5448	3484	69	45	3187	611	228	213	78	67
Germany	2000	11037	8356	127	72	7783	.	446	409	308	302
	2010	13245	9705	195	121	9015	.	494	448	498	477
	2011	15695	11454	197	115	10681	.	576	524	598	568
	2012	13889	10056	184	111	9300	.	572	522	564	534
	2013	14443	10416	181	104	9618	.	617	566	563	530
Developed Economies - North America 2/	2000	13157	6733	440	284	1449	194	4844	2013	27	23
	2010	14064	5871	426	228	1347	265	4099	1668	36	34
	2011	15805	6283	457	243	1428	278	4398	1786	44	42
	2012	15480	6340	505	282	1335	260	4501	1811	39	37
	2013	15910	6341	585	342	1393	253	4362	1707	72	67
United States	2000	10952	4618	424	279	1362	184	2832	.	24	21
	2010	12157	4110	407	225	1273	252	2430	.	34	32
	2011	13781	4415	440	239	1364	270	2611	.	41	40
	2012	13462	4466	489	276	1287	256	2690	.	36	34
	2013	14004	4575	573	337	1348	249	2654	.	69	65
South-Eastern Europe	2000	410	299	3	2	270	57	27	23	27	26
	2010	1585	1298	2	0	1278	215	18	17	84	81
	2011	1928	1595	1	1	1579	273	14	13	106	104
	2012	1790	1462	2	1	1447	245	14	12	103	101
	2013	2043	1634	2	1	1615	283	17	15	122	120
Commonwealth of Independent States	2000	1283	502	15	15	424	67	63	61	542	499
	2010	2298	538	4	3	497	121	37	35	1064	972
	2011	2463	521	4	3	494	129	23	22	1426	1281
	2012	2751	444	5	4	426	102	13	12	1698	1393
	2013	3056	469	6	4	449	99	14	13	1813	1483
Russian Federation	2000	394	237	0	0	208	21	29	28	97	65
	2010	230	85	1	1	80	24	4	3	92	67
	2011	282	100	1	0	96	31	4	3	109	80
	2012	426	78	2	1	74	32	2	2	294	168
	2013	453	89	2	2	83	28	4	4	314	178

Textile yarn and fabrics (SITC, Rev. 3, 65)

For general note and footnotes see end of table

Exportations mondiales par provenance et destination (Tableau D)

En millions de dollars E.-U. f.o.b.

South-Eastern Europe Europe du Sud-est	Northern Africa Afrique septentrio-nale	Sub-Saharan Africa Afrique du Nord	Latin America and the Caribbean Amérique latine et Caraïbes	Eastern Asia Asie orientale	Southern Asia Asie méridionale	South-eastern Asia Asie du Sud-est	Western Asia Asie occidentale	Oceania Océanie	Others 4/ Autre 4/	Année	Exportations en provence de ↓
2510	3580	3439	11575	34984	5146	10757	8694	473	785	2000	Monde 1/
4752	7566	9207	20830	40252	15962	24088	17210	177	765	2010	
5805	8629	11616	25161	42537	18753	30287	20629	199	745	2011	
5469	8634	11335	24205	40986	18218	31908	19440	202	825	2012	
6032	9064	12289	24252	43474	21050	37140	21053	196	734	2013	
1	5	32	64	4333	137	933	291	81	0	2000	Economies Développées -
5	13	45	55	4137	161	1230	380	43	0	2010	Asie-Pacifique 2/
9	15	60	50	4537	195	1591	379	52	0	2011	
9	17	52	59	4227	199	1712	425	47	0	2012	
10	15	37	49	3513	200	1555	412	43	1	2013	
1	4	27	60	4271	122	877	287	31	...	2000	Japon
4	13	40	51	4100	154	1196	376	2	...	2010	
9	15	55	45	4497	188	1546	374	3	...	2011	
9	17	44	54	4189	192	1661	420	3	...	2012	
10	14	33	44	3485	191	1507	407	2	...	2013	
2155	2672	551	758	1586	276	585	1898	20	388	2000	Economies Développées -
3563	3590	916	1027	2456	540	683	2442	20	124	2010	Europe 2/
4413	3829	1065	1207	2813	677	803	2815	20	127	2011	
4017	3345	1081	1237	2622	572	778	2599	18	110	2012	
4320	3383	1151	1193	2735	577	813	2740	18	136	2013	
169	943	98	69	148	19	56	214	8	0	2000	France
290	1000	118	72	169	43	67	185	13	0	2010	
335	1071	147	65	168	34	79	184	12	0	2011	
292	895	158	74	157	38	73	174	12	0	2012	
307	865	184	76	156	30	83	170	12	1	2013	
800	355	69	100	180	58	132	386	3	290	2000	Allemagne
930	309	171	211	504	120	203	592	1	0	2010	
1158	346	179	249	583	165	240	720	1	1	2011	
1021	277	156	257	563	128	225	637	1	2	2012	
1092	307	163	249	625	141	238	645	1	4	2013	
8	18	57	5245	627	65	181	194	4	0	2000	Economies Développées -
3	15	63	6291	1150	142	255	234	4	...	2010	Amérique du Nord 2/
5	24	65	7526	1228	156	266	200	7	0	2011	
5	17	69	7211	1163	123	310	199	3	0	2012	
9	16	67	7454	1320	125	295	207	5	0	2013	
6	16	49	5209	607	64	173	183	4	...	2000	Etats-Unis
3	13	59	6243	1093	136	245	220	1	...	2010	
5	21	61	7464	1171	151	256	192	4	...	2011	
5	14	64	7141	1120	119	301	193	2	...	2012	
8	13	62	7381	1284	122	286	198	5	...	2013	
49	3	3	2	4	2	0	19	...	3	2000	Europe du Sud-est
107	12	1	2	10	5	3	62	0	2	2010	
117	14	1	2	10	7	3	69	0	4	2011	
109	17	1	6	11	3	2	72	0	2	2012	
141	13	1	10	10	6	3	103	0	0	2013	
10	1	3	4	78	32	4	106	0	0	2000	Communauté d'Etats
20	5	3	8	186	42	1	430	0	0	2010	Indépendants
22	14	3	6	141	47	4	278	0	1	2011	
19	13	5	16	283	39	4	229	0	1	2012	
32	8	4	9	380	39	9	293	0	0	2013	
3	1	3	3	30	10	1	8	...	...	2000	Fédération de Russie
4	0	2	5	14	12	1	14	0	0	2010	
5	8	3	3	16	21	1	15	...	1	2011	
3	7	4	2	7	19	1	9	...	1	2012	
3	0	2	2	6	21	3	12	...	0	2013	

Fils et tissus de matières textiles (CTCI, Rev. 3, 65)

Voir la fin du tableau pour la remarque générale et les notes.

World exports by provenance and destination (Table D)

In million U.S. dollars f.o.b.

| Exports from | Year | World 1/ Monde 1/ | Developed economies 2/ Economies développées 2/ | | | | | | | Commonwealth of Independent States Communauté d'Etats Indépendants | |
| | | | Total | Asia-Pacific Asie-Pacifique | | Europe | | North America Amérique du Nord | | | |
				Total	Japan Japon	Total	Germany Allemagne	Total	U.S.A. É.-U.	Total	Europe

Textile yarn and fabrics (SITC, Rev. 3, 65) [cont.]

Exports from	Year	World 1/ Monde 1/	Total	Total	Japan Japon	Total	Germany Allemagne	Total	U.S.A. É.-U.	Total	Europe
Northern Africa	2000	688	592	2	0	502	41	87	84	0	0
	2010	2075	1545	16	8	1239	88	290	267	12	12
	2011	2405	1785	17	9	1460	130	309	286	17	17
	2012	2144	1533	17	10	1233	101	283	259	19	18
	2013	2267	1575	17	8	1273	104	285	262	11	11
Sub-Saharan Africa	2000	669	310	18	3	234	31	58	54	1	1
	2010	1206	209	25	4	136	12	48	39	2	2
	2011	1419	255	25	5	188	18	42	31	1	1
	2012	1436	394	26	5	331	77	38	36	1	1
	2013	1358	281	24	3	237	54	20	19	2	1
South Africa	2000	237	122	15	1	71	10	36	33	1	1
	2010	415	111	23	3	69	9	19	17	2	2
	2011	448	106	23	4	64	7	19	17	0	0
	2012	426	96	23	2	56	8	18	16	0	0
	2013	425	93	22	2	54	14	17	15	1	0
Latin America and the Caribbean	2000	4607	2826	69	52	233	52	2524	2417	1	1
	2010	5727	2197	26	19	191	29	1981	1912	3	3
	2011	6319	2272	31	22	224	30	2017	1949	2	2
	2012	5857	2315	31	20	203	26	2082	2022	3	3
	2013	6049	2542	30	18	209	23	2303	2237	3	3
Brazil	2000	895	373	46	41	122	26	205	182	0	0
	2010	1094	295	18	16	64	14	213	209	2	2
	2011	1108	182	20	18	58	10	104	98	2	2
	2012	996	162	15	14	49	7	98	93	2	2
	2013	949	167	15	13	53	7	98	93	2	2
Eastern Asia	2000	54516	10743	3254	2639	3564	615	3925	3460	429	318
	2010	108902	27995	5926	4699	11138	2028	10931	9926	4583	2259
	2011	129100	32633	7415	5912	12999	2528	12219	11095	5709	2871
	2012	128276	32154	7253	5741	12236	2396	12665	11525	6286	3463
	2013	139568	33586	7120	5579	13023	2638	13443	12239	6679	3923
China	2000	16135	5077	2059	1786	1618	349	1400	1233	208	115
	2010	76871	24106	4987	3939	9780	1787	9338	8473	4303	2079
	2011	94411	28145	6281	4958	11448	2242	10416	9446	5414	2689
	2012	95450	27765	6205	4855	10760	2126	10800	9822	5985	3282
	2013	106578	29289	6159	4769	11498	2359	11632	10576	6377	3748
Southern Asia	2000	11712	6651	579	351	3506	843	2565	2305	167	112
	2010	23801	10536	561	237	5598	1150	4377	4078	288	196
	2011	27870	12670	782	391	6863	1481	5026	4671	314	226
	2012	27244	11537	735	325	5655	1141	5147	4793	333	254
	2013	31562	13370	859	346	6619	1278	5892	5483	355	275
South-Eastern Asia	2000	8304	2841	843	650	1157	142	842	760	8	7
	2010	13645	3540	1362	1172	1284	224	894	827	45	42
	2011	15740	4257	1728	1519	1505	304	1023	952	57	54
	2012	14766	3902	1616	1388	1254	249	1032	960	55	52
	2013	16147	4441	1814	1514	1415	276	1213	1118	51	49
Western Asia	2000	5834	3096	33	20	2415	565	648	610	268	166
	2010	12936	5487	98	46	4391	1046	999	901	1531	1205
	2011	14864	6412	137	65	5281	1265	994	904	1853	1501
	2012	14999	5931	137	63	4694	1038	1099	991	2102	1703
	2013	16553	6598	166	69	5272	1160	1160	1101	2194	1756
Oceania	2000	76	15	13	0	1	0	1	1	...	...
	2010	14	5	5	0	1	0	0	0	0	...
	2011	9	5	5	0	0	0	0	0	...	...
	2012	10	6	5	0	0	0	0	0	...	...
	2013	11	5	4	0	0	0	0	0	...	...

For general note and footnotes see end of table

Exportations mondiales par provenance et destination (Tableau D)

En millions de dollars E.-U. f.o.b.

South-Eastern Europe Europe du Sud-est	Northern Africa Afrique septentrionale	Sub-Saharan Africa Afrique du Nord	Latin America and the Caribbean Amérique latine et Caraïbes	Eastern Asia Asie orientale	Southern Asia Asie méridionale	South-eastern Asia Asie du Sud-est	Western Asia Asie occidentale	Oceania Océanie	Others 4/ Autre 4/	Année	Exportations en provence de ↓
Fils et tissus de matières textiles (CTCI, Rev. 3, 65) [suite]

South-Eastern Europe	Northern Africa	Sub-Saharan Africa	Latin America and the Caribbean	Eastern Asia	Southern Asia	South-eastern Asia	Western Asia	Oceania	Others 4/	Année	Exportations en provence de
2	9	7	3	10	1	1	35	0	28	2000	Afrique du Nord
3	71	53	29	15	24	5	288	0	30	2010	
3	66	68	38	14	18	6	340	0	49	2011	
4	100	44	25	13	29	8	318	...	51	2012	
3	95	55	32	14	33	7	392	0	49	2013	
0	1	273	24	19	7	12	16	0	7	2000	Afrique subsaharienne
0	7	707	184	14	11	21	38	1	11	2010	
0	7	1025	18	13	14	6	45	1	33	2011	
7	3	913	21	14	14	11	33	1	22	2012	
9	2	927	10	22	20	10	46	1	30	2013	
0	0	61	22	11	4	8	9	0	0	2000	Afrique du sud
0	1	275	5	1	4	1	12	0	1	2010	
0	1	322	5	1	1	1	9	0	0	2011	
0	0	308	6	1	2	1	10	0	1	2012	
0	0	305	9	1	1	2	11	0	2	2013	
0	5	8	1539	188	4	10	16	0	9	2000	Amérique latine et Caraïbes
4	7	20	3383	62	9	19	10	1	13	2010	
6	10	25	3887	57	8	25	12	1	14	2011	
5	6	23	3351	92	7	30	11	0	13	2012	
6	4	20	3341	60	13	28	14	0	17	2013	
0	2	5	497	7	1	1	8	0	...	2000	Brésil
4	4	15	746	11	2	11	3	0	...	2010	
6	5	20	868	8	2	15	2	0	...	2011	
4	2	19	779	8	2	14	3	0	...	2012	
6	2	17	725	13	5	10	2	...	...	2013	
69	396	1406	3285	24870	3212	6889	2826	309	80	2000	Asie orientale
241	1972	5344	7345	26749	9640	18072	6907	54	1	2010	
359	2435	6925	9503	27728	11788	23123	8828	68	1	2011	
393	2752	6990	9368	25403	11467	24737	8650	75	0	2012	
465	2987	7473	9336	26486	13437	29596	9444	79	0	2013	
30	152	702	739	6310	865	1228	807	17	...	2000	Chine
208	1793	4995	6040	11418	8059	10539	5372	38	...	2010	
313	2225	6524	8103	12351	9970	14168	7146	52	...	2011	
344	2509	6600	8031	11648	9617	15772	7124	54	...	2012	
410	2771	7107	8071	13088	11480	19991	7941	53	...	2013	
9	188	649	303	1483	537	361	1356	7	1	2000	Asie méridionale
53	620	1235	1442	2461	3046	841	3089	13	177	2010	
69	854	1656	1716	2698	3267	972	3464	14	174	2011	
65	874	1462	1717	3810	3326	1004	2894	15	206	2012	
68	803	1708	1721	5065	3851	1190	3188	15	228	2013	
3	62	323	298	1675	576	1744	724	48	0	2000	Asie Sud-est
13	253	527	873	2699	1135	2881	1636	35	8	2010	
19	312	407	992	3033	1235	3354	2012	31	32	2011	
20	337	389	925	2963	1060	3186	1883	30	15	2012	
25	310	460	873	3532	1155	3470	1781	30	18	2013	
203	219	127	49	56	296	38	1214	0	269	2000	Asie occidentale
741	1001	293	191	312	1206	75	1694	4	400	2010	
784	1048	315	217	263	1340	132	2188	1	311	2011	
815	1152	306	268	383	1378	125	2126	9	404	2012	
944	1428	386	221	337	1595	161	2435	0	254	2013	
1	...	0	1	57	0	0	...	3	0	2000	Océanie
0	...	0	0	0	3	1	0	4	0	2010	
0	...	0	0	0	0	0	0	4	0	2011	
0	...	0	0	0	0	0	0	4	0	2012	
0	...	0	2	0	0	0	0	4	0	2013	

Voir la fin du tableau pour la remarque générale et les notes.

World exports by provenance and destination (Table D)

In million U.S. dollars f.o.b.

Exports from	Year	World 1/ Monde 1/	Developed economies 2/ Economies développées 2/	Asia-Pacific Asie-Pacifique Total	Japan Japon	Europe Total	Germany Allemagne	North America Amérique du Nord Total	U.S.A. É.-U.	Commonwealth of Independent States Communauté d'Etats Indépendants Total	Europe
World 1/	2000	140147	88375	4448	3400	61340	12136	22587	17437	2280	1686
	2010	416633	205907	12393	8453	153140	31634	40374	29527	12920	9865
	2011	516938	264441	16787	12297	195399	42371	52254	39259	18748	14618
	2012	478251	232555	15286	10199	162875	34589	54394	40983	20294	13345
	2013	448515	216862	12269	7971	156033	32712	48559	36695	20409	12445
Developed Economies - Asia-Pacific 2/	2000	15647	2932	406	32	693	64	1833	1594	46	28
	2010	43548	5018	879	36	1387	155	2751	2425	369	332
	2011	48242	6178	969	32	1691	165	3517	3242	519	429
	2012	44882	5939	813	13	1421	147	3705	3376	455	364
	2013	39901	4839	770	10	1039	125	3030	2785	473	335
Japan	2000	14833	2510	259	.	609	63	1642	1415	46	28
	2010	41974	4247	577	.	1281	153	2389	2087	369	332
	2011	46578	5318	634	.	1585	164	3098	2850	518	429
	2012	43789	5389	500	.	1389	146	3501	3186	452	362
	2013	38868	4304	477	.	998	124	2829	2604	471	334
Developed Economies - Europe 2/	2000	65514	57580	425	200	51823	11073	5332	4610	512	433
	2010	160965	128011	847	359	119657	26900	7507	6560	3393	3082
	2011	202636	161996	1140	490	151035	35593	9821	8525	4912	4342
	2012	177083	138817	1196	473	127104	29267	10518	9316	3249	2907
	2013	169803	133211	1103	405	123454	28883	8655	7653	3045	2700
France	2000	8850	7853	52	22	6883	1841	919	756	12	7
	2010	16198	13051	71	51	12373	3661	607	543	219	213
	2011	19405	15543	82	54	14685	4606	776	674	270	252
	2012	16947	13467	83	48	12667	3668	717	620	140	132
	2013	16099	12480	53	31	11769	3666	657	593	112	105
Germany	2000	13445	11343	64	32	10039	.	1240	1071	122	109
	2010	31731	25394	117	40	23567	.	1710	1444	910	838
	2011	39417	31600	193	71	29127	.	2280	1959	1628	1547
	2012	34761	27394	260	81	24675	.	2459	2164	675	610
	2013	32792	26045	321	52	23691	.	2034	1761	528	440
Developed Economies - North America 2/	2000	9535	7205	206	169	749	146	6250	3071	30	21
	2010	24250	16177	261	146	1763	312	14153	6151	61	51
	2011	27867	18107	305	152	2111	344	15691	6556	72	51
	2012	28410	18100	343	162	1887	313	15871	6603	77	50
	2013	26762	16640	276	137	1668	277	14696	5995	93	75
United States	2000	6319	4075	195	161	701	142	3179	.	29	21
	2010	17198	9803	220	132	1580	306	8002	.	57	50
	2011	20323	11331	257	135	1939	338	9135	.	65	47
	2012	20817	11286	289	152	1728	309	9268	.	73	46
	2013	19881	10445	242	128	1503	271	8701	.	85	71
South-Eastern Europe	2000	1634	1069	0	0	864	148	205	174	24	16
	2010	5366	2816	3	1	2575	531	238	160	104	99
	2011	7009	3719	4	1	3377	695	337	193	276	272
	2012	5288	2598	6	1	2300	434	292	216	140	130
	2013	4843	2434	4	2	2191	474	239	162	156	142
Commonwealth of Independent States	2000	11626	3308	60	58	2128	356	1120	1045	1614	1176
	2010	39702	14228	748	733	11825	2108	1654	1624	6279	4729
	2011	50327	18965	1228	1209	15586	2903	2151	2106	9290	7148
	2012	48456	17518	1383	1354	13982	2342	2153	2067	11962	7656
	2013	42140	14558	711	704	11926	1533	1922	1795	11754	6753
Russian Federation	2000	6146	2251	40	40	1537	288	674	639	379	91
	2010	18570	8473	193	191	7376	1143	904	894	1715	1003
	2011	21816	10647	197	194	9180	1514	1270	1258	2287	1289
	2012	23310	10450	224	222	8818	1096	1408	1352	5245	2418
	2013	21017	8641	217	213	7207	929	1217	1102	5584	2131

Iron and steel (SITC, Rev. 3, 67)

For general note and footnotes see end of table

Exportations mondiales par provenance et destination (Tableau D)

En millions de dollars E.-U. f.o.b.

← Exportations vers

South-Eastern Europe Europe du Sud-est	Northern Africa Afrique septentrio-nale	Sub-Saharan Africa Afrique du Nord	Latin America and the Caribbean Amérique latine et Caraïbes	Eastern Asia Asie orientale	Southern Asia Asie méridionale	South-eastern Asia Asie du Sud-est	Western Asia Asie occidentale	Oceania Océanie	Others 4/ Autre 4/	Année	Exportations en provence de ↓
				Fer et acier (CTCI, Rev. 3, 67)							
994	1777	1605	6631	20633	2612	9017	5865	107	252	2000	Monde 1/
5048	9049	8894	25262	57363	21294	37846	31212	354	1485	2010	
6940	8624	11796	29816	64436	23606	47047	39310	750	1424	2011	
5680	9686	11834	30960	55402	20364	49458	40226	617	1177	2012	
5784	9773	13220	29314	51146	15503	48054	37676	337	437	2013	
1	57	172	704	7099	468	3634	479	54	0	2000	Economies Développées -
11	127	492	2085	20638	1985	11160	1533	102	29	2010	Asie-Pacifique 2/
81	114	537	2127	21267	2376	12821	2059	157	6	2011	
45	102	561	2084	17561	2075	13100	2814	145	0	2012	
9	178	815	2169	15349	1966	11875	2103	118	7	2013	
1	57	159	651	6971	456	3517	460	6	...	2000	Japon
11	126	470	1978	20469	1972	10871	1452	7	...	2010	
81	113	521	2010	21188	2350	12469	1976	34	...	2011	
44	99	547	2035	17508	2056	12864	2770	24	...	2012	
8	178	804	2129	15289	1958	11639	2076	11	...	2013	
341	776	525	1186	1286	685	658	1760	20	185	2000	Economies Développées -
2544	4266	1888	3787	4529	3121	1653	6771	33	969	2010	Europe 2/
3215	4606	2072	4229	5789	3419	2543	8885	64	908	2011	
2909	5251	2214	4617	4918	2870	3180	8439	52	567	2012	
3019	5025	2038	3996	5567	1880	3325	8640	38	18	2013	
11	180	92	150	146	82	80	230	13	0	2000	France
102	406	299	289	467	351	123	877	13	1	2010	
153	310	291	309	625	526	254	1110	14	...	2011	
115	507	327	261	523	456	146	990	15	0	2012	
138	411	230	308	704	236	109	1357	15	1	2013	
50	111	101	317	441	233	141	422	0	163	2000	Allemagne
273	326	280	835	1408	848	333	1123	0	0	2010	
353	253	337	931	1758	764	444	1337	14	0	2011	
323	317	331	995	1568	1039	661	1453	3	3	2012	
299	204	298	887	1762	514	917	1335	0	3	2013	
1	23	40	1681	254	80	139	82	2	0	2000	Economies Développées -
16	97	227	4931	1092	477	666	492	15	...	2010	Amérique du Nord 2/
43	190	232	6383	1241	442	547	597	14	...	2011	
14	58	372	7313	993	433	420	605	23	...	2012	
21	86	365	7124	1065	353	401	609	4	...	2013	
1	22	39	1642	239	62	132	77	2	...	2000	Etats-Unis
8	86	211	4575	1030	341	625	448	15	...	2010	
26	177	215	5935	1137	348	532	544	13	...	2011	
10	52	365	6847	918	293	395	556	22	...	2012	
19	72	351	6736	976	234	372	587	4	...	2013	
101	19	1	58	47	19	12	279	0	3	2000	Europe du Sud-est
1013	173	23	29	99	79	11	1019	0	0	2010	
1402	158	60	21	205	68	8	1091	0	0	2011	
1221	111	8	91	258	54	12	793	0	0	2012	
1207	92	18	75	142	52	18	633	...	16	2013	
472	586	207	428	2221	552	787	1448	1	0	2000	Communauté d'Etats
875	1016	555	893	3078	4488	2128	6161	1	0	2010	Indépendants
1313	815	805	736	3544	4849	1916	8066	5	23	2011	
734	1184	752	688	3462	2604	1737	7807	10	0	2012	
695	1604	699	837	2626	1469	1119	6772	6	...	2013	
122	235	103	271	1360	377	403	644	...	0	2000	Fédération de Russie
105	337	81	474	1857	2631	1194	1701	1	...	2010	
156	244	139	237	2013	2988	725	2351	5	23	2011	
108	299	110	400	1976	1636	913	2165	7	0	2012	
73	327	88	633	1911	711	507	2536	6	...	2013	

Voir la fin du tableau pour la remarque générale et les notes.

World exports by provenance and destination (Table D)

In million U.S. dollars f.o.b.

Exports from	Year	World 1/ Monde 1/	Developed economies 2/ Économies développées 2/	Asia-Pacific Asie-Pacifique Total	Asia-Pacific Japan Japon	Europe Total	Europe Germany Allemagne	North America Amérique du Nord Total	North America U.S.A. É.-U.	Commonwealth of Independent States Communauté d'Etats Indépendants Total	Commonwealth of Independent States Europe

Iron and steel (SITC, Rev. 3, 67) [cont.]

Exports from	Year	World 1/ Monde 1/	Total	Total	Japan Japon	Total	Germany Allemagne	Total	U.S.A. É.-U.	Total	Europe
Northern Africa	2000	331	201	8	8	185	5	8	5	7	0
	2010	1517	510	3	3	504	22	2	2	16	16
	2011	1849	496	0	0	492	13	3	2	27	27
	2012	1564	388	0	0	376	36	11	11	22	22
	2013	1357	292	0	0	288	1	4	4	9	9
Sub-Saharan Africa	2000	3026	1814	315	284	941	101	557	487	1	1
	2010	8840	3797	587	512	2360	525	849	813	18	17
	2011	8918	3425	531	471	2031	406	862	849	12	12
	2012	7743	3024	409	360	1712	396	904	890	15	15
	2013	7332	2506	382	353	1378	274	745	720	28	27
South Africa	2000	2758	1709	275	245	877	81	557	486	1	1
	2010	7997	3633	578	503	2230	506	825	788	18	17
	2011	7927	3293	528	468	1927	389	838	828	11	11
	2012	6699	2899	407	359	1611	380	881	868	15	15
	2013	6213	2473	381	353	1356	274	736	711	27	27
Latin America and the Caribbean	2000	8156	5017	176	162	1351	109	3490	3186	3	1
	2010	19120	7909	442	422	2329	232	5138	4754	65	16
	2011	24611	11935	509	486	3526	802	7900	7393	57	31
	2012	21760	10854	446	429	2698	536	7710	7200	103	57
	2013	19598	10078	430	420	1980	141	7668	7401	106	75
Brazil	2000	3633	2261	145	137	716	89	1400	1273	0	0
	2010	8893	3367	336	334	1340	125	1690	1570	7	7
	2011	12539	6417	384	381	2442	754	3591	3453	3	3
	2012	11149	5965	377	373	1800	479	3788	3654	6	6
	2013	9025	5093	350	348	1342	104	3401	3332	44	43
Eastern Asia	2000	17592	6217	2503	2249	1136	38	2577	2213	29	6
	2010	76943	19069	7007	5411	6427	461	5635	4814	2047	1310
	2011	102068	28429	10434	8627	9608	828	8387	7126	2681	1834
	2012	97144	24786	8647	6721	7063	600	9075	7778	3169	1635
	2013	93939	21831	6611	5144	6818	561	8402	7320	3735	1867
China	2000	4391	1673	627	597	385	12	661	566	17	3
	2010	39565	8944	2747	1959	3889	307	2307	1801	1639	1000
	2011	55462	14334	4557	3581	6186	625	3590	2795	2104	1382
	2012	53833	11441	3270	2272	4436	439	3735	2964	2596	1188
	2013	54689	9653	2191	1546	4017	378	3445	2820	3135	1438
Southern Asia	2000	1591	787	51	44	308	25	428	361	3	0
	2010	11756	3763	426	389	2071	199	1266	1209	117	75
	2011	12057	4182	291	229	2455	308	1436	1330	232	133
	2012	12243	3936	479	255	2043	257	1414	1308	257	172
	2013	13907	4400	409	319	2728	232	1263	1166	246	186
South-Eastern Asia	2000	2644	947	227	127	284	22	435	385	1	1
	2010	10624	1987	1004	267	571	41	412	359	145	58
	2011	13350	2770	1124	367	754	60	892	807	222	192
	2012	14322	3251	1424	310	658	65	1169	1048	57	52
	2013	12605	2758	1444	375	566	29	748	642	78	54
Western Asia	2000	2481	1072	6	3	748	49	319	275	9	3
	2010	13311	2223	22	11	1486	149	715	602	305	79
	2011	17149	3768	30	10	2553	254	1185	1059	449	148
	2012	18675	3026	22	2	1493	196	1511	1110	788	284
	2013	15775	3028	33	10	1870	182	1125	990	687	223
Oceania	2000	371	227	65	63	130	1	32	32	...	...
	2010	690	399	162	162	183	...	54	54	...	...
	2011	853	471	221	221	178	0	72	72	...	...
	2012	682	317	118	116	138	0	61	61	...	...
	2013	556	287	95	93	129	0	62	62	...	...

For general note and footnotes see end of table

Exportations mondiales par provenance et destination (Tableau D)

En millions de dollars E.-U. f.o.b.

← Exportations vers

South-Eastern Europe Europe du Sud-est	Northern Africa Afrique septentrio-nale	Sub-Saharan Africa Afrique du Nord	Latin America and the Caribbean Amérique latine et Caraïbes	Eastern Asia Asie orientale	Southern Asia Asie méridionale	South-eastern Asia Asie du Sud-est	Western Asia Asie occidentale	Oceania Océanie	Others 4/ Autre 4/	Année	Exportations en provenance de ↓
						Fer et acier (CTCI, Rev. 3, 67) [suite]					
0	72	12	0	5	0	5	28	...	1	2000	Afrique du Nord
0	287	83	2	1	37	17	560	0	4	2010	
4	286	94	5	3	4	9	916	0	5	2011	
1	419	119	4	1	2	41	561	1	6	2012	
7	215	99	12	3	1	0	712	0	7	2013	
0	2	298	164	424	75	131	116	0	2	2000	Afrique subsaharienne
1	23	2060	322	1859	283	207	265	1	4	2010	
11	18	2431	279	1996	251	245	245	2	4	2011	
8	6	2309	239	1377	177	246	330	2	8	2012	
9	15	2404	181	1676	121	216	171	0	5	2013	
0	2	190	164	408	74	131	79	0	1	2000	Afrique du sud
1	22	1451	303	1827	274	203	261	1	3	2010	
11	11	1627	271	1983	238	239	238	2	1	2011	
0	5	1443	227	1374	163	240	326	1	6	2012	
1	10	1387	153	1667	111	211	168	0	4	2013	
0	65	94	1935	646	50	199	147	0	1	2000	Amérique latine et Caraïbes
2	313	352	6150	2744	326	909	345	0	5	2010	
23	182	544	7314	2839	231	1010	470	2	4	2011	
17	125	408	6569	2133	208	913	423	3	4	2012	
38	131	483	5782	1542	112	594	730	0	2	2013	
...	39	21	666	383	21	160	81	0	...	2000	Brésil
0	26	117	2503	1776	232	773	91	0	...	2010	
0	48	203	2817	1907	161	840	142	0	...	2011	
0	13	87	2690	1323	155	790	119	0	...	2012	
4	18	133	2117	918	46	495	158	...	...	2013	
51	40	81	341	7803	343	2191	481	14	0	2000	Asie orientale
190	953	1732	6014	19673	7157	14626	5383	97	2	2010	
286	718	2570	7320	24147	8530	19705	7571	110	0	2011	
227	784	2754	7687	20642	7926	21429	7618	120	3	2012	
266	786	3742	7483	20153	6487	21837	7511	108	1	2013	
15	12	35	62	1717	81	581	196	0	...	2000	Chine
95	688	1506	3623	8988	4076	6671	3271	63	...	2010	
170	552	2281	4697	13121	4386	9220	4539	59	...	2011	
126	619	2457	4969	11607	4122	11452	4366	78	...	2012	
179	648	3354	5150	11491	3640	12623	4748	67	...	2013	
1	6	114	27	136	136	167	213	0	0	2000	Asie méridionale
48	101	744	433	1379	1651	492	2936	1	91	2010	
64	90	1013	408	1451	1496	955	1969	2	196	2011	
77	104	944	575	1094	1606	1095	2445	1	109	2012	
68	151	1288	650	1260	1694	1710	2361	0	78	2013	
0	14	10	30	423	126	1012	68	14	0	2000	Asie Sud-est
1	88	210	107	1186	734	5554	512	99	0	2010	
3	43	225	170	1352	838	6777	546	390	13	2011	
1	45	204	146	1737	1102	7048	469	257	4	2012	
4	58	295	98	1449	609	6662	533	58	2	2013	
26	118	48	78	151	73	83	763	...	59	2000	Asie occidentale
347	1606	498	510	835	950	420	5235	1	380	2010	
494	1405	1181	823	268	1093	509	6894	1	265	2011	
426	1497	1148	947	924	1286	235	7921	1	475	2012	
442	1431	944	906	112	731	293	6900	1	301	2013	
0	...	0	...	138	4	0	...	1	0	2000	Océanie
...	...	30	0	250	6	2	0	3	...	2010	
...	...	31	0	335	10	2	...	4	0	2011	
...	...	39	0	301	20	2	...	3	...	2012	
...	...	30	0	202	28	4	...	4	0	2013	

Voir la fin du tableau pour la remarque générale et les notes.

World exports by provenance and destination (Table D)

In million U.S. dollars f.o.b.

| Exports from | Year | World 1/ Monde 1/ | Developed economies 2/ Economies développées 2/ | | | | | | | Commonwealth of Independent States Communauté d'Etats Indépendants | |
| | | | | Asia-Pacific Asie-Pacifique | | Europe | | North America Amérique du Nord | | | |
			Total	Total	Japan Japon	Total	Germany Allemagne	Total	U.S.A. É.-U.	Total	Europe

Non-ferrous metals (SITC, Rev. 3, 68)

Exports from	Year	World 1/ Monde 1/	Total	Total (A-P)	Japan Japon	Total (Eur)	Germany Allemagne	Total (NA)	U.S.A. É.-U.	Total (CIS)	Europe
World 1/	2000	112704	79471	8866	8228	50017	9556	20588	17562	801	711
	2010	330458	192412	21457	16671	130205	26369	40751	35354	2434	2078
	2011	403430	237193	27150	21666	158666	33155	51377	44712	3646	3164
	2012	364203	207421	19889	15704	141774	27608	45758	39646	4264	3718
	2013	347831	191935	18624	14245	130510	26806	42802	37152	3770	3091
Developed Economies - Asia-Pacific 2/	2000	10460	3592	1685	1488	878	175	1029	984	18	3
	2010	24571	4890	2498	2084	1309	213	1084	1049	11	6
	2011	28122	5580	2604	2162	1542	200	1434	1399	12	10
	2012	26033	5460	2047	1695	2027	156	1387	1353	9	7
	2013	24702	4865	1758	1425	1909	158	1199	1159	5	5
Japan	2000	4854	990	31	.	348	105	612	588	18	3
	2010	14365	1385	26	.	631	191	728	718	8	4
	2011	15291	1726	25	.	801	177	900	883	5	3
	2012	14920	1995	25	.	1072	147	898	878	4	3
	2013	13893	1751	28	.	836	143	887	857	3	2
Developed Economies - Europe 2/	2000	45180	40165	1546	1395	34148	8196	4471	4289	307	296
	2010	109177	91908	1911	1574	83113	21025	6883	6183	898	832
	2011	136995	112961	2907	1856	100762	26221	9293	8470	1141	1050
	2012	119916	98061	1587	1298	89280	21751	7194	6571	960	907
	2013	114569	90325	1412	1055	83001	21040	5911	5423	928	858
France	2000	3859	3505	50	43	3256	922	198	183	7	6
	2010	6573	5297	62	37	4901	1532	334	314	27	25
	2011	8083	6659	94	66	6159	1762	406	379	35	29
	2012	6847	5494	74	64	5003	1391	417	383	35	32
	2013	6680	5422	67	52	4974	1447	382	353	19	15
Germany	2000	10368	8668	319	266	7379	.	969	912	122	119
	2010	26283	21234	381	283	18842	.	2012	1912	373	332
	2011	33280	26258	396	295	23161	.	2701	2574	414	389
	2012	28407	22290	345	254	19800	.	2144	2032	352	336
	2013	27582	21570	299	216	18914	.	2357	2212	326	295
Developed Economies - North America 2/	2000	16445	12861	1067	1006	2325	298	9469	6794	8	8
	2010	32402	22422	1439	1294	4742	996	16241	12508	12	10
	2011	39902	27717	1745	1591	5470	1160	20503	15781	21	16
	2012	35725	23959	1442	1296	5211	1031	17306	12890	24	11
	2013	34436	23002	1370	1200	4345	777	17287	13345	40	19
United States	2000	8272	5132	729	685	1728	289	2675	.	8	8
	2010	15918	8025	977	845	3316	979	3733	.	11	10
	2011	19439	9539	1235	1114	3583	1053	4721	.	17	12
	2012	19051	9000	1040	944	3545	975	4415	.	23	10
	2013	17818	7852	1010	862	2900	735	3941	.	38	17
South-Eastern Europe	2000	1376	1092	3	3	1069	73	21	13	9	8
	2010	4525	3073	1	0	3041	548	31	26	77	77
	2011	6417	4581	3	0	4513	1069	66	55	133	132
	2012	5480	3629	5	0	3549	622	75	63	116	116
	2013	5701	3933	4	0	3866	1113	63	53	115	115
Commonwealth of Independent States	2000	9320	7842	1129	1128	5567	411	1146	1142	423	372
	2010	23933	16028	915	910	13106	1468	2007	1995	903	758
	2011	26813	16486	1101	1093	13455	1789	1929	1923	1668	1468
	2012	30413	18525	1483	1480	14851	2026	2192	2190	2495	2212
	2013	25885	16027	1177	1175	12691	1700	2159	2152	1927	1567
Russian Federation	2000	8137	7079	1096	1095	4927	283	1056	1053	76	32
	2010	17655	13817	848	843	11128	1180	1841	1838	333	217
	2011	17985	13790	1014	1008	11160	1448	1616	1614	457	328
	2012	20028	15862	1405	1403	12515	1874	1942	1941	909	712
	2013	17818	14075	1134	1131	10930	1605	2011	2009	924	673

For general note and footnotes see end of table

Exportations mondiales par provenance et destination (Tableau D)

En millions de dollars E.-U. f.o.b.

South-Eastern Europe Europe du Sud-est	Northern Africa Afrique septentrio-nale	Sub-Saharan Africa Afrique du Nord	Latin America and the Caribbean Amérique latine et Caraïbes	Eastern Asia Asie orientale	Southern Asia Asie méridionale	South-eastern Asia Asie du Sud-est	Western Asia Asie occidentale	Oceania Océanie	Others 4/ Autre 4/	Année	← Exportations vers Exportations en provence de ↓
						Metaux non ferreux (CTCI, Rev. 3, 68)					
318	428	759	4412	16503	1304	5747	2522	19	420	2000	Monde 1/
2361	2815	2575	12944	72535	6526	22007	13201	45	603	2010	
3105	3153	3427	16947	80870	10497	25709	17228	68	1586	2011	
2778	3099	3072	15902	75135	8195	24820	18004	91	1423	2012	
2844	3100	3297	14525	72591	11316	26657	15852	78	1866	2013	
0	2	81	51	4508	135	1964	99	8	0	2000	Economies Développées -
1	74	66	95	12945	431	5809	228	21	0	2010	Asie-Pacifique 2/
1	113	66	364	14485	501	6688	290	22	0	2011	
2	51	106	153	12315	394	7233	287	22	0	2012	
1	35	52	88	12508	301	6630	204	13	0	2013	
0	2	14	32	2576	49	1118	53	0	...	2000	Japon
1	7	9	58	9063	138	3580	115	0	...	2010	
1	8	12	60	9638	163	3552	127	0	...	2011	
1	7	16	54	8788	171	3684	200	0	...	2012	
1	6	11	50	8037	142	3785	107	0	...	2013	
187	297	223	563	1498	423	395	759	6	356	2000	Economies Développées -
1500	1666	411	1221	6062	1474	1225	2426	11	375	2010	Europe 2/
1994	1966	542	1437	8257	3257	1581	2953	14	893	2011	
1819	1856	577	1315	8519	1833	1335	2905	15	722	2012	
2015	1808	573	1293	8229	3273	1771	3276	11	1066	2013	
3	74	32	24	88	9	35	77	3	3	2000	France
31	230	81	62	327	45	111	356	7	1	2010	
35	266	86	81	428	46	83	334	8	23	2011	
32	263	99	70	345	80	90	317	8	14	2012	
40	263	95	79	301	53	93	293	7	15	2013	
35	55	73	308	433	56	152	207	0	259	2000	Allemagne
383	261	133	696	1436	339	695	732	1	0	2010	
505	255	156	778	2089	368	869	1096	3	489	2011	
472	168	158	709	2051	342	692	798	2	372	2012	
496	139	162	636	1684	275	811	948	2	532	2013	
2	6	186	1752	1153	21	258	198	1	0	2000	Economies Développées -
6	10	41	4699	4158	196	478	379	1	...	2010	Amérique du Nord 2/
7	20	82	5853	4554	270	532	843	2		2011	
13	29	55	6039	4175	226	482	720	1	0	2012	
11	18	41	6087	3787	242	510	695	4	...	2013	
2	5	185	1692	870	17	176	185	1	...	2000	Etats-Unis
6	9	40	4359	2651	141	340	335	1	...	2010	
7	19	71	5453	3063	171	403	695	2	...	2011	
13	29	53	5689	3090	159	357	637	1	...	2012	
10	18	34	5782	2894	146	402	639	2	...	2013	
94	19	2	20	7	4	2	125	...	3	2000	Europe du Sud-est
446	75	5	3	163	1	19	663	0	0	2010	
480	128	5	4	293	1	25	767	...	0	2011	
398	80	4	3	577	0	26	646	...	0	2012	
332	104	4	3	552	3	57	598	0	0	2013	
11	0	6	79	696	25	19	217	...	0	2000	Communauté d'Etats
172	5	3	129	2587	115	101	3889	0	...	2010	Indépendants
282	9	7	265	3307	80	44	4665	0	0	2011	
224	93	6	223	3354	168	44	5281	0	0	2012	
160	53	9	150	2816	201	55	4485	0	...	2013	
4	0	6	73	678	21	18	181	...	...	2000	Fédération de Russie
152	1	2	104	741	36	63	2406	...	...	2010	
259	6	4	251	851	46	13	2308	...	0	2011	
147	74	4	207	755	128	21	1922	...	0	2012	
134	41	8	131	612	185	47	1660	0	...	2013	

Voir la fin du tableau pour la remarque générale et les notes.

World exports by provenance and destination (Table D)

In million U.S. dollars f.o.b.

Exports from	Year	World 1/ Monde 1/	Developed economies 2/ Economies développées 2/							Commonwealth of Independent States Communauté d'Etats Indépendants	
			Total	Asia-Pacific Asie-Pacifique		Europe		North America Amérique du Nord			
				Total	Japan Japon	Total	Germany Allemagne	Total	U.S.A. É.-U.	Total	Europe

Non-ferrous metals (SITC, Rev. 3, 68) [cont.]

Exports from	Year	World 1/ Monde 1/	Total	Total	Japan Japon	Total	Germany Allemagne	Total	U.S.A. É.-U.	Total	Europe
Northern Africa	2000	266	214	8	8	202	4	4	4	0	0
	2010	1639	814	5	4	787	83	21	21	0	...
	2011	1832	1052	9	9	994	128	49	49	...	...
	2012	1545	873	6	6	831	107	36	36	...	...
	2013	1183	710	8	8	688	70	14	14	0	0
Sub-Saharan Africa	2000	2282	1367	315	311	913	32	139	130	0	0
	2010	22158	15797	4077	4055	9487	774	2233	2220	14	14
	2011	26480	19238	4728	4703	12146	916	2364	2352	10	10
	2012	22584	14639	3054	3038	9811	637	1774	1733	9	9
	2013	23840	15750	3232	3221	10759	747	1760	1750	4	4
South Africa	2000	1209	526	246	242	169	7	110	102	0	0
	2010	11926	10031	3913	3896	4006	712	2112	2102	9	9
	2011	13877	11804	4652	4637	4931	889	2221	2209	8	8
	2012	10163	8207	2939	2928	3525	582	1742	1702	8	8
	2013	10956	8717	2953	2943	4106	601	1657	1647	4	4
Latin America and the Caribbean	2000	11193	7835	1142	1135	3436	170	3257	3236	2	2
	2010	41292	18409	1645	1182	8537	239	8226	7732	0	0
	2011	49062	24301	2522	1860	10144	388	11635	11139	0	0
	2012	42138	20794	2138	1107	7251	264	11405	10957	2	2
	2013	37841	17690	1470	869	5918	165	10302	9662	2	2
Brazil	2000	1757	1477	391	388	735	11	350	348	1	1
	2010	2668	1784	538	536	904	26	341	338	0	0
	2011	3169	2101	619	617	1099	56	383	380	0	0
	2012	2444	1447	502	501	609	52	336	331	1	1
	2013	2598	1247	483	482	461	33	302	299	0	0
Eastern Asia	2000	9406	2290	965	854	672	75	653	593	9	8
	2010	38324	10106	4008	3123	3081	419	3016	2663	383	317
	2011	50251	13710	5812	5151	5193	614	2705	2205	479	401
	2012	46165	12434	4332	3773	5470	421	2632	2210	459	372
	2013	44180	10880	4119	3534	3919	439	2841	2406	530	434
China	2000	3363	1340	563	498	500	29	278	252	6	5
	2010	17945	6939	2296	1543	2235	332	2408	2178	369	308
	2011	23480	7809	2837	2313	3178	390	1793	1535	453	379
	2012	21694	6084	1953	1519	2309	294	1822	1520	437	352
	2013	22655	6419	1992	1561	2384	307	2042	1724	512	421
Southern Asia	2000	499	100	4	2	64	18	32	29	4	3
	2010	8363	422	82	63	277	22	64	55	6	5
	2011	6341	441	91	68	254	26	97	88	9	3
	2012	5738	276	30	11	144	18	101	96	3	2
	2013	6461	384	47	31	189	35	148	139	13	1
South-Eastern Asia	2000	3876	1079	769	683	160	9	150	140	3	2
	2010	15282	3935	2494	2346	756	158	685	654	8	8
	2011	19468	5554	3231	3044	1445	118	879	835	9	7
	2012	15703	3840	2058	1845	868	100	914	830	17	16
	2013	17567	3507	1846	1523	825	64	836	787	14	14
Western Asia	2000	2401	1033	232	215	585	96	216	209	18	9
	2010	6396	2215	122	36	1834	425	259	248	121	50
	2011	9447	3279	232	128	2621	526	425	415	163	67
	2012	11263	3440	269	154	2429	475	742	716	168	64
	2013	9492	2897	284	204	2331	496	281	262	190	72
Oceania	2000	1	0	0	...	0	...	0	0	...	...
	2010	2396	2393	2260	0	133	0	0	0	...	...
	2011	2300	2293	2166	0	127	0	0	0	...	...
	2012	1500	1493	1440	0	53	0	0	0	...	...
	2013	1974	1965	1896	0	70	0	.	.	...	...

For general note and footnotes see end of table

Exportations mondiales par provenance et destination (Tableau D)

En millions de dollars E.-U. f.o.b.

← Exportations vers

South-Eastern Europe Europe du Sud-est	Northern Africa Afrique septentrionale	Sub-Saharan Africa Afrique du Nord	Latin America and the Caribbean Amérique latine et Caraïbes	Eastern Asia Asie orientale	Southern Asia Asie méridionale	South-eastern Asia Asie du Sud-est	Western Asia Asie occidentale	Oceania Océanie	Others 4/ Autre 4/	Année	Exportations en provence de
				Metaux non ferreux (CTCI, Rev. 3, 68) [suite]							
0	18	2	0	2	0	11	19	...	0	2000	Afrique du Nord
9	166	135	2	48	15	7	442	...	1	2010	
9	126	60	3	46	12	6	515	...	1	2011	
19	134	47	2	30	22	5	411	...	3	2012	
2	138	42	3	36	13	4	231	...	4	2013	
0	1	174	82	425	10	145	78	0	0	2000	Afrique subsaharienne
0	60	865	203	4200	234	286	499	0	0	2010	
1	24	1154	159	4549	247	293	672	4	129	2011	
0	75	730	176	5298	373	278	983	22	2	2012	
0	28	904	98	5051	378	516	1095	14	1	2013	
0	0	40	48	394	9	143	49	0	0	2000	Afrique du sud
...	9	157	154	1146	98	255	67	0	0	2010	
0	4	172	131	1247	149	272	90	0	0	2011	
0	4	134	154	1207	91	260	75	22	2	2012	
0	4	133	93	1386	100	338	166	14	1	2013	
0	7	17	1784	1242	13	58	210	...	23	2000	Amérique latine et Caraïbes
3	67	43	5662	16223	48	476	358	...	2	2010	
29	16	33	6242	17159	31	669	581	0	0	2011	
0	4	49	5326	14805	74	566	517	...	1	2012	
3	11	88	4995	14092	117	454	388	0	2	2013	
...	3	10	207	17	6	13	23	...	...	2000	Brésil
1	16	34	497	244	5	15	72	...	...	2010	
0	8	26	695	250	7	37	46	...	...	2011	
0	1	40	726	190	6	12	23	...	0	2012	
0	8	78	615	622	7	3	19	...	...	2013	
2	6	25	68	5432	289	1123	160	1	0	2000	Asie orientale
29	218	651	820	17559	1919	5491	1142	6	0	2010	
45	231	991	2335	20517	3335	6933	1668	9	...	2011	
41	259	1012	2297	18379	2216	7449	1610	9	0	2012	
50	259	1115	1245	16308	2892	9280	1604	15	1	2013	
2	2	15	21	1541	32	352	52	0	...	2000	Chine
28	169	589	753	5320	738	2145	891	5	...	2010	
44	188	885	2242	6683	996	2910	1263	8	...	2011	
40	226	881	2178	5895	1009	3629	1309	7	...	2012	
48	229	1009	1139	5460	1078	5407	1348	7	...	2013	
0	3	10	1	97	55	126	104	0	0	2000	Asie méridionale
0	7	156	29	4638	455	1219	1427	0	2	2010	
5	52	194	48	2762	421	864	1541	0	4	2011	
7	31	202	134	2999	397	494	1192	0	4	2012	
33	32	203	330	3063	371	1036	996	0	0	2013	
1	5	17	5	1015	259	1430	61	1	0	2000	Asie Sud-est
0	54	85	62	3304	962	6487	378	4	1	2010	
0	49	128	82	4463	1143	7422	611	5	3	2011	
1	47	86	70	3993	1052	6121	465	8	3	2012	
6	45	79	87	5594	1904	5930	392	6	1	2013	
20	65	16	6	428	70	217	491	0	36	2000	Asie occidentale
193	411	113	17	648	677	409	1369	0	222	2010	
251	419	165	154	478	1200	653	2122	8	555	2011	
253	440	198	163	686	1441	788	2988	9	690	2012	
231	568	187	146	551	1620	414	1886	11	791	2013	
...	...	0	...	0	...	...	...	0	0	2000	Océanie
...	...	...	1	0	0	0	...	1	...	2010	
...	...	0	1	1	0	1	0	5	...	2011	
...	...	...	0	3	0	1	0	4	...	2012	
...	...	0	...	4	0	0	0	4	0	2013	

Voir la fin du tableau pour la remarque générale et les notes.

World exports by provenance and destination (Table D)

In million U.S. dollars f.o.b.

| Exports from | Year | World 1/ Monde 1/ | Developed economies 2/ Economies développées 2/ | | | | | North America Amérique du Nord | | Commonwealth of Independent States Communauté d'Etats Indépendants | |
| | | | Total | Asia-Pacific Asie-Pacifique | | Europe | | | | | |
				Total	Japan Japon	Total	Germany Allemagne	Total	U.S.A. É.-U.	Total	Europe
Other manufactured metal products (SITC, Rev. 3, 691-695, 699 and 812)											
World 1/	2000	117510	88500	4453	3151	57073	12703	26975	19396	1305	990
	2010	280330	179233	13063	8289	126728	26472	39441	29630	9874	7772
	2011	335366	215757	16063	10179	153693	33661	46001	34712	12413	9847
	2012	337232	210171	16988	10568	141885	31290	51297	38951	14247	10951
	2013	354918	220338	18699	10749	149338	33241	52301	39992	15288	11715
Developed Economies - Asia-Pacific 2/	2000	6630	2982	252	23	861	168	1870	1762	8	6
	2010	12506	3652	489	36	1276	251	1888	1748	47	38
	2011	13855	4107	532	33	1435	298	2140	2028	82	71
	2012	14502	4587	501	31	1467	302	2619	2458	110	99
	2013	12824	3927	446	31	1206	260	2275	2159	147	133
Japan	2000	6114	2675	70	.	820	162	1785	1692	8	5
	2010	11289	3086	105	.	1186	236	1795	1666	44	36
	2011	12495	3468	110	.	1333	283	2026	1930	76	68
	2012	13126	3962	97	.	1366	285	2500	2353	105	96
	2013	11524	3359	78	.	1115	244	2166	2062	139	128
Developed Economies - Europe 2/	2000	59895	52072	900	547	47121	10410	4051	3602	740	634
	2010	137634	108809	1877	943	100468	21080	6464	5681	4720	4204
	2011	164539	131673	2182	1134	121612	26498	7879	6837	5796	5231
	2012	153482	121089	2054	1035	110623	24614	8412	7330	6077	5490
	2013	165172	128797	2286	1058	117561	26299	8950	7974	6496	5917
France	2000	6147	5280	64	44	4751	1283	464	384	32	25
	2010	10508	7413	189	83	6696	1674	528	451	149	77
	2011	11457	8294	134	76	7481	1912	679	580	172	122
	2012	10387	7546	116	71	6761	1707	669	582	159	130
	2013	10746	7655	130	61	6846	1765	678	572	171	137
Germany	2000	15167	13206	266	161	11808	.	1132	1036	217	190
	2010	38471	30307	606	316	27513	.	2188	1974	1576	1454
	2011	46327	36321	675	330	32873	.	2773	2483	1939	1809
	2012	43115	33114	677	339	29519	.	2918	2660	2037	1888
	2013	45657	34355	705	355	30597	.	3053	2796	2029	1892
Developed Economies - North America 2/	2000	20273	13612	580	410	2211	425	10821	4367	32	24
	2010	27137	16146	1112	686	3742	738	11292	4129	212	167
	2011	30797	18189	1248	713	4559	845	12382	4339	263	212
	2012	33422	19196	1330	757	4472	799	13394	4642	268	218
	2013	34340	19208	1313	799	4570	786	13325	4518	274	217
United States	2000	15573	9038	550	392	2037	402	6451	.	25	18
	2010	22051	11606	1031	653	3417	663	7157	.	171	137
	2011	25398	13405	1164	683	4201	782	8039	.	218	178
	2012	27635	14093	1242	733	4103	741	8749	.	222	179
	2013	28795	14276	1250	770	4225	722	8801	.	230	181
South-Eastern Europe	2000	356	269	0	0	254	58	14	14	8	5
	2010	2317	1761	2	1	1729	426	30	27	116	106
	2011	3154	2382	4	2	2338	594	40	36	150	138
	2012	2943	2245	7	5	2203	546	35	30	164	153
	2013	3239	2428	7	4	2374	582	48	41	203	185
Commonwealth of Independent States	2000	2115	1624	24	24	1505	639	95	92	360	244
	2010	2577	720	7	4	506	128	207	203	1415	1086
	2011	3391	892	5	2	723	166	163	159	1776	1413
	2012	4068	1004	5	3	821	220	178	172	2577	1827
	2013	4278	981	8	4	802	235	171	160	2668	1818
Russian Federation	2000	1780	1527	24	24	1416	626	87	85	147	52
	2010	1154	428	4	2	229	57	194	192	392	241
	2011	1622	564	4	1	416	99	144	142	445	261
	2012	2183	737	3	2	576	164	158	155	1052	518
	2013	2265	675	3	2	531	178	141	138	1118	504

For general note and footnotes see end of table

Exportations mondiales par provenance et destination (Tableau D)

En millions de dollars E.-U. f.o.b.

←—— Exportations vers

South-Eastern Europe Europe du Sud-est	Northern Africa Afrique septentrio-nale	Sub-Saharan Africa Afrique du Nord	Latin America and the Caribbean Amérique latine et Caraïbes	Eastern Asia Asie orientale	Southern Asia Asie méridionale	South-eastern Asia Asie du Sud-est	Western Asia Asie occidentale	Oceania Océanie	Others 4/ Autre 4/	Année	Exportations en provence de ↓
	**Autres produits en metal manufacturés (CTCI, Rev. 3, 691-695, 699 et 812)**

South-Eastern Europe	Northern Africa	Sub-Saharan Africa	Latin America and the Caribbean	Eastern Asia	Southern Asia	South-eastern Asia	Western Asia	Oceania	Others 4/	Année	Exportations en provence de
669	933	1606	8305	6602	1035	5165	3062	159	166	2000	Monde 1/
3727	4607	8431	16829	21906	6370	15974	11755	509	1116	2010	
4675	3880	9581	20243	24194	8159	20230	14877	620	736	2011	
4530	3916	10177	22686	24682	7406	22703	15041	747	926	2012	
4681	4357	10653	24471	24696	7749	23392	17855	560	879	2013	
1	14	51	222	1615	165	1420	83	68	0	2000	Economies Développées -
15	31	148	434	4525	414	2828	218	177	18	2010	Asie-Pacifique 2/
13	48	167	544	4912	426	3108	211	232	6	2011	
16	33	162	634	4501	434	3586	219	210	9	2012	
10	18	157	651	3995	346	3188	198	168	19	2013	
1	13	45	218	1585	158	1336	71	5	...	2000	Japon
13	27	43	413	4471	390	2608	187	7	...	2010	
12	46	63	520	4833	410	2876	182	8	...	2011	
14	30	54	602	4380	423	3351	192	12	...	2012	
8	17	61	629	3864	334	2932	172	8	...	2013	
553	663	750	1371	980	321	727	1569	48	101	2000	Economies Développées -
2920	2233	2747	3383	4225	1445	2045	4531	108	466	2010	Europe 2/
3571	1989	2747	4207	4851	1723	2317	5355	110	200	2011	
3527	1940	2643	4247	4889	1386	2166	5206	129	182	2012	
3614	2231	3000	4894	5619	1420	2125	6427	106	443	2013	
15	165	161	120	79	47	52	157	37	0	2000	France
221	485	732	276	388	163	206	394	79	2	2010	
250	532	572	362	391	168	234	403	79	0	2011	
225	479	467	362	367	119	185	405	72	0	2012	
230	514	449	499	449	134	145	421	74	5	2013	
99	77	126	425	362	76	186	378	1	15	2000	Allemagne
663	192	399	1063	2052	455	512	1248	2	1	2010	
833	199	456	1288	2447	591	611	1632	4	5	2011	
841	180	427	1236	2517	483	640	1628	3	9	2012	
892	211	449	1369	2830	440	651	2424	4	4	2013	
8	52	87	5140	616	52	407	259	9	0	2000	Economies Développées -
27	151	374	6705	1639	226	877	764	15	0	2010	Amérique du Nord 2/
34	128	459	7618	1878	273	1029	915	11	0	2011	
30	112	451	8964	1967	294	1093	1031	16	0	2012	
41	115	474	9688	2040	258	1067	1152	22	0	2013	
7	50	82	5084	590	51	394	244	8	...	2000	Etats-Unis
19	137	341	6483	1544	209	824	704	14	...	2010	
23	115	391	7375	1774	261	968	857	10	...	2011	
23	100	381	8663	1837	279	1049	973	14	...	2012	
28	96	430	9438	1931	236	1020	1088	21	...	2013	
51	4	1	0	1	1	0	17	...	4	2000	Europe du Sud-est
226	46	17	27	15	18	4	86	0	0	2010	
357	37	20	30	10	48	5	115	0	1	2011	
293	43	17	22	11	25	4	118	0	1	2012	
297	83	13	36	10	18	5	143	0	3	2013	
9	4	3	10	47	40	2	17	0	0	2000	Communauté d'Etats
36	13	14	43	113	152	19	52	0	0	2010	Indépendants
67	34	21	43	104	211	164	64	0	14	2011	
50	9	13	40	141	155	21	57	0	0	2012	
61	7	24	30	154	246	28	79	0	0	2013	
3	1	1	8	46	37	2	8	...	0	2000	Fédération de Russie
8	10	8	33	96	128	16	36	0	0	2010	
33	32	15	30	91	193	161	45	0	14	2011	
27	7	6	21	134	142	18	39	0	0	2012	
24	5	16	16	138	199	27	48	0	0	2013	

Voir la fin du tableau pour la remarque générale et les notes.

World exports by provenance and destination (Table D)

In million U.S. dollars f.o.b.

Exports from	Year	World 1/ Monde 1/	Developed economies 2/ Economies développées 2/		Asia-Pacific Asie-Pacifique		Europe		North America Amérique du Nord		Commonwealth of Independent States Communauté d'Etats Indépendants	
			Total	Total	Japan Japon	Total	Germany Allemagne	Total	U.S.A. É.-U.	Total	Europe

Other manufactured metal products (SITC, Rev. 3, 691-695, 699 and 812) [cont.]

Exports from	Year	World	Dev. Total	AP Total	Japan	Eur Total	Germany	NA Total	USA	CIS Total	CIS Europe
Northern Africa	2000	465	411	1	1	408	4	2	1	0	0
	2010	1006	341	0	0	337	9	4	3	4	2
	2011	980	398	0	0	392	12	6	6	8	4
	2012	1020	366	1	0	357	15	9	9	9	5
	2013	1162	375	0	0	365	15	10	9	8	4
Sub-Saharan Africa	2000	637	264	49	31	173	14	41	32	0	0
	2010	2472	468	69	32	292	29	108	97	1	0
	2011	2621	559	46	10	406	22	107	85	2	1
	2012	2660	337	54	17	169	23	114	91	1	1
	2013	2224	279	43	19	145	20	91	80	4	0
South Africa	2000	442	172	30	12	104	13	38	29	0	0
	2010	1728	294	67	32	127	27	100	90	0	0
	2011	1774	261	45	10	117	20	99	77	1	0
	2012	1826	242	48	13	90	16	104	82	1	0
	2013	1602	210	40	18	94	17	76	66	1	0
Latin America and the Caribbean	2000	4857	3809	17	7	156	23	3636	3581	0	0
	2010	8983	5940	44	30	1148	127	4748	4612	2	2
	2011	10187	6595	82	42	1170	150	5344	5205	5	3
	2012	11253	7790	85	72	1369	115	6336	6186	7	4
	2013	11322	7853	86	73	1263	106	6504	6348	11	7
Brazil	2000	531	200	12	4	63	9	126	120	0	0
	2010	2168	1246	32	25	938	82	276	266	1	1
	2011	2429	1357	34	27	966	96	357	345	1	1
	2012	2745	1574	37	32	1159	66	378	370	2	1
	2013	2436	1373	42	37	1006	50	324	313	4	1
Eastern Asia	2000	16395	10611	1974	1604	3084	668	5553	5130	62	44
	2010	60487	31273	6689	4769	11965	2433	12619	11224	2467	1852
	2011	75932	38846	9050	6215	14536	3182	15260	13593	3138	2356
	2012	81506	40310	9433	6494	13960	2952	16917	15068	3658	2633
	2013	85774	41949	9945	6129	14455	3083	17550	15662	4001	2817
China	2000	5952	3677	780	653	1193	248	1704	1585	33	18
	2010	41329	21137	4224	2786	8486	1640	8428	7430	2116	1553
	2011	51697	26312	5759	3879	10145	2084	10408	9171	2653	1963
	2012	56731	27767	6432	4087	9885	1993	11450	10085	3180	2226
	2013	61571	29054	6599	3960	10357	2085	12099	10710	3397	2314
Southern Asia	2000	894	515	34	9	236	40	245	233	14	3
	2010	3885	1931	103	28	1170	302	658	595	58	18
	2011	5773	3098	171	51	1801	506	1125	1001	86	41
	2012	6404	3521	174	62	1809	531	1539	1348	94	58
	2013	6907	3594	188	70	1994	547	1412	1228	126	96
South-Eastern Asia	2000	3185	1309	578	468	382	96	349	317	6	2
	2010	12447	5058	2512	1681	1689	330	857	767	45	29
	2011	13637	4959	2530	1903	1517	427	912	833	57	42
	2012	14968	5909	3167	2027	1702	350	1041	961	61	46
	2013	16328	6902	4198	2503	1505	453	1198	1119	63	53
Western Asia	2000	1799	1016	43	27	677	156	296	263	73	27
	2010	8843	3107	134	77	2407	620	566	543	788	267
	2011	10459	4029	184	72	3201	960	644	590	1052	335
	2012	10963	3790	153	66	2933	822	704	658	1220	417
	2013	11306	4022	156	62	3099	855	767	693	1287	468
Oceania	2000	9	7	2	0	3	2	2	2	0	...
	2010	35	26	25	1	1	0	0	0	0	0
	2011	42	30	28	1	1	0	0	0	0	0
	2012	42	25	23	0	1	0	0	0	...	...
	2013	42	24	23	0	1	0	0	0	0	0

For general note and footnotes see end of table

Exportations mondiales par provenance et destination (Tableau D)

← Exportations vers

South-Eastern Europe Europe du Sud-est	Northern Africa Afrique septentrio-nale	Sub-Saharan Africa Afrique du Nord	Latin America and the Caribbean Amérique latine et Caraïbes	Eastern Asia Asie orientale	Southern Asia Asie méridionale	South-eastern Asia Asie du Sud-est	Western Asia Asie occidentale	Oceania Océanie	Others 4/ Autre 4/	Année	Exportations en provenance de ↓

Autres produits en metal manufacturés (CTCI, Rev. 3, 691-695, 699 et 812) [suite]

South-Eastern Europe	Northern Africa	Sub-Saharan Africa	Latin America	Eastern Asia	Southern Asia	South-eastern Asia	Western Asia	Oceania	Others 4/	Année	Exportations en provenance de
0	18	11	7	1	0	0	13	0	3	2000	Afrique du Nord
3	328	140	1	4	2	1	176	0	6	2010	
3	177	180	2	2	2	1	200	0	7	2011	
2	245	169	6	2	1	4	205	0	10	2012	
6	256	166	3	1	2	1	330	0	14	2013	
0	1	306	17	14	5	13	15	0	1	2000	Afrique subsaharienne
1	8	1712	65	121	18	30	33	2	14	2010	
0	2	1791	54	85	15	35	63	1	12	2011	
5	2	1984	54	160	12	33	52	1	20	2012	
5	2	1684	41	79	9	37	72	1	11	2013	
0	1	211	16	11	5	12	11	0	1	2000	Afrique du sud
0	4	1315	42	10	9	23	23	2	4	2010	
0	1	1376	52	21	10	24	25	1	2	2011	
0	1	1437	52	14	7	26	35	0	11	2012	
0	1	1262	40	16	7	30	30	0	4	2013	
0	4	18	981	7	10	12	12	1	2	2000	Amérique latine et Caraïbes
3	8	78	2690	145	28	46	34	1	9	2010	
8	7	97	3057	267	24	72	41	2	15	2011	
8	5	78	3042	128	15	125	32	2	21	2012	
6	6	95	3045	119	20	130	29	2	6	2013	
0	2	14	294	4	2	4	10	1	...	2000	Brésil
1	6	65	755	34	13	31	14	1	...	2010	
3	5	75	868	39	13	52	13	2	...	2011	
3	3	52	950	49	8	85	16	2	...	2012	
3	5	65	811	47	11	102	13	2	...	2013	
11	89	244	482	2909	269	1232	468	18	0	2000	Asie orientale
176	1013	2196	2950	9004	2678	5514	3089	126	0	2010	
216	841	2708	3974	10294	3679	7914	4194	128	0	2011	
232	919	3191	4849	10414	3441	9676	4640	167	8	2012	
252	933	3434	5207	10724	3726	10331	5046	164	6	2013	
7	57	146	195	1095	108	387	242	4	...	2000	Chine
137	678	2023	2284	4813	1934	3664	2438	105	...	2010	
160	612	2529	3209	5566	2729	4969	2857	100	...	2011	
178	757	2990	3888	5823	2542	6384	3081	141	...	2012	
204	802	3209	4044	6136	3041	7724	3819	140	...	2013	
1	17	51	20	27	41	57	149	0	0	2000	Asie méridionale
8	92	405	110	73	265	192	684	1	65	2010	
11	77	643	166	113	327	318	892	5	36	2011	
13	77	616	230	110	327	304	1087	3	22	2012	
17	93	638	255	128	330	365	1332	6	22	2013	
2	13	37	26	346	81	1284	68	13	0	2000	Asie Sud-est
18	95	226	290	1456	477	4342	371	68	2	2010	
46	57	291	342	1504	650	5172	429	124	6	2011	
13	53	336	395	1535	517	5551	392	199	6	2012	
10	38	342	432	1626	512	5973	344	81	6	2013	
34	54	47	28	41	51	11	392	...	54	2000	Asie occidentale
294	590	373	131	585	647	75	1715	3	535	2010	
349	483	459	205	172	780	92	2398	1	438	2011	
340	479	517	202	823	799	133	2002	11	647	2012	
360	575	624	188	199	864	134	2701	3	350	2013	
...	...	0	0	0	0	0	...	2	0	2000	Océanie
0	0	0	0	1	0	1	0	6	0	2010	
0	...	0	0	1	0	3	...	7	0	2011	
0	...	0	0	1	0	8	0	8	0	2012	
0	...	0	0	1	0	9	0	7	0	2013	

Voir la fin du tableau pour la remarque générale et les notes.

World exports by provenance and destination (Table D)

In million U.S. dollars f.o.b.

| Exports from | Year | World 1/ Monde 1/ | Developed economies 2/ Economies développées 2/ | | | | | | | Commonwealth of Independent States Communauté d'Etats Indépendants | |
| | | | | Asia-Pacific Asie-Pacifique | | Europe | | North America Amérique du Nord | | | |
			Total	Total	Japan Japon	Total	Germany Allemagne	Total	U.S.A. É.-U.	Total	Europe
Clothing (SITC, Rev. 3, 84)											
World 1/	2000	201719	161759	20949	18560	83449	19964	57361	53808	3158	2789
	2010	372234	287743	29994	24629	173168	34556	84581	76578	17540	11470
	2011	436351	332171	36448	29936	202938	42405	92785	83610	20429	14326
	2012	431153	315444	37694	30781	183786	37288	93964	85096	21690	15693
	2013	468992	336159	38843	31468	197665	40350	99651	89979	26509	19333
Developed Economies - Asia-Pacific 2/	2000	846	450	169	7	138	26	142	136	1	1
	2010	934	530	294	5	151	22	86	76	3	3
	2011	1058	573	330	5	146	22	97	87	4	4
	2012	1008	549	323	5	135	19	91	80	4	3
	2013	944	563	343	5	127	22	93	85	4	4
Japan	2000	534	222	5	.	119	21	98	92	1	0
	2010	531	191	8	.	121	19	62	58	3	3
	2011	595	188	9	.	111	19	68	64	4	3
	2012	557	177	11	.	100	17	66	59	3	3
	2013	487	178	9	.	100	19	69	63	3	3
Developed Economies - Europe 2/	2000	53018	47097	1561	1442	42397	9608	3139	2881	993	955
	2010	96712	82157	1748	1484	77530	12605	2878	2427	4539	4207
	2011	114118	95872	2112	1726	90308	15386	3453	2925	5856	5429
	2012	106795	88299	2370	1851	82175	14224	3753	3238	6015	5520
	2013	116533	95772	2438	1927	89223	15920	4111	3551	6696	6116
France	2000	5303	4353	329	318	3698	610	325	291	66	63
	2010	9996	8145	355	322	7326	1029	464	395	336	297
	2011	11043	8828	371	331	7917	1157	540	465	384	339
	2012	10355	8104	399	361	7105	1088	600	538	362	314
	2013	11109	8609	414	370	7536	1215	659	589	347	293
Germany	2000	6852	6348	96	80	6043	.	209	166	165	156
	2010	16971	15413	115	54	15108	.	189	113	838	785
	2011	20086	17799	146	69	17390	.	264	167	1274	1193
	2012	18312	15965	156	76	15532	.	277	188	1349	1257
	2013	18984	16428	158	73	15993	.	277	187	1482	1375
Developed Economies - North America 2/	2000	10706	3691	509	477	429	55	2754	1997	7	5
	2010	5850	3688	405	301	804	105	2479	951	25	20
	2011	6539	4144	451	331	896	119	2796	1038	29	24
	2012	6922	4448	504	367	1016	116	2928	1021	46	25
	2013	7078	4561	488	349	1000	128	3072	1008	50	35
United States	2000	8629	1635	495	465	383	50	757	.	5	3
	2010	4674	2574	379	289	671	79	1525	.	20	16
	2011	5223	2902	422	313	725	90	1755	.	23	19
	2012	5579	3183	474	349	806	85	1903	.	35	16
	2013	5782	3344	451	327	832	106	2061	.	39	25
South-Eastern Europe	2000	3689	3635	1	1	3393	1091	240	233	7	6
	2010	5980	5759	3	2	5724	1564	32	25	28	26
	2011	7122	6828	3	2	6783	1894	43	34	45	43
	2012	6530	6209	8	7	6139	1695	61	52	95	93
	2013	6977	6544	9	8	6462	1807	73	64	171	169
Commonwealth of Independent States	2000	1068	887	0	0	700	318	188	183	131	123
	2010	1763	898	0	0	881	273	16	15	767	750
	2011	2131	963	0	0	954	292	9	8	1040	1008
	2012	2397	816	0	0	812	233	4	3	1461	1257
	2013	2567	857	0	0	851	245	5	4	1571	1253
Russian Federation	2000	234	208	0	0	140	53	68	68	10	4
	2010	89	68	0	0	67	15	1	0	15	11
	2011	112	72	0	0	71	10	1	0	27	22
	2012	247	66	0	0	65	1	1	1	170	89
	2013	337	78	0	0	76	5	2	2	243	106

For general note and footnotes see end of table

Exportations mondiales par provenance et destination (Tableau D)

En millions de dollars E.-U. f.o.b.

← Exportations vers

South-Eastern Europe Europe du Sud-est	Northern Africa Afrique septentrionale	Sub-Saharan Africa Afrique du Nord	Latin America and the Caribbean Amérique latine et Caraïbes	Eastern Asia Asie orientale	Southern Asia Asie méridionale	South-eastern Asia Asie du Sud-est	Western Asia Asie occidentale	Oceania Océanie	Others 4/ Autre 4/	Année	Exportations en provenance de ↓
1087	1489	1280	11330	13959	310	2318	4726	105	198	2000	Monde 1/
2527	2845	4745	13499	18013	1980	6960	14828	152	1402	2010	
2802	3057	5835	18067	22562	2765	9054	17978	182	1449	2011	
2653	4040	6474	17504	24042	3489	14644	19556	175	1444	2012	
2901	3992	6891	16705	28657	4231	18320	23016	180	1431	2013	
0	1	2	2	336	2	35	6	12	0	2000	Economies Développées -
0	0	6	3	298	2	58	12	21	0	2010	Asie-Pacifique 2/
0	0	10	5	357	3	68	13	23	1	2011	
0	0	8	6	319	1	83	16	21	0	2012	
0	0	7	4	259	1	68	14	23	0	2013	
0	1	1	2	280	1	23	4	0	...	2000	Japon
0	0	1	2	284	1	43	6	0	...	2010	
0	0	1	4	336	2	53	7	0	...	2011	
0	0	1	4	297	0	64	10	0	...	2012	
0	0	1	2	241	0	52	8	0	...	2013	
924	842	128	436	1050	45	143	1296	32	33	2000	Economies Développées -
1668	851	284	820	2596	133	400	3197	43	25	2010	Europe 2/
1921	824	349	1049	3703	173	529	3770	48	24	2011	
1749	791	357	1128	3954	141	544	3751	41	26	2012	
1942	811	409	1199	4589	155	687	4203	46	24	2013	
101	194	41	48	235	2	29	214	21	0	2000	France
70	266	101	43	479	12	74	429	38	2	2010	
74	259	111	62	688	15	102	474	44	1	2011	
71	240	102	67	795	15	105	454	39	3	2012	
74	237	111	66	964	13	129	510	43	6	2013	
64	35	9	20	83	4	15	96	0	12	2000	Allemagne
161	48	22	39	181	14	29	225	0	0	2010	
215	47	30	57	310	19	47	285	1	0	2011	
202	43	34	67	286	18	47	299	0	1	2012	
209	44	44	75	323	15	52	308	1	3	2013	
2	6	10	6778	89	6	46	66	3	0	2000	Economies Développées -
2	7	30	1539	250	30	62	210	6	0	2010	Amérique du Nord 2/
3	5	39	1642	309	32	80	251	5	0	2011	
3	7	40	1643	329	28	92	283	4	...	2012	
4	7	45	1676	333	18	86	293	5	...	2013	
2	6	10	6772	85	5	46	59	3	...	2000	Etats-Unis
2	5	28	1527	231	29	58	194	6	...	2010	
2	4	38	1626	282	30	74	236	5	...	2011	
2	6	38	1626	311	25	86	264	4	...	2012	
3	6	44	1658	311	17	81	273	5	...	2013	
33	0	0	1	1	0	0	13	...	1	2000	Europe du Sud-est
140	1	1	0	10	1	1	39	0	0	2010	
165	1	1	1	16	4	5	55	0	0	2011	
151	1	1	2	16	3	5	48	0	0	2012	
164	11	1	2	15	1	3	63	0	0	2013	
1	0	0	5	14	0	1	29	0	0	2000	Communauté d'Etats
35	0	0	2	2	1	1	54	0	2	2010	Indépendants
56	2	0	1	5	2	2	54	0	4	2011	
43	0	1	1	2	4	0	64	0	3	2012	
47	2	0	9	2	3	1	72	0	2	2013	
0	0	0	0	14	0	1	1	...	0	2000	Fédération de Russie
0	0	0	0	1	0	1	1	0	1	2010	
0	1	0	0	1	0	2	6	...	2	2011	
0	0	1	1	1	1	0	4	0	1	2012	
0	1	0	8	1	1	0	3	...	1	2013	

Vêtements (CTCI, Rev. 3, 84)

Voir la fin du tableau pour la remarque générale et les notes.

STAFFS UNIVERSITY LIBRARY

World exports by provenance and destination (Table D)

In million U.S. dollars f.o.b.

Exports from	Year	World 1/ Monde 1/	Developed economies 2/ Economies développées 2/							Commonwealth of Independent States Communauté d'Etats Indépendants	
			Asia-Pacific Asie-Pacifique			Europe		North America Amérique du Nord			
			Total	Total	Japan Japon	Total	Germany Allemagne	Total	U.S.A. É.-U.	Total	Europe

Clothing (SITC, Rev. 3, 84) [cont.]

Exports from	Year	World	Total	Total	Japan	Total	Germany	Total	U.S.A.	Total	Europe
Northern Africa	2000	4942	4857	4	4	4579	640	274	268	0	0
	2010	7374	7205	5	3	6457	591	742	730	1	1
	2011	8144	7933	7	4	7048	786	878	860	4	4
	2012	7207	6972	7	4	6237	595	727	710	5	4
	2013	7322	7006	8	5	6235	646	762	747	7	6
Sub-Saharan Africa	2000	1992	1784	6	4	937	72	842	830	0	0
	2010	2422	1585	11	3	744	86	830	706	1	1
	2011	3135	1991	15	4	924	111	1052	877	2	2
	2012	2695	1721	16	4	734	93	972	951	1	1
	2013	2590	1658	16	2	755	106	887	868	1	1
South Africa	2000	218	181	2	1	62	2	117	117	0	0
	2010	425	28	3	0	17	1	8	8	0	0
	2011	491	25	2	0	15	1	8	7	0	0
	2012	478	22	2	0	12	1	8	8	0	0
	2013	503	23	3	0	14	1	7	6	0	0
Latin America and the Caribbean	2000	11231	10371	49	11	202	56	10119	10063	1	1
	2010	12716	9257	38	22	308	48	8912	8785	2	1
	2011	14359	9936	53	30	340	65	9543	9404	4	2
	2012	13605	10803	60	35	302	52	10441	10289	4	2
	2013	13501	11194	65	36	304	61	10825	10647	4	3
Brazil	2000	282	140	4	4	35	12	101	99	...	...
	2010	157	51	7	6	27	2	17	15	0	0
	2011	193	61	11	7	26	2	24	22	1	1
	2012	167	50	12	8	17	2	21	20	1	0
	2013	163	47	9	5	13	1	25	24	1	1
Eastern Asia	2000	70341	50636	16462	14772	13827	2997	20347	18846	1325	1171
	2010	156726	108236	24479	20433	45152	10352	38604	34864	11076	5684
	2011	181345	122427	28987	24287	51868	12442	41572	37520	12074	6789
	2012	185305	115573	29321	24414	44453	9762	41800	38099	12413	7598
	2013	202650	120665	29544	24343	47366	9920	43756	39777	16081	10343
China	2000	36071	22838	12571	11513	4943	923	5324	4780	1230	1087
	2010	129820	85789	21737	18450	35988	8208	28065	25208	10897	5517
	2011	153774	100353	25940	22041	43102	10309	31312	28175	11820	6547
	2012	159614	95461	26391	22262	37180	7996	31891	29029	12170	7368
	2013	177435	101429	26549	22107	40700	8292	34180	30989	15856	10133
Southern Asia	2000	15372	13550	264	167	6094	1367	7192	6746	417	283
	2010	33780	29752	638	371	17725	4135	11389	10279	184	84
	2011	42855	37223	1065	592	23383	5786	12775	11402	277	159
	2012	42049	35991	1132	637	22286	5383	12572	11203	319	175
	2013	47430	40132	1233	690	24844	5982	14055	12562	436	235
South-Eastern Asia	2000	18862	16449	1456	1312	5121	1190	9873	9448	63	60
	2010	31127	26760	2289	1986	7187	1664	17285	16457	277	233
	2011	37538	31327	3332	2930	8833	2163	19161	18118	353	303
	2012	38251	31377	3847	3423	8382	2117	19147	18053	350	338
	2013	41581	33900	4583	4072	8861	2310	20457	19206	358	349
Western Asia	2000	8580	7574	14	9	5378	2544	2182	2109	212	184
	2010	15763	11863	33	19	10504	3110	1327	1261	638	459
	2011	16890	12903	47	25	11449	3336	1407	1336	741	560
	2012	17245	12636	57	34	11114	2999	1466	1397	977	676
	2013	18634	13250	61	31	11635	3201	1555	1460	1130	818
Oceania	2000	1071	778	455	354	254	1	68	68	0	0
	2010	1088	53	51	0	1	0	1	1	0	0
	2011	1117	51	47	0	4	0	1	1	0	0
	2012	1146	51	49	0	2	0	0	0	0	0
	2013	1186	56	54	0	2	0	0	0	0	0

For general note and footnotes see end of table

Exportations mondiales par provenance et destination (Tableau D)

En millions de dollars E.-U. f.o.b.

⟵ Exportations vers

South-Eastern Europe / Europe du Sud-est	Northern Africa / Afrique septentrionale	Sub-Saharan Africa / Afrique du Nord	Latin America and the Caribbean / Amérique latine et Caraïbes	Eastern Asia / Asie orientale	Southern Asia / Asie méridionale	South-eastern Asia / Asie du Sud-est	Western Asia / Asie occidentale	Oceania / Océanie	Others 4/ / Autre 4/	Année	Exportations en provenance de ↓
				Vêtements (CTCI, Rev. 3, 84) [suite]							
0	10	19	1	1	0	0	13	0	40	2000	Afrique du Nord
1	15	34	5	11	1	1	75	0	25	2010	
1	15	35	7	17	1	2	111	0	20	2011	
2	29	22	9	17	1	1	131	0	18	2012	
1	27	21	11	17	0	2	216	0	15	2013	
0	0	161	6	4	1	1	32	0	3	2000	Afrique subsaharienne
1	1	792	7	10	5	1	18	0	1	2010	
0	1	1098	9	10	5	1	16	0	1	2011	
2	0	923	16	11	2	1	15	0	2	2012	
2	0	882	13	7	3	2	21	0	1	2013	
0	0	26	3	1	0	0	7	0	0	2000	Afrique du sud
0	0	382	1	1	1	0	10	0	0	2010	
0	0	452	1	2	2	0	9	0	0	2011	
0	0	445	0	2	0	0	7	0	1	2012	
0	0	462	1	1	0	1	14	0	0	2013	
0	0	2	827	6	0	1	8	0	17	2000	Amérique latine et Caraïbes
0	0	11	3400	20	0	5	9	0	10	2010	
0	0	15	4334	23	1	4	13	0	28	2011	
1	0	16	2692	40	1	14	13	0	21	2012	
0	0	17	2197	38	1	10	18	0	20	2013	
0	0	1	139	0	0	0	1	0	...	2000	Brésil
0	0	10	90	1	0	0	5	0	...	2010	
0	0	12	112	1	0	1	6	0	0	2011	
0	0	14	95	1	0	1	5	0	...	2012	
0	0	14	96	0	0	1	3	0	...	2013	
83	388	530	2581	11820	126	1385	1431	27	8	2000	Asie orientale
234	1441	2859	6302	13261	1205	5283	6788	41	0	2010	
285	1672	3354	8882	15374	1858	6889	8467	62	1	2011	
318	2554	4097	9829	16104	2570	12148	9635	63	0	2012	
239	2466	4307	9313	19248	3240	15658	11373	61	1	2013	
81	277	287	1316	8384	52	611	991	5	...	2000	Chine
227	1415	2670	5928	11189	1086	4268	6329	22	...	2010	
279	1649	3193	8433	12620	1709	5694	7987	35	1	2011	
312	2528	3947	9391	13313	2425	10875	9157	36	...	2012	
233	2444	4189	8882	16201	3090	14206	10869	35	...	2013	
3	9	129	157	84	48	85	882	6	1	2000	Asie méridionale
18	27	346	515	244	206	207	2263	7	13	2010	
25	26	526	904	476	310	269	2804	6	9	2011	
23	49	569	1006	509	350	266	2950	8	10	2012	
31	58	752	1156	592	355	353	3547	9	11	2013	
8	51	241	262	515	45	611	593	22	4	2000	Asie Sud-est
16	63	235	887	1219	113	931	589	27	10	2010	
20	73	240	1208	2179	135	1192	764	30	19	2011	
14	99	253	1140	2573	133	1473	789	33	17	2012	
17	80	229	1084	3428	161	1423	844	28	29	2013	
33	183	58	8	19	37	7	357	0	92	2000	Asie occidentale
410	438	146	19	90	283	12	1574	0	289	2010	
326	438	168	25	93	240	12	1659	0	285	2011	
345	510	186	33	168	254	17	1860	0	259	2012	
453	531	221	41	128	293	28	2352	0	206	2013	
...	...	0	266	21	0	3	0	3	1	2000	Océanie
0	...	0	0	2	0	0	0	7	1026	2010	
0	...	0	0	1	0	1	0	7	1057	2011	
0	0	0	0	0	0	0	0	6	1088	2012	
0	0	0	0	0	0	0	0	8	1121	2013	

Voir la fin du tableau pour la remarque générale et les notes.

World exports by provenance and destination (Table D)

General Note

Table D is based on data of UN Comtrade as of mid November 2014. An earlier version of this table has been published in Volume I of the 2013 ITSY which has been produced earlier this year. The totals of imports and exports presented in table A and D are not necessarily identical as table A is mainly based on the data of the IMF's International Financial Statistics (IFS) which is a different data collection system with different aims, procedures, timetable and sources for update and maintenance than UN Comtrade (see the introduction for details). Nevertheless, discrepancies between both tables are in general minor and usually do not affect the overall information provided. A systematic comparison of the figures from both sources (which includes the description of known and relevant conceptual differences) is available at http://unstats.un.org/unsd/trade/imts/annual%20totals.htm.

Overall, the discrepancies in the world total or world aggregate of exports in table A and table D is around 1.0 percent for all years shown, which is minor, given the differences between the two sources. For further information on sources and presentation of table D as well as for a brief table description please see the introduction.

1/ Exports for which country of destination is not available are included in the totals for the 'World' and in region "Others" (see footnote number 4 for further explanation).
2/ This classification is intended for statistical convenience and does not, necessarily, express a judgment about the stage reached by a particular country in the development process.
3/ Section 9 of the SITC, which comprises commodities and transactions not classified elsewhere, is included in the total trade but is not shown.
4/ The region "Others" as destination for exports contains the following trading partners: Antarctica, bunkers, free zones, confidential and not elsewhere specified countries

Exportations mondiales par provenance et destination (Tableau D)

Remarque générale

Tableau D est basée sur les données de UN Comtrade telles que disponible mi-novembre 2014. Une version antérieure de cette table est publiée dans le volume I de l'annuaire 2013 ITSY qui a été produit plus tôt cette année. Les importations et exportations totales présentées dans les tableaux A et D ne sont pas nécessairement identiques du fait que le tableau A est basé principalement sur les données des Statistiques Financières Internationales (IFS) du FMI qui est un différent système de collecte des données avec des objectifs, des procédures, un calendrier et des sources de mise à jour et de maintenance différents de ceux de UN Comtrade sur lequel le tableau D est basé (voir l'introduction pour les détails). Toutefois, les écarts entre les deux tableaux sont en général mineurs et n'affectent pas substantiellement l'information fournie. Une comparaison systématique des données de ces deux sources (incluant une description des différences conceptuelles pertinentes connues) est disponible à http://unstats.un.org/unsd/trade/imts/annual%20totals.htm.

En général, la différence entre les totaux des exportations mondiales présentés dans les tableaux A et D est d'environ 1,0 pour cent pur chacune des années publiées, ce qui est mineur étant donné les différences entre les deux sources. Pour plus d'information sur les sources et la présentation du tableau D ainsi qu'une brève description, se il vous plaît se référer à l'introduction.

1/ Pour la composition des régions géographiques, se référer à http://unstats.un.org/unsd/mdg/default.aspx
2/ Cette classification est utilisée pour plus de commodité dans la présentation des statistiques et n'implique pas nécessairement un jugement quant au stade de développement auquel est parvenu un pays donné.
3/ Section 9 de la CTCI, qui représente les articles et transactions non classes ailleurs est comprise dans le commerce total mais n'est pas présentée séparément dans ce tableau.
4/ La région "Autres" comme destination des exportations comprend les partenaires commerciaux suivants: Antarctique, combustibles de soute, zones franches, partenaires confidentiels ou non specifiés ailleurs

Growth of world exports by provenance and destination (Table E)

Annual average rate: in per cent

| Exports from | Year | World 1/ Monde 1/ | Developed economies 2/ Economies développées 2/ | | | | | | | Commonwealth of Independent States Communauté d'Etats Indépendants | |
| | | | Total | Asia-Pacific Asie-Pacifique | | Europe | | North America Amérique du Nord | | | |
				Total	Japan Japon	Total	Germany Allemagne	Total	U.S.A. É.-U.	Total	Europe
Origin of exports of major commodity classes											
0-9 All commodities 3/	2000/2013	8.6	6.5	4.7	3.1	7.3	7.8	5.2	5.6	13.7	13.2
	2009/2010	21.6	16.4	32.7	32.6	12.5	12.7	21.3	20.9	30.5	30.6
	2010/2011	19.9	16.1	12.2	6.9	16.9	16.6	16.0	15.9	32.9	31.5
	2011/2012	0.5	-2.3	-3.4	-3.0	-3.9	-4.5	3.6	4.4	2.0	2.3
	2012/2013	2.7	2.7	-7.8	-10.5	5.0	3.0	1.8	2.1	-2.2	-1.7
0&1 Food, live animals, beverages and tobacco	2000/2013	9.5	8.4	8.1	6.0	8.8	10.5	7.0	7.1	20.6	20.8
	2009/2010	10.9	8.0	16.4	18.5	5.9	3.6	13.4	15.1	-0.4	-4.7
	2010/2011	20.5	18.9	23.9	-2.8	18.1	20.1	19.9	22.2	29.3	33.9
	2011/2012	0.9	-1.3	1.8	-1.2	-2.1	-3.6	0.3	-0.8	35.3	38.2
	2012/2013	6.8	8.5	3.8	0.3	9.5	8.8	7.0	6.8	0.8	0.1
2&4 Crude maerials, oils and fats, (fuels excluded)	2000/2013	11.1	9.7	15.7	10.6	9.0	9.1	7.4	8.7	11.7	11.9
	2009/2010	40.6	36.3	58.6	22.1	29.4	33.5	33.0	31.2	35.6	34.3
	2010/2011	28.9	26.1	39.8	12.5	25.9	28.0	17.0	13.7	38.2	38.0
	2011/2012	-5.6	-4.9	-7.5	8.8	-6.3	-9.7	-0.7	-1.0	3.1	3.4
	2012/2013	-0.5	0.7	9.0	-6.9	0.1	-4.2	-4.8	-6.2	-4.8	-0.5
3 Mineral fuels, lubricants and related material	2000/2013	13.1	12.5	14.0	20.2	11.8	13.7	13.8	20.4	16.9	16.3
	2009/2010	30.8	28.9	30.1	23.9	25.5	3.3	36.3	47.5	34.2	35.5
	2010/2011	39.3	36.8	26.7	24.9	36.4	39.3	41.9	60.1	36.9	35.2
	2011/2012	5.3	3.1	-6.3	-17.4	4.7	15.2	3.3	6.3	4.0	6.0
	2012/2013	-1.6	4.0	-5.4	24.0	4.6	7.5	5.8	8.0	-0.4	-0.5
5 Chemicals	2000/2013	10.0	8.8	6.2	6.1	9.4	9.1	7.6	7.6	12.0	10.8
	2009/2010	17.3	12.4	25.9	27.7	9.9	8.9	18.5	18.4	31.1	29.8
	2010/2011	16.7	12.5	8.4	7.8	13.2	13.8	11.1	9.7	41.2	47.8
	2011/2012	-1.8	-3.1	-5.1	-6.6	-3.4	-4.2	-1.1	0.0	11.2	10.6
	2012/2013	2.9	4.2	-4.7	-4.0	5.8	6.0	1.1	0.8	-15.0	-16.4
7 Machinery and transport equipment	2000/2013	6.6	4.2	1.9	1.8	5.9	7.3	1.7	2.0	11.5	10.9
	2009/2010	22.2	18.0	35.0	35.6	13.3	16.5	22.0	22.4	18.6	16.4
	2010/2011	13.2	13.8	5.3	4.9	16.7	19.0	11.0	11.5	25.1	23.3
	2011/2012	0.5	-2.7	-0.7	-0.9	-5.8	-4.5	6.7	6.2	27.5	26.2
	2012/2013	3.5	0.8	-12.7	-13.0	4.4	2.8	-0.5	0.1	-1.6	-1.7
6&8 Other manufactured goods	2000/2013	7.8	5.8	4.1	4.0	6.5	7.6	4.0	4.7	9.8	8.8
	2009/2010	20.0	15.3	31.3	32.5	12.7	11.7	18.7	18.1	23.8	22.7
	2010/2011	18.3	16.8	12.2	11.1	18.8	19.1	11.3	11.6	21.5	17.7
	2011/2012	-0.9	-5.4	-4.4	-3.5	-7.1	-8.6	1.8	3.7	8.7	7.9
	2012/2013	3.4	2.5	-10.3	-11.5	4.3	2.9	1.9	2.7	-7.2	-3.5
Destination of exports of major commodity classes											
0-9 All commodities 3/	2000/2013	8.6	6.3	6.1	5.1	7.0	6.8	5.0	4.6	16.7	16.2
	2009/2010	21.6	16.5	23.9	25.0	13.2	15.4	22.8	23.1	24.0	28.7
	2010/2011	19.9	17.3	21.9	22.3	17.6	15.3	15.1	14.4	39.4	42.5
	2011/2012	0.5	-2.0	4.0	3.5	-5.0	-4.7	3.5	3.4	3.7	2.0
	2012/2013	2.7	1.1	-6.9	-8.1	2.4	3.1	0.8	0.4	2.2	0.2
0&1 Food, live animals, beverages and tobacco	2000/2013	9.5	7.8	4.6	3.4	8.6	7.8	7.4	7.1	14.8	14.0
	2009/2010	10.9	6.2	13.1	12.4	3.9	4.4	11.7	11.8	20.9	24.6
	2010/2011	20.5	17.6	23.3	23.0	17.1	18.7	16.5	17.3	17.9	15.5
	2011/2012	0.9	-1.6	1.3	0.5	-3.3	-3.8	3.0	2.5	6.4	2.9
	2012/2013	6.8	6.6	-2.6	-5.3	8.4	8.0	5.1	5.6	7.9	6.9
2&4 Crude maerials, oils and fats, (fuels excluded)	2000/2013	11.1	7.2	7.3	7.4	7.9	8.4	4.7	4.6	13.7	12.9
	2009/2010	40.6	37.7	52.6	54.1	35.3	37.9	33.6	34.7	27.9	33.8
	2010/2011	28.9	25.2	21.8	21.2	25.5	23.9	28.0	29.8	34.4	34.9
	2011/2012	-5.6	-8.4	-11.1	-11.3	-9.8	-6.2	0.5	2.3	4.2	-3.2
	2012/2013	-0.5	-3.2	-2.5	-1.9	-2.5	-1.9	-6.5	-6.6	1.6	3.6
3 Mineral fuels, lubricants and related material	2000/2013	13.1	10.7	8.8	7.9	12.5	11.3	8.3	5.7	14.0	13.5
	2009/2010	30.8	27.3	26.8	27.0	26.0	24.7	30.0	32.2	17.2	27.6
	2010/2011	39.3	35.6	42.6	40.9	37.2	41.9	29.9	25.3	51.6	55.9
	2011/2012	5.3	3.6	14.8	16.7	5.2	4.7	-4.4	-7.4	20.9	13.0
	2012/2013	-1.6	-1.7	-1.7	-2.1	0.2	23.8	-6.2	-12.0	-11.0	-14.8
5 Chemicals	2000/2013	10.0	8.8	8.4	8.1	9.1	9.7	8.0	8.2	18.2	18.2
	2009/2010	17.3	11.7	23.2	25.2	10.1	7.9	13.8	14.2	25.6	30.6
	2010/2011	16.7	14.4	20.1	20.9	14.1	12.7	13.3	13.9	24.2	24.6
	2011/2012	-1.8	-3.6	-1.3	-2.2	-4.7	-3.9	-0.6	-1.2	8.4	5.2
	2012/2013	2.9	2.6	-4.9	-5.6	4.1	4.1	0.6	0.3	7.7	7.0
7 Machinery and transport equipment	2000/2013	6.6	4.2	5.3	4.2	4.5	5.6	3.5	3.6	19.7	19.9
	2009/2010	22.2	17.4	25.3	24.1	12.7	16.5	25.1	24.8	36.1	46.1
	2010/2011	13.2	12.2	13.1	11.1	12.9	14.5	10.7	10.7	41.1	43.2
	2011/2012	0.5	-2.4	7.5	6.6	-9.0	-7.3	7.8	8.5	12.0	9.3
	2012/2013	3.5	2.5	-2.5	0.9	3.4	2.1	2.5	2.9	-1.5	-3.4
6&8 Other manufactured goods	2000/2013	7.8	6.0	6.0	4.9	6.6	6.3	4.7	4.6	17.0	16.0
	2009/2010	20.0	16.5	19.5	20.4	14.2	17.1	21.9	22.2	18.7	32.3
	2010/2011	18.3	17.2	21.1	21.9	18.2	23.3	13.5	14.0	26.2	29.0
	2011/2012	-0.9	-4.5	1.4	0.2	-8.5	-10.1	4.0	3.9	11.1	7.8
	2012/2013	3.4	2.6	-1.9	-3.6	3.2	3.1	2.8	3.6	8.3	7.7

For general note and footnotes see end of Special Table F.

Croissance des exportations mondiales par provenance et destination (Tableau E)

Taux annuel moyen: en pourcentage

← Exportations vers

South-Eastern Europe / Europe du Sud-est	Northern Africa / Afrique du Nord	Sub-Saharan Africa / Afrique subsahari-enne	Latin America and the Caribbean / Amérique latine et Caraïbes	Eastern Asia / Asie orientale	Southern Asia / Asie méridionale	South-eastern Asia / Asie du Sud-est	Western Asia / Asie occidentale	Oceania / Océanie	Others 4/ Autre 4/	Exportations Année	
Provenance des exportations de grandes catégories de marchandises												
15.2	10.2	11.8	9.1	12.6	13.6	8.7	14.1	6.0	0.0	2000/2013 0-9	Tous produits 3/
22.2	23.1	37.2	26.4	29.6	19.2	29.6	23.9	9.0	0.0	2009/2010	
28.4	5.5	35.7	24.2	18.3	39.1	18.3	36.5	6.6	0.0	2010/2011	
-7.0	22.2	0.5	0.3	5.4	-9.6	0.1	10.4	-10.4	0.0	2011/2012	
14.3	-10.5	-12.1	-0.2	6.4	8.2	1.3	3.6	13.8	0.0	2012/2013	
19.8	11.8	10.2	10.6	10.3	14.2	10.0	12.4	8.9	0.0	2000/2013 0&1	Produits alimentaires, boissons et tabacs
20.2	7.3	15.3	15.0	23.9	21.1	16.4	12.3	17.7	0.0	2009/2010	
20.1	8.4	19.5	23.4	21.9	32.0	25.7	11.5	10.0	0.0	2010/2011	
4.7	-7.2	11.1	0.8	3.8	4.5	0.2	1.4	-3.4	0.0	2011/2012	
19.3	14.0	-8.4	3.1	5.0	19.3	1.2	12.6	1.8	0.0	2012/2013	
13.4	9.6	14.2	14.6	8.2	17.2	13.0	15.6	5.1	0.0	2000/2013 2&4	Matières premières huiles & graisses (combust. exclu.)
47.0	19.1	42.0	48.6	38.1	45.1	51.6	40.9	34.0	0.0	2009/2010	
38.3	29.5	43.2	29.4	32.5	7.9	34.6	41.0	2.6	0.0	2010/2011	
-18.6	-6.7	5.1	-8.2	-6.4	10.4	-15.8	7.5	-5.2	0.0	2011/2012	
12.1	-12.5	-10.8	3.5	-1.9	-13.7	-3.6	10.2	21.6	0.0	2012/2013	
16.2	10.1	12.1	10.8	14.5	12.8	12.8	13.7	-2.4	0.0	2000/2013 3	Combustibles minéraux et produits
29.1	26.9	38.4	27.4	32.8	22.0	33.7	31.1	47.3	0.0	2009/2010	
29.9	0.4	42.7	38.8	40.0	51.9	39.6	48.3	18.4	0.0	2010/2011	
-0.8	37.7	-0.1	2.6	6.9	-18.5	-2.4	13.6	-9.2	0.0	2011/2012	
9.5	-15.8	-18.0	-7.7	0.6	4.8	-3.7	0.2	6.5	0.0	2012/2013	
15.2	12.3	11.4	9.7	13.8	18.7	13.3	16.2	29.2	0.0	2000/2013 5	Produits chimiques
39.1	31.5	41.6	18.0	35.7	21.4	34.7	34.3	30.6	0.0	2009/2010	
36.8	17.0	19.1	24.5	24.0	31.2	30.7	29.6	172.7	0.0	2010/2011	
-4.1	3.5	3.3	-5.6	-1.6	1.6	2.5	8.6	56.7	0.0	2011/2012	
7.4	-8.9	-3.3	-2.0	4.9	9.9	-1.6	-6.5	26.3	0.0	2012/2013	
22.3	16.4	14.6	6.6	13.4	22.0	5.8	13.7	6.8	0.0	2000/2013 7	Machines et matèriels de transports
18.9	26.6	31.7	31.6	31.0	18.1	24.1	6.6	-70.5	0.0	2009/2010	
25.8	21.5	20.7	12.8	13.6	28.5	4.6	9.7	7.2	0.0	2010/2011	
-6.8	-0.6	0.3	6.1	4.0	-5.8	6.4	5.4	-18.3	0.0	2011/2012	
22.9	12.9	7.5	6.5	6.8	14.6	4.6	11.4	18.6	0.0	2012/2013	
10.9	6.9	9.8	6.1	11.0	11.2	8.8	11.7	6.4	0.0	2000/2013 6&8	Articles manufacturés divers
20.1	7.9	55.3	21.5	27.0	18.2	24.0	23.6	13.9	0.0	2009/2010	
28.2	10.4	9.6	15.3	20.4	26.9	18.7	19.2	2.5	0.0	2010/2011	
-9.7	-7.2	-8.3	-5.4	7.5	-3.8	0.5	5.1	-21.1	0.0	2011/2012	
7.6	-0.6	3.0	-1.6	5.1	8.0	5.6	6.7	12.0	0.0	2012/2013	
Destination des exportations de grandes catégories de marchandises												
13.6	11.5	14.2	9.1	12.9	15.6	9.9	12.4	13.2	20.3	2000/2013 0-9	Tous produits 3/
11.6	11.2	22.2	30.6	35.5	28.1	30.8	14.7	1.1	33.9	2009/2010	
26.8	11.3	25.4	25.3	22.1	24.7	20.2	20.3	30.2	20.7	2010/2011	
-4.2	8.6	5.0	3.0	4.3	-1.5	7.3	4.4	-7.0	-17.2	2011/2012	
2.4	2.5	4.8	-1.6	4.1	-3.0	3.5	7.4	1.2	75.6	2012/2013	
14.2	11.2	14.6	9.8	12.3	13.8	13.5	12.3	9.5	5.4	2000/2013 0&1	Produits alimentaires, boissons et tabacs
2.8	26.2	17.5	14.4	28.8	17.8	28.3	10.2	11.7	-9.6	2009/2010	
14.3	31.0	30.5	23.9	28.0	10.2	30.2	27.0	18.4	-10.4	2010/2011	
-0.3	3.7	5.3	6.0	8.9	1.9	5.1	-3.3	7.9	34.1	2011/2012	
5.9	-1.2	5.3	1.3	10.0	7.7	10.1	11.5	-1.5	-10.6	2012/2013	
16.2	12.1	12.4	8.9	18.8	14.6	11.8	14.3	9.5	-1.3	2000/2013 2&4	Matières premières huiles & graisses (combust. exclu.)
52.3	37.1	40.8	38.0	44.7	38.0	41.6	52.0	5.0	5.7	2009/2010	
45.3	25.8	32.2	28.9	32.5	23.9	33.9	35.0	27.8	1.2	2010/2011	
-6.9	-8.6	-5.2	-3.5	-4.4	1.4	-2.8	-3.9	3.9	16.0	2011/2012	
4.6	-6.8	-0.9	-6.8	5.5	-9.3	-5.1	-1.6	-5.8	40.9	2012/2013	
13.7	14.5	20.4	13.1	18.2	19.4	17.5	15.1	12.2	13.3	2000/2013 3	Combustibles minéraux et produits
36.8	27.9	28.0	34.0	39.9	26.2	38.7	31.5	19.3	25.7	2009/2010	
31.5	50.7	29.9	60.5	39.2	54.7	35.1	22.9	94.2	73.7	2010/2011	
8.1	19.9	17.4	-1.2	11.3	6.7	9.8	15.4	-5.1	-38.7	2011/2012	
-24.8	-1.6	1.4	-12.7	1.2	-4.6	2.6	-0.6	-19.8	11.9	2012/2013	
16.3	13.0	13.7	10.8	11.2	15.7	11.7	13.0	10.1	-4.6	2000/2013 5	Produits chimiques
7.5	11.2	24.7	25.2	32.2	26.4	32.4	15.9	14.6	45.8	2009/2010	
22.3	10.4	23.3	22.9	17.0	20.1	21.6	20.7	18.5	41.8	2010/2011	
-1.8	9.5	1.4	4.2	-1.8	-4.4	3.6	-1.3	6.5	-3.3	2011/2012	
9.4	9.9	13.1	2.1	-1.5	2.0	8.8	14.3	-30.8	-61.8	2012/2013	
14.2	9.9	12.4	7.9	11.6	13.5	6.6	11.5	17.4	0.6	2000/2013 7	Machines et matèriels de transports
7.8	4.3	19.3	35.5	35.4	23.5	25.0	15.4	-9.5	-27.4	2009/2010	
24.0	-11.8	24.2	16.2	10.8	14.1	12.1	14.0	16.3	57.8	2010/2011	
-6.5	15.0	-4.0	2.6	3.2	-10.8	8.9	6.5	-18.7	-22.6	2011/2012	
10.4	4.3	8.3	3.1	7.1	-3.4	0.7	7.8	18.3	-20.7	2012/2013	
11.5	10.9	14.1	7.9	9.6	15.6	11.8	12.5	5.7	4.6	2000/2013 6&8	Articles manufacturés divers
10.0	2.9	21.4	31.1	30.7	39.8	31.1	12.4	15.3	25.4	2009/2010	
22.7	-1.1	23.7	19.9	17.1	21.5	20.7	24.3	28.3	29.7	2010/2011	
-8.5	11.7	8.3	4.3	2.7	-5.5	11.0	3.6	6.6	-20.2	2011/2012	
6.7	5.8	6.6	-1.1	2.2	9.1	9.3	4.6	-13.5	-2.0	2012/2013	

Voir la fin du Tableau Spécial F pour la remarque générale et les notes.

Structure of world exports by provenance and destination (Table F)

in per cent

| SITC Commodity classes | Year | World 1/ Monde 1/ | Developed economies 2/ Economies développées 2/ | | | | | | | Commonwealth of Independent States Communauté d'Etats Indépendants | |
| | | | Asia-Pacific Asie-Pacifique | | | Europe | | North America Amérique du Nord | | | |
			Total	Total	Japan Japon	Total	Germany Allemagne	Total	U.S.A. É.-U.	Total	Europe
Origin of exports of major commodity classes											
0-9 All commodities 3/	2000	100.0	65.2	8.8	7.5	39.8	8.7	16.7	12.3	2.3	2.0
	2010	100.0	53.1	6.7	5.1	35.4	8.4	11.0	8.5	3.8	3.2
	2011	100.0	51.4	6.2	4.6	34.5	8.2	10.7	8.2	4.2	3.5
	2012	100.0	50.0	6.0	4.4	33.0	7.8	11.0	8.5	4.3	3.5
	2013	100.0	50.0	5.4	3.8	33.7	7.8	10.9	8.5	4.1	3.4
0&1 Food, live animals, beverages and tobacco	2000	100.0	67.6	5.1	0.5	46.1	5.6	16.4	12.2	0.8	0.7
	2010	100.0	60.4	4.3	0.5	43.8	6.5	12.2	9.1	2.2	1.7
	2011	100.0	59.6	4.4	0.4	43.0	6.5	12.2	9.3	2.4	1.9
	2012	100.0	58.3	4.5	0.4	41.7	6.2	12.1	9.1	3.2	2.7
	2013	100.0	59.2	4.4	0.4	42.7	6.3	12.1	9.1	3.0	2.5
2&4 Crude materials, oils and fats, (fuels excluded)	2000	100.0	61.7	8.1	1.6	28.7	4.4	24.9	14.3	4.3	3.4
	2010	100.0	52.0	11.8	1.6	22.8	3.7	17.5	12.3	4.1	3.1
	2011	100.0	50.9	12.7	1.4	22.3	3.7	15.9	10.9	4.4	3.4
	2012	100.0	51.3	12.5	1.6	22.1	3.5	16.7	11.4	4.8	3.7
	2013	100.0	51.9	13.7	1.5	22.2	3.4	16.0	10.7	4.6	3.7
3 Mineral fuels, lubricants and related material	2000	100.0	29.9	2.3	0.2	20.0	1.2	7.6	2.0	9.6	8.3
	2010	100.0	27.3	3.3	0.6	16.4	1.1	7.6	3.6	14.9	12.0
	2011	100.0	26.8	3.0	0.5	16.1	1.1	7.8	4.1	14.6	11.6
	2012	100.0	26.3	2.7	0.4	16.0	1.2	7.6	4.1	14.5	11.7
	2013	100.0	27.8	2.5	0.5	17.0	1.3	8.2	4.5	14.6	11.8
5 Chemicals	2000	100.0	79.7	6.9	6.2	56.1	12.3	16.8	14.1	1.5	1.5
	2010	100.0	72.0	5.2	4.7	53.3	11.3	13.4	11.4	1.7	1.4
	2011	100.0	69.4	4.9	4.4	51.8	11.0	12.7	10.7	2.0	1.8
	2012	100.0	68.4	4.7	4.2	50.9	10.8	12.8	10.9	2.3	2.0
	2013	100.0	69.3	4.4	3.9	52.4	11.1	12.6	10.7	1.9	1.6
7 Machinery and transport equipment	2000	100.0	71.8	12.9	12.6	38.9	10.4	20.0	15.7	0.4	0.4
	2010	100.0	56.3	9.2	8.9	36.4	11.4	10.7	8.8	0.5	0.5
	2011	100.0	56.6	8.5	8.3	37.6	12.0	10.5	8.6	0.6	0.5
	2012	100.0	54.9	8.5	8.2	35.2	11.4	11.2	9.1	0.7	0.7
	2013	100.0	53.4	7.1	6.9	35.6	11.3	10.7	8.8	0.7	0.6
6&8 Other manufactured goods	2000	100.0	61.1	6.3	5.5	41.3	7.8	13.6	10.1	1.9	1.8
	2010	100.0	51.2	5.0	4.4	37.2	8.2	9.0	7.1	2.4	2.1
	2011	100.0	50.6	4.8	4.1	37.3	8.3	8.5	6.7	2.5	2.0
	2012	100.0	48.3	4.6	4.0	35.0	7.6	8.7	7.0	2.7	2.2
	2013	100.0	47.9	4.0	3.5	35.3	7.6	8.6	6.9	2.4	2.1
Destination of exports of major commodity classes											
0-9 All commodities 3/	2000	100.0	69.1	6.5	5.3	40.4	7.5	22.2	18.5	1.2	1.0
	2010	100.0	55.7	5.0	3.7	36.0	6.6	14.7	11.8	2.6	2.1
	2011	100.0	54.5	5.1	3.8	35.3	6.3	14.1	11.3	3.0	2.5
	2012	100.0	53.2	5.3	3.9	33.4	6.0	14.5	11.6	3.1	2.5
	2013	100.0	52.4	4.8	3.5	33.3	6.0	14.3	11.4	3.1	2.5
0&1 Food, live animals, beverages and tobacco	2000	100.0	70.2	10.5	9.5	45.3	8.4	14.3	11.4	2.5	2.2
	2010	100.0	60.8	6.2	5.0	43.0	7.3	11.6	8.7	4.5	3.9
	2011	100.0	59.4	6.4	5.1	41.8	7.2	11.2	8.5	4.4	3.7
	2012	100.0	57.9	6.4	5.1	40.1	6.8	11.4	8.6	4.7	3.8
	2013	100.0	57.8	5.8	4.5	40.7	6.9	11.2	8.5	4.7	3.8
2&4 Crude materials, oils and fats, (fuels excluded)	2000	100.0	63.4	10.0	9.3	39.4	7.1	14.0	10.9	1.5	1.4
	2010	100.0	43.1	7.3	6.8	29.3	5.5	6.5	4.8	1.8	1.5
	2011	100.0	41.9	6.9	6.4	28.5	5.3	6.4	4.9	1.8	1.6
	2012	100.0	40.6	6.5	6.0	27.3	5.2	6.9	5.3	2.0	1.6
	2013	100.0	39.5	6.3	5.9	26.7	5.2	6.4	4.9	2.1	1.7
3 Mineral fuels, lubricants and related material	2000	100.0	67.4	10.9	10.1	33.9	4.5	22.5	20.9	1.7	1.5
	2010	100.0	53.0	5.9	4.9	31.4	2.8	15.7	12.3	1.7	1.5
	2011	100.0	51.6	6.0	4.9	30.9	2.9	14.7	11.0	1.8	1.7
	2012	100.0	50.8	6.6	5.5	30.9	2.9	13.3	9.7	2.1	1.8
	2013	100.0	50.7	6.5	5.4	31.5	3.6	12.7	8.7	1.9	1.5
5 Chemicals	2000	100.0	66.4	5.2	3.8	46.1	7.6	15.1	11.7	1.3	1.1
	2010	100.0	60.2	4.5	3.1	43.4	7.6	12.4	9.9	2.7	2.3
	2011	100.0	59.0	4.6	3.3	42.4	7.4	12.0	9.6	2.8	2.5
	2012	100.0	57.9	4.6	3.2	41.1	7.2	12.2	9.7	3.1	2.6
	2013	100.0	57.7	4.3	3.0	41.6	7.3	11.9	9.5	3.3	2.8
7 Machinery and transport equipment	2000	100.0	68.7	5.2	3.9	37.6	7.2	25.8	21.2	0.8	0.6
	2010	100.0	53.5	4.4	2.8	32.2	6.9	16.9	13.9	2.6	2.2
	2011	100.0	53.0	4.4	2.8	32.1	7.0	16.5	13.6	3.2	2.7
	2012	100.0	51.5	4.7	3.0	29.1	6.4	17.7	14.6	3.6	3.0
	2013	100.0	51.1	4.5	2.9	29.0	6.4	17.6	14.6	3.4	2.8
6&8 Other manufactured goods	2000	100.0	70.6	6.4	5.2	41.6	8.4	22.7	19.1	1.2	1.0
	2010	100.0	59.8	5.2	3.8	39.1	7.4	15.5	12.8	2.9	2.2
	2011	100.0	59.2	5.3	3.9	39.1	7.8	14.8	12.4	3.1	2.4
	2012	100.0	57.1	5.4	3.9	36.1	7.0	15.6	13.0	3.5	2.6
	2013	100.0	56.7	5.2	3.7	36.0	7.0	15.5	13.0	3.6	2.7

For general note and footnotes see end of Special Table F.

Structure des exportations mondiales par provenance et destination (Tableau F)

en pourcentage

← En provenance ou vers

South-Eastern Europe / Europe du Sud-est	Northern Africa / Afrique du Nord	Sub-Saharan Africa / Afrique subsaharienne	Latin America and the Caribbean / Amérique latine et Caraïbes	Eastern Asia / Asie orientale	Southern Asia / Asie méridionale	South-eastern Asia / Asie du Sud-est	Western Asia / Asie occidentale	Oceania / Océanie	Others 4/ Autre 4/	Année	CTCI: Classes de marchandises
Provenance des exportations de grandes catégories de marchandises											
0.3	0.8	1.5	5.6	12.2	1.4	6.7	4.0	0.1	0.0	2000	0-9 Tous produits 3/
0.6	1.0	2.2	5.8	18.1	2.4	7.0	5.9	0.1	0.0	2010	
0.6	0.9	2.5	6.0	17.8	2.7	6.9	6.8	0.1	0.0	2011	
0.6	1.1	2.5	6.0	18.7	2.5	6.9	7.4	0.1	0.0	2012	
0.7	1.0	2.2	5.9	19.4	2.6	6.8	7.5	0.1	0.0	2013	
0.3	0.6	2.7	12.2	5.4	2.2	6.1	1.9	0.1	0.0	2000	0&1 Produits alimentaires, boissons et tabacs
0.9	0.9	3.1	14.1	5.9	2.9	6.7	2.8	0.1	0.0	2010	
0.9	0.8	3.1	14.5	5.9	3.2	6.9	2.6	0.1	0.0	2011	
0.9	0.7	3.4	14.5	6.1	3.3	6.9	2.6	0.1	0.0	2012	
1.0	0.8	2.9	14.0	6.0	3.7	6.5	2.7	0.1	0.0	2013	
0.8	0.7	3.5	11.8	5.3	1.2	8.5	1.2	0.8	0.0	2000	2&4 Matières premières huiles & graisses (combust. exclu.)
1.0	0.6	4.6	17.3	3.7	2.9	11.8	1.5	0.4	0.0	2010	
1.1	0.6	5.1	17.4	3.8	2.4	12.3	1.6	0.3	0.0	2011	
0.9	0.6	5.6	16.9	3.8	2.8	11.0	1.9	0.3	0.0	2012	
1.1	0.6	5.0	17.6	3.8	2.4	10.6	2.1	0.4	0.0	2013	
0.2	5.2	6.9	9.5	3.0	4.1	6.9	24.7	0.1	0.0	2000	3 Combustibles minéraux et produits
0.3	4.5	7.5	7.9	3.3	4.4	7.3	22.4	0.0	0.0	2010	
0.3	3.3	7.7	7.9	3.4	4.8	7.3	23.9	0.0	0.0	2011	
0.3	4.3	7.3	7.7	3.4	3.7	6.8	25.8	0.0	0.0	2012	
0.3	3.6	6.1	7.2	3.5	3.9	6.6	26.2	0.0	0.0	2013	
0.2	0.4	0.5	2.9	8.1	0.9	3.7	2.0	0.0	0.0	2000	5 Produits chimiques
0.4	0.6	0.6	2.9	11.5	1.9	4.9	3.6	0.0	0.0	2010	
0.4	0.6	0.6	3.1	12.2	2.2	5.5	4.0	0.0	0.0	2011	
0.4	0.6	0.6	3.0	12.2	2.2	5.7	4.4	0.0	0.0	2012	
0.4	0.5	0.6	2.8	12.5	2.4	5.5	4.0	0.0	0.0	2013	
0.1	0.1	0.2	4.7	13.3	0.1	8.6	0.7	0.0	0.0	2000	7 Machines et matèriels de transports
0.5	0.2	0.5	4.3	27.6	0.7	7.9	1.5	0.0	0.0	2010	
0.6	0.2	0.5	4.3	27.7	0.8	7.3	1.5	0.0	0.0	2011	
0.5	0.2	0.5	4.5	28.7	0.7	7.7	1.5	0.0	0.0	2012	
0.6	0.2	0.5	4.7	29.6	0.8	7.8	1.7	0.0	0.0	2013	
0.6	0.5	1.1	4.5	20.0	2.7	5.1	2.4	0.1	0.0	2000	6&8 Articles manufacturés divers
0.9	0.5	1.6	4.1	26.2	3.7	5.6	3.5	0.1	0.0	2010	
1.0	0.5	1.5	4.0	26.7	4.0	5.6	3.5	0.1	0.0	2011	
0.9	0.5	1.4	3.8	29.0	3.9	5.7	3.7	0.1	0.0	2012	
0.9	0.4	1.4	3.6	29.5	4.0	5.8	3.8	0.1	0.0	2013	
Destination des exportations de grandes catégories de marchandises											
0.4	0.9	1.2	5.7	11.0	1.3	5.6	3.0	0.1	0.5	2000	0-9 Tous produits 3/
0.8	1.2	2.0	5.9	17.0	3.0	6.1	4.3	0.2	1.2	2010	
0.8	1.1	2.1	6.1	17.4	3.1	6.1	4.3	0.2	1.3	2011	
0.8	1.2	2.2	6.3	18.0	3.0	6.5	4.5	0.2	1.0	2012	
0.8	1.2	2.2	6.0	18.3	2.9	6.5	4.7	0.2	1.8	2013	
0.6	1.9	2.1	5.8	6.1	1.3	4.1	4.6	0.2	0.5	2000	0&1 Produits alimentaires, boissons et tabacs
1.2	2.2	3.5	5.8	7.2	2.4	5.7	6.1	0.2	0.3	2010	
1.1	2.4	3.8	6.0	7.7	2.2	6.2	6.4	0.2	0.2	2011	
1.1	2.5	3.9	6.3	8.3	2.2	6.4	6.1	0.2	0.3	2012	
1.1	2.3	3.9	6.0	8.5	2.2	6.6	6.4	0.2	0.3	2013	
0.5	1.3	1.4	4.8	15.4	3.3	4.3	3.0	0.0	1.0	2000	2&4 Matières premières huiles & graisses (combust. exclu.)
0.8	1.6	1.6	3.9	33.2	5.2	4.5	4.1	0.0	0.2	2010	
0.9	1.6	1.7	3.9	34.2	5.0	4.7	4.3	0.0	0.1	2011	
0.9	1.5	1.7	3.9	34.6	5.4	4.8	4.4	0.0	0.2	2012	
1.0	1.4	1.7	3.7	36.6	4.9	4.6	4.3	0.0	0.2	2013	
0.5	1.1	0.9	5.2	13.5	1.8	3.9	1.9	0.2	1.9	2000	3 Combustibles minéraux et produits
0.7	1.1	1.8	5.3	22.0	3.4	6.1	2.4	0.1	2.3	2010	
0.7	1.2	1.7	6.1	21.9	3.7	5.9	2.1	0.2	2.9	2011	
0.7	1.3	1.9	5.8	23.2	3.8	6.2	2.4	0.2	1.7	2012	
0.5	1.3	2.0	5.1	23.9	3.7	6.4	2.4	0.2	1.9	2013	
0.5	0.8	1.4	6.9	12.0	1.6	4.9	3.0	0.1	1.3	2000	5 Produits chimiques
0.9	1.0	1.7	6.8	14.3	3.1	5.1	3.7	0.1	0.5	2010	
0.9	1.0	1.8	7.2	14.4	3.2	5.3	3.8	0.1	0.6	2011	
0.9	1.1	1.9	7.6	14.4	3.1	5.6	3.8	0.1	0.5	2012	
1.0	1.1	2.1	7.5	13.8	3.0	5.9	4.3	0.1	0.2	2013	
0.3	0.7	1.1	6.1	11.0	0.9	7.6	2.7	0.1	0.2	2000	7 Machines et matèriels de transports
0.6	1.1	2.0	6.8	19.1	2.3	7.2	4.4	0.3	0.1	2010	
0.7	0.9	2.2	7.0	18.7	2.4	7.1	4.4	0.3	0.2	2011	
0.6	1.0	2.1	7.1	19.2	2.1	7.7	4.7	0.2	0.1	2012	
0.7	1.0	2.2	7.1	19.9	2.0	7.5	4.9	0.3	0.1	2013	
0.6	0.8	1.1	5.3	11.0	1.4	4.1	3.5	0.1	0.3	2000	6&8 Articles manufacturés divers
0.9	1.2	2.0	5.3	13.5	3.3	5.4	5.4	0.1	0.2	2010	
1.0	1.0	2.0	5.3	13.4	3.4	5.5	5.7	0.1	0.3	2011	
0.9	1.2	2.2	5.6	13.8	3.2	6.2	5.9	0.1	0.2	2012	
0.9	1.2	2.3	5.4	13.7	3.4	6.6	6.0	0.1	0.2	2013	

Voir la fin du Tableau Spécial F pour la remarque générale et les notes.

Structure of world exports by provenance and destination (Table F)

in per cent

SITC Commodity classes	Year	World 1/ Monde 1/	Developed economies 2/ Économies développées 2/	Asia-Pacific Asie-Pacifique		Europe		North America Amérique du Nord		Commonwealth of Independent States Communauté d'Etats Indépendants	
Origin or destination →			Total	Total	Japan Japon	Total	Germany Allemagne	Total	U.S.A. É.-U.	Total	Europe
Commodity composition of the total exports of selected regions											
0-9 All commodities 3/	2000	100.0	100.0	100.0	100.0	100.0	100.0	100.0	100.0	100.0	100.0
	2010	100.0	100.0	100.0	100.0	100.0	100.0	100.0	100.0	100.0	100.0
	2011	100.0	100.0	100.0	100.0	100.0	100.0	100.0	100.0	100.0	100.0
	2012	100.0	100.0	100.0	100.0	100.0	100.0	100.0	100.0	100.0	100.0
	2013	100.0	100.0	100.0	100.0	100.0	100.0	100.0	100.0	100.0	100.0
0&1 Food, live animals, beverages and tobacco	2000	6.1	6.3	3.6	0.4	7.1	4.0	6.0	6.0	2.3	2.1
	2010	6.4	7.3	4.1	0.6	7.9	5.0	7.1	6.9	3.7	3.5
	2011	6.4	7.5	4.6	0.5	8.0	5.1	7.3	7.3	3.6	3.6
	2012	6.5	7.5	4.8	0.6	8.2	5.1	7.1	6.9	4.8	4.9
	2013	6.7	8.0	5.4	0.6	8.5	5.4	7.5	7.2	4.9	5.0
2&4 Crude materials, oils and fats, (fuels excluded)	2000	3.4	3.2	3.1	0.7	2.4	1.7	5.0	3.9	6.5	5.7
	2010	4.6	4.5	8.1	1.4	3.0	2.0	7.3	6.7	5.0	4.6
	2011	4.9	4.9	10.1	1.5	3.2	2.2	7.3	6.6	5.2	4.8
	2012	4.6	4.8	9.6	1.7	3.1	2.1	7.0	6.2	5.2	4.9
	2013	4.5	4.7	11.4	1.8	3.0	2.0	6.6	5.7	5.1	4.9
3 Mineral fuels, lubricants and related material	2000	10.3	4.7	2.7	0.3	5.2	1.4	4.7	1.7	44.0	43.4
	2010	15.0	7.7	7.4	1.7	7.0	1.9	10.4	6.3	58.8	57.1
	2011	17.4	9.1	8.3	2.0	8.1	2.2	12.7	8.7	60.5	58.7
	2012	18.3	9.6	8.1	1.7	8.9	2.7	12.7	8.9	61.7	60.8
	2013	17.5	9.7	8.3	2.3	8.8	2.8	13.2	9.4	62.9	61.6
5 Chemicals	2000	8.9	10.9	7.0	7.3	12.6	12.7	9.0	10.3	6.0	6.7
	2010	11.0	14.9	8.6	10.2	16.6	14.7	13.3	14.8	4.9	4.9
	2011	10.7	14.4	8.3	10.3	16.0	14.4	12.8	14.0	5.2	5.5
	2012	10.5	14.3	8.2	9.9	16.1	14.4	12.2	13.4	5.6	6.0
	2013	10.5	14.5	8.5	10.6	16.3	14.9	12.1	13.2	4.9	5.1
7 Machinery and transport equipment	2000	41.2	45.4	60.8	68.8	40.3	49.6	49.5	52.8	7.3	8.0
	2010	34.0	36.1	46.8	59.5	35.0	46.0	33.1	35.2	4.7	5.3
	2011	32.1	35.4	43.9	58.3	35.0	47.0	31.6	33.9	4.5	4.9
	2012	32.1	35.2	45.1	59.6	34.3	46.9	32.6	34.4	5.6	6.1
	2013	32.3	34.6	42.7	57.9	34.1	46.8	31.9	33.8	5.6	6.1
6&8 Other manufactured goods	2000	25.8	24.2	18.4	18.8	26.8	23.3	21.1	21.2	21.8	23.9
	2010	23.8	22.9	17.9	20.6	25.0	23.2	19.4	19.8	15.0	15.5
	2011	23.4	23.0	17.9	21.4	25.4	23.6	18.6	19.1	13.7	13.8
	2012	23.1	22.3	17.7	21.2	24.5	22.6	18.3	19.0	14.6	14.6
	2013	23.3	22.3	17.2	21.0	24.4	22.6	18.3	19.1	13.8	14.3
Commodity composition of the world exports to selected regions											
0-9 All commodities 3/	2000	100.0	100.0	100.0	100.0	100.0	100.0	100.0	100.0	100.0	100.0
	2010	100.0	100.0	100.0	100.0	100.0	100.0	100.0	100.0	100.0	100.0
	2011	100.0	100.0	100.0	100.0	100.0	100.0	100.0	100.0	100.0	100.0
	2012	100.0	100.0	100.0	100.0	100.0	100.0	100.0	100.0	100.0	100.0
	2013	100.0	100.0	100.0	100.0	100.0	100.0	100.0	100.0	100.0	100.0
0&1 Food, live animals, beverages and tobacco	2000	6.1	6.2	9.8	10.9	6.8	6.8	3.9	3.7	12.7	13.3
	2010	6.4	7.0	7.9	8.7	7.7	7.1	5.0	4.7	11.2	11.9
	2011	6.4	7.0	8.0	8.8	7.6	7.3	5.1	4.8	9.5	9.6
	2012	6.5	7.0	7.8	8.5	7.8	7.4	5.1	4.8	9.7	9.7
	2013	6.7	7.4	8.2	8.8	8.2	7.7	5.3	5.1	10.3	10.4
2&4 Crude materials, oils and fats, (fuels excluded)	2000	3.4	3.1	5.1	5.8	3.3	3.2	2.1	2.0	4.2	4.5
	2010	4.6	3.6	6.6	8.5	3.7	3.8	2.0	1.9	3.1	3.3
	2011	4.9	3.8	6.6	8.4	4.0	4.1	2.3	2.1	3.0	3.1
	2012	4.6	3.5	5.7	7.2	3.8	4.1	2.2	2.1	3.0	3.0
	2013	4.5	3.4	5.9	7.7	3.6	3.9	2.0	2.0	3.0	3.1
3 Mineral fuels, lubricants and related material	2000	10.3	10.1	17.4	19.7	8.7	6.1	10.5	11.7	14.4	14.9
	2010	15.0	14.3	17.5	19.9	13.1	6.4	16.1	15.6	9.7	10.6
	2011	17.4	16.5	20.5	22.9	15.3	7.9	18.1	17.1	10.5	11.6
	2012	18.3	17.5	22.6	25.8	16.9	8.7	16.8	15.3	12.3	12.9
	2013	17.5	17.0	23.9	27.5	16.6	10.4	15.6	13.4	10.7	11.0
5 Chemicals	2000	8.9	8.6	7.1	6.3	10.2	9.0	6.1	5.6	9.4	9.4
	2010	11.0	11.9	9.8	9.3	13.2	12.8	9.2	9.2	11.3	12.2
	2011	10.7	11.6	9.6	9.2	12.8	12.5	9.1	9.1	10.1	10.7
	2012	10.5	11.4	9.1	8.7	12.9	12.6	8.7	8.7	10.6	11.0
	2013	10.5	11.6	9.3	9.0	13.1	12.7	8.7	8.7	11.1	11.8
7 Machinery and transport equipment	2000	41.2	41.0	33.1	30.4	38.4	39.6	47.9	47.1	25.5	24.3
	2010	34.0	32.6	29.9	26.1	30.4	35.7	39.1	39.8	33.7	35.3
	2011	32.1	31.2	27.7	23.7	29.2	35.5	37.6	38.6	34.1	35.5
	2012	32.1	31.1	28.7	24.5	27.9	34.5	39.2	40.5	36.8	38.1
	2013	32.3	31.5	30.1	26.9	28.2	34.1	39.8	41.5	35.5	36.7
6&8 Other manufactured goods	2000	25.8	26.4	25.3	25.1	26.6	29.0	26.3	26.7	26.4	25.9
	2010	23.8	25.5	24.5	24.2	25.8	26.9	25.0	25.8	26.6	24.8
	2011	23.4	25.5	24.3	24.1	25.9	28.8	24.6	25.7	24.0	22.4
	2012	23.1	24.8	23.7	23.4	25.0	27.2	24.8	25.8	25.8	23.7
	2013	23.3	25.2	25.0	24.5	25.2	27.2	25.3	26.7	27.3	25.5

For general note and footnotes see end of Special Table F.

Structure des exportations mondiales par provenance et destination (Tableau F)

en pourcentage

En provenance ou vers ←

South-Eastern Europe Europe du Sud-est	Northern Africa Afrique du Nord	Sub-Saharan Africa Afrique subsaharienne	Latin America and the Caribbean Amérique latine et Caraïbes	Eastern Asia Asie orientale	Southern Asia Asie méridionale	South-eastern Asia Asie du Sud-est	Western Asia Asie occidentale	Oceania Océanie	Others 4/ Autre 4/	Année		CTCI: Classes de marchandises ↓
Composition par marchandises des exportations mondiales des régions selectionnées												
100.0	100.0	100.0	100.0	100.0	100.0	100.0	100.0	100.0	0.0	2000	0-9	Tous produits 3/
100.0	100.0	100.0	100.0	100.0	100.0	100.0	100.0	100.0	0.0	2010		
100.0	100.0	100.0	100.0	100.0	100.0	100.0	100.0	100.0	0.0	2011		
100.0	100.0	100.0	100.0	100.0	100.0	100.0	100.0	100.0	0.0	2012		
100.0	100.0	100.0	100.0	100.0	100.0	100.0	100.0	100.0	0.0	2013		
6.3	4.5	11.1	13.4	2.7	9.1	5.6	3.0	9.3	0.0	2000	0&1	Produits alimentaires, boissons et tabacs
9.6	5.5	9.1	15.5	2.1	8.0	6.1	3.0	13.3	0.0	2010		
9.0	5.7	8.0	15.4	2.1	7.6	6.5	2.4	13.7	0.0	2011		
10.1	4.3	8.8	15.5	2.1	8.8	6.5	2.2	14.7	0.0	2012		
10.5	5.5	9.2	16.0	2.1	9.7	6.5	2.4	13.2	0.0	2013		
8.9	2.8	7.9	7.1	1.5	2.8	4.3	1.1	35.1	0.0	2000	2&4	Matières premières huiles & graisses (combust. exclu.)
7.8	2.9	9.4	13.6	1.0	5.6	7.8	1.2	28.6	0.0	2010		
8.4	3.5	9.9	14.2	1.1	4.4	8.8	1.2	27.5	0.0	2011		
7.4	2.7	10.4	13.0	0.9	5.3	7.4	1.2	29.1	0.0	2012		
7.2	2.6	10.5	13.5	0.9	4.2	7.1	1.2	31.1	0.0	2013		
7.4	68.2	47.9	17.6	2.5	29.3	10.6	64.4	14.0	0.0	2000	3	Combustibles minéraux et produits
8.0	66.3	50.9	20.4	2.8	27.9	15.7	56.7	4.5	0.0	2010		
8.1	63.1	53.5	22.8	3.3	30.4	18.6	61.7	5.0	0.0	2011		
8.6	71.1	53.2	23.3	3.3	27.4	18.1	63.4	5.1	0.0	2012		
8.2	66.9	49.6	21.6	3.2	26.6	17.2	61.4	4.8	0.0	2013		
6.9	4.7	3.0	4.7	5.9	5.5	4.9	4.5	0.3	0.0	2000	5	Produits chimiques
6.6	6.3	2.9	5.4	7.0	9.0	7.7	6.7	0.9	0.0	2010		
7.1	7.0	2.6	5.4	7.3	8.5	8.5	6.3	2.2	0.0	2011		
7.3	5.9	2.6	5.1	6.8	9.5	8.7	6.2	3.8	0.0	2012		
6.8	6.0	2.9	5.0	6.7	9.7	8.5	5.6	4.2	0.0	2013		
14.3	3.5	5.6	34.6	44.8	4.0	52.8	7.5	3.1	0.0	2000	7	Machines et matèriels de transports
29.5	6.0	7.1	25.1	52.0	9.8	38.4	8.6	3.5	0.0	2010		
28.9	6.9	6.3	22.8	49.9	9.0	34.0	6.9	3.5	0.0	2011		
29.0	5.6	6.3	24.1	49.2	9.4	36.1	6.6	3.2	0.0	2012		
31.2	7.1	7.7	25.7	49.4	10.0	37.3	7.1	3.3	0.0	2013		
54.3	16.0	18.9	20.7	42.2	48.2	19.8	15.7	35.9	0.0	2000	6&8	Articles manufacturés divers
36.4	12.2	17.3	16.8	34.5	37.5	19.2	13.9	44.8	0.0	2010		
36.3	12.8	14.0	15.6	35.1	34.2	19.2	12.2	43.1	0.0	2011		
35.3	9.7	12.8	14.7	35.8	36.4	19.3	11.6	37.9	0.0	2012		
33.2	10.8	15.0	14.5	35.4	36.3	20.1	11.9	37.3	0.0	2013		
Composition par marchandises des exportations mondiales vers régions selectionnées												
100.0	100.0	100.0	100.0	100.0	100.0	100.0	100.0	100.0	100.0	2000	0-9	Tous produits 3/
100.0	100.0	100.0	100.0	100.0	100.0	100.0	100.0	100.0	100.0	2010		
100.0	100.0	100.0	100.0	100.0	100.0	100.0	100.0	100.0	100.0	2011		
100.0	100.0	100.0	100.0	100.0	100.0	100.0	100.0	100.0	100.0	2012		
100.0	100.0	100.0	100.0	100.0	100.0	100.0	100.0	100.0	100.0	2013		
9.1	13.4	11.1	6.1	3.4	6.4	4.5	9.3	12.5	5.9	2000	0&1	Produits alimentaires, boissons et tabacs
10.0	12.1	11.1	6.4	2.7	5.1	6.0	9.0	7.9	1.7	2010		
9.0	14.2	11.6	6.3	2.8	4.5	6.5	9.5	7.1	1.3	2011		
9.4	13.6	11.6	6.5	3.0	4.7	6.4	8.8	8.3	2.1	2012		
9.7	13.1	11.6	6.7	3.1	5.2	6.8	9.1	8.1	1.1	2013		
4.2	5.0	4.1	2.8	4.7	8.5	2.6	3.3	1.3	7.2	2000	2&4	Matières premières huiles & graisses (combust. exclu.)
4.9	6.2	3.7	3.0	9.0	8.0	3.4	4.4	0.8	0.6	2010		
5.6	7.0	3.9	3.1	9.7	8.0	3.8	4.9	0.8	0.5	2011		
5.4	5.9	3.5	2.9	8.9	8.2	3.5	4.5	0.9	0.7	2012		
5.6	5.4	3.3	2.8	9.0	7.7	3.2	4.1	0.9	0.6	2013		
11.8	13.7	7.7	9.3	12.7	14.5	7.3	6.5	17.5	41.8	2000	3	Combustibles minéraux et produits
13.8	13.5	13.8	13.6	19.4	16.9	15.2	8.5	12.9	28.3	2010		
14.4	18.3	14.3	17.5	22.1	21.0	17.0	8.6	19.2	40.7	2011		
16.2	20.2	15.9	16.8	23.6	22.7	17.4	9.5	19.6	30.2	2012		
11.9	19.4	15.4	14.9	22.9	22.3	17.3	8.8	15.6	19.2	2013		
9.9	8.3	10.3	10.7	9.7	10.9	7.7	8.9	5.1	24.5	2000	5	Produits chimiques
12.6	9.3	9.4	12.7	9.3	11.3	9.2	9.4	5.0	4.0	2010		
12.2	9.2	9.3	12.5	8.9	10.9	9.4	9.4	4.5	4.7	2011		
12.5	9.3	8.9	12.6	8.3	10.6	9.0	8.9	5.2	5.5	2012		
13.3	10.0	9.7	13.1	7.9	11.1	9.5	9.4	3.5	1.2	2013		
27.0	32.2	38.7	43.6	41.0	27.8	55.8	37.2	31.7	17.4	2000	7	Machines et matèriels de transports
28.1	31.3	33.8	39.3	38.2	26.7	40.4	34.3	55.7	3.1	2010		
27.5	24.8	33.5	36.4	34.6	24.5	37.7	32.5	49.7	4.0	2011		
26.8	26.3	30.6	36.3	34.3	22.2	38.3	33.1	43.5	3.8	2012		
28.9	26.8	31.6	38.0	35.2	22.1	37.2	33.2	50.8	1.7	2013		
36.0	25.0	24.1	23.9	25.8	27.6	18.8	29.6	25.8	16.4	2000	6&8	Articles manufacturés divers
29.3	24.8	23.1	21.2	18.8	26.2	21.3	29.7	10.9	4.6	2010		
28.3	22.1	22.8	20.3	18.0	25.6	21.4	30.7	10.7	4.9	2011		
27.0	22.7	23.5	20.6	17.8	24.5	22.1	30.4	12.3	4.7	2012		
28.2	23.4	23.9	20.7	17.4	27.6	23.3	29.6	10.5	2.6	2013		

Voir la fin du Tableau Spécial F pour la remarque générale et les notes.

Growth and structure of world exports by provenance and destination (Tables E and F)
Croissance et structure des exportations mondiales par provenance et destination (Tableaux E et F)

General note

The figures in tables E and F are derived from the data in Special Table D.

The commodity classification is in accordance with the United Nations' Standard International Trade Classification (SITC), Revision 3, except for countries which report trade data only in terms of the SITC, Revision 2, or the SITC, Revised.

The data approximate total exports of all countries and areas of the world. They are based on official export figures converted, where necessary, to U.S. dollars according to conversion factors published in Table C for each country in this volume. Where official figures are not available, estimates based on the imports reported by partner countries and on other subsidiary data are used. Some official national data have been adjusted
(a) to approximate the commodity groupings of the SITC and
(b) to approximate calendar years.

The data include special category (confidential) exports, ships' stores and bunkers and exports of minor importance, the destination of which cannot be determined. These data are included in the world totals for each commodity group and in total exports, and are available separately in region "Others"

1/ For the country composition of geographical regions, please refer to http://mdgs.un.org/unsd/mdg/Host.aspx?Content=Data/RegionalGroupings.htm
2/ This classification is intended for statistical convenience and does not, necessarily, express a judgment about the stage reached by a particular country in the development process.
3/ Section 9 of the SITC, which comprises commodities and transactions not classified elsewhere, is included in the total trade but is not shown separately in this table.
4/ The region "Others" as destination for exports contains the following trading partners: Antarctica, bunkers, free zones, confidential and not elsewhere specified countries

Remarque générale

Les données des tables E et F sont derivées de celles publiées dans le Tableau Spécial D.

La classification par marchandise utilisée est la Classification Type pour le Commerce International (CTCI), Revision 3,) en dehors des pays qui rapportent exclusivement les données du commerce en accord avec la CTCI, Revision 2, ou la CTCI, Revisée.

Les données sont une estimation des exportations totales de tous les pays et régions du monde. Elles sont basées sur les chiffres des exportations officielles nationales convertis en dollars E.-U. selon les facteurs de conversion pour chaque pays publiés dans le Tableau C de ce volume. Quand les chiffres officiels ne sont pas disponibles, des estimations basées sur les importations rapportées par les pays partenaires ou sur d'autres données subsidiaries sont utilisées. Quelques données officielles nationales ont été ajustées afin
(a) qu'elles correspondent aux groupes des marchandises de la CTCI et
(b) qu'elles correspondent aux années civiles.

Les données comprennent les exportations de 'special category' (confidentielles), les approvisionnments des navires et combustible de soute et autres exportations de moindre importance dont la destination n'a pu être déterminée. Ces donnés sont comprises dans le total pour chaque groupe de marchandise et dans les exportations totales, et sont disponibles separemment dans la région "Autres".

1/ Pour la composition des régions géographiques, se référer à http://mdgs.un.org/unsd/mdg/Host.aspx?Content=Data/RegionalGroupings.htm
2/ Cette classification est utilisée pour plus de commodité dans la présentation des statistiques et n'implique pas nécessairement un jugement quant au stade de développement auquel est parvenu un pays donné.
3/ Section 9 de la CTCI, qui représente les articles et transactions non ailleurs est comprise dans le commerce total mais n'est pas présentée séparément dans ce tableau.
4/ La région "Autres" comme destination des exportations comprend les partenaires commerciaux suivants: Antarctique, combustibles de soute, zones franches, partenaires confidentiels ou non specifiés ailleurs.

Indices of total exports and imports by countries or areas (Table G)

Quantum and unit value indices and terms of trade in US dollars (2000 = 100)

Indices des exportations et importations totales par pays ou zones (Tableau G)

Indices du quantum et de la valeur unitaire et termes de l'échange en dollars É.-U. (2000 = 100)

Countries	2004	2005	2006	2007	2008	2009	2010	2011	2012	2013	Pays
Argentina											**Argentine**
Imp: Quantum	87	108	125	150	177	137	188	232	204	212	Imp: quantum
Imp: Unit Value	102	105	108	115	128	111	119	130	144	151	Imp: valeur unitaire
Exp: Quantum	118	135	143	154	156	142	165	...	166	172	Exp: quantum
Exp: Unit Value	111	113	122	137	213	178	157	183	198	194	Exp: valeur unitaire
Terms of Trade	*110*	*107*	*114*	*119*	*167*	*161*	*133*	*141*	*137*	*129*	*Termes de l'échange*
Purchasing Power of Exports	*129*	*145*	*163*	*183*	*260*	*228*	*218*	*...*	*227*	*221*	*Pouvoir d'achat des export.*
Australia											**Australie**
Imp: Quantum	116	129	145	155	186	164	173	192	208	211	Imp: quantum
Imp: Unit Value[1]	111	117	120	128	141	132	145	164	167	159	Imp: valeur unitaire[1]
Exp: Quantum	101	119	141	145	191	168	198	229	212	225	Exp: quantum
Exp: Unit Value[1]	129	153	175	196	245	214	260	329	304	282	Exp: valeur unitaire[1]
Terms of Trade	*116*	*131*	*146*	*153*	*174*	*162*	*179*	*201*	*182*	*177*	*Termes de l'échange*
Purchasing Power of Exports	*117*	*156*	*206*	*220*	*331*	*272*	*354*	*461*	*386*	*398*	*Pouvoir d'achat des export.*
Austria											**Autriche**
Imp: Quantum	122	130	137	149	148	125	137	147	148	148	Imp: quantum
Imp: Unit Value[1]	125	136	142	158	174	161	164	177	167	169	Imp: valeur unitaire[1]
Exp: Quantum	127	135	145	159	159	129	145	158	157	162	Exp: quantum
Exp: Unit Value[1]	126	137	142	158	174	162	156	170	158	161	Exp: valeur unitaire[1]
Terms of Trade	*101*	*101*	*100*	*100*	*100*	*100*	*95*	*96*	*95*	*95*	*Termes de l'échange*
Purchasing Power of Exports	*128*	*136*	*145*	*159*	*159*	*130*	*138*	*151*	*148*	*154*	*Pouvoir d'achat des export.*
Belgium											**Belgique**
Imp: Quantum	121	126	132	138	139	123	130	136	133	134	Imp: quantum
Imp: Unit Value	134	143	151	169	191	164	172	196	186	192	Imp: valeur unitaire
Exp: Quantum	121	126	131	135	132	117	126	130	129	131	Exp: quantum
Exp: Unit Value	135	142	149	170	190	169	174	196	185	191	Exp: valeur unitaire
Terms of Trade	*101*	*99*	*99*	*101*	*100*	*103*	*101*	*100*	*99*	*99*	*Termes de l'échange*
Purchasing Power of Exports	*122*	*125*	*129*	*136*	*132*	*121*	*126*	*130*	*128*	*131*	*Pouvoir d'achat des export.*
Bolivia (Plurinational State of)											**Bolivie (État plurinational de)**
Imp: Quantum	...	...	...	...	...	...	...	...	...	...	Imp: quantum
Imp: Unit Value	...	...	...	...	...	...	...	...	...	...	Imp: valeur unitaire
Exp: Quantum	237	278	300	315	358	325	394	373	415	470	Exp: quantum
Exp: Unit Value	115	151	257	289	321	259	298	432	456	425	Exp: valeur unitaire
Terms of Trade	*...*	*...*	*...*	*...*	*...*	*...*	*...*	*...*	*...*	*...*	*Termes de l'échange*
Purchasing Power of Exports	*...*	*...*	*...*	*...*	*...*	*...*	*...*	*...*	*...*	*...*	*Pouvoir d'achat des export.*
Brazil											**Brésil**
Imp: Quantum	111	101	110	128	134	112	149	160	153	172	Imp: quantum
Imp: Unit Value	101	130	149	167	230	204	217	251	262	249	Imp: valeur unitaire
Exp: Quantum	154	162	173	189	192	186	213	222	223	228	Exp: quantum
Exp: Unit Value	116	132	145	154	188	149	171	208	198	192	Exp: valeur unitaire
Terms of Trade	*114*	*101*	*97*	*92*	*82*	*73*	*79*	*83*	*76*	*77*	*Termes de l'échange*
Purchasing Power of Exports	*176*	*164*	*169*	*174*	*157*	*136*	*167*	*184*	*169*	*176*	*Pouvoir d'achat des export.*
Bulgaria											**Bulgarie**
Imp: Quantum	...	...	...	...	...	...	...	...	...	...	Imp: quantum
Imp: Unit Value[1]	130	140	156	182	208	178	177	199	188	189	Imp: valeur unitaire[1]
Exp: Quantum	...	...	...	...	...	...	...	...	...	...	Exp: quantum
Exp: Unit Value[1]	133	142	162	194	227	188	197	232	225	227	Exp: valeur unitaire[1]
Terms of Trade	*102*	*102*	*104*	*107*	*109*	*106*	*112*	*117*	*120*	*120*	*Termes de l'échange*
Purchasing Power of Exports	*...*	*...*	*...*	*...*	*...*	*...*	*...*	*...*	*...*	*...*	*Pouvoir d'achat des export.*

Indices of total exports and imports by countries or areas (Table G)

Quantum and unit value indices and terms of trade in US dollars (2000 = 100)

Indices des exportations et importations totales par pays ou zones (Tableau G)

Indices du quantum et de la valeur unitaire et termes de l'échange en dollars É.-U. (2000 = 100)

Countries	2004	2005	2006	2007	2008	2009	2010	2011	2012	2013	Pays
Canada											**Canada**
Imp: Quantum	108	116	123	130	130	110	127	135	138	142	Imp: quantum
Imp: Unit Value	104	111	119	125	134	125	132	143	142	139	Imp: valeur unitaire
Exp: Quantum	100	102	103	105	100	85	91	96	100	102	Exp: quantum
Exp: Unit Value	120	133	143	154	175	142	163	180	175	173	Exp: valeur unitaire
Terms of Trade	*116*	*120*	*120*	*123*	*130*	*114*	*123*	*126*	*123*	*125*	*Termes de l'échange*
Purchasing Power of Exports	*116*	*123*	*124*	*129*	*130*	*97*	*113*	*121*	*123*	*127*	*Pouvoir d'achat des export.*
China, Hong Kong SAR											**Chine, Hong Kong RAS**
Imp: Quantum	136	147	162	179	184	167	198	206	208	216	Imp: quantum
Imp: Unit Value	95	98	100	102	107	107	114	123	127	129	Imp: valeur unitaire
Exp: Quantum	138	154	169	184	189	166	196	201	201	206	Exp: quantum
Exp: Unit Value	95	96	97	99	103	105	109	118	122	124	Exp: valeur unitaire
Terms of Trade	*99*	*98*	*97*	*97*	*96*	*97*	*96*	*96*	*96*	*96*	*Termes de l'échange*
Purchasing Power of Exports	*137*	*151*	*164*	*178*	*182*	*162*	*188*	*193*	*192*	*199*	*Pouvoir d'achat des export.*
Colombia											**Colombie**
Imp: Quantum	...	...	...	...	...	...	...	...	...	...	Imp: quantum
Imp: Unit Value[1]	103	114	114	117	125	116	...	...	...	...	Imp: valeur unitaire[1]
Exp: Quantum	...	...	...	...	...	...	...	...	...	...	Exp: quantum
Exp: Unit Value[1]	96	111	119	130	159	151	...	...	...	...	Exp: valeur unitaire[1]
Terms of Trade	*93*	*97*	*104*	*111*	*128*	*130*	*...*	*...*	*...*	*...*	*Termes de l'échange*
Purchasing Power of Exports	*...*	*...*	*...*	*...*	*...*	*...*	*...*	*...*	*...*	*...*	*Pouvoir d'achat des export.*
Czech Republic											**République tchèque**
Imp: Quantum	...	...	...	...	...	...	...	...	...	...	Imp: quantum
Imp: Unit Value	137	148	158	175	201	173	175	197	186	185	Imp: valeur unitaire
Exp: Quantum	...	...	...	...	...	...	...	...	...	...	Exp: quantum
Exp: Unit Value	147	155	164	185	210	189	185	203	189	191	Exp: valeur unitaire
Terms of Trade	*107*	*105*	*104*	*106*	*105*	*109*	*106*	*103*	*102*	*103*	*Termes de l'échange*
Purchasing Power of Exports	*...*	*...*	*...*	*...*	*...*	*...*	*...*	*...*	*...*	*...*	*Pouvoir d'achat des export.*
Denmark											**Danemark**
Imp: Quantum	113	122	135	147	141	114	123	134	138	143	Imp: quantum
Imp: Unit Value	133	138	143	160	173	154	150	163	152	153	Imp: valeur unitaire
Exp: Quantum	110	116	123	131	130	114	120	128	128	131	Exp: quantum
Exp: Unit Value	136	143	148	160	178	160	159	173	166	168	Exp: valeur unitaire
Terms of Trade	*103*	*104*	*103*	*100*	*103*	*103*	*106*	*106*	*109*	*110*	*Termes de l'échange*
Purchasing Power of Exports	*113*	*121*	*128*	*132*	*133*	*118*	*127*	*135*	*139*	*144*	*Pouvoir d'achat des export.*
Ecuador											**Equateur**
Imp: Quantum	168	204	229	262	280	274	331	350	345	381	Imp: quantum
Imp: Unit Value	...	...	...	...	...	...	...	...	...	...	Imp: valeur unitaire
Exp: Quantum	133	117	143	139	141	137	133	138	140	147	Exp: quantum
Exp: Unit Value	118	152	184	212	289	202	267	369	346	...	Exp: valeur unitaire
Terms of Trade	*...*	*...*	*...*	*...*	*...*	*...*	*...*	*...*	*...*	*...*	*Termes de l'échange*
Purchasing Power of Exports	*...*	*...*	*...*	*...*	*...*	*...*	*...*	*...*	*...*	*...*	*Pouvoir d'achat des export.*
Estonia											**Estonie**
Imp: Quantum	...	...	...	...	...	...	...	...	...	...	Imp: quantum
Imp: Unit Value	135	140	148	166	189	170	176	206	197	200	Imp: valeur unitaire
Exp: Quantum	...	...	...	...	...	...	...	...	...	...	Exp: quantum
Exp: Unit Value	194	199	211	247	276	252	254	292	275	281	Exp: valeur unitaire
Terms of Trade	*144*	*143*	*142*	*148*	*146*	*149*	*144*	*142*	*139*	*140*	*Termes de l'échange*
Purchasing Power of Exports	*...*	*...*	*...*	*...*	*...*	*...*	*...*	*...*	*...*	*...*	*Pouvoir d'achat des export.*

Indices of total exports and imports by countries or areas (Table G)

Quantum and unit value indices and terms of trade in US dollars (2000 = 100)

Indices des exportations et importations totales par pays ou zones (Tableau G)

Indices du quantum et de la valeur unitaire et termes de l'échange en dollars É.-U. (2000 = 100)

Countries	2004	2005	2006	2007	2008	2009	2010	2011	2012	2013	Pays
Finland											**Finlande**
Imp: Quantum	108	114	127	128	130	100	109	118	108	98	Imp: quantum
Imp: Unit Value[1]	131	146	149	166	184	159	160	182	173	175	Imp: valeur unitaire[1]
Exp: Quantum	112	111	124	120	121	88	94	94	94	97	Exp: quantum
Exp: Unit Value[1]	117	127	122	134	145	126	124	137	127	129	Exp: valeur unitaire[1]
Terms of Trade	*89*	*87*	*82*	*81*	*79*	*79*	*78*	*75*	*73*	*74*	*Termes de l'échange*
Purchasing Power of Exports	*99*	*96*	*102*	*98*	*96*	*70*	*73*	*71*	*69*	*72*	*Pouvoir d'achat des export.*
France											**France**
Imp: Quantum	105	111	117	121	121	109	120	122	121	121	Imp: quantum
Imp: Unit Value[1]	135	141	149	165	187	161	163	185	176	178	Imp: valeur unitaire[1]
Exp: Quantum	101	104	112	114	114	99	110	114	116	115	Exp: quantum
Exp: Unit Value[1]	139	141	145	161	179	161	156	171	160	165	Exp: valeur unitaire[1]
Terms of Trade	*103*	*100*	*97*	*97*	*96*	*100*	*96*	*92*	*91*	*93*	*Termes de l'échange*
Purchasing Power of Exports	*103*	*104*	*109*	*111*	*109*	*99*	*105*	*105*	*106*	*106*	*Pouvoir d'achat des export.*
Germany											**Allemagne**
Imp: Quantum	120	128	144	148	150	131	148	158	155	156	Imp: quantum
Imp: Unit Value[1]	131	136	143	157	177	153	156	174	164	165	Imp: valeur unitaire[1]
Exp: Quantum	128	137	155	164	166	136	155	168	169	169	Exp: quantum
Exp: Unit Value[1]	137	138	142	156	171	158	155	168	158	162	Exp: valeur unitaire[1]
Terms of Trade	*104*	*102*	*99*	*99*	*97*	*104*	*100*	*97*	*96*	*98*	*Termes de l'échange*
Purchasing Power of Exports	*133*	*139*	*153*	*163*	*161*	*140*	*154*	*162*	*162*	*166*	*Pouvoir d'achat des export.*
Greece											**Grèce**
Imp: Quantum	...	...	...	...	...	...	...	...	...	...	Imp: quantum
Imp: Unit Value[1]	144	158	165	185	213	198	201	227	219	220	Imp: valeur unitaire[1]
Exp: Quantum	...	...	...	...	...	...	...	...	...	...	Exp: quantum
Exp: Unit Value[1]	143	149	158	177	202	180	187	213	205	208	Exp: valeur unitaire[1]
Terms of Trade	*99*	*95*	*95*	*96*	*95*	*91*	*93*	*94*	*93*	*94*	*Termes de l'échange*
Purchasing Power of Exports	*...*	*...*	*...*	*...*	*...*	*...*	*...*	*...*	*...*	*...*	*Pouvoir d'achat des export.*
Guyana											**Guyana**
Imp: Quantum	...	...	...	...	...	...	...	...	...	...	Imp: quantum
Imp: Unit Value	...	...	...	...	...	...	...	...	...	...	Imp: valeur unitaire
Exp: Quantum	84	75	76	99	86	77	78	90	100	...	Exp: quantum
Exp: Unit Value	...	...	...	...	...	...	...	...	...	...	Exp: valeur unitaire
Terms of Trade	*...*	*...*	*...*	*...*	*...*	*...*	*...*	*...*	*...*	*...*	*Termes de l'échange*
Purchasing Power of Exports	*...*	*...*	*...*	*...*	*...*	*...*	*...*	*...*	*...*	*...*	*Pouvoir d'achat des export.*
Honduras											**Honduras**
Imp: Quantum	...	...	...	...	...	...	...	...	...	...	Imp: quantum
Imp: Unit Value	...	...	...	...	...	...	...	...	...	...	Imp: valeur unitaire
Exp: Quantum	113	105	110	119	123	113	116	131	165	144	Exp: quantum
Exp: Unit Value[1]	88	125	128	135	162	152	183	263	224	174	Exp: valeur unitaire[1]
Terms of Trade	*...*	*...*	*...*	*...*	*...*	*...*	*...*	*...*	*...*	*...*	*Termes de l'échange*
Purchasing Power of Exports	*...*	*...*	*...*	*...*	*...*	*...*	*...*	*...*	*...*	*...*	*Pouvoir d'achat des export.*
Hungary											**Hongrie**
Imp: Quantum	139	148	169	189	198	165	185	198	198	208	Imp: quantum
Imp: Unit Value[1]	135	138	142	156	171	147	144	157	146	146	Imp: valeur unitaire[1]
Exp: Quantum	148	165	194	225	235	206	235	258	260	273	Exp: quantum
Exp: Unit Value[1]	134	134	136	149	160	140	138	147	135	136	Exp: valeur unitaire[1]
Terms of Trade	*99*	*97*	*95*	*95*	*94*	*96*	*95*	*94*	*93*	*93*	*Termes de l'échange*
Purchasing Power of Exports	*146*	*159*	*186*	*215*	*220*	*197*	*224*	*242*	*241*	*254*	*Pouvoir d'achat des export.*

Indices of total exports and imports by countries or areas (Table G)
Quantum and unit value indices and terms of trade in US dollars (2000 = 100)

Indices des exportations et importations totales par pays ou zones (Tableau G)
Indices du quantum et de la valeur unitaire et termes de l'échange en dollars É.-U. (2000 = 100)

Countries	2004	2005	2006	2007	2008	2009	2010	2011	2012	2013	Pays
Iceland											Islande
Imp: Quantum	113	140	154	154	132	96	101	...	...	...	Imp: quantum
Imp: Unit Value	130	139	146	166	185	148	157	...	...	...	Imp: valeur unitaire
Exp: Quantum	126	120	117	129	161	166	170	...	...	...	Exp: quantum
Exp: Unit Value	123	132	148	167	167	125	144	...	...	...	Exp: valeur unitaire
Terms of Trade	95	95	101	101	91	84	92	...	...	...	Termes de l'échange
Purchasing Power of Exports	119	114	118	130	146	140	156	...	...	...	Pouvoir d'achat des export.
India											Inde
Imp: Quantum	155	197	239	290	241	236	282	247	231	...	Imp: quantum
Imp: Unit Value	135	124	124	139	150	121	145	248	234	246	Imp: valeur unitaire
Exp: Quantum	152	185	193	212	206	193	230	274	264	...	Exp: quantum
Exp: Unit Value	116	130	137	159	177	160	192	226	210	224	Exp: valeur unitaire
Terms of Trade	86	105	111	114	118	132	133	91	90	91	Termes de l'échange
Purchasing Power of Exports	131	195	215	242	243	254	305	250	236	...	Pouvoir d'achat des export.
Indonesia											Indonésie
Imp: Quantum	...	...	...	...	...	...	...	...	...	...	Imp: quantum
Imp: Unit Value	...	...	...	...	...	...	...	...	...	...	Imp: valeur unitaire
Exp: Quantum	101	64	...	...	...	...	...	...	...	...	Exp: quantum
Exp: Unit Value	120	81	...	...	...	...	...	...	...	...	Exp: valeur unitaire
Terms of Trade	...	...	...	...	...	...	...	...	...	...	Termes de l'échange
Purchasing Power of Exports	...	...	...	...	...	...	...	...	...	...	Pouvoir d'achat des export.
Ireland											Irlande
Imp: Quantum	104	116	119	122	110	90	89	85	84	86	Imp: quantum
Imp: Unit Value	120	121	126	137	150	134	134	149	146	149	Imp: valeur unitaire
Exp: Quantum	112	114	114	120	121	116	122	127	119	114	Exp: quantum
Exp: Unit Value	122	123	124	132	137	130	127	133	129	131	Exp: valeur unitaire
Terms of Trade	102	102	99	97	91	97	94	89	88	88	Termes de l'échange
Purchasing Power of Exports	114	116	113	116	110	112	115	112	105	100	Pouvoir d'achat des export.
Israel											Israël
Imp: Quantum	103	105	105	114	116	99	115	126	128	127	Imp: quantum
Imp: Unit Value	112	120	127	138	158	134	144	165	160	159	Imp: valeur unitaire
Exp: Quantum	116	119	124	136	134	112	132	144	128	134	Exp: quantum
Exp: Unit Value	106	114	119	127	147	136	141	151	157	160	Exp: valeur unitaire
Terms of Trade	95	95	94	92	93	102	98	91	98	101	Termes de l'échange
Purchasing Power of Exports	110	113	116	125	124	114	130	132	125	135	Pouvoir d'achat des export.
Italy											Italie
Imp: Quantum	107	108	113	116	109	94	105	104	94	91	Imp: quantum
Imp: Unit Value	139	149	165	185	218	185	194	226	218	221	Imp: valeur unitaire
Exp: Quantum	103	104	110	115	110	89	97	100	100	99	Exp: quantum
Exp: Unit Value	142	149	158	181	206	191	192	217	209	219	Exp: valeur unitaire
Terms of Trade	103	100	96	98	95	103	99	96	96	99	Termes de l'échange
Purchasing Power of Exports	106	104	105	112	104	92	96	96	96	97	Pouvoir d'achat des export.
Jamaica											Jamaïque
Imp: Quantum	...	...	...	...	...	...	...	...	...	...	Imp: quantum
Imp: Unit Value	...	...	...	...	...	...	...	...	...	...	Imp: valeur unitaire
Exp: Quantum	112	117	118	107	116	60	54	67	60	61	Exp: quantum
Exp: Unit Value	115	115	125	139	140	119	136	138	144	138	Exp: valeur unitaire
Terms of Trade	...	...	...	...	...	...	...	...	...	...	Termes de l'échange
Purchasing Power of Exports	...	...	...	...	...	...	...	...	...	...	Pouvoir d'achat des export.

Indices of total exports and imports by countries or areas (Table G)
Quantum and unit value indices and terms of trade in US dollars (2000 = 100)

Indices des exportations et importations totales par pays ou zones (Tableau G)
Indices du quantum et de la valeur unitaire et termes de l'échange en dollars É.-U. (2000 = 100)

Countries	2004	2005	2006	2007	2008	2009	2010	2011	2012	2013	Pays
Japan											Japon
Imp: Quantum	115	118	123	119	119	102	116	119	121	122	Imp: quantum
Imp: Unit Value[1]	104	115	125	133	163	135	154	183	182	170	Imp: valeur unitaire[1]
Exp: Quantum	113	114	123	130	128	94	117	112	107	105	Exp: quantum
Exp: Unit Value[1]	96	96	94	95	101	101	105	112	110	100	Exp: valeur unitaire[1]
Terms of Trade	92	83	75	72	62	74	68	62	60	59	Termes de l'échange
Purchasing Power of Exports	104	95	92	93	79	70	79	69	65	62	Pouvoir d'achat des export.
Jordan											Jordanie
Imp: Quantum	136	155	154	162	166	155	138	132	151	155	Imp: quantum
Imp: Unit Value	130	148	162	184	221	197	243	305	300	303	Imp: valeur unitaire
Exp: Quantum	190	182	188	173	158	142	188	190	175	195	Exp: quantum
Exp: Unit Value	114	131	143	170	261	237	207	233	252	230	Exp: valeur unitaire
Terms of Trade	87	88	88	92	118	120	85	77	84	76	Termes de l'échange
Purchasing Power of Exports	166	161	166	160	186	171	160	145	146	148	Pouvoir d'achat des export.
Korea, Republic of											Corée, République de
Imp: Quantum	129	138	151	149	214	139	177	186	187	195	Imp: quantum
Imp: Unit Value[1]	107	124	134	144	168	137	159	185	181	172	Imp: valeur unitaire[1]
Exp: Quantum	159	169	196	221	232	232	283	322	340	356	Exp: quantum
Exp: Unit Value[1]	92	96	94	95	99	84	90	94	91	89	Exp: valeur unitaire[1]
Terms of Trade	85	77	70	66	59	61	57	51	50	52	Termes de l'échange
Purchasing Power of Exports	136	131	138	146	137	142	161	164	171	185	Pouvoir d'achat des export.
Latvia											Lettonie
Imp: Quantum	...	...	...	...	...	...	...	...	...	...	Imp: quantum
Imp: Unit Value	...	...	...	...	...	...	...	...	...	...	Imp: valeur unitaire
Exp: Quantum	...	...	...	...	...	...	...	...	...	...	Exp: quantum
Exp: Unit Value	145	152	169	209	242	207	212	253	240	252	Exp: valeur unitaire
Terms of Trade	...	...	...	...	...	...	...	...	...	...	Termes de l'échange
Purchasing Power of Exports	...	...	...	...	...	...	...	...	...	...	Pouvoir d'achat des export.
Lithuania											Lituanie
Imp: Quantum	182	209	233	257	280	197	239	271	285	310	Imp: quantum
Imp: Unit Value	127	138	151	174	211	169	178	214	207	209	Imp: valeur unitaire
Exp: Quantum	185	214	234	250	284	251	296	336	373	405	Exp: quantum
Exp: Unit Value	137	151	160	185	216	179	191	227	218	221	Exp: valeur unitaire
Terms of Trade	108	109	106	106	102	106	107	106	105	105	Termes de l'échange
Purchasing Power of Exports	199	233	247	266	289	265	316	357	392	427	Pouvoir d'achat des export.
Malta											Malte
Imp: Quantum	...	...	...	...	...	...	...	...	...	...	Imp: quantum
Imp: Unit Value	113	...	...	...	...	...	...	...	...	...	Imp: valeur unitaire
Exp: Quantum	...	...	...	...	...	...	...	...	...	...	Exp: quantum
Exp: Unit Value	97	...	...	...	...	...	...	...	...	...	Exp: valeur unitaire
Terms of Trade	85	...	...	...	...	...	...	...	...	...	Termes de l'échange
Purchasing Power of Exports	...	...	...	...	...	...	...	...	...	...	Pouvoir d'achat des export.
Mauritius											Maurice
Imp: Quantum	102	108	111	114	114	108	115	119	122	...	Imp: quantum
Imp: Unit Value[1]	90	98	102	111	133	112	124	141	143	...	Imp: valeur unitaire[1]
Exp: Quantum	89	96	106	95	96	87	101	104	106	...	Exp: quantum
Exp: Unit Value[1]	92	90	89	96	102	91	91	101	103	...	Exp: valeur unitaire[1]
Terms of Trade	101	92	87	87	77	81	73	72	72	...	Termes de l'échange
Purchasing Power of Exports	90	89	93	83	73	71	74	75	77	...	Pouvoir d'achat des export.

Indices of total exports and imports by countries or areas (Table G)

Quantum and unit value indices and terms of trade in US dollars (2000 = 100)

Indices des exportations et importations totales par pays ou zones (Tableau G)

Indices du quantum et de la valeur unitaire et termes de l'échange en dollars É.-U. (2000 = 100)

Countries	2004	2005	2006	2007	2008	2009	2010	2011	2012	2013	Pays
Mexico											**Mexique**
Imp: Quantum	...	...	...	...	...	...	...	...	...	...	Imp: quantum
Imp: Unit Value[1]	108	99	103	109	117	92	102	112	106	109	Imp: valeur unitaire[1]
Exp: Quantum	...	...	...	...	...	...	...	...	...	...	Exp: quantum
Exp: Unit Value[1]	117	110	119	124	135	94	113	132	121	125	Exp: valeur unitaire[1]
Terms of Trade	108	112	115	114	116	103	111	118	114	114	Termes de l'échange
Purchasing Power of Exports	...	...	...	...	...	...	...	...	...	...	Pouvoir d'achat des export.
Morocco											**Maroc**
Imp: Quantum	127	140	155	176	...	...	...	...	228	...	Imp: quantum
Imp: Unit Value	122	129	134	152	...	...	...	...	164	...	Imp: valeur unitaire
Exp: Quantum	105	118	127	131	...	...	...	...	148	...	Exp: quantum
Exp: Unit Value	127	128	135	150	...	...	...	...	186	...	Exp: valeur unitaire
Terms of Trade	105	99	100	98	...	...	...	...	114	...	Termes de l'échange
Purchasing Power of Exports	110	117	128	129	...	...	...	...	168	...	Pouvoir d'achat des export.
Netherlands											**Pays-Bas**
Imp: Quantum	114	121	133	141	146	130	147	154	160	161	Imp: quantum
Imp: Unit Value	125	129	135	150	169	147	150	165	156	159	Imp: valeur unitaire
Exp: Quantum	115	122	134	144	147	134	151	158	163	165	Exp: quantum
Exp: Unit Value	130	134	140	155	175	151	153	169	160	163	Exp: valeur unitaire
Terms of Trade	103	104	104	103	103	103	103	103	102	103	Termes de l'échange
Purchasing Power of Exports	119	127	139	149	151	138	155	162	166	169	Pouvoir d'achat des export.
New Zealand											**Nouvelle-Zélande**
Imp: Quantum	143	151	152	166	164	148	164	174	176	195	Imp: quantum
Imp: Unit Value[1]	118	125	123	134	147	121	138	153	153	147	Imp: valeur unitaire[1]
Exp: Quantum	118	117	121	129	124	134	136	139	150	150	Exp: quantum
Exp: Unit Value[1]	129	134	134	157	178	133	170	193	180	198	Exp: valeur unitaire[1]
Terms of Trade	109	107	109	117	122	109	124	127	118	135	Termes de l'échange
Purchasing Power of Exports	129	125	131	151	150	146	168	176	176	202	Pouvoir d'achat des export.
Norway											**Norvège**
Imp: Quantum[2]	119	130	143	157	158	139	149	157	159	161	Imp: quantum[2]
Imp: Unit Value[2]	126	131	138	158	172	152	156	175	169	171	Imp: valeur unitaire[2]
Exp: Quantum[2]	108	107	105	106	107	103	101	98	98	94	Exp: quantum[2]
Exp: Unit Value[2]	128	162	195	214	270	189	217	276	275	277	Exp: valeur unitaire[2]
Terms of Trade	102	123	141	136	157	124	139	158	162	162	Termes de l'échange
Purchasing Power of Exports	110	132	148	144	168	128	140	154	159	151	Pouvoir d'achat des export.
Oman											**Oman**
Imp: Quantum	...	...	...	...	...	...	...	...	...	...	Imp: quantum
Imp: Unit Value	115	121	...	...	...	...	...	...	...	...	Imp: valeur unitaire
Exp: Quantum	...	...	...	...	...	...	...	...	...	...	Exp: quantum
Exp: Unit Value	129	188	231	244	378	212	...	...	...	...	Exp: valeur unitaire
Terms of Trade	112	156	...	...	...	...	...	...	...	...	Termes de l'échange
Purchasing Power of Exports	...	...	...	...	...	...	...	...	...	...	Pouvoir d'achat des export.
Pakistan											**Pakistan**
Imp: Quantum	142	165	153	169	184	178	173	161	157	...	Imp: quantum
Imp: Unit Value	122	138	151	167	216	178	203	251	263	...	Imp: valeur unitaire
Exp: Quantum	103	126	127	124	133	126	131	126	132	...	Exp: quantum
Exp: Unit Value	103	103	106	110	124	115	131	156	156	...	Exp: valeur unitaire
Terms of Trade	85	75	70	66	57	65	65	62	59	...	Termes de l'échange
Purchasing Power of Exports	87	95	89	81	76	82	85	78	78	...	Pouvoir d'achat des export.

Indices of total exports and imports by countries or areas (Table G)
Quantum and unit value indices and terms of trade in US dollars (2000 = 100)

Indices des exportations et importations totales par pays ou zones (Tableau G)
Indices du quantum et de la valeur unitaire et termes de l'échange en dollars É.-U. (2000 = 100)

Countries	2004	2005	2006	2007	2008	2009	2010	2011	2012	2013	Pays
Panama											**Panama**
Imp: Quantum	...	...	...	...	...	...	...	...	...	...	Imp: quantum
Imp: Unit Value	...	...	...	...	...	...	...	...	...	...	Imp: valeur unitaire
Exp: Quantum	80	88	94	96	75	62	60	...	...	...	Exp: quantum
Exp: Unit Value	...	...	...	...	...	...	...	...	...	...	Exp: valeur unitaire
Terms of Trade	...	...	...	...	...	...	...	...	...	...	Termes de l'échange
Purchasing Power of Exports	...	...	...	...	...	...	...	...	...	...	Pouvoir d'achat des export.
Papua New Guinea											**Papouasie-Nouvelle-Guinée**
Imp: Quantum	...	...	...	...	...	...	...	...	...	...	Imp: quantum
Imp: Unit Value	...	...	...	...	...	...	...	...	...	...	Imp: valeur unitaire
Exp: Quantum	99	106	92	94	100	102	102	103	88	91	Exp: quantum
Exp: Unit Value	126	157	247	271	329	222	291	379	373	344	Exp: valeur unitaire
Terms of Trade	...	...	...	...	...	...	...	...	...	...	Termes de l'échange
Purchasing Power of Exports	...	...	...	...	...	...	...	...	...	...	Pouvoir d'achat des export.
Peru											**Pérou**
Imp: Quantum	...	...	...	...	...	...	...	...	...	...	Imp: quantum
Imp: Unit Value	...	...	...	...	...	...	...	...	...	...	Imp: valeur unitaire
Exp: Quantum	127	144	137	150	163	162	159	159	172	169	Exp: quantum
Exp: Unit Value	134	175	287	316	298	231	336	402	369	353	Exp: valeur unitaire
Terms of Trade	...	...	...	...	...	...	...	...	...	...	Termes de l'échange
Purchasing Power of Exports	...	...	...	...	...	...	...	...	...	...	Pouvoir d'achat des export.
Philippines											**Philippines**
Imp: Quantum	136	121	124	...	...	...	...	...	...	...	Imp: quantum
Imp: Unit Value[1]	81	94	114	...	...	...	...	...	...	...	Imp: valeur unitaire[1]
Exp: Quantum	109	104	124	...	...	...	...	...	...	...	Exp: quantum
Exp: Unit Value[1]	75	84	88	...	...	...	...	...	...	...	Exp: valeur unitaire[1]
Terms of Trade	92	89	77	...	...	...	...	...	...	...	Termes de l'échange
Purchasing Power of Exports	101	92	95	...	...	...	...	...	...	...	Pouvoir d'achat des export.
Poland											**Pologne**
Imp: Quantum	141	149	174	200	218	186	211	223	207	223	Imp: quantum
Imp: Unit Value[1]	131	141	151	171	198	172	...	192	...	...	Imp: valeur unitaire[1]
Exp: Quantum	173	191	222	243	260	238	270	291	278	318	Exp: quantum
Exp: Unit Value[1]	139	150	160	186	213	185	...	207	...	...	Exp: valeur unitaire[1]
Terms of Trade	107	107	107	109	107	107	...	108	...	...	Termes de l'échange
Purchasing Power of Exports	184	204	236	264	279	255	...	314	...	...	Pouvoir d'achat des export.
Portugal											**Portugal**
Imp: Quantum	103	90	91	99	92	80	96	...	...	...	Imp: quantum
Imp: Unit Value[1]	126	128	130	137	153	125	138	...	...	...	Imp: valeur unitaire[1]
Exp: Quantum	97	88	95	93	88	76	87	...	...	...	Exp: quantum
Exp: Unit Value[1]	128	130	135	144	155	136	143	...	...	...	Exp: valeur unitaire[1]
Terms of Trade	102	101	103	105	101	109	104	...	...	...	Termes de l'échange
Purchasing Power of Exports	99	89	98	97	89	83	90	...	...	...	Pouvoir d'achat des export.
Republic of Moldova											**République de Moldova**
Imp: Quantum	204	237	255	317	364	271	311	383	393	419	Imp: quantum
Imp: Unit Value	113	122	127	152	208	176	161	187	179	170	Imp: valeur unitaire
Exp: Quantum	208	226	208	244	268	248	290	399	406	462	Exp: quantum
Exp: Unit Value	105	104	104	124	159	131	121	138	129	121	Exp: valeur unitaire
Terms of Trade	93	86	82	81	77	74	75	74	72	71	Termes de l'échange
Purchasing Power of Exports	193	194	171	199	205	184	218	294	293	329	Pouvoir d'achat des export.

Indices of total exports and imports by countries or areas (Table G)

Quantum and unit value indices and terms of trade in US dollars (2000 = 100)

Indices des exportations et importations totales par pays ou zones (Tableau G)

Indices du quantum et de la valeur unitaire et termes de l'échange en dollars É.-U. (2000 = 100)

Countries	2004	2005	2006	2007	2008	2009	2010	2011	2012	2013	Pays
Romania											**Roumanie**
Imp: Quantum	207	244	293	369	394	299	345	381	376	387	Imp: quantum
Imp: Unit Value	106	112	116	100	103	92	96	102	102	100	Imp: valeur unitaire
Exp: Quantum	166	179	191	204	225	216	259	291	279	316	Exp: quantum
Exp: Unit Value	125	137	148	107	111	100	107	115	120	116	Exp: valeur unitaire
Terms of Trade	*118*	*122*	*127*	*108*	*108*	*109*	*112*	*113*	*117*	*116*	*Termes de l'échange*
Purchasing Power of Exports	*195*	*218*	*244*	*221*	*243*	*235*	*289*	*330*	*326*	*366*	*Pouvoir d'achat des export.*
Russian Federation											**Fédération de Russie**
Imp: Quantum	222	288	398	...	470	492	672	902	934	947	Imp: quantum
Imp: Unit Value	...	...	...	...	...	...	...	...	...	...	Imp: valeur unitaire
Exp: Quantum	180	240	303	...	261	291	387	501	509	513	Exp: quantum
Exp: Unit Value	...	...	...	...	...	...	...	...	...	...	Exp: valeur unitaire
Terms of Trade	...	...	...	...	...	...	...	...	...	...	*Termes de l'échange*
Purchasing Power of Exports	...	...	...	...	...	...	...	...	...	...	*Pouvoir d'achat des export.*
Saudi Arabia											**Arabie saoudite**
Imp: Quantum	...	...	...	...	...	...	...	...	...	...	Imp: quantum
Imp: Unit Value	...	...	...	...	...	...	...	...	...	...	Imp: valeur unitaire
Exp: Quantum	...	...	...	...	...	...	...	...	...	...	Exp: quantum
Exp: Unit Value	143	206	248	284	397	252	331	460	438	433	Exp: valeur unitaire
Terms of Trade	...	...	...	...	...	...	...	...	...	...	*Termes de l'échange*
Purchasing Power of Exports	...	...	...	...	...	...	...	...	...	...	*Pouvoir d'achat des export.*
Serbia											**Serbie**
Imp: Quantum	.	.	...	129	109	85	108	178	299	349	Imp: quantum
Imp: Unit Value	.	.	...	106	113	79	96	138	145	134	Imp: valeur unitaire
Exp: Quantum	.	.	...	126	112	90	122	168	236	306	Exp: quantum
Exp: Unit Value	.	.	...	110	110	83	97	155	187	185	Exp: valeur unitaire
Terms of Trade	.	.	...	*104*	*97*	*104*	*102*	*112*	*129*	*139*	*Termes de l'échange*
Purchasing Power of Exports	.	.	...	*131*	*109*	*94*	*125*	*188*	*304*	*425*	*Pouvoir d'achat des export.*
Singapore											**Singapour**
Imp: Quantum	117	134	148	158	175	150	177	183	190	192	Imp: quantum
Imp: Unit Value[1]	104	111	119	124	136	122	131	148	149	144	Imp: valeur unitaire[1]
Exp: Quantum	156	174	192	208	217	195	235	247	248	256	Exp: quantum
Exp: Unit Value[1]	93	96	103	104	113	101	109	120	120	116	Exp: valeur unitaire[1]
Terms of Trade	*89*	*87*	*86*	*84*	*83*	*83*	*83*	*81*	*81*	*81*	*Termes de l'échange*
Purchasing Power of Exports	*139*	*151*	*165*	*176*	*180*	*161*	*196*	*200*	*200*	*207*	*Pouvoir d'achat des export.*
Slovakia											**Slovaquie**
Imp: Quantum	...	...	...	...	...	...	...	...	...	...	Imp: quantum
Imp: Unit Value[1]	147	157	177	196	235	197	194	219	197	202	Imp: valeur unitaire[1]
Exp: Quantum	...	...	...	...	...	...	...	...	...	...	Exp: quantum
Exp: Unit Value[1]	174	191	204	221	248	220	243	270	243	245	Exp: valeur unitaire[1]
Terms of Trade	*118*	*121*	*115*	*112*	*106*	*111*	*125*	*123*	*123*	*121*	*Termes de l'échange*
Purchasing Power of Exports	...	...	...	...	...	...	...	...	...	...	*Pouvoir d'achat des export.*
Slovenia											**Slovénie**
Imp: Quantum	...	...	...	...	...	...	...	...	...	...	Imp: quantum
Imp: Unit Value	141	152	164	175	183	166	179	194	198	...	Imp: valeur unitaire
Exp: Quantum	...	...	...	...	...	...	...	...	...	...	Exp: quantum
Exp: Unit Value	142	149	159	168	171	163	172	184	186	...	Exp: valeur unitaire
Terms of Trade	*101*	*98*	*97*	*96*	*94*	*98*	*96*	*94*	*94*	...	*Termes de l'échange*
Purchasing Power of Exports	...	...	...	...	...	...	...	...	...	...	*Pouvoir d'achat des export.*

Indices of total exports and imports by countries or areas (Table G)
Quantum and unit value indices and terms of trade in US dollars (2000 = 100)

Indices des exportations et importations totales par pays ou zones (Tableau G)
Indices du quantum et de la valeur unitaire et termes de l'échange en dollars É.-U. (2000 = 100)

Countries	2004	2005	2006	2007	2008	2009	2010	2011	2012	2013	Pays
South Africa											**Afrique du Sud**
Imp: Quantum	131	144	...	...	...	...	...	...	...	...	Imp: quantum
Imp: Unit Value	136	144	...	...	...	...	...	...	...	...	Imp: valeur unitaire
Exp: Quantum	105	112	...	...	...	...	...	...	...	...	Exp: quantum
Exp: Unit Value	148	156	...	...	...	...	...	...	...	...	Exp: valeur unitaire
Terms of Trade	*108*	*109*	...	...	...	...	...	...	...	...	*Termes de l'échange*
Purchasing Power of Exports	*114*	*122*	...	...	...	...	...	...	...	...	*Pouvoir d'achat des export.*
Spain											**Espagne**
Imp: Quantum	129	137	148	158	153	128	140	141	131	135	Imp: quantum
Imp: Unit Value	131	138	144	159	179	149	148	168	162	161	Imp: valeur unitaire
Exp: Quantum	120	121	128	133	136	122	142	157	157	166	Exp: quantum
Exp: Unit Value	134	140	148	166	181	160	154	169	160	165	Exp: valeur unitaire
Terms of Trade	*102*	*102*	*102*	*104*	*101*	*107*	*104*	*101*	*98*	*102*	*Termes de l'échange*
Purchasing Power of Exports	*123*	*123*	*131*	*139*	*138*	*132*	*148*	*158*	*155*	*170*	*Pouvoir d'achat des export.*
Sri Lanka											**Sri Lanka**
Imp: Quantum	122	126	135	140	147	131	149	...	...	...	Imp: quantum
Imp: Unit Value	...	...	113	53	48	56	...	...	...	...	Imp: valeur unitaire
Exp: Quantum	106	113	97	126	126	111	130	...	...	...	Exp: quantum
Exp: Unit Value	101	104	109	113	119	118	132	...	...	...	Exp: valeur unitaire
Terms of Trade	...	...	*96*	*213*	*250*	*211*	...	...	...	...	*Termes de l'échange*
Purchasing Power of Exports	...	...	*93*	*268*	*315*	*234*	...	...	...	...	*Pouvoir d'achat des export.*
Sweden											**Suède**
Imp: Quantum	109	117	127	140	142	119	140	152	150	146	Imp: quantum
Imp: Unit Value[1]	131	138	149	166	183	155	164	185	175	175	Imp: valeur unitaire[1]
Exp: Quantum	117	123	132	136	138	114	131	142	140	136	Exp: quantum
Exp: Unit Value[1]	121	124	131	148	158	139	145	161	152	151	Exp: valeur unitaire[1]
Terms of Trade	*92*	*90*	*88*	*89*	*87*	*89*	*89*	*87*	*87*	*86*	*Termes de l'échange*
Purchasing Power of Exports	*108*	*110*	*117*	*122*	*120*	*102*	*116*	*124*	*122*	*117*	*Pouvoir d'achat des export.*
Switzerland											**Suisse**
Imp: Quantum	107	111	117	124	126	113	123	127	127	126	Imp: quantum
Imp: Unit Value	135	142	148	161	179	171	179	204	195	200	Imp: valeur unitaire
Exp: Quantum	114	121	132	141	143	122	131	141	142	142	Exp: quantum
Exp: Unit Value	137	139	143	156	178	182	190	210	201	203	Exp: valeur unitaire
Terms of Trade	*101*	*98*	*96*	*96*	*99*	*107*	*106*	*103*	*103*	*102*	*Termes de l'échange*
Purchasing Power of Exports	*116*	*118*	*127*	*136*	*142*	*130*	*139*	*146*	*147*	*145*	*Pouvoir d'achat des export.*
Thailand											**Thaïlande**
Imp: Quantum	137	162	164	170	191	146	186	211	224	228	Imp: quantum
Imp: Unit Value	110	116	124	131	147	144	155	171	173	173	Imp: valeur unitaire
Exp: Quantum	133	143	159	178	186	160	186	202	207	208	Exp: quantum
Exp: Unit Value	105	113	119	126	139	139	152	160	161	158	Exp: valeur unitaire
Terms of Trade	*96*	*97*	*96*	*96*	*94*	*97*	*98*	*94*	*93*	*91*	*Termes de l'échange*
Purchasing Power of Exports	*128*	*138*	*152*	*171*	*176*	*155*	*183*	*190*	*193*	*190*	*Pouvoir d'achat des export.*
Turkey											**Turquie**
Imp: Quantum	131	146	159	179	177	154	181	204	206	223	Imp: quantum
Imp: Unit Value	127	136	148	162	195	157	170	195	190	187	Imp: valeur unitaire
Exp: Quantum	181	200	224	250	266	246	274	291	338	336	Exp: quantum
Exp: Unit Value	126	133	138	155	180	151	156	174	169	169	Exp: valeur unitaire
Terms of Trade	*99*	*98*	*93*	*96*	*92*	*96*	*92*	*89*	*89*	*90*	*Termes de l'échange*
Purchasing Power of Exports	*179*	*195*	*209*	*240*	*246*	*236*	*251*	*259*	*301*	*304*	*Pouvoir d'achat des export.*

Indices of total exports and imports by countries or areas (Table G)
Quantum and unit value indices and terms of trade in US dollars (2000 = 100)

Indices des exportations et importations totales par pays ou zones (Tableau G)
Indices du quantum et de la valeur unitaire et termes de l'échange en dollars É.-U. (2000 = 100)

Countries	2004	2005	2006	2007	2008	2009	2010	2011	2012	2013	Pays
United Kingdom											**Royaume-Uni**
Imp: Quantum	120	129	144	139	137	121	134	135	139	140	Imp: quantum
Imp: Unit Value[1]	115	119	124	135	143	123	129	145	143	142	Imp: valeur unitaire[1]
Exp: Quantum	103	112	127	115	117	105	115	120	122	123	Exp: quantum
Exp: Unit Value[1]	120	123	126	137	145	124	131	147	144	143	Exp: valeur unitaire[1]
Terms of Trade	*104*	*103*	*102*	*102*	*101*	*101*	*102*	*101*	*100*	*101*	*Termes de l'échange*
Purchasing Power of Exports	*107*	*115*	*129*	*117*	*118*	*105*	*117*	*121*	*123*	*124*	*Pouvoir d'achat des export.*
United States											**Etats-Unis**
Imp: Quantum	118	125	132	133	129	107	123	128	132	133	Imp: quantum
Imp: Unit Value[1]	102	110	115	120	134	119	127	141	141	139	Imp: valeur unitaire[1]
Exp: Quantum[3]	101	108	119	126	134	115	133	142	148	152	Exp: quantum[3]
Exp: Unit Value[1,3]	104	107	111	116	123	117	123	133	134	133	Exp: valeur unitaire[1,3]
Terms of Trade	*101*	*97*	*96*	*97*	*92*	*99*	*97*	*95*	*95*	*95*	*Termes de l'échange*
Purchasing Power of Exports	*102*	*105*	*114*	*122*	*123*	*114*	*129*	*135*	*140*	*145*	*Pouvoir d'achat des export.*
Venezuela (Bolivarian Rep. of)											**Venezuela (Rép. bolivarienne du)**
Imp: Quantum	...	...	...	...	...	...	...	...	...	...	Imp: quantum
Imp: Unit Value[1]	123	126	132	150	179	227	236	171	185	185	Imp: valeur unitaire[1]
Exp: Quantum	...	...	...	...	...	...	...	...	...	...	Exp: quantum
Exp: Unit Value	...	...	...	...	...	...	...	...	...	...	Exp: valeur unitaire
Terms of Trade	*...*	*...*	*...*	*...*	*...*	*...*	*...*	*...*	*...*	*...*	*Termes de l'échange*
Purchasing Power of Exports	*...*	*...*	*...*	*...*	*...*	*...*	*...*	*...*	*...*	*...*	*Pouvoir d'achat des export.*

General Note:

The volume and unit value/price indices are as compiled by countries. They show the changes in the volume (volume index) and the average price (unit value/price index) of total imports and exports. Using these indices UNSD calculates the terms of trade indices (export unit value/price indices divided by the corresponding import unit value/price indices), and the index of the purchasing power of exports (the terms of trade multiplied by the volume index of exports). Country footnotes which appear in Special Table B of this volume also apply to the country indices published in this table.

For further information on sources and presentation as well as for a brief table description please see the introduction.

Remarque générale :

Les indices du volume et les indices de la valeur unitaire/prix sont comme compilées par les pays. Ils indiquent les variations des quantitées (indice du volume) et des prix moyens (indice de la valeur unitaire/prix) des importations ou exportations totales. Utilisant ces indices la Division de Statistique des Nations Unies calcule les indices des termes de l'échange (sont obtenus en divisant les indices de la valeur unitaire à l'exportation par ceux à l'importation), et l'indice du pouvoir d'achat des exportations (sont obtenu en multipliant l'indice des termes de l'échange du volume des exportations). Les notes se rapportant aux pays qui apparaissent dans le Tableau Spécial B de ce tome s'appliquent aussi aux indices de ce tableau.

Pour plus d'information sur les sources et la présentation ainsi qu'une brève description du tableau, se il vous plaît se référer à l'introduction.

1 Price indices.
2 Index numbers exclude ships.
3 Excluding military goods.

1 Les indices des prix.
2 Les indices ne comprennent pas de navires.
3 Non compris les importations des economats militaires.

Indices of total exports and imports by regions (Table H)
Quantum and unit value indices and terms of trade in US dollars (2000 = 100)
Indices des exportations et importations totales par région (Tableau H)
Indices du quantum et de la valeur unitaire et termes de l'échange en dollars É.-U. (2000 = 100)

Regions - Régions	2002	2003	2004	2005	2006	2007	2008	2009	2010	2011	2012	2013
Exports - Unit value index / Exportations - Indice de la valeur unitaire[1]												
Total - Totaux	98	108	117	121	125	135	147	133	138	150	144	143
Developed economies - Economies développées[2]	100	112	122	127	131	143	157	143	146	161	155	155
North America - Amérique du Nord	98	102	108	113	118	124	133	122	131	142	141	140
Europe	102	119	133	138	143	159	176	158	159	175	166	169
Asia-Pacific - Asie-Pacifique	90	94	100	102	102	105	115	114	121	136	131	123
Africa - Afrique	95	109	122	123	123	127	122	119	127	136	121	112
Northern Africa - Afrique du Nord	93	95	99	100	102	110	116	114	112	127	117	116
Sub-Saharan Africa - Afrique subsaharienne	97	119	141	149	148	146	128	124	140	140	125	109
Latin America & The Caribbean - Amérique latine et	96	101	110	111	120	126	142	115	127	124	117	108
Latin America - Amérique latine	96	101	110	111	120	126	142	115	127	124	117	108
Western Asia - Asie Occidentale[3]	96	105	117	126	131	145	170	148	152	167	167	168
Other Asia - Autres Pays d'Asie	90	92	97	102	105	108	116	106	115	125	124	124
Eastern Asia - Asie Orientale	90	92	98	101	101	102	107	97	104	111	110	110
Southern Asia - Asie Méridionale	92	103	114	126	133	151	170	154	185	219	205	216
South-eastern Asia - Asie du Sud-est	89	91	93	99	105	110	120	111	120	131	131	127
Imports - Unit value index / Importations - Indice de la valeur unitaire[1]												
Total - Totaux	96	105	115	123	130	141	160	144	148	168	164	163
Developed economies - Economies développées[2]	97	108	118	125	132	143	162	141	148	166	161	160
North America - Amérique du Nord	94	97	103	110	116	121	134	120	128	141	141	139
Europe	100	116	130	136	143	159	178	154	159	177	169	170
Asia-Pacific - Asie-Pacifique	89	96	106	116	124	132	158	134	152	177	177	167
Africa - Afrique	94	113	131	137	...	...	...	...	...	...	...	...
Northern Africa - Afrique du Nord	76	83	87	95	101	117	123	111	108	123	99	97
Latin America & The Caribbean - Amérique latine et	91	90	101	121	134	148	184	175	184	193	202	206
Western Asia - Asie Occidentale	99	108	123	132	143	157	186	153	166	191	186	184
Other Asia - Autres Pays d'Asie	93	96	105	110	116	124	...	...	138	166	166	164
Eastern Asia - Asie Orientale	91	95	104	111	118	123	137	122	136	153	154	151
Southern Asia - Asie Méridionale	102	108	133	126	127	142	155	126	149	248	236	247
South-eastern Asia - Asie du Sud-est	95	98	101	110	120	125	138	127	137	153	154	152
Terms of trade / Termes de l'échange[4]												
Developed economies - Economies développées[2]	103	104	104	102	99	100	97	102	99	97	96	97
North America - Amérique du Nord	105	105	105	103	102	103	99	102	102	100	100	101
Europe	102	103	102	101	100	100	99	103	100	99	98	100
Asia-Pacific - Asie-Pacifique	101	98	95	88	83	80	73	85	80	77	74	74
Africa - Afrique	101	97	93	90	...	...	...	...	...	...	...	...
Northern Africa - Afrique du Nord	122	114	114	105	101	94	94	103	104	103	118	120
Latin America & The Caribbean - Amérique latine et	105	113	109	91	89	85	77	66	69	64	58	52
Western Asia - Asie Occidentale	97	97	96	95	92	93	92	97	92	87	90	91
Other Asia - Autres Pays d'Asie	97	96	93	93	90	87	...	...	83	75	75	76
Eastern Asia - Asie Orientale	99	97	94	90	86	83	78	80	77	72	72	73
Southern Asia - Asie Méridionale	90	95	86	100	104	107	109	122	124	88	87	88
South-eastern Asia - Asie du Sud-est	94	93	92	90	88	88	87	87	88	86	85	84

Indices of total exports and imports by regions (Table H)
Quantum and unit value indices and terms of trade in US dollars (2000 = 100)

Indices des exportations et importations totales par région (Tableau H)
Indices du quantum et de la valeur unitaire et termes de l'échange en dollars É.-U. (2000 = 100)

Regions - Régions	2002	2003	2004	2005	2006	2007	2008	2009	2010	2011	2012	2013
Exports - Volume index / Exportations - Indice du volume[5]												
Total - Totaux	103	109	121	133	148	158	167	144	169	185	192	198
Developed economies - Economies développées[2]	101	104	112	117	128	135	137	116	132	140	142	143
North America - Amérique du Nord	91	92	99	105	113	119	123	106	121	129	134	137
Europe	106	108	115	120	132	137	138	120	133	142	143	144
Asia-Pacific - Asie-Pacifique	99	107	121	127	139	151	155	120	150	150	149	148
Africa - Afrique	103	112	132	178	206	236	326	230	277	303	355	374
Northern Africa - Afrique du Nord	104	131	163	221	257	280	360	236	296	256	343	306
Sub-Saharan Africa - Afrique subsaharienne	102	102	114	146	168	203	303	223	258	328	356	415
Latin America & The Caribbean - Amérique latine et	101	105	118	143	158	170	177	167	192	245	261	286
Latin America - Amérique latine	102	105	118	143	157	169	176	167	193	245	261	285
Western Asia - Asie Occidentale	102	115	137	168	191	195	236	190	231	287	308	319
Other Asia - Autres Pays d'Asie	113	132	158	180	210	237	253	232	278	304	314	329
Eastern Asia - Asie Orientale	117	141	170	197	235	276	298	277	337	372	392	415
Southern Asia - Asie Méridionale	114	124	140	163	194	197	227	202	222	247	243	234
South-eastern Asia - Asie du Sud-est	106	116	142	154	171	183	192	170	204	221	223	232
Imports - Volume index / Importations - Indice du volume[5]												
Total - Totaux	104	111	123	131	142	150	152	130	154	162	166	169
Developed economies - Economies développées[2]	103	107	117	123	132	137	136	117	130	136	137	138
North America - Amérique du Nord	101	106	117	124	131	133	128	107	124	129	132	134
Europe	104	107	116	122	133	139	139	122	133	139	137	138
Asia-Pacific - Asie-Pacifique	103	110	119	124	130	133	136	119	131	138	144	144
Africa - Afrique	112	112	124	143	...	...	...	...	...	...	...	...
Northern Africa - Afrique du Nord	141	138	167	180	182	206	285	282	319	316	446	465
Latin America & The Caribbean - Amérique latine et	101	106	114	113	122	132	130	103	126	145	142	145
Western Asia - Asie Occidentale	111	119	140	157	170	195	206	202	217	229	248	267
Other Asia - Autres Pays d'Asie	109	127	150	168	185	200	...	...	236	239	248	258
Eastern Asia - Asie Orientale	114	136	160	171	189	209	217	206	250	268	275	293
Southern Asia - Asie Méridionale	111	128	139	198	233	255	316	318	358	272	294	267
South-eastern Asia - Asie du Sud-est	98	107	130	144	151	164	179	151	184	199	209	216

Indices of total exports and imports by regions (Table H)

Quantum and unit value indices and terms of trade in US dollars (2000 = 100)

Indices des exportations et importations totales par région (Tableau H)

Indices du quantum et de la valeur unitaire et termes de l'échange en dollars É.-U. (2000 = 100)

Source:

Compiled by the United Nations Statistics Division from international and national publications.For the composition of the regions, see Special Table A of this issue.

For further information on sources and presentation as well as for brief table description, please see the introduction.

1   Regional aggregates are current period weighted.

2   This classification is intended for statistical convenience and does not, necessarily, express a judgement about the stage reached by a particular country in the development process.

3   Index does not include data of the major oil producing countries.

4   Unit value index of exports divided by unit value index of imports.

5   Volume indices are derived from value data and unit value indices. They are base period weighted.

Source:

Compilé par la Division de statistique des Nations Unies à partir de publications internationales et nationales. Pour la composition des régions, voir tableau special A du présent numéro.

Pour plus d'informaton sur les sources et présentation ainsi qu'une brève description de la table, se il vous plaît se référer à l'introduction.

1   Les totaux généraux ont été pondérés selon la période en cours.

2   Cette classification est utilisée pour plus de commodité dans la présentation des statistiques et n'implique pas nécessairement un jugement quant au stade de développement auquel est parvenu un pays donné.

3   L'indice ne comprend pas les données des principaux pays producteurs de pétrole.

4   Indice de la valeur unitaire des exportations divisé par l'indice de la valeur unitaire des importations.

5   Les indices de volume proviennent des données sur la valeur et des indices de la valeur unitaire. Ils sont pondérés selon la période de base.

Indices and values of manufactured goods exports (Table I)
Unit value and volume indices (2000=100) and value in thousand million U.S. dollars
Indices et valeurs des exportations des produits manufacturés (Tableau I)
Indices de valeur unitaire et de volume (2000=100), et valeur en milliards de dollars E.-U.

Region, country or area	2002	2003	2004	2005	2006	2007	2008	2009	2010	2011	2012	2013
Unit value indices in U.S. dollars - Indices de valeur unitaire en dollars des E.-U. 2000 = 100												
Total 1/	**98**	**105**	**111**	**112**	**115**	**126**	**133**	**123**	**125**	**136**	**123**	**133**
Developed economies	**99**	**110**	**119**	**121**	**125**	**135**	**142**	**135**	**136**	**148**	**145**	**153**
America	100	103	106	108	111	115	118	112	118	127	125	132
Canada	96	104	112	119	128	135	...	...	...	...	...	...
United States 2/	102	103	104	104	107	110	116	113	117	124	122	128
Europe	100	115	126	128	132	146	155	143	142	154	150	164
Austria	100	...	...	...	...	...	...	...	...	...	...	...
Belgium	106	126	141	148	156	179	186	173	173	195	185	189
Denmark	102	124	136	138	141	145	157	155	147	156	144	148
Finland	100	117	120	130	141	166	178	158	163	185		
France	84	101	111	111	109	118	124					
Germany	104	118	128	128	132	144	155	145	140	149	144	150
Greece	...	...	...	...	...	...	...	...	...	...	...	...
Iceland	...	...	...	...	...	...	...	...	...	...	...	...
Ireland	...	...	...	...	...	...	...	...	...	...	...	...
Italy	103	122	138	143	150	174	195	184	183	202	191	198
Netherlands	104	120	131	139	144	176	...	...	...	...	...	...
Norway	101	111	126	131	145	169	176	148	155	174	164	161
Portugal	...	...	...	...	...	...	...	...	...	...	...	...
Spain	...	...	...	...	...	...	...	...	...	...	...	...
Sweden	...	...	...	...	...	...	...	...	...	...	...	...
Switzerland	109	...	...	...	...	...	...	...	...	...	...	...
United Kingdom	98	108	120	120	123	133	136	124	125	132	132	130
Other developed economies	91	98	107	112	114	119	128	129	138	151	153	139
Australia	92	101	133	151	203	245	223	155	205	235	225	213
Israel	95	95	99	109	118	124	126	120	121	129	131	133
Japan	92	98	107	111	112	117	129	133	141	155	158	144
New Zealand	99	112	125	136	140	155	163	131	152	171	166	164
South Africa	...	...	...	...	...	...	...	...	...	...	...	...
Developing economies	**96**	**97**	**99**	**98**	**102**	**110**	**117**	**103**	**108**	**117**	**96**	**108**
China, Hong Kong SAR	93	93	94	96	93	94	99	100	105	110	116	119
India	98	107	120	143	...	...	144	132	166	...	188	...
Korea, Republic of 3/	82	83	92	96	101	106	99	84	90	98	90	89
Pakistan	96	101	108	106	108	108	108	101	118	150	149	147
Singapore	83	80	79	77	79	79	80	77	79	82	81	80
Turkey 4/	96	108	124	130	127	137	171	...	153	170	163	165
Unit value indices in 'SDR' - Indices de valeur unitaire en 'DTS' 2000 = 100												
Total	99	100	98	99	103	108	111	105	108	113	106	115
Developed economies	**100**	**104**	**104**	**108**	**112**	**116**	**119**	**115**	**118**	**123**	**124**	**132**
Developing economies	**98**	**92**	**87**	**87**	**91**	**94**	**97**	**88**	**93**	**97**	**82**	**93**

For general note and footnotes see end of Table K.

Indices and values of manufactured goods exports (Table I)
Unit value and volume indices (2000=100) and value in thousand million U.S. dollars
Indices et valeurs des exportations des produits manufacturés (Tableau I)
Indices de valeur unitaire et de volume (2000=100), et valeur en milliards de dollars E.-U.

2002	2003	2004	2005	2006	2007	2008	2009	2010	2011	2012	2013	Région, pays ou zones

Unit value indices in national currency - Indices de valeur unitaire en monnaie nationale
2000 = 100

2002	2003	2004	2005	2006	2007	2008	2009	2010	2011	2012	2013	Région, pays ou zones
...	...	...	...	...	...	...	...	...	...	...	...	**Totaux 1/**
...	...	...	...	...	...	...	...	...	...	...	...	**Economies dévelopeées**
102	98	98	97	98	97	...	...	...	...	...	...	Amérique
102	103	104	104	107	110	116	113	117	124	122	128	Canada
												Etats-Unis 2/
98	...	...	...	...	...	...	...	...	...	...	...	Europe
103	103	105	110	115	120	116	114	121	130	133	131	Autriche
100	101	101	102	103	97	98	102	102	104	103	103	Belgique
98	96	89	97	104	112	111	105	114	123	...	...	Danemark
83	83	82	82	81	80	78	...	...	...	...	...	Finlande
102	96	95	95	97	97	97	96	97	99	104	104	France
...	...	...	...	...	...	...	...	...	...	...	...	Allemagne
...	...	...	...	...	...	...	...	...	...	...	...	Grèce
...	...	...	...	...	...	...	...	...	...	...	...	Islande
102	101	103	107	111	118	123	123	128	135	138	139	Irlande
102	98	97	103	106	118							Italie
91	89	96	96	106	112	111	105	106	110	108	107	Pays-Bas
												Norvège
...	...	...	...	...	...	...	...	...	...	...	...	Portugal
...	...	...	...	...	...	...	...	...	...	...	...	Espagne
...	...	...	...	...	...	...	...	...	...	...	...	Suède
99	100	99	100	101	101	111	120	122	125	126	126	Suisse
...	...	...	...	...	...	...	...	...	...	...	...	Royaume-Uni
97	89	104	114	156	169	153	114	129	131	125	127	Autres économies dévelopées
...	...	...	...	...	...	...	...	...	...	...	...	Australie
106	105	107	114	121	127	124	115	115	115	117	131	Israël
97	88	86	88	98	96	104	95	95	98	93	91	Japon
...	...	...	...	...	...	...	...	...	...	...	...	Nouvelle-Zélande
...	...	...	...	...	...	...	...	...	...	...	...	Afrique du Sud
93	93	94	96	93	94	99	99	104	110	115	119	**Economies en voie de développement**
106	111	121	140	...	...	138	141	169		224		Chine, Hong-Kong RAS
91	87	93	87	85	87	94	95	92	96	90	86	Inde
108	111	119	119	123	124	143	156	191	244	264	282	Corée, République de 3/
86	81	78	75	73	69	65	64	63	60	59	58	Pakistan
...	...	...	...	...	...	...	...	...	...	...	...	Singapour
...	...	...	...	...	...	...	...	...	...	...	...	Turquie 4/

Voir à la fin du Tableau K pour la remarque générale et les notes.

Indices and values of manufactured goods exports (Table I)
Unit value and volume indices (2000=100) and value in thousand million U.S. dollars
Indices et valeurs des exportations des produits manufacturés (Tableau I)
Indices de valeur unitaire et de volume (2000=100), et valeur en milliards de dollars E.-U.

Region, country or area	2002	2003	2004	2005	2006	2007	2008	2009	2010	2011	2012	2013
					Volume indices - Indices de volume 2000 = 100							
Total..	103	110	126	138	152	144	144	125	143	148	161	153
Developed economies........................	101	104	113	118	128	134	133	111	126	131	130	124
America....................................	88	88	97	104	113	120	120	99	110	114	120	114
Canada....................................	94	91	97	100	99	100	...	...	...	...	...	...
United States	86	87	97	105	118	126	126	104	117	121	130	124
Europe	107	111	120	126	136	141	140	120	136	144	140	132
Austria	118	...	...	...	...	...	...	...	...	...	...	...
Belgium....................................	99	99	106	107	107	109	111	83	92	94	91	92
Denmark	114	117	119	129	137	148	153	125	135	149	151	153
Finland	98	98	109	108	116	116	115	84	85	83	...	...
France	120	118	127	133	149	152	159	...	...	...	...	...
Germany	107	113	128	138	152	165	153	138	165	180	176	174
Greece	...	...	...	...	...	...	...	...	...	...	...	...
Iceland	...	...	...	...	...	...	...	...	...	...	...	...
Ireland	...	...	...	...	...	...	...	...	...	...	...	...
Italy	102	99	104	106	112	116	110	87	95	100	100	101
Netherlands	116	121	134	135	147	147	...	...	...	...	...	...
Norway	109	110	112	119	129	141	149	134	139	133	132	136
Portugal	...	...	...	...	...	...	...	...	...	...	...	...
Spain	...	...	...	...	...	...	...	...	...	...	...	...
Sweden	...	...	...	...	...	...	...	...	...	...	...	...
Switzerland	99	...	...	...	...	...	...	...	...	...	...	...
United Kingdom	102	102	104	111	124	112	113	96	107	116	116	119
Other developed economies	96	102	112	112	120	127	128	94	115	113	109	109
Australia	104	103	89	88	73	73	85	93	86	86	88	88
Israel	98	105	124	125	123	134	135	123	145	151	146	148
Japan	94	99	110	110	117	123	121	86	108	105	101	98
New Zealand	105	109	116	115	117	119	113	112	113	117	118	117
South Africa	...	...	...	...	...	...	...	...	...	...	...	...
Developing economies	107	124	157	185	208	167	169	156	181	187	231	220
China, Hong Kong SAR	93	70	71	75	77	60	45	27	31	26	22	19
India	116	130	141	148	...	...	233	...	...	...	...	...
Korea, Republic of	97	117	145	175	188	203	241	249	297	315	333	351
Pakistan	114	139	137	155	160	163	176	163	165	151	148	150
Singapore	108	130	161	191	230	250	253	223	274	289	296	307
Turkey	138	162	189	204	240	279	268	...	259	277	301	314

For general note and footnotes see end of Table K

Indices and values of manufactured goods exports (Table I)
Unit value and volume indices (2000=100) and value in thousand million U.S. dollars
Indices et valeurs des exportations des produits manufacturés (Tableau I)
Indices de valeur unitaire et de volume (2000=100), et valeur en milliards de dollars E.-U.

In thousand million U.S. dollars | | | | | | | | | | | En milliards de dollars E.-U.

2002	2003	2004	2005	2006	2007	2008	2009	2010	2011	2012	2013	Région, pays ou zones

Value - Valeur
In thousand million U.S. dollars - En milliards de dollars E.-U.

2002	2003	2004	2005	2006	2007	2008	2009	2010	2011	2012	2013	Région, pays ou zones
4647.84	5350.28	6492.49	7143.91	8110.93	8385.88	8879.06	7057.63	8272.16	9301.19	9154.44	9418.42	**Totaux**
3197.84	3650.28	4312.49	4593.91	5130.93	5795.88	6099.06	4777.63	5522.16	6231.19	6044.44	6088.42	**Economies dévelopées**
686	704	803	872	983	1071	1105	870	1017	1123	1169	1175	Amérique
167	174	200	219	235	248	235	170	203	225	228	225	Canada
519	530	603	653	748	823	870	700	814	898	941	950	Etats-Unis
2051.84	2423.55	2877.49	3058.41	3429.65	3929.33	4135.75	3273.29	3668.95	4206.11	3997.33	4114.16	Europe
59	76.82	96.74	100	114	134	150	112	121	145	135	143.57	Autriche
139	166	199	210	222	258	275	191	213	243	223	231	Belgique
37.16	46.38	51.39	56.59	61.09	68.42	76.18	61.4	63.34	73.81	68.99	72.12	Danemark
38.87	45.44	51.83	56.06	65.09	76.79	81.29	52.6	55.4	61.02	55.38	54.69	Finlande
252	298	352	365	405	449	490	384	419	470	454		France
535	644	790	849	970	1140	1140	962	1110	1290	1220	1256.82	Allemagne
5.66	8.65	8.48	10.72	11.98	14	15.43	11.68					Grèce
0.73	0.8	0.95	1.06	1.25	1.85	2.9	1.97	2.55	2.88	2.6	2.42	Islande
77.65	79.42	88.69	94	96.45	102	108	98.19	98.63	110	100	97.19	Irlande
226	261	309	324	362	433	462	343	376	435	410	432.26	Italie
155	186	225	240	271	331	351	286	324	357	337	344	Pays-Bas
18.26	20.25	23.49	25.9	31.11	39.53	43.61	33.11	35.61	38.46	36.02	36.22	Norvège
22.4	27.49	30.54	28.83	32.14	32.93	39.73	30.34	35.05	44.18	42.83	45.73	Portugal
99.02	124	143	150	167	197	209	166	182	212	197	218.37	Espagne
66.86	82.36	101	111	124	143	151	107	128	151	134	128	Suède
84.48	96.76	114	123	138	158	182				202	208	Suisse
233	258	290	311	355	348	356	278	311	359	358	360.8	Royaume-Uni
460	522.73	631.99	663.51	718.29	795.55	858.31	634.34	836.21	902.08	878.11	799.25	Autres économies dévelopées
20.23	22	25	28.17	31.61	38.06	40.31	30.57	37.16	43.01	41.88	39.59	Australie
27.53	29.52	36.53	40.47	43.33	49.36	50.67	44.06	52.12	57.88	56.74	58.26	Israël
392	443	534	554	597	654	708	519	695	741	725	640.97	Japon
4.91	5.72	6.78	7.32	7.68	8.64	8.65	6.88	8.04	9.38	9.22	9	Nouvelle-Zélande
15.33	22.51	29.68	33.54	38.67	45.49	50.68	33.83		50.8	45.27	51.44	Afrique du Sud
1450	1700	2180	2550	2980	2590	2780	2280	2750	3070	3110	3330	**Economies en voie de développement**
19.42	14.7	15.07	16.3	16.01	12.52	10.03	6.14	7.21	6.38	5.66	5.15	Chine, Hong-Kong RAS
39.86	48.79	59.07	74.07	86.12	96.89	117						Inde
125	153	208	263	297	339	373	329	420	485	473	491.21	Corée, République de
8.42	10.88	11.4	12.69	13.37	13.61	14.66	12.68	15.06	17.49	17.12	16.94	Pakistan
107	123	152	176	217	234	240	203	259	284	286	293	Singapour
30.79	40.31	54.24	61.13	70.89	88.65	106	80.3	91.65	109	113	120	Turquie

Voir à la fin du Tableau K pour la remarque générale et les notes

Indices and values of fuel imports - Developed economies (Table J)

Unit value and volume indices (2000=100) and value in thousand million U.S. dollars

Indices et valeurs des importations de produits énergétiques - Pays à économies développées (Tableau J)

Indices de valeur unitaire et de volume (2000=100), et valeur en milliards de dollars E.-U.

Region, country or area	2002	2003	2004	2005	2006	2007	2008	2009	2010	2011	2012	2013
Unit Value Indices in U.S. dollars - Indices de valeur unitaire en dollars des E.-U. 2000 = 100												
Developed economies	89	104	129	175	192	207	294	200	248	317	315	304
America	85	102	129	187	220	243	329	206	263	340	332	322
Canada	109	134	161	215	255	279	...	...	...	...	...	...
United States 1/..............	83	100	127	185	217	240	328	204	259	346	342	336
Europe 2/	94	109	133	175	203	217	299	200	238	298	296	289
Austria	92	111	141	190	227	244	347	231	268	348	339	
Belgium...........................	90	108	135	188	210	217	316	194	248	344	323	320
Denmark	99	119	147	188	220	241	333	211	249	327	316	300
Finland	91	108	122	167	205	224	317	212	261	362	...	...
France	100	104	128	198	240	263	370	...	...	...	...	...
Germany	102	117	141	189	228	234	341	227	255	347	402	397
Greece	...	...	...	...	...	...	...	...	...	...	...	...
Iceland	...	...	...	...	...	...	...	...	...	...	...	...
Ireland	...	...	...	...	...	...	...	...	...	...	...	...
Italy	90	113	135	178	218	249	340	225	296	398	403	385
Netherlands	...	...	...	...	...	...	...	...	...	...	...	...
Norway	99	120	137	182	221	242	331	221	276	362	359	348
Portugal	...	...	...	...	...	...	...	...	...	...	...	...
Spain	73	88	107	135	161	174	231	150	179	236	240	227
Sweden	...	...	...	...	...	...	...	...	...	...	...	...
Switzerland	88	109	138	...	...	...	...	...	...	...	...	...
United Kingdom	100	119	157	222	275	300	402	267	338	451	458	465
Other developed economies ..	88	97	120	158	138	150	242	190	252	337	346	324
Australia	86	121	153	214	265	285	405	250	327	454	452	431
Israel	90	90	117	190	205	228	349	227	285	397	379	367
Japan	89	95	116	153	128	138	234	186	249	338	353	331
New Zealand	92	110	144	196	244	266	364	211	277	377	397	381
South Africa	...	...	...	...	...	...	...	...	...	...	...	...

For general note and footnotes see end of Table K.

Indices and values of fuel imports - Developed economies (Table J)

Unit value and volume indices (2000=100) and value in thousand million U.S. dollars

Indices et valeurs des importations de produits énergétiques - Pays à économies développées (Tableau J)

Indices de valeur unitaire et de volume (2000=100), et valeur en milliards de dollars E.-U.

In thousand million U.S. dollars

En milliards de dollars E.-U.

2002	2003	2004	2005	2006	2007	2008	2009	2010	2011	2012	2013	Région, pays ou zones

Unit value indices in national currency - Indices de valeur unitaire en monnaie nationale
2000 = 100

2002	2003	2004	2005	2006	2007	2008	2009	2010	2011	2012	2013	Région, pays ou zones
...	...	...	...	...	...	...	...	...	...	...	...	**Economies dévelopeées**
...	...	...	...	...	...	...	...	...	...	...	...	Amérique
115	126	141	176	195	201							Canada
83	100	127	185	217	240	328	204	259	346	342	336	Etats-Unis 1/
												Europe 2/
90	91	105	141	167	165	218	153	187	231	244		Autriche
88	88	100	139	154	146	198	129	173	228	232	223	Belgique
97	97	109	139	161	162	209	140	173	217	227	208	Danemark
89	88	90	124	151	151	198	140	182	240	...	...	Finlande
98	85	95	147	176	177	232	...	...	...	...	...	France
100	95	105	140	167	158	214	151	178	231	289	276	Allemagne
...	...	...	...	...	...	...	...	...	...	...	...	Grece
...	...	...	...	...	...	...	...	...	...	...	...	Islande
...	...	...	...	...	...	...	...	...	...	...	...	Irlande
89	93	101	133	162	169	214	150	207	266	292	270	Italie
...	...	...	...	...	...	...	...	...	...	...	...	Pays-Bas
89	97	105	133	161	160	210	156	189	230	237	232	Norvège
...	...	...	...	...	...	...	...	...	...	...	...	Portugal
72	72	79	100	119	117	145	100	125	157	172	158	Espagne
...	...	...	...	...	...	...	...	...	...	...	...	Suède
81	86	101	...	...	...	...	...	...	...	...	...	Suisse
101	110	130	185	226	227	327	258	331	426	437	450	Royaume-Uni
...	...	...	...	...	...	...	...	...	...	...	...	Autres économies dévelopées
91	108	121	163	204	197	277	183	207	255	253	259	Australie
...	...	...	...	...	...	...	...	...	...	...	...	Israël
104	102	116	157	138	151	225	161	202	250	261	300	Japon
89	85	98	126	170	163	232	150	173	215	222	210	Nouvelle-Zélande
...	...	...	...	...	...	...	...	...	...	...	...	Afrique du Sud

Voir à la fin du Tableau K pour la remarque générale et les notes.

Indices and values of fuel imports - Developed economies (Table J)
Unit value and volume indices (2000=100) and value in thousand million U.S. dollars

Indices et valeurs des importations de produits énergétiques - Pays à économies développées (Tableau J)
Indices de valeur unitaire et de volume (2000=100), et valeur en milliards de dollars E.-U.

Region, country or area	2002	2003	2004	2005	2006	2007	2008	2009	2010	2011	2012	2013
Volume indices - indices de volume 2000 = 100												
Developed economies	102	111	117	121	134	133	133	116	118	123	128	125
America	103	110	115	110	109	107	107	96	98	98	94	86
Canada	80	91	96	107	100	102	...	...	...	...	...	...
United States	105	112	116	111	110	108	106	95	98	94	89	81
Europe	102	113	122	133	142	140	144	133	138	147	156	155
Austria	138	175	194	205	218	172	163	166	160	168	177	
Belgium	110	123	132	132	132	131	145	126	128	127	131	145
Denmark	78	86	95	106	100	91	109	110	110	121	125	152
Finland	106	118	125	118	129	126	127	120	120	125	...	...
France	91	115	124	109	110	106	108	...	...	...	...	...
Germany	90	103	108	110	114	111	111	107	112	111	100	102
Greece	...	...	...	...	...	...	...	...	...	...	...	...
Iceland	...	...	...	...	...	...	...	...	...	...	...	...
Ireland	...	...	...	...	...	...	...	...	...	...	...	...
Italy	106	102	108	148	153	145	144	140	132	120	117	107
Netherlands	...	...	...	...	...	...	...	...	...	...	...	...
Norway	89	112	115	92	97	105	97	116	139	122	115	138
Portugal	...	...	...	...	...	...	...	...	...	...	...	...
Spain	132	132	147	163	173	181	189	170	175	177	179	180
Sweden	...	...	...	...	...	...	...	...	...	...	...	...
Switzerland	104	101	100	...	...	...	...	...	...	...	...	...
United Kingdom	97	105	129	130	133	134	139	126	127	136	154	141
Other developed economies ..	102	109	111	111	159	161	151	113	110	114	123	123
Australia	102	100	113	113	120	130	135	144	143	155	167	169
Israel	96	116	107	99	90	105	100	85	96	96	118	110
Japan	102	110	110	110	162	162	147	106	103	104	110	110
New Zealand	101	104	107	105	105	111	110	120	110	111	113	116
South Africa	...	...	...	...	...	...	...	...	...	...	...	...

For general note and footnotes see end of Table K.

Indices and values of fuel imports - Developed economies (Table J)

Unit value and volume indices (2000=100) and value in thousand million U.S. dollars

Indices et valeurs des importations de produits énergétiques - Pays à économies développées (Tableau J)

Indices de valeur unitaire et de volume (2000=100), et valeur en milliards de dollars E.-U.

In thousand million U.S. dollars

En milliards de dollars E.-U.

2002	2003	2004	2005	2006	2007	2008	2009	2010	2011	2012	2013	Région, pays ou zones

Value - Valeur

In thousand million U.S. dollars - En milliards de dollars E.-U.

2002	2003	2004	2005	2006	2007	2008	2009	2010	2011	2012	2013	Région, pays ou zones
404.07	510.42	668.93	937.04	1136.83	1218.46	1723.95	1024.1	1295.42	1728.04	1777.96	1675.26	**Economies dévelopeées**
132.88	171.14	225.39	314.86	365.39	396.39	538.47	300.13	393.06	508.15	476.37	422.44	Amérique
10.88	15.14	19.39	28.86	31.9	35.39	50.47	30.13	39.06	53.15	51.37	42.44	Canada
122	156	206	286	333.49	361	488	270	354	455	425	380	Etats-Unis
187.98	241.52	321.17	459.51	569.86	599.76	849.35	526.51	647.21	865.05	909.72	884.77	Europe
4.7	7.23	10.2	14.44	18.33	15.57	21.05	14.29	15.92	21.77	22.3	19.61	Autriche
15.21	20.31	27.41	38.21	42.6	43.79	70.49	37.63	48.98	67.06	64.85	71.18	Belgique
1.96	2.56	3.53	5.01	5.56	5.54	9.19	5.86	6.9	10	9.99	11.53	Danemark
3.86	5.07	6.08	7.87	10.52	11.24	16.08	10.13	12.54	17.98	16.7	17.73	Finlande
27.84	36.26	48.37	65.94	80.29	84.83	122	76.07	88.5	121	121		France
39.79	51.97	65.91	89.55	112	112	164	105	123	166	173	174.45	Allemagne
4.35	6.16	6.69	9.82	12.21	11.51	7.61	3.05	...	...	...	...	Grèce
0.18	0.21	0.36	0.48	0.5	0.55	0.71	0.42	0.51	0.72	0.72	0.72	Islande
1.69	1.99	3.14	4.77	5.59	6.47	10.24	6.44	7.41	9.39	9.02	9.14	Irlande
21.94	26.69	33.68	61.09	77.26	83.18	113	72.75	89.93	110	109	95.15	Italie
19.53	24.39	33.3	45.25	59	66.27	90.4	59.89	80.1	110	127	128	Pays-Bas
1.21	1.84	2.17	2.29	2.95	3.5	4.42	3.53	5.28	6.07	5.68	6.59	Norvège
3.85	4.77	6.15	8.97	9.95	9.16	14.99	9.02	11.01	14.17	14.77	14.67	Portugal
17.96	21.63	29.12	40.76	51.8	58.4	81.33	47.36	58.23	77.65	79.66	75.91	Espagne
5.86	7.68	9.77	13.04	15.74	16.89	24.38	13.97	20.02	25.1	26.42	22.94	Suède
3.51	4.19	5.27	9.05	11.24	11.15	16.21	11.15	...	...	18.95	16.51	Suisse
14.31	18.29	29.72	42.56	53.94	59.13	82.38	49.52	63.33	90.68	104	96.48	Royaume-Uni
83.21	97.76	122.38	162.67	201.58	222.31	336.12	197.46	255.15	354.84	391.88	368.06	Autres économies dévelopées
5.05	6.99	9.96	13.94	18.45	21.39	31.57	20.88	27.05	40.66	43.51	41.94	Australie
3.12	3.76	4.5	6.76	6.6	8.58	12.5	6.9	9.78	13.63	16.08	14.55	Israël
70.36	81.17	98.71	131	160	173	266	152	198	273	302	281.58	Japon
1.4	1.74	2.34	3.12	3.86	4.46	6.06	3.84	4.61	6.36	6.78	6.67	Nouvelle-Zélande
3.27	4.11	6.86	7.85	12.68	14.88	20	13.84	15.71	21.19	...	...	Afrique du Sud

Voir à la fin du Tableau K pour la remarque générale et les notes.

Some indicators on fuel imports - Developed economies (Table K)

Fuel imports as a percentage of total imports and exports, and ratio of unit value indices of manufactured goods exports and fuel imports

Quelques indicateurs sur les importations de produits énergétiques - Pays à économies développées (Tableau K)

Importation des produits énergétiques en pourcentage des importations et des exportations totales,
et quotient des indices de la valeur unitaire des exportations des produits manufacturés et des importations des produits énergétiques

Region, country or area	2002	2003	2004	2005	2006	2007	2008	2009	2010	2011	2012	2013
Fuel Imports as percent of total imports												
Importation des produits énergétiques en pourcentage des importations totales												
Developed economies	9.4	10.2	11.3	14.2	15.2	14.6	18.5	14.6	15.8	18.1	19.0	17.9
America	9.3	11.1	12.5	15.3	16.1	16.5	20.9	15.6	16.6	18.7	17.0	15.1
Canada	4.9	6.3	7.1	8.9	9.1	9.3	12.4	9.4	10.0	11.8	10.9	9.2
United States	10.2	12.0	13.5	16.4	17.4	17.9	22.5	16.8	18.0	20.0	18.2	16.3
Europe	7.8	8.4	9.3	12.1	13.2	12.0	15.2	12.4	13.6	15.6	17.5	16.7
Austria	6.5	7.9	9.0	12.0	14.0	9.9	12.0	10.5	10.6	12.1	13.2	11.3
Belgium	7.7	8.6	9.5	11.9	12.1	10.6	15.1	10.7	12.6	14.5	14.9	15.7
Denmark	4.0	4.6	5.3	6.7	6.5	5.7	8.4	7.3	8.3	10.4	10.8	11.7
Finland	11.5	12.2	12.0	13.5	15.2	13.8	17.4	16.6	18.4	21.5	22.2	23.0
France	8.9	9.8	10.9	13.4	14.7	13.4	17.0	13.6	14.8	17.2	18.3	
Germany	8.1	8.6	9.2	11.5	12.1	10.6	13.8	11.3	11.6	13.2	14.8	14.7
Greece	13.8	13.7	12.7	18.0	19.2	15.1	8.5	4.5	...	...	...	...
Iceland	7.9	7.7	10.0	10.5	9.9	8.7	12.7	11.7	13.1	15.3	15.4	15.0
Ireland	3.3	3.7	5.1	6.9	6.7	7.6	12.4	10.3	12.3	14.1	14.3	13.9
Italy	8.9	9.0	9.5	15.9	17.5	16.3	20.1	17.5	18.5	19.7	22.4	19.9
Netherlands	10.1	10.4	11.7	14.5	16.4	15.7	18.3	15.7	18.2	21.8	25.5	25.2
Norway	3.5	4.7	4.5	4.1	4.6	4.4	4.9	5.1	6.9	6.7	6.6	7.3
Portugal	10.0	11.7	12.5	16.8	15.2	12.0	15.8	12.6	14.6	17.8	20.5	19.5
Spain	10.9	10.3	11.3	14.2	15.9	15.2	19.5	16.3	18.4	21.4	24.4	22.7
Sweden	8.7	9.1	9.7	11.8	12.4	11.0	14.4	11.6	13.5	14.3	16.4	14.4
Switzerland	4.3	4.4	4.8	7.5	8.5	7.3	9.3	7.5	...	...	10.0	8.6
United Kingdom	4.3	4.8	6.6	8.8	9.8	9.5	12.9	10.2	11.3	14.2	16.1	14.9
Other developed economies	17.1	17.4	18.1	21.2	23.3	23.3	29.0	23.1	24.0	27.1	28.8	28.6
Australia	6.9	7.8	9.1	11.2	13.3	13.0	15.7	12.7	13.4	16.7	16.7	17.3
Israel	8.8	10.4	10.5	14.3	13.1	14.5	18.5	14.0	16.0	18.1	21.3	19.9
Japan	20.9	21.2	21.7	25.4	27.6	27.9	34.9	27.6	28.6	32.0	34.1	33.8
New Zealand	9.3	9.4	10.1	11.9	14.6	14.4	17.6	15.0	15.6	17.1	17.7	16.8
South Africa	12.6	12.0	14.5	14.3	18.7	18.6	21.1	21.5	19.6	21.3	...	...
Fuel imports as percent of total exports												
Importations des produits énergétiques en pourcentage des exportations totales												
Developed economies	10.0	11.0	12.3	15.8	17.1	16.1	20.5	15.7	17.1	19.7	20.7	19.3
America	14.1	17.1	20.1	24.9	25.6	25.2	30.7	21.8	23.6	26.3	23.7	20.7
Canada	4.3	5.5	6.4	8.0	8.2	8.5	11.2	9.6	10.1	11.8	11.1	9.3
United States	17.6	21.5	25.2	31.5	32.1	31.1	37.5	25.5	27.7	30.7	27.4	24.1
Europe	7.4	8.0	9.0	12.0	13.2	12.0	15.4	12.3	13.6	15.5	17.0	16.1
Austria	6.4	8.1	9.1	12.2	14.1	9.9	12.2	10.9	11.1	12.8	14.0	11.7
Belgium	7.0	7.9	8.9	11.4	11.6	10.2	14.9	10.2	11.9	14.1	14.5	15.1
Denmark	3.5	3.9	4.7	6.0	6.1	5.4	7.9	6.4	7.2	8.9	9.4	10.4
Finland	8.6	9.6	10.0	12.1	13.6	12.5	16.6	16.1	18.1	22.8	23.0	23.9
France	9.0	10.0	11.6	14.9	16.4	15.4	20.0	16.0	17.3	20.8	21.8	...
Germany	6.5	6.9	7.2	9.2	10.0	8.5	11.3	9.4	9.8	11.2	12.3	12.0
Greece	41.7	46.0	43.7	56.8	58.8	48.8	29.7	14.9	...	...	...	...
Iceland	8.0	9.0	12.3	16.2	15.6	12.2	13.7	10.4	11.2	13.4	14.3	14.3
Ireland	1.9	2.2	3.0	4.3	5.3	5.3	8.1	5.5	6.2	7.3	7.6	7.9
Italy	8.6	8.9	9.5	16.4	18.6	16.6	20.7	17.9	20.1	21.0	21.8	18.4
Netherlands	8.9	9.2	10.5	12.9	14.7	13.9	16.7	13.9	16.3	19.5	22.8	22.5
Norway	2.0	2.7	2.7	2.2	2.4	2.6	2.6	2.9	4.1	3.8	3.6	4.3
Portugal	15.1	15.5	18.6	27.9	23.2	18.2	26.0	20.4	22.6	24.1	25.3	23.3
Spain	14.5	13.9	16.0	21.3	24.3	23.6	29.3	21.4	23.7	26.1	27.9	24.4
Sweden	7.1	7.5	7.9	10.0	10.7	10.0	13.3	10.7	12.6	13.4	15.4	13.7
Switzerland	4.0	4.2	4.5	7.2	7.9	6.8	8.4	6.7	...	...	8.7	7.6
United Kingdom	5.2	6.0	8.7	11.5	12.6	13.6	17.6	13.9	15.4	18.9	21.8	20.2
Other developed economies	15.0	15.6	16.2	19.9	22.5	22.1	29.4	22.7	22.1	27.4	31.5	31.8
Australia	7.8	9.8	11.5	13.2	15.0	15.2	16.9	13.6	12.8	14.9	16.6	16.6
Israel	10.6	11.8	11.7	15.8	14.1	15.9	20.5	14.4	16.8	21.1	25.4	21.9
Japan	16.9	17.2	17.4	22.0	24.7	24.2	34.0	26.2	25.7	33.2	37.8	39.4
New Zealand	9.8	10.5	11.5	14.4	17.2	16.5	19.8	15.4	15.3	16.9	18.2	16.9
South Africa	11.0	11.2	14.9	15.2	21.8	21.3	23.7	22.1	19.2	21.9	...	...

For general note and footnotes see end of table.

Some indicators on fuel imports - Developed economies (Table K)

Fuel imports as a percentage of total imports and exports, and ratio of unit value indices of manufactured goods exports and fuel imports

Quelques indicateurs sur les importations de produits énergétiques - Pays à économies développées (Tableau K)

Importation des produits énergétiques en pourcentage des importations et des exportations totales,
et quotient des indices de la valeur unitaire des exportations des produits manufacturés et des importations des produits énergétiques

2002	2003	2004	2005	2006	2007	2008	2009	2010	2011	2012	2013	Région, pays ou zones

Ratio of unit value indices of manufactured goods exports and fuel imports
Quotient des indices de la valeur unitaire des exportations des produits manufacturés et des importations des produits énergétiques
2000 = 100

2002	2003	2004	2005	2006	2007	2008	2009	2010	2011	2012	2013	Région, pays ou zones
110.0	105.0	92.0	69.0	65.0	65.0	48.0	67.0	55.0	47.0	46.0	50.0	Economies dévelopeées
118.0	101.0	82.0	58.0	50.0	47.0	36.0	55.0	45.0	37.0	38.0	41.0	Amérique
89.0	77.0	69.0	55.0	50.0	48.0	...	...	...	...	...	...	Canada
122.0	103.0	82.0	57.0	49.0	46.0	35.0	55.0	45.0	36.0	36.0	38.0	Etats-Unis
107.0	106.0	95.0	73.0	65.0	67.0	52.0	72.0	60.0	51.0	51.0	57.0	Europe
109.0												Autriche
117.0	116.0	104.0	79.0	75.0	82.0	59.0	89.0	70.0	57.0	57.0	59.0	Belgique
103.0	105.0	93.0	74.0	64.0	60.0	47.0	73.0	59.0	48.0	45.0	49.0	Danemark
109.0	109.0	99.0	78.0	69.0	74.0	56.0	75.0	63.0	51.0	...	...	Finlande
84.0	98.0	87.0	56.0	46.0	45.0	33.0	...	...	...	...	...	France
102.0	101.0	91.0	68.0	58.0	61.0	45.0	64.0	55.0	43.0	36.0	38.0	Allemagne
												Grèce
...	...	...	...	...	...	...	...	...	...	...	...	Islande
...	...	...	...	...	...	...	...	...	...	...	...	Irlande
115.0	108.0	102.0	80.0	69.0	70.0	57.0	82.0	62.0	51.0	47.0	52.0	Italie
												Pays-Bas
101.0	92.0	92.0	72.0	66.0	70.0	53.0	67.0	56.0	48.0	46.0	46.0	Norvège
...	...	...	...	...	...	...	...	...	...	...	...	Portugal
...	...	...	...	...	...	...	...	...	...	...	...	Espagne
...	...	...	...	...	...	...	...	...	...	...	...	Suède
124.0												Suisse
98.0	91.0	76.0	54.0	45.0	44.0	34.0	47.0	37.0	29.0	29.0	28.0	Royaume-Uni
103.0	101.0	90.0	71.0	83.0	80.0	53.0	68.0	55.0	45.0	44.0	43.0	Autres économies développées
107.0	83.0	87.0	71.0	77.0	86.0	55.0	62.0	63.0	52.0	50.0	49.0	Australie
105.0	105.0	84.0	57.0	58.0	54.0	36.0	53.0	42.0	33.0	35.0	36.0	Israël
103.0	103.0	92.0	72.0	88.0	84.0	55.0	71.0	57.0	46.0	45.0	44.0	Japon
108.0	102.0	86.0	70.0	58.0	58.0	45.0	62.0	55.0	45.0	42.0	43.0	Nouvelle-Zélande
...	...	...	...	...	...	...	...	...	...	...	...	Afrique du Sud

Voir la fin du tableau pour la remarque générale et les notes.

Tables I, J and K

General note:

Manufactured goods are here defined to comprise sections 5 through 8 of the Standard International Trade Classification (SITC). These sections are: chemicals and related products, manufactured goods classified chiefly by material, machinery and transport equipment and miscellaneous manufactured articles. Fuels are here defined to comprise all the products in section 3 of the SITC. These products are: coal, coke and briquettes, petroleum, petroleum products and related materials gas and electric current. The unit value indices are obtained from national sources, except those of a few countries which the United Nations Statistics Division compiles using their quantity and value figures. For countries that do not compile indices for manufactured goods exports and fuel imports conforming to the above definition, sub-indices are aggregated to approximate an index of SITC sections 5-8 and SITC section 3 respectively. Unit value indices obtained from national indices are rebased, where necessary, so that 2000=100. Indices in national currency are converted into U.S. dollars using conversion factors obtained by dividing the weighted average exchange rate of a given currency in the current period by the weighted average exchange rate in the base period. All aggregate unit value indices are current period weighted. The indices in SDRs are calculated by multiplying the equivalent aggregate indices in U.S. dollars by conversion factors obtained by dividing the SDR/$US exchange rate in the current period by the rate in the base period. The quantum indices are derived from the value data and the unit value indices. All aggregate quantum indices are base period weighted. The figures in Table K are calculated from those prepared for Tables I and J. Total imports and exports used in the calculations are, in general, those published in Table A.

Table I:

1/ Excludes trade of the countries of Eastern Europe and Commonwealth of Independent States.
2/ Beginning 1989, derived from price indices; national unit value index is discontinued.
3/ Average price indexes of manufacturing industry products.
4/ Industrial product.

Table J:

1/ Beginning 1989, derived from price indices; national unit value index is discontinued.
2/ In December 2011, estimates of 2010 unit value indices for certain European economies were revised.

Remarque générale:

Les produits manufacturéscomprennent les sections 5 à 8 de la Classificationtype pour le commerce international (CTCI). Ces sections sont produits chimiques et produits connexes, articles manufacturés classés principalement d'après la matière première, machines et matérial de transport et articles manufacturés divers. Les produits énergétiques comprennent tous les produits appartenant à la section 3 de la CTCI. Ces produits sont huilles, cokes et briquettes, pétrole, produits dérives du pétrole et produits connexes, gaz et énergie électrique. Les indices de la valeur unitaire sont obtenus de sources nationales, á l'exception de quelque pays pour lesquels la Division de Statistique des Nations Unies calcule ces indices en utilisant le chiffres de la valeur et du volume fournis par ces pays. Pour les pays ne calculant pas leurs indices des exportations des produits manufacturés et importations des produits énergétiques selon la definition décrite ci-dessus les sous-indices sont agrégés en un indice qui se rapproche les sections 5 à 8 de la CTCI et la section 3 de la CTCI respectivement. Les indices en monnaie nationale son convertis en dollars des E.-U. en les multipliant par un facteur de conversion obtenu en divisant le taux de change courant, moyenne pondérés, d'une monnaie donnée par celui de la période de base. Tous les agrégés des indices de la valeur unitaire, sont à coéfficients de pondération correspondant à la période indiquée. Les indices indices en DTS son calculés en multipliant les indices totaux equivlents en dollars E.-U. par un facteur de conversion obtenu en divisant le taux de change cournat du DTS/$E-U d'une monnaie donnée par celui de la période de base. Les indices du quantum sont calculés à partir de chiffres de la valeur et lés indices de la valeur unitaire. Tous les agrégés des indices du quantum sont à coéfficients de pondération correspondant à la période en base. Les chiffres dans le tableau K sont calculés selon des données preparées pour les tableaux I et J. Les totaux des importations et exportations utilisées dans les calculs sont, en général, celles publiées dans le Tableau A.

Tableau I:

1/ Non compris le commerce des pays de l'Europe de l'Est et Communauté des États indépendants.

2/ A partir de 1989, calculés à partir des indices des prix; l'indice de valeur unitaire national est discontinué.

3/ Les indices moyens de prix des produits de l'industrie manufacturiere.

4/ Produit industriel.

Tableau J:

1/ A partir de 1989, calculés à partir des indices des prix; l'indice de valeur unitaire national est discontinué.

2/ En décembre 2011, les estimations des indices de valeur unitaire 2010 pour certaines économies européennes ont été mises à jour.

2013
International Trade
Statistics Yearbook

Volume II
Trade by Product

Part 2 – Commodity Trade Profiles

- Food and live animals (SITC Section 0)
- Beverages and tobacco (SITC Section 1)
- Crude materials, inedible, except fuels (SITC Section 2)
- Mineral fuels, lubricants and related materials (SITC Section 3)
- Animal and vegetable oils, fats and waxes (SITC Section 4)
- Chemicals and related products, n.e.s. (SITC Section 5)
- Manufactured goods classified chiefly by material (SITC Section 6)
- Machinery and transport equipment (SITC Section 7)
- Miscellaneous manufactured articles (SITC Section 8)
- Commodities and transactions not classified elsewhere in SITC (SITC Section 9)

Food and live animals

(SITC Section 0)

001 Live animals other than animals of division 03

In 2013, the value (in current US$) of exports of "live animals other than animals of division 03" (SITC group 001) increased by 2.2 percent (compared to 6.8 percent average growth rate from 2009-2013) to reach 22.4 bln US$ (see table 2), while imports increased by 0.3 percent to reach 21.8 bln US$ (see table 3). Exports of this commodity accounted for 1.8 percent of world exports of SITC sections 0+1, and 0.1 percent of total world merchandise exports (see table 1). Netherlands, France and Canada were the top exporters in 2013 (see table 2). They accounted for 13.3, 10.8 and 8.2 percent of world exports, respectively. USA, Germany and Italy were the top destinations, with respectively 12.2, 10.6 and 8.1 percent of world imports (see table 3).

The top 15 countries/areas accounted for 76.2 and 67.3 percent of total world exports and imports, respectively (see tables 2 and 3). In 2013, France was the country/area with the highest value of net exports (+2.1 bln US$), followed by Canada (+1.6 bln US$). By MDG regions (see graph 2), the largest surpluses in this product group were recorded by Developed Europe (+2.5 bln US$), Sub-Saharan Africa (+959.9 mln US$) and Developed Asia-Pacific (+861.7 mln US$). The largest trade deficits were recorded by Western Asia (-2.2 bln US$), Northern Africa (-647.0 mln US$) and Commonwealth of Independent States (-590.2 mln US$).

Table 1: Imports (Imp.) and exports (Exp.), 1999-2013, in current US$

		1999	2000	2001	2002	2003	2004	2005	2006	2007	2008	2009	2010	2011	2012	2013
Values in Bln US$	Imp.	9.3	9.4	8.8	9.5	9.5	10.6	12.7	14.4	15.5	17.0	16.5	18.7	20.5	21.7	21.8
	Exp.	8.8	9.0	8.9	9.8	10.2	11.3	13.1	14.5	16.0	17.6	17.2	18.2	21.1	21.9	22.4
As a percentage of SITC section (%)	Imp.	2.2	2.3	2.1	2.1	1.9	1.8	2.0	2.1	1.9	1.7	1.8	1.9	1.7	1.8	1.8
	Exp.	2.2	2.3	2.2	2.3	2.1	2.0	2.2	2.2	2.0	1.9	2.0	1.9	1.8	1.9	1.8
As a percentage of world trade (%)	Imp.	0.2	0.1	0.1	0.1	0.1	0.1	0.1	0.1	0.1	0.1	0.1	0.1	0.1	0.1	0.1
	Exp.	0.2	0.1	0.1	0.2	0.1	0.1	0.1	0.1	0.1	0.1	0.1	0.1	0.1	0.1	0.1

Graph 1: Annual growth rates of exports, 1999–2013
(In percentage by year)

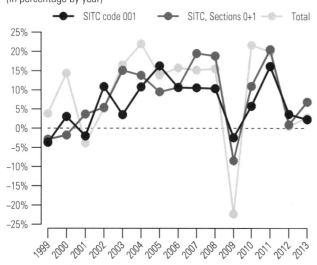

Table 2: Top exporting countries or areas in 2013

Country or area	Value (million US$)	Avg. Growth (%) 09-13	Growth (%) 12-13	World share %	Cum.
World........................	22 373.6	6.8	2.2	100.0	
Netherlands................	2 978.8	8.8	12.9	13.3	13.3
France......................	2 427.0	1.5	-2.2	10.8	24.2
Canada.....................	1 835.7	6.4	13.2	8.2	32.4
Germany....................	1 745.6	9.8	7.5	7.8	40.2
Denmark....................	1 142.7	5.0	0.2	5.1	45.3
USA.........................	1 018.1	6.3	-14.5	4.6	49.8
Australia...................	1 007.2	2.7	-7.1	4.5	54.3
Brazil......................	782.6	13.5	21.8	3.5	57.8
Spain.......................	635.8	12.3	9.4	2.8	60.7
Belgium....................	628.0	3.1	22.2	2.8	63.5
United Kingdom...........	618.3	-2.1	6.9	2.8	66.2
Ireland.....................	583.5	9.1	37.8	2.6	68.8
China.......................	580.6	7.1	-0.4	2.6	71.4
Mexico.....................	543.1	8.0	-28.0	2.4	73.9
Somalia.....................	*532.1*	18.2	9.7	2.4	76.2

Graph 2: Trade Balance by MDG regions 2013
(Bln US$)

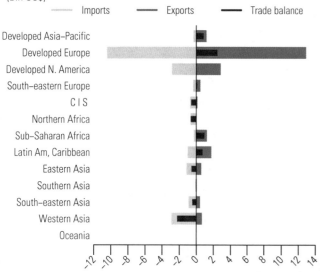

Table 3: Top importing countries or areas in 2013

Country or area	Value (million US$)	Avg. Growth (%) 09-13	Growth (%) 12-13	World share %	Cum.
World........................	21 769.4	7.2	0.3	100.0	
USA.........................	2 666.5	7.0	0.8	12.2	12.2
Germany....................	2 300.3	8.3	10.3	10.6	22.8
Italy........................	1 773.1	0.4	-4.5	8.1	31.0
Netherlands................	1 397.9	11.7	2.0	6.4	37.4
Saudi Arabia...............	968.4	15.5	24.1	4.4	41.8
Belgium....................	848.4	3.7	12.1	3.9	45.7
Poland......................	798.4	29.5	47.4	3.7	49.4
Venezuela..................	641.0	0.6	-42.8	2.9	52.3
United Kingdom...........	638.5	-1.8	0.4	2.9	55.3
China, Hong Kong SAR........	593.2	6.3	-5.1	2.7	58.0
Spain.......................	479.8	2.8	21.8	2.2	60.2
China.......................	432.7	32.5	-13.4	2.0	62.2
Russian Federation........	413.4	-3.2	-37.6	1.9	64.1
Turkey......................	346.4	79.1	-59.3	1.6	65.7
Indonesia...................	342.0	-6.0	19.4	1.6	67.3

In 2013, the value (in current US$) of exports of "meat of bovine animals, fresh, chilled or frozen" (SITC group 011) increased by 10.1 percent (compared to 10.6 percent average growth rate from 2009-2013) to reach 43.3 bln US$ (see table 2), while imports increased by 7.6 percent to reach 39.5 bln US$ (see table 3). Exports of this commodity accounted for 3.4 percent of world exports of SITC sections 0+1, and 0.2 percent of total world merchandise exports (see table 1). Australia, Brazil and USA were the top exporters in 2013 (see table 2). They accounted for 12.7, 12.4 and 12.1 percent of world exports, respectively. USA, Russian Federation and Japan were the top destinations, with respectively 9.0, 7.3 and 6.9 percent of world imports (see table 3).

The top 15 countries/areas accounted for 85.8 and 69.5 percent of total world exports and imports, respectively (see tables 2 and 3). In 2013, Australia was the country/area with the highest value of net exports (+5.5 bln US$), followed by Brazil (+5.1 bln US$). By MDG regions (see graph 2), the largest surpluses in this product group were recorded by Latin America and the Caribbean (+6.7 bln US$), Developed Asia-Pacific (+4.5 bln US$) and Southern Asia (+4.0 bln US$). The largest trade deficits were recorded by Eastern Asia (-4.7 bln US$), Commonwealth of Independent States (-2.3 bln US$) and Western Asia (-2.0 bln US$).

Table 1: Imports (Imp.) and exports (Exp.), 1999-2013, in current US$

		1999	2000	2001	2002	2003	2004	2005	2006	2007	2008	2009	2010	2011	2012	2013
Values in Bln US$	Imp.	14.4	14.5	12.8	14.2	16.6	18.3	20.6	23.3	26.1	30.4	28.4	30.4	35.5	36.7	39.5
	Exp.	14.3	14.3	12.7	14.3	16.6	18.7	21.5	24.2	26.7	32.5	28.9	32.4	39.0	39.3	43.3
As a percentage of	Imp.	3.5	3.5	3.0	3.2	3.2	3.1	3.2	3.3	3.1	3.1	3.2	3.1	3.0	3.1	3.2
SITC section (%)	Exp.	3.6	3.7	3.2	3.4	3.4	3.4	3.6	3.6	3.3	3.4	3.3	3.4	3.4	3.3	3.4
As a percentage of	Imp.	0.3	0.2	0.2	0.2	0.2	0.2	0.2	0.2	0.2	0.2	0.2	0.2	0.2	0.2	0.2
world trade (%)	Exp.	0.3	0.2	0.2	0.2	0.2	0.2	0.2	0.2	0.2	0.2	0.2	0.2	0.2	0.2	0.2

Graph 1: Annual growth rates of exports, 1999–2013
(In percentage by year)

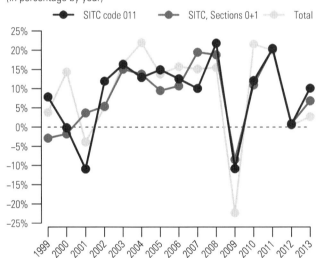

Table 2: Top exporting countries or areas in 2013

Country or area	Value (million US$)	Avg. Growth (%) 09-13	Growth (%) 12-13	World share %	Cum.
World	43 262.9	10.6	10.1	100.0	
Australia	5 507.8	13.0	11.9	12.7	12.7
Brazil	5 358.7	15.4	19.2	12.4	25.1
USA	5 239.0	20.5	12.5	12.1	37.2
India	4 486.6	46.1	49.8	10.4	47.6
Netherlands	3 010.0	3.6	0.5	7.0	54.6
Ireland	2 081.2	4.6	3.5	4.8	59.4
Germany	1 888.2	-0.9	-2.6	4.4	63.7
New Zealand	1 722.8	11.2	2.3	4.0	67.7
Uruguay	1 300.7	8.2	-7.2	3.0	70.7
France	1 296.3	-1.0	-5.2	3.0	73.7
Poland	1 254.8	12.1	15.7	2.9	76.6
Canada	1 108.9	2.5	5.2	2.6	79.2
Paraguay	1 004.7	16.1	33.0	2.3	81.5
Argentina	993.1	-10.2	0.0	2.3	83.8
Belgium	846.6	5.2	8.2	2.0	85.8

Graph 2: Trade Balance by MDG regions 2013
(Bln US$)

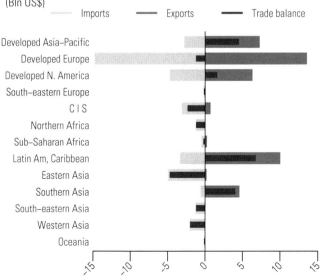

Table 3: Top importing countries or areas in 2013

Country or area	Value (million US$)	Avg. Growth (%) 09-13	Growth (%) 12-13	World share %	Cum.
World	39 478.1	8.6	7.6	100.0	
USA	3 550.4	9.5	1.8	9.0	9.0
Russian Federation	2 874.1	5.6	-2.8	7.3	16.3
Japan	2 729.1	8.1	-1.1	6.9	23.2
Italy	2 655.5	-1.6	-1.2	6.7	29.9
Germany	2 161.4	8.3	4.2	5.5	35.4
Netherlands	1 969.4	8.2	-0.9	5.0	40.4
France	1 864.4	3.4	5.3	4.7	45.1
China, Hong Kong SAR	1 632.5	36.2	108.9	4.1	49.2
United Kingdom	1 490.5	5.2	11.9	3.8	53.0
Rep. of Korea	1 395.7	15.0	10.8	3.5	56.5
China	1 270.1	131.7	398.8	3.2	59.8
Canada	1 145.3	14.7	-1.9	2.9	62.7
Chile	904.7	17.9	7.1	2.3	65.0
Mexico	894.4	1.6	7.5	2.3	67.2
Venezuela	890.1	0.6	13.5	2.3	69.5

012 Other meat, meat offal, fresh, chilled, frozen (for human)

In 2013, the value (in current US$) of exports of "other meat, meat offal, fresh, chilled, frozen (for human)" (SITC group 012) increased by 3.6 percent (compared to 8.3 percent average growth rate from 2009-2013) to reach 74.1 bln US$ (see table 2), while imports increased by 2.5 percent to reach 70.6 bln US$ (see table 3). Exports of this commodity accounted for 5.9 percent of world exports of SITC sections 0+1, and 0.4 percent of total world merchandise exports (see table 1). USA, Brazil and Germany were the top exporters in 2013 (see table 2). They accounted for 14.5, 12.0 and 10.1 percent of world exports, respectively. Japan, China and Germany were the top destinations, with respectively 8.4, 6.6 and 6.5 percent of world imports (see table 3).

The top 15 countries/areas accounted for 85.5 and 66.2 percent of total world exports and imports, respectively (see tables 2 and 3). In 2013, Brazil was the country/area with the highest value of net exports (+8.8 bln US$), followed by USA (+8.5 bln US$). By MDG regions (see graph 2), the largest surpluses in this product group were recorded by Developed North America (+10.6 bln US$), Developed Europe (+9.4 bln US$) and Latin America and the Caribbean (+6.3 bln US$). The largest trade deficits were recorded by Eastern Asia (-7.9 bln US$), Western Asia (-4.8 bln US$) and Commonwealth of Independent States (-4.2 bln US$).

Table 1: Imports (Imp.) and exports (Exp.), 1999-2013, in current US$

		1999	2000	2001	2002	2003	2004	2005	2006	2007	2008	2009	2010	2011	2012	2013
Values in Bln US$	Imp.	22.6	23.7	26.0	26.1	29.6	34.5	38.8	39.8	46.3	57.9	53.1	57.1	68.6	68.9	70.6
	Exp.	22.0	23.0	26.1	24.7	28.6	34.1	39.3	40.0	47.4	59.7	53.9	58.8	71.1	71.5	74.1
As a percentage of SITC section (%)	Imp.	5.4	5.7	6.1	5.8	5.8	5.9	6.1	5.7	5.6	5.9	5.9	5.8	5.8	5.8	5.7
	Exp.	5.6	5.9	6.5	5.8	5.9	6.2	6.5	6.0	5.9	6.3	6.2	6.1	6.1	6.1	5.9
As a percentage of world trade (%)	Imp.	0.4	0.4	0.4	0.4	0.4	0.4	0.4	0.3	0.3	0.4	0.4	0.4	0.4	0.4	0.4
	Exp.	0.4	0.4	0.4	0.4	0.4	0.4	0.4	0.3	0.3	0.4	0.4	0.4	0.4	0.4	0.4

Graph 1: Annual growth rates of exports, 1999–2013
(In percentage by year)

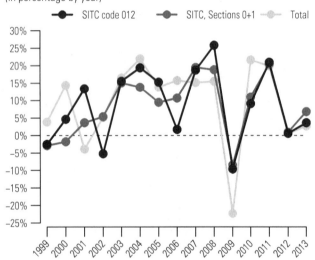

Legend: SITC code 012 — SITC, Sections 0+1 — Total

Graph 2: Trade Balance by MDG regions 2013
(Bln US$)

Legend: Imports — Exports — Trade balance

Regions (top to bottom): Developed Asia–Pacific, Developed Europe, Developed N. America, South–eastern Europe, CIS, Northern Africa, Sub-Saharan Africa, Latin Am, Caribbean, Eastern Asia, Southern Asia, South–eastern Asia, Western Asia, Oceania

Axis: -30, -20, -10, 0, 10, 20, 30, 40

Table 2: Top exporting countries or areas in 2013

Country or area	Value (million US$)	Avg. Growth (%) 09-13	Growth (%) 12-13	World share %	World share % Cum.
World	74 132.0	8.3	3.6	100.0	
USA	10 759.7	8.2	-3.6	14.5	14.5
Brazil	8 883.0	8.8	2.3	12.0	26.5
Germany	7 501.4	7.7	6.2	10.1	36.6
Netherlands	5 898.7	9.3	2.0	8.0	44.6
Spain	3 972.5	9.2	5.5	5.4	49.9
Denmark	3 957.3	2.5	1.6	5.3	55.3
Belgium	3 629.1	5.2	12.4	4.9	60.2
Canada	3 313.7	8.2	-1.7	4.5	64.6
France	3 070.8	3.9	3.3	4.1	68.8
Poland	2 952.3	22.9	19.3	4.0	72.8
Australia	2 789.4	12.2	13.5	3.8	76.5
New Zealand	2 607.8	5.5	4.4	3.5	80.0
United Kingdom	1 610.0	9.4	12.9	2.2	82.2
China, Hong Kong SAR	1 288.5	-5.4	-1.3	1.7	84.0
Hungary	1 134.9	8.6	2.5	1.5	85.5

Table 3: Top importing countries or areas in 2013

Country or area	Value (million US$)	Avg. Growth (%) 09-13	Growth (%) 12-13	World share %	World share % Cum.
World	70 572.8	7.4	2.5	100.0	
Japan	5 945.1	2.8	-15.6	8.4	8.4
China	4 652.8	28.8	21.0	6.6	15.0
Germany	4 607.7	3.4	3.6	6.5	21.5
China, Hong Kong SAR	3 805.2	3.8	5.2	5.4	26.9
France	3 624.5	3.7	4.4	5.1	32.1
Russian Federation	3 473.4	-0.5	-11.7	4.9	37.0
United Kingdom	3 405.5	3.1	6.1	4.8	41.8
Italy	3 251.1	4.9	8.3	4.6	46.4
Mexico	2 900.8	13.0	12.9	4.1	50.5
Saudi Arabia	2 305.0	15.1	12.2	3.3	53.8
USA	2 304.6	10.9	8.3	3.3	57.1
Netherlands	2 072.0	10.2	1.5	2.9	60.0
Poland	1 801.1	6.2	13.5	2.6	62.6
Belgium	1 324.5	2.9	5.7	1.9	64.4
Rep. of Korea	1 280.2	10.0	-19.7	1.8	66.2

Meat, edible offal, salted, in brine, dried, etc; flours, meals 016

In 2013, the value (in current US$) of exports of "meat, edible offal, salted, in brine, dried, etc; flours, meals" (SITC group 016) increased by 10.1 percent (compared to 6.0 percent average growth rate from 2009-2013) to reach 5.1 bln US$ (see table 2), while imports increased by 10.0 percent to reach 4.6 bln US$ (see table 3). Exports of this commodity accounted for 0.4 percent of world exports of SITC sections 0+1, and less than 0.1 percent of total world merchandise exports (see table 1). Italy, Netherlands and Brazil were the top exporters in 2013 (see table 2). They accounted for 18.5, 18.5 and 10.6 percent of world exports, respectively. United Kingdom, Netherlands and France were the top destinations, with respectively 25.7, 11.8 and 10.4 percent of world imports (see table 3).

The top 15 countries/areas accounted for 94.9 and 83.8 percent of total world exports and imports, respectively (see tables 2 and 3). In 2013, Italy was the country/area with the highest value of net exports (+816.2 mln US$), followed by Brazil (+530.7 mln US$). By MDG regions (see graph 2), the largest surpluses in this product group were recorded by Latin America and the Caribbean (+388.7 mln US$), Developed Europe (+159.8 mln US$) and South-eastern Asia (+112.3 mln US$). The largest trade deficits were recorded by Developed Asia-Pacific (-83.6 mln US$), Sub-Saharan Africa (-61.6 mln US$) and Eastern Asia (-47.3 mln US$).

Table 1: Imports (Imp.) and exports (Exp.), 1999-2013, in current US$

		1999	2000	2001	2002	2003	2004	2005	2006	2007	2008	2009	2010	2011	2012	2013
Values in Bln US$	Imp.	1.6	1.8	2.3	2.2	2.6	2.6	2.5	2.9	3.7	4.1	3.9	4.0	4.4	4.2	4.6
	Exp.	1.6	1.7	1.9	1.9	2.5	2.7	2.5	3.0	3.9	4.7	4.1	4.3	4.9	4.7	5.1
As a percentage of	Imp.	0.4	0.4	0.5	0.5	0.5	0.4	0.4	0.4	0.4	0.4	0.4	0.4	0.4	0.4	0.4
SITC section (%)	Exp.	0.4	0.4	0.5	0.5	0.5	0.5	0.4	0.4	0.5	0.5	0.5	0.4	0.4	0.4	0.4
As a percentage of	Imp.	0.0	0.0	0.0	0.0	0.0	0.0	0.0	0.0	0.0	0.0	0.0	0.0	0.0	0.0	0.0
world trade (%)	Exp.	0.0	0.0	0.0	0.0	0.0	0.0	0.0	0.0	0.0	0.0	0.0	0.0	0.0	0.0	0.0

Graph 1: Annual growth rates of exports, 1999–2013
(In percentage by year)

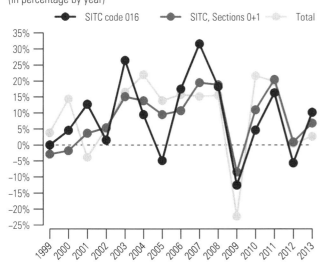

- SITC code 016   - SITC, Sections 0+1   - Total

Graph 2: Trade Balance by MDG regions 2013
(Bln US$)

— Imports   — Exports   — Trade balance

Developed Asia-Pacific
Developed Europe
Developed N. America
South-eastern Europe
CIS
Northern Africa
Sub-Saharan Africa
Latin Am, Caribbean
Eastern Asia
Southern Asia
South-eastern Asia
Western Asia
Oceania

Table 2: Top exporting countries or areas in 2013

Country or area	Value (million US$)	Avg. Growth (%) 09-13	Growth (%) 12-13	World share %	Cum.
World	5 140.6	6.0	10.1	100.0	
Italy	950.8	6.8	9.3	18.5	18.5
Netherlands	950.2	9.7	26.7	18.5	37.0
Brazil	543.4	0.6	4.0	10.6	47.6
Germany	489.9	7.7	8.5	9.5	57.1
Spain	476.7	11.9	22.5	9.3	66.4
Denmark	355.1	-2.6	-7.0	6.9	73.3
USA	247.0	4.2	-2.2	4.8	78.1
Thailand	168.0	157.7	100.7	3.3	81.3
Poland	142.1	7.7	29.5	2.8	84.1
Belgium	135.6	-3.3	-2.6	2.6	86.7
France	112.7	-3.7	9.5	2.2	88.9
Canada	110.8	-0.1	3.0	2.2	91.1
United Kingdom	90.7	0.2	1.2	1.8	92.8
Austria	60.0	3.6	22.8	1.2	94.0
Switzerland	46.7	3.3	-12.2	0.9	94.9

Table 3: Top importing countries or areas in 2013

Country or area	Value (million US$)	Avg. Growth (%) 09-13	Growth (%) 12-13	World share %	Cum.
World	4 636.2	4.4	10.0	100.0	
United Kingdom	1 190.1	-2.1	2.7	25.7	25.7
Netherlands	545.0	11.0	21.9	11.8	37.4
France	480.0	3.8	6.4	10.4	47.8
Germany	458.6	1.7	13.8	9.9	57.7
Belgium	202.8	2.1	18.0	4.4	62.0
USA	165.5	3.2	2.5	3.6	65.6
Italy	134.6	5.0	10.0	2.9	68.5
Denmark	129.6	1.8	4.3	2.8	71.3
Ireland	104.0	23.9	45.7	2.2	73.6
Canada	102.9	18.3	-11.9	2.2	75.8
Mexico	100.3	12.1	14.1	2.2	77.9
Portugal	70.8	13.1	45.5	1.5	79.5
Austria	68.7	10.0	20.7	1.5	80.9
Sweden	68.6	10.0	7.5	1.5	82.4
Switzerland	62.8	3.7	5.8	1.4	83.8

017 Meat and edible meat offal, prepared or preserved, nes

In 2013, the value (in current US$) of exports of "meat and edible meat offal, prepared or preserved, nes" (SITC group 017) increased by 6.6 percent (compared to 8.1 percent average growth rate from 2009-2013) to reach 21.2 bln US$ (see table 2), while imports increased by 4.8 percent to reach 20.6 bln US$ (see table 3). Exports of this commodity accounted for 1.7 percent of world exports of SITC sections 0+1, and 0.1 percent of total world merchandise exports (see table 1). Germany, Thailand and China were the top exporters in 2013 (see table 2). They accounted for 11.6, 10.9 and 9.8 percent of world exports, respectively. Japan, United Kingdom and Germany were the top destinations, with respectively 15.7, 15.1 and 8.1 percent of world imports (see table 3).

The top 15 countries/areas accounted for 83.2 and 76.5 percent of total world exports and imports, respectively (see tables 2 and 3). In 2013, Thailand was the country/area with the highest value of net exports (+2.3 bln US$), followed by China (+2.1 bln US$). By MDG regions (see graph 2), the largest surpluses in this product group were recorded by South-eastern Asia (+2.2 bln US$), Latin America and the Caribbean (+1.1 bln US$) and Eastern Asia (+951.1 mln US$). The largest trade deficits were recorded by Developed Asia-Pacific (-3.1 bln US$), Sub-Saharan Africa (-320.5 mln US$) and Developed Europe (-264.2 mln US$).

Table 1: Imports (Imp.) and exports (Exp.), 1999-2013, in current US$

		1999	2000	2001	2002	2003	2004	2005	2006	2007	2008	2009	2010	2011	2012	2013
Values in Bln US$	Imp.	5.4	5.5	6.0	6.4	7.5	8.9	10.4	11.6	13.5	15.9	15.3	15.7	19.3	19.6	20.6
	Exp.	5.4	5.5	6.0	6.5	7.5	8.9	10.7	11.7	13.9	16.8	15.6	16.3	19.3	19.9	21.2
As a percentage of SITC section (%)	Imp.	1.3	1.3	1.4	1.4	1.5	1.5	1.6	1.7	1.6	1.6	1.7	1.6	1.6	1.7	1.7
	Exp.	1.4	1.4	1.5	1.5	1.5	1.6	1.8	1.8	1.7	1.8	1.8	1.7	1.7	1.7	1.7
As a percentage of world trade (%)	Imp.	0.1	0.1	0.1	0.1	0.1	0.1	0.1	0.1	0.1	0.1	0.1	0.1	0.1	0.1	0.1
	Exp.	0.1	0.1	0.1	0.1	0.1	0.1	0.1	0.1	0.1	0.1	0.1	0.1	0.1	0.1	0.1

Graph 1: Annual growth rates of exports, 1999–2013
(In percentage by year)

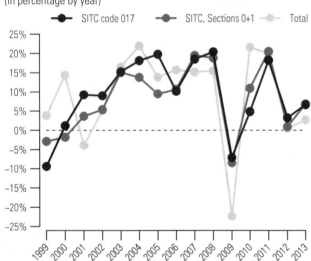

Legend: SITC code 017 — SITC, Sections 0+1 — Total

Table 2: Top exporting countries or areas in 2013

Country or area	Value (million US$)	Avg. Growth (%) 09-13	Growth (%) 12-13	World share %	Cum.
World	21 229.3	8.1	6.6	100.0	
Germany	2 463.5	4.1	6.2	11.6	11.6
Thailand	2 306.0	8.4	-0.3	10.9	22.5
China	2 074.5	15.7	-3.5	9.8	32.2
USA	1 719.8	13.4	16.7	8.1	40.3
Brazil	1 515.4	-1.6	-4.8	7.1	47.5
Netherlands	1 221.9	13.5	34.9	5.8	53.2
Belgium	928.6	3.1	6.1	4.4	57.6
Poland	860.8	19.7	38.7	4.1	61.7
France	822.9	2.2	3.7	3.9	65.5
Italy	816.9	7.5	10.5	3.8	69.4
Ireland	779.6	6.5	8.8	3.7	73.1
Denmark	729.1	4.8	4.4	3.4	76.5
Spain	563.3	8.8	-5.0	2.7	79.1
Austria	498.6	8.9	14.6	2.3	81.5
Belarus	366.6	38.2	-5.2	1.7	83.2

Graph 2: Trade Balance by MDG regions 2013
(Bln US$)

Legend: Imports — Exports — Trade balance

Developed Asia–Pacific
Developed Europe
Developed N. America
South–eastern Europe
C I S
Northern Africa
Sub–Saharan Africa
Latin Am, Caribbean
Eastern Asia
Southern Asia
South–eastern Asia
Western Asia
Oceania

-12 -10 -8 -6 -4 -2 0 2 4 6 8 10 12

Table 3: Top importing countries or areas in 2013

Country or area	Value (million US$)	Avg. Growth (%) 09-13	Growth (%) 12-13	World share %	Cum.
World	20 595.0	7.8	4.8	100.0	
Japan	3 242.7	9.7	-5.9	15.7	15.7
United Kingdom	3 106.6	5.7	-2.4	15.1	30.8
Germany	1 677.8	1.4	2.3	8.1	39.0
Netherlands	1 100.5	6.6	1.8	5.3	44.3
China, Hong Kong SAR	1 065.6	19.4	26.5	5.2	49.5
Canada	886.3	16.4	14.5	4.3	53.8
France	881.3	4.8	12.6	4.3	58.1
Belgium	840.9	9.3	19.9	4.1	62.2
USA	677.5	2.2	8.1	3.3	65.4
Denmark	458.4	10.4	20.3	2.2	67.7
Sweden	398.5	11.5	11.0	1.9	69.6
Ireland	367.9	4.8	-3.5	1.8	71.4
Russian Federation	365.6	26.1	9.1	1.8	73.2
Spain	351.1	3.8	-1.3	1.7	74.9
Italy	335.8	0.7	1.2	1.6	76.5

In 2013, the value (in current US$) of exports of "milk and cream and milk products other than butter or cheese" (SITC group 022) increased by 16.0 percent (compared to 14.7 percent average growth rate from 2009-2013) to reach 48.3 bln US$ (see table 2), while imports increased by 14.6 percent to reach 47.1 bln US$ (see table 3). Exports of this commodity accounted for 3.9 percent of world exports of SITC sections 0+1, and 0.3 percent of total world merchandise exports (see table 1). New Zealand, Germany and France were the top exporters in 2013 (see table 2). They accounted for 16.7, 12.0 and 8.5 percent of world exports, respectively. China, Netherlands and Italy were the top destinations, with respectively 10.2, 5.3 and 5.3 percent of world imports (see table 3).

The top 15 countries/areas accounted for 76.6 and 57.6 percent of total world exports and imports, respectively (see tables 2 and 3). In 2013, New Zealand was the country/area with the highest value of net exports (+7.9 bln US$), followed by Germany (+3.3 bln US$). By MDG regions (see graph 2), the largest surpluses in this product group were recorded by Developed Asia-Pacific (+8.7 bln US$), Developed Europe (+7.0 bln US$) and Developed North America (+3.0 bln US$). The largest trade deficits were recorded by Eastern Asia (-6.5 bln US$), South-eastern Asia (-3.7 bln US$) and Western Asia (-2.3 bln US$).

Table 1: Imports (Imp.) and exports (Exp.), 1999-2013, in current US$

		1999	2000	2001	2002	2003	2004	2005	2006	2007	2008	2009	2010	2011	2012	2013
Values in Bln US$	Imp.	14.3	14.3	15.0	14.5	17.1	20.5	22.3	23.8	31.8	35.3	28.1	33.5	42.3	41.0	47.1
	Exp.	13.9	14.1	15.2	14.3	17.0	20.5	22.3	23.8	32.1	36.0	27.9	34.1	42.1	41.7	48.3
As a percentage of SITC section (%)	Imp.	3.4	3.5	3.5	3.2	3.3	3.5	3.5	3.4	3.8	3.6	3.1	3.4	3.6	3.5	3.8
	Exp.	3.5	3.6	3.8	3.4	3.5	3.7	3.7	3.5	4.0	3.8	3.2	3.5	3.6	3.5	3.9
As a percentage of world trade (%)	Imp.	0.3	0.2	0.2	0.2	0.2	0.2	0.2	0.2	0.2	0.2	0.2	0.2	0.2	0.2	0.3
	Exp.	0.2	0.2	0.2	0.2	0.2	0.2	0.2	0.2	0.2	0.2	0.2	0.2	0.2	0.2	0.3

Graph 1: Annual growth rates of exports, 1999–2013
(In percentage by year)

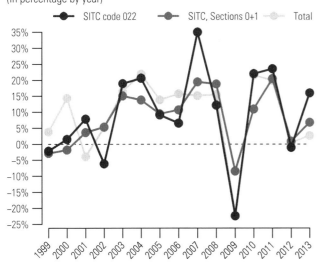

Graph 2: Trade Balance by MDG regions 2013
(Bln US$)

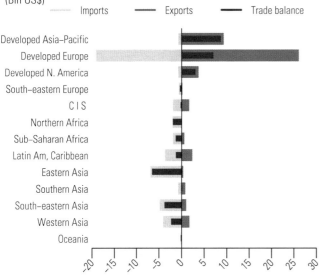

Table 2: Top exporting countries or areas in 2013

Country or area	Value (million US$)	Avg. Growth (%) 09-13	Growth (%) 12-13	World share %	Cum.
World	48 305.4	14.7	16.0	100.0	
New Zealand	8 062.1	25.4	24.1	16.7	16.7
Germany	5 803.6	9.1	18.5	12.0	28.7
France	4 084.6	9.1	7.6	8.5	37.2
USA	3 601.0	33.1	39.4	7.5	44.6
Netherlands	3 538.0	12.5	20.1	7.3	51.9
Belgium	2 769.8	9.1	18.6	5.7	57.7
Belarus	1 265.7	35.0	38.4	2.6	60.3
Australia	1 262.4	7.4	-1.2	2.6	62.9
Poland	1 167.5	13.3	18.4	2.4	65.3
Argentina	1 121.5	25.0	14.9	2.3	67.6
United Kingdom	1 089.9	11.8	16.1	2.3	69.9
Denmark	852.8	7.8	8.3	1.8	71.7
Austria	848.6	6.3	13.6	1.8	73.4
Spain	788.7	4.6	3.2	1.6	75.1
Ireland	725.1	12.5	22.0	1.5	76.6

Table 3: Top importing countries or areas in 2013

Country or area	Value (million US$)	Avg. Growth (%) 09-13	Growth (%) 12-13	World share %	Cum.
World	47 053.2	13.7	14.6	100.0	
China	4 785.0	51.5	66.5	10.2	10.2
Netherlands	2 516.2	10.9	10.5	5.3	15.5
Italy	2 505.2	6.1	11.9	5.3	20.8
Germany	2 502.8	7.8	11.9	5.3	26.2
Belgium	2 080.3	12.7	22.0	4.4	30.6
France	1 753.0	6.0	12.1	3.7	34.3
United Kingdom	1 558.3	5.9	14.9	3.3	37.6
China, Hong Kong SAR	1 460.1	30.8	21.5	3.1	40.7
Russian Federation	1 353.1	74.8	62.0	2.9	43.6
Spain	1 239.6	0.1	7.9	2.6	46.2
Mexico	1 137.5	14.9	6.5	2.4	48.6
Indonesia	1 131.0	22.1	18.2	2.4	51.1
Saudi Arabia	1 090.1	11.6	-1.7	2.3	53.4
Algeria	1 083.0	7.8	-1.4	2.3	55.7
Singapore	907.2	17.0	21.4	1.9	57.6

023 Butter and other fats and oils derived from milk

In 2013, the value (in current US$) of exports of "butter and other fats and oils derived from milk" (SITC group 023) increased by 22.9 percent (compared to 15.2 percent average growth rate from 2009-2013) to reach 8.3 bln US$ (see table 2), while imports increased by 18.5 percent to reach 8.0 bln US$ (see table 3). Exports of this commodity accounted for 0.7 percent of world exports of SITC sections 0+1, and less than 0.1 percent of total world merchandise exports (see table 1). New Zealand, Netherlands and Ireland were the top exporters in 2013 (see table 2). They accounted for 22.0, 14.9 and 9.8 percent of world exports, respectively. France, Belgium and Germany were the top destinations, with respectively 11.4, 8.9 and 8.8 percent of world imports (see table 3).

The top 15 countries/areas accounted for 91.6 and 69.6 percent of total world exports and imports, respectively (see tables 2 and 3). In 2013, New Zealand was the country/area with the highest value of net exports (+1.8 bln US$), followed by Ireland (+777.6 mln US$). By MDG regions (see graph 2), the largest surpluses in this product group were recorded by Developed Asia-Pacific (+1.9 bln US$), Developed Europe (+633.8 mln US$) and Developed North America (+279.3 mln US$). The largest trade deficits were recorded by Western Asia (-515.3 mln US$), Commonwealth of Independent States (-483.8 mln US$) and South-eastern Asia (-431.7 mln US$).

Table 1: Imports (Imp.) and exports (Exp.), 1999-2013, in current US$

		1999	2000	2001	2002	2003	2004	2005	2006	2007	2008	2009	2010	2011	2012	2013
Values in Bln US$	Imp.	3.0	2.8	2.9	2.8	3.9	4.3	4.4	4.5	5.4	5.6	4.7	6.4	7.8	6.7	8.0
	Exp.	3.0	2.7	2.7	2.6	3.4	4.1	4.2	4.0	5.3	6.0	4.7	6.7	8.2	6.8	8.3
As a percentage of SITC section (%)	Imp.	0.7	0.7	0.7	0.6	0.8	0.7	0.7	0.6	0.6	0.6	0.5	0.6	0.7	0.6	0.6
	Exp.	0.8	0.7	0.7	0.6	0.7	0.7	0.7	0.6	0.7	0.6	0.5	0.7	0.7	0.6	0.7
As a percentage of world trade (%)	Imp.	0.1	0.0	0.0	0.0	0.1	0.0	0.0	0.0	0.0	0.0	0.0	0.0	0.0	0.0	0.0
	Exp.	0.1	0.0	0.0	0.0	0.0	0.0	0.0	0.0	0.0	0.0	0.0	0.0	0.0	0.0	0.0

Graph 1: Annual growth rates of exports, 1999–2013
(In percentage by year)

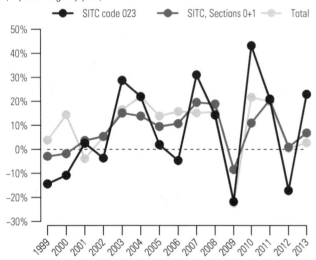

Graph 2: Trade Balance by MDG regions 2013
(Bln US$)

Table 2: Top exporting countries or areas in 2013

Country or area	Value (million US$)	Avg. Growth (%) 09-13	Growth (%) 12-13	World share %	Cum.
World	8 293.8	15.2	22.9	100.0	
New Zealand	1 824.7	17.7	13.1	22.0	22.0
Netherlands	1 232.0	18.5	30.5	14.9	36.9
Ireland	816.6	20.5	29.4	9.8	46.7
Germany	715.6	20.4	38.3	8.6	55.3
Belgium	705.4	7.5	36.1	8.5	63.8
France	426.8	10.2	4.0	5.1	69.0
USA	363.3	44.8	106.9	4.4	73.4
Belarus	358.0	11.4	17.5	4.3	77.7
Denmark	236.1	-3.6	-17.7	2.8	80.5
United Kingdom	227.4	26.0	41.4	2.7	83.3
Australia	207.5	4.0	4.5	2.5	85.8
Poland	162.2	30.3	37.9	2.0	87.7
Finland	136.2	3.4	17.1	1.6	89.4
Uruguay	103.4	27.3	0.4	1.2	90.6
Spain	84.7	14.6	7.6	1.0	91.6

Table 3: Top importing countries or areas in 2013

Country or area	Value (million US$)	Avg. Growth (%) 09-13	Growth (%) 12-13	World share %	Cum.
World	7 985.5	14.3	18.5	100.0	
France	912.3	16.1	36.1	11.4	11.4
Belgium	711.1	18.2	48.6	8.9	20.3
Germany	702.4	15.0	26.9	8.8	29.1
Russian Federation	698.0	44.0	51.5	8.7	37.9
United Kingdom	498.3	7.3	5.6	6.2	44.1
Netherlands	455.2	17.8	17.7	5.7	49.8
Italy	318.8	12.3	28.1	4.0	53.8
China	226.2	36.2	15.6	2.8	56.6
Saudi Arabia	198.4	16.4	-5.7	2.5	59.1
Iran	180.1	-3.5	-13.3	2.3	61.4
Egypt	176.1	5.4	-13.4	2.2	63.6
Mexico	159.7	1.3	36.2	2.0	65.6
Singapore	113.2	17.9	5.4	1.4	67.0
United Arab Emirates	108.3	18.0	11.4	1.4	68.3
Indonesia	102.7	29.5	69.6	1.3	69.6

In 2013, the value (in current US$) of exports of "cheese and curd" (SITC group 024) increased by 11.5 percent (compared to 8.7 percent average growth rate from 2009-2013) to reach 32.2 bln US$ (see table 2), while imports increased by 12.7 percent to reach 31.5 bln US$ (see table 3). Exports of this commodity accounted for 2.6 percent of world exports of SITC sections 0+1, and 0.2 percent of total world merchandise exports (see table 1). Germany, Netherlands and France were the top exporters in 2013 (see table 2). They accounted for 16.0, 13.7 and 12.4 percent of world exports, respectively. Germany, Italy and United Kingdom were the top destinations, with respectively 13.8, 7.7 and 7.2 percent of world imports (see table 3).

The top 15 countries/areas accounted for 82.7 and 70.7 percent of total world exports and imports, respectively (see tables 2 and 3). In 2013, Netherlands was the country/area with the highest value of net exports (+3.0 bln US$), followed by France (+2.3 bln US$). By MDG regions (see graph 2), the largest surpluses in this product group were recorded by Developed Europe (+5.1 bln US$), Developed Asia-Pacific (+366.0 mln US$) and Southern Asia (+48.9 mln US$). The largest trade deficits were recorded by Commonwealth of Independent States (-1.4 bln US$), Western Asia (-1.1 bln US$) and Eastern Asia (-843.6 mln US$).

Table 1: Imports (Imp.) and exports (Exp.), 1999-2013, in current US$

		1999	2000	2001	2002	2003	2004	2005	2006	2007	2008	2009	2010	2011	2012	2013
Values in Bln US$	Imp.	10.5	9.7	10.5	11.2	13.3	15.7	16.6	17.8	21.3	25.7	22.4	24.4	28.1	28.0	31.5
	Exp.	10.4	9.9	11.0	11.2	13.6	16.1	17.2	18.5	22.2	27.0	23.0	25.6	29.7	28.9	32.2
As a percentage of	Imp.	2.5	2.4	2.5	2.5	2.6	2.7	2.6	2.6	2.6	2.6	2.5	2.5	2.4	2.4	2.5
SITC section (%)	Exp.	2.6	2.6	2.7	2.6	2.8	2.9	2.8	2.8	2.8	2.8	2.6	2.6	2.5	2.5	2.6
As a percentage of	Imp.	0.2	0.1	0.2	0.2	0.2	0.2	0.2	0.1	0.2	0.2	0.2	0.2	0.2	0.2	0.2
world trade (%)	Exp.	0.2	0.2	0.2	0.2	0.2	0.2	0.2	0.2	0.2	0.2	0.2	0.2	0.2	0.2	0.2

Graph 1: Annual growth rates of exports, 1999–2013
(In percentage by year)

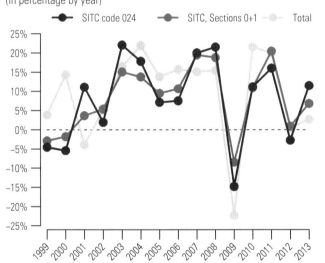

Graph 2: Trade Balance by MDG regions 2013
(Bln US$)

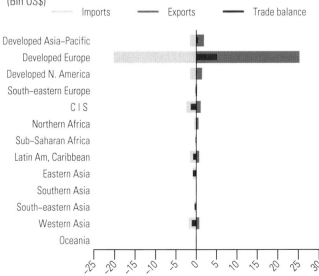

Table 2: Top exporting countries or areas in 2013

Country or area	Value (million US$)	Avg. Growth (%) 09-13	Growth (%) 12-13	World share %	Cum.
World	32 176.6	8.7	11.5	100.0	
Germany	5 147.5	9.3	14.1	16.0	16.0
Netherlands	4 423.0	12.7	18.1	13.7	29.7
France	4 001.9	3.6	7.9	12.4	42.2
Italy	2 733.8	8.0	7.6	8.5	50.7
Denmark	1 575.8	3.1	10.3	4.9	55.6
USA	1 364.3	32.9	21.8	4.2	59.8
New Zealand	1 156.1	7.8	-1.7	3.6	63.4
Belgium	1 030.0	9.5	20.2	3.2	66.6
Ireland	966.7	8.6	10.8	3.0	69.6
Poland	915.3	15.9	30.4	2.8	72.5
Australia	755.5	8.3	-1.7	2.3	74.8
United Kingdom	692.6	11.4	9.0	2.2	77.0
Belarus	649.4	13.2	11.9	2.0	79.0
Switzerland	615.4	4.2	5.9	1.9	80.9
Austria	597.6	4.8	9.7	1.9	82.7

Table 3: Top importing countries or areas in 2013

Country or area	Value (million US$)	Avg. Growth (%) 09-13	Growth (%) 12-13	World share %	Cum.
World	31 534.2	8.9	12.7	100.0	
Germany	4 343.7	6.3	11.3	13.8	13.8
Italy	2 435.9	7.1	16.5	7.7	21.5
United Kingdom	2 266.8	3.8	12.8	7.2	28.7
Russian Federation	2 167.5	24.9	19.2	6.9	35.6
France	1 654.6	4.2	10.9	5.2	40.8
Belgium	1 593.7	5.6	14.9	5.1	45.9
Netherlands	1 440.3	16.9	27.5	4.6	50.4
Spain	1 196.6	3.1	8.4	3.8	54.2
USA	1 191.3	3.3	4.7	3.8	58.0
Japan	1 119.6	8.3	-3.8	3.6	61.6
Sweden	705.4	12.0	30.5	2.2	63.8
Saudi Arabia	613.9	7.6	1.4	1.9	65.7
Greece	568.9	2.5	12.9	1.8	67.5
Austria	527.0	6.3	6.5	1.7	69.2
Mexico	480.2	16.4	17.7	1.5	70.7

025 Eggs, birds', egg yolks, fresh, dried or preserved; egg albumin

In 2013, the value (in current US$) of exports of "eggs, birds', egg yolks, fresh, dried or preserved; egg albumin" (SITC group 025) increased by 5.9 percent (compared to 6.4 percent average growth rate from 2009-2013) to reach 5.8 bln US$ (see table 2), while imports increased by 5.7 percent to reach 5.4 bln US$ (see table 3). Exports of this commodity accounted for 0.5 percent of world exports of SITC sections 0+1, and less than 0.1 percent of total world merchandise exports (see table 1). Netherlands, USA and Turkey were the top exporters in 2013 (see table 2). They accounted for 24.8, 10.7 and 7.0 percent of world exports, respectively. Germany, Netherlands and United Kingdom were the top destinations, with respectively 16.0, 9.4 and 5.2 percent of world imports (see table 3).

The top 15 countries/areas accounted for 83.6 and 68.9 percent of total world exports and imports, respectively (see tables 2 and 3). In 2013, Netherlands was the country/area with the highest value of net exports (+925.7 mln US$), followed by USA (+578.4 mln US$). By MDG regions (see graph 2), the largest surpluses in this product group were recorded by Developed Europe (+563.2 mln US$), Developed North America (+525.1 mln US$) and Southern Asia (+43.5 mln US$). The largest trade deficits were recorded by Latin America and the Caribbean (-268.3 mln US$), Developed Asia-Pacific (-184.5 mln US$) and Commonwealth of Independent States (-98.8 mln US$).

Table 1: Imports (Imp.) and exports (Exp.), 1999-2013, in current US$

		1999	2000	2001	2002	2003	2004	2005	2006	2007	2008	2009	2010	2011	2012	2013
Values in Bln US$	Imp.	1.4	1.4	1.5	1.6	1.9	2.2	2.3	2.5	3.1	3.8	4.1	4.2	4.4	5.1	5.4
	Exp.	1.4	1.4	1.5	1.5	2.0	2.1	2.2	2.4	3.2	4.1	4.5	4.5	4.8	5.5	5.8
As a percentage of	Imp.	0.3	0.3	0.4	0.4	0.4	0.4	0.4	0.4	0.4	0.4	0.5	0.4	0.4	0.4	0.4
SITC section (%)	Exp.	0.4	0.4	0.4	0.4	0.4	0.4	0.4	0.4	0.4	0.4	0.5	0.5	0.4	0.5	0.5
As a percentage of	Imp.	0.0	0.0	0.0	0.0	0.0	0.0	0.0	0.0	0.0	0.0	0.0	0.0	0.0	0.0	0.0
world trade (%)	Exp.	0.0	0.0	0.0	0.0	0.0	0.0	0.0	0.0	0.0	0.0	0.0	0.0	0.0	0.0	0.0

Graph 1: Annual growth rates of exports, 1999–2013
(In percentage by year)

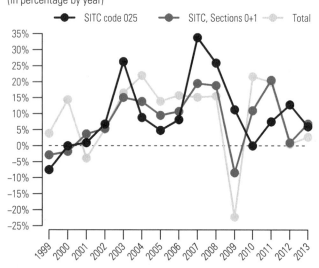

Legend: SITC code 025 — SITC, Sections 0+1 — Total

Table 2: Top exporting countries or areas in 2013

Country or area	Value (million US$)	Avg. Growth (%) 09-13	Growth (%) 12-13	World share %	Cum.
World................................	5790.4	6.4	5.9	100.0	
Netherlands.........................	1436.7	7.2	8.2	24.8	24.8
USA..................................	621.3	15.7	24.9	10.7	35.5
Turkey...............................	406.4	33.8	15.9	7.0	42.6
Germany.............................	362.9	4.0	-2.7	6.3	48.8
Poland...............................	339.4	8.7	-4.8	5.9	54.7
France...............................	304.8	0.0	2.5	5.3	60.0
Belgium.............................	252.3	10.9	18.0	4.4	64.3
Spain................................	206.2	-4.4	2.1	3.6	67.9
China................................	179.0	10.0	0.4	3.1	71.0
Ukraine..............................	142.3	18.5	44.0	2.5	73.4
United Kingdom.....................	140.3	18.4	55.6	2.4	75.8
Malaysia............................	137.2	11.3	1.9	2.4	78.2
Italy.................................	135.2	-2.0	-7.7	2.3	80.5
India................................	100.6	6.7	-5.2	1.7	82.3
Saudi Arabia........................	79.0	3.1	3.7	1.4	83.6

Graph 2: Trade Balance by MDG regions 2013
(Bln US$)

Legend: Imports — Exports — Trade balance

Developed Asia–Pacific
Developed Europe
Developed N. America
South–eastern Europe
C I S
Northern Africa
Sub–Saharan Africa
Latin Am, Caribbean
Eastern Asia
Southern Asia
South–eastern Asia
Western Asia
Oceania

-4 -3 -2 -1 0 1 2 3 4

Table 3: Top importing countries or areas in 2013

Country or area	Value (million US$)	Avg. Growth (%) 09-13	Growth (%) 12-13	World share %	Cum.
World................................	5408.6	7.1	5.7	100.0	
Germany.............................	867.6	-3.2	-5.5	16.0	16.0
Netherlands.........................	511.0	21.6	13.2	9.4	25.5
United Kingdom.....................	281.6	4.0	4.7	5.2	30.7
Russian Federation.................	251.3	33.3	23.7	4.6	35.3
Mexico..............................	228.2	61.8	197.6	4.2	39.6
Belgium.............................	207.8	7.3	11.4	3.8	43.4
China, Hong Kong SAR.........	200.1	12.3	13.1	3.7	47.1
France...............................	189.6	-0.6	-33.9	3.5	50.6
Japan................................	186.2	7.6	1.9	3.4	54.1
Iraq.................................	184.0	1.2	-0.9	3.4	57.5
Italy.................................	173.9	21.3	42.7	3.2	60.7
Singapore...........................	129.5	8.5	11.5	2.4	63.1
Switzerland.........................	106.6	0.2	6.1	2.0	65.0
United Arab Emirates...........	106.2	9.7	11.4	2.0	67.0
Canada..............................	103.0	10.0	27.6	1.9	68.9

In 2013, the value (in current US$) of exports of "fish, fresh (live or dead), chilled or frozen" (SITC group 034) increased by 7.3 percent (compared to 9.4 percent average growth rate from 2009-2013) to reach 62.2 bln US$ (see table 2), while imports increased by 3.3 percent to reach 63.0 bln US$ (see table 3). Exports of this commodity accounted for 5.0 percent of world exports of SITC sections 0+1, and 0.3 percent of total world merchandise exports (see table 1). Norway, China and Chile were the top exporters in 2013 (see table 2). They accounted for 14.8, 12.1 and 6.1 percent of world exports, respectively. USA, Japan and China were the top destinations, with respectively 11.6, 11.4 and 5.9 percent of world imports (see table 3).

The top 15 countries/areas accounted for 70.7 and 72.1 percent of total world exports and imports, respectively (see tables 2 and 3). In 2013, Norway was the country/area with the highest value of net exports (+9.0 bln US$), followed by Chile (+3.8 bln US$). By MDG regions (see graph 2), the largest surpluses in this product group were recorded by Latin America and the Caribbean (+3.5 bln US$), Eastern Asia (+3.3 bln US$) and Developed Europe (+2.1 bln US$). The largest trade deficits were recorded by Developed Asia-Pacific (-5.9 bln US$), Developed North America (-3.3 bln US$) and Commonwealth of Independent States (-1.1 bln US$).

Table 1: Imports (Imp.) and exports (Exp.), 1999-2013, in current US$

		1999	2000	2001	2002	2003	2004	2005	2006	2007	2008	2009	2010	2011	2012	2013
Values in Bln US$	Imp.	25.1	25.1	26.3	27.2	29.8	33.5	38.1	42.5	47.2	51.1	47.0	53.3	62.4	61.0	63.0
	Exp.	20.8	21.1	22.4	23.2	25.9	29.7	33.9	37.4	40.3	43.9	43.4	50.7	58.8	58.0	62.2
As a percentage of	Imp.	6.0	6.1	6.2	6.0	5.8	5.7	6.0	6.1	5.7	5.2	5.3	5.4	5.3	5.2	5.1
SITC section (%)	Exp.	5.3	5.5	5.6	5.5	5.3	5.4	5.6	5.6	5.0	4.6	5.0	5.2	5.0	4.9	5.0
As a percentage of	Imp.	0.4	0.4	0.4	0.4	0.4	0.4	0.4	0.3	0.3	0.3	0.4	0.3	0.3	0.3	0.3
world trade (%)	Exp.	0.4	0.3	0.4	0.4	0.3	0.3	0.3	0.3	0.3	0.3	0.3	0.3	0.3	0.3	0.3

Graph 1: Annual growth rates of exports, 1999–2013
(In percentage by year)

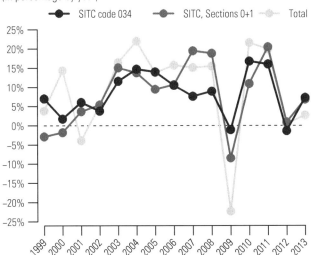

Table 2: Top exporting countries or areas in 2013

Country or area	Value (million US$)	Avg. Growth (%) 09-13	Growth (%) 12-13	World share %	Cum.
World	62 174.1	9.4	7.3	100.0	
Norway	9 191.7	11.6	21.7	14.8	14.8
China	7 513.0	13.8	4.5	12.1	26.9
Chile	3 798.5	12.2	21.0	6.1	33.0
USA	3 577.0	9.3	3.2	5.8	38.7
Sweden	3 148.7	18.4	34.4	5.1	43.8
Viet Nam	2 531.5	9.3	-6.3	4.1	47.9
Russian Federation	2 387.4	13.3	12.6	3.8	51.7
Spain	1 901.7	5.3	0.9	3.1	54.8
Netherlands	1 878.7	7.9	-0.8	3.0	57.8
Denmark	1 563.6	6.9	15.9	2.5	60.3
Iceland	1 468.5	9.9	5.5	2.4	62.7
United Kingdom	1 382.5	13.6	19.0	2.2	64.9
Canada	1 256.5	3.3	-0.4	2.0	66.9
Other Asia, nes	1 223.9	5.3	-33.0	2.0	68.9
Rep. of Korea	1 162.9	7.6	-13.2	1.9	70.7

Graph 2: Trade Balance by MDG regions 2013
(Bln US$)

Imports   Exports   Trade balance

Developed Asia-Pacific
Developed Europe
Developed N. America
South-eastern Europe
C I S
Northern Africa
Sub-Saharan Africa
Latin Am, Caribbean
Eastern Asia
Southern Asia
South-eastern Asia
Western Asia
Oceania

-25 -20 -15 -10 -5 0 5 10 15 20 25 30

Table 3: Top importing countries or areas in 2013

Country or area	Value (million US$)	Avg. Growth (%) 09-13	Growth (%) 12-13	World share %	Cum.
World	63 019.6	7.6	3.3	100.0	
USA	7 335.8	7.9	5.1	11.6	11.6
Japan	7 166.9	1.8	-18.7	11.4	23.0
China	3 735.3	7.0	2.7	5.9	28.9
Sweden	3 646.1	17.4	32.5	5.8	34.7
France	3 051.0	3.7	8.2	4.8	39.6
Spain	2 662.1	0.7	5.2	4.2	43.8
Germany	2 658.9	3.1	7.9	4.2	48.0
Thailand	2 481.2	10.6	-2.5	3.9	51.9
Russian Federation	2 341.5	12.7	18.8	3.7	55.7
Italy	1 995.1	2.6	4.3	3.2	58.8
United Kingdom	1 977.9	30.6	4.2	3.1	62.0
Rep. of Korea	1 948.3	6.2	-3.5	3.1	65.1
Poland	1 720.1	14.1	30.1	2.7	67.8
Netherlands	1 464.6	5.0	-5.0	2.3	70.1
Denmark	1 261.2	6.9	20.3	2.0	72.1

035 Fish, dried, salted or in brine; smoked fish; flours, meals, etc

In 2013, the value (in current US$) of exports of "fish, dried, salted or in brine; smoked fish; flours, meals, etc" (SITC group 035) increased by 1.6 percent (compared to 7.2 percent average growth rate from 2009-2013) to reach 5.6 bln US$ (see table 2), while imports increased by 1.0 percent to reach 5.6 bln US$ (see table 3). Exports of this commodity accounted for 0.4 percent of world exports of SITC sections 0+1, and less than 0.1 percent of total world merchandise exports (see table 1). Norway, Poland and China were the top exporters in 2013 (see table 2). They accounted for 15.4, 14.0 and 8.5 percent of world exports, respectively. Germany, Italy and China, Hong Kong SAR were the top destinations, with respectively 15.9, 7.9 and 6.7 percent of world imports (see table 3).

The top 15 countries/areas accounted for 77.3 and 76.3 percent of total world exports and imports, respectively (see tables 2 and 3). In 2013, Norway was the country/area with the highest value of net exports (+850.5 mln US$), followed by Poland (+763.8 mln US$). By MDG regions (see graph 2), the largest surpluses in this product group were recorded by Developed Europe (+599.3 mln US$), South-eastern Asia (+259.9 mln US$) and Eastern Asia (+78.7 mln US$). The largest trade deficits were recorded by Developed Asia-Pacific (-312.4 mln US$), Latin America and the Caribbean (-249.0 mln US$) and Sub-Saharan Africa (-234.7 mln US$).

Table 1: Imports (Imp.) and exports (Exp.), 1999-2013, in current US$

		1999	2000	2001	2002	2003	2004	2005	2006	2007	2008	2009	2010	2011	2012	2013
Values in Bln US$	Imp.	2.8	2.8	2.8	2.7	2.9	3.3	3.6	3.9	4.6	4.9	4.6	5.1	5.8	5.6	5.6
	Exp.	2.7	2.7	2.8	2.8	3.0	3.5	3.7	4.0	4.5	4.8	4.2	4.8	5.7	5.5	5.6
As a percentage of SITC section (%)	Imp.	0.7	0.7	0.7	0.6	0.6	0.6	0.6	0.6	0.6	0.5	0.5	0.5	0.5	0.5	0.5
	Exp.	0.7	0.7	0.7	0.7	0.6	0.6	0.6	0.6	0.6	0.5	0.5	0.5	0.5	0.5	0.4
As a percentage of world trade (%)	Imp.	0.0	0.0	0.0	0.0	0.0	0.0	0.0	0.0	0.0	0.0	0.0	0.0	0.0	0.0	0.0
	Exp.	0.0	0.0	0.0	0.0	0.0	0.0	0.0	0.0	0.0	0.0	0.0	0.0	0.0	0.0	0.0

Graph 1: Annual growth rates of exports, 1999–2013
(In percentage by year)

Legend: SITC code 035 — SITC, Sections 0+1 — Total

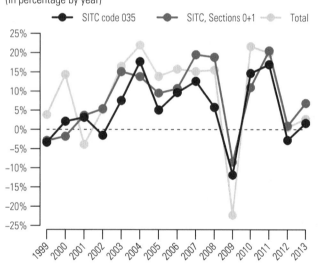

Table 2: Top exporting countries or areas in 2013

Country or area	Value (million US$)	Avg. Growth (%) 09-13	Growth (%) 12-13	World share %	Cum.
World	5 582.1	7.2	1.6	100.0	
Norway	860.1	2.2	-10.7	15.4	15.4
Poland	782.2	17.6	38.2	14.0	29.4
China	472.2	13.4	4.7	8.5	37.9
Denmark	336.2	5.3	11.1	6.0	43.9
Iceland	334.7	-2.9	-8.2	6.0	49.9
Germany	304.7	12.1	17.1	5.5	55.4
Sweden	237.0	-1.8	-29.3	4.2	59.6
Lithuania	179.5	112.7	31.7	3.2	62.8
Thailand	150.8	22.5	20.4	2.7	65.5
Canada	135.5	-3.2	-2.0	2.4	67.9
Netherlands	132.1	16.5	11.2	2.4	70.3
Chile	103.8	7.1	-1.4	1.9	72.2
France	97.5	3.4	2.8	1.7	73.9
United Kingdom	96.7	3.2	-1.7	1.7	75.7
Portugal	94.1	5.1	1.6	1.7	77.3

Graph 2: Trade Balance by MDG regions 2013
(Bln US$)

Legend: Imports — Exports — Trade balance

Developed Asia–Pacific
Developed Europe
Developed N. America
South–eastern Europe
CIS
Northern Africa
Sub–Saharan Africa
Latin Am, Caribbean
Eastern Asia
Southern Asia
South–eastern Asia
Western Asia
Oceania

(axis: -4 -3 -2 -1 0 1 2 3 4)

Table 3: Top importing countries or areas in 2013

Country or area	Value (million US$)	Avg. Growth (%) 09-13	Growth (%) 12-13	World share %	Cum.
World	5 609.0	4.8	1.0	100.0	
Germany	894.4	10.1	14.8	15.9	15.9
Italy	442.5	2.7	10.8	7.9	23.8
China, Hong Kong SAR	377.4	-1.5	-14.4	6.7	30.6
Portugal	375.0	4.7	-7.1	6.7	37.3
USA	281.2	3.0	-2.1	5.0	42.3
Brazil	272.8	6.2	-15.6	4.9	47.1
Japan	270.1	1.1	-10.5	4.8	51.9
Sweden	261.4	-0.3	-21.2	4.7	56.6
France	223.0	9.7	8.5	4.0	60.6
Spain	203.2	-7.4	-5.4	3.6	64.2
Nigeria	174.4	0.3	-3.9	3.1	67.3
Netherlands	173.6	2.4	1.6	3.1	70.4
Belgium	141.4	11.3	32.8	2.5	72.9
Denmark	100.5	7.9	26.5	1.8	74.7
Sri Lanka	87.1	6.2	24.3	1.6	76.3

In 2013, the value (in current US$) of exports of "crustaceans, molluscs, aquatic invertebrates; flours and pellets" (SITC group 036) increased by 13.0 percent (compared to 12.3 percent average growth rate from 2009-2013) to reach 34.4 bln US$ (see table 2), while imports increased by 5.4 percent to reach 31.7 bln US$ (see table 3). Exports of this commodity accounted for 2.7 percent of world exports of SITC sections 0+1, and 0.2 percent of total world merchandise exports (see table 1). China, India and Canada were the top exporters in 2013 (see table 2). They accounted for 13.2, 10.4 and 7.2 percent of world exports, respectively. USA, Japan and Spain were the top destinations, with respectively 22.4, 13.7 and 7.8 percent of world imports (see table 3).

The top 15 countries/areas accounted for 71.9 and 85.1 percent of total world exports and imports, respectively (see tables 2 and 3). In 2013, India was the country/area with the highest value of net exports (+3.6 bln US$), followed by China (+2.3 bln US$). By MDG regions (see graph 2), the largest surpluses in this product group were recorded by Latin America and the Caribbean (+4.8 bln US$), South-eastern Asia (+4.8 bln US$) and Southern Asia (+4.3 bln US$). The largest trade deficits were recorded by Developed Europe (-5.2 bln US$), Developed North America (-3.8 bln US$) and Developed Asia-Pacific (-3.1 bln US$).

Table 1: Imports (Imp.) and exports (Exp.), 1999-2013, in current US$

		1999	2000	2001	2002	2003	2004	2005	2006	2007	2008	2009	2010	2011	2012	2013
Values in Bln US$	Imp.	17.6	19.2	18.2	18.3	20.2	21.3	21.9	23.5	24.6	25.3	22.8	26.1	31.4	30.1	31.7
	Exp.	15.5	17.2	16.3	16.6	18.2	18.9	19.3	20.8	21.9	22.5	21.6	25.6	30.9	30.4	34.4
As a percentage of SITC section (%)	Imp.	4.2	4.7	4.3	4.1	3.9	3.6	3.4	3.4	3.0	2.6	2.6	2.7	2.7	2.6	2.6
	Exp.	3.9	4.4	4.1	3.9	3.7	3.4	3.2	3.1	2.7	2.4	2.5	2.6	2.7	2.6	2.7
As a percentage of world trade (%)	Imp.	0.3	0.3	0.3	0.3	0.3	0.2	0.2	0.2	0.2	0.2	0.2	0.2	0.2	0.2	0.2
	Exp.	0.3	0.3	0.3	0.3	0.2	0.2	0.2	0.2	0.2	0.1	0.2	0.2	0.2	0.2	0.2

Graph 1: Annual growth rates of exports, 1999–2013
(In percentage by year)

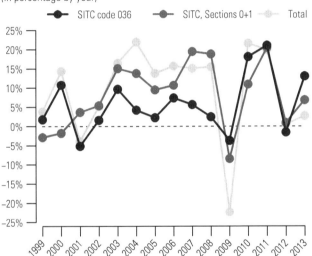

Graph 2: Trade Balance by MDG regions 2013
(Bln US$)

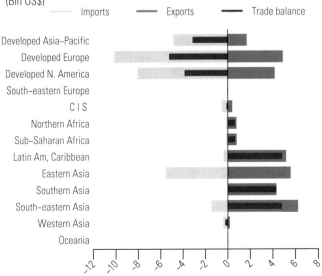

Table 2: Top exporting countries or areas in 2013

Country or area	Value (million US$)	Avg. Growth (%) 09-13	Growth (%) 12-13	World share %	Cum.
World	34 419.5	12.3	13.0	100.0	
China	4 540.1	22.3	23.4	13.2	13.2
India	3 592.5	37.5	54.0	10.4	23.6
Canada	2 466.7	10.8	7.3	7.2	30.8
Viet Nam	2 456.4	8.4	18.1	7.1	37.9
Ecuador	1 797.1	28.1	40.2	5.2	43.2
Indonesia	1 673.1	15.8	18.5	4.9	48.0
USA	1 508.4	11.9	1.6	4.4	52.4
Thailand	1 453.2	-5.0	-27.9	4.2	56.6
Argentina	919.2	20.9	30.5	2.7	59.3
Spain	895.2	3.6	-0.6	2.6	61.9
Netherlands	816.9	7.6	0.0	2.4	64.3
Australia	715.5	7.9	8.9	2.1	66.3
Morocco	703.9	6.8	5.6	2.0	68.4
United Kingdom	608.4	2.2	2.5	1.8	70.2
China, Hong Kong SAR	601.8	41.7	38.6	1.7	71.9

Table 3: Top importing countries or areas in 2013

Country or area	Value (million US$)	Avg. Growth (%) 09-13	Growth (%) 12-13	World share %	Cum.
World	31 738.7	8.6	5.4	100.0	
USA	7 096.7	9.2	16.7	22.4	22.4
Japan	4 345.9	4.9	-9.9	13.7	36.1
Spain	2 460.3	1.7	-2.9	7.8	43.8
China	2 240.4	33.9	22.3	7.1	50.9
China, Hong Kong SAR	1 881.5	9.4	4.3	5.9	56.8
Italy	1 791.0	3.1	-1.4	5.6	62.4
France	1 697.7	4.5	3.6	5.3	67.8
Rep. of Korea	1 117.7	9.8	-0.5	3.5	71.3
Canada	928.0	11.4	6.3	2.9	74.2
Belgium	839.7	6.1	6.1	2.6	76.9
United Kingdom	603.0	7.8	18.3	1.9	78.8
Germany	560.2	9.8	2.4	1.8	80.5
Netherlands	548.9	10.0	3.8	1.7	82.3
Thailand	457.4	24.1	42.2	1.4	83.7
Russian Federation	444.1	21.0	30.4	1.4	85.1

037 Fish, crustaceans, molluscs, aquatic invertebrates, prepared, nes

In 2013, the value (in current US$) of exports of "fish, crustaceans, molluscs, aquatic invertebrates, prepared, nes" (SITC group 037) increased by 5.2 percent (compared to 10.6 percent average growth rate from 2009-2013) to reach 28.0 bln US$ (see table 2), while imports increased by 3.8 percent to reach 25.1 bln US$ (see table 3). Exports of this commodity accounted for 2.2 percent of world exports of SITC sections 0+1, and 0.2 percent of total world merchandise exports (see table 1). China, Thailand and Viet Nam were the top exporters in 2013 (see table 2). They accounted for 24.7, 17.2 and 5.7 percent of world exports, respectively. USA, Japan and United Kingdom were the top destinations, with respectively 16.2, 12.6 and 6.6 percent of world imports (see table 3).

The top 15 countries/areas accounted for 79.9 and 72.7 percent of total world exports and imports, respectively (see tables 2 and 3). In 2013, China was the country/area with the highest value of net exports (+6.7 bln US$), followed by Thailand (+4.6 bln US$). By MDG regions (see graph 2), the largest surpluses in this product group were recorded by South-eastern Asia (+7.6 bln US$), Eastern Asia (+6.1 bln US$) and Latin America and the Caribbean (+712.2 mln US$). The largest trade deficits were recorded by Developed Europe (-4.6 bln US$), Developed North America (-3.6 bln US$) and Developed Asia-Pacific (-3.1 bln US$).

Table 1: Imports (Imp.) and exports (Exp.), 1999-2013, in current US$

		1999	2000	2001	2002	2003	2004	2005	2006	2007	2008	2009	2010	2011	2012	2013
Values in Bln US$	Imp.	9.5	9.9	9.9	10.6	11.6	13.1	14.2	15.6	17.2	19.8	18.2	19.3	22.9	24.2	25.1
	Exp.	9.0	9.4	9.6	10.1	11.5	13.1	14.6	17.1	18.9	21.7	18.8	20.6	25.1	26.6	28.0
As a percentage of SITC section (%)	Imp.	2.3	2.4	2.3	2.4	2.3	2.2	2.2	2.2	2.1	2.0	2.0	2.0	1.9	2.1	2.0
	Exp.	2.3	2.4	2.4	2.4	2.4	2.4	2.4	2.5	2.4	2.3	2.2	2.1	2.2	2.3	2.2
As a percentage of world trade (%)	Imp.	0.2	0.2	0.2	0.2	0.2	0.1	0.1	0.1	0.1	0.1	0.1	0.1	0.1	0.1	0.1
	Exp.	0.2	0.1	0.2	0.2	0.2	0.1	0.1	0.1	0.1	0.1	0.2	0.1	0.1	0.1	0.2

Graph 1: Annual growth rates of exports, 1999–2013
(In percentage by year)

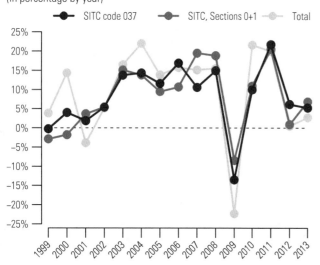

— SITC code 037   — SITC, Sections 0+1   — Total

Table 2: Top exporting countries or areas in 2013

Country or area	Value (million US$)	Avg. Growth (%) 09-13	Growth (%) 12-13	World share %	Cum.
World	28 016.1	10.6	5.2	100.0	
China	6 907.7	19.2	1.6	24.7	24.7
Thailand	4 809.6	6.6	-7.6	17.2	41.8
Viet Nam	1 604.4	26.1	31.5	5.7	47.6
Ecuador	1 351.9	20.9	20.1	4.8	52.4
Indonesia	989.0	16.4	17.6	3.5	55.9
Germany	944.9	5.9	13.8	3.4	59.3
Spain	907.8	7.8	2.3	3.2	62.5
Denmark	779.3	1.2	5.7	2.8	65.3
Morocco	700.3	2.6	4.9	2.5	67.8
Philippines	678.2	22.7	73.5	2.4	70.2
Japan	611.9	5.5	-0.2	2.2	72.4
Netherlands	598.5	2.1	20.7	2.1	74.5
Poland	525.5	9.9	7.1	1.9	76.4
USA	504.9	1.3	3.3	1.8	78.2
Canada	466.1	10.2	-2.4	1.7	79.9

Graph 2: Trade Balance by MDG regions 2013
(Bln US$)

— Imports   — Exports   — Trade balance

Developed Asia–Pacific
Developed Europe
Developed N. America
South–eastern Europe
C I S
Northern Africa
Sub–Saharan Africa
Latin Am, Caribbean
Eastern Asia
Southern Asia
South–eastern Asia
Western Asia
Oceania

-12 -10 -8 -6 -4 -2 0 2 4 6 8 10

Table 3: Top importing countries or areas in 2013

Country or area	Value (million US$)	Avg. Growth (%) 09-13	Growth (%) 12-13	World share %	Cum.
World	25 126.2	8.4	3.8	100.0	
USA	4 058.8	7.0	0.5	16.2	16.2
Japan	3 156.7	6.9	-12.3	12.6	28.7
United Kingdom	1 652.5	5.9	7.4	6.6	35.3
France	1 454.3	3.8	14.0	5.8	41.1
Italy	1 408.4	3.6	9.4	5.6	46.7
Germany	1 244.6	8.4	12.3	5.0	51.6
Spain	974.5	7.9	7.3	3.9	55.5
Netherlands	682.1	9.4	10.9	2.7	58.2
Australia	668.5	9.8	4.1	2.7	60.9
Canada	604.3	6.5	1.2	2.4	63.3
China, Hong Kong SAR	560.0	23.3	4.0	2.2	65.5
Denmark	524.9	8.1	2.3	2.1	67.6
Belgium	487.5	1.2	18.6	1.9	69.6
Rep. of Korea	428.5	12.3	0.7	1.7	71.3
Sweden	350.9	5.2	6.2	1.4	72.7

In 2013, the value (in current US$) of exports of "wheat (including spelt) and meslin, unmilled" (SITC group 041) increased by 0.5 percent (compared to 11.3 percent average growth rate from 2009-2013) to reach 49.0 bln US$ (see table 2), while imports decreased by 2.6 percent to reach 46.4 bln US$ (see table 3). Exports of this commodity accounted for 3.9 percent of world exports of SITC sections 0+1, and 0.3 percent of total world merchandise exports (see table 1). USA, Canada and France were the top exporters in 2013 (see table 2). They accounted for 21.5, 13.3 and 12.6 percent of world exports, respectively. Indonesia, Brazil and Japan were the top destinations, with respectively 5.3, 5.2 and 4.9 percent of world imports (see table 3).

The top 15 countries/areas accounted for 90.5 and 52.7 percent of total world exports and imports, respectively (see tables 2 and 3). In 2013, USA was the country/area with the highest value of net exports (+9.5 bln US$), followed by Canada (+6.5 bln US$). By MDG regions (see graph 2), the largest surpluses in this product group were recorded by Developed North America (+16.0 bln US$), Commonwealth of Independent States (+5.4 bln US$) and Developed Europe (+3.7 bln US$). The largest trade deficits were recorded by Western Asia (-5.3 bln US$), Latin America and the Caribbean (-5.1 bln US$) and Northern Africa (-4.9 bln US$).

Table 1: Imports (Imp.) and exports (Exp.), 1999-2013, in current US$

		1999	2000	2001	2002	2003	2004	2005	2006	2007	2008	2009	2010	2011	2012	2013
Values in Bln US$	Imp.	15.4	15.2	15.7	16.6	17.4	21.5	20.8	22.2	33.3	48.1	33.9	35.9	51.8	47.6	46.4
	Exp.	14.3	13.6	14.6	15.4	15.8	19.3	17.7	20.7	30.3	44.7	32.0	32.6	47.5	48.8	49.0
As a percentage of	Imp.	3.7	3.7	3.7	3.7	3.4	3.7	3.3	3.2	4.0	4.9	3.8	3.7	4.4	4.0	3.7
SITC section (%)	Exp.	3.6	3.5	3.6	3.7	3.2	3.5	2.9	3.1	3.8	4.7	3.7	3.4	4.1	4.2	3.9
As a percentage of	Imp.	0.3	0.2	0.2	0.3	0.2	0.2	0.2	0.2	0.2	0.3	0.3	0.2	0.3	0.3	0.3
world trade (%)	Exp.	0.3	0.2	0.2	0.2	0.2	0.2	0.2	0.2	0.2	0.3	0.3	0.2	0.3	0.3	0.3

Graph 1: Annual growth rates of exports, 1999–2013
(In percentage by year)

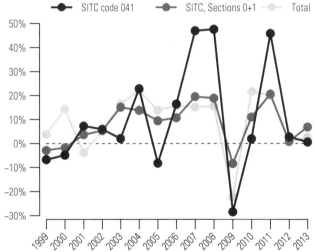

Table 2: Top exporting countries or areas in 2013

Country or area	Value (million US$)	Avg. Growth (%) 09-13	Growth (%) 12-13	World share %	Cum.
World	49 042.1	11.3	0.5	100.0	
USA	10 542.8	18.3	29.0	21.5	21.5
Canada	6 538.9	5.4	6.3	13.3	34.8
France	6 171.8	13.2	22.1	12.6	47.4
Australia	5 875.6	12.0	-13.1	12.0	59.4
Russian Federation	3 482.7	6.1	-23.0	7.1	66.5
Germany	2 678.9	5.1	24.4	5.5	72.0
Ukraine	1 891.5	1.6	-18.8	3.9	75.8
Romania	1 303.0	32.9	87.9	2.7	78.5
India	1 260.3	830.2	-6.6	2.6	81.0
Kazakhstan	1 235.0	18.2	-22.8	2.5	83.6
Bulgaria	950.8	33.1	32.7	1.9	85.5
Argentina	725.4	-7.8	-75.4	1.5	87.0
Hungary	660.9	18.3	71.8	1.3	88.3
Lithuania	594.0	22.1	5.6	1.2	89.5
Poland	477.4	5.0	52.7	1.0	90.5

Graph 2: Trade Balance by MDG regions 2013
(Bln US$)

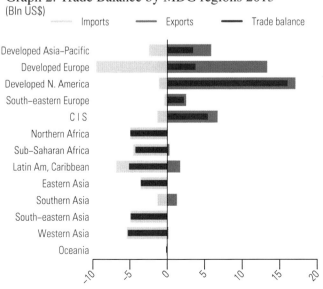

Table 3: Top importing countries or areas in 2013

Country or area	Value (million US$)	Avg. Growth (%) 09-13	Growth (%) 12-13	World share %	Cum.
World	46 364.7	8.1	-2.6	100.0	
Indonesia	2 440.0	16.7	8.3	5.3	5.3
Brazil	2 414.8	18.9	40.3	5.2	10.5
Japan	2 277.8	12.0	5.7	4.9	15.4
Algeria	2 123.4	3.8	-0.3	4.6	20.0
Italy	1 984.8	3.4	-3.0	4.3	24.2
China	1 865.9	73.8	69.4	4.0	28.3
Rep. of Korea	1 615.6	14.2	-8.9	3.5	31.8
Mexico	1 354.5	16.8	82.7	2.9	34.7
Nigeria	1 294.9	4.0	-13.2	2.8	37.5
Turkey	1 289.2	9.3	14.5	2.8	40.2
Netherlands	1 232.5	6.4	3.0	2.7	42.9
Belgium	1 229.0	11.5	0.5	2.7	45.6
Germany	1 193.4	8.9	16.1	2.6	48.1
USA	1 082.9	10.6	27.2	2.3	50.5
Yemen	1 048.4	9.3	6.6	2.3	52.7

042 Rice

In 2013, the value (in current US$) of exports of "rice" (SITC group 042) increased by 7.5 percent (compared to 7.7 percent average growth rate from 2009-2013) to reach 25.7 bln US$ (see table 2), while imports decreased by 6.4 percent to reach 22.7 bln US$ (see table 3). Exports of this commodity accounted for 2.0 percent of world exports of SITC sections 0+1, and 0.1 percent of total world merchandise exports (see table 1). India, Thailand and Viet Nam were the top exporters in 2013 (see table 2). They accounted for 31.8, 17.2 and 11.4 percent of world exports, respectively. United Arab Emirates, Saudi Arabia and China were the top destinations, with respectively 6.3, 6.1 and 4.6 percent of world imports (see table 3).

The top 15 countries/areas accounted for 92.6 and 47.5 percent of total world exports and imports, respectively (see tables 2 and 3). In 2013, India was the country/area with the highest value of net exports (+8.2 bln US$), followed by Thailand (+4.4 bln US$). By MDG regions (see graph 2), the largest surpluses in this product group were recorded by Southern Asia (+8.7 bln US$), South-eastern Asia (+6.4 bln US$) and Developed North America (+1.1 bln US$). The largest trade deficits were recorded by Sub-Saharan Africa (-5.1 bln US$), Western Asia (-4.1 bln US$) and Eastern Asia (-1.5 bln US$).

Table 1: Imports (Imp.) and exports (Exp.), 1999-2013, in current US$

		1999	2000	2001	2002	2003	2004	2005	2006	2007	2008	2009	2010	2011	2012	2013
Values in Bln US$	Imp.	8.2	6.6	6.5	6.6	7.5	9.1	10.0	10.7	13.4	21.0	19.2	19.9	23.0	24.3	22.7
	Exp.	7.9	6.5	6.9	6.7	7.3	8.7	10.1	10.5	13.2	21.3	19.1	20.3	24.0	23.9	25.7
As a percentage of SITC section (%)	Imp.	2.0	1.6	1.5	1.5	1.5	1.6	1.6	1.5	1.6	2.1	2.1	2.0	1.9	2.1	1.8
	Exp.	2.0	1.7	1.7	1.6	1.5	1.6	1.7	1.6	1.6	2.2	2.2	2.1	2.1	2.0	2.0
As a percentage of world trade (%)	Imp.	0.1	0.1	0.1	0.1	0.1	0.1	0.1	0.1	0.1	0.1	0.2	0.1	0.1	0.1	0.1
	Exp.	0.1	0.1	0.1	0.1	0.1	0.1	0.1	0.1	0.1	0.1	0.2	0.1	0.1	0.1	0.1

Graph 1: Annual growth rates of exports, 1999–2013
(In percentage by year)

Legend: SITC code 042 — SITC, Sections 0+1 — Total

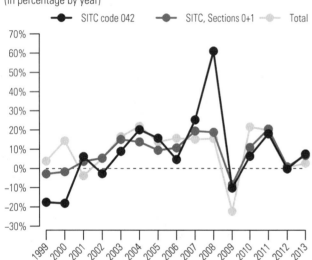

Graph 2: Trade Balance by MDG regions 2013
(Bln US$)

Legend: Imports — Exports — Trade balance

Developed Asia–Pacific, Developed Europe, Developed N. America, South–eastern Europe, CIS, Northern Africa, Sub–Saharan Africa, Latin Am, Caribbean, Eastern Asia, Southern Asia, South–eastern Asia, Western Asia, Oceania

Table 2: Top exporting countries or areas in 2013

Country or area	Value (million US$)	Avg. Growth (%) 09-13	Growth (%) 12-13	World share %	Cum.
World	25 699.7	7.7	7.5	100.0	
India	8 169.5	35.9	33.3	31.8	31.8
Thailand	4 420.4	-3.3	-4.6	17.2	49.0
Viet Nam	2 926.3	2.4	-20.4	11.4	60.4
USA	2 176.3	-0.1	4.9	8.5	68.8
Pakistan	2 111.0	4.4	12.2	8.2	77.1
Italy	646.1	-3.4	2.8	2.5	79.6
United Arab Emirates	566.7	2.3	21.7	2.2	81.8
Uruguay	508.0	2.6	-9.3	2.0	83.8
China	416.7	-5.5	53.2	1.6	85.4
Brazil	400.6	10.6	-26.6	1.6	86.9
Australia	369.9	95.8	4.2	1.4	88.4
Belgium	315.5	2.8	34.2	1.2	89.6
Argentina	291.0	1.7	-3.8	1.1	90.7
Cambodia	258.2	120.1	85.2	1.0	91.7
Guyana	216.7	17.6	10.5	0.8	92.6

Table 3: Top importing countries or areas in 2013

Country or area	Value (million US$)	Avg. Growth (%) 09-13	Growth (%) 12-13	World share %	Cum.
World	22 706.5	4.3	-6.4	100.0	
United Arab Emirates	1 428.6	3.4	11.4	6.3	6.3
Saudi Arabia	1 387.4	0.0	28.0	6.1	12.4
China	1 052.0	51.2	-6.5	4.6	17.0
USA	796.5	5.9	10.8	3.5	20.5
Iran	699.6	-5.4	-13.3	3.1	23.6
South Africa	667.7	10.7	-2.7	2.9	26.6
Bangladesh	662.0	100.0	-1.6	2.9	29.5
Benin	594.0	59.6	88.4	2.6	32.1
United Kingdom	566.9	-2.6	5.5	2.5	34.6
France	508.6	0.4	11.0	2.2	36.8
Malaysia	503.3	-2.3	-16.9	2.2	39.0
Japan	492.3	-6.0	5.2	2.2	41.2
Rep. of Korea	486.1	17.7	187.9	2.1	43.4
Côte d'Ivoire	472.5	-5.7	-31.0	2.1	45.4
Senegal	461.6	9.0	2.7	2.0	47.5

In 2013, the value (in current US$) of exports of "barley, unmilled" (SITC group 043) increased by 9.7 percent (compared to 17.6 percent average growth rate from 2009-2013) to reach 8.7 bln US$ (see table 2), while imports increased by 14.7 percent to reach 9.4 bln US$ (see table 3). Exports of this commodity accounted for 0.7 percent of world exports of SITC sections 0+1, and less than 0.1 percent of total world merchandise exports (see table 1). France, Australia and Argentina were the top exporters in 2013 (see table 2). They accounted for 21.6, 17.0 and 10.5 percent of world exports, respectively. Saudi Arabia, China and Belgium were the top destinations, with respectively 34.6, 8.5 and 6.3 percent of world imports (see table 3).

The top 15 countries/areas accounted for 91.3 and 80.5 percent of total world exports and imports, respectively (see tables 2 and 3). In 2013, France was the country/area with the highest value of net exports (+1.9 bln US$), followed by Australia (+1.5 bln US$). By MDG regions (see graph 2), the largest surpluses in this product group were recorded by Developed Europe (+1.7 bln US$), Commonwealth of Independent States (+1.1 bln US$) and Developed Asia-Pacific (+1.0 bln US$). The largest trade deficits were recorded by Western Asia (-4.1 bln US$), Eastern Asia (-820.0 mln US$) and Northern Africa (-647.4 mln US$).

Table 1: Imports (Imp.) and exports (Exp.), 1999-2013, in current US$

		1999	2000	2001	2002	2003	2004	2005	2006	2007	2008	2009	2010	2011	2012	2013
Values in Bln US$	Imp.	2.5	3.0	2.7	2.7	2.8	3.5	4.0	3.9	6.0	8.7	5.0	5.6	7.5	8.2	9.4
	Exp.	2.4	2.8	2.4	2.5	2.9	3.3	3.6	3.5	5.4	7.7	4.5	4.9	7.4	7.9	8.7
As a percentage of SITC section (%)	Imp.	0.6	0.7	0.6	0.6	0.6	0.6	0.6	0.6	0.7	0.9	0.6	0.6	0.6	0.7	0.8
	Exp.	0.6	0.7	0.6	0.6	0.6	0.6	0.6	0.5	0.7	0.8	0.5	0.5	0.6	0.7	0.7
As a percentage of world trade (%)	Imp.	0.0	0.0	0.0	0.0	0.0	0.0	0.0	0.0	0.1	0.0	0.0	0.0	0.0	0.0	0.1
	Exp.	0.0	0.0	0.0	0.0	0.0	0.0	0.0	0.0	0.0	0.0	0.0	0.0	0.0	0.0	0.0

Graph 1: Annual growth rates of exports, 1999–2013
(In percentage by year)

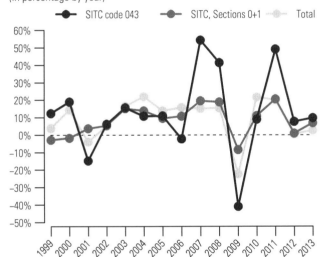

Graph 2: Trade Balance by MDG regions 2013
(Bln US$)

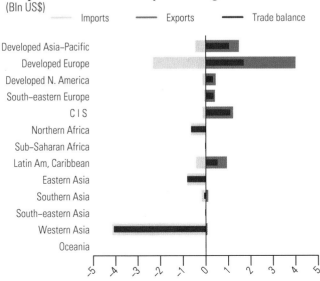

Table 2: Top exporting countries or areas in 2013

Country or area	Value (million US$)	Avg. Growth (%) 09-13	Growth (%) 12-13	World share %	Cum.
World	8 675.5	17.6	9.7	100.0	
France	1 874.3	15.6	40.6	21.6	21.6
Australia	1 478.3	25.2	8.5	17.0	38.6
Argentina	912.3	48.2	8.2	10.5	49.2
Germany	823.6	40.9	88.6	9.5	58.7
Ukraine	575.7	-5.8	-17.0	6.6	65.3
Russian Federation	553.7	6.0	-38.3	6.4	71.7
Canada	393.2	0.4	-18.9	4.5	76.2
Romania	297.3	36.8	55.1	3.4	79.6
Denmark	252.5	34.8	-23.2	2.9	82.5
United Kingdom	220.7	6.5	26.1	2.5	85.1
Hungary	117.4	30.5	29.5	1.4	86.4
Sweden	112.0	20.5	-20.9	1.3	87.7
India	108.1	98.8	202.0	1.2	89.0
Bulgaria	103.8	13.7	13.5	1.2	90.2
Belgium	101.5	30.4	3.1	1.2	91.3

Table 3: Top importing countries or areas in 2013

Country or area	Value (million US$)	Avg. Growth (%) 09-13	Growth (%) 12-13	World share %	Cum.
World	9 387.5	17.3	14.7	100.0	
Saudi Arabia	3 249.6	26.1	29.3	34.6	34.6
China	798.6	16.4	2.2	8.5	43.1
Belgium	591.9	13.3	12.7	6.3	49.4
Netherlands	545.1	17.8	20.2	5.8	55.2
Japan	439.9	10.5	6.6	4.7	59.9
Germany	341.1	1.1	-15.3	3.6	63.6
Tunisia	241.3	112.6	334.8	2.6	66.1
Jordan	228.1	26.0	-4.1	2.4	68.6
Libya	192.4	56.3	23.2	2.0	70.6
Iran	184.0	17.6	-13.3	2.0	72.6
Italy	180.6	10.9	26.4	1.9	74.5
United Arab Emirates	157.0	58.2	11.4	1.7	76.2
Algeria	152.4	52.1	33.8	1.6	77.8
USA	130.1	-2.2	-20.8	1.4	79.2
Brazil	128.3	4.1	66.8	1.4	80.5

044 Maize (not including sweet corn), unmilled

In 2013, the value (in current US$) of exports of "maize (not including sweet corn), unmilled" (SITC group 044) decreased by 2.2 percent (compared to 15.2 percent average growth rate from 2009-2013) to reach 35.0 bln US$ (see table 2), while imports increased by 0.2 percent to reach 38.4 bln US$ (see table 3). Exports of this commodity accounted for 2.8 percent of world exports of SITC sections 0+1, and 0.2 percent of total world merchandise exports (see table 1). USA, Brazil and Argentina were the top exporters in 2013 (see table 2). They accounted for 19.7, 18.0 and 16.7 percent of world exports, respectively. Japan, Rep. of Korea and Mexico were the top destinations, with respectively 12.4, 7.0 and 5.3 percent of world imports (see table 3).

The top 15 countries/areas accounted for 92.0 and 63.6 percent of total world exports and imports, respectively (see tables 2 and 3). In 2013, Brazil was the country/area with the highest value of net exports (+6.1 bln US$), followed by Argentina (+5.8 bln US$). By MDG regions (see graph 2), the largest surpluses in this product group were recorded by Latin America and the Caribbean (+6.8 bln US$), Developed North America (+5.5 bln US$) and Commonwealth of Independent States (+3.9 bln US$). The largest trade deficits were recorded by Eastern Asia (-4.8 bln US$), Developed Asia-Pacific (-4.7 bln US$) and Northern Africa (-3.8 bln US$).

Table 1: Imports (Imp.) and exports (Exp.), 1999-2013, in current US$

		1999	2000	2001	2002	2003	2004	2005	2006	2007	2008	2009	2010	2011	2012	2013
Values in Bln US$	Imp.	9.9	10.2	10.1	11.1	12.6	14.5	13.6	15.1	23.9	31.1	22.7	25.7	36.5	38.3	38.4
	Exp.	8.7	8.8	8.9	9.9	11.1	11.7	11.2	13.2	20.5	27.2	19.8	23.2	33.9	35.8	35.0
As a percentage of	Imp.	2.4	2.5	2.4	2.5	2.5	2.5	2.1	2.2	2.9	3.2	2.5	2.6	3.1	3.3	3.1
SITC section (%)	Exp.	2.2	2.3	2.2	2.3	2.3	2.1	1.8	2.0	2.6	2.9	2.3	2.4	2.9	3.0	2.8
As a percentage of	Imp.	0.2	0.2	0.2	0.2	0.2	0.2	0.1	0.1	0.2	0.2	0.2	0.2	0.2	0.2	0.2
world trade (%)	Exp.	0.2	0.1	0.1	0.2	0.1	0.1	0.1	0.1	0.1	0.2	0.2	0.2	0.2	0.2	0.2

Graph 1: Annual growth rates of exports, 1999–2013
(In percentage by year)

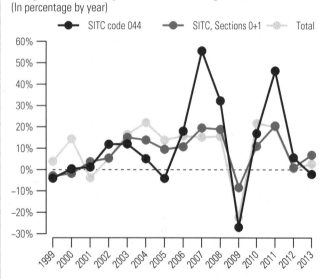

Legend: SITC code 044 — SITC, Sections 0+1 — Total

Graph 2: Trade Balance by MDG regions 2013
(Bln US$)

Legend: Imports — Exports — Trade balance

Developed Asia–Pacific, Developed Europe, Developed N. America, South-eastern Europe, CIS, Northern Africa, Sub-Saharan Africa, Latin Am, Caribbean, Eastern Asia, Southern Asia, South-eastern Asia, Western Asia, Oceania

Table 2: Top exporting countries or areas in 2013

Country or area	Value (million US$)	Avg. Growth (%) 09-13	Growth (%) 12-13	World share %	Cum.
World	34 976.4	15.2	-2.2	100.0	
USA	6 882.9	-6.7	-29.1	19.7	19.7
Brazil	6 307.6	48.4	17.2	18.0	37.7
Argentina	5 848.0	38.0	20.8	16.7	54.4
Ukraine	3 833.3	39.5	-1.5	11.0	65.4
France	2 643.6	9.3	10.2	7.6	73.0
India	1 258.5	24.0	11.1	3.6	76.5
Romania	977.4	29.8	26.4	2.8	79.3
Hungary	807.0	-0.7	-37.9	2.3	81.7
South Africa	764.9	14.2	40.3	2.2	83.8
Russian Federation	590.1	33.1	2.9	1.7	85.5
Canada	578.7	56.4	95.4	1.7	87.2
Bulgaria	490.5	49.1	124.2	1.4	88.6
Paraguay	463.7	18.6	-15.5	1.3	89.9
Chile	362.2	16.7	40.6	1.0	90.9
Germany	360.6	15.9	-2.4	1.0	92.0

Table 3: Top importing countries or areas in 2013

Country or area	Value (million US$)	Avg. Growth (%) 09-13	Growth (%) 12-13	World share %	Cum.
World	38 377.5	14.1	0.2	100.0	
Japan	4 750.4	5.9	-7.3	12.4	12.4
Rep. of Korea	2 676.6	13.1	2.8	7.0	19.4
Mexico	2 053.0	9.3	-31.5	5.3	24.7
Egypt	1 985.0	24.2	1.4	5.2	29.9
USA	1 693.5	52.1	66.4	4.4	34.3
Spain	1 674.1	15.6	-7.3	4.4	38.6
Netherlands	1 466.8	19.9	17.4	3.8	42.5
Italy	1 229.2	25.0	49.1	3.2	45.7
Other Asia, nes	1 182.7	5.4	-16.2	3.1	48.8
Colombia	1 022.4	11.1	1.8	2.7	51.4
Malaysia	995.0	15.0	6.9	2.6	54.0
China	936.5	160.0	-44.5	2.4	56.5
Iran	928.1	2.1	-13.3	2.4	58.9
Indonesia	918.9	85.4	83.1	2.4	61.3
Algeria	892.6	21.7	-5.2	2.3	63.6

Cereals, unmilled (other than wheat, rice, barley and maize) 045

In 2013, the value (in current US$) of exports of "cereals, unmilled (other than wheat, rice, barley and maize)" (SITC group 045) increased by 12.5 percent (compared to 13.0 percent average growth rate from 2009-2013) to reach 3.8 bln US$ (see table 2), while imports increased by 14.5 percent to reach 4.2 bln US$ (see table 3). Exports of this commodity accounted for 0.3 percent of world exports of SITC sections 0+1, and less than 0.1 percent of total world merchandise exports (see table 1). USA, Canada and Argentina were the top exporters in 2013 (see table 2). They accounted for 17.7, 16.2 and 13.8 percent of world exports, respectively. USA, Japan and Mexico were the top destinations, with respectively 16.0, 14.3 and 10.2 percent of world imports (see table 3).

The top 15 countries/areas accounted for 87.7 and 80.4 percent of total world exports and imports, respectively (see tables 2 and 3). In 2013, Canada was the country/area with the highest value of net exports (+563.1 mln US$), followed by Argentina (+524.4 mln US$). By MDG regions (see graph 2), the largest surpluses in this product group were recorded by Developed North America (+554.1 mln US$), Commonwealth of Independent States (+81.8 mln US$) and Latin America and the Caribbean (+68.2 mln US$). The largest trade deficits were recorded by Eastern Asia (-380.8 mln US$), Developed Asia-Pacific (-362.5 mln US$) and Developed Europe (-174.4 mln US$).

Table 1: Imports (Imp.) and exports (Exp.), 1999-2013, in current US$

		1999	2000	2001	2002	2003	2004	2005	2006	2007	2008	2009	2010	2011	2012	2013
Values in Bln US$	Imp.	1.5	1.6	1.6	1.7	1.8	1.9	1.8	2.0	3.0	4.3	2.6	2.9	3.8	3.7	4.2
	Exp.	1.3	1.4	1.4	1.5	1.5	1.6	1.6	1.8	2.8	3.5	2.3	2.6	3.5	3.4	3.8
As a percentage of SITC section (%)	Imp.	0.4	0.4	0.4	0.4	0.3	0.3	0.3	0.3	0.4	0.4	0.3	0.3	0.3	0.3	0.3
	Exp.	0.3	0.4	0.4	0.3	0.3	0.3	0.3	0.3	0.3	0.4	0.3	0.3	0.3	0.3	0.3
As a percentage of world trade (%)	Imp.	0.0	0.0	0.0	0.0	0.0	0.0	0.0	0.0	0.0	0.0	0.0	0.0	0.0	0.0	0.0
	Exp.	0.0	0.0	0.0	0.0	0.0	0.0	0.0	0.0	0.0	0.0	0.0	0.0	0.0	0.0	0.0

Graph 1: Annual growth rates of exports, 1999–2013
(In percentage by year)

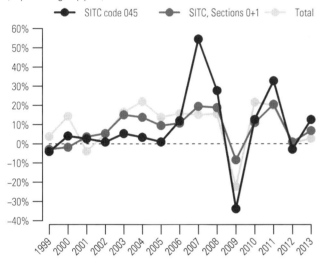

— SITC code 045 — SITC, Sections 0+1 — Total

Table 2: Top exporting countries or areas in 2013

Country or area	Value (million US$)	Avg. Growth (%) 09-13	Growth (%) 12-13	World share %	Cum.
World	3 798.5	13.0	12.5	100.0	
USA	670.7	-2.1	8.4	17.7	17.7
Canada	617.2	8.7	5.2	16.2	33.9
Argentina	525.4	39.7	-11.2	13.8	47.7
Australia	279.0	47.1	160.8	7.3	55.1
Poland	273.3	22.2	127.5	7.2	62.3
Germany	203.5	12.8	55.0	5.4	67.6
Bolivia	158.4	36.4	84.9	4.2	71.8
France	100.6	11.5	-3.5	2.6	74.5
Finland	94.7	8.9	-9.1	2.5	76.9
Peru	83.5	73.0	137.1	2.2	79.1
Lithuania	70.4	9.7	11.6	1.9	81.0
Sweden	66.6	11.6	-13.6	1.8	82.7
India	65.5	7.8	-21.0	1.7	84.5
China	62.6	2.6	-8.0	1.6	86.1
Ukraine	58.6	14.6	42.6	1.5	87.7

Graph 2: Trade Balance by MDG regions 2013
(Bln US$)

— Imports — Exports — Trade balance

- Developed Asia–Pacific
- Developed Europe
- Developed N. America
- South–eastern Europe
- C I S
- Northern Africa
- Sub–Saharan Africa
- Latin Am, Caribbean
- Eastern Asia
- Southern Asia
- South–eastern Asia
- Western Asia
- Oceania

-1.5   -1   -0.5   0   0.5   1   1.5

Table 3: Top importing countries or areas in 2013

Country or area	Value (million US$)	Avg. Growth (%) 09-13	Growth (%) 12-13	World share %	Cum.
World	4 249.7	12.8	14.5	100.0	
USA	679.3	16.3	23.9	16.0	16.0
Japan	607.0	8.4	8.1	14.3	30.3
Mexico	433.0	-2.7	-4.6	10.2	40.5
China	400.8	127.1	646.4	9.4	49.9
Germany	302.0	17.0	12.4	7.1	57.0
Netherlands	172.4	8.4	19.9	4.1	61.1
Spain	168.1	7.7	15.2	4.0	65.0
Colombia	134.2	32.5	-15.6	3.2	68.2
Belgium	119.6	15.5	44.2	2.8	71.0
Italy	109.1	22.9	51.6	2.6	73.5
Chile	68.3	-4.9	-52.6	1.6	75.2
United Kingdom	61.8	28.6	40.4	1.5	76.6
Ethiopia	59.6	22.6	215.3	1.4	78.0
Canada	54.1	42.6	63.0	1.3	79.3
France	47.6	9.9	21.8	1.1	80.4

046 Meal and flour of wheat and flour of meslin

In 2013, the value (in current US$) of exports of "meal and flour of wheat and flour of meslin" (SITC group 046) increased by 4.5 percent (compared to 8.3 percent average growth rate from 2009-2013) to reach 5.9 bln US$ (see table 2), while imports increased by 5.4 percent to reach 5.5 bln US$ (see table 3). Exports of this commodity accounted for 0.5 percent of world exports of SITC sections 0+1, and less than 0.1 percent of total world merchandise exports (see table 1). Turkey, Kazakhstan and Germany were the top exporters in 2013 (see table 2). They accounted for 16.3, 9.7 and 6.5 percent of world exports, respectively. Afghanistan, Netherlands and Uzbekistan were the top destinations, with respectively 7.8, 5.9 and 5.5 percent of world imports (see table 3).

The top 15 countries/areas accounted for 68.0 and 50.4 percent of total world exports and imports, respectively (see tables 2 and 3). In 2013, Turkey was the country/area with the highest value of net exports (+962.0 mln US$), followed by Kazakhstan (+573.4 mln US$). By MDG regions (see graph 2), the largest surpluses in this product group were recorded by Western Asia (+709.0 mln US$), Developed Europe (+578.1 mln US$) and Commonwealth of Independent States (+201.5 mln US$). The largest trade deficits were recorded by Sub-Saharan Africa (-682.3 mln US$), South-eastern Asia (-316.0 mln US$) and Latin America and the Caribbean (-102.5 mln US$).

Table 1: Imports (Imp.) and exports (Exp.), 1999-2013, in current US$

		1999	2000	2001	2002	2003	2004	2005	2006	2007	2008	2009	2010	2011	2012	2013
Values in Bln US$	Imp.	1.7	1.8	1.6	1.7	1.8	2.2	2.4	2.4	3.5	5.1	4.3	4.1	5.4	5.2	5.5
	Exp.	1.9	1.8	1.8	1.9	2.1	2.3	2.5	2.5	3.8	5.7	4.3	4.2	6.0	5.7	5.9
As a percentage of SITC section (%)	Imp.	0.4	0.4	0.4	0.4	0.4	0.4	0.4	0.3	0.4	0.5	0.5	0.4	0.5	0.4	0.4
	Exp.	0.5	0.5	0.4	0.4	0.4	0.4	0.4	0.4	0.5	0.6	0.5	0.4	0.5	0.5	0.5
As a percentage of world trade (%)	Imp.	0.0	0.0	0.0	0.0	0.0	0.0	0.0	0.0	0.0	0.0	0.0	0.0	0.0	0.0	0.0
	Exp.	0.0	0.0	0.0	0.0	0.0	0.0	0.0	0.0	0.0	0.0	0.0	0.0	0.0	0.0	0.0

Graph 1: Annual growth rates of exports, 1999–2013
(In percentage by year)

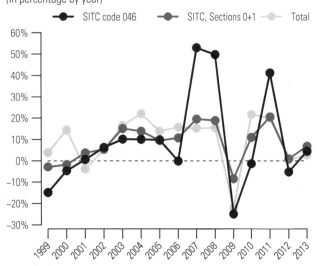

Legend: SITC code 046 — SITC, Sections 0+1 — Total

Graph 2: Trade Balance by MDG regions 2013
(Bln US$)

Legend: Imports — Exports — Trade balance

Regions: Developed Asia–Pacific, Developed Europe, Developed N. America, South–eastern Europe, CIS, Northern Africa, Sub–Saharan Africa, Latin Am, Caribbean, Eastern Asia, Southern Asia, South–eastern Asia, Western Asia, Oceania

Table 2: Top exporting countries or areas in 2013

Country or area	Value (million US$)	Avg. Growth (%) 09-13	Growth (%) 12-13	World share %	Cum.
World	5 914.7	8.3	4.5	100.0	
Turkey	962.2	12.7	10.5	16.3	16.3
Kazakhstan	575.6	0.0	-5.2	9.7	26.0
Germany	385.2	12.1	20.5	6.5	32.5
France	343.6	1.5	8.4	5.8	38.3
Belgium	288.3	2.9	16.1	4.9	43.2
Pakistan	209.0	286.7	-15.9	3.5	46.7
Oman	189.7	69.7	437.8	3.2	49.9
United Kingdom	176.2	12.5	11.1	3.0	52.9
China	149.4	11.7	-0.1	2.5	55.4
India	147.8	86.4	85.2	2.5	57.9
USA	147.0	0.7	-7.5	2.5	60.4
Italy	140.3	13.4	22.7	2.4	62.8
Canada	121.4	1.7	11.5	2.1	64.9
Spain	107.3	8.3	5.4	1.8	66.7
Hungary	80.7	14.2	20.9	1.4	68.0

Table 3: Top importing countries or areas in 2013

Country or area	Value (million US$)	Avg. Growth (%) 09-13	Growth (%) 12-13	World share %	Cum.
World	5 466.6	6.3	5.4	100.0	
Afghanistan	429.1	4.5	144.5	7.8	7.8
Netherlands	323.7	21.7	9.3	5.9	13.8
Uzbekistan	298.3	4.8	-1.3	5.5	19.2
Angola	245.1	10.0	10.5	4.5	23.7
Iraq	194.7	13.5	8.8	3.6	27.3
France	176.0	9.0	16.1	3.2	30.5
USA	153.4	7.0	9.0	2.8	33.3
Malaysia	149.7	30.0	44.8	2.7	36.0
Belgium	130.3	5.8	26.6	2.4	38.4
China, Hong Kong SAR	125.3	7.6	0.9	2.3	40.7
Brazil	115.1	-13.2	-55.7	2.1	42.8
Dem.Rep. of the Congo	115.1	21.5	9.8	2.1	44.9
Saudi Arabia	101.6	13.5	34.7	1.9	46.8
Ireland	98.0	-0.9	19.1	1.8	48.6
Syria	97.7	172.6	2808.0	1.8	50.4

In 2013, the value (in current US$) of exports of "other cereal meals and flours" (SITC group 047) increased by 10.3 percent (compared to 7.9 percent average growth rate from 2009-2013) to reach 1.5 bln US$ (see table 2), while imports increased by 6.3 percent to reach 1.6 bln US$ (see table 3). Exports of this commodity accounted for 0.1 percent of world exports of SITC sections 0+1, and less than 0.1 percent of total world merchandise exports (see table 1). USA, Thailand and South Africa were the top exporters in 2013 (see table 2). They accounted for 11.5, 9.3 and 9.2 percent of world exports, respectively. USA, Malaysia and Angola were the top destinations, with respectively 12.0, 7.9 and 6.1 percent of world imports (see table 3).

The top 15 countries/areas accounted for 76.2 and 60.8 percent of total world exports and imports, respectively (see tables 2 and 3). In 2013, Thailand was the country/area with the highest value of net exports (+131.4 mln US$), followed by South Africa (+130.7 mln US$). By MDG regions (see graph 2), the largest surpluses in this product group were recorded by Developed North America (+39.4 mln US$), Southern Asia (+34.5 mln US$) and Latin America and the Caribbean (+20.9 mln US$). The largest trade deficits were recorded by Sub-Saharan Africa (-68.6 mln US$), Eastern Asia (-42.1 mln US$) and Western Asia (-39.0 mln US$).

Table 1: Imports (Imp.) and exports (Exp.), 1999-2013, in current US$

		1999	2000	2001	2002	2003	2004	2005	2006	2007	2008	2009	2010	2011	2012	2013
Values in Bln US$	Imp.	0.5	0.5	0.5	0.6	0.6	0.7	0.7	0.8	1.0	1.4	1.4	1.2	1.6	1.5	1.6
	Exp.	0.5	0.4	0.5	0.5	0.5	0.6	0.7	0.7	0.9	1.2	1.1	1.1	1.4	1.3	1.5
As a percentage of	Imp.	0.1	0.1	0.1	0.1	0.1	0.1	0.1	0.1	0.1	0.1	0.2	0.1	0.1	0.1	0.1
SITC section (%)	Exp.	0.1	0.1	0.1	0.1	0.1	0.1	0.1	0.1	0.1	0.1	0.1	0.1	0.1	0.1	0.1
As a percentage of	Imp.	0.0	0.0	0.0	0.0	0.0	0.0	0.0	0.0	0.0	0.0	0.0	0.0	0.0	0.0	0.0
world trade (%)	Exp.	0.0	0.0	0.0	0.0	0.0	0.0	0.0	0.0	0.0	0.0	0.0	0.0	0.0	0.0	0.0

Graph 1: Annual growth rates of exports, 1999–2013

(In percentage by year)

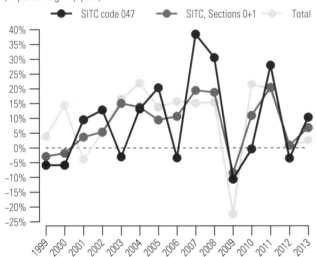

Table 2: Top exporting countries or areas in 2013

Country or area	Value (million US$)	Avg. Growth (%) 09-13	Growth (%) 12-13	World share %	Cum.
World	1 465.4	7.9	10.3	100.0	
USA	168.0	-1.8	-3.0	11.5	11.5
Thailand	135.8	10.4	-2.6	9.3	20.7
South Africa	135.0	19.9	20.0	9.2	29.9
Canada	123.7	7.7	16.1	8.4	38.4
France	105.4	5.7	13.0	7.2	45.6
Italy	88.4	-2.0	-9.7	6.0	51.6
Germany	67.9	16.9	17.4	4.6	56.2
Turkey	48.2	30.7	138.8	3.3	59.5
Mexico	44.5	6.3	14.3	3.0	62.6
Brazil	41.6	3.5	9.5	2.8	65.4
El Salvador	39.2	3.5	-9.1	2.7	68.1
Poland	38.8	54.2	93.6	2.6	70.7
India	32.1	19.1	18.3	2.2	72.9
Netherlands	24.1	4.0	-0.9	1.6	74.6
Belgium	23.6	29.0	15.2	1.6	76.2

Graph 2: Trade Balance by MDG regions 2013

(Mln US$)

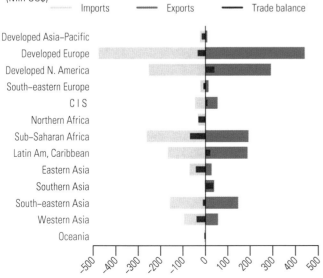

Table 3: Top importing countries or areas in 2013

Country or area	Value (million US$)	Avg. Growth (%) 09-13	Growth (%) 12-13	World share %	Cum.
World	1 617.1	4.5	6.3	100.0	
USA	193.5	9.7	17.8	12.0	12.0
Malaysia	127.0	36.3	33.9	7.9	19.8
Angola	98.5	5.7	2.6	6.1	25.9
Spain	93.2	7.2	6.9	5.8	31.7
Canada	58.1	2.6	5.9	3.6	35.3
Germany	55.6	7.9	13.3	3.4	38.7
Netherlands	55.2	23.9	12.3	3.4	42.1
Mexico	51.3	19.6	8.1	3.2	45.3
Lesotho	43.8	2.5	-15.2	2.7	48.0
United Kingdom	42.2	18.8	56.4	2.6	50.6
France	41.8	7.7	16.6	2.6	53.2
Belgium	37.1	11.3	19.4	2.3	55.5
China	32.1	20.3	11.2	2.0	57.5
Egypt	27.1	8.5	-7.0	1.7	59.1
China, Hong Kong SAR	26.2	9.4	2.1	1.6	60.8

048 Cereal, flour or starch preparations of fruits or vegetables

In 2013, the value (in current US$) of exports of "cereal, flour or starch preparations of fruits or vegetables" (SITC group 048) increased by 8.5 percent (compared to 7.8 percent average growth rate from 2009-2013) to reach 50.3 bln US$ (see table 2), while imports increased by 8.0 percent to reach 49.7 bln US$ (see table 3). Exports of this commodity accounted for 4.0 percent of world exports of SITC sections 0+1, and 0.3 percent of total world merchandise exports (see table 1). Germany, Italy and France were the top exporters in 2013 (see table 2). They accounted for 11.2, 8.9 and 7.6 percent of world exports, respectively. USA, Germany and France were the top destinations, with respectively 11.0, 6.5 and 6.4 percent of world imports (see table 3).

The top 15 countries/areas accounted for 73.0 and 58.4 percent of total world exports and imports, respectively (see tables 2 and 3). In 2013, Italy was the country/area with the highest value of net exports (+3.0 bln US$), followed by Germany (+2.4 bln US$). By MDG regions (see graph 2), the largest surpluses in this product group were recorded by Developed Europe (+5.9 bln US$), Southern Asia (+553.8 mln US$) and South-eastern Asia (+383.5 mln US$). The largest trade deficits were recorded by Sub-Saharan Africa (-1.4 bln US$), Developed North America (-1.2 bln US$) and Developed Asia-Pacific (-1.1 bln US$).

Table 1: Imports (Imp.) and exports (Exp.), 1999-2013, in current US$

		1999	2000	2001	2002	2003	2004	2005	2006	2007	2008	2009	2010	2011	2012	2013
Values in Bln US$	Imp.	14.0	13.7	14.8	16.7	20.0	23.2	25.0	27.3	33.0	39.6	37.8	38.4	44.7	46.0	49.7
	Exp.	13.9	13.6	14.6	16.6	19.9	23.1	25.0	27.5	32.7	39.5	37.3	38.1	44.7	46.4	50.3
As a percentage of SITC section (%)	Imp.	3.4	3.3	3.5	3.7	3.9	4.0	3.9	3.9	4.0	4.0	4.2	3.9	3.8	3.9	4.0
	Exp.	3.5	3.5	3.6	3.9	4.1	4.2	4.1	4.1	4.1	4.2	4.3	3.9	3.8	3.9	4.0
As a percentage of world trade (%)	Imp.	0.2	0.2	0.2	0.3	0.3	0.2	0.2	0.2	0.2	0.2	0.3	0.3	0.2	0.3	0.3
	Exp.	0.3	0.2	0.2	0.3	0.3	0.3	0.2	0.2	0.2	0.2	0.3	0.3	0.2	0.3	0.3

Graph 1: Annual growth rates of exports, 1999–2013
(In percentage by year)

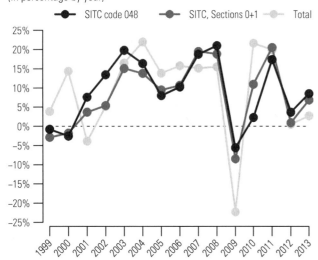

Legend: SITC code 048 — SITC, Sections 0+1 — Total

Table 2: Top exporting countries or areas in 2013

Country or area	Value (million US$)	Avg. Growth (%) 09-13	Growth (%) 12-13	World share %	Cum.
World	50 300.9	7.8	8.5	100.0	
Germany	5 646.4	5.4	7.2	11.2	11.2
Italy	4 459.8	4.9	7.5	8.9	20.1
France	3 833.8	5.7	7.9	7.6	27.7
Belgium	3 831.2	7.3	18.8	7.6	35.3
USA	3 722.6	8.8	7.5	7.4	42.7
Canada	3 027.2	5.7	2.9	6.0	48.7
United Kingdom	2 235.0	3.5	2.9	4.4	53.2
Netherlands	2 194.2	10.4	9.3	4.4	57.6
Turkey	1 525.5	23.1	21.3	3.0	60.6
Poland	1 292.9	10.5	22.3	2.6	63.2
Spain	1 289.1	10.3	17.0	2.6	65.7
Mexico	1 057.6	10.1	1.5	2.1	67.8
Austria	985.7	7.3	11.2	2.0	69.8
China	904.3	11.7	-2.0	1.8	71.6
Sweden	739.5	7.1	8.7	1.5	73.0

Graph 2: Trade Balance by MDG regions 2013
(Bln US$)

Legend: Imports — Exports — Trade balance

- Developed Asia–Pacific
- Developed Europe
- Developed N. America
- South–eastern Europe
- C I S
- Northern Africa
- Sub–Saharan Africa
- Latin Am, Caribbean
- Eastern Asia
- Southern Asia
- South–eastern Asia
- Western Asia
- Oceania

(axis: -25, -20, -15, -10, -5, 0, 5, 10, 15, 20, 25, 30, 35)

Table 3: Top importing countries or areas in 2013

Country or area	Value (million US$)	Avg. Growth (%) 09-13	Growth (%) 12-13	World share %	Cum.
World	49 661.3	7.1	8.0	100.0	
USA	5 474.6	7.6	4.5	11.0	11.0
Germany	3 247.5	5.4	11.1	6.5	17.6
France	3 198.5	3.7	7.7	6.4	24.0
United Kingdom	3 105.0	5.1	8.5	6.3	30.3
Canada	2 395.1	8.4	6.7	4.8	35.1
Belgium	1 941.2	3.2	7.7	3.9	39.0
Netherlands	1 831.7	8.5	7.5	3.7	42.7
Italy	1 487.0	5.3	5.8	3.0	45.7
Japan	1 200.3	2.6	-6.3	2.4	48.1
Spain	1 092.5	1.1	2.3	2.2	50.3
Austria	922.7	2.7	6.2	1.9	52.1
Ireland	831.0	3.7	6.6	1.7	53.8
Australia	790.1	15.0	11.8	1.6	55.4
Russian Federation	783.9	22.8	13.7	1.6	57.0
Mexico	720.2	5.1	6.8	1.5	58.4

In 2013, the value (in current US$) of exports of "vegetables, fresh, chilled , frozen, simply preserved; roots" (SITC group 054) increased by 13.3 percent (compared to 7.0 percent average growth rate from 2009-2013) to reach 62.8 bln US$ (see table 2), while imports increased by 11.3 percent to reach 65.7 bln US$ (see table 3). Exports of this commodity accounted for 5.0 percent of world exports of SITC sections 0+1, and 0.3 percent of total world merchandise exports (see table 1). Netherlands, Spain and China were the top exporters in 2013 (see table 2). They accounted for 12.4, 10.1 and 9.6 percent of world exports, respectively. USA, Germany and United Kingdom were the top destinations, with respectively 13.2, 9.6 and 6.8 percent of world imports (see table 3).

The top 15 countries/areas accounted for 77.5 and 69.5 percent of total world exports and imports, respectively (see tables 2 and 3). In 2013, Netherlands was the country/area with the highest value of net exports (+5.1 bln US$), followed by Spain (+5.0 bln US$). By MDG regions (see graph 2), the largest surpluses in this product group were recorded by Latin America and the Caribbean (+5.2 bln US$), Eastern Asia (+2.3 bln US$) and Sub-Saharan Africa (+734.6 mln US$). The largest trade deficits were recorded by Developed North America (-2.9 bln US$), Developed Europe (-2.8 bln US$) and Commonwealth of Independent States (-2.3 bln US$).

Table 1: Imports (Imp.) and exports (Exp.), 1999-2013, in current US$

		1999	2000	2001	2002	2003	2004	2005	2006	2007	2008	2009	2010	2011	2012	2013
Values in Bln US$	Imp.	22.3	21.5	23.1	24.6	28.1	31.3	34.2	38.5	45.5	50.0	47.9	54.6	59.8	59.1	65.7
	Exp.	20.6	19.6	21.6	22.8	27.0	29.6	32.4	37.3	43.9	48.6	48.0	54.3	59.9	55.5	62.8
As a percentage of SITC section (%)	Imp.	5.3	5.2	5.4	5.5	5.5	5.3	5.4	5.5	5.5	5.1	5.4	5.6	5.0	5.0	5.3
	Exp.	5.2	5.1	5.4	5.4	5.6	5.3	5.3	5.6	5.5	5.1	5.5	5.6	5.1	4.7	5.0
As a percentage of world trade (%)	Imp.	0.4	0.3	0.4	0.4	0.4	0.3	0.3	0.3	0.3	0.3	0.4	0.4	0.3	0.3	0.4
	Exp.	0.4	0.3	0.4	0.4	0.4	0.3	0.3	0.3	0.3	0.3	0.4	0.4	0.3	0.3	0.3

Graph 1: Annual growth rates of exports, 1999–2013
(In percentage by year)

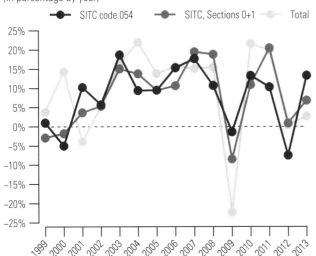

Table 2: Top exporting countries or areas in 2013

Country or area	Value (million US$)	Avg. Growth (%) 09-13	Growth (%) 12-13	World share %	World share % Cum.
World	62 840.1	7.0	13.3	100.0	
Netherlands	7 809.5	7.3	12.6	12.4	12.4
Spain	6 343.0	3.5	13.8	10.1	22.5
China	6 017.2	9.4	5.0	9.6	32.1
Mexico	5 390.9	9.9	15.5	8.6	40.7
Canada	4 284.2	9.1	34.0	6.8	47.5
USA	4 248.5	6.6	8.6	6.8	54.3
Belgium	2 789.2	5.3	20.6	4.4	58.7
France	2 678.2	6.2	16.9	4.3	63.0
Italy	1 706.4	6.1	13.4	2.7	65.7
Thailand	1 585.5	16.7	16.1	2.5	68.2
Germany	1 379.2	7.1	29.5	2.2	70.4
India	1 268.9	13.3	68.2	2.0	72.4
Poland	1 155.3	9.5	24.2	1.8	74.2
Egypt	1 028.6	6.7	30.5	1.6	75.9
Australia	990.3	15.5	-23.3	1.6	77.5

Graph 2: Trade Balance by MDG regions 2013
(Bln US$)

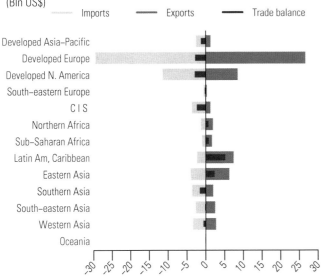

Table 3: Top importing countries or areas in 2013

Country or area	Value (million US$)	Avg. Growth (%) 09-13	Growth (%) 12-13	World share %	World share % Cum.
World	65 708.0	8.2	11.3	100.0	
USA	8 664.2	10.9	10.5	13.2	13.2
Germany	6 332.8	5.5	16.8	9.6	22.8
United Kingdom	4 479.8	5.7	18.0	6.8	29.6
France	3 347.0	4.4	10.7	5.1	34.7
Russian Federation	2 858.4	14.6	16.1	4.4	39.1
Canada	2 725.9	7.0	12.8	4.1	43.2
Netherlands	2 725.5	11.5	10.8	4.1	47.4
China	2 631.1	25.0	6.4	4.0	51.4
India	2 304.7	2.7	1.2	3.5	54.9
Belgium	2 266.6	9.5	26.7	3.4	58.3
Japan	2 265.8	10.1	-6.9	3.4	61.8
Italy	1 791.3	3.0	12.7	2.7	64.5
Spain	1 333.5	3.7	6.5	2.0	66.5
United Arab Emirates	1 131.6	11.1	11.4	1.7	68.3
Malaysia	788.7	11.6	16.7	1.2	69.5

STAFFS UNIVERSITY LIBRARY

056 Vegetables, roots and tubers, prepared or preserved, nes

In 2013, the value (in current US$) of exports of "vegetables, roots and tubers, prepared or preserved, nes" (SITC group 056) increased by 13.2 percent (compared to 7.6 percent average growth rate from 2009-2013) to reach 31.1 bln US$ (see table 2), while imports increased by 7.6 percent to reach 27.9 bln US$ (see table 3). Exports of this commodity accounted for 2.5 percent of world exports of SITC sections 0+1, and 0.2 percent of total world merchandise exports (see table 1). China, Netherlands and USA were the top exporters in 2013 (see table 2). They accounted for 19.7, 9.6 and 8.5 percent of world exports, respectively. USA, Germany and Japan were the top destinations, with respectively 10.6, 8.4 and 8.3 percent of world imports (see table 3).

The top 15 countries/areas accounted for 82.5 and 67.5 percent of total world exports and imports, respectively (see tables 2 and 3). In 2013, China was the country/area with the highest value of net exports (+5.9 bln US$), followed by Netherlands (+1.9 bln US$). By MDG regions (see graph 2), the largest surpluses in this product group were recorded by Eastern Asia (+5.2 bln US$), Developed Europe (+2.8 bln US$) and Southern Asia (+482.9 mln US$). The largest trade deficits were recorded by Developed Asia-Pacific (-2.7 bln US$), Commonwealth of Independent States (-853.4 mln US$) and Latin America and the Caribbean (-546.3 mln US$).

Table 1: Imports (Imp.) and exports (Exp.), 1999-2013, in current US$

		1999	2000	2001	2002	2003	2004	2005	2006	2007	2008	2009	2010	2011	2012	2013
Values in Bln US$	Imp.	10.9	10.0	10.1	11.1	12.7	14.6	15.5	17.0	20.2	22.6	22.0	22.9	26.1	25.9	27.9
	Exp.	10.7	9.8	10.2	11.3	13.2	15.1	15.9	17.7	21.4	24.1	23.2	24.8	28.8	27.5	31.1
As a percentage of SITC section (%)	Imp.	2.6	2.4	2.4	2.5	2.5	2.5	2.4	2.4	2.4	2.3	2.5	2.3	2.2	2.2	2.3
	Exp.	2.7	2.5	2.5	2.7	2.7	2.7	2.6	2.6	2.7	2.5	2.7	2.6	2.5	2.3	2.5
As a percentage of world trade (%)	Imp.	0.2	0.2	0.2	0.2	0.2	0.2	0.1	0.1	0.1	0.1	0.2	0.2	0.1	0.1	0.2
	Exp.	0.2	0.2	0.2	0.2	0.2	0.2	0.2	0.1	0.2	0.2	0.2	0.2	0.2	0.2	0.2

Graph 1: Annual growth rates of exports, 1999–2013
(In percentage by year)

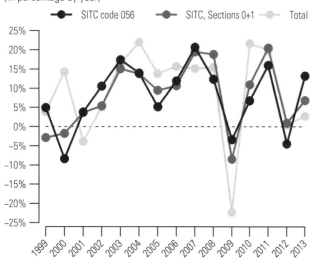

Table 2: Top exporting countries or areas in 2013

Country or area	Value (million US$)	Avg. Growth (%) 09-13	Growth (%) 12-13	World share %	Cum.
World	31 110.7	7.6	13.2	100.0	
China	6 113.8	16.8	24.5	19.7	19.7
Netherlands	3 001.6	5.0	11.9	9.6	29.3
USA	2 649.0	9.5	7.6	8.5	37.8
Italy	2 632.6	2.3	11.3	8.5	46.3
Belgium	2 619.4	9.6	21.7	8.4	54.7
Spain	1 794.9	3.0	5.5	5.8	60.5
Germany	1 324.4	4.7	10.0	4.3	64.7
France	1 281.9	4.1	4.3	4.1	68.8
Canada	1 081.3	2.0	5.0	3.5	72.3
Turkey	748.4	2.4	15.4	2.4	74.7
Greece	623.6	4.7	9.4	2.0	76.7
Poland	550.8	11.5	21.8	1.8	78.5
Peru	450.5	6.0	-6.4	1.4	79.9
Portugal	400.1	7.7	16.4	1.3	81.2
India	398.2	15.9	10.4	1.3	82.5

Graph 2: Trade Balance by MDG regions 2013
(Bln US$)

Imports — Exports — Trade balance

Developed Asia–Pacific
Developed Europe
Developed N. America
South–eastern Europe
C I S
Northern Africa
Sub–Saharan Africa
Latin Am, Caribbean
Eastern Asia
Southern Asia
South–eastern Asia
Western Asia
Oceania

-15 -10 -5 0 5 10 15 20

Table 3: Top importing countries or areas in 2013

Country or area	Value (million US$)	Avg. Growth (%) 09-13	Growth (%) 12-13	World share %	Cum.
World	27 877.8	6.1	7.6	100.0	
USA	2 946.5	5.0	1.6	10.6	10.6
Germany	2 332.8	1.1	6.5	8.4	18.9
Japan	2 302.7	7.0	-5.8	8.3	27.2
France	2 065.9	2.9	9.4	7.4	34.6
United Kingdom	1 925.7	7.5	11.6	6.9	41.5
Netherlands	1 092.3	7.6	10.0	3.9	45.4
Italy	907.9	-0.4	9.5	3.3	48.7
Canada	832.0	8.0	0.4	3.0	51.7
Belgium	815.0	5.9	13.8	2.9	54.6
Russian Federation	791.4	5.4	5.7	2.8	57.4
Spain	692.0	4.3	13.1	2.5	59.9
Brazil	623.3	19.9	35.7	2.2	62.2
Australia	504.4	8.7	4.2	1.8	64.0
Saudi Arabia	500.4	14.5	11.6	1.8	65.8
Rep. of Korea	486.8	12.2	7.0	1.7	67.5

Fruit and nuts (not including oil nuts), fresh or dried 057

In 2013, the value (in current US$) of exports of "fruit and nuts (not including oil nuts), fresh or dried" (SITC group 057) increased by 10.2 percent (compared to 9.4 percent average growth rate from 2009-2013) to reach 94.3 bln US$ (see table 2), while imports increased by 10.0 percent to reach 101.0 bln US$ (see table 3). Exports of this commodity accounted for 7.5 percent of world exports of SITC sections 0+1, and 0.5 percent of total world merchandise exports (see table 1). USA, Spain and Chile were the top exporters in 2013 (see table 2). They accounted for 15.1, 9.7 and 5.4 percent of world exports, respectively. USA, Germany and Russian Federation were the top destinations, with respectively 11.7, 8.9 and 6.3 percent of world imports (see table 3).

The top 15 countries/areas accounted for 68.1 and 70.2 percent of total world exports and imports, respectively (see tables 2 and 3). In 2013, Spain was the country/area with the highest value of net exports (+6.8 bln US$), followed by Chile (+5.0 bln US$). By MDG regions (see graph 2), the largest surpluses in this product group were recorded by Latin America and the Caribbean (+15.1 bln US$), Sub-Saharan Africa (+4.1 bln US$) and South-eastern Asia (+1.7 bln US$). The largest trade deficits were recorded by Developed Europe (-15.8 bln US$), Commonwealth of Independent States (-7.0 bln US$) and Eastern Asia (-3.8 bln US$).

Table 1: Imports (Imp.) and exports (Exp.), 1999-2013, in current US$

		1999	2000	2001	2002	2003	2004	2005	2006	2007	2008	2009	2010	2011	2012	2013
Values in Bln US$	Imp.	33.1	31.4	32.1	34.8	41.2	46.7	52.6	57.0	65.7	75.5	72.3	79.0	89.6	91.9	101.0
	Exp.	28.5	27.3	27.8	29.7	35.8	40.4	46.9	50.2	58.8	68.4	65.9	72.7	83.6	85.5	94.3
As a percentage of	Imp.	7.9	7.6	7.5	7.7	8.0	8.0	8.2	8.2	7.9	7.7	8.1	8.0	7.6	7.8	8.2
SITC section (%)	Exp.	7.2	7.0	6.9	7.0	7.4	7.3	7.7	7.5	7.3	7.2	7.6	7.5	7.2	7.3	7.5
As a percentage of	Imp.	0.6	0.5	0.5	0.5	0.5	0.5	0.5	0.5	0.5	0.6	0.5	0.5	0.5	0.5	0.5
world trade (%)	Exp.	0.5	0.4	0.5	0.5	0.5	0.4	0.5	0.4	0.4	0.4	0.5	0.5	0.5	0.5	0.5

Graph 1: Annual growth rates of exports, 1999–2013
(In percentage by year)

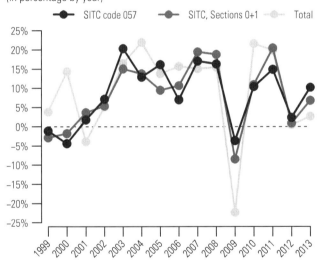

Graph 2: Trade Balance by MDG regions 2013
(Bln US$)

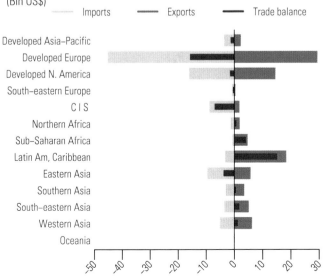

Table 2: Top exporting countries or areas in 2013

Country or area	Value (million US$)	Avg. Growth (%) 09-13	Growth (%) 12-13	World share %	Cum.
World....................	94 263.5	9.4	10.2	100.0	
USA.......................	14 259.0	13.7	9.7	15.1	15.1
Spain....................	9 144.7	7.9	15.0	9.7	24.8
Chile....................	5 115.5	11.9	11.8	5.4	30.3
Netherlands..........	5 085.3	9.9	16.4	5.4	35.6
Italy.....................	3 938.6	5.3	6.2	4.2	39.8
Turkey..................	3 910.1	7.2	4.4	4.1	44.0
China...................	3 827.2	15.3	12.4	4.1	48.0
Belgium................	3 217.6	1.1	14.0	3.4	51.4
Mexico.................	3 203.7	11.2	13.8	3.4	54.8
South Africa.........	2 630.9	13.0	12.0	2.8	57.6
Ecuador...............	2 403.4	3.8	11.3	2.5	60.2
France..................	2 036.1	3.2	1.4	2.2	62.3
Viet Nam..............	2 024.3	17.5	3.0	2.1	64.5
China, Hong Kong SAR........	1 715.9	15.5	-6.5	1.8	66.3
Costa Rica............	1 702.9	14.5	6.1	1.8	68.1

Table 3: Top importing countries or areas in 2013

Country or area	Value (million US$)	Avg. Growth (%) 09-13	Growth (%) 12-13	World share %	Cum.
World....................	101 022.9	8.7	10.0	100.0	
USA.......................	11 776.2	8.3	10.1	11.7	11.7
Germany...............	8 981.9	6.3	20.0	8.9	20.5
Russian Federation............	6 329.5	9.8	1.9	6.3	26.8
Netherlands..........	5 670.2	8.0	12.6	5.6	32.4
United Kingdom.....	5 622.2	5.1	7.9	5.6	38.0
France..................	4 884.0	5.7	12.4	4.8	42.8
Canada.................	4 274.6	9.1	5.0	4.2	47.1
China...................	3 983.2	24.7	8.4	3.9	51.0
Belgium................	3 771.3	1.8	14.7	3.7	54.7
China, Hong Kong SAR........	3 670.1	16.6	5.6	3.6	58.4
Italy.....................	3 087.3	4.3	17.0	3.1	61.4
Japan...................	2 692.1	2.5	-7.6	2.7	64.1
Spain....................	2 349.5	6.3	19.3	2.3	66.4
India....................	2 132.5	17.9	14.9	2.1	68.5
United Arab Emirates..........	*1 644.5*	11.7	11.4	1.6	70.2

058 Fruits, preserved, and fruit preparations (excluding fruit juices)

In 2013, the value (in current US$) of exports of "fruits, preserved, and fruit preparations (excluding fruit juices)" (SITC group 058) increased by 6.3 percent (compared to 10.4 percent average growth rate from 2009-2013) to reach 20.8 bln US$ (see table 2), while imports increased by 6.4 percent to reach 20.2 bln US$ (see table 3). Exports of this commodity accounted for 1.7 percent of world exports of SITC sections 0+1, and 0.1 percent of total world merchandise exports (see table 1). China, USA and Germany were the top exporters in 2013 (see table 2). They accounted for 15.0, 8.7 and 5.2 percent of world exports, respectively. USA, Germany and France were the top destinations, with respectively 17.2, 10.8 and 7.5 percent of world imports (see table 3).

The top 15 countries/areas accounted for 71.5 and 72.6 percent of total world exports and imports, respectively (see tables 2 and 3). In 2013, China was the country/area with the highest value of net exports (+2.8 bln US$), followed by Turkey (+992.1 mln US$). By MDG regions (see graph 2), the largest surpluses in this product group were recorded by Eastern Asia (+2.2 bln US$), Latin America and the Caribbean (+1.5 bln US$) and South-eastern Asia (+1.4 bln US$). The largest trade deficits were recorded by Developed North America (-2.1 bln US$), Developed Europe (-2.1 bln US$) and Developed Asia-Pacific (-1.5 bln US$).

Table 1: Imports (Imp.) and exports (Exp.), 1999-2013, in current US$

		1999	2000	2001	2002	2003	2004	2005	2006	2007	2008	2009	2010	2011	2012	2013
Values in Bln US$	Imp.	6.7	6.3	6.3	6.8	8.3	9.5	10.6	11.8	13.6	15.7	13.9	14.9	18.3	19.0	20.2
	Exp.	6.1	5.7	6.0	6.6	7.9	9.0	10.0	11.3	13.8	16.1	14.0	15.2	18.7	19.5	20.8
As a percentage of SITC section (%)	Imp.	1.6	1.5	1.5	1.5	1.6	1.6	1.7	1.7	1.6	1.6	1.6	1.5	1.5	1.6	1.6
	Exp.	1.5	1.5	1.5	1.6	1.6	1.6	1.7	1.7	1.7	1.7	1.6	1.6	1.6	1.7	1.7
As a percentage of world trade (%)	Imp.	0.1	0.1	0.1	0.1	0.1	0.1	0.1	0.1	0.1	0.1	0.1	0.1	0.1	0.1	0.1
	Exp.	0.1	0.1	0.1	0.1	0.1	0.1	0.1	0.1	0.1	0.1	0.1	0.1	0.1	0.1	0.1

Graph 1: Annual growth rates of exports, 1999–2013
(In percentage by year)

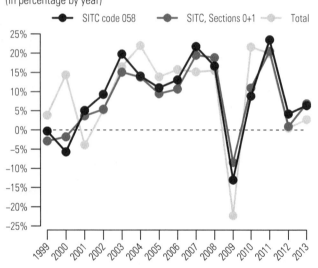

Legend: SITC code 058 — SITC, Sections 0+1 — Total

Table 2: Top exporting countries or areas in 2013

Country or area	Value (million US$)	Avg. Growth (%) 09-13	Growth (%) 12-13	World share %	Cum.
World	20 759.1	10.4	6.3	100.0	
China	3 123.5	14.0	1.3	15.0	15.0
USA	1 797.8	14.6	12.4	8.7	23.7
Germany	1 072.8	5.3	9.6	5.2	28.9
Netherlands	1 063.6	8.6	9.7	5.1	34.0
Turkey	1 032.9	13.5	1.3	5.0	39.0
Thailand	967.7	3.4	-0.5	4.7	43.6
Belgium	742.4	10.9	19.2	3.6	47.2
Poland	737.5	8.4	3.6	3.6	50.8
Chile	689.1	12.9	6.9	3.3	54.1
France	650.1	7.1	19.3	3.1	57.2
Canada	636.4	12.6	-2.6	3.1	60.3
Spain	627.9	6.2	17.6	3.0	63.3
Italy	611.6	6.1	-2.3	2.9	66.3
Greece	557.0	6.6	2.7	2.7	68.9
Mexico	542.3	15.0	10.4	2.6	71.5

Graph 2: Trade Balance by MDG regions 2013
(Bln US$)

Legend: Imports — Exports — Trade balance

Developed Asia–Pacific
Developed Europe
Developed N. America
South–eastern Europe
C I S
Northern Africa
Sub–Saharan Africa
Latin Am, Caribbean
Eastern Asia
Southern Asia
South–eastern Asia
Western Asia
Oceania

-10 -8 -6 -4 -2 0 2 4 6 8

Table 3: Top importing countries or areas in 2013

Country or area	Value (million US$)	Avg. Growth (%) 09-13	Growth (%) 12-13	World share %	Cum.
World	20 224.2	9.9	6.4	100.0	
USA	3 482.2	11.5	5.0	17.2	17.2
Germany	2 186.7	5.4	1.7	10.8	28.0
France	1 511.4	5.8	7.8	7.5	35.5
Japan	1 188.6	10.2	-6.5	5.9	41.4
Canada	1 034.4	14.2	11.8	5.1	46.5
United Kingdom	922.8	7.3	6.8	4.6	51.1
Netherlands	904.9	7.2	12.8	4.5	55.5
Belgium	688.9	11.7	15.0	3.4	58.9
Russian Federation	441.7	11.0	12.1	2.2	61.1
Italy	427.5	7.5	2.6	2.1	63.2
Rep. of Korea	414.6	21.6	8.3	2.1	65.3
Austria	398.4	7.1	5.8	2.0	67.3
Poland	376.4	13.1	16.1	1.9	69.1
China	349.6	15.0	-1.8	1.7	70.8
Australia	345.2	15.3	6.4	1.7	72.6

Fruit and vegetable juices, unfermented and without added spirit 059

In 2013, the value (in current US$) of exports of "fruit and vegetable juices, unfermented and without added spirit" (SITC group 059) increased by 1.2 percent (compared to 7.7 percent average growth rate from 2009-2013) to reach 17.1 bln US$ (see table 2), while imports increased by 0.1 percent to reach 17.1 bln US$ (see table 3). Exports of this commodity accounted for 1.4 percent of world exports of SITC sections 0+1, and 0.1 percent of total world merchandise exports (see table 1). Brazil, Netherlands and USA were the top exporters in 2013 (see table 2). They accounted for 14.4, 8.7 and 7.2 percent of world exports, respectively. USA, Germany and Netherlands were the top destinations, with respectively 11.4, 9.4 and 9.1 percent of world imports (see table 3).

The top 15 countries/areas accounted for 77.1 and 73.5 percent of total world exports and imports, respectively (see tables 2 and 3). In 2013, Brazil was the country/area with the highest value of net exports (+2.4 bln US$), followed by China (+813.0 mln US$). By MDG regions (see graph 2), the largest surpluses in this product group were recorded by Latin America and the Caribbean (+3.7 bln US$), Eastern Asia (+562.1 mln US$) and South-eastern Asia (+405.9 mln US$). The largest trade deficits were recorded by Developed Europe (-2.1 bln US$), Developed North America (-1.3 bln US$) and Developed Asia-Pacific (-933.7 mln US$).

Table 1: Imports (Imp.) and exports (Exp.), 1999-2013, in current US$

		1999	2000	2001	2002	2003	2004	2005	2006	2007	2008	2009	2010	2011	2012	2013
Values in Bln US$	Imp.	7.0	6.8	6.2	6.9	8.2	8.6	9.5	11.4	14.7	16.4	13.3	13.8	17.3	17.0	17.1
	Exp.	6.6	6.4	5.9	6.4	7.7	7.9	8.9	10.8	14.2	15.3	12.7	13.6	17.2	16.9	17.1
As a percentage of SITC section (%)	Imp.	1.7	1.6	1.5	1.5	1.6	1.5	1.5	1.6	1.8	1.7	1.5	1.4	1.5	1.4	1.4
	Exp.	1.7	1.6	1.5	1.5	1.6	1.4	1.5	1.6	1.8	1.6	1.5	1.4	1.5	1.4	1.4
As a percentage of world trade (%)	Imp.	0.1	0.1	0.1	0.1	0.1	0.1	0.1	0.1	0.1	0.1	0.1	0.1	0.1	0.1	0.1
	Exp.	0.1	0.1	0.1	0.1	0.1	0.1	0.1	0.1	0.1	0.1	0.1	0.1	0.1	0.1	0.1

Graph 1: Annual growth rates of exports, 1999–2013
(In percentage by year)

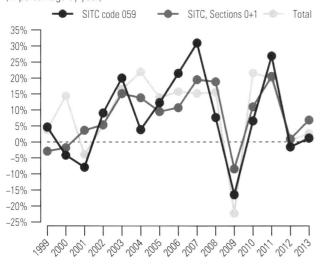

Table 2: Top exporting countries or areas in 2013

Country or area	Value (million US$)	Avg. Growth (%) 09-13	Growth (%) 12-13	World share %	Cum.
World	17 117.7	7.7	1.2	100.0	
Brazil	2 460.2	8.9	0.4	14.4	14.4
Netherlands	1 496.9	6.6	3.2	8.7	23.1
USA	1 237.6	4.8	-0.9	7.2	30.3
Belgium	1 155.6	1.8	-8.0	6.8	37.1
China	1 042.5	8.1	-20.1	6.1	43.2
Germany	971.4	0.2	2.1	5.7	48.9
Spain	887.2	7.6	4.8	5.2	54.0
Poland	784.0	15.9	10.2	4.6	58.6
Italy	683.6	5.1	-4.2	4.0	62.6
Thailand	465.5	9.5	8.9	2.7	65.3
Mexico	457.5	14.4	47.2	2.7	68.0
Argentina	439.4	7.8	-10.4	2.6	70.6
Austria	401.7	7.5	11.1	2.3	72.9
Saudi Arabia	394.9	11.1	16.0	2.3	75.2
South Africa	313.1	17.1	1.0	1.8	77.1

Graph 2: Trade Balance by MDG regions 2013
(Bln US$)

Imports   Exports   Trade balance

Developed Asia–Pacific
Developed Europe
Developed N. America
South–eastern Europe
C I S
Northern Africa
Sub–Saharan Africa
Latin Am, Caribbean
Eastern Asia
Southern Asia
South–eastern Asia
Western Asia
Oceania

-10 -8 -6 -4 -2 0 2 4 6 8

Table 3: Top importing countries or areas in 2013

Country or area	Value (million US$)	Avg. Growth (%) 09-13	Growth (%) 12-13	World share %	Cum.
World	17 050.9	6.3	0.1	100.0	
USA	1 944.1	5.6	-4.9	11.4	11.4
Germany	1 605.1	6.1	-8.7	9.4	20.8
Netherlands	1 555.5	7.1	0.7	9.1	29.9
France	1 273.3	2.6	1.1	7.5	37.4
Belgium	1 233.5	5.8	35.7	7.2	44.6
United Kingdom	1 116.5	3.8	1.7	6.5	51.2
Japan	883.1	9.6	-5.9	5.2	56.4
Canada	721.4	4.1	-4.9	4.2	60.6
Russian Federation	458.6	9.9	-9.3	2.7	63.3
Austria	372.3	9.3	-9.4	2.2	65.5
Saudi Arabia	309.8	8.3	15.5	1.8	67.3
Spain	294.2	1.6	6.7	1.7	69.0
Italy	294.1	6.0	-2.3	1.7	70.7
Poland	240.5	16.5	7.9	1.4	72.1
China	229.5	12.9	5.3	1.3	73.5

061 Sugars, molasses and honey

In 2013, the value (in current US$) of exports of "sugars, molasses and honey" (SITC group 061) decreased by 3.6 percent (compared to 11.8 percent average growth rate from 2009-2013) to reach 42.3 bln US$ (see table 2), while imports decreased by 7.1 percent to reach 41.1 bln US$ (see table 3). Exports of this commodity accounted for 3.4 percent of world exports of SITC sections 0+1, and 0.2 percent of total world merchandise exports (see table 1). Brazil, Thailand and USA were the top exporters in 2013 (see table 2). They accounted for 28.1, 7.1 and 4.7 percent of world exports, respectively. USA, China and Indonesia were the top destinations, with respectively 6.9, 5.6 and 4.7 percent of world imports (see table 3).

The top 15 countries/areas accounted for 71.1 and 51.9 percent of total world exports and imports, respectively (see tables 2 and 3). In 2013, Brazil was the country/area with the highest value of net exports (+11.8 bln US$), followed by Thailand (+2.9 bln US$). By MDG regions (see graph 2), the largest surpluses in this product group were recorded by Latin America and the Caribbean (+15.9 bln US$), South-eastern Asia (+261.2 mln US$) and Oceania (+19.9 mln US$). The largest trade deficits were recorded by Developed Europe (-4.0 bln US$), Eastern Asia (-2.5 bln US$) and Western Asia (-1.8 bln US$).

Table 1: Imports (Imp.) and exports (Exp.), 1999-2013, in current US$

		1999	2000	2001	2002	2003	2004	2005	2006	2007	2008	2009	2010	2011	2012	2013
Values in Bln US$	Imp.	13.1	11.4	14.2	13.6	15.0	16.0	19.9	24.1	24.7	27.1	28.7	37.4	48.7	44.3	41.1
	Exp.	11.0	9.8	12.1	12.0	13.2	14.1	17.4	22.6	22.1	24.1	27.1	36.2	44.7	43.9	42.3
As a percentage of SITC section (%)	Imp.	3.1	2.8	3.3	3.0	2.9	2.7	3.1	3.5	3.0	2.8	3.2	3.8	4.1	3.8	3.3
	Exp.	2.8	2.5	3.0	2.8	2.7	2.6	2.9	3.4	2.8	2.5	3.1	3.8	3.8	3.7	3.4
As a percentage of world trade (%)	Imp.	0.2	0.2	0.2	0.2	0.2	0.2	0.2	0.2	0.2	0.2	0.2	0.2	0.3	0.2	0.2
	Exp.	0.2	0.2	0.2	0.2	0.2	0.2	0.2	0.2	0.2	0.2	0.2	0.2	0.2	0.2	0.2

Graph 1: Annual growth rates of exports, 1999–2013
(In percentage by year)

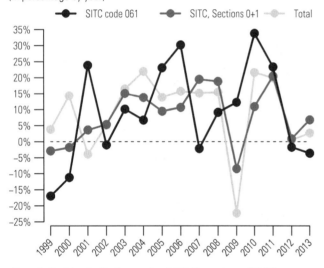

Legend: SITC code 061 — SITC, Sections 0+1 — Total

Table 2: Top exporting countries or areas in 2013

Country or area	Value (million US$)	Avg. Growth (%) 09-13	Growth (%) 12-13	World share %	Cum.
World	42 334.3	11.8	-3.6	100.0	
Brazil	11 903.1	8.9	-6.4	28.1	28.1
Thailand	2 994.5	12.2	-27.0	7.1	35.2
USA	1 976.2	23.6	-5.8	4.7	39.9
France	1 702.0	0.2	-13.1	4.0	43.9
Mexico	1 599.9	24.5	70.3	3.8	47.7
Germany	1 529.6	6.3	-3.9	3.6	51.3
Cuba	1 443.0	27.0	14.6	3.4	54.7
India	1 161.4	94.3	-46.8	2.7	57.4
Netherlands	1 035.7	13.8	34.5	2.4	59.9
Guatemala	988.1	14.6	17.5	2.3	62.2
United Arab Emirates	974.8	14.8	21.7	2.3	64.5
China	954.8	17.9	14.0	2.3	66.8
Belgium	761.2	5.8	-7.5	1.8	68.6
Pakistan	569.0	61.9	180.6	1.3	69.9
Poland	512.8	27.1	-8.4	1.2	71.1

Graph 2: Trade Balance by MDG regions 2013
(Bln US$)

Legend: Imports — Exports — Trade balance

- Developed Asia–Pacific
- Developed Europe
- Developed N. America
- South–eastern Europe
- CIS
- Northern Africa
- Sub–Saharan Africa
- Latin Am, Caribbean
- Eastern Asia
- Southern Asia
- South–eastern Asia
- Western Asia
- Oceania

(axis: -15, -10, -5, 0, 5, 10, 15, 20)

Table 3: Top importing countries or areas in 2013

Country or area	Value (million US$)	Avg. Growth (%) 09-13	Growth (%) 12-13	World share %	Cum.
World	41 122.3	9.4	-7.1	100.0	
USA	2 854.4	8.8	-17.3	6.9	6.9
China	2 294.1	51.3	-7.2	5.6	12.5
Indonesia	1 951.1	29.1	5.1	4.7	17.3
Germany	1 714.0	7.9	7.7	4.2	21.4
Italy	1 591.2	11.1	-3.2	3.9	25.3
United Kingdom	1 539.3	2.0	10.3	3.7	29.0
Spain	1 255.4	14.3	18.5	3.1	32.1
Rep. of Korea	1 183.0	9.5	-7.6	2.9	35.0
Belgium	1 074.6	9.5	8.1	2.6	37.6
Japan	1 037.5	9.1	-13.7	2.5	40.1
Malaysia	1 030.5	11.9	-9.0	2.5	42.6
Saudi Arabia	1 003.7	13.3	53.3	2.4	45.1
Bangladesh	955.6	12.7	-1.6	2.3	47.4
Nigeria	940.5	24.4	-7.2	2.3	49.7
Netherlands	923.2	15.6	14.2	2.2	51.9

In 2013, the value (in current US$) of exports of "sugar confectionery" (SITC group 062) increased by 10.5 percent (compared to 8.5 percent average growth rate from 2009-2013) to reach 11.9 bln US$ (see table 2), while imports increased by 9.7 percent to reach 10.8 bln US$ (see table 3). Exports of this commodity accounted for 0.9 percent of world exports of SITC sections 0+1, and 0.1 percent of total world merchandise exports (see table 1). Germany, China and Belgium were the top exporters in 2013 (see table 2). They accounted for 8.9, 8.4 and 6.3 percent of world exports, respectively. USA, Germany and United Kingdom were the top destinations, with respectively 15.5, 6.7 and 6.3 percent of world imports (see table 3).

The top 15 countries/areas accounted for 67.5 and 58.0 percent of total world exports and imports, respectively (see tables 2 and 3). In 2013, China was the country/area with the highest value of net exports (+877.2 mln US$), followed by Turkey (+477.5 mln US$). By MDG regions (see graph 2), the largest surpluses in this product group were recorded by Developed Europe (+923.8 mln US$), Eastern Asia (+736.9 mln US$) and South-eastern Asia (+469.2 mln US$). The largest trade deficits were recorded by Developed North America (-1.0 bln US$), Developed Asia-Pacific (-237.6 mln US$) and Sub-Saharan Africa (-186.1 mln US$).

Table 1: Imports (Imp.) and exports (Exp.), 1999-2013, in current US$

		1999	2000	2001	2002	2003	2004	2005	2006	2007	2008	2009	2010	2011	2012	2013
Values in Bln US$	Imp.	4.0	4.1	4.2	4.5	5.4	6.0	6.5	6.7	7.6	8.4	8.0	8.5	9.7	9.8	10.8
	Exp.	4.2	4.4	4.4	4.6	5.5	6.2	6.5	7.0	8.2	9.1	8.6	9.3	10.6	10.8	11.9
As a percentage of SITC section (%)	Imp.	1.0	1.0	1.0	1.0	1.1	1.0	1.0	1.0	0.9	0.9	0.9	0.9	0.8	0.8	0.9
	Exp.	1.1	1.1	1.1	1.1	1.1	1.1	1.1	1.0	1.0	1.0	1.0	1.0	0.9	0.9	0.9
As a percentage of world trade (%)	Imp.	0.1	0.1	0.1	0.1	0.1	0.1	0.1	0.1	0.1	0.1	0.1	0.1	0.1	0.1	0.1
	Exp.	0.1	0.1	0.1	0.1	0.1	0.1	0.1	0.1	0.1	0.1	0.1	0.1	0.1	0.1	0.1

Graph 1: Annual growth rates of exports, 1999–2013
(In percentage by year)

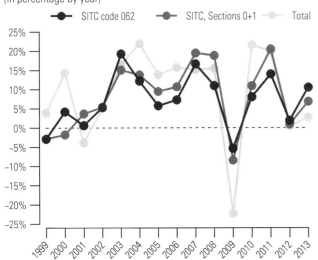

Table 2: Top exporting countries or areas in 2013

Country or area	Value (million US$)	Avg. Growth (%) 09-13	Growth (%) 12-13	World share %	Cum.
World	11 910.5	8.5	10.5	100.0	
Germany	1 060.6	6.9	9.7	8.9	8.9
China	997.2	16.6	15.0	8.4	17.3
Belgium	748.0	7.0	21.8	6.3	23.6
Netherlands	723.8	16.1	19.2	6.1	29.6
Mexico	576.1	3.6	8.3	4.8	34.5
Spain	545.8	6.0	9.0	4.6	39.1
USA	529.8	7.8	10.6	4.4	43.5
Canada	514.9	7.4	3.6	4.3	47.8
Turkey	491.4	17.4	21.5	4.1	51.9
Thailand	417.1	14.1	9.2	3.5	55.5
Colombia	314.3	7.7	12.1	2.6	58.1
Poland	299.8	6.5	25.3	2.5	60.6
United Kingdom	278.5	5.6	5.8	2.3	62.9
France	272.0	6.1	0.4	2.3	65.2
Italy	265.3	12.2	22.4	2.2	67.5

Graph 2: Trade Balance by MDG regions 2013
(Bln US$)

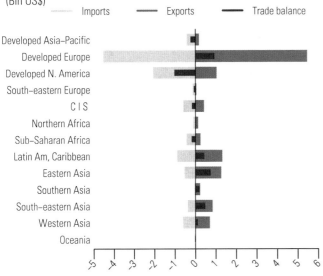

Table 3: Top importing countries or areas in 2013

Country or area	Value (million US$)	Avg. Growth (%) 09-13	Growth (%) 12-13	World share %	Cum.
World	10 754.5	7.8	9.7	100.0	
USA	1 670.9	7.4	7.2	15.5	15.5
Germany	725.6	5.1	8.6	6.7	22.3
United Kingdom	679.9	6.2	15.3	6.3	28.6
France	426.2	3.6	3.0	4.0	32.6
Canada	386.7	7.3	2.7	3.6	36.2
Netherlands	351.5	8.2	16.6	3.3	39.4
Belgium	333.4	7.2	21.0	3.1	42.5
Sweden	265.4	9.2	31.0	2.5	45.0
Russian Federation	247.1	9.3	3.2	2.3	47.3
Australia	211.8	11.3	8.5	2.0	49.3
Venezuela	208.0	19.3	20.7	1.9	51.2
China, Hong Kong SAR	195.7	5.3	1.2	1.8	53.0
Poland	186.4	9.4	17.9	1.7	54.8
Italy	179.4	2.8	7.5	1.7	56.4
Spain	173.8	9.0	9.9	1.6	58.0

071 Coffee and coffee substitutes

In 2013, the value (in current US$) of exports of "coffee and coffee substitutes" (SITC group 071) decreased by 10.7 percent (compared to 9.7 percent average growth rate from 2009-2013) to reach 35.7 bln US$ (see table 2), while imports decreased by 10.9 percent to reach 35.7 bln US$ (see table 3). Exports of this commodity accounted for 2.8 percent of world exports of SITC sections 0+1, and 0.2 percent of total world merchandise exports (see table 1). Brazil, Germany and Viet Nam were the top exporters in 2013 (see table 2). They accounted for 14.8, 9.6 and 8.1 percent of world exports, respectively. USA, Germany and France were the top destinations, with respectively 16.7, 11.3 and 7.5 percent of world imports (see table 3).

The top 15 countries/areas accounted for 72.4 and 71.3 percent of total world exports and imports, respectively (see tables 2 and 3). In 2013, Brazil was the country/area with the highest value of net exports (+5.2 bln US$), followed by Viet Nam (+2.8 bln US$). By MDG regions (see graph 2), the largest surpluses in this product group were recorded by Latin America and the Caribbean (+10.7 bln US$), South-eastern Asia (+4.1 bln US$) and Sub-Saharan Africa (+1.8 bln US$). The largest trade deficits were recorded by Developed North America (-5.7 bln US$), Developed Europe (-5.4 bln US$) and Developed Asia-Pacific (-2.3 bln US$).

Table 1: Imports (Imp.) and exports (Exp.), 1999-2013, in current US$

		1999	2000	2001	2002	2003	2004	2005	2006	2007	2008	2009	2010	2011	2012	2013
Values in Bln US$	Imp.	13.6	12.4	9.6	9.1	10.9	12.3	16.2	18.5	22.2	27.1	25.1	29.3	42.8	40.1	35.7
	Exp.	13.1	11.5	8.7	8.5	10.0	11.7	15.5	18.3	22.0	26.9	24.6	29.5	42.6	40.0	35.7
As a percentage of	Imp.	3.2	3.0	2.3	2.0	2.1	2.1	2.5	2.7	2.7	2.8	2.8	3.0	3.6	3.4	2.9
SITC section (%)	Exp.	3.3	3.0	2.2	2.0	2.1	2.1	2.6	2.7	2.8	2.8	2.8	3.1	3.7	3.4	2.8
As a percentage of	Imp.	0.2	0.2	0.2	0.1	0.1	0.1	0.2	0.2	0.2	0.2	0.2	0.2	0.2	0.2	0.2
world trade (%)	Exp.	0.2	0.2	0.1	0.1	0.1	0.1	0.1	0.2	0.2	0.2	0.2	0.2	0.2	0.2	0.2

Graph 1: Annual growth rates of exports, 1999–2013
(In percentage by year)

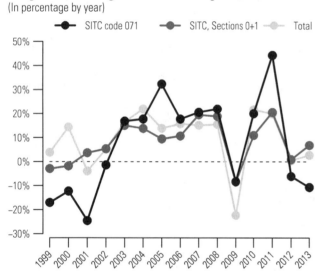

Table 2: Top exporting countries or areas in 2013

Country or area	Value (million US$)	Avg. Growth (%) 09-13	Growth (%) 12-13	World share %	Cum.
World	35 717.7	9.7	-10.7	100.0	
Brazil	5 275.7	5.4	-18.4	14.8	14.8
Germany	3 438.5	8.1	-6.9	9.6	24.4
Viet Nam	2 883.2	13.1	-21.5	8.1	32.5
Switzerland	2 414.0	21.2	18.4	6.8	39.2
Colombia	2 166.3	4.8	-1.8	6.1	45.3
Indonesia	1 468.4	12.4	-6.3	4.1	49.4
Italy	1 443.0	10.7	7.0	4.0	53.4
USA	1 148.8	11.5	-10.0	3.2	56.7
France	900.9	17.5	34.4	2.5	59.2
Belgium	870.2	-3.9	-36.3	2.4	61.6
India	863.9	20.5	-4.2	2.4	64.0
Honduras	796.9	11.4	-40.5	2.2	66.3
Ethiopia	770.8	20.2	-13.5	2.2	68.4
Guatemala	721.0	5.0	-25.6	2.0	70.4
Mexico	709.7	10.4	-22.7	2.0	72.4

Graph 2: Trade Balance by MDG regions 2013
(Bln US$)

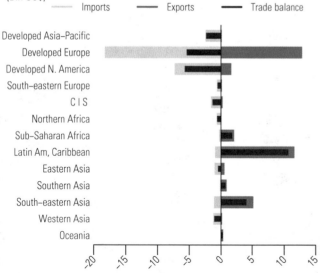

Table 3: Top importing countries or areas in 2013

Country or area	Value (million US$)	Avg. Growth (%) 09-13	Growth (%) 12-13	World share %	Cum.
World	35 702.9	9.2	-10.9	100.0	
USA	5 973.2	9.2	-17.8	16.7	16.7
Germany	4 026.4	5.3	-21.0	11.3	28.0
France	2 677.5	12.7	1.8	7.5	35.5
Japan	1 773.9	8.4	-5.4	5.0	40.5
Italy	1 732.7	7.4	-12.7	4.9	45.3
Canada	1 341.0	10.2	-14.8	3.8	49.1
Belgium	1 242.6	3.7	-16.5	3.5	52.6
Spain	1 119.6	7.0	-11.0	3.1	55.7
United Kingdom	1 085.9	4.7	-14.3	3.0	58.7
Russian Federation	971.0	12.6	-1.0	2.7	61.5
Netherlands	919.4	11.2	-5.2	2.6	64.0
Switzerland	749.4	13.7	-11.9	2.1	66.1
Poland	712.9	6.7	-10.8	2.0	68.1
Sweden	559.5	10.8	-20.0	1.6	69.7
Australia	559.4	13.0	-9.1	1.6	71.3

In 2013, the value (in current US$) of exports of "cocoa" (SITC group 072) decreased by 11.7 percent (compared to 2.3 percent average growth rate from 2009-2013) to reach 17.2 bln US$ (see table 2), while imports decreased by 1.1 percent to reach 17.3 bln US$ (see table 3). Exports of this commodity accounted for 1.4 percent of world exports of SITC sections 0+1, and 0.1 percent of total world merchandise exports (see table 1). Côte d'Ivoire, Netherlands and Nigeria were the top exporters in 2013 (see table 2). They accounted for 18.1, 16.7 and 11.7 percent of world exports, respectively. Netherlands, USA and Germany were the top destinations, with respectively 14.1, 12.1 and 11.1 percent of world imports (see table 3).

The top 15 countries/areas accounted for 90.6 and 79.8 percent of total world exports and imports, respectively (see tables 2 and 3). In 2013, Côte d'Ivoire was the country/area with the highest value of net exports (+3.1 bln US$), followed by Nigeria (+2.0 bln US$). By MDG regions (see graph 2), the largest surpluses in this product group were recorded by Sub-Saharan Africa (+7.1 bln US$), South-eastern Asia (+917.1 mln US$) and Latin America and the Caribbean (+648.2 mln US$). The largest trade deficits were recorded by Developed Europe (-4.1 bln US$), Developed North America (-2.2 bln US$) and Commonwealth of Independent States (-945.7 mln US$).

Table 1: Imports (Imp.) and exports (Exp.), 1999-2013, in current US$

		1999	2000	2001	2002	2003	2004	2005	2006	2007	2008	2009	2010	2011	2012	2013
Values in Bln US$	Imp.	6.0	4.6	4.9	6.8	9.8	9.3	9.9	10.1	12.2	15.4	16.1	19.2	23.4	17.5	17.3
	Exp.	5.1	3.9	4.3	6.6	8.0	8.5	8.4	9.0	10.5	13.1	15.7	17.9	19.7	19.5	17.2
As a percentage of SITC section (%)	Imp.	1.4	1.1	1.2	1.5	1.9	1.6	1.5	1.4	1.5	1.6	1.8	2.0	2.0	1.5	1.4
	Exp.	1.3	1.0	1.1	1.6	1.7	1.5	1.4	1.3	1.3	1.4	1.8	1.9	1.7	1.7	1.4
As a percentage of world trade (%)	Imp.	0.1	0.1	0.1	0.1	0.1	0.1	0.1	0.1	0.1	0.1	0.1	0.1	0.1	0.1	0.1
	Exp.	0.1	0.1	0.1	0.1	0.1	0.1	0.1	0.1	0.1	0.1	0.1	0.1	0.1	0.1	0.1

Graph 1: Annual growth rates of exports, 1999–2013
(In percentage by year)

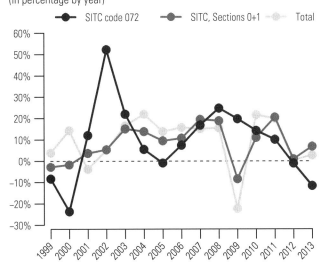

Table 2: Top exporting countries or areas in 2013

Country or area	Value (million US$)	Avg. Growth (%) 09-13	Growth (%) 12-13	World share %	Cum.
World	17 230.6	2.3	-11.7	100.0	
Côte d'Ivoire	3 113.7	-3.6	-5.3	18.1	18.1
Netherlands	2 870.7	2.8	4.1	16.7	34.7
Nigeria	2 023.4	9.1	-46.6	11.7	46.5
Ghana	1 449.5	5.9	-28.6	8.4	54.9
Indonesia	1 103.5	-5.5	10.5	6.4	61.3
Malaysia	983.9	4.2	-6.4	5.7	67.0
Germany	783.8	10.9	5.2	4.5	71.6
France	746.6	2.7	4.7	4.3	75.9
Cameroon	540.9	-3.0	13.3	3.1	79.0
Ecuador	509.4	6.4	19.3	3.0	82.0
Belgium	422.9	3.4	-3.8	2.5	84.4
USA	325.8	9.5	-4.4	1.9	86.3
Singapore	294.0	2.4	-10.9	1.7	88.0
Estonia	235.5	11.1	5.9	1.4	89.4
Spain	213.4	7.0	-20.7	1.2	90.6

Graph 2: Trade Balance by MDG regions 2013
(Bln US$)

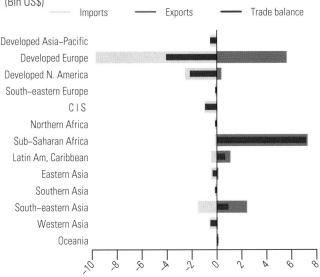

Table 3: Top importing countries or areas in 2013

Country or area	Value (million US$)	Avg. Growth (%) 09-13	Growth (%) 12-13	World share %	Cum.
World	17 333.5	1.8	-1.1	100.0	
Netherlands	2 449.1	0.7	3.0	14.1	14.1
USA	2 100.0	-1.0	-2.0	12.1	26.2
Germany	1 920.7	0.2	-2.7	11.1	37.3
Belgium	1 308.4	5.5	19.4	7.5	44.9
France	1 149.8	-0.9	4.0	6.6	51.5
Malaysia	947.7	4.4	-8.5	5.5	57.0
Russian Federation	625.3	4.4	9.9	3.6	60.6
Italy	541.2	3.9	-2.9	3.1	63.7
United Kingdom	510.8	-12.2	-5.7	2.9	66.7
Canada	430.0	3.4	1.4	2.5	69.1
Spain	422.3	6.0	-9.6	2.4	71.6
Turkey	400.7	15.0	10.0	2.3	73.9
China	362.0	22.2	4.0	2.1	76.0
Poland	342.0	6.1	2.7	2.0	77.9
Japan	315.7	-3.5	-17.5	1.8	79.8

073 Chocolate and other food preparations containing cocoa, nes

In 2013, the value (in current US$) of exports of "chocolate and other food preparations containing cocoa, nes" (SITC group 073) increased by 9.5 percent (compared to 9.7 percent average growth rate from 2009-2013) to reach 26.4 bln US$ (see table 2), while imports increased by 9.8 percent to reach 25.6 bln US$ (see table 3). Exports of this commodity accounted for 2.1 percent of world exports of SITC sections 0+1, and 0.1 percent of total world merchandise exports (see table 1). Germany, Belgium and Netherlands were the top exporters in 2013 (see table 2). They accounted for 16.8, 11.0 and 7.0 percent of world exports, respectively. Germany, USA and United Kingdom were the top destinations, with respectively 8.6, 8.5 and 7.5 percent of world imports (see table 3).

The top 15 countries/areas accounted for 79.3 and 61.2 percent of total world exports and imports, respectively (see tables 2 and 3). In 2013, Germany was the country/area with the highest value of net exports (+2.2 bln US$), followed by Belgium (+2.1 bln US$). By MDG regions (see graph 2), the largest surpluses in this product group were recorded by Developed Europe (+4.8 bln US$) and South-eastern Asia (+41.5 mln US$). The largest trade deficits were recorded by Developed Asia-Pacific (-896.2 mln US$), Eastern Asia (-706.2 mln US$) and Western Asia (-658.6 mln US$).

Table 1: Imports (Imp.) and exports (Exp.), 1999-2013, in current US$

		1999	2000	2001	2002	2003	2004	2005	2006	2007	2008	2009	2010	2011	2012	2013
Values in Bln US$	Imp.	6.9	6.7	7.2	8.0	9.7	11.3	12.3	13.6	16.3	18.7	17.6	19.3	22.9	23.3	25.6
	Exp.	7.1	6.9	7.6	8.2	10.0	11.7	12.6	14.0	16.9	19.3	18.2	20.0	23.6	24.1	26.4
As a percentage of SITC section (%)	Imp.	1.7	1.6	1.7	1.8	1.9	1.9	1.9	2.0	2.0	1.9	2.0	2.0	1.9	2.0	2.1
	Exp.	1.8	1.8	1.9	1.9	2.1	2.1	2.1	2.1	2.1	2.0	2.1	2.1	2.0	2.1	2.1
As a percentage of world trade (%)	Imp.	0.1	0.1	0.1	0.1	0.1	0.1	0.1	0.1	0.1	0.1	0.1	0.1	0.1	0.1	0.1
	Exp.	0.1	0.1	0.1	0.1	0.1	0.1	0.1	0.1	0.1	0.1	0.1	0.1	0.1	0.1	0.1

Graph 1: Annual growth rates of exports, 1999–2013
(In percentage by year)

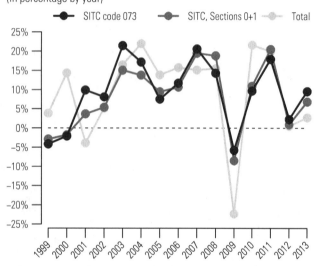

Graph 2: Trade Balance by MDG regions 2013
(Bln US$)

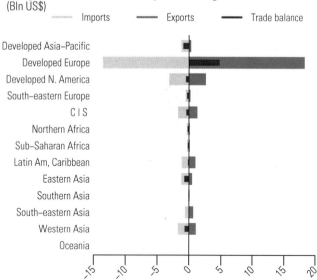

Table 2: Top exporting countries or areas in 2013

Country or area	Value (million US$)	Avg. Growth (%) 09-13	Growth (%) 12-13	World share %	Cum.
World	26 395.4	9.7	9.5	100.0	
Germany	4 434.8	9.1	12.3	16.8	16.8
Belgium	2 909.1	6.9	17.0	11.0	27.8
Netherlands	1 847.7	9.7	8.4	7.0	34.8
Italy	1 608.4	7.8	0.1	6.1	40.9
France	1 552.2	5.1	1.4	5.9	46.8
USA	1 543.7	13.4	12.4	5.8	52.6
Poland	1 414.1	20.5	28.6	5.4	58.0
Canada	1 070.5	12.6	5.0	4.1	62.1
United Kingdom	894.1	11.6	9.4	3.4	65.4
Switzerland	822.3	4.7	7.8	3.1	68.6
Russian Federation	666.8	23.1	20.0	2.5	71.1
Mexico	598.4	11.1	-1.3	2.3	73.4
Turkey	542.7	13.4	13.3	2.1	75.4
Ukraine	526.6	5.2	-16.8	2.0	77.4
Austria	512.4	5.1	22.0	1.9	79.3

Table 3: Top importing countries or areas in 2013

Country or area	Value (million US$)	Avg. Growth (%) 09-13	Growth (%) 12-13	World share %	Cum.
World	25 557.4	9.8	9.8	100.0	
Germany	2 202.2	10.5	11.2	8.6	8.6
USA	2 167.9	11.4	4.5	8.5	17.1
United Kingdom	1 905.4	6.7	11.2	7.5	24.6
France	1 900.3	4.5	5.8	7.4	32.0
Netherlands	1 095.9	10.3	18.3	4.3	36.3
Canada	908.8	7.3	6.1	3.6	39.8
Russian Federation	779.0	14.2	-5.7	3.0	42.9
Belgium	772.8	10.3	21.9	3.0	45.9
Japan	614.8	7.9	-1.8	2.4	48.3
Italy	595.0	5.3	3.4	2.3	50.6
Spain	589.2	1.4	11.1	2.3	52.9
Poland	574.5	16.2	26.3	2.2	55.2
Saudi Arabia	540.9	19.5	3.5	2.1	57.3
Austria	533.0	6.0	12.1	2.1	59.4
Mexico	453.4	12.6	-0.2	1.8	61.2

In 2013, the value (in current US$) of exports of "tea and mate" (SITC group 074) increased by 9.5 percent (compared to 9.3 percent average growth rate from 2009-2013) to reach 8.9 bln US$ (see table 2), while imports increased by 6.2 percent to reach 8.1 bln US$ (see table 3). Exports of this commodity accounted for 0.7 percent of world exports of SITC sections 0+1, and less than 0.1 percent of total world merchandise exports (see table 1). Sri Lanka, China and Kenya were the top exporters in 2013 (see table 2). They accounted for 17.3, 15.0 and 13.7 percent of world exports, respectively. Russian Federation, USA and United Arab Emirates were the top destinations, with respectively 8.4, 8.0 and 6.9 percent of world imports (see table 3).

The top 15 countries/areas accounted for 82.5 and 60.9 percent of total world exports and imports, respectively (see tables 2 and 3). In 2013, Sri Lanka was the country/area with the highest value of net exports (+1.5 bln US$), followed by China (+1.3 bln US$). By MDG regions (see graph 2), the largest surpluses in this product group were recorded by Southern Asia (+1.8 bln US$), Sub-Saharan Africa (+1.4 bln US$) and Eastern Asia (+1.2 bln US$). The largest trade deficits were recorded by Western Asia (-1.1 bln US$), Commonwealth of Independent States (-1.0 bln US$) and Northern Africa (-533.1 mln US$).

Table 1: Imports (Imp.) and exports (Exp.), 1999-2013, in current US$

		1999	2000	2001	2002	2003	2004	2005	2006	2007	2008	2009	2010	2011	2012	2013
Values in Bln US$	Imp.	3.1	3.1	3.1	3.1	3.3	3.7	4.0	4.4	4.9	6.0	5.8	6.8	7.6	7.7	8.1
	Exp.	3.1	3.2	3.2	2.8	3.4	3.8	4.2	4.7	5.3	6.4	6.3	7.2	8.1	8.2	8.9
As a percentage of	Imp.	0.7	0.8	0.7	0.7	0.6	0.6	0.6	0.6	0.6	0.6	0.7	0.7	0.6	0.6	0.7
SITC section (%)	Exp.	0.8	0.8	0.8	0.7	0.7	0.7	0.7	0.7	0.7	0.7	0.7	0.7	0.7	0.7	0.7
As a percentage of	Imp.	0.1	0.0	0.0	0.0	0.0	0.0	0.0	0.0	0.0	0.0	0.0	0.0	0.0	0.0	0.0
world trade (%)	Exp.	0.1	0.1	0.1	0.0	0.0	0.0	0.0	0.0	0.0	0.0	0.1	0.0	0.0	0.0	0.0

Graph 1: Annual growth rates of exports, 1999–2013
(In percentage by year)

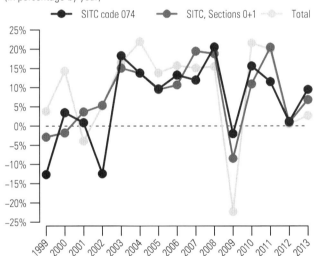

Table 2: Top exporting countries or areas in 2013

Country or area	Value (million US$)	Avg. Growth (%) 09-13	Growth (%) 12-13	World share %	Cum.
World...............................	8936.9	9.3	9.5	100.0	
Sri Lanka...........................	1544.0	6.8	9.2	17.3	17.3
China..............................	1340.6	16.0	19.6	15.0	32.3
Kenya..............................	1221.4	8.1	-9.6	13.7	45.9
India..............................	858.8	10.2	18.9	9.6	55.6
USA................................	336.1	14.7	11.0	3.8	59.3
Germany............................	324.9	6.6	16.2	3.6	63.0
Netherlands........................	299.2	5.7	14.5	3.3	66.3
Viet Nam...........................	230.2	6.3	1.9	2.6	68.9
United Kingdom.....................	218.4	-7.1	4.7	2.4	71.3
Poland.............................	214.8	34.6	19.9	2.4	73.7
Ireland............................	202.2	37.9	18.5	2.3	76.0
Argentina..........................	202.1	16.0	13.8	2.3	78.2
Indonesia..........................	160.8	-2.0	0.3	1.8	80.0
Brazil.............................	109.1	20.4	37.1	1.2	81.3
Canada.............................	106.7	2.0	-4.0	1.2	82.5

Graph 2: Trade Balance by MDG regions 2013
(Bln US$)

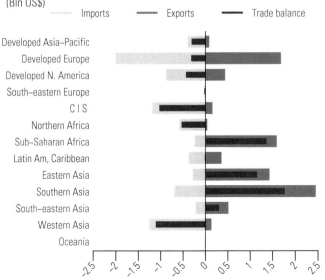

Table 3: Top importing countries or areas in 2013

Country or area	Value (million US$)	Avg. Growth (%) 09-13	Growth (%) 12-13	World share %	Cum.
World...............................	8122.5	8.7	6.2	100.0	
Russian Federation.................	685.5	6.5	1.6	8.4	8.4
USA................................	653.2	9.0	6.0	8.0	16.5
United Arab Emirates...............	563.1	11.7	11.4	6.9	23.4
United Kingdom.....................	437.3	3.6	-3.1	5.4	28.8
Pakistan...........................	318.5	9.2	-11.9	3.9	32.7
Egypt..............................	307.6	7.8	-7.0	3.8	36.5
Germany............................	284.1	9.5	13.7	3.5	40.0
Netherlands........................	251.0	20.4	32.4	3.1	43.1
Japan..............................	239.4	5.0	-1.9	2.9	46.0
France.............................	238.2	9.3	12.3	2.9	49.0
Saudi Arabia.......................	237.2	6.2	-5.3	2.9	51.9
Canada.............................	222.2	3.7	-4.8	2.7	54.6
Morocco............................	189.6	15.1	13.3	2.3	57.0
Ukraine............................	166.3	11.1	1.5	2.0	59.0
Kazakhstan.........................	154.9	13.4	6.0	1.9	60.9

075 Spices

In 2013, the value (in current US$) of exports of "spices" (SITC group 075) increased by 5.7 percent (compared to 12.8 percent average growth rate from 2009-2013) to reach 8.3 bln US$ (see table 2), while imports increased by 4.2 percent to reach 7.6 bln US$ (see table 3). Exports of this commodity accounted for 0.7 percent of world exports of SITC sections 0+1, and less than 0.1 percent of total world merchandise exports (see table 1). India, Viet Nam and China were the top exporters in 2013 (see table 2). They accounted for 15.7, 12.0 and 9.5 percent of world exports, respectively. USA, Germany and Netherlands were the top destinations, with respectively 16.4, 7.2 and 4.7 percent of world imports (see table 3).

The top 15 countries/areas accounted for 76.0 and 67.0 percent of total world exports and imports, respectively (see tables 2 and 3). In 2013, India was the country/area with the highest value of net exports (+1.0 bln US$), followed by Viet Nam (+868.6 mln US$). By MDG regions (see graph 2), the largest surpluses in this product group were recorded by Southern Asia (+1.4 bln US$), South-eastern Asia (+1.2 bln US$) and Eastern Asia (+642.0 mln US$). The largest trade deficits were recorded by Developed North America (-1.2 bln US$), Developed Europe (-1.0 bln US$) and Western Asia (-390.8 mln US$).

Table 1: Imports (Imp.) and exports (Exp.), 1999-2013, in current US$

		1999	2000	2001	2002	2003	2004	2005	2006	2007	2008	2009	2010	2011	2012	2013
Values in Bln US$	Imp.	2.8	2.9	2.7	2.7	3.0	3.2	3.1	3.3	4.1	4.9	4.7	5.8	7.7	7.3	7.6
	Exp.	2.6	2.7	2.5	2.6	2.8	3.1	3.0	3.4	4.4	5.2	5.1	6.0	8.1	7.8	8.3
As a percentage of	Imp.	0.7	0.7	0.6	0.6	0.6	0.6	0.5	0.5	0.5	0.5	0.5	0.6	0.6	0.6	0.6
SITC section (%)	Exp.	0.7	0.7	0.6	0.6	0.6	0.6	0.5	0.5	0.6	0.6	0.6	0.6	0.7	0.7	0.7
As a percentage of	Imp.	0.0	0.0	0.0	0.0	0.0	0.0	0.0	0.0	0.0	0.0	0.0	0.0	0.0	0.0	0.0
world trade (%)	Exp.	0.0	0.0	0.0	0.0	0.0	0.0	0.0	0.0	0.0	0.0	0.0	0.0	0.0	0.0	0.0

Graph 1: Annual growth rates of exports, 1999–2013
(In percentage by year)

Legend: SITC code 075 — SITC, Sections 0+1 — Total

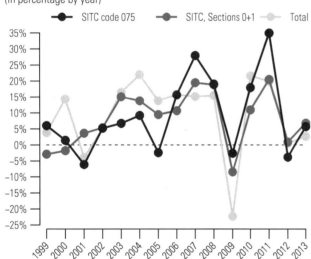

Table 2: Top exporting countries or areas in 2013

Country or area	Value (million US$)	Avg. Growth (%) 09-13	Growth (%) 12-13	World share %	Cum.
World	8 274.5	12.8	5.7	100.0	
India	1 295.4	16.5	-7.2	15.7	15.7
Viet Nam	989.6	26.1	13.9	12.0	27.6
China	782.3	6.1	17.1	9.5	37.1
Indonesia	617.0	24.5	-9.4	7.5	44.5
Netherlands	371.1	13.4	3.0	4.5	49.0
Sri Lanka	334.8	29.8	39.4	4.0	53.1
Germany	307.2	14.5	22.0	3.7	56.8
Brazil	253.5	16.1	22.6	3.1	59.8
Spain	231.4	1.8	-0.5	2.8	62.6
Guatemala	221.3	-7.8	-12.3	2.7	65.3
Iran	*207.0*	-10.4	-14.1	2.5	67.8
Singapore	197.0	13.2	-15.2	2.4	70.2
United Arab Emirates	*180.6*	33.3	21.7	2.2	72.4
Madagascar	157.9	12.6	-15.1	1.9	74.3
USA	142.5	12.1	5.3	1.7	76.0

Graph 2: Trade Balance by MDG regions 2013
(Bln US$)

Legend: Imports — Exports — Trade balance

Developed Asia–Pacific
Developed Europe
Developed N. America
South–eastern Europe
CIS
Northern Africa
Sub–Saharan Africa
Latin Am, Caribbean
Eastern Asia
Southern Asia
South–eastern Asia
Western Asia
Oceania

(axis: -2.5, -2, -1.5, -1, -0.5, 0, 0.5, 1, 1.5, 2, 2.5)

Table 3: Top importing countries or areas in 2013

Country or area	Value (million US$)	Avg. Growth (%) 09-13	Growth (%) 12-13	World share %	Cum.
World	7 570.2	12.5	4.2	100.0	
USA	1 243.3	16.1	7.2	16.4	16.4
Germany	548.8	16.7	19.3	7.2	23.7
Netherlands	354.5	19.4	15.8	4.7	28.4
United Arab Emirates	*349.7*	22.0	11.4	4.6	33.0
Saudi Arabia	313.1	15.6	2.9	4.1	37.1
Japan	311.1	8.1	-2.1	4.1	41.2
United Kingdom	307.7	14.2	12.9	4.1	45.3
India	274.0	12.6	-5.6	3.6	48.9
Singapore	261.0	14.5	5.2	3.4	52.4
France	233.1	10.7	17.4	3.1	55.4
Spain	231.7	4.0	-1.4	3.1	58.5
Malaysia	209.9	3.9	0.2	2.8	61.3
Canada	163.3	11.4	14.2	2.2	63.4
Mexico	149.4	5.2	23.0	2.0	65.4
Viet Nam	120.9	39.7	-5.0	1.6	67.0

In 2013, the value (in current US$) of exports of "feeding stuff for animals (not including unmilled cereals)" (SITC group 081) increased by 11.1 percent (compared to 12.0 percent average growth rate from 2009-2013) to reach 83.1 bln US$ (see table 2), while imports increased by 8.8 percent to reach 85.4 bln US$ (see table 3). Exports of this commodity accounted for 6.6 percent of world exports of SITC sections 0+1, and 0.4 percent of total world merchandise exports (see table 1). USA, Argentina and Brazil were the top exporters in 2013 (see table 2). They accounted for 15.8, 14.5 and 8.6 percent of world exports, respectively. Netherlands, Germany and Japan were the top destinations, with respectively 6.2, 5.3 and 4.9 percent of world imports (see table 3).

The top 15 countries/areas accounted for 79.0 and 55.8 percent of total world exports and imports, respectively (see tables 2 and 3). In 2013, Argentina was the country/area with the highest value of net exports (+12.0 bln US$), followed by USA (+10.1 bln US$). By MDG regions (see graph 2), the largest surpluses in this product group were recorded by Latin America and the Caribbean (+16.0 bln US$), Developed North America (+10.7 bln US$) and Southern Asia (+2.2 bln US$). The largest trade deficits were recorded by South-eastern Asia (-7.6 bln US$), Developed Europe (-7.3 bln US$) and Eastern Asia (-4.5 bln US$).

Table 1: Imports (Imp.) and exports (Exp.), 1999-2013, in current US$

		1999	2000	2001	2002	2003	2004	2005	2006	2007	2008	2009	2010	2011	2012	2013
Values in Bln US$	Imp.	20.6	22.4	23.8	24.9	27.9	33.2	33.5	36.2	45.2	60.5	56.1	61.8	71.3	78.5	85.4
	Exp.	18.9	20.2	21.9	23.0	25.5	29.5	30.0	33.0	41.4	54.6	52.8	57.5	67.3	74.8	83.1
As a percentage of	Imp.	4.9	5.4	5.6	5.6	5.4	5.7	5.2	5.2	5.4	6.2	6.3	6.3	6.0	6.7	6.9
SITC section (%)	Exp.	4.8	5.2	5.5	5.4	5.2	5.3	5.0	4.9	5.2	5.7	6.1	6.0	5.8	6.4	6.6
As a percentage of	Imp.	0.4	0.3	0.4	0.4	0.4	0.4	0.3	0.3	0.3	0.4	0.4	0.4	0.4	0.4	0.5
world trade (%)	Exp.	0.3	0.3	0.4	0.4	0.3	0.3	0.3	0.3	0.3	0.3	0.4	0.4	0.4	0.4	0.4

Graph 1: Annual growth rates of exports, 1999–2013
(In percentage by year)

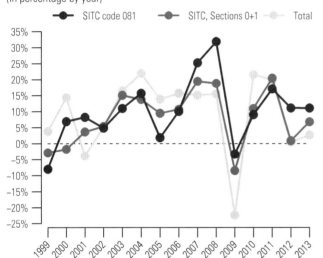

— SITC code 081 — SITC, Sections 0+1 Total

Graph 2: Trade Balance by MDG regions 2013
(Bln US$)

Imports — Exports — Trade balance

Developed Asia–Pacific
Developed Europe
Developed N. America
South–eastern Europe
CIS
Northern Africa
Sub–Saharan Africa
Latin Am, Caribbean
Eastern Asia
Southern Asia
South–eastern Asia
Western Asia
Oceania

Table 2: Top exporting countries or areas in 2013

Country or area	Value (million US$)	Avg. Growth (%) 09-13	Growth (%) 12-13	World share %	Cum.
World	83 073.9	12.0	11.1	100.0	
USA	13 140.7	13.1	18.1	15.8	15.8
Argentina	12 038.7	8.7	9.5	14.5	30.3
Brazil	7 140.6	10.0	3.5	8.6	38.9
Netherlands	6 610.1	11.2	12.8	8.0	46.9
Germany	4 738.1	9.0	8.6	5.7	52.6
India	3 697.6	21.3	40.1	4.5	57.0
France	3 494.2	5.7	9.8	4.2	61.2
China	2 756.9	11.5	-6.9	3.3	64.5
Belgium	2 684.1	14.1	19.2	3.2	67.8
Canada	2 325.4	25.1	8.8	2.8	70.6
Peru	1 514.6	0.0	-22.0	1.8	72.4
Spain	1 479.0	15.7	6.3	1.8	74.2
United Kingdom	1 458.0	12.2	15.1	1.8	75.9
Thailand	1 432.2	16.6	12.4	1.7	77.7
Denmark	1 089.6	2.3	8.7	1.3	79.0

Table 3: Top importing countries or areas in 2013

Country or area	Value (million US$)	Avg. Growth (%) 09-13	Growth (%) 12-13	World share %	Cum.
World	85 388.5	11.0	8.8	100.0	
Netherlands	5 280.5	14.1	8.2	6.2	6.2
Germany	4 520.0	6.3	4.9	5.3	11.5
Japan	4 152.5	4.3	-5.0	4.9	16.3
China	3 958.7	20.8	22.5	4.6	21.0
France	3 607.1	5.5	8.4	4.2	25.2
United Kingdom	3 263.0	7.4	18.1	3.8	29.0
Viet Nam	3 084.6	15.0	25.3	3.6	32.6
Indonesia	3 044.1	16.0	8.7	3.6	36.2
USA	3 004.8	22.2	8.5	3.5	39.7
Rep. of Korea	2 749.9	12.8	15.4	3.2	42.9
Italy	2 583.1	5.2	8.9	3.0	46.0
Belgium	2 397.0	7.9	16.7	2.8	48.8
Thailand	2 261.3	13.0	10.5	2.6	51.4
Spain	2 000.6	1.3	-4.0	2.3	53.8
Canada	1 729.2	6.0	0.1	2.0	55.8

091 Margarine and shortening

In 2013, the value (in current US$) of exports of "margarine and shortening" (SITC group 091) increased by 0.4 percent (compared to 6.8 percent average growth rate from 2009-2013) to reach 6.2 bln US$ (see table 2), while imports decreased by 2.1 percent to reach 5.4 bln US$ (see table 3). Exports of this commodity accounted for 0.5 percent of world exports of SITC sections 0+1, and less than 0.1 percent of total world merchandise exports (see table 1). Belgium, Netherlands and Indonesia were the top exporters in 2013 (see table 2). They accounted for 13.7, 11.2 and 9.6 percent of world exports, respectively. France, Germany and China were the top destinations, with respectively 8.3, 6.4 and 5.1 percent of world imports (see table 3).

The top 15 countries/areas accounted for 78.6 and 53.5 percent of total world exports and imports, respectively (see tables 2 and 3). In 2013, Belgium was the country/area with the highest value of net exports (+714.1 mln US$), followed by Indonesia (+560.4 mln US$). By MDG regions (see graph 2), the largest surpluses in this product group were recorded by South-eastern Asia (+885.3 mln US$), Developed Europe (+800.6 mln US$) and Developed North America (+225.3 mln US$). The largest trade deficits were recorded by Eastern Asia (-374.4 mln US$), Latin America and the Caribbean (-196.9 mln US$) and Sub-Saharan Africa (-166.5 mln US$).

Table 1: Imports (Imp.) and exports (Exp.), 1999-2013, in current US$

		1999	2000	2001	2002	2003	2004	2005	2006	2007	2008	2009	2010	2011	2012	2013
Values in Bln US$	Imp.	1.4	1.4	1.4	1.5	1.7	2.2	2.3	2.6	3.4	4.8	4.0	4.2	5.6	5.5	5.4
	Exp.	1.6	1.4	1.4	1.6	2.0	2.4	2.6	3.0	4.0	5.9	4.8	4.9	6.7	6.2	6.2
As a percentage of	Imp.	0.3	0.3	0.3	0.3	0.3	0.4	0.4	0.4	0.4	0.5	0.4	0.4	0.5	0.5	0.4
SITC section (%)	Exp.	0.4	0.4	0.3	0.4	0.4	0.4	0.4	0.4	0.5	0.6	0.5	0.5	0.6	0.5	0.5
As a percentage of	Imp.	0.0	0.0	0.0	0.0	0.0	0.0	0.0	0.0	0.0	0.0	0.0	0.0	0.0	0.0	0.0
world trade (%)	Exp.	0.0	0.0	0.0	0.0	0.0	0.0	0.0	0.0	0.0	0.0	0.0	0.0	0.0	0.0	0.0

Graph 1: Annual growth rates of exports, 1999–2013
(In percentage by year)

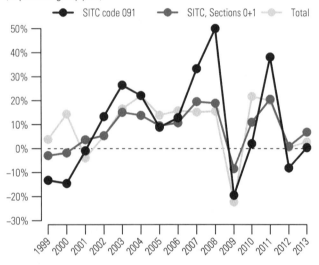

Legend: SITC code 091 — SITC, Sections 0+1 — Total

Table 2: Top exporting countries or areas in 2013

Country or area	Value (million US$)	Avg. Growth (%) 09-13	Growth (%) 12-13	World share %	Cum.
World	6 220.2	6.8	0.4	100.0	
Belgium	851.8	8.7	15.9	13.7	13.7
Netherlands	697.1	1.6	8.7	11.2	24.9
Indonesia	600.1	22.8	-25.6	9.6	34.5
USA	452.6	9.9	-0.5	7.3	41.8
Germany	384.4	6.0	-2.9	6.2	48.0
Sweden	320.5	12.2	27.3	5.2	53.2
Malaysia	307.1	-7.2	-0.9	4.9	58.1
Argentina	191.2	6.2	-19.3	3.1	61.2
Russian Federation	191.0	12.8	3.2	3.1	64.2
Turkey	189.1	19.4	23.9	3.0	67.3
Poland	186.8	11.1	0.3	3.0	70.3
Canada	155.1	10.1	28.4	2.5	72.8
Denmark	154.5	-6.0	-10.1	2.5	75.3
Spain	110.7	10.3	-0.9	1.8	77.0
Australia	97.1	8.8	-10.0	1.6	78.6

Graph 2: Trade Balance by MDG regions 2013
(Bln US$)

Legend: Imports — Exports — Trade balance

Regions (top to bottom): Developed Asia–Pacific, Developed Europe, Developed N. America, South–eastern Europe, CIS, Northern Africa, Sub-Saharan Africa, Latin Am, Caribbean, Eastern Asia, Southern Asia, South–eastern Asia, Western Asia, Oceania

Axis: -2.5 -2 -1.5 -1 -0.5 0 0.5 1 1.5 2 2.5 3 3.5

Table 3: Top importing countries or areas in 2013

Country or area	Value (million US$)	Avg. Growth (%) 09-13	Growth (%) 12-13	World share %	Cum.
World	5 392.4	7.8	-2.1	100.0	
France	445.4	3.0	-2.8	8.3	8.3
Germany	347.0	9.9	-2.6	6.4	14.7
China	273.7	54.3	-28.9	5.1	19.8
Chile	249.5	2.6	-26.3	4.6	24.4
USA	219.5	8.1	16.8	4.1	28.5
Netherlands	205.2	9.1	-4.7	3.8	32.3
Canada	159.3	9.2	3.8	3.0	35.2
Poland	153.5	20.8	-14.1	2.8	38.1
Russian Federation	144.5	12.8	14.3	2.7	40.8
United Kingdom	140.2	4.9	-5.9	2.6	43.4
Belgium	137.8	4.2	16.0	2.6	45.9
Italy	109.7	9.6	4.5	2.0	47.9
Spain	103.7	4.4	3.5	1.9	49.9
Ukraine	98.7	2.7	-16.3	1.8	51.7
Czech Rep	96.9	13.0	2.5	1.8	53.5

In 2013, the value (in current US$) of exports of "edible products and preparations, nes" (SITC group 098) increased by 13.5 percent (compared to 10.8 percent average growth rate from 2009-2013) to reach 71.7 bln US$ (see table 2), while imports increased by 11.5 percent to reach 72.3 bln US$ (see table 3). Exports of this commodity accounted for 5.7 percent of world exports of SITC sections 0+1, and 0.4 percent of total world merchandise exports (see table 1). USA, Netherlands and Germany were the top exporters in 2013 (see table 2). They accounted for 11.5, 9.1 and 8.0 percent of world exports, respectively. USA, United Kingdom and Germany were the top destinations, with respectively 6.0, 5.7 and 4.5 percent of world imports (see table 3).

The top 15 countries/areas accounted for 68.4 and 50.2 percent of total world exports and imports, respectively (see tables 2 and 3). In 2013, Netherlands was the country/area with the highest value of net exports (+4.2 bln US$), followed by USA (+3.9 bln US$). By MDG regions (see graph 2), the largest surpluses in this product group were recorded by Developed Europe (+10.7 bln US$), Developed North America (+2.7 bln US$) and South-eastern Asia (+1.4 bln US$). The largest trade deficits were recorded by Western Asia (-3.1 bln US$), Sub-Saharan Africa (-2.6 bln US$) and Commonwealth of Independent States (-2.4 bln US$).

Table 1: Imports (Imp.) and exports (Exp.), 1999-2013, in current US$

		1999	2000	2001	2002	2003	2004	2005	2006	2007	2008	2009	2010	2011	2012	2013
Values in Bln US$	Imp.	18.9	18.5	20.0	22.1	26.2	31.0	34.3	37.6	44.2	51.9	51.0	54.5	67.2	64.9	72.3
	Exp.	17.5	17.7	19.1	20.8	24.7	29.2	32.6	35.7	41.9	49.3	47.7	52.2	61.2	63.2	71.7
As a percentage of	Imp.	4.5	4.5	4.7	4.9	5.1	5.3	5.4	5.4	5.3	5.3	5.7	5.6	5.7	5.5	5.8
SITC section (%)	Exp.	4.4	4.6	4.8	4.9	5.1	5.3	5.4	5.3	5.2	5.2	5.5	5.4	5.3	5.4	5.7
As a percentage of	Imp.	0.3	0.3	0.3	0.3	0.3	0.3	0.3	0.3	0.3	0.3	0.4	0.4	0.4	0.4	0.4
world trade (%)	Exp.	0.3	0.3	0.3	0.3	0.3	0.3	0.3	0.3	0.3	0.3	0.4	0.3	0.3	0.3	0.4

Graph 1: Annual growth rates of exports, 1999–2013
(In percentage by year)

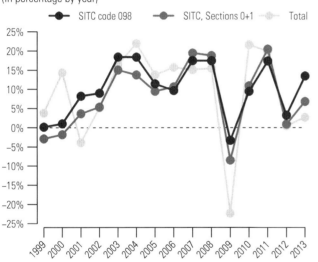

Graph 2: Trade Balance by MDG regions 2013
(Bln US$)

Table 2: Top exporting countries or areas in 2013

Country or area	Value (million US$)	Avg. Growth (%) 09-13	Growth (%) 12-13	World share %	Cum.
World	71 706.6	10.8	13.5	100.0	
USA	8 256.4	11.9	11.2	11.5	11.5
Netherlands	6 528.4	11.3	13.8	9.1	20.6
Germany	5 761.0	6.9	13.1	8.0	28.7
France	3 909.5	8.6	10.6	5.5	34.1
China	3 181.0	14.9	9.6	4.4	38.5
Italy	2 789.1	6.2	10.2	3.9	42.4
Singapore	2 577.6	22.7	33.8	3.6	46.0
Belgium	2 389.1	12.1	17.4	3.3	49.4
Thailand	2 186.0	13.7	10.5	3.0	52.4
Ireland	2 169.0	4.1	18.1	3.0	55.4
Denmark	2 133.2	8.8	19.7	3.0	58.4
United Kingdom	2 090.8	9.6	16.9	2.9	61.3
Canada	1 732.8	7.9	5.2	2.4	63.7
Spain	1 676.3	6.5	13.1	2.3	66.1
Poland	1 660.7	14.6	27.2	2.3	68.4

Table 3: Top importing countries or areas in 2013

Country or area	Value (million US$)	Avg. Growth (%) 09-13	Growth (%) 12-13	World share %	Cum.
World	72 345.8	9.2	11.5	100.0	
USA	4 341.6	8.9	6.7	6.0	6.0
United Kingdom	4 107.0	5.4	9.4	5.7	11.7
Germany	3 245.2	-1.3	13.8	4.5	16.2
China	3 137.3	24.1	29.7	4.3	20.5
Canada	2 811.3	9.1	7.0	3.9	24.4
France	2 666.6	4.9	8.9	3.7	28.1
Netherlands	2 328.7	12.6	16.0	3.2	31.3
Japan	2 097.1	5.8	-6.6	2.9	34.2
Australia	1 950.8	12.0	5.8	2.7	36.9
Saudi Arabia	1 923.8	15.6	2.8	2.7	39.5
Russian Federation	1 881.5	16.6	20.1	2.6	42.1
Belgium	1 634.0	7.2	16.9	2.3	44.4
Spain	1 502.1	-3.8	-4.5	2.1	46.5
Malaysia	1 376.4	18.2	10.7	1.9	48.4
Thailand	1 330.4	23.0	22.4	1.8	50.2

Beverages and tobacco

(SITC Section 1)

111 Non-alcoholic beverages, nes

In 2013, the value (in current US$) of exports of "non-alcoholic beverages, nes" (SITC group 111) increased by 9.9 percent (compared to 8.2 percent average growth rate from 2009-2013) to reach 21.1 bln US$ (see table 2), while imports increased by 8.0 percent to reach 19.9 bln US$ (see table 3). Exports of this commodity accounted for 1.7 percent of world exports of SITC sections 0+1, and 0.1 percent of total world merchandise exports (see table 1). Austria, Germany and Switzerland were the top exporters in 2013 (see table 2). They accounted for 8.7, 8.5 and 8.4 percent of world exports, respectively. USA, United Kingdom and Germany were the top destinations, with respectively 14.9, 6.3 and 5.8 percent of world imports (see table 3).

The top 15 countries/areas accounted for 74.9 and 61.8 percent of total world exports and imports, respectively (see tables 2 and 3). In 2013, Austria was the country/area with the highest value of net exports (+1.6 bln US$), followed by Switzerland (+1.5 bln US$). By MDG regions (see graph 2), the largest surpluses in this product group were recorded by Developed Europe (+5.3 bln US$), South-eastern Asia (+841.8 mln US$) and Eastern Asia (+79.1 mln US$). The largest trade deficits were recorded by Developed North America (-2.4 bln US$), Western Asia (-611.1 mln US$) and Developed Asia-Pacific (-593.5 mln US$).

Table 1: Imports (Imp.) and exports (Exp.), 1999-2013, in current US$

		1999	2000	2001	2002	2003	2004	2005	2006	2007	2008	2009	2010	2011	2012	2013
Values in Bln US$	Imp.	5.0	5.2	5.7	6.6	7.9	9.2	10.4	12.0	14.8	16.6	14.9	15.4	18.0	18.4	19.9
	Exp.	5.1	5.2	5.8	6.6	8.4	9.8	10.8	12.7	15.0	17.7	15.4	16.0	18.7	19.2	21.1
As a percentage of SITC section (%)	Imp.	1.2	1.3	1.3	1.5	1.5	1.6	1.6	1.7	1.8	1.7	1.7	1.6	1.5	1.6	1.6
	Exp.	1.3	1.3	1.4	1.5	1.7	1.8	1.8	1.9	1.9	1.9	1.8	1.7	1.6	1.6	1.7
As a percentage of world trade (%)	Imp.	0.1	0.1	0.1	0.1	0.1	0.1	0.1	0.1	0.1	0.1	0.1	0.1	0.1	0.1	0.1
	Exp.	0.1	0.1	0.1	0.1	0.1	0.1	0.1	0.1	0.1	0.1	0.1	0.1	0.1	0.1	0.1

Graph 1: Annual growth rates of exports, 1999–2013
(In percentage by year)

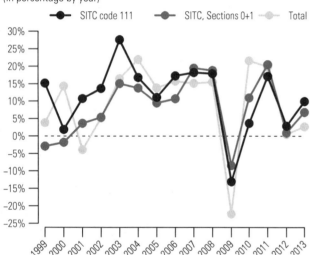

Graph 2: Trade Balance by MDG regions 2013
(Bln US$)

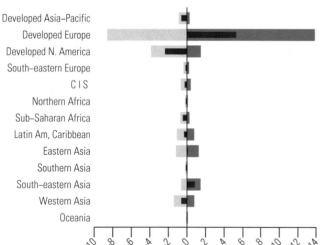

Table 2: Top exporting countries or areas in 2013

Country or area	Value (million US$)	Avg. Growth (%) 09-13	Growth (%) 12-13	World share %	Cum.
World	21 133.4	8.2	9.9	100.0	
Austria	1 839.4	3.4	-6.7	8.7	8.7
Germany	1 800.3	3.1	10.5	8.5	17.2
Switzerland	1 785.6	8.9	8.3	8.4	25.7
Netherlands	1 723.6	7.6	9.0	8.2	33.8
France	1 710.4	2.7	8.3	8.1	41.9
USA	1 314.7	10.0	11.2	6.2	48.1
Belgium	1 222.9	8.5	22.5	5.8	53.9
Italy	851.5	8.8	15.3	4.0	58.0
Thailand	798.6	31.2	21.2	3.8	61.7
China	706.9	12.7	9.4	3.3	65.1
United Kingdom	638.3	6.2	11.2	3.0	68.1
Denmark	442.1	36.3	67.5	2.1	70.2
Malaysia	368.4	27.8	18.5	1.7	71.9
Rep. of Korea	316.5	28.4	6.1	1.5	73.4
Poland	312.0	6.5	32.4	1.5	74.9

Table 3: Top importing countries or areas in 2013

Country or area	Value (million US$)	Avg. Growth (%) 09-13	Growth (%) 12-13	World share %	Cum.
World	19 861.3	7.4	8.0	100.0	
USA	2 958.7	13.8	13.1	14.9	14.9
United Kingdom	1 243.0	2.1	12.1	6.3	21.2
Germany	1 148.5	7.3	3.3	5.8	26.9
Belgium	990.7	4.0	2.9	5.0	31.9
France	975.0	2.8	6.7	4.9	36.8
Netherlands	881.7	1.4	6.8	4.4	41.3
Canada	870.5	7.6	7.6	4.4	45.7
China, Hong Kong SAR	749.1	7.6	9.9	3.8	49.4
Japan	530.2	1.0	-3.1	2.7	52.1
Spain	429.8	5.2	5.2	2.2	54.3
Switzerland	332.4	9.6	4.7	1.7	55.9
Ireland	322.1	-0.4	6.4	1.6	57.6
Russian Federation	292.2	21.2	42.1	1.5	59.0
Saudi Arabia	278.4	18.1	17.7	1.4	60.4
Australia	274.7	11.6	1.8	1.4	61.8

In 2013, the value (in current US$) of exports of "alcoholic beverages" (SITC group 112) increased by 5.5 percent (compared to 8.9 percent average growth rate from 2009-2013) to reach 81.6 bln US$ (see table 2), while imports increased by 5.3 percent to reach 80.1 bln US$ (see table 3). Exports of this commodity accounted for 6.5 percent of world exports of SITC sections 0+1, and 0.4 percent of total world merchandise exports (see table 1). France, United Kingdom and Italy were the top exporters in 2013 (see table 2). They accounted for 19.4, 12.5 and 9.9 percent of world exports, respectively. USA, United Kingdom and Germany were the top destinations, with respectively 20.8, 8.7 and 7.4 percent of world imports (see table 3).

The top 15 countries/areas accounted for 81.0 and 73.0 percent of total world exports and imports, respectively (see tables 2 and 3). In 2013, France was the country/area with the highest value of net exports (+12.9 bln US$), followed by Italy (+6.6 bln US$). By MDG regions (see graph 2), the largest surpluses in this product group were recorded by Developed Europe (+22.3 bln US$) and Latin America and the Caribbean (+4.4 bln US$). The largest trade deficits were recorded by Developed North America (-15.4 bln US$), Eastern Asia (-4.3 bln US$) and Commonwealth of Independent States (-2.8 bln US$).

Table 1: Imports (Imp.) and exports (Exp.), 1999-2013, in current US$

		1999	2000	2001	2002	2003	2004	2005	2006	2007	2008	2009	2010	2011	2012	2013
Values in Bln US$	Imp.	30.4	30.5	31.8	34.4	39.6	45.0	48.4	53.0	62.4	67.5	59.5	64.3	74.8	76.1	80.1
	Exp.	30.0	29.1	29.8	32.9	38.9	43.5	46.0	50.9	60.9	65.8	58.0	64.0	75.0	77.4	81.6
As a percentage of	Imp.	7.3	7.4	7.5	7.7	7.7	7.7	7.6	7.6	7.5	6.9	6.7	6.6	6.3	6.5	6.5
SITC section (%)	Exp.	7.6	7.5	7.4	7.8	8.0	7.9	7.6	7.6	7.6	6.9	6.7	6.6	6.4	6.6	6.5
As a percentage of	Imp.	0.5	0.5	0.5	0.5	0.5	0.5	0.5	0.4	0.4	0.4	0.5	0.4	0.4	0.4	0.4
world trade (%)	Exp.	0.5	0.5	0.5	0.5	0.5	0.5	0.4	0.4	0.4	0.4	0.5	0.4	0.4	0.4	0.4

Graph 1: Annual growth rates of exports, 1999–2013
(In percentage by year)

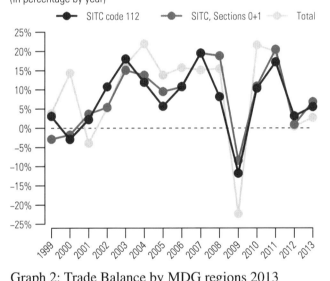

Graph 2: Trade Balance by MDG regions 2013
(Bln US$)

— Imports — Exports — Trade balance

Developed Asia–Pacific
Developed Europe
Developed N. America
South–eastern Europe
C I S
Northern Africa
Sub–Saharan Africa
Latin Am, Caribbean
Eastern Asia
Southern Asia
South–eastern Asia
Western Asia
Oceania

Table 2: Top exporting countries or areas in 2013

Country or area	Value (million US$)	Avg. Growth (%) 09-13	Growth (%) 12-13	World share %	Cum.
World	81 631.5	8.9	5.5	100.0	
France	15 859.6	9.0	3.2	19.4	19.4
United Kingdom	10 214.5	8.5	0.4	12.5	31.9
Italy	8 069.5	8.2	11.1	9.9	41.8
Spain	4 501.3	8.5	6.2	5.5	47.3
Germany	4 467.4	6.3	4.8	5.5	52.8
USA	3 999.3	13.5	7.2	4.9	57.7
Mexico	3 365.6	7.6	6.8	4.1	61.8
Netherlands	3 199.3	6.3	3.8	3.9	65.8
Singapore	2 656.3	17.9	5.1	3.3	69.0
Belgium	2 025.9	10.2	17.6	2.5	71.5
Chile	2 004.0	9.2	8.8	2.5	73.9
Australia	1 928.3	0.4	-7.4	2.4	76.3
Ireland	1 294.2	0.1	-2.2	1.6	77.9
Portugal	1 282.7	5.9	1.6	1.6	79.5
South Africa	1 217.6	9.8	12.2	1.5	81.0

Table 3: Top importing countries or areas in 2013

Country or area	Value (million US$)	Avg. Growth (%) 09-13	Growth (%) 12-13	World share %	Cum.
World	80 096.7	7.7	5.3	100.0	
USA	16 634.0	6.4	3.7	20.8	20.8
United Kingdom	6 964.4	0.8	1.7	8.7	29.5
Germany	5 955.1	6.3	9.3	7.4	36.9
Canada	3 487.8	7.5	2.9	4.4	41.3
Russian Federation	3 102.5	17.4	7.8	3.9	45.1
France	2 997.6	4.8	4.9	3.7	48.9
China	2 866.3	28.5	-3.3	3.6	52.4
Japan	2 574.5	9.2	-3.3	3.2	55.7
Singapore	2 530.8	19.0	13.5	3.2	58.8
Netherlands	2 495.6	8.7	5.4	3.1	61.9
Belgium	2 204.5	5.2	11.5	2.8	64.7
Spain	1 791.0	1.1	1.9	2.2	66.9
China, Hong Kong SAR	1 663.3	15.7	-3.0	2.1	69.0
Switzerland	1 626.3	5.8	6.7	2.0	71.0
Australia	1 584.1	12.5	7.0	2.0	73.0

121 Tobacco, unmanufactured; tobacco refuse

In 2013, the value (in current US$) of exports of "tobacco, unmanufactured; tobacco refuse" (SITC group 121) increased by 5.1 percent (compared to 3.4 percent average growth rate from 2009-2013) to reach 12.9 bln US$ (see table 2), while imports decreased by 1.0 percent to reach 13.3 bln US$ (see table 3). Exports of this commodity accounted for 1.0 percent of world exports of SITC sections 0+1, and 0.1 percent of total world merchandise exports (see table 1). Brazil, USA and Zimbabwe were the top exporters in 2013 (see table 2). They accounted for 24.7, 9.4 and 6.7 percent of world exports, respectively. China, Russian Federation and USA were the top destinations, with respectively 10.0, 8.7 and 7.6 percent of world imports (see table 3).

The top 15 countries/areas accounted for 80.2 and 68.4 percent of total world exports and imports, respectively (see tables 2 and 3). In 2013, Brazil was the country/area with the highest value of net exports (+3.2 bln US$), followed by India (+833.0 mln US$). By MDG regions (see graph 2), the largest surpluses in this product group were recorded by Latin America and the Caribbean (+3.3 bln US$), Sub-Saharan Africa (+1.5 bln US$) and Southern Asia (+832.6 mln US$). The largest trade deficits were recorded by Developed Europe (-1.9 bln US$), Commonwealth of Independent States (-1.5 bln US$) and Eastern Asia (-1.1 bln US$).

Table 1: Imports (Imp.) and exports (Exp.), 1999-2013, in current US$

		1999	2000	2001	2002	2003	2004	2005	2006	2007	2008	2009	2010	2011	2012	2013
Values in Bln US$	Imp.	7.5	7.0	7.3	7.4	7.6	7.9	7.9	8.0	9.3	10.6	11.9	11.8	13.1	13.4	13.3
	Exp.	6.3	5.5	5.8	5.3	5.7	6.8	7.0	7.4	8.6	10.2	11.3	10.8	11.4	12.3	12.9
As a percentage of SITC section (%)	Imp.	1.8	1.7	1.7	1.7	1.5	1.3	1.2	1.1	1.1	1.1	1.3	1.2	1.1	1.1	1.1
	Exp.	1.6	1.4	1.5	1.3	1.2	1.2	1.1	1.1	1.1	1.1	1.3	1.1	1.0	1.0	1.0
As a percentage of world trade (%)	Imp.	0.1	0.1	0.1	0.1	0.1	0.1	0.1	0.1	0.1	0.1	0.1	0.1	0.1	0.1	0.1
	Exp.	0.1	0.1	0.1	0.1	0.1	0.1	0.1	0.1	0.1	0.1	0.1	0.1	0.1	0.1	0.1

Graph 1: Annual growth rates of exports, 1999–2013
(In percentage by year)

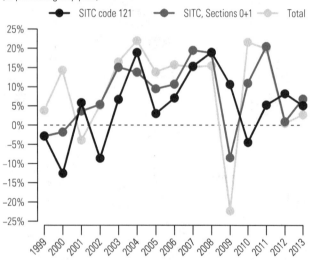

Graph 2: Trade Balance by MDG regions 2013
(Bln US$)

Table 2: Top exporting countries or areas in 2013

Country or area	Value (million US$)	Avg. Growth (%) 09-13	Growth (%) 12-13	World share %	Cum.
World	12 903.5	3.4	5.1	100.0	
Brazil	3 192.5	1.6	-0.1	24.7	24.7
USA	1 216.7	1.1	7.9	9.4	34.2
Zimbabwe	869.9	37.7	11.8	6.7	40.9
India	842.9	3.3	20.5	6.5	47.4
China	644.4	4.8	-2.0	5.0	52.4
Malawi	562.6	-7.2	11.7	4.4	56.8
Belgium	469.0	4.4	5.5	3.6	60.4
Turkey	439.4	-2.7	2.9	3.4	63.8
Germany	382.0	3.4	9.7	3.0	66.8
Netherlands	361.4	27.4	10.9	2.8	69.6
Argentina	325.0	-2.5	-12.2	2.5	72.1
Italy	320.2	3.0	-6.8	2.5	74.6
Mozambique	257.3	9.4	12.9	2.0	76.6
Greece	248.0	-10.7	-14.7	1.9	78.5
Bulgaria	221.4	-6.5	32.1	1.7	80.2

Table 3: Top importing countries or areas in 2013

Country or area	Value (million US$)	Avg. Growth (%) 09-13	Growth (%) 12-13	World share %	Cum.
World	13 299.7	2.9	-1.0	100.0	
China	1 334.3	15.8	11.5	10.0	10.0
Russian Federation	1 152.0	2.6	-0.2	8.7	18.7
USA	1 012.0	2.3	2.9	7.6	26.3
Germany	973.1	-0.2	-1.8	7.3	33.6
Netherlands	770.0	0.2	-8.9	5.8	39.4
Indonesia	627.3	21.3	-4.8	4.7	44.1
Belgium	610.0	0.8	14.6	4.6	48.7
Poland	474.5	9.8	7.6	3.6	52.3
Turkey	378.6	6.9	5.2	2.8	55.1
Japan	375.6	-2.0	-3.4	2.8	58.0
Rep. of Korea	308.0	6.1	22.3	2.3	60.3
United Kingdom	295.5	-13.3	-12.7	2.2	62.5
Ukraine	275.6	0.3	-22.5	2.1	64.6
Malaysia	273.4	7.3	-22.7	2.1	66.6
Viet Nam	233.5	2.1	16.7	1.8	68.4

Tobacco, manufactured (whether or not containing tobacco substitutes) 122

In 2013, the value (in current US$) of exports of "tobacco, manufactured (whether or not containing tobacco substitutes)" (SITC group 122) increased by 5.2 percent (compared to 6.6 percent average growth rate from 2009-2013) to reach 30.2 bln US$ (see table 2), while imports increased by 1.9 percent to reach 31.3 bln US$ (see table 3). Exports of this commodity accounted for 2.4 percent of world exports of SITC sections 0+1, and 0.2 percent of total world merchandise exports (see table 1). Germany, Netherlands and Poland were the top exporters in 2013 (see table 2). They accounted for 15.1, 14.5 and 6.5 percent of world exports, respectively. Japan, Italy and France were the top destinations, with respectively 13.2, 8.5 and 7.4 percent of world imports (see table 3).

The top 15 countries/areas accounted for 66.7 and 65.0 percent of total world exports and imports, respectively (see tables 2 and 3). In 2013, Netherlands was the country/area with the highest value of net exports (+3.6 bln US$), followed by Germany (+3.1 bln US$). By MDG regions (see graph 2), the largest surpluses in this product group were recorded by Developed Europe (+3.0 bln US$), Latin America and the Caribbean (+1.8 bln US$) and South-eastern Asia (+1.1 bln US$). The largest trade deficits were recorded by Developed Asia-Pacific (-4.3 bln US$), Sub-Saharan Africa (-1.3 bln US$) and Western Asia (-1.3 bln US$).

Table 1: Imports (Imp.) and exports (Exp.), 1999-2013, in current US$

		1999	2000	2001	2002	2003	2004	2005	2006	2007	2008	2009	2010	2011	2012	2013
Values in Bln US$	Imp.	13.8	13.9	14.6	15.2	16.7	19.3	21.0	20.9	22.8	24.3	24.7	25.8	32.3	30.8	31.3
	Exp.	16.2	16.0	15.2	15.8	16.0	17.0	18.2	19.3	21.6	23.7	23.4	24.4	29.1	28.8	30.2
As a percentage of SITC section (%)	Imp.	3.3	3.4	3.4	3.4	3.2	3.3	3.3	3.0	2.7	2.5	2.8	2.6	2.7	2.6	2.5
	Exp.	4.1	4.1	3.8	3.7	3.3	3.1	3.0	2.9	2.7	2.5	2.7	2.5	2.5	2.4	2.4
As a percentage of world trade (%)	Imp.	0.2	0.2	0.2	0.2	0.2	0.2	0.2	0.2	0.2	0.1	0.2	0.2	0.2	0.2	0.2
	Exp.	0.3	0.3	0.2	0.2	0.2	0.2	0.2	0.2	0.2	0.1	0.2	0.2	0.2	0.2	0.2

Graph 1: Annual growth rates of exports, 1999–2013
(In percentage by year)

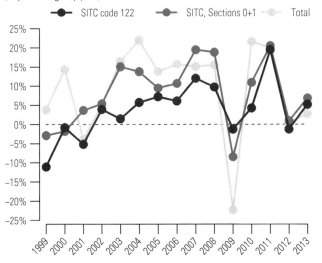

Legend: SITC code 122 — SITC, Sections 0+1 — Total

Table 2: Top exporting countries or areas in 2013

Country or area	Value (million US$)	Avg. Growth (%) 09-13	Growth (%) 12-13	World share %	Cum.
World	30 239.2	6.6	5.2	100.0	
Germany	4 552.0	1.9	-8.5	15.1	15.1
Netherlands	4 393.3	2.4	4.5	14.5	29.6
Poland	1 961.4	8.4	8.6	6.5	36.1
China, Hong Kong SAR	1 053.5	10.2	8.1	3.5	39.6
Cuba	973.3	22.8	53.4	3.2	42.8
Belgium	907.2	5.4	7.4	3.0	45.8
United Arab Emirates	859.7	15.6	21.7	2.8	48.6
Singapore	840.1	14.5	4.4	2.8	51.4
Indonesia	731.8	14.7	15.3	2.4	53.8
Russian Federation	702.8	11.7	6.8	2.3	56.1
Romania	679.3	7.5	14.7	2.2	58.4
China	677.3	18.4	12.0	2.2	60.6
USA	653.9	5.2	24.3	2.2	62.8
France	613.7	1.8	-3.8	2.0	64.8
Switzerland	579.3	-2.9	-5.8	1.9	66.7

Graph 2: Trade Balance by MDG regions 2013
(Bln US$)

Legend: Imports — Exports — Trade balance

Developed Asia–Pacific
Developed Europe
Developed N. America
South–eastern Europe
CIS
Northern Africa
Sub-Saharan Africa
Latin Am, Caribbean
Eastern Asia
Southern Asia
South–eastern Asia
Western Asia
Oceania

Table 3: Top importing countries or areas in 2013

Country or area	Value (million US$)	Avg. Growth (%) 09-13	Growth (%) 12-13	World share %	Cum.
World	31 343.9	6.1	1.9	100.0	
Japan	4 142.9	4.1	-23.4	13.2	13.2
Italy	2 678.6	-2.9	-3.8	8.5	21.8
France	2 334.1	2.4	-0.9	7.4	29.2
Spain	1 718.3	-1.6	9.2	5.5	34.7
Germany	1 412.4	0.8	3.9	4.5	39.2
Nigeria	1 345.5	236.7	10510.9	4.3	43.5
USA	1 207.4	15.0	35.9	3.9	47.3
Saudi Arabia	1 003.6	15.8	9.4	3.2	50.5
Belgium	843.2	9.0	14.4	2.7	53.2
Netherlands	812.1	6.0	-20.8	2.6	55.8
China, Hong Kong SAR	758.2	10.2	6.7	2.4	58.2
Singapore	675.0	12.7	2.1	2.2	60.4
Other Asia, nes	530.5	4.4	-2.5	1.7	62.1
Australia	474.6	41.5	60.9	1.5	63.6
United Kingdom	438.2	5.8	-54.0	1.4	65.0

Crude materials, inedible, except fuels

(SITC Section 2)

211 Hides and skins (except furskins), raw

In 2013, the value (in current US$) of exports of "hides and skins (except furskins), raw" (SITC group 211) increased by 16.4 percent (compared to 21.9 percent average growth rate from 2009-2013) to reach 9.1 bln US$ (see table 2), while imports increased by 14.9 percent to reach 9.1 bln US$ (see table 3). Exports of this commodity accounted for 1.1 percent of world exports of SITC sections 2+4, and less than 0.1 percent of total world merchandise exports (see table 1). USA, Australia and France were the top exporters in 2013 (see table 2). They accounted for 27.7, 10.9 and 5.9 percent of world exports, respectively. China, Italy and Rep. of Korea were the top destinations, with respectively 39.1, 16.8 and 5.3 percent of world imports (see table 3).

The top 15 countries/areas accounted for 80.7 and 88.6 percent of total world exports and imports, respectively (see tables 2 and 3). In 2013, USA was the country/area with the highest value of net exports (+2.5 bln US$), followed by Australia (+987.9 mln US$). By MDG regions (see graph 2), the largest surpluses in this product group were recorded by Developed North America (+2.8 bln US$), Developed Asia-Pacific (+1.3 bln US$) and Developed Europe (+380.7 mln US$). The largest trade deficits were recorded by Eastern Asia (-4.4 bln US$), South-eastern Asia (-345.9 mln US$) and Western Asia (-306.4 mln US$).

Table 1: Imports (Imp.) and exports (Exp.), 1999-2013, in current US$

		1999	2000	2001	2002	2003	2004	2005	2006	2007	2008	2009	2010	2011	2012	2013
Values in Bln US$	Imp.	4.1	5.2	5.8	5.5	5.5	5.6	5.6	5.9	6.3	6.2	4.2	6.3	8.0	8.0	9.1
	Exp.	3.9	5.1	5.7	5.4	5.6	5.7	5.7	6.0	6.3	5.9	4.1	6.4	8.1	7.8	9.1
As a percentage of SITC section (%)	Imp.	1.8	2.1	2.5	2.3	1.9	1.5	1.3	1.2	1.0	0.8	0.8	0.8	0.8	0.9	1.0
	Exp.	2.0	2.4	2.8	2.5	2.2	1.8	1.6	1.3	1.1	0.9	0.8	0.9	0.9	0.9	1.1
As a percentage of world trade (%)	Imp.	0.1	0.1	0.1	0.1	0.1	0.1	0.1	0.0	0.0	0.0	0.0	0.0	0.0	0.0	0.0
	Exp.	0.1	0.1	0.1	0.1	0.1	0.1	0.1	0.1	0.0	0.0	0.0	0.0	0.0	0.0	0.0

Graph 1: Annual growth rates of exports, 1999–2013
(In percentage by year)

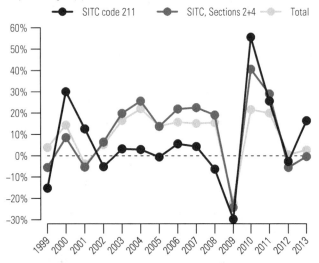

— SITC code 211   — SITC, Sections 2+4   — Total

Table 2: Top exporting countries or areas in 2013

Country or area	Value (million US$)	Avg. Growth (%) 09-13	Growth (%) 12-13	World share %	Cum.
World	9 120.5	21.9	16.4	100.0	
USA	2 524.2	18.0	12.1	27.7	27.7
Australia	990.3	24.7	16.9	10.9	38.5
France	541.9	23.8	20.7	5.9	44.5
Spain	438.1	25.4	26.5	4.8	49.3
Germany	364.8	22.1	-0.5	4.0	53.3
United Kingdom	350.6	25.2	11.1	3.8	57.1
Netherlands	346.1	18.9	-6.4	3.8	60.9
Italy	327.3	23.2	19.2	3.6	64.5
Canada	326.9	19.4	10.5	3.6	68.1
New Zealand	287.7	28.9	1.3	3.2	71.2
South Africa	239.6	38.1	111.6	2.6	73.9
Ireland	171.2	24.1	27.3	1.9	75.7
Mexico	163.5	77.6	67.2	1.8	77.5
Japan	158.2	16.5	4.5	1.7	79.3
Belgium	127.3	29.6	39.4	1.4	80.7

Graph 2: Trade Balance by MDG regions 2013
(Bln US$)

— Imports   — Exports   — Trade balance

Developed Asia–Pacific
Developed Europe
Developed N. America
South–eastern Europe
C I S
Northern Africa
Sub–Saharan Africa
Latin Am, Caribbean
Eastern Asia
Southern Asia
South–eastern Asia
Western Asia
Oceania

-5 -4 -3 -2 -1 0 1 2 3 4

Table 3: Top importing countries or areas in 2013

Country or area	Value (million US$)	Avg. Growth (%) 09-13	Growth (%) 12-13	World share %	Cum.
World	9 135.8	21.6	14.9	100.0	
China	3 567.9	25.4	18.4	39.1	39.1
Italy	1 535.1	26.6	23.2	16.8	55.9
Rep. of Korea	480.1	13.6	-2.6	5.3	61.1
Turkey	375.4	32.4	-6.7	4.1	65.2
China, Hong Kong SAR	274.8	-2.2	1.5	3.0	68.2
Austria	251.0	42.1	42.0	2.7	71.0
Germany	243.8	26.3	32.9	2.7	73.6
Thailand	237.7	18.9	6.4	2.6	76.2
Other Asia, nes	212.6	7.2	8.0	2.3	78.6
Netherlands	195.7	26.6	24.4	2.1	80.7
France	189.5	25.6	22.5	2.1	82.8
Mexico	149.3	8.9	-11.6	1.6	84.4
Japan	138.1	9.2	-11.7	1.5	85.9
Spain	132.6	14.0	17.4	1.5	87.4
Slovakia	107.3	28.8	24.8	1.2	88.6

In 2013, the value (in current US$) of exports of "furskins, raw (including heads, tails, paws, etc), other than those of 211" (SITC group 212) increased by 30.3 percent (compared to 32.2 percent average growth rate from 2009-2013) to reach 7.4 bln US$ (see table 2), while imports increased by 37.8 percent to reach 4.9 bln US$ (see table 3). Exports of this commodity accounted for 0.9 percent of world exports of SITC sections 2+4, and less than 0.1 percent of total world merchandise exports (see table 1). Denmark, China, Hong Kong SAR and Finland were the top exporters in 2013 (see table 2). They accounted for 31.1, 15.6 and 14.7 percent of world exports, respectively. China, Hong Kong SAR, China and Finland were the top destinations, with respectively 35.1, 16.7 and 9.4 percent of world imports (see table 3).

The top 15 countries/areas accounted for 97.1 and 98.0 percent of total world exports and imports, respectively (see tables 2 and 3). In 2013, Denmark was the country/area with the highest value of net exports (+1.9 bln US$), followed by Finland (+632.0 mln US$). By MDG regions (see graph 2), the largest surpluses in this product group were recorded by Developed Europe (+2.8 bln US$), Developed North America (+927.3 mln US$) and Commonwealth of Independent States (+240.3 mln US$). The largest trade deficits were recorded by Eastern Asia (-1.5 bln US$), South-eastern Asia (-22.5 mln US$) and Developed Asia-Pacific (-9.1 mln US$).

Table 1: Imports (Imp.) and exports (Exp.), 1999-2013, in current US$

		1999	2000	2001	2002	2003	2004	2005	2006	2007	2008	2009	2010	2011	2012	2013
Values in Bln US$	Imp.	0.9	1.0	1.1	1.2	1.3	1.6	1.7	2.1	1.9	2.1	1.7	2.5	3.2	3.6	4.9
	Exp.	1.1	1.4	1.5	1.6	1.8	2.2	2.3	3.0	2.5	3.1	2.4	3.8	4.7	5.7	7.4
As a percentage of SITC section (%)	Imp.	0.4	0.4	0.5	0.5	0.5	0.4	0.4	0.4	0.3	0.3	0.3	0.3	0.3	0.4	0.5
	Exp.	0.6	0.7	0.7	0.7	0.7	0.7	0.6	0.7	0.5	0.5	0.5	0.6	0.5	0.7	0.9
As a percentage of world trade (%)	Imp.	0.0	0.0	0.0	0.0	0.0	0.0	0.0	0.0	0.0	0.0	0.0	0.0	0.0	0.0	0.0
	Exp.	0.0	0.0	0.0	0.0	0.0	0.0	0.0	0.0	0.0	0.0	0.0	0.0	0.0	0.0	0.0

Graph 1: Annual growth rates of exports, 1999–2013
(In percentage by year)

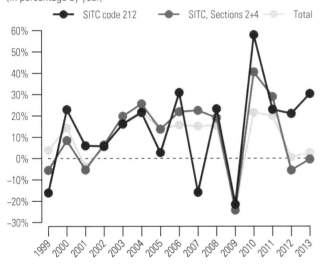

Table 2: Top exporting countries or areas in 2013

Country or area	Value (million US$)	Avg. Growth (%) 09-13	Growth (%) 12-13	World share %	Cum.
World	7 398.3	32.2	30.3	100.0	
Denmark	2 303.7	31.8	22.5	31.1	31.1
China, Hong Kong SAR	1 156.9	22.8	31.3	15.6	46.8
Finland	1 090.8	36.5	30.5	14.7	61.5
Canada	918.1	37.4	37.3	12.4	73.9
USA	613.5	38.0	15.9	8.3	82.2
Poland	270.8	37.4	123.9	3.7	85.9
Netherlands	215.2	23.0	43.1	2.9	88.8
Russian Federation	211.3	42.8	45.4	2.9	91.6
Norway	79.4	22.1	34.4	1.1	92.7
Lithuania	65.4	41.9	81.8	0.9	93.6
France	60.7	54.0	41.4	0.8	94.4
Greece	51.1	69.5	29.5	0.7	95.1
Spain	50.5	66.8	24.7	0.7	95.8
Sweden	48.5	27.1	26.4	0.7	96.4
Belarus	46.8	25.3	1.6	0.6	97.1

Graph 2: Trade Balance by MDG regions 2013
(Bln US$)

Imports — Exports — Trade balance

Developed Asia–Pacific
Developed Europe
Developed N. America
South–eastern Europe
CIS
Northern Africa
Sub–Saharan Africa
Latin Am, Caribbean
Eastern Asia
Southern Asia
South–eastern Asia
Western Asia
Oceania

Table 3: Top importing countries or areas in 2013

Country or area	Value (million US$)	Avg. Growth (%) 09-13	Growth (%) 12-13	World share %	Cum.
World	4 899.1	30.9	37.8	100.0	
China, Hong Kong SAR	1 718.8	29.2	26.2	35.1	35.1
China	817.8	33.1	28.3	16.7	51.8
Finland	458.8	26.8	70.1	9.4	61.1
Denmark	446.4	30.3	153.2	9.1	70.3
Canada	371.3	42.7	98.5	7.6	77.8
Italy	237.2	40.5	39.6	4.8	82.7
USA	232.9	28.4	30.9	4.8	87.4
Greece	190.5	32.4	3.7	3.9	91.3
Rep. of Korea	112.5	12.4	-24.1	2.3	93.6
Poland	64.8	36.4	16.5	1.3	94.9
Germany	45.6	53.2	17.8	0.9	95.9
Estonia	44.7	40.2	138.5	0.9	96.8
Malaysia	21.3	86.3	-2.8	0.4	97.2
Lithuania	20.5	58.7	22.1	0.4	97.6
France	16.9	16.8	39.5	0.3	98.0

222 Oil-seeds and oleaginous fruits used for extraction of 'soft' fixed oils

In 2013, the value (in current US$) of exports of "oil-seeds and oleaginous fruits used for extraction of 'soft' fixed oils" (SITC group 222) increased by 6.8 percent (compared to 14.9 percent average growth rate from 2009-2013) to reach 79.9 bln US$ (see table 2), while imports increased by 5.9 percent to reach 84.4 bln US$ (see table 3). Exports of this commodity accounted for 9.5 percent of world exports of SITC sections 2+4, and 0.4 percent of total world merchandise exports (see table 1). Brazil, USA and Canada were the top exporters in 2013 (see table 2). They accounted for 28.7, 28.2 and 7.8 percent of world exports, respectively. China, Germany and Netherlands were the top destinations, with respectively 48.9, 6.5 and 4.8 percent of world imports (see table 3).

The top 15 countries/areas accounted for 91.3 and 85.3 percent of total world exports and imports, respectively (see tables 2 and 3). In 2013, Brazil was the country/area with the highest value of net exports (+22.8 bln US$), followed by USA (+21.2 bln US$). By MDG regions (see graph 2), the largest surpluses in this product group were recorded by Latin America and the Caribbean (+28.2 bln US$), Developed North America (+27.0 bln US$) and Sub-Saharan Africa (+1.9 bln US$). The largest trade deficits were recorded by Eastern Asia (-41.6 bln US$), Developed Europe (-12.5 bln US$) and South-eastern Asia (-3.8 bln US$).

Table 1: Imports (Imp.) and exports (Exp.), 1999-2013, in current US$

		1999	2000	2001	2002	2003	2004	2005	2006	2007	2008	2009	2010	2011	2012	2013
Values in Bln US$	Imp.	14.2	15.4	16.6	16.7	22.4	26.3	25.3	24.9	35.8	60.2	50.7	58.9	73.4	79.7	84.4
	Exp.	12.5	13.6	14.5	14.8	20.4	21.4	21.4	22.7	32.3	50.3	45.8	54.2	65.6	74.8	79.9
As a percentage of	Imp.	6.3	6.2	7.1	6.9	7.8	7.0	6.1	5.0	5.8	7.9	9.3	7.7	7.4	8.6	9.2
SITC section (%)	Exp.	6.3	6.4	7.2	6.9	7.9	6.6	5.8	5.1	5.9	7.7	9.3	7.8	7.3	8.9	9.5
As a percentage of	Imp.	0.2	0.2	0.3	0.3	0.3	0.3	0.2	0.2	0.3	0.4	0.4	0.4	0.4	0.4	0.5
world trade (%)	Exp.	0.2	0.2	0.2	0.2	0.3	0.2	0.2	0.2	0.2	0.3	0.4	0.4	0.4	0.4	0.4

Graph 1: Annual growth rates of exports, 1999–2013
(In percentage by year)

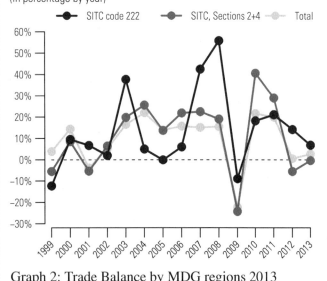

— SITC code 222   — SITC, Sections 2+4   — Total

Graph 2: Trade Balance by MDG regions 2013
(Bln US$)

Imports   Exports   Trade balance

Developed Asia–Pacific
Developed Europe
Developed N. America
South–eastern Europe
C I S
Northern Africa
Sub–Saharan Africa
Latin Am, Caribbean
Eastern Asia
Southern Asia
South–eastern Asia
Western Asia
Oceania

Table 2: Top exporting countries or areas in 2013

Country or area	Value (million US$)	Avg. Growth (%) 09-13	Growth (%) 12-13	World share %	Cum.
World	79 935.4	14.9	6.8	100.0	
Brazil	22 923.2	18.8	32.0	28.7	28.7
USA	22 550.0	7.2	-11.6	28.2	56.9
Canada	6 252.7	10.5	-16.8	7.8	64.7
Argentina	4 534.3	23.5	22.3	5.7	70.4
Paraguay	2 570.1	30.0	56.3	3.2	73.6
Australia	2 431.2	42.6	32.7	3.0	76.6
Ukraine	2 002.3	19.6	19.4	2.5	79.1
Uruguay	1 874.5	42.2	35.9	2.3	81.5
Netherlands	1 707.4	19.0	-3.4	2.1	83.6
France	1 266.7	9.9	-7.7	1.6	85.2
India	1 231.4	25.3	-16.3	1.5	86.7
Romania	1 026.1	18.2	88.7	1.3	88.0
Bulgaria	929.0	20.0	43.2	1.2	89.2
Nigeria	862.2	45.1	71.3	1.1	90.3
China	841.5	6.2	-7.0	1.1	91.3

Table 3: Top importing countries or areas in 2013

Country or area	Value (million US$)	Avg. Growth (%) 09-13	Growth (%) 12-13	World share %	Cum.
World	84 386.9	13.6	5.9	100.0	
China	41 292.6	19.0	9.7	48.9	48.9
Germany	5 454.0	13.3	8.7	6.5	55.4
Netherlands	4 038.4	11.4	11.6	4.8	60.2
Japan	3 938.7	7.3	3.0	4.7	64.8
Mexico	3 193.2	11.0	55.2	3.8	68.6
Spain	2 310.4	9.2	-3.6	2.7	71.4
Belgium	1 608.6	9.1	-16.2	1.9	73.3
Indonesia	1 447.4	15.9	0.1	1.7	75.0
France	1 402.8	13.8	49.0	1.7	76.7
Turkey	1 397.1	12.5	-1.0	1.7	78.3
USA	1 378.0	20.7	49.9	1.6	79.9
Egypt	1 154.2	12.9	-8.3	1.4	81.3
Italy	1 129.5	6.3	16.0	1.3	82.6
Thailand	1 114.0	11.4	-17.7	1.3	84.0
Russian Federation	1 086.9	13.5	33.6	1.3	85.3

Oil seeds and oleaginous fruits used for the extraction of other fixed oils 223

In 2013, the value (in current US$) of exports of "oil seeds and oleaginous fruits used for the extraction of other fixed oils" (SITC group 223) increased by 9.1 percent (compared to 18.9 percent average growth rate from 2009-2013) to reach 4.3 bln US$ (see table 2), while imports increased by 14.2 percent to reach 2.9 bln US$ (see table 3). Exports of this commodity accounted for 0.5 percent of world exports of SITC sections 2+4, and less than 0.1 percent of total world merchandise exports (see table 1). USA, Canada and Netherlands were the top exporters in 2013 (see table 2). They accounted for 35.3, 10.7 and 5.1 percent of world exports, respectively. Belgium, USA and Germany were the top destinations, with respectively 12.9, 12.0 and 7.7 percent of world imports (see table 3).

The top 15 countries/areas accounted for 81.6 and 68.6 percent of total world exports and imports, respectively (see tables 2 and 3). In 2013, USA was the country/area with the highest value of net exports (+1.2 bln US$), followed by Canada (+398.5 mln US$). By MDG regions (see graph 2), the largest surpluses in this product group were recorded by Developed North America (+1.6 bln US$), Commonwealth of Independent States (+250.7 mln US$) and Southern Asia (+68.7 mln US$). The largest trade deficits were recorded by Developed Europe (-480.5 mln US$), Eastern Asia (-54.7 mln US$) and South-eastern Asia (-31.0 mln US$).

Table 1: Imports (Imp.) and exports (Exp.), 1999-2013, in current US$

		1999	2000	2001	2002	2003	2004	2005	2006	2007	2008	2009	2010	2011	2012	2013
Values in Bln US$	Imp.	0.9	0.8	0.8	0.9	1.0	1.2	1.3	1.4	1.8	2.6	2.1	2.3	2.4	2.6	2.9
	Exp.	0.7	0.7	0.7	0.8	0.9	1.2	1.5	1.5	1.9	2.8	2.2	2.2	2.6	4.0	4.3
As a percentage of SITC section (%)	Imp.	0.4	0.3	0.3	0.4	0.4	0.3	0.3	0.3	0.3	0.3	0.4	0.3	0.2	0.3	0.3
	Exp.	0.4	0.3	0.4	0.4	0.3	0.4	0.4	0.3	0.4	0.4	0.4	0.3	0.3	0.5	0.5
As a percentage of world trade (%)	Imp.	0.0	0.0	0.0	0.0	0.0	0.0	0.0	0.0	0.0	0.0	0.0	0.0	0.0	0.0	0.0
	Exp.	0.0	0.0	0.0	0.0	0.0	0.0	0.0	0.0	0.0	0.0	0.0	0.0	0.0	0.0	0.0

Graph 1: Annual growth rates of exports, 1999–2013
(In percentage by year)

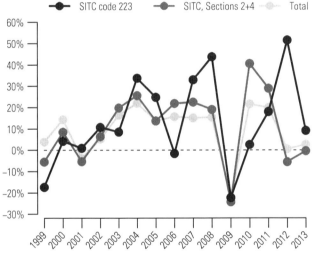

SITC code 223 — SITC, Sections 2+4 — Total

Graph 2: Trade Balance by MDG regions 2013
(Bln US$)

Imports — Exports — Trade balance

Developed Asia–Pacific
Developed Europe
Developed N. America
South–eastern Europe
CIS
Northern Africa
Sub–Saharan Africa
Latin Am, Caribbean
Eastern Asia
Southern Asia
South–eastern Asia
Western Asia
Oceania

Table 2: Top exporting countries or areas in 2013

Country or area	Value (million US$)	Avg. Growth (%) 09-13	Growth (%) 12-13	World share %	Cum.
World	4 329.4	18.9	9.1	100.0	
USA	1 527.9	30.1	5.9	35.3	35.3
Canada	462.9	13.6	30.5	10.7	46.0
Netherlands	222.8	-1.4	-37.9	5.1	51.1
Russian Federation	210.0	53.9	2.8	4.9	56.0
India	188.1	35.8	234.8	4.3	60.3
China	176.6	24.5	8.7	4.1	64.4
Belgium	134.3	-7.7	21.0	3.1	67.5
Italy	93.5	52.0	43.7	2.2	69.7
Bolivia	90.6	27.6	172.9	2.1	71.8
Turkey	88.2	16.6	66.3	2.0	73.8
Kazakhstan	85.5	75.8	-52.7	2.0	75.8
Czech Rep	76.3	15.6	0.2	1.8	77.5
Austria	73.6	8.5	22.8	1.7	79.2
France	55.0	30.0	45.1	1.3	80.5
Germany	46.0	16.0	21.8	1.1	81.6

Table 3: Top importing countries or areas in 2013

Country or area	Value (million US$)	Avg. Growth (%) 09-13	Growth (%) 12-13	World share %	Cum.
World	2 926.8	8.7	14.2	100.0	
Belgium	377.3	9.0	11.0	12.9	12.9
USA	350.5	20.1	41.6	12.0	24.9
Germany	225.6	6.7	13.1	7.7	32.6
China	145.9	11.8	35.3	5.0	37.6
Netherlands	142.5	21.0	24.2	4.9	42.4
United Kingdom	88.9	14.1	28.8	3.0	45.5
Nigeria	86.3	180.4	211.4	2.9	48.4
Dominican Rep	83.7	-15.0	34.2	2.9	51.3
Spain	79.8	19.2	-10.1	2.7	54.0
Turkey	77.1	15.4	-11.9	2.6	56.6
France	77.0	16.3	15.3	2.6	59.3
Rep. of Korea	76.7	10.9	12.4	2.6	61.9
India	67.8	5.0	38.7	2.3	64.2
Sweden	64.5	56.0	27.3	2.2	66.4
Canada	64.4	15.6	35.8	2.2	68.6

231 Natural rubber, balata, gutta-percha, chicle, etc, in primary forms

In 2013, the value (in current US$) of exports of "natural rubber, balata, gutta-percha, chicle, etc, in primary forms" (SITC group 231) decreased by 28.2 percent (compared to 21.2 percent average growth rate from 2009-2013) to reach 25.6 bln US$ (see table 2), while imports decreased by 10.4 percent to reach 24.9 bln US$ (see table 3). Exports of this commodity accounted for 3.1 percent of world exports of SITC sections 2+4, and 0.1 percent of total world merchandise exports (see table 1). Thailand, Indonesia and Nigeria were the top exporters in 2013 (see table 2). They accounted for 32.1, 27.0 and 9.5 percent of world exports, respectively. China, USA and Malaysia were the top destinations, with respectively 25.7, 10.9 and 10.0 percent of world imports (see table 3).

The top 15 countries/areas accounted for 96.5 and 83.0 percent of total world exports and imports, respectively (see tables 2 and 3). In 2013, Thailand was the country/area with the highest value of net exports (+8.2 bln US$), followed by Indonesia (+6.9 bln US$). By MDG regions (see graph 2), the largest surpluses in this product group were recorded by South-eastern Asia (+17.4 bln US$), Sub-Saharan Africa (+2.4 bln US$) and Oceania (+25.6 mln US$). The largest trade deficits were recorded by Eastern Asia (-7.8 bln US$), Developed Europe (-3.2 bln US$) and Developed North America (-3.0 bln US$).

Table 1: Imports (Imp.) and exports (Exp.), 1999-2013, in current US$

		1999	2000	2001	2002	2003	2004	2005	2006	2007	2008	2009	2010	2011	2012	2013
Values in Bln US$	Imp.	3.9	4.8	4.1	4.7	6.8	9.0	9.9	14.5	15.9	19.9	11.8	23.8	39.4	27.8	24.9
	Exp.	3.4	3.9	3.3	4.3	6.5	8.6	9.8	14.9	16.3	19.7	11.9	24.5	45.6	35.7	25.6
As a percentage of SITC section (%)	Imp.	1.7	1.9	1.7	1.9	2.4	2.4	2.4	2.9	2.6	2.6	2.2	3.1	4.0	3.0	2.7
	Exp.	1.7	1.8	1.6	2.0	2.5	2.7	2.7	3.3	3.0	3.0	2.4	3.5	5.1	4.2	3.1
As a percentage of world trade (%)	Imp.	0.1	0.1	0.1	0.1	0.1	0.1	0.1	0.1	0.1	0.1	0.1	0.2	0.2	0.2	0.1
	Exp.	0.1	0.1	0.1	0.1	0.1	0.1	0.1	0.1	0.1	0.1	0.1	0.2	0.3	0.2	0.1

Graph 1: Annual growth rates of exports, 1999–2013
(In percentage by year)

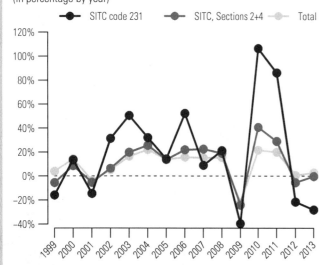

Graph 2: Trade Balance by MDG regions 2013
(Bln US$)

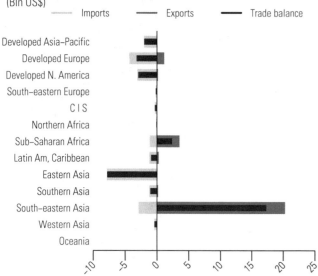

Table 2: Top exporting countries or areas in 2013

Country or area	Value (million US$)	Avg. Growth (%) 09-13	Growth (%) 12-13	World share %	Cum.
World	25 632.0	21.2	-28.2	100.0	
Thailand	8 233.5	17.6	-5.9	32.1	32.1
Indonesia	6 910.7	20.8	-12.1	27.0	59.1
Nigeria	2 427.3	94.3	-75.9	9.5	68.6
Viet Nam	2 378.7	21.0	-4.7	9.3	77.8
Malaysia	2 228.4	15.2	-12.5	8.7	86.5
Côte d'Ivoire	759.6	21.8	-6.1	3.0	89.5
Germany	336.8	30.2	-15.6	1.3	90.8
Belgium	296.0	46.9	30.1	1.2	92.0
Guatemala	238.8	15.1	-18.8	0.9	92.9
Singapore	187.4	1.1	-40.6	0.7	93.6
Cambodia	176.9	38.1	6.0	0.7	94.3
Luxembourg	174.1	54.1	-22.6	0.7	95.0
France	129.1	19.6	14.0	0.5	95.5
USA	127.9	9.3	-26.8	0.5	96.0
Cameroon	122.2	21.0	0.5	0.5	96.5

Table 3: Top importing countries or areas in 2013

Country or area	Value (million US$)	Avg. Growth (%) 09-13	Growth (%) 12-13	World share %	Cum.
World	24 894.6	20.5	-10.4	100.0	
China	6 392.7	22.8	-6.2	25.7	25.7
USA	2 707.6	18.8	-23.6	10.9	36.6
Malaysia	2 481.9	18.3	-0.4	10.0	46.5
Japan	2 020.5	14.5	-19.4	8.1	54.6
Rep. of Korea	1 108.8	16.6	-19.2	4.5	59.1
Germany	1 059.8	22.3	-16.7	4.3	63.4
Nigeria	981.7	379.2	78498.7	3.9	67.3
India	902.0	35.3	-6.7	3.6	70.9
Brazil	645.1	22.9	-2.6	2.6	73.5
France	483.9	16.4	-21.8	1.9	75.5
Spain	426.6	14.7	-18.8	1.7	77.2
Turkey	396.1	18.3	-14.1	1.6	78.8
Canada	389.7	17.1	-26.1	1.6	80.3
Italy	345.6	15.3	-13.4	1.4	81.7
Poland	327.8	25.5	-10.6	1.3	83.0

In 2013, the value (in current US$) of exports of "synthetic and reclaimed rubber; waste, scrap of unhardened rubber" (SITC group 232) decreased by 11.5 percent (compared to 14.3 percent average growth rate from 2009-2013) to reach 23.5 bln US$ (see table 2), while imports decreased by 12.9 percent to reach 26.1 bln US$ (see table 3). Exports of this commodity accounted for 2.8 percent of world exports of SITC sections 2+4, and 0.1 percent of total world merchandise exports (see table 1). USA, Rep. of Korea and Japan were the top exporters in 2013 (see table 2). They accounted for 13.9, 12.7 and 12.0 percent of world exports, respectively. China, USA and Germany were the top destinations, with respectively 17.1, 6.8 and 6.1 percent of world imports (see table 3).

The top 15 countries/areas accounted for 88.1 and 69.2 percent of total world exports and imports, respectively (see tables 2 and 3). In 2013, Japan was the country/area with the highest value of net exports (+2.3 bln US$), followed by Rep. of Korea (+2.3 bln US$). By MDG regions (see graph 2), the largest surpluses in this product group were recorded by Developed Asia-Pacific (+2.2 bln US$), Commonwealth of Independent States (+1.8 bln US$) and Developed North America (+1.4 bln US$). The largest trade deficits were recorded by South-eastern Asia (-2.6 bln US$), Southern Asia (-1.4 bln US$) and Latin America and the Caribbean (-1.2 bln US$).

Table 1: Imports (Imp.) and exports (Exp.), 1999-2013, in current US$

		1999	2000	2001	2002	2003	2004	2005	2006	2007	2008	2009	2010	2011	2012	2013
Values in Bln US$	Imp.	7.1	7.8	7.5	7.8	9.1	11.0	13.3	15.3	17.5	21.4	15.3	22.6	31.8	29.9	26.1
	Exp.	5.5	6.2	6.2	6.5	7.5	9.4	11.7	13.7	15.8	18.7	13.8	20.4	28.5	26.6	23.5
As a percentage of	Imp.	3.1	3.2	3.2	3.3	3.2	2.9	3.2	3.1	2.8	2.8	2.8	3.0	3.2	3.2	2.8
SITC section (%)	Exp.	2.8	2.9	3.1	3.0	2.9	2.9	3.2	3.1	2.9	2.9	2.8	2.9	3.2	3.1	2.8
As a percentage of	Imp.	0.1	0.1	0.1	0.1	0.1	0.1	0.1	0.1	0.1	0.1	0.1	0.1	0.2	0.2	0.1
world trade (%)	Exp.	0.1	0.1	0.1	0.1	0.1	0.1	0.1	0.1	0.1	0.1	0.1	0.1	0.2	0.1	0.1

Graph 1: Annual growth rates of exports, 1999–2013
(In percentage by year)

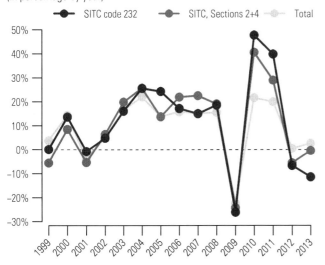

— SITC code 232   — SITC, Sections 2+4   — Total

Graph 2: Trade Balance by MDG regions 2013
(Bln US$)

— Imports   — Exports   — Trade balance

Developed Asia–Pacific
Developed Europe
Developed N. America
South–eastern Europe
C I S
Northern Africa
Sub–Saharan Africa
Latin Am, Caribbean
Eastern Asia
Southern Asia
South–eastern Asia
Western Asia
Oceania

Table 2: Top exporting countries or areas in 2013

Country or area	Value (million US$)	Avg. Growth (%) 09-13	Growth (%) 12-13	World share %	Cum.
World..................	23 511.2	14.3	-11.5	100.0	
USA....................	3 277.4	9.3	-17.6	13.9	13.9
Rep. of Korea..........	2 975.1	17.3	-20.8	12.7	26.6
Japan..................	2 814.1	14.8	-5.7	12.0	38.6
Russian Federation.....	2 377.4	20.2	-11.2	10.1	48.7
Belgium................	1 922.2	15.4	8.3	8.2	56.9
Germany................	1 877.6	14.1	-10.2	8.0	64.8
Other Asia, nes........	1 125.5	9.3	-15.4	4.8	69.6
France.................	903.6	7.2	-18.3	3.8	73.5
Netherlands............	746.8	18.4	67.3	3.2	76.6
China..................	653.6	26.3	-20.3	2.8	79.4
Canada.................	509.5	14.9	-9.1	2.2	81.6
Poland.................	494.0	27.9	-18.6	2.1	83.7
Italy..................	372.7	3.3	-12.4	1.6	85.3
Czech Rep..............	334.3	32.1	-16.9	1.4	86.7
Spain..................	333.0	12.9	-5.7	1.4	88.1

Table 3: Top importing countries or areas in 2013

Country or area	Value (million US$)	Avg. Growth (%) 09-13	Growth (%) 12-13	World share %	Cum.
World..................	26 059.0	14.3	-12.9	100.0	
China..................	4 463.6	10.3	-12.9	17.1	17.1
USA....................	1 771.9	15.4	-17.8	6.8	23.9
Germany................	1 593.5	13.8	-8.0	6.1	30.0
India..................	1 239.1	21.9	-17.9	4.8	34.8
Belgium................	1 229.4	15.7	-2.8	4.7	39.5
Thailand...............	1 157.8	24.1	-14.8	4.4	44.0
France.................	791.8	9.0	-10.2	3.0	47.0
Malaysia...............	779.4	20.9	-12.7	3.0	50.0
Italy..................	776.7	9.3	-6.9	3.0	53.0
Indonesia..............	756.5	19.4	-18.2	2.9	55.9
Brazil.................	722.1	13.5	-7.4	2.8	58.6
Turkey.................	706.3	17.9	-10.8	2.7	61.4
Rep. of Korea..........	704.3	14.8	-1.1	2.7	64.1
Spain..................	686.5	13.1	-16.4	2.6	66.7
Poland.................	650.7	20.6	-11.4	2.5	69.2

244 Cork, natural, raw, and waste (including natural cork in blocks or sheets)

In 2013, the value (in current US$) of exports of "cork, natural, raw, and waste (including natural cork in blocks or sheets)" (SITC group 244) decreased by 8.7 percent (compared to 5.2 percent average growth rate from 2009-2013) to reach 175.2 mln US$ (see table 2), while imports decreased by 1.3 percent to reach 265.6 mln US$ (see table 3). Exports of this commodity accounted for less than 0.1 percent of world exports of SITC sections 2+4, and less than 0.1 percent of total world merchandise exports (see table 1). Spain, Portugal and Morocco were the top exporters in 2013 (see table 2). They accounted for 43.4, 42.0 and 4.3 percent of world exports, respectively. Portugal, Spain and Italy were the top destinations, with respectively 56.1, 11.8 and 6.0 percent of world imports (see table 3).

The top 15 countries/areas accounted for 98.9 and 94.5 percent of total world exports and imports, respectively (see tables 2 and 3). In 2013, Spain was the country/area with the highest value of net exports (+44.7 mln US$), followed by Morocco (+6.9 mln US$). By MDG regions (see graph 2), the largest surplus in this product group was recorded solely by Northern Africa (+9.9 mln US$). The largest trade deficits were recorded by Developed Europe (-72.1 mln US$), Eastern Asia (-11.2 mln US$) and Latin America and the Caribbean (-4.1 mln US$).

Table 1: Imports (Imp.) and exports (Exp.), 1999-2013, in current US$

		1999	2000	2001	2002	2003	2004	2005	2006	2007	2008	2009	2010	2011	2012	2013
Values in Mln US$	Imp.	198.0	255.8	216.9	202.5	264.6	243.8	231.7	225.6	255.8	260.3	173.3	197.9	286.1	268.9	265.6
	Exp.	178.5	245.7	203.0	190.8	254.4	234.5	230.4	234.8	247.1	244.7	143.1	146.1	193.9	192.0	175.2
As a percentage of	Imp.	0.1	0.1	0.1	0.1	0.1	0.1	0.1	0.0	0.0	0.0	0.0	0.0	0.0	0.0	0.0
SITC section (%)	Exp.	0.1	0.1	0.1	0.1	0.1	0.1	0.1	0.1	0.0	0.0	0.0	0.0	0.0	0.0	0.0
As a percentage of	Imp.	0.0	0.0	0.0	0.0	0.0	0.0	0.0	0.0	0.0	0.0	0.0	0.0	0.0	0.0	0.0
world trade (%)	Exp.	0.0	0.0	0.0	0.0	0.0	0.0	0.0	0.0	0.0	0.0	0.0	0.0	0.0	0.0	0.0

Graph 1: Annual growth rates of exports, 1999–2013
(In percentage by year)

● SITC code 244   ● SITC, Sections 2+4   ○ Total

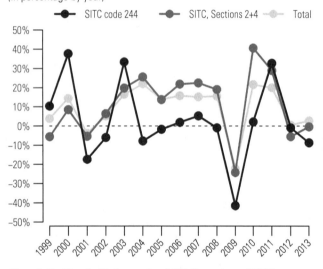

Graph 2: Trade Balance by MDG regions 2013
(Mln US$)

— Imports   — Exports   — Trade balance

Developed Asia–Pacific
Developed Europe
Developed N. America
South–eastern Europe
CIS
Northern Africa
Sub–Saharan Africa
Latin Am, Caribbean
Eastern Asia
Southern Asia
South–eastern Asia
Western Asia
Oceania

Table 2: Top exporting countries or areas in 2013

Country or area	Value (million US$)	Avg. Growth (%) 09-13	Growth (%) 12-13	World share %	Cum.
World	175.2	5.2	-8.7	100.0	
Spain	76.0	1.8	-16.0	43.4	43.4
Portugal	73.6	9.5	0.5	42.0	85.4
Morocco	7.5	23.0	3.0	4.3	89.6
Italy	6.3	18.1	1.4	3.6	93.2
USA	2.7	-8.6	0.8	1.5	94.8
Tunisia	2.2	1.2	-17.0	1.2	96.0
United Kingdom	1.4	42.0	78.9	0.8	96.8
Algeria	0.9	17.9	-49.1	0.5	97.3
France	0.5	-17.8	-27.3	0.3	97.6
Belgium	0.5	50.5	68.8	0.3	97.9
Canada	0.5	1.2	-16.1	0.3	98.2
Germany	0.4	-15.2	-23.9	0.2	98.4
Netherlands	0.3	3.2	-47.5	0.2	98.6
Japan	0.3	6.9	-6.8	0.2	98.7
Czech Rep	0.3	50.6	6.0	0.2	98.9

Table 3: Top importing countries or areas in 2013

Country or area	Value (million US$)	Avg. Growth (%) 09-13	Growth (%) 12-13	World share %	Cum.
World	265.6	11.3	-1.3	100.0	
Portugal	149.0	20.0	13.7	56.1	56.1
Spain	31.2	12.3	-5.1	11.8	67.9
Italy	15.9	-0.2	-39.7	6.0	73.9
France	10.6	3.2	36.4	4.0	77.8
China	10.0	3.4	0.4	3.7	81.6
Slovakia	5.9	29.5	15.7	2.2	83.8
United Kingdom	4.9	-0.1	26.7	1.8	85.6
Germany	4.0	0.6	12.4	1.5	87.2
India	3.6	8.8	-7.0	1.4	88.5
Belgium	3.5	8.2	17.6	1.3	89.8
Netherlands	3.0	-0.2	1.3	1.1	91.0
Japan	2.9	8.4	12.9	1.1	92.1
USA	2.5	-25.0	25.8	0.9	93.0
Brazil	2.3	6.8	-25.6	0.8	93.9
Saudi Arabia	1.6	10.2	56.0	0.6	94.5

In 2013, the value (in current US$) of exports of "fuel wood (excluding wood waste) and wood charcoal" (SITC group 245) increased by 20.1 percent (compared to 11.3 percent average growth rate from 2009-2013) to reach 1.5 bln US$ (see table 2), while imports increased by 12.3 percent to reach 1.7 bln US$ (see table 3). Exports of this commodity accounted for 0.2 percent of world exports of SITC sections 2+4, and less than 0.1 percent of total world merchandise exports (see table 1). Indonesia, Cuba and Ukraine were the top exporters in 2013 (see table 2). They accounted for 7.8, 6.9 and 6.5 percent of world exports, respectively. Germany, Japan and Italy were the top destinations, with respectively 9.8, 7.6 and 7.1 percent of world imports (see table 3).

The top 15 countries/areas accounted for 61.2 and 68.1 percent of total world exports and imports, respectively (see tables 2 and 3). In 2013, Indonesia was the country/area with the highest value of net exports (+117.0 mln US$), followed by Cuba (+106.4 mln US$). By MDG regions (see graph 2), the largest surpluses in this product group were recorded by South-eastern Asia (+200.9 mln US$), Latin America and the Caribbean (+176.9 mln US$) and Sub-Saharan Africa (+110.7 mln US$). The largest trade deficits were recorded by Developed Europe (-400.6 mln US$), Western Asia (-162.0 mln US$) and Developed Asia-Pacific (-135.8 mln US$).

Table 1: Imports (Imp.) and exports (Exp.), 1999-2013, in current US$

		1999	2000	2001	2002	2003	2004	2005	2006	2007	2008	2009	2010	2011	2012	2013
Values in Bln US$	Imp.	0.3	0.4	0.4	0.4	0.5	0.6	0.7	0.8	0.9	1.0	1.1	1.2	1.5	1.5	1.7
	Exp.	0.3	0.3	0.3	0.3	0.5	0.5	0.6	0.6	0.8	0.9	1.0	1.0	1.3	1.3	1.5
As a percentage of	Imp.	0.1	0.2	0.2	0.2	0.2	0.2	0.2	0.2	0.1	0.1	0.2	0.2	0.2	0.2	0.2
SITC section (%)	Exp.	0.1	0.2	0.2	0.2	0.2	0.2	0.2	0.1	0.1	0.1	0.2	0.2	0.1	0.2	0.2
As a percentage of	Imp.	0.0	0.0	0.0	0.0	0.0	0.0	0.0	0.0	0.0	0.0	0.0	0.0	0.0	0.0	0.0
world trade (%)	Exp.	0.0	0.0	0.0	0.0	0.0	0.0	0.0	0.0	0.0	0.0	0.0	0.0	0.0	0.0	0.0

Graph 1: Annual growth rates of exports, 1999–2013
(In percentage by year)

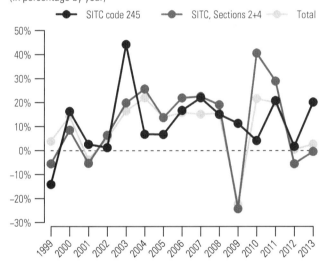

Table 2: Top exporting countries or areas in 2013

Country or area	Value (million US$)	Avg. Growth (%) 09-13	Growth (%) 12-13	World share %	Cum.
World	1 540.3	11.3	20.1	100.0	
Indonesia	120.7	16.4	14.0	7.8	7.8
Cuba	106.4	65.0	82.1	6.9	14.7
Ukraine	100.4	14.9	28.6	6.5	21.3
Poland	100.3	14.2	28.3	6.5	27.8
Nigeria	76.5	32.7	339.5	5.0	32.7
China	64.5	25.3	45.0	4.2	36.9
Bosnia Herzegovina	59.8	11.9	27.4	3.9	40.8
Philippines	51.6	42.8	84.8	3.4	44.2
Croatia	43.8	14.5	27.4	2.8	47.0
USA	42.3	15.8	-20.0	2.7	49.7
France	37.6	3.5	6.6	2.4	52.2
Belgium	36.0	-4.2	10.9	2.3	54.5
Paraguay	35.5	-1.6	2.5	2.3	56.8
Slovenia	33.7	11.8	29.4	2.2	59.0
Netherlands	33.3	9.1	34.5	2.2	61.2

Graph 2: Trade Balance by MDG regions 2013
(Mln US$)

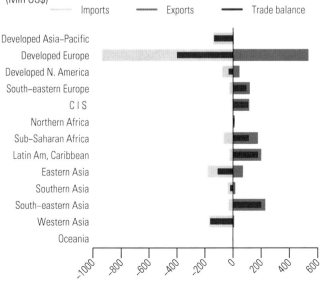

Table 3: Top importing countries or areas in 2013

Country or area	Value (million US$)	Avg. Growth (%) 09-13	Growth (%) 12-13	World share %	Cum.
World	1 702.3	11.2	12.3	100.0	
Germany	166.5	11.2	15.3	9.8	9.8
Japan	129.9	3.9	-0.8	7.6	17.4
Italy	121.4	3.9	11.6	7.1	24.5
Rep. of Korea	101.0	10.9	5.3	5.9	30.5
Austria	93.4	12.5	27.6	5.5	36.0
Belgium	75.6	11.5	17.9	4.4	40.4
France	67.9	10.2	18.6	4.0	44.4
China	64.4	37.7	10.6	3.8	48.2
USA	59.5	12.5	17.4	3.5	51.7
United Kingdom	57.3	90.6	27.5	3.4	55.0
Greece	54.3	5.1	-11.8	3.2	58.2
Sweden	44.5	4.7	23.3	2.6	60.8
Norway	41.6	11.0	12.9	2.4	63.3
Netherlands	41.5	11.7	6.5	2.4	65.7
Nigeria	39.8	1452.1	37082.4	2.3	68.1

246 Wood in chips or particles and wood waste

In 2013, the value (in current US$) of exports of "wood in chips or particles and wood waste" (SITC group 246) increased by 15.6 percent (compared to 14.3 percent average growth rate from 2009-2013) to reach 7.0 bln US$ (see table 2), while imports increased by 8.6 percent to reach 8.3 bln US$ (see table 3). Exports of this commodity accounted for 0.8 percent of world exports of SITC sections 2+4, and less than 0.1 percent of total world merchandise exports (see table 1). Viet Nam, Australia and USA were the top exporters in 2013 (see table 2). They accounted for 16.1, 9.1 and 8.9 percent of world exports, respectively. Japan, China and United Kingdom were the top destinations, with respectively 27.0, 18.6 and 7.9 percent of world imports (see table 3).

The top 15 countries/areas accounted for 75.4 and 90.2 percent of total world exports and imports, respectively (see tables 2 and 3). In 2013, Viet Nam was the country/area with the highest value of net exports (+1.1 bln US$), followed by Australia (+634.1 mln US$). By MDG regions (see graph 2), the largest surpluses in this product group were recorded by South-eastern Asia (+1.7 bln US$), Developed North America (+762.5 mln US$) and Latin America and the Caribbean (+526.0 mln US$). The largest trade deficits were recorded by Eastern Asia (-1.9 bln US$), Developed Asia-Pacific (-1.6 bln US$) and Developed Europe (-1.4 bln US$).

Table 1: Imports (Imp.) and exports (Exp.), 1999-2013, in current US$

		1999	2000	2001	2002	2003	2004	2005	2006	2007	2008	2009	2010	2011	2012	2013
Values in Bln US$	Imp.	2.6	2.6	2.5	2.4	2.8	3.3	3.7	4.2	5.0	6.0	5.1	6.5	7.8	7.7	8.3
	Exp.	1.8	1.8	1.8	1.8	2.1	2.5	2.9	3.3	3.9	4.7	4.1	5.3	6.2	6.1	7.0
As a percentage of SITC section (%)	Imp.	1.2	1.0	1.0	1.0	1.0	0.9	0.9	0.8	0.8	0.8	0.9	0.8	0.8	0.8	0.9
	Exp.	0.9	0.9	0.9	0.8	0.8	0.8	0.8	0.7	0.7	0.7	0.8	0.8	0.7	0.7	0.8
As a percentage of world trade (%)	Imp.	0.0	0.0	0.0	0.0	0.0	0.0	0.0	0.0	0.0	0.0	0.0	0.0	0.0	0.0	0.0
	Exp.	0.0	0.0	0.0	0.0	0.0	0.0	0.0	0.0	0.0	0.0	0.0	0.0	0.0	0.0	0.0

Graph 1: Annual growth rates of exports, 1999–2013
(In percentage by year)

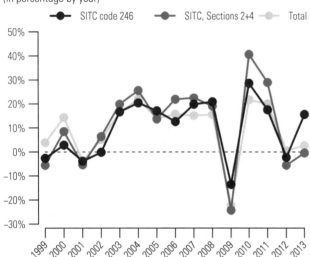

Legend: ● SITC code 246 ● SITC, Sections 2+4 ○ Total

Table 2: Top exporting countries or areas in 2013

Country or area	Value (million US$)	Avg. Growth (%) 09-13	Growth (%) 12-13	World share %	Cum.
World	6 994.7	14.3	15.6	100.0	
Viet Nam	1 124.2	47.4	35.5	16.1	16.1
Australia	638.0	-1.4	-7.8	9.1	25.2
USA	620.2	20.9	28.7	8.9	34.1
Germany	385.9	6.1	7.7	5.5	39.6
Canada	340.5	5.6	1.6	4.9	44.4
Thailand	320.1	34.5	-9.5	4.6	49.0
Chile	314.8	3.4	-15.0	4.5	53.5
Latvia	290.6	16.8	14.3	4.2	57.7
Russian Federation	257.2	12.5	14.7	3.7	61.4
Austria	201.2	10.7	21.0	2.9	64.2
South Africa	165.9	-3.0	-3.7	2.4	66.6
Indonesia	164.6	46.9	31.7	2.4	69.0
Estonia	159.8	19.0	43.9	2.3	71.2
Portugal	152.0	23.3	37.1	2.2	73.4
Romania	137.8	55.7	55.7	2.0	75.4

Graph 2: Trade Balance by MDG regions 2013
(Bln US$)

Legend: Imports — Exports — Trade balance

Developed Asia–Pacific
Developed Europe
Developed N. America
South–eastern Europe
C I S
Northern Africa
Sub–Saharan Africa
Latin Am, Caribbean
Eastern Asia
Southern Asia
South–eastern Asia
Western Asia
Oceania

Table 3: Top importing countries or areas in 2013

Country or area	Value (million US$)	Avg. Growth (%) 09-13	Growth (%) 12-13	World share %	Cum.
World	8 349.3	13.4	8.6	100.0	
Japan	2 256.9	1.4	-11.2	27.0	27.0
China	1 554.8	44.6	16.7	18.6	45.7
United Kingdom	658.6	93.7	119.7	7.9	53.5
Italy	546.8	26.9	52.2	6.5	60.1
Denmark	451.8	19.8	8.5	5.4	65.5
Germany	270.6	22.9	41.9	3.2	68.7
Austria	264.3	13.8	43.5	3.2	71.9
Belgium	260.7	-2.0	-13.4	3.1	75.0
Sweden	233.1	0.0	-0.4	2.8	77.8
Finland	209.1	3.4	0.9	2.5	80.3
Turkey	205.6	13.1	-32.3	2.5	82.8
Rep. of Korea	199.4	29.1	57.8	2.4	85.2
Netherlands	179.0	-2.6	-31.4	2.1	87.3
Canada	118.8	1.9	12.3	1.4	88.7
Other Asia, nes	118.8	13.0	3.1	1.4	90.2

In 2013, the value (in current US$) of exports of "wood in the rough or roughly squared" (SITC group 247) increased by 22.1 percent (compared to 11.6 percent average growth rate from 2009-2013) to reach 14.5 bln US$ (see table 2), while imports increased by 17.7 percent to reach 20.0 bln US$ (see table 3). Exports of this commodity accounted for 1.7 percent of world exports of SITC sections 2+4, and 0.1 percent of total world merchandise exports (see table 1). USA, New Zealand and Russian Federation were the top exporters in 2013 (see table 2). They accounted for 16.8, 13.3 and 11.3 percent of world exports, respectively. China, India and Japan were the top destinations, with respectively 46.5, 10.1 and 5.5 percent of world imports (see table 3).

The top 15 countries/areas accounted for 73.1 and 88.9 percent of total world exports and imports, respectively (see tables 2 and 3). In 2013, USA was the country/area with the highest value of net exports (+2.3 bln US$), followed by New Zealand (+1.9 bln US$). By MDG regions (see graph 2), the largest surpluses in this product group were recorded by Developed North America (+2.9 bln US$), Commonwealth of Independent States (+1.9 bln US$) and Developed Asia-Pacific (+1.1 bln US$). The largest trade deficits were recorded by Eastern Asia (-10.2 bln US$), Southern Asia (-2.1 bln US$) and Developed Europe (-720.3 mln US$).

Table 1: Imports (Imp.) and exports (Exp.), 1999-2013, in current US$

		1999	2000	2001	2002	2003	2004	2005	2006	2007	2008	2009	2010	2011	2012	2013
Values in Bln US$	Imp.	9.5	10.4	9.5	9.5	10.6	12.4	13.2	14.2	17.6	16.6	11.4	15.0	18.8	17.0	20.0
	Exp.	7.3	7.7	6.9	7.5	7.6	9.2	10.5	11.3	14.5	13.6	9.4	12.1	14.9	11.9	14.5
As a percentage of SITC section (%)	Imp.	4.2	4.2	4.0	4.0	3.7	3.3	3.2	2.9	2.8	2.2	2.1	2.0	1.9	1.8	2.2
	Exp.	3.7	3.6	3.4	3.5	3.0	2.8	2.9	2.5	2.7	2.1	1.9	1.8	1.7	1.4	1.7
As a percentage of world trade (%)	Imp.	0.2	0.2	0.2	0.1	0.1	0.1	0.1	0.1	0.1	0.1	0.1	0.1	0.1	0.1	0.1
	Exp.	0.1	0.1	0.1	0.1	0.1	0.1	0.1	0.1	0.1	0.1	0.1	0.1	0.1	0.1	0.1

Graph 1: Annual growth rates of exports, 1999–2013
(In percentage by year)

Legend: SITC code 247 — SITC, Sections 2+4 — Total

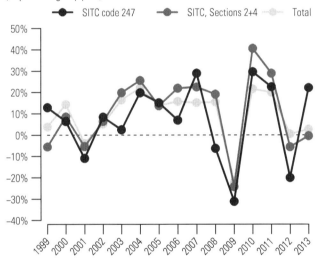

Graph 2: Trade Balance by MDG regions 2013
(Bln US$)

Legend: Imports — Exports — Trade balance

Developed Asia–Pacific, Developed Europe, Developed N. America, South–eastern Europe, CIS, Northern Africa, Sub–Saharan Africa, Latin Am, Caribbean, Eastern Asia, Southern Asia, South–eastern Asia, Western Asia, Oceania

Table 2: Top exporting countries or areas in 2013

Country or area	Value (million US$)	Avg. Growth (%) 09-13	Growth (%) 12-13	World share %	Cum.
World....................	14518.8	11.6	22.1	100.0	
USA......................	2444.1	15.1	22.4	16.8	16.8
New Zealand..........	1931.3	34.0	51.3	13.3	30.1
Russian Federation....	1640.9	-2.7	7.2	11.3	41.4
Canada.................	886.5	31.9	29.2	6.1	47.5
Malaysia...............	591.5	0.6	8.1	4.1	51.6
Czech Rep..............	501.4	18.0	25.5	3.5	55.1
Germany................	358.2	0.8	0.6	2.5	57.5
France..................	346.5	3.5	6.3	2.4	59.9
Papua New Guinea....	316.8	17.2	31.7	2.2	62.1
Uruguay................	298.2	10.9	10.6	2.1	64.2
Lao People's Dem. Rep.......	297.8	66.4	76.8	2.1	66.2
Poland..................	265.8	33.4	40.4	1.8	68.0
Latvia..................	247.8	15.2	1.2	1.7	69.7
Slovakia................	244.1	4.2	6.0	1.7	71.4
Ukraine.................	237.5	19.1	11.7	1.6	73.1

Table 3: Top importing countries or areas in 2013

Country or area	Value (million US$)	Avg. Growth (%) 09-13	Growth (%) 12-13	World share %	Cum.
World....................	20047.8	15.1	17.7	100.0	
China...................	9320.1	22.9	28.5	46.5	46.5
India...................	2032.5	15.6	1.1	10.1	56.6
Japan...................	1105.0	7.8	7.3	5.5	62.1
Austria.................	842.1	5.9	13.4	4.2	66.3
Rep. of Korea..........	739.0	4.3	12.7	3.7	70.0
Germany................	736.0	21.9	25.8	3.7	73.7
Sweden.................	576.7	17.7	12.4	2.9	76.6
Finland.................	460.3	15.3	19.5	2.3	78.9
Viet Nam...............	427.2	14.3	31.8	2.1	81.0
Canada.................	310.7	0.7	5.0	1.6	82.6
Italy...................	298.4	-2.4	0.4	1.5	84.0
Belgium................	295.0	10.8	22.5	1.5	85.5
Portugal................	235.3	46.3	39.8	1.2	86.7
Czech Rep..............	225.8	18.8	12.9	1.1	87.8
Other Asia, nes........	209.6	10.3	4.7	1.0	88.9

248 Wood, simply worked, and railway sleepers of wood

In 2013, the value (in current US$) of exports of "wood, simply worked, and railway sleepers of wood" (SITC group 248) increased by 11.7 percent (compared to 9.7 percent average growth rate from 2009-2013) to reach 40.4 bln US$ (see table 2), while imports increased by 9.9 percent to reach 42.1 bln US$ (see table 3). Exports of this commodity accounted for 4.8 percent of world exports of SITC sections 2+4, and 0.2 percent of total world merchandise exports (see table 1). Canada, Russian Federation and USA were the top exporters in 2013 (see table 2). They accounted for 18.7, 9.2 and 8.7 percent of world exports, respectively. China, USA and Japan were the top destinations, with respectively 16.3, 15.3 and 8.2 percent of world imports (see table 3).

The top 15 countries/areas accounted for 76.9 and 71.8 percent of total world exports and imports, respectively (see tables 2 and 3). In 2013, Canada was the country/area with the highest value of net exports (+6.6 bln US$), followed by Russian Federation (+3.6 bln US$). By MDG regions (see graph 2), the largest surpluses in this product group were recorded by Developed North America (+3.7 bln US$), Commonwealth of Independent States (+3.0 bln US$) and Developed Europe (+1.7 bln US$). The largest trade deficits were recorded by Eastern Asia (-7.1 bln US$), Developed Asia-Pacific (-3.3 bln US$) and Northern Africa (-2.2 bln US$).

Table 1: Imports (Imp.) and exports (Exp.), 1999-2013, in current US$

		1999	2000	2001	2002	2003	2004	2005	2006	2007	2008	2009	2010	2011	2012	2013
Values in Bln US$	Imp.	29.3	29.2	26.8	27.8	30.1	36.7	38.4	40.5	43.7	38.1	28.7	35.0	39.3	38.3	42.1
	Exp.	25.2	26.4	24.4	25.4	27.5	33.7	35.1	38.3	41.8	36.4	27.9	33.7	37.0	36.2	40.4
As a percentage of SITC section (%)	Imp.	12.8	11.8	11.4	11.5	10.4	9.8	9.2	8.2	7.1	5.0	5.3	4.6	4.0	4.1	4.6
	Exp.	12.8	12.4	12.1	11.8	10.7	10.4	9.6	8.6	7.6	5.6	5.7	4.9	4.1	4.3	4.8
As a percentage of world trade (%)	Imp.	0.5	0.4	0.4	0.4	0.4	0.4	0.4	0.3	0.3	0.2	0.2	0.2	0.2	0.2	0.2
	Exp.	0.5	0.4	0.4	0.4	0.4	0.4	0.3	0.3	0.3	0.2	0.2	0.2	0.2	0.2	0.2

Graph 1: Annual growth rates of exports, 1999–2013
(In percentage by year)

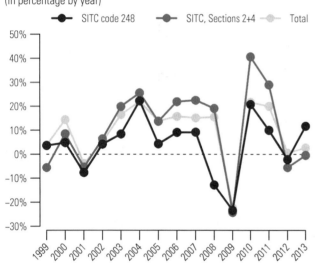

Graph 2: Trade Balance by MDG regions 2013
(Bln US$)

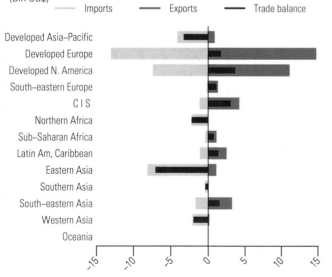

Table 2: Top exporting countries or areas in 2013

Country or area	Value (million US$)	Avg. Growth (%) 09-13	Growth (%) 12-13	World share %	Cum.
World	40 420.8	9.7	11.7	100.0	
Canada	7 572.2	20.6	25.3	18.7	18.7
Russian Federation	3 737.4	8.8	8.8	9.2	28.0
USA	3 517.7	17.1	15.3	8.7	36.7
Sweden	3 377.8	2.5	3.4	8.4	45.0
Germany	2 173.5	3.3	8.2	5.4	50.4
Finland	1 933.5	10.7	17.9	4.8	55.2
Austria	1 573.2	0.9	4.9	3.9	59.1
Chile	1 087.8	17.5	16.5	2.7	61.8
Malaysia	1 003.5	3.2	-2.6	2.5	64.3
China	973.4	0.8	-4.9	2.4	66.7
Romania	970.9	13.3	8.9	2.4	69.1
Thailand	912.2	23.9	26.6	2.3	71.3
Brazil	825.5	1.1	-4.2	2.0	73.4
New Zealand	756.5	9.8	3.9	1.9	75.2
Latvia	679.6	15.8	15.7	1.7	76.9

Table 3: Top importing countries or areas in 2013

Country or area	Value (million US$)	Avg. Growth (%) 09-13	Growth (%) 12-13	World share %	Cum.
World	42 056.1	10.0	9.9	100.0	
China	6 858.6	30.8	23.5	16.3	16.3
USA	6 447.1	15.7	24.5	15.3	31.6
Japan	3 454.4	12.8	20.6	8.2	39.9
United Kingdom	2 112.6	7.3	12.1	5.0	44.9
Germany	1 657.7	5.3	4.6	3.9	48.8
Italy	1 503.5	-4.4	-2.8	3.6	52.4
France	1 315.1	-1.5	-1.2	3.1	55.5
Netherlands	1 111.9	2.3	-0.8	2.6	58.2
Egypt	1 019.6	5.9	-15.8	2.4	60.6
Canada	939.5	6.6	1.3	2.2	62.8
Belgium	933.4	4.6	4.3	2.2	65.0
Viet Nam	806.6	21.5	31.5	1.9	67.0
Austria	689.0	4.5	1.2	1.6	68.6
Saudi Arabia	670.8	19.3	-0.4	1.6	70.2
Rep. of Korea	666.5	16.9	10.1	1.6	71.8

In 2013, the value (in current US$) of exports of "pulp and waste paper" (SITC group 251) increased by 2.3 percent (compared to 10.2 percent average growth rate from 2009-2013) to reach 45.4 bln US$ (see table 2), while imports increased by 1.8 percent to reach 50.5 bln US$ (see table 3). Exports of this commodity accounted for 5.4 percent of world exports of SITC sections 2+4, and 0.2 percent of total world merchandise exports (see table 1). USA, Canada and Brazil were the top exporters in 2013 (see table 2). They accounted for 19.9, 14.9 and 11.4 percent of world exports, respectively. China, Germany and USA were the top destinations, with respectively 34.3, 8.8 and 7.5 percent of world imports (see table 3).

The top 15 countries/areas accounted for 85.9 and 83.3 percent of total world exports and imports, respectively (see tables 2 and 3). In 2013, Canada was the country/area with the highest value of net exports (+6.5 bln US$), followed by USA (+5.3 bln US$). By MDG regions (see graph 2), the largest surpluses in this product group were recorded by Developed North America (+11.7 bln US$), Latin America and the Caribbean (+6.3 bln US$) and Commonwealth of Independent States (+841.2 mln US$). The largest trade deficits were recorded by Eastern Asia (-19.6 bln US$), Developed Europe (-2.0 bln US$) and Southern Asia (-1.7 bln US$).

Table 1: Imports (Imp.) and exports (Exp.), 1999-2013, in current US$

		1999	2000	2001	2002	2003	2004	2005	2006	2007	2008	2009	2010	2011	2012	2013
Values in Bln US$	Imp.	19.8	27.2	21.7	21.2	24.2	28.4	30.3	33.3	40.4	46.6	34.0	49.2	57.2	49.6	50.5
	Exp.	16.8	24.3	19.0	18.8	21.9	24.8	25.9	29.7	36.7	40.6	30.8	43.7	49.7	44.4	45.4
As a percentage of	Imp.	8.7	11.0	9.3	8.8	8.4	7.6	7.3	6.7	6.6	6.1	6.3	6.5	5.8	5.4	5.5
SITC section (%)	Exp.	8.6	11.4	9.4	8.8	8.5	7.7	7.1	6.6	6.7	6.2	6.2	6.3	5.6	5.3	5.4
As a percentage of	Imp.	0.3	0.4	0.3	0.3	0.3	0.3	0.3	0.3	0.3	0.3	0.3	0.3	0.3	0.3	0.3
world trade (%)	Exp.	0.3	0.4	0.3	0.3	0.3	0.3	0.2	0.2	0.3	0.3	0.2	0.3	0.3	0.2	0.2

Graph 1: Annual growth rates of exports, 1999–2013
(In percentage by year)

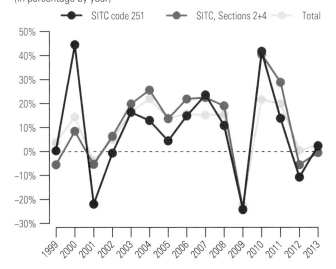

Graph 2: Trade Balance by MDG regions 2013
(Bln US$)

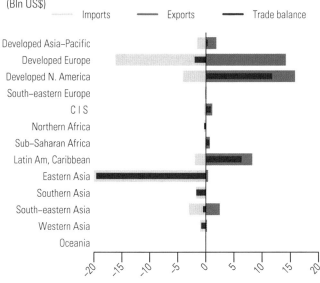

Table 2: Top exporting countries or areas in 2013

Country or area	Value (million US$)	Avg. Growth (%) 09-13	Growth (%) 12-13	World share %	World share % Cum.
World	45411.0	10.2	2.3	100.0	
USA	9035.4	7.4	-3.2	19.9	19.9
Canada	6783.2	10.0	0.4	14.9	34.8
Brazil	5186.0	11.8	10.2	11.4	46.3
Chile	2806.2	8.6	10.9	6.2	52.4
Sweden	2665.9	7.4	3.7	5.9	58.3
Finland	2093.2	27.0	19.4	4.6	62.9
Indonesia	1845.8	20.7	19.3	4.1	67.0
Germany	1461.1	8.4	4.3	3.2	70.2
Netherlands	1143.5	6.4	-21.7	2.5	72.7
Japan	1135.9	10.1	-0.6	2.5	75.2
Russian Federation	1125.2	12.1	-7.4	2.5	77.7
Spain	1092.9	14.2	3.4	2.4	80.1
Belgium	941.0	2.8	-1.3	2.1	82.2
France	907.4	10.0	-9.6	2.0	84.2
United Kingdom	784.6	9.0	-7.7	1.7	85.9

Table 3: Top importing countries or areas in 2013

Country or area	Value (million US$)	Avg. Growth (%) 09-13	Growth (%) 12-13	World share %	World share % Cum.
World	50494.5	10.4	1.8	100.0	
China	17305.5	12.9	0.3	34.3	34.3
Germany	4456.7	9.3	1.2	8.8	43.1
USA	3778.6	10.3	7.9	7.5	50.6
Italy	2387.8	7.4	8.0	4.7	55.3
Rep. of Korea	1930.6	7.3	3.1	3.8	59.1
Indonesia	1733.2	16.2	11.7	3.4	62.6
France	1644.8	8.2	10.2	3.3	65.8
Netherlands	1542.0	14.2	-8.8	3.1	68.9
Japan	1394.9	7.4	-3.8	2.8	71.6
India	1370.4	15.5	6.6	2.7	74.4
Spain	1040.9	12.0	17.2	2.1	76.4
Mexico	957.8	4.2	0.7	1.9	78.3
Belgium	898.3	1.8	6.4	1.8	80.1
United Kingdom	815.8	0.3	-3.6	1.6	81.7
Austria	781.3	9.4	-5.3	1.5	83.3

261 Silk

In 2013, the value (in current US$) of exports of "silk" (SITC group 261) increased by 8.2 percent (compared to 13.4 percent average growth rate from 2009-2013) to reach 525.5 mln US$ (see table 2), while imports increased by 2.4 percent to reach 539.3 mln US$ (see table 3). Exports of this commodity accounted for 0.1 percent of world exports of SITC sections 2+4, and less than 0.1 percent of total world merchandise exports (see table 1). China, Italy and Uzbekistan were the top exporters in 2013 (see table 2). They accounted for 79.5, 4.9 and 4.2 percent of world exports, respectively. India, Romania and Italy were the top destinations, with respectively 31.7, 15.8 and 13.6 percent of world imports (see table 3).

The top 15 countries/areas accounted for 99.5 and 96.8 percent of total world exports and imports, respectively (see tables 2 and 3). In 2013, China was the country/area with the highest value of net exports (+408.9 mln US$), followed by Uzbekistan (+22.0 mln US$). By MDG regions (see graph 2), the largest surpluses in this product group were recorded by Eastern Asia (+385.2 mln US$), Commonwealth of Independent States (+21.7 mln US$) and Developed North America (+1.9 mln US$). The largest trade deficits were recorded by Southern Asia (-156.4 mln US$), South-eastern Europe (-80.6 mln US$) and Developed Europe (-73.7 mln US$).

Table 1: Imports (Imp.) and exports (Exp.), 1999-2013, in current US$

		1999	2000	2001	2002	2003	2004	2005	2006	2007	2008	2009	2010	2011	2012	2013
Values in Mln US$	Imp.	471.4	502.8	426.7	398.6	359.5	365.9	449.0	490.2	459.0	476.8	374.3	456.9	539.6	526.6	539.3
	Exp.	384.3	433.6	359.2	333.5	301.7	314.9	350.2	340.3	452.3	437.2	317.9	476.0	491.1	485.7	525.5
As a percentage of	Imp.	0.2	0.2	0.2	0.2	0.1	0.1	0.1	0.1	0.1	0.1	0.1	0.1	0.1	0.1	0.1
SITC section (%)	Exp.	0.2	0.2	0.2	0.2	0.1	0.1	0.1	0.1	0.1	0.1	0.1	0.1	0.1	0.1	0.1
As a percentage of	Imp.	0.0	0.0	0.0	0.0	0.0	0.0	0.0	0.0	0.0	0.0	0.0	0.0	0.0	0.0	0.0
world trade (%)	Exp.	0.0	0.0	0.0	0.0	0.0	0.0	0.0	0.0	0.0	0.0	0.0	0.0	0.0	0.0	0.0

Graph 1: Annual growth rates of exports, 1999–2013
(In percentage by year)

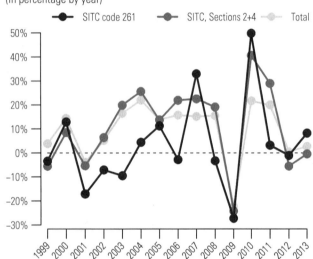

Legend: SITC code 261 — SITC, Sections 2+4 — Total

Table 2: Top exporting countries or areas in 2013

Country or area	Value (million US$)	Avg. Growth (%) 09-13	Growth (%) 12-13	World share %	Cum.
World	525.5	13.4	8.2	100.0	
China	418.0	12.3	4.9	79.5	79.5
Italy	25.6	30.7	24.4	4.9	84.4
Uzbekistan	22.0	11.2	8.0	4.2	88.6
India	20.6	42.0	80.8	3.9	92.5
Germany	18.4	24.8	11.8	3.5	96.0
Romania	7.3	24.7	29.6	1.4	97.4
USA	2.6	6.8	1.5	0.5	97.9
Viet Nam	2.1	22.6	11.2	0.4	98.3
United Kingdom	1.7	16.3	43.4	0.3	98.6
Japan	1.2	15.4	-23.7	0.2	98.8
United Arab Emirates	1.0	-2.7	21.7	0.2	99.0
Brazil	0.8	11.1	88.6	0.2	99.2
Belgium	0.8	47.7	121.5	0.2	99.3
Tajikistan	0.6	-19.4	-46.2	0.1	99.4
Turkmenistan	0.5	-9.2	99.3	0.1	99.5

Graph 2: Trade Balance by MDG regions 2013
(Mln US$)

Legend: Imports — Exports — Trade balance

Developed Asia–Pacific
Developed Europe
Developed N. America
South–eastern Europe
CIS
Northern Africa
Sub–Saharan Africa
Latin Am, Caribbean
Eastern Asia
Southern Asia
South–eastern Asia
Western Asia
Oceania

-200 -150 -100 -50 0 50 100 150 200 250 300 350 400 450

Table 3: Top importing countries or areas in 2013

Country or area	Value (million US$)	Avg. Growth (%) 09-13	Growth (%) 12-13	World share %	Cum.
World	539.3	9.6	2.4	100.0	
India	170.7	-3.7	-27.7	31.7	31.7
Romania	85.3	46.8	64.8	15.8	47.5
Italy	73.4	26.3	27.0	13.6	61.1
Viet Nam	57.1	21.9	16.8	10.6	71.7
Japan	40.7	12.9	8.3	7.6	79.2
Rep. of Korea	23.9	1.7	-8.4	4.4	83.7
France	21.3	42.4	99.2	4.0	87.6
Germany	19.1	25.6	18.3	3.5	91.1
China	9.1	16.5	-14.3	1.7	92.8
Brazil	5.7	43.8	139.6	1.1	93.9
Tunisia	3.5	19.0	36.4	0.6	94.5
Bangladesh	3.4	-10.9	-1.6	0.6	95.1
Turkey	3.3	20.8	42.4	0.6	95.8
Thailand	2.9	14.3	24.9	0.5	96.3
Bulgaria	2.8	49.3	55.9	0.5	96.8

In 2013, the value (in current US$) of exports of "cotton" (SITC group 263) decreased by 8.2 percent (compared to 19.8 percent average growth rate from 2009-2013) to reach 21.0 bln US$ (see table 2), while imports decreased by 12.1 percent to reach 21.0 bln US$ (see table 3). Exports of this commodity accounted for 2.5 percent of world exports of SITC sections 2+4, and 0.1 percent of total world merchandise exports (see table 1). USA, India and Australia were the top exporters in 2013 (see table 2). They accounted for 27.3, 22.2 and 12.0 percent of world exports, respectively. China, Bangladesh and Turkey were the top destinations, with respectively 41.4, 9.4 and 8.0 percent of world imports (see table 3).

The top 15 countries/areas accounted for 89.3 and 90.9 percent of total world exports and imports, respectively (see tables 2 and 3). In 2013, USA was the country/area with the highest value of net exports (+5.7 bln US$), followed by India (+4.3 bln US$). By MDG regions (see graph 2), the largest surpluses in this product group were recorded by Developed North America (+5.7 bln US$), Developed Asia-Pacific (+2.3 bln US$) and Commonwealth of Independent States (+2.2 bln US$). The largest trade deficits were recorded by Eastern Asia (-9.8 bln US$), South-eastern Asia (-3.3 bln US$) and Western Asia (-1.3 bln US$).

Table 1: Imports (Imp.) and exports (Exp.), 1999-2013, in current US$

		1999	2000	2001	2002	2003	2004	2005	2006	2007	2008	2009	2010	2011	2012	2013
Values in Bln US$	Imp.	7.8	8.1	8.2	6.9	8.8	12.0	10.8	12.6	12.5	14.0	9.8	17.2	25.8	24.0	21.0
	Exp.	7.2	7.6	7.3	6.6	9.5	11.6	10.4	11.8	12.4	12.7	10.2	17.4	23.6	22.9	21.0
As a percentage of	Imp.	3.4	3.3	3.5	2.9	3.0	3.2	2.6	2.5	2.0	1.8	1.8	2.3	2.6	2.6	2.3
SITC section (%)	Exp.	3.7	3.6	3.6	3.1	3.7	3.6	2.8	2.6	2.3	1.9	2.1	2.5	2.6	2.7	2.5
As a percentage of	Imp.	0.1	0.1	0.1	0.1	0.1	0.1	0.1	0.1	0.1	0.1	0.1	0.1	0.1	0.1	0.1
world trade (%)	Exp.	0.1	0.1	0.1	0.1	0.1	0.1	0.1	0.1	0.1	0.1	0.1	0.1	0.1	0.1	0.1

Graph 1: Annual growth rates of exports, 1999–2013
(In percentage by year)

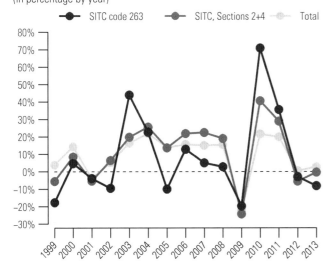

Graph 2: Trade Balance by MDG regions 2013
(Bln US$)

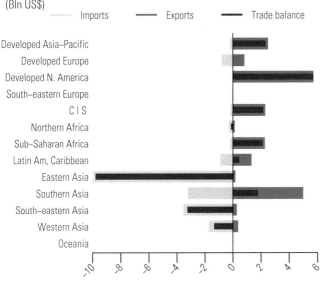

Table 2: Top exporting countries or areas in 2013

Country or area	Value (million US$)	Avg. Growth (%) 09-13	Growth (%) 12-13	World share %	Cum.
World	21 016.7	19.8	-8.2	100.0	
USA	5 733.4	12.9	-9.8	27.3	27.3
India	4 672.0	45.7	24.0	22.2	49.5
Australia	2 512.4	56.2	-7.6	12.0	61.5
Uzbekistan	1 896.6	11.8	-14.8	9.0	70.5
Brazil	1 113.4	12.4	-47.6	5.3	75.8
Greece	500.9	3.9	-11.9	2.4	78.2
Burkina Faso	441.1	15.3	49.8	2.1	80.3
Mali	384.3	26.5	-0.4	1.8	82.1
Pakistan	313.4	9.2	-33.0	1.5	83.6
Côte d'Ivoire	272.1	41.2	21.8	1.3	84.9
Benin	236.0	16.4	58.7	1.1	86.0
Turkey	200.1	13.2	-9.4	1.0	87.0
Malaysia	177.8	31.4	-60.7	0.8	87.8
Cameroon	173.7	17.8	20.7	0.8	88.6
Tajikistan	148.0	15.1	-8.5	0.7	89.3

Table 3: Top importing countries or areas in 2013

Country or area	Value (million US$)	Avg. Growth (%) 09-13	Growth (%) 12-13	World share %	Cum.
World	21 045.9	21.0	-12.1	100.0	
China	8 718.1	40.9	-27.4	41.4	41.4
Bangladesh	1 978.6	14.1	-1.6	9.4	50.8
Turkey	1 689.2	13.8	32.0	8.0	58.9
Indonesia	1 348.7	14.5	0.8	6.4	65.3
Viet Nam	1 170.0	31.2	32.8	5.6	70.8
Pakistan	758.3	12.0	34.1	3.6	74.4
Thailand	750.4	11.2	-9.3	3.6	78.0
Rep. of Korea	610.7	20.2	-11.4	2.9	80.9
Mexico	463.2	2.6	0.6	2.2	83.1
Other Asia, nes	439.5	13.4	5.2	2.1	85.2
India	402.1	21.1	-14.9	1.9	87.1
Malaysia	230.8	10.2	-63.2	1.1	88.2
China, Hong Kong SAR	199.5	11.9	26.8	0.9	89.1
Japan	194.0	11.5	-6.8	0.9	90.1
Germany	172.2	14.8	6.2	0.8	90.9

264 Jute, other textile bast fibres, nes, not spun; tow and waste

In 2013, the value (in current US$) of exports of "jute, other textile bast fibres, nes, not spun; tow and waste" (SITC group 264) increased by 5.7 percent (compared to 16.8 percent average growth rate from 2009-2013) to reach 380.5 mln US$ (see table 2), while imports decreased by 28.0 percent to reach 198.4 mln US$ (see table 3). Exports of this commodity accounted for less than 0.1 percent of world exports of SITC sections 2+4, and less than 0.1 percent of total world merchandise exports (see table 1). Bangladesh, United Rep. of Tanzania and Kenya were the top exporters in 2013 (see table 2). They accounted for 86.3, 4.8 and 3.1 percent of world exports, respectively. Pakistan, India and China were the top destinations, with respectively 21.9, 19.5 and 15.1 percent of world imports (see table 3).

The top 15 countries/areas accounted for 99.6 and 89.9 percent of total world exports and imports, respectively (see tables 2 and 3). In 2013, Bangladesh was the country/area with the highest value of net exports (+328.2 mln US$), followed by United Rep. of Tanzania (+18.4 mln US$). By MDG regions (see graph 2), the largest surpluses in this product group were recorded by Southern Asia (+236.0 mln US$) and Sub-Saharan Africa (+14.3 mln US$). The largest trade deficits were recorded by Eastern Asia (-34.4 mln US$), Developed Europe (-6.8 mln US$) and Commonwealth of Independent States (-6.2 mln US$).

Table 1: Imports (Imp.) and exports (Exp.), 1999-2013, in current US$

		1999	2000	2001	2002	2003	2004	2005	2006	2007	2008	2009	2010	2011	2012	2013
Values in Mln US$	Imp.	87.4	95.3	84.3	115.0	101.8	96.5	116.8	160.6	182.7	206.7	207.9	299.5	351.6	275.4	198.4
	Exp.	59.9	79.9	55.5	62.5	61.5	103.3	139.3	155.9	228.4	207.6	204.6	352.1	362.1	360.0	380.5
As a percentage of SITC section (%)	Imp.	0.0	0.0	0.0	0.0	0.0	0.0	0.0	0.0	0.0	0.0	0.0	0.0	0.0	0.0	0.0
	Exp.	0.0	0.0	0.0	0.0	0.0	0.0	0.0	0.0	0.0	0.0	0.0	0.1	0.0	0.0	0.0
As a percentage of world trade (%)	Imp.	0.0	0.0	0.0	0.0	0.0	0.0	0.0	0.0	0.0	0.0	0.0	0.0	0.0	0.0	0.0
	Exp.	0.0	0.0	0.0	0.0	0.0	0.0	0.0	0.0	0.0	0.0	0.0	0.0	0.0	0.0	0.0

Graph 1: Annual growth rates of exports, 1999–2013
(In percentage by year)

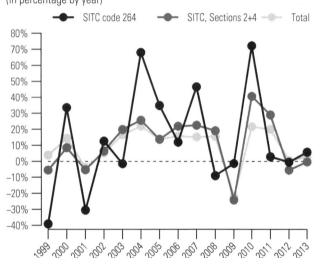

Graph 2: Trade Balance by MDG regions 2013
(Mln US$)

Table 2: Top exporting countries or areas in 2013

Country or area	Value (million US$)	Avg. Growth (%) 09-13	Growth (%) 12-13	World share %	Cum.
World....................	380.5	16.8	5.7	100.0	
Bangladesh..................	328.4	19.2	7.6	86.3	86.3
United Rep. of Tanzania.......	18.4	21.1	7.3	4.8	91.1
Kenya....................	11.8	-8.2	-9.6	3.1	94.2
India....................	9.1	6.6	-10.4	2.4	96.6
Belgium....................	3.8	28.1	7.8	1.0	97.6
Viet Nam..................	1.3	5.2	-50.9	0.3	98.0
Spain....................	1.2	80.2	872.4	0.3	98.3
Mozambique..................	1.0	-2.4	16.5	0.3	98.5
Nepal....................	0.9	176.3	45.8	0.2	98.8
Germany....................	0.6	52.7	14.2	0.2	98.9
United Arab Emirates..........	0.6	10.3	21.7	0.2	99.1
France....................	0.6	7.0	52.6	0.2	99.2
USA....................	0.5	-16.1	-56.6	0.1	99.4
Netherlands..................	0.4	17.9	-74.6	0.1	99.5
Lao People's Dem. Rep.........	0.3	0.2	91.0	0.1	99.6

Table 3: Top importing countries or areas in 2013

Country or area	Value (million US$)	Avg. Growth (%) 09-13	Growth (%) 12-13	World share %	Cum.
World....................	198.4	-1.2	-28.0	100.0	
Pakistan....................	43.5	-5.2	-8.0	21.9	21.9
India....................	38.7	0.3	-47.7	19.5	41.4
China....................	30.0	-10.3	-37.4	15.1	56.6
Nepal....................	19.9	4.9	-26.6	10.0	66.6
Côte d'Ivoire.................	10.7	19.8	-27.3	5.4	72.0
Russian Federation.............	5.7	36.1	-2.9	2.9	74.9
Rep. of Korea................	4.6	13.3	-5.5	2.3	77.2
Ethiopia....................	4.5	11.9	100.0	2.2	79.5
Germany....................	4.4	35.5	-9.9	2.2	81.7
Saudi Arabia.................	3.9	26.2	7.8	2.0	83.6
Indonesia....................	3.6	30.0	-13.5	1.8	85.4
USA....................	2.5	5.7	-14.1	1.2	86.7
United Kingdom...............	2.4	-17.9	-12.9	1.2	87.9
Viet Nam..................	2.4	0.2	-40.2	1.2	89.1
Cuba....................	1.7	...	-13.6	0.8	89.9

In 2013, the value (in current US$) of exports of "vegetable textile fibres (other than cotton or jute) not spun; waste" (SITC group 265) increased by 14.8 percent (compared to 15.6 percent average growth rate from 2009-2013) to reach 1.0 bln US$ (see table 2), while imports increased by 12.0 percent to reach 992.1 mln US$ (see table 3). Exports of this commodity accounted for 0.1 percent of world exports of SITC sections 2+4, and less than 0.1 percent of total world merchandise exports (see table 1). France, Belgium and India were the top exporters in 2013 (see table 2). They accounted for 30.5, 20.1 and 13.3 percent of world exports, respectively. China, Belgium and USA were the top destinations, with respectively 51.9, 10.2 and 3.8 percent of world imports (see table 3).

The top 15 countries/areas accounted for 94.4 and 88.1 percent of total world exports and imports, respectively (see tables 2 and 3). In 2013, France was the country/area with the highest value of net exports (+294.2 mln US$), followed by Sri Lanka (+111.4 mln US$). By MDG regions (see graph 2), the largest surpluses in this product group were recorded by Developed Europe (+285.6 mln US$), Southern Asia (+217.2 mln US$) and South-eastern Asia (+74.0 mln US$). The largest trade deficits were recorded by Eastern Asia (-506.7 mln US$), Developed North America (-29.8 mln US$) and Developed Asia-Pacific (-21.1 mln US$).

Table 1: Imports (Imp.) and exports (Exp.), 1999-2013, in current US$

		1999	2000	2001	2002	2003	2004	2005	2006	2007	2008	2009	2010	2011	2012	2013
Values in Bln US$	Imp.	0.5	0.6	0.6	0.5	0.7	0.8	0.7	0.7	0.8	0.7	0.6	0.8	1.0	0.9	1.0
	Exp.	0.5	0.6	0.5	0.5	0.7	0.8	0.7	0.7	0.7	0.6	0.6	0.8	0.9	0.9	1.0
As a percentage of SITC section (%)	Imp.	0.2	0.2	0.2	0.2	0.3	0.2	0.2	0.1	0.1	0.1	0.1	0.1	0.1	0.1	0.1
	Exp.	0.3	0.3	0.3	0.3	0.3	0.2	0.2	0.2	0.1	0.1	0.1	0.1	0.1	0.1	0.1
As a percentage of world trade (%)	Imp.	0.0	0.0	0.0	0.0	0.0	0.0	0.0	0.0	0.0	0.0	0.0	0.0	0.0	0.0	0.0
	Exp.	0.0	0.0	0.0	0.0	0.0	0.0	0.0	0.0	0.0	0.0	0.0	0.0	0.0	0.0	0.0

Graph 1: Annual growth rates of exports, 1999–2013

(In percentage by year)

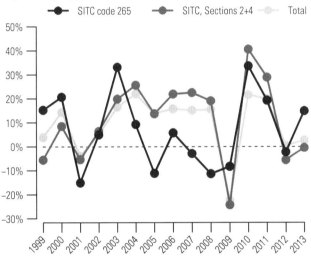

SITC code 265 — SITC, Sections 2+4 — Total

Table 2: Top exporting countries or areas in 2013

Country or area	Value (million US$)	Avg. Growth (%) 09-13	Growth (%) 12-13	World share %	Cum.
World	1 033.2	15.6	14.8	100.0	
France	314.6	15.9	26.8	30.5	30.5
Belgium	207.4	21.3	33.3	20.1	50.5
India	137.9	32.0	20.0	13.3	63.9
Sri Lanka	111.6	9.7	-0.8	10.8	74.7
Brazil	29.2	12.1	-10.7	2.8	77.5
Philippines	28.1	25.0	127.6	2.7	80.2
Viet Nam	27.6	1.5	-6.7	2.7	82.9
Kenya	22.2	411.2	-9.6	2.1	85.0
Belarus	19.5	34.8	13.8	1.9	86.9
Thailand	14.6	5.8	-5.4	1.4	88.3
Ecuador	13.9	1.9	-18.0	1.3	89.7
Lithuania	13.5	21.3	1.0	1.3	91.0
Netherlands	13.3	-4.8	-45.9	1.3	92.3
Canada	11.7	-7.0	20.7	1.1	93.4
China	9.9	8.8	-0.1	1.0	94.4

Graph 2: Trade Balance by MDG regions 2013

(Mln US$)

Imports — Exports — Trade balance

Developed Asia–Pacific
Developed Europe
Developed N. America
South–eastern Europe
CIS
Northern Africa
Sub–Saharan Africa
Latin Am, Caribbean
Eastern Asia
Southern Asia
South–eastern Asia
Western Asia
Oceania

-600 -500 -400 -300 -200 -100 0 100 200 300 400 500 600

Table 3: Top importing countries or areas in 2013

Country or area	Value (million US$)	Avg. Growth (%) 09-13	Growth (%) 12-13	World share %	Cum.
World	992.1	15.1	12.0	100.0	
China	514.9	18.5	19.6	51.9	51.9
Belgium	101.3	12.4	56.6	10.2	62.1
USA	37.5	2.0	-17.1	3.8	65.9
Netherlands	28.9	3.7	-10.5	2.9	68.8
India	27.4	29.0	22.3	2.8	71.6
United Kingdom	22.5	107.2	-5.2	2.3	73.8
Spain	22.0	-1.4	-26.7	2.2	76.1
France	20.5	8.2	-7.6	2.1	78.1
Japan	18.1	5.7	10.0	1.8	79.9
Poland	16.7	20.3	129.1	1.7	81.6
Germany	15.4	15.0	-15.1	1.5	83.2
Lithuania	14.8	18.1	4.5	1.5	84.7
Mexico	12.6	24.8	-2.3	1.3	85.9
Russian Federation	12.2	52.3	20.0	1.2	87.2
Tunisia	9.7	17.3	-45.9	1.0	88.1

266 Synthetic fibres suitable for spinning

In 2013, the value (in current US$) of exports of "synthetic fibres suitable for spinning" (SITC group 266) increased by 5.0 percent (compared to 12.9 percent average growth rate from 2009-2013) to reach 8.5 bln US$ (see table 2), while imports increased by 4.7 percent to reach 10.1 bln US$ (see table 3). Exports of this commodity accounted for 1.0 percent of world exports of SITC sections 2+4, and less than 0.1 percent of total world merchandise exports (see table 1). Rep. of Korea, China and Japan were the top exporters in 2013 (see table 2). They accounted for 15.4, 14.7 and 11.2 percent of world exports, respectively. China, USA and Germany were the top destinations, with respectively 11.4, 9.8 and 7.8 percent of world imports (see table 3).

The top 15 countries/areas accounted for 85.9 and 67.5 percent of total world exports and imports, respectively (see tables 2 and 3). In 2013, Rep. of Korea was the country/area with the highest value of net exports (+1.3 bln US$), followed by Other Asia, nes (+853.5 mln US$). By MDG regions (see graph 2), the largest surpluses in this product group were recorded by Eastern Asia (+2.2 bln US$) and Developed Asia-Pacific (+737.3 mln US$). The largest trade deficits were recorded by Developed Europe (-1.5 bln US$), Developed North America (-685.2 mln US$) and Western Asia (-644.4 mln US$).

Table 1: Imports (Imp.) and exports (Exp.), 1999-2013, in current US$

		1999	2000	2001	2002	2003	2004	2005	2006	2007	2008	2009	2010	2011	2012	2013
Values in Bln US$	Imp.	5.1	5.8	5.3	5.5	6.3	7.2	7.7	7.4	8.1	8.3	6.6	8.7	10.9	9.6	10.1
	Exp.	4.2	4.6	4.0	4.3	4.8	5.4	5.9	5.9	6.8	6.8	5.2	7.2	9.1	8.1	8.5
As a percentage of	Imp.	2.2	2.3	2.2	2.3	2.2	1.9	1.9	1.5	1.3	1.1	1.2	1.1	1.1	1.0	1.1
SITC section (%)	Exp.	2.2	2.2	2.0	2.0	1.9	1.7	1.6	1.3	1.2	1.0	1.1	1.0	1.0	1.0	1.0
As a percentage of	Imp.	0.1	0.1	0.1	0.1	0.1	0.1	0.1	0.1	0.1	0.1	0.1	0.1	0.1	0.1	0.1
world trade (%)	Exp.	0.1	0.1	0.1	0.1	0.1	0.1	0.1	0.0	0.0	0.0	0.0	0.0	0.1	0.0	0.0

Graph 1: Annual growth rates of exports, 1999–2013
(In percentage by year)

● SITC code 266   ● SITC, Sections 2+4   ● Total

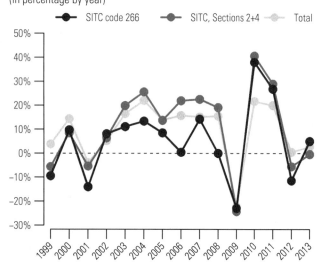

Graph 2: Trade Balance by MDG regions 2013
(Bln US$)

— Imports   — Exports   — Trade balance

Developed Asia–Pacific
Developed Europe
Developed N. America
South–eastern Europe
C I S
Northern Africa
Sub–Saharan Africa
Latin Am, Caribbean
Eastern Asia
Southern Asia
South–eastern Asia
Western Asia
Oceania

Table 2: Top exporting countries or areas in 2013

Country or area	Value (million US$)	Avg. Growth (%) 09-13	Growth (%) 12-13	World share %	Cum.
World.................................	8464.5	12.9	5.0	100.0	
Rep. of Korea.......................	1306.0	13.5	3.3	15.4	15.4
China.................................	1242.2	22.8	4.0	14.7	30.1
Japan.................................	952.1	11.6	1.6	11.2	41.4
Other Asia, nes....................	910.8	6.0	-5.0	10.8	52.1
Thailand..............................	576.1	11.0	12.7	6.8	58.9
USA...................................	465.3	13.2	-5.3	5.5	64.4
Belgium..............................	411.7	18.3	17.5	4.9	69.3
India..................................	395.6	22.3	36.1	4.7	74.0
Belarus..............................	191.6	4.2	-8.8	2.3	76.2
Malaysia.............................	153.3	17.4	8.6	1.8	78.0
Ireland...............................	150.9	10.7	1.4	1.8	79.8
Portugal.............................	148.9	7.1	6.9	1.8	81.6
Germany.............................	147.8	6.0	36.8	1.7	83.3
Viet Nam............................	108.1	26.8	3.1	1.3	84.6
United Kingdom....................	107.8	12.5	1.9	1.3	85.9

Table 3: Top importing countries or areas in 2013

Country or area	Value (million US$)	Avg. Growth (%) 09-13	Growth (%) 12-13	World share %	Cum.
World.................................	10083.6	11.3	4.7	100.0	
China.................................	1154.4	13.3	14.5	11.4	11.4
USA...................................	987.4	13.4	-2.0	9.8	21.2
Germany.............................	789.6	11.7	8.0	7.8	29.1
Turkey................................	517.6	14.9	5.0	5.1	34.2
Italy...................................	478.8	7.0	6.5	4.7	39.0
Indonesia............................	459.8	22.2	11.8	4.6	43.5
Viet Nam............................	441.0	17.1	1.8	4.4	47.9
Iran....................................	*328.1*	-3.1	-13.3	3.3	51.1
United Kingdom....................	284.9	10.4	3.6	2.8	54.0
Spain.................................	271.2	20.7	60.1	2.7	56.7
Mexico...............................	244.3	9.7	-5.3	2.4	59.1
France................................	236.1	6.0	-2.5	2.3	61.4
Russian Federation...............	218.4	45.9	20.7	2.2	63.6
Pakistan.............................	200.4	1.7	-9.1	2.0	65.6
India..................................	195.6	38.2	36.2	1.9	67.5

Source: UN Comtrade and UN Service Trade

In 2013, the value (in current US$) of exports of "other man-made fibres suitable for spinning; waste of man-made fibres" (SITC group 267) increased by 1.3 percent (compared to 8.7 percent average growth rate from 2009-2013) to reach 5.1 bln US$ (see table 2), while imports decreased by 4.6 percent to reach 5.7 bln US$ (see table 3). Exports of this commodity accounted for 0.6 percent of world exports of SITC sections 2+4, and less than 0.1 percent of total world merchandise exports (see table 1). USA, Germany and Japan were the top exporters in 2013 (see table 2). They accounted for 24.3, 14.6 and 11.4 percent of world exports, respectively. China, Turkey and Indonesia were the top destinations, with respectively 19.7, 10.9 and 6.9 percent of world imports (see table 3).

The top 15 countries/areas accounted for 96.4 and 70.2 percent of total world exports and imports, respectively (see tables 2 and 3). In 2013, USA was the country/area with the highest value of net exports (+1.0 bln US$), followed by Japan (+510.8 mln US$). By MDG regions (see graph 2), the largest surpluses in this product group were recorded by Developed North America (+998.1 mln US$), Developed Asia-Pacific (+498.9 mln US$) and Developed Europe (+186.6 mln US$). The largest trade deficits were recorded by Eastern Asia (-693.0 mln US$), Western Asia (-693.0 mln US$) and Commonwealth of Independent States (-289.5 mln US$).

Table 1: Imports (Imp.) and exports (Exp.), 1999-2013, in current US$

		1999	2000	2001	2002	2003	2004	2005	2006	2007	2008	2009	2010	2011	2012	2013
Values in Bln US$	Imp.	2.1	2.2	2.1	2.3	2.5	3.0	3.0	3.1	4.1	4.6	4.4	5.1	6.1	6.0	5.7
	Exp.	2.1	2.3	2.2	2.6	2.7	3.3	3.2	3.5	4.4	4.4	3.6	4.3	5.0	5.0	5.1
As a percentage of	Imp.	0.9	0.9	0.9	1.0	0.9	0.8	0.7	0.6	0.7	0.6	0.8	0.7	0.6	0.6	0.6
SITC section (%)	Exp.	1.1	1.1	1.1	1.2	1.1	1.0	0.9	0.8	0.8	0.7	0.7	0.6	0.6	0.6	0.6
As a percentage of	Imp.	0.0	0.0	0.0	0.0	0.0	0.0	0.0	0.0	0.0	0.0	0.0	0.0	0.0	0.0	0.0
world trade (%)	Exp.	0.0	0.0	0.0	0.0	0.0	0.0	0.0	0.0	0.0	0.0	0.0	0.0	0.0	0.0	0.0

Graph 1: Annual growth rates of exports, 1999–2013
(In percentage by year)

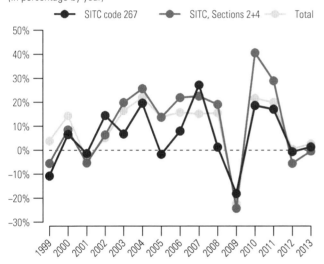

── SITC code 267   ── SITC, Sections 2+4   ── Total

Table 2: Top exporting countries or areas in 2013

Country or area	Value (million US$)	Avg. Growth (%) 09-13	Growth (%) 12-13	World share %	Cum.
World	5076.8	8.7	1.3	100.0	
USA	1235.3	6.5	9.6	24.3	24.3
Germany	740.8	7.3	10.3	14.6	38.9
Japan	577.2	9.2	8.0	11.4	50.3
Belgium	483.6	13.5	33.5	9.5	59.8
Indonesia	403.2	11.2	0.4	7.9	67.8
China	397.0	14.6	-33.8	7.8	75.6
India	240.5	18.7	4.6	4.7	80.3
Other Asia, nes	180.2	-0.5	9.7	3.5	83.9
Thailand	174.3	7.7	-31.6	3.4	87.3
Rep. of Korea	128.1	122.9	15.7	2.5	89.8
United Kingdom	114.0	-9.0	-44.2	2.2	92.1
Mexico	112.4	13.6	5.9	2.2	94.3
Brazil	51.0	-0.8	39.5	1.0	95.3
Singapore	35.3	9.6	63.6	0.7	96.0
Zambia	20.2	1075.0	>	0.4	96.4

Graph 2: Trade Balance by MDG regions 2013
(Bln US$)

── Imports   ── Exports   ── Trade balance

Developed Asia–Pacific
Developed Europe
Developed N. America
South–eastern Europe
C I S
Northern Africa
Sub–Saharan Africa
Latin Am, Caribbean
Eastern Asia
Southern Asia
South–eastern Asia
Western Asia
Oceania

Table 3: Top importing countries or areas in 2013

Country or area	Value (million US$)	Avg. Growth (%) 09-13	Growth (%) 12-13	World share %	Cum.
World	5679.8	6.8	-4.6	100.0	
China	1119.6	11.4	-5.9	19.7	19.7
Turkey	618.2	6.7	-16.0	10.9	30.6
Indonesia	394.2	21.9	-10.8	6.9	37.5
Germany	274.8	9.7	2.8	4.8	42.4
USA	201.4	-3.0	-12.6	3.5	45.9
Russian Federation	197.9	4.8	4.9	3.5	49.4
Pakistan	195.9	9.8	-3.0	3.4	52.9
Rep. of Korea	184.7	0.7	-16.9	3.3	56.1
Belgium	148.9	4.5	24.4	2.6	58.7
India	135.5	8.8	13.0	2.4	61.1
Italy	120.3	0.3	-4.9	2.1	63.2
Poland	110.5	12.6	5.7	1.9	65.2
France	108.5	6.4	5.1	1.9	67.1
Viet Nam	99.7	9.4	-19.1	1.8	68.8
Other Asia, nes	76.4	5.7	-7.9	1.3	70.2

268 Wool and other animal hair (including wool tops)

In 2013, the value (in current US$) of exports of "wool and other animal hair (including wool tops)" (SITC group 268) increased by 1.3 percent (compared to 14.8 percent average growth rate from 2009-2013) to reach 6.8 bln US$ (see table 2), while imports increased by 2.4 percent to reach 7.0 bln US$ (see table 3). Exports of this commodity accounted for 0.8 percent of world exports of SITC sections 2+4, and less than 0.1 percent of total world merchandise exports (see table 1). Australia, China and New Zealand were the top exporters in 2013 (see table 2). They accounted for 36.8, 14.0 and 8.5 percent of world exports, respectively. China, Italy and Germany were the top destinations, with respectively 42.6, 14.3 and 4.8 percent of world imports (see table 3).

The top 15 countries/areas accounted for 90.9 and 88.3 percent of total world exports and imports, respectively (see tables 2 and 3). In 2013, Australia was the country/area with the highest value of net exports (+2.5 bln US$), followed by New Zealand (+576.8 mln US$). By MDG regions (see graph 2), the largest surpluses in this product group were recorded by Developed Asia-Pacific (+2.9 bln US$), Latin America and the Caribbean (+420.7 mln US$) and Sub-Saharan Africa (+327.6 mln US$). The largest trade deficits were recorded by Eastern Asia (-2.0 bln US$), Developed Europe (-1.1 bln US$) and Southern Asia (-308.0 mln US$).

Table 1: Imports (Imp.) and exports (Exp.), 1999-2013, in current US$

		1999	2000	2001	2002	2003	2004	2005	2006	2007	2008	2009	2010	2011	2012	2013
Values in Bln US$	Imp.	4.4	5.1	4.8	4.8	5.0	5.3	5.1	5.2	6.0	5.6	4.0	5.6	7.9	6.8	7.0
	Exp.	4.2	4.7	4.3	4.7	4.7	5.0	4.9	5.2	6.1	5.4	3.9	5.5	7.9	6.7	6.8
As a percentage of SITC section (%)	Imp.	1.9	2.1	2.0	2.0	1.7	1.4	1.2	1.1	1.0	0.7	0.7	0.7	0.8	0.7	0.8
	Exp.	2.1	2.2	2.1	2.2	1.8	1.6	1.3	1.2	1.1	0.8	0.8	0.8	0.9	0.8	0.8
As a percentage of world trade (%)	Imp.	0.1	0.1	0.1	0.1	0.1	0.1	0.0	0.0	0.0	0.0	0.0	0.0	0.0	0.0	0.0
	Exp.	0.1	0.1	0.1	0.1	0.1	0.1	0.0	0.0	0.0	0.0	0.0	0.0	0.0	0.0	0.0

Graph 1: Annual growth rates of exports, 1999–2013
(In percentage by year)

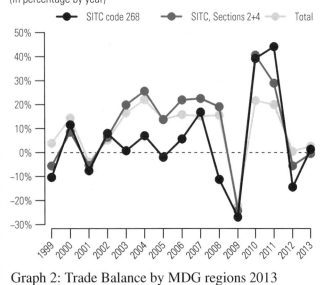

Legend: SITC code 268 — SITC, Sections 2+4 — Total

Table 2: Top exporting countries or areas in 2013

Country or area	Value (million US$)	Avg. Growth (%) 09-13	Growth (%) 12-13	World share %	Cum.
World	6 839.5	14.8	1.3	100.0	
Australia	2 517.8	14.9	-3.7	36.8	36.8
China	959.4	19.5	6.1	14.0	50.8
New Zealand	584.1	14.7	-0.4	8.5	59.4
South Africa	385.8	13.5	5.4	5.6	65.0
Germany	270.6	8.7	-22.7	4.0	69.0
Mongolia	255.0	30.5	-2.6	3.7	72.7
Uruguay	254.8	13.1	8.8	3.7	76.4
Czech Rep	220.9	20.3	0.8	3.2	79.7
Italy	207.5	6.8	15.5	3.0	82.7
Argentina	192.4	7.2	-3.2	2.8	85.5
United Kingdom	149.0	19.6	58.4	2.2	87.7
Peru	64.1	13.0	29.0	0.9	88.6
India	59.8	13.0	-8.0	0.9	89.5
Belgium	51.1	8.8	22.9	0.7	90.2
Malaysia	47.6	33.2	62.5	0.7	90.9

Graph 2: Trade Balance by MDG regions 2013
(Bln US$)

Legend: Imports — Exports — Trade balance

Developed Asia–Pacific
Developed Europe
Developed N. America
South–eastern Europe
C I S
Northern Africa
Sub–Saharan Africa
Latin Am, Caribbean
Eastern Asia
Southern Asia
South–eastern Asia
Western Asia
Oceania

Table 3: Top importing countries or areas in 2013

Country or area	Value (million US$)	Avg. Growth (%) 09-13	Growth (%) 12-13	World share %	Cum.
World	7 013.2	15.3	2.4	100.0	
China	2 990.7	16.6	5.3	42.6	42.6
Italy	1 005.9	14.5	6.5	14.3	57.0
Germany	337.0	14.1	-25.6	4.8	61.8
India	336.1	14.9	-6.1	4.8	66.6
Czech Rep	292.7	25.4	10.7	4.2	70.8
Rep. of Korea	228.3	7.4	3.5	3.3	74.0
Japan	177.4	20.2	-8.2	2.5	76.5
Turkey	150.9	9.3	-10.6	2.2	78.7
United Kingdom	125.5	13.9	33.8	1.8	80.5
Romania	120.5	13.8	4.6	1.7	82.2
Poland	110.6	6.5	-12.9	1.6	83.8
Bulgaria	105.3	22.5	14.4	1.5	85.3
Malaysia	75.8	41.0	29.0	1.1	86.4
Mexico	73.3	11.6	-13.2	1.0	87.4
Belgium	62.1	4.2	-5.9	0.9	88.3

In 2013, the value (in current US$) of exports of "worn clothing and other worn textile articles; rags" (SITC group 269) increased by 6.4 percent (compared to 13.5 percent average growth rate from 2009-2013) to reach 5.1 bln US$ (see table 2), while imports increased by 7.1 percent to reach 4.2 bln US$ (see table 3). Exports of this commodity accounted for 0.6 percent of world exports of SITC sections 2+4, and less than 0.1 percent of total world merchandise exports (see table 1). USA, United Kingdom and Germany were the top exporters in 2013 (see table 2). They accounted for 15.2, 12.1 and 10.2 percent of world exports, respectively. India, Russian Federation and Pakistan were the top destinations, with respectively 4.3, 4.0 and 3.8 percent of world imports (see table 3).

The top 15 countries/areas accounted for 77.2 and 44.5 percent of total world exports and imports, respectively (see tables 2 and 3). In 2013, USA was the country/area with the highest value of net exports (+682.5 mln US$), followed by United Kingdom (+581.7 mln US$). By MDG regions (see graph 2), the largest surpluses in this product group were recorded by Developed Europe (+1.5 bln US$), Developed North America (+784.4 mln US$) and Eastern Asia (+349.2 mln US$). The largest trade deficits were recorded by Sub-Saharan Africa (-1.0 bln US$), Commonwealth of Independent States (-360.8 mln US$) and Latin America and the Caribbean (-260.9 mln US$).

Table 1: Imports (Imp.) and exports (Exp.), 1999-2013, in current US$

		1999	2000	2001	2002	2003	2004	2005	2006	2007	2008	2009	2010	2011	2012	2013
Values in Bln US$	Imp.	1.4	1.4	1.4	1.6	1.6	1.7	1.9	2.0	2.2	2.6	2.8	2.9	3.6	3.9	4.2
	Exp.	1.5	1.5	1.5	1.7	1.7	1.9	2.1	2.4	2.9	3.1	3.1	3.5	4.5	4.8	5.1
As a percentage of SITC section (%)	Imp.	0.6	0.6	0.6	0.7	0.5	0.5	0.5	0.4	0.4	0.3	0.5	0.4	0.4	0.4	0.5
	Exp.	0.8	0.7	0.8	0.8	0.7	0.6	0.6	0.5	0.5	0.5	0.6	0.5	0.5	0.6	0.6
As a percentage of world trade (%)	Imp.	0.0	0.0	0.0	0.0	0.0	0.0	0.0	0.0	0.0	0.0	0.0	0.0	0.0	0.0	0.0
	Exp.	0.0	0.0	0.0	0.0	0.0	0.0	0.0	0.0	0.0	0.0	0.0	0.0	0.0	0.0	0.0

Graph 1: Annual growth rates of exports, 1999–2013
(In percentage by year)

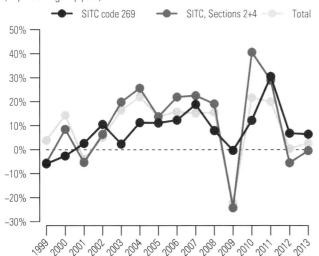

Legend: ● SITC code 269 ● SITC, Sections 2+4 ○ Total

Table 2: Top exporting countries or areas in 2013

Country or area	Value (million US$)	Avg. Growth (%) 09-13	Growth (%) 12-13	World share %	Cum.
World	5 117.7	13.5	6.4	100.0	
USA	777.1	13.8	6.0	15.2	15.2
United Kingdom	621.3	12.6	7.3	12.1	27.3
Germany	523.4	9.0	18.5	10.2	37.6
Rep. of Korea	366.4	11.0	3.5	7.2	44.7
Netherlands	268.2	14.4	9.8	5.2	50.0
Canada	205.7	5.3	-3.2	4.0	54.0
Belgium	203.2	11.8	24.1	4.0	57.9
Italy	178.9	11.5	6.3	3.5	61.4
Poland	158.0	23.6	24.0	3.1	64.5
Japan	127.6	9.8	-5.1	2.5	67.0
China	114.7	97.6	62.5	2.2	69.3
Malaysia	114.5	26.9	2.2	2.2	71.5
India	105.8	6.8	31.5	2.1	73.6
France	97.6	13.2	19.4	1.9	75.5
Indonesia	89.8	61.4	-31.1	1.8	77.2

Graph 2: Trade Balance by MDG regions 2013
(Bln US$)

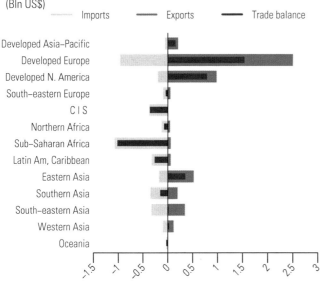

Legend: Imports · Exports · Trade balance

Regions (top to bottom): Developed Asia–Pacific, Developed Europe, Developed N. America, South–eastern Europe, C I S, Northern Africa, Sub–Saharan Africa, Latin Am, Caribbean, Eastern Asia, Southern Asia, South–eastern Asia, Western Asia, Oceania

Table 3: Top importing countries or areas in 2013

Country or area	Value (million US$)	Avg. Growth (%) 09-13	Growth (%) 12-13	World share %	Cum.
World	4 178.8	10.6	7.1	100.0	
India	181.6	10.1	4.7	4.3	4.3
Russian Federation	165.3	16.8	5.6	4.0	8.3
Pakistan	160.5	14.6	4.1	3.8	12.1
Malaysia	149.2	11.8	8.2	3.6	15.7
Poland	145.5	10.5	49.3	3.5	19.2
Netherlands	141.5	23.3	40.9	3.4	22.6
Ukraine	129.0	22.5	10.5	3.1	25.7
China	112.9	46.9	-8.7	2.7	28.4
Canada	103.5	12.1	-8.1	2.5	30.8
Hungary	101.1	24.9	57.0	2.4	33.3
Kenya	96.9	13.3	0.7	2.3	35.6
Tunisia	95.7	6.1	2.1	2.3	37.9
Angola	95.4	-0.5	-7.9	2.3	40.2
USA	94.6	6.1	-22.1	2.3	42.4
Belgium	86.1	16.5	24.7	2.1	44.5

In 2013, the value (in current US$) of exports of "fertilizers crude, other than those of division 56" (SITC group 272) decreased by 14.4 percent (compared to 10.7 percent average growth rate from 2009-2013) to reach 4.2 bln US$ (see table 2), while imports decreased by 25.4 percent to reach 4.6 bln US$ (see table 3). Exports of this commodity accounted for 0.5 percent of world exports of SITC sections 2+4, and less than 0.1 percent of total world merchandise exports (see table 1). Morocco, Russian Federation and Peru were the top exporters in 2013 (see table 2). They accounted for 25.6, 10.5 and 10.0 percent of world exports, respectively. India, USA and Belgium were the top destinations, with respectively 21.9, 8.6 and 5.5 percent of world imports (see table 3).

The top 15 countries/areas accounted for 90.2 and 73.1 percent of total world exports and imports, respectively (see tables 2 and 3). In 2013, Morocco was the country/area with the highest value of net exports (+1.1 bln US$), followed by Russian Federation (+419.1 mln US$). By MDG regions (see graph 2), the largest surpluses in this product group were recorded by Northern Africa (+1.4 bln US$), Western Asia (+532.9 mln US$) and Commonwealth of Independent States (+270.1 mln US$). The largest trade deficits were recorded by Southern Asia (-1.1 bln US$), Developed Europe (-491.2 mln US$) and Developed North America (-341.8 mln US$).

Table 1: Imports (Imp.) and exports (Exp.), 1999-2013, in current US$

		1999	2000	2001	2002	2003	2004	2005	2006	2007	2008	2009	2010	2011	2012	2013
Values in Bln US$	Imp.	1.9	1.7	1.6	1.6	1.6	1.9	2.2	2.2	2.7	7.2	3.2	3.8	5.6	6.1	4.6
	Exp.	1.6	1.2	1.3	1.4	1.4	1.7	1.8	1.8	1.9	5.7	2.8	3.4	4.6	4.9	4.2
As a percentage of	Imp.	0.8	0.7	0.7	0.6	0.6	0.5	0.5	0.4	0.4	0.9	0.6	0.5	0.6	0.7	0.5
SITC section (%)	Exp.	0.8	0.5	0.7	0.6	0.5	0.5	0.5	0.4	0.3	0.9	0.6	0.5	0.5	0.6	0.5
As a percentage of	Imp.	0.0	0.0	0.0	0.0	0.0	0.0	0.0	0.0	0.0	0.0	0.0	0.0	0.0	0.0	0.0
world trade (%)	Exp.	0.0	0.0	0.0	0.0	0.0	0.0	0.0	0.0	0.0	0.0	0.0	0.0	0.0	0.0	0.0

Graph 1: Annual growth rates of exports, 1999–2013
(In percentage by year)

SITC code 272 — SITC, Sections 2+4 — Total

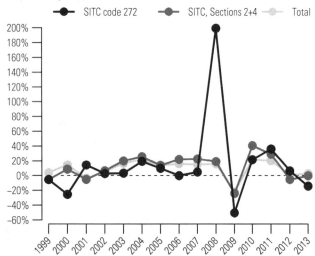

Graph 2: Trade Balance by MDG regions 2013
(Bln US$)

Imports — Exports — Trade balance

Developed Asia–Pacific
Developed Europe
Developed N. America
South–eastern Europe
CIS
Northern Africa
Sub–Saharan Africa
Latin Am, Caribbean
Eastern Asia
Southern Asia
South–eastern Asia
Western Asia
Oceania

Table 2: Top exporting countries or areas in 2013

Country or area	Value (million US$)	Avg. Growth (%) 09-13	Growth (%) 12-13	World share %	Cum.
World	4227.0	10.7	-14.4	100.0	
Morocco	1082.1	18.2	-29.9	25.6	25.6
Russian Federation	444.9	4.9	15.3	10.5	36.1
Peru	420.9	179.7	-3.9	10.0	46.1
Jordan	376.9	0.3	-37.4	8.9	55.0
Egypt	253.0	0.4	-17.2	6.0	61.0
Netherlands	206.2	20.9	15.0	4.9	65.9
Syria	198.8	9.2	178.3	4.7	70.6
Italy	190.2	8.4	9.8	4.5	75.1
Israel	109.4	10.0	-7.2	2.6	77.7
Belgium	104.3	4.5	18.4	2.5	80.1
China	99.6	-1.7	-25.1	2.4	82.5
Algeria	96.7	6.3	-36.8	2.3	84.8
USA	95.7	39.0	73.6	2.3	87.0
Chile	68.4	-0.1	-50.4	1.6	88.6
Germany	64.7	17.1	2.3	1.5	90.2

Table 3: Top importing countries or areas in 2013

Country or area	Value (million US$)	Avg. Growth (%) 09-13	Growth (%) 12-13	World share %	Cum.
World	4555.6	9.6	-25.4	100.0	
India	999.7	9.3	-45.0	21.9	21.9
USA	392.5	26.4	-23.4	8.6	30.6
Belgium	252.1	14.7	-10.9	5.5	36.1
Brazil	248.2	26.7	4.9	5.4	41.5
Lithuania	231.9	8.3	-9.7	5.1	46.6
Indonesia	172.7	0.5	-6.1	3.8	50.4
New Zealand	141.4	26.5	-2.9	3.1	53.5
Poland	138.7	24.9	-37.1	3.0	56.6
Mexico	132.1	59.4	-10.7	2.9	59.5
Belarus	124.8	14.1	-23.0	2.7	62.2
Japan	118.5	-16.5	-8.9	2.6	64.8
Turkey	103.0	6.1	-8.1	2.3	67.1
Netherlands	100.7	7.5	-35.9	2.2	69.3
France	88.4	10.4	-17.7	1.9	71.2
Rep. of Korea	85.7	-3.8	-38.2	1.9	73.1

In 2013, the value (in current US$) of exports of "stone, sand and gravel" (SITC group 273) increased by 8.0 percent (compared to 6.7 percent average growth rate from 2009-2013) to reach 10.5 bln US$ (see table 2), while imports increased by 5.6 percent to reach 13.0 bln US$ (see table 3). Exports of this commodity accounted for 1.3 percent of world exports of SITC sections 2+4, and 0.1 percent of total world merchandise exports (see table 1). Turkey, India and Italy were the top exporters in 2013 (see table 2). They accounted for 12.1, 9.3 and 5.7 percent of world exports, respectively. China, India and Singapore were the top destinations, with respectively 22.8, 4.9 and 4.7 percent of world imports (see table 3).

The top 15 countries/areas accounted for 70.4 and 70.2 percent of total world exports and imports, respectively (see tables 2 and 3). In 2013, Turkey was the country/area with the highest value of net exports (+1.2 bln US$), followed by Spain (+390.1 mln US$). By MDG regions (see graph 2), the largest surpluses in this product group were recorded by Western Asia (+1.0 bln US$), Southern Asia (+455.1 mln US$) and Developed Europe (+230.3 mln US$). The largest trade deficits were recorded by Eastern Asia (-3.4 bln US$), South-eastern Asia (-491.5 mln US$) and Commonwealth of Independent States (-265.7 mln US$).

Table 1: Imports (Imp.) and exports (Exp.), 1999-2013, in current US$

		1999	2000	2001	2002	2003	2004	2005	2006	2007	2008	2009	2010	2011	2012	2013
Values in Bln US$	Imp.	4.8	5.2	4.8	5.1	6.0	7.0	7.8	8.9	10.7	12.4	10.3	10.8	12.2	12.3	13.0
	Exp.	3.7	3.8	3.8	4.1	4.7	5.5	5.9	7.3	8.4	9.6	8.1	8.5	9.8	9.8	10.5
As a percentage of SITC section (%)	Imp.	2.1	2.1	2.1	2.1	2.1	1.9	1.9	1.8	1.7	1.6	1.9	1.4	1.2	1.3	1.4
	Exp.	1.9	1.8	1.9	1.9	1.8	1.7	1.6	1.6	1.5	1.5	1.6	1.2	1.1	1.2	1.3
As a percentage of world trade (%)	Imp.	0.1	0.1	0.1	0.1	0.1	0.1	0.1	0.1	0.1	0.1	0.1	0.1	0.1	0.1	0.1
	Exp.	0.1	0.1	0.1	0.1	0.1	0.1	0.1	0.1	0.1	0.1	0.1	0.1	0.1	0.1	0.1

Graph 1: Annual growth rates of exports, 1999–2013

(In percentage by year)

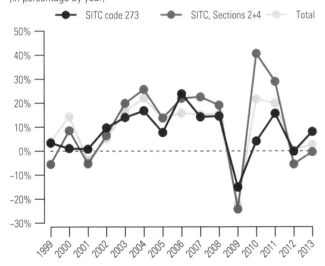

Table 2: Top exporting countries or areas in 2013

Country or area	Value (million US$)	Avg. Growth (%) 09-13	Growth (%) 12-13	World share %	Cum.
World	10532.8	6.7	8.0	100.0	
Turkey	1277.4	21.5	18.4	12.1	12.1
India	976.7	14.0	7.8	9.3	21.4
Italy	602.3	8.7	9.3	5.7	27.1
Germany	597.4	-3.9	-1.3	5.7	32.8
USA	542.8	12.5	6.6	5.2	37.9
Spain	496.6	7.6	5.9	4.7	42.7
Belgium	422.5	1.7	9.4	4.0	46.7
United Arab Emirates	420.2	5.3	21.7	4.0	50.7
Ukraine	365.3	13.1	-0.1	3.5	54.1
China	363.5	16.9	98.0	3.5	57.6
Norway	321.0	6.9	-2.6	3.0	60.6
Brazil	288.8	19.9	19.4	2.7	63.4
Netherlands	269.0	12.0	3.5	2.6	65.9
France	261.3	1.1	6.6	2.5	68.4
Thailand	212.9	12.2	10.9	2.0	70.4

Graph 2: Trade Balance by MDG regions 2013

(Bln US$)

Imports — Exports — Trade balance

Developed Asia–Pacific
Developed Europe
Developed N. America
South–eastern Europe
CIS
Northern Africa
Sub–Saharan Africa
Latin Am, Caribbean
Eastern Asia
Southern Asia
South–eastern Asia
Western Asia
Oceania

Table 3: Top importing countries or areas in 2013

Country or area	Value (million US$)	Avg. Growth (%) 09-13	Growth (%) 12-13	World share %	Cum.
World	13039.5	6.0	5.6	100.0	
China	2975.7	19.2	9.5	22.8	22.8
India	634.0	22.2	10.9	4.9	27.7
Singapore	618.9	-12.7	15.7	4.7	32.4
Other Asia, nes	573.9	6.9	9.8	4.4	36.8
Netherlands	534.2	-2.2	-3.9	4.1	40.9
Russian Federation	526.5	31.7	5.3	4.0	45.0
Germany	506.8	-1.5	-1.2	3.9	48.9
Italy	443.7	-2.6	-0.4	3.4	52.3
Belgium	431.8	0.6	-0.8	3.3	55.6
USA	363.1	3.1	-3.2	2.8	58.3
France	336.1	-0.1	0.4	2.6	60.9
Qatar	333.1	13.2	-0.7	2.6	63.5
United Kingdom	304.0	7.2	5.5	2.3	65.8
Switzerland	288.8	7.6	7.8	2.2	68.0
Canada	277.0	18.8	30.4	2.1	70.2

274 Sulphur and unroasted iron pyrites

In 2013, the value (in current US$) of exports of "sulphur and unroasted iron pyrites" (SITC group 274) decreased by 30.3 percent (compared to 27.3 percent average growth rate from 2009-2013) to reach 2.5 bln US$ (see table 2), while imports decreased by 32.8 percent to reach 4.2 bln US$ (see table 3). Exports of this commodity accounted for 0.3 percent of world exports of SITC sections 2+4, and less than 0.1 percent of total world merchandise exports (see table 1). Canada, Russian Federation and Qatar were the top exporters in 2013 (see table 2). They accounted for 13.8, 12.0 and 10.6 percent of world exports, respectively. China, Morocco and Brazil were the top destinations, with respectively 34.9, 12.5 and 7.1 percent of world imports (see table 3).

The top 15 countries/areas accounted for 87.1 and 83.3 percent of total world exports and imports, respectively (see tables 2 and 3). In 2013, Canada was the country/area with the highest value of net exports (+340.1 mln US$), followed by Russian Federation (+289.4 mln US$). By MDG regions (see graph 2), the largest surpluses in this product group were recorded by Commonwealth of Independent States (+520.8 mln US$), Developed North America (+331.6 mln US$) and Western Asia (+186.8 mln US$). The largest trade deficits were recorded by Eastern Asia (-1.3 bln US$), Northern Africa (-713.4 mln US$) and Latin America and the Caribbean (-362.7 mln US$).

Table 1: Imports (Imp.) and exports (Exp.), 1999-2013, in current US$

		1999	2000	2001	2002	2003	2004	2005	2006	2007	2008	2009	2010	2011	2012	2013
Values in Bln US$	Imp.	0.9	1.0	0.8	0.9	1.5	2.0	2.2	2.0	3.0	12.5	1.9	3.5	6.0	6.2	4.2
	Exp.	0.5	0.6	0.4	0.5	0.7	0.9	1.1	1.1	1.4	6.5	1.0	1.9	3.8	3.6	2.5
As a percentage of	Imp.	0.4	0.4	0.3	0.4	0.5	0.5	0.5	0.4	0.5	1.6	0.4	0.5	0.6	0.7	0.5
SITC section (%)	Exp.	0.2	0.3	0.2	0.2	0.3	0.3	0.3	0.2	0.3	1.0	0.2	0.3	0.4	0.4	0.3
As a percentage of	Imp.	0.0	0.0	0.0	0.0	0.0	0.0	0.0	0.0	0.1	0.0	0.0	0.0	0.0	0.0	0.0
world trade (%)	Exp.	0.0	0.0	0.0	0.0	0.0	0.0	0.0	0.0	0.0	0.0	0.0	0.0	0.0	0.0	0.0

Graph 1: Annual growth rates of exports, 1999–2013
(In percentage by year)

— SITC code 274 — SITC, Sections 2+4 — Total

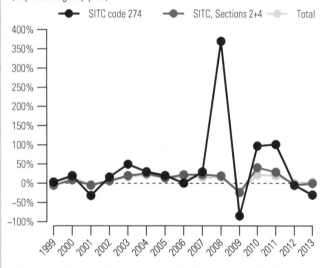

Table 2: Top exporting countries or areas in 2013

Country or area	Value (million US$)	Avg. Growth (%) 09-13	Growth (%) 12-13	World share %	Cum.
World..............................	2 537.3	27.3	-30.3	100.0	
Canada............................	349.8	7.9	-36.1	13.8	13.8
Russian Federation..............	304.1	77.4	-46.6	12.0	25.8
Qatar..............................	270.2	53.7	-30.4	10.6	36.4
Kazakhstan........................	268.2	43.8	-39.4	10.6	47.0
USA................................	223.0	29.7	-38.1	8.8	55.8
Germany...........................	153.3	15.5	-14.1	6.0	61.8
Japan..............................	109.5	23.1	-27.8	4.3	66.1
India..............................	93.3	76.7	158.3	3.7	69.8
Mexico.............................	78.1	247.3	-18.2	3.1	72.9
Rep. of Korea.....................	77.8	43.1	-37.9	3.1	76.0
South Africa......................	72.6	138.2	-9.4	2.9	78.8
Netherlands.......................	60.2	26.9	-33.3	2.4	81.2
Spain..............................	52.7	48.4	-26.7	2.1	83.3
Poland.............................	52.2	45.5	-37.3	2.1	85.3
Greece.............................	45.8	22.9	80.8	1.8	87.1

Graph 2: Trade Balance by MDG regions 2013
(Bln US$)

— Imports — Exports — Trade balance

Developed Asia–Pacific
Developed Europe
Developed N. America
South–eastern Europe
C I S
Northern Africa
Sub–Saharan Africa
Latin Am, Caribbean
Eastern Asia
Southern Asia
South–eastern Asia
Western Asia
Oceania

-1.6 -1.4 -1.2 -1 -0.8 -0.6 -0.4 -0.2 0 0.2 0.4 0.6

Table 3: Top importing countries or areas in 2013

Country or area	Value (million US$)	Avg. Growth (%) 09-13	Growth (%) 12-13	World share %	Cum.
World..............................	4 188.0	21.1	-32.8	100.0	
China..............................	1 460.9	19.6	-36.4	34.9	34.9
Morocco............................	522.5	29.2	-36.9	12.5	47.4
Brazil.............................	298.7	11.0	-27.9	7.1	54.5
USA................................	231.5	38.8	-12.1	5.5	60.0
India..............................	161.3	9.6	-63.4	3.9	63.9
Tunisia............................	156.1	6.4	-23.9	3.7	67.6
Australia..........................	116.9	36.6	-25.3	2.8	70.4
Israel.............................	108.9	33.7	-18.9	2.6	73.0
Belgium............................	108.1	44.2	-0.8	2.6	75.6
Indonesia..........................	58.7	13.6	-18.0	1.4	77.0
Madagascar.........................	55.4	402.2	124.8	1.3	78.3
South Africa.......................	55.1	7.2	-48.1	1.3	79.6
Zambia.............................	53.2	55.3	-27.0	1.3	80.9
Mexico.............................	52.1	31.9	-38.3	1.2	82.1
Egypt..............................	50.3	43.0	-9.7	1.2	83.3

In 2013, the value (in current US$) of exports of "natural abrasives, nes (including industrial diamonds)" (SITC group 277) decreased by 8.2 percent (compared to 10.2 percent average growth rate from 2009-2013) to reach 1.8 bln US$ (see table 2), while imports increased by 17.2 percent to reach 1.7 bln US$ (see table 3). Exports of this commodity accounted for 0.2 percent of world exports of SITC sections 2+4, and less than 0.1 percent of total world merchandise exports (see table 1). Singapore, India and Zimbabwe were the top exporters in 2013 (see table 2). They accounted for 25.8, 10.6 and 10.4 percent of world exports, respectively. Singapore, USA and India were the top destinations, with respectively 30.9, 10.1 and 8.0 percent of world imports (see table 3).

The top 15 countries/areas accounted for 90.4 and 80.5 percent of total world exports and imports, respectively (see tables 2 and 3). In 2013, Zimbabwe was the country/area with the highest value of net exports (+188.1 mln US$), followed by China (+107.4 mln US$). By MDG regions (see graph 2), the largest surpluses in this product group were recorded by Sub-Saharan Africa (+303.0 mln US$), Commonwealth of Independent States (+88.3 mln US$) and Eastern Asia (+73.5 mln US$). The largest trade deficits were recorded by Developed Europe (-183.1 mln US$), Western Asia (-101.1 mln US$) and South-eastern Asia (-88.7 mln US$).

Table 1: Imports (Imp.) and exports (Exp.), 1999-2013, in current US$

		1999	2000	2001	2002	2003	2004	2005	2006	2007	2008	2009	2010	2011	2012	2013
Values in Bln US$	Imp.	1.7	1.4	1.0	1.0	1.2	1.2	1.2	1.4	1.3	1.3	1.0	1.2	1.4	1.5	1.7
	Exp.	1.0	1.0	0.9	1.0	1.2	1.1	1.2	1.1	1.2	1.2	1.2	1.4	1.7	2.0	1.8
As a percentage of	Imp.	0.7	0.6	0.4	0.4	0.4	0.3	0.3	0.3	0.2	0.2	0.2	0.2	0.1	0.2	0.2
SITC section (%)	Exp.	0.5	0.5	0.5	0.5	0.5	0.3	0.3	0.2	0.2	0.2	0.2	0.2	0.2	0.2	0.2
As a percentage of	Imp.	0.0	0.0	0.0	0.0	0.0	0.0	0.0	0.0	0.0	0.0	0.0	0.0	0.0	0.0	0.0
world trade (%)	Exp.	0.0	0.0	0.0	0.0	0.0	0.0	0.0	0.0	0.0	0.0	0.0	0.0	0.0	0.0	0.0

Graph 1: Annual growth rates of exports, 1999–2013
(In percentage by year)

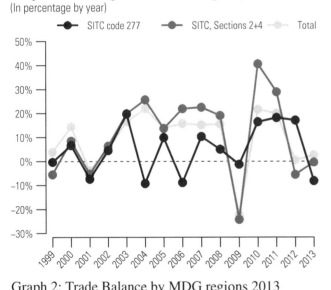

SITC code 277 — SITC, Sections 2+4 — Total

Table 2: Top exporting countries or areas in 2013

Country or area	Value (million US$)	Avg. Growth (%) 09-13	Growth (%) 12-13	World share %	Cum.
World....................	1 813.5	10.2	-8.2	100.0	
Singapore...............	468.4	12.9	152.4	25.8	25.8
India.....................	192.7	-3.9	64.8	10.6	36.5
Zimbabwe..............	188.1	111.2	-71.4	10.4	46.8
China....................	150.4	20.0	-0.7	8.3	55.1
USA......................	141.3	11.6	-6.4	7.8	62.9
Russian Federation....	103.6	34.3	-9.1	5.7	68.6
Botswana...............	80.8	129.7	207.3	4.5	73.1
Australia................	67.9	19.9	1.0	3.7	76.8
United Kingdom.......	54.8	10.7	-8.5	3.0	79.8
Belgium.................	45.4	6.5	-4.7	2.5	82.3
China, Hong Kong SAR........	44.8	18.4	-24.7	2.5	84.8
Rep. of Korea..........	27.2	4.5	-24.9	1.5	86.3
Viet Nam...............	25.3	88.4	67.6	1.4	87.7
Switzerland............	24.1	13.5	-11.9	1.3	89.0
South Africa...........	24.0	20.6	-49.1	1.3	90.4

Graph 2: Trade Balance by MDG regions 2013
(Mln US$)

Imports — Exports — Trade balance

Developed Asia–Pacific
Developed Europe
Developed N. America
South–eastern Europe
C I S
Northern Africa
Sub–Saharan Africa
Latin Am, Caribbean
Eastern Asia
Southern Asia
South–eastern Asia
Western Asia
Oceania

-700 -600 -500 -400 -300 -200 -100 0 100 200 300 400 500 600

Table 3: Top importing countries or areas in 2013

Country or area	Value (million US$)	Avg. Growth (%) 09-13	Growth (%) 12-13	World share %	Cum.
World....................	1 728.2	14.1	17.2	100.0	
Singapore...............	534.2	17.3	129.0	30.9	30.9
USA......................	175.3	15.9	-7.0	10.1	41.1
India.....................	138.3	43.6	388.6	8.0	49.1
United Kingdom.......	72.4	30.5	-57.8	4.2	53.2
Italy......................	60.4	14.9	33.5	3.5	56.7
Japan....................	55.6	9.5	-10.8	3.2	60.0
Rep. of Korea..........	53.6	12.5	-2.0	3.1	63.1
Belgium.................	52.8	-1.4	-33.1	3.1	66.1
China....................	43.0	21.2	10.8	2.5	68.6
Qatar....................	36.8	10.6	72.8	2.1	70.7
China, Hong Kong SAR........	35.6	0.8	-30.1	2.1	72.8
Malaysia................	35.6	29.4	-17.1	2.1	74.9
Switzerland............	32.9	18.0	15.7	1.9	76.8
Germany................	32.7	16.4	6.1	1.9	78.6
United Arab Emirates..........	*32.7*	12.7	11.4	1.9	80.5

278 Other crude minerals

In 2013, the value (in current US$) of exports of "other crude minerals" (SITC group 278) increased by 2.5 percent (compared to 10.8 percent average growth rate from 2009-2013) to reach 17.2 bln US$ (see table 2), while imports decreased by 1.4 percent to reach 21.9 bln US$ (see table 3). Exports of this commodity accounted for 2.0 percent of world exports of SITC sections 2+4, and 0.1 percent of total world merchandise exports (see table 1). China, USA and Germany were the top exporters in 2013 (see table 2). They accounted for 13.6, 9.5 and 6.0 percent of world exports, respectively. China, USA and Japan were the top destinations, with respectively 9.8, 8.5 and 7.4 percent of world imports (see table 3).

The top 15 countries/areas accounted for 70.6 and 62.4 percent of total world exports and imports, respectively (see tables 2 and 3). In 2013, South Africa was the country/area with the highest value of net exports (+537.4 mln US$), followed by Turkey (+494.7 mln US$). By MDG regions (see graph 2), the largest surpluses in this product group were recorded by Southern Asia (+266.8 mln US$), Latin America and the Caribbean (+196.2 mln US$) and Sub-Saharan Africa (+165.9 mln US$). The largest trade deficits were recorded by Developed Europe (-2.0 bln US$), Developed Asia-Pacific (-1.3 bln US$) and South-eastern Asia (-1.2 bln US$).

Table 1: Imports (Imp.) and exports (Exp.), 1999-2013, in current US$

		1999	2000	2001	2002	2003	2004	2005	2006	2007	2008	2009	2010	2011	2012	2013
Values in Bln US$	Imp.	9.0	9.3	9.3	9.5	10.5	13.2	13.7	14.9	16.4	20.5	15.7	19.5	23.5	22.2	21.9
	Exp.	6.9	6.8	7.0	7.1	8.2	9.6	10.1	11.2	12.0	14.6	11.4	14.9	16.8	16.8	17.2
As a percentage of	Imp.	4.0	3.7	4.0	3.9	3.6	3.5	3.3	3.0	2.7	2.7	2.9	2.6	2.4	2.4	2.4
SITC section (%)	Exp.	3.5	3.2	3.5	3.3	3.2	3.0	2.8	2.5	2.2	2.2	2.3	2.1	1.9	2.0	2.0
As a percentage of	Imp.	0.2	0.1	0.1	0.1	0.1	0.1	0.1	0.1	0.1	0.1	0.1	0.1	0.1	0.1	0.1
world trade (%)	Exp.	0.1	0.1	0.1	0.1	0.1	0.1	0.1	0.1	0.1	0.1	0.1	0.1	0.1	0.1	0.1

Graph 1: Annual growth rates of exports, 1999–2013
(In percentage by year)

— SITC code 278   — SITC, Sections 2+4   — Total

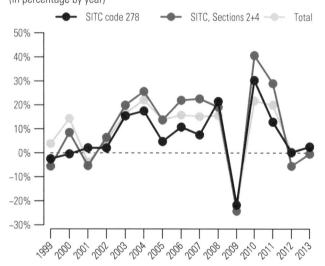

Graph 2: Trade Balance by MDG regions 2013
(Bln US$)

Imports   Exports   Trade balance

Developed Asia–Pacific
Developed Europe
Developed N. America
South–eastern Europe
C I S
Northern Africa
Sub-Saharan Africa
Latin Am, Caribbean
Eastern Asia
Southern Asia
South–eastern Asia
Western Asia
Oceania

Table 2: Top exporting countries or areas in 2013

Country or area	Value (million US$)	Avg. Growth (%) 09-13	Growth (%) 12-13	World share %	Cum.
World	17 208.8	10.8	2.5	100.0	
China	2 348.2	17.1	-4.9	13.6	13.6
USA	1 639.2	5.7	0.5	9.5	23.2
Germany	1 026.5	4.6	2.6	6.0	29.1
Netherlands	882.0	11.0	4.4	5.1	34.3
India	806.8	26.9	14.4	4.7	38.9
Turkey	719.5	29.0	18.7	4.2	43.1
South Africa	627.2	27.9	-11.2	3.6	46.8
Belgium	615.1	2.9	6.4	3.6	50.3
Spain	567.7	8.9	8.9	3.3	53.6
Canada	547.1	4.7	13.9	3.2	56.8
Brazil	496.7	3.2	-3.7	2.9	59.7
France	493.6	2.2	5.0	2.9	62.6
Russian Federation	480.1	12.7	-17.5	2.8	65.4
Mexico	447.3	11.1	-2.2	2.6	68.0
United Kingdom	445.3	-4.5	5.3	2.6	70.6

Table 3: Top importing countries or areas in 2013

Country or area	Value (million US$)	Avg. Growth (%) 09-13	Growth (%) 12-13	World share %	Cum.
World	21 851.4	8.7	-1.4	100.0	
China	2 142.6	34.7	13.3	9.8	9.8
USA	1 862.0	7.2	-2.6	8.5	18.3
Japan	1 610.3	4.0	-8.7	7.4	25.7
Germany	1 422.1	9.2	-0.2	6.5	32.2
Italy	766.9	5.9	-5.1	3.5	35.7
Belgium	706.8	4.1	6.9	3.2	38.9
Rep. of Korea	702.5	7.2	0.3	3.2	42.2
France	659.6	3.0	8.5	3.0	45.2
Netherlands	604.7	11.5	-9.1	2.8	47.9
United Kingdom	567.8	5.6	38.6	2.6	50.5
Russian Federation	546.9	22.0	0.2	2.5	53.0
Other Asia, nes	537.4	6.8	3.3	2.5	55.5
Canada	506.6	5.4	-3.1	2.3	57.8
India	500.7	6.1	-23.2	2.3	60.1
Indonesia	498.7	14.5	-3.8	2.3	62.4

In 2013, the value (in current US$) of exports of "iron ore and concentrates" (SITC group 281) increased by 10.4 percent (compared to 25.3 percent average growth rate from 2009-2013) to reach 138.6 bln US$ (see table 2), while imports increased by 4.2 percent to reach 163.9 bln US$ (see table 3). Exports of this commodity accounted for 16.5 percent of world exports of SITC sections 2+4, and 0.7 percent of total world merchandise exports (see table 1). Australia, Brazil and South Africa were the top exporters in 2013 (see table 2). They accounted for 48.5, 23.4 and 6.1 percent of world exports, respectively. China, Japan and Rep. of Korea were the top destinations, with respectively 64.8, 10.6 and 5.1 percent of world imports (see table 3).

The top 15 countries/areas accounted for 96.4 and 93.2 percent of total world exports and imports, respectively (see tables 2 and 3). In 2013, Australia was the country/area with the highest value of net exports (+67.1 bln US$), followed by Brazil (+32.5 bln US$). By MDG regions (see graph 2), the largest surpluses in this product group were recorded by Developed Asia-Pacific (+49.8 bln US$), Latin America and the Caribbean (+33.7 bln US$) and Sub-Saharan Africa (+11.3 bln US$). The largest trade deficits were recorded by Eastern Asia (-116.7 bln US$), Developed Europe (-13.0 bln US$) and Western Asia (-2.8 bln US$).

Table 1: Imports (Imp.) and exports (Exp.), 1999-2013, in current US$

		1999	2000	2001	2002	2003	2004	2005	2006	2007	2008	2009	2010	2011	2012	2013
Values in Bln US$	Imp.	11.3	13.1	12.7	13.0	16.8	29.5	40.6	47.5	65.7	108.4	77.6	131.9	184.6	157.3	163.9
	Exp.	8.2	9.2	9.1	9.9	11.3	16.5	28.0	33.2	40.0	66.0	56.3	104.0	149.9	125.6	138.6
As a percentage of	Imp.	4.9	5.3	5.4	5.4	5.8	7.9	9.8	9.6	10.7	14.2	14.3	17.4	18.7	17.0	17.9
SITC section (%)	Exp.	4.2	4.3	4.5	4.6	4.4	5.1	7.6	7.4	7.3	10.1	11.4	15.0	16.8	14.9	16.5
As a percentage of	Imp.	0.2	0.2	0.2	0.2	0.2	0.3	0.4	0.4	0.5	0.7	0.6	0.9	1.0	0.9	0.9
world trade (%)	Exp.	0.1	0.1	0.1	0.2	0.2	0.2	0.3	0.3	0.3	0.4	0.5	0.7	0.8	0.7	0.7

Graph 1: Annual growth rates of exports, 1999–2013
(In percentage by year)

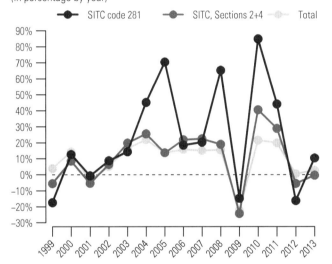

Table 2: Top exporting countries or areas in 2013

Country or area	Value (million US$)	Avg. Growth (%) 09-13	Growth (%) 12-13	World share %	Cum.
World....................	138 603.1	25.3	10.4	100.0	
Australia..............................	67 209.0	29.9	18.5	48.5	48.5
Brazil..................................	32 491.5	25.1	4.8	23.4	71.9
South Africa........................	8 428.3	28.0	8.7	6.1	78.0
Canada................................	4 427.2	10.6	7.0	3.2	81.2
Ukraine...............................	3 739.1	31.7	19.4	2.7	83.9
Sweden................................	2 942.3	22.3	-12.4	2.1	86.0
Russian Federation..............	2 388.5	27.2	-4.2	1.7	87.8
Bahrain...............................	*2 025.4*	67.0	-14.6	1.5	89.2
India...................................	1 635.2	-25.5	-32.6	1.2	90.4
Kazakhstan..........................	1 561.5	13.6	-35.4	1.1	91.5
USA....................................	1 483.3	42.8	3.3	1.1	92.6
Chile...................................	1 378.8	26.8	3.1	1.0	93.6
Sierra Leone........................	*1 361.0*	2678.0	182.8	1.0	94.6
Mauritania...........................	1 269.2	...	25.5	0.9	95.5
Oman..................................	1 259.6	473.9	54.2	0.9	96.4

Graph 2: Trade Balance by MDG regions 2013
(Bln US$)

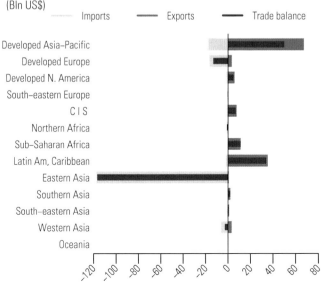

Table 3: Top importing countries or areas in 2013

Country or area	Value (million US$)	Avg. Growth (%) 09-13	Growth (%) 12-13	World share %	Cum.
World....................	163 921.3	20.6	4.2	100.0	
China..................................	106 175.4	20.6	11.0	64.8	64.8
Japan..................................	17 391.5	18.9	-9.6	10.6	75.4
Rep. of Korea......................	8 354.2	24.0	-12.4	5.1	80.5
Germany..............................	5 243.4	16.6	-2.7	3.2	83.7
Other Asia, nes....................	2 888.4	28.4	9.9	1.8	85.4
France.................................	1 879.4	21.9	4.0	1.1	86.6
United Kingdom...................	1 772.4	24.7	34.7	1.1	87.7
Italy....................................	1 434.4	17.1	-20.9	0.9	88.5
Oman..................................	1 235.9	1568.5	19.4	0.8	89.3
Austria................................	1 214.7	17.8	-19.1	0.7	90.0
Saudi Arabia........................	1 206.6	14.5	-16.2	0.7	90.8
Turkey.................................	1 159.5	6.5	0.9	0.7	91.5
Bahrain...............................	*994.4*	47.2	-12.8	0.6	92.1
United Arab Emirates...........	*937.5*	127.9	11.4	0.6	92.7
Belgium...............................	919.0	31.7	8.9	0.6	93.2

282 Ferrous waste and scrap; remelting scrap ingots of iron or steel

In 2013, the value (in current US$) of exports of "ferrous waste and scrap; remelting scrap ingots of iron or steel" (SITC group 282) decreased by 13.7 percent (compared to 9.0 percent average growth rate from 2009-2013) to reach 42.5 bln US$ (see table 2), while imports decreased by 15.7 percent to reach 44.5 bln US$ (see table 3). Exports of this commodity accounted for 5.1 percent of world exports of SITC sections 2+4, and 0.2 percent of total world merchandise exports (see table 1). USA, Germany and Japan were the top exporters in 2013 (see table 2). They accounted for 17.8, 10.7 and 8.9 percent of world exports, respectively. Turkey, Rep. of Korea and India were the top destinations, with respectively 16.9, 8.6 and 7.1 percent of world imports (see table 3).

The top 15 countries/areas accounted for 78.3 and 79.5 percent of total world exports and imports, respectively (see tables 2 and 3). In 2013, USA was the country/area with the highest value of net exports (+6.1 bln US$), followed by Japan (+3.5 bln US$). By MDG regions (see graph 2), the largest surpluses in this product group were recorded by Developed North America (+7.6 bln US$), Developed Asia-Pacific (+4.5 bln US$) and Developed Europe (+3.9 bln US$). The largest trade deficits were recorded by Eastern Asia (-7.7 bln US$), Western Asia (-6.3 bln US$) and Southern Asia (-3.9 bln US$).

Table 1: Imports (Imp.) and exports (Exp.), 1999-2013, in current US$

		1999	2000	2001	2002	2003	2004	2005	2006	2007	2008	2009	2010	2011	2012	2013
Values in Bln US$	Imp.	6.9	9.0	8.4	9.8	14.9	27.1	27.0	32.8	44.9	58.1	31.3	45.3	58.5	52.8	44.5
	Exp.	6.0	7.5	7.4	8.7	12.8	23.1	23.9	30.8	41.5	51.3	30.2	43.9	55.2	49.3	42.5
As a percentage of SITC section (%)	Imp.	3.0	3.6	3.6	4.1	5.2	7.2	6.5	6.6	7.3	7.6	5.8	6.0	5.9	5.7	4.8
	Exp.	3.1	3.5	3.7	4.1	5.0	7.2	6.5	6.9	7.6	7.9	6.1	6.3	6.2	5.8	5.1
As a percentage of world trade (%)	Imp.	0.1	0.1	0.1	0.1	0.2	0.3	0.3	0.3	0.3	0.4	0.2	0.3	0.3	0.3	0.2
	Exp.	0.1	0.1	0.1	0.1	0.2	0.3	0.2	0.3	0.3	0.3	0.2	0.3	0.3	0.3	0.2

Graph 1: Annual growth rates of exports, 1999–2013
(In percentage by year)

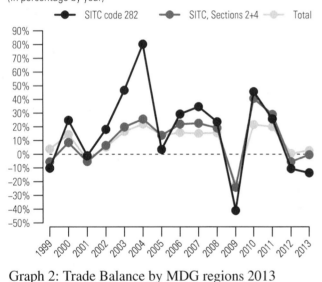

Table 2: Top exporting countries or areas in 2013

Country or area	Value (million US$)	Avg. Growth (%) 09-13	Growth (%) 12-13	World share %	Cum.
World	42 542.2	9.0	-13.7	100.0	
USA	7 574.2	1.5	-19.7	17.8	17.8
Germany	4 551.4	14.5	-14.6	10.7	28.5
Japan	3 805.2	3.6	-11.6	8.9	37.4
Netherlands	3 227.1	11.0	-16.4	7.6	45.0
United Kingdom	2 945.1	12.2	-12.1	6.9	52.0
France	2 476.7	12.1	-11.0	5.8	57.8
Canada	1 807.3	14.2	-5.2	4.2	62.0
Russian Federation	1 370.2	24.1	-3.0	3.2	65.2
Belgium	1 292.0	8.6	-10.5	3.0	68.3
Australia	852.9	12.0	-14.4	2.0	70.3
Poland	825.9	23.7	-8.0	1.9	72.2
Romania	721.4	1.2	-8.1	1.7	73.9
Czech Rep.	686.2	16.4	-14.0	1.6	75.5
Singapore	593.8	12.9	12.2	1.4	76.9
South Africa	565.5	14.2	-21.9	1.3	78.3

Graph 2: Trade Balance by MDG regions 2013
(Bln US$)

Imports — Exports — Trade balance

- Developed Asia-Pacific
- Developed Europe
- Developed N. America
- South-eastern Europe
- CIS
- Northern Africa
- Sub-Saharan Africa
- Latin Am, Caribbean
- Eastern Asia
- Southern Asia
- South-eastern Asia
- Western Asia
- Oceania

Table 3: Top importing countries or areas in 2013

Country or area	Value (million US$)	Avg. Growth (%) 09-13	Growth (%) 12-13	World share %	Cum.
World	44 482.8	9.2	-15.7	100.0	
Turkey	7 511.2	15.4	-20.3	16.9	16.9
Rep. of Korea	3 806.9	9.8	-21.8	8.6	25.4
India	3 139.1	13.9	-29.9	7.1	32.5
Belgium	2 611.3	13.7	-2.3	5.9	38.4
China	2 598.5	-15.5	-15.9	5.8	44.2
Germany	2 328.6	16.9	-13.9	5.2	49.4
Spain	2 085.5	8.3	-1.1	4.7	54.1
Italy	1 968.8	22.2	-14.5	4.4	58.6
Other Asia, nes	1 909.9	5.5	-23.8	4.3	62.9
Netherlands	1 611.4	8.3	-20.0	3.6	66.5
USA	1 497.6	15.1	-9.2	3.4	69.8
Viet Nam	1 247.1	16.3	-11.9	2.8	72.6
Egypt	1 069.0	22.5	14.4	2.4	75.1
Finland	1 028.9	10.3	-17.3	2.3	77.4
Indonesia	963.2	20.9	12.7	2.2	79.5

In 2013, the value (in current US$) of exports of "copper ores and concentrates; copper mattes, cement copper" (SITC group 283) increased by 2.2 percent (compared to 14.0 percent average growth rate from 2009-2013) to reach 52.8 bln US$ (see table 2), while imports increased by 8.6 percent to reach 57.2 bln US$ (see table 3). Exports of this commodity accounted for 6.3 percent of world exports of SITC sections 2+4, and 0.3 percent of total world merchandise exports (see table 1). Chile, Peru and Australia were the top exporters in 2013 (see table 2). They accounted for 32.3, 14.5 and 9.4 percent of world exports, respectively. China, Japan and India were the top destinations, with respectively 34.8, 18.6 and 13.0 percent of world imports (see table 3).

The top 15 countries/areas accounted for 91.6 and 97.1 percent of total world exports and imports, respectively (see tables 2 and 3). In 2013, Chile was the country/area with the highest value of net exports (+16.6 bln US$), followed by Peru (+7.6 bln US$). By MDG regions (see graph 2), the largest surpluses in this product group were recorded by Latin America and the Caribbean (+27.4 bln US$), Developed North America (+5.3 bln US$) and South-eastern Asia (+2.9 bln US$). The largest trade deficits were recorded by Eastern Asia (-22.9 bln US$), Southern Asia (-7.4 bln US$) and Developed Asia-Pacific (-5.7 bln US$).

Table 1: Imports (Imp.) and exports (Exp.), 1999-2013, in current US$

		1999	2000	2001	2002	2003	2004	2005	2006	2007	2008	2009	2010	2011	2012	2013
Values in Bln US$	Imp.	5.4	6.5	6.4	6.0	7.3	12.2	16.4	32.8	37.8	38.2	30.8	46.5	53.8	52.7	57.2
	Exp.	5.0	6.5	6.3	6.2	8.2	13.3	19.3	32.4	37.4	34.3	31.2	44.4	51.6	51.6	52.8
As a percentage of SITC section (%)	Imp.	2.4	2.6	2.7	2.5	2.5	3.3	3.9	6.6	6.1	5.0	5.7	6.1	5.4	5.7	6.2
	Exp.	2.6	3.1	3.1	2.9	3.2	4.1	5.3	7.3	6.8	5.3	6.3	6.4	5.8	6.1	6.3
As a percentage of world trade (%)	Imp.	0.1	0.1	0.1	0.1	0.1	0.1	0.2	0.3	0.3	0.2	0.2	0.3	0.3	0.3	0.3
	Exp.	0.1	0.1	0.1	0.1	0.1	0.1	0.2	0.3	0.3	0.2	0.3	0.3	0.3	0.3	0.3

Graph 1: Annual growth rates of exports, 1999–2013
(In percentage by year)

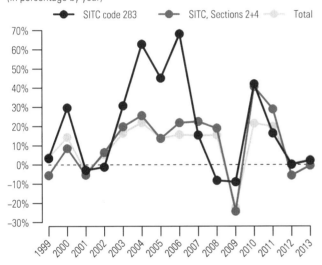

— SITC code 283   — SITC, Sections 2+4   — Total

Table 2: Top exporting countries or areas in 2013

Country or area	Value (million US$)	Avg. Growth (%) 09-13	Growth (%) 12-13	World share %	Cum.
World	52756.8	14.0	2.2	100.0	
Chile	17026.1	14.5	5.0	32.3	32.3
Peru	7625.8	18.1	-9.5	14.5	46.7
Australia	4969.2	13.7	-9.1	9.4	56.1
Canada	3116.0	24.2	-3.5	5.9	62.1
Indonesia	3007.0	-12.4	15.9	5.7	67.8
USA	2623.2	25.8	9.2	5.0	72.7
Brazil	1842.6	23.1	16.7	3.5	76.2
Mexico	1542.6	51.0	7.2	2.9	79.1
Spain	1422.3	75.7	23.9	2.7	81.8
Dem.Rep. of the Congo	1132.6	22.8	44.3	2.1	84.0
Philippines	968.0	59.4	323.5	1.8	85.8
Argentina	954.0	-4.1	-37.0	1.8	87.6
Mongolia	949.0	8.0	-2.6	1.8	89.4
Kazakhstan	592.8	6.7	-28.0	1.1	90.5
Papua New Guinea	535.1	10.7	31.7	1.0	91.6

Graph 2: Trade Balance by MDG regions 2013
(Bln US$)

— Imports   — Exports   — Trade balance

Developed Asia–Pacific
Developed Europe
Developed N. America
South–eastern Europe
CIS
Northern Africa
Sub–Saharan Africa
Latin Am, Caribbean
Eastern Asia
Southern Asia
South–eastern Asia
Western Asia
Oceania

-25 -20 -15 -10 -5 0 5 10 15 20 25 30

Table 3: Top importing countries or areas in 2013

Country or area	Value (million US$)	Avg. Growth (%) 09-13	Growth (%) 12-13	World share %	Cum.
World	57220.7	16.7	8.6	100.0	
China	19908.0	23.1	15.2	34.8	34.8
Japan	10651.1	6.7	-7.9	18.6	53.4
India	7443.4	25.2	52.4	13.0	66.4
Rep. of Korea	4001.5	4.9	-13.4	7.0	73.4
Spain	3076.8	25.2	-4.0	5.4	78.8
Germany	2389.4	9.2	-19.9	4.2	83.0
Bulgaria	1950.4	27.0	23.6	3.4	86.4
Zambia	1389.4	52.7	64.0	2.4	88.8
Philippines	1127.5	5.5	34.4	2.0	90.8
Brazil	1062.1	14.2	87.9	1.9	92.6
Finland	779.6	15.8	-14.7	1.4	94.0
Sweden	556.8	2.4	-23.2	1.0	95.0
Namibia	478.7	335.3	37.4	0.8	95.8
Chile	427.2	44.2	-4.4	0.7	96.5
Russian Federation	342.5	49.8	16.3	0.6	97.1

284 Nickel ores and concentrates; nickel mattes, nickel oxide sinters

In 2013, the value (in current US$) of exports of "nickel ores and concentrates; nickel mattes, nickel oxide sinters" (SITC group 284) decreased by 1.5 percent (compared to 16.7 percent average growth rate from 2009-2013) to reach 9.8 bln US$ (see table 2), while imports decreased by 6.3 percent to reach 13.2 bln US$ (see table 3). Exports of this commodity accounted for 1.2 percent of world exports of SITC sections 2+4, and 0.1 percent of total world merchandise exports (see table 1). Indonesia, Canada and Australia were the top exporters in 2013 (see table 2). They accounted for 26.6, 21.6 and 10.8 percent of world exports, respectively. China, Norway and Japan were the top destinations, with respectively 47.8, 14.0 and 13.0 percent of world imports (see table 3).

The top 15 countries/areas accounted for 99.3 and 98.6 percent of total world exports and imports, respectively (see tables 2 and 3). In 2013, Indonesia was the country/area with the highest value of net exports (+2.6 bln US$), followed by Canada (+1.8 bln US$). By MDG regions (see graph 2), the largest surpluses in this product group were recorded by South-eastern Asia (+3.6 bln US$), Developed North America (+1.8 bln US$) and Sub-Saharan Africa (+1.1 bln US$). The largest trade deficits were recorded by Eastern Asia (-7.0 bln US$), Developed Europe (-3.0 bln US$) and Developed Asia-Pacific (-732.2 mln US$).

Table 1: Imports (Imp.) and exports (Exp.), 1999-2013, in current US$

		1999	2000	2001	2002	2003	2004	2005	2006	2007	2008	2009	2010	2011	2012	2013
Values in Bln US$	Imp.	1.7	2.7	2.3	2.2	3.2	5.1	6.0	8.9	18.5	13.3	6.7	11.5	16.8	14.1	13.2
	Exp.	1.6	2.4	2.0	2.0	2.7	5.0	5.4	5.9	12.1	9.4	5.3	9.1	11.4	9.9	9.8
As a percentage of SITC section (%)	Imp.	0.7	1.1	1.0	0.9	1.1	1.4	1.4	1.8	3.0	1.7	1.2	1.5	1.7	1.5	1.4
	Exp.	0.8	1.1	1.0	0.9	1.1	1.6	1.5	1.3	2.2	1.4	1.1	1.3	1.3	1.2	1.2
As a percentage of world trade (%)	Imp.	0.0	0.0	0.0	0.0	0.0	0.1	0.1	0.1	0.1	0.1	0.1	0.1	0.1	0.1	0.1
	Exp.	0.0	0.0	0.0	0.0	0.0	0.1	0.1	0.0	0.1	0.1	0.0	0.1	0.1	0.1	0.1

Graph 1: Annual growth rates of exports, 1999–2013
(In percentage by year)

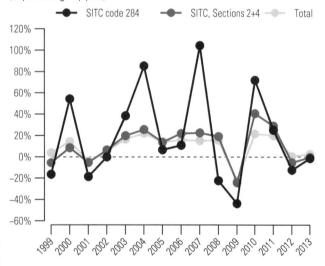

- SITC code 284
- SITC, Sections 2+4
- Total

Graph 2: Trade Balance by MDG regions 2013
(Bln US$)

- Imports
- Exports
- Trade balance

Developed Asia–Pacific
Developed Europe
Developed N. America
South–eastern Europe
C I S
Northern Africa
Sub–Saharan Africa
Latin Am, Caribbean
Eastern Asia
Southern Asia
South–eastern Asia
Western Asia
Oceania

Table 2: Top exporting countries or areas in 2013

Country or area	Value (million US$)	Avg. Growth (%) 09-13	Growth (%) 12-13	World share %	Cum.
World	9794.8	16.7	-1.5	100.0	
Indonesia	2607.1	32.0	5.5	26.6	26.6
Canada	2120.0	12.5	-13.5	21.6	48.3
Australia	1061.8	14.8	-30.4	10.8	59.1
Philippines	1032.2	64.8	56.1	10.5	69.6
Zimbabwe	738.0	15.0	3.8	7.5	77.2
Cuba	542.1	-4.0	-10.8	5.5	82.7
New Caledonia	454.4	7.1	1.8	4.6	87.3
Botswana	418.7	-1.0	25.7	4.3	91.6
Finland	208.6	...	14.6	2.1	93.8
Brazil	201.0	33.1	-34.6	2.1	95.8
South Africa	144.7	-5.1	754.3	1.5	97.3
Spain	94.6	2.0	330.8	1.0	98.2
Germany	45.0	21.4	-8.7	0.5	98.7
Guatemala	28.8	...	240.1	0.3	99.0
USA	27.2	6.9	-9.2	0.3	99.3

Table 3: Top importing countries or areas in 2013

Country or area	Value (million US$)	Avg. Growth (%) 09-13	Growth (%) 12-13	World share %	Cum.
World	13211.8	18.7	-6.3	100.0	
China	6320.0	32.8	-2.8	47.8	47.8
Norway	1846.3	7.0	-19.0	14.0	61.8
Japan	1718.4	8.2	-7.0	13.0	74.8
United Kingdom	652.7	23.5	-8.7	4.9	79.8
Finland	598.9	15.4	-10.4	4.5	84.3
Rep. of Korea	464.8	7.1	2.0	3.5	87.8
Canada	287.3	4.2	-35.4	2.2	90.0
Other Asia, nes	266.6	9.0	-1.9	2.0	92.0
Russian Federation	199.6	...	-3.9	1.5	93.5
France	187.1	-2.7	-11.9	1.4	94.9
Ukraine	130.9	21.6	29.0	1.0	95.9
Zimbabwe	112.0	-5.9	239.7	0.8	96.8
TFYR of Macedonia	100.0	...	-31.5	0.8	97.5
Australia	78.7	557.0	71.9	0.6	98.1
Belgium	66.3	96.1	180.6	0.5	98.6

In 2013, the value (in current US$) of exports of "aluminium ores and concentrates (including alumina)" (SITC group 285) increased by 10.1 percent (compared to 12.1 percent average growth rate from 2009-2013) to reach 15.4 bln US$ (see table 2), while imports increased by 11.1 percent to reach 18.4 bln US$ (see table 3). Exports of this commodity accounted for 1.8 percent of world exports of SITC sections 2+4, and 0.1 percent of total world merchandise exports (see table 1). Australia, Brazil and Indonesia were the top exporters in 2013 (see table 2). They accounted for 37.0, 13.9 and 8.7 percent of world exports, respectively. China, United Arab Emirates and Canada were the top destinations, with respectively 28.1, 7.9 and 7.7 percent of world imports (see table 3).

The top 15 countries/areas accounted for 94.5 and 82.5 percent of total world exports and imports, respectively (see tables 2 and 3). In 2013, Australia was the country/area with the highest value of net exports (+5.7 bln US$), followed by Brazil (+2.1 bln US$). By MDG regions (see graph 2), the largest surpluses in this product group were recorded by Developed Asia-Pacific (+5.5 bln US$), Latin America and the Caribbean (+2.6 bln US$) and South-eastern Asia (+841.5 mln US$). The largest trade deficits were recorded by Eastern Asia (-5.3 bln US$), Western Asia (-2.4 bln US$) and Developed North America (-1.8 bln US$).

Table 1: Imports (Imp.) and exports (Exp.), 1999-2013, in current US$

		1999	2000	2001	2002	2003	2004	2005	2006	2007	2008	2009	2010	2011	2012	2013
Values in Bln US$	Imp.	5.9	7.3	6.9	6.5	7.6	9.8	12.4	15.0	16.6	18.9	11.7	14.6	16.3	16.6	18.4
	Exp.	5.0	5.9	5.7	5.3	6.3	8.0	9.9	12.5	13.8	14.9	9.8	13.4	14.8	14.0	15.4
As a percentage of	Imp.	2.6	2.9	3.0	2.7	2.6	2.6	3.0	3.0	2.7	2.5	2.2	1.9	1.6	1.8	2.0
SITC section (%)	Exp.	2.6	2.8	2.8	2.4	2.4	2.5	2.7	2.8	2.5	2.3	2.0	1.9	1.7	1.7	1.8
As a percentage of	Imp.	0.1	0.1	0.1	0.1	0.1	0.1	0.1	0.1	0.1	0.1	0.1	0.1	0.1	0.1	0.1
world trade (%)	Exp.	0.1	0.1	0.1	0.1	0.1	0.1	0.1	0.1	0.1	0.1	0.1	0.1	0.1	0.1	0.1

Graph 1: Annual growth rates of exports, 1999–2013
(In percentage by year)

— SITC code 285 — SITC, Sections 2+4 — Total

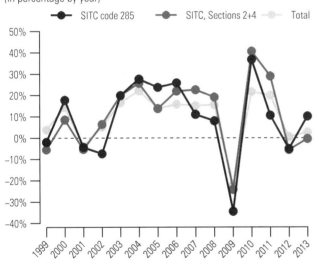

Table 2: Top exporting countries or areas in 2013

Country or area	Value (million US$)	Avg. Growth (%) 09-13	Growth (%) 12-13	World share %	Cum.
World	15437.4	12.1	10.1	100.0	
Australia	5706.3	11.0	4.6	37.0	37.0
Brazil	2149.5	10.2	-4.1	13.9	50.9
Indonesia	1349.7	52.5	115.6	8.7	59.6
USA	894.4	18.9	15.6	5.8	65.4
Jamaica	659.3	10.1	3.1	4.3	69.7
India	595.1	33.1	48.4	3.9	73.6
Ireland	588.9	30.0	23.4	3.8	77.4
Ukraine	584.8	15.6	4.2	3.8	81.2
Guinea	*538.2*	-8.3	-28.6	3.5	84.6
Germany	341.7	5.3	-0.2	2.2	86.9
Kazakhstan	305.8	0.4	0.2	2.0	88.8
France	257.9	6.9	-4.7	1.7	90.5
Netherlands	254.3	24.2	751.4	1.6	92.2
Spain	214.3	2.6	43.3	1.4	93.5
Japan	152.6	4.1	-3.4	1.0	94.5

Graph 2: Trade Balance by MDG regions 2013
(Bln US$)

— Imports — Exports — Trade balance

Developed Asia–Pacific
Developed Europe
Developed N. America
South–eastern Europe
CIS
Northern Africa
Sub–Saharan Africa
Latin Am, Caribbean
Eastern Asia
Southern Asia
South–eastern Asia
Western Asia
Oceania

-6 -5 -4 -3 -2 -1 0 1 2 3 4 5 6

Table 3: Top importing countries or areas in 2013

Country or area	Value (million US$)	Avg. Growth (%) 09-13	Growth (%) 12-13	World share %	Cum.
World	18434.5	12.1	11.1	100.0	
China	5172.5	26.7	39.7	28.1	28.1
United Arab Emirates	*1464.5*	21.7	11.4	7.9	36.0
Canada	1421.7	3.5	1.0	7.7	43.7
Russian Federation	1388.8	4.7	-16.8	7.5	51.2
USA	1278.5	8.4	2.0	6.9	58.2
Norway	709.8	5.5	-0.8	3.9	62.0
India	580.3	47.3	61.0	3.1	65.2
South Africa	563.3	10.9	30.2	3.1	68.2
Germany	520.1	8.6	20.4	2.8	71.1
Iceland	502.5	4.3	-1.1	2.7	73.8
Qatar	363.0	34.3	-14.2	2.0	75.8
France	340.6	1.5	-9.4	1.8	77.6
Malaysia	327.1	37.4	178.2	1.8	79.4
Argentina	302.8	8.1	3.5	1.6	81.0
Netherlands	275.5	8.1	-5.2	1.5	82.5

287 Ores and concentrates of base metals, nes

In 2013, the value (in current US$) of exports of "ores and concentrates of base metals, nes" (SITC group 287) decreased by 5.4 percent (compared to 13.3 percent average growth rate from 2009-2013) to reach 29.2 bln US$ (see table 2), while imports decreased by 9.1 percent to reach 33.6 bln US$ (see table 3). Exports of this commodity accounted for 3.5 percent of world exports of SITC sections 2+4, and 0.2 percent of total world merchandise exports (see table 1). Australia, South Africa and USA were the top exporters in 2013 (see table 2). They accounted for 14.8, 14.5 and 9.4 percent of world exports, respectively. China, Rep. of Korea and Belgium were the top destinations, with respectively 35.1, 9.8 and 7.2 percent of world imports (see table 3).

The top 15 countries/areas accounted for 80.9 and 86.4 percent of total world exports and imports, respectively (see tables 2 and 3). In 2013, South Africa was the country/area with the highest value of net exports (+4.1 bln US$), followed by Australia (+4.1 bln US$). By MDG regions (see graph 2), the largest surpluses in this product group were recorded by Sub-Saharan Africa (+6.2 bln US$), Latin America and the Caribbean (+5.8 bln US$) and Developed Asia-Pacific (+1.8 bln US$). The largest trade deficits were recorded by Eastern Asia (-14.8 bln US$), Developed Europe (-4.7 bln US$) and South-eastern Asia (-529.8 mln US$).

Table 1: Imports (Imp.) and exports (Exp.), 1999-2013, in current US$

		1999	2000	2001	2002	2003	2004	2005	2006	2007	2008	2009	2010	2011	2012	2013
Values in Bln US$	Imp.	5.8	6.3	6.4	6.1	7.5	13.3	20.8	25.1	33.7	36.8	21.1	31.8	38.8	36.9	33.6
	Exp.	5.2	5.3	5.2	5.0	5.7	10.8	17.7	22.8	29.3	29.4	17.7	27.5	33.1	30.9	29.2
As a percentage of SITC section (%)	Imp.	2.5	2.5	2.7	2.5	2.6	3.5	5.0	5.1	5.5	4.8	3.9	4.2	3.9	4.0	3.7
	Exp.	2.6	2.5	2.6	2.3	2.2	3.3	4.8	5.1	5.3	4.5	3.6	4.0	3.7	3.7	3.5
As a percentage of world trade (%)	Imp.	0.1	0.1	0.1	0.1	0.1	0.1	0.2	0.2	0.2	0.2	0.2	0.2	0.2	0.2	0.2
	Exp.	0.1	0.1	0.1	0.1	0.1	0.1	0.2	0.2	0.2	0.2	0.1	0.2	0.2	0.2	0.2

Graph 1: Annual growth rates of exports, 1999–2013
(In percentage by year)

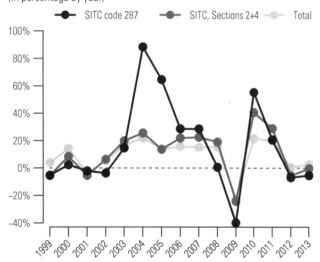

Legend: ● SITC code 287   ● SITC, Sections 2+4   ● Total

Table 2: Top exporting countries or areas in 2013

Country or area	Value (million US$)	Avg. Growth (%) 09-13	Growth (%) 12-13	World share %	Cum.
World	29 187.5	13.3	-5.4	100.0	
Australia	4 331.9	16.6	0.7	14.8	14.8
South Africa	4 241.6	20.7	6.3	14.5	29.4
USA	2 730.9	11.9	1.3	9.4	38.7
Peru	2 539.7	2.2	-27.0	8.7	47.4
Mexico	1 892.2	35.4	-20.4	6.5	53.9
Belgium	1 362.9	14.5	1.7	4.7	58.6
Bolivia	1 000.5	3.2	1.3	3.4	62.0
Turkey	939.1	24.0	19.1	3.2	65.2
Chile	896.4	-6.4	-28.7	3.1	68.3
Gabon	802.4	50.2	90.4	2.7	71.0
Netherlands	675.3	23.0	-3.5	2.3	73.4
Russian Federation	636.8	40.0	-10.2	2.2	75.5
Canada	564.8	3.5	-23.1	1.9	77.5
Kazakhstan	526.4	13.4	-25.5	1.8	79.3
Ireland	483.0	8.2	-8.1	1.7	80.9

Graph 2: Trade Balance by MDG regions 2013
(Bln US$)

Legend: Imports   Exports   Trade balance

Developed Asia–Pacific
Developed Europe
Developed N. America
South–eastern Europe
C I S
Northern Africa
Sub–Saharan Africa
Latin Am, Caribbean
Eastern Asia
Southern Asia
South–eastern Asia
Western Asia
Oceania

Table 3: Top importing countries or areas in 2013

Country or area	Value (million US$)	Avg. Growth (%) 09-13	Growth (%) 12-13	World share %	Cum.
World	33 558.6	12.3	-9.1	100.0	
China	11 776.2	7.7	-3.3	35.1	35.1
Rep. of Korea	3 302.9	17.3	-16.9	9.8	44.9
Belgium	2 404.5	33.8	11.6	7.2	52.1
Japan	2 241.6	8.0	-14.1	6.7	58.8
Canada	1 498.3	30.4	10.6	4.5	63.2
Germany	1 306.3	13.9	0.7	3.9	67.1
USA	1 286.1	19.2	-8.5	3.8	71.0
Spain	1 048.8	13.5	1.0	3.1	74.1
Netherlands	882.1	8.3	-26.9	2.6	76.7
India	741.6	27.6	-31.0	2.2	78.9
Russian Federation	623.5	16.8	-14.9	1.9	80.8
Finland	566.5	13.8	-7.6	1.7	82.5
Malaysia	461.2	24.1	10.9	1.4	83.9
Italy	449.1	9.9	-4.5	1.3	85.2
France	420.9	19.5	-22.6	1.3	86.4

In 2013, the value (in current US$) of exports of "non-ferrous base metal waste and scrap, nes" (SITC group 288) decreased by 7.6 percent (compared to 14.0 percent average growth rate from 2009-2013) to reach 40.0 bln US$ (see table 2), while imports decreased by 8.2 percent to reach 50.2 bln US$ (see table 3). Exports of this commodity accounted for 4.8 percent of world exports of SITC sections 2+4, and 0.2 percent of total world merchandise exports (see table 1). USA, Germany and United Kingdom were the top exporters in 2013 (see table 2). They accounted for 19.2, 9.8 and 5.8 percent of world exports, respectively. China, Germany and Rep. of Korea were the top destinations, with respectively 35.3, 9.4 and 6.3 percent of world imports (see table 3).

The top 15 countries/areas accounted for 71.2 and 88.0 percent of total world exports and imports, respectively (see tables 2 and 3). In 2013, USA was the country/area with the highest value of net exports (+5.6 bln US$), followed by France (+1.3 bln US$). By MDG regions (see graph 2), the largest surpluses in this product group were recorded by Developed North America (+6.8 bln US$), Latin America and the Caribbean (+2.6 bln US$) and Western Asia (+1.9 bln US$). The largest trade deficits were recorded by Eastern Asia (-21.1 bln US$), Southern Asia (-2.3 bln US$) and Developed Europe (-297.3 mln US$).

Table 1: Imports (Imp.) and exports (Exp.), 1999-2013, in current US$

		1999	2000	2001	2002	2003	2004	2005	2006	2007	2008	2009	2010	2011	2012	2013
Values in Bln US$	Imp.	9.1	11.0	10.4	9.6	11.0	16.2	19.2	32.0	40.4	38.4	26.2	46.2	59.5	54.7	50.2
	Exp.	7.3	8.3	7.7	8.0	9.4	12.9	17.0	30.0	35.7	34.6	23.7	37.4	46.2	43.3	40.0
As a percentage of	Imp.	4.0	4.4	4.4	4.0	3.8	4.3	4.6	6.5	6.5	5.0	4.8	6.1	6.0	5.9	5.5
SITC section (%)	Exp.	3.7	3.9	3.8	3.7	3.7	4.0	4.6	6.7	6.5	5.3	4.8	5.4	5.2	5.1	4.8
As a percentage of	Imp.	0.2	0.2	0.2	0.1	0.1	0.2	0.2	0.3	0.3	0.2	0.2	0.3	0.3	0.3	0.3
world trade (%)	Exp.	0.1	0.1	0.1	0.1	0.1	0.1	0.2	0.2	0.3	0.2	0.2	0.2	0.3	0.2	0.2

Graph 1: Annual growth rates of exports, 1999–2013

(In percentage by year)

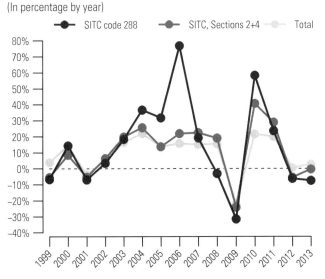

Table 2: Top exporting countries or areas in 2013

Country or area	Value (million US$)	Avg. Growth (%) 09-13	Growth (%) 12-13	World share %	Cum.
World	40 020.5	14.0	-7.6	100.0	
USA	7 703.9	15.1	-6.5	19.2	19.2
Germany	3 935.3	12.5	-11.4	9.8	29.1
United Kingdom	2 331.3	6.2	-20.6	5.8	34.9
France	2 184.5	16.5	-8.0	5.5	40.4
Canada	1 894.2	14.0	-17.5	4.7	45.1
Netherlands	1 807.1	11.6	-12.1	4.5	49.6
Japan	1 286.2	8.4	-2.1	3.2	52.8
Belgium	1 177.7	16.9	-10.3	2.9	55.8
Mexico	1 120.2	14.6	-10.1	2.8	58.6
Australia	970.9	18.7	-8.7	2.4	61.0
Spain	949.4	8.1	-8.3	2.4	63.4
Italy	887.3	9.5	-11.7	2.2	65.6
Chile	827.7	9.3	86.3	2.1	67.7
Saudi Arabia	784.3	55.3	159.0	2.0	69.6
Switzerland	636.2	15.1	-5.9	1.6	71.2

Graph 2: Trade Balance by MDG regions 2013

(Bln US$)

Imports   Exports   Trade balance

Developed Asia–Pacific
Developed Europe
Developed N. America
South–eastern Europe
CIS
Northern Africa
Sub–Saharan Africa
Latin Am, Caribbean
Eastern Asia
Southern Asia
South–eastern Asia
Western Asia
Oceania

Table 3: Top importing countries or areas in 2013

Country or area	Value (million US$)	Avg. Growth (%) 09-13	Growth (%) 12-13	World share %	Cum.
World	50 198.8	17.6	-8.2	100.0	
China	17 730.3	18.8	-6.9	35.3	35.3
Germany	4 700.0	16.8	-10.6	9.4	44.7
Rep. of Korea	3 183.6	24.8	-3.8	6.3	51.0
Belgium	2 902.3	21.3	-0.8	5.8	56.8
India	2 416.9	30.2	-11.3	4.8	61.6
USA	2 104.5	17.6	-6.6	4.2	65.8
Japan	2 095.9	6.7	-21.2	4.2	70.0
Italy	1 827.5	25.0	3.7	3.6	73.6
United Kingdom	1 543.2	12.2	4.3	3.1	76.7
Austria	1 168.4	11.0	-20.0	2.3	79.0
Netherlands	974.0	7.8	-26.5	1.9	81.0
Spain	923.8	22.9	-5.6	1.8	82.8
Other Asia, nes	898.7	18.0	1.2	1.8	84.6
Sweden	883.6	14.4	-13.7	1.8	86.4
France	846.9	11.6	-11.1	1.7	88.0

289 Ores, concentrates of precious metals; waste, scrap and sweepings (no gold)

In 2013, the value (in current US$) of exports of "ores, concentrates of precious metals; waste, scrap and sweepings (no gold)" (SITC group 289) decreased by 12.7 percent (compared to 7.7 percent average growth rate from 2009-2013) to reach 15.6 bln US$ (see table 2), while imports decreased by 1.2 percent to reach 15.5 bln US$ (see table 3). Exports of this commodity accounted for 1.9 percent of world exports of SITC sections 2+4, and 0.1 percent of total world merchandise exports (see table 1). USA, Germany and Australia were the top exporters in 2013 (see table 2). They accounted for 19.9, 8.8 and 6.7 percent of world exports, respectively. Germany, United Kingdom and China were the top destinations, with respectively 23.3, 14.8 and 11.7 percent of world imports (see table 3).

The top 15 countries/areas accounted for 72.7 and 95.8 percent of total world exports and imports, respectively (see tables 2 and 3). In 2013, USA was the country/area with the highest value of net exports (+1.6 bln US$), followed by Australia (+1.0 bln US$). By MDG regions (see graph 2), the largest surpluses in this product group were recorded by Latin America and the Caribbean (+2.8 bln US$), Developed North America (+1.2 bln US$) and South-eastern Asia (+557.2 mln US$). The largest trade deficits were recorded by Developed Europe (-3.8 bln US$) and Eastern Asia (-2.7 bln US$).

Table 1: Imports (Imp.) and exports (Exp.), 1999-2013, in current US$

		1999	2000	2001	2002	2003	2004	2005	2006	2007	2008	2009	2010	2011	2012	2013
Values in Bln US$	Imp.	2.9	3.9	4.0	3.4	3.5	3.5	4.6	7.2	10.1	13.1	8.4	11.1	15.7	15.7	15.5
	Exp.	2.8	3.5	2.9	2.7	2.9	3.2	3.8	6.4	9.6	14.3	11.6	16.9	19.7	17.9	15.6
As a percentage of	Imp.	1.3	1.6	1.7	1.4	1.2	0.9	1.1	1.5	1.6	1.7	1.5	1.5	1.6	1.7	1.7
SITC section (%)	Exp.	1.4	1.7	1.4	1.2	1.1	1.0	1.0	1.4	1.8	2.2	2.3	2.4	2.2	2.1	1.9
As a percentage of	Imp.	0.1	0.1	0.1	0.1	0.0	0.0	0.0	0.1	0.1	0.1	0.1	0.1	0.1	0.1	0.1
world trade (%)	Exp.	0.1	0.1	0.0	0.0	0.0	0.0	0.0	0.1	0.1	0.1	0.1	0.1	0.1	0.1	0.1

Graph 1: Annual growth rates of exports, 1999–2013
(In percentage by year)

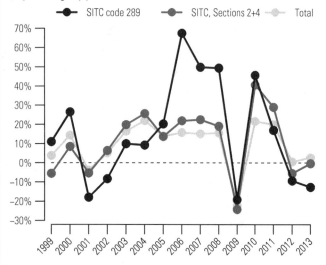

- SITC code 289
- SITC, Sections 2+4
- Total

Graph 2: Trade Balance by MDG regions 2013
(Bln US$)

- Imports
- Exports
- Trade balance

Developed Asia–Pacific
Developed Europe
Developed N. America
South–eastern Europe
CIS
Northern Africa
Sub–Saharan Africa
Latin Am, Caribbean
Eastern Asia
Southern Asia
South–eastern Asia
Western Asia
Oceania

Table 2: Top exporting countries or areas in 2013

Country or area	Value (million US$)	Avg. Growth (%) 09-13	Growth (%) 12-13	World share %	Cum.
World	15 589.7	7.7	-12.7	100.0	
USA	3 099.6	-11.4	-4.2	19.9	19.9
Germany	1 366.6	10.2	-24.6	8.8	28.6
Australia	1 047.3	58.1	-15.5	6.7	35.4
Bolivia	866.6	9.8	-14.5	5.6	40.9
United Kingdom	718.8	42.0	-0.2	4.6	45.5
Indonesia	621.6	673.3	4.4	4.0	49.5
Peru	503.1	23.2	-20.6	3.2	52.7
Guatemala	468.6	8.7	-19.8	3.0	55.8
Japan	464.5	12.9	-31.5	3.0	58.7
Russian Federation	443.1	2294.5	-13.0	2.8	61.6
Papua New Guinea	422.3	15.3	31.7	2.7	64.3
Bulgaria	356.2	25.3	-16.2	2.3	66.6
Belgium	324.5	83.2	18.7	2.1	68.7
Mexico	323.6	21.7	-1.7	2.1	70.7
India	314.7	33.6	-36.5	2.0	72.7

Table 3: Top importing countries or areas in 2013

Country or area	Value (million US$)	Avg. Growth (%) 09-13	Growth (%) 12-13	World share %	Cum.
World	15 484.5	16.7	-1.2	100.0	
Germany	3 604.0	15.9	6.9	23.3	23.3
United Kingdom	2 295.0	13.0	-0.2	14.8	38.1
China	1 809.8	57.5	41.7	11.7	49.8
Japan	1 487.5	31.8	13.3	9.6	59.4
USA	1 456.7	18.3	-6.4	9.4	68.8
Italy	1 170.5	11.8	-20.8	7.6	76.4
Rep. of Korea	1 131.7	14.2	-4.5	7.3	83.7
Canada	720.0	8.9	-16.1	4.6	88.3
Singapore	354.2	116.4	15.1	2.3	90.6
Russian Federation	152.3	48.4	33.9	1.0	91.6
South Africa	151.2	258.4	-23.4	1.0	92.6
Kazakhstan	141.4	1365.2	-66.9	0.9	93.5
Other Asia, nes	128.0	28.6	-33.8	0.8	94.3
Malaysia	127.0	67.7	1009.2	0.8	95.1
Mexico	98.7	-3.3	-36.5	0.6	95.8

In 2013, the value (in current US$) of exports of "crude animal materials, nes" (SITC group 291) increased by 10.4 percent (compared to 12.2 percent average growth rate from 2009-2013) to reach 10.3 bln US$ (see table 2), while imports increased by 7.3 percent to reach 9.8 bln US$ (see table 3). Exports of this commodity accounted for 1.2 percent of world exports of SITC sections 2+4, and 0.1 percent of total world merchandise exports (see table 1). China, Germany and USA were the top exporters in 2013 (see table 2). They accounted for 21.3, 10.2 and 9.9 percent of world exports, respectively. Germany, USA and Japan were the top destinations, with respectively 11.5, 10.4 and 8.0 percent of world imports (see table 3).

The top 15 countries/areas accounted for 78.7 and 72.2 percent of total world exports and imports, respectively (see tables 2 and 3). In 2013, China was the country/area with the highest value of net exports (+1.7 bln US$), followed by Brazil (+478.0 mln US$). By MDG regions (see graph 2), the largest surpluses in this product group were recorded by Eastern Asia (+1.6 bln US$), Latin America and the Caribbean (+383.0 mln US$) and Southern Asia (+182.9 mln US$). The largest trade deficits were recorded by Developed Europe (-721.5 mln US$), South-eastern Asia (-350.4 mln US$) and Developed Asia-Pacific (-347.5 mln US$).

Table 1: Imports (Imp.) and exports (Exp.), 1999-2013, in current US$

		1999	2000	2001	2002	2003	2004	2005	2006	2007	2008	2009	2010	2011	2012	2013
Values in Bln US$	Imp.	4.0	4.1	3.8	3.9	4.3	5.0	5.3	5.4	6.0	7.1	6.5	7.1	8.6	9.1	9.8
	Exp.	3.3	3.4	3.3	3.6	4.0	4.7	5.1	5.3	6.0	7.3	6.5	7.0	8.8	9.4	10.3
As a percentage of	Imp.	1.7	1.7	1.6	1.6	1.5	1.3	1.3	1.1	1.0	0.9	1.2	0.9	0.9	1.0	1.1
SITC section (%)	Exp.	1.7	1.6	1.6	1.7	1.5	1.5	1.4	1.2	1.1	1.1	1.3	1.0	1.0	1.1	1.2
As a percentage of	Imp.	0.1	0.1	0.1	0.1	0.1	0.1	0.0	0.0	0.0	0.0	0.1	0.0	0.0	0.0	0.1
world trade (%)	Exp.	0.1	0.1	0.1	0.1	0.1	0.1	0.0	0.0	0.0	0.0	0.1	0.0	0.0	0.1	0.1

Graph 1: Annual growth rates of exports, 1999–2013
(In percentage by year)

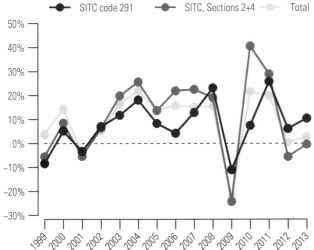

Table 2: Top exporting countries or areas in 2013

Country or area	Value (million US$)	Avg. Growth (%) 09-13	Growth (%) 12-13	World share %	Cum.
World..................................	10 339.1	12.2	10.4	100.0	
China.................................	2 200.3	15.9	6.9	21.3	21.3
Germany............................	1 056.4	10.8	12.8	10.2	31.5
USA...................................	1 021.7	7.0	14.2	9.9	41.4
Brazil.................................	639.0	13.1	11.0	6.2	47.6
Netherlands........................	612.5	4.4	2.1	5.9	53.5
New Zealand......................	367.7	14.0	3.7	3.6	57.0
Other Asia, nes..................	319.2	26.4	22.9	3.1	60.1
France...............................	307.3	8.5	9.0	3.0	63.1
Spain.................................	298.6	8.8	8.1	2.9	66.0
Poland...............................	284.6	14.5	24.3	2.8	68.7
Rep. of Korea.....................	275.2	82.4	68.1	2.7	71.4
Canada..............................	244.4	9.0	6.9	2.4	73.8
Denmark............................	180.4	1.0	2.7	1.7	75.5
United Kingdom..................	172.2	13.1	-4.3	1.7	77.2
Belgium.............................	161.2	9.0	15.1	1.6	78.7

Graph 2: Trade Balance by MDG regions 2013
(Bln US$)

Imports — Exports — Trade balance

Developed Asia–Pacific
Developed Europe
Developed N. America
South–eastern Europe
C I S
Northern Africa
Sub–Saharan Africa
Latin Am, Caribbean
Eastern Asia
Southern Asia
South–eastern Asia
Western Asia
Oceania

Table 3: Top importing countries or areas in 2013

Country or area	Value (million US$)	Avg. Growth (%) 09-13	Growth (%) 12-13	World share %	Cum.
World..................................	9 760.6	10.5	7.3	100.0	
Germany............................	1 119.7	9.5	5.5	11.5	11.5
USA...................................	1 015.0	10.8	9.8	10.4	21.9
Japan.................................	780.0	8.0	-8.9	8.0	29.9
France...............................	564.5	11.0	10.6	5.8	35.6
Netherlands........................	528.1	7.8	-1.6	5.4	41.1
China.................................	498.1	16.0	11.5	5.1	46.2
Rep. of Korea.....................	383.4	38.0	34.2	3.9	50.1
Other Asia, nes..................	335.5	27.4	9.5	3.4	53.5
Italy...................................	293.2	4.0	2.8	3.0	56.5
Denmark............................	291.7	12.3	12.9	3.0	59.5
Viet Nam............................	264.9	46.1	71.5	2.7	62.2
Poland...............................	261.2	-1.5	4.5	2.7	64.9
Spain.................................	248.4	9.8	8.7	2.5	67.5
Mexico...............................	242.5	9.4	15.4	2.5	69.9
Belgium.............................	223.8	16.9	14.0	2.3	72.2

292 Crude vegetable materials, nes

In 2013, the value (in current US$) of exports of "crude vegetable materials, nes" (SITC group 292) decreased by 2.6 percent (compared to 9.2 percent average growth rate from 2009-2013) to reach 42.1 bln US$ (see table 2), while imports increased by 0.1 percent to reach 39.0 bln US$ (see table 3). Exports of this commodity accounted for 5.0 percent of world exports of SITC sections 2+4, and 0.2 percent of total world merchandise exports (see table 1). Netherlands, India and China were the top exporters in 2013 (see table 2). They accounted for 29.6, 8.2 and 7.0 percent of world exports, respectively. USA, Germany and Netherlands were the top destinations, with respectively 15.0, 11.0 and 7.5 percent of world imports (see table 3).

The top 15 countries/areas accounted for 79.4 and 72.0 percent of total world exports and imports, respectively (see tables 2 and 3). In 2013, Netherlands was the country/area with the highest value of net exports (+9.6 bln US$), followed by India (+3.1 bln US$). By MDG regions (see graph 2), the largest surpluses in this product group were recorded by Southern Asia (+3.2 bln US$), Developed Europe (+2.2 bln US$) and Latin America and the Caribbean (+2.1 bln US$). The largest trade deficits were recorded by Developed North America (-3.7 bln US$), Commonwealth of Independent States (-1.6 bln US$) and Developed Asia-Pacific (-1.5 bln US$).

Table 1: Imports (Imp.) and exports (Exp.), 1999-2013, in current US$

		1999	2000	2001	2002	2003	2004	2005	2006	2007	2008	2009	2010	2011	2012	2013
Values in Bln US$	Imp.	16.6	15.7	15.7	17.0	19.4	22.0	23.3	24.7	28.1	31.0	28.1	31.1	37.2	39.0	39.0
	Exp.	15.2	14.4	14.5	16.1	19.2	21.1	22.6	25.1	28.1	31.4	29.6	31.6	39.2	43.2	42.1
As a percentage of SITC section (%)	Imp.	7.3	6.3	6.7	7.0	6.7	5.9	5.6	5.0	4.6	4.1	5.2	4.1	3.8	4.2	4.3
	Exp.	7.8	6.8	7.2	7.5	7.5	6.6	6.2	5.6	5.1	4.8	6.0	4.6	4.4	5.1	5.0
As a percentage of world trade (%)	Imp.	0.3	0.2	0.2	0.3	0.3	0.2	0.2	0.2	0.2	0.2	0.2	0.2	0.2	0.2	0.2
	Exp.	0.3	0.2	0.2	0.3	0.3	0.2	0.2	0.2	0.2	0.2	0.2	0.2	0.2	0.2	0.2

Graph 1: Annual growth rates of exports, 1999–2013
(In percentage by year)

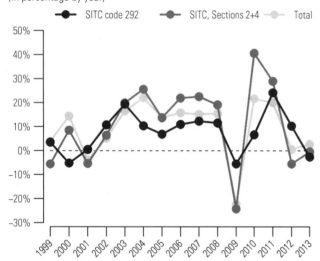

Table 2: Top exporting countries or areas in 2013

Country or area	Value (million US$)	Avg. Growth (%) 09-13	Growth (%) 12-13	World share %	Cum.
World..................	42 068.3	9.2	-2.6	100.0	
Netherlands..........................	12 469.4	6.5	2.7	29.6	29.6
India..................	3 455.9	55.8	-50.1	8.2	37.9
China.................	2 951.0	19.2	18.2	7.0	44.9
Germany..............	2 348.5	7.1	10.7	5.6	50.5
USA...................	2 322.9	5.2	-2.8	5.5	56.0
Belgium...............	1 384.3	6.2	10.4	3.3	59.3
Italy.................	1 375.2	4.6	1.7	3.3	62.5
Colombia..............	1 364.3	6.4	5.2	3.2	65.8
France................	1 166.0	5.1	6.4	2.8	68.5
Denmark...............	987.4	-0.9	-2.2	2.3	70.9
Ecuador...............	846.1	11.3	8.4	2.0	72.9
Spain.................	823.3	8.7	9.1	2.0	74.9
Canada................	717.5	9.2	6.5	1.7	76.6
Ethiopia..............	607.0	39.2	200.2	1.4	78.0
Kenya.................	586.8	1.1	-9.6	1.4	79.4

Graph 2: Trade Balance by MDG regions 2013
(Bln US$)

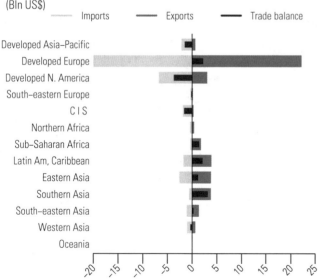

Table 3: Top importing countries or areas in 2013

Country or area	Value (million US$)	Avg. Growth (%) 09-13	Growth (%) 12-13	World share %	Cum.
World..................	39 014.6	8.6	0.1	100.0	
USA...................	5 862.9	16.7	-20.6	15.0	15.0
Germany...............	4 299.8	4.7	3.4	11.0	26.0
Netherlands...........	2 915.6	7.5	6.8	7.5	33.5
United Kingdom........	2 330.2	21.2	11.5	6.0	39.5
France................	2 219.3	-0.1	3.6	5.7	45.2
Japan.................	1 761.3	8.0	-6.0	4.5	49.7
Russian Federation....	1 327.1	9.1	-6.0	3.4	53.1
China.................	1 309.4	25.8	27.2	3.4	56.5
Italy.................	1 241.8	4.3	2.1	3.2	59.6
Belgium...............	1 087.4	3.1	10.2	2.8	62.4
Canada................	876.2	8.4	-2.0	2.2	64.7
Switzerland...........	799.5	4.8	3.5	2.0	66.7
Spain.................	764.0	1.4	-0.4	2.0	68.7
Poland................	653.6	7.7	15.0	1.7	70.4
Mexico................	633.4	6.8	-2.1	1.6	72.0

Mineral fuels, lubricants and related materials

(SITC Section 3)

321 Coal, whether or not pulverized, but not agglomerated

In 2013, the value (in current US$) of exports of "coal, whether or not pulverized, but not agglomerated" (SITC group 321) decreased by 12.0 percent (compared to 8.2 percent average growth rate from 2009-2013) to reach 110.8 bln US$ (see table 2), while imports decreased by 11.8 percent to reach 127.9 bln US$ (see table 3). Exports of this commodity accounted for 3.5 percent of world exports of SITC section 3, and 0.6 percent of total world merchandise exports (see table 1). Australia, Indonesia and Russian Federation were the top exporters in 2013 (see table 2). They accounted for 34.7, 20.5 and 10.7 percent of world exports, respectively. China, Japan and India were the top destinations, with respectively 20.3, 18.4 and 11.7 percent of world imports (see table 3).

The top 15 countries/areas accounted for 98.3 and 86.1 percent of total world exports and imports, respectively (see tables 2 and 3). In 2013, Australia was the country/area with the highest value of net exports (+38.4 bln US$), followed by Indonesia (+22.7 bln US$). By MDG regions (see graph 2), the largest surpluses in this product group were recorded by South-eastern Asia (+19.6 bln US$), Developed North America (+14.9 bln US$) and Developed Asia-Pacific (+14.8 bln US$). The largest trade deficits were recorded by Eastern Asia (-44.2 bln US$), Developed Europe (-20.3 bln US$) and Southern Asia (-15.3 bln US$).

Table 1: Imports (Imp.) and exports (Exp.), 1999-2013, in current US$

		1999	2000	2001	2002	2003	2004	2005	2006	2007	2008	2009	2010	2011	2012	2013
Values in Bln US$	Imp.	19.9	21.0	25.1	25.5	28.1	43.8	58.3	60.5	70.0	123.5	96.5	115.2	151.9	145.1	127.9
	Exp.	15.9	16.6	20.7	20.4	21.9	31.7	46.1	49.6	52.4	94.4	80.9	103.3	138.6	125.9	110.8
As a percentage of SITC section (%)	Imp.	4.8	3.1	4.0	4.1	3.6	4.2	4.1	3.4	3.6	4.4	5.4	4.9	4.8	4.4	4.0
	Exp.	3.8	2.5	3.5	3.4	3.0	3.2	3.2	2.9	2.7	3.4	4.7	4.6	4.4	3.8	3.5
As a percentage of world trade (%)	Imp.	0.3	0.3	0.4	0.4	0.4	0.5	0.6	0.5	0.5	0.8	0.8	0.8	0.8	0.8	0.7
	Exp.	0.3	0.3	0.3	0.3	0.3	0.3	0.4	0.4	0.4	0.6	0.7	0.7	0.8	0.7	0.6

Graph 1: Annual growth rates of exports, 1999–2013
(In percentage by year)

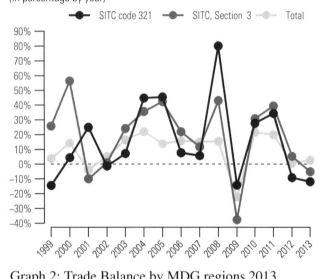

— SITC code 321   — SITC, Section 3   — Total

Graph 2: Trade Balance by MDG regions 2013
(Bln US$)

Imports   Exports   Trade balance

- Developed Asia–Pacific
- Developed Europe
- Developed N. America
- South–eastern Europe
- C I S
- Northern Africa
- Sub–Saharan Africa
- Latin Am, Caribbean
- Eastern Asia
- Southern Asia
- South–eastern Asia
- Western Asia
- Oceania

Table 2: Top exporting countries or areas in 2013

Country or area	Value (million US$)	Avg. Growth (%) 09-13	Growth (%) 12-13	World share %	Cum.
World	110814.8	8.2	-12.0	100.0	
Australia	38422.8	5.6	-10.0	34.7	34.7
Indonesia	22759.7	13.3	-6.3	20.5	55.2
Russian Federation	11821.2	12.5	-9.2	10.7	65.9
USA	11169.3	16.8	-24.9	10.1	76.0
Colombia	6253.8	4.4	-14.3	5.6	81.6
South Africa	5879.5	8.7	-11.9	5.3	86.9
Canada	5279.6	4.9	-16.6	4.8	91.7
Poland	1239.6	6.7	29.1	1.1	92.8
Netherlands	1176.3	18.3	-22.7	1.1	93.9
Mongolia	1116.2	33.0	-2.6	1.0	94.9
China	1018.5	-19.0	-34.0	0.9	95.8
Viet Nam	904.0	-9.0	-24.8	0.8	96.6
Ukraine	737.0	20.8	20.9	0.7	97.3
Czech Rep	589.6	-8.5	-28.7	0.5	97.8
Kazakhstan	571.1	1.5	-40.9	0.5	98.3

Table 3: Top importing countries or areas in 2013

Country or area	Value (million US$)	Avg. Growth (%) 09-13	Growth (%) 12-13	World share %	Cum.
World	127941.4	7.3	-11.8	100.0	
China	25926.8	25.1	2.5	20.3	20.3
Japan	23570.9	1.7	-18.7	18.4	38.7
India	14931.1	18.4	-1.4	11.7	50.4
Rep. of Korea	12940.4	7.0	-18.6	10.1	60.5
Other Asia, nes	6833.7	4.0	-13.9	5.3	65.8
Germany	5478.6	4.6	-6.6	4.3	70.1
United Kingdom	4498.6	1.7	-8.7	3.5	73.6
Brazil	2448.0	4.3	-18.6	1.9	75.5
France	2380.1	2.8	-17.5	1.9	77.4
Netherlands	2314.6	5.0	-4.6	1.8	79.2
Italy	2285.1	-2.3	-37.8	1.8	81.0
Ukraine	1980.9	25.6	-24.9	1.5	82.5
Malaysia	1854.7	14.5	-14.0	1.4	84.0
Spain	1399.9	-4.8	-41.8	1.1	85.1
Thailand	1342.2	6.8	-8.7	1.0	86.1

In 2013, the value (in current US$) of exports of "briquettes, lignite and peat" (SITC group 322) decreased by 4.3 percent (compared to 25.5 percent average growth rate from 2009-2013) to reach 3.6 bln US$ (see table 2), while imports decreased by 4.2 percent to reach 6.9 bln US$ (see table 3). Exports of this commodity accounted for 0.1 percent of world exports of SITC section 3, and less than 0.1 percent of total world merchandise exports (see table 1). Indonesia, Germany and Canada were the top exporters in 2013 (see table 2). They accounted for 48.4, 10.4 and 8.3 percent of world exports, respectively. China, Afghanistan and Netherlands were the top destinations, with respectively 45.6, 21.0 and 6.3 percent of world imports (see table 3).

The top 15 countries/areas accounted for 94.1 and 90.0 percent of total world exports and imports, respectively (see tables 2 and 3). In 2013, Indonesia was the country/area with the highest value of net exports (+1.8 bln US$), followed by Canada (+291.8 mln US$). By MDG regions (see graph 2), the largest surpluses in this product group were recorded by South-eastern Asia (+1.8 bln US$), Commonwealth of Independent States (+111.3 mln US$) and Developed North America (+42.8 mln US$). The largest trade deficits were recorded by Eastern Asia (-3.1 bln US$), Southern Asia (-1.4 bln US$) and Developed Europe (-228.6 mln US$).

Table 1: Imports (Imp.) and exports (Exp.), 1999-2013, in current US$

		1999	2000	2001	2002	2003	2004	2005	2006	2007	2008	2009	2010	2011	2012	2013
Values in Bln US$	Imp.	0.8	0.7	0.7	0.8	0.9	1.0	1.1	1.2	1.4	1.8	1.8	2.9	5.2	7.2	6.9
	Exp.	0.7	0.7	0.7	0.7	0.8	0.8	0.9	1.0	1.2	1.5	1.5	1.9	3.7	3.8	3.6
As a percentage of SITC section (%)	Imp.	0.2	0.1	0.1	0.1	0.1	0.1	0.1	0.1	0.1	0.1	0.1	0.1	0.2	0.2	0.2
	Exp.	0.2	0.1	0.1	0.1	0.1	0.1	0.1	0.1	0.1	0.1	0.1	0.1	0.1	0.1	0.1
As a percentage of world trade (%)	Imp.	0.0	0.0	0.0	0.0	0.0	0.0	0.0	0.0	0.0	0.0	0.0	0.0	0.0	0.0	0.0
	Exp.	0.0	0.0	0.0	0.0	0.0	0.0	0.0	0.0	0.0	0.0	0.0	0.0	0.0	0.0	0.0

Graph 1: Annual growth rates of exports, 1999–2013
(In percentage by year)

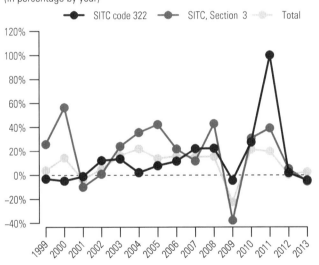

— SITC code 322 — SITC, Section 3 — Total

Table 2: Top exporting countries or areas in 2013

Country or area	Value (million US$)	Avg. Growth (%) 09-13	Growth (%) 12-13	World share %	Cum.
World....................	3 627.4	25.5	-4.3	100.0	
Indonesia................	1 755.2	168.8	-6.8	48.4	48.4
Germany..................	376.2	3.5	-0.6	10.4	58.8
Canada...................	301.4	1.3	3.2	8.3	67.1
Latvia...................	154.0	9.4	14.2	4.2	71.3
Netherlands..............	136.7	6.5	-4.8	3.8	75.1
Czech Rep................	114.5	3.3	-0.7	3.2	78.2
Ireland..................	93.8	6.8	13.7	2.6	80.8
Russian Federation.......	93.4	27.1	13.5	2.6	83.4
Belgium..................	77.0	9.5	26.3	2.1	85.5
Estonia..................	65.6	3.5	-13.5	1.8	87.3
Lithuania................	63.7	9.5	5.4	1.8	89.1
South Africa.............	54.4	273.9	-20.7	1.5	90.6
United Kingdom...........	43.7	8.9	-39.8	1.2	91.8
China....................	43.5	30.6	-2.0	1.2	93.0
Kazakhstan...............	39.6	40.1	-33.4	1.1	94.1

Graph 2: Trade Balance by MDG regions 2013
(Bln US$)

.... Imports — Exports — Trade balance

Developed Asia–Pacific
Developed Europe
Developed N. America
South–eastern Europe
C I S
Northern Africa
Sub–Saharan Africa
Latin Am, Caribbean
Eastern Asia
Southern Asia
South–eastern Asia
Western Asia
Oceania

Table 3: Top importing countries or areas in 2013

Country or area	Value (million US$)	Avg. Growth (%) 09-13	Growth (%) 12-13	World share %	Cum.
World....................	6 928.5	39.9	-4.2	100.0	
China....................	3 156.2	75.0	-8.0	45.6	45.6
Afghanistan..............	1 452.5	...	-4.3	21.0	66.5
Netherlands..............	437.5	38.0	12.7	6.3	72.8
USA......................	282.2	1.6	2.5	4.1	76.9
Cayman Isds..............	138.9	666.7	-27.0	2.0	78.9
France...................	133.4	-1.0	1.0	1.9	80.8
Belgium..................	112.4	12.9	23.4	1.6	82.5
Germany..................	105.6	10.1	12.2	1.5	84.0
Italy....................	80.3	0.6	2.5	1.2	85.1
Japan....................	80.0	15.9	7.0	1.2	86.3
United Kingdom...........	56.2	7.1	2.4	0.8	87.1
Slovenia.................	55.3	1.3	-22.3	0.8	87.9
Slovakia.................	52.1	-4.1	-27.4	0.8	88.7
Czech Rep................	50.2	36.3	6.9	0.7	89.4
Poland...................	45.5	19.0	30.6	0.7	90.0

325 Coke, semi-coke of coal, lignite or peat, agglomerated or not; retort carbon

In 2013, the value (in current US$) of exports of "coke, semi-coke of coal, lignite or peat, agglomerated or not; retort carbon" (SITC group 325) decreased by 12.1 percent (compared to 13.9 percent average growth rate from 2009-2013) to reach 6.5 bln US$ (see table 2), while imports decreased by 19.2 percent to reach 6.6 bln US$ (see table 3). Exports of this commodity accounted for 0.2 percent of world exports of SITC section 3, and less than 0.1 percent of total world merchandise exports (see table 1). Poland, China and Mozambique were the top exporters in 2013 (see table 2). They accounted for 26.6, 17.4 and 8.1 percent of world exports, respectively. India, Germany and Iran were the top destinations, with respectively 12.8, 11.5 and 7.5 percent of world imports (see table 3).

The top 15 countries/areas accounted for 95.1 and 75.6 percent of total world exports and imports, respectively (see tables 2 and 3). In 2013, Poland was the country/area with the highest value of net exports (+1.7 bln US$), followed by China (+1.1 bln US$). By MDG regions (see graph 2), the largest surpluses in this product group were recorded by Eastern Asia (+985.4 mln US$), Sub-Saharan Africa (+462.3 mln US$) and Commonwealth of Independent States (+383.5 mln US$). The largest trade deficits were recorded by Southern Asia (-1.4 bln US$), Latin America and the Caribbean (-215.0 mln US$) and South-eastern Europe (-207.5 mln US$).

Table 1: Imports (Imp.) and exports (Exp.), 1999-2013, in current US$

		1999	2000	2001	2002	2003	2004	2005	2006	2007	2008	2009	2010	2011	2012	2013
Values in Bln US$	Imp.	2.1	2.6	2.6	2.9	4.1	9.8	7.4	6.7	8.2	14.8	4.8	9.1	11.0	8.2	6.6
	Exp.	1.7	2.2	2.3	2.4	3.7	8.4	6.1	7.5	7.4	13.5	3.9	8.0	9.2	7.4	6.5
As a percentage of	Imp.	0.5	0.4	0.4	0.5	0.5	0.9	0.5	0.4	0.4	0.5	0.3	0.4	0.3	0.2	0.2
SITC section (%)	Exp.	0.4	0.3	0.4	0.4	0.5	0.8	0.4	0.4	0.4	0.5	0.2	0.4	0.3	0.2	0.2
As a percentage of	Imp.	0.0	0.0	0.0	0.0	0.1	0.1	0.1	0.1	0.1	0.1	0.0	0.1	0.1	0.0	0.0
world trade (%)	Exp.	0.0	0.0	0.0	0.0	0.0	0.1	0.1	0.1	0.1	0.1	0.0	0.1	0.1	0.0	0.0

Graph 1: Annual growth rates of exports, 1999–2013
(In percentage by year)

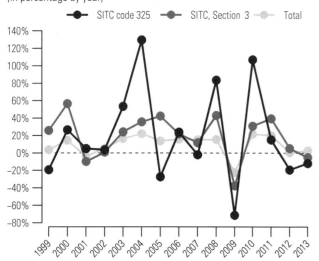

Table 2: Top exporting countries or areas in 2013

Country or area	Value (million US$)	Avg. Growth (%) 09-13	Growth (%) 12-13	World share %	Cum.
World	6516.2	13.9	-12.1	100.0	
Poland	1735.4	12.6	-10.5	26.6	26.6
China	1134.2	53.5	154.8	17.4	44.0
Mozambique	526.6	...	21.0	8.1	52.1
Russian Federation	506.1	8.8	-12.7	7.8	59.9
Colombia	433.9	28.5	-14.3	6.7	66.5
Ukraine	404.9	24.9	-35.3	6.2	72.8
Japan	330.6	12.1	-29.8	5.1	77.8
Australia	194.5	11.4	-35.6	3.0	80.8
USA	185.6	2.9	-11.2	2.8	83.7
Czech Rep.	171.3	6.2	-8.1	2.6	86.3
Belgium	144.1	-6.2	-63.4	2.2	88.5
Hungary	123.2	24.1	29.1	1.9	90.4
Italy	113.2	7.2	-20.8	1.7	92.1
Germany	108.8	18.6	10.6	1.7	93.8
Spain	83.9	5.2	-59.9	1.3	95.1

Graph 2: Trade Balance by MDG regions 2013
(Bln US$)

Imports — Exports — Trade balance

Developed Asia–Pacific
Developed Europe
Developed N. America
South–eastern Europe
CIS
Northern Africa
Sub–Saharan Africa
Latin Am, Caribbean
Eastern Asia
Southern Asia
South–eastern Asia
Western Asia
Oceania

Table 3: Top importing countries or areas in 2013

Country or area	Value (million US$)	Avg. Growth (%) 09-13	Growth (%) 12-13	World share %	Cum.
World	6610.8	8.3	-19.2	100.0	
India	847.0	8.7	-26.0	12.8	12.8
Germany	757.9	-1.5	-29.3	11.5	24.3
Iran	494.5	6.9	-13.3	7.5	31.8
Japan	485.5	37.1	42.0	7.3	39.1
Brazil	461.9	24.3	-22.2	7.0	46.1
Austria	459.3	26.0	9.1	6.9	53.0
Romania	205.1	7.8	-15.1	3.1	56.1
Kazakhstan	196.4	15.4	-22.6	3.0	59.1
Ukraine	193.4	29.6	32.4	2.9	62.0
Italy	186.3	111.7	983.0	2.8	64.9
United Kingdom	173.5	62.3	302.6	2.6	67.5
France	136.9	-9.3	-40.7	2.1	69.5
Norway	134.7	13.5	-20.5	2.0	71.6
Turkey	131.5	22.5	13.5	2.0	73.6
Mexico	131.1	16.4	-18.2	2.0	75.6

"Petroleum oils and oils obtained from bituminous minerals, crude" (SITC group 333) is the top exported commodities in 2013 with 8.5 percent of total exports (see table 1). The value (in current US$) of exports of this commodity decreased by 5.2 percent (compared to 16.6 percent average growth rate from 2009-2013) to reach 1579.3 bln US$ (see table 2), while imports decreased by 5.9 percent to reach 1626.4 bln US$ (see table 3). One contributing factor is the increased oil production in USA, which reduced imports to USA by 13.3 percent in 2013. Another factor is the fall in crude oil prices of around 3.0 percent in 2013. Saudi Arabia, Russian Federation and United Arab Emirates were the top exporters in 2013 (see table 2). They accounted for 18.6, 11.0 and 8.4 percent of world exports, respectively. USA, China and India were the top destinations, with respectively 17.2, 13.5 and 9.1 percent of world imports (see table 3).

The top 15 countries/areas accounted for 84.1 and 81.9 percent of total world exports and imports, respectively (see tables 2 and 3). In 2013, Saudi Arabia was the country/area with the highest value of net exports (+294.0 bln US$), followed by Russian Federation (+173.5 bln US$). By MDG regions (see graph 2), the largest surplus in this product group was recorded by Western Asia (+613.6 bln US$). The largest trade deficit was recorded by Eastern Asia (-350.8 bln US$).

Table 1: Imports (Imp.) and exports (Exp.), 1999-2013, in current US$

		1999	2000	2001	2002	2003	2004	2005	2006	2007	2008	2009	2010	2011	2012	2013
Values in Bln US$	Imp.	225.1	389.2	340.3	340.0	427.5	576.7	799.7	993.2	1084.3	1566.9	921.5	1223.6	1638.2	1729.1	1626.4
	Exp.	232.2	374.7	314.6	324.3	399.9	535.5	765.5	942.2	1053.8	1478.2	854.7	1123.4	1576.2	1666.6	1579.3
As a percentage of	Imp.	54.4	58.1	54.5	55.1	54.6	55.3	55.6	56.0	55.2	55.4	51.6	52.4	51.4	52.0	50.3
SITC section (%)	Exp.	55.3	57.1	53.2	54.4	54.0	53.4	53.6	54.2	54.2	53.2	49.3	49.6	49.9	50.2	50.1
As a percentage of	Imp.	3.9	5.9	5.4	5.2	5.6	6.2	7.6	8.2	7.7	9.6	7.3	8.0	9.0	9.5	8.8
world trade (%)	Exp.	4.2	5.9	5.2	5.1	5.3	5.9	7.4	7.8	7.6	9.3	6.9	7.4	8.7	9.2	8.5

Graph 1: Annual growth rates of exports, 1999–2013
(In percentage by year)

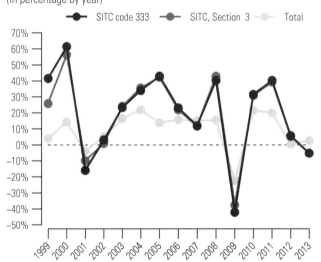

Table 2: Top exporting countries or areas in 2013

Country or area	Value (million US$)	Avg. Growth (%) 09-13	Growth (%) 12-13	World share %	Cum.
World	1579307.7	16.6	-5.2	100.0	
Saudi Arabia	293994.6	19.9	-3.7	18.6	18.6
Russian Federation	173669.6	16.7	-4.0	11.0	29.6
United Arab Emirates	132867.8	32.2	21.7	8.4	38.0
Iraq	89214.5	20.9	-5.1	5.6	43.7
Canada	79344.8	20.5	6.6	5.0	48.7
Kuwait	79041.0	27.8	-0.8	5.0	53.7
Nigeria	74953.8	15.4	-24.3	4.7	58.4
Venezuela	74850.6	20.2	8.6	4.7	63.2
Angola	62804.1	13.5	-4.6	4.0	67.2
Kazakhstan	55221.4	20.5	-2.2	3.5	70.7
Iran	53003.5	4.8	-14.1	3.4	74.0
Norway	48748.6	5.1	-10.8	3.1	77.1
Mexico	42723.2	13.6	-8.7	2.7	79.8
Libya	35277.0	12.6	-28.6	2.2	82.0
Oman	32087.1	23.2	4.6	2.0	84.1

Graph 2: Trade Balance by MDG regions 2013
(Bln US$)

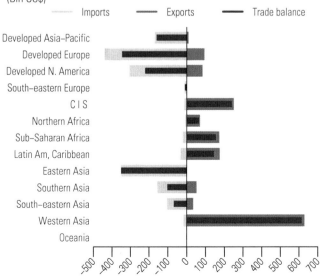

Table 3: Top importing countries or areas in 2013

Country or area	Value (million US$)	Avg. Growth (%) 09-13	Growth (%) 12-13	World share %	Cum.
World	1626401.1	15.3	-5.9	100.0	
USA	279133.6	8.6	-13.3	17.2	17.2
China	219660.4	25.3	-0.5	13.5	30.7
India	148046.7	22.9	-0.5	9.1	39.8
Japan	145720.8	16.2	-4.8	9.0	48.7
Rep. of Korea	99333.2	18.3	-8.3	6.1	54.8
Germany	74284.1	14.4	-2.6	4.6	59.4
Netherlands	52164.0	19.1	-2.1	3.2	62.6
Italy	46460.4	8.5	-18.4	2.9	65.5
France	45627.9	9.5	-4.1	2.8	68.3
Spain	45308.1	18.7	-2.0	2.8	71.1
United Kingdom	40092.0	14.6	-16.3	2.5	73.5
Thailand	38916.9	19.6	8.6	2.4	75.9
Singapore	35538.7	15.3	-10.9	2.2	78.1
Other Asia, nes	33463.8	14.2	-6.1	2.1	80.2
Belgium	28484.2	18.8	-1.9	1.8	81.9

334 Petroleum oils and oils obtained from bituminous minerals, (not crude)

"Petroleum oils and oils obtained from bituminous minerals, (not crude)" (SITC group 334) is the second most exported commodities in 2013 with 5.4 percent of total exports (see table 1). The value (in current US$) of exports of this commodity decreased by 1.0 percent (compared to 18.2 percent average growth rate from 2009-2013) to reach 1001.8 bln US$ (see table 2), while imports increased by 1.8 percent to reach 914.5 bln US$ (see table 3). Exports of this commodity accounted for 31.8 percent of world exports of SITC section 3 (see table 1). USA, Russian Federation and Netherlands were the top exporters in 2013 (see table 2). They accounted for 11.2, 10.9 and 7.5 percent of world exports, respectively. USA, Singapore and Netherlands were the top destinations, with respectively 9.7, 8.2 and 5.5 percent of world imports. but imports by USA and Singapore decreased by respectively 4.0 and 3.5 percent in 2013 (see table 3).

The top 15 countries/areas accounted for 70.7 and 60.0 percent of total world exports and imports, respectively (see tables 2 and 3). In 2013, Russian Federation was the country/area with the highest value of net exports (+107.6 bln US$), followed by India (+62.7 bln US$). By MDG regions (see graph 2), the largest surpluses in this product group were recorded by Commonwealth of Independent States (+111.6 bln US$), Southern Asia (+48.7 bln US$) and Western Asia (+42.3 bln US$). The largest trade deficit was recorded by Latin America and the Caribbean (-55.7 bln US$).

Table 1: Imports (Imp.) and exports (Exp.), 1999-2013, in current US$

		1999	2000	2001	2002	2003	2004	2005	2006	2007	2008	2009	2010	2011	2012	2013
Values in Bln US$	Imp.	98.7	156.9	141.8	136.8	171.7	236.6	342.5	428.3	500.9	701.6	448.7	611.5	874.7	898.2	914.5
	Exp.	101.7	161.4	147.0	147.8	178.0	261.7	385.0	469.8	541.9	781.2	513.6	683.4	958.4	1012.3	1001.8
As a percentage of SITC section (%)	Imp.	23.9	23.4	22.7	22.2	21.9	22.7	23.8	24.2	25.5	24.8	25.1	26.2	27.5	27.0	28.3
	Exp.	24.2	24.6	24.9	24.8	24.1	26.1	27.0	27.0	27.9	28.1	29.7	30.2	30.4	30.5	31.8
As a percentage of world trade (%)	Imp.	1.7	2.4	2.2	2.1	2.2	2.5	3.2	3.5	3.6	4.3	3.6	4.0	4.8	4.9	4.9
	Exp.	1.8	2.5	2.4	2.3	2.4	2.9	3.7	3.9	3.9	4.9	4.1	4.5	5.3	5.6	5.4

Graph 1: Annual growth rates of exports, 1999–2013
(In percentage by year)

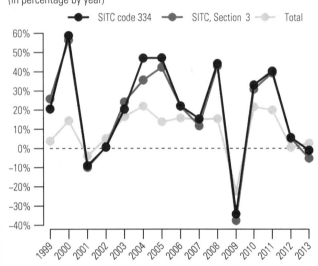

Graph 2: Trade Balance by MDG regions 2013
(Bln US$)

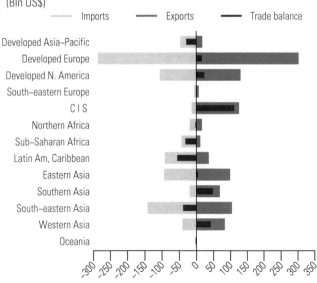

Table 2: Top exporting countries or areas in 2013

Country or area	Value (million US$)	Avg. Growth (%) 09-13	Growth (%) 12-13	World share %	Cum.
World	1001837.8	18.2	-1.0	100.0	
USA	111798.5	32.3	8.8	11.2	11.2
Russian Federation	109415.4	23.6	5.6	10.9	22.1
Netherlands	75502.3	23.9	5.7	7.5	29.6
Singapore	69253.4	14.7	-5.4	6.9	36.5
India	67075.2	30.4	27.1	6.7	43.2
Rep. of Korea	51003.4	23.2	-6.8	5.1	48.3
Belgium	48750.5	28.6	30.8	4.9	53.2
United Kingdom	25963.0	13.7	-6.9	2.6	55.8
Kuwait	24980.5	12.4	-14.6	2.5	58.3
China	24505.0	18.2	15.0	2.4	60.7
Other Asia, nes.	22425.7	19.6	6.8	2.2	63.0
Italy	20432.8	14.1	-18.2	2.0	65.0
Malaysia	19433.7	37.0	26.0	1.9	66.9
Saudi Arabia	19060.0	5.9	-16.2	1.9	68.8
Canada	18337.7	14.9	-6.9	1.8	70.7

Table 3: Top importing countries or areas in 2013

Country or area	Value (million US$)	Avg. Growth (%) 09-13	Growth (%) 12-13	World share %	Cum.
World	914478.4	19.5	1.8	100.0	
USA	88759.8	12.9	-4.0	9.7	9.7
Singapore	74603.6	17.9	-3.5	8.2	17.9
Netherlands	50573.8	26.8	1.9	5.5	23.4
Belgium	36991.2	25.4	34.9	4.0	27.4
Germany	36623.5	19.5	7.7	4.0	31.4
France	34791.5	18.5	-6.4	3.8	35.2
China	32025.7	17.2	-3.0	3.5	38.8
Rep. of Korea	28842.4	23.4	12.2	3.2	41.9
Indonesia	27850.9	26.6	-0.7	3.0	45.0
United Kingdom	27621.7	17.9	-1.6	3.0	48.0
Japan	26882.1	20.6	-10.5	2.9	50.9
Mexico	25329.9	21.2	-7.0	2.8	53.7
Malaysia	22082.0	52.4	41.6	2.4	56.1
Brazil	17757.0	40.6	8.5	1.9	58.0
Australia	17592.8	21.2	7.0	1.9	60.0

In 2013, the value (in current US$) of exports of "residual petroleum products, nes, and related materials" (SITC group 335) increased by 1.9 percent (compared to 16.3 percent average growth rate from 2009-2013) to reach 49.8 bln US$ (see table 2), while imports decreased by 1.8 percent to reach 52.3 bln US$ (see table 3). Exports of this commodity accounted for 1.6 percent of world exports of SITC section 3, and 0.3 percent of total world merchandise exports (see table 1). USA, Netherlands and Indonesia were the top exporters in 2013 (see table 2). They accounted for 14.7, 7.2 and 5.9 percent of world exports, respectively. China, Netherlands and Rep. of Korea were the top destinations, with respectively 17.7, 9.9 and 5.5 percent of world imports (see table 3).

The top 15 countries/areas accounted for 73.0 and 68.2 percent of total world exports and imports, respectively (see tables 2 and 3). In 2013, USA was the country/area with the highest value of net exports (+4.6 bln US$), followed by Indonesia (+2.1 bln US$). By MDG regions (see graph 2), the largest surpluses in this product group were recorded by Developed North America (+5.2 bln US$), South-eastern Asia (+4.1 bln US$) and Northern Africa (+1.0 bln US$). The largest trade deficits were recorded by Eastern Asia (-8.1 bln US$), Latin America and the Caribbean (-4.2 bln US$) and Sub-Saharan Africa (-902.7 mln US$).

Table 1: Imports (Imp.) and exports (Exp.), 1999-2013, in current US$

		1999	2000	2001	2002	2003	2004	2005	2006	2007	2008	2009	2010	2011	2012	2013
Values in Bln US$	Imp.	7.6	9.6	9.9	10.5	13.0	18.2	21.3	27.0	39.3	43.4	28.2	38.4	50.7	53.3	52.3
	Exp.	7.7	8.3	8.5	9.0	11.6	14.8	17.5	22.4	27.6	38.8	27.2	36.9	51.4	48.9	49.8
As a percentage of	Imp.	1.8	1.4	1.6	1.7	1.7	1.7	1.5	1.5	2.0	1.5	1.6	1.6	1.6	1.6	1.6
SITC section (%)	Exp.	1.8	1.3	1.4	1.5	1.6	1.5	1.2	1.3	1.4	1.4	1.6	1.6	1.6	1.5	1.6
As a percentage of	Imp.	0.1	0.1	0.2	0.2	0.2	0.2	0.2	0.2	0.3	0.3	0.2	0.3	0.3	0.3	0.3
world trade (%)	Exp.	0.1	0.1	0.1	0.1	0.2	0.2	0.2	0.2	0.2	0.2	0.2	0.2	0.3	0.3	0.3

Graph 1: Annual growth rates of exports, 1999–2013
(In percentage by year)

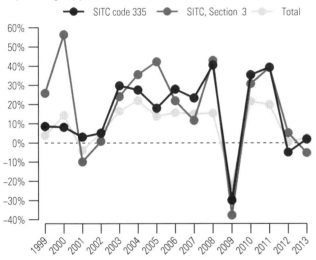

Table 2: Top exporting countries or areas in 2013

Country or area	Value (million US$)	Avg. Growth (%) 09-13	Growth (%) 12-13	World share %	Cum.
World....................	49 793.1	16.3	1.9	100.0	
USA.......................	7 315.9	11.1	-9.4	14.7	14.7
Netherlands...........	3 595.6	31.9	-3.9	7.2	21.9
Indonesia...............	2 935.5	18.3	12.6	5.9	27.8
Germany................	2 852.6	13.4	-2.4	5.7	33.5
Rep. of Korea.........	2 790.4	16.4	15.6	5.6	39.1
Belgium.................	2 208.7	14.9	8.5	4.4	43.6
China....................	2 021.6	16.8	-6.8	4.1	47.6
Spain....................	2 017.0	18.3	13.9	4.1	51.7
India.....................	1 977.1	36.1	73.6	4.0	55.7
Singapore..............	1 870.2	20.9	-3.2	3.8	59.4
Canada..................	1 558.4	13.1	-12.4	3.1	62.5
Japan....................	1 484.5	14.2	25.7	3.0	65.5
Thailand................	1 332.2	39.0	-15.9	2.7	68.2
Italy......................	1 211.9	12.5	-7.6	2.4	70.6
France...................	1 171.8	12.4	5.7	2.4	73.0

Graph 2: Trade Balance by MDG regions 2013
(Bln US$)

Imports — Exports — Trade balance

Developed Asia–Pacific
Developed Europe
Developed N. America
South–eastern Europe
CIS
Northern Africa
Sub–Saharan Africa
Latin Am, Caribbean
Eastern Asia
Southern Asia
South–eastern Asia
Western Asia
Oceania

-20 -15 -10 -5 0 5 10 15 20

Table 3: Top importing countries or areas in 2013

Country or area	Value (million US$)	Avg. Growth (%) 09-13	Growth (%) 12-13	World share %	Cum.
World....................	52 291.7	16.7	-1.8	100.0	
China....................	9 262.3	31.4	-6.6	17.7	17.7
Netherlands...........	5 202.8	21.3	-9.2	9.9	27.7
Rep. of Korea.........	2 861.0	20.9	25.1	5.5	33.1
USA.......................	2 746.0	9.3	-3.2	5.3	38.4
Belgium.................	2 207.2	30.7	67.1	4.2	42.6
Ecuador.................	2 153.8	29.4	2.9	4.1	46.7
Germany................	1 905.9	13.8	3.1	3.6	50.4
India.....................	1 654.1	17.2	14.3	3.2	53.5
Japan....................	1 513.5	13.4	-17.3	2.9	56.4
France...................	1 426.3	11.3	-17.8	2.7	59.2
Other Asia, nes.......	1 149.3	13.1	-18.6	2.2	61.4
Mexico..................	1 017.7	25.1	-0.8	1.9	63.3
Canada..................	926.4	7.8	-20.1	1.8	65.1
Indonesia...............	835.3	25.9	12.4	1.6	66.7
Australia................	826.6	18.5	2.3	1.6	68.2

342 Liquefied propane and butane

In 2013, the value (in current US$) of exports of "liquefied propane and butane" (SITC group 342) decreased by 2.6 percent (compared to 10.4 percent average growth rate from 2009-2013) to reach 42.7 bln US$ (see table 2), while imports decreased by 0.7 percent to reach 60.1 bln US$ (see table 3). Exports of this commodity accounted for 1.4 percent of world exports of SITC section 3, and 0.2 percent of total world merchandise exports (see table 1). Saudi Arabia, USA and Algeria were the top exporters in 2013 (see table 2). They accounted for 14.7, 13.0 and 11.8 percent of world exports, respectively. Japan, Rep. of Korea and India were the top destinations, with respectively 18.3, 8.5 and 8.5 percent of world imports (see table 3).

The top 15 countries/areas accounted for 86.2 and 76.0 percent of total world exports and imports, respectively (see tables 2 and 3). In 2013, Saudi Arabia was the country/area with the highest value of net exports (+6.3 bln US$), followed by Algeria (+5.1 bln US$). By MDG regions (see graph 2), the largest surpluses in this product group were recorded by Western Asia (+9.7 bln US$), Developed North America (+5.0 bln US$) and Commonwealth of Independent States (+2.5 bln US$). The largest trade deficits were recorded by Developed Asia-Pacific (-10.2 bln US$), Eastern Asia (-9.0 bln US$) and South-eastern Asia (-5.4 bln US$).

Table 1: Imports (Imp.) and exports (Exp.), 1999-2013, in current US$

		1999	2000	2001	2002	2003	2004	2005	2006	2007	2008	2009	2010	2011	2012	2013
Values in Bln US$	Imp.	10.7	16.0	14.3	12.7	17.4	21.3	27.2	33.6	37.6	47.8	30.7	43.3	58.3	60.5	60.1
	Exp.	6.3	10.5	9.6	8.9	15.1	18.9	24.6	28.1	32.8	43.0	28.7	42.5	56.3	43.9	42.7
As a percentage of SITC section (%)	Imp.	2.6	2.4	2.3	2.1	2.2	2.0	1.9	1.9	1.9	1.7	1.7	1.9	1.8	1.8	1.9
	Exp.	1.5	1.6	1.6	1.5	2.0	1.9	1.7	1.6	1.7	1.5	1.7	1.9	1.8	1.3	1.4
As a percentage of world trade (%)	Imp.	0.2	0.2	0.2	0.2	0.2	0.2	0.3	0.3	0.3	0.3	0.2	0.3	0.3	0.3	0.3
	Exp.	0.1	0.2	0.2	0.1	0.2	0.2	0.2	0.2	0.2	0.3	0.2	0.3	0.3	0.2	0.2

Graph 1: Annual growth rates of exports, 1999–2013
(In percentage by year)

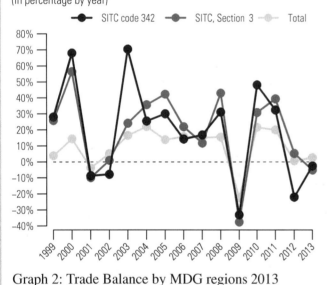

— SITC code 342   — SITC, Section 3   — Total

Table 2: Top exporting countries or areas in 2013

Country or area	Value (million US$)	Avg. Growth (%) 09-13	Growth (%) 12-13	World share %	Cum.
World	42 724.7	10.4	-2.6	100.0	
Saudi Arabia	6 289.0	10.5	-8.8	14.7	14.7
USA	5 575.1	40.8	64.1	13.0	27.8
Algeria	5 055.2	11.0	5.7	11.8	39.6
Kuwait	3 764.7	24.4	-1.7	8.8	48.4
Norway	3 241.9	9.7	-14.0	7.6	56.0
Iran	1 975.4	0.0	-14.1	4.6	60.6
Canada	1 812.2	1.8	-0.6	4.2	64.9
United Kingdom	1 536.4	6.9	-11.5	3.6	68.5
Russian Federation	1 412.1	33.1	4.2	3.3	71.8
Kazakhstan	1 261.7	34.2	2.2	3.0	74.7
China	1 209.3	28.6	-1.4	2.8	77.5
Australia	1 064.4	7.9	-4.4	2.5	80.0
Netherlands	999.2	35.8	-16.1	2.3	82.4
France	879.6	12.4	-15.3	2.1	84.4
Belgium	764.1	14.1	3.1	1.8	86.2

Graph 2: Trade Balance by MDG regions 2013
(Bln US$)

— Imports   — Exports   — Trade balance

Developed Asia–Pacific
Developed Europe
Developed N. America
South–eastern Europe
CIS
Northern Africa
Sub–Saharan Africa
Latin Am, Caribbean
Eastern Asia
Southern Asia
South–eastern Asia
Western Asia
Oceania

-14 -12 -10 -8 -6 -4 -2 0 2 4 6 8 10 12

Table 3: Top importing countries or areas in 2013

Country or area	Value (million US$)	Avg. Growth (%) 09-13	Growth (%) 12-13	World share %	Cum.
World	60 065.8	18.3	-0.7	100.0	
Japan	10 962.3	14.7	-14.0	18.3	18.3
Rep. of Korea	5 089.1	13.7	-8.7	8.5	26.7
India	5 084.1	42.0	-0.3	8.5	35.2
China	3 784.1	16.7	24.4	6.3	41.5
Indonesia	3 073.2	60.8	1.5	5.1	46.6
France	2 461.2	20.8	3.0	4.1	50.7
Netherlands	2 278.6	40.5	28.8	3.8	54.5
USA	1 978.7	-3.4	-8.5	3.3	57.8
Thailand	1 946.1	41.7	28.4	3.2	61.0
Morocco	1 811.3	16.1	-7.4	3.0	64.0
Italy	1 803.6	17.9	-2.4	3.0	67.0
Egypt	1 573.5	5.1	-29.5	2.6	69.7
Belgium	1 339.2	21.7	-1.7	2.2	71.9
Poland	1 311.3	24.1	-6.3	2.2	74.1
Brazil	1 159.1	14.6	20.0	1.9	76.0

"Natural gas, whether or not liquefied" (SITC group 343) is amongst the top exported commodities in 2013 with 2.1 percent of total exports (see table 1). The value (in current US$) of exports of this commodity increased by 11.3 percent (compared to 21.0 percent average growth rate from 2009-2013) to reach 397.3 bln US$ (see table 2), while imports increased by 6.5 percent to reach 394.5 bln US$ (see table 3). Exports of this commodity accounted for 12.6 percent of world exports of SITC section 3 (see table 1). Qatar, Russian Federation and Norway were the top exporters in 2013 (see table 2). They accounted for 22.0, 18.3 and 10.7 percent of world exports, respectively. Despite a decrease in import by 3.8 percent Japan is still the largest importer, followed by Germany and Rep. of Korea, with respectively 18.3, 12.7 and 7.8 percent of world imports (see table 3).

The top 15 countries/areas accounted for 89.4 and 82.9 percent of total world exports and imports, respectively (see tables 2 and 3). In 2013, Qatar was the country/area with the highest value of net exports (+87.5 bln US$), followed by Russian Federation (+72.5 bln US$). By MDG regions (see graph 2), the largest surpluses in this product group were recorded by Western Asia (+98.1 bln US$), Commonwealth of Independent States (+64.4 bln US$) and South-eastern Asia (+30.7 bln US$). The largest trade deficits were recorded by Developed Europe (-82.5 bln US$), Eastern Asia (-60.9 bln US$) and Developed Asia-Pacific (-60.5 bln US$).

Table 1: Imports (Imp.) and exports (Exp.), 1999-2013, in current US$

		1999	2000	2001	2002	2003	2004	2005	2006	2007	2008	2009	2010	2011	2012	2013
Values in Bln US$	Imp.	39.4	60.8	73.7	71.5	99.6	112.7	149.9	183.8	186.0	279.7	215.8	249.4	342.1	370.3	394.5
	Exp.	42.7	68.1	71.0	65.8	85.7	101.3	145.6	174.1	181.8	274.5	185.2	222.7	309.4	357.1	397.3
As a percentage of	Imp.	9.5	9.1	11.8	11.6	12.7	10.8	10.4	10.4	9.5	9.9	12.1	10.7	10.7	11.1	12.2
SITC section (%)	Exp.	10.2	10.4	12.0	11.0	11.6	10.1	10.2	10.0	9.4	9.9	10.7	9.8	9.8	10.8	12.6
As a percentage of	Imp.	0.7	0.9	1.2	1.1	1.3	1.2	1.4	1.5	1.3	1.7	1.7	1.6	1.9	2.0	2.1
world trade (%)	Exp.	0.8	1.1	1.2	1.0	1.1	1.1	1.4	1.4	1.3	1.7	1.5	1.5	1.7	2.0	2.1

Graph 1: Annual growth rates of exports, 1999–2013
(In percentage by year)

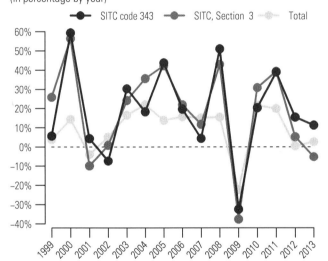

Table 2: Top exporting countries or areas in 2013

Country or area	Value (million US$)	Avg. Growth (%) 09-13	Growth (%) 12-13	World share %	Cum.
World	397 318.1	21.0	11.3	100.0	
Qatar	87 538.4	58.1	5.9	22.0	22.0
Russian Federation	72 743.3	15.9	8.7	18.3	40.3
Norway	42 352.5	14.8	-2.4	10.7	51.0
Netherlands	23 271.1	...		5.9	56.9
Algeria	20 621.4	9.2	-7.2	5.2	62.0
Malaysia	18 890.6	20.8	4.0	4.8	66.8
Indonesia	18 118.6	19.9	-11.7	4.6	71.4
Australia	14 187.7	24.1	1.0	3.6	74.9
Germany	14 059.3	42.1	20.7	3.5	78.5
Belgium	10 748.2	16.5	43.0	2.7	81.2
Canada	10 102.3	-7.9	17.1	2.5	83.7
Bolivia	6 113.4	32.8	11.6	1.5	85.3
USA	6 028.2	18.3	24.7	1.5	86.8
Brunei Darussalam	5 930.9	12.0	-4.0	1.5	88.3
Trinidad and Tobago	*4 507.4*	5.0	197.9	1.1	89.4

Graph 2: Trade Balance by MDG regions 2013
(Bln US$)

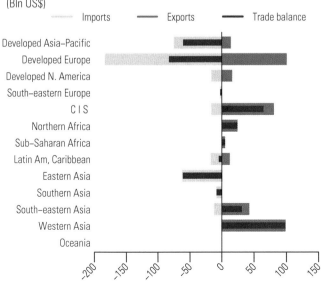

Table 3: Top importing countries or areas in 2013

Country or area	Value (million US$)	Avg. Growth (%) 09-13	Growth (%) 12-13	World share %	Cum.
World	394 485.3	16.3	6.5	100.0	
Japan	72 347.7	24.3	-3.8	18.3	18.3
Germany	50 230.4	10.9	2.7	12.7	31.1
Rep. of Korea	30 645.2	21.9	12.0	7.8	38.8
Italy	27 233.6	2.9	-12.9	6.9	45.7
France	22 244.2	7.7	2.0	5.6	51.4
China	20 566.5	100.2	22.1	5.2	56.6
Belgium	18 333.4	15.3	32.7	4.6	61.2
Spain	13 590.9	7.8	-0.8	3.4	64.7
United Kingdom	12 983.1	14.8	6.0	3.3	68.0
USA	12 171.1	-5.1	32.8	3.1	71.1
Ukraine	11 538.2	9.7	-17.7	2.9	74.0
Netherlands	10 303.0	...		2.6	76.6
Other Asia, nes	9 693.7	24.3	-0.3	2.5	79.1
India	8 311.5	34.7	6.6	2.1	81.2
Brazil	6 712.6	41.3	37.4	1.7	82.9

344 Petroleum gases and other gaseous hydrocarbons, nes

In 2013, the value (in current US$) of exports of "petroleum gases and other gaseous hydrocarbons, nes" (SITC group 344) decreased by 38.4 percent (compared to 16.2 percent average growth rate from 2009-2013) to reach 10.3 bln US$ (see table 2), while imports decreased by 3.0 percent to reach 14.1 bln US$ (see table 3). Exports of this commodity accounted for 0.3 percent of world exports of SITC section 3, and 0.1 percent of total world merchandise exports (see table 1). Iran, Malaysia and USA were the top exporters in 2013 (see table 2). They accounted for 14.6, 12.5 and 9.2 percent of world exports, respectively. Turkey, Germany and Belgium were the top destinations, with respectively 18.7, 8.0 and 7.9 percent of world imports (see table 3).

The top 15 countries/areas accounted for 78.0 and 81.6 percent of total world exports and imports, respectively (see tables 2 and 3). In 2013, Iran was the country/area with the highest value of net exports (+1.5 bln US$), followed by Malaysia (+1.1 bln US$). By MDG regions (see graph 2), the largest surpluses in this product group were recorded by Commonwealth of Independent States (+559.6 mln US$), Sub-Saharan Africa (+456.6 mln US$) and Developed North America (+391.9 mln US$). The largest trade deficits were recorded by Western Asia (-2.5 bln US$), Northern Africa (-1.0 bln US$) and Eastern Asia (-793.9 mln US$).

Table 1: Imports (Imp.) and exports (Exp.), 1999-2013, in current US$

		1999	2000	2001	2002	2003	2004	2005	2006	2007	2008	2009	2010	2011	2012	2013
Values in Bln US$	Imp.	2.8	4.2	3.8	3.7	4.8	5.3	7.4	8.4	9.9	13.3	7.9	11.3	14.1	14.6	14.1
	Exp.	2.6	4.2	4.9	4.8	7.6	11.4	12.4	14.8	16.8	13.9	5.7	10.0	12.0	16.8	10.3
As a percentage of SITC section (%)	Imp.	0.7	0.6	0.6	0.6	0.6	0.5	0.5	0.5	0.5	0.5	0.4	0.5	0.4	0.4	0.4
	Exp.	0.6	0.6	0.8	0.8	1.0	1.1	0.9	0.8	0.9	0.5	0.3	0.4	0.5	0.5	0.3
As a percentage of world trade (%)	Imp.	0.0	0.1	0.1	0.1	0.1	0.1	0.1	0.1	0.1	0.1	0.1	0.1	0.1	0.1	0.1
	Exp.	0.0	0.1	0.1	0.1	0.1	0.1	0.1	0.1	0.1	0.1	0.0	0.1	0.1	0.1	0.1

Graph 1: Annual growth rates of exports, 1999–2013
(In percentage by year)

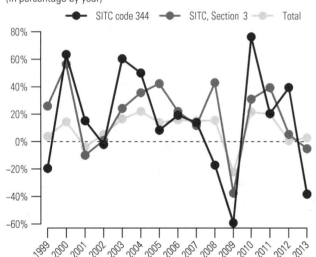

Graph 2: Trade Balance by MDG regions 2013
(Bln US$)

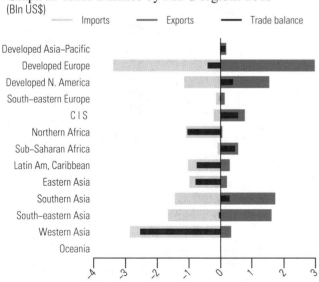

Table 2: Top exporting countries or areas in 2013

Country or area	Value (million US$)	Avg. Growth (%) 09-13	Growth (%) 12-13	World share %	Cum.
World	10 336.2	16.2	-38.4	100.0	
Iran	1 507.5	10.7	-14.1	14.6	14.6
Malaysia	1 294.2	14.4	3.7	12.5	27.1
USA	946.7	32.7	69.7	9.2	36.3
Canada	598.9	10.2	-28.7	5.8	42.1
Netherlands	485.3	5.4	13.0	4.7	46.8
Russian Federation	483.8	27.5	-11.6	4.7	51.4
Belgium	478.8	23.8	-11.0	4.6	56.1
Norway	472.9	19.3	-28.4	4.6	60.6
Equatorial Guinea	448.7	93.6	>	4.3	65.0
Germany	289.1	18.5	31.9	2.8	67.8
Turkey	265.3	27.7	-15.7	2.6	70.3
India	219.0	39.7	26.4	2.1	72.5
France	208.0	68.8	-9.8	2.0	74.5
United Kingdom	194.9	-3.1	-32.6	1.9	76.4
Japan	168.3	18.2	28.3	1.6	78.0

Table 3: Top importing countries or areas in 2013

Country or area	Value (million US$)	Avg. Growth (%) 09-13	Growth (%) 12-13	World share %	Cum.
World	14 132.8	15.8	-3.0	100.0	
Turkey	2 646.1	13.8	-6.9	18.7	18.7
Germany	1 130.6	26.8	9.3	8.0	26.7
Belgium	1 116.2	9.7	-2.3	7.9	34.6
Tunisia	1 029.8	31.5	11.4	7.3	41.9
USA	957.0	10.4	-23.2	6.8	48.7
India	877.1	28.2	-21.0	6.2	54.9
Singapore	664.1	312.6	33858.6	4.7	59.6
Mexico	633.4	3.1	-11.7	4.5	64.1
Rep. of Korea	586.4	27.0	-34.4	4.1	68.2
Philippines	433.3	19.8	-8.1	3.1	71.3
China	376.3	66.4	18.9	2.7	73.9
Viet Nam	328.9	10.0	13.6	2.3	76.3
Netherlands	316.2	22.2	-17.5	2.2	78.5
Nepal	221.8	22.6	-8.4	1.6	80.1
Israel	217.4	19.9	-24.1	1.5	81.6

In 2013, the value (in current US$) of exports of "electric current" (SITC group 351) decreased by 11.1 percent (compared to 3.1 percent average growth rate from 2009-2013) to reach 34.7 bln US$ (see table 2), while imports decreased by 10.9 percent to reach 33.1 bln US$ (see table 3). Exports of this commodity accounted for 1.1 percent of world exports of SITC section 3, and 0.2 percent of total world merchandise exports (see table 1). Germany, France and Switzerland were the top exporters in 2013 (see table 2). They accounted for 14.4, 8.9 and 7.3 percent of world exports, respectively. Italy, Germany and USA were the top destinations, with respectively 9.2, 7.3 and 6.9 percent of world imports (see table 3).

The top 15 countries/areas accounted for 74.3 and 69.0 percent of total world exports and imports, respectively (see tables 2 and 3). In 2013, Germany was the country/area with the highest value of net exports (+2.6 bln US$), followed by France (+2.3 bln US$). By MDG regions (see graph 2), the largest surpluses in this product group were recorded by Latin America and the Caribbean (+2.1 bln US$), Commonwealth of Independent States (+1.1 bln US$) and South-eastern Europe (+631.4 mln US$). The largest trade deficits were recorded by Developed Europe (-1.1 bln US$), Western Asia (-868.1 mln US$) and Northern Africa (-277.7 mln US$).

Table 1: Imports (Imp.) and exports (Exp.), 1999-2013, in current US$

		1999	2000	2001	2002	2003	2004	2005	2006	2007	2008	2009	2010	2011	2012	2013
Values in Bln US$	Imp.	6.9	8.4	12.2	12.2	15.4	17.8	24.4	30.3	25.0	35.2	28.8	31.1	38.2	37.2	33.1
	Exp.	8.3	9.9	11.8	12.2	15.7	18.8	23.7	30.2	27.4	38.7	30.7	33.5	40.6	39.0	34.7
As a percentage of	Imp.	1.7	1.3	1.9	2.0	2.0	1.7	1.7	1.7	1.3	1.2	1.6	1.3	1.2	1.1	1.0
SITC section (%)	Exp.	2.0	1.5	2.0	2.0	2.1	1.9	1.7	1.7	1.4	1.4	1.8	1.5	1.3	1.2	1.1
As a percentage of	Imp.	0.1	0.1	0.2	0.2	0.2	0.2	0.2	0.2	0.2	0.2	0.2	0.2	0.2	0.2	0.2
world trade (%)	Exp.	0.2	0.2	0.2	0.2	0.2	0.2	0.2	0.3	0.2	0.2	0.2	0.2	0.2	0.2	0.2

Graph 1: Annual growth rates of exports, 1999–2013
(In percentage by year)

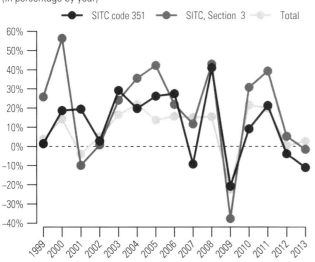

Table 2: Top exporting countries or areas in 2013

Country or area	Value (million US$)	Avg. Growth (%) 09-13	Growth (%) 12-13	World share %	Cum.
World	34 665.1	3.1	-11.1	100.0	
Germany	4 989.0	2.6	5.7	14.4	14.4
France	3 094.9	7.4	-2.3	8.9	23.3
Switzerland	2 528.1	-11.8	-60.7	7.3	30.6
Canada	2 373.0	3.2	23.0	6.8	37.5
Paraguay	2 236.6	...	0.2	6.5	43.9
Czech Rep.	1 801.5	-0.2	-22.5	5.2	49.1
China	1 394.3	6.6	13.1	4.0	53.1
Austria	1 245.4	-4.5	-34.6	3.6	56.7
Sweden	1 192.0	27.5	-5.0	3.4	60.2
Netherlands	1 016.3	6.0	2.0	2.9	63.1
Russian Federation	992.1	10.7	-2.7	2.9	66.0
Norway	749.2	1.6	-14.2	2.2	68.1
Poland	726.1	1.6	-6.8	2.1	70.2
Spain	717.6	5.5	-6.3	2.1	72.3
Hungary	697.9	-2.5	-32.0	2.0	74.3

Graph 2: Trade Balance by MDG regions 2013
(Bln US$)

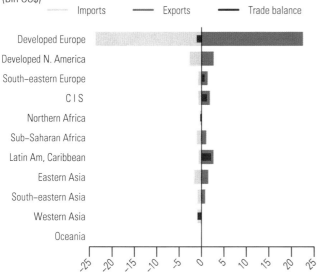

Table 3: Top importing countries or areas in 2013

Country or area	Value (million US$)	Avg. Growth (%) 09-13	Growth (%) 12-13	World share %	Cum.
World	33 096.9	3.5	-10.9	100.0	
Italy	3 034.5	-6.7	-9.8	9.2	9.2
Germany	2 409.0	-6.9	-18.6	7.3	16.4
USA	2 293.2	2.6	19.8	6.9	23.4
Switzerland	2 178.2	-6.1	-61.2	6.6	30.0
Netherlands	1 944.1	...	22.3	5.9	35.8
Belgium	1 751.5	34.8	78.7	5.3	41.1
Hungary	1 476.2	2.7	-4.4	4.5	45.6
United Kingdom	1 465.3	37.8	37.1	4.4	50.0
Austria	1 427.3	-2.0	-6.5	4.3	54.3
Czech Rep.	1 166.5	2.3	-24.8	3.5	57.8
Finland	940.9	8.8	-3.7	2.8	60.7
France	816.3	-12.6	-12.7	2.5	63.2
Sweden	692.7	-1.4	14.6	2.1	65.3
Croatia	624.6	2.3	-2.5	1.9	67.1
China, Hong Kong SAR	617.9	-1.2	-1.2	1.9	69.0

Animal and vegetable oils, fats and waxes

(SITC Section 4)

411 Animal oils and fats

In 2013, the value (in current US$) of exports of "animal oils and fats" (SITC group 411) decreased by 6.0 percent (compared to 10.8 percent average growth rate from 2009-2013) to reach 5.9 bln US$ (see table 2), while imports decreased by 11.5 percent to reach 5.2 bln US$ (see table 3). Exports of this commodity accounted for 0.7 percent of world exports of SITC sections 2+4, and less than 0.1 percent of total world merchandise exports (see table 1). USA, Germany and Netherlands were the top exporters in 2013 (see table 2). They accounted for 13.3, 8.0 and 6.8 percent of world exports, respectively. Mexico, Russian Federation and Norway were the top destinations, with respectively 8.3, 8.1 and 7.1 percent of world imports (see table 3).

The top 15 countries/areas accounted for 78.7 and 70.2 percent of total world exports and imports, respectively (see tables 2 and 3). In 2013, USA was the country/area with the highest value of net exports (+515.1 mln US$), followed by Australia (+335.2 mln US$). By MDG regions (see graph 2), the largest surpluses in this product group were recorded by Developed Europe (+655.8 mln US$), Developed North America (+597.9 mln US$) and Developed Asia-Pacific (+331.5 mln US$). The largest trade deficits were recorded by Commonwealth of Independent States (-513.8 mln US$), Western Asia (-142.6 mln US$) and Eastern Asia (-117.0 mln US$).

Table 1: Imports (Imp.) and exports (Exp.), 1999-2013, in current US$

		1999	2000	2001	2002	2003	2004	2005	2006	2007	2008	2009	2010	2011	2012	2013
Values in Bln US$	Imp.	2.0	1.7	1.6	1.8	2.2	2.7	2.6	2.8	3.6	5.4	4.0	4.5	6.3	5.9	5.2
	Exp.	1.6	1.4	1.4	1.7	2.0	2.7	2.5	2.7	3.6	5.5	3.9	4.6	6.3	6.3	5.9
As a percentage of SITC section (%)	Imp.	0.9	0.7	0.7	0.7	0.8	0.7	0.6	0.6	0.6	0.7	0.7	0.6	0.6	0.6	0.6
	Exp.	0.8	0.7	0.7	0.8	0.8	0.8	0.7	0.6	0.7	0.8	0.8	0.7	0.7	0.7	0.7
As a percentage of world trade (%)	Imp.	0.0	0.0	0.0	0.0	0.0	0.0	0.0	0.0	0.0	0.0	0.0	0.0	0.0	0.0	0.0
	Exp.	0.0	0.0	0.0	0.0	0.0	0.0	0.0	0.0	0.0	0.0	0.0	0.0	0.0	0.0	0.0

Graph 1: Annual growth rates of exports, 1999–2013
(In percentage by year)

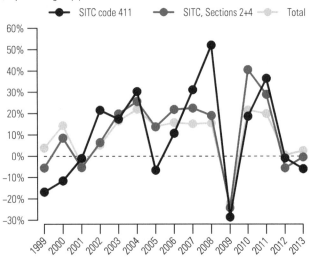

Legend: SITC code 411 — SITC, Sections 2+4 — Total

Graph 2: Trade Balance by MDG regions 2013
(Bln US$)

Legend: Imports — Exports — Trade balance

Developed Asia–Pacific, Developed Europe, Developed N. America, South–eastern Europe, CIS, Northern Africa, Sub–Saharan Africa, Latin Am, Caribbean, Eastern Asia, Southern Asia, South–eastern Asia, Western Asia, Oceania

Table 2: Top exporting countries or areas in 2013

Country or area	Value (million US$)	Avg. Growth (%) 09-13	Growth (%) 12-13	World share %	Cum.
World	5 891.0	10.8	-6.0	100.0	
USA	782.1	1.8	-14.6	13.3	13.3
Germany	472.9	7.7	-12.0	8.0	21.3
Netherlands	400.3	20.7	8.2	6.8	28.1
Australia	390.6	16.3	10.8	6.6	34.7
France	387.5	9.8	-7.3	6.6	41.3
Denmark	366.7	14.8	-0.6	6.2	47.5
Peru	343.0	7.4	-36.7	5.8	53.4
Spain	250.8	9.7	4.6	4.3	57.6
Canada	236.2	5.4	-19.2	4.0	61.6
China	204.9	30.3	14.2	3.5	65.1
Belgium	188.7	6.6	3.3	3.2	68.3
United Kingdom	187.7	14.6	-6.5	3.2	71.5
Norway	146.0	8.1	2.8	2.5	74.0
Italy	139.2	6.3	-7.5	2.4	76.3
Chile	137.6	18.3	5.3	2.3	78.7

Table 3: Top importing countries or areas in 2013

Country or area	Value (million US$)	Avg. Growth (%) 09-13	Growth (%) 12-13	World share %	Cum.
World	5 201.9	7.0	-11.5	100.0	
Mexico	432.9	5.4	63.8	8.3	8.3
Russian Federation	423.8	2.0	-17.4	8.1	16.5
Norway	369.3	9.1	6.8	7.1	23.6
Netherlands	358.9	24.7	-3.5	6.9	30.5
USA	267.0	16.0	7.2	5.1	35.6
China	244.9	-2.5	-19.8	4.7	40.3
Denmark	234.2	9.2	-28.9	4.5	44.8
Belgium	225.2	5.9	-11.2	4.3	49.1
Germany	182.7	7.5	5.7	3.5	52.7
United Kingdom	163.0	1.4	-16.1	3.1	55.8
Japan	160.4	4.6	-30.1	3.1	58.9
Spain	157.9	3.1	-14.0	3.0	61.9
Canada	153.1	14.6	-4.2	2.9	64.8
France	148.3	12.0	5.3	2.9	67.7
Turkey	129.9	5.1	-18.8	2.5	70.2

Fixed vegetable fats and oils, 'soft', crude, refined or fractionated 421

In 2013, the value (in current US$) of exports of "fixed vegetable fats and oils, 'soft', crude, refined or fractionated" (SITC group 421) decreased by 3.2 percent (compared to 11.7 percent average growth rate from 2009-2013) to reach 38.4 bln US$ (see table 2), while imports decreased by 1.6 percent to reach 38.6 bln US$ (see table 3). Exports of this commodity accounted for 4.6 percent of world exports of SITC sections 2+4, and 0.2 percent of total world merchandise exports (see table 1). Argentina, Spain and Ukraine were the top exporters in 2013 (see table 2). They accounted for 12.5, 9.5 and 8.9 percent of world exports, respectively. China, USA and India were the top destinations, with respectively 10.4, 8.0 and 6.6 percent of world imports (see table 3).

The top 15 countries/areas accounted for 78.6 and 60.7 percent of total world exports and imports, respectively (see tables 2 and 3). In 2013, Argentina was the country/area with the highest value of net exports (+4.7 bln US$), followed by Ukraine (+3.4 bln US$). By MDG regions (see graph 2), the largest surpluses in this product group were recorded by Commonwealth of Independent States (+4.9 bln US$), Latin America and the Caribbean (+4.1 bln US$) and Developed Europe (+2.2 bln US$). The largest trade deficits were recorded by Eastern Asia (-4.5 bln US$), Southern Asia (-4.5 bln US$) and Northern Africa (-1.7 bln US$).

Table 1: Imports (Imp.) and exports (Exp.), 1999-2013, in current US$

		1999	2000	2001	2002	2003	2004	2005	2006	2007	2008	2009	2010	2011	2012	2013
Values in Bln US$	Imp.	11.5	8.9	9.0	10.9	13.8	16.3	17.0	20.0	24.8	34.7	25.8	28.0	38.3	39.3	38.6
	Exp.	11.0	8.3	8.6	10.6	13.3	15.6	16.6	19.8	24.7	34.5	24.7	28.5	38.5	39.6	38.4
As a percentage of	Imp.	5.0	3.6	3.8	4.5	4.8	4.3	4.1	4.0	4.0	4.5	4.7	3.7	3.9	4.3	4.2
SITC section (%)	Exp.	5.6	3.9	4.3	5.0	5.2	4.8	4.5	4.4	4.5	5.3	5.0	4.1	4.3	4.7	4.6
As a percentage of	Imp.	0.2	0.1	0.1	0.2	0.2	0.2	0.2	0.2	0.2	0.2	0.2	0.2	0.2	0.2	0.2
world trade (%)	Exp.	0.2	0.1	0.1	0.2	0.2	0.2	0.2	0.2	0.2	0.2	0.2	0.2	0.2	0.2	0.2

Graph 1: Annual growth rates of exports, 1999–2013
(In percentage by year)

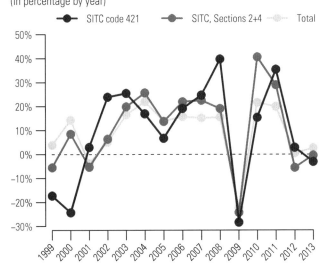

Graph 2: Trade Balance by MDG regions 2013
(Bln US$)

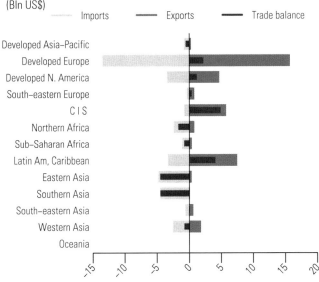

Table 2: Top exporting countries or areas in 2013

Country or area	Value (million US$)	Avg. Growth (%) 09-13	Growth (%) 12-13	World share %	Cum.
World	38 361.7	11.7	-3.2	100.0	
Argentina	4 798.6	3.4	-12.2	12.5	12.5
Spain	3 635.3	9.2	1.6	9.5	22.0
Ukraine	3 405.8	19.8	-15.1	8.9	30.9
Canada	2 905.4	19.8	-17.1	7.6	38.4
Italy	2 023.8	7.5	12.4	5.3	43.7
Netherlands	1 989.5	4.4	19.7	5.2	48.9
Russian Federation	1 976.2	26.4	-4.0	5.2	54.1
Germany	1 942.9	22.8	8.7	5.1	59.1
USA	1 750.3	-0.6	-26.4	4.6	63.7
Brazil	1 494.3	3.4	-32.2	3.9	67.6
France	1 006.7	3.0	-17.5	2.6	70.2
Belgium	906.4	7.0	13.5	2.4	72.6
Turkey	864.5	38.4	57.2	2.3	74.8
Hungary	741.0	34.0	49.5	1.9	76.7
Greece	722.8	14.7	56.2	1.9	78.6

Table 3: Top importing countries or areas in 2013

Country or area	Value (million US$)	Avg. Growth (%) 09-13	Growth (%) 12-13	World share %	Cum.
World	38 634.1	10.6	-1.6	100.0	
China	4 012.0	13.3	-5.6	10.4	10.4
USA	3 086.8	10.5	-4.1	8.0	18.4
India	2 533.5	19.8	-11.4	6.6	24.9
Italy	2 200.6	0.9	3.5	5.7	30.6
Netherlands	1 962.7	28.0	19.8	5.1	35.7
Belgium	1 244.3	7.8	6.0	3.2	38.9
France	1 191.4	-5.3	-9.1	3.1	42.0
Germany	1 085.7	2.4	6.0	2.8	44.8
Turkey	974.0	15.1	-5.7	2.5	47.3
United Kingdom	972.9	4.9	0.9	2.5	49.9
Spain	953.7	13.6	31.6	2.5	52.3
Bangladesh	*905.9*	14.0	-1.6	2.3	54.7
Egypt	903.6	25.3	-17.8	2.3	57.0
Algeria	731.5	13.3	-8.4	1.9	58.9
Iran	*692.0*	8.9	-13.3	1.8	60.7

422 Fixed vegetable fats and oils, crude, refined or fractionated, not 'soft'

In 2013, the value (in current US$) of exports of "fixed vegetable fats and oils, crude, refined or fractionated, not 'soft'" (SITC group 422) decreased by 11.3 percent (compared to 9.9 percent average growth rate from 2009-2013) to reach 41.1 bln US$ (see table 2), while imports decreased by 10.0 percent to reach 45.4 bln US$ (see table 3). Exports of this commodity accounted for 4.9 percent of world exports of SITC sections 2+4, and 0.2 percent of total world merchandise exports (see table 1). Indonesia, Malaysia and Netherlands were the top exporters in 2013 (see table 2). They accounted for 43.0, 32.0 and 5.0 percent of world exports, respectively. India, China and Netherlands were the top destinations, with respectively 16.0, 13.0 and 7.5 percent of world imports (see table 3).

The top 15 countries/areas accounted for 93.7 and 70.9 percent of total world exports and imports, respectively (see tables 2 and 3). In 2013, Indonesia was the country/area with the highest value of net exports (+17.6 bln US$), followed by Malaysia (+12.2 bln US$). By MDG regions (see graph 2), the largest surpluses in this product group were recorded by South-eastern Asia (+30.4 bln US$) and Oceania (+797.9 mln US$). The largest trade deficits were recorded by Southern Asia (-11.0 bln US$), Developed Europe (-8.0 bln US$) and Eastern Asia (-6.5 bln US$).

Table 1: Imports (Imp.) and exports (Exp.), 1999-2013, in current US$

		1999	2000	2001	2002	2003	2004	2005	2006	2007	2008	2009	2010	2011	2012	2013
Values in Bln US$	Imp.	8.4	7.0	6.5	8.8	11.9	14.8	15.0	16.9	23.4	36.8	29.9	37.8	53.2	50.5	45.4
	Exp.	7.8	6.4	5.8	8.3	10.7	13.0	13.3	15.4	24.2	37.1	28.2	37.1	50.3	46.3	41.1
As a percentage of SITC section (%)	Imp.	3.7	2.8	2.8	3.7	4.1	4.0	3.6	3.4	3.8	4.8	5.5	5.0	5.4	5.5	5.0
	Exp.	4.0	3.0	2.9	3.9	4.2	4.0	3.6	3.4	4.4	5.7	5.7	5.4	5.6	5.5	4.9
As a percentage of world trade (%)	Imp.	0.1	0.1	0.1	0.1	0.2	0.2	0.1	0.1	0.2	0.2	0.2	0.2	0.3	0.3	0.2
	Exp.	0.1	0.1	0.1	0.1	0.1	0.1	0.1	0.1	0.2	0.2	0.2	0.2	0.3	0.3	0.2

Graph 1: Annual growth rates of exports, 1999–2013
(In percentage by year)

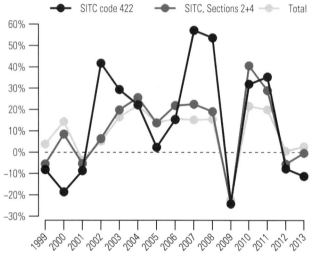

Graph 2: Trade Balance by MDG regions 2013
(Bln US$)

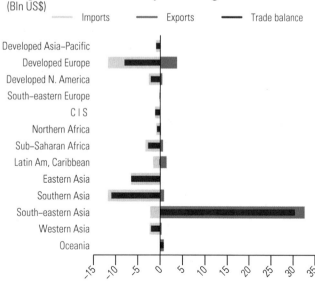

Table 2: Top exporting countries or areas in 2013

Country or area	Value (million US$)	Avg. Growth (%) 09-13	Growth (%) 12-13	World share %	Cum.
World..................................	41110.1	9.9	-11.3	100.0	
Indonesia.............................	17670.6	10.5	-11.9	43.0	43.0
Malaysia...............................	13146.0	7.4	-19.9	32.0	75.0
Netherlands..........................	2053.0	9.2	1.0	5.0	80.0
Philippines...........................	1056.5	15.4	-0.1	2.6	82.5
India....................................	807.0	14.6	5.9	2.0	84.5
Papua New Guinea...............	*774.5*	5.0	31.7	1.9	86.4
Thailand...............................	583.1	39.5	30.2	1.4	87.8
Germany...............................	544.2	18.9	20.5	1.3	89.1
USA.....................................	370.2	4.1	-0.3	0.9	90.0
Guatemala............................	291.3	28.3	2.4	0.7	90.7
Italy.....................................	270.9	11.5	16.3	0.7	91.4
Honduras..............................	267.7	12.2	-15.4	0.7	92.0
Ecuador................................	231.4	11.7	-25.7	0.6	92.6
Belgium................................	226.6	8.9	35.9	0.6	93.1
Colombia..............................	224.9	8.7	-8.3	0.5	93.7

Table 3: Top importing countries or areas in 2013

Country or area	Value (million US$)	Avg. Growth (%) 09-13	Growth (%) 12-13	World share %	Cum.
World..................................	45411.7	11.0	-10.0	100.0	
India....................................	7246.4	18.3	-10.6	16.0	16.0
China...................................	5911.6	5.2	-23.6	13.0	29.0
Netherlands..........................	3397.9	17.6	-5.1	7.5	36.5
USA.....................................	2364.4	12.1	-1.2	5.2	41.7
Germany...............................	2205.3	8.2	-1.1	4.9	46.5
Bangladesh...........................	*1977.2*	11.1	-1.6	4.4	50.9
Pakistan...............................	1858.8	10.2	-13.7	4.1	55.0
Italy.....................................	1519.4	13.2	17.4	3.3	58.3
Malaysia...............................	916.4	-5.1	-63.0	2.0	60.3
Spain...................................	912.1	12.5	27.3	2.0	62.3
France..................................	867.4	13.3	5.7	1.9	64.2
Russian Federation...............	814.9	6.4	-8.2	1.8	66.0
Belgium................................	776.4	11.0	32.1	1.7	67.8
Japan...................................	766.1	5.4	-18.0	1.7	69.4
Egypt...................................	657.7	7.9	39.6	1.4	70.9

Source: UN Comtrade and UN Service Trade

In 2013, the value (in current US$) of exports of "animal or vegetable fats and oils, processed; waxes of; inedible" (SITC group 431) decreased by 5.4 percent (compared to 14.6 percent average growth rate from 2009-2013) to reach 13.4 bln US$ (see table 2), while imports decreased by 4.8 percent to reach 11.9 bln US$ (see table 3). Exports of this commodity accounted for 1.6 percent of world exports of SITC sections 2+4, and 0.1 percent of total world merchandise exports (see table 1). Malaysia, Indonesia and Netherlands were the top exporters in 2013 (see table 2). They accounted for 25.0, 16.8 and 13.1 percent of world exports, respectively. Germany, Netherlands and China were the top destinations, with respectively 10.3, 10.0 and 7.0 percent of world imports (see table 3).

The top 15 countries/areas accounted for 84.0 and 61.0 percent of total world exports and imports, respectively (see tables 2 and 3). In 2013, Malaysia was the country/area with the highest value of net exports (+3.0 bln US$), followed by Indonesia (+2.2 bln US$). By MDG regions (see graph 2), the largest surpluses in this product group were recorded by South-eastern Asia (+5.1 bln US$), Developed North America (+143.0 mln US$) and Southern Asia (+47.4 mln US$). The largest trade deficits were recorded by Developed Europe (-1.5 bln US$), Eastern Asia (-1.0 bln US$) and Sub-Saharan Africa (-321.1 mln US$).

Table 1: Imports (Imp.) and exports (Exp.), 1999-2013, in current US$

		1999	2000	2001	2002	2003	2004	2005	2006	2007	2008	2009	2010	2011	2012	2013
Values in Bln US$	Imp.	3.3	3.0	2.9	3.3	4.0	4.8	5.0	5.6	7.3	10.2	7.3	8.9	13.2	12.5	11.9
	Exp.	3.5	3.0	2.9	3.8	4.5	5.6	5.6	6.2	8.1	11.3	7.8	9.8	14.3	14.2	13.4
As a percentage of SITC section (%)	Imp.	1.4	1.2	1.2	1.4	1.4	1.3	1.2	1.1	1.2	1.3	1.3	1.2	1.3	1.3	1.3
	Exp.	1.8	1.4	1.4	1.8	1.8	1.7	1.5	1.4	1.5	1.7	1.6	1.4	1.6	1.7	1.6
As a percentage of world trade (%)	Imp.	0.1	0.0	0.0	0.1	0.1	0.1	0.0	0.0	0.1	0.1	0.1	0.1	0.1	0.1	0.1
	Exp.	0.1	0.0	0.0	0.1	0.1	0.1	0.1	0.1	0.1	0.1	0.1	0.1	0.1	0.1	0.1

Graph 1: Annual growth rates of exports, 1999–2013
(In percentage by year)

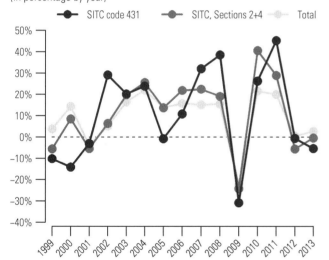

Table 2: Top exporting countries or areas in 2013

Country or area	Value (million US$)	Avg. Growth (%) 09-13	Growth (%) 12-13	World share %	Cum.
World	13 435.4	14.6	-5.4	100.0	
Malaysia	3 365.1	9.5	-10.7	25.0	25.0
Indonesia	2 251.3	47.6	15.3	16.8	41.8
Netherlands	1 759.3	18.5	-10.2	13.1	54.9
Germany	868.7	4.9	-16.9	6.5	61.4
USA	669.6	7.4	-13.9	5.0	66.3
Belgium	446.3	8.5	-13.6	3.3	69.7
Turkey	347.9	17.2	-29.9	2.6	72.3
Philippines	267.4	119.3	178.4	2.0	74.2
India	238.7	23.1	37.4	1.8	76.0
Argentina	193.2	13.9	-19.3	1.4	77.5
Sweden	190.4	6.4	-7.8	1.4	78.9
Brazil	186.9	13.4	-11.7	1.4	80.3
United Kingdom	180.2	10.8	-11.3	1.3	81.6
China	172.6	19.4	9.7	1.3	82.9
Thailand	152.1	7.1	13.3	1.1	84.0

Graph 2: Trade Balance by MDG regions 2013
(Bln US$)

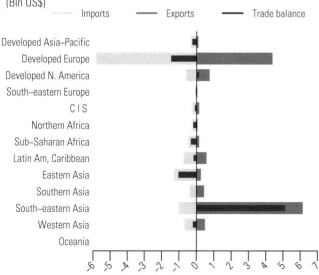

Table 3: Top importing countries or areas in 2013

Country or area	Value (million US$)	Avg. Growth (%) 09-13	Growth (%) 12-13	World share %	Cum.
World	11 854.7	12.9	-4.8	100.0	
Germany	1 217.5	16.6	12.7	10.3	10.3
Netherlands	1 182.4	28.8	-5.7	10.0	20.2
China	828.7	33.4	-12.4	7.0	27.2
United Kingdom	573.5	12.9	9.9	4.8	32.1
USA	427.3	22.0	4.4	3.6	35.7
Belgium	351.1	5.4	-4.1	3.0	38.6
Malaysia	344.1	31.9	-22.5	2.9	41.5
Spain	340.5	7.5	-4.5	2.9	44.4
Rep. of Korea	334.8	18.4	-8.5	2.8	47.2
Finland	325.0	108.7	1404.0	2.7	50.0
Italy	294.1	1.5	-16.5	2.5	52.5
France	289.6	5.7	-3.5	2.4	54.9
Poland	253.7	14.4	7.4	2.1	57.0
Japan	246.6	10.3	-14.1	2.1	59.1
Denmark	222.6	9.4	-4.5	1.9	61.0

Chemicals and related products, n.e.s.

(SITC Section 5)

511 Hydrocarbons, nes, and their derivatives

In 2013, the value (in current US$) of exports of "hydrocarbons, nes, and their derivatives" (SITC group 511) increased by 6.6 percent (compared to 17.5 percent average growth rate from 2009-2013) to reach 99.3 bln US$ (see table 2), while imports increased by 9.9 percent to reach 105.9 bln US$ (see table 3). Exports of this commodity accounted for 5.1 percent of world exports of SITC section 5, and 0.5 percent of total world merchandise exports (see table 1). Rep. of Korea, Japan and USA were the top exporters in 2013 (see table 2). They accounted for 14.4, 13.6 and 10.6 percent of world exports, respectively. China, Belgium and USA were the top destinations, with respectively 29.9, 9.1 and 6.8 percent of world imports (see table 3).

The top 15 countries/areas accounted for 86.3 and 83.7 percent of total world exports and imports, respectively (see tables 2 and 3). In 2013, Japan was the country/area with the highest value of net exports (+12.4 bln US$), followed by Rep. of Korea (+9.1 bln US$). By MDG regions (see graph 2), the largest surpluses in this product group were recorded by Developed Asia-Pacific (+12.3 bln US$), Developed North America (+4.6 bln US$) and Western Asia (+2.9 bln US$). The largest trade deficits were recorded by Eastern Asia (-21.1 bln US$), Latin America and the Caribbean (-4.2 bln US$) and Developed Europe (-4.1 bln US$).

Table 1: Imports (Imp.) and exports (Exp.), 1999-2013, in current US$

		1999	2000	2001	2002	2003	2004	2005	2006	2007	2008	2009	2010	2011	2012	2013
Values in Bln US$	Imp.	18.3	26.4	22.0	23.5	31.5	46.4	53.2	61.2	72.8	77.3	54.4	75.6	97.9	96.3	105.9
	Exp.	16.6	23.2	19.7	21.9	29.4	43.6	48.5	57.2	68.4	70.4	52.1	71.9	93.3	93.2	99.3
As a percentage of SITC section (%)	Imp.	3.2	4.3	3.5	3.3	3.8	4.6	4.6	4.8	4.8	4.5	3.7	4.3	4.8	4.8	5.1
	Exp.	3.2	4.1	3.4	3.3	3.7	4.5	4.5	4.7	4.7	4.3	3.7	4.3	4.8	4.9	5.1
As a percentage of world trade (%)	Imp.	0.3	0.4	0.3	0.4	0.4	0.5	0.5	0.5	0.5	0.5	0.4	0.5	0.5	0.5	0.6
	Exp.	0.3	0.4	0.3	0.3	0.4	0.5	0.5	0.5	0.5	0.4	0.4	0.5	0.5	0.5	0.5

Graph 1: Annual growth rates of exports, 1999–2013
(In percentage by year)

Legend: SITC code 511 — SITC, Section 5 — Total

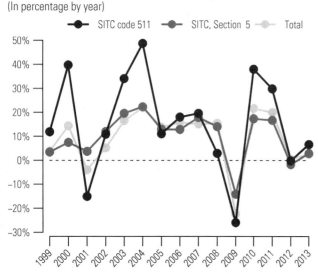

Graph 2: Trade Balance by MDG regions 2013
(Bln US$)

Legend: Imports — Exports — Trade balance

Developed Asia–Pacific
Developed Europe
Developed N. America
South–eastern Europe
CIS
Northern Africa
Sub-Saharan Africa
Latin Am, Caribbean
Eastern Asia
Southern Asia
South–eastern Asia
Western Asia
Oceania

Table 2: Top exporting countries or areas in 2013

Country or area	Value (million US$)	Avg. Growth (%) 09-13	Growth (%) 12-13	World share %	World share % Cum.
World	99 344.4	17.5	6.6	100.0	
Rep. of Korea	14 313.4	25.6	10.0	14.4	14.4
Japan	13 529.1	17.4	31.8	13.6	28.0
USA	10 561.0	14.0	8.4	10.6	38.7
Netherlands	9 378.9	14.1	-10.8	9.4	48.1
Germany	5 481.2	14.5	6.2	5.5	53.6
Other Asia, nes	4 984.9	22.9	49.1	5.0	58.6
Belgium	3 717.1	18.4	10.3	3.7	62.4
Singapore	3 665.0	22.3	13.9	3.7	66.1
United Kingdom	3 500.2	21.1	4.4	3.5	69.6
Saudi Arabia	3 111.2	16.3	-8.1	3.1	72.7
India	3 109.3	21.9	4.0	3.1	75.8
Thailand	3 100.7	31.1	30.5	3.1	79.0
China	2 667.9	9.4	-14.7	2.7	81.7
Canada	2 618.1	13.7	9.2	2.6	84.3
Russian Federation	2 018.6	27.3	0.7	2.0	86.3

Table 3: Top importing countries or areas in 2013

Country or area	Value (million US$)	Avg. Growth (%) 09-13	Growth (%) 12-13	World share %	World share % Cum.
World	105 875.7	18.1	9.9	100.0	
China	31 680.2	27.1	33.8	29.9	29.9
Belgium	9 624.2	17.1	7.1	9.1	39.0
USA	7 203.2	17.3	8.8	6.8	45.8
Other Asia, nes	5 582.4	13.6	-0.8	5.3	51.1
Netherlands	5 462.4	18.4	7.4	5.2	56.2
Rep. of Korea	5 174.2	12.7	1.2	4.9	61.1
Germany	4 951.1	11.8	0.2	4.7	65.8
India	3 702.7	24.4	15.0	3.5	69.3
Mexico	3 519.6	13.3	-8.0	3.3	72.6
France	3 176.1	19.7	6.2	3.0	75.6
Indonesia	3 057.8	14.2	-1.9	2.9	78.5
Malaysia	1 447.0	14.8	5.3	1.4	79.9
Spain	1 363.8	9.2	5.3	1.3	81.2
Canada	1 333.3	9.8	8.2	1.3	82.4
United Kingdom	1 315.8	20.7	11.2	1.2	83.7

In 2013, the value (in current US$) of exports of "alcohols, phenols, phenol-alcohols and their derivatives" (SITC group 512) decreased by 3.0 percent (compared to 14.6 percent average growth rate from 2009-2013) to reach 53.8 bln US$ (see table 2), while imports increased by 2.2 percent to reach 66.7 bln US$ (see table 3). Exports of this commodity accounted for 2.8 percent of world exports of SITC section 5, and 0.3 percent of total world merchandise exports (see table 1). USA, Belgium and Saudi Arabia were the top exporters in 2013 (see table 2). They accounted for 10.2, 6.6 and 6.6 percent of world exports, respectively. China, USA and Germany were the top destinations, with respectively 24.2, 9.3 and 6.3 percent of world imports (see table 3).

The top 15 countries/areas accounted for 71.7 and 77.3 percent of total world exports and imports, respectively (see tables 2 and 3). In 2013, Saudi Arabia was the country/area with the highest value of net exports (+3.2 bln US$), followed by Singapore (+1.7 bln US$). By MDG regions (see graph 2), the largest surpluses in this product group were recorded by Western Asia (+3.6 bln US$), South-eastern Asia (+2.0 bln US$) and Latin America and the Caribbean (+1.6 bln US$). The largest trade deficits were recorded by Eastern Asia (-14.4 bln US$), Developed Europe (-5.3 bln US$) and Southern Asia (-680.7 mln US$).

Table 1: Imports (Imp.) and exports (Exp.), 1999-2013, in current US$

		1999	2000	2001	2002	2003	2004	2005	2006	2007	2008	2009	2010	2011	2012	2013
Values in Bln US$	Imp.	13.7	16.5	16.9	16.8	22.0	28.4	33.6	38.1	46.1	52.7	35.7	51.2	68.3	65.3	66.7
	Exp.	11.7	14.2	14.5	15.0	18.8	25.0	29.3	32.7	39.3	44.9	31.1	44.0	59.3	55.4	53.8
As a percentage of SITC section (%)	Imp.	2.4	2.7	2.7	2.4	2.6	2.8	2.9	3.0	3.1	3.1	2.4	2.9	3.3	3.3	3.2
	Exp.	2.2	2.5	2.5	2.3	2.4	2.6	2.7	2.7	2.7	2.7	2.2	2.7	3.1	2.9	2.8
As a percentage of world trade (%)	Imp.	0.2	0.3	0.3	0.3	0.3	0.3	0.3	0.3	0.3	0.3	0.3	0.3	0.4	0.4	0.4
	Exp.	0.2	0.2	0.2	0.2	0.3	0.3	0.3	0.3	0.3	0.3	0.3	0.3	0.3	0.3	0.3

Graph 1: Annual growth rates of exports, 1999–2013
(In percentage by year)

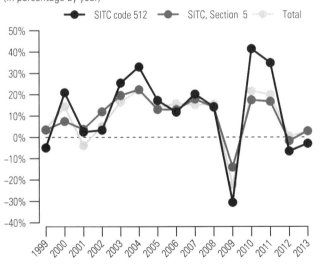

Table 2: Top exporting countries or areas in 2013

Country or area	Value (million US$)	Avg. Growth (%) 09-13	Growth (%) 12-13	World share %	Cum.
World..................	53774.8	14.6	-3.0	100.0	
USA.....................	5499.2	17.7	-9.0	10.2	10.2
Belgium...............	3573.5	20.1	11.9	6.6	16.9
Saudi Arabia........	3530.4	8.8	-32.4	6.6	23.4
Netherlands.........	3498.4	8.7	-6.8	6.5	29.9
Germany..............	3382.3	8.1	-2.3	6.3	36.2
Singapore............	2843.3	30.4	11.6	5.3	41.5
Other Asia, nes....	2736.7	13.0	0.4	5.1	46.6
Brazil..................	2100.5	8.7	-13.6	3.9	50.5
Japan..................	1941.4	6.9	2.3	3.6	54.1
China..................	1810.3	18.8	19.2	3.4	57.5
Malaysia..............	1735.1	21.3	-14.7	3.2	60.7
Rep. of Korea.......	1700.1	14.8	17.4	3.2	63.9
Canada................	1692.8	18.8	12.4	3.1	67.0
India...................	1275.7	31.7	-13.5	2.4	69.4
France.................	1258.7	4.4	-8.1	2.3	71.7

Graph 2: Trade Balance by MDG regions 2013
(Bln US$)

Table 3: Top importing countries or areas in 2013

Country or area	Value (million US$)	Avg. Growth (%) 09-13	Growth (%) 12-13	World share %	Cum.
World..................	66698.4	16.9	2.2	100.0	
China..................	16123.9	17.9	0.8	24.2	24.2
USA.....................	6218.5	20.6	-2.5	9.3	33.5
Germany..............	4198.6	14.9	1.3	6.3	39.8
Netherlands.........	3734.1	10.6	-2.1	5.6	45.4
Rep. of Korea.......	2801.4	18.5	5.8	4.2	49.6
India...................	2786.3	18.4	12.9	4.2	53.8
Belgium...............	2780.8	17.6	17.9	4.2	57.9
Japan..................	2116.3	10.8	-10.1	3.2	61.1
United Kingdom....	1936.5	24.4	23.8	2.9	64.0
Italy....................	1868.9	14.9	2.6	2.8	66.8
Other Asia, nes....	1691.4	19.8	8.7	2.5	69.4
France.................	1386.6	8.1	1.7	2.1	71.4
Thailand..............	1383.8	17.6	-2.5	2.1	73.5
Canada................	1356.8	24.1	7.7	2.0	75.5
Singapore............	1177.2	15.7	-5.0	1.8	77.3

513 Carboxylic acids, and their derivatives

In 2013, the value (in current US$) of exports of "carboxylic acids, and their derivatives" (SITC group 513) decreased by 2.9 percent (compared to 9.1 percent average growth rate from 2009-2013) to reach 46.6 bln US$ (see table 2), while imports decreased by 1.2 percent to reach 52.0 bln US$ (see table 3). Exports of this commodity accounted for 2.4 percent of world exports of SITC section 5, and 0.2 percent of total world merchandise exports (see table 1). China, Rep. of Korea and USA were the top exporters in 2013 (see table 2). They accounted for 13.5, 11.7 and 10.8 percent of world exports, respectively. China, USA and Germany were the top destinations, with respectively 11.0, 7.6 and 7.2 percent of world imports (see table 3).

The top 15 countries/areas accounted for 86.6 and 69.2 percent of total world exports and imports, respectively (see tables 2 and 3). In 2013, Rep. of Korea was the country/area with the highest value of net exports (+4.2 bln US$), followed by Belgium (+1.6 bln US$). By MDG regions (see graph 2), the largest surpluses in this product group were recorded by Eastern Asia (+6.0 bln US$), South-eastern Asia (+880.9 mln US$) and Developed North America (+348.5 mln US$). The largest trade deficits were recorded by Developed Europe (-3.5 bln US$), Western Asia (-2.4 bln US$) and Latin America and the Caribbean (-2.3 bln US$).

Table 1: Imports (Imp.) and exports (Exp.), 1999-2013, in current US$

		1999	2000	2001	2002	2003	2004	2005	2006	2007	2008	2009	2010	2011	2012	2013
Values in Bln US$	Imp.	17.6	20.1	20.5	22.0	25.7	32.3	36.7	40.1	43.7	45.4	36.7	47.4	57.1	52.7	52.0
	Exp.	14.6	16.5	16.4	17.9	22.1	28.4	33.0	37.0	40.1	41.2	32.9	42.3	52.5	48.0	46.6
As a percentage of SITC section (%)	Imp.	3.1	3.3	3.2	3.1	3.1	3.2	3.2	3.1	2.9	2.6	2.5	2.7	2.8	2.6	2.5
	Exp.	2.8	2.9	2.8	2.7	2.8	3.0	3.0	3.0	2.8	2.5	2.3	2.6	2.7	2.5	2.4
As a percentage of world trade (%)	Imp.	0.3	0.3	0.3	0.3	0.3	0.3	0.3	0.3	0.3	0.3	0.3	0.3	0.3	0.3	0.3
	Exp.	0.3	0.3	0.3	0.3	0.3	0.3	0.3	0.3	0.3	0.3	0.3	0.3	0.3	0.3	0.2

Graph 1: Annual growth rates of exports, 1999–2013
(In percentage by year)

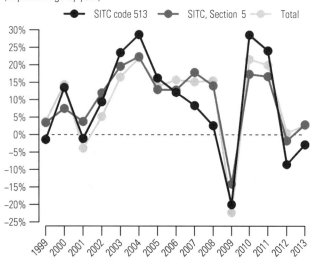

SITC code 513 — SITC, Section 5 — Total

Table 2: Top exporting countries or areas in 2013

Country or area	Value (million US$)	Avg. Growth (%) 09-13	Growth (%) 12-13	World share %	Cum.
World	46 603.7	9.1	-2.9	100.0	
China	6 311.1	19.8	4.6	13.5	13.5
Rep. of Korea	5 436.6	7.3	-4.1	11.7	25.2
USA	5 014.4	7.8	-1.7	10.8	36.0
Belgium	4 881.2	21.7	8.6	10.5	46.4
Germany	3 791.8	11.3	5.7	8.1	54.6
Netherlands	2 585.1	10.2	4.3	5.5	60.1
Other Asia, nes	2 160.3	-6.5	-40.3	4.6	64.8
Thailand	1 602.6	5.4	-18.3	3.4	68.2
Japan	1 581.1	0.0	-7.4	3.4	71.6
Mexico	1 337.2	11.5	4.8	2.9	74.5
Singapore	1 287.7	6.8	-2.3	2.8	77.2
India	1 283.9	30.1	25.8	2.8	80.0
Malaysia	1 271.6	9.9	-8.1	2.7	82.7
Italy	980.8	8.9	4.5	2.1	84.8
United Kingdom	823.7	9.3	-29.2	1.8	86.6

Graph 2: Trade Balance by MDG regions 2013
(Bln US$)

— Imports — Exports — Trade balance

Developed Asia–Pacific
Developed Europe
Developed N. America
South–eastern Europe
CIS
Northern Africa
Sub–Saharan Africa
Latin Am, Caribbean
Eastern Asia
Southern Asia
South–eastern Asia
Western Asia
Oceania

-20 -15 -10 -5 0 5 10 15 20

Table 3: Top importing countries or areas in 2013

Country or area	Value (million US$)	Avg. Growth (%) 09-13	Growth (%) 12-13	World share %	Cum.
World	52 024.9	9.1	-1.2	100.0	
China	5 705.5	-5.9	-32.8	11.0	11.0
USA	3 951.8	13.4	3.6	7.6	18.6
Germany	3 749.9	9.3	7.9	7.2	25.8
Belgium	3 306.7	12.3	15.8	6.4	32.1
India	3 185.3	21.8	18.6	6.1	38.2
Italy	2 351.7	10.3	2.0	4.5	42.8
Netherlands	1 994.9	14.3	10.3	3.8	46.6
Japan	1 863.3	17.1	4.7	3.6	50.2
France	1 666.1	8.3	-1.5	3.2	53.4
Brazil	1 551.1	10.3	-5.9	3.0	56.4
Spain	1 538.1	17.2	38.5	3.0	59.3
United Kingdom	1 390.7	8.0	-2.7	2.7	62.0
Turkey	1 363.2	17.1	9.4	2.6	64.6
Rep. of Korea	1 254.9	12.3	-0.7	2.4	67.0
Mexico	1 112.1	5.3	-0.7	2.1	69.2

In 2013, the value (in current US$) of exports of "nitrogen-function compounds" (SITC group 514) decreased by 0.5 percent (compared to 8.4 percent average growth rate from 2009-2013) to reach 52.4 bln US$ (see table 2), while imports decreased by 4.0 percent to reach 54.2 bln US$ (see table 3). Exports of this commodity accounted for 2.7 percent of world exports of SITC section 5, and 0.3 percent of total world merchandise exports (see table 1). China, Belgium and USA were the top exporters in 2013 (see table 2). They accounted for 15.3, 13.2 and 10.7 percent of world exports, respectively. Germany, USA and Belgium were the top destinations, with respectively 13.3, 9.8 and 8.4 percent of world imports (see table 3).

The top 15 countries/areas accounted for 87.0 and 73.8 percent of total world exports and imports, respectively (see tables 2 and 3). In 2013, China was the country/area with the highest value of net exports (+4.3 bln US$), followed by Singapore (+2.8 bln US$). By MDG regions (see graph 2), the largest surpluses in this product group were recorded by Eastern Asia (+4.1 bln US$), South-eastern Asia (+1.7 bln US$) and Developed Europe (+263.0 mln US$). The largest trade deficits were recorded by Latin America and the Caribbean (-3.0 bln US$), Southern Asia (-1.2 bln US$) and Western Asia (-984.6 mln US$).

Table 1: Imports (Imp.) and exports (Exp.), 1999-2013, in current US$

		1999	2000	2001	2002	2003	2004	2005	2006	2007	2008	2009	2010	2011	2012	2013
Values in Bln US$	Imp.	21.8	21.5	21.5	22.4	26.7	31.5	35.0	37.1	45.4	48.8	40.8	48.3	56.0	56.4	54.2
	Exp.	19.8	19.8	20.1	21.1	26.1	31.0	33.7	34.7	41.9	44.6	38.0	45.6	52.5	52.7	52.4
As a percentage of	Imp.	3.9	3.5	3.4	3.2	3.2	3.1	3.0	2.9	3.0	2.8	2.8	2.8	2.7	2.8	2.6
SITC section (%)	Exp.	3.8	3.5	3.4	3.2	3.3	3.2	3.1	2.8	2.9	2.7	2.7	2.7	2.7	2.8	2.7
As a percentage of	Imp.	0.4	0.3	0.3	0.3	0.3	0.3	0.3	0.3	0.3	0.3	0.3	0.3	0.3	0.3	0.3
world trade (%)	Exp.	0.4	0.3	0.3	0.3	0.3	0.3	0.3	0.3	0.3	0.3	0.3	0.3	0.3	0.3	0.3

Graph 1: Annual growth rates of exports, 1999–2013
(In percentage by year)

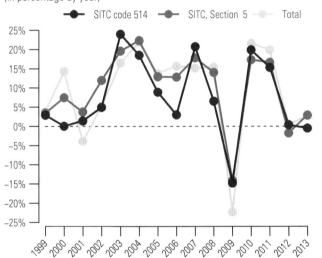

Table 2: Top exporting countries or areas in 2013

Country or area	Value (million US$)	Avg. Growth (%) 09-13	Growth (%) 12-13	World share %	Cum.
World	52441.0	8.4	-0.5	100.0	
China	8040.2	18.2	8.7	15.3	15.3
Belgium	6932.8	16.5	29.2	13.2	28.6
USA	5602.5	6.7	-13.6	10.7	39.2
Switzerland	3984.2	1.4	-6.9	7.6	46.8
Germany	3878.9	4.9	3.6	7.4	54.2
Singapore	3325.1	4.7	-37.8	6.3	60.6
Japan	2312.4	2.0	-2.2	4.4	65.0
Netherlands	2035.0	8.3	20.2	3.9	68.9
United Kingdom	1917.0	2.2	-14.8	3.7	72.5
Rep. of Korea	1862.4	8.4	5.8	3.6	76.1
Ireland	1642.8	6.4	7.6	3.1	79.2
India	1444.7	23.6	34.0	2.8	82.0
Italy	1042.2	0.4	1.4	2.0	83.9
France	841.5	5.3	7.1	1.6	85.5
Norway	785.9	11.4	21.7	1.5	87.0

Graph 2: Trade Balance by MDG regions 2013
(Bln US$)

Imports — Exports — Trade balance

Developed Asia–Pacific
Developed Europe
Developed N. America
South–eastern Europe
CIS
Northern Africa
Sub–Saharan Africa
Latin Am, Caribbean
Eastern Asia
Southern Asia
South–eastern Asia
Western Asia
Oceania

Table 3: Top importing countries or areas in 2013

Country or area	Value (million US$)	Avg. Growth (%) 09-13	Growth (%) 12-13	World share %	Cum.
World	54190.8	7.4	-4.0	100.0	
Germany	7230.8	7.9	-7.1	13.3	13.3
USA	5333.4	5.0	-5.7	9.8	23.2
Belgium	4574.7	13.4	3.9	8.4	31.6
China	3718.3	9.1	2.1	6.9	38.5
Japan	2320.9	3.9	-7.1	4.3	42.8
India	2090.9	15.2	8.2	3.9	46.6
Netherlands	1950.0	8.9	-2.6	3.6	50.2
Italy	1823.5	2.9	-9.6	3.4	53.6
France	1804.6	-4.3	-27.6	3.3	56.9
United Kingdom	1798.0	-0.1	-33.4	3.3	60.2
Brazil	1690.8	16.2	7.9	3.1	63.4
Switzerland	1602.0	7.6	13.0	3.0	66.3
Rep. of Korea	1598.9	11.5	1.2	3.0	69.3
Spain	1524.3	14.6	11.9	2.8	72.1
Other Asia, nes	919.6	12.3	1.0	1.7	73.8

515 Organo-inorganic and heterocyclic compounds, nucleic acids; salts

In 2013, the value (in current US$) of exports of "organo-inorganic and heterocyclic compounds, nucleic acids; salts" (SITC group 515) increased by 2.3 percent (compared to 5.1 percent average growth rate from 2009-2013) to reach 114.2 bln US$ (see table 2), while imports decreased by 2.1 percent to reach 126.7 bln US$ (see table 3). Exports of this commodity accounted for 5.8 percent of world exports of SITC section 5, and 0.6 percent of total world merchandise exports (see table 1). Ireland, Belgium and China were the top exporters in 2013 (see table 2). They accounted for 19.6, 13.2 and 12.6 percent of world exports, respectively. USA, Belgium and Switzerland were the top destinations, with respectively 21.6, 9.1 and 6.8 percent of world imports (see table 3).

The top 15 countries/areas accounted for 94.4 and 81.8 percent of total world exports and imports, respectively (see tables 2 and 3). In 2013, Ireland was the country/area with the highest value of net exports (+20.1 bln US$), followed by China (+9.7 bln US$). By MDG regions (see graph 2), the largest surpluses in this product group were recorded by Developed Europe (+10.7 bln US$), Eastern Asia (+7.2 bln US$) and South-eastern Asia (+935.9 mln US$). The largest trade deficits were recorded by Developed North America (-17.2 bln US$), Latin America and the Caribbean (-8.7 bln US$) and Developed Asia-Pacific (-2.6 bln US$).

Table 1: Imports (Imp.) and exports (Exp.), 1999-2013, in current US$

		1999	2000	2001	2002	2003	2004	2005	2006	2007	2008	2009	2010	2011	2012	2013
Values in Bln US$	Imp.	51.5	54.1	61.2	61.2	68.3	81.5	88.9	94.8	108.7	113.3	110.7	112.7	129.4	129.3	126.7
	Exp.	41.4	46.6	47.0	54.8	62.7	71.2	79.2	86.0	96.1	100.0	93.6	99.1	110.8	111.6	114.2
As a percentage of SITC section (%)	Imp.	9.1	8.9	9.7	8.7	8.2	8.0	7.7	7.4	7.2	6.6	7.5	6.5	6.3	6.5	6.1
	Exp.	7.9	8.2	8.0	8.3	8.0	7.4	7.3	7.0	6.7	6.1	6.6	6.0	5.7	5.9	5.8
As a percentage of world trade (%)	Imp.	0.9	0.8	1.0	0.9	0.9	0.9	0.8	0.8	0.8	0.7	0.9	0.7	0.7	0.7	0.7
	Exp.	0.7	0.7	0.8	0.9	0.8	0.8	0.8	0.7	0.7	0.6	0.8	0.7	0.6	0.6	0.6

Graph 1: Annual growth rates of exports, 1999–2013
(In percentage by year)

SITC code 515 — SITC, Section 5 — Total

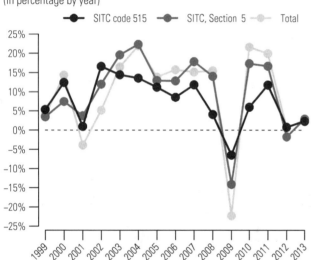

Table 2: Top exporting countries or areas in 2013

Country or area	Value (million US$)	Avg. Growth (%) 09-13	Growth (%) 12-13	World share %	Cum.
World................	114 186.9	5.1	2.3	100.0	
Ireland................	22 351.6	0.6	-7.0	19.6	19.6
Belgium................	15 080.5	4.8	17.7	13.2	32.8
China................	14 352.3	17.7	8.2	12.6	45.4
USA................	11 811.4	12.9	12.1	10.3	55.7
Germany................	8 134.8	3.1	9.8	7.1	62.8
Switzerland................	7 952.5	4.2	-1.6	7.0	69.8
Japan................	5 097.5	2.0	-2.0	4.5	74.2
Singapore................	4 663.9	6.6	-26.5	4.1	78.3
Netherlands................	4 250.7	21.0	45.3	3.7	82.1
United Kingdom................	3 668.8	-18.4	-30.1	3.2	85.3
France................	3 638.5	0.9	1.8	3.2	88.5
India................	2 568.1	35.4	71.8	2.2	90.7
Italy................	2 466.0	7.8	9.1	2.2	92.9
Spain................	1 132.3	6.6	13.2	1.0	93.9
Rep. of Korea................	642.4	12.4	-1.3	0.6	94.4

Graph 2: Trade Balance by MDG regions 2013
(Bln US$)

Imports — Exports — Trade balance

Developed Asia–Pacific
Developed Europe
Developed N. America
South–eastern Europe
CIS
Northern Africa
Sub-Saharan Africa
Latin Am, Caribbean
Eastern Asia
Southern Asia
South–eastern Asia
Western Asia
Oceania

-80 -60 -40 -20 0 20 40 60 80

Table 3: Top importing countries or areas in 2013

Country or area	Value (million US$)	Avg. Growth (%) 09-13	Growth (%) 12-13	World share %	Cum.
World................	126 666.9	3.4	-2.1	100.0	
USA................	27 376.3	0.1	-1.1	21.6	21.6
Belgium................	11 463.5	1.2	-4.0	9.1	30.7
Switzerland................	8 613.1	18.5	5.9	6.8	37.5
Germany................	8 400.7	0.9	3.6	6.6	44.1
Italy................	6 670.3	6.9	24.7	5.3	49.4
Japan................	6 659.6	-2.1	-16.3	5.3	54.6
France................	6 412.0	2.2	-15.2	5.1	59.7
Brazil................	4 696.9	9.8	13.7	3.7	63.4
China................	4 653.9	8.7	-11.9	3.7	67.1
United Kingdom................	4 286.6	-14.3	-38.9	3.4	70.4
Netherlands................	4 014.2	20.8	48.2	3.2	73.6
Spain................	3 879.6	4.1	6.4	3.1	76.7
Mexico................	2 240.3	17.1	31.0	1.8	78.4
Ireland................	2 219.6	13.8	0.8	1.8	80.2
Rep. of Korea................	2 043.2	8.5	-2.1	1.6	81.8

In 2013, the value (in current US$) of exports of "other organic chemicals" (SITC group 516) increased by 0.2 percent (compared to 12.2 percent average growth rate from 2009-2013) to reach 42.6 bln US$ (see table 2), while imports increased by 1.4 percent to reach 39.1 bln US$ (see table 3). Exports of this commodity accounted for 2.2 percent of world exports of SITC section 5, and 0.2 percent of total world merchandise exports (see table 1). USA, Saudi Arabia and Germany were the top exporters in 2013 (see table 2). They accounted for 14.5, 13.6 and 11.0 percent of world exports, respectively. China, USA and Netherlands were the top destinations, with respectively 9.4, 8.1 and 7.4 percent of world imports (see table 3).

The top 15 countries/areas accounted for 88.2 and 73.8 percent of total world exports and imports, respectively (see tables 2 and 3). In 2013, Saudi Arabia was the country/area with the highest value of net exports (+5.6 bln US$), followed by USA (+3.0 bln US$). By MDG regions (see graph 2), the largest surpluses in this product group were recorded by Western Asia (+4.6 bln US$), Developed North America (+2.9 bln US$) and Developed Europe (+461.7 mln US$). The largest trade deficits were recorded by Latin America and the Caribbean (-2.2 bln US$), Eastern Asia (-1.0 bln US$) and South-eastern Asia (-639.5 mln US$).

Table 1: Imports (Imp.) and exports (Exp.), 1999-2013, in current US$

		1999	2000	2001	2002	2003	2004	2005	2006	2007	2008	2009	2010	2011	2012	2013
Values in Bln US$	Imp.	12.8	14.4	14.0	14.3	16.5	20.1	24.6	26.6	29.8	32.7	26.6	33.0	39.5	38.6	39.1
	Exp.	12.2	13.7	13.4	14.3	16.6	19.6	23.6	26.2	29.2	31.7	26.9	33.1	38.7	42.6	42.6
As a percentage of	Imp.	2.3	2.4	2.2	2.0	2.0	2.0	2.1	2.1	2.0	1.9	1.8	1.9	1.9	1.9	1.9
SITC section (%)	Exp.	2.3	2.4	2.3	2.2	2.1	2.0	2.2	2.1	2.0	1.9	1.9	2.0	2.0	2.2	2.2
As a percentage of	Imp.	0.2	0.2	0.2	0.2	0.2	0.2	0.2	0.2	0.2	0.2	0.2	0.2	0.2	0.2	0.2
world trade (%)	Exp.	0.2	0.2	0.2	0.2	0.2	0.2	0.2	0.2	0.2	0.2	0.2	0.2	0.2	0.2	0.2

Graph 1: Annual growth rates of exports, 1999–2013
(In percentage by year)

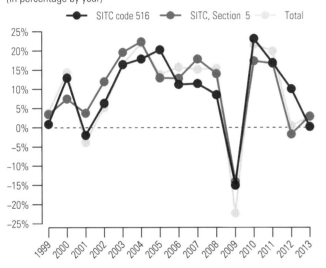

● SITC code 516 ● SITC, Section 5 ● Total

Table 2: Top exporting countries or areas in 2013

Country or area	Value (million US$)	Avg. Growth (%) 09-13	Growth (%) 12-13	World share %	Cum.
World	42 642.0	12.2	0.2	100.0	
USA	6 198.0	14.6	-0.5	14.5	14.5
Saudi Arabia	5 799.4	73.0	57.5	13.6	28.1
Germany	4 698.5	9.4	4.2	11.0	39.2
Netherlands	3 508.5	2.9	-13.0	8.2	47.4
China	3 237.4	15.0	-3.7	7.6	55.0
Belgium	2 517.3	11.0	11.8	5.9	60.9
India	2 488.9	0.0	-29.0	5.8	66.7
France	1 807.0	8.3	-1.7	4.2	71.0
Japan	1 657.7	4.0	3.0	3.9	74.8
Singapore	1 325.5	13.4	12.1	3.1	77.9
Denmark	1 214.1	5.3	9.0	2.8	80.8
Other Asia, nes	1 095.0	9.2	-10.9	2.6	83.4
Thailand	912.8	48.8	2.1	2.1	85.5
Rep. of Korea	588.3	23.3	35.9	1.4	86.9
Brazil	558.0	8.1	-2.7	1.3	88.2

Graph 2: Trade Balance by MDG regions 2013
(Bln US$)

Imports Exports Trade balance

Developed Asia–Pacific
Developed Europe
Developed N. America
South–eastern Europe
CIS
Northern Africa
Sub–Saharan Africa
Latin Am, Caribbean
Eastern Asia
Southern Asia
South–eastern Asia
Western Asia
Oceania

-20 -15 -10 -5 0 5 10 15 20

Table 3: Top importing countries or areas in 2013

Country or area	Value (million US$)	Avg. Growth (%) 09-13	Growth (%) 12-13	World share %	Cum.
World	39 146.4	10.1	1.4	100.0	
China	3 662.5	14.0	1.6	9.4	9.4
USA	3 178.0	11.5	3.1	8.1	17.5
Netherlands	2 891.7	12.7	14.6	7.4	24.9
Germany	2 869.8	10.5	7.5	7.3	32.2
India	2 186.5	14.4	2.1	5.6	37.8
Belgium	2 107.8	10.7	12.2	5.4	43.2
Singapore	1 792.0	21.4	5.7	4.6	47.7
Japan	1 738.7	19.8	-4.6	4.4	52.2
Rep. of Korea	1 404.7	13.1	-9.1	3.6	55.8
Italy	1 376.5	2.7	-14.5	3.5	59.3
France	1 341.7	-0.9	-4.1	3.4	62.7
Mexico	1 219.3	10.9	7.7	3.1	65.8
United Kingdom	1 152.1	12.2	11.0	2.9	68.8
Spain	1 086.5	8.9	-14.5	2.8	71.5
Other Asia, nes	890.3	13.7	-14.6	2.3	73.8

522 Inorganic chemical elements, oxides and halogen salts

In 2013, the value (in current US$) of exports of "inorganic chemical elements, oxides and halogen salts" (SITC group 522) decreased by 4.4 percent (compared to 11.4 percent average growth rate from 2009-2013) to reach 54.0 bln US$ (see table 2), while imports decreased by 7.0 percent to reach 60.2 bln US$ (see table 3). Exports of this commodity accounted for 2.8 percent of world exports of SITC section 5, and 0.3 percent of total world merchandise exports (see table 1). China, USA and Germany were the top exporters in 2013 (see table 2). They accounted for 13.3, 10.6 and 8.3 percent of world exports, respectively. USA, Japan and China were the top destinations, with respectively 13.2, 6.1 and 6.0 percent of world imports (see table 3).

The top 15 countries/areas accounted for 70.4 and 66.2 percent of total world exports and imports, respectively (see tables 2 and 3). In 2013, China was the country/area with the highest value of net exports (+3.6 bln US$), followed by Russian Federation (+2.3 bln US$). By MDG regions (see graph 2), the largest surpluses in this product group were recorded by Commonwealth of Independent States (+3.0 bln US$), Northern Africa (+1.7 bln US$) and Eastern Asia (+1.3 bln US$). The largest trade deficits were recorded by Developed Europe (-4.6 bln US$), Southern Asia (-3.1 bln US$) and South-eastern Asia (-2.2 bln US$).

Table 1: Imports (Imp.) and exports (Exp.), 1999-2013, in current US$

		1999	2000	2001	2002	2003	2004	2005	2006	2007	2008	2009	2010	2011	2012	2013
Values in Bln US$	Imp.	17.5	18.7	19.2	18.6	21.9	27.0	32.7	37.2	44.4	66.1	41.4	53.3	70.0	64.8	60.2
	Exp.	15.2	16.3	16.7	16.2	18.8	24.0	28.5	32.3	39.0	58.1	35.1	47.5	61.6	56.5	54.0
As a percentage of SITC section (%)	Imp.	3.1	3.1	3.0	2.6	2.6	2.7	2.8	2.9	2.9	3.8	2.8	3.1	3.4	3.2	2.9
	Exp.	2.9	2.9	2.8	2.5	2.4	2.5	2.6	2.6	2.7	3.5	2.5	2.9	3.2	3.0	2.8
As a percentage of world trade (%)	Imp.	0.3	0.3	0.3	0.3	0.3	0.3	0.3	0.3	0.3	0.4	0.3	0.3	0.4	0.4	0.3
	Exp.	0.3	0.3	0.3	0.3	0.3	0.3	0.3	0.3	0.3	0.4	0.3	0.3	0.3	0.3	0.3

Graph 1: Annual growth rates of exports, 1999–2013
(In percentage by year)

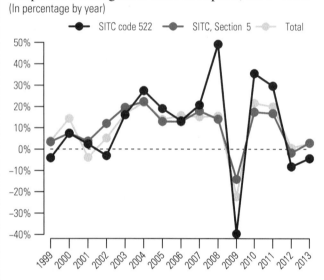

Legend: SITC code 522 — SITC, Section 5 — Total

Table 2: Top exporting countries or areas in 2013

Country or area	Value (million US$)	Avg. Growth (%) 09-13	Growth (%) 12-13	World share %	Cum.
World	54 035.4	11.4	-4.4	100.0	
China	7 207.9	18.9	-0.8	13.3	13.3
USA	5 754.2	2.6	-11.3	10.6	24.0
Germany	4 489.6	4.7	-5.6	8.3	32.3
Russian Federation	2 775.3	22.2	3.7	5.1	37.4
Japan	2 259.2	0.4	-10.0	4.2	41.6
Canada	2 069.8	14.1	-1.4	3.8	45.4
Rep. of Korea	2 026.3	6.0	-8.8	3.7	49.2
Belgium	1 988.8	10.2	19.2	3.7	52.9
Netherlands	1 843.6	10.8	1.5	3.4	56.3
Saudi Arabia	1 660.5	51.9	59.3	3.1	59.4
Trinidad and Tobago	*1 508.2*	45.3	-13.8	2.8	62.2
Morocco	1 446.7	9.1	-13.5	2.7	64.8
Other Asia, nes	1 192.6	12.6	3.6	2.2	67.0
Chile	1 022.9	18.8	-8.6	1.9	68.9
France	811.0	4.4	10.4	1.5	70.4

Graph 2: Trade Balance by MDG regions 2013
(Bln US$)

Legend: Imports — Exports — Trade balance

Developed Asia–Pacific
Developed Europe
Developed N. America
South–eastern Europe
CIS
Northern Africa
Sub–Saharan Africa
Latin Am, Caribbean
Eastern Asia
Southern Asia
South–eastern Asia
Western Asia
Oceania

Table 3: Top importing countries or areas in 2013

Country or area	Value (million US$)	Avg. Growth (%) 09-13	Growth (%) 12-13	World share %	Cum.
World	60 248.4	9.8	-7.0	100.0	
USA	7 924.4	14.0	-5.6	13.2	13.2
Japan	3 648.2	4.3	-16.3	6.1	19.2
China	3 634.3	2.8	-16.9	6.0	25.2
India	3 536.5	9.0	-15.7	5.9	31.1
Germany	3 338.0	5.7	-4.0	5.5	36.7
Rep. of Korea	3 177.4	13.5	-6.7	5.3	41.9
Belgium	2 360.5	11.8	6.7	3.9	45.8
Other Asia, nes	2 298.2	11.0	3.0	3.8	49.7
France	2 222.2	8.6	-2.3	3.7	53.3
Netherlands	1 518.1	9.6	2.9	2.5	55.9
Spain	1 343.5	14.1	-5.6	2.2	58.1
Brazil	1 318.1	11.7	-8.7	2.2	60.3
United Kingdom	1 317.0	5.5	-3.3	2.2	62.5
Turkey	1 129.7	12.2	-1.9	1.9	64.3
Italy	1 120.9	6.6	2.0	1.9	66.2

In 2013, the value (in current US$) of exports of "metal salts and peroxysalts, of inorganic acids" (SITC group 523) increased by 1.6 percent (compared to 9.2 percent average growth rate from 2009-2013) to reach 21.7 bln US$ (see table 2), while imports decreased by 0.5 percent to reach 25.8 bln US$ (see table 3). Exports of this commodity accounted for 1.1 percent of world exports of SITC section 5, and 0.1 percent of total world merchandise exports (see table 1). China, USA and Germany were the top exporters in 2013 (see table 2). They accounted for 20.2, 15.5 and 8.0 percent of world exports, respectively. USA, Germany and Rep. of Korea were the top destinations, with respectively 7.9, 4.4 and 3.6 percent of world imports (see table 3).

The top 15 countries/areas accounted for 74.8 and 51.4 percent of total world exports and imports, respectively (see tables 2 and 3). In 2013, China was the country/area with the highest value of net exports (+3.4 bln US$), followed by USA (+1.3 bln US$). By MDG regions (see graph 2), the largest surpluses in this product group were recorded by Eastern Asia (+2.9 bln US$), Developed North America (+1.3 bln US$) and South-eastern Europe (+255.8 mln US$). The largest trade deficits were recorded by Latin America and the Caribbean (-2.0 bln US$), South-eastern Asia (-1.6 bln US$) and Developed Europe (-1.3 bln US$).

Table 1: Imports (Imp.) and exports (Exp.), 1999-2013, in current US$

		1999	2000	2001	2002	2003	2004	2005	2006	2007	2008	2009	2010	2011	2012	2013
Values in Bln US$	Imp.	9.4	9.5	9.6	10.0	10.7	12.4	14.1	15.7	18.6	24.3	19.3	21.9	25.7	25.9	25.8
	Exp.	7.5	7.5	8.1	8.2	9.0	10.5	12.1	13.9	16.3	20.9	15.3	18.1	21.4	21.4	21.7
As a percentage of SITC section (%)	Imp.	1.7	1.6	1.5	1.4	1.3	1.2	1.2	1.2	1.2	1.4	1.3	1.3	1.3	1.3	1.3
	Exp.	1.4	1.3	1.4	1.2	1.1	1.1	1.1	1.1	1.1	1.3	1.1	1.1	1.1	1.1	1.1
As a percentage of world trade (%)	Imp.	0.2	0.1	0.2	0.2	0.1	0.1	0.1	0.1	0.1	0.1	0.2	0.1	0.1	0.1	0.1
	Exp.	0.1	0.1	0.1	0.1	0.1	0.1	0.1	0.1	0.1	0.1	0.1	0.1	0.1	0.1	0.1

Graph 1: Annual growth rates of exports, 1999–2013
(In percentage by year)

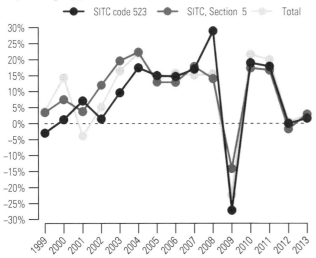

SITC code 523 — SITC, Section 5 — Total

Table 2: Top exporting countries or areas in 2013

Country or area	Value (million US$)	Avg. Growth (%) 09-13	Growth (%) 12-13	World share %	Cum.
World	21 714.5	9.2	1.6	100.0	
China	4 375.8	8.4	-2.0	20.2	20.2
USA	3 359.0	10.9	1.8	15.5	35.6
Germany	1 732.2	5.4	2.4	8.0	43.6
Belgium	1 077.5	12.2	15.8	5.0	48.6
Canada	634.6	2.8	-3.3	2.9	51.5
Netherlands	625.0	12.6	49.0	2.9	54.4
Chile	616.3	16.2	-12.5	2.8	57.2
Spain	610.1	10.4	43.5	2.8	60.0
Russian Federation	598.7	17.5	2.7	2.8	62.8
Rep. of Korea	519.9	13.7	5.6	2.4	65.2
Japan	510.6	3.9	-12.0	2.4	67.5
India	446.7	14.3	8.1	2.1	69.6
France	437.5	5.4	2.7	2.0	71.6
Mexico	373.4	9.3	-2.7	1.7	73.3
Finland	328.9	51.1	-11.7	1.5	74.8

Graph 2: Trade Balance by MDG regions 2013
(Bln US$)

Imports — Exports — Trade balance

Developed Asia–Pacific
Developed Europe
Developed N. America
South–eastern Europe
C I S
Northern Africa
Sub–Saharan Africa
Latin Am, Caribbean
Eastern Asia
Southern Asia
South–eastern Asia
Western Asia
Oceania

-8 -6 -4 -2 0 2 4 6 8

Table 3: Top importing countries or areas in 2013

Country or area	Value (million US$)	Avg. Growth (%) 09-13	Growth (%) 12-13	World share %	Cum.
World	25 781.5	7.5	-0.5	100.0	
USA	2 034.7	7.1	-5.9	7.9	7.9
Germany	1 129.9	4.4	1.5	4.4	12.3
Rep. of Korea	935.5	11.0	-3.2	3.6	15.9
China	927.7	13.5	3.4	3.6	19.5
Belgium	859.4	11.5	14.8	3.3	22.8
Japan	842.4	5.7	-15.0	3.3	26.1
Netherlands	839.5	9.8	12.2	3.3	29.4
France	793.1	1.8	-2.6	3.1	32.4
Brazil	791.7	5.2	-4.5	3.1	35.5
Mexico	740.8	9.8	3.6	2.9	38.4
India	703.2	12.9	1.5	2.7	41.1
Russian Federation	691.8	19.8	17.6	2.7	43.8
Indonesia	670.8	10.9	-6.1	2.6	46.4
Spain	660.4	6.9	24.9	2.6	49.0
Canada	638.4	8.0	0.0	2.5	51.4

524 Other inorganic chemicals; organic, inorganic compounds precious metals

In 2013, the value (in current US$) of exports of "other inorganic chemicals; organic, inorganic compounds precious metals" (SITC group 524) increased by 1.0 percent (compared to 13.9 percent average growth rate from 2009-2013) to reach 12.4 bln US$ (see table 2), while imports decreased by 3.3 percent to reach 11.4 bln US$ (see table 3). Exports of this commodity accounted for 0.6 percent of world exports of SITC section 5, and 0.1 percent of total world merchandise exports (see table 1). Germany, Russian Federation and China were the top exporters in 2013 (see table 2). They accounted for 13.6, 11.5 and 10.0 percent of world exports, respectively. Germany, Italy and France were the top destinations, with respectively 15.1, 9.1 and 6.8 percent of world imports (see table 3).

The top 15 countries/areas accounted for 86.7 and 75.3 percent of total world exports and imports, respectively (see tables 2 and 3). In 2013, Russian Federation was the country/area with the highest value of net exports (+1.4 bln US$), followed by China (+672.6 mln US$). By MDG regions (see graph 2), the largest surpluses in this product group were recorded by Commonwealth of Independent States (+1.4 bln US$), Developed North America (+370.5 mln US$) and Western Asia (+236.1 mln US$). The largest trade deficits were recorded by South-eastern Asia (-486.5 mln US$), Latin America and the Caribbean (-283.6 mln US$) and Southern Asia (-279.2 mln US$).

Table 1: Imports (Imp.) and exports (Exp.), 1999-2013, in current US$

		1999	2000	2001	2002	2003	2004	2005	2006	2007	2008	2009	2010	2011	2012	2013
Values in Bln US$	Imp.	3.9	5.0	4.8	3.9	4.1	5.5	6.7	7.9	9.7	10.8	7.0	11.1	13.7	11.8	11.4
	Exp.	3.4	4.6	4.5	3.6	3.9	5.3	6.7	8.1	10.3	12.1	7.4	11.9	14.1	12.3	12.4
As a percentage of SITC section (%)	Imp.	0.7	0.8	0.8	0.6	0.5	0.5	0.6	0.6	0.6	0.6	0.5	0.6	0.7	0.6	0.6
	Exp.	0.6	0.8	0.8	0.6	0.5	0.6	0.6	0.7	0.7	0.7	0.5	0.7	0.7	0.6	0.6
As a percentage of world trade (%)	Imp.	0.1	0.1	0.1	0.1	0.1	0.1	0.1	0.1	0.1	0.1	0.1	0.1	0.1	0.1	0.1
	Exp.	0.1	0.1	0.1	0.1	0.1	0.1	0.1	0.1	0.1	0.1	0.1	0.1	0.1	0.1	0.1

Graph 1: Annual growth rates of exports, 1999–2013
(In percentage by year)

— SITC code 524   — SITC, Section 5   — Total

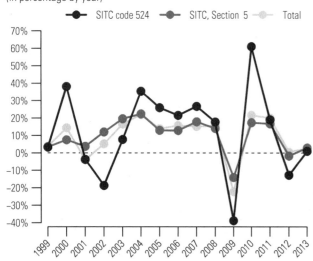

Graph 2: Trade Balance by MDG regions 2013
(Bln US$)

— Imports   — Exports   — Trade balance

Developed Asia–Pacific
Developed Europe
Developed N. America
South–eastern Europe
CIS
Northern Africa
Sub–Saharan Africa
Latin Am, Caribbean
Eastern Asia
Southern Asia
South–eastern Asia
Western Asia
Oceania

Table 2: Top exporting countries or areas in 2013

Country or area	Value (million US$)	Avg. Growth (%) 09-13	Growth (%) 12-13	World share %	Cum.
World	12 446.3	13.9	1.0	100.0	
Germany	1 698.9	15.3	0.3	13.6	13.6
Russian Federation	1 426.8	36.0	16.5	11.5	25.1
China	1 249.4	13.4	-6.3	10.0	35.2
USA	1 173.1	9.2	2.4	9.4	44.6
Italy	954.3	15.5	6.3	7.7	52.2
Japan	796.8	6.7	-9.8	6.4	58.6
United Kingdom	662.9	1.9	-1.7	5.3	64.0
Rep. of Korea	518.9	53.4	24.0	4.2	68.1
Switzerland	502.7	7.6	-14.4	4.0	72.2
Israel	439.3	18.3	27.4	3.5	75.7
Belgium	435.8	15.5	67.8	3.5	79.2
Netherlands	280.4	13.5	0.8	2.3	81.5
China, Hong Kong SAR	259.9	18.4	-6.7	2.1	83.6
Ireland	213.2	60.5	5.1	1.7	85.3
Brazil	178.2	-1.4	-19.5	1.4	86.7

Table 3: Top importing countries or areas in 2013

Country or area	Value (million US$)	Avg. Growth (%) 09-13	Growth (%) 12-13	World share %	Cum.
World	11 448.1	13.0	-3.3	100.0	
Germany	1 723.2	15.7	2.4	15.1	15.1
Italy	1 040.2	54.2	14.0	9.1	24.1
France	778.0	8.8	-11.3	6.8	30.9
Japan	710.2	16.0	-6.4	6.2	37.1
USA	681.5	9.6	-15.3	6.0	43.1
Rep. of Korea	603.9	13.3	-16.2	5.3	48.4
China	576.8	12.7	5.3	5.0	53.4
Other Asia, nes	396.2	7.8	-12.8	3.5	56.9
China, Hong Kong SAR	372.9	8.2	-6.2	3.3	60.1
Switzerland	337.7	-0.9	3.5	2.9	63.1
Singapore	335.4	10.8	-10.5	2.9	66.0
India	315.6	15.3	2.2	2.8	68.8
Mexico	259.9	16.3	2.8	2.3	71.0
Belgium	247.0	-6.5	6.3	2.2	73.2
Canada	241.4	26.2	5.8	2.1	75.3

In 2013, the value (in current US$) of exports of "radioactive and associated materials" (SITC group 525) decreased by 13.8 percent (compared to -0.6 percent average growth rate from 2009-2013) to reach 13.0 bln US$ (see table 2), while imports decreased by 3.8 percent to reach 19.6 bln US$ (see table 3). Exports of this commodity accounted for 0.7 percent of world exports of SITC section 5, and 0.1 percent of total world merchandise exports (see table 1). Kazakhstan, Canada and Netherlands were the top exporters in 2013 (see table 2). They accounted for 18.0, 17.6 and 10.6 percent of world exports, respectively. USA, France and China were the top destinations, with respectively 21.1, 16.1 and 14.9 percent of world imports (see table 3).

The top 15 countries/areas accounted for 95.3 and 95.9 percent of total world exports and imports, respectively (see tables 2 and 3). In 2013, Kazakhstan was the country/area with the highest value of net exports (+2.2 bln US$), followed by Canada (+1.3 bln US$). By MDG regions (see graph 2), the largest surpluses in this product group were recorded by Commonwealth of Independent States (+2.8 bln US$), Sub-Saharan Africa (+52.7 mln US$) and Southern Asia (less than 0.1 mln US$). The largest trade deficits were recorded by Developed Europe (-3.5 bln US$), Eastern Asia (-3.4 bln US$) and Developed North America (-1.5 bln US$).

Table 1: Imports (Imp.) and exports (Exp.), 1999-2013, in current US$

		1999	2000	2001	2002	2003	2004	2005	2006	2007	2008	2009	2010	2011	2012	2013
Values in Bln US$	Imp.	6.3	6.9	6.9	7.4	9.3	10.1	11.2	13.6	17.8	18.5	18.2	21.0	25.0	20.4	19.6
	Exp.	4.3	5.0	4.5	5.0	5.8	6.3	7.4	9.4	14.8	14.5	13.3	14.8	19.2	15.1	13.0
As a percentage of	Imp.	1.1	1.1	1.1	1.1	1.1	1.0	1.0	1.1	1.2	1.1	1.2	1.2	1.2	1.0	1.0
SITC section (%)	Exp.	0.8	0.9	0.8	0.8	0.7	0.7	0.7	0.8	1.0	0.9	0.9	0.9	1.0	0.8	0.7
As a percentage of	Imp.	0.1	0.1	0.1	0.1	0.1	0.1	0.1	0.1	0.1	0.1	0.1	0.1	0.1	0.1	0.1
world trade (%)	Exp.	0.1	0.1	0.1	0.1	0.1	0.1	0.1	0.1	0.1	0.1	0.1	0.1	0.1	0.1	0.1

Graph 1: Annual growth rates of exports, 1999–2013
(In percentage by year)

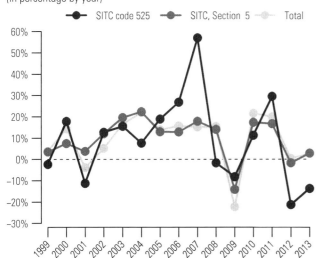

Graph 2: Trade Balance by MDG regions 2013
(Bln US$)

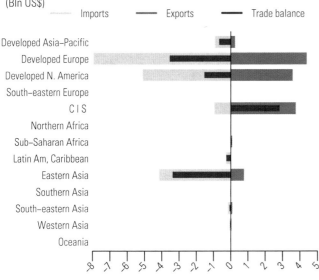

Table 2: Top exporting countries or areas in 2013

Country or area	Value (million US$)	Avg. Growth (%) 09-13	Growth (%) 12-13	World share %	Cum.
World....................................	13017.7	-0.6	-13.8	100.0	
Kazakhstan............................	2343.6	9.7	-15.0	18.0	18.0
Canada..................................	2288.3	10.5	24.0	17.6	35.6
Netherlands...........................	1382.8	0.0	-26.5	10.6	46.2
France...................................	1340.4	-19.8	-32.4	10.3	56.5
USA.......................................	1288.6	-13.5	-34.2	9.9	66.4
Germany................................	1073.7	-4.9	-29.5	8.2	74.6
Uzbekistan.............................	*984.8*	8.2	40.0	7.6	82.2
China....................................	664.7	28.4	-18.4	5.1	87.3
Japan....................................	231.8	20.3	-18.9	1.8	89.1
Ukraine.................................	221.0	445.8	52.9	1.7	90.8
Russian Federation.................	208.0	-3.3	-4.3	1.6	92.4
Belgium.................................	103.5	-6.3	-34.1	0.8	93.2
United Kingdom.....................	102.3	3.2	-2.2	0.8	94.0
China, Hong Kong SAR...........	91.5	117.0	44.8	0.7	94.7
Sweden.................................	85.8	90.6	1235.1	0.7	95.3

Table 3: Top importing countries or areas in 2013

Country or area	Value (million US$)	Avg. Growth (%) 09-13	Growth (%) 12-13	World share %	Cum.
World....................................	19593.5	1.9	-3.8	100.0	
USA.......................................	4133.8	-2.5	-12.0	21.1	21.1
France...................................	3151.7	0.0	11.9	16.1	37.2
China....................................	2917.2	38.9	36.4	14.9	52.1
Germany................................	1325.9	-9.6	-11.7	6.8	58.8
Rep. of Korea........................	1114.0	9.5	34.8	5.7	64.5
Canada..................................	967.7	13.6	1.0	4.9	69.5
United Kingdom.....................	911.9	-3.7	-24.3	4.7	74.1
Japan....................................	887.1	-9.8	-43.5	4.5	78.6
Russian Federation.................	797.5	18.7	56.6	4.1	82.7
Netherlands...........................	782.8	6.5	-7.8	4.0	86.7
Sweden.................................	703.1	1.6	-36.4	3.6	90.3
Spain....................................	510.1	-3.6	-21.8	2.6	92.9
Belgium.................................	266.1	-26.5	-24.2	1.4	94.3
Brazil....................................	176.0	12.5	4.0	0.9	95.2
Kazakhstan............................	137.7	22.3	60.5	0.7	95.9

531 Synthetic organic colouring matter and preparations based thereon

In 2013, the value (in current US$) of exports of "synthetic organic colouring matter and preparations based thereon" (SITC group 531) increased by 6.4 percent (compared to 6.6 percent average growth rate from 2009-2013) to reach 12.7 bln US$ (see table 2), while imports increased by 5.1 percent to reach 13.3 bln US$ (see table 3). Exports of this commodity accounted for 0.7 percent of world exports of SITC section 5, and 0.1 percent of total world merchandise exports (see table 1). China, India and Germany were the top exporters in 2013 (see table 2). They accounted for 21.9, 15.4 and 13.1 percent of world exports, respectively. Germany, USA and Rep. of Korea were the top destinations, with respectively 8.0, 7.3 and 6.0 percent of world imports (see table 3).

The top 15 countries/areas accounted for 87.1 and 61.9 percent of total world exports and imports, respectively (see tables 2 and 3). In 2013, China was the country/area with the highest value of net exports (+2.1 bln US$), followed by India (+1.6 bln US$). By MDG regions (see graph 2), the largest surpluses in this product group were recorded by Eastern Asia (+1.7 bln US$), Southern Asia (+1.2 bln US$) and Developed Europe (+101.0 mln US$). The largest trade deficits were recorded by Latin America and the Caribbean (-976.7 mln US$), South-eastern Asia (-729.0 mln US$) and Western Asia (-701.7 mln US$).

Table 1: Imports (Imp.) and exports (Exp.), 1999-2013, in current US$

		1999	2000	2001	2002	2003	2004	2005	2006	2007	2008	2009	2010	2011	2012	2013
Values in Bln US$	Imp.	9.8	9.6	8.7	9.1	9.9	10.5	10.4	11.2	12.1	12.6	10.1	12.5	13.2	12.6	13.3
	Exp.	9.2	8.9	8.4	9.1	9.8	10.4	10.4	11.1	12.1	12.4	9.9	12.2	12.5	12.0	12.7
As a percentage of SITC section (%)	Imp.	1.7	1.6	1.4	1.3	1.2	1.0	0.9	0.9	0.8	0.7	0.7	0.7	0.6	0.6	0.6
	Exp.	1.7	1.6	1.4	1.4	1.2	1.1	1.0	0.9	0.8	0.8	0.7	0.7	0.6	0.6	0.7
As a percentage of world trade (%)	Imp.	0.2	0.1	0.1	0.1	0.1	0.1	0.1	0.1	0.1	0.1	0.1	0.1	0.1	0.1	0.1
	Exp.	0.2	0.1	0.1	0.1	0.1	0.1	0.1	0.1	0.1	0.1	0.1	0.1	0.1	0.1	0.1

Graph 1: Annual growth rates of exports, 1999–2013
(In percentage by year)

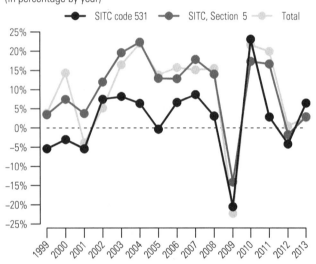

Legend: SITC code 531 — SITC, Section 5 — Total

Table 2: Top exporting countries or areas in 2013

Country or area	Value (million US$)	Avg. Growth (%) 09-13	Growth (%) 12-13	World share %	Cum.
World	12 742.3	6.6	6.4	100.0	
China	2 785.2	12.4	10.6	21.9	21.9
India	1 957.6	21.4	31.0	15.4	37.2
Germany	1 664.8	2.3	2.7	13.1	50.3
USA	735.1	5.1	0.2	5.8	56.1
Switzerland	516.8	-6.9	-9.5	4.1	60.1
Belgium	486.4	-0.4	3.4	3.8	63.9
Rep. of Korea	454.1	10.9	14.4	3.6	67.5
Japan	435.2	-1.2	-22.9	3.4	70.9
Other Asia, nes.	359.6	8.9	11.1	2.8	73.7
United Kingdom	334.4	2.1	1.0	2.6	76.4
France	303.0	1.2	-4.9	2.4	78.7
Spain	286.4	7.3	4.9	2.2	81.0
Netherlands	265.9	2.3	7.0	2.1	83.1
Italy	259.5	-0.5	-8.9	2.0	85.1
Singapore	250.1	2.5	-5.6	2.0	87.1

Graph 2: Trade Balance by MDG regions 2013
(Bln US$)

Legend: Imports — Exports — Trade balance

- Developed Asia–Pacific
- Developed Europe
- Developed N. America
- South–eastern Europe
- CIS
- Northern Africa
- Sub–Saharan Africa
- Latin Am, Caribbean
- Eastern Asia
- Southern Asia
- South–eastern Asia
- Western Asia
- Oceania

Table 3: Top importing countries or areas in 2013

Country or area	Value (million US$)	Avg. Growth (%) 09-13	Growth (%) 12-13	World share %	Cum.
World	13 261.7	7.1	5.1	100.0	
Germany	1 061.9	6.0	8.4	8.0	8.0
USA	973.9	12.3	-0.6	7.3	15.4
Rep. of Korea	795.1	14.6	17.0	6.0	21.3
China	680.0	4.2	3.0	5.1	26.5
Turkey	551.6	10.6	14.9	4.2	30.6
Italy	533.4	1.6	11.2	4.0	34.7
Japan	514.2	10.3	-7.8	3.9	38.5
Indonesia	448.6	16.3	16.9	3.4	41.9
France	437.8	5.7	2.6	3.3	45.2
Belgium	435.3	5.5	15.1	3.3	48.5
Other Asia, nes.	410.5	15.9	6.8	3.1	51.6
Brazil	364.7	9.9	6.8	2.7	54.3
Mexico	358.6	10.3	2.6	2.7	57.0
India	326.7	13.6	10.2	2.5	59.5
Thailand	321.5	14.4	10.9	2.4	61.9

In 2013, the value (in current US$) of exports of "dyeing and tanning extracts, and synthetic tanning materials" (SITC group 532) increased by 1.5 percent (compared to 9.0 percent average growth rate from 2009-2013) to reach 2.1 bln US$ (see table 2), while imports decreased by 4.8 percent to reach 2.5 bln US$ (see table 3). Exports of this commodity accounted for 0.1 percent of world exports of SITC section 5, and less than 0.1 percent of total world merchandise exports (see table 1). Italy, Germany and Netherlands were the top exporters in 2013 (see table 2). They accounted for 12.6, 10.4 and 7.6 percent of world exports, respectively. China, USA and Japan were the top destinations, with respectively 9.8, 7.8 and 6.3 percent of world imports (see table 3).

The top 15 countries/areas accounted for 80.6 and 65.1 percent of total world exports and imports, respectively (see tables 2 and 3). In 2013, Italy was the country/area with the highest value of net exports (+123.3 mln US$), followed by Germany (+102.7 mln US$). By MDG regions (see graph 2), the largest surpluses in this product group were recorded by Developed Europe (+329.5 mln US$), Sub-Saharan Africa (+40.3 mln US$) and Western Asia (+28.7 mln US$). The largest trade deficits were recorded by Eastern Asia (-267.1 mln US$), Developed Asia-Pacific (-162.5 mln US$) and Developed North America (-107.6 mln US$).

Table 1: Imports (Imp.) and exports (Exp.), 1999-2013, in current US$

		1999	2000	2001	2002	2003	2004	2005	2006	2007	2008	2009	2010	2011	2012	2013
Values in Bln US$	Imp.	1.0	1.1	1.1	1.1	1.3	1.4	1.5	1.6	1.8	1.9	1.8	2.3	2.9	2.7	2.5
	Exp.	0.9	0.9	0.9	1.0	1.1	1.3	1.4	1.5	1.6	1.6	1.5	1.9	2.2	2.1	2.1
As a percentage of	Imp.	0.2	0.2	0.2	0.2	0.2	0.1	0.1	0.1	0.1	0.1	0.1	0.1	0.1	0.1	0.1
SITC section (%)	Exp.	0.2	0.2	0.2	0.1	0.1	0.1	0.1	0.1	0.1	0.1	0.1	0.1	0.1	0.1	0.1
As a percentage of	Imp.	0.0	0.0	0.0	0.0	0.0	0.0	0.0	0.0	0.0	0.0	0.0	0.0	0.0	0.0	0.0
world trade (%)	Exp.	0.0	0.0	0.0	0.0	0.0	0.0	0.0	0.0	0.0	0.0	0.0	0.0	0.0	0.0	0.0

Graph 1: Annual growth rates of exports, 1999–2013
(In percentage by year)

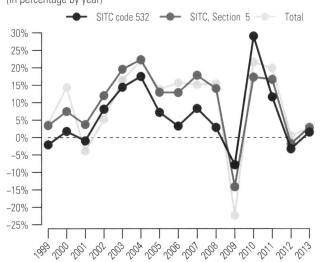

Table 2: Top exporting countries or areas in 2013

Country or area	Value (million US$)	Avg. Growth (%) 09-13	Growth (%) 12-13	World share %	Cum.
World	2 117.7	9.0	1.5	100.0	
Italy	266.4	10.7	13.1	12.6	12.6
Germany	219.4	8.6	6.2	10.4	22.9
Netherlands	161.8	11.5	9.2	7.6	30.6
France	147.5	10.2	6.3	7.0	37.5
Spain	138.7	5.2	-15.3	6.5	44.1
USA	116.2	6.2	-3.3	5.5	49.6
South Africa	97.7	11.9	8.5	4.6	54.2
Denmark	88.7	16.3	-2.3	4.2	58.4
Turkey	86.1	11.1	16.1	4.1	62.4
Argentina	85.9	10.2	-3.9	4.1	66.5
India	74.8	15.3	10.7	3.5	70.0
Brazil	73.5	9.5	1.3	3.5	73.5
Ireland	52.1	11.1	1.3	2.5	76.0
China	49.9	14.1	11.6	2.4	78.3
United Kingdom	47.7	3.5	-17.6	2.3	80.6

Graph 2: Trade Balance by MDG regions 2013
(Bln US$)

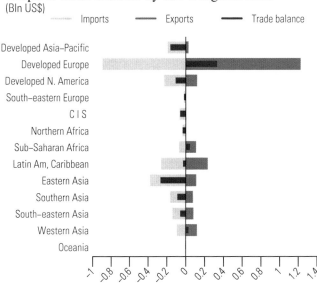

Table 3: Top importing countries or areas in 2013

Country or area	Value (million US$)	Avg. Growth (%) 09-13	Growth (%) 12-13	World share %	Cum.
World	2 543.3	9.7	-4.8	100.0	
China	248.8	9.2	-0.9	9.8	9.8
USA	198.3	10.7	-0.7	7.8	17.6
Japan	160.1	4.0	-9.3	6.3	23.9
Italy	143.0	12.1	1.0	5.6	29.5
Germany	116.7	9.0	-7.5	4.6	34.1
France	102.6	13.8	12.1	4.0	38.1
Spain	101.1	11.9	-6.4	4.0	42.1
India	99.9	4.1	20.8	3.9	46.0
Netherlands	89.6	37.7	-3.3	3.5	49.5
United Kingdom	85.8	13.9	-1.2	3.4	52.9
Mexico	84.5	2.7	-32.9	3.3	56.2
Brazil	61.6	15.3	-12.6	2.4	58.7
Turkey	59.4	13.5	13.2	2.3	61.0
Rep. of Korea	56.3	4.1	-6.8	2.2	63.2
Denmark	48.2	16.0	-14.1	1.9	65.1

533 Pigments, paints, varnishes and related materials

In 2013, the value (in current US$) of exports of "pigments, paints, varnishes and related materials" (SITC group 533) decreased by 2.8 percent (compared to 8.0 percent average growth rate from 2009-2013) to reach 60.3 bln US$ (see table 2), while imports increased by 2.4 percent to reach 59.2 bln US$ (see table 3). Exports of this commodity accounted for 3.1 percent of world exports of SITC section 5, and 0.3 percent of total world merchandise exports (see table 1). Germany, USA and Belgium were the top exporters in 2013 (see table 2). They accounted for 16.4, 11.6 and 6.5 percent of world exports, respectively. Germany, China and USA were the top destinations, with respectively 6.7, 5.7 and 4.7 percent of world imports (see table 3).

The top 15 countries/areas accounted for 77.6 and 53.6 percent of total world exports and imports, respectively (see tables 2 and 3). In 2013, Germany was the country/area with the highest value of net exports (+5.9 bln US$), followed by USA (+4.2 bln US$). By MDG regions (see graph 2), the largest surpluses in this product group were recorded by Developed Europe (+10.0 bln US$), Developed North America (+3.0 bln US$) and Developed Asia-Pacific (+2.9 bln US$). The largest trade deficits were recorded by Latin America and the Caribbean (-3.7 bln US$), Commonwealth of Independent States (-3.0 bln US$) and South-eastern Asia (-2.1 bln US$).

Table 1: Imports (Imp.) and exports (Exp.), 1999-2013, in current US$

		1999	2000	2001	2002	2003	2004	2005	2006	2007	2008	2009	2010	2011	2012	2013
Values in Bln US$	Imp.	23.0	24.5	24.1	25.9	30.0	35.0	38.0	42.3	47.8	51.7	43.9	50.9	60.2	57.8	59.2
	Exp.	23.3	24.6	24.1	25.9	30.2	35.5	38.6	43.1	48.9	52.1	44.3	52.1	63.4	62.1	60.3
As a percentage of SITC section (%)	Imp.	4.1	4.0	3.8	3.7	3.6	3.5	3.3	3.3	3.2	3.0	3.0	2.9	2.9	2.9	2.9
	Exp.	4.4	4.4	4.1	3.9	3.8	3.7	3.6	3.5	3.4	3.2	3.1	3.1	3.3	3.3	3.1
As a percentage of world trade (%)	Imp.	0.4	0.4	0.4	0.4	0.4	0.4	0.4	0.3	0.3	0.3	0.3	0.3	0.3	0.3	0.3
	Exp.	0.4	0.4	0.4	0.4	0.4	0.4	0.4	0.4	0.4	0.3	0.4	0.3	0.4	0.3	0.3

Graph 1: Annual growth rates of exports, 1999–2013
(In percentage by year)

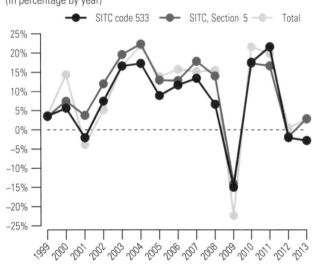

- SITC code 533
- SITC, Section 5
- Total

Table 2: Top exporting countries or areas in 2013

Country or area	Value (million US$)	Avg. Growth (%) 09-13	Growth (%) 12-13	World share %	Cum.
World	60 316.6	8.0	-2.8	100.0	
Germany	9 899.0	6.1	2.5	16.4	16.4
USA	6 973.4	8.6	-4.5	11.6	28.0
Belgium	3 893.3	7.2	3.7	6.5	34.4
Japan	3 862.2	6.0	-12.1	6.4	40.8
Netherlands	2 994.4	8.6	17.7	5.0	45.8
China	2 838.5	22.9	2.8	4.7	50.5
Italy	2 797.4	7.6	7.5	4.6	55.1
United Kingdom	2 757.1	4.4	1.4	4.6	59.7
Spain	2 385.7	8.5	12.2	4.0	63.7
France	2 357.4	4.2	4.7	3.9	67.6
Rep. of Korea	1 896.4	21.2	15.4	3.1	70.7
Other Asia, nes	1 153.5	5.5	-10.9	1.9	72.6
Sweden	1 115.0	6.2	6.3	1.8	74.5
Switzerland	948.1	10.3	5.3	1.6	76.1
Singapore	943.1	3.4	-6.6	1.6	77.6

Graph 2: Trade Balance by MDG regions 2013
(Bln US$)

Imports — Exports — Trade balance

Developed Asia–Pacific
Developed Europe
Developed N. America
South–eastern Europe
CIS
Northern Africa
Sub–Saharan Africa
Latin Am, Caribbean
Eastern Asia
Southern Asia
South–eastern Asia
Western Asia
Oceania

-25 -20 -15 -10 -5 0 5 10 15 20 25 30 35

Table 3: Top importing countries or areas in 2013

Country or area	Value (million US$)	Avg. Growth (%) 09-13	Growth (%) 12-13	World share %	Cum.
World	59 179.1	7.8	2.4	100.0	
Germany	3 988.4	9.2	1.8	6.7	6.7
China	3 346.6	4.3	4.2	5.7	12.4
USA	2 783.4	12.1	3.2	4.7	17.1
France	2 615.3	5.3	0.3	4.4	21.5
Russian Federation	2 427.0	13.1	0.7	4.1	25.6
Canada	2 063.1	9.3	-1.1	3.5	29.1
Italy	1 852.0	4.4	0.6	3.1	32.2
United Kingdom	1 811.7	3.9	4.9	3.1	35.3
Belgium	1 799.3	4.0	13.5	3.0	38.3
Netherlands	1 679.6	8.5	5.5	2.8	41.2
Rep. of Korea	1 620.6	8.7	-4.7	2.7	43.9
Mexico	1 568.2	13.4	2.4	2.6	46.6
Poland	1 519.2	5.3	7.0	2.6	49.1
Turkey	1 350.6	11.5	4.1	2.3	51.4
Spain	1 295.0	-1.1	6.8	2.2	53.6

In 2013, the value (in current US$) of exports of "medicinal and pharmaceutical products, other than medicament of 542" (SITC group 541) increased by 9.0 percent (compared to 9.3 percent average growth rate from 2009-2013) to reach 176.2 bln US$ (see table 2), while imports increased by 8.2 percent to reach 175.8 bln US$ (see table 3). Exports of this commodity accounted for 9.0 percent of world exports of SITC section 5, and 0.9 percent of total world merchandise exports (see table 1). Switzerland, Germany and Belgium were the top exporters in 2013 (see table 2). They accounted for 16.8, 14.9 and 11.2 percent of world exports, respectively. Germany, Belgium and USA were the top destinations, with respectively 12.8, 10.6 and 10.5 percent of world imports (see table 3).

The top 15 countries/areas accounted for 92.3 and 77.1 percent of total world exports and imports, respectively (see tables 2 and 3). In 2013, Switzerland was the country/area with the highest value of net exports (+21.3 bln US$), followed by Ireland (+8.1 bln US$). By MDG regions (see graph 2), the largest surpluses in this product group were recorded by Developed Europe (+30.0 bln US$) and Eastern Asia (+2.5 bln US$). The largest trade deficits were recorded by Latin America and the Caribbean (-9.5 bln US$), Developed Asia-Pacific (-7.2 bln US$) and Commonwealth of Independent States (-4.3 bln US$).

Table 1: Imports (Imp.) and exports (Exp.), 1999-2013, in current US$

		1999	2000	2001	2002	2003	2004	2005	2006	2007	2008	2009	2010	2011	2012	2013
Values in Bln US$	Imp.	32.4	33.6	37.9	43.9	52.2	60.6	66.7	75.4	95.6	108.4	116.8	133.0	159.4	162.5	175.8
	Exp.	31.1	31.0	34.9	40.7	49.9	59.4	65.5	73.6	93.5	111.7	123.5	134.7	151.9	161.7	176.2
As a percentage of	Imp.	5.7	5.5	6.0	6.3	6.3	6.0	5.8	5.9	6.3	6.3	7.9	7.7	7.8	8.1	8.5
SITC section (%)	Exp.	5.9	5.5	6.0	6.2	6.3	6.2	6.0	6.0	6.5	6.8	8.7	8.1	7.9	8.5	9.0
As a percentage of	Imp.	0.6	0.5	0.6	0.7	0.7	0.6	0.6	0.6	0.7	0.7	0.9	0.9	0.9	0.9	0.9
world trade (%)	Exp.	0.6	0.5	0.6	0.6	0.7	0.7	0.6	0.6	0.7	0.7	1.0	0.9	0.8	0.9	0.9

Graph 1: Annual growth rates of exports, 1999–2013
(In percentage by year)

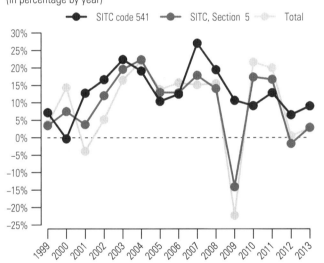

Table 2: Top exporting countries or areas in 2013

Country or area	Value (million US$)	Avg. Growth (%) 09-13	Growth (%) 12-13	World share %	Cum.
World	176 249.8	9.3	9.0	100.0	
Switzerland	29 674.1	12.4	9.5	16.8	16.8
Germany	26 232.1	8.3	14.3	14.9	31.7
Belgium	19 657.7	11.0	16.8	11.2	42.9
USA	19 101.4	-0.4	2.3	10.8	53.7
Ireland	10 017.9	8.2	-15.0	5.7	59.4
Netherlands	9 828.4	43.4	107.2	5.6	65.0
France	9 551.8	13.1	20.5	5.4	70.4
China	9 336.3	5.9	2.6	5.3	75.7
United Kingdom	9 295.9	16.3	-13.7	5.3	81.0
Austria	4 306.9	9.5	15.6	2.4	83.4
Italy	3 711.2	3.5	11.6	2.1	85.5
Spain	3 491.7	16.5	7.7	2.0	87.5
Denmark	3 404.1	12.2	20.1	1.9	89.4
Singapore	2 749.6	10.9	-30.4	1.6	91.0
India	2 329.7	15.2	24.5	1.3	92.3

Graph 2: Trade Balance by MDG regions 2013
(Bln US$)

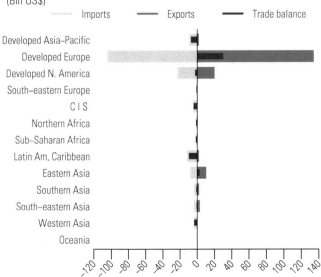

Table 3: Top importing countries or areas in 2013

Country or area	Value (million US$)	Avg. Growth (%) 09-13	Growth (%) 12-13	World share %	Cum.
World	175 784.4	10.8	8.2	100.0	
Germany	22 430.7	7.5	5.7	12.8	12.8
Belgium	18 584.8	17.7	15.0	10.6	23.3
USA	18 462.4	7.6	-2.5	10.5	33.8
France	11 317.4	11.2	8.7	6.4	40.3
United Kingdom	9 771.7	15.8	1.2	5.6	45.8
Italy	8 915.3	4.7	5.4	5.1	50.9
Switzerland	8 369.2	15.2	19.7	4.8	55.7
Japan	6 791.8	11.0	-7.2	3.9	59.5
Austria	5 296.7	13.0	12.6	3.0	62.5
Netherlands	5 195.6	31.2	122.3	3.0	65.5
China	5 120.3	31.7	38.3	2.9	68.4
Brazil	4 391.8	16.0	10.9	2.5	70.9
Canada	4 111.2	11.1	8.5	2.3	73.2
Spain	3 602.1	-4.0	-1.6	2.0	75.3
Russian Federation	3 152.8	18.1	11.4	1.8	77.1

542 Medicaments (including veterinary medicaments)

"Medicaments (including veterinary medicaments)" (SITC group 542) is amongst the top exported commodities in 2013 with 1.8 percent of total exports (see table 1). After a decrease in the export value of 3.2 percent in 2012, the value (in current US$) of exports of this commodity increased by 3.3 percent (compared to 2.2 percent average growth rate from 2009-2013) to reach 337.5 bln US$ (see table 2), while imports increased by 2.1 percent to reach 357.3 bln US$ (see table 3). Exports of this commodity accounted for 17.3 percent of world exports of SITC section 5 (see table 1). Germany, Belgium and Switzerland were the top exporters in 2013 (see table 2). They accounted for 14.5, 10.0 and 9.7 percent of world exports, respectively. India and Italy recorded a strong growth of 20.6 and 18.2 percent, increasing their share of world export. USA, Belgium and Germany were the top destinations, with respectively 13.7, 7.4 and 6.8 percent of world imports (see table 3).

The top 15 countries/areas accounted for 85.8 and 70.2 percent of total world exports and imports, respectively (see tables 2 and 3). In 2013, Germany was the country/area with the highest value of net exports (+24.6 bln US$), followed by Switzerland (+17.2 bln US$). By MDG regions (see graph 2), the largest surpluses in this product group were recorded by Developed Europe (+81.6 bln US$) and Southern Asia (+8.4 bln US$). The largest trade deficit was recorded by Developed North America (-28.5 bln US$).

Table 1: Imports (Imp.) and exports (Exp.), 1999-2013, in current US$

		1999	2000	2001	2002	2003	2004	2005	2006	2007	2008	2009	2010	2011	2012	2013
Values in Bln US$	Imp.	75.7	79.0	96.4	132.2	161.2	191.8	216.4	245.2	283.3	318.2	323.0	335.8	357.3	349.9	357.3
	Exp.	73.8	75.7	97.9	125.8	151.7	187.0	206.8	237.3	274.6	304.0	309.4	320.1	337.6	326.7	337.5
As a percentage of SITC section (%)	Imp.	13.4	12.9	15.2	18.8	19.3	18.9	18.9	19.1	18.8	18.5	21.8	19.3	17.4	17.5	17.3
	Exp.	14.0	13.4	16.7	19.1	19.3	19.4	19.1	19.4	19.0	18.5	21.9	19.3	17.5	17.2	17.3
As a percentage of world trade (%)	Imp.	1.3	1.2	1.5	2.0	2.1	2.1	2.0	2.0	2.0	2.0	2.6	2.2	2.0	1.9	1.9
	Exp.	1.3	1.2	1.6	2.0	2.0	2.1	2.0	2.0	2.0	1.9	2.5	2.1	1.9	1.8	1.8

Graph 1: Annual growth rates of exports, 1999–2013
(In percentage by year)

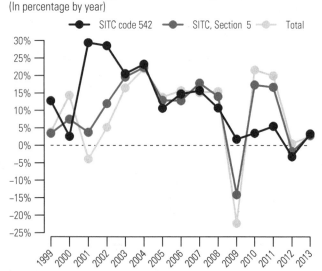

Graph 2: Trade Balance by MDG regions 2013
(Bln US$)

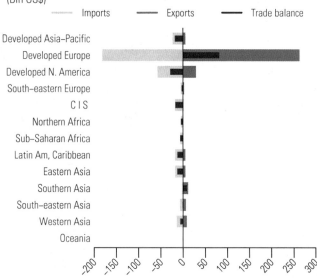

Table 2: Top exporting countries or areas in 2013

Country or area	Value (million US$)	Avg. Growth (%) 09-13	Growth (%) 12-13	World share %	Cum.
World	337 484.2	2.2	3.3	100.0	
Germany	48 876.3	2.1	6.8	14.5	14.5
Belgium	33 813.8	-3.2	12.1	10.0	24.5
Switzerland	32 708.8	5.9	3.0	9.7	34.2
France	28 178.9	-0.2	1.8	8.3	42.5
USA	24 643.7	0.0	-4.9	7.3	49.8
United Kingdom	23 572.2	-3.1	-7.9	7.0	56.8
Italy	21 210.7	13.4	18.2	6.3	63.1
Ireland	18 498.6	-4.3	-5.3	5.5	68.6
Netherlands	13 814.3	9.8	2.8	4.1	72.7
India	10 844.7	23.9	20.6	3.2	75.9
Spain	10 259.9	3.1	8.5	3.0	78.9
Sweden	6 372.7	-4.1	-0.2	1.9	80.8
Israel	5 876.1	7.4	-7.7	1.7	82.6
Austria	5 666.7	4.9	2.1	1.7	84.3
Singapore	5 124.5	6.7	-0.8	1.5	85.8

Table 3: Top importing countries or areas in 2013

Country or area	Value (million US$)	Avg. Growth (%) 09-13	Growth (%) 12-13	World share %	Cum.
World	357 296.0	2.6	2.1	100.0	
USA	48 883.4	1.3	-1.7	13.7	13.7
Belgium	26 324.0	-5.3	20.6	7.4	21.0
Germany	24 233.0	-5.1	-1.8	6.8	27.8
United Kingdom	18 899.1	4.5	2.9	5.3	33.1
France	18 378.4	-1.8	-5.6	5.1	38.3
Italy	15 972.8	3.4	3.0	4.5	42.7
Switzerland	15 504.9	5.4	4.8	4.3	47.1
Japan	15 039.1	11.5	-11.2	4.2	51.3
Netherlands	12 389.0	4.3	1.4	3.5	54.8
Russian Federation	11 804.9	13.6	9.5	3.3	58.1
Spain	11 418.1	-2.7	1.8	3.2	61.3
China	11 075.4	22.0	8.9	3.1	64.4
Canada	8 621.4	-2.0	-5.1	2.4	66.8
Australia	7 548.7	5.6	-10.8	2.1	68.9
Poland	4 582.8	2.1	9.6	1.3	70.2

In 2013, the value (in current US$) of exports of "essential oils, perfume and flavour materials" (SITC group 551) increased by 2.6 percent (compared to 8.1 percent average growth rate from 2009-2013) to reach 26.1 bln US$ (see table 2), while imports increased by 8.0 percent to reach 25.0 bln US$ (see table 3). Exports of this commodity accounted for 1.3 percent of world exports of SITC section 5, and 0.1 percent of total world merchandise exports (see table 1). Ireland, France and USA were the top exporters in 2013 (see table 2). They accounted for 28.4, 9.3 and 8.8 percent of world exports, respectively. USA, France and United Kingdom were the top destinations, with respectively 12.1, 11.3 and 5.3 percent of world imports (see table 3).

The top 15 countries/areas accounted for 89.0 and 62.5 percent of total world exports and imports, respectively (see tables 2 and 3). In 2013, Ireland was the country/area with the highest value of net exports (+7.0 bln US$), followed by Switzerland (+1.6 bln US$). By MDG regions (see graph 2), the largest surpluses in this product group were recorded by Developed Europe (+7.3 bln US$) and Southern Asia (+572.3 mln US$). The largest trade deficits were recorded by Latin America and the Caribbean (-1.5 bln US$), Developed North America (-1.1 bln US$) and Sub-Saharan Africa (-1.0 bln US$).

Table 1: Imports (Imp.) and exports (Exp.), 1999-2013, in current US$

		1999	2000	2001	2002	2003	2004	2005	2006	2007	2008	2009	2010	2011	2012	2013
Values in Bln US$	Imp.	7.1	7.7	8.2	9.1	11.7	13.8	14.9	15.7	17.6	19.3	18.3	20.4	22.6	23.2	25.0
	Exp.	8.0	7.8	8.6	10.0	12.9	14.9	15.6	16.6	18.7	20.9	19.1	21.2	24.7	25.4	26.1
As a percentage of	Imp.	1.3	1.3	1.3	1.3	1.4	1.4	1.3	1.2	1.2	1.1	1.2	1.2	1.1	1.2	1.2
SITC section (%)	Exp.	1.5	1.4	1.5	1.5	1.6	1.5	1.4	1.4	1.3	1.3	1.3	1.3	1.3	1.3	1.3
As a percentage of	Imp.	0.1	0.1	0.1	0.1	0.2	0.1	0.1	0.1	0.1	0.1	0.1	0.1	0.1	0.1	0.1
world trade (%)	Exp.	0.1	0.1	0.1	0.2	0.2	0.2	0.2	0.1	0.1	0.1	0.2	0.1	0.1	0.1	0.1

Graph 1: Annual growth rates of exports, 1999–2013

(In percentage by year)

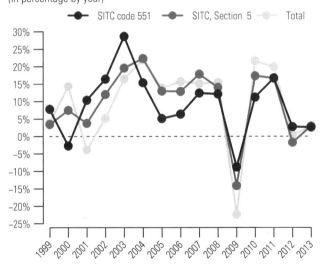

Graph 2: Trade Balance by MDG regions 2013

(Bln US$)

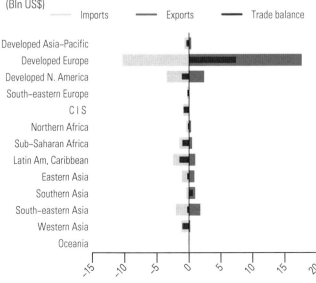

Table 2: Top exporting countries or areas in 2013

Country or area	Value (million US$)	Avg. Growth (%) 09-13	Growth (%) 12-13	World share %	Cum.
World	26 067.5	8.1	2.6	100.0	
Ireland	7 402.5	2.9	1.5	28.4	28.4
France	2 423.5	7.8	6.0	9.3	37.7
USA	2 284.8	7.9	3.6	8.8	46.5
Germany	2 147.3	5.6	11.0	8.2	54.7
Switzerland	1 952.3	7.3	-0.1	7.5	62.2
Singapore	1 429.1	18.9	-25.4	5.5	67.7
United Kingdom	1 113.4	8.7	6.6	4.3	71.9
Netherlands	1 053.6	14.6	11.4	4.0	76.0
India	956.0	25.5	-0.1	3.7	79.6
Spain	648.3	10.1	16.7	2.5	82.1
China	643.6	22.5	21.6	2.5	84.6
Swaziland	*322.7*	14.1	-28.0	1.2	85.8
Mexico	279.2	12.6	6.0	1.1	86.9
Egypt	272.1	55.6	62.1	1.0	88.0
Brazil	267.2	12.2	-13.0	1.0	89.0

Table 3: Top importing countries or areas in 2013

Country or area	Value (million US$)	Avg. Growth (%) 09-13	Growth (%) 12-13	World share %	Cum.
World	25 014.0	8.2	8.0	100.0	
USA	3 020.2	5.5	13.0	12.1	12.1
France	2 833.7	6.7	5.7	11.3	23.4
United Kingdom	1 319.1	5.7	9.6	5.3	28.7
Germany	1 180.7	7.3	9.4	4.7	33.4
Mexico	1 089.0	11.1	5.8	4.4	37.7
Spain	946.4	4.1	21.2	3.8	41.5
Italy	832.5	1.8	7.7	3.3	44.9
China	698.5	15.7	11.3	2.8	47.7
Russian Federation	657.3	9.9	6.0	2.6	50.3
Indonesia	559.9	16.9	32.7	2.2	52.5
Japan	540.2	3.2	-14.4	2.2	54.7
South Africa	527.1	42.5	12.5	2.1	56.8
Thailand	483.3	12.8	0.3	1.9	58.7
Netherlands	481.1	6.9	2.8	1.9	60.6
Canada	469.8	4.1	-1.0	1.9	62.5

553 Perfumery, cosmetic or toilet preparations (excluding soaps)

In 2013, the value (in current US$) of exports of "perfumery, cosmetic or toilet preparations (excluding soaps)" (SITC group 553) increased by 9.1 percent (the same as the average growth rate from 2009-2013) to reach 84.8 bln US$ (see table 2), while imports increased by 8.4 percent to reach 82.1 bln US$ (see table 3). Exports of this commodity accounted for 4.3 percent of world exports of SITC section 5, and 0.5 percent of total world merchandise exports (see table 1). France, Germany and USA were the top exporters in 2013 (see table 2). They accounted for 16.8, 10.4 and 10.3 percent of world exports, respectively. USA, Germany and United Kingdom were the top destinations, with respectively 9.5, 6.9 and 5.9 percent of world imports (see table 3).

The top 15 countries/areas accounted for 77.1 and 58.7 percent of total world exports and imports, respectively (see tables 2 and 3). In 2013, France was the country/area with the highest value of net exports (+11.5 bln US$), followed by Germany (+3.2 bln US$). By MDG regions (see graph 2), the largest surpluses in this product group were recorded by Developed Europe (+16.5 bln US$), South-eastern Asia (+1.2 bln US$) and Southern Asia (+63.4 mln US$). The largest trade deficits were recorded by Commonwealth of Independent States (-4.2 bln US$), Western Asia (-3.5 bln US$) and Developed Asia-Pacific (-2.4 bln US$).

Table 1: Imports (Imp.) and exports (Exp.), 1999-2013, in current US$

		1999	2000	2001	2002	2003	2004	2005	2006	2007	2008	2009	2010	2011	2012	2013
Values in Bln US$	Imp.	21.6	22.6	24.5	27.5	33.0	39.0	43.0	47.8	56.2	63.1	58.7	65.0	74.0	75.7	82.1
	Exp.	22.4	23.4	25.7	28.5	34.4	40.4	44.1	49.5	58.4	65.7	59.7	67.3	77.6	77.7	84.8
As a percentage of SITC section (%)	Imp.	3.8	3.7	3.9	3.9	4.0	3.9	3.7	3.7	3.7	3.7	4.0	3.7	3.6	3.8	4.0
	Exp.	4.3	4.1	4.4	4.3	4.4	4.2	4.1	4.0	4.0	4.0	4.2	4.1	4.0	4.1	4.3
As a percentage of world trade (%)	Imp.	0.4	0.3	0.4	0.4	0.4	0.4	0.4	0.4	0.4	0.4	0.5	0.4	0.4	0.4	0.4
	Exp.	0.4	0.4	0.4	0.4	0.5	0.4	0.4	0.4	0.4	0.4	0.5	0.4	0.4	0.4	0.5

Graph 1: Annual growth rates of exports, 1999–2013
(In percentage by year)

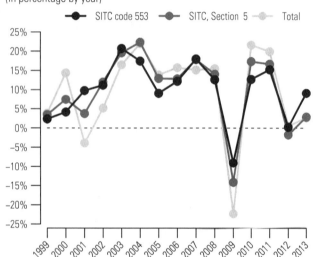

Graph 2: Trade Balance by MDG regions 2013
(Bln US$)

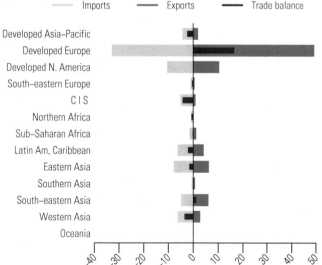

Table 2: Top exporting countries or areas in 2013

Country or area	Value (million US$)	Avg. Growth (%) 09-13	Growth (%) 12-13	World share %	Cum.
World	84 785.0	9.1	9.1	100.0	
France	14 216.8	4.6	5.3	16.8	16.8
Germany	8 848.5	6.4	5.2	10.4	27.2
USA	8 765.9	8.2	6.8	10.3	37.5
United Kingdom	5 016.4	6.5	11.5	5.9	43.5
Italy	4 100.0	10.0	13.3	4.8	48.3
Spain	3 388.6	9.9	16.9	4.0	52.3
Singapore	3 070.1	21.2	11.7	3.6	55.9
China	2 977.1	15.9	7.5	3.5	59.4
Poland	2 832.8	7.3	9.3	3.3	62.8
Belgium	2 697.2	8.5	18.1	3.2	65.9
Mexico	2 265.6	8.9	12.3	2.7	68.6
Netherlands	2 114.1	11.0	16.4	2.5	71.1
Thailand	1 896.8	15.1	-0.8	2.2	73.4
Canada	1 662.8	7.7	5.5	2.0	75.3
China, Hong Kong SAR	1 507.8	22.4	5.0	1.8	77.1

Table 3: Top importing countries or areas in 2013

Country or area	Value (million US$)	Avg. Growth (%) 09-13	Growth (%) 12-13	World share %	Cum.
World	82 059.6	8.7	8.4	100.0	
USA	7 776.4	12.9	10.3	9.5	9.5
Germany	5 634.8	8.5	14.9	6.9	16.3
United Kingdom	4 845.2	5.3	8.2	5.9	22.2
China, Hong Kong SAR	3 330.5	19.6	5.3	4.1	26.3
Russian Federation	3 243.8	10.8	6.8	4.0	30.3
France	2 759.7	4.3	3.3	3.4	33.6
Canada	2 646.7	6.7	6.9	3.2	36.8
Japan	2 616.5	8.1	-6.8	3.2	40.0
Netherlands	2 444.0	7.1	18.1	3.0	43.0
Singapore	2 370.0	16.7	12.1	2.9	45.9
Belgium	2 313.0	8.7	24.9	2.8	48.7
Italy	2 222.0	2.7	4.5	2.7	51.4
Spain	2 139.0	2.5	13.4	2.6	54.0
United Arab Emirates	*2 134.5*	9.7	11.4	2.6	56.6
China	1 686.3	21.0	10.7	2.1	58.7

In 2013, the value (in current US$) of exports of "soap, cleansing and polishing preparations" (SITC group 554) increased by 4.9 percent (compared to 7.5 percent average growth rate from 2009-2013) to reach 42.0 bln US$ (see table 2), while imports increased by 5.2 percent to reach 41.1 bln US$ (see table 3). Exports of this commodity accounted for 2.1 percent of world exports of SITC section 5, and 0.2 percent of total world merchandise exports (see table 1). Germany, USA and Belgium were the top exporters in 2013 (see table 2). They accounted for 12.5, 11.3 and 5.5 percent of world exports, respectively. Germany, France and USA were the top destinations, with respectively 6.9, 5.3 and 4.8 percent of world imports (see table 3).

The top 15 countries/areas accounted for 70.6 and 51.2 percent of total world exports and imports, respectively (see tables 2 and 3). In 2013, USA was the country/area with the highest value of net exports (+2.8 bln US$), followed by Germany (+2.4 bln US$). By MDG regions (see graph 2), the largest surpluses in this product group were recorded by Developed Europe (+4.2 bln US$), Developed North America (+1.5 bln US$) and South-eastern Asia (+890.6 mln US$). The largest trade deficits were recorded by Commonwealth of Independent States (-1.6 bln US$), Latin America and the Caribbean (-1.4 bln US$) and Sub-Saharan Africa (-896.5 mln US$).

Table 1: Imports (Imp.) and exports (Exp.), 1999-2013, in current US$

		1999	2000	2001	2002	2003	2004	2005	2006	2007	2008	2009	2010	2011	2012	2013
Values in Bln US$	Imp.	12.6	12.7	13.4	15.1	17.9	20.4	22.2	24.7	28.3	33.2	31.0	34.0	39.2	39.1	41.1
	Exp.	13.0	13.0	13.6	15.4	18.3	20.8	22.4	25.0	29.0	34.3	31.4	34.4	39.9	40.0	42.0
As a percentage of SITC section (%)	Imp.	2.2	2.1	2.1	2.1	2.2	2.0	1.9	1.9	1.9	1.9	2.1	2.0	1.9	2.0	2.0
	Exp.	2.5	2.3	2.3	2.3	2.3	2.2	2.1	2.0	2.0	2.1	2.2	2.1	2.1	2.1	2.1
As a percentage of world trade (%)	Imp.	0.2	0.2	0.2	0.2	0.2	0.2	0.2	0.2	0.2	0.2	0.2	0.2	0.2	0.2	0.2
	Exp.	0.2	0.2	0.2	0.2	0.2	0.2	0.2	0.2	0.2	0.2	0.3	0.2	0.2	0.2	0.2

Graph 1: Annual growth rates of exports, 1999–2013
(In percentage by year)

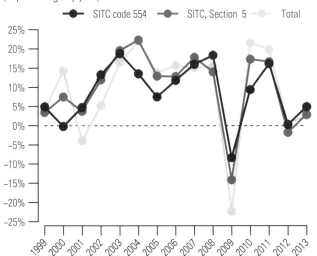

Graph 2: Trade Balance by MDG regions 2013
(Bln US$)

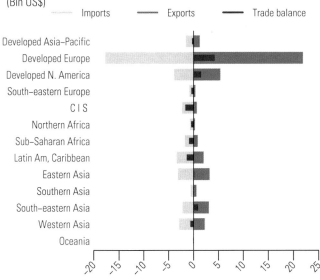

Table 2: Top exporting countries or areas in 2013

Country or area	Value (million US$)	Avg. Growth (%) 09-13	Growth (%) 12-13	World share %	Cum.
World	41 993.5	7.5	4.9	100.0	
Germany	5 253.7	6.0	5.2	12.5	12.5
USA	4 733.6	7.1	2.7	11.3	23.8
Belgium	2 324.9	4.3	26.4	5.5	29.3
China	2 311.6	24.3	10.3	5.5	34.8
France	2 253.2	2.8	-0.8	5.4	40.2
United Kingdom	2 119.5	4.5	5.5	5.0	45.2
Netherlands	2 005.2	14.4	8.2	4.8	50.0
Italy	1 816.1	4.6	6.0	4.3	54.3
Poland	1 272.7	10.4	16.5	3.0	57.4
Spain	1 137.3	4.3	15.0	2.7	60.1
Japan	1 071.5	7.4	-9.9	2.6	62.6
Indonesia	916.2	14.5	3.6	2.2	64.8
Turkey	878.7	9.4	6.2	2.1	66.9
Mexico	768.9	7.6	15.7	1.8	68.7
Malaysia	766.3	8.4	-0.7	1.8	70.6

Table 3: Top importing countries or areas in 2013

Country or area	Value (million US$)	Avg. Growth (%) 09-13	Growth (%) 12-13	World share %	Cum.
World	41 129.7	7.4	5.2	100.0	
Germany	2 838.5	6.9	8.4	6.9	6.9
France	2 169.4	2.7	1.7	5.3	12.2
USA	1 973.7	9.7	4.2	4.8	17.0
Canada	1 898.5	5.4	2.9	4.6	21.6
United Kingdom	1 858.6	2.4	2.4	4.5	26.1
Belgium	1 572.1	5.4	20.7	3.8	29.9
China	1 563.0	10.7	5.5	3.8	33.7
Netherlands	1 435.9	11.5	4.8	3.5	37.2
Italy	1 061.1	4.5	2.5	2.6	39.8
Russian Federation	1 038.5	14.4	7.4	2.5	42.3
Poland	842.7	8.9	11.3	2.0	44.4
Spain	799.9	0.4	-0.5	1.9	46.3
Japan	793.0	5.6	-6.6	1.9	48.2
Other Asia, nes	616.9	10.2	-6.4	1.5	49.7
Turkey	606.6	14.7	5.5	1.5	51.2

562 Fertilizers (other than those of group 272)

In 2013, the value (in current US$) of exports of "fertilizers (other than those of group 272)" (SITC group 562) decreased by 13.7 percent (compared to 12.1 percent average growth rate from 2009-2013) to reach 62.5 bln US$ (see table 2), while imports decreased by 6.3 percent to reach 75.9 bln US$ (see table 3). Exports of this commodity accounted for 3.2 percent of world exports of SITC section 5, and 0.3 percent of total world merchandise exports (see table 1). Russian Federation, Canada and China were the top exporters in 2013 (see table 2). They accounted for 14.6, 10.5 and 9.9 percent of world exports, respectively. Brazil, USA and India were the top destinations, with respectively 11.7, 11.0 and 7.8 percent of world imports (see table 3).

The top 15 countries/areas accounted for 75.0 and 60.9 percent of total world exports and imports, respectively (see tables 2 and 3). In 2013, Russian Federation was the country/area with the highest value of net exports (+9.1 bln US$), followed by Canada (+5.2 bln US$). By MDG regions (see graph 2), the largest surpluses in this product group were recorded by Commonwealth of Independent States (+12.1 bln US$), Western Asia (+3.3 bln US$) and Northern Africa (+3.2 bln US$). The largest trade deficits were recorded by Latin America and the Caribbean (-13.3 bln US$), Southern Asia (-8.1 bln US$) and South-eastern Asia (-6.2 bln US$).

Table 1: Imports (Imp.) and exports (Exp.), 1999-2013, in current US$

		1999	2000	2001	2002	2003	2004	2005	2006	2007	2008	2009	2010	2011	2012	2013
Values in Bln US$	Imp.	17.4	17.7	17.4	17.7	21.5	28.0	33.0	33.4	46.0	87.7	44.9	57.6	84.2	81.0	75.9
	Exp.	15.0	12.4	12.3	12.5	15.4	19.2	23.8	24.5	35.8	73.3	39.5	53.2	73.4	72.3	62.5
As a percentage of SITC section (%)	Imp.	3.1	2.9	2.7	2.5	2.6	2.8	2.9	2.6	3.0	5.1	3.0	3.3	4.1	4.0	3.7
	Exp.	2.9	2.2	2.1	1.9	2.0	2.0	2.2	2.0	2.5	4.5	2.8	3.2	3.8	3.8	3.2
As a percentage of world trade (%)	Imp.	0.3	0.3	0.3	0.3	0.3	0.3	0.3	0.3	0.3	0.5	0.4	0.4	0.5	0.4	0.4
	Exp.	0.3	0.2	0.2	0.2	0.2	0.2	0.2	0.2	0.3	0.5	0.3	0.4	0.4	0.4	0.3

Graph 1: Annual growth rates of exports, 1999–2013
(In percentage by year)

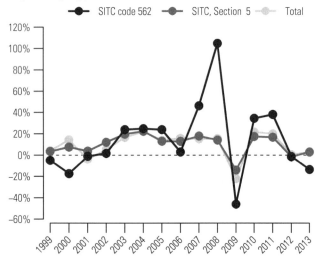

Table 2: Top exporting countries or areas in 2013

Country or area	Value (million US$)	Avg. Growth (%) 09-13	Growth (%) 12-13	World share %	Cum.
World.................................	62 454.2	12.1	-13.7	100.0	
Russian Federation..............	9 118.5	13.5	-18.4	14.6	14.6
Canada................................	6 570.9	12.0	-10.5	10.5	25.1
China..................................	6 213.3	24.9	-13.7	9.9	35.1
USA....................................	4 969.6	4.9	-7.0	8.0	43.0
Belgium..............................	2 878.2	17.7	18.6	4.6	47.6
Germany.............................	2 770.6	6.7	-10.2	4.4	52.1
Netherlands.........................	2 733.3	13.8	-5.0	4.4	56.4
Belarus...............................	2 463.8	11.9	-18.1	3.9	60.4
Morocco.............................	1 924.2	28.8	-20.4	3.1	63.5
Israel..................................	1 729.3	11.6	-3.6	2.8	66.2
Egypt.................................	1 185.6	1.0	-7.7	1.9	68.1
Ukraine...............................	1 166.0	8.3	-34.5	1.9	70.0
Lithuania............................	1 058.0	9.9	-16.7	1.7	71.7
Saudi Arabia.......................	1 035.0	-0.8	-36.0	1.7	73.4
Spain..................................	995.8	16.3	0.2	1.6	75.0

Graph 2: Trade Balance by MDG regions 2013
(Bln US$)

Developed Asia–Pacific
Developed Europe
Developed N. America
South–eastern Europe
CIS
Northern Africa
Sub–Saharan Africa
Latin Am, Caribbean
Eastern Asia
Southern Asia
South–eastern Asia
Western Asia
Oceania

Table 3: Top importing countries or areas in 2013

Country or area	Value (million US$)	Avg. Growth (%) 09-13	Growth (%) 12-13	World share %	Cum.
World.................................	75 886.8	14.0	-6.3	100.0	
Brazil.................................	8 857.3	22.8	3.6	11.7	11.7
USA....................................	8 375.4	17.9	-8.7	11.0	22.7
India..................................	5 944.3	-0.5	-24.4	7.8	30.5
China..................................	3 371.0	14.1	-16.2	4.4	35.0
France................................	2 761.2	14.6	-6.6	3.6	38.6
Thailand..............................	2 483.7	16.9	-8.5	3.3	41.9
Germany.............................	1 769.4	13.4	-2.2	2.3	44.2
Indonesia............................	1 740.2	20.3	-33.4	2.3	46.5
Viet Nam............................	1 692.3	4.6	0.7	2.2	48.7
Belgium..............................	1 674.1	11.7	10.1	2.2	51.0
Bangladesh.........................	*1 615.2*	31.0	-1.6	2.1	53.1
Malaysia.............................	1 555.1	8.1	-9.1	2.0	55.1
Turkey................................	1 484.5	9.0	7.9	2.0	57.1
Australia.............................	1 472.1	18.5	-13.7	1.9	59.0
Mexico...............................	1 403.9	14.4	-14.0	1.9	60.9

In 2013, the value (in current US$) of exports of "polymers of ethylene, in primary forms" (SITC group 571) increased by 2.3 percent (compared to 10.2 percent average growth rate from 2009-2013) to reach 72.6 bln US$ (see table 2), while imports increased by 7.9 percent to reach 79.6 bln US$ (see table 3). Exports of this commodity accounted for 3.7 percent of world exports of SITC section 5, and 0.4 percent of total world merchandise exports (see table 1). Saudi Arabia, USA and Belgium were the top exporters in 2013 (see table 2). They accounted for 12.8, 11.0 and 9.3 percent of world exports, respectively. China, Germany and USA were the top destinations, with respectively 18.7, 5.9 and 5.5 percent of world imports (see table 3).

The top 15 countries/areas accounted for 80.2 and 63.1 percent of total world exports and imports, respectively (see tables 2 and 3). In 2013, Saudi Arabia was the country/area with the highest value of net exports (+8.9 bln US$), followed by Rep. of Korea (+3.8 bln US$). By MDG regions (see graph 2), the largest surpluses in this product group were recorded by Western Asia (+6.8 bln US$), Developed North America (+6.7 bln US$) and South-eastern Asia (+2.4 bln US$). The largest trade deficits were recorded by Eastern Asia (-9.9 bln US$), Latin America and the Caribbean (-5.1 bln US$) and Sub-Saharan Africa (-2.0 bln US$).

Table 1: Imports (Imp.) and exports (Exp.), 1999-2013, in current US$

		1999	2000	2001	2002	2003	2004	2005	2006	2007	2008	2009	2010	2011	2012	2013
Values in Bln US$	Imp.	17.5	20.5	20.1	20.2	24.4	33.2	41.2	47.6	55.9	61.7	48.5	63.0	75.6	73.8	79.6
	Exp.	16.7	19.1	18.8	18.6	22.6	31.1	40.0	46.1	55.2	60.3	49.2	60.3	72.2	71.0	72.6
As a percentage of	Imp.	3.1	3.4	3.2	2.9	2.9	3.3	3.6	3.7	3.7	3.6	3.3	3.6	3.7	3.7	3.9
SITC section (%)	Exp.	3.2	3.4	3.2	2.8	2.9	3.2	3.7	3.8	3.8	3.7	3.5	3.6	3.7	3.7	3.7
As a percentage of	Imp.	0.3	0.3	0.3	0.3	0.3	0.4	0.4	0.4	0.4	0.4	0.4	0.4	0.4	0.4	0.4
world trade (%)	Exp.	0.3	0.3	0.3	0.3	0.3	0.3	0.4	0.4	0.4	0.4	0.4	0.4	0.4	0.4	0.4

Graph 1: Annual growth rates of exports, 1999–2013
(In percentage by year)

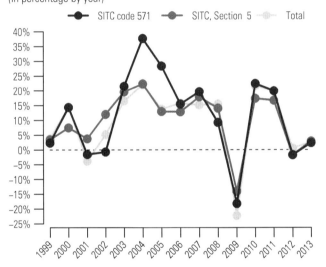

Graph 2: Trade Balance by MDG regions 2013
(Bln US$)

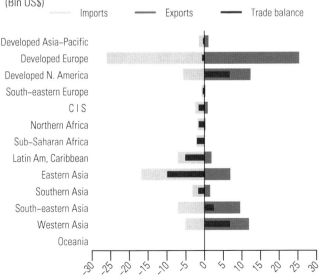

Table 2: Top exporting countries or areas in 2013

Country or area	Value (million US$)	Avg. Growth (%) 09-13	Growth (%) 12-13	World share %	Cum.
World	72 585.9	10.2	2.3	100.0	
Saudi Arabia	9 299.1	28.3	12.6	12.8	12.8
USA	8 007.7	6.0	6.2	11.0	23.8
Belgium	6 770.2	9.4	8.2	9.3	33.2
Singapore	4 776.8	26.4	11.5	6.6	39.8
Canada	4 388.5	11.1	13.9	6.0	45.8
Rep. of Korea	4 267.6	9.6	14.4	5.9	51.7
Germany	4 113.2	9.2	4.9	5.7	57.3
Netherlands	3 701.2	9.5	6.4	5.1	62.4
Thailand	3 686.6	34.1	4.6	5.1	67.5
France	2 585.4	6.9	4.8	3.6	71.1
Kuwait	1 419.2	-10.4	97.7	2.0	73.0
Spain	1 344.2	13.5	13.9	1.9	74.9
Brazil	1 305.1	8.0	-6.4	1.8	76.7
Iran	*1 303.3*	-6.5	-14.1	1.8	78.5
Other Asia, nes	1 213.9	3.6	18.8	1.7	80.2

Table 3: Top importing countries or areas in 2013

Country or area	Value (million US$)	Avg. Growth (%) 09-13	Growth (%) 12-13	World share %	Cum.
World	79 601.8	13.2	7.9	100.0	
China	14 855.5	12.4	16.5	18.7	18.7
Germany	4 706.1	12.5	6.5	5.9	24.6
USA	4 367.1	14.2	10.7	5.5	30.1
Belgium	3 936.2	14.5	17.0	4.9	35.0
Italy	2 898.4	8.9	4.3	3.6	38.6
Turkey	2 557.5	22.0	11.0	3.2	41.9
France	2 482.8	8.4	2.2	3.1	45.0
United Kingdom	2 238.6	6.0	1.6	2.8	47.8
Mexico	2 186.9	13.3	9.6	2.7	50.5
India	2 129.0	13.9	-1.7	2.7	53.2
Singapore	1 850.2	32.3	-15.4	2.3	55.5
Viet Nam	1 674.5	17.8	20.1	2.1	57.6
Spain	1 645.9	10.3	16.3	2.1	59.7
Netherlands	1 356.7	17.3	1.4	1.7	61.4
Brazil	1 346.2	18.3	20.1	1.7	63.1

572 Polymers of styrene, in primary forms

In 2013, the value (in current US$) of exports of "polymers of styrene, in primary forms" (SITC group 572) increased by 3.3 percent (compared to 9.8 percent average growth rate from 2009-2013) to reach 25.5 bln US$ (see table 2), while imports increased by 3.0 percent to reach 26.8 bln US$ (see table 3). Exports of this commodity accounted for 1.3 percent of world exports of SITC section 5, and 0.1 percent of total world merchandise exports (see table 1). Rep. of Korea, Other Asia, nes and Belgium were the top exporters in 2013 (see table 2). They accounted for 16.5, 15.3 and 9.8 percent of world exports, respectively. China, China, Hong Kong SAR and Germany were the top destinations, with respectively 23.9, 6.7 and 6.3 percent of world imports (see table 3).

The top 15 countries/areas accounted for 86.5 and 68.7 percent of total world exports and imports, respectively (see tables 2 and 3). In 2013, Rep. of Korea was the country/area with the highest value of net exports (+4.0 bln US$), followed by Other Asia, nes (+3.8 bln US$). By MDG regions (see graph 2), the largest surpluses in this product group were recorded by Eastern Asia (+2.7 bln US$), Developed Asia-Pacific (+308.4 mln US$) and Developed Europe (+62.8 mln US$). The largest trade deficits were recorded by Western Asia (-1.3 bln US$), Latin America and the Caribbean (-901.6 mln US$) and Commonwealth of Independent States (-608.9 mln US$).

Table 1: Imports (Imp.) and exports (Exp.), 1999-2013, in current US$

		1999	2000	2001	2002	2003	2004	2005	2006	2007	2008	2009	2010	2011	2012	2013
Values in Bln US$	Imp.	9.9	12.3	10.8	11.7	13.3	16.7	18.7	22.8	23.6	24.1	18.5	24.3	27.1	26.0	26.8
	Exp.	9.4	12.1	10.2	11.3	13.0	16.9	19.1	20.9	24.5	24.2	17.6	23.7	25.9	24.7	25.5
As a percentage of SITC section (%)	Imp.	1.8	2.0	1.7	1.7	1.6	1.6	1.6	1.8	1.6	1.4	1.2	1.4	1.3	1.3	1.3
	Exp.	1.8	2.1	1.7	1.7	1.7	1.8	1.8	1.7	1.7	1.5	1.2	1.4	1.3	1.3	1.3
As a percentage of world trade (%)	Imp.	0.2	0.2	0.2	0.2	0.2	0.2	0.2	0.2	0.2	0.1	0.1	0.2	0.1	0.1	0.1
	Exp.	0.2	0.2	0.2	0.2	0.2	0.2	0.2	0.2	0.2	0.2	0.1	0.2	0.1	0.1	0.1

Graph 1: Annual growth rates of exports, 1999–2013
(In percentage by year)

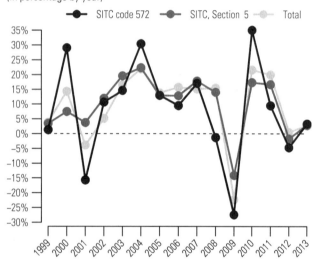

Graph 2: Trade Balance by MDG regions 2013
(Bln US$)

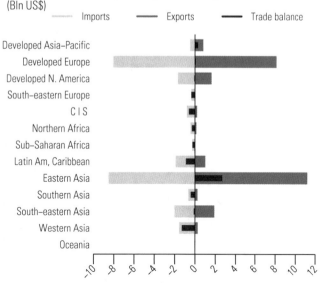

Table 2: Top exporting countries or areas in 2013

Country or area	Value (million US$)	Avg. Growth (%) 09-13	Growth (%) 12-13	World share %	Cum.
World..........................	25 538.1	9.8	3.3	100.0	
Rep. of Korea......................	4 208.6	10.4	4.9	16.5	16.5
Other Asia, nes....................	3 903.2	9.9	1.4	15.3	31.8
Belgium............................	2 495.5	12.4	15.2	9.8	41.5
China, Hong Kong SAR.........	2 315.4	1.5	-7.0	9.1	50.6
USA.................................	1 476.4	9.4	-0.5	5.8	56.4
Netherlands.......................	1 259.9	11.2	5.3	4.9	61.3
France..............................	1 038.1	12.7	16.5	4.1	65.4
Germany...........................	856.4	3.7	-8.9	3.4	68.7
Japan...............................	800.8	1.9	-14.0	3.1	71.9
China...............................	787.7	15.2	8.6	3.1	75.0
Singapore.........................	660.3	9.6	13.5	2.6	77.5
Mexico.............................	626.4	15.4	8.6	2.5	80.0
Thailand...........................	587.0	7.0	8.9	2.3	82.3
Malaysia...........................	556.2	3.5	-21.4	2.2	84.5
Spain...............................	513.0	16.2	11.8	2.0	86.5

Table 3: Top importing countries or areas in 2013

Country or area	Value (million US$)	Avg. Growth (%) 09-13	Growth (%) 12-13	World share %	Cum.
World..........................	26 837.2	9.8	3.0	100.0	
China...............................	6 408.0	4.3	1.4	23.9	23.9
China, Hong Kong SAR.........	1 802.7	-2.1	-10.9	6.7	30.6
Germany...........................	1 691.1	17.1	9.3	6.3	36.9
USA.................................	1 246.1	15.9	2.9	4.6	41.5
Turkey..............................	1 074.8	21.4	6.2	4.0	45.5
Italy................................	1 048.5	7.1	2.5	3.9	49.5
Mexico.............................	904.1	11.7	2.3	3.4	52.8
Poland..............................	701.3	14.3	10.1	2.6	55.4
France..............................	683.8	8.5	-1.7	2.5	58.0
Viet Nam...........................	531.8	19.9	12.9	2.0	60.0
United Kingdom...................	521.0	14.8	26.7	1.9	61.9
Thailand...........................	503.2	16.9	-13.3	1.9	63.8
Canada.............................	448.5	9.1	-1.6	1.7	65.5
Indonesia..........................	447.0	24.8	3.9	1.7	67.1
Russian Federation..............	428.2	17.5	-1.2	1.6	68.7

In 2013, the value (in current US$) of exports of "polymers of vinyl choride or of other halogenated olefins" (SITC group 573) decreased by 0.2 percent (compared to 9.8 percent average growth rate from 2009-2013) to reach 18.9 bln US$ (see table 2), while imports increased by 3.4 percent to reach 20.3 bln US$ (see table 3). Exports of this commodity accounted for 1.0 percent of world exports of SITC section 5, and 0.1 percent of total world merchandise exports (see table 1). USA, Germany and Belgium were the top exporters in 2013 (see table 2). They accounted for 21.8, 11.7 and 6.5 percent of world exports, respectively. China, India and Germany were the top destinations, with respectively 7.9, 7.7 and 6.1 percent of world imports (see table 3).

The top 15 countries/areas accounted for 84.4 and 64.3 percent of total world exports and imports, respectively (see tables 2 and 3). In 2013, USA was the country/area with the highest value of net exports (+3.1 bln US$), followed by Other Asia, nes (+1.0 bln US$). By MDG regions (see graph 2), the largest surpluses in this product group were recorded by Developed North America (+2.7 bln US$), Developed Europe (+1.4 bln US$) and Eastern Asia (+930.3 mln US$). The largest trade deficits were recorded by Southern Asia (-1.8 bln US$), Western Asia (-1.7 bln US$) and Latin America and the Caribbean (-1.3 bln US$).

Table 1: Imports (Imp.) and exports (Exp.), 1999-2013, in current US$

		1999	2000	2001	2002	2003	2004	2005	2006	2007	2008	2009	2010	2011	2012	2013
Values in Bln US$	Imp.	7.7	9.1	8.0	8.2	9.2	11.6	12.6	13.8	16.0	17.6	13.5	17.4	20.8	19.6	20.3
	Exp.	7.3	8.6	7.9	7.9	8.9	11.6	12.3	13.4	16.1	17.2	13.0	17.1	20.2	18.9	18.9
As a percentage of	Imp.	1.4	1.5	1.3	1.2	1.1	1.2	1.1	1.1	1.1	1.0	0.9	1.0	1.0	1.0	1.0
SITC section (%)	Exp.	1.4	1.5	1.3	1.2	1.1	1.2	1.1	1.1	1.1	1.0	0.9	1.0	1.0	1.0	1.0
As a percentage of	Imp.	0.1	0.1	0.1	0.1	0.1	0.1	0.1	0.1	0.1	0.1	0.1	0.1	0.1	0.1	0.1
world trade (%)	Exp.	0.1	0.1	0.1	0.1	0.1	0.1	0.1	0.1	0.1	0.1	0.1	0.1	0.1	0.1	0.1

Graph 1: Annual growth rates of exports, 1999–2013
(In percentage by year)

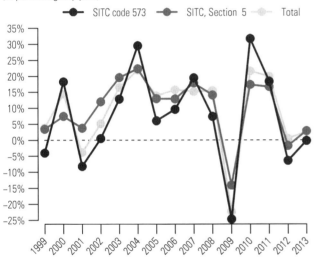

●— SITC code 573   ●— SITC, Section 5   ●— Total

Table 2: Top exporting countries or areas in 2013

Country or area	Value (million US$)	Avg. Growth (%) 09-13	Growth (%) 12-13	World share %	Cum.
World....................	18868.2	9.8	-0.2	100.0	
USA......................	4106.0	12.2	-0.3	21.8	21.8
Germany...............	2204.8	8.5	1.9	11.7	33.4
Belgium................	1218.4	13.7	13.5	6.5	39.9
Other Asia, nes......	1148.6	10.6	9.9	6.1	46.0
China...................	1093.2	30.1	22.9	5.8	51.8
Japan...................	1076.6	2.6	5.3	5.7	57.5
France..................	978.9	5.7	0.2	5.2	62.7
Netherlands..........	884.1	2.0	-22.6	4.7	67.4
Rep. of Korea........	771.2	6.5	-5.1	4.1	71.5
Italy.....................	589.2	13.6	4.7	3.1	74.6
Mexico.................	407.3	25.7	14.0	2.2	76.7
Thailand...............	400.6	2.7	2.7	2.1	78.9
Spain...................	371.4	20.3	8.3	2.0	80.8
Colombia..............	353.9	9.5	2.8	1.9	82.7
United Kingdom.....	324.5	6.1	-8.4	1.7	84.4

Graph 2: Trade Balance by MDG regions 2013
(Bln US$)

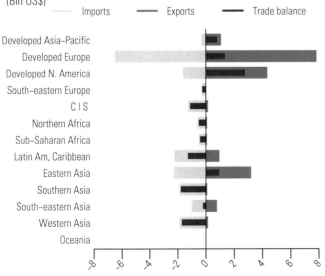

····· Imports   — Exports   — Trade balance

Developed Asia–Pacific
Developed Europe
Developed N. America
South–eastern Europe
CIS
Northern Africa
Sub–Saharan Africa
Latin Am, Caribbean
Eastern Asia
Southern Asia
South–eastern Asia
Western Asia
Oceania

Table 3: Top importing countries or areas in 2013

Country or area	Value (million US$)	Avg. Growth (%) 09-13	Growth (%) 12-13	World share %	Cum.
World....................	20292.9	10.8	3.4	100.0	
China...................	1595.2	-4.2	-9.6	7.9	7.9
India....................	1558.3	24.3	13.5	7.7	15.5
Germany...............	1245.5	9.5	-0.1	6.1	21.7
Turkey..................	1116.5	16.6	21.6	5.5	27.2
Italy.....................	1054.4	7.8	2.3	5.2	32.4
USA......................	992.6	18.1	-2.4	4.9	37.3
Belgium................	882.4	13.6	13.9	4.3	41.6
Russian Federation...	713.9	19.6	-6.9	3.5	45.1
Brazil...................	683.7	19.4	13.7	3.4	48.5
Mexico.................	639.1	14.7	5.0	3.1	51.7
Canada.................	618.7	7.1	-4.5	3.0	54.7
France..................	565.3	5.0	0.9	2.8	57.5
United Kingdom.....	536.7	11.8	15.3	2.6	60.1
Netherlands..........	437.0	13.3	8.1	2.2	62.3
Poland..................	401.3	5.1	7.0	2.0	64.3

574 Polyacetals, epoxide resins, etc, and other polyethers in primary forms

In 2013, the value (in current US$) of exports of "polyacetals, epoxide resins, etc, and other polyethers in primary forms" (SITC group 574) increased by 3.8 percent (compared to 10.7 percent average growth rate from 2009-2013) to reach 55.8 bln US$ (see table 2), while imports increased by 3.4 percent to reach 57.9 bln US$ (see table 3). Exports of this commodity accounted for 2.9 percent of world exports of SITC section 5, and 0.3 percent of total world merchandise exports (see table 1). USA, Rep. of Korea and China were the top exporters in 2013 (see table 2). They accounted for 10.2, 9.1 and 9.0 percent of world exports, respectively. China, Germany and USA were the top destinations, with respectively 14.5, 6.8 and 4.6 percent of world imports (see table 3).

The top 15 countries/areas accounted for 82.2 and 59.3 percent of total world exports and imports, respectively (see tables 2 and 3). In 2013, Rep. of Korea was the country/area with the highest value of net exports (+4.1 bln US$), followed by Netherlands (+3.4 bln US$). By MDG regions (see graph 2), the largest surpluses in this product group were recorded by Eastern Asia (+3.9 bln US$), Developed North America (+2.7 bln US$) and Developed Europe (+1.3 bln US$). The largest trade deficits were recorded by Latin America and the Caribbean (-3.7 bln US$), Commonwealth of Independent States (-1.6 bln US$) and Western Asia (-1.3 bln US$).

Table 1: Imports (Imp.) and exports (Exp.), 1999-2013, in current US$

		1999	2000	2001	2002	2003	2004	2005	2006	2007	2008	2009	2010	2011	2012	2013
Values in Bln US$	Imp.	17.6	20.1	19.2	20.2	24.4	30.3	36.9	41.2	47.5	49.2	37.3	49.2	57.8	56.0	57.9
	Exp.	16.2	18.7	18.2	19.4	23.4	29.2	35.4	39.6	45.6	46.7	37.1	47.9	56.3	53.7	55.8
As a percentage of SITC section (%)	Imp.	3.1	3.3	3.0	2.9	2.9	3.0	3.2	3.2	3.1	2.9	2.5	2.8	2.8	2.8	2.8
	Exp.	3.1	3.3	3.1	2.9	3.0	3.0	3.3	3.2	3.2	2.8	2.6	2.9	2.9	2.8	2.9
As a percentage of world trade (%)	Imp.	0.3	0.3	0.3	0.3	0.3	0.3	0.3	0.3	0.3	0.3	0.3	0.3	0.3	0.3	0.3
	Exp.	0.3	0.3	0.3	0.3	0.3	0.3	0.3	0.3	0.3	0.3	0.3	0.3	0.3	0.3	0.3

Graph 1: Annual growth rates of exports, 1999–2013
(In percentage by year)

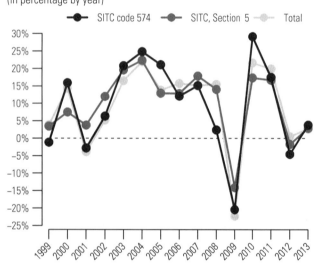

Legend: SITC code 574, SITC, Section 5, Total

Table 2: Top exporting countries or areas in 2013

Country or area	Value (million US$)	Avg. Growth (%) 09-13	Growth (%) 12-13	World share %	Cum.
World	55 777.0	10.7	3.8	100.0	
USA	5 695.7	10.3	-0.4	10.2	10.2
Rep. of Korea	5 074.8	12.1	7.9	9.1	19.3
China	5 028.5	26.8	22.9	9.0	28.3
Netherlands	4 659.4	10.0	2.6	8.4	36.7
Germany	4 421.8	2.6	2.6	7.9	44.6
Other Asia, nes	4 191.2	14.4	1.6	7.5	52.1
Belgium	2 868.9	11.8	19.9	5.1	57.3
Japan	2 426.3	5.5	-7.7	4.3	61.6
Italy	2 029.4	9.0	3.1	3.6	65.3
Spain	1 954.8	10.2	-1.7	3.5	68.8
Thailand	1 943.6	5.9	-0.8	3.5	72.2
Singapore	1 895.9	12.6	-5.9	3.4	75.6
China, Hong Kong SAR	1 809.6	6.0	0.2	3.2	78.9
France	1 008.6	8.2	6.0	1.8	80.7
India	863.4	25.2	67.2	1.5	82.2

Graph 2: Trade Balance by MDG regions 2013
(Bln US$)

Legend: Imports, Exports, Trade balance

Developed Asia–Pacific
Developed Europe
Developed N. America
South–eastern Europe
CIS
Northern Africa
Sub–Saharan Africa
Latin Am, Caribbean
Eastern Asia
Southern Asia
South–eastern Asia
Western Asia
Oceania

(axis: -20, -15, -10, -5, 0, 5, 10, 15, 20, 25)

Table 3: Top importing countries or areas in 2013

Country or area	Value (million US$)	Avg. Growth (%) 09-13	Growth (%) 12-13	World share %	Cum.
World	57 873.3	11.6	3.4	100.0	
China	8 380.9	8.1	0.2	14.5	14.5
Germany	3 953.5	12.3	4.5	6.8	21.3
USA	2 642.8	12.2	2.7	4.6	25.9
Japan	2 257.2	14.1	1.3	3.9	29.8
Italy	2 201.7	6.7	7.3	3.8	33.6
France	2 110.3	7.3	5.1	3.6	37.2
Belgium	1 892.9	9.2	12.6	3.3	40.5
China, Hong Kong SAR	1 842.1	3.3	-5.6	3.2	43.7
Mexico	1 583.2	13.6	3.2	2.7	46.4
Turkey	1 438.0	20.0	12.4	2.5	48.9
United Kingdom	1 308.8	11.4	13.8	2.3	51.2
Netherlands	1 284.9	13.0	1.4	2.2	53.4
India	1 244.6	24.6	7.9	2.2	55.5
Viet Nam	1 119.6	25.5	16.5	1.9	57.5
Brazil	1 074.1	14.4	11.8	1.9	59.3

Source: UN Comtrade and UN Service Trade   2013 International Trade Statistics Yearbook, Vol. II

In 2013, the value (in current US$) of exports of "other plastics, in primary forms" (SITC group 575) increased by 5.9 percent (compared to 12.3 percent average growth rate from 2009-2013) to reach 114.7 bln US$ (see table 2), while imports increased by 4.6 percent to reach 120.0 bln US$ (see table 3). Exports of this commodity accounted for 5.9 percent of world exports of SITC section 5, and 0.6 percent of total world merchandise exports (see table 1). USA, Germany and Belgium were the top exporters in 2013 (see table 2). They accounted for 13.3, 10.3 and 10.2 percent of world exports, respectively. China, Germany and Italy were the top destinations, with respectively 14.9, 7.2 and 4.8 percent of world imports (see table 3).

The top 15 countries/areas accounted for 81.9 and 62.5 percent of total world exports and imports, respectively (see tables 2 and 3). In 2013, USA was the country/area with the highest value of net exports (+10.2 bln US$), followed by Belgium (+6.5 bln US$). By MDG regions (see graph 2), the largest surpluses in this product group were recorded by Developed North America (+8.2 bln US$), Developed Europe (+5.3 bln US$) and Developed Asia-Pacific (+2.7 bln US$). The largest trade deficits were recorded by Latin America and the Caribbean (-6.8 bln US$), Eastern Asia (-4.8 bln US$) and Commonwealth of Independent States (-2.4 bln US$).

Table 1: Imports (Imp.) and exports (Exp.), 1999-2013, in current US$

		1999	2000	2001	2002	2003	2004	2005	2006	2007	2008	2009	2010	2011	2012	2013
Values in Bln US$	Imp.	32.2	34.6	34.3	37.5	44.7	55.5	64.7	73.8	86.7	94.1	75.5	99.1	117.4	114.7	120.0
	Exp.	30.4	33.2	32.5	36.5	44.2	55.2	64.9	74.6	87.5	94.2	72.1	94.4	110.8	108.3	114.7
As a percentage of	Imp.	5.7	5.7	5.4	5.3	5.4	5.5	5.6	5.7	5.7	5.5	5.1	5.7	5.7	5.7	5.8
SITC section (%)	Exp.	5.8	5.9	5.5	5.6	5.6	5.7	6.0	6.1	6.1	5.7	5.1	5.7	5.7	5.7	5.9
As a percentage of	Imp.	0.6	0.5	0.5	0.6	0.6	0.6	0.6	0.6	0.6	0.6	0.6	0.6	0.6	0.6	0.6
world trade (%)	Exp.	0.5	0.5	0.5	0.6	0.6	0.6	0.6	0.6	0.6	0.6	0.6	0.6	0.6	0.6	0.6

Graph 1: Annual growth rates of exports, 1999–2013
(In percentage by year)

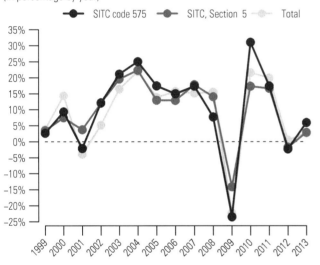

Table 2: Top exporting countries or areas in 2013

Country or area	Value (million US$)	Avg. Growth (%) 09-13	Growth (%) 12-13	World share %	Cum.
World..................	114693.9	12.3	5.9	100.0	
USA....................	15248.9	10.2	3.9	13.3	13.3
Germany.............	11869.7	6.1	5.9	10.3	23.6
Belgium..............	11672.4	11.6	14.2	10.2	33.8
Rep. of Korea......	8015.4	17.7	10.6	7.0	40.8
Netherlands.........	6372.0	13.0	6.9	5.6	46.4
Japan.................	5857.7	6.1	-6.1	5.1	51.5
Saudi Arabia........	5807.0	34.2	10.1	5.1	56.5
France................	5115.5	9.0	4.5	4.5	61.0
China.................	4950.3	26.7	8.6	4.3	65.3
Singapore............	4657.1	19.0	1.0	4.1	69.4
Other Asia, nes.....	4235.6	11.8	11.9	3.7	73.1
Italy...................	3105.6	8.5	2.2	2.7	75.8
United Kingdom.....	2467.7	1.3	-6.6	2.2	77.9
Spain.................	2413.0	13.0	11.4	2.1	80.0
China, Hong Kong SAR........	2155.5	2.5	-7.4	1.9	81.9

Graph 2: Trade Balance by MDG regions 2013
(Bln US$)

Imports — Exports — Trade balance

Developed Asia–Pacific
Developed Europe
Developed N. America
South–eastern Europe
C I S
Northern Africa
Sub-Saharan Africa
Latin Am, Caribbean
Eastern Asia
Southern Asia
South–eastern Asia
Western Asia
Oceania

-50 -40 -30 -20 -10 0 10 20 30 40 50 60

Table 3: Top importing countries or areas in 2013

Country or area	Value (million US$)	Avg. Growth (%) 09-13	Growth (%) 12-13	World share %	Cum.
World..................	120023.1	12.3	4.6	100.0	
China.................	17856.3	10.4	5.1	14.9	14.9
Germany.............	8646.5	11.9	4.4	7.2	22.1
Italy...................	5729.9	10.2	4.3	4.8	26.9
Belgium..............	5188.0	11.0	9.9	4.3	31.2
USA....................	5049.0	14.8	4.6	4.2	35.4
Turkey................	4761.1	19.3	8.6	4.0	39.4
France................	4682.0	4.4	2.1	3.9	43.3
Mexico...............	3503.3	14.4	4.0	2.9	46.2
United Kingdom.....	3237.7	9.6	5.1	2.7	48.9
Netherlands.........	3222.8	13.9	7.7	2.7	51.6
Canada...............	2960.6	12.3	3.6	2.5	54.0
Indonesia............	2642.6	22.1	7.9	2.2	56.2
Japan.................	2586.0	12.9	-10.6	2.2	58.4
Rep. of Korea......	2506.5	15.3	5.5	2.1	60.5
Poland................	2478.3	14.6	12.9	2.1	62.5

579 Waste, parings and scrap, of plastics

In 2013, the value (in current US$) of exports of "waste, parings and scrap, of plastics" (SITC group 579) decreased by 6.1 percent (compared to 6.8 percent average growth rate from 2009-2013) to reach 6.7 bln US$ (see table 2), while imports decreased by 3.2 percent to reach 9.5 bln US$ (see table 3). Exports of this commodity accounted for 0.3 percent of world exports of SITC section 5, and less than 0.1 percent of total world merchandise exports (see table 1). USA, Japan and China, Hong Kong SAR were the top exporters in 2013 (see table 2). They accounted for 13.0, 12.1 and 11.4 percent of world exports, respectively. China, China, Hong Kong SAR and USA were the top destinations, with respectively 63.4, 11.1 and 2.7 percent of world imports (see table 3).

The top 15 countries/areas accounted for 79.2 and 91.9 percent of total world exports and imports, respectively (see tables 2 and 3). In 2013, Japan was the country/area with the highest value of net exports (+807.8 mln US$), followed by USA (+607.4 mln US$). By MDG regions (see graph 2), the largest surpluses in this product group were recorded by Developed Europe (+1.1 bln US$), Developed Asia-Pacific (+862.9 mln US$) and Developed North America (+636.8 mln US$). The largest trade deficits were recorded by Eastern Asia (-6.3 bln US$), Southern Asia (-83.0 mln US$) and Sub-Saharan Africa (-1.7 mln US$).

Table 1: Imports (Imp.) and exports (Exp.), 1999-2013, in current US$

		1999	2000	2001	2002	2003	2004	2005	2006	2007	2008	2009	2010	2011	2012	2013
Values in Bln US$	Imp.	1.2	1.6	1.6	1.6	2.0	3.1	4.4	5.6	6.4	7.9	6.4	8.4	10.0	9.9	9.5
	Exp.	1.1	1.4	1.4	1.5	1.9	2.6	3.6	4.4	5.3	5.7	5.2	6.2	7.2	7.2	6.7
As a percentage of SITC section (%)	Imp.	0.2	0.3	0.3	0.2	0.2	0.3	0.4	0.4	0.4	0.5	0.4	0.5	0.5	0.5	0.5
	Exp.	0.2	0.2	0.2	0.2	0.2	0.3	0.3	0.4	0.4	0.3	0.4	0.4	0.4	0.4	0.3
As a percentage of world trade (%)	Imp.	0.0	0.0	0.0	0.0	0.0	0.0	0.0	0.0	0.0	0.0	0.1	0.1	0.1	0.1	0.1
	Exp.	0.0	0.0	0.0	0.0	0.0	0.0	0.0	0.0	0.0	0.0	0.0	0.0	0.0	0.0	0.0

Graph 1: Annual growth rates of exports, 1999–2013
(In percentage by year)

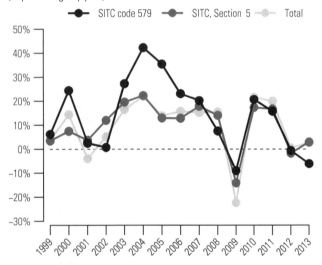

Graph 2: Trade Balance by MDG regions 2013
(Bln US$)

Table 2: Top exporting countries or areas in 2013

Country or area	Value (million US$)	Avg. Growth (%) 09-13	Growth (%) 12-13	World share %	Cum.
World....................	6715.5	6.8	-6.1	100.0	
USA......................	869.7	1.2	-8.2	13.0	13.0
Japan....................	810.7	6.3	-12.4	12.1	25.0
China, Hong Kong SAR.........	763.7	-9.4	-27.3	11.4	36.4
Germany.................	676.0	8.8	-1.5	10.1	46.5
Mexico..................	285.8	11.1	-3.6	4.3	50.7
France..................	273.2	11.6	-5.2	4.1	54.8
Netherlands.............	271.6	17.1	14.1	4.0	58.8
Thailand................	260.8	34.6	22.6	3.9	62.7
Belgium.................	234.8	9.1	14.1	3.5	66.2
United Kingdom..........	223.5	1.6	-25.0	3.3	69.5
Indonesia...............	173.3	59.7	11.6	2.6	72.1
Malaysia................	147.4	24.7	12.9	2.2	74.3
Viet Nam................	126.1	81.8	33.7	1.9	76.2
Canada..................	106.2	2.4	-10.2	1.6	77.8
Spain...................	98.3	11.0	-2.5	1.5	79.2

Table 3: Top importing countries or areas in 2013

Country or area	Value (million US$)	Avg. Growth (%) 09-13	Growth (%) 12-13	World share %	Cum.
World....................	9544.6	10.4	-3.2	100.0	
China...................	6048.9	14.3	-5.5	63.4	63.4
China, Hong Kong SAR.........	1057.7	-8.9	-17.7	11.1	74.5
USA.....................	262.3	6.2	17.3	2.7	77.2
Netherlands.............	248.8	28.3	19.6	2.6	79.8
Germany.................	175.4	23.2	-4.6	1.8	81.6
India...................	158.8	17.1	37.4	1.7	83.3
Belgium.................	151.3	3.7	-0.7	1.6	84.9
Malaysia................	99.9	39.9	52.4	1.0	85.9
Italy...................	98.6	14.9	-5.8	1.0	87.0
Ireland.................	89.8	9.9	-0.6	0.9	87.9
Indonesia...............	81.5	187.9	22.3	0.9	88.8
Other Asia, nes.........	81.4	17.4	8.7	0.9	89.6
Canada..................	76.8	4.7	-20.0	0.8	90.4
United Kingdom..........	73.1	24.5	25.5	0.8	91.2
Austria.................	68.8	29.8	-3.8	0.7	91.9

In 2013, the value (in current US$) of exports of "tubes, pipes and hoses, and fittings therefore of plastics" (SITC group 581) increased by 6.8 percent (compared to 9.8 percent average growth rate from 2009-2013) to reach 23.1 bln US$ (see table 2), while imports increased by 7.5 percent to reach 22.9 bln US$ (see table 3). Exports of this commodity accounted for 1.2 percent of world exports of SITC section 5, and 0.1 percent of total world merchandise exports (see table 1). Germany, USA and China were the top exporters in 2013 (see table 2). They accounted for 17.1, 11.1 and 9.4 percent of world exports, respectively. USA, Germany and Mexico were the top destinations, with respectively 8.3, 7.0 and 5.7 percent of world imports (see table 3).

The top 15 countries/areas accounted for 75.1 and 54.6 percent of total world exports and imports, respectively (see tables 2 and 3). In 2013, Germany was the country/area with the highest value of net exports (+2.4 bln US$), followed by China (+1.3 bln US$). By MDG regions (see graph 2), the largest surpluses in this product group were recorded by Developed Europe (+3.0 bln US$), Eastern Asia (+1.3 bln US$) and Developed North America (+399.6 mln US$). The largest trade deficits were recorded by Latin America and the Caribbean (-1.6 bln US$), Commonwealth of Independent States (-1.1 bln US$) and Sub-Saharan Africa (-706.6 mln US$).

Table 1: Imports (Imp.) and exports (Exp.), 1999-2013, in current US$

		1999	2000	2001	2002	2003	2004	2005	2006	2007	2008	2009	2010	2011	2012	2013
Values in Bln US$	Imp.	6.5	6.8	6.8	7.5	8.9	10.8	11.9	14.0	16.7	18.8	15.6	17.4	20.7	21.3	22.9
	Exp.	6.2	6.7	6.6	7.1	8.5	10.4	11.9	14.0	17.3	19.2	15.9	18.0	21.5	21.6	23.1
As a percentage of	Imp.	1.1	1.1	1.1	1.1	1.1	1.1	1.0	1.1	1.1	1.1	1.1	1.0	1.0	1.1	1.1
SITC section (%)	Exp.	1.2	1.2	1.1	1.1	1.1	1.1	1.1	1.1	1.2	1.2	1.1	1.1	1.1	1.1	1.2
As a percentage of	Imp.	0.1	0.1	0.1	0.1	0.1	0.1	0.1	0.1	0.1	0.1	0.1	0.1	0.1	0.1	0.1
world trade (%)	Exp.	0.1	0.1	0.1	0.1	0.1	0.1	0.1	0.1	0.1	0.1	0.1	0.1	0.1	0.1	0.1

Graph 1: Annual growth rates of exports, 1999–2013
(In percentage by year)

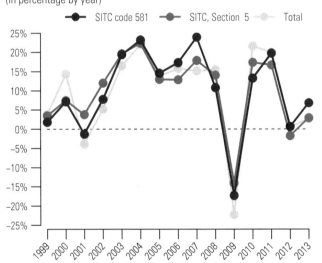

Table 2: Top exporting countries or areas in 2013

Country or area	Value (million US$)	Avg. Growth (%) 09-13	Growth (%) 12-13	World share %	Cum.
World	23 105.7	9.8	6.8	100.0	
Germany	3 955.2	8.1	4.7	17.1	17.1
USA	2 573.0	9.9	6.4	11.1	28.3
China	2 163.4	25.6	14.8	9.4	37.6
Italy	1 378.6	5.9	5.4	6.0	43.6
Turkey	899.0	11.5	6.7	3.9	47.5
Czech Rep.	884.6	8.5	8.6	3.8	51.3
Poland	769.1	13.5	12.1	3.3	54.6
United Kingdom	761.2	3.3	-0.6	3.3	57.9
Netherlands	628.8	8.7	6.9	2.7	60.6
Switzerland	604.7	6.2	5.7	2.6	63.3
Spain	597.1	5.6	9.9	2.6	65.8
France	593.4	7.1	9.7	2.6	68.4
Japan	567.5	7.8	-12.8	2.5	70.9
Austria	510.7	7.5	15.8	2.2	73.1
Mexico	466.2	12.0	9.3	2.0	75.1

Graph 2: Trade Balance by MDG regions 2013
(Bln US$)

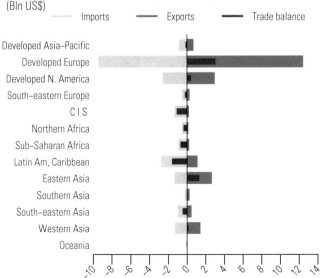

Table 3: Top importing countries or areas in 2013

Country or area	Value (million US$)	Avg. Growth (%) 09-13	Growth (%) 12-13	World share %	Cum.
World	22 865.2	10.0	7.5	100.0	
USA	1 895.1	19.0	21.7	8.3	8.3
Germany	1 602.1	7.0	6.4	7.0	15.3
Mexico	1 298.2	10.8	6.8	5.7	21.0
France	1 107.6	7.6	2.6	4.8	25.8
China	856.7	15.3	15.9	3.7	29.6
Russian Federation	700.8	14.4	-22.6	3.1	32.6
Canada	676.5	10.7	-5.7	3.0	35.6
Czech Rep.	663.0	10.5	7.6	2.9	38.5
United Kingdom	584.2	6.2	15.7	2.6	41.0
Belgium	582.1	7.2	17.2	2.5	43.6
Poland	574.2	9.4	12.4	2.5	46.1
Italy	527.1	2.5	1.3	2.3	48.4
Netherlands	492.0	8.1	6.4	2.2	50.6
Switzerland	487.5	8.0	3.7	2.1	52.7
Austria	448.5	8.0	10.8	2.0	54.6

582 Plates, sheets, film, foil and strip, of plastics

In 2013, the value (in current US$) of exports of "plates, sheets, film, foil and strip, of plastics" (SITC group 582) increased by 4.6 percent (compared to 10.2 percent average growth rate from 2009-2013) to reach 102.1 bln US$ (see table 2), while imports increased by 5.0 percent to reach 101.5 bln US$ (see table 3). Exports of this commodity accounted for 5.2 percent of world exports of SITC section 5, and 0.5 percent of total world merchandise exports (see table 1). Germany, Japan and USA were the top exporters in 2013 (see table 2). They accounted for 12.3, 10.2 and 9.5 percent of world exports, respectively. China, USA and Germany were the top destinations, with respectively 11.6, 7.0 and 6.4 percent of world imports (see table 3).

The top 15 countries/areas accounted for 76.2 and 62.7 percent of total world exports and imports, respectively (see tables 2 and 3). In 2013, Japan was the country/area with the highest value of net exports (+8.2 bln US$), followed by Germany (+6.0 bln US$). By MDG regions (see graph 2), the largest surpluses in this product group were recorded by Developed Asia-Pacific (+7.0 bln US$), Developed Europe (+5.5 bln US$) and Developed North America (+2.0 bln US$). The largest trade deficits were recorded by Latin America and the Caribbean (-5.5 bln US$), Commonwealth of Independent States (-3.0 bln US$) and Sub-Saharan Africa (-2.0 bln US$).

Table 1: Imports (Imp.) and exports (Exp.), 1999-2013, in current US$

		1999	2000	2001	2002	2003	2004	2005	2006	2007	2008	2009	2010	2011	2012	2013
Values in Bln US$	Imp.	31.5	33.2	32.3	35.6	42.0	50.5	57.3	64.4	73.8	80.3	68.7	86.0	99.4	96.7	101.5
	Exp.	31.0	33.3	32.4	35.5	42.0	50.8	57.5	65.8	76.2	82.8	69.1	85.6	99.6	97.6	102.1
As a percentage of SITC section (%)	Imp.	5.6	5.4	5.1	5.1	5.0	5.0	5.0	5.0	4.9	4.7	4.6	4.9	4.9	4.8	4.9
	Exp.	5.9	5.9	5.5	5.4	5.3	5.3	5.3	5.4	5.3	5.0	4.9	5.2	5.2	5.1	5.2
As a percentage of world trade (%)	Imp.	0.6	0.5	0.5	0.5	0.5	0.5	0.5	0.5	0.5	0.5	0.5	0.6	0.5	0.5	0.5
	Exp.	0.6	0.5	0.5	0.6	0.6	0.6	0.6	0.5	0.6	0.5	0.6	0.6	0.6	0.5	0.5

Graph 1: Annual growth rates of exports, 1999–2013
(In percentage by year)

— SITC code 582   — SITC, Section 5   — Total

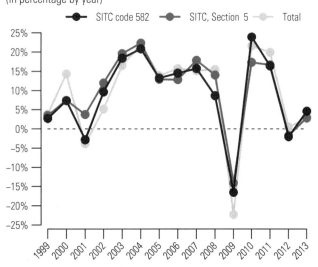

Table 2: Top exporting countries or areas in 2013

Country or area	Value (million US$)	Avg. Growth (%) 09-13	Growth (%) 12-13	World share %	Cum.
World...............................	102 065.1	10.2	4.6	100.0	
Germany...........................	12 530.8	7.0	5.4	12.3	12.3
Japan..............................	10 428.5	3.6	-12.7	10.2	22.5
USA................................	9 743.5	9.0	3.7	9.5	32.0
China..............................	8 754.1	27.1	12.3	8.6	40.6
Rep. of Korea.....................	5 659.5	20.2	16.1	5.5	46.2
Italy.............................	5 639.4	4.5	5.4	5.5	51.7
Belgium...........................	3 801.6	5.2	9.4	3.7	55.4
Other Asia, nes...................	3 598.8	9.7	-1.0	3.5	58.9
China, Hong Kong SAR..............	3 424.4	29.1	29.0	3.4	62.3
Netherlands.......................	2 909.5	8.9	8.7	2.9	65.1
France............................	2 888.6	5.1	7.1	2.8	68.0
United Kingdom....................	2 743.1	7.2	9.4	2.7	70.7
Canada............................	2 052.6	5.6	-1.7	2.0	72.7
Spain.............................	1 823.1	7.9	7.3	1.8	74.5
Austria...........................	1 794.6	3.4	2.6	1.8	76.2

Graph 2: Trade Balance by MDG regions 2013
(Bln US$)

— Imports   — Exports   — Trade balance

Developed Asia–Pacific
Developed Europe
Developed N. America
South–eastern Europe
CIS
Northern Africa
Sub–Saharan Africa
Latin Am, Caribbean
Eastern Asia
Southern Asia
South–eastern Asia
Western Asia
Oceania

-40 -30 -20 -10 0 10 20 30 40 50

Table 3: Top importing countries or areas in 2013

Country or area	Value (million US$)	Avg. Growth (%) 09-13	Growth (%) 12-13	World share %	Cum.
World...............................	101 481.1	10.2	5.0	100.0	
China..............................	11 752.2	15.9	2.4	11.6	11.6
USA................................	7 130.2	11.7	2.7	7.0	18.6
Germany...........................	6 523.8	9.2	7.6	6.4	25.0
France............................	4 656.0	4.8	3.2	4.6	29.6
Mexico............................	4 139.4	15.2	4.3	4.1	33.7
Rep. of Korea.....................	4 064.2	4.8	-11.5	4.0	37.7
United Kingdom....................	3 857.2	7.0	10.6	3.8	41.5
Other Asia, nes...................	3 115.3	6.1	-8.7	3.1	44.6
China, Hong Kong SAR..............	3 065.1	16.8	4.3	3.0	47.6
Belgium...........................	2 823.7	7.2	12.5	2.8	50.4
Italy.............................	2 791.1	6.4	3.6	2.8	53.1
Canada............................	2 633.4	8.6	4.1	2.6	55.7
Netherlands.......................	2 440.8	10.8	12.4	2.4	58.1
Poland............................	2 374.4	9.5	11.9	2.3	60.5
Russian Federation...............	2 268.4	15.5	1.6	2.2	62.7

Monofilament of any cross-sectional dimension exceed 1 mm, of plastics 583

In 2013, the value (in current US$) of exports of "monofilament of any cross-sectional dimension exceed 1 mm, of plastics" (SITC group 583) increased by 5.5 percent (compared to 5.4 percent average growth rate from 2009-2013) to reach 5.4 bln US$ (see table 2), while imports increased by 6.9 percent to reach 4.9 bln US$ (see table 3). Exports of this commodity accounted for 0.3 percent of world exports of SITC section 5, and less than 0.1 percent of total world merchandise exports (see table 1). Germany, Turkey and China were the top exporters in 2013 (see table 2). They accounted for 34.3, 7.6 and 7.1 percent of world exports, respectively. Germany, France and USA were the top destinations, with respectively 7.5, 7.1 and 5.9 percent of world imports (see table 3).

The top 15 countries/areas accounted for 85.6 and 58.5 percent of total world exports and imports, respectively (see tables 2 and 3). In 2013, Germany was the country/area with the highest value of net exports (+1.5 bln US$), followed by Turkey (+344.3 mln US$). By MDG regions (see graph 2), the largest surpluses in this product group were recorded by Developed Europe (+1.0 bln US$), Eastern Asia (+306.4 mln US$) and Western Asia (+266.0 mln US$). The largest trade deficits were recorded by Commonwealth of Independent States (-427.5 mln US$), South-eastern Europe (-204.1 mln US$) and Latin America and the Caribbean (-189.8 mln US$).

Table 1: Imports (Imp.) and exports (Exp.), 1999-2013, in current US$

		1999	2000	2001	2002	2003	2004	2005	2006	2007	2008	2009	2010	2011	2012	2013
Values in Bln US$	Imp.	1.9	1.9	2.0	2.2	2.7	3.2	3.5	4.2	4.7	5.3	3.9	4.2	4.8	4.5	4.9
	Exp.	1.8	1.9	1.9	2.2	2.7	3.3	3.7	4.3	4.9	5.2	4.3	4.7	5.6	5.1	5.4
As a percentage of SITC section (%)	Imp.	0.3	0.3	0.3	0.3	0.3	0.3	0.3	0.3	0.3	0.3	0.3	0.2	0.2	0.2	0.2
	Exp.	0.3	0.3	0.3	0.3	0.3	0.3	0.3	0.3	0.3	0.3	0.3	0.3	0.3	0.3	0.3
As a percentage of world trade (%)	Imp.	0.0	0.0	0.0	0.0	0.0	0.0	0.0	0.0	0.0	0.0	0.0	0.0	0.0	0.0	0.0
	Exp.	0.0	0.0	0.0	0.0	0.0	0.0	0.0	0.0	0.0	0.0	0.0	0.0	0.0	0.0	0.0

Graph 1: Annual growth rates of exports, 1999–2013
(In percentage by year)

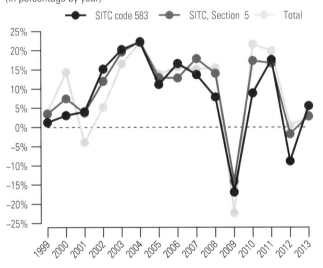

● SITC code 583　　● SITC, Section 5　　○ Total

Table 2: Top exporting countries or areas in 2013

Country or area	Value (million US$)	Avg. Growth (%) 09-13	Growth (%) 12-13	World share %	Cum.
World	5 350.9	5.4	5.5	100.0	
Germany	1 837.2	0.7	2.5	34.3	34.3
Turkey	405.2	16.9	14.2	7.6	41.9
China	377.9	26.3	16.6	7.1	49.0
Belgium	337.0	1.4	7.2	6.3	55.3
USA	277.9	11.7	1.8	5.2	60.5
Poland	234.0	0.5	3.0	4.4	64.8
Italy	191.1	7.1	6.5	3.6	68.4
Canada	182.5	5.0	2.2	3.4	71.8
United Kingdom	172.1	7.9	8.5	3.2	75.0
Austria	160.9	1.5	-0.2	3.0	78.0
Netherlands	101.8	9.1	23.4	1.9	79.9
France	91.8	-5.0	-7.1	1.7	81.7
Russian Federation	73.7	30.3	22.0	1.4	83.0
Denmark	69.9	7.5	2.8	1.3	84.3
Bulgaria	65.9	10.6	-2.5	1.2	85.6

Graph 2: Trade Balance by MDG regions 2013
(Bln US$)

Imports ── Exports ── Trade balance

Developed Asia–Pacific
Developed Europe
Developed N. America
South–eastern Europe
CIS
Northern Africa
Sub–Saharan Africa
Latin Am, Caribbean
Eastern Asia
Southern Asia
South–eastern Asia
Western Asia
Oceania

-3 -2.5 -2 -1.5 -1 -0.5 0 0.5 1 1.5 2 2.5 3 3.5 4

Table 3: Top importing countries or areas in 2013

Country or area	Value (million US$)	Avg. Growth (%) 09-13	Growth (%) 12-13	World share %	Cum.
World	4 862.9	5.9	6.9	100.0	
Germany	362.7	8.6	2.0	7.5	7.5
France	345.9	0.3	1.0	7.1	14.6
USA	289.2	7.7	2.5	5.9	20.5
Poland	217.6	2.2	5.2	4.5	25.0
Czech Rep.	194.2	-3.4	-0.4	4.0	29.0
Italy	183.4	10.9	19.4	3.8	32.8
United Kingdom	153.2	1.6	15.0	3.2	35.9
Austria	147.7	2.7	5.3	3.0	38.9
Romania	147.1	0.0	5.7	3.0	42.0
Russian Federation	145.8	2.6	-6.3	3.0	45.0
Belgium	143.6	-1.8	12.9	3.0	47.9
Canada	139.7	10.0	3.7	2.9	50.8
Ukraine	128.8	-2.0	-2.9	2.6	53.4
Netherlands	122.9	8.0	15.3	2.5	56.0
Switzerland	120.4	3.1	1.5	2.5	58.5

591 Pesticides, disinfectant, put up in preparation, articles or packings for retail

In 2013, the value (in current US$) of exports of "pesticides, disinfectant, put up in preparation, articles or packings for retail" (SITC group 591) increased by 14.5 percent (compared to 13.1 percent average growth rate from 2009-2013) to reach 33.2 bln US$ (see table 2), while imports increased by 10.6 percent to reach 33.9 bln US$ (see table 3). Exports of this commodity accounted for 1.7 percent of world exports of SITC section 5, and 0.2 percent of total world merchandise exports (see table 1). Germany, USA and France were the top exporters in 2013 (see table 2). They accounted for 12.5, 11.8 and 11.4 percent of world exports, respectively. Brazil, France and Germany were the top destinations, with respectively 8.9, 7.3 and 5.4 percent of world imports (see table 3).

The top 15 countries/areas accounted for 83.0 and 54.1 percent of total world exports and imports, respectively (see tables 2 and 3). In 2013, China was the country/area with the highest value of net exports (+3.1 bln US$), followed by USA (+2.9 bln US$). By MDG regions (see graph 2), the largest surpluses in this product group were recorded by Developed Europe (+4.7 bln US$), Eastern Asia (+3.1 bln US$) and Developed North America (+1.4 bln US$). The largest trade deficits were recorded by Latin America and the Caribbean (-5.1 bln US$), Commonwealth of Independent States (-1.5 bln US$) and Sub-Saharan Africa (-1.4 bln US$).

Table 1: Imports (Imp.) and exports (Exp.), 1999-2013, in current US$

		1999	2000	2001	2002	2003	2004	2005	2006	2007	2008	2009	2010	2011	2012	2013
Values in Bln US$	Imp.	11.5	10.7	10.9	11.6	13.1	15.8	16.5	16.6	19.9	25.2	22.8	24.7	29.7	30.6	33.9
	Exp.	11.3	10.6	10.6	10.9	12.7	15.0	16.3	16.3	18.2	24.7	20.3	23.0	27.6	29.0	33.2
As a percentage of SITC section (%)	Imp.	2.0	1.8	1.7	1.7	1.6	1.6	1.4	1.3	1.3	1.5	1.5	1.4	1.5	1.5	1.6
	Exp.	2.1	1.9	1.8	1.7	1.6	1.6	1.5	1.3	1.3	1.5	1.4	1.4	1.4	1.5	1.7
As a percentage of world trade (%)	Imp.	0.2	0.2	0.2	0.2	0.2	0.2	0.2	0.1	0.1	0.2	0.2	0.2	0.2	0.2	0.2
	Exp.	0.2	0.2	0.2	0.2	0.2	0.2	0.2	0.1	0.1	0.2	0.2	0.2	0.2	0.2	0.2

Graph 1: Annual growth rates of exports, 1999–2013
(In percentage by year)

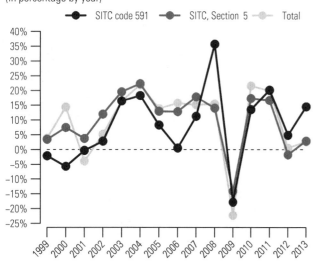

Graph 2: Trade Balance by MDG regions 2013
(Bln US$)

Table 2: Top exporting countries or areas in 2013

Country or area	Value (million US$)	Avg. Growth (%) 09-13	Growth (%) 12-13	World share %	Cum.
World	33 174.1	13.1	14.5	100.0	
Germany	4 140.9	8.0	13.5	12.5	12.5
USA	3 908.6	12.9	18.2	11.8	24.3
France	3 787.3	8.6	7.5	11.4	35.7
China	3 744.2	27.5	31.3	11.3	47.0
Belgium	2 153.4	4.5	20.4	6.5	53.5
India	2 133.2	19.7	28.4	6.4	59.9
United Kingdom	1 601.3	...	7.6	4.8	64.7
Spain	1 209.2	15.8	5.6	3.6	68.4
Switzerland	1 052.1	6.9	8.3	3.2	71.5
Netherlands	896.7	8.6	1.5	2.7	74.2
Italy	767.1	5.7	6.9	2.3	76.5
Israel	754.9	7.5	0.8	2.3	78.8
Argentina	555.9	10.1	35.9	1.7	80.5
Colombia	442.0	15.8	56.7	1.3	81.8
Japan	390.1	1.2	-8.5	1.2	83.0

Table 3: Top importing countries or areas in 2013

Country or area	Value (million US$)	Avg. Growth (%) 09-13	Growth (%) 12-13	World share %	Cum.
World	33 879.2	10.4	10.6	100.0	
Brazil	2 999.8	23.2	33.6	8.9	8.9
France	2 467.1	4.0	10.7	7.3	16.1
Germany	1 840.1	6.1	4.8	5.4	21.6
Canada	1 546.2	6.4	29.1	4.6	26.1
USA	998.3	6.5	12.7	2.9	29.1
Belgium	979.5	2.6	10.8	2.9	32.0
United Kingdom	948.6	...	-2.9	2.8	34.8
Spain	904.7	5.8	10.2	2.7	37.4
Italy	884.7	2.0	-2.4	2.6	40.1
Netherlands	822.3	11.2	11.6	2.4	42.5
Thailand	799.2	14.4	27.6	2.4	44.8
India	792.6	15.9	9.4	2.3	47.2
Viet Nam	786.2	12.1	12.4	2.3	49.5
Poland	778.0	8.9	11.6	2.3	51.8
Ukraine	769.5	29.9	2.0	2.3	54.1

In 2013, the value (in current US$) of exports of "starches, insulin and wheat gluten; albuminoidal substances; glues" (SITC group 592) increased by 9.1 percent (compared to 11.2 percent average growth rate from 2009-2013) to reach 27.3 bln US$ (see table 2), while imports increased by 6.6 percent to reach 29.2 bln US$ (see table 3). Exports of this commodity accounted for 1.4 percent of world exports of SITC section 5, and 0.1 percent of total world merchandise exports (see table 1). Germany, USA and China were the top exporters in 2013 (see table 2). They accounted for 13.8, 10.5 and 8.8 percent of world exports, respectively. China, USA and Germany were the top destinations, with respectively 12.4, 8.3 and 7.8 percent of world imports (see table 3).

The top 15 countries/areas accounted for 77.7 and 63.6 percent of total world exports and imports, respectively (see tables 2 and 3). In 2013, Thailand was the country/area with the highest value of net exports (+1.6 bln US$), followed by Germany (+1.5 bln US$). By MDG regions (see graph 2), the largest surpluses in this product group were recorded by Developed Europe (+1.8 bln US$), South-eastern Asia (+1.0 bln US$) and Developed Asia-Pacific (+611.1 mln US$). The largest trade deficits were recorded by Eastern Asia (-1.6 bln US$), Latin America and the Caribbean (-1.1 bln US$) and Commonwealth of Independent States (-793.7 mln US$).

Table 1: Imports (Imp.) and exports (Exp.), 1999-2013, in current US$

		1999	2000	2001	2002	2003	2004	2005	2006	2007	2008	2009	2010	2011	2012	2013
Values in Bln US$	Imp.	9.0	9.4	9.8	10.2	11.8	13.9	15.0	16.4	19.4	22.4	19.3	22.4	27.1	27.4	29.2
	Exp.	8.4	8.8	9.3	9.7	11.0	12.7	13.7	15.0	17.8	20.3	17.9	20.8	24.9	25.0	27.3
As a percentage of SITC section (%)	Imp.	1.6	1.5	1.5	1.4	1.4	1.4	1.3	1.3	1.3	1.3	1.3	1.3	1.3	1.4	1.4
	Exp.	1.6	1.6	1.6	1.5	1.4	1.3	1.3	1.2	1.2	1.2	1.3	1.3	1.3	1.3	1.4
As a percentage of world trade (%)	Imp.	0.2	0.1	0.2	0.2	0.2	0.1	0.1	0.1	0.1	0.1	0.2	0.1	0.1	0.2	0.2
	Exp.	0.2	0.1	0.2	0.2	0.1	0.1	0.1	0.1	0.1	0.1	0.1	0.1	0.1	0.1	0.1

Graph 1: Annual growth rates of exports, 1999–2013

(In percentage by year)

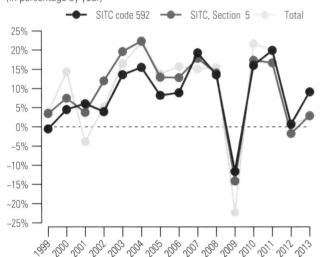

Table 2: Top exporting countries or areas in 2013

Country or area	Value (million US$)	Avg. Growth (%) 09-13	Growth (%) 12-13	World share %	Cum.
World	27 327.8	11.2	9.1	100.0	
Germany	3 782.1	8.9	5.4	13.8	13.8
USA	2 878.4	9.6	4.1	10.5	24.4
China	2 403.6	14.3	12.1	8.8	33.2
Netherlands	2 026.5	16.1	59.3	7.4	40.6
Thailand	1 926.3	20.2	12.1	7.0	47.6
France	1 820.3	7.0	7.3	6.7	54.3
New Zealand	1 031.2	11.2	4.4	3.8	58.1
Belgium	881.3	6.3	18.4	3.2	61.3
Italy	826.7	7.5	10.5	3.0	64.3
Viet Nam	790.2	28.4	-8.6	2.9	67.2
Japan	784.7	6.1	-15.2	2.9	70.1
Other Asia, nes	543.6	11.3	-9.9	2.0	72.1
Australia	537.0	6.6	12.1	2.0	74.0
Ireland	512.7	11.0	6.4	1.9	75.9
China, Hong Kong SAR	482.3	17.0	14.1	1.8	77.7

Graph 2: Trade Balance by MDG regions 2013

(Bln US$)

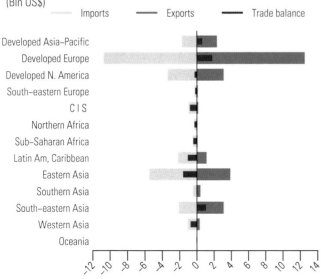

Table 3: Top importing countries or areas in 2013

Country or area	Value (million US$)	Avg. Growth (%) 09-13	Growth (%) 12-13	World share %	Cum.
World	29 220.5	11.0	6.6	100.0	
China	3 615.2	21.1	9.4	12.4	12.4
USA	2 428.7	9.4	3.6	8.3	20.7
Germany	2 291.6	9.6	5.9	7.8	28.5
Japan	1 338.3	8.8	-0.3	4.6	33.1
France	1 027.4	5.6	9.7	3.5	36.6
United Kingdom	970.5	6.1	11.2	3.3	39.9
Canada	950.3	10.3	8.9	3.3	43.2
Netherlands	924.2	8.5	13.8	3.2	46.4
Belgium	828.1	9.6	23.0	2.8	49.2
Mexico	794.1	9.8	2.6	2.7	51.9
Rep. of Korea	751.6	12.7	7.0	2.6	54.5
Other Asia, nes	702.0	9.4	-5.8	2.4	56.9
Poland	679.7	9.1	7.9	2.3	59.2
Italy	646.6	6.3	14.1	2.2	61.4
Russian Federation	634.9	13.9	11.4	2.2	63.6

593 Explosives and pyrotechnic products

In 2013, the value (in current US$) of exports of "explosives and pyrotechnic products" (SITC group 593) increased by 5.0 percent (compared to 9.8 percent average growth rate from 2009-2013) to reach 3.8 bln US$ (see table 2), while imports increased by 4.6 percent to reach 4.2 bln US$ (see table 3). Exports of this commodity accounted for 0.2 percent of world exports of SITC section 5, and less than 0.1 percent of total world merchandise exports (see table 1). China, USA and Canada were the top exporters in 2013 (see table 2). They accounted for 23.0, 21.0 and 7.6 percent of world exports, respectively. USA, France and Mexico were the top destinations, with respectively 15.8, 7.1 and 6.3 percent of world imports (see table 3).

The top 15 countries/areas accounted for 85.2 and 61.4 percent of total world exports and imports, respectively (see tables 2 and 3). In 2013, China was the country/area with the highest value of net exports (+763.4 mln US$), followed by Czech Rep. (+176.9 mln US$). By MDG regions (see graph 2), the largest surpluses in this product group were recorded by Eastern Asia (+696.9 mln US$), Developed North America (+200.0 mln US$) and Southern Asia (+13.3 mln US$). The largest trade deficits were recorded by Latin America and the Caribbean (-339.4 mln US$), Sub-Saharan Africa (-249.0 mln US$) and Developed Asia-Pacific (-184.4 mln US$).

Table 1: Imports (Imp.) and exports (Exp.), 1999-2013, in current US$

		1999	2000	2001	2002	2003	2004	2005	2006	2007	2008	2009	2010	2011	2012	2013
Values in Bln US$	Imp.	1.4	1.4	1.3	1.5	1.8	2.1	2.2	2.6	3.0	3.2	3.0	3.3	3.7	4.1	4.2
	Exp.	1.2	1.2	1.1	1.2	1.5	1.8	1.9	2.3	2.5	2.8	2.6	3.1	3.5	3.6	3.8
As a percentage of SITC section (%)	Imp.	0.2	0.2	0.2	0.2	0.2	0.2	0.2	0.2	0.2	0.2	0.2	0.2	0.2	0.2	0.2
	Exp.	0.2	0.2	0.2	0.2	0.2	0.2	0.2	0.2	0.2	0.2	0.2	0.2	0.2	0.2	0.2
As a percentage of world trade (%)	Imp.	0.0	0.0	0.0	0.0	0.0	0.0	0.0	0.0	0.0	0.0	0.0	0.0	0.0	0.0	0.0
	Exp.	0.0	0.0	0.0	0.0	0.0	0.0	0.0	0.0	0.0	0.0	0.0	0.0	0.0	0.0	0.0

Graph 1: Annual growth rates of exports, 1999–2013
(In percentage by year)

● SITC code 593 ● SITC, Section 5 ● Total

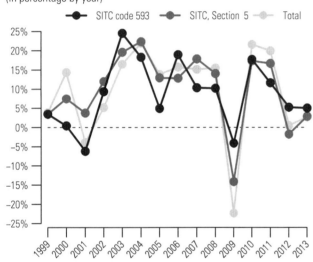

Graph 2: Trade Balance by MDG regions 2013
(Bln US$)

— Imports — Exports — Trade balance

Developed Asia-Pacific
Developed Europe
Developed N. America
South-eastern Europe
C I S
Northern Africa
Sub-Saharan Africa
Latin Am, Caribbean
Eastern Asia
Southern Asia
South-eastern Asia
Western Asia
Oceania

Table 2: Top exporting countries or areas in 2013

Country or area	Value (million US$)	Avg. Growth (%) 09-13	Growth (%) 12-13	World share %	Cum.
World	3830.4	9.8	5.0	100.0	
China	880.1	8.8	6.4	23.0	23.0
USA	803.4	7.8	-4.1	21.0	44.0
Canada	289.7	16.0	16.1	7.6	51.5
Germany	232.9	2.7	-5.3	6.1	57.6
Czech Rep.	208.1	9.9	4.6	5.4	63.0
France	163.0	14.1	-7.1	4.3	67.3
South Africa	134.8	14.3	-4.8	3.5	70.8
Russian Federation	115.8	22.3	-1.0	3.0	73.8
Mexico	112.3	8.8	4.0	2.9	76.8
Spain	81.2	43.2	478.8	2.1	78.9
Chile	56.1	21.5	41.6	1.5	80.3
Netherlands	50.3	10.0	40.5	1.3	81.7
Switzerland	46.9	-1.5	4.8	1.2	82.9
Italy	46.3	9.8	15.6	1.2	84.1
Philippines	43.7	51.4	58.4	1.1	85.2

Table 3: Top importing countries or areas in 2013

Country or area	Value (million US$)	Avg. Growth (%) 09-13	Growth (%) 12-13	World share %	Cum.
World	4242.1	9.3	4.6	100.0	
USA	669.0	5.3	-0.4	15.8	15.8
France	300.9	42.0	2.3	7.1	22.9
Mexico	269.2	5.7	1.7	6.3	29.2
Germany	248.8	2.1	-6.4	5.9	35.1
Canada	222.1	12.9	11.6	5.2	40.3
Australia	137.6	11.4	-1.3	3.2	43.6
Indonesia	126.8	19.4	8.7	3.0	46.5
China	116.8	29.1	9.6	2.8	49.3
Japan	97.1	1.2	-10.0	2.3	51.6
Norway	82.0	11.4	13.9	1.9	53.5
Chile	77.9	34.6	51.7	1.8	55.4
Italy	74.3	-0.1	1.0	1.8	57.1
Zambia	67.6	32.5	86.4	1.6	58.7
Netherlands	57.8	-2.8	-6.5	1.4	60.1
Russian Federation	57.4	32.5	1.9	1.4	61.4

Source: UN Comtrade and UN Service Trade

In 2013, the value (in current US$) of exports of "prepared additives, de-icing and liquid for transmissions; lubricant, etc" (SITC group 597) increased by 0.4 percent (compared to 10.7 percent average growth rate from 2009-2013) to reach 23.4 bln US$ (see table 2), while imports increased by 5.3 percent to reach 24.9 bln US$ (see table 3). Exports of this commodity accounted for 1.2 percent of world exports of SITC section 5, and 0.1 percent of total world merchandise exports (see table 1). USA, France and Germany were the top exporters in 2013 (see table 2). They accounted for 22.5, 14.3 and 14.2 percent of world exports, respectively. China, Germany and Belgium were the top destinations, with respectively 12.0, 6.1 and 5.1 percent of world imports (see table 3).

The top 15 countries/areas accounted for 90.1 and 60.4 percent of total world exports and imports, respectively (see tables 2 and 3). In 2013, USA was the country/area with the highest value of net exports (+4.4 bln US$), followed by France (+2.2 bln US$). By MDG regions (see graph 2), the largest surpluses in this product group were recorded by Developed Europe (+4.1 bln US$), Developed North America (+3.8 bln US$) and Developed Asia-Pacific (+316.3 mln US$). The largest trade deficits were recorded by Eastern Asia (-3.5 bln US$), Latin America and the Caribbean (-1.8 bln US$) and Commonwealth of Independent States (-1.1 bln US$).

Table 1: Imports (Imp.) and exports (Exp.), 1999-2013, in current US$

		1999	2000	2001	2002	2003	2004	2005	2006	2007	2008	2009	2010	2011	2012	2013
Values in Bln US$	Imp.	7.3	7.0	7.2	7.9	8.8	10.4	12.0	13.9	16.1	18.7	16.5	19.8	23.4	23.6	24.9
	Exp.	6.7	6.8	6.8	7.2	8.2	9.8	11.2	13.0	15.2	18.1	15.6	19.0	22.9	23.3	23.4
As a percentage of	Imp.	1.3	1.1	1.1	1.1	1.1	1.0	1.0	1.1	1.1	1.1	1.1	1.1	1.1	1.2	1.2
SITC section (%)	Exp.	1.3	1.2	1.2	1.1	1.0	1.0	1.0	1.1	1.1	1.1	1.1	1.1	1.2	1.2	1.2
As a percentage of	Imp.	0.1	0.1	0.1	0.1	0.1	0.1	0.1	0.1	0.1	0.1	0.1	0.1	0.1	0.1	0.1
world trade (%)	Exp.	0.1	0.1	0.1	0.1	0.1	0.1	0.1	0.1	0.1	0.1	0.1	0.1	0.1	0.1	0.1

Graph 1: Annual growth rates of exports, 1999–2013
(In percentage by year)

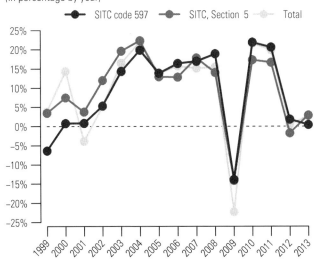

Table 2: Top exporting countries or areas in 2013

Country or area	Value (million US$)	Avg. Growth (%) 09-13	Growth (%) 12-13	World share %	Cum.
World	23 426.5	10.7	0.4	100.0	
USA	5 271.5	11.6	0.7	22.5	22.5
France	3 338.7	8.4	6.0	14.3	36.8
Germany	3 317.9	12.8	12.6	14.2	50.9
Singapore	2 068.0	14.6	8.4	8.8	59.7
Belgium	1 553.3	13.0	12.5	6.6	66.4
Italy	1 335.4	13.1	7.3	5.7	72.1
Japan	1 189.5	11.2	-1.5	5.1	77.2
Netherlands	940.0	4.7	0.3	4.0	81.2
United Kingdom	669.4	3.3	-6.5	2.9	84.0
Spain	289.8	14.2	3.8	1.2	85.3
Canada	288.3	12.3	3.1	1.2	86.5
China	254.0	13.4	10.3	1.1	87.6
Switzerland	209.5	9.7	3.5	0.9	88.5
Sweden	194.4	6.5	13.4	0.8	89.3
Finland	190.6	8.2	1.1	0.8	90.1

Graph 2: Trade Balance by MDG regions 2013
(Bln US$)

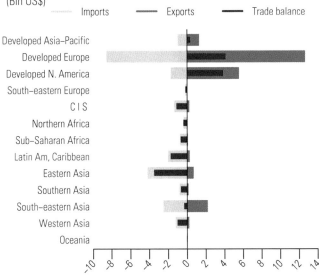

Table 3: Top importing countries or areas in 2013

Country or area	Value (million US$)	Avg. Growth (%) 09-13	Growth (%) 12-13	World share %	Cum.
World	24 894.2	10.8	5.3	100.0	
China	2 982.6	19.0	17.8	12.0	12.0
Germany	1 519.5	12.0	3.6	6.1	18.1
Belgium	1 274.4	10.6	6.7	5.1	23.2
France	1 114.0	9.6	12.2	4.5	27.7
Singapore	1 067.4	10.6	17.9	4.3	32.0
Russian Federation	941.9	15.3	2.8	3.8	35.8
USA	882.1	14.6	3.5	3.5	39.3
Canada	856.9	12.2	1.3	3.4	42.7
Italy	798.6	10.8	5.7	3.2	45.9
Netherlands	733.4	8.6	3.8	2.9	48.9
Rep. of Korea	688.0	10.6	0.3	2.8	51.7
Japan	644.8	6.4	-4.5	2.6	54.2
Mexico	550.3	15.4	9.1	2.2	56.5
United Kingdom	495.5	7.6	7.0	2.0	58.4
India	476.0	16.9	0.0	1.9	60.4

598 Miscellaneous chemical products, nes

In 2013, the value (in current US$) of exports of "miscellaneous chemical products, nes" (SITC group 598) increased by 4.8 percent (compared to 9.4 percent average growth rate from 2009-2013) to reach 127.5 bln US$ (see table 2), while imports increased by 0.7 percent to reach 130.5 bln US$ (see table 3). Exports of this commodity accounted for 6.5 percent of world exports of SITC section 5, and 0.7 percent of total world merchandise exports (see table 1). USA, Germany and Japan were the top exporters in 2013 (see table 2). They accounted for 15.0, 14.4 and 7.5 percent of world exports, respectively. China, Germany and USA were the top destinations, with respectively 9.9, 8.3 and 8.1 percent of world imports (see table 3).

The top 15 countries/areas accounted for 79.1 and 66.3 percent of total world exports and imports, respectively (see tables 2 and 3). In 2013, USA was the country/area with the highest value of net exports (+8.6 bln US$), followed by Germany (+7.6 bln US$). By MDG regions (see graph 2), the largest surpluses in this product group were recorded by Developed Europe (+11.5 bln US$), Developed North America (+7.3 bln US$) and Developed Asia-Pacific (+4.4 bln US$). The largest trade deficits were recorded by Eastern Asia (-10.9 bln US$), Latin America and the Caribbean (-5.9 bln US$) and Commonwealth of Independent States (-2.5 bln US$).

Table 1: Imports (Imp.) and exports (Exp.), 1999-2013, in current US$

		1999	2000	2001	2002	2003	2004	2005	2006	2007	2008	2009	2010	2011	2012	2013
Values in Bln US$	Imp.	35.8	40.4	40.4	43.9	51.5	60.1	67.9	79.1	93.5	108.5	92.1	112.2	136.2	129.6	130.5
	Exp.	35.3	38.0	37.7	41.2	48.3	57.0	63.5	75.2	89.1	109.6	88.9	108.2	128.7	121.7	127.5
As a percentage of SITC section (%)	Imp.	6.3	6.6	6.4	6.3	6.2	5.9	5.9	6.2	6.2	6.3	6.2	6.5	6.6	6.5	6.3
	Exp.	6.7	6.7	6.4	6.3	6.1	5.9	5.9	6.1	6.2	6.7	6.3	6.5	6.7	6.4	6.5
As a percentage of world trade (%)	Imp.	0.6	0.6	0.6	0.7	0.7	0.6	0.6	0.6	0.7	0.7	0.7	0.7	0.7	0.7	0.7
	Exp.	0.6	0.6	0.6	0.6	0.6	0.6	0.6	0.6	0.6	0.7	0.7	0.7	0.7	0.7	0.7

Graph 1: Annual growth rates of exports, 1999–2013
(In percentage by year)

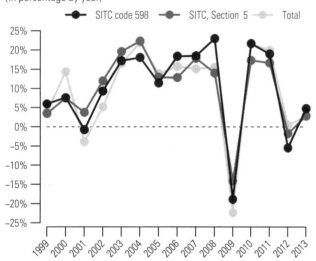

Table 2: Top exporting countries or areas in 2013

Country or area	Value (million US$)	Avg. Growth (%) 09-13	Growth (%) 12-13	World share %	Cum.
World	127 463.9	9.4	4.8	100.0	
USA	19 178.1	10.1	6.1	15.0	15.0
Germany	18 412.6	9.1	8.2	14.4	29.5
Japan	9 507.1	4.1	-15.5	7.5	36.9
China	8 256.0	14.1	5.0	6.5	43.4
Netherlands	7 276.4	10.0	6.7	5.7	49.1
Belgium	5 551.1	5.2	16.3	4.4	53.5
France	5 524.3	6.4	5.2	4.3	57.8
United Kingdom	5 078.1	2.7	2.1	4.0	61.8
Israel	4 108.3	19.1	81.1	3.2	65.0
Ireland	3 669.3	-3.3	2.4	2.9	67.9
Italy	3 243.5	5.9	1.8	2.5	70.5
Other Asia, nes	3 225.4	13.6	4.8	2.5	73.0
Rep. of Korea	3 140.0	15.4	6.7	2.5	75.4
Singapore	2 452.8	9.3	-13.7	1.9	77.4
Spain	2 166.5	16.3	14.5	1.7	79.1

Graph 2: Trade Balance by MDG regions 2013
(Bln US$)

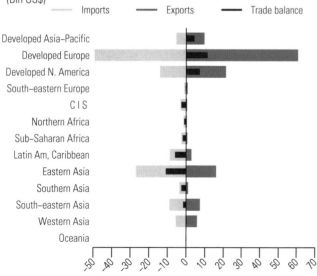

Table 3: Top importing countries or areas in 2013

Country or area	Value (million US$)	Avg. Growth (%) 09-13	Growth (%) 12-13	World share %	Cum.
World	130 548.0	9.1	0.7	100.0	
China	12 984.9	13.9	1.2	9.9	9.9
Germany	10 817.7	6.1	-0.1	8.3	18.2
USA	10 627.4	13.6	9.4	8.1	26.4
Other Asia, nes	6 479.6	9.0	6.1	5.0	31.3
Rep. of Korea	6 105.9	7.0	-1.2	4.7	36.0
France	5 224.1	6.2	1.1	4.0	40.0
Netherlands	4 940.1	8.4	-6.4	3.8	43.8
Italy	4 521.8	5.1	-9.4	3.5	47.3
United Kingdom	4 174.5	-2.6	3.6	3.2	50.5
Japan	4 117.0	5.5	-14.8	3.2	53.6
Belgium	3 835.3	4.9	2.1	2.9	56.6
Canada	3 429.4	14.3	4.1	2.6	59.2
Mexico	3 304.4	13.8	7.8	2.5	61.7
Spain	3 124.4	3.4	-21.8	2.4	64.1
Singapore	2 855.9	13.8	-10.7	2.2	66.3

Manufactured goods classified chiefly by material

material

(SITC Section 6)

611 Leather

In 2013, the value (in current US$) of exports of "leather" (SITC group 611) increased by 9.9 percent (compared to 12.3 percent average growth rate from 2009-2013) to reach 26.2 bln US$ (see table 2), while imports increased by 11.3 percent to reach 24.4 bln US$ (see table 3). Exports of this commodity accounted for 1.2 percent of world exports of SITC section 6, and 0.1 percent of total world merchandise exports (see table 1). Italy, Brazil and China, Hong Kong SAR were the top exporters in 2013 (see table 2). They accounted for 19.7, 9.5 and 9.3 percent of world exports, respectively. China, China, Hong Kong SAR and Italy were the top destinations, with respectively 18.3, 13.2 and 12.4 percent of world imports (see table 3).

The top 15 countries/areas accounted for 75.7 and 77.1 percent of total world exports and imports, respectively (see tables 2 and 3). In 2013, Brazil was the country/area with the highest value of net exports (+2.5 bln US$), followed by Italy (+2.2 bln US$). By MDG regions (see graph 2), the largest surpluses in this product group were recorded by Latin America and the Caribbean (+3.2 bln US$), Southern Asia (+1.8 bln US$) and Sub-Saharan Africa (+1.3 bln US$). The largest trade deficits were recorded by Eastern Asia (-3.9 bln US$), South-eastern Asia (-1.2 bln US$) and South-eastern Europe (-1.0 bln US$).

Table 1: Imports (Imp.) and exports (Exp.), 1999-2013, in current US$

		1999	2000	2001	2002	2003	2004	2005	2006	2007	2008	2009	2010	2011	2012	2013
Values in Bln US$	Imp.	13.2	15.2	16.4	16.2	18.0	19.8	19.9	21.7	23.1	21.6	15.1	19.7	23.3	21.9	24.4
	Exp.	14.1	16.4	17.3	16.8	18.5	20.5	20.6	22.8	25.0	23.1	16.4	23.4	24.2	23.8	26.2
As a percentage of SITC section (%)	Imp.	1.6	1.7	1.9	1.8	1.8	1.5	1.4	1.3	1.2	1.0	1.0	1.0	1.0	1.0	1.1
	Exp.	1.8	1.9	2.1	1.9	1.8	1.6	1.5	1.4	1.3	1.1	1.1	1.2	1.0	1.1	1.2
As a percentage of world trade (%)	Imp.	0.2	0.2	0.3	0.2	0.2	0.2	0.2	0.2	0.2	0.1	0.1	0.1	0.1	0.1	0.1
	Exp.	0.3	0.3	0.3	0.3	0.2	0.2	0.2	0.2	0.2	0.1	0.1	0.2	0.1	0.1	0.1

Graph 1: Annual growth rates of exports, 1999–2013
(In percentage by year)

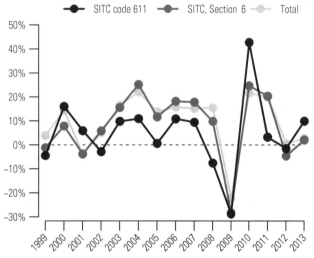

Graph 2: Trade Balance by MDG regions 2013
(Bln US$)

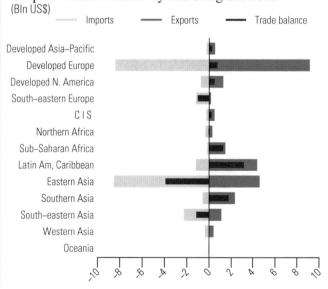

Table 2: Top exporting countries or areas in 2013

Country or area	Value (million US$)	Avg. Growth (%) 09-13	Growth (%) 12-13	World share %	Cum.
World.................................	26 172.5	12.3	9.9	100.0	
Italy..................................	5 165.6	9.0	11.4	19.7	19.7
Brazil................................	2 492.1	21.3	20.3	9.5	29.3
China, Hong Kong SAR.........	2 422.7	10.9	4.4	9.3	38.5
India.................................	1 344.5	25.4	25.4	5.1	43.7
USA..................................	1 232.5	21.7	25.4	4.7	48.4
Rep. of Korea......................	998.1	10.3	8.1	3.8	52.2
Germany.............................	921.2	11.9	8.5	3.5	55.7
Nigeria...............................	921.1	15.8	-18.5	3.5	59.2
Argentina............................	905.4	8.6	9.6	3.5	62.7
Other Asia, nes....................	723.8	4.4	1.5	2.8	65.4
Spain.................................	601.3	11.7	8.2	2.3	67.7
Thailand.............................	552.3	14.0	8.1	2.1	69.8
Austria...............................	552.2	8.0	23.9	2.1	72.0
Pakistan.............................	529.0	18.3	15.7	2.0	74.0
China.................................	449.2	17.3	3.8	1.7	75.7

Table 3: Top importing countries or areas in 2013

Country or area	Value (million US$)	Avg. Growth (%) 09-13	Growth (%) 12-13	World share %	Cum.
World.................................	24 388.4	12.8	11.3	100.0	
China.................................	4 457.8	10.2	8.4	18.3	18.3
China, Hong Kong SAR.........	3 228.5	13.8	8.0	13.2	31.5
Italy..................................	3 012.5	18.2	18.2	12.4	43.9
Viet Nam............................	1 103.6	15.3	21.7	4.5	48.4
Germany.............................	869.5	8.1	7.3	3.6	52.0
Mexico...............................	863.3	30.1	20.5	3.5	55.5
Spain.................................	744.6	16.3	21.8	3.1	58.6
Romania.............................	682.5	3.3	8.1	2.8	61.4
USA..................................	681.2	11.3	4.6	2.8	64.1
Portugal.............................	587.6	19.3	24.4	2.4	66.6
France...............................	566.3	12.0	-1.0	2.3	68.9
Rep. of Korea......................	546.1	16.5	23.3	2.2	71.1
Poland...............................	517.6	11.2	10.8	2.1	73.2
India.................................	475.1	10.3	13.4	1.9	75.2
Thailand.............................	466.0	17.1	10.2	1.9	77.1

Manufactures of leather or of composition leather, nes; saddlery, harness 612

In 2013, the value (in current US$) of exports of "manufactures of leather or of composition leather, nes; saddlery, harness" (SITC group 612) increased by 8.6 percent (compared to 11.1 percent average growth rate from 2009-2013) to reach 4.1 bln US$ (see table 2), while imports increased by 9.3 percent to reach 3.5 bln US$ (see table 3). Exports of this commodity accounted for 0.2 percent of world exports of SITC section 6, and less than 0.1 percent of total world merchandise exports (see table 1). China, France and Italy were the top exporters in 2013 (see table 2). They accounted for 21.7, 8.8 and 5.8 percent of world exports, respectively. USA, Germany and Italy were the top destinations, with respectively 17.3, 5.6 and 4.9 percent of world imports (see table 3).

The top 15 countries/areas accounted for 78.3 and 69.3 percent of total world exports and imports, respectively (see tables 2 and 3). In 2013, China was the country/area with the highest value of net exports (+811.0 mln US$), followed by India (+213.3 mln US$). By MDG regions (see graph 2), the largest surpluses in this product group were recorded by Eastern Asia (+879.5 mln US$), Developed Europe (+288.1 mln US$) and Southern Asia (+245.0 mln US$). The largest trade deficits were recorded by Developed North America (-438.2 mln US$), South-eastern Europe (-157.9 mln US$) and Developed Asia-Pacific (-157.4 mln US$).

Table 1: Imports (Imp.) and exports (Exp.), 1999-2013, in current US$

		1999	2000	2001	2002	2003	2004	2005	2006	2007	2008	2009	2010	2011	2012	2013
Values in Bln US$	Imp.	1.1	1.3	1.4	1.6	1.9	2.4	2.4	2.5	2.7	2.8	2.2	2.7	3.2	3.2	3.5
	Exp.	1.5	1.7	1.7	2.0	2.3	2.9	3.1	3.4	3.5	3.4	2.7	3.1	3.6	3.8	4.1
As a percentage of SITC section (%)	Imp.	0.1	0.1	0.2	0.2	0.2	0.2	0.2	0.2	0.1	0.1	0.1	0.1	0.1	0.1	0.2
	Exp.	0.2	0.2	0.2	0.2	0.2	0.2	0.2	0.2	0.2	0.2	0.2	0.2	0.2	0.2	0.2
As a percentage of world trade (%)	Imp.	0.0	0.0	0.0	0.0	0.0	0.0	0.0	0.0	0.0	0.0	0.0	0.0	0.0	0.0	0.0
	Exp.	0.0	0.0	0.0	0.0	0.0	0.0	0.0	0.0	0.0	0.0	0.0	0.0	0.0	0.0	0.0

Graph 1: Annual growth rates of exports, 1999–2013
(In percentage by year)

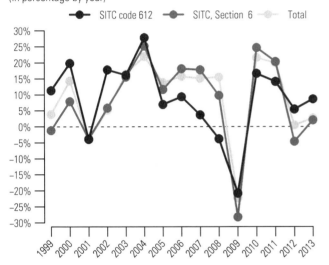

Legend: ● SITC code 612　● SITC, Section 6　○ Total

Table 2: Top exporting countries or areas in 2013

Country or area	Value (million US$)	Avg. Growth (%) 09-13	Growth (%) 12-13	World share %	Cum.
World	4108.0	11.1	8.6	100.0	
China	892.7	16.0	12.6	21.7	21.7
France	363.3	0.0	-10.5	8.8	30.6
Italy	239.4	18.6	35.8	5.8	36.4
USA	238.4	16.5	3.7	5.8	42.2
India	228.7	16.3	46.5	5.6	47.8
Hungary	210.6	17.8	14.6	5.1	52.9
Germany	203.6	3.7	2.2	5.0	57.9
China, Hong Kong SAR	177.2	25.1	20.4	4.3	62.2
Mexico	121.7	2.5	-29.8	3.0	65.1
Poland	107.6	13.8	24.5	2.6	67.8
Austria	103.4	9.6	2.5	2.5	70.3
Croatia	95.9	10.2	-17.0	2.3	72.6
Thailand	95.4	11.3	30.5	2.3	74.9
Slovakia	72.6	26.0	3.4	1.8	76.7
United Kingdom	67.2	8.6	18.6	1.6	78.3

Graph 2: Trade Balance by MDG regions 2013
(Bln US$)

Legend: ┈ Imports　━ Exports　━ Trade balance

Developed Asia-Pacific
Developed Europe
Developed N. America
South-eastern Europe
CIS
Northern Africa
Sub-Saharan Africa
Latin Am, Caribbean
Eastern Asia
Southern Asia
South-eastern Asia
Western Asia
Oceania

-2　-1.5　-1　-0.5　0　0.5　1　1.5　2

Table 3: Top importing countries or areas in 2013

Country or area	Value (million US$)	Avg. Growth (%) 09-13	Growth (%) 12-13	World share %	Cum.
World	3512.7	12.5	9.3	100.0	
USA	608.8	10.4	1.5	17.3	17.3
Germany	196.3	8.4	4.9	5.6	22.9
Italy	171.9	29.6	36.6	4.9	27.8
France	169.7	7.8	-1.9	4.8	32.6
United Kingdom	156.6	7.3	25.1	4.5	37.1
Mexico	140.6	8.0	-10.6	4.0	41.1
China, Hong Kong SAR	138.7	19.8	14.5	3.9	45.0
Poland	135.6	22.7	36.6	3.9	48.9
Singapore	123.0	18.7	24.1	3.5	52.4
Romania	113.9	22.9	9.2	3.2	55.7
Japan	108.6	6.4	4.0	3.1	58.7
Czech Rep.	102.9	5.4	17.6	2.9	61.7
Canada	97.8	7.8	1.2	2.8	64.5
Netherlands	88.7	13.6	25.2	2.5	67.0
China	81.7	13.0	-7.9	2.3	69.3

613 Furskins, tanned or dressed, other than those of heading 848.31

In 2013, the value (in current US$) of exports of "furskins, tanned or dressed, other than those of heading 848.31" (SITC group 613) increased by 27.1 percent (compared to 20.4 percent average growth rate from 2009-2013) to reach 2.9 bln US$ (see table 2), while imports increased by 18.0 percent to reach 2.9 bln US$ (see table 3). Exports of this commodity accounted for 0.1 percent of world exports of SITC section 6, and less than 0.1 percent of total world merchandise exports (see table 1). China, China, Hong Kong SAR and Italy were the top exporters in 2013 (see table 2). They accounted for 28.4, 23.0 and 6.7 percent of world exports, respectively. China, Hong Kong SAR, China and Greece were the top destinations, with respectively 49.4, 11.4 and 6.1 percent of world imports (see table 3).

The top 15 countries/areas accounted for 90.1 and 92.2 percent of total world exports and imports, respectively (see tables 2 and 3). In 2013, China was the country/area with the highest value of net exports (+480.2 mln US$), followed by Poland (+94.6 mln US$). By MDG regions (see graph 2), the largest surpluses in this product group were recorded by Developed Europe (+239.3 mln US$), Commonwealth of Independent States (+60.2 mln US$) and Latin America and the Caribbean (+42.5 mln US$). The largest trade deficits were recorded by Eastern Asia (-414.0 mln US$), South-eastern Asia (-47.6 mln US$) and South-eastern Europe (-3.5 mln US$).

Table 1: Imports (Imp.) and exports (Exp.), 1999-2013, in current US$

		1999	2000	2001	2002	2003	2004	2005	2006	2007	2008	2009	2010	2011	2012	2013
Values in Bln US$	Imp.	0.9	1.1	1.1	1.2	1.4	1.6	1.7	1.9	1.9	2.0	1.5	2.0	2.4	2.5	2.9
	Exp.	1.0	1.1	1.1	1.2	1.3	1.5	1.7	1.8	1.7	1.8	1.4	1.6	2.0	2.3	2.9
As a percentage of SITC section (%)	Imp.	0.1	0.1	0.1	0.1	0.1	0.1	0.1	0.1	0.1	0.1	0.1	0.1	0.1	0.1	0.1
	Exp.	0.1	0.1	0.1	0.1	0.1	0.1	0.1	0.1	0.1	0.1	0.1	0.1	0.1	0.1	0.1
As a percentage of world trade (%)	Imp.	0.0	0.0	0.0	0.0	0.0	0.0	0.0	0.0	0.0	0.0	0.0	0.0	0.0	0.0	0.0
	Exp.	0.0	0.0	0.0	0.0	0.0	0.0	0.0	0.0	0.0	0.0	0.0	0.0	0.0	0.0	0.0

Graph 1: Annual growth rates of exports, 1999–2013
(In percentage by year)

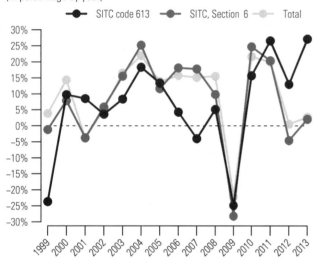

Legend: SITC code 613 — SITC, Section 6 — Total

Table 2: Top exporting countries or areas in 2013

Country or area	Value (million US$)	Avg. Growth (%) 09-13	Growth (%) 12-13	World share %	Cum.
World	2 863.6	20.4	27.1	100.0	
China	813.4	28.4	35.2	28.4	28.4
China, Hong Kong SAR	657.6	12.6	42.4	23.0	51.4
Italy	192.7	22.1	27.9	6.7	58.1
Spain	114.5	5.9	-1.7	4.0	62.1
Turkey	107.1	55.3	26.7	3.7	65.8
Netherlands	103.5	23.9	22.1	3.6	69.4
Poland	102.9	16.3	84.1	3.6	73.0
Germany	99.2	18.7	9.0	3.5	76.5
Russian Federation	97.2	268.5	29.5	3.4	79.9
Greece	67.9	17.2	19.9	2.4	82.3
USA	58.3	39.2	13.3	2.0	84.3
Estonia	50.7	33.2	48.3	1.8	86.1
Lithuania	42.4	39.1	5.1	1.5	87.6
Argentina	37.5	14.4	-17.0	1.3	88.9
Brazil	36.7	15.5	12.2	1.3	90.1

Graph 2: Trade Balance by MDG regions 2013
(Bln US$)

Legend: Imports — Exports — Trade balance

Developed Asia–Pacific
Developed Europe
Developed N. America
South–eastern Europe
CIS
Northern Africa
Sub–Saharan Africa
Latin Am, Caribbean
Eastern Asia
Southern Asia
South–eastern Asia
Western Asia
Oceania

(axis: -2, -1.5, -1, -0.5, 0, 0.5, 1, 1.5)

Table 3: Top importing countries or areas in 2013

Country or area	Value (million US$)	Avg. Growth (%) 09-13	Growth (%) 12-13	World share %	Cum.
World	2 923.8	17.3	18.0	100.0	
China, Hong Kong SAR	1 444.3	16.1	23.5	49.4	49.4
China	333.2	14.8	31.7	11.4	60.8
Greece	178.8	23.7	22.3	6.1	66.9
Italy	163.5	24.2	8.2	5.6	72.5
Rep. of Korea	109.4	24.6	6.6	3.7	76.2
Turkey	88.5	19.7	2.6	3.0	79.3
Germany	70.8	6.2	-12.4	2.4	81.7
France	52.0	22.6	11.6	1.8	83.5
Viet Nam	51.6	47.2	16.3	1.8	85.2
Netherlands	50.5	27.3	41.0	1.7	87.0
USA	34.7	16.5	8.0	1.2	88.2
United Kingdom	33.4	13.5	-9.4	1.1	89.3
Anguilla	32.9	...		1.1	90.4
Russian Federation	29.9	5.9	-19.2	1.0	91.4
Spain	23.4	19.9	12.3	0.8	92.2

In 2013, the value (in current US$) of exports of "materials of rubber (e.g., pastes, plates, rods, threads, tubes of rubber)" (SITC group 621) decreased by 2.0 percent (compared to 12.7 percent average growth rate from 2009-2013) to reach 25.0 bln US$ (see table 2), while imports decreased by 0.7 percent to reach 25.6 bln US$ (see table 3). Exports of this commodity accounted for 1.1 percent of world exports of SITC section 6, and 0.1 percent of total world merchandise exports (see table 1). Germany, Thailand and USA were the top exporters in 2013 (see table 2). They accounted for 15.0, 11.2 and 8.9 percent of world exports, respectively. China, USA and Germany were the top destinations, with respectively 20.9, 9.3 and 7.8 percent of world imports (see table 3).

The top 15 countries/areas accounted for 80.7 and 70.4 percent of total world exports and imports, respectively (see tables 2 and 3). In 2013, Thailand was the country/area with the highest value of net exports (+2.5 bln US$), followed by Germany (+1.7 bln US$). By MDG regions (see graph 2), the largest surpluses in this product group were recorded by South-eastern Asia (+4.0 bln US$), Developed Europe (+2.1 bln US$) and Developed Asia-Pacific (+391.3 mln US$). The largest trade deficits were recorded by Eastern Asia (-4.0 bln US$), Latin America and the Caribbean (-1.2 bln US$) and Commonwealth of Independent States (-675.5 mln US$).

Table 1: Imports (Imp.) and exports (Exp.), 1999-2013, in current US$

		1999	2000	2001	2002	2003	2004	2005	2006	2007	2008	2009	2010	2011	2012	2013
Values in Bln US$	Imp.	7.2	7.5	7.6	8.2	9.8	11.8	12.9	15.3	18.0	19.7	15.8	21.1	26.6	25.8	25.6
	Exp.	7.1	7.4	7.4	7.8	9.5	12.0	13.0	15.4	18.3	19.7	15.5	20.3	25.9	25.5	25.0
As a percentage of SITC section (%)	Imp.	0.9	0.8	0.9	0.9	1.0	0.9	0.9	0.9	0.9	0.9	1.0	1.1	1.2	1.2	1.2
	Exp.	0.9	0.9	0.9	0.9	0.9	0.9	0.9	0.9	0.9	0.9	1.0	1.0	1.1	1.1	1.1
As a percentage of world trade (%)	Imp.	0.1	0.1	0.1	0.1	0.1	0.1	0.1	0.1	0.1	0.1	0.1	0.1	0.1	0.1	0.1
	Exp.	0.1	0.1	0.1	0.1	0.1	0.1	0.1	0.1	0.1	0.1	0.1	0.1	0.1	0.1	0.1

Graph 1: Annual growth rates of exports, 1999–2013
(In percentage by year)

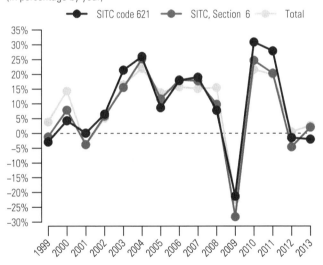

Table 2: Top exporting countries or areas in 2013

Country or area	Value (million US$)	Avg. Growth (%) 09-13	Growth (%) 12-13	World share %	Cum.
World	25 004.3	12.7	-2.0	100.0	
Germany	3 749.0	12.1	-0.3	15.0	15.0
Thailand	2 794.6	23.7	1.2	11.2	26.2
USA	2 220.3	13.5	2.0	8.9	35.0
Malaysia	1 830.5	14.4	-20.4	7.3	42.4
Italy	1 519.2	8.2	3.0	6.1	48.4
China	1 273.4	25.9	13.3	5.1	53.5
France	1 087.5	4.3	2.3	4.3	57.9
Japan	996.7	8.1	-13.7	4.0	61.9
United Kingdom	858.5	8.2	2.3	3.4	65.3
Czech Rep	729.7	14.6	4.3	2.9	68.2
Belgium	726.2	6.3	6.2	2.9	71.1
Canada	624.2	18.2	-3.8	2.5	73.6
Poland	612.8	21.9	15.3	2.5	76.1
Spain	610.1	3.0	7.7	2.4	78.5
Turkey	547.3	25.1	5.3	2.2	80.7

Graph 2: Trade Balance by MDG regions 2013
(Bln US$)

Imports — Exports — Trade balance

Developed Asia–Pacific
Developed Europe
Developed N. America
South–eastern Europe
C I S
Northern Africa
Sub–Saharan Africa
Latin Am, Caribbean
Eastern Asia
Southern Asia
South–eastern Asia
Western Asia
Oceania

Table 3: Top importing countries or areas in 2013

Country or area	Value (million US$)	Avg. Growth (%) 09-13	Growth (%) 12-13	World share %	Cum.
World	25 644.8	12.9	-0.7	100.0	
China	5 359.8	20.0	-2.3	20.9	20.9
USA	2 393.6	19.2	2.9	9.3	30.2
Germany	1 999.6	10.2	5.0	7.8	38.0
France	1 009.4	7.1	-8.1	3.9	42.0
Canada	925.8	12.9	-0.8	3.6	45.6
United Kingdom	884.8	10.7	2.4	3.5	49.0
Mexico	794.9	15.6	5.9	3.1	52.1
Poland	753.2	12.4	12.0	2.9	55.1
Spain	705.8	6.1	-9.6	2.8	57.8
Belgium	643.9	10.0	10.9	2.5	60.3
Italy	591.3	10.0	6.9	2.3	62.6
Brazil	563.2	19.5	13.7	2.2	64.8
Russian Federation	540.1	25.2	5.1	2.1	66.9
Czech Rep	482.9	13.4	2.5	1.9	68.8
Netherlands	413.9	4.8	-18.6	1.6	70.4

625 Rubber tyres, interchangeable tyre treads, tyre flaps and inner tubes

In 2013, the value (in current US$) of exports of "rubber tyres, interchangeable tyre treads, tyre flaps and inner tubes" (SITC group 625) decreased by 0.5 percent (compared to 12.5 percent average growth rate from 2009-2013) to reach 91.4 bln US$ (see table 2), while imports increased by 0.1 percent to reach 90.7 bln US$ (see table 3). Exports of this commodity accounted for 4.0 percent of world exports of SITC section 6, and 0.5 percent of total world merchandise exports (see table 1). China, Japan and Germany were the top exporters in 2013 (see table 2). They accounted for 18.6, 8.1 and 7.6 percent of world exports, respectively. USA, Germany and France were the top destinations, with respectively 16.9, 8.8 and 4.8 percent of world imports (see table 3).

The top 15 countries/areas accounted for 73.6 and 63.5 percent of total world exports and imports, respectively (see tables 2 and 3). In 2013, China was the country/area with the highest value of net exports (+16.0 bln US$), followed by Japan (+6.2 bln US$). By MDG regions (see graph 2), the largest surpluses in this product group were recorded by Eastern Asia (+20.3 bln US$), South-eastern Asia (+3.8 bln US$) and Developed Asia-Pacific (+3.3 bln US$). The largest trade deficits were recorded by Developed North America (-10.8 bln US$), Latin America and the Caribbean (-6.7 bln US$) and Sub-Saharan Africa (-3.0 bln US$).

Table 1: Imports (Imp.) and exports (Exp.), 1999-2013, in current US$

		1999	2000	2001	2002	2003	2004	2005	2006	2007	2008	2009	2010	2011	2012	2013
Values in Bln US$	Imp.	25.5	25.6	24.8	26.9	31.8	38.6	44.3	50.2	60.7	66.7	57.0	69.3	89.8	90.6	90.7
	Exp.	25.7	24.9	24.0	26.0	31.0	37.9	43.6	49.9	60.0	66.5	57.1	70.6	92.7	91.9	91.4
As a percentage of SITC section (%)	Imp.	3.1	2.9	2.9	3.0	3.1	3.0	3.1	3.0	3.1	3.1	3.7	3.6	3.9	4.2	4.1
	Exp.	3.2	2.9	2.9	3.0	3.0	3.0	3.1	3.0	3.0	3.1	3.7	3.6	4.0	4.1	4.0
As a percentage of world trade (%)	Imp.	0.4	0.4	0.4	0.4	0.4	0.4	0.4	0.4	0.4	0.4	0.5	0.5	0.5	0.5	0.5
	Exp.	0.5	0.4	0.4	0.4	0.4	0.4	0.4	0.4	0.4	0.4	0.5	0.5	0.5	0.5	0.5

Graph 1: Annual growth rates of exports, 1999–2013
(In percentage by year)

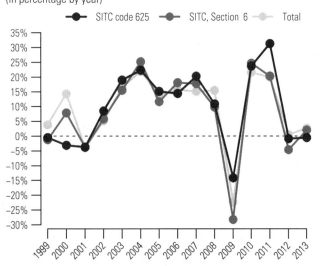

— SITC code 625 — SITC, Section 6 — Total

Graph 2: Trade Balance by MDG regions 2013
(Bln US$)

— Imports — Exports — Trade balance

Developed Asia–Pacific
Developed Europe
Developed N. America
South–eastern Europe
C I S
Northern Africa
Sub–Saharan Africa
Latin Am, Caribbean
Eastern Asia
Southern Asia
South–eastern Asia
Western Asia
Oceania

-40 -30 -20 -10 0 10 20 30 40

Table 2: Top exporting countries or areas in 2013

Country or area	Value (million US$)	Avg. Growth (%) 09-13	Growth (%) 12-13	World share %	Cum.
World	91 436.5	12.5	-0.5	100.0	
China	17 008.9	20.2	1.4	18.6	18.6
Japan	7 440.5	7.2	-10.0	8.1	26.7
Germany	6 907.2	11.0	3.3	7.6	34.3
USA	5 877.9	10.4	-5.2	6.4	40.7
Rep. of Korea	4 439.2	12.4	-7.4	4.9	45.6
France	3 914.1	4.0	-7.1	4.3	49.9
Thailand	3 625.4	17.7	3.9	4.0	53.8
Spain	2 887.9	6.9	1.9	3.2	57.0
Netherlands	2 654.8	11.3	8.2	2.9	59.9
Poland	2 514.6	13.1	10.1	2.8	62.6
Czech Rep.	2 353.1	9.2	-1.0	2.6	65.2
Canada	2 139.8	7.4	-5.6	2.3	67.5
India	1 942.7	27.8	4.2	2.1	69.7
Belgium	1 822.4	5.5	9.1	2.0	71.7
Italy	1 729.5	6.4	-3.0	1.9	73.6

Table 3: Top importing countries or areas in 2013

Country or area	Value (million US$)	Avg. Growth (%) 09-13	Growth (%) 12-13	World share %	Cum.
World	90 723.1	12.3	0.1	100.0	
USA	15 346.7	15.6	0.0	16.9	16.9
Germany	8 026.7	11.2	0.0	8.8	25.8
France	4 394.9	8.0	4.6	4.8	30.6
Canada	3 507.6	6.9	-7.6	3.9	34.5
Mexico	3 197.0	22.4	1.0	3.5	38.0
United Kingdom	3 186.7	7.1	3.1	3.5	41.5
Netherlands	2 775.9	11.9	3.7	3.1	44.6
Russian Federation	2 729.4	33.9	-1.6	3.0	47.6
Italy	2 662.5	4.3	5.6	2.9	50.5
Australia	2 643.2	14.9	-16.4	2.9	53.4
Belgium	2 356.2	5.9	4.6	2.6	56.0
Spain	1 997.5	5.3	10.8	2.2	58.2
Saudi Arabia	1 813.6	12.5	-3.3	2.0	60.2
Brazil	1 742.7	25.2	7.1	1.9	62.1
Chile	1 239.2	17.0	-2.3	1.4	63.5

In 2013, the value (in current US$) of exports of "articles of rubber, nes" (SITC group 629) increased by 8.3 percent (compared to 12.3 percent average growth rate from 2009-2013) to reach 32.6 bln US$ (see table 2), while imports increased by 5.3 percent to reach 35.1 bln US$ (see table 3). Exports of this commodity accounted for 1.4 percent of world exports of SITC section 6, and 0.2 percent of total world merchandise exports (see table 1). Germany, China and USA were the top exporters in 2013 (see table 2). They accounted for 13.9, 11.1 and 9.3 percent of world exports, respectively. USA, Germany and China were the top destinations, with respectively 12.4, 10.0 and 7.2 percent of world imports (see table 3).

The top 15 countries/areas accounted for 75.1 and 62.2 percent of total world exports and imports, respectively (see tables 2 and 3). In 2013, Japan was the country/area with the highest value of net exports (+1.3 bln US$), followed by China (+1.1 bln US$). By MDG regions (see graph 2), the largest surpluses in this product group were recorded by Developed Europe (+2.6 bln US$), Eastern Asia (+1.4 bln US$) and Developed Asia-Pacific (+741.5 mln US$). The largest trade deficits were recorded by Latin America and the Caribbean (-2.6 bln US$), Developed North America (-1.8 bln US$) and Commonwealth of Independent States (-1.3 bln US$).

Table 1: Imports (Imp.) and exports (Exp.), 1999-2013, in current US$

		1999	2000	2001	2002	2003	2004	2005	2006	2007	2008	2009	2010	2011	2012	2013
Values in Bln US$	Imp.	11.9	12.6	12.6	13.6	15.8	18.5	20.0	22.1	25.9	28.0	22.4	28.8	33.2	33.3	35.1
	Exp.	10.7	11.3	11.3	12.2	14.5	17.1	18.3	20.5	24.1	25.8	20.5	25.7	30.3	30.1	32.6
As a percentage of SITC section (%)	Imp.	1.5	1.4	1.5	1.5	1.5	1.4	1.4	1.3	1.3	1.3	1.4	1.5	1.4	1.5	1.6
	Exp.	1.3	1.3	1.4	1.4	1.4	1.3	1.3	1.2	1.2	1.2	1.3	1.3	1.3	1.4	1.4
As a percentage of world trade (%)	Imp.	0.2	0.2	0.2	0.2	0.2	0.2	0.2	0.2	0.2	0.2	0.2	0.2	0.2	0.2	0.2
	Exp.	0.2	0.2	0.2	0.2	0.2	0.2	0.2	0.2	0.2	0.2	0.2	0.2	0.2	0.2	0.2

Graph 1: Annual growth rates of exports, 1999–2013
(In percentage by year)

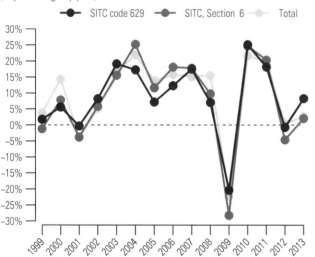

Table 2: Top exporting countries or areas in 2013

Country or area	Value (million US$)	Avg. Growth (%) 09-13	Growth (%) 12-13	World share %	Cum.
World	32 600.0	12.3	8.3	100.0	
Germany	4 541.5	9.4	9.7	13.9	13.9
China	3 617.7	26.7	26.3	11.1	25.0
USA	3 033.2	14.3	3.2	9.3	34.3
Japan	2 184.4	6.7	-11.6	6.7	41.0
France	1 630.7	4.0	5.0	5.0	46.0
Poland	1 620.4	16.6	26.6	5.0	51.0
Italy	1 570.6	11.7	9.3	4.8	55.8
Belgium	1 013.1	6.8	20.1	3.1	58.9
Thailand	1 011.5	8.0	2.9	3.1	62.0
Spain	817.5	11.4	5.8	2.5	64.5
United Kingdom	792.7	6.9	2.5	2.4	67.0
Canada	700.6	6.5	-2.8	2.1	69.1
Turkey	686.7	14.7	13.6	2.1	71.2
Mexico	646.9	20.9	15.6	2.0	73.2
Sweden	622.9	8.2	6.7	1.9	75.1

Graph 2: Trade Balance by MDG regions 2013
(Bln US$)

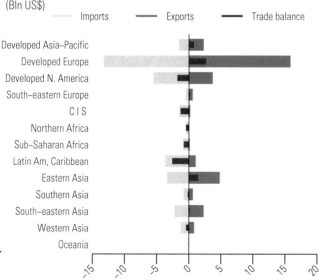

Table 3: Top importing countries or areas in 2013

Country or area	Value (million US$)	Avg. Growth (%) 09-13	Growth (%) 12-13	World share %	Cum.
World	35 124.1	11.9	5.3	100.0	
USA	4 351.1	13.9	1.3	12.4	12.4
Germany	3 519.2	12.8	8.9	10.0	22.4
China	2 545.5	14.7	12.6	7.2	29.7
Mexico	1 583.3	16.3	2.2	4.5	34.2
France	1 302.0	3.6	5.9	3.7	37.9
Canada	1 184.6	10.4	-2.4	3.4	41.2
United Kingdom	1 055.8	9.7	8.2	3.0	44.2
Japan	901.0	10.2	-7.2	2.6	46.8
Russian Federation	870.1	27.7	0.9	2.5	49.3
Belgium	860.2	9.7	20.8	2.4	51.7
Brazil	836.6	16.5	11.9	2.4	54.1
Italy	768.8	6.0	4.9	2.2	56.3
Poland	760.4	7.3	13.1	2.2	58.5
Czech Rep.	721.9	11.3	3.9	2.1	60.5
India	594.0	14.4	-4.4	1.7	62.2

633 Cork manufacture

In 2013, the value (in current US$) of exports of "cork manufacture" (SITC group 633) increased by 4.8 percent (compared to 3.9 percent average growth rate from 2009-2013) to reach 1.6 bln US$ (see table 2), while imports decreased by 0.2 percent to reach 1.5 bln US$ (see table 3). Exports of this commodity accounted for 0.1 percent of world exports of SITC section 6, and less than 0.1 percent of total world merchandise exports (see table 1). Portugal, Spain and France were the top exporters in 2013 (see table 2). They accounted for 65.6, 13.0 and 4.8 percent of world exports, respectively. France, USA and Italy were the top destinations, with respectively 18.7, 16.6 and 9.9 percent of world imports (see table 3).

The top 15 countries/areas accounted for 96.9 and 80.7 percent of total world exports and imports, respectively (see tables 2 and 3). In 2013, Portugal was the country/area with the highest value of net exports (+1.0 bln US$), followed by Spain (+112.0 mln US$). By MDG regions (see graph 2), the largest surpluses in this product group were recorded by Developed Europe (+631.3 mln US$) and Northern Africa (+12.7 mln US$). The largest trade deficits were recorded by Developed North America (-248.5 mln US$), Latin America and the Caribbean (-107.5 mln US$) and Commonwealth of Independent States (-92.5 mln US$).

Table 1: Imports (Imp.) and exports (Exp.), 1999-2013, in current US$

		1999	2000	2001	2002	2003	2004	2005	2006	2007	2008	2009	2010	2011	2012	2013
Values in Bln US$	Imp.	1.2	1.2	1.2	1.2	1.4	1.5	1.5	1.5	1.7	1.6	1.3	1.5	1.6	1.5	1.5
	Exp.	1.2	1.2	1.2	1.3	1.5	1.6	1.5	1.6	1.7	1.6	1.4	1.4	1.6	1.5	1.6
As a percentage of SITC section (%)	Imp.	0.1	0.1	0.1	0.1	0.1	0.1	0.1	0.1	0.1	0.1	0.1	0.1	0.1	0.1	0.1
	Exp.	0.2	0.1	0.1	0.1	0.1	0.1	0.1	0.1	0.1	0.1	0.1	0.1	0.1	0.1	0.1
As a percentage of world trade (%)	Imp.	0.0	0.0	0.0	0.0	0.0	0.0	0.0	0.0	0.0	0.0	0.0	0.0	0.0	0.0	0.0
	Exp.	0.0	0.0	0.0	0.0	0.0	0.0	0.0	0.0	0.0	0.0	0.0	0.0	0.0	0.0	0.0

Graph 1: Annual growth rates of exports, 1999–2013
(In percentage by year)

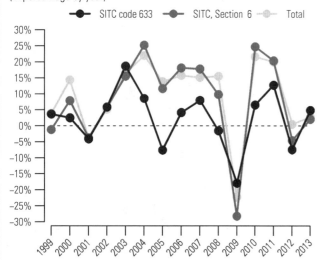

Graph 2: Trade Balance by MDG regions 2013
(Bln US$)

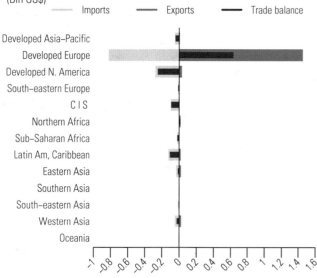

Table 2: Top exporting countries or areas in 2013

Country or area	Value (million US$)	Avg. Growth (%) 09-13	Growth (%) 12-13	World share %	Cum.
World	1 573.9	3.9	4.8	100.0	
Portugal	1 032.3	4.9	3.1	65.6	65.6
Spain	203.9	6.7	14.6	13.0	78.5
France	76.0	7.5	9.6	4.8	83.4
Italy	53.1	-0.1	3.1	3.4	86.7
Germany	32.7	-3.7	-9.5	2.1	88.8
USA	26.2	-7.9	-8.0	1.7	90.5
United Arab Emirates	20.1	23.0	21.7	1.3	91.8
China	16.8	4.8	10.9	1.1	92.8
Belgium	12.2	-2.0	56.4	0.8	93.6
Chile	11.9	16.2	28.6	0.8	94.4
Austria	9.8	-7.7	-7.5	0.6	95.0
Morocco	9.1	0.5	29.5	0.6	95.6
Switzerland	7.6	-30.4	16.7	0.5	96.1
Poland	6.9	22.1	15.7	0.4	96.5
United Kingdom	6.8	6.5	6.1	0.4	96.9

Table 3: Top importing countries or areas in 2013

Country or area	Value (million US$)	Avg. Growth (%) 09-13	Growth (%) 12-13	World share %	Cum.
World	1 503.2	3.3	-0.2	100.0	
France	280.8	0.3	0.1	18.7	18.7
USA	248.8	4.7	0.6	16.6	35.2
Italy	149.5	7.2	1.2	9.9	45.2
Germany	103.7	0.0	-3.7	6.9	52.1
Spain	91.9	0.4	9.6	6.1	58.2
Russian Federation	55.8	18.0	-12.2	3.7	61.9
Argentina	46.3	5.8	12.1	3.1	65.0
Chile	36.1	1.3	4.3	2.4	67.4
United Kingdom	32.0	12.3	12.2	2.1	69.5
Switzerland	30.7	-0.9	11.1	2.0	71.6
Canada	29.7	-1.7	-8.9	2.0	73.5
Portugal	28.2	-2.2	-28.0	1.9	75.4
United Arab Emirates	27.2	21.7	11.4	1.8	77.2
China	27.1	2.7	-23.0	1.8	79.0
Mexico	24.8	12.2	-10.2	1.6	80.7

Veneers, plywood, particle board,and other wood, worked, nes 634

In 2013, the value (in current US$) of exports of "veneers, plywood, particle board,and other wood, worked, nes" (SITC group 634) increased by 5.7 percent (compared to 9.0 percent average growth rate from 2009-2013) to reach 36.2 bln US$ (see table 2), while imports increased by 4.2 percent to reach 34.7 bln US$ (see table 3). Exports of this commodity accounted for 1.6 percent of world exports of SITC section 6, and 0.2 percent of total world merchandise exports (see table 1). China, Germany and Indonesia were the top exporters in 2013 (see table 2). They accounted for 19.0 and 9.0 and 6.3 percent of world exports, respectively. USA, Japan and Germany were the top destinations, with respectively 13.9, 8.2 and 6.5 percent of world imports (see table 3).

The top 15 countries/areas accounted for 75.8 and 60.3 percent of total world exports and imports, respectively (see tables 2 and 3). In 2013, China was the country/area with the highest value of net exports (+6.4 bln US$), followed by Indonesia (+2.0 bln US$). By MDG regions (see graph 2), the largest surpluses in this product group were recorded by Eastern Asia (+4.9 bln US$), South-eastern Asia (+4.2 bln US$) and Developed Europe (+986.5 mln US$). The largest trade deficits were recorded by Developed Asia-Pacific (-2.8 bln US$), Developed North America (-2.4 bln US$) and Western Asia (-2.4 bln US$).

Table 1: Imports (Imp.) and exports (Exp.), 1999-2013, in current US$

		1999	2000	2001	2002	2003	2004	2005	2006	2007	2008	2009	2010	2011	2012	2013
Values in Bln US$	Imp.	18.0	18.2	17.4	19.0	22.5	28.7	30.0	32.1	33.9	33.4	23.6	29.0	33.3	33.3	34.7
	Exp.	17.7	17.2	16.7	18.7	21.8	27.8	29.8	32.3	35.5	34.6	25.7	30.0	34.0	34.3	36.2
As a percentage of	Imp.	2.2	2.0	2.0	2.1	2.2	2.2	2.1	1.9	1.7	1.5	1.5	1.5	1.4	1.5	1.6
SITC section (%)	Exp.	2.2	2.0	2.0	2.1	2.1	2.2	2.1	1.9	1.8	1.6	1.6	1.5	1.5	1.5	1.6
As a percentage of	Imp.	0.3	0.3	0.3	0.3	0.3	0.3	0.3	0.3	0.2	0.2	0.2	0.2	0.2	0.2	0.2
world trade (%)	Exp.	0.3	0.3	0.3	0.3	0.3	0.3	0.3	0.3	0.3	0.2	0.2	0.2	0.2	0.2	0.2

Graph 1: Annual growth rates of exports, 1999–2013
(In percentage by year)

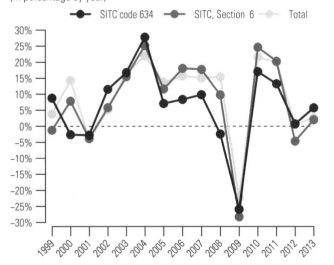

Table 2: Top exporting countries or areas in 2013

Country or area	Value (million US$)	Avg. Growth (%) 09-13	Growth (%) 12-13	World share %	Cum.
World	36243.9	9.0	5.7	100.0	
China	6897.7	17.4	2.6	19.0	19.0
Germany	3244.0	0.4	5.3	9.0	28.0
Indonesia	2285.8	16.0	8.6	6.3	34.3
Malaysia	2227.8	4.4	-1.8	6.1	40.4
Canada	2185.5	14.1	27.3	6.0	46.5
Austria	1519.3	2.7	3.8	4.2	50.7
Russian Federation	1470.5	18.4	9.9	4.1	54.7
Belgium	1288.4	1.7	6.7	3.6	58.3
USA	1235.4	7.5	1.2	3.4	61.7
France	1036.2	3.4	0.5	2.9	64.5
Poland	983.5	7.8	12.7	2.7	67.3
Romania	890.0	24.5	28.2	2.5	69.7
Spain	771.1	3.0	4.4	2.1	71.8
Thailand	729.7	10.0	5.1	2.0	73.8
Finland	699.3	6.8	10.1	1.9	75.8

Graph 2: Trade Balance by MDG regions 2013
(Bln US$)

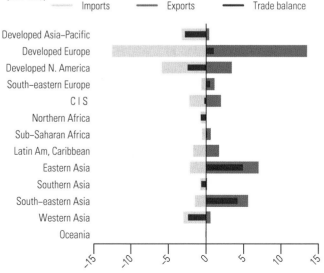

Table 3: Top importing countries or areas in 2013

Country or area	Value (million US$)	Avg. Growth (%) 09-13	Growth (%) 12-13	World share %	Cum.
World	34694.9	10.2	4.2	100.0	
USA	4818.9	11.9	16.8	13.9	13.9
Japan	2834.0	12.1	-0.4	8.2	22.1
Germany	2253.9	7.7	0.7	6.5	28.6
United Kingdom	1376.4	82.5	12.9	4.0	32.5
France	1274.5	2.2	-0.5	3.7	36.2
Canada	1023.1	6.5	-1.1	2.9	39.1
Rep. of Korea	1001.8	7.3	10.1	2.9	42.0
Italy	985.8	3.9	7.6	2.8	44.9
Netherlands	908.6	3.7	1.0	2.6	47.5
Russian Federation	901.9	25.4	10.6	2.6	50.1
Belgium	812.8	5.2	8.2	2.3	52.4
Turkey	792.0	26.8	1.2	2.3	54.7
Mexico	662.7	8.7	7.5	1.9	56.6
Saudi Arabia	643.2	23.7	-10.5	1.9	58.5
Poland	615.6	3.4	13.5	1.8	60.3

635 Wood manufactures, nes

In 2013, the value (in current US$) of exports of "wood manufactures, nes" (SITC group 635) increased by 11.2 percent (compared to 8.4 percent average growth rate from 2009-2013) to reach 28.6 bln US$ (see table 2), while imports increased by 7.1 percent to reach 27.1 bln US$ (see table 3). Exports of this commodity accounted for 1.3 percent of world exports of SITC section 6, and 0.2 percent of total world merchandise exports (see table 1). China, Philippines and Germany were the top exporters in 2013 (see table 2). They accounted for 16.8, 10.8 and 7.5 percent of world exports, respectively. USA, Japan and Germany were the top destinations, with respectively 16.9, 9.9 and 9.8 percent of world imports (see table 3).

The top 15 countries/areas accounted for 73.9 and 75.2 percent of total world exports and imports, respectively (see tables 2 and 3). In 2013, China was the country/area with the highest value of net exports (+4.3 bln US$), followed by Philippines (+3.1 bln US$). By MDG regions (see graph 2), the largest surpluses in this product group were recorded by South-eastern Asia (+4.1 bln US$), Eastern Asia (+4.1 bln US$) and South-eastern Europe (+299.1 mln US$). The largest trade deficits were recorded by Developed Asia-Pacific (-3.1 bln US$), Developed North America (-2.9 bln US$) and Commonwealth of Independent States (-442.8 mln US$).

Table 1: Imports (Imp.) and exports (Exp.), 1999-2013, in current US$

		1999	2000	2001	2002	2003	2004	2005	2006	2007	2008	2009	2010	2011	2012	2013
Values in Bln US$	Imp.	13.3	13.8	13.6	14.6	16.8	19.6	21.1	23.2	26.1	26.5	21.1	23.1	25.7	25.3	27.1
	Exp.	13.9	14.3	13.9	14.7	16.8	20.0	21.2	24.0	26.1	26.0	20.8	22.4	25.9	25.7	28.6
As a percentage of SITC section (%)	Imp.	1.6	1.5	1.6	1.6	1.6	1.5	1.5	1.4	1.3	1.2	1.4	1.2	1.1	1.2	1.2
	Exp.	1.7	1.7	1.7	1.7	1.7	1.6	1.5	1.4	1.3	1.2	1.3	1.2	1.1	1.2	1.3
As a percentage of world trade (%)	Imp.	0.2	0.2	0.2	0.2	0.2	0.2	0.2	0.2	0.2	0.2	0.2	0.2	0.1	0.1	0.1
	Exp.	0.2	0.2	0.2	0.2	0.2	0.2	0.2	0.2	0.2	0.2	0.2	0.1	0.1	0.1	0.2

Graph 1: Annual growth rates of exports, 1999–2013
(In percentage by year)

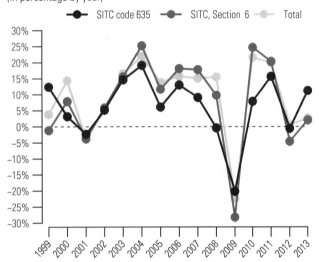

Table 2: Top exporting countries or areas in 2013

Country or area	Value (million US$)	Avg. Growth (%) 09-13	Growth (%) 12-13	World share %	World share % Cum.
World	28 614.5	8.4	11.2	100.0	
China	4 797.6	11.5	6.2	16.8	16.8
Philippines	3 085.2	39.3	42.9	10.8	27.5
Germany	2 159.8	4.6	8.2	7.5	35.1
Poland	1 984.1	8.7	17.9	6.9	42.0
Austria	1 553.7	4.8	4.9	5.4	47.5
Canada	1 359.7	5.5	10.4	4.8	52.2
USA	1 096.9	3.5	3.1	3.8	56.0
Italy	856.2	4.2	8.8	3.0	59.0
France	824.8	0.0	4.4	2.9	61.9
Sweden	672.3	6.4	5.6	2.3	64.3
Netherlands	601.5	13.6	14.3	2.1	66.4
Denmark	593.4	-0.6	25.3	2.1	68.4
Czech Rep.	543.2	7.5	6.9	1.9	70.3
Indonesia	508.2	-2.7	-6.6	1.8	72.1
Belgium	504.9	3.0	3.8	1.8	73.9

Graph 2: Trade Balance by MDG regions 2013
(Bln US$)

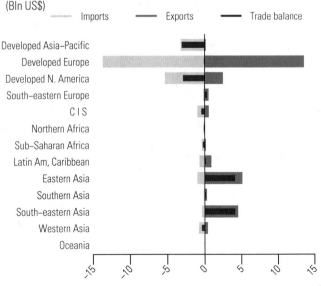

Table 3: Top importing countries or areas in 2013

Country or area	Value (million US$)	Avg. Growth (%) 09-13	Growth (%) 12-13	World share %	World share % Cum.
World	27 121.0	6.5	7.1	100.0	
USA	4 574.5	6.4	10.8	16.9	16.9
Japan	2 687.2	11.9	5.8	9.9	26.8
Germany	2 650.8	6.4	7.7	9.8	36.5
United Kingdom	1 474.2	4.9	8.3	5.4	42.0
France	1 392.6	-0.5	-3.0	5.1	47.1
Switzerland	1 148.2	9.9	8.1	4.2	51.4
Italy	1 033.7	1.5	-2.2	3.8	55.2
Netherlands	779.3	6.0	1.4	2.9	58.0
Canada	762.3	6.9	5.7	2.8	60.8
Belgium	759.7	2.8	5.1	2.8	63.6
Norway	755.9	12.1	6.6	2.8	66.4
Austria	698.8	5.1	12.4	2.6	69.0
Russian Federation	601.3	24.4	17.6	2.2	71.2
Denmark	541.1	-0.3	-0.2	2.0	73.2
Sweden	523.4	10.3	8.8	1.9	75.2

In 2013, the value (in current US$) of exports of "paper and paperboard" (SITC group 641) increased by 2.6 percent (compared to 4.2 percent average growth rate from 2009-2013) to reach 116.3 bln US$ (see table 2), while imports increased by 0.9 percent to reach 118.0 bln US$ (see table 3). Exports of this commodity accounted for 5.1 percent of world exports of SITC section 6, and 0.6 percent of total world merchandise exports (see table 1). Germany, USA and Sweden were the top exporters in 2013 (see table 2). They accounted for 13.0, 9.8 and 8.5 percent of world exports, respectively. USA, Germany and United Kingdom were the top destinations, with respectively 8.8, 8.6 and 5.4 percent of world imports (see table 3).

The top 15 countries/areas accounted for 78.2 and 58.5 percent of total world exports and imports, respectively (see tables 2 and 3). In 2013, Sweden was the country/area with the highest value of net exports (+8.8 bln US$), followed by Finland (+8.8 bln US$). By MDG regions (see graph 2), the largest surpluses in this product group were recorded by Developed Europe (+15.9 bln US$), Developed North America (+4.8 bln US$) and Eastern Asia (+3.9 bln US$). The largest trade deficits were recorded by Latin America and the Caribbean (-6.8 bln US$), Western Asia (-5.6 bln US$) and Southern Asia (-3.4 bln US$).

Table 1: Imports (Imp.) and exports (Exp.), 1999-2013, in current US$

		1999	2000	2001	2002	2003	2004	2005	2006	2007	2008	2009	2010	2011	2012	2013
Values in Bln US$	Imp.	69.0	72.2	69.9	76.1	85.7	96.1	100.1	106.4	116.1	122.9	101.4	112.9	125.1	116.9	118.0
	Exp.	66.5	70.6	67.6	73.8	83.0	93.1	95.8	103.2	113.0	119.6	98.5	110.5	123.3	113.4	116.3
As a percentage of SITC section (%)	Imp.	8.4	8.1	8.2	8.5	8.3	7.5	7.0	6.4	5.9	5.7	6.5	5.9	5.4	5.4	5.4
	Exp.	8.3	8.2	8.1	8.4	8.2	7.3	6.7	6.1	5.7	5.5	6.3	5.7	5.3	5.1	5.1
As a percentage of world trade (%)	Imp.	1.2	1.1	1.1	1.2	1.1	1.0	0.9	0.9	0.8	0.8	0.8	0.7	0.7	0.6	0.6
	Exp.	1.2	1.1	1.1	1.2	1.1	1.0	0.9	0.9	0.8	0.7	0.8	0.7	0.7	0.6	0.6

Graph 1: Annual growth rates of exports, 1999–2013
(In percentage by year)

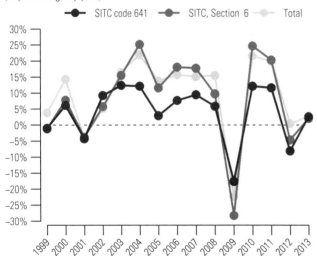

Table 2: Top exporting countries or areas in 2013

Country or area	Value (million US$)	Avg. Growth (%) 09-13	Growth (%) 12-13	World share %	Cum.
World	116272.2	4.2	2.6	100.0	
Germany	15090.1	2.1	-0.8	13.0	13.0
USA	11441.0	5.9	1.2	9.8	22.8
Sweden	9828.3	2.7	0.4	8.5	31.3
Finland	9327.9	2.1	2.0	8.0	39.3
Canada	6898.6	-1.5	1.5	5.9	45.2
China	6812.9	21.4	19.8	5.9	51.1
France	5077.1	-0.7	-0.7	4.4	55.5
Italy	4521.0	6.7	5.9	3.9	59.3
Austria	3541.6	1.6	-0.6	3.0	62.4
Belgium	3489.7	4.4	9.2	3.0	65.4
Indonesia	3275.3	2.5	-4.8	2.8	68.2
Spain	3095.6	5.3	7.4	2.7	70.9
Netherlands	3069.0	3.1	8.0	2.6	73.5
Rep. of Korea	2807.0	10.7	7.2	2.4	75.9
Poland	2628.7	11.0	8.0	2.3	78.2

Graph 2: Trade Balance by MDG regions 2013
(Bln US$)

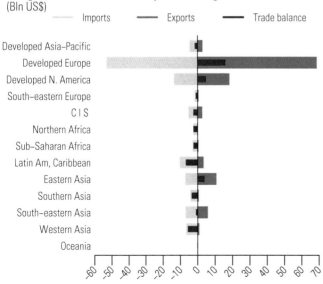

Table 3: Top importing countries or areas in 2013

Country or area	Value (million US$)	Avg. Growth (%) 09-13	Growth (%) 12-13	World share %	Cum.
World	117980.6	3.8	0.9	100.0	
USA	10381.6	0.7	1.7	8.8	8.8
Germany	10171.1	0.9	-0.7	8.6	17.4
United Kingdom	6318.7	-0.6	0.2	5.4	22.8
France	5637.0	-1.8	-2.5	4.8	27.6
Italy	4824.1	2.6	2.6	4.1	31.6
Belgium	3894.3	3.1	4.9	3.3	34.9
China	3660.3	3.9	-4.5	3.1	38.0
Poland	3404.4	7.7	10.1	2.9	40.9
Mexico	3274.7	10.2	4.3	2.8	43.7
Netherlands	3207.3	1.5	4.3	2.7	46.4
Canada	3129.7	2.0	1.7	2.7	49.1
Spain	3092.7	-0.2	2.3	2.6	51.7
Russian Federation	2900.0	10.3	1.6	2.5	54.2
Turkey	2792.2	9.8	8.1	2.4	56.5
Japan	2294.4	0.6	-22.8	1.9	58.5

642 Paper and paperboard, cut to size or shape; articles of paper or paperboard

In 2013, the value (in current US$) of exports of "paper and paperboard, cut to size or shape; articles of paper or paperboard" (SITC group 642) increased by 7.1 percent (compared to 7.5 percent average growth rate from 2009-2013) to reach 63.9 bln US$ (see table 2), while imports increased by 4.6 percent to reach 62.2 bln US$ (see table 3). Exports of this commodity accounted for 2.8 percent of world exports of SITC section 6, and 0.3 percent of total world merchandise exports (see table 1). China, Germany and USA were the top exporters in 2013 (see table 2). They accounted for 15.2, 12.3 and 8.1 percent of world exports, respectively. USA, Germany and France were the top destinations, with respectively 10.6, 7.0 and 6.4 percent of world imports (see table 3).

The top 15 countries/areas accounted for 72.1 and 58.5 percent of total world exports and imports, respectively (see tables 2 and 3). In 2013, China was the country/area with the highest value of net exports (+8.8 bln US$), followed by Germany (+3.5 bln US$). By MDG regions (see graph 2), the largest surpluses in this product group were recorded by Eastern Asia (+8.6 bln US$), Developed Europe (+2.3 bln US$) and South-eastern Asia (+245.4 mln US$). The largest trade deficits were recorded by Commonwealth of Independent States (-2.4 bln US$), Developed North America (-2.1 bln US$) and Latin America and the Caribbean (-1.6 bln US$).

Table 1: Imports (Imp.) and exports (Exp.), 1999-2013, in current US$

		1999	2000	2001	2002	2003	2004	2005	2006	2007	2008	2009	2010	2011	2012	2013
Values in Bln US$	Imp.	27.8	29.3	30.2	27.1	31.0	34.8	37.1	39.9	48.1	53.8	48.9	52.8	59.0	59.5	62.2
	Exp.	27.6	28.8	29.8	26.9	30.7	34.2	36.4	39.6	47.3	52.1	47.9	52.0	59.2	59.7	63.9
As a percentage of SITC section (%)	Imp.	3.4	3.3	3.6	3.0	3.0	2.7	2.6	2.4	2.5	2.5	3.1	2.7	2.6	2.7	2.8
	Exp.	3.4	3.3	3.6	3.1	3.0	2.7	2.6	2.4	2.4	2.4	3.1	2.7	2.5	2.7	2.8
As a percentage of world trade (%)	Imp.	0.5	0.4	0.5	0.4	0.4	0.4	0.4	0.3	0.3	0.3	0.4	0.3	0.3	0.3	0.3
	Exp.	0.5	0.5	0.5	0.4	0.4	0.4	0.4	0.3	0.3	0.3	0.4	0.3	0.3	0.3	0.3

Graph 1: Annual growth rates of exports, 1999–2013
(In percentage by year)

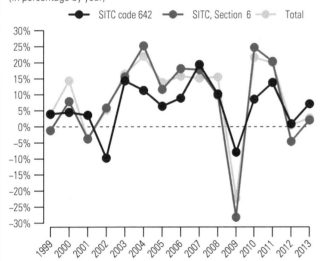

Graph 2: Trade Balance by MDG regions 2013
(Bln US$)

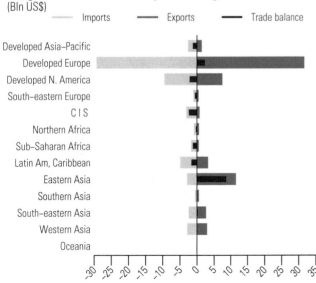

Table 2: Top exporting countries or areas in 2013

Country or area	Value (million US$)	Avg. Growth (%) 09-13	Growth (%) 12-13	World share %	Cum.
World	63905.9	7.5	7.1	100.0	
China	9732.5	24.4	14.7	15.2	15.2
Germany	7879.7	2.4	4.9	12.3	27.6
USA	5189.9	5.9	4.0	8.1	35.7
Italy	3253.4	3.2	6.2	5.1	40.8
Poland	2697.9	11.5	13.0	4.2	45.0
Netherlands	2552.0	5.2	9.5	4.0	49.0
Belgium	2422.8	4.8	15.8	3.8	52.8
Canada	2223.1	2.9	3.9	3.5	56.3
France	1953.0	-0.7	3.7	3.1	59.3
United Kingdom	1446.7	1.3	0.3	2.3	61.6
Spain	1414.5	3.0	4.1	2.2	63.8
Turkey	1401.1	16.8	18.3	2.2	66.0
Mexico	1334.1	8.3	36.7	2.1	68.1
Sweden	1305.4	0.7	-7.3	2.0	70.1
Czech Rep.	1239.0	6.0	11.6	1.9	72.1

Table 3: Top importing countries or areas in 2013

Country or area	Value (million US$)	Avg. Growth (%) 09-13	Growth (%) 12-13	World share %	Cum.
World	62172.8	6.2	4.6	100.0	
USA	6590.6	6.1	2.9	10.6	10.6
Germany	4367.2	6.2	8.3	7.0	17.6
France	3995.6	2.6	1.6	6.4	24.1
United Kingdom	3200.5	5.9	10.6	5.1	29.2
Canada	2918.1	6.9	4.9	4.7	33.9
Netherlands	2370.1	8.6	9.8	3.8	37.7
Belgium	2124.9	4.4	12.1	3.4	41.1
Mexico	1801.4	4.0	3.6	2.9	44.0
Russian Federation	1674.3	6.9	2.3	2.7	46.7
Japan	1360.9	8.5	-1.3	2.2	48.9
Switzerland	1315.4	3.4	5.7	2.1	51.0
Spain	1230.0	1.0	6.6	2.0	53.0
Poland	1191.5	7.0	11.2	1.9	54.9
China, Hong Kong SAR	1121.8	7.1	-2.3	1.8	56.7
Italy	1093.4	3.3	4.0	1.8	58.5

In 2013, the value (in current US$) of exports of "textile yarn" (SITC group 651) increased by 7.4 percent (compared to 11.7 percent average growth rate from 2009-2013) to reach 58.7 bln US$ (see table 2), while imports increased by 7.2 percent to reach 55.2 bln US$ (see table 3). Exports of this commodity accounted for 2.6 percent of world exports of SITC section 6, and 0.3 percent of total world merchandise exports (see table 1). China, India and USA were the top exporters in 2013 (see table 2). They accounted for 20.8, 12.1 and 5.8 percent of world exports, respectively. China, China, Hong Kong SAR and Turkey were the top destinations, with respectively 17.4, 5.9 and 5.5 percent of world imports (see table 3).

The top 15 countries/areas accounted for 78.2 and 65.6 percent of total world exports and imports, respectively (see tables 2 and 3). In 2013, India was the country/area with the highest value of net exports (+6.0 bln US$), followed by China (+2.6 bln US$). By MDG regions (see graph 2), the largest surpluses in this product group were recorded by Southern Asia (+6.0 bln US$), Eastern Asia (+3.5 bln US$) and South-eastern Asia (+3.4 bln US$). The largest trade deficits were recorded by Latin America and the Caribbean (-3.7 bln US$), Developed Europe (-3.2 bln US$) and Western Asia (-1.3 bln US$).

Table 1: Imports (Imp.) and exports (Exp.), 1999-2013, in current US$

		1999	2000	2001	2002	2003	2004	2005	2006	2007	2008	2009	2010	2011	2012	2013
Values in Bln US$	Imp.	31.9	34.2	32.3	32.6	35.6	38.8	38.8	41.3	44.8	45.3	36.5	47.3	54.9	51.5	55.2
	Exp.	30.3	32.7	30.9	31.5	35.3	40.3	40.3	43.7	47.5	46.9	37.7	50.2	58.0	54.6	58.7
As a percentage of SITC section (%)	Imp.	3.9	3.8	3.8	3.6	3.5	3.0	2.7	2.5	2.3	2.1	2.3	2.5	2.4	2.4	2.5
	Exp.	3.8	3.8	3.7	3.6	3.5	3.2	2.8	2.6	2.4	2.2	2.4	2.6	2.5	2.5	2.6
As a percentage of world trade (%)	Imp.	0.6	0.5	0.5	0.5	0.5	0.4	0.4	0.3	0.3	0.3	0.3	0.3	0.3	0.3	0.3
	Exp.	0.5	0.5	0.5	0.5	0.5	0.4	0.4	0.4	0.3	0.3	0.3	0.3	0.3	0.3	0.3

Graph 1: Annual growth rates of exports, 1999–2013
(In percentage by year)

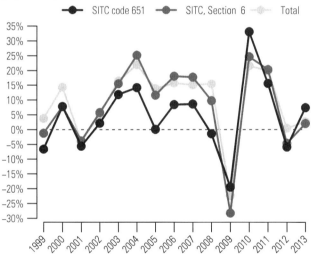

Table 2: Top exporting countries or areas in 2013

Country or area	Value (million US$)	Avg. Growth (%) 09-13	Growth (%) 12-13	World share %	Cum.
World..................	58673.8	11.7	7.4	100.0	
China..................	12176.9	14.7	6.0	20.8	20.8
India..................	7086.0	34.1	33.6	12.1	32.8
USA..................	3388.3	12.0	1.0	5.8	38.6
China, Hong Kong SAR........	3015.7	2.1	5.0	5.1	43.7
Italy..................	2644.3	4.7	-0.3	4.5	48.3
Indonesia..................	2425.0	10.9	9.2	4.1	52.4
Pakistan..................	2275.5	14.4	3.5	3.9	56.3
Other Asia, nes..................	2198.6	5.3	-4.8	3.7	60.0
Viet Nam..................	2071.0	26.0	17.4	3.5	63.5
Turkey..................	1777.4	14.0	6.8	3.0	66.6
Rep. of Korea..................	1735.1	10.2	-1.6	3.0	69.5
Germany..................	1698.1	1.1	0.1	2.9	72.4
Japan..................	1286.9	10.0	-9.5	2.2	74.6
Netherlands..................	1120.2	12.8	19.2	1.9	76.5
Thailand..................	993.1	6.1	15.5	1.7	78.2

Graph 2: Trade Balance by MDG regions 2013
(Bln US$)

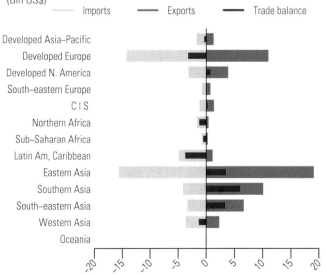

Table 3: Top importing countries or areas in 2013

Country or area	Value (million US$)	Avg. Growth (%) 09-13	Growth (%) 12-13	World share %	Cum.
World..................	55212.5	10.9	7.2	100.0	
China..................	9615.6	21.5	25.5	17.4	17.4
China, Hong Kong SAR........	3280.4	2.5	2.6	5.9	23.4
Turkey..................	3061.7	13.9	2.5	5.5	28.9
Italy..................	2721.3	5.9	4.1	4.9	33.8
USA..................	2664.8	9.8	0.6	4.8	38.7
Germany..................	2474.3	7.3	5.4	4.5	43.1
Rep. of Korea..................	2251.2	9.6	9.3	4.1	47.2
Bangladesh..................	*1713.0*	17.1	-1.6	3.1	50.3
Brazil..................	1579.0	7.9	-4.3	2.9	53.2
Japan..................	1400.4	12.5	-5.6	2.5	55.7
Viet Nam..................	1128.9	17.9	15.1	2.0	57.8
India..................	1127.6	13.1	15.1	2.0	59.8
France..................	1095.3	2.5	-3.0	2.0	61.8
United Kingdom..................	1079.8	14.7	8.6	2.0	63.7
Egypt..................	1048.8	10.9	1.7	1.9	65.6

652 Cotton fabrics, woven (not including narrow or special fabrics)

In 2013, the value (in current US$) of exports of "cotton fabrics, woven (not including narrow or special fabrics)" (SITC group 652) increased by 9.0 percent (the same as the average growth rate from 2009-2013) to reach 34.0 bln US$ (see table 2), while imports increased by 1.0 percent to reach 24.4 bln US$ (see table 3). Exports of this commodity accounted for 1.5 percent of world exports of SITC section 6, and 0.2 percent of total world merchandise exports (see table 1). China, Pakistan and India were the top exporters in 2013 (see table 2). They accounted for 45.4, 8.2 and 5.4 percent of world exports, respectively. Bangladesh, China and China, Hong Kong SAR were the top destinations, with respectively 10.2, 7.3 and 6.5 percent of world imports (see table 3).

The top 15 countries/areas accounted for 87.5 and 62.1 percent of total world exports and imports, respectively (see tables 2 and 3). In 2013, China was the country/area with the highest value of net exports (+13.7 bln US$), followed by Pakistan (+2.7 bln US$). By MDG regions (see graph 2), the largest surpluses in this product group were recorded by Eastern Asia (+14.0 bln US$), Southern Asia (+1.4 bln US$) and Developed Europe (+892.9 mln US$). The largest trade deficits were recorded by South-eastern Asia (-2.2 bln US$), Latin America and the Caribbean (-1.4 bln US$) and Northern Africa (-1.2 bln US$).

Table 1: Imports (Imp.) and exports (Exp.), 1999-2013, in current US$

		1999	2000	2001	2002	2003	2004	2005	2006	2007	2008	2009	2010	2011	2012	2013
Values in Bln US$	Imp.	19.3	19.7	19.6	21.2	22.6	24.9	24.8	23.8	24.6	26.9	20.5	23.7	28.1	24.2	24.4
	Exp.	21.1	22.0	22.2	24.4	26.5	28.8	28.9	30.1	30.0	30.7	24.1	28.6	33.6	31.2	34.0
As a percentage of	Imp.	2.4	2.2	2.3	2.4	2.2	1.9	1.7	1.4	1.3	1.2	1.3	1.2	1.2	1.1	1.1
SITC section (%)	Exp.	2.6	2.5	2.7	2.8	2.6	2.3	2.0	1.8	1.5	1.4	1.6	1.5	1.4	1.4	1.5
As a percentage of	Imp.	0.3	0.3	0.3	0.3	0.3	0.3	0.2	0.2	0.2	0.2	0.2	0.2	0.2	0.1	0.1
world trade (%)	Exp.	0.4	0.3	0.4	0.4	0.4	0.3	0.3	0.3	0.2	0.2	0.2	0.2	0.2	0.2	0.2

Graph 1: Annual growth rates of exports, 1999–2013
(In percentage by year)

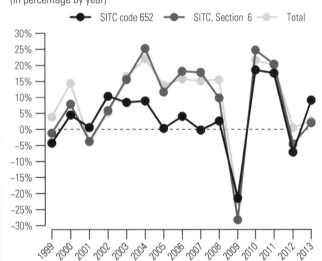

Table 2: Top exporting countries or areas in 2013

Country or area	Value (million US$)	Avg. Growth (%) 09-13	Growth (%) 12-13	World share %	Cum.
World	34033.2	9.0	9.0	100.0	
China	15446.8	16.2	16.8	45.4	45.4
Pakistan	2790.0	13.4	6.7	8.2	53.6
India	1836.9	20.4	13.0	5.4	59.0
China, Hong Kong SAR	1794.0	-2.3	-3.5	5.3	64.3
Italy	1658.2	-1.8	-3.4	4.9	69.1
Turkey	1293.0	8.8	12.7	3.8	72.9
Germany	1036.9	1.7	1.0	3.0	76.0
Japan	635.3	-0.8	-10.1	1.9	77.8
Spain	610.5	2.1	0.7	1.8	79.6
USA	583.2	0.5	-10.3	1.7	81.3
Thailand	499.7	7.5	10.8	1.5	82.8
Rep. of Korea	449.3	3.7	-5.1	1.3	84.1
Netherlands	406.5	6.8	8.3	1.2	85.3
Dominican Rep.	376.9	7.6	63.3	1.1	86.4
France	366.6	-9.1	-9.9	1.1	87.5

Graph 2: Trade Balance by MDG regions 2013
(Bln US$)

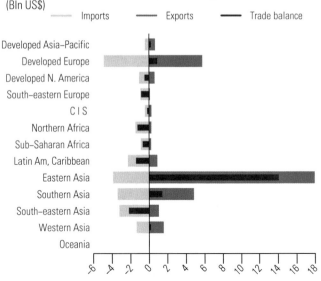

Table 3: Top importing countries or areas in 2013

Country or area	Value (million US$)	Avg. Growth (%) 09-13	Growth (%) 12-13	World share %	Cum.
World	24439.0	4.5	1.0	100.0	
Bangladesh	2490.7	14.0	-1.6	10.2	10.2
China	1780.3	1.1	-3.0	7.3	17.5
China, Hong Kong SAR	1592.6	-2.8	-3.6	6.5	24.0
Viet Nam	1499.3	10.0	12.0	6.1	30.1
Indonesia	1084.9	14.0	0.8	4.4	34.6
Italy	995.4	3.2	9.4	4.1	38.6
USA	965.4	7.9	-3.9	4.0	42.6
Turkey	849.9	0.8	10.7	3.5	46.1
Germany	814.6	5.9	6.7	3.3	49.4
Tunisia	712.8	-3.7	0.6	2.9	52.3
Mexico	553.1	2.7	-8.3	2.3	54.6
Romania	503.5	1.1	7.0	2.1	56.6
Morocco	454.6	-1.1	-8.7	1.9	58.5
Sri Lanka	448.3	3.7	-15.9	1.8	60.3
Rep. of Korea	431.9	7.0	5.5	1.8	62.1

Fabrics, woven, of man-made textile materials (not narrow or special fabrics) 653

In 2013, the value (in current US$) of exports of "fabrics, woven, of man-made textile materials (not narrow or special fabrics)" (SITC group 653) increased by 7.1 percent (compared to 9.7 percent average growth rate from 2009-2013) to reach 45.6 bln US$ (see table 2), while imports increased by 3.2 percent to reach 33.8 bln US$ (see table 3). Exports of this commodity accounted for 2.0 percent of world exports of SITC section 6, and 0.2 percent of total world merchandise exports (see table 1). China, Rep. of Korea and Other Asia, nes were the top exporters in 2013 (see table 2). They accounted for 42.5, 5.8 and 4.7 percent of world exports, respectively. Viet Nam, China and United Arab Emirates were the top destinations, with respectively 8.6, 7.8 and 4.4 percent of world imports (see table 3).

The top 15 countries/areas accounted for 88.3 and 53.5 percent of total world exports and imports, respectively (see tables 2 and 3). In 2013, China was the country/area with the highest value of net exports (+16.7 bln US$), followed by Rep. of Korea (+2.3 bln US$). By MDG regions (see graph 2), the largest surpluses in this product group were recorded by Eastern Asia (+20.8 bln US$), Southern Asia (+1.2 bln US$) and Developed Asia-Pacific (+963.4 mln US$). The largest trade deficits were recorded by Latin America and the Caribbean (-3.2 bln US$), South-eastern Asia (-3.1 bln US$) and Northern Africa (-1.7 bln US$).

Table 1: Imports (Imp.) and exports (Exp.), 1999-2013, in current US$

		1999	2000	2001	2002	2003	2004	2005	2006	2007	2008	2009	2010	2011	2012	2013
Values in Bln US$	Imp.	28.8	29.3	26.6	26.0	26.9	28.9	28.3	28.8	30.4	31.2	25.6	28.9	34.5	32.7	33.8
	Exp.	30.2	31.6	28.3	27.7	29.8	32.7	32.4	33.5	36.4	37.5	31.5	36.2	44.0	42.6	45.6
As a percentage of	Imp.	3.5	3.3	3.1	2.9	2.6	2.3	2.0	1.7	1.5	1.4	1.6	1.5	1.5	1.5	1.5
SITC section (%)	Exp.	3.8	3.7	3.4	3.1	2.9	2.6	2.3	2.0	1.8	1.7	2.0	1.9	1.9	1.9	2.0
As a percentage of	Imp.	0.5	0.4	0.4	0.4	0.4	0.3	0.3	0.2	0.2	0.2	0.2	0.2	0.2	0.2	0.2
world trade (%)	Exp.	0.5	0.5	0.5	0.4	0.4	0.4	0.3	0.3	0.3	0.2	0.3	0.2	0.2	0.2	0.2

Graph 1: Annual growth rates of exports, 1999–2013
(In percentage by year)

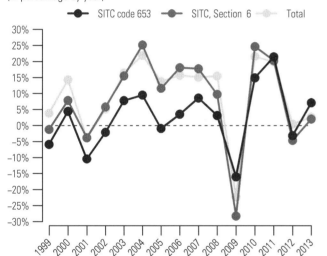

Table 2: Top exporting countries or areas in 2013

Country or area	Value (million US$)	Avg. Growth (%) 09-13	Growth (%) 12-13	World share %	Cum.
World	45635.6	9.7	7.1	100.0	
China	19383.5	18.4	13.0	42.5	42.5
Rep. of Korea	2667.4	9.2	2.8	5.8	48.3
Other Asia, nes	2144.7	4.8	-3.3	4.7	53.0
India	2126.1	2.7	16.2	4.7	57.7
Italy	1809.0	4.1	4.3	4.0	61.6
United Arab Emirates	*1781.7*	13.4	21.7	3.9	65.5
Turkey	1745.3	8.5	9.7	3.8	69.4
Japan	1637.7	1.2	-14.1	3.6	73.0
Germany	1499.1	1.6	2.4	3.3	76.2
Indonesia	1146.5	8.5	-11.3	2.5	78.8
USA	1088.0	9.9	5.3	2.4	81.1
Spain	862.9	7.4	20.1	1.9	83.0
Belgium	834.9	2.5	14.4	1.8	84.9
China, Hong Kong SAR	822.0	-0.2	-8.0	1.8	86.7
France	739.0	-1.2	4.3	1.6	88.3

Graph 2: Trade Balance by MDG regions 2013
(Bln US$)

Imports ▬ Exports ▬ Trade balance

Developed Asia–Pacific
Developed Europe
Developed N. America
South–eastern Europe
C I S
Northern Africa
Sub–Saharan Africa
Latin Am, Caribbean
Eastern Asia
Southern Asia
South–eastern Asia
Western Asia
Oceania

Table 3: Top importing countries or areas in 2013

Country or area	Value (million US$)	Avg. Growth (%) 09-13	Growth (%) 12-13	World share %	Cum.
World	33778.4	7.1	3.2	100.0	
Viet Nam	2900.0	16.8	14.0	8.6	8.6
China	2648.9	0.5	-6.1	7.8	16.4
United Arab Emirates	*1490.5*	5.9	11.4	4.4	20.8
USA	1394.7	11.3	3.9	4.1	25.0
Indonesia	1187.8	24.9	2.2	3.5	28.5
Germany	1171.4	4.8	7.8	3.5	32.0
China, Hong Kong SAR	919.6	-1.6	-10.5	2.7	34.7
Turkey	906.3	7.5	0.3	2.7	37.4
Mexico	898.3	10.3	-1.1	2.7	40.0
Italy	856.6	7.4	5.6	2.5	42.6
Brazil	828.9	23.5	9.6	2.5	45.0
United Kingdom	762.3	4.5	9.9	2.3	47.3
Romania	724.8	6.5	2.1	2.1	49.4
Bangladesh	*703.9*	8.0	-1.6	2.1	51.5
Cambodia	667.4	24.2	14.9	2.0	53.5

654 Other textile fabrics, woven

In 2013, the value (in current US$) of exports of "other textile fabrics, woven" (SITC group 654) decreased by 0.8 percent (compared to 4.2 percent average growth rate from 2009-2013) to reach 10.5 bln US$ (see table 2), while imports decreased by 2.7 percent to reach 9.0 bln US$ (see table 3). Exports of this commodity accounted for 0.5 percent of world exports of SITC section 6, and 0.1 percent of total world merchandise exports (see table 1). China, Italy and Germany were the top exporters in 2013 (see table 2). They accounted for 28.1, 19.4 and 5.5 percent of world exports, respectively. China, USA and Germany were the top destinations, with respectively 10.1, 7.0 and 6.7 percent of world imports (see table 3).

The top 15 countries/areas accounted for 86.0 and 63.2 percent of total world exports and imports, respectively (see tables 2 and 3). In 2013, China was the country/area with the highest value of net exports (+2.0 bln US$), followed by Italy (+1.5 bln US$). By MDG regions (see graph 2), the largest surpluses in this product group were recorded by Eastern Asia (+2.1 bln US$), Developed Europe (+1.7 bln US$) and Southern Asia (+149.9 mln US$). The largest trade deficits were recorded by Developed North America (-449.9 mln US$), South-eastern Asia (-400.5 mln US$) and South-eastern Europe (-369.2 mln US$).

Table 1: Imports (Imp.) and exports (Exp.), 1999-2013, in current US$

		1999	2000	2001	2002	2003	2004	2005	2006	2007	2008	2009	2010	2011	2012	2013
Values in Bln US$	Imp.	8.3	8.5	8.1	7.9	8.5	10.1	10.4	10.6	11.0	11.1	8.0	8.7	10.1	9.2	9.0
	Exp.	9.3	9.9	9.1	8.6	9.3	11.1	11.1	11.5	11.9	12.0	8.9	9.9	11.2	10.6	10.5
As a percentage of	Imp.	1.0	1.0	1.0	0.9	0.8	0.8	0.7	0.6	0.6	0.5	0.5	0.5	0.4	0.4	0.4
SITC section (%)	Exp.	1.2	1.1	1.1	1.0	0.9	0.9	0.8	0.7	0.6	0.6	0.6	0.5	0.5	0.5	0.5
As a percentage of	Imp.	0.1	0.1	0.1	0.1	0.1	0.1	0.1	0.1	0.1	0.1	0.1	0.1	0.1	0.1	0.0
world trade (%)	Exp.	0.2	0.2	0.1	0.1	0.1	0.1	0.1	0.1	0.1	0.1	0.1	0.1	0.1	0.1	0.1

Graph 1: Annual growth rates of exports, 1999–2013
(In percentage by year)

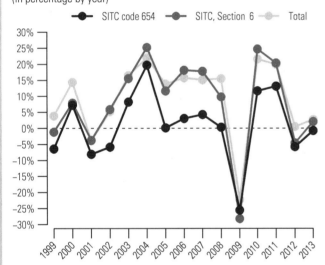

Graph 2: Trade Balance by MDG regions 2013
(Bln US$)

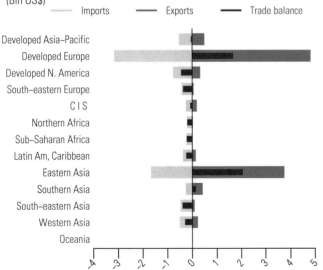

Table 2: Top exporting countries or areas in 2013

Country or area	Value (million US$)	Avg. Growth (%) 09-13	Growth (%) 12-13	World share %	Cum.
World	10516.1	4.2	-0.8	100.0	
China	2952.0	11.1	1.9	28.1	28.1
Italy	2044.7	2.0	-2.5	19.4	47.5
Germany	574.2	-0.6	-4.9	5.5	53.0
Japan	472.7	1.0	-12.2	4.5	57.5
United Kingdom	451.8	3.7	-4.7	4.3	61.8
France	342.0	-2.4	-2.9	3.3	65.0
India	340.8	-3.7	1.2	3.2	68.3
Other Asia, nes	299.1	14.5	1.8	2.8	71.1
China, Hong Kong SAR	290.2	-7.4	-8.6	2.8	73.9
USA	288.0	4.6	0.6	2.7	76.6
Czech Rep	282.1	9.9	5.3	2.7	79.3
Belgium	231.0	8.0	11.7	2.2	81.5
Rep. of Korea	192.8	2.7	-8.2	1.8	83.3
Turkey	157.1	4.0	-2.1	1.5	84.8
Spain	127.0	-8.2	-8.1	1.2	86.0

Table 3: Top importing countries or areas in 2013

Country or area	Value (million US$)	Avg. Growth (%) 09-13	Growth (%) 12-13	World share %	Cum.
World	8960.4	2.8	-2.7	100.0	
China	902.2	2.1	-8.1	10.1	10.1
USA	625.3	9.1	-1.6	7.0	17.0
Germany	604.3	3.5	-0.6	6.7	23.8
Italy	539.2	4.9	-3.4	6.0	29.8
Japan	472.5	10.1	-2.7	5.3	35.1
China, Hong Kong SAR	399.5	-5.2	-4.8	4.5	39.5
France	365.1	-1.1	-1.3	4.1	43.6
Rep. of Korea	312.7	7.8	-1.6	3.5	47.1
Turkey	308.1	7.1	-3.0	3.4	50.5
Romania	231.7	-0.2	-3.7	2.6	53.1
United Kingdom	227.1	1.5	2.5	2.5	55.7
Viet Nam	182.9	10.8	10.1	2.0	57.7
Spain	169.6	-9.1	-4.3	1.9	59.6
India	166.9	-7.2	-9.8	1.9	61.5
Poland	153.4	-1.5	-2.2	1.7	63.2

In 2013, the value (in current US$) of exports of "knitted or crocheted fabrics, nes," (SITC group 655) increased by 8.6 percent (compared to 10.7 percent average growth rate from 2009-2013) to reach 32.8 bln US$ (see table 2), while imports increased by 7.8 percent to reach 24.9 bln US$ (see table 3). Exports of this commodity accounted for 1.4 percent of world exports of SITC section 6, and 0.2 percent of total world merchandise exports (see table 1). China, Rep. of Korea and Other Asia, nes were the top exporters in 2013 (see table 2). They accounted for 39.3, 12.5 and 8.0 percent of world exports, respectively. Viet Nam, China and China, Hong Kong SAR were the top destinations, with respectively 11.0, 9.3 and 9.1 percent of world imports (see table 3).

The top 15 countries/areas accounted for 90.8 and 65.1 percent of total world exports and imports, respectively (see tables 2 and 3). In 2013, China was the country/area with the highest value of net exports (+10.6 bln US$), followed by Rep. of Korea (+4.0 bln US$). By MDG regions (see graph 2), the largest surpluses in this product group were recorded by Eastern Asia (+17.4 bln US$), Developed Europe (+957.6 mln US$) and Western Asia (+631.5 mln US$). The largest trade deficits were recorded by South-eastern Asia (-5.8 bln US$), Latin America and the Caribbean (-2.0 bln US$) and Southern Asia (-972.0 mln US$).

Table 1: Imports (Imp.) and exports (Exp.), 1999-2013, in current US$

		1999	2000	2001	2002	2003	2004	2005	2006	2007	2008	2009	2010	2011	2012	2013
Values in Bln US$	Imp.	12.5	13.6	12.6	12.8	14.2	15.5	16.6	17.5	19.4	19.9	17.0	19.9	22.8	23.1	24.9
	Exp.	14.5	15.8	14.9	16.0	17.7	19.4	19.8	21.8	24.3	24.9	21.8	26.3	30.7	30.2	32.8
As a percentage of	Imp.	1.5	1.5	1.5	1.4	1.4	1.2	1.2	1.1	1.0	0.9	1.1	1.0	1.0	1.1	1.1
SITC section (%)	Exp.	1.8	1.8	1.8	1.8	1.7	1.5	1.4	1.3	1.2	1.1	1.4	1.4	1.3	1.4	1.4
As a percentage of	Imp.	0.2	0.2	0.2	0.2	0.2	0.2	0.2	0.1	0.1	0.1	0.1	0.1	0.1	0.1	0.1
world trade (%)	Exp.	0.3	0.2	0.2	0.2	0.2	0.2	0.2	0.2	0.2	0.2	0.2	0.2	0.2	0.2	0.2

Graph 1: Annual growth rates of exports, 1999–2013
(In percentage by year)

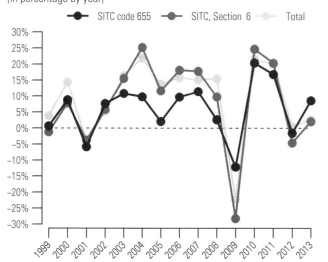

Table 2: Top exporting countries or areas in 2013

Country or area	Value (million US$)	Avg. Growth (%) 09-13	Growth (%) 12-13	World share %	Cum.
World	32 800.4	10.7	8.6	100.0	
China	12 900.4	19.0	15.0	39.3	39.3
Rep. of Korea	4 087.7	6.7	0.4	12.5	51.8
Other Asia, nes	2 612.2	11.7	6.8	8.0	59.8
China, Hong Kong SAR	2 560.0	3.0	4.1	7.8	67.6
Turkey	1 681.9	14.5	7.7	5.1	72.7
Italy	1 312.4	4.8	9.0	4.0	76.7
USA	1 074.4	4.2	4.1	3.3	80.0
Germany	992.0	3.0	4.7	3.0	83.0
Japan	611.3	-0.1	-20.6	1.9	84.9
France	510.4	1.1	3.2	1.6	86.4
Spain	364.6	9.9	8.6	1.1	87.5
Thailand	317.9	14.4	20.2	1.0	88.5
Viet Nam	267.6	27.8	18.9	0.8	89.3
India	256.5	23.8	22.5	0.8	90.1
Belgium	230.3	5.7	23.6	0.7	90.8

Graph 2: Trade Balance by MDG regions 2013
(Bln US$)

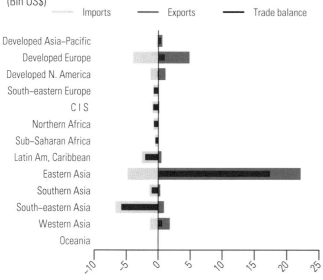

Table 3: Top importing countries or areas in 2013

Country or area	Value (million US$)	Avg. Growth (%) 09-13	Growth (%) 12-13	World share %	Cum.
World	24 910.2	10.1	7.8	100.0	
Viet Nam	2 744.6	28.4	27.2	11.0	11.0
China	2 322.0	2.1	-1.6	9.3	20.3
China, Hong Kong SAR	2 274.8	2.3	4.1	9.1	29.5
Cambodia	1 604.7	21.4	15.0	6.4	35.9
Indonesia	1 336.6	20.8	3.4	5.4	41.3
USA	1 019.0	10.0	-0.2	4.1	45.4
Mexico	742.2	3.3	1.3	3.0	48.3
Italy	741.0	8.6	15.1	3.0	51.3
Sri Lanka	620.3	10.5	-7.7	2.5	53.8
Russian Federation	561.8	19.0	14.5	2.3	56.1
Germany	501.6	5.6	4.1	2.0	58.1
Brazil	448.2	7.3	-7.2	1.8	59.9
Turkey	446.7	18.0	26.1	1.8	61.7
France	440.0	2.0	9.4	1.8	63.4
Thailand	419.2	7.5	8.6	1.7	65.1

656 Tulles, lace, embroidery, ribbons, trimmings and other smallwares

In 2013, the value (in current US$) of exports of "tulles, lace, embroidery, ribbons, trimmings and other smallwares" (SITC group 656) increased by 7.5 percent (compared to 8.4 percent average growth rate from 2009-2013) to reach 10.3 bln US$ (see table 2), while imports increased by 5.2 percent to reach 8.2 bln US$ (see table 3). Exports of this commodity accounted for 0.5 percent of world exports of SITC section 6, and 0.1 percent of total world merchandise exports (see table 1). China, China, Hong Kong SAR and Other Asia, nes were the top exporters in 2013 (see table 2). They accounted for 32.9, 9.8 and 6.4 percent of world exports, respectively. China, Viet Nam and USA were the top destinations, with respectively 7.8, 7.5 and 7.3 percent of world imports (see table 3).

The top 15 countries/areas accounted for 85.3 and 59.3 percent of total world exports and imports, respectively (see tables 2 and 3). In 2013, China was the country/area with the highest value of net exports (+2.7 bln US$), followed by Other Asia, nes (+631.5 mln US$). By MDG regions (see graph 2), the largest surpluses in this product group were recorded by Eastern Asia (+4.2 bln US$), Developed Europe (+506.0 mln US$) and Developed Asia-Pacific (+18.6 mln US$). The largest trade deficits were recorded by South-eastern Asia (-854.2 mln US$), Latin America and the Caribbean (-614.7 mln US$) and Northern Africa (-239.8 mln US$).

Table 1: Imports (Imp.) and exports (Exp.), 1999-2013, in current US$

		1999	2000	2001	2002	2003	2004	2005	2006	2007	2008	2009	2010	2011	2012	2013
Values in Bln US$	Imp.	4.9	5.3	5.0	5.4	6.0	6.6	7.1	7.3	7.5	7.5	6.1	7.2	8.0	7.8	8.2
	Exp.	5.3	5.9	5.7	6.2	6.8	7.6	8.2	9.0	9.5	9.5	7.5	8.7	9.6	9.6	10.3
As a percentage of SITC section (%)	Imp.	0.6	0.6	0.6	0.6	0.6	0.5	0.5	0.4	0.4	0.3	0.4	0.4	0.3	0.4	0.4
	Exp.	0.7	0.7	0.7	0.7	0.7	0.6	0.6	0.5	0.5	0.4	0.5	0.4	0.4	0.4	0.5
As a percentage of world trade (%)	Imp.	0.1	0.1	0.1	0.1	0.1	0.1	0.1	0.1	0.1	0.0	0.0	0.0	0.0	0.0	0.0
	Exp.	0.1	0.1	0.1	0.1	0.1	0.1	0.1	0.1	0.1	0.1	0.1	0.1	0.1	0.1	0.1

Graph 1: Annual growth rates of exports, 1999–2013
(In percentage by year)

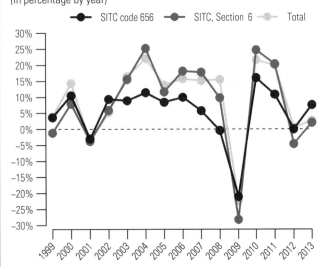

Table 2: Top exporting countries or areas in 2013

Country or area	Value (million US$)	Avg. Growth (%) 09-13	Growth (%) 12-13	World share %	Cum.
World..	10 328.0	8.4	7.5	100.0	
China..	3 394.1	13.4	9.6	32.9	32.9
China, Hong Kong SAR........	1 011.7	11.6	9.4	9.8	42.7
Other Asia, nes.....................	656.9	7.7	2.1	6.4	49.0
USA...	456.5	2.4	3.1	4.4	53.4
Italy...	455.6	7.3	7.1	4.4	57.9
France.....................................	446.4	0.8	7.5	4.3	62.2
Rep. of Korea........................	440.6	1.4	-0.6	4.3	66.4
Germany..................................	434.7	4.0	6.9	4.2	70.6
Turkey......................................	361.9	9.8	2.7	3.5	74.2
India..	350.6	20.5	49.5	3.4	77.5
Thailand..................................	215.7	7.4	9.3	2.1	79.6
Japan.......................................	185.8	0.2	-16.9	1.8	81.4
Austria....................................	146.8	1.3	0.6	1.4	82.9
Spain.......................................	137.1	3.7	8.5	1.3	84.2
Belgium...................................	118.9	3.9	26.8	1.2	85.3

Graph 2: Trade Balance by MDG regions 2013
(Bln US$)

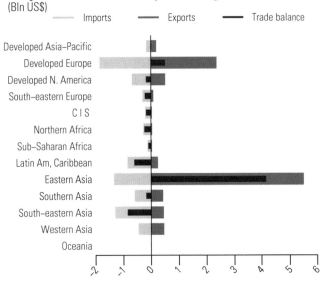

Table 3: Top importing countries or areas in 2013

Country or area	Value (million US$)	Avg. Growth (%) 09-13	Growth (%) 12-13	World share %	Cum.
World..	8 226.2	7.6	5.2	100.0	
China..	644.2	5.6	2.4	7.8	7.8
Viet Nam.................................	612.9	14.6	23.3	7.5	15.3
USA...	597.1	9.7	0.2	7.3	22.5
China, Hong Kong SAR........	593.2	7.3	7.1	7.2	29.8
Mexico.....................................	374.0	9.1	0.5	4.5	34.3
Germany..................................	278.9	2.6	3.2	3.4	37.7
Italy...	271.1	6.3	6.6	3.3	41.0
Indonesia................................	260.9	12.9	4.6	3.2	44.2
France.....................................	221.2	3.0	5.4	2.7	46.8
Sri Lanka................................	183.8	10.4	-5.5	2.2	49.1
Romania..................................	182.5	7.3	6.6	2.2	51.3
Brazil.......................................	176.6	41.5	2.6	2.1	53.4
Turkey......................................	168.2	13.5	13.4	2.0	55.5
United Arab Emirates...........	*162.3*	13.5	11.4	2.0	57.5
Afghanistan............................	151.4	8.7	37.3	1.8	59.3

In 2013, the value (in current US$) of exports of "special yarns, special textile fabrics and related products" (SITC group 657) increased by 5.5 percent (compared to 9.1 percent average growth rate from 2009-2013) to reach 48.2 bln US$ (see table 2), while imports increased by 4.7 percent to reach 41.8 bln US$ (see table 3). Exports of this commodity accounted for 2.1 percent of world exports of SITC section 6, and 0.3 percent of total world merchandise exports (see table 1). China, Germany and USA were the top exporters in 2013 (see table 2). They accounted for 23.5, 11.0 and 9.6 percent of world exports, respectively. USA, China and Germany were the top destinations, with respectively 10.1, 7.6 and 6.4 percent of world imports (see table 3).

The top 15 countries/areas accounted for 78.0 and 58.3 percent of total world exports and imports, respectively (see tables 2 and 3). In 2013, China was the country/area with the highest value of net exports (+8.1 bln US$), followed by Germany (+2.6 bln US$). By MDG regions (see graph 2), the largest surpluses in this product group were recorded by Eastern Asia (+10.7 bln US$), Developed Europe (+4.6 bln US$) and Developed Asia-Pacific (+106.4 mln US$). The largest trade deficits were recorded by Latin America and the Caribbean (-2.8 bln US$), South-eastern Asia (-2.0 bln US$) and Commonwealth of Independent States (-1.2 bln US$).

Table 1: Imports (Imp.) and exports (Exp.), 1999-2013, in current US$

		1999	2000	2001	2002	2003	2004	2005	2006	2007	2008	2009	2010	2011	2012	2013
Values in Bln US$	Imp.	18.5	19.1	18.8	20.0	22.6	25.4	27.5	29.8	34.0	36.1	30.5	36.4	41.3	40.0	41.8
	Exp.	21.5	22.0	21.1	22.2	25.2	27.7	29.6	32.1	35.9	39.6	34.0	41.2	48.0	45.6	48.2
As a percentage of	Imp.	2.3	2.1	2.2	2.2	2.2	2.0	1.9	1.8	1.7	1.7	2.0	1.9	1.8	1.8	1.9
SITC section (%)	Exp.	2.7	2.5	2.5	2.5	2.5	2.2	2.1	1.9	1.8	1.8	2.2	2.1	2.1	2.0	2.1
As a percentage of	Imp.	0.3	0.3	0.3	0.3	0.3	0.3	0.3	0.2	0.2	0.2	0.2	0.2	0.2	0.2	0.2
world trade (%)	Exp.	0.4	0.3	0.3	0.3	0.3	0.3	0.3	0.3	0.3	0.2	0.3	0.3	0.3	0.3	0.3

Graph 1: Annual growth rates of exports, 1999–2013

(In percentage by year)

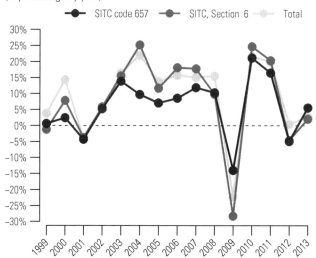

Graph 2: Trade Balance by MDG regions 2013

(Bln US$)

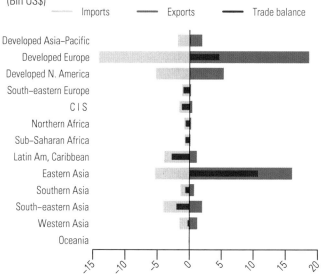

Table 2: Top exporting countries or areas in 2013

Country or area	Value (million US$)	Avg. Growth (%) 09-13	Growth (%) 12-13	World share %	Cum.
World	48 162.9	9.1	5.5	100.0	
China	11 309.1	18.0	10.5	23.5	23.5
Germany	5 293.4	7.3	6.9	11.0	34.5
USA	4 623.5	11.4	7.6	9.6	44.1
Italy	2 634.7	4.7	5.2	5.5	49.5
Rep. of Korea	2 110.9	7.9	2.8	4.4	53.9
Japan	1 858.6	4.6	-11.0	3.9	57.8
Other Asia, nes	1 780.4	4.5	-3.2	3.7	61.5
France	1 378.4	2.5	5.4	2.9	64.3
Belgium	1 120.5	5.0	12.4	2.3	66.7
Netherlands	1 076.8	4.9	2.7	2.2	68.9
United Kingdom	1 004.2	3.1	1.3	2.1	71.0
Spain	955.7	7.8	6.3	2.0	73.0
China, Hong Kong SAR	842.9	3.6	-0.1	1.8	74.7
Czech Rep.	813.7	9.6	4.3	1.7	76.4
Turkey	767.3	16.7	12.1	1.6	78.0

Table 3: Top importing countries or areas in 2013

Country or area	Value (million US$)	Avg. Growth (%) 09-13	Growth (%) 12-13	World share %	Cum.
World	41 822.2	8.2	4.7	100.0	
USA	4 214.6	10.6	5.6	10.1	10.1
China	3 173.9	7.1	2.6	7.6	17.7
Germany	2 671.5	3.1	3.4	6.4	24.1
Mexico	1 872.5	15.6	11.5	4.5	28.5
Viet Nam	1 482.5	17.9	12.4	3.5	32.1
Japan	1 367.6	10.7	-1.1	3.3	35.3
France	1 360.6	2.2	2.4	3.3	38.6
United Kingdom	1 200.3	2.7	5.6	2.9	41.5
Poland	1 193.6	8.0	8.9	2.9	44.3
Italy	1 057.6	4.5	7.4	2.5	46.9
Canada	1 019.6	6.5	3.0	2.4	49.3
Indonesia	992.8	26.4	6.6	2.4	51.7
Russian Federation	942.5	11.4	6.8	2.3	53.9
India	933.8	12.9	3.3	2.2	56.2
Rep. of Korea	890.3	9.3	-1.8	2.1	58.3

658 Made-up articles, wholly or chiefly of textile materials, nes

In 2013, the value (in current US$) of exports of "made-up articles, wholly or chiefly of textile materials, nes" (SITC group 658) increased by 12.2 percent (compared to 10.1 percent average growth rate from 2009-2013) to reach 57.2 bln US$ (see table 2), while imports increased by 5.8 percent to reach 47.7 bln US$ (see table 3). Exports of this commodity accounted for 2.5 percent of world exports of SITC section 6, and 0.3 percent of total world merchandise exports (see table 1). China, India and Pakistan were the top exporters in 2013 (see table 2). They accounted for 46.3, 8.1 and 6.4 percent of world exports, respectively. USA, Germany and Japan were the top destinations, with respectively 27.8, 8.0 and 7.8 percent of world imports (see table 3).

The top 15 countries/areas accounted for 84.5 and 73.9 percent of total world exports and imports, respectively (see tables 2 and 3). In 2013, China was the country/area with the highest value of net exports (+26.2 bln US$), followed by India (+4.4 bln US$). By MDG regions (see graph 2), the largest surpluses in this product group were recorded by Eastern Asia (+25.8 bln US$), Southern Asia (+9.2 bln US$) and South-eastern Asia (+1.2 bln US$). The largest trade deficits were recorded by Developed North America (-13.0 bln US$), Developed Europe (-7.5 bln US$) and Developed Asia-Pacific (-4.9 bln US$).

Table 1: Imports (Imp.) and exports (Exp.), 1999-2013, in current US$

		1999	2000	2001	2002	2003	2004	2005	2006	2007	2008	2009	2010	2011	2012	2013
Values in Bln US$	Imp.	16.0	17.2	17.6	19.3	23.1	27.2	30.1	33.4	37.3	39.9	36.9	41.3	46.9	45.1	47.7
	Exp.	16.2	17.2	17.5	19.2	23.5	27.3	31.6	34.2	37.6	41.7	39.0	44.5	51.1	51.0	57.2
As a percentage of SITC section (%)	Imp.	2.0	1.9	2.1	2.2	2.3	2.1	2.1	2.0	1.9	1.8	2.4	2.1	2.0	2.1	2.2
	Exp.	2.0	2.0	2.1	2.2	2.3	2.1	2.2	2.0	1.9	1.9	2.5	2.3	2.2	2.3	2.5
As a percentage of world trade (%)	Imp.	0.3	0.3	0.3	0.3	0.3	0.3	0.3	0.3	0.3	0.2	0.3	0.3	0.3	0.2	0.3
	Exp.	0.3	0.3	0.3	0.3	0.3	0.3	0.3	0.3	0.3	0.3	0.3	0.3	0.3	0.3	0.3

Graph 1: Annual growth rates of exports, 1999–2013
(In percentage by year)

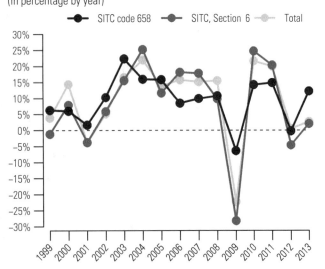

Legend: SITC code 658 — SITC, Section 6 — Total

Table 2: Top exporting countries or areas in 2013

Country or area	Value (million US$)	Avg. Growth (%) 09-13	Growth (%) 12-13	World share %	Cum.
World	57 204.1	10.1	12.2	100.0	
China	26 475.9	12.3	11.7	46.3	46.3
India	4 607.0	19.8	18.3	8.1	54.3
Pakistan	3 645.9	5.9	12.2	6.4	60.7
Germany	2 228.0	8.0	6.4	3.9	64.6
Turkey	2 176.8	7.3	15.0	3.8	68.4
USA	1 369.5	7.8	9.6	2.4	70.8
Viet Nam	1 158.0	21.2	31.7	2.0	72.8
Bangladesh	*1 146.3*	22.1	7.6	2.0	74.8
Mexico	913.1	9.4	18.2	1.6	76.4
Belgium	908.8	1.8	7.1	1.6	78.0
Netherlands	837.0	10.4	15.1	1.5	79.5
Portugal	738.1	6.7	15.1	1.3	80.8
France	737.8	1.8	3.8	1.3	82.1
Poland	722.5	5.3	12.9	1.3	83.3
Italy	688.7	5.8	9.6	1.2	84.5

Graph 2: Trade Balance by MDG regions 2013
(Bln US$)

Legend: Imports — Exports — Trade balance

Developed Asia–Pacific
Developed Europe
Developed N. America
South–eastern Europe
CIS
Northern Africa
Sub–Saharan Africa
Latin Am, Caribbean
Eastern Asia
Southern Asia
South–eastern Asia
Western Asia
Oceania

Table 3: Top importing countries or areas in 2013

Country or area	Value (million US$)	Avg. Growth (%) 09-13	Growth (%) 12-13	World share %	Cum.
World	47 715.6	6.7	5.8	100.0	
USA	13 246.4	7.9	5.8	27.8	27.8
Germany	3 838.1	6.5	7.5	8.0	35.8
Japan	3 707.5	2.5	-1.8	7.8	43.6
France	2 401.0	2.8	4.0	5.0	48.6
United Kingdom	2 265.5	1.6	6.9	4.7	53.4
Canada	1 295.8	8.2	2.4	2.7	56.1
Netherlands	1 186.1	7.0	7.5	2.5	58.6
Belgium	1 177.0	5.7	13.8	2.5	61.0
Australia	1 173.0	13.1	1.9	2.5	63.5
Italy	1 112.0	3.9	8.2	2.3	65.8
Spain	1 023.0	1.1	9.4	2.1	68.0
Russian Federation	927.2	19.5	-16.3	1.9	69.9
Switzerland	666.5	5.2	3.5	1.4	71.3
Rep. of Korea	633.3	20.0	20.4	1.3	72.6
Poland	613.4	7.0	19.6	1.3	73.9

In 2013, the value (in current US$) of exports of "floor coverings, etc" (SITC group 659) increased by 7.5 percent (compared to 6.9 percent average growth rate from 2009-2013) to reach 16.5 bln US$ (see table 2), while imports increased by 5.0 percent to reach 13.9 bln US$ (see table 3). Exports of this commodity accounted for 0.7 percent of world exports of SITC section 6, and 0.1 percent of total world merchandise exports (see table 1). China, Turkey and Belgium were the top exporters in 2013 (see table 2). They accounted for 15.4, 13.3 and 12.1 percent of world exports, respectively. USA, Germany and United Kingdom were the top destinations, with respectively 16.7, 9.1 and 8.5 percent of world imports (see table 3).

The top 15 countries/areas accounted for 85.2 and 68.6 percent of total world exports and imports, respectively (see tables 2 and 3). In 2013, China was the country/area with the highest value of net exports (+2.4 bln US$), followed by Turkey (+2.0 bln US$). By MDG regions (see graph 2), the largest surpluses in this product group were recorded by Southern Asia (+2.4 bln US$), Eastern Asia (+2.3 bln US$) and Western Asia (+1.4 bln US$). The largest trade deficits were recorded by Developed North America (-1.9 bln US$), Developed Asia-Pacific (-1.1 bln US$) and Latin America and the Caribbean (-472.2 mln US$).

Table 1: Imports (Imp.) and exports (Exp.), 1999-2013, in current US$

		1999	2000	2001	2002	2003	2004	2005	2006	2007	2008	2009	2010	2011	2012	2013
Values in Bln US$	Imp.	8.3	8.3	8.1	8.2	9.1	10.5	11.1	12.0	13.2	13.4	11.2	12.3	13.5	13.3	13.9
	Exp.	9.1	8.8	8.2	8.4	9.5	10.7	11.7	12.6	14.5	15.1	12.6	14.1	15.7	15.3	16.5
As a percentage of SITC section (%)	Imp.	1.0	0.9	0.9	0.9	0.9	0.8	0.8	0.7	0.7	0.6	0.7	0.6	0.6	0.6	0.6
	Exp.	1.1	1.0	1.0	1.0	0.9	0.8	0.8	0.8	0.7	0.7	0.8	0.7	0.7	0.7	0.7
As a percentage of world trade (%)	Imp.	0.1	0.1	0.1	0.1	0.1	0.1	0.1	0.1	0.1	0.1	0.1	0.1	0.1	0.1	0.1
	Exp.	0.2	0.1	0.1	0.1	0.1	0.1	0.1	0.1	0.1	0.1	0.1	0.1	0.1	0.1	0.1

Graph 1: Annual growth rates of exports, 1999–2013
(In percentage by year)

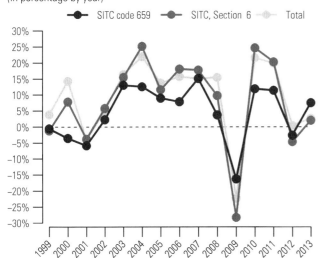

Graph 2: Trade Balance by MDG regions 2013
(Bln US$)

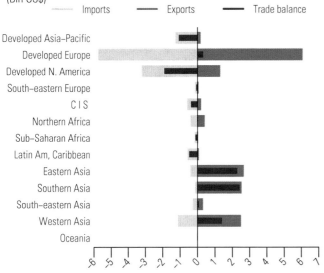

Table 2: Top exporting countries or areas in 2013

Country or area	Value (million US$)	Avg. Growth (%) 09-13	Growth (%) 12-13	World share %	Cum.
World	16 460.5	6.9	7.5	100.0	
China	2 539.2	13.6	4.4	15.4	15.4
Turkey	2 189.3	19.4	9.5	13.3	28.7
Belgium	1 990.2	-0.8	6.9	12.1	40.8
India	1 716.4	15.1	27.0	10.4	51.2
Netherlands	1 336.5	7.4	22.7	8.1	59.4
USA	1 132.3	6.9	1.4	6.9	66.2
Germany	686.6	2.5	-1.6	4.2	70.4
Iran	538.4	-10.1	-14.1	3.3	73.7
Egypt	405.2	7.6	4.0	2.5	76.1
United Kingdom	384.3	2.0	13.3	2.3	78.5
France	271.7	-0.1	5.5	1.7	80.1
Poland	244.9	15.8	12.3	1.5	81.6
Italy	216.5	1.4	7.7	1.3	82.9
Denmark	188.4	1.2	2.8	1.1	84.1
Thailand	184.5	6.7	7.0	1.1	85.2

Table 3: Top importing countries or areas in 2013

Country or area	Value (million US$)	Avg. Growth (%) 09-13	Growth (%) 12-13	World share %	Cum.
World	13 944.0	5.7	5.0	100.0	
USA	2 328.8	9.6	5.9	16.7	16.7
Germany	1 262.0	0.5	5.8	9.1	25.8
United Kingdom	1 186.6	0.9	6.3	8.5	34.3
Canada	868.0	5.3	0.1	6.2	40.5
Japan	682.6	7.9	-6.3	4.9	45.4
France	517.6	-0.6	-0.4	3.7	49.1
Australia	467.2	15.0	5.6	3.4	52.4
Netherlands	380.6	0.8	-1.8	2.7	55.2
Saudi Arabia	337.0	19.8	14.0	2.4	57.6
Russian Federation	292.9	19.1	-1.6	2.1	59.7
Libya	268.9	101.1	788.3	1.9	61.6
Belgium	258.6	2.6	4.9	1.9	63.5
Poland	245.8	3.0	8.9	1.8	65.2
Sweden	239.5	7.3	8.5	1.7	67.0
Switzerland	234.7	3.3	4.9	1.7	68.6

661 Lime, cement, and fabricated construction materials (except glass and clay)

In 2013, the value (in current US$) of exports of "lime, cement, and fabricated construction materials (except glass and clay)" (SITC group 661) increased by 8.3 percent (compared to 7.5 percent average growth rate from 2009-2013) to reach 32.6 bln US$ (see table 2), while imports increased by 6.1 percent to reach 31.8 bln US$ (see table 3). Exports of this commodity accounted for 1.4 percent of world exports of SITC section 6, and 0.2 percent of total world merchandise exports (see table 1). China, Italy and Turkey were the top exporters in 2013 (see table 2). They accounted for 22.0, 7.9 and 5.8 percent of world exports, respectively. USA, France and Japan were the top destinations, with respectively 13.0, 3.7 and 3.3 percent of world imports (see table 3).

The top 15 countries/areas accounted for 69.0 and 46.6 percent of total world exports and imports, respectively (see tables 2 and 3). In 2013, China was the country/area with the highest value of net exports (+7.1 bln US$), followed by Italy (+2.3 bln US$). By MDG regions (see graph 2), the largest surpluses in this product group were recorded by Eastern Asia (+6.3 bln US$), Developed Europe (+2.5 bln US$) and Southern Asia (+726.9 mln US$). The largest trade deficits were recorded by Developed North America (-3.4 bln US$), Sub-Saharan Africa (-2.3 bln US$) and Developed Asia-Pacific (-1.0 bln US$).

Table 1: Imports (Imp.) and exports (Exp.), 1999-2013, in current US$

		1999	2000	2001	2002	2003	2004	2005	2006	2007	2008	2009	2010	2011	2012	2013
Values in Bln US$	Imp.	11.9	12.2	12.7	13.1	15.1	17.9	21.9	25.2	29.3	31.3	25.1	27.5	29.0	29.9	31.8
	Exp.	10.9	10.9	11.1	12.2	13.3	15.7	19.0	22.8	25.9	30.4	24.4	25.7	28.4	30.0	32.6
As a percentage of	Imp.	1.5	1.4	1.5	1.5	1.5	1.4	1.5	1.5	1.5	1.4	1.6	1.4	1.3	1.4	1.4
SITC section (%)	Exp.	1.4	1.3	1.3	1.4	1.3	1.2	1.3	1.4	1.3	1.4	1.6	1.3	1.2	1.3	1.4
As a percentage of	Imp.	0.2	0.2	0.2	0.2	0.2	0.2	0.2	0.2	0.2	0.2	0.2	0.2	0.2	0.2	0.2
world trade (%)	Exp.	0.2	0.2	0.2	0.2	0.2	0.2	0.2	0.2	0.2	0.2	0.2	0.2	0.2	0.2	0.2

Graph 1: Annual growth rates of exports, 1999–2013
(In percentage by year)

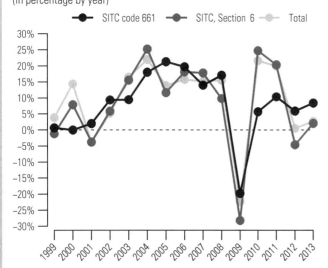

Graph 2: Trade Balance by MDG regions 2013
(Bln US$)

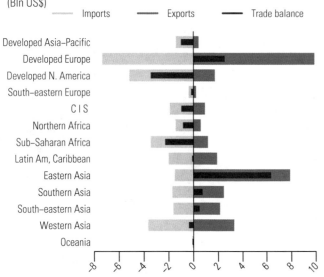

Table 2: Top exporting countries or areas in 2013

Country or area	Value (million US$)	Avg. Growth (%) 09-13	Growth (%) 12-13	World share %	Cum.
World	32 550.1	7.5	8.3	100.0	
China	7 154.9	13.2	17.9	22.0	22.0
Italy	2 578.0	4.9	8.7	7.9	29.9
Turkey	1 882.8	-1.4	3.5	5.8	35.7
India	1 399.1	12.5	27.4	4.3	40.0
Spain	1 398.5	7.7	-1.5	4.3	44.3
Germany	1 091.4	-2.1	-5.6	3.4	47.6
Brazil	1 031.2	13.4	22.5	3.2	50.8
USA	975.8	14.2	2.6	3.0	53.8
Viet Nam	972.0	68.8	35.0	3.0	56.8
Belgium	787.2	-0.7	8.1	2.4	59.2
Canada	756.7	5.8	0.2	2.3	61.5
Thailand	693.9	0.8	-12.7	2.1	63.7
United Arab Emirates	622.3	31.5	21.7	1.9	65.6
Portugal	577.5	11.9	22.4	1.8	67.3
Pakistan	552.6	0.6	-5.8	1.7	69.0

Table 3: Top importing countries or areas in 2013

Country or area	Value (million US$)	Avg. Growth (%) 09-13	Growth (%) 12-13	World share %	Cum.
World	31 750.2	6.0	6.1	100.0	
USA	4 142.7	9.2	15.3	13.0	13.0
France	1 159.3	1.5	2.3	3.7	16.7
Japan	1 035.4	5.1	0.0	3.3	20.0
Germany	1 015.8	3.4	-4.7	3.2	23.2
Canada	1 006.7	12.5	0.6	3.2	26.3
Rep. of Korea	815.6	-2.0	-4.8	2.6	28.9
Russian Federation	801.1	24.9	-10.3	2.5	31.4
Saudi Arabia	759.6	27.8	43.5	2.4	33.8
United Kingdom	671.6	5.4	15.2	2.1	35.9
Netherlands	642.8	2.7	-1.9	2.0	38.0
Libya	626.9	18.9	38.0	2.0	39.9
Belgium	579.0	0.8	-0.5	1.8	41.8
United Arab Emirates	540.1	-9.2	11.4	1.7	43.5
Sri Lanka	529.3	32.4	30.4	1.7	45.1
Singapore	485.5	5.5	4.2	1.5	46.6

In 2013, the value (in current US$) of exports of "clay construction materials and refractory construction materials" (SITC group 662) increased by 9.7 percent (compared to 10.5 percent average growth rate from 2009-2013) to reach 30.0 bln US$ (see table 2), while imports increased by 4.1 percent to reach 25.4 bln US$ (see table 3). Exports of this commodity accounted for 1.3 percent of world exports of SITC section 6, and 0.2 percent of total world merchandise exports (see table 1). China, Italy and Spain were the top exporters in 2013 (see table 2). They accounted for 34.0, 15.7 and 10.8 percent of world exports, respectively. USA, France and Russian Federation were the top destinations, with respectively 7.9, 5.6 and 4.5 percent of world imports (see table 3).

The top 15 countries/areas accounted for 85.4 and 45.6 percent of total world exports and imports, respectively (see tables 2 and 3). In 2013, China was the country/area with the highest value of net exports (+9.9 bln US$), followed by Italy (+4.4 bln US$). By MDG regions (see graph 2), the largest surpluses in this product group were recorded by Eastern Asia (+9.0 bln US$) and Developed Europe (+6.1 bln US$). The largest trade deficits were recorded by Developed North America (-1.9 bln US$), Sub-Saharan Africa (-1.6 bln US$) and Commonwealth of Independent States (-1.5 bln US$).

Table 1: Imports (Imp.) and exports (Exp.), 1999-2013, in current US$

		1999	2000	2001	2002	2003	2004	2005	2006	2007	2008	2009	2010	2011	2012	2013
Values in Bln US$	Imp.	10.5	10.4	10.3	11.1	13.2	15.6	17.1	19.2	22.1	24.1	19.3	21.6	23.9	24.4	25.4
	Exp.	10.4	10.1	10.3	11.2	13.3	16.0	16.9	19.3	22.2	24.8	20.1	22.1	25.5	27.3	30.0
As a percentage of	Imp.	1.3	1.2	1.2	1.2	1.3	1.2	1.2	1.2	1.1	1.1	1.2	1.1	1.0	1.1	1.2
SITC section (%)	Exp.	1.3	1.2	1.2	1.3	1.3	1.3	1.2	1.1	1.1	1.1	1.3	1.1	1.1	1.2	1.3
As a percentage of	Imp.	0.2	0.2	0.2	0.2	0.2	0.2	0.2	0.2	0.2	0.1	0.2	0.1	0.1	0.1	0.1
world trade (%)	Exp.	0.2	0.2	0.2	0.2	0.2	0.2	0.2	0.2	0.2	0.2	0.2	0.1	0.1	0.2	0.2

Graph 1: Annual growth rates of exports, 1999–2013

(In percentage by year)

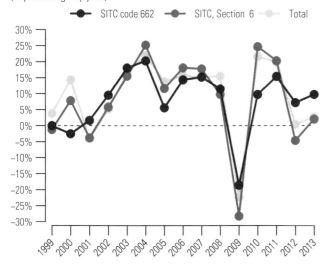

— SITC code 662 — SITC, Section 6 — Total

Table 2: Top exporting countries or areas in 2013

Country or area	Value (million US$)	Avg. Growth (%) 09-13	Growth (%) 12-13	World share %	Cum.
World	29 988.0	10.5	9.7	100.0	
China	10 188.5	25.0	19.6	34.0	34.0
Italy	4 703.9	2.8	8.4	15.7	49.7
Spain	3 239.1	5.9	10.7	10.8	60.5
Germany	1 976.6	2.2	2.6	6.6	67.1
United Arab Emirates	778.6	37.2	21.7	2.6	69.7
Turkey	760.2	11.2	4.6	2.5	72.2
USA	553.8	2.6	-10.6	1.8	74.0
Austria	511.4	6.9	1.9	1.7	75.7
Poland	505.3	13.2	18.3	1.7	77.4
France	477.5	-4.2	-12.2	1.6	79.0
Mexico	461.1	8.6	5.7	1.5	80.6
Portugal	387.7	3.0	2.1	1.3	81.8
India	362.5	32.6	34.8	1.2	83.1
Brazil	353.8	2.6	2.8	1.2	84.2
Belgium	344.7	7.2	11.2	1.1	85.4

Graph 2: Trade Balance by MDG regions 2013

(Bln US$)

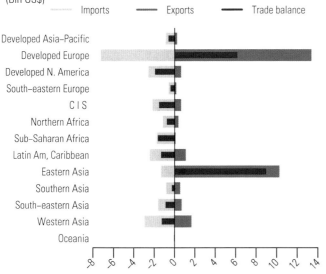

Imports — Exports — Trade balance

Developed Asia–Pacific
Developed Europe
Developed N. America
South–eastern Europe
C I S
Northern Africa
Sub–Saharan Africa
Latin Am, Caribbean
Eastern Asia
Southern Asia
South–eastern Asia
Western Asia
Oceania

Table 3: Top importing countries or areas in 2013

Country or area	Value (million US$)	Avg. Growth (%) 09-13	Growth (%) 12-13	World share %	Cum.
World	25 384.8	7.1	4.1	100.0	
USA	1 994.3	8.7	15.5	7.9	7.9
France	1 418.5	-1.9	-1.8	5.6	13.4
Russian Federation	1 138.9	25.7	9.8	4.5	17.9
Germany	1 085.2	4.0	1.0	4.3	22.2
Saudi Arabia	889.8	11.5	6.8	3.5	25.7
United Kingdom	686.9	1.4	17.7	2.7	28.4
Rep. of Korea	587.8	4.8	0.4	2.3	30.7
Canada	560.1	9.1	4.6	2.2	32.9
Belgium	523.1	-0.4	8.2	2.1	35.0
India	522.9	12.0	-18.0	2.1	37.1
Libya	475.3	51.5	98.0	1.9	38.9
Japan	454.5	-0.3	-15.8	1.8	40.7
Thailand	429.9	23.2	15.1	1.7	42.4
Brazil	407.0	34.1	12.3	1.6	44.0
Mexico	397.2	17.3	-1.7	1.6	45.6

663 Mineral manufactures, nes

In 2013, the value (in current US$) of exports of "mineral manufactures, nes" (SITC group 663) increased by 8.2 percent (compared to 11.9 percent average growth rate from 2009-2013) to reach 37.9 bln US$ (see table 2), while imports increased by 4.7 percent to reach 35.8 bln US$ (see table 3). Exports of this commodity accounted for 1.7 percent of world exports of SITC section 6, and 0.2 percent of total world merchandise exports (see table 1). Germany, China and USA were the top exporters in 2013 (see table 2). They accounted for 14.2, 14.0 and 10.5 percent of world exports, respectively. USA, Germany and China were the top destinations, with respectively 12.6, 8.9 and 4.9 percent of world imports (see table 3).

The top 15 countries/areas accounted for 77.0 and 60.7 percent of total world exports and imports, respectively (see tables 2 and 3). In 2013, China was the country/area with the highest value of net exports (+3.5 bln US$), followed by Japan (+2.2 bln US$). By MDG regions (see graph 2), the largest surpluses in this product group were recorded by Developed Europe (+3.7 bln US$), Eastern Asia (+2.8 bln US$) and Developed Asia-Pacific (+1.7 bln US$). The largest trade deficits were recorded by Latin America and the Caribbean (-1.3 bln US$), Commonwealth of Independent States (-1.2 bln US$) and Developed North America (-980.3 mln US$).

Table 1: Imports (Imp.) and exports (Exp.), 1999-2013, in current US$

		1999	2000	2001	2002	2003	2004	2005	2006	2007	2008	2009	2010	2011	2012	2013
Values in Bln US$	Imp.	13.1	13.5	13.4	13.9	15.8	18.9	21.1	24.3	28.7	30.8	23.8	28.8	34.8	34.1	35.8
	Exp.	13.6	13.8	13.4	13.6	15.7	19.2	21.4	24.9	29.5	31.7	24.1	29.4	35.3	35.0	37.9
As a percentage of SITC section (%)	Imp.	1.6	1.5	1.6	1.6	1.5	1.5	1.5	1.5	1.5	1.4	1.5	1.5	1.5	1.6	1.6
	Exp.	1.7	1.6	1.6	1.6	1.5	1.5	1.5	1.5	1.5	1.5	1.6	1.5	1.5	1.6	1.7
As a percentage of world trade (%)	Imp.	0.2	0.2	0.2	0.2	0.2	0.2	0.2	0.2	0.2	0.2	0.2	0.2	0.2	0.2	0.2
	Exp.	0.2	0.2	0.2	0.2	0.2	0.2	0.2	0.2	0.2	0.2	0.2	0.2	0.2	0.2	0.2

Graph 1: Annual growth rates of exports, 1999–2013
(In percentage by year)

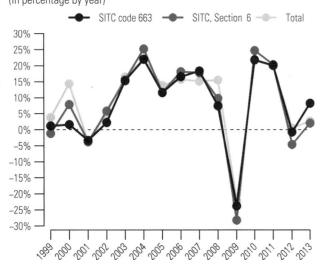

Table 2: Top exporting countries or areas in 2013

Country or area	Value (million US$)	Avg. Growth (%) 09-13	Growth (%) 12-13	World share %	Cum.
World	37 895.1	11.9	8.2	100.0	
Germany	5 394.5	6.9	4.9	14.2	14.2
China	5 301.7	32.7	22.5	14.0	28.2
USA	3 966.7	14.7	6.9	10.5	38.7
Japan	3 375.7	9.3	-5.1	8.9	47.6
Italy	1 307.2	7.5	11.3	3.4	51.1
Poland	1 304.7	10.4	11.4	3.4	54.5
United Kingdom	1 254.9	6.7	1.1	3.3	57.8
France	1 234.3	7.9	4.2	3.3	61.1
Belgium	1 208.3	4.3	17.1	3.2	64.3
Netherlands	1 017.1	15.3	15.5	2.7	66.9
Spain	910.7	5.9	15.1	2.4	69.3
Austria	816.7	4.2	2.1	2.2	71.5
Mexico	708.4	20.0	11.9	1.9	73.4
Canada	699.7	5.2	5.1	1.8	75.2
Rep. of Korea	685.5	15.1	12.3	1.8	77.0

Graph 2: Trade Balance by MDG regions 2013
(Bln US$)

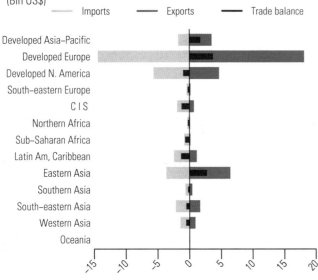

Table 3: Top importing countries or areas in 2013

Country or area	Value (million US$)	Avg. Growth (%) 09-13	Growth (%) 12-13	World share %	Cum.
World	35 753.3	10.7	4.7	100.0	
USA	4 510.2	12.9	-0.1	12.6	12.6
Germany	3 192.1	11.5	12.9	8.9	21.5
China	1 754.0	18.4	8.3	4.9	26.4
France	1 577.7	5.7	3.0	4.4	30.9
United Kingdom	1 256.1	5.9	15.7	3.5	34.4
Japan	1 153.7	17.0	2.9	3.2	37.6
Canada	1 110.2	9.5	3.3	3.1	40.7
Russian Federation	1 109.7	31.0	17.5	3.1	43.8
Italy	1 045.6	4.1	6.1	2.9	46.7
Netherlands	1 016.0	7.8	6.9	2.8	49.6
Rep. of Korea	926.0	10.6	-7.7	2.6	52.2
Belgium	861.1	8.3	14.8	2.4	54.6
Mexico	811.0	15.6	-2.6	2.3	56.8
Switzerland	703.7	6.9	7.3	2.0	58.8
Austria	671.9	7.3	3.7	1.9	60.7

In 2013, the value (in current US$) of exports of "glass" (SITC group 664) increased by 3.7 percent (compared to 7.7 percent average growth rate from 2009-2013) to reach 39.7 bln US$ (see table 2), while imports increased by 3.3 percent to reach 42.2 bln US$ (see table 3). Exports of this commodity accounted for 1.7 percent of world exports of SITC section 6, and 0.2 percent of total world merchandise exports (see table 1). China, USA and Germany were the top exporters in 2013 (see table 2). They accounted for 17.5, 10.2 and 9.6 percent of world exports, respectively. China, Germany and USA were the top destinations, with respectively 12.4, 7.5 and 6.8 percent of world imports (see table 3).

The top 15 countries/areas accounted for 81.1 and 66.5 percent of total world exports and imports, respectively (see tables 2 and 3). In 2013, Japan was the country/area with the highest value of net exports (+1.8 bln US$), followed by China (+1.7 bln US$). By MDG regions (see graph 2), the largest surpluses in this product group were recorded by Developed Asia-Pacific (+1.5 bln US$), Developed Europe (+835.8 mln US$) and Eastern Asia (+293.4 mln US$). The largest trade deficits were recorded by Latin America and the Caribbean (-1.2 bln US$), Western Asia (-971.6 mln US$) and South-eastern Asia (-891.5 mln US$).

Table 1: Imports (Imp.) and exports (Exp.), 1999-2013, in current US$

		1999	2000	2001	2002	2003	2004	2005	2006	2007	2008	2009	2010	2011	2012	2013
Values in Bln US$	Imp.	15.7	17.0	17.0	18.3	20.9	24.7	26.6	29.5	33.5	36.0	29.8	36.2	41.4	40.9	42.2
	Exp.	15.3	16.8	16.7	18.0	20.5	24.1	25.3	27.9	32.3	36.5	29.6	33.9	39.2	38.3	39.7
As a percentage of	Imp.	1.9	1.9	2.0	2.0	2.0	1.9	1.9	1.8	1.7	1.7	1.9	1.9	1.8	1.9	1.9
SITC section (%)	Exp.	1.9	1.9	2.0	2.0	2.0	1.9	1.8	1.7	1.6	1.7	1.9	1.7	1.7	1.7	1.7
As a percentage of	Imp.	0.3	0.3	0.3	0.3	0.3	0.3	0.3	0.2	0.2	0.2	0.2	0.2	0.2	0.2	0.2
world trade (%)	Exp.	0.3	0.3	0.3	0.3	0.3	0.3	0.2	0.2	0.2	0.2	0.2	0.2	0.2	0.2	0.2

Graph 1: Annual growth rates of exports, 1999–2013
(In percentage by year)

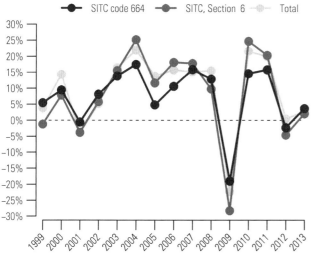

Table 2: Top exporting countries or areas in 2013

Country or area	Value (million US$)	Avg. Growth (%) 09-13	Growth (%) 12-13	World share %	Cum.
World	39 708.7	7.7	3.7	100.0	
China	6 961.8	19.3	13.5	17.5	17.5
USA	4 036.8	8.7	8.1	10.2	27.7
Germany	3 816.8	4.9	9.4	9.6	37.3
Japan	3 477.3	0.0	-27.3	8.8	46.1
China, Hong Kong SAR	2 467.4	74.8	53.3	6.2	52.3
Belgium	1 801.6	-1.5	9.2	4.5	56.8
Other Asia, nes	1 539.1	23.0	-14.8	3.9	60.7
France	1 321.9	1.1	2.7	3.3	64.0
Italy	1 271.5	3.5	4.7	3.2	67.2
Spain	1 187.5	13.4	73.3	3.0	70.2
Poland	1 168.8	12.8	28.3	2.9	73.2
Rep. of Korea	979.3	21.9	21.1	2.5	75.6
Czech Rep.	821.2	0.9	0.3	2.1	77.7
Mexico	702.8	4.8	-0.7	1.8	79.5
United Kingdom	665.3	-0.3	-8.3	1.7	81.1

Graph 2: Trade Balance by MDG regions 2013
(Bln US$)

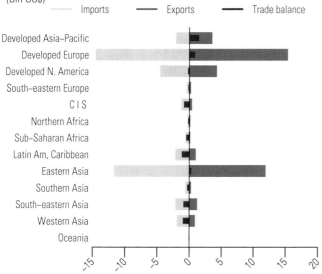

Table 3: Top importing countries or areas in 2013

Country or area	Value (million US$)	Avg. Growth (%) 09-13	Growth (%) 12-13	World share %	Cum.
World	42 249.9	9.1	3.3	100.0	
China	5 229.0	35.7	11.5	12.4	12.4
Germany	3 185.5	6.2	7.8	7.5	19.9
USA	2 893.6	6.8	0.3	6.8	26.8
Rep. of Korea	2 780.7	9.0	-11.5	6.6	33.3
China, Hong Kong SAR	1 899.3	56.8	50.6	4.5	37.8
Other Asia, nes	1 718.6	4.7	-20.4	4.1	41.9
France	1 651.2	-0.1	5.1	3.9	45.8
Japan	1 649.5	7.2	-4.4	3.9	49.7
Canada	1 610.1	8.4	3.9	3.8	53.5
United Kingdom	1 251.3	5.7	0.1	3.0	56.5
Belgium	1 189.1	4.8	13.0	2.8	59.3
Italy	884.8	2.0	8.8	2.1	61.4
Mexico	813.8	12.7	4.3	1.9	63.3
Netherlands	677.8	0.2	3.9	1.6	64.9
Russian Federation	663.0	22.9	4.0	1.6	66.5

665 Glassware

In 2013, the value (in current US$) of exports of "glassware" (SITC group 665) increased by 5.2 percent (compared to 9.7 percent average growth rate from 2009-2013) to reach 28.2 bln US$ (see table 2), while imports increased by 2.3 percent to reach 24.6 bln US$ (see table 3). Exports of this commodity accounted for 1.2 percent of world exports of SITC section 6, and 0.2 percent of total world merchandise exports (see table 1). China, Germany and France were the top exporters in 2013 (see table 2). They accounted for 29.1, 8.5 and 6.4 percent of world exports, respectively. USA, China and France were the top destinations, with respectively 12.8, 6.8 and 6.6 percent of world imports (see table 3).

The top 15 countries/areas accounted for 75.9 and 59.6 percent of total world exports and imports, respectively (see tables 2 and 3). In 2013, China was the country/area with the highest value of net exports (+6.5 bln US$), followed by Germany (+1.1 bln US$). By MDG regions (see graph 2), the largest surpluses in this product group were recorded by Eastern Asia (+5.8 bln US$), Developed Europe (+1.9 bln US$) and Developed Asia-Pacific (+111.6 mln US$). The largest trade deficits were recorded by Developed North America (-2.6 bln US$), Commonwealth of Independent States (-685.1 mln US$) and Sub-Saharan Africa (-410.2 mln US$).

Table 1: Imports (Imp.) and exports (Exp.), 1999-2013, in current US$

		1999	2000	2001	2002	2003	2004	2005	2006	2007	2008	2009	2010	2011	2012	2013
Values in Bln US$	Imp.	10.3	10.8	10.7	11.4	13.2	15.6	16.7	18.2	21.4	23.1	19.2	22.3	24.9	24.1	24.6
	Exp.	10.3	10.8	11.0	11.7	13.6	16.1	17.2	19.6	21.8	22.5	19.4	23.1	25.9	26.8	28.2
As a percentage of SITC section (%)	Imp.	1.3	1.2	1.3	1.3	1.3	1.2	1.2	1.1	1.1	1.1	1.2	1.2	1.1	1.1	1.1
	Exp.	1.3	1.3	1.3	1.3	1.3	1.3	1.2	1.2	1.1	1.0	1.2	1.2	1.1	1.2	1.2
As a percentage of world trade (%)	Imp.	0.2	0.2	0.2	0.2	0.2	0.2	0.2	0.1	0.2	0.1	0.2	0.1	0.1	0.1	0.1
	Exp.	0.2	0.2	0.2	0.2	0.2	0.2	0.2	0.2	0.2	0.1	0.2	0.2	0.1	0.1	0.2

Graph 1: Annual growth rates of exports, 1999–2013
(In percentage by year)

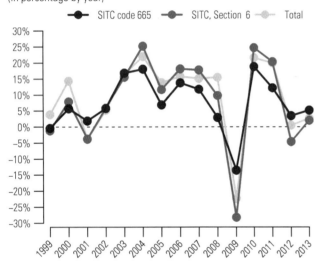

Graph 2: Trade Balance by MDG regions 2013
(Bln US$)

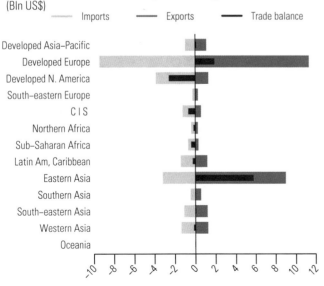

Table 2: Top exporting countries or areas in 2013

Country or area	Value (million US$)	Avg. Growth (%) 09-13	Growth (%) 12-13	World share %	Cum.
World	28 162.7	9.7	5.2	100.0	
China	8 194.1	23.6	7.1	29.1	29.1
Germany	2 387.0	2.9	3.9	8.5	37.6
France	1 804.2	1.5	3.2	6.4	44.0
Italy	1 501.3	4.2	5.6	5.3	49.3
USA	1 089.4	3.7	-4.3	3.9	53.2
Japan	1 049.3	5.5	-6.2	3.7	56.9
Czech Rep.	774.5	6.2	2.1	2.8	59.7
Mexico	726.3	12.8	7.6	2.6	62.2
Netherlands	585.4	9.5	9.5	2.1	64.3
Austria	561.6	2.3	14.7	2.0	66.3
United Arab Emirates	555.6	16.5	21.7	2.0	68.3
Portugal	545.6	4.0	7.0	1.9	70.2
Turkey	538.9	3.1	1.4	1.9	72.1
Poland	538.7	9.2	9.6	1.9	74.0
Spain	536.4	6.0	8.2	1.9	75.9

Table 3: Top importing countries or areas in 2013

Country or area	Value (million US$)	Avg. Growth (%) 09-13	Growth (%) 12-13	World share %	Cum.
World	24 614.5	6.5	2.3	100.0	
USA	3 159.6	10.5	8.4	12.8	12.8
China	1 684.4	10.3	-18.0	6.8	19.7
France	1 626.7	4.3	3.7	6.6	26.3
Germany	1 248.5	4.9	4.0	5.1	31.4
United Kingdom	925.3	11.0	18.3	3.8	35.1
Italy	855.9	2.0	1.4	3.5	38.6
Spain	739.3	1.7	5.8	3.0	41.6
Canada	702.0	3.2	-1.5	2.9	44.5
Belgium	651.4	3.2	11.0	2.6	47.1
China, Hong Kong SAR	635.1	-4.7	-10.1	2.6	49.7
Japan	566.4	2.1	-7.2	2.3	52.0
Netherlands	490.7	7.3	6.5	2.0	54.0
Russian Federation	483.3	16.2	-0.3	2.0	55.9
Switzerland	462.9	0.3	2.7	1.9	57.8
Rep. of Korea	436.2	5.8	-6.7	1.8	59.6

In 2013, the value (in current US$) of exports of "pottery" (SITC group 666) decreased by 0.3 percent (compared to 11.4 percent average growth rate from 2009-2013) to reach 9.7 bln US$ (see table 2), while imports decreased by 2.1 percent to reach 8.1 bln US$ (see table 3). Exports of this commodity accounted for 0.4 percent of world exports of SITC section 6, and 0.1 percent of total world merchandise exports (see table 1). China, Germany and United Kingdom were the top exporters in 2013 (see table 2). They accounted for 58.1, 6.5 and 2.8 percent of world exports, respectively. USA, Germany and United Kingdom were the top destinations, with respectively 21.9, 6.2 and 5.3 percent of world imports (see table 3).

The top 15 countries/areas accounted for 88.5 and 65.5 percent of total world exports and imports, respectively (see tables 2 and 3). In 2013, China was the country/area with the highest value of net exports (+5.6 bln US$), followed by Portugal (+220.4 mln US$). By MDG regions (see graph 2), the largest surpluses in this product group were recorded by Eastern Asia (+5.4 bln US$), South-eastern Asia (+347.4 mln US$) and South-eastern Europe (+34.9 mln US$). The largest trade deficits were recorded by Developed North America (-1.8 bln US$), Developed Europe (-499.5 mln US$) and Developed Asia-Pacific (-468.4 mln US$).

Table 1: Imports (Imp.) and exports (Exp.), 1999-2013, in current US$

		1999	2000	2001	2002	2003	2004	2005	2006	2007	2008	2009	2010	2011	2012	2013
Values in Bln US$	Imp.	5.9	6.1	5.7	5.7	6.4	6.9	7.3	7.4	8.2	8.3	6.7	7.9	8.4	8.2	8.1
	Exp.	5.4	5.5	4.9	5.1	5.7	6.2	6.4	6.7	6.8	6.8	6.3	7.7	9.1	9.7	9.7
As a percentage of SITC section (%)	Imp.	0.7	0.7	0.7	0.6	0.6	0.5	0.5	0.4	0.4	0.4	0.4	0.4	0.4	0.4	0.4
	Exp.	0.7	0.6	0.6	0.6	0.6	0.5	0.4	0.4	0.3	0.3	0.4	0.4	0.4	0.4	0.4
As a percentage of world trade (%)	Imp.	0.1	0.1	0.1	0.1	0.1	0.1	0.1	0.1	0.1	0.1	0.1	0.1	0.0	0.0	0.0
	Exp.	0.1	0.1	0.1	0.1	0.1	0.1	0.1	0.1	0.0	0.0	0.1	0.1	0.1	0.1	0.1

Graph 1: Annual growth rates of exports, 1999–2013
(In percentage by year)

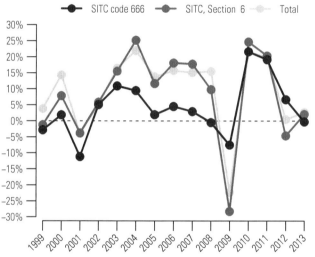

● SITC code 666   ● SITC, Section 6   ○ Total

Table 2: Top exporting countries or areas in 2013

Country or area	Value (million US$)	Avg. Growth (%) 09-13	Growth (%) 12-13	World share %	Cum.
World	9 706.9	11.4	-0.3	100.0	
China	5 643.8	18.4	-4.2	58.1	58.1
Germany	633.5	2.5	6.4	6.5	64.7
United Kingdom	269.7	4.7	2.9	2.8	67.4
Portugal	256.3	8.9	15.0	2.6	70.1
France	222.7	-0.4	-9.0	2.3	72.4
United Arab Emirates	221.6	16.1	21.7	2.3	74.7
Thailand	220.4	7.7	3.4	2.3	76.9
Italy	183.6	5.0	8.9	1.9	78.8
USA	168.3	5.2	4.0	1.7	80.6
Netherlands	157.7	2.4	2.1	1.6	82.2
Belgium	147.2	-2.4	4.3	1.5	83.7
Indonesia	131.5	10.3	4.0	1.4	85.1
Spain	117.4	-0.4	6.7	1.2	86.3
Poland	111.7	7.2	24.9	1.2	87.4
Czech Rep.	108.2	-4.1	10.2	1.1	88.5

Graph 2: Trade Balance by MDG regions 2013
(Bln US$)

Imports   Exports   Trade balance

Developed Asia–Pacific
Developed Europe
Developed N. America
South–eastern Europe
CIS
Northern Africa
Sub–Saharan Africa
Latin Am, Caribbean
Eastern Asia
Southern Asia
South–eastern Asia
Western Asia
Oceania

Table 3: Top importing countries or areas in 2013

Country or area	Value (million US$)	Avg. Growth (%) 09-13	Growth (%) 12-13	World share %	Cum.
World	8 070.7	4.8	-2.1	100.0	
USA	1 771.1	8.0	6.5	21.9	21.9
Germany	501.6	-0.8	-14.0	6.2	28.2
United Kingdom	425.2	0.6	-6.9	5.3	33.4
Japan	358.9	7.9	4.1	4.4	37.9
France	327.0	-6.1	-15.1	4.1	41.9
Russian Federation	265.8	20.6	-14.2	3.3	45.2
Italy	256.8	-8.0	-18.1	3.2	48.4
Canada	247.7	5.6	-0.4	3.1	51.5
Turkey	189.9	11.4	11.2	2.4	53.8
Netherlands	181.2	-1.2	-16.9	2.2	56.1
Belgium	167.5	-2.2	-5.1	2.1	58.1
Rep. of Korea	155.8	21.4	20.6	1.9	60.1
Australia	155.6	7.8	-0.1	1.9	62.0
Spain	144.4	-4.2	-2.1	1.8	63.8
United Arab Emirates	141.1	10.0	11.4	1.7	65.5

667 Pearls and precious or semiprecious stones, unworked or worked

In 2013, the value (in current US$) of exports of "pearls and precious or semiprecious stones, unworked or worked" (SITC group 667) increased by 14.6 percent (compared to 17.4 percent average growth rate from 2009-2013) to reach 172.5 bln US$ (see table 2), while imports increased by 12.1 percent to reach 154.3 bln US$ (see table 3). Exports of this commodity accounted for 7.6 percent of world exports of SITC section 6, and 0.9 percent of total world merchandise exports (see table 1). India, United Arab Emirates and USA were the top exporters in 2013 (see table 2). They accounted for 17.5, 14.4 and 12.1 percent of world exports, respectively. USA, India and China, Hong Kong SAR were the top destinations, with respectively 16.3, 15.6 and 13.9 percent of world imports (see table 3).

The top 15 countries/areas accounted for 95.9 and 96.7 percent of total world exports and imports, respectively (see tables 2 and 3). In 2013, Israel was the country/area with the highest value of net exports (+10.1 bln US$), followed by India (+6.2 bln US$). By MDG regions (see graph 2), the largest surpluses in this product group were recorded by Western Asia (+15.9 bln US$), Sub-Saharan Africa (+8.6 bln US$) and Southern Asia (+6.4 bln US$). The largest trade deficits were recorded by Eastern Asia (-12.4 bln US$), Developed North America (-2.6 bln US$) and Developed Europe (-2.3 bln US$).

Table 1: Imports (Imp.) and exports (Exp.), 1999-2013, in current US$

		1999	2000	2001	2002	2003	2004	2005	2006	2007	2008	2009	2010	2011	2012	2013
Values in Bln US$	Imp.	52.6	60.7	47.0	59.9	62.7	76.3	90.2	85.6	96.7	107.1	82.8	124.5	159.4	137.7	154.3
	Exp.	45.9	54.9	47.5	58.7	63.2	75.9	92.3	89.7	104.5	114.9	90.9	129.5	166.1	150.5	172.5
As a percentage of SITC section (%)	Imp.	6.4	6.8	5.5	6.7	6.1	6.0	6.3	5.1	4.9	5.0	5.3	6.5	6.9	6.3	7.0
	Exp.	5.7	6.3	5.7	6.7	6.2	6.0	6.5	5.3	5.3	5.3	5.8	6.7	7.1	6.8	7.6
As a percentage of world trade (%)	Imp.	0.9	0.9	0.7	0.9	0.8	0.8	0.9	0.7	0.7	0.7	0.7	0.8	0.9	0.8	0.8
	Exp.	0.8	0.9	0.8	0.9	0.8	0.8	0.9	0.7	0.8	0.7	0.7	0.9	0.9	0.8	0.9

Graph 1: Annual growth rates of exports, 1999–2013

(In percentage by year)

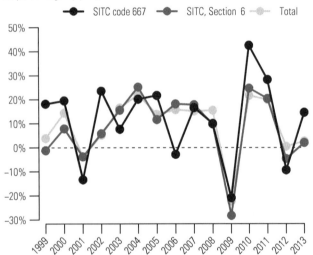

- SITC code 667
- SITC, Section 6
- Total

Table 2: Top exporting countries or areas in 2013

Country or area	Value (million US$)	Avg. Growth (%) 09-13	Growth (%) 12-13	World share %	Cum.
World	172 464.1	17.4	14.6	100.0	
India	30 207.8	15.5	32.8	17.5	17.5
United Arab Emirates	24 802.1	33.7	21.7	14.4	31.9
USA	20 952.3	18.8	15.2	12.1	44.0
Belgium	20 847.5	17.1	15.4	12.1	56.1
Israel	19 143.7	13.2	9.0	11.1	67.2
China, Hong Kong SAR	16 693.5	16.5	12.0	9.7	76.9
United Kingdom	6 956.9	5.0	-22.3	4.0	80.9
Botswana	6 198.7	30.1	31.4	3.6	84.5
Russian Federation	4 940.1	43.6	7.7	2.9	87.4
China	3 768.1	20.5	8.9	2.2	89.6
Switzerland	2 634.8	9.8	7.6	1.5	91.1
Thailand	2 581.3	19.1	15.5	1.5	92.6
Canada	2 154.7	5.6	-11.4	1.2	93.9
South Africa	2 107.2	12.7	4.1	1.2	95.1
Namibia	1 338.8	14.0	-0.4	0.8	95.9

Graph 2: Trade Balance by MDG regions 2013

(Bln US$)

- Imports
- Exports
- Trade balance

Developed Asia-Pacific
Developed Europe
Developed N. America
South-eastern Europe
CIS
Northern Africa
Sub-Saharan Africa
Latin Am, Caribbean
Eastern Asia
Southern Asia
South-eastern Asia
Western Asia
Oceania

Table 3: Top importing countries or areas in 2013

Country or area	Value (million US$)	Avg. Growth (%) 09-13	Growth (%) 12-13	World share %	Cum.
World	154 323.1	16.8	12.1	100.0	
USA	25 107.5	16.5	16.1	16.3	16.3
India	24 003.0	11.7	11.9	15.6	31.8
China, Hong Kong SAR	21 491.2	17.1	9.5	13.9	45.7
Belgium	20 920.8	18.0	11.1	13.6	59.3
United Arab Emirates	18 823.7	26.8	11.4	12.2	71.5
China	11 079.8	40.3	63.5	7.2	78.7
Israel	9 052.0	14.1	9.5	5.9	84.5
United Kingdom	6 854.4	2.9	-16.5	4.4	89.0
Switzerland	3 460.3	13.1	10.7	2.2	91.2
Botswana	2 024.5	53.2	-6.3	1.3	92.5
Thailand	1 801.3	14.0	23.5	1.2	93.7
Japan	1 470.3	8.0	-2.1	1.0	94.7
Singapore	1 171.3	13.3	53.6	0.8	95.4
France	1 107.6	16.7	-5.8	0.7	96.1
Italy	821.9	16.2	8.7	0.5	96.7

Pig iron, spiegeleisen, sponge iron, iron or steel granules and powders 671

In 2013, the value (in current US$) of exports of "pig iron, spiegeleisen, sponge iron, iron or steel granules and powders" (SITC group 671) decreased by 12.9 percent (compared to 11.6 percent average growth rate from 2009-2013) to reach 34.2 bln US$ (see table 2), while imports decreased by 11.8 percent to reach 37.4 bln US$ (see table 3). Exports of this commodity accounted for 1.5 percent of world exports of SITC section 6, and 0.2 percent of total world merchandise exports (see table 1). Russian Federation, South Africa and Brazil were the top exporters in 2013 (see table 2). They accounted for 12.4, 11.6 and 10.1 percent of world exports, respectively. USA, China and Japan were the top destinations, with respectively 14.2, 10.2 and 8.0 percent of world imports (see table 3).

The top 15 countries/areas accounted for 74.4 and 79.9 percent of total world exports and imports, respectively (see tables 2 and 3). In 2013, South Africa was the country/area with the highest value of net exports (+3.8 bln US$), followed by Russian Federation (+3.7 bln US$). By MDG regions (see graph 2), the largest surpluses in this product group were recorded by Commonwealth of Independent States (+6.9 bln US$), Latin America and the Caribbean (+4.4 bln US$) and Sub-Saharan Africa (+3.9 bln US$). The largest trade deficits were recorded by Developed Europe (-6.2 bln US$), Eastern Asia (-5.9 bln US$) and Developed North America (-4.8 bln US$).

Table 1: Imports (Imp.) and exports (Exp.), 1999-2013, in current US$

		1999	2000	2001	2002	2003	2004	2005	2006	2007	2008	2009	2010	2011	2012	2013
Values in Bln US$	Imp.	9.8	11.6	10.1	10.9	14.2	26.2	30.8	31.3	43.5	59.1	26.5	40.2	47.6	42.4	37.4
	Exp.	7.8	8.9	8.0	8.8	11.8	21.2	25.8	25.8	36.1	47.8	22.1	35.2	43.0	39.2	34.2
As a percentage of	Imp.	1.2	1.3	1.2	1.2	1.4	2.0	2.2	1.9	2.2	2.7	1.7	2.1	2.1	2.0	1.7
SITC section (%)	Exp.	1.0	1.0	1.0	1.0	1.2	1.7	1.8	1.5	1.8	2.2	1.4	1.8	1.8	1.8	1.5
As a percentage of	Imp.	0.2	0.2	0.2	0.2	0.2	0.3	0.3	0.3	0.3	0.4	0.2	0.3	0.3	0.2	0.2
world trade (%)	Exp.	0.1	0.1	0.1	0.1	0.2	0.2	0.2	0.2	0.3	0.3	0.2	0.2	0.2	0.2	0.2

Graph 1: Annual growth rates of exports, 1999–2013
(In percentage by year)

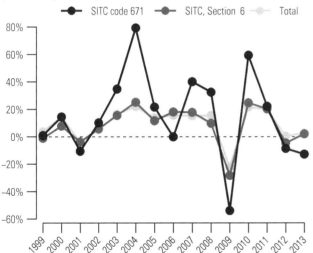

Table 2: Top exporting countries or areas in 2013

Country or area	Value (million US$)	Avg. Growth (%) 09-13	Growth (%) 12-13	World share %	Cum.
World	34 187.6	11.6	-12.9	100.0	
Russian Federation	4 246.9	10.3	-6.3	12.4	12.4
South Africa	3 966.9	8.0	1.6	11.6	24.0
Brazil	3 438.1	8.0	-17.3	10.1	34.1
India	2 466.7	25.5	14.5	7.2	41.3
Ukraine	1 750.0	12.5	0.8	5.1	46.4
Kazakhstan	1 715.8	9.6	-55.9	5.0	51.4
China	1 471.9	1.9	-37.1	4.3	55.7
Netherlands	1 269.1	12.2	-16.8	3.7	59.5
Japan	913.9	5.3	-17.5	2.7	62.1
Belgium	874.7	9.6	-1.4	2.6	64.7
Norway	739.3	13.5	-1.7	2.2	66.8
Colombia	683.2	-1.5	-22.5	2.0	68.8
Sweden	655.8	69.4	-8.9	1.9	70.8
Oman	619.3	555.4	41.3	1.8	72.6
Germany	614.2	5.9	-8.0	1.8	74.4

Graph 2: Trade Balance by MDG regions 2013
(Bln US$)

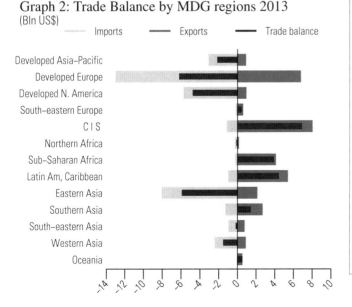

Table 3: Top importing countries or areas in 2013

Country or area	Value (million US$)	Avg. Growth (%) 09-13	Growth (%) 12-13	World share %	Cum.
World	37 379.5	9.0	-11.8	100.0	
USA	5 323.9	20.8	-14.9	14.2	14.2
China	3 812.1	-5.9	-14.9	10.2	24.4
Japan	2 995.6	9.8	-7.8	8.0	32.5
Germany	2 906.9	7.2	-14.0	7.8	40.2
Italy	2 709.6	16.1	-2.3	7.2	47.5
Rep. of Korea	2 622.4	9.8	-9.1	7.0	54.5
Other Asia, nes	1 598.0	6.9	-5.0	4.3	58.8
Belgium	1 321.0	12.6	-1.3	3.5	62.3
Turkey	1 153.3	13.5	-17.0	3.1	65.4
Netherlands	1 136.7	5.5	-6.4	3.0	68.4
Spain	1 074.0	9.6	-1.6	2.9	71.3
India	950.9	23.0	-20.0	2.5	73.8
Saudi Arabia	935.6	31.2	-5.5	2.5	76.4
France	732.9	6.9	-0.1	2.0	78.3
Russian Federation	580.2	9.0	2.1	1.6	79.9

672 Ingots and other primary forms, of iron or steel; semi-finished products

In 2013, the value (in current US$) of exports of "ingots and other primary forms, of iron or steel; semi-finished products" (SITC group 672) decreased by 15.5 percent (compared to 8.3 percent average growth rate from 2009-2013) to reach 33.6 bln US$ (see table 2), while imports decreased by 15.7 percent to reach 34.5 bln US$ (see table 3). Exports of this commodity accounted for 1.5 percent of world exports of SITC section 6, and 0.2 percent of total world merchandise exports (see table 1). Russian Federation, Ukraine and Japan were the top exporters in 2013 (see table 2). They accounted for 20.5, 15.8 and 8.5 percent of world exports, respectively. USA, Turkey and Indonesia were the top destinations, with respectively 11.2, 8.4 and 6.2 percent of world imports (see table 3).

The top 15 countries/areas accounted for 84.7 and 73.4 percent of total world exports and imports, respectively (see tables 2 and 3). In 2013, Russian Federation was the country/area with the highest value of net exports (+6.8 bln US$), followed by Ukraine (+5.2 bln US$). By MDG regions (see graph 2), the largest surpluses in this product group were recorded by Commonwealth of Independent States (+12.3 bln US$), Developed Asia-Pacific (+2.7 bln US$) and Latin America and the Caribbean (+2.5 bln US$). The largest trade deficits were recorded by Western Asia (-3.6 bln US$), South-eastern Asia (-3.5 bln US$) and Developed North America (-3.2 bln US$).

Table 1: Imports (Imp.) and exports (Exp.), 1999-2013, in current US$

		1999	2000	2001	2002	2003	2004	2005	2006	2007	2008	2009	2010	2011	2012	2013
Values in Bln US$	Imp.	11.1	13.8	12.2	13.9	17.5	28.9	31.7	32.9	40.7	57.3	28.5	36.2	45.6	40.9	34.5
	Exp.	9.6	11.5	10.6	12.2	15.3	26.0	28.5	31.0	39.2	54.4	24.4	34.6	43.1	39.7	33.6
As a percentage of SITC section (%)	Imp.	1.4	1.5	1.4	1.6	1.7	2.3	2.2	2.0	2.1	2.7	1.8	1.9	2.0	1.9	1.6
	Exp.	1.2	1.3	1.3	1.4	1.5	2.0	2.0	1.8	2.0	2.5	1.6	1.8	1.8	1.8	1.5
As a percentage of world trade (%)	Imp.	0.2	0.2	0.2	0.2	0.2	0.3	0.3	0.3	0.3	0.4	0.2	0.2	0.3	0.2	0.2
	Exp.	0.2	0.2	0.2	0.2	0.2	0.3	0.3	0.3	0.3	0.3	0.2	0.2	0.2	0.2	0.2

Graph 1: Annual growth rates of exports, 1999–2013
(In percentage by year)

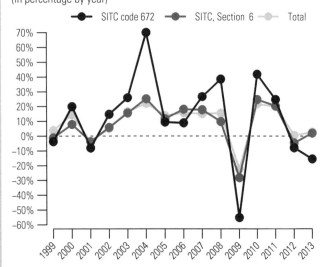

Graph 2: Trade Balance by MDG regions 2013
(Bln US$)

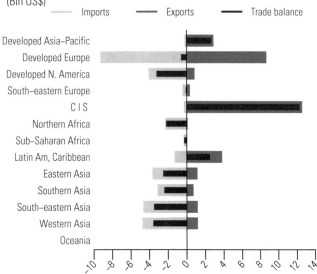

Table 2: Top exporting countries or areas in 2013

Country or area	Value (million US$)	Avg. Growth (%) 09-13	Growth (%) 12-13	World share %	Cum.
World	33553.9	8.3	-15.5	100.0	
Russian Federation	6870.9	8.7	-15.6	20.5	20.5
Ukraine	5296.5	7.5	-3.3	15.8	36.3
Japan	2849.4	4.8	-6.7	8.5	44.8
Brazil	2710.2	11.8	-29.5	8.1	52.8
United Kingdom	2456.6	12.7	32.1	7.3	60.2
Germany	1416.3	6.9	3.3	4.2	64.4
France	957.5	-3.6	-43.0	2.9	67.2
Turkey	920.9	-2.0	-50.2	2.7	70.0
Italy	836.7	14.3	-16.8	2.5	72.5
Thailand	812.3	91.1	-37.6	2.4	74.9
Mexico	755.9	14.7	32.1	2.3	77.1
Rep. of Korea	707.2	46.1	-40.8	2.1	79.2
India	704.1	19.6	76.3	2.1	81.3
USA	625.8	0.7	-30.8	1.9	83.2
Netherlands	498.1	31.0	-38.4	1.5	84.7

Table 3: Top importing countries or areas in 2013

Country or area	Value (million US$)	Avg. Growth (%) 09-13	Growth (%) 12-13	World share %	Cum.
World	34482.4	4.9	-15.7	100.0	
USA	3866.0	36.2	-18.8	11.2	11.2
Turkey	2910.7	18.5	45.7	8.4	19.7
Indonesia	2136.9	23.0	-10.8	6.2	25.9
Iran	2059.3	-2.8	-13.3	6.0	31.8
Thailand	2000.3	5.3	-16.6	5.8	37.6
Italy	1931.9	7.9	-9.2	5.6	43.2
Other Asia, nes	1778.7	-0.4	-23.7	5.2	48.4
Egypt	1528.1	16.5	-6.0	4.4	52.8
France	1395.9	10.2	-4.9	4.0	56.9
Rep. of Korea	1329.2	-15.2	-22.8	3.9	60.7
Germany	1254.1	6.8	-14.1	3.6	64.4
Saudi Arabia	972.8	48.3	-40.1	2.8	67.2
Belgium	962.1	0.1	-34.7	2.8	70.0
Hungary	596.3	84.1	72.2	1.7	71.7
China	578.2	-27.8	7.1	1.7	73.4

Flat-rolled products of iron or non-alloy steel, not clad, plated or coated 673

In 2013, the value (in current US$) of exports of "flat-rolled products of iron or non-alloy steel, not clad, plated or coated" (SITC group 673) decreased by 6.3 percent (compared to 5.7 percent average growth rate from 2009-2013) to reach 74.0 bln US$ (see table 2), while imports decreased by 5.5 percent to reach 83.0 bln US$ (see table 3). Exports of this commodity accounted for 3.3 percent of world exports of SITC section 6, and 0.4 percent of total world merchandise exports (see table 1). Japan, Rep. of Korea and Germany were the top exporters in 2013 (see table 2). They accounted for 15.5, 10.8 and 6.4 percent of world exports, respectively. China, Rep. of Korea and Germany were the top destinations, with respectively 5.7, 5.7 and 5.6 percent of world imports (see table 3).

The top 15 countries/areas accounted for 79.5 and 58.5 percent of total world exports and imports, respectively (see tables 2 and 3). In 2013, Japan was the country/area with the highest value of net exports (+9.6 bln US$), followed by Rep. of Korea (+3.3 bln US$). By MDG regions (see graph 2), the largest surpluses in this product group were recorded by Developed Asia-Pacific (+9.8 bln US$), Commonwealth of Independent States (+5.9 bln US$) and Eastern Asia (+3.4 bln US$). The largest trade deficits were recorded by South-eastern Asia (-11.5 bln US$), Western Asia (-5.4 bln US$) and Latin America and the Caribbean (-3.7 bln US$).

Table 1: Imports (Imp.) and exports (Exp.), 1999-2013, in current US$

		1999	2000	2001	2002	2003	2004	2005	2006	2007	2008	2009	2010	2011	2012	2013
Values in Bln US$	Imp.	27.4	32.7	28.0	29.5	40.0	58.0	69.6	74.2	91.2	118.5	65.6	83.3	99.2	87.8	83.0
	Exp.	25.1	29.5	24.6	27.7	36.9	55.4	65.5	71.8	88.8	112.2	59.4	79.9	92.2	79.0	74.0
As a percentage of	Imp.	3.4	3.7	3.3	3.3	3.9	4.5	4.9	4.5	4.7	5.5	4.2	4.3	4.3	4.0	3.8
SITC section (%)	Exp.	3.1	3.4	3.0	3.1	3.6	4.4	4.6	4.3	4.5	5.2	3.8	4.1	3.9	3.5	3.3
As a percentage of	Imp.	0.5	0.5	0.4	0.4	0.5	0.6	0.7	0.6	0.7	0.7	0.5	0.5	0.5	0.5	0.4
world trade (%)	Exp.	0.5	0.5	0.4	0.4	0.5	0.6	0.6	0.6	0.6	0.7	0.5	0.5	0.5	0.4	0.4

Graph 1: Annual growth rates of exports, 1999–2013
(In percentage by year)

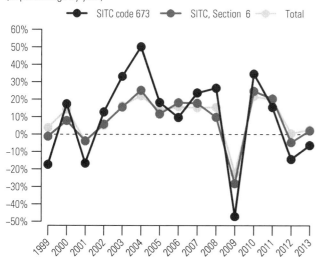

Table 2: Top exporting countries or areas in 2013

Country or area	Value (million US$)	Avg. Growth (%) 09-13	Growth (%) 12-13	World share %	Cum.
World	73 990.5	5.7	-6.3	100.0	
Japan	11 453.1	6.3	-7.7	15.5	15.5
Rep. of Korea	8 025.6	7.8	-20.1	10.8	26.3
Germany	4 756.2	4.4	-12.4	6.4	32.8
Belgium	4 310.7	2.1	-0.5	5.8	38.6
Russian Federation	3 816.3	-0.2	-11.5	5.2	43.7
France	3 712.4	24.9	46.1	5.0	48.8
Other Asia, nes	3 368.7	8.9	-0.8	4.6	53.3
Ukraine	3 304.4	7.8	-8.1	4.5	57.8
USA	2 896.5	10.6	-4.2	3.9	61.7
Italy	2 789.2	7.4	-20.8	3.8	65.5
India	2 423.9	29.5	75.5	3.3	68.7
Netherlands	2 324.2	5.8	-10.7	3.1	71.9
China	2 315.7	-13.2	-15.1	3.1	75.0
Slovakia	1 760.8	14.5	8.9	2.4	77.4
Austria	1 548.8	1.8	-8.1	2.1	79.5

Graph 2: Trade Balance by MDG regions 2013
(Bln US$)

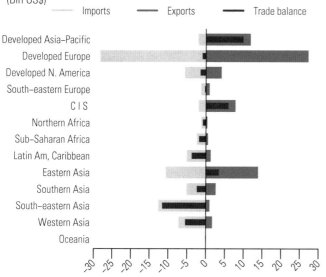

Table 3: Top importing countries or areas in 2013

Country or area	Value (million US$)	Avg. Growth (%) 09-13	Growth (%) 12-13	World share %	Cum.
World	82 973.7	6.1	-5.5	100.0	
China	4 763.5	-5.3	-2.2	5.7	5.7
Rep. of Korea	4 754.7	-10.0	-27.5	5.7	11.5
Germany	4 624.6	5.3	-7.9	5.6	17.0
Thailand	3 954.7	28.2	34.4	4.8	21.8
USA	3 895.3	17.4	-11.6	4.7	26.5
Italy	3 773.2	9.5	33.7	4.5	31.1
Turkey	3 127.5	5.9	5.9	3.8	34.8
Belgium	3 085.4	15.3	41.6	3.7	38.5
France	3 047.5	4.2	-0.4	3.7	42.2
Viet Nam	2 963.4	2.7	10.5	3.6	45.8
Indonesia	2 533.4	24.5	-14.1	3.1	48.8
Mexico	2 094.8	20.3	-11.3	2.5	51.4
India	2 030.6	-9.3	-31.6	2.4	53.8
Spain	1 942.5	11.7	-1.0	2.3	56.2
Poland	1 917.2	12.6	-10.2	2.3	58.5

674 Flat-rolled products of iron or non-alloy steel, clad, plated or coated

In 2013, the value (in current US$) of exports of "flat-rolled products of iron or non-alloy steel, clad, plated or coated" (SITC group 674) decreased by 0.3 percent (compared to 10.7 percent average growth rate from 2009-2013) to reach 54.1 bln US$ (see table 2), while imports decreased by 0.8 percent to reach 54.5 bln US$ (see table 3). Exports of this commodity accounted for 2.4 percent of world exports of SITC section 6, and 0.3 percent of total world merchandise exports (see table 1). China, Rep. of Korea and Belgium were the top exporters in 2013 (see table 2). They accounted for 18.0, 10.8 and 7.9 percent of world exports, respectively. Germany, USA and China were the top destinations, with respectively 8.3, 6.0 and 5.8 percent of world imports (see table 3).

The top 15 countries/areas accounted for 83.8 and 57.3 percent of total world exports and imports, respectively (see tables 2 and 3). In 2013, China was the country/area with the highest value of net exports (+6.6 bln US$), followed by Rep. of Korea (+4.4 bln US$). By MDG regions (see graph 2), the largest surpluses in this product group were recorded by Eastern Asia (+12.5 bln US$), Developed Asia-Pacific (+3.2 bln US$) and Southern Asia (+379.3 mln US$). The largest trade deficits were recorded by South-eastern Asia (-4.7 bln US$), Latin America and the Caribbean (-3.4 bln US$) and Commonwealth of Independent States (-2.4 bln US$).

Table 1: Imports (Imp.) and exports (Exp.), 1999-2013, in current US$

		1999	2000	2001	2002	2003	2004	2005	2006	2007	2008	2009	2010	2011	2012	2013
Values in Bln US$	Imp.	17.9	19.8	18.2	19.7	24.9	32.7	36.2	41.4	50.5	56.7	38.6	51.1	59.4	54.9	54.5
	Exp.	17.3	19.0	16.9	18.7	23.5	30.9	34.2	40.1	48.3	56.1	36.1	49.3	58.7	54.3	54.1
As a percentage of SITC section (%)	Imp.	2.2	2.2	2.1	2.2	2.4	2.6	2.5	2.5	2.6	2.6	2.5	2.7	2.6	2.5	2.5
	Exp.	2.2	2.2	2.0	2.1	2.3	2.4	2.4	2.4	2.4	2.6	2.3	2.5	2.5	2.4	2.4
As a percentage of world trade (%)	Imp.	0.3	0.3	0.3	0.3	0.3	0.3	0.3	0.3	0.4	0.3	0.3	0.3	0.3	0.3	0.3
	Exp.	0.3	0.3	0.3	0.3	0.3	0.3	0.3	0.3	0.3	0.4	0.3	0.3	0.3	0.3	0.3

Graph 1: Annual growth rates of exports, 1999–2013
(In percentage by year)

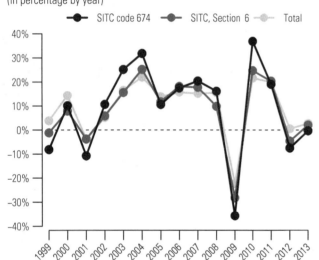

Graph 2: Trade Balance by MDG regions 2013
(Bln US$)

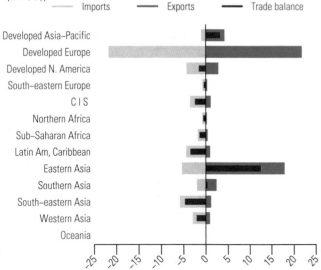

Table 2: Top exporting countries or areas in 2013

Country or area	Value (million US$)	Avg. Growth (%) 09-13	Growth (%) 12-13	World share %	Cum.
World	54 098.0	10.7	-0.3	100.0	
China	9 761.2	36.3	-0.3	18.0	18.0
Rep. of Korea	5 817.7	13.0	-2.3	10.8	28.8
Belgium	4 249.7	1.3	-1.8	7.9	36.7
Germany	4 139.4	1.0	-3.6	7.7	44.3
Japan	4 102.6	3.7	-15.3	7.6	51.9
France	2 434.9	6.3	19.9	4.5	56.4
Netherlands	2 332.3	8.0	5.3	4.3	60.7
India	2 254.9	15.8	35.3	4.2	64.9
Italy	2 195.3	27.1	-2.2	4.1	68.9
Other Asia, nes	1 965.4	8.1	-8.8	3.6	72.6
USA	1 798.5	7.9	-8.2	3.3	75.9
Austria	1 381.9	7.0	-4.9	2.6	78.4
Slovakia	1 084.5	2.9	2.9	2.0	80.4
Canada	1 009.6	11.0	5.9	1.9	82.3
United Kingdom	832.1	6.4	25.4	1.5	83.8

Table 3: Top importing countries or areas in 2013

Country or area	Value (million US$)	Avg. Growth (%) 09-13	Growth (%) 12-13	World share %	Cum.
World	54 498.2	9.0	-0.8	100.0	
Germany	4 505.1	8.8	-0.2	8.3	8.3
USA	3 290.3	19.0	5.3	6.0	14.3
China	3 184.5	0.4	-6.0	5.8	20.1
Thailand	2 690.7	22.5	-4.1	4.9	25.1
France	1 959.3	-2.5	-9.1	3.6	28.7
Poland	1 907.0	6.9	5.6	3.5	32.2
Spain	1 865.6	12.5	9.7	3.4	35.6
Russian Federation	1 769.0	22.1	-11.9	3.2	38.8
Italy	1 747.2	1.3	1.9	3.2	42.1
Mexico	1 733.5	9.0	-9.5	3.2	45.2
Belgium	1 516.5	1.5	3.1	2.8	48.0
Rep. of Korea	1 375.1	34.0	-0.7	2.5	50.5
United Kingdom	1 348.9	6.3	-2.6	2.5	53.0
Czech Rep.	1 266.5	7.8	-1.1	2.3	55.3
Indonesia	1 060.6	26.7	6.8	1.9	57.3

In 2013, the value (in current US$) of exports of "flat-rolled products of alloy steel" (SITC group 675) decreased by 6.6 percent (compared to 9.2 percent average growth rate from 2009-2013) to reach 61.1 bln US$ (see table 2), while imports decreased by 5.1 percent to reach 57.4 bln US$ (see table 3). Exports of this commodity accounted for 2.7 percent of world exports of SITC section 6, and 0.3 percent of total world merchandise exports (see table 1). China, Japan and Germany were the top exporters in 2013 (see table 2). They accounted for 16.7, 11.8 and 8.7 percent of world exports, respectively. Germany, China and Italy were the top destinations, with respectively 8.6, 7.0 and 6.0 percent of world imports (see table 3).

The top 15 countries/areas accounted for 88.8 and 66.4 percent of total world exports and imports, respectively (see tables 2 and 3). In 2013, Japan was the country/area with the highest value of net exports (+6.7 bln US$), followed by China (+6.2 bln US$). By MDG regions (see graph 2), the largest surpluses in this product group were recorded by Eastern Asia (+7.4 bln US$), Developed Asia-Pacific (+6.3 bln US$) and Developed Europe (+5.1 bln US$). The largest trade deficits were recorded by South-eastern Asia (-5.1 bln US$), Latin America and the Caribbean (-3.6 bln US$) and Western Asia (-2.5 bln US$).

Table 1: Imports (Imp.) and exports (Exp.), 1999-2013, in current US$

		1999	2000	2001	2002	2003	2004	2005	2006	2007	2008	2009	2010	2011	2012	2013
Values in Bln US$	Imp.	16.7	20.0	18.2	20.4	26.5	37.7	43.1	54.4	70.1	69.1	41.1	55.5	68.3	60.5	57.4
	Exp.	17.5	21.1	18.5	21.3	28.0	39.4	44.3	56.6	72.2	73.0	43.0	59.4	75.0	65.4	61.1
As a percentage of SITC section (%)	Imp.	2.0	2.2	2.1	2.3	2.6	2.9	3.0	3.3	3.6	3.2	2.6	2.9	3.0	2.8	2.6
	Exp.	2.2	2.4	2.2	2.4	2.8	3.1	3.1	3.4	3.7	3.4	2.8	3.1	3.2	2.9	2.7
As a percentage of world trade (%)	Imp.	0.3	0.3	0.3	0.3	0.3	0.4	0.4	0.4	0.5	0.4	0.3	0.4	0.4	0.3	0.3
	Exp.	0.3	0.3	0.3	0.3	0.4	0.4	0.4	0.5	0.5	0.5	0.3	0.4	0.4	0.4	0.3

Graph 1: Annual growth rates of exports, 1999–2013
(In percentage by year)

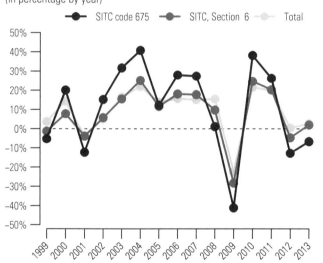

Table 2: Top exporting countries or areas in 2013

Country or area	Value (million US$)	Avg. Growth (%) 09-13	Growth (%) 12-13	World share %	Cum.
World	61 084.2	9.2	-6.6	100.0	
China	10 218.4	56.6	4.1	16.7	16.7
Japan	7 206.0	3.5	-14.2	11.8	28.5
Germany	5 336.5	2.8	-5.2	8.7	37.3
Belgium	5 318.2	10.5	7.3	8.7	46.0
Rep. of Korea	3 650.6	9.5	-2.3	6.0	51.9
Finland	3 279.9	15.4	-0.9	5.4	57.3
USA	2 914.4	9.9	-2.8	4.8	62.1
France	2 842.7	-11.1	-33.6	4.7	66.7
Other Asia, nes	2 676.9	5.3	-0.7	4.4	71.1
Sweden	2 642.4	3.4	-15.2	4.3	75.4
Netherlands	2 384.1	12.8	-5.2	3.9	79.3
Italy	2 074.5	4.5	-22.4	3.4	82.7
Austria	1 525.5	9.6	6.0	2.5	85.2
Spain	1 318.0	6.8	-8.0	2.2	87.4
India	866.5	41.5	14.8	1.4	88.8

Graph 2: Trade Balance by MDG regions 2013
(Bln US$)

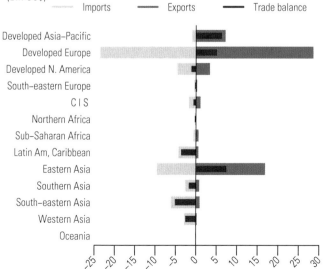

Table 3: Top importing countries or areas in 2013

Country or area	Value (million US$)	Avg. Growth (%) 09-13	Growth (%) 12-13	World share %	Cum.
World	57 439.6	8.7	-5.1	100.0	
Germany	4 912.5	11.6	0.7	8.6	8.6
China	4 044.9	-4.7	-11.9	7.0	15.6
Italy	3 446.9	4.8	-11.3	6.0	21.6
USA	3 170.4	15.4	-14.6	5.5	27.1
Rep. of Korea	2 720.0	14.3	12.6	4.7	31.9
Netherlands	2 516.1	12.2	-0.2	4.4	36.2
France	2 419.3	5.5	0.6	4.2	40.4
Other Asia, nes	2 344.0	27.3	3.7	4.1	44.5
Mexico	2 217.9	11.9	-11.8	3.9	48.4
Thailand	2 078.3	25.4	-15.2	3.6	52.0
India	2 027.9	8.0	-17.5	3.5	55.5
Turkey	1 762.6	11.5	-6.5	3.1	58.6
Viet Nam	1 702.2	30.7	7.9	3.0	61.6
Canada	1 393.3	11.0	-3.7	2.4	64.0
Belgium	1 367.3	-2.1	-14.6	2.4	66.4

676 Iron and steel bars, rods, angles, shapes and sections

In 2013, the value (in current US$) of exports of "iron and steel bars, rods, angles, shapes and sections" (SITC group 676) decreased by 4.8 percent (compared to 13.0 percent average growth rate from 2009-2013) to reach 83.1 bln US$ (see table 2), while imports decreased by 4.6 percent to reach 83.0 bln US$ (see table 3). Exports of this commodity accounted for 3.7 percent of world exports of SITC section 6, and 0.4 percent of total world merchandise exports (see table 1). China, Germany and Turkey were the top exporters in 2013 (see table 2). They accounted for 15.7, 8.4 and 8.1 percent of world exports, respectively. Germany, USA and Rep. of Korea were the top destinations, with respectively 7.7, 6.2 and 4.2 percent of world imports (see table 3).

The top 15 countries/areas accounted for 75.0 and 49.2 percent of total world exports and imports, respectively (see tables 2 and 3). In 2013, China was the country/area with the highest value of net exports (+11.1 bln US$), followed by Turkey (+5.5 bln US$). By MDG regions (see graph 2), the largest surpluses in this product group were recorded by Eastern Asia (+9.0 bln US$), Developed Europe (+7.7 bln US$) and Developed Asia-Pacific (+3.3 bln US$). The largest trade deficits were recorded by South-eastern Asia (-6.8 bln US$), Northern Africa (-3.5 bln US$) and Latin America and the Caribbean (-3.4 bln US$).

Table 1: Imports (Imp.) and exports (Exp.), 1999-2013, in current US$

		1999	2000	2001	2002	2003	2004	2005	2006	2007	2008	2009	2010	2011	2012	2013
Values in Bln US$	Imp.	22.4	24.0	23.3	24.0	29.8	46.4	52.4	63.5	84.8	108.6	52.3	68.0	90.3	87.0	83.0
	Exp.	21.4	23.1	22.8	23.3	29.6	46.5	52.0	64.1	88.3	112.9	50.9	68.6	91.5	87.4	83.1
As a percentage of SITC section (%)	Imp.	2.7	2.7	2.7	2.7	2.9	3.6	3.7	3.8	4.3	5.0	3.4	3.5	3.9	4.0	3.8
	Exp.	2.7	2.7	2.7	2.7	2.9	3.7	3.7	3.8	4.5	5.2	3.3	3.5	3.9	3.9	3.7
As a percentage of world trade (%)	Imp.	0.4	0.4	0.4	0.4	0.4	0.5	0.5	0.5	0.6	0.7	0.4	0.4	0.5	0.5	0.4
	Exp.	0.4	0.4	0.4	0.4	0.4	0.5	0.5	0.5	0.6	0.7	0.4	0.5	0.5	0.5	0.4

Graph 1: Annual growth rates of exports, 1999–2013
(In percentage by year)

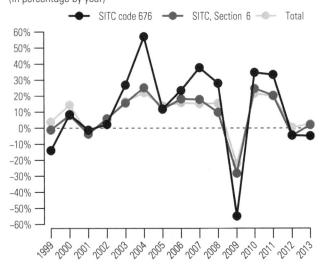

Table 2: Top exporting countries or areas in 2013

Country or area	Value (million US$)	Avg. Growth (%) 09-13	Growth (%) 12-13	World share %	Cum.
World	83 137.6	13.0	-4.8	100.0	
China	13 040.9	51.6	23.5	15.7	15.7
Germany	6 979.0	10.3	-4.3	8.4	24.1
Turkey	6 766.4	5.7	-9.9	8.1	32.2
Italy	4 852.4	10.6	-2.4	5.8	38.1
Spain	4 837.0	9.2	-8.2	5.8	43.9
Japan	4 393.2	12.0	-6.9	5.3	49.2
Ukraine	3 416.3	13.3	-11.1	4.1	53.3
USA	3 161.4	14.0	-16.4	3.8	57.1
France	2 525.5	10.6	-7.4	3.0	60.1
Rep. of Korea	2 487.9	5.1	-5.8	3.0	63.1
Russian Federation	2 261.7	8.6	-10.5	2.7	65.8
Poland	2 120.8	15.7	-6.5	2.6	68.4
United Kingdom	1 901.4	8.8	-6.7	2.3	70.7
Czech Rep.	1 892.4	14.1	-7.6	2.3	72.9
Luxembourg	1 700.1	-0.5	-9.9	2.0	75.0

Graph 2: Trade Balance by MDG regions 2013
(Bln US$)

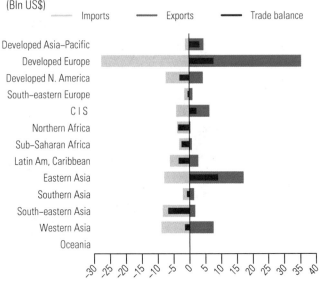

Table 3: Top importing countries or areas in 2013

Country or area	Value (million US$)	Avg. Growth (%) 09-13	Growth (%) 12-13	World share %	Cum.
World	82 972.7	12.2	-4.6	100.0	
Germany	6 421.8	13.0	-5.9	7.7	7.7
USA	5 121.1	19.3	-7.8	6.2	13.9
Rep. of Korea	3 459.8	14.4	-6.4	4.2	18.1
France	2 811.3	6.1	-6.6	3.4	21.5
Algeria	2 559.2	6.9	-6.8	3.1	24.6
Italy	2 407.4	8.7	-2.4	2.9	27.5
United Arab Emirates	2 272.6	9.3	11.4	2.7	30.2
Canada	2 253.4	15.5	-17.6	2.7	32.9
Netherlands	2 221.2	10.2	-0.9	2.7	35.6
Thailand	2 072.5	24.0	-0.9	2.5	38.1
China	1 985.5	8.2	2.8	2.4	40.5
Singapore	1 954.7	19.0	7.7	2.4	42.8
Russian Federation	1 881.7	37.4	7.0	2.3	45.1
United Kingdom	1 822.4	15.6	-2.0	2.2	47.3
Saudi Arabia	1 594.5	25.2	-29.6	1.9	49.2

In 2013, the value (in current US$) of exports of "rails or railway track construction material, of iron or steel" (SITC group 677) decreased by 1.4 percent (compared to 3.4 percent average growth rate from 2009-2013) to reach 4.3 bln US$ (see table 2), while imports increased by 0.9 percent to reach 4.9 bln US$ (see table 3). Exports of this commodity accounted for 0.2 percent of world exports of SITC section 6, and less than 0.1 percent of total world merchandise exports (see table 1). Japan, Austria and China were the top exporters in 2013 (see table 2). They accounted for 15.0, 14.2 and 8.9 percent of world exports, respectively. USA, Russian Federation and Kazakhstan were the top destinations, with respectively 9.9, 8.9 and 6.0 percent of world imports (see table 3).

The top 15 countries/areas accounted for 91.0 and 61.1 percent of total world exports and imports, respectively (see tables 2 and 3). In 2013, Japan was the country/area with the highest value of net exports (+631.7 mln US$), followed by Austria (+581.2 mln US$). By MDG regions (see graph 2), the largest surpluses in this product group were recorded by Developed Europe (+749.4 mln US$), Developed Asia-Pacific (+622.3 mln US$) and Eastern Asia (+180.1 mln US$). The largest trade deficits were recorded by Latin America and the Caribbean (-450.4 mln US$), Commonwealth of Independent States (-385.7 mln US$) and Western Asia (-307.9 mln US$).

Table 1: Imports (Imp.) and exports (Exp.), 1999-2013, in current US$

		1999	2000	2001	2002	2003	2004	2005	2006	2007	2008	2009	2010	2011	2012	2013
Values in Bln US$	Imp.	1.4	1.2	1.4	1.5	1.8	2.1	2.6	2.9	3.8	5.2	4.0	4.3	4.8	4.9	4.9
	Exp.	1.2	1.0	1.2	1.3	1.6	2.0	2.2	2.5	3.3	4.3	3.8	3.8	4.4	4.4	4.3
As a percentage of SITC section (%)	Imp.	0.2	0.1	0.2	0.2	0.2	0.2	0.2	0.2	0.2	0.2	0.3	0.2	0.2	0.2	0.2
	Exp.	0.1	0.1	0.1	0.2	0.2	0.2	0.2	0.1	0.2	0.2	0.2	0.2	0.2	0.2	0.2
As a percentage of world trade (%)	Imp.	0.0	0.0	0.0	0.0	0.0	0.0	0.0	0.0	0.0	0.0	0.0	0.0	0.0	0.0	0.0
	Exp.	0.0	0.0	0.0	0.0	0.0	0.0	0.0	0.0	0.0	0.0	0.0	0.0	0.0	0.0	0.0

Graph 1: Annual growth rates of exports, 1999–2013
(In percentage by year)

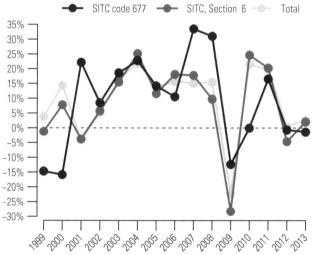

Table 2: Top exporting countries or areas in 2013

Country or area	Value (million US$)	Avg. Growth (%) 09-13	Growth (%) 12-13	World share %	Cum.
World	4310.2	3.4	-1.4	100.0	
Japan	645.0	14.3	-3.7	15.0	15.0
Austria	610.6	5.9	-3.1	14.2	29.1
China	381.7	-7.4	-26.3	8.9	38.0
USA	379.5	14.8	11.8	8.8	46.8
Germany	289.6	-6.5	9.4	6.7	53.5
Ukraine	268.8	50.3	20.4	6.2	59.7
Russian Federation	250.5	16.8	41.1	5.8	65.6
Czech Rep.	242.8	2.1	-1.7	5.6	71.2
Spain	209.8	2.0	31.2	4.9	76.1
Italy	157.0	-0.9	-31.1	3.6	79.7
United Kingdom	105.7	0.5	2.2	2.5	82.2
Canada	102.2	11.8	-3.9	2.4	84.5
Belgium	100.4	-10.8	-26.9	2.3	86.9
Poland	93.7	-12.5	3.5	2.2	89.0
Luxembourg	85.2	-5.2	-1.2	2.0	91.0

Graph 2: Trade Balance by MDG regions 2013
(Bln US$)

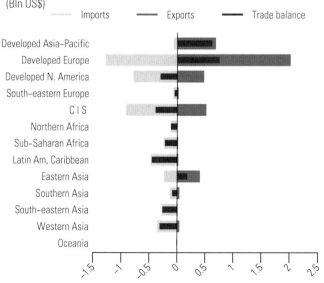

Table 3: Top importing countries or areas in 2013

Country or area	Value (million US$)	Avg. Growth (%) 09-13	Growth (%) 12-13	World share %	Cum.
World	4926.7	5.6	0.9	100.0	
USA	490.0	9.6	3.1	9.9	9.9
Russian Federation	439.0	164.0	7.5	8.9	18.9
Kazakhstan	293.6	41.0	57.4	6.0	24.8
Canada	291.0	15.6	-2.9	5.9	30.7
Germany	249.7	-0.6	5.3	5.1	35.8
Saudi Arabia	216.9	-3.0	11.3	4.4	40.2
Brazil	177.8	-0.5	-14.2	3.6	43.8
Mexico	152.6	13.8	17.8	3.1	46.9
Switzerland	149.2	11.6	28.6	3.0	49.9
Belgium	114.6	-9.4	-29.7	2.3	52.3
France	106.2	0.8	24.7	2.2	54.4
Indonesia	87.0	37.1	-11.7	1.8	56.2
Poland	83.3	23.1	29.4	1.7	57.9
Sweden	82.0	-2.5	-7.4	1.7	59.5
China	77.9	-11.1	29.7	1.6	61.1

678 Wire of iron or steel

In 2013, the value (in current US$) of exports of "wire of iron or steel" (SITC group 678) decreased by 2.7 percent (compared to 10.3 percent average growth rate from 2009-2013) to reach 11.5 bln US$ (see table 2), while imports decreased by 2.9 percent to reach 11.5 bln US$ (see table 3). Exports of this commodity accounted for 0.5 percent of world exports of SITC section 6, and 0.1 percent of total world merchandise exports (see table 1). China, Rep. of Korea and Germany were the top exporters in 2013 (see table 2). They accounted for 17.8, 8.0 and 7.5 percent of world exports, respectively. USA, Germany and China were the top destinations, with respectively 9.2, 9.1 and 4.0 percent of world imports (see table 3).

The top 15 countries/areas accounted for 73.8 and 55.1 percent of total world exports and imports, respectively (see tables 2 and 3). In 2013, China was the country/area with the highest value of net exports (+1.6 bln US$), followed by Rep. of Korea (+603.3 mln US$). By MDG regions (see graph 2), the largest surpluses in this product group were recorded by Eastern Asia (+2.3 bln US$), Developed Asia-Pacific (+137.8 mln US$) and Developed Europe (+94.5 mln US$). The largest trade deficits were recorded by Developed North America (-650.8 mln US$), Latin America and the Caribbean (-540.0 mln US$) and South-eastern Asia (-472.7 mln US$).

Table 1: Imports (Imp.) and exports (Exp.), 1999-2013, in current US$

		1999	2000	2001	2002	2003	2004	2005	2006	2007	2008	2009	2010	2011	2012	2013
Values in Bln US$	Imp.	4.0	4.3	4.1	4.2	5.0	7.0	7.9	8.7	10.8	12.8	8.0	10.7	13.2	11.8	11.5
	Exp.	3.6	3.8	3.5	3.8	4.5	6.6	7.2	8.2	10.3	12.7	7.8	10.8	13.3	11.9	11.5
As a percentage of	Imp.	0.5	0.5	0.5	0.5	0.5	0.6	0.6	0.5	0.6	0.6	0.5	0.6	0.6	0.5	0.5
SITC section (%)	Exp.	0.4	0.4	0.4	0.4	0.4	0.5	0.5	0.5	0.5	0.6	0.5	0.6	0.6	0.5	0.5
As a percentage of	Imp.	0.1	0.1	0.1	0.1	0.1	0.1	0.1	0.1	0.1	0.1	0.1	0.1	0.1	0.1	0.1
world trade (%)	Exp.	0.1	0.1	0.1	0.1	0.1	0.1	0.1	0.1	0.1	0.1	0.1	0.1	0.1	0.1	0.1

Graph 1: Annual growth rates of exports, 1999–2013
(In percentage by year)

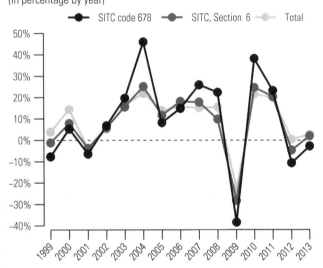

Table 2: Top exporting countries or areas in 2013

Country or area	Value (million US$)	Avg. Growth (%) 09-13	Growth (%) 12-13	World share %	Cum.
World	11 541.7	10.3	-2.7	100.0	
China	2 057.1	17.1	-0.7	17.8	17.8
Rep. of Korea	925.6	9.9	-3.6	8.0	25.8
Germany	869.4	7.1	-4.9	7.5	33.4
Japan	696.8	8.0	-13.7	6.0	39.4
Italy	580.1	9.4	-7.4	5.0	44.4
Czech Rep.	513.7	11.0	-1.0	4.5	48.9
France	490.0	11.3	-2.6	4.2	53.1
USA	394.7	8.6	-5.4	3.4	56.6
Slovakia	342.3	10.3	22.8	3.0	59.5
India	332.7	25.2	4.6	2.9	62.4
Spain	322.1	5.8	-8.0	2.8	65.2
Sweden	262.7	5.5	0.8	2.3	67.5
Other Asia, nes	258.5	7.6	-4.8	2.2	69.7
Malaysia	238.8	6.5	-2.5	2.1	71.8
Canada	229.0	6.1	-0.2	2.0	73.8

Graph 2: Trade Balance by MDG regions 2013
(Bln US$)

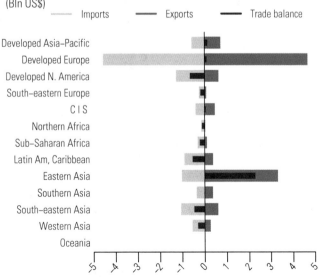

Table 3: Top importing countries or areas in 2013

Country or area	Value (million US$)	Avg. Growth (%) 09-13	Growth (%) 12-13	World share %	Cum.
World	11 482.4	9.5	-2.9	100.0	
USA	1 061.9	12.8	-4.7	9.2	9.2
Germany	1 039.9	6.8	-4.6	9.1	18.3
China	463.4	1.5	-4.8	4.0	22.3
France	459.7	2.0	-2.4	4.0	26.3
Japan	437.7	8.2	-16.6	3.8	30.2
Poland	368.1	12.4	8.6	3.2	33.4
Rep. of Korea	322.3	17.7	-4.3	2.8	36.2
Brazil	311.6	17.2	2.2	2.7	38.9
Italy	300.5	7.1	0.6	2.6	41.5
Thailand	284.0	11.1	-7.0	2.5	44.0
Netherlands	274.1	16.0	8.9	2.4	46.4
United Kingdom	261.4	10.5	-5.7	2.3	48.6
Mexico	248.1	17.4	-1.7	2.2	50.8
Belgium	247.5	10.3	3.5	2.2	53.0
Indonesia	246.4	14.9	-2.3	2.1	55.1

Tubes, pipes and hollow profiles, and tube or pipe fittings of iron or steel 679

In 2013, the value (in current US$) of exports of "tubes, pipes and hollow profiles, and tube or pipe fittings of iron or steel" (SITC group 679) decreased by 4.6 percent (compared to 7.1 percent average growth rate from 2009-2013) to reach 92.6 bln US$ (see table 2), while imports decreased by 3.0 percent to reach 95.7 bln US$ (see table 3). Exports of this commodity accounted for 4.1 percent of world exports of SITC section 6, and 0.5 percent of total world merchandise exports (see table 1). China, Germany and Italy were the top exporters in 2013 (see table 2). They accounted for 16.7, 9.1 and 8.4 percent of world exports, respectively. USA, Germany and Canada were the top destinations, with respectively 13.6, 4.7 and 4.4 percent of world imports (see table 3).

The top 15 countries/areas accounted for 74.8 and 54.8 percent of total world exports and imports, respectively (see tables 2 and 3). In 2013, China was the country/area with the highest value of net exports (+12.9 bln US$), followed by Italy (+6.0 bln US$). By MDG regions (see graph 2), the largest surpluses in this product group were recorded by Eastern Asia (+15.2 bln US$), Developed Europe (+10.3 bln US$) and Developed Asia-Pacific (+3.7 bln US$). The largest trade deficits were recorded by Western Asia (-9.3 bln US$), Developed North America (-8.1 bln US$) and South-eastern Asia (-4.4 bln US$).

Table 1: Imports (Imp.) and exports (Exp.), 1999-2013, in current US$

		1999	2000	2001	2002	2003	2004	2005	2006	2007	2008	2009	2010	2011	2012	2013
Values in Bln US$	Imp.	22.1	23.2	26.4	27.3	30.2	41.2	54.2	70.0	87.6	106.8	78.1	76.9	95.3	98.7	95.7
	Exp.	21.3	22.2	25.0	26.5	29.5	41.3	54.1	69.7	86.3	106.5	70.4	75.2	95.8	97.0	92.6
As a percentage of SITC section (%)	Imp.	2.7	2.6	3.1	3.1	2.9	3.2	3.8	4.2	4.5	4.9	5.0	4.0	4.1	4.5	4.4
	Exp.	2.7	2.6	3.0	3.0	2.9	3.2	3.8	4.2	4.4	4.9	4.5	3.9	4.1	4.4	4.1
As a percentage of world trade (%)	Imp.	0.4	0.4	0.4	0.4	0.4	0.4	0.5	0.6	0.6	0.7	0.6	0.5	0.5	0.5	0.5
	Exp.	0.4	0.3	0.4	0.4	0.4	0.5	0.5	0.6	0.6	0.7	0.6	0.5	0.5	0.5	0.5

Graph 1: Annual growth rates of exports, 1999–2013
(In percentage by year)

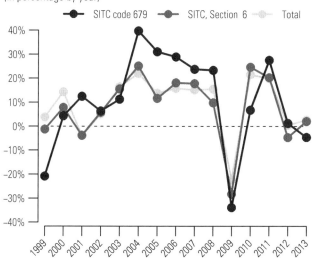

Table 2: Top exporting countries or areas in 2013

Country or area	Value (million US$)	Avg. Growth (%) 09-13	Growth (%) 12-13	World share %	Cum.
World	92 611.7	7.1	-4.6	100.0	
China	15 437.7	12.7	-3.5	16.7	16.7
Germany	8 391.3	1.0	-5.7	9.1	25.7
Italy	7 786.7	3.7	-1.8	8.4	34.1
USA	7 245.5	11.9	4.8	7.8	42.0
Japan	6 608.1	4.5	-15.2	7.1	49.1
Rep. of Korea	4 480.3	19.9	-11.0	4.8	53.9
France	2 726.9	0.1	-2.3	2.9	56.9
India	2 489.6	4.7	-20.8	2.7	59.6
Netherlands	2 310.9	10.1	25.2	2.5	62.1
United Kingdom	2 147.8	7.2	-12.7	2.3	64.4
Russian Federation	2 052.5	-2.1	6.5	2.2	66.6
Mexico	2 028.0	16.6	13.2	2.2	68.8
Spain	1 927.2	8.5	5.3	2.1	70.9
Canada	1 876.0	9.6	-11.3	2.0	72.9
Austria	1 779.6	6.7	2.5	1.9	74.8

Graph 2: Trade Balance by MDG regions 2013
(Bln US$)

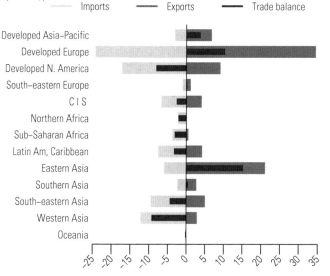

Table 3: Top importing countries or areas in 2013

Country or area	Value (million US$)	Avg. Growth (%) 09-13	Growth (%) 12-13	World share %	Cum.
World	95 742.2	5.2	-3.0	100.0	
USA	13 011.3	9.6	-16.3	13.6	13.6
Germany	4 532.2	7.3	-1.1	4.7	18.3
Canada	4 173.6	12.4	-11.7	4.4	22.7
Saudi Arabia	3 777.9	16.9	12.1	3.9	26.6
United Arab Emirates	*3 741.3*	12.1	11.4	3.9	30.5
Kazakhstan	2 759.2	-3.6	27.4	2.9	33.4
Rep. of Korea	2 541.4	13.7	11.2	2.7	36.1
China	2 532.9	-7.9	2.4	2.6	38.7
France	2 355.7	5.3	-0.5	2.5	41.2
Indonesia	2 302.6	14.6	-9.9	2.4	43.6
United Kingdom	2 244.8	10.4	-4.1	2.3	45.9
Malaysia	2 202.3	12.7	7.6	2.3	48.2
Singapore	2 160.1	3.5	-5.6	2.3	50.5
Netherlands	2 140.3	9.8	10.5	2.2	52.7
Russian Federation	1 987.0	15.5	9.9	2.1	54.8

681 Silver, platinum and other metals of the platinum group

In 2013, the value (in current US$) of exports of "silver, platinum and other metals of the platinum group" (SITC group 681) decreased by 11.2 percent (compared to 12.7 percent average growth rate from 2009-2013) to reach 58.3 bln US$ (see table 2), while imports decreased by 7.0 percent to reach 57.6 bln US$ (see table 3). Exports of this commodity accounted for 2.6 percent of world exports of SITC section 6, and 0.3 percent of total world merchandise exports (see table 1). South Africa, United Kingdom and Germany were the top exporters in 2013 (see table 2). They accounted for 14.5, 11.4 and 7.9 percent of world exports, respectively. USA, United Kingdom and China were the top destinations, with respectively 18.0, 13.6 and 9.9 percent of world imports (see table 3).

The top 15 countries/areas accounted for 83.2 and 90.5 percent of total world exports and imports, respectively (see tables 2 and 3). In 2013, South Africa was the country/area with the highest value of net exports (+8.4 bln US$), followed by Mexico (+3.0 bln US$). By MDG regions (see graph 2), the largest surpluses in this product group were recorded by Sub-Saharan Africa (+8.6 bln US$), Latin America and the Caribbean (+3.9 bln US$) and Commonwealth of Independent States (+2.4 bln US$). The largest trade deficits were recorded by Developed North America (-5.4 bln US$), Southern Asia (-4.8 bln US$) and Eastern Asia (-4.4 bln US$).

Table 1: Imports (Imp.) and exports (Exp.), 1999-2013, in current US$

		1999	2000	2001	2002	2003	2004	2005	2006	2007	2008	2009	2010	2011	2012	2013
Values in Bln US$	Imp.	13.9	21.6	20.3	14.8	15.2	19.3	23.0	37.0	45.4	56.1	39.1	54.2	78.4	62.0	57.6
	Exp.	10.7	12.1	14.3	10.5	13.3	18.1	21.8	37.2	45.6	51.0	36.1	50.1	74.2	65.7	58.3
As a percentage of SITC section (%)	Imp.	1.7	2.4	2.4	1.7	1.5	1.5	1.6	2.2	2.3	2.6	2.5	2.8	3.4	2.9	2.6
	Exp.	1.3	1.4	1.7	1.2	1.3	1.4	1.5	2.2	2.3	2.4	2.3	2.6	3.2	3.0	2.6
As a percentage of world trade (%)	Imp.	0.2	0.3	0.3	0.2	0.2	0.2	0.2	0.3	0.3	0.3	0.3	0.4	0.4	0.3	0.3
	Exp.	0.2	0.2	0.2	0.2	0.2	0.2	0.2	0.3	0.3	0.3	0.3	0.3	0.4	0.4	0.3

Graph 1: Annual growth rates of exports, 1999–2013
(In percentage by year)

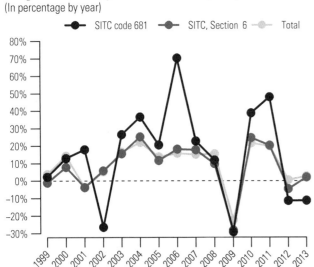

Graph 2: Trade Balance by MDG regions 2013
(Bln US$)

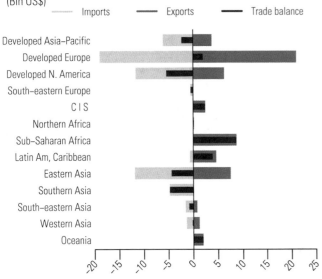

Table 2: Top exporting countries or areas in 2013

Country or area	Value (million US$)	Avg. Growth (%) 09-13	Growth (%) 12-13	World share %	Cum.
World	58 325.0	12.7	-11.2	100.0	
South Africa	8 442.5	5.7	6.5	14.5	14.5
United Kingdom	6 658.1	23.9	13.6	11.4	25.9
Germany	4 614.4	11.3	-10.9	7.9	33.8
Switzerland	3 772.6	7.5	-14.5	6.5	40.3
USA	3 750.8	8.8	-21.5	6.4	46.7
China, Hong Kong SAR	3 307.3	12.6	-21.7	5.7	52.4
Mexico	3 125.0	22.0	-26.9	5.4	57.7
Japan	3 031.4	14.9	-1.3	5.2	62.9
Canada	2 473.5	36.0	2.2	4.2	67.2
Papua New Guinea	1 967.3	1.7	31.7	3.4	70.5
Rep. of Korea	1 966.2	26.9	-26.7	3.4	73.9
Russian Federation	1 795.9	...	-32.9	3.1	77.0
Italy	1 382.6	26.1	5.5	2.4	79.4
China	1 174.7	-9.3	20.4	2.0	81.4
United Arab Emirates	1 039.6	88.6	21.7	1.8	83.2

Table 3: Top importing countries or areas in 2013

Country or area	Value (million US$)	Avg. Growth (%) 09-13	Growth (%) 12-13	World share %	Cum.
World	57 643.4	10.2	-7.0	100.0	
USA	10 387.9	19.2	-6.1	18.0	18.0
United Kingdom	7 845.5	8.6	-37.7	13.6	31.6
China	5 710.6	16.5	11.1	9.9	41.5
Japan	5 491.9	6.8	-4.7	9.5	51.1
India	4 704.0	10.3	105.9	8.2	59.2
Germany	4 406.0	9.2	-0.3	7.6	66.9
China, Hong Kong SAR	3 560.1	-0.3	-1.4	6.2	73.0
Switzerland	2 650.1	-8.9	-1.7	4.6	77.6
Other Asia, nes	1 384.3	8.8	-50.8	2.4	80.0
Canada	1 238.2	12.3	-28.8	2.1	82.2
Rep. of Korea	1 223.6	22.0	5.1	2.1	84.3
United Arab Emirates	1 094.3	61.1	11.4	1.9	86.2
Italy	1 042.4	-1.2	1.8	1.8	88.0
Thailand	797.8	10.0	8.2	1.4	89.4
France	638.9	20.6	-10.7	1.1	90.5

In 2013, the value (in current US$) of exports of "copper" (SITC group 682) decreased by 4.6 percent (compared to 10.4 percent average growth rate from 2009-2013) to reach 131.1 bln US$ (see table 2), while imports decreased by 3.1 percent to reach 131.7 bln US$ (see table 3). Exports of this commodity accounted for 5.8 percent of world exports of SITC section 6, and 0.7 percent of total world merchandise exports (see table 1). Chile, Germany and Japan were the top exporters in 2013 (see table 2). They accounted for 17.5, 8.0 and 5.7 percent of world exports, respectively. China, USA and Germany were the top destinations, with respectively 26.6, 7.2 and 6.9 percent of world imports (see table 3).

The top 15 countries/areas accounted for 69.3 and 74.4 percent of total world exports and imports, respectively (see tables 2 and 3). In 2013, Chile was the country/area with the highest value of net exports (+22.8 bln US$), followed by Zambia (+6.8 bln US$). By MDG regions (see graph 2), the largest surpluses in this product group were recorded by Latin America and the Caribbean (+21.9 bln US$), Sub-Saharan Africa (+8.9 bln US$) and Commonwealth of Independent States (+8.4 bln US$). The largest trade deficits were recorded by Eastern Asia (-30.2 bln US$), Western Asia (-8.8 bln US$) and South-eastern Asia (-4.5 bln US$).

Table 1: Imports (Imp.) and exports (Exp.), 1999-2013, in current US$

		1999	2000	2001	2002	2003	2004	2005	2006	2007	2008	2009	2010	2011	2012	2013
Values in Bln US$	Imp.	27.4	33.1	29.7	29.3	33.4	50.8	62.4	107.1	121.3	121.4	83.6	123.5	147.0	135.9	131.7
	Exp.	28.0	32.1	29.8	28.9	32.8	51.3	63.5	111.8	123.4	121.3	88.1	129.2	149.0	137.4	131.1
As a percentage of SITC section (%)	Imp.	3.3	3.7	3.5	3.3	3.3	4.0	4.4	6.4	6.2	5.6	5.4	6.4	6.4	6.3	6.0
	Exp.	3.5	3.7	3.6	3.3	3.2	4.0	4.5	6.7	6.2	5.6	5.7	6.7	6.4	6.2	5.8
As a percentage of world trade (%)	Imp.	0.5	0.5	0.5	0.4	0.4	0.5	0.6	0.9	0.9	0.7	0.7	0.8	0.8	0.7	0.7
	Exp.	0.5	0.5	0.5	0.4	0.4	0.6	0.6	0.9	0.9	0.8	0.7	0.9	0.8	0.8	0.7

Graph 1: Annual growth rates of exports, 1999–2013
(In percentage by year)

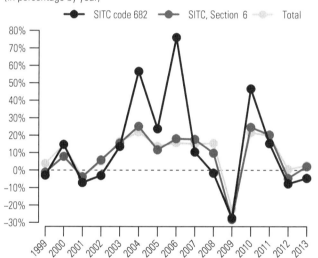

- ● SITC code 682
- ● SITC, Section 6
- ● Total

Table 2: Top exporting countries or areas in 2013

Country or area	Value (million US$)	Avg. Growth (%) 09-13	Growth (%) 12-13	World share %	Cum.
World	131 071.0	10.4	-4.6	100.0	
Chile	22 909.8	4.0	-11.8	17.5	17.5
Germany	10 513.6	10.5	-4.6	8.0	25.5
Japan	7 472.6	7.9	-5.3	5.7	31.2
Zambia	6 877.3	24.2	8.0	5.2	36.4
China	6 442.9	19.5	-1.0	4.9	41.4
Russian Federation	4 842.6	8.2	-14.6	3.7	45.1
Poland	4 140.0	12.7	-0.9	3.2	48.2
Rep. of Korea	4 079.0	11.6	2.2	3.1	51.3
USA	4 054.0	13.6	-5.4	3.1	54.4
Belgium	4 006.8	11.9	2.4	3.1	57.5
Malaysia	3 282.4	42.7	134.2	2.5	60.0
Australia	3 243.1	13.4	-6.1	2.5	62.5
Other Asia, nes	3 057.7	9.9	0.3	2.3	64.8
Italy	3 001.7	9.2	-3.7	2.3	67.1
Bulgaria	2 934.6	20.1	8.2	2.2	69.3

Graph 2: Trade Balance by MDG regions 2013
(Bln US$)

Imports — Exports — Trade balance

Developed Asia–Pacific
Developed Europe
Developed N. America
South–eastern Europe
C I S
Northern Africa
Sub–Saharan Africa
Latin Am, Caribbean
Eastern Asia
Southern Asia
South–eastern Asia
Western Asia
Oceania

-50 -40 -30 -20 -10 0 10 20 30 40

Table 3: Top importing countries or areas in 2013

Country or area	Value (million US$)	Avg. Growth (%) 09-13	Growth (%) 12-13	World share %	Cum.
World	131 695.9	12.0	-3.1	100.0	
China	34 993.0	11.5	-9.4	26.6	26.6
USA	9 439.9	13.6	4.6	7.2	33.7
Germany	9 026.6	13.0	3.3	6.9	40.6
Italy	6 532.9	10.7	-7.4	5.0	45.6
Malaysia	5 431.5	31.6	68.4	4.1	49.7
Other Asia, nes	4 621.1	8.2	-6.3	3.5	53.2
Rep. of Korea	4 135.9	2.8	-4.9	3.1	56.3
France	4 037.4	9.4	-3.3	3.1	59.4
Turkey	3 636.8	16.8	-4.7	2.8	62.2
Thailand	3 297.4	13.8	-3.8	2.5	64.7
Saudi Arabia	3 209.6	25.7	-0.4	2.4	67.1
Belgium	2 764.5	7.2	-7.8	2.1	69.2
United Arab Emirates	*2564.0*	37.9	11.4	1.9	71.1
Brazil	2 195.6	14.3	-13.3	1.7	72.8
Mexico	2 072.9	10.0	-4.4	1.6	74.4

683 Nickel

In 2013, the value (in current US$) of exports of "nickel" (SITC group 683) increased by 2.7 percent (compared to 11.2 percent average growth rate from 2009-2013) to reach 20.3 bln US$ (see table 2), while imports decreased by 3.4 percent to reach 20.0 bln US$ (see table 3). Exports of this commodity accounted for 0.9 percent of world exports of SITC section 6, and 0.1 percent of total world merchandise exports (see table 1). Russian Federation, Canada and USA were the top exporters in 2013 (see table 2). They accounted for 18.2, 11.8 and 7.5 percent of world exports, respectively. China, USA and Germany were the top destinations, with respectively 16.0, 12.6 and 8.0 percent of world imports (see table 3).

The top 15 countries/areas accounted for 85.9 and 86.0 percent of total world exports and imports, respectively (see tables 2 and 3). In 2013, Russian Federation was the country/area with the highest value of net exports (+3.6 bln US$), followed by Canada (+2.3 bln US$). By MDG regions (see graph 2), the largest surpluses in this product group were recorded by Commonwealth of Independent States (+3.4 bln US$), Developed North America (+1.3 bln US$) and Sub-Saharan Africa (+714.3 mln US$). The largest trade deficits were recorded by Eastern Asia (-2.9 bln US$), South-eastern Asia (-1.9 bln US$) and Southern Asia (-566.6 mln US$).

Table 1: Imports (Imp.) and exports (Exp.), 1999-2013, in current US$

		1999	2000	2001	2002	2003	2004	2005	2006	2007	2008	2009	2010	2011	2012	2013
Values in Bln US$	Imp.	5.5	8.3	6.2	6.7	9.1	12.9	14.6	21.9	32.8	22.5	13.7	20.3	25.8	20.7	20.0
	Exp.	5.2	7.4	6.2	7.0	8.0	12.2	13.3	20.9	31.7	20.9	13.3	19.2	23.1	19.8	20.3
As a percentage of SITC section (%)	Imp.	0.7	0.9	0.7	0.8	0.9	1.0	1.0	1.3	1.7	1.0	0.9	1.1	1.1	1.0	0.9
	Exp.	0.7	0.9	0.7	0.8	0.8	1.0	0.9	1.2	1.6	1.0	0.9	1.0	1.0	0.9	0.9
As a percentage of world trade (%)	Imp.	0.1	0.1	0.1	0.1	0.1	0.1	0.1	0.2	0.2	0.1	0.1	0.1	0.1	0.1	0.1
	Exp.	0.1	0.1	0.1	0.1	0.1	0.1	0.1	0.2	0.2	0.1	0.1	0.1	0.1	0.1	0.1

Graph 1: Annual growth rates of exports, 1999–2013
(In percentage by year)

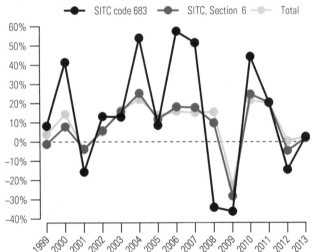

Legend: SITC code 683 — SITC, Section 6 — Total

Table 2: Top exporting countries or areas in 2013

Country or area	Value (million US$)	Avg. Growth (%) 09-13	Growth (%) 12-13	World share %	Cum.
World....................	20 325.8	11.2	2.7	100.0	
Russian Federation..............	3 701.6	0.4	-4.4	18.2	18.2
Canada........................	2 390.2	9.8	-11.1	11.8	30.0
USA...........................	1 521.7	10.7	-7.1	7.5	37.5
Norway........................	1 381.0	2.4	-15.3	6.8	44.3
United Kingdom.................	1 224.0	16.2	-4.3	6.0	50.3
Germany.......................	1 103.5	11.2	-6.5	5.4	55.7
China.........................	966.5	11.3	13.8	4.8	60.5
Netherlands....................	761.6	107.5	-12.8	3.7	64.2
Singapore.....................	761.3	33.5	164.1	3.7	68.0
Japan.........................	690.6	9.4	-14.3	3.4	71.3
France........................	685.4	8.7	-8.4	3.4	74.7
Australia......................	630.1	6.0	3.5	3.1	77.8
Belgium.......................	583.5	18.9	54.1	2.9	80.7
Finland.......................	561.4	2.6	-15.0	2.8	83.5
India.........................	494.8	139.0	78.1	2.4	85.9

Graph 2: Trade Balance by MDG regions 2013
(Bln US$)

Legend: Imports — Exports — Trade balance

Developed Asia–Pacific
Developed Europe
Developed N. America
South–eastern Europe
CIS
Northern Africa
Sub–Saharan Africa
Latin Am, Caribbean
Eastern Asia
Southern Asia
South–eastern Asia
Western Asia
Oceania

Table 3: Top importing countries or areas in 2013

Country or area	Value (million US$)	Avg. Growth (%) 09-13	Growth (%) 12-13	World share %	Cum.
World....................	20 011.8	9.9	-3.4	100.0	
China.........................	3 201.5	-5.5	-6.4	16.0	16.0
USA...........................	2 523.9	10.8	-14.7	12.6	28.6
Germany.......................	1 595.5	12.5	-23.3	8.0	36.6
Malaysia......................	1 370.9	153.2	105.7	6.9	43.4
Singapore.....................	1 147.8	25.2	40.3	5.7	49.2
India.........................	1 013.2	28.9	27.4	5.1	54.2
France........................	929.4	15.0	-11.7	4.6	58.9
Italy.........................	885.6	9.4	-5.0	4.4	63.3
Japan.........................	874.4	12.1	-13.5	4.4	67.7
Rep. of Korea.................	763.7	5.5	0.1	3.8	71.5
Belgium.......................	730.0	22.2	32.6	3.6	75.1
Netherlands....................	717.6	93.5	0.6	3.6	78.7
United Kingdom.................	657.6	8.5	-12.2	3.3	82.0
Spain.........................	411.1	10.9	-12.1	2.1	84.1
Sweden........................	379.0	7.0	-7.9	1.9	86.0

In 2013, the value (in current US$) of exports of "aluminium" (SITC group 684) decreased by 1.7 percent (compared to 8.7 percent average growth rate from 2009-2013) to reach 105.1 bln US$ (see table 2), while imports decreased by 1.1 percent to reach 107.7 bln US$ (see table 3). Exports of this commodity accounted for 4.6 percent of world exports of SITC section 6, and 0.6 percent of total world merchandise exports (see table 1). China, Germany and USA were the top exporters in 2013 (see table 2). They accounted for 11.1, 9.4 and 7.0 percent of world exports, respectively. Germany, USA and Japan were the top destinations, with respectively 11.2, 10.4 and 5.6 percent of world imports (see table 3).

The top 15 countries/areas accounted for 67.1 and 64.5 percent of total world exports and imports, respectively (see tables 2 and 3). In 2013, China was the country/area with the highest value of net exports (+7.6 bln US$), followed by Russian Federation (+6.1 bln US$). By MDG regions (see graph 2), the largest surpluses in this product group were recorded by Commonwealth of Independent States (+6.6 bln US$), Eastern Asia (+4.3 bln US$) and Sub-Saharan Africa (+1.3 bln US$). The largest trade deficits were recorded by South-eastern Asia (-4.7 bln US$), Latin America and the Caribbean (-4.0 bln US$) and Developed Europe (-3.9 bln US$).

Table 1: Imports (Imp.) and exports (Exp.), 1999-2013, in current US$

		1999	2000	2001	2002	2003	2004	2005	2006	2007	2008	2009	2010	2011	2012	2013
Values in Bln US$	Imp.	44.0	50.8	48.2	49.8	56.7	70.2	78.2	103.8	117.1	115.5	76.3	100.3	122.5	108.9	107.7
	Exp.	43.3	48.9	47.5	48.4	55.2	67.4	76.1	99.9	113.5	116.4	75.2	100.5	118.8	106.9	105.1
As a percentage of SITC section (%)	Imp.	5.4	5.7	5.7	5.6	5.5	5.5	5.5	6.2	6.0	5.3	4.9	5.2	5.3	5.0	4.9
	Exp.	5.4	5.7	5.7	5.5	5.4	5.3	5.4	6.0	5.7	5.4	4.8	5.2	5.1	4.8	4.6
As a percentage of world trade (%)	Imp.	0.8	0.8	0.8	0.8	0.7	0.8	0.7	0.9	0.8	0.7	0.6	0.7	0.7	0.6	0.6
	Exp.	0.8	0.8	0.8	0.8	0.7	0.7	0.7	0.8	0.8	0.7	0.6	0.7	0.7	0.6	0.6

Graph 1: Annual growth rates of exports, 1999–2013
(In percentage by year)

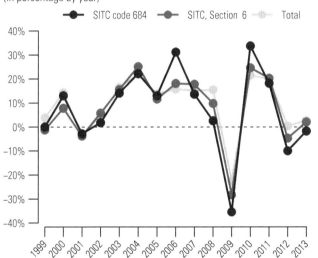

Table 2: Top exporting countries or areas in 2013

Country or area	Value (million US$)	Avg. Growth (%) 09-13	Growth (%) 12-13	World share %	Cum.
World	105 116.1	8.7	-1.7	100.0	
China	11 685.8	23.0	3.7	11.1	11.1
Germany	9 872.7	6.2	4.5	9.4	20.5
USA	7 316.0	12.9	2.8	7.0	27.5
Canada	7 094.9	6.7	-0.3	6.7	34.2
Russian Federation	6 944.6	5.1	-2.7	6.6	40.8
Norway	3 765.9	2.0	-9.0	3.6	44.4
Australia	3 606.3	3.0	-8.2	3.4	47.8
Italy	3 553.2	11.0	5.1	3.4	51.2
France	2 992.5	4.5	2.4	2.8	54.1
Netherlands	2 661.3	5.2	2.2	2.5	56.6
Belgium	2 559.2	10.4	21.2	2.4	59.0
Austria	2 354.6	6.6	-0.9	2.2	61.3
Spain	2 322.7	9.3	6.6	2.2	63.5
Rep. of Korea	1 952.8	7.8	4.0	1.9	65.3
Iceland	1 865.2	7.4	-0.6	1.8	67.1

Graph 2: Trade Balance by MDG regions 2013
(Bln US$)

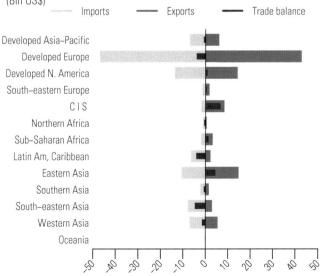

Table 3: Top importing countries or areas in 2013

Country or area	Value (million US$)	Avg. Growth (%) 09-13	Growth (%) 12-13	World share %	Cum.
World	107 711.4	9.0	-1.1	100.0	
Germany	12 042.1	11.1	0.4	11.2	11.2
USA	11 189.9	5.9	-3.0	10.4	21.6
Japan	6 003.2	12.4	-11.0	5.6	27.1
France	4 556.7	7.7	5.8	4.2	31.4
Italy	4 225.2	11.6	8.6	3.9	35.3
Rep. of Korea	4 214.7	12.7	2.9	3.9	39.2
China	4 036.3	-6.8	-15.7	3.7	43.0
Mexico	3 812.9	14.7	-15.3	3.5	46.5
United Kingdom	3 363.4	5.5	8.8	3.1	49.6
Turkey	2 966.4	19.4	7.2	2.8	52.4
Netherlands	2 954.4	7.9	-15.8	2.7	55.1
Belgium	2 678.5	9.6	6.9	2.5	57.6
Poland	2 583.8	13.7	10.5	2.4	60.0
Canada	2 438.4	11.7	-1.5	2.3	62.3
Thailand	2 382.5	15.8	3.5	2.2	64.5

685 Lead

In 2013, the value (in current US$) of exports of "lead" (SITC group 685) increased by 8.4 percent (compared to 9.5 percent average growth rate from 2009-2013) to reach 6.5 bln US$ (see table 2), while imports increased by 12.6 percent to reach 6.7 bln US$ (see table 3). Exports of this commodity accounted for 0.3 percent of world exports of SITC section 6, and less than 0.1 percent of total world merchandise exports (see table 1). Australia, Canada and Rep. of Korea were the top exporters in 2013 (see table 2). They accounted for 13.7, 9.1 and 7.3 percent of world exports, respectively. USA, United Kingdom and Rep. of Korea were the top destinations, with respectively 15.6, 7.9 and 6.5 percent of world imports (see table 3).

The top 15 countries/areas accounted for 75.9 and 75.2 percent of total world exports and imports, respectively (see tables 2 and 3). In 2013, Australia was the country/area with the highest value of net exports (+880.4 mln US$), followed by Canada (+585.9 mln US$). By MDG regions (see graph 2), the largest surpluses in this product group were recorded by Developed Asia-Pacific (+852.2 mln US$), Commonwealth of Independent States (+336.9 mln US$) and Latin America and the Caribbean (+251.1 mln US$). The largest trade deficits were recorded by South-eastern Asia (-541.4 mln US$), Developed North America (-385.1 mln US$) and Developed Europe (-320.5 mln US$).

Table 1: Imports (Imp.) and exports (Exp.), 1999-2013, in current US$

		1999	2000	2001	2002	2003	2004	2005	2006	2007	2008	2009	2010	2011	2012	2013
Values in Bln US$	Imp.	1.6	1.6	1.5	1.5	1.6	2.6	3.0	3.9	6.4	6.2	4.6	5.8	7.0	6.0	6.7
	Exp.	1.5	1.4	1.4	1.4	1.5	2.3	2.8	3.8	6.2	5.8	4.5	5.6	6.9	6.0	6.5
As a percentage of	Imp.	0.2	0.2	0.2	0.2	0.2	0.2	0.2	0.2	0.3	0.3	0.3	0.3	0.3	0.3	0.3
SITC section (%)	Exp.	0.2	0.2	0.2	0.2	0.1	0.2	0.2	0.2	0.3	0.3	0.3	0.3	0.3	0.3	0.3
As a percentage of	Imp.	0.0	0.0	0.0	0.0	0.0	0.0	0.0	0.0	0.0	0.0	0.0	0.0	0.0	0.0	0.0
world trade (%)	Exp.	0.0	0.0	0.0	0.0	0.0	0.0	0.0	0.0	0.0	0.0	0.0	0.0	0.0	0.0	0.0

Graph 1: Annual growth rates of exports, 1999–2013
(In percentage by year)

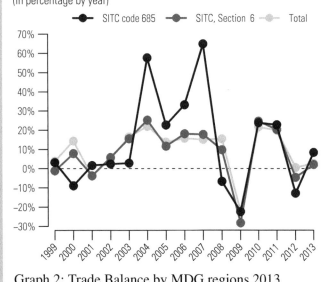

● SITC code 685   ● SITC, Section 6   ● Total

Table 2: Top exporting countries or areas in 2013

Country or area	Value (million US$)	Avg. Growth (%) 09-13	Growth (%) 12-13	World share %	Cum.
World	6 489.3	9.5	8.4	100.0	
Australia	890.6	7.6	-3.7	13.7	13.7
Canada	593.1	9.0	0.4	9.1	22.9
Rep. of Korea	475.0	21.3	16.1	7.3	30.2
Germany	451.2	-0.7	-8.2	7.0	37.1
United Kingdom	423.6	3.7	-4.9	6.5	43.7
Belgium	375.8	15.9	47.4	5.8	49.5
Malaysia	282.8	59.5	79.7	4.4	53.8
Mexico	233.0	-3.4	6.8	3.6	57.4
India	211.5	30.5	99.1	3.3	60.7
Russian Federation	191.5	7.8	-2.4	3.0	63.6
Bulgaria	170.5	6.2	22.8	2.6	66.2
Peru	161.1	34.9	916.0	2.5	68.7
Sweden	159.9	16.7	47.3	2.5	71.2
Kazakhstan	159.2	8.0	-50.9	2.5	73.6
China	146.8	6.0	195.6	2.3	75.9

Graph 2: Trade Balance by MDG regions 2013
(Bln US$)

—— Imports   —— Exports   —— Trade balance

Developed Asia–Pacific
Developed Europe
Developed N. America
South–eastern Europe
CIS
Northern Africa
Sub–Saharan Africa
Latin Am, Caribbean
Eastern Asia
Southern Asia
South–eastern Asia
Western Asia
Oceania

-2.5 -2 -1.5 -1 -0.5 0 0.5 1 1.5 2 2.5

Table 3: Top importing countries or areas in 2013

Country or area	Value (million US$)	Avg. Growth (%) 09-13	Growth (%) 12-13	World share %	Cum.
World	6 723.4	10.2	12.6	100.0	
USA	1 046.3	25.5	45.3	15.6	15.6
United Kingdom	532.7	9.8	-4.1	7.9	23.5
Rep. of Korea	434.8	6.2	53.9	6.5	30.0
India	421.2	5.0	-0.5	6.3	36.2
Germany	366.8	17.6	12.3	5.5	41.7
Spain	288.4	5.7	6.9	4.3	46.0
Viet Nam	276.9	14.0	22.8	4.1	50.1
Czech Rep	248.9	15.1	76.9	3.7	53.8
Thailand	247.2	14.1	15.0	3.7	57.5
Indonesia	232.9	14.1	19.9	3.5	60.9
Other Asia, nes	224.4	1.3	8.0	3.3	64.3
Turkey	218.3	11.3	-2.5	3.2	67.5
Brazil	191.8	9.4	21.1	2.9	70.4
Italy	188.2	3.5	-7.9	2.8	73.2
Malaysia	137.9	12.6	-18.5	2.1	75.2

Zinc 686

In 2013, the value (in current US$) of exports of "zinc" (SITC group 686) decreased by 9.0 percent (compared to 8.2 percent average growth rate from 2009-2013) to reach 11.2 bln US$ (see table 2), while imports increased by 2.5 percent to reach 11.6 bln US$ (see table 3). Exports of this commodity accounted for 0.5 percent of world exports of SITC section 6, and 0.1 percent of total world merchandise exports (see table 1). Canada, Rep. of Korea and Belgium were the top exporters in 2013 (see table 2). They accounted for 9.8, 9.1 and 8.8 percent of world exports, respectively. China, USA and Germany were the top destinations, with respectively 13.6, 12.6 and 9.4 percent of world imports (see table 3).

The top 15 countries/areas accounted for 81.3 and 73.7 percent of total world exports and imports, respectively (see tables 2 and 3). In 2013, Canada was the country/area with the highest value of net exports (+1.1 bln US$), followed by Rep. of Korea (+832.8 mln US$). By MDG regions (see graph 2), the largest surpluses in this product group were recorded by Developed Asia-Pacific (+1.0 bln US$), Latin America and the Caribbean (+708.7 mln US$) and Commonwealth of Independent States (+596.3 mln US$). The largest trade deficits were recorded by Eastern Asia (-1.2 bln US$), Western Asia (-854.2 mln US$) and South-eastern Asia (-675.1 mln US$).

Table 1: Imports (Imp.) and exports (Exp.), 1999-2013, in current US$

		1999	2000	2001	2002	2003	2004	2005	2006	2007	2008	2009	2010	2011	2012	2013
Values in Bln US$	Imp.	5.4	6.0	5.1	4.7	5.0	6.5	7.7	15.8	19.0	11.3	8.5	11.8	13.1	11.3	11.6
	Exp.	4.9	5.3	4.6	4.3	4.8	5.9	6.9	15.7	17.9	10.9	8.1	11.8	13.5	12.3	11.2
As a percentage of SITC section (%)	Imp.	0.7	0.7	0.6	0.5	0.5	0.5	0.5	1.0	1.0	0.5	0.5	0.6	0.6	0.5	0.5
	Exp.	0.6	0.6	0.6	0.5	0.5	0.5	0.5	0.9	0.9	0.5	0.5	0.6	0.6	0.6	0.5
As a percentage of world trade (%)	Imp.	0.1	0.1	0.1	0.1	0.1	0.1	0.1	0.1	0.1	0.1	0.1	0.1	0.1	0.1	0.1
	Exp.	0.1	0.1	0.1	0.1	0.1	0.1	0.1	0.1	0.1	0.1	0.1	0.1	0.1	0.1	0.1

Graph 1: Annual growth rates of exports, 1999–2013
(In percentage by year)

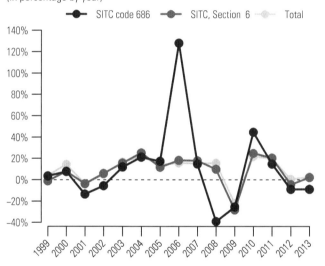

Table 2: Top exporting countries or areas in 2013

Country or area	Value (million US$)	Avg. Growth (%) 09-13	Growth (%) 12-13	World share %	Cum.
World	11 152.8	8.2	-9.0	100.0	
Canada	1 092.5	2.8	0.0	9.8	9.8
Rep. of Korea	1 014.1	11.9	-1.1	9.1	18.9
Belgium	978.6	56.6	-8.2	8.8	27.7
Australia	834.8	4.6	-6.4	7.5	35.1
Spain	744.4	12.4	-12.0	6.7	41.8
Netherlands	712.3	16.9	24.0	6.4	48.2
Peru	616.3	30.4	12.6	5.5	53.7
Finland	582.3	5.0	-0.7	5.2	59.0
India	486.4	9.4	-1.8	4.4	63.3
Kazakhstan	456.3	3.3	-55.8	4.1	67.4
Mexico	383.0	0.3	-3.4	3.4	70.8
Poland	311.5	18.0	21.1	2.8	73.6
Norway	291.5	5.1	-5.0	2.6	76.2
Japan	288.2	-0.2	-13.2	2.6	78.8
Namibia	274.6	-0.8	0.7	2.5	81.3

Graph 2: Trade Balance by MDG regions 2013
(Bln US$)

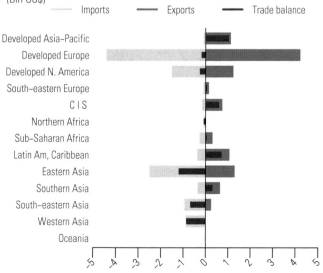

Table 3: Top importing countries or areas in 2013

Country or area	Value (million US$)	Avg. Growth (%) 09-13	Growth (%) 12-13	World share %	Cum.
World	11 631.0	8.2	2.5	100.0	
China	1 576.5	4.5	13.8	13.6	13.6
USA	1 466.7	6.0	0.1	12.6	26.2
Germany	1 095.5	11.2	-0.5	9.4	35.6
Belgium	682.5	8.5	-6.5	5.9	41.5
Turkey	512.9	20.0	7.0	4.4	45.9
Other Asia, nes	499.2	9.0	6.5	4.3	50.2
France	456.0	5.7	1.3	3.9	54.1
Netherlands	433.2	9.8	-8.9	3.7	57.8
Italy	433.1	11.9	-3.5	3.7	61.5
Indonesia	298.2	13.2	-0.3	2.6	64.1
United Kingdom	251.0	6.5	16.7	2.2	66.2
China, Hong Kong SAR	245.2	0.9	20.5	2.1	68.4
Austria	245.0	13.2	19.5	2.1	70.5
Viet Nam	195.8	16.8	23.0	1.7	72.1
Rep. of Korea	181.3	11.2	-7.1	1.6	73.7

687 Tin

In 2013, the value (in current US$) of exports of "tin" (SITC group 687) decreased by 3.7 percent (compared to 15.3 percent average growth rate from 2009-2013) to reach 6.8 bln US$ (see table 2), while imports decreased by 4.0 percent to reach 6.8 bln US$ (see table 3). Exports of this commodity accounted for 0.3 percent of world exports of SITC section 6, and less than 0.1 percent of total world merchandise exports (see table 1). Indonesia, Malaysia and Singapore were the top exporters in 2013 (see table 2). They accounted for 31.3, 12.4 and 11.2 percent of world exports, respectively. USA, Singapore and Japan were the top destinations, with respectively 12.2, 11.8 and 9.2 percent of world imports (see table 3).

The top 15 countries/areas accounted for 90.4 and 83.9 percent of total world exports and imports, respectively (see tables 2 and 3). In 2013, Indonesia was the country/area with the highest value of net exports (+2.1 bln US$), followed by Malaysia (+479.4 mln US$). By MDG regions (see graph 2), the largest surpluses in this product group were recorded by South-eastern Asia (+2.5 bln US$), Latin America and the Caribbean (+509.0 mln US$) and Sub-Saharan Africa (+23.8 mln US$). The largest trade deficits were recorded by Eastern Asia (-741.7 mln US$), Developed North America (-719.0 mln US$) and Developed Europe (-683.4 mln US$).

Table 1: Imports (Imp.) and exports (Exp.), 1999-2013, in current US$

		1999	2000	2001	2002	2003	2004	2005	2006	2007	2008	2009	2010	2011	2012	2013
Values in Bln US$	Imp.	1.4	1.5	1.3	1.2	1.6	3.3	3.4	3.7	5.1	6.2	4.3	6.3	9.0	7.1	6.8
	Exp.	1.6	1.7	1.3	1.3	1.6	3.0	3.2	3.4	4.7	6.1	3.8	5.6	7.9	7.0	6.8
As a percentage of SITC section (%)	Imp.	0.2	0.2	0.2	0.1	0.2	0.3	0.2	0.2	0.3	0.3	0.3	0.3	0.4	0.3	0.3
	Exp.	0.2	0.2	0.2	0.1	0.2	0.2	0.2	0.2	0.2	0.3	0.2	0.3	0.3	0.3	0.3
As a percentage of world trade (%)	Imp.	0.0	0.0	0.0	0.0	0.0	0.0	0.0	0.0	0.0	0.0	0.0	0.0	0.0	0.0	0.0
	Exp.	0.0	0.0	0.0	0.0	0.0	0.0	0.0	0.0	0.0	0.0	0.0	0.0	0.0	0.0	0.0

Graph 1: Annual growth rates of exports, 1999–2013
(In percentage by year)

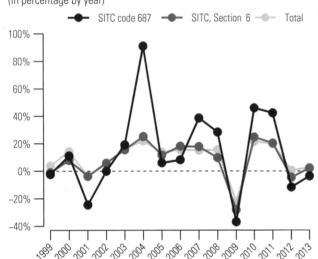

Table 2: Top exporting countries or areas in 2013

Country or area	Value (million US$)	Avg. Growth (%) 09-13	Growth (%) 12-13	World share %	World share % Cum.
World	6 750.1	15.3	-3.7	100.0	
Indonesia	2 114.3	13.7	2.3	31.3	31.3
Malaysia	837.3	22.2	-2.6	12.4	43.7
Singapore	758.6	6.1	-18.3	11.2	55.0
Thailand	449.4	18.1	4.2	6.7	61.6
Bolivia	336.6	12.9	12.8	5.0	66.6
Belgium	311.0	23.2	14.7	4.6	71.2
Netherlands	203.2	37.5	14.3	3.0	74.2
Peru	197.2	-6.8	-24.9	2.9	77.1
Other Asia, nes	153.4	8.8	-7.4	2.3	79.4
USA	148.7	15.3	0.4	2.2	81.6
Brazil	143.7	31.2	2.9	2.1	83.8
China, Hong Kong SAR	137.9	8.7	2.2	2.0	85.8
China	114.1	51.3	71.7	1.7	87.5
Germany	106.2	13.4	0.8	1.6	89.1
India	87.1	60.6	1830.1	1.3	90.4

Graph 2: Trade Balance by MDG regions 2013
(Bln US$)

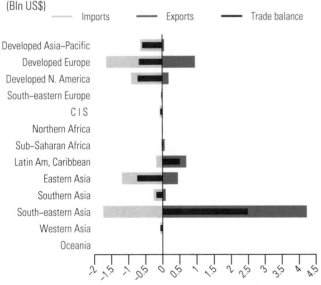

Table 3: Top importing countries or areas in 2013

Country or area	Value (million US$)	Avg. Growth (%) 09-13	Growth (%) 12-13	World share %	World share % Cum.
World	6 810.4	12.5	-4.0	100.0	
USA	832.7	15.9	4.2	12.2	12.2
Singapore	800.5	2.3	-4.3	11.8	24.0
Japan	629.0	18.6	6.0	9.2	33.2
Thailand	531.4	39.2	7.5	7.8	41.0
China	500.8	3.7	-42.1	7.4	48.4
Germany	461.6	21.9	6.4	6.8	55.1
Malaysia	357.9	-0.2	-37.6	5.3	60.4
Rep. of Korea	352.5	11.9	-3.8	5.2	65.6
Netherlands	276.7	16.7	66.3	4.1	69.6
India	240.0	28.7	44.1	3.5	73.2
Other Asia, nes	224.1	9.0	-6.4	3.3	76.5
France	142.3	11.9	9.5	2.1	78.5
Spain	127.4	12.0	5.9	1.9	80.4
Mexico	126.5	19.9	8.9	1.9	82.3
United Kingdom	112.9	6.0	-19.8	1.7	83.9

Miscellaneous non-ferrous base metals employed in metallurgy and cermets 689

In 2013, the value (in current US$) of exports of "miscellaneous non-ferrous base metals employed in metallurgy and cermets" (SITC group 689) decreased by 5.6 percent (compared to 12.3 percent average growth rate from 2009-2013) to reach 8.6 bln US$ (see table 2), while imports decreased by 10.9 percent to reach 9.7 bln US$ (see table 3). Exports of this commodity accounted for 0.4 percent of world exports of SITC section 6, and less than 0.1 percent of total world merchandise exports (see table 1). China, USA and Germany were the top exporters in 2013 (see table 2). They accounted for 24.3, 9.3 and 8.1 percent of world exports, respectively. USA, Germany and China were the top destinations, with respectively 19.1, 10.0 and 9.6 percent of world imports (see table 3).

The top 15 countries/areas accounted for 80.7 and 80.3 percent of total world exports and imports, respectively (see tables 2 and 3). In 2013, China was the country/area with the highest value of net exports (+1.2 bln US$), followed by Dem.Rep. of the Congo (+501.1 mln US$). By MDG regions (see graph 2), the largest surpluses in this product group were recorded by Eastern Asia (+739.6 mln US$), Sub-Saharan Africa (+713.8 mln US$) and Commonwealth of Independent States (+353.3 mln US$). The largest trade deficits were recorded by Developed Europe (-1.2 bln US$), Developed North America (-908.7 mln US$) and Developed Asia-Pacific (-300.4 mln US$).

Table 1: Imports (Imp.) and exports (Exp.), 1999-2013, in current US$

		1999	2000	2001	2002	2003	2004	2005	2006	2007	2008	2009	2010	2011	2012	2013
Values in Bln US$	Imp.	3.7	4.1	4.1	3.4	4.0	6.6	8.1	8.7	10.5	13.1	6.1	9.9	12.7	10.8	9.7
	Exp.	3.4	3.8	3.8	3.1	3.9	6.3	7.2	8.4	9.7	11.9	5.4	8.5	10.1	9.1	8.6
As a percentage of	Imp.	0.4	0.5	0.5	0.4	0.4	0.5	0.6	0.5	0.5	0.6	0.4	0.5	0.6	0.5	0.4
SITC section (%)	Exp.	0.4	0.4	0.5	0.4	0.4	0.5	0.5	0.5	0.5	0.5	0.3	0.4	0.4	0.4	0.4
As a percentage of	Imp.	0.1	0.1	0.1	0.1	0.1	0.1	0.1	0.1	0.1	0.1	0.0	0.1	0.1	0.1	0.1
world trade (%)	Exp.	0.1	0.1	0.1	0.0	0.1	0.1	0.1	0.1	0.1	0.1	0.0	0.1	0.1	0.1	0.0

Graph 1: Annual growth rates of exports, 1999–2013

(In percentage by year)

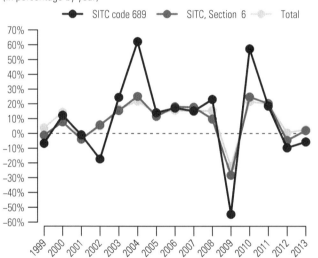

— SITC code 689   — SITC, Section 6   — Total

Table 2: Top exporting countries or areas in 2013

Country or area	Value (million US$)	Avg. Growth (%) 09-13	Growth (%) 12-13	World share %	Cum.
World	8 601.5	12.3	-5.6	100.0	
China	2 094.4	13.7	7.6	24.3	24.3
USA	799.8	11.8	1.1	9.3	33.6
Germany	700.3	19.3	-6.8	8.1	41.8
Dem.Rep. of the Congo	*501.1*	8.7	0.8	5.8	47.6
Japan	485.5	10.0	-31.9	5.6	53.3
Canada	361.6	0.6	-11.4	4.2	57.5
United Kingdom	322.0	7.9	-8.7	3.7	61.2
Russian Federation	289.4	2.3	-21.5	3.4	64.6
France	232.7	19.8	-10.5	2.7	67.3
Netherlands	219.8	12.7	-10.4	2.6	69.8
Kazakhstan	212.3	13.2	-32.6	2.5	72.3
Rep. of Korea	208.7	14.1	7.5	2.4	74.7
Finland	199.8	131.2	-13.8	2.3	77.1
Belgium	161.7	2.7	-4.8	1.9	78.9
South Africa	156.3	20.1	21.5	1.8	80.7

Graph 2: Trade Balance by MDG regions 2013

(Bln US$)

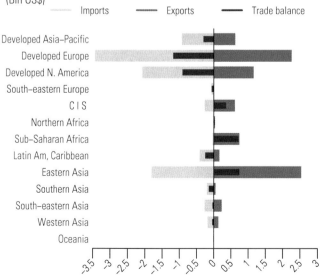

···· Imports   — Exports   — Trade balance

Table 3: Top importing countries or areas in 2013

Country or area	Value (million US$)	Avg. Growth (%) 09-13	Growth (%) 12-13	World share %	Cum.
World	9 667.6	12.3	-10.9	100.0	
USA	1 842.7	12.8	-19.7	19.1	19.1
Germany	963.8	15.8	-12.8	10.0	29.0
China	930.4	13.0	16.8	9.6	38.7
Japan	884.8	2.7	-18.3	9.2	47.8
Rep. of Korea	577.7	12.6	-21.5	6.0	53.8
United Kingdom	534.8	7.4	-19.3	5.5	59.3
France	351.3	14.7	-1.0	3.6	62.9
Netherlands	247.2	5.8	-20.2	2.6	65.5
Canada	227.5	16.5	-10.6	2.4	67.9
Other Asia, nes	223.2	11.2	1.8	2.3	70.2
Mexico	219.5	25.1	3.3	2.3	72.4
Russian Federation	201.2	33.0	0.1	2.1	74.5
Austria	195.5	15.9	-5.4	2.0	76.5
Finland	182.8	11.7	-14.2	1.9	78.4
Belgium	180.2	16.4	3.7	1.9	80.3

691 Structures and parts of structures, nes, of iron, steel or aluminium

In 2013, the value (in current US$) of exports of "structures and parts of structures, nes, of iron, steel or aluminium" (SITC group 691) increased by 8.5 percent (compared to 5.9 percent average growth rate from 2009-2013) to reach 60.5 bln US$ (see table 2), while imports increased by 3.9 percent to reach 53.1 bln US$ (see table 3). Exports of this commodity accounted for 2.7 percent of world exports of SITC section 6, and 0.3 percent of total world merchandise exports (see table 1). China, Germany and Rep. of Korea were the top exporters in 2013 (see table 2). They accounted for 22.2, 11.4 and 4.2 percent of world exports, respectively. Germany, USA and Australia were the top destinations, with respectively 7.2, 6.5 and 4.8 percent of world imports (see table 3).

The top 15 countries/areas accounted for 73.2 and 54.7 percent of total world exports and imports, respectively (see tables 2 and 3). In 2013, China was the country/area with the highest value of net exports (+12.7 bln US$), followed by Germany (+3.1 bln US$). By MDG regions (see graph 2), the largest surpluses in this product group were recorded by Eastern Asia (+12.7 bln US$), Developed Europe (+10.5 bln US$) and South-eastern Asia (+330.0 mln US$). The largest trade deficits were recorded by Developed Asia-Pacific (-4.2 bln US$), Sub-Saharan Africa (-2.4 bln US$) and Western Asia (-2.3 bln US$).

Table 1: Imports (Imp.) and exports (Exp.), 1999-2013, in current US$

		1999	2000	2001	2002	2003	2004	2005	2006	2007	2008	2009	2010	2011	2012	2013
Values in Bln US$	Imp.	13.2	12.4	13.0	14.2	16.4	20.3	24.1	31.0	40.6	51.2	42.3	41.8	48.0	51.1	53.1
	Exp.	13.7	13.4	14.0	15.5	17.8	22.4	27.1	34.5	45.6	57.4	48.2	44.2	53.3	55.8	60.5
As a percentage of SITC section (%)	Imp.	1.6	1.4	1.5	1.6	1.6	1.6	1.7	1.9	2.1	2.4	2.7	2.2	2.1	2.4	2.4
	Exp.	1.7	1.6	1.7	1.8	1.8	1.8	1.9	2.1	2.3	2.6	3.1	2.3	2.3	2.5	2.7
As a percentage of world trade (%)	Imp.	0.2	0.2	0.2	0.2	0.2	0.2	0.2	0.3	0.3	0.3	0.3	0.3	0.3	0.3	0.3
	Exp.	0.2	0.2	0.2	0.2	0.2	0.2	0.3	0.3	0.3	0.4	0.4	0.3	0.3	0.3	0.3

Graph 1: Annual growth rates of exports, 1999–2013
(In percentage by year)

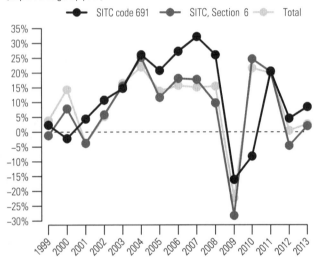

Legend: SITC code 691 — SITC, Section 6 — Total

Table 2: Top exporting countries or areas in 2013

Country or area	Value (million US$)	Avg. Growth (%) 09-13	Growth (%) 12-13	World share %	Cum.
World	60497.9	5.9	8.5	100.0	
China	13438.2	10.4	3.6	22.2	22.2
Germany	6920.7	5.7	14.9	11.4	33.7
Rep. of Korea	2531.0	-0.7	-13.9	4.2	37.8
Italy	2495.2	2.6	22.7	4.1	42.0
Poland	2455.1	8.4	11.9	4.1	46.0
USA	2362.2	10.7	-5.8	3.9	49.9
Spain	1994.1	18.6	29.7	3.3	53.2
Netherlands	1857.2	8.8	14.6	3.1	56.3
Turkey	1649.5	8.7	4.4	2.7	59.0
Belgium	1597.6	1.4	11.8	2.6	61.7
Denmark	1587.8	2.4	13.1	2.6	64.3
Czech Rep.	1517.4	8.1	8.8	2.5	66.8
Austria	1477.0	5.5	3.0	2.4	69.2
Thailand	1344.5	-13.2	13.5	2.2	71.5
Canada	1069.3	-1.9	-5.4	1.8	73.2

Graph 2: Trade Balance by MDG regions 2013
(Bln US$)

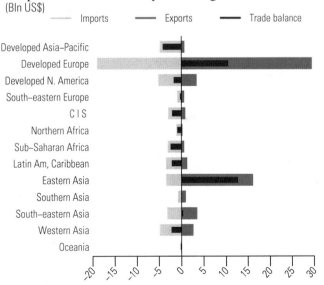

Legend: Imports — Exports — Trade balance

Developed Asia–Pacific, Developed Europe, Developed N. America, South–eastern Europe, CIS, Northern Africa, Sub–Saharan Africa, Latin Am, Caribbean, Eastern Asia, Southern Asia, South–eastern Asia, Western Asia, Oceania

Table 3: Top importing countries or areas in 2013

Country or area	Value (million US$)	Avg. Growth (%) 09-13	Growth (%) 12-13	World share %	Cum.
World	53145.9	5.9	3.9	100.0	
Germany	3832.4	7.8	3.9	7.2	7.2
USA	3480.2	0.0	-17.6	6.5	13.8
Australia	2556.0	43.8	30.7	4.8	18.6
Japan	2193.7	0.2	-2.9	4.1	22.7
France	2106.4	2.6	-3.5	4.0	26.7
Rep. of Korea	1919.3	1.7	-7.8	3.6	30.3
Saudi Arabia	1881.3	11.1	22.9	3.5	33.8
United Kingdom	1720.8	6.1	14.0	3.2	37.0
Canada	1629.7	20.5	4.4	3.1	40.1
Switzerland	1569.0	11.0	15.0	3.0	43.1
Russian Federation	1452.8	17.0	5.1	2.7	45.8
Norway	1302.5	9.0	-6.6	2.5	48.3
Austria	1246.5	6.4	3.7	2.3	50.6
United Arab Emirates	1092.4	-4.8	11.4	2.1	52.7
Singapore	1088.5	8.0	15.0	2.0	54.7

In 2013, the value (in current US$) of exports of "metal containers for storage or transport" (SITC group 692) increased by 2.2 percent (compared to 5.5 percent average growth rate from 2009-2013) to reach 20.3 bln US$ (see table 2), while imports increased by 4.0 percent to reach 19.5 bln US$ (see table 3). Exports of this commodity accounted for 0.9 percent of world exports of SITC section 6, and 0.1 percent of total world merchandise exports (see table 1). Germany, China and USA were the top exporters in 2013 (see table 2). They accounted for 10.4, 10.3 and 9.1 percent of world exports, respectively. USA, Germany and France were the top destinations, with respectively 7.6, 5.8 and 5.0 percent of world imports (see table 3).

The top 15 countries/areas accounted for 70.0 and 53.9 percent of total world exports and imports, respectively (see tables 2 and 3). In 2013, China was the country/area with the highest value of net exports (+1.7 bln US$), followed by Germany (+992.5 mln US$). By MDG regions (see graph 2), the largest surpluses in this product group were recorded by Developed Europe (+2.5 bln US$), Eastern Asia (+2.3 bln US$) and South-eastern Europe (+17.1 mln US$). The largest trade deficits were recorded by Western Asia (-905.9 mln US$), Sub-Saharan Africa (-600.0 mln US$) and Latin America and the Caribbean (-547.6 mln US$).

Table 1: Imports (Imp.) and exports (Exp.), 1999-2013, in current US$

		1999	2000	2001	2002	2003	2004	2005	2006	2007	2008	2009	2010	2011	2012	2013
Values in Bln US$	Imp.	6.6	6.4	6.7	7.2	8.2	9.4	10.7	12.3	15.2	17.6	16.3	16.1	18.8	18.7	19.5
	Exp.	7.0	6.8	6.8	7.2	8.5	9.9	11.3	13.6	17.0	19.5	16.4	17.2	19.9	19.8	20.3
As a percentage of SITC section (%)	Imp.	0.8	0.7	0.8	0.8	0.8	0.7	0.7	0.7	0.8	0.8	1.1	0.8	0.8	0.9	0.9
	Exp.	0.9	0.8	0.8	0.8	0.8	0.8	0.8	0.8	0.9	0.9	1.1	0.9	0.9	0.9	0.9
As a percentage of world trade (%)	Imp.	0.1	0.1	0.1	0.1	0.1	0.1	0.1	0.1	0.1	0.1	0.1	0.1	0.1	0.1	0.1
	Exp.	0.1	0.1	0.1	0.1	0.1	0.1	0.1	0.1	0.1	0.1	0.1	0.1	0.1	0.1	0.1

Graph 1: Annual growth rates of exports, 1999–2013
(In percentage by year)

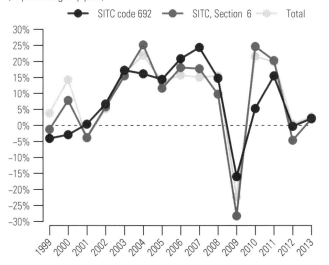

Table 2: Top exporting countries or areas in 2013

Country or area	Value (million US$)	Avg. Growth (%) 09-13	Growth (%) 12-13	World share %	Cum.
World	20270.7	5.5	2.2	100.0	
Germany	2112.4	1.0	-1.7	10.4	10.4
China	2089.7	21.4	10.2	10.3	20.7
USA	1848.4	7.6	8.1	9.1	29.8
Italy	1240.9	-0.7	4.4	6.1	36.0
Rep. of Korea	895.5	-0.7	-15.7	4.4	40.4
Spain	829.7	4.4	4.9	4.1	44.5
France	802.7	-2.3	-4.7	4.0	48.4
United Kingdom	699.5	3.2	0.2	3.5	51.9
Czech Rep.	658.1	7.5	2.1	3.2	55.1
Poland	647.6	9.0	6.0	3.2	58.3
Netherlands	610.2	4.0	11.2	3.0	61.3
Austria	485.8	6.7	14.6	2.4	63.7
Turkey	470.2	10.0	16.9	2.3	66.1
Thailand	422.1	17.0	-1.6	2.1	68.1
Mexico	383.6	9.7	13.1	1.9	70.0

Graph 2: Trade Balance by MDG regions 2013
(Bln US$)

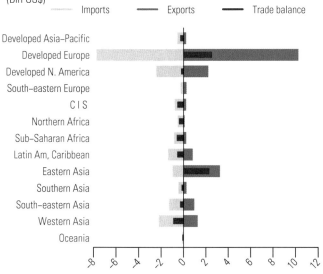

Table 3: Top importing countries or areas in 2013

Country or area	Value (million US$)	Avg. Growth (%) 09-13	Growth (%) 12-13	World share %	Cum.
World	19470.8	4.5	4.0	100.0	
USA	1475.8	2.7	0.5	7.6	7.6
Germany	1119.9	4.3	1.8	5.8	13.3
France	978.4	2.1	-2.5	5.0	18.4
Canada	946.2	10.0	7.2	4.9	23.2
United Arab Emirates	868.2	30.8	11.4	4.5	27.7
Netherlands	833.4	7.5	19.0	4.3	32.0
Belgium	775.3	4.0	15.7	4.0	35.9
United Kingdom	657.8	7.7	10.7	3.4	39.3
Switzerland	440.2	3.4	5.2	2.3	41.6
Saudi Arabia	429.1	10.3	25.1	2.2	43.8
Thailand	418.0	8.6	-2.3	2.1	45.9
Rep. of Korea	417.6	-6.4	-0.6	2.1	48.1
Russian Federation	404.5	15.4	25.6	2.1	50.1
Poland	378.4	1.9	2.7	1.9	52.1
China	360.6	6.6	4.5	1.9	53.9

693 Wire products (excluding insulated electrical wiring) and fencing grills

In 2013, the value (in current US$) of exports of "wire products (excluding insulated electrical wiring) and fencing grills" (SITC group 693) increased by 1.7 percent (compared to 9.7 percent average growth rate from 2009-2013) to reach 15.6 bln US$ (see table 2), while imports increased by 0.2 percent to reach 15.4 bln US$ (see table 3). Exports of this commodity accounted for 0.7 percent of world exports of SITC section 6, and 0.1 percent of total world merchandise exports (see table 1). China, Germany and USA were the top exporters in 2013 (see table 2). They accounted for 17.7, 9.2 and 6.9 percent of world exports, respectively. USA, Germany and France were the top destinations, with respectively 10.5, 6.5 and 5.6 percent of world imports (see table 3).

The top 15 countries/areas accounted for 72.1 and 53.5 percent of total world exports and imports, respectively (see tables 2 and 3). In 2013, China was the country/area with the highest value of net exports (+2.2 bln US$), followed by Turkey (+600.7 mln US$). By MDG regions (see graph 2), the largest surpluses in this product group were recorded by Eastern Asia (+2.6 bln US$), Developed Europe (+355.8 mln US$) and Western Asia (+91.7 mln US$). The largest trade deficits were recorded by Latin America and the Caribbean (-989.3 mln US$), Developed North America (-918.2 mln US$) and Sub-Saharan Africa (-465.4 mln US$).

Table 1: Imports (Imp.) and exports (Exp.), 1999-2013, in current US$

		1999	2000	2001	2002	2003	2004	2005	2006	2007	2008	2009	2010	2011	2012	2013
Values in Bln US$	Imp.	4.6	4.7	4.7	4.8	5.7	7.6	8.8	10.6	12.7	15.4	10.8	12.5	15.3	15.4	15.4
	Exp.	4.8	4.8	4.8	4.9	5.7	7.9	9.0	10.7	13.0	15.7	10.7	12.8	15.6	15.3	15.6
As a percentage of SITC section (%)	Imp.	0.6	0.5	0.6	0.5	0.6	0.6	0.6	0.6	0.7	0.7	0.7	0.7	0.7	0.7	0.7
	Exp.	0.6	0.6	0.6	0.6	0.6	0.6	0.6	0.6	0.7	0.7	0.7	0.7	0.7	0.7	0.7
As a percentage of world trade (%)	Imp.	0.1	0.1	0.1	0.1	0.1	0.1	0.1	0.1	0.1	0.1	0.1	0.1	0.1	0.1	0.1
	Exp.	0.1	0.1	0.1	0.1	0.1	0.1	0.1	0.1	0.1	0.1	0.1	0.1	0.1	0.1	0.1

Graph 1: Annual growth rates of exports, 1999–2013
(In percentage by year)

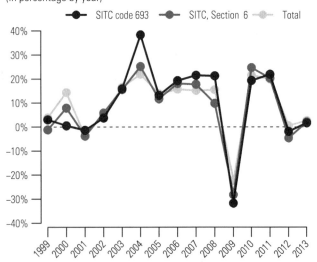

Table 2: Top exporting countries or areas in 2013

Country or area	Value (million US$)	Avg. Growth (%) 09-13	Growth (%) 12-13	World share %	Cum.
World	15 583.2	9.7	1.7	100.0	
China	2 760.3	12.6	-0.6	17.7	17.7
Germany	1 428.3	3.4	-2.4	9.2	26.9
USA	1 068.4	14.1	5.7	6.9	33.7
Italy	804.6	6.4	5.0	5.2	38.9
Rep. of Korea	748.7	7.5	0.0	4.8	43.7
Turkey	734.6	21.0	-0.2	4.7	48.4
Netherlands	655.0	19.0	3.5	4.2	52.6
Spain	540.6	8.2	0.5	3.5	56.1
Belgium	479.8	6.6	19.1	3.1	59.2
France	398.0	2.3	7.0	2.6	61.7
Poland	378.6	24.8	28.0	2.4	64.2
India	361.3	14.3	20.8	2.3	66.5
United Kingdom	332.1	1.8	3.5	2.1	68.6
Japan	283.2	-1.7	-16.6	1.8	70.4
Thailand	255.8	11.3	-31.5	1.6	72.1

Graph 2: Trade Balance by MDG regions 2013
(Bln US$)

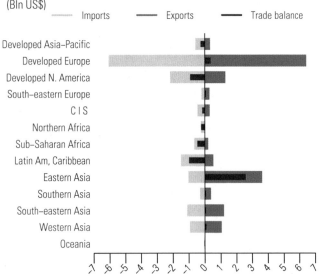

Table 3: Top importing countries or areas in 2013

Country or area	Value (million US$)	Avg. Growth (%) 09-13	Growth (%) 12-13	World share %	Cum.
World	15 419.9	9.2	0.2	100.0	
USA	1 622.0	9.2	-5.7	10.5	10.5
Germany	997.4	8.3	1.0	6.5	17.0
France	863.8	8.1	2.0	5.6	22.6
Canada	565.7	17.0	4.8	3.7	26.3
China	550.5	5.5	-0.2	3.6	29.8
Mexico	511.1	21.2	3.3	3.3	33.1
United Kingdom	470.8	11.3	27.7	3.1	36.2
Belgium	400.7	6.1	3.6	2.6	38.8
Saudi Arabia	353.7	5.5	27.7	2.3	41.1
Netherlands	337.3	5.0	-7.8	2.2	43.3
Spain	336.6	4.2	-30.6	2.2	45.5
Italy	322.7	3.2	0.0	2.1	47.6
Singapore	312.0	8.5	9.7	2.0	49.6
Japan	306.5	9.6	-10.8	2.0	51.6
Rep. of Korea	295.1	11.3	-1.9	1.9	53.5

Nails, screws, nuts, bolts, and the like of iron, steel, copper, aluminium 694

In 2013, the value (in current US$) of exports of "nails, screws, nuts, bolts, and the like of iron, steel, copper, aluminium" (SITC group 694) increased by 4.8 percent (compared to 13.7 percent average growth rate from 2009-2013) to reach 39.0 bln US$ (see table 2), while imports increased by 3.7 percent to reach 43.4 bln US$ (see table 3). Exports of this commodity accounted for 1.7 percent of world exports of SITC section 6, and 0.2 percent of total world merchandise exports (see table 1). Germany, China and USA were the top exporters in 2013 (see table 2). They accounted for 15.5, 15.4 and 10.0 percent of world exports, respectively. USA, Germany and China were the top destinations, with respectively 13.2, 8.6 and 7.6 percent of world imports (see table 3).

The top 15 countries/areas accounted for 83.4 and 64.3 percent of total world exports and imports, respectively (see tables 2 and 3). In 2013, Other Asia, nes was the country/area with the highest value of net exports (+3.7 bln US$), followed by China (+2.7 bln US$). By MDG regions (see graph 2), the largest surpluses in this product group were recorded by Eastern Asia (+6.7 bln US$), Developed Asia-Pacific (+1.5 bln US$) and Developed Europe (+355.1 mln US$). The largest trade deficits were recorded by Latin America and the Caribbean (-4.2 bln US$), Developed North America (-3.0 bln US$) and South-eastern Asia (-1.5 bln US$).

Table 1: Imports (Imp.) and exports (Exp.), 1999-2013, in current US$

		1999	2000	2001	2002	2003	2004	2005	2006	2007	2008	2009	2010	2011	2012	2013
Values in Bln US$	Imp.	13.6	14.9	14.3	14.8	17.4	22.0	25.0	28.2	33.8	38.1	27.6	35.1	42.3	41.8	43.4
	Exp.	11.5	12.5	11.7	12.5	14.8	18.8	21.3	24.5	29.3	33.2	23.3	30.8	37.8	37.2	39.0
As a percentage of SITC section (%)	Imp.	1.7	1.7	1.7	1.7	1.7	1.7	1.7	1.7	1.7	1.8	1.8	1.8	1.8	1.9	2.0
	Exp.	1.4	1.4	1.4	1.4	1.5	1.5	1.5	1.5	1.5	1.5	1.5	1.6	1.6	1.7	1.7
As a percentage of world trade (%)	Imp.	0.2	0.2	0.2	0.2	0.2	0.2	0.2	0.2	0.2	0.2	0.2	0.2	0.2	0.2	0.2
	Exp.	0.2	0.2	0.2	0.2	0.2	0.2	0.2	0.2	0.2	0.2	0.2	0.2	0.2	0.2	0.2

Graph 1: Annual growth rates of exports, 1999–2013
(In percentage by year)

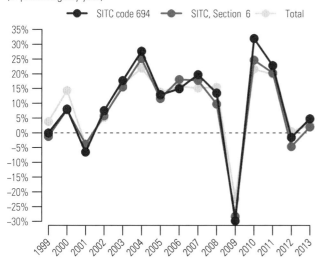

SITC code 694 — SITC, Section 6 — Total

Table 2: Top exporting countries or areas in 2013

Country or area	Value (million US$)	Avg. Growth (%) 09-13	Growth (%) 12-13	World share %	Cum.
World	39 008.4	13.7	4.8	100.0	
Germany	6 048.9	13.2	6.6	15.5	15.5
China	6 016.7	16.4	1.6	15.4	30.9
USA	3 899.5	15.0	7.7	10.0	40.9
Other Asia, nes	3 857.7	17.0	1.6	9.9	50.8
Japan	3 094.8	10.4	-9.5	7.9	58.8
Italy	1 943.0	10.7	4.6	5.0	63.7
France	1 604.7	7.9	11.8	4.1	67.8
Switzerland	1 079.6	9.0	4.4	2.8	70.6
United Kingdom	876.5	11.8	6.7	2.2	72.9
India	836.1	36.2	38.6	2.1	75.0
Netherlands	835.6	17.4	17.7	2.1	77.1
Rep. of Korea	750.7	27.1	9.4	1.9	79.1
Spain	603.9	13.0	-0.2	1.5	80.6
Belgium	594.6	7.2	15.7	1.5	82.1
Thailand	499.5	18.4	4.4	1.3	83.4

Graph 2: Trade Balance by MDG regions 2013
(Bln US$)

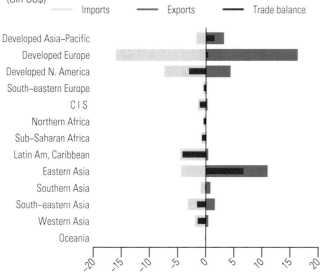

······ Imports —— Exports —— Trade balance

Table 3: Top importing countries or areas in 2013

Country or area	Value (million US$)	Avg. Growth (%) 09-13	Growth (%) 12-13	World share %	Cum.
World	43 355.3	11.9	3.7	100.0	
USA	5 731.5	15.7	-1.6	13.2	13.2
Germany	3 728.9	11.9	3.1	8.6	21.8
China	3 298.5	9.4	4.9	7.6	29.4
Mexico	2 478.0	16.8	5.7	5.7	35.1
France	1 781.6	7.8	5.3	4.1	39.3
Canada	1 662.8	12.0	-2.7	3.8	43.1
United Kingdom	1 491.8	10.9	8.2	3.4	46.5
Thailand	1 146.4	13.9	-8.8	2.6	49.2
Japan	1 123.9	12.8	4.8	2.6	51.8
Brazil	1 049.1	17.1	13.1	2.4	54.2
Russian Federation	948.0	32.6	10.7	2.2	56.4
Netherlands	943.3	14.1	7.7	2.2	58.5
Czech Rep.	863.6	11.3	8.1	2.0	60.5
Italy	822.7	9.9	3.4	1.9	62.4
Austria	804.8	10.8	11.3	1.9	64.3

695 Tools for use in the hand or in machines

In 2013, the value (in current US$) of exports of "tools for use in the hand or in machines" (SITC group 695) increased by 2.7 percent (compared to 11.9 percent average growth rate from 2009-2013) to reach 51.0 bln US$ (see table 2), while imports increased by 0.9 percent to reach 50.8 bln US$ (see table 3). Exports of this commodity accounted for 2.2 percent of world exports of SITC section 6, and 0.3 percent of total world merchandise exports (see table 1). China, Germany and USA were the top exporters in 2013 (see table 2). They accounted for 17.0, 15.2 and 9.7 percent of world exports, respectively. USA, Germany and China were the top destinations, with respectively 13.6, 8.5 and 6.0 percent of world imports (see table 3).

The top 15 countries/areas accounted for 81.8 and 64.1 percent of total world exports and imports, respectively (see tables 2 and 3). In 2013, China was the country/area with the highest value of net exports (+5.6 bln US$), followed by Germany (+3.4 bln US$). By MDG regions (see graph 2), the largest surpluses in this product group were recorded by Eastern Asia (+8.7 bln US$), Developed Europe (+2.4 bln US$) and Developed Asia-Pacific (+1.9 bln US$). The largest trade deficits were recorded by Developed North America (-3.1 bln US$), Latin America and the Caribbean (-3.0 bln US$) and Commonwealth of Independent States (-2.5 bln US$).

Table 1: Imports (Imp.) and exports (Exp.), 1999-2013, in current US$

		1999	2000	2001	2002	2003	2004	2005	2006	2007	2008	2009	2010	2011	2012	2013
Values in Bln US$	Imp.	19.3	20.3	20.2	20.5	23.5	28.4	30.9	34.5	39.8	45.0	32.8	40.8	48.4	50.3	50.8
	Exp.	19.7	20.7	20.6	21.0	23.3	27.5	30.1	34.1	39.0	44.1	32.5	40.6	49.2	49.6	51.0
As a percentage of SITC section (%)	Imp.	2.4	2.3	2.4	2.3	2.3	2.2	2.2	2.1	2.0	2.1	2.1	2.1	2.1	2.3	2.3
	Exp.	2.5	2.4	2.5	2.4	2.3	2.2	2.1	2.0	2.0	2.0	2.1	2.1	2.1	2.2	2.2
As a percentage of world trade (%)	Imp.	0.3	0.3	0.3	0.3	0.3	0.3	0.3	0.3	0.3	0.3	0.3	0.3	0.3	0.3	0.3
	Exp.	0.4	0.3	0.3	0.3	0.3	0.3	0.3	0.3	0.3	0.3	0.3	0.3	0.3	0.3	0.3

Graph 1: Annual growth rates of exports, 1999–2013
(In percentage by year)

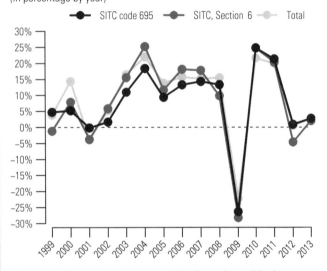

Table 2: Top exporting countries or areas in 2013

Country or area	Value (million US$)	Avg. Growth (%) 09-13	Growth (%) 12-13	World share %	Cum.
World	50 987.5	11.9	2.7	100.0	
China	8 681.1	21.0	8.8	17.0	17.0
Germany	7 739.9	9.2	5.3	15.2	32.2
USA	4 968.6	11.6	0.4	9.7	42.0
Japan	3 708.4	12.3	-10.2	7.3	49.2
Other Asia, nes	2 519.8	13.4	0.6	4.9	54.2
Netherlands	2 185.3	12.0	7.1	4.3	58.5
Rep. of Korea	1 781.1	13.8	2.4	3.5	61.9
Italy	1 593.2	8.1	3.4	3.1	65.1
Belgium	1 457.5	10.4	14.5	2.9	67.9
Sweden	1 429.7	14.5	-1.2	2.8	70.7
Singapore	1 344.5	9.8	-1.9	2.6	73.4
Switzerland	1 179.9	8.6	1.4	2.3	75.7
France	1 083.6	3.9	6.8	2.1	77.8
United Kingdom	1 082.7	2.4	0.9	2.1	79.9
Austria	969.3	6.3	5.1	1.9	81.8

Graph 2: Trade Balance by MDG regions 2013
(Bln US$)

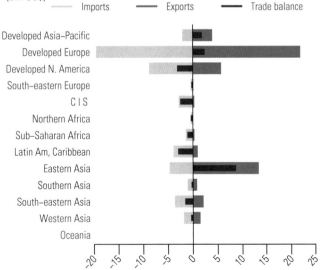

Table 3: Top importing countries or areas in 2013

Country or area	Value (million US$)	Avg. Growth (%) 09-13	Growth (%) 12-13	World share %	Cum.
World	50 777.4	11.5	0.9	100.0	
USA	6 913.1	14.7	4.5	13.6	13.6
Germany	4 292.8	9.8	-0.1	8.5	22.1
China	3 035.4	11.5	2.2	6.0	28.0
Netherlands	2 208.9	13.0	0.3	4.4	32.4
Russian Federation	2 132.2	42.7	-21.5	4.2	36.6
Canada	1 881.3	9.6	-0.7	3.7	40.3
France	1 699.6	4.8	1.9	3.3	43.6
Mexico	1 638.3	17.0	1.4	3.2	46.9
United Kingdom	1 502.7	6.9	5.1	3.0	49.8
Belgium	1 421.0	8.4	14.4	2.8	52.6
Italy	1 275.6	6.2	4.2	2.5	55.1
Singapore	1 268.4	12.0	-9.2	2.5	57.6
Japan	1 231.2	14.9	-5.1	2.4	60.1
Thailand	1 155.8	18.7	-5.1	2.3	62.3
Switzerland	898.3	7.7	5.9	1.8	64.1

In 2013, the value (in current US$) of exports of "cutlery" (SITC group 696) increased by 5.6 percent (compared to 12.0 percent average growth rate from 2009-2013) to reach 12.1 bln US$ (see table 2), while imports increased by 4.8 percent to reach 11.3 bln US$ (see table 3). Exports of this commodity accounted for 0.5 percent of world exports of SITC section 6, and 0.1 percent of total world merchandise exports (see table 1). China, Poland and Germany were the top exporters in 2013 (see table 2). They accounted for 36.2, 9.8 and 8.9 percent of world exports, respectively. USA, Germany and Poland were the top destinations, with respectively 17.8, 6.3 and 4.5 percent of world imports (see table 3).

The top 15 countries/areas accounted for 85.9 and 64.0 percent of total world exports and imports, respectively (see tables 2 and 3). In 2013, China was the country/area with the highest value of net exports (+4.2 bln US$), followed by Poland (+684.7 mln US$). By MDG regions (see graph 2), the largest surpluses in this product group were recorded by Eastern Asia (+4.3 bln US$), Developed Europe (+139.4 mln US$) and South-eastern Asia (+127.7 mln US$). The largest trade deficits were recorded by Developed North America (-1.8 bln US$), Western Asia (-479.6 mln US$) and Commonwealth of Independent States (-476.3 mln US$).

Table 1: Imports (Imp.) and exports (Exp.), 1999-2013, in current US$

		1999	2000	2001	2002	2003	2004	2005	2006	2007	2008	2009	2010	2011	2012	2013
Values in Bln US$	Imp.	5.2	5.4	5.4	5.7	6.2	7.0	7.6	8.0	9.1	9.5	8.2	9.8	11.2	10.7	11.3
	Exp.	4.8	5.0	5.2	5.5	6.0	6.8	7.2	8.0	8.4	9.2	7.7	9.6	11.5	11.5	12.1
As a percentage of SITC section (%)	Imp.	0.6	0.6	0.6	0.6	0.6	0.5	0.5	0.5	0.5	0.4	0.5	0.5	0.5	0.5	0.5
	Exp.	0.6	0.6	0.6	0.6	0.6	0.5	0.5	0.5	0.4	0.4	0.5	0.5	0.5	0.5	0.5
As a percentage of world trade (%)	Imp.	0.1	0.1	0.1	0.1	0.1	0.1	0.1	0.1	0.1	0.1	0.1	0.1	0.1	0.1	0.1
	Exp.	0.1	0.1	0.1	0.1	0.1	0.1	0.1	0.1	0.1	0.1	0.1	0.1	0.1	0.1	0.1

Graph 1: Annual growth rates of exports, 1999–2013
(In percentage by year)

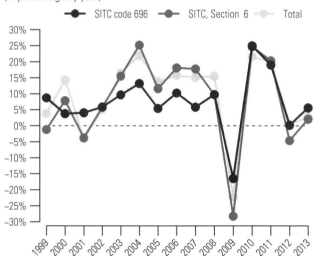

Graph 2: Trade Balance by MDG regions 2013
(Bln US$)

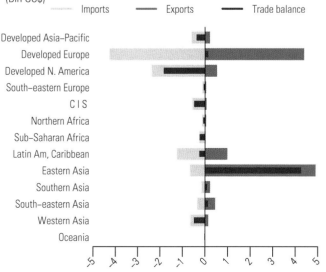

Table 2: Top exporting countries or areas in 2013

Country or area	Value (million US$)	Avg. Growth (%) 09-13	Growth (%) 12-13	World share %	Cum.
World	12 106.7	12.0	5.6	100.0	
China	4 380.6	17.2	6.3	36.2	36.2
Poland	1 189.0	14.6	16.3	9.8	46.0
Germany	1 075.0	6.4	2.9	8.9	54.9
Mexico	736.0	38.0	7.6	6.1	61.0
USA	517.0	2.1	2.6	4.3	65.2
Belgium	502.0	11.2	33.5	4.1	69.4
China, Hong Kong SAR	305.3	0.3	-10.6	2.5	71.9
France	239.9	3.2	9.8	2.0	73.9
Netherlands	237.9	3.9	-12.0	2.0	75.8
Brazil	231.1	13.1	3.7	1.9	77.8
Viet Nam	211.3	22.7	19.5	1.7	79.5
United Kingdom	206.0	8.2	3.6	1.7	81.2
Japan	196.6	5.2	-8.3	1.6	82.8
Czech Rep.	186.8	7.3	-25.7	1.5	84.4
Switzerland	179.8	4.7	-8.8	1.5	85.9

Table 3: Top importing countries or areas in 2013

Country or area	Value (million US$)	Avg. Growth (%) 09-13	Growth (%) 12-13	World share %	Cum.
World	11 255.4	8.1	4.8	100.0	
USA	2 007.7	9.4	6.8	17.8	17.8
Germany	708.2	1.5	2.6	6.3	24.1
Poland	504.2	41.8	17.4	4.5	28.6
United Kingdom	467.1	1.8	-0.9	4.1	32.8
Belgium	436.7	10.5	27.2	3.9	36.6
Mexico	431.8	30.3	15.1	3.8	40.5
France	419.8	1.5	-3.9	3.7	44.2
Russian Federation	372.6	14.8	2.4	3.3	47.5
Japan	361.0	9.2	-3.6	3.2	50.7
Canada	349.6	6.3	4.6	3.1	53.8
China, Hong Kong SAR	291.8	4.0	-6.1	2.6	56.4
Netherlands	264.0	6.9	-6.6	2.3	58.8
Italy	234.2	0.1	-0.7	2.1	60.8
Spain	182.5	-1.8	0.5	1.6	62.5
Australia	176.6	4.6	-5.7	1.6	64.0

697 Household equipment of base metal, nes

In 2013, the value (in current US$) of exports of "household equipment of base metal, nes" (SITC group 697) increased by 7.2 percent (compared to 10.8 percent average growth rate from 2009-2013) to reach 32.7 bln US$ (see table 2), while imports increased by 5.5 percent to reach 30.2 bln US$ (see table 3). Exports of this commodity accounted for 1.4 percent of world exports of SITC section 6, and 0.2 percent of total world merchandise exports (see table 1). China, Italy and Germany were the top exporters in 2013 (see table 2). They accounted for 45.0, 7.4 and 5.4 percent of world exports, respectively. USA, Germany and France were the top destinations, with respectively 23.7, 7.0 and 4.7 percent of world imports (see table 3).

The top 15 countries/areas accounted for 81.1 and 67.0 percent of total world exports and imports, respectively (see tables 2 and 3). In 2013, China was the country/area with the highest value of net exports (+14.5 bln US$), followed by Italy (+1.7 bln US$). By MDG regions (see graph 2), the largest surpluses in this product group were recorded by Eastern Asia (+15.0 bln US$), Southern Asia (+597.2 mln US$) and South-eastern Asia (+416.1 mln US$). The largest trade deficits were recorded by Developed North America (-7.0 bln US$), Developed Asia-Pacific (-1.7 bln US$) and Developed Europe (-1.4 bln US$).

Table 1: Imports (Imp.) and exports (Exp.), 1999-2013, in current US$

		1999	2000	2001	2002	2003	2004	2005	2006	2007	2008	2009	2010	2011	2012	2013
Values in Bln US$	Imp.	11.5	12.5	12.5	13.8	16.0	18.6	20.2	22.3	25.2	26.9	23.0	26.2	28.9	28.6	30.2
	Exp.	10.9	12.0	11.9	12.9	14.9	17.4	18.7	21.3	23.7	25.2	21.7	25.3	29.1	30.5	32.7
As a percentage of SITC section (%)	Imp.	1.4	1.4	1.5	1.5	1.6	1.5	1.4	1.3	1.3	1.2	1.5	1.4	1.3	1.3	1.4
	Exp.	1.4	1.4	1.4	1.5	1.5	1.4	1.3	1.3	1.2	1.2	1.4	1.3	1.2	1.4	1.4
As a percentage of world trade (%)	Imp.	0.2	0.2	0.2	0.2	0.2	0.2	0.2	0.2	0.2	0.2	0.2	0.2	0.2	0.2	0.2
	Exp.	0.2	0.2	0.2	0.2	0.2	0.2	0.2	0.2	0.2	0.2	0.2	0.2	0.2	0.2	0.2

Graph 1: Annual growth rates of exports, 1999–2013
(In percentage by year)

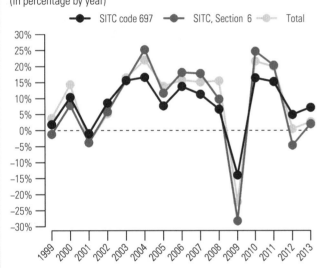

Table 2: Top exporting countries or areas in 2013

Country or area	Value (million US$)	Avg. Growth (%) 09-13	Growth (%) 12-13	World share %	Cum.
World	32 724.9	10.8	7.2	100.0	
China	14 718.9	19.0	8.8	45.0	45.0
Italy	2 420.9	4.9	7.5	7.4	52.4
Germany	1 766.3	5.5	9.0	5.4	57.8
USA	1 040.0	7.1	0.2	3.2	61.0
France	904.7	3.6	6.3	2.8	63.7
Turkey	825.2	9.3	7.8	2.5	66.2
India	773.7	9.2	13.5	2.4	68.6
Other Asia, nes	582.9	3.0	-5.5	1.8	70.4
Mexico	568.5	7.7	14.0	1.7	72.1
Netherlands	545.9	4.3	-2.6	1.7	73.8
Belgium	516.2	2.1	19.2	1.6	75.4
Thailand	502.9	13.7	17.4	1.5	76.9
Spain	498.9	3.0	0.7	1.5	78.4
United Arab Emirates	*452.5*	20.1	21.7	1.4	79.8
Poland	436.1	5.6	5.9	1.3	81.1

Graph 2: Trade Balance by MDG regions 2013
(Bln US$)

Developed Asia–Pacific
Developed Europe
Developed N. America
South–eastern Europe
CIS
Northern Africa
Sub–Saharan Africa
Latin Am, Caribbean
Eastern Asia
Southern Asia
South–eastern Asia
Western Asia
Oceania

Table 3: Top importing countries or areas in 2013

Country or area	Value (million US$)	Avg. Growth (%) 09-13	Growth (%) 12-13	World share %	Cum.
World	30 182.0	7.1	5.5	100.0	
USA	7 153.9	8.1	9.3	23.7	23.7
Germany	2 125.6	5.6	10.7	7.0	30.7
France	1 404.7	2.7	8.5	4.7	35.4
United Kingdom	1 310.0	2.3	9.1	4.3	39.7
Russian Federation	1 228.0	15.2	-8.2	4.1	43.8
Canada	1 099.0	5.8	-0.3	3.6	47.4
Japan	1 055.7	5.7	-2.3	3.5	50.9
Netherlands	762.3	5.9	9.4	2.5	53.5
Belgium	733.2	6.2	22.7	2.4	55.9
Australia	721.8	9.7	-1.5	2.4	58.3
Italy	699.5	4.2	10.1	2.3	60.6
Spain	543.2	1.0	6.9	1.8	62.4
United Arab Emirates	*479.7*	11.4	11.4	1.6	64.0
Switzerland	463.0	2.3	-2.0	1.5	65.5
Austria	450.5	3.7	4.1	1.5	67.0

In 2013, the value (in current US$) of exports of "manufactures of base metal, nes" (SITC group 699) increased by 5.1 percent (compared to 10.0 percent average growth rate from 2009-2013) to reach 152.0 bln US$ (see table 2), while imports increased by 4.3 percent to reach 149.8 bln US$ (see table 3). Exports of this commodity accounted for 6.7 percent of world exports of SITC section 6, and 0.8 percent of total world merchandise exports (see table 1). China, Germany and USA were the top exporters in 2013 (see table 2). They accounted for 17.3, 12.5 and 9.2 percent of world exports, respectively. USA, Germany and France were the top destinations, with respectively 12.4, 8.5 and 4.7 percent of world imports (see table 3).

The top 15 countries/areas accounted for 75.1 and 60.8 percent of total world exports and imports, respectively (see tables 2 and 3). In 2013, China was the country/area with the highest value of net exports (+19.8 bln US$), followed by Germany (+6.2 bln US$). By MDG regions (see graph 2), the largest surpluses in this product group were recorded by Eastern Asia (+22.7 bln US$), Developed Europe (+11.0 bln US$) and Southern Asia (+1.3 bln US$). The largest trade deficits were recorded by Developed North America (-7.1 bln US$), Latin America and the Caribbean (-5.9 bln US$) and South-eastern Asia (-4.6 bln US$).

Table 1: Imports (Imp.) and exports (Exp.), 1999-2013, in current US$

		1999	2000	2001	2002	2003	2004	2005	2006	2007	2008	2009	2010	2011	2012	2013
Values in Bln US$	Imp.	51.5	54.2	52.9	56.2	64.5	77.6	89.2	103.6	123.4	138.5	105.3	123.3	143.1	143.6	149.8
	Exp.	50.0	53.2	52.3	55.7	64.3	78.9	90.7	107.0	128.0	141.4	104.0	121.1	144.3	144.7	152.0
As a percentage of SITC section (%)	Imp.	6.3	6.1	6.2	6.3	6.3	6.1	6.2	6.2	6.3	6.4	6.8	6.4	6.2	6.6	6.8
	Exp.	6.2	6.2	6.3	6.3	6.3	6.2	6.4	6.4	6.5	6.5	6.7	6.2	6.2	6.5	6.7
As a percentage of world trade (%)	Imp.	0.9	0.8	0.8	0.9	0.8	0.8	0.8	0.9	0.9	0.9	0.8	0.8	0.8	0.8	0.8
	Exp.	0.9	0.8	0.9	0.9	0.9	0.9	0.9	0.9	0.9	0.9	0.8	0.8	0.8	0.8	0.8

Graph 1: Annual growth rates of exports, 1999–2013
(In percentage by year)

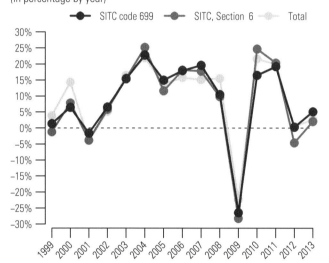

Table 2: Top exporting countries or areas in 2013

Country or area	Value (million US$)	Avg. Growth (%) 09-13	Growth (%) 12-13	World share %	Cum.
World	152 007.7	10.0	5.1	100.0	
China	26 248.8	17.8	9.7	17.3	17.3
Germany	18 947.8	7.4	5.2	12.5	29.7
USA	14 048.4	11.8	5.9	9.2	39.0
Italy	10 059.1	3.4	4.4	6.6	45.6
France	5 343.9	2.5	3.1	3.5	49.1
Czech Rep.	4 604.5	13.0	8.2	3.0	52.1
Austria	4 504.4	9.5	4.6	3.0	55.1
Mexico	4 256.7	11.0	8.1	2.8	57.9
Other Asia, nes	4 031.1	9.5	-2.6	2.7	60.6
Japan	3 880.3	4.2	-13.9	2.6	63.1
Poland	3 756.0	13.2	11.7	2.5	65.6
United Kingdom	3 723.6	5.9	12.8	2.4	68.0
Spain	3 686.6	8.0	12.3	2.4	70.5
Rep. of Korea	3 580.6	11.5	-1.0	2.4	72.8
India	3 469.7	26.7	7.0	2.3	75.1

Graph 2: Trade Balance by MDG regions 2013
(Bln US$)

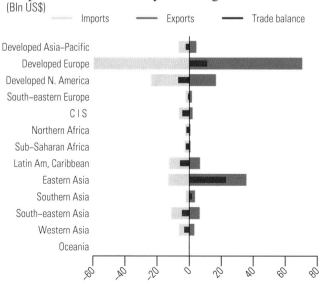

Table 3: Top importing countries or areas in 2013

Country or area	Value (million US$)	Avg. Growth (%) 09-13	Growth (%) 12-13	World share %	Cum.
World	149 776.9	9.2	4.3	100.0	
USA	18 636.9	12.3	2.2	12.4	12.4
Germany	12 711.8	9.0	4.6	8.5	20.9
France	7 036.8	4.0	0.7	4.7	25.6
Mexico	6 657.1	11.4	2.7	4.4	30.1
China	6 418.0	11.1	0.0	4.3	34.4
United Kingdom	5 239.0	6.7	6.8	3.5	37.9
Canada	4 955.0	8.8	-1.1	3.3	41.2
Japan	4 150.6	8.6	-2.8	2.8	43.9
Thailand	4 149.9	13.8	-2.7	2.8	46.7
Russian Federation	3 936.0	20.9	3.0	2.6	49.3
Italy	3 922.4	6.4	3.4	2.6	52.0
Rep. of Korea	3 769.6	10.5	14.8	2.5	54.5
Poland	3 440.0	7.8	12.5	2.3	56.8
Austria	3 014.8	7.2	3.2	2.0	58.8
Czech Rep.	3 003.0	9.6	8.2	2.0	60.8

Machinery and transport equipment

(SITC Section 7)

711 Steam boilers, superheated water boiler; auxiliary plants; parts thereof

In 2013, the value (in current US$) of exports of "steam boilers, superheated water boiler; auxiliary plants; parts thereof" (SITC group 711) decreased by 1.4 percent (compared to 0.2 percent average growth rate from 2009-2013) to reach 9.2 bln US$ (see table 2), while imports increased by 26.7 percent to reach 9.4 bln US$ (see table 3). Exports of this commodity accounted for 0.2 percent of world exports of SITC section 7, and less than 0.1 percent of total world merchandise exports (see table 1). China, Rep. of Korea and Japan were the top exporters in 2013 (see table 2). They accounted for 27.9, 9.1 and 8.0 percent of world exports, respectively. Turkey, USA and Indonesia were the top destinations, with respectively 8.9, 7.0 and 6.9 percent of world imports (see table 3).

The top 15 countries/areas accounted for 81.2 and 62.5 percent of total world exports and imports, respectively (see tables 2 and 3). In 2013, China was the country/area with the highest value of net exports (+2.5 bln US$), followed by Japan (+658.9 mln US$). By MDG regions (see graph 2), the largest surpluses in this product group were recorded by Eastern Asia (+2.8 bln US$), Developed Europe (+1.1 bln US$) and Developed Asia-Pacific (+608.3 mln US$). The largest trade deficits were recorded by South-eastern Asia (-1.8 bln US$), Western Asia (-1.7 bln US$) and Latin America and the Caribbean (-643.8 mln US$).

Table 1: Imports (Imp.) and exports (Exp.), 1999-2013, in current US$

		1999	2000	2001	2002	2003	2004	2005	2006	2007	2008	2009	2010	2011	2012	2013
Values in Bln US$	Imp.	3.1	2.8	3.1	2.9	2.6	2.9	3.6	3.5	5.4	8.0	8.8	6.8	7.4	7.4	9.4
	Exp.	2.7	2.5	2.8	2.5	2.7	3.1	3.9	4.1	5.7	9.1	9.1	8.1	9.8	9.3	9.2
As a percentage of SITC section (%)	Imp.	0.1	0.1	0.1	0.1	0.1	0.1	0.1	0.1	0.1	0.1	0.2	0.1	0.1	0.1	0.2
	Exp.	0.1	0.1	0.1	0.1	0.1	0.1	0.1	0.1	0.1	0.2	0.2	0.2	0.2	0.2	0.2
As a percentage of world trade (%)	Imp.	0.1	0.0	0.0	0.0	0.0	0.0	0.0	0.0	0.0	0.0	0.1	0.0	0.0	0.0	0.1
	Exp.	0.0	0.0	0.0	0.0	0.0	0.0	0.0	0.0	0.0	0.1	0.1	0.1	0.1	0.1	0.0

Graph 1: Annual growth rates of exports, 1999–2013
(In percentage by year)

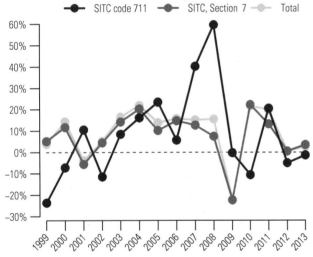

Table 2: Top exporting countries or areas in 2013

Country or area	Value (million US$)	Avg. Growth (%) 09-13	Growth (%) 12-13	World share %	Cum.
World	9 160.9	0.2	-1.4	100.0	
China	2 555.0	-3.3	-7.6	27.9	27.9
Rep. of Korea	829.7	-7.9	-45.3	9.1	36.9
Japan	732.1	4.8	66.6	8.0	44.9
USA	656.2	6.6	5.3	7.2	52.1
Italy	507.1	2.7	-7.4	5.5	57.6
Germany	391.5	-1.0	7.8	4.3	61.9
India	323.8	22.3	18.7	3.5	65.4
Canada	266.9	8.6	71.5	2.9	68.4
Finland	212.2	4.4	-9.9	2.3	70.7
Belgium	192.8	10.1	161.8	2.1	72.8
Poland	175.9	-10.4	-5.6	1.9	74.7
Russian Federation	162.2	9.3	-6.9	1.8	76.5
Other Asia, nes	161.9	13.3	39.8	1.8	78.2
France	137.4	-3.4	93.8	1.5	79.7
Spain	137.2	14.4	-35.3	1.5	81.2

Graph 2: Trade Balance by MDG regions 2013
(Bln US$)

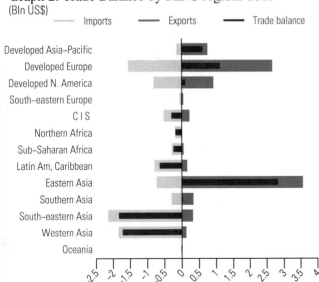

Table 3: Top importing countries or areas in 2013

Country or area	Value (million US$)	Avg. Growth (%) 09-13	Growth (%) 12-13	World share %	Cum.
World	9 410.8	1.6	26.7	100.0	
Turkey	834.8	22.6	108.8	8.9	8.9
USA	657.8	-7.5	45.3	7.0	15.9
Indonesia	652.3	-1.2	6.5	6.9	22.8
Viet Nam	620.1	104.5	43.2	6.6	29.4
Saudi Arabia	575.0	15.9	-13.7	6.1	35.5
Rep. of Korea	525.7	21.1	158.0	5.6	41.1
Malaysia	334.3	72.5	151.6	3.6	44.6
France	250.0	15.2	109.1	2.7	47.3
Russian Federation	235.7	12.9	45.8	2.5	49.8
Singapore	214.3	8.7	-0.8	2.3	52.1
Slovenia	212.2	215.0	133.5	2.3	54.3
United Kingdom	210.0	0.4	93.9	2.2	56.6
United Arab Emirates	205.4	-11.1	11.4	2.2	58.7
Argentina	180.6	10.4	337.2	1.9	60.7
India	175.2	-22.7	-10.0	1.9	62.5

Steam turbines and other vapour turbines and parts thereof, nes 712

In 2013, the value (in current US$) of exports of "steam turbines and other vapour turbines and parts thereof, nes" (SITC group 712) decreased by 3.0 percent (compared to -2.5 percent average growth rate from 2009-2013) to reach 7.5 bln US$ (see table 2), while imports decreased by 10.0 percent to reach 7.5 bln US$ (see table 3). Exports of this commodity accounted for 0.1 percent of world exports of SITC section 7, and less than 0.1 percent of total world merchandise exports (see table 1). Japan, China and Germany were the top exporters in 2013 (see table 2). They accounted for 21.7, 18.8 and 13.2 percent of world exports, respectively. Rep. of Korea, South Africa and Turkey were the top destinations, with respectively 9.4, 6.6 and 6.6 percent of world imports (see table 3).

The top 15 countries/areas accounted for 90.4 and 65.7 percent of total world exports and imports, respectively (see tables 2 and 3). In 2013, Japan was the country/area with the highest value of net exports (+1.4 bln US$), followed by China (+1.1 bln US$). By MDG regions (see graph 2), the largest surpluses in this product group were recorded by Developed Europe (+1.6 bln US$), Developed Asia-Pacific (+1.4 bln US$) and Eastern Asia (+471.7 mln US$). The largest trade deficits were recorded by Western Asia (-1.0 bln US$), South-eastern Asia (-991.6 mln US$) and Sub-Saharan Africa (-570.0 mln US$).

Table 1: Imports (Imp.) and exports (Exp.), 1999-2013, in current US$

		1999	2000	2001	2002	2003	2004	2005	2006	2007	2008	2009	2010	2011	2012	2013
Values in Bln US$	Imp.	2.9	3.1	3.3	3.3	2.7	3.3	4.6	4.6	5.0	6.1	8.0	7.8	8.5	8.3	7.5
	Exp.	2.4	2.5	3.0	3.1	2.7	3.2	4.1	4.3	5.1	6.8	8.3	8.1	8.7	7.7	7.5
As a percentage of SITC section (%)	Imp.	0.1	0.1	0.1	0.1	0.1	0.1	0.1	0.1	0.1	0.1	0.2	0.1	0.1	0.1	0.1
	Exp.	0.1	0.1	0.1	0.1	0.1	0.1	0.1	0.1	0.1	0.1	0.2	0.2	0.2	0.1	0.1
As a percentage of world trade (%)	Imp.	0.1	0.0	0.1	0.1	0.0	0.0	0.0	0.0	0.0	0.0	0.1	0.1	0.0	0.0	0.0
	Exp.	0.0	0.0	0.0	0.0	0.0	0.0	0.0	0.0	0.0	0.0	0.1	0.1	0.0	0.0	0.0

Graph 1: Annual growth rates of exports, 1999–2013
(In percentage by year)

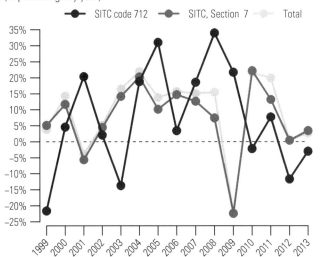

Graph 2: Trade Balance by MDG regions 2013
(Bln US$)

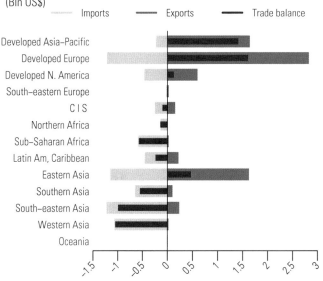

Table 2: Top exporting countries or areas in 2013

Country or area	Value (million US$)	Avg. Growth (%) 09-13	Growth (%) 12-13	World share %	Cum.
World	7 469.1	-2.5	-3.0	100.0	
Japan	1 617.6	0.8	3.1	21.7	21.7
China	1 402.0	3.3	9.0	18.8	40.4
Germany	986.2	-5.6	-23.8	13.2	53.6
USA	570.5	-10.5	-16.7	7.6	61.3
Italy	527.8	0.8	29.8	7.1	68.3
Czech Rep.	220.9	-4.3	-8.1	3.0	71.3
Rep. of Korea	217.3	9.1	-14.8	2.9	74.2
France	201.4	-10.8	-37.7	2.7	76.9
United Kingdom	194.5	-5.9	24.9	2.6	79.5
Poland	188.1	-6.6	39.1	2.5	82.0
Singapore	141.6	28.0	13.9	1.9	83.9
Mexico	135.7	2.6	18.5	1.8	85.7
Austria	126.8	-7.2	12.4	1.7	87.4
Sweden	122.2	-21.8	-37.8	1.6	89.1
India	97.6	5.6	25.2	1.3	90.4

Table 3: Top importing countries or areas in 2013

Country or area	Value (million US$)	Avg. Growth (%) 09-13	Growth (%) 12-13	World share %	Cum.
World	7 487.6	-1.6	-10.0	100.0	
Rep. of Korea	703.9	23.8	222.9	9.4	9.4
South Africa	494.9	8.8	-52.3	6.6	16.0
Turkey	490.8	16.6	215.2	6.6	22.6
USA	370.6	-10.6	-5.7	4.9	27.5
Viet Nam	367.5	57.4	91.8	4.9	32.4
Indonesia	366.3	-1.6	-16.7	4.9	37.3
India	350.3	-6.9	-43.5	4.7	42.0
China	337.5	-12.6	-54.7	4.5	46.5
Saudi Arabia	288.6	54.8	79.3	3.9	50.4
Brazil	231.6	42.1	-57.8	3.1	53.4
Germany	227.1	-18.2	-26.8	3.0	56.5
Italy	223.5	29.1	-22.1	3.0	59.5
Japan	173.2	-1.6	32.8	2.3	61.8
Singapore	153.2	7.3	-22.6	2.0	63.8
Switzerland	143.5	-9.8	81.2	1.9	65.7

713 Internal combustion piston engines and parts thereof, nes

In 2013, the value (in current US$) of exports of "internal combustion piston engines and parts thereof, nes" (SITC group 713) increased by 2.8 percent (compared to 11.6 percent average growth rate from 2009-2013) to reach 163.7 bln US$ (see table 2), while imports decreased by 0.1 percent to reach 159.5 bln US$ (see table 3). Exports of this commodity accounted for 2.7 percent of world exports of SITC section 7, and 0.9 percent of total world merchandise exports (see table 1). Germany, USA and Japan were the top exporters in 2013 (see table 2). They accounted for 16.2, 11.0 and 10.8 percent of world exports, respectively. USA, Germany and Mexico were the top destinations, with respectively 15.6, 10.8 and 5.9 percent of world imports (see table 3).

The top 15 countries/areas accounted for 82.4 and 70.2 percent of total world exports and imports, respectively (see tables 2 and 3). In 2013, Japan was the country/area with the highest value of net exports (+14.7 bln US$), followed by Germany (+9.3 bln US$). By MDG regions (see graph 2), the largest surpluses in this product group were recorded by Developed Europe (+22.0 bln US$), Developed Asia-Pacific (+13.7 bln US$) and South-eastern Europe (+201.3 mln US$). The largest trade deficits were recorded by Developed North America (-10.9 bln US$), Commonwealth of Independent States (-4.9 bln US$) and Latin America and the Caribbean (-4.8 bln US$).

Table 1: Imports (Imp.) and exports (Exp.), 1999-2013, in current US$

		1999	2000	2001	2002	2003	2004	2005	2006	2007	2008	2009	2010	2011	2012	2013
Values in Bln US$	Imp.	67.6	71.0	68.3	75.2	85.6	101.4	113.4	123.1	144.6	151.8	106.3	138.7	167.7	159.8	159.5
	Exp.	66.1	69.2	66.2	71.9	83.7	101.1	113.2	125.2	145.8	151.0	105.5	137.0	166.4	159.2	163.7
As a percentage of SITC section (%)	Imp.	2.9	2.7	2.7	2.9	2.9	2.8	2.9	2.8	2.9	2.8	2.5	2.7	2.8	2.7	2.6
	Exp.	2.8	2.6	2.7	2.8	2.8	2.9	2.9	2.8	2.9	2.8	2.5	2.7	2.9	2.7	2.7
As a percentage of world trade (%)	Imp.	1.2	1.1	1.1	1.1	1.1	1.1	1.1	1.0	1.0	0.9	0.8	0.9	0.9	0.9	0.9
	Exp.	1.2	1.1	1.1	1.1	1.1	1.1	1.1	1.0	1.1	0.9	0.9	0.9	0.9	0.9	0.9

Graph 1: Annual growth rates of exports, 1999–2013
(In percentage by year)

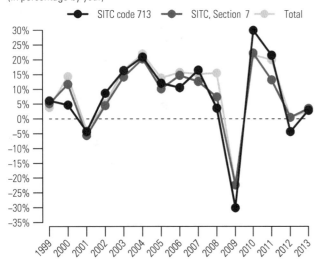

Legend: SITC code 713 — SITC, Section 7 — Total

Table 2: Top exporting countries or areas in 2013

Country or area	Value (million US$)	Avg. Growth (%) 09-13	Growth (%) 12-13	World share %	Cum.
World	163 692.9	11.6	2.8	100.0	
Germany	26 440.4	11.1	4.3	16.2	16.2
USA	18 041.2	13.7	-0.1	11.0	27.2
Japan	17 660.9	8.3	-11.4	10.8	38.0
Mexico	8 736.6	26.6	7.0	5.3	43.3
United Kingdom	8 596.6	11.3	12.4	5.3	48.6
France	8 269.5	8.0	9.3	5.1	53.6
China	7 705.3	20.3	9.4	4.7	58.3
Hungary	7 558.9	9.2	9.3	4.6	62.9
Italy	6 112.5	9.7	8.8	3.7	66.7
Austria	6 109.9	6.4	3.1	3.7	70.4
Poland	4 727.2	7.8	7.7	2.9	73.3
Rep. of Korea	4 575.7	5.6	-13.0	2.8	76.1
Spain	3 747.2	17.1	17.7	2.3	78.4
Thailand	3 347.6	20.8	4.5	2.0	80.4
Canada	3 206.8	4.5	-18.2	2.0	82.4

Graph 2: Trade Balance by MDG regions 2013
(Bln US$)

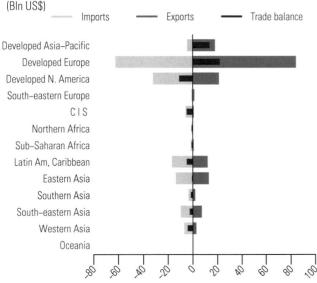

Legend: Imports — Exports — Trade balance

Regions listed: Developed Asia–Pacific, Developed Europe, Developed N. America, South–eastern Europe, CIS, Northern Africa, Sub–Saharan Africa, Latin Am, Caribbean, Eastern Asia, Southern Asia, South–eastern Asia, Western Asia, Oceania

Table 3: Top importing countries or areas in 2013

Country or area	Value (million US$)	Avg. Growth (%) 09-13	Growth (%) 12-13	World share %	Cum.
World	159 531.7	10.7	-0.1	100.0	
USA	24 903.9	19.4	-4.4	15.6	15.6
Germany	17 151.3	7.4	0.6	10.8	26.4
Mexico	9 483.2	22.6	-3.2	5.9	32.3
China	9 290.1	3.9	-4.7	5.8	38.1
Canada	7 262.0	8.0	-9.5	4.6	42.7
United Kingdom	7 159.9	12.0	-2.0	4.5	47.2
France	5 556.3	2.9	-0.2	3.5	50.7
Spain	4 476.5	4.5	15.7	2.8	53.5
Russian Federation	4 445.6	46.7	8.5	2.8	56.2
Belgium	4 083.0	7.9	6.1	2.6	58.8
Thailand	3 958.8	27.8	-0.4	2.5	61.3
Italy	3 921.5	5.2	4.3	2.5	63.7
Turkey	3 691.9	10.4	13.7	2.3	66.1
Brazil	3 595.8	21.2	17.3	2.3	68.3
Hungary	3 077.2	11.2	24.5	1.9	70.2

In 2013, the value (in current US$) of exports of "engines and motors, non-electric; parts, nes (not those of 712, 713 and 718)" (SITC group 714) increased by 6.5 percent (compared to 7.3 percent average growth rate from 2009-2013) to reach 98.3 bln US$ (see table 2), while imports increased by 7.0 percent to reach 117.4 bln US$ (see table 3). Exports of this commodity accounted for 1.6 percent of world exports of SITC section 7, and 0.5 percent of total world merchandise exports (see table 1). United Kingdom, France and Germany were the top exporters in 2013 (see table 2). They accounted for 22.5, 11.9 and 10.7 percent of world exports, respectively. USA, United Kingdom and Germany were the top destinations, with respectively 17.0, 14.0 and 8.7 percent of world imports (see table 3).

The top 15 countries/areas accounted for 88.2 and 81.1 percent of total world exports and imports, respectively (see tables 2 and 3). In 2013, United Kingdom was the country/area with the highest value of net exports (+5.8 bln US$), followed by France (+2.6 bln US$). By MDG regions (see graph 2), the largest surpluses in this product group were recorded by Developed Europe (+12.5 bln US$), Commonwealth of Independent States (+1.7 bln US$) and South-eastern Europe (+7.9 mln US$). The largest trade deficits were recorded by Developed North America (-10.0 bln US$), South-eastern Asia (-5.9 bln US$) and Eastern Asia (-5.6 bln US$).

Table 1: Imports (Imp.) and exports (Exp.), 1999-2013, in current US$

		1999	2000	2001	2002	2003	2004	2005	2006	2007	2008	2009	2010	2011	2012	2013
Values in Bln US$	Imp.	42.6	45.5	50.2	48.2	47.8	54.5	60.5	68.8	75.6	87.7	88.7	90.6	100.8	109.7	117.4
	Exp.	44.8	47.6	55.4	52.4	53.5	61.8	68.0	78.4	83.2	95.0	74.1	76.2	85.7	92.3	98.3
As a percentage of SITC section (%)	Imp.	1.8	1.7	2.0	1.9	1.6	1.5	1.5	1.5	1.5	1.6	2.1	1.7	1.7	1.8	1.9
	Exp.	1.9	1.8	2.2	2.0	1.8	1.7	1.7	1.8	1.7	1.8	1.8	1.5	1.5	1.6	1.6
As a percentage of world trade (%)	Imp.	0.7	0.7	0.8	0.7	0.6	0.6	0.6	0.6	0.5	0.5	0.7	0.6	0.6	0.6	0.6
	Exp.	0.8	0.7	0.9	0.8	0.7	0.7	0.7	0.7	0.6	0.6	0.6	0.5	0.5	0.5	0.5

Graph 1: Annual growth rates of exports, 1999–2013
(In percentage by year)

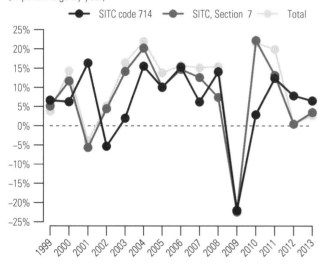

Table 2: Top exporting countries or areas in 2013

Country or area	Value (million US$)	Avg. Growth (%) 09-13	Growth (%) 12-13	World share %	Cum.
World	98 333.9	7.3	6.5	100.0	
United Kingdom	22 166.4	10.2	10.2	22.5	22.5
France	11 662.2	5.8	2.5	11.9	34.4
Germany	10 547.7	7.3	-2.7	10.7	45.1
USA	9 971.4	0.4	-7.5	10.1	55.3
Japan	4 519.3	4.6	-2.0	4.6	59.9
Canada	4 347.3	2.5	-2.8	4.4	64.3
Italy	4 273.8	2.8	18.6	4.3	68.6
Singapore	3 751.5	22.9	32.3	3.8	72.4
China, Hong Kong SAR	3 649.2	9.4	27.4	3.7	76.2
Netherlands	2 369.6	0.1	17.0	2.4	78.6
China	2 183.7	16.8	14.7	2.2	80.8
Russian Federation	2 131.3	19.1	27.7	2.2	83.0
Switzerland	1 918.3	-3.9	8.2	2.0	84.9
Mexico	1 790.8	10.7	-11.0	1.8	86.7
Poland	1 414.6	20.7	18.1	1.4	88.2

Graph 2: Trade Balance by MDG regions 2013
(Bln US$)

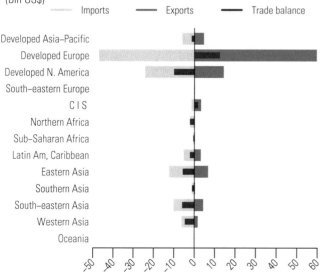

Table 3: Top importing countries or areas in 2013

Country or area	Value (million US$)	Avg. Growth (%) 09-13	Growth (%) 12-13	World share %	Cum.
World	117 419.3	7.3	7.0	100.0	
USA	19 906.6	8.6	3.0	17.0	17.0
United Kingdom	16 401.4	10.2	9.6	14.0	30.9
Germany	10 233.0	10.4	17.2	8.7	39.6
France	9 081.6	5.1	9.4	7.7	47.4
Singapore	7 720.4	21.3	22.5	6.6	53.9
China, Hong Kong SAR	5 120.4	5.9	2.8	4.4	58.3
China	4 778.1	20.8	7.1	4.1	62.4
Japan	4 585.7	0.6	3.1	3.9	66.3
Canada	4 346.8	2.2	4.5	3.7	70.0
United Arab Emirates	3 033.0	8.0	11.4	2.6	72.6
Brazil	2 328.0	3.2	6.8	2.0	74.5
Netherlands	2 150.1	-3.5	10.8	1.8	76.4
Rep. of Korea	2 067.7	16.6	47.8	1.8	78.1
Italy	1 881.1	2.4	6.2	1.6	79.7
Mexico	1 618.9	13.1	-3.1	1.4	81.1

STAFFS UNIVERSITY LIBRARY

716 Rotating electric plant and parts thereof, nes

In 2013, the value (in current US$) of exports of "rotating electric plant and parts thereof, nes" (SITC group 716) decreased by 3.3 percent (compared to 6.9 percent average growth rate from 2009-2013) to reach 94.1 bln US$ (see table 2), while imports decreased by 2.2 percent to reach 96.7 bln US$ (see table 3). Exports of this commodity accounted for 1.6 percent of world exports of SITC section 7, and 0.5 percent of total world merchandise exports (see table 1). China, Germany and USA were the top exporters in 2013 (see table 2). They accounted for 19.0, 13.8 and 9.5 percent of world exports, respectively. USA, Germany and China were the top destinations, with respectively 11.8, 7.1 and 7.0 percent of world imports (see table 3).

The top 15 countries/areas accounted for 77.6 and 59.1 percent of total world exports and imports, respectively (see tables 2 and 3). In 2013, China was the country/area with the highest value of net exports (+11.1 bln US$), followed by Germany (+6.1 bln US$). By MDG regions (see graph 2), the largest surpluses in this product group were recorded by Developed Europe (+15.3 bln US$), Eastern Asia (+10.2 bln US$) and Developed Asia-Pacific (+1.3 bln US$). The largest trade deficits were recorded by Western Asia (-5.6 bln US$), Developed North America (-4.8 bln US$) and Latin America and the Caribbean (-4.8 bln US$).

Table 1: Imports (Imp.) and exports (Exp.), 1999-2013, in current US$

		1999	2000	2001	2002	2003	2004	2005	2006	2007	2008	2009	2010	2011	2012	2013
Values in Bln US$	Imp.	31.2	32.7	34.7	36.6	39.9	45.6	53.2	62.5	76.0	89.6	77.1	82.7	97.3	98.9	96.7
	Exp.	29.0	30.8	32.5	33.0	37.6	44.6	51.6	61.1	72.9	87.3	72.1	80.7	93.8	97.3	94.1
As a percentage of SITC section (%)	Imp.	1.3	1.2	1.4	1.4	1.4	1.3	1.4	1.4	1.5	1.7	1.8	1.6	1.6	1.7	1.6
	Exp.	1.2	1.2	1.3	1.3	1.3	1.3	1.3	1.4	1.4	1.6	1.7	1.6	1.6	1.7	1.6
As a percentage of world trade (%)	Imp.	0.5	0.5	0.6	0.6	0.5	0.5	0.5	0.5	0.5	0.6	0.6	0.5	0.5	0.5	0.5
	Exp.	0.5	0.5	0.5	0.5	0.5	0.5	0.5	0.5	0.5	0.5	0.6	0.5	0.5	0.5	0.5

Graph 1: Annual growth rates of exports, 1999–2013
(In percentage by year)

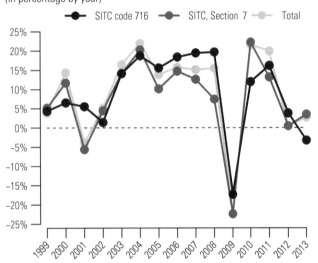

Table 2: Top exporting countries or areas in 2013

Country or area	Value (million US$)	Avg. Growth (%) 09-13	Growth (%) 12-13	World share %	World share % Cum.
World..................................	94 115.8	6.9	-3.3	100.0	
China..................................	17 906.6	17.5	6.0	19.0	19.0
Germany............................	12 996.0	6.7	-1.7	13.8	32.8
USA....................................	8 925.8	6.9	-9.5	9.5	42.3
Japan.................................	4 844.0	-0.2	-19.8	5.1	47.5
Denmark.............................	3 504.4	3.0	51.0	3.7	51.2
Italy...................................	3 336.2	0.8	-11.8	3.5	54.7
Mexico...............................	3 071.5	8.0	-5.8	3.3	58.0
United Kingdom...................	2 905.6	2.5	-12.6	3.1	61.1
France................................	2 825.6	-0.2	-3.5	3.0	64.1
Spain.................................	2 792.3	-2.9	-23.5	3.0	67.1
China, Hong Kong SAR.........	2 459.6	7.6	-7.0	2.6	69.7
Czech Rep..........................	2 041.4	8.6	-2.4	2.2	71.8
Switzerland.........................	1 907.2	8.8	7.5	2.0	73.9
Finland...............................	1 863.0	-0.9	6.5	2.0	75.8
Rep. of Korea......................	1 631.3	7.4	-17.7	1.7	77.6

Graph 2: Trade Balance by MDG regions 2013
(Bln US$)

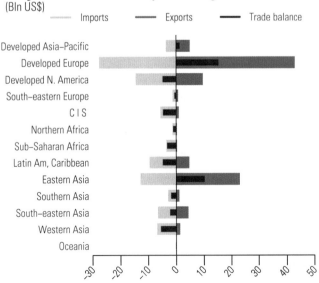

Table 3: Top importing countries or areas in 2013

Country or area	Value (million US$)	Avg. Growth (%) 09-13	Growth (%) 12-13	World share %	World share % Cum.
World..................................	96 668.2	5.8	-2.2	100.0	
USA....................................	11 434.2	4.0	-7.9	11.8	11.8
Germany............................	6 852.0	6.3	0.9	7.1	18.9
China.................................	6 766.0	4.3	-1.7	7.0	25.9
Russian Federation..............	4 368.8	13.6	30.3	4.5	30.4
Mexico...............................	3 216.1	15.8	-8.4	3.3	33.8
Canada..............................	2 862.8	7.0	-1.3	3.0	36.7
China, Hong Kong SAR.........	2 743.2	8.9	-5.9	2.8	39.6
France................................	2 718.5	3.7	-2.6	2.8	42.4
United Kingdom...................	2 668.9	3.9	-10.2	2.8	45.1
Italy...................................	2 601.6	0.6	-22.5	2.7	47.8
Rep. of Korea......................	2 422.8	8.1	9.4	2.5	50.3
Brazil.................................	2 264.9	19.9	28.2	2.3	52.7
Turkey................................	2 214.9	8.4	7.6	2.3	55.0
Japan.................................	2 131.9	5.3	-11.9	2.2	57.2
Thailand.............................	1 841.5	11.3	-31.8	1.9	59.1

In 2013, the value (in current US$) of exports of "power generating machinery and parts thereof, nes" (SITC group 718) decreased by 1.2 percent (compared to 9.4 percent average growth rate from 2009-2013) to reach 24.5 bln US$ (see table 2), while imports decreased by 2.7 percent to reach 26.2 bln US$ (see table 3). Exports of this commodity accounted for 0.4 percent of world exports of SITC section 7, and 0.1 percent of total world merchandise exports (see table 1). USA, Germany and China were the top exporters in 2013 (see table 2). They accounted for 15.4, 13.3 and 8.4 percent of world exports, respectively. USA, Germany and China were the top destinations, with respectively 15.4, 9.9 and 8.4 percent of world imports (see table 3).

The top 15 countries/areas accounted for 83.1 and 67.2 percent of total world exports and imports, respectively (see tables 2 and 3). In 2013, Russian Federation was the country/area with the highest value of net exports (+973.8 mln US$), followed by Sweden (+965.3 mln US$). By MDG regions (see graph 2), the largest surpluses in this product group were recorded by Developed Europe (+2.2 bln US$), Commonwealth of Independent States (+207.8 mln US$) and Developed Asia-Pacific (+197.9 mln US$). The largest trade deficits were recorded by Latin America and the Caribbean (-1.2 bln US$), Developed North America (-865.4 mln US$) and Sub-Saharan Africa (-605.0 mln US$).

Table 1: Imports (Imp.) and exports (Exp.), 1999-2013, in current US$

		1999	2000	2001	2002	2003	2004	2005	2006	2007	2008	2009	2010	2011	2012	2013
Values in Bln US$	Imp.	6.9	7.3	7.1	7.5	9.2	10.6	11.8	13.3	17.0	21.8	18.7	22.1	26.2	26.9	26.2
	Exp.	6.3	6.1	6.1	6.7	8.1	9.7	11.4	13.1	16.2	20.7	17.1	20.5	24.3	24.8	24.5
As a percentage of	Imp.	0.3	0.3	0.3	0.3	0.3	0.3	0.3	0.3	0.3	0.4	0.4	0.4	0.4	0.5	0.4
SITC section (%)	Exp.	0.3	0.2	0.2	0.3	0.3	0.3	0.3	0.3	0.3	0.4	0.4	0.4	0.4	0.4	0.4
As a percentage of	Imp.	0.1	0.1	0.1	0.1	0.1	0.1	0.1	0.1	0.1	0.1	0.1	0.1	0.1	0.1	0.1
world trade (%)	Exp.	0.1	0.1	0.1	0.1	0.1	0.1	0.1	0.1	0.1	0.1	0.1	0.1	0.1	0.1	0.1

Graph 1: Annual growth rates of exports, 1999–2013
(In percentage by year)

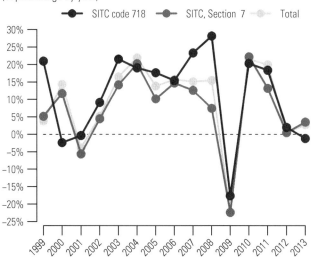

Table 2: Top exporting countries or areas in 2013

Country or area	Value (million US$)	Avg. Growth (%) 09-13	Growth (%) 12-13	World share %	Cum.
World....................	24 498.1	9.4	-1.2	100.0	
USA.....................	3 776.4	22.6	20.4	15.4	15.4
Germany..............	3 254.9	-0.7	-17.6	13.3	28.7
China...................	2 062.5	18.6	-4.5	8.4	37.1
Sweden................	1 608.5	10.2	5.1	6.6	43.7
Russian Federation..............	1 580.9	6.5	18.7	6.5	50.1
Japan...................	1 271.2	7.4	-27.7	5.2	55.3
Spain...................	1 118.2	12.9	8.9	4.6	59.9
France.................	1 065.9	12.5	-23.1	4.4	64.2
Denmark...............	837.2	9.5	-25.6	3.4	67.7
Canada................	707.2	2.3	-7.5	2.9	70.5
Italy.....................	692.5	7.8	17.9	2.8	73.4
United Kingdom....................	665.9	11.6	-6.3	2.7	76.1
Netherlands..........	647.3	12.6	24.3	2.6	78.7
Singapore............	605.3	30.1	94.5	2.5	81.2
Rep. of Korea.......................	457.0	23.1	3.1	1.9	83.1

Graph 2: Trade Balance by MDG regions 2013
(Bln US$)

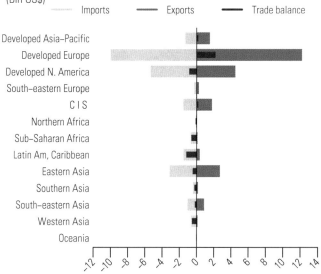

Table 3: Top importing countries or areas in 2013

Country or area	Value (million US$)	Avg. Growth (%) 09-13	Growth (%) 12-13	World share %	Cum.
World....................	26 168.7	8.7	-2.7	100.0	
USA.....................	4 032.7	11.9	-17.6	15.4	15.4
Germany..............	2 586.9	5.9	-21.6	9.9	25.3
China...................	2 201.4	0.5	-7.5	8.4	33.7
France.................	1 442.0	-4.1	-15.5	5.5	39.2
Canada................	1 315.5	23.4	14.6	5.0	44.2
United Kingdom.....................	906.5	24.9	-6.7	3.5	47.7
Japan...................	758.7	-2.5	16.8	2.9	50.6
Ukraine................	691.2	7.0	-0.5	2.6	53.2
Sweden................	643.3	13.3	31.6	2.5	55.7
Russian Federation..............	607.1	25.4	4.3	2.3	58.0
Brazil..................	539.9	23.9	16.3	2.1	60.1
Australia..............	534.2	26.6	40.6	2.0	62.1
Netherlands..........	465.4	12.7	17.3	1.8	63.9
Italy.....................	456.2	15.2	5.3	1.7	65.7
Rep. of Korea.......................	416.9	1.5	11.9	1.6	67.2

721 Agricultural machinery (excluding tractors) and parts thereof

In 2013, the value (in current US$) of exports of "agricultural machinery (excluding tractors) and parts thereof" (SITC group 721) increased by 2.6 percent (compared to 10.6 percent average growth rate from 2009-2013) to reach 39.5 bln US$ (see table 2), while imports increased by 1.6 percent to reach 39.0 bln US$ (see table 3). Exports of this commodity accounted for 0.7 percent of world exports of SITC section 7, and 0.2 percent of total world merchandise exports (see table 1). Germany, USA and Italy were the top exporters in 2013 (see table 2). They accounted for 18.3, 15.5 and 7.7 percent of world exports, respectively. USA, France and Germany were the top destinations, with respectively 10.4, 8.2 and 7.7 percent of world imports (see table 3).

The top 15 countries/areas accounted for 82.5 and 62.6 percent of total world exports and imports, respectively (see tables 2 and 3). In 2013, Germany was the country/area with the highest value of net exports (+4.3 bln US$), followed by Italy (+2.4 bln US$). By MDG regions (see graph 2), the largest surpluses in this product group were recorded by Developed Europe (+6.9 bln US$), Eastern Asia (+1.6 bln US$) and Developed North America (+882.6 mln US$). The largest trade deficits were recorded by Commonwealth of Independent States (-3.1 bln US$), Latin America and the Caribbean (-1.7 bln US$) and Developed Asia-Pacific (-843.3 mln US$).

Table 1: Imports (Imp.) and exports (Exp.), 1999-2013, in current US$

		1999	2000	2001	2002	2003	2004	2005	2006	2007	2008	2009	2010	2011	2012	2013
Values in Bln US$	Imp.	11.4	10.8	11.0	12.5	14.9	17.6	20.0	22.2	26.9	34.6	25.9	28.2	37.2	38.3	39.0
	Exp.	11.1	10.8	11.0	12.5	14.9	17.9	20.5	22.5	27.8	35.5	26.4	28.8	37.1	38.5	39.5
As a percentage of	Imp.	0.5	0.4	0.4	0.5	0.5	0.5	0.5	0.5	0.5	0.6	0.6	0.5	0.6	0.6	0.6
SITC section (%)	Exp.	0.5	0.4	0.4	0.5	0.5	0.5	0.5	0.5	0.6	0.7	0.6	0.6	0.6	0.7	0.7
As a percentage of	Imp.	0.2	0.2	0.2	0.2	0.2	0.2	0.2	0.2	0.2	0.2	0.2	0.2	0.2	0.2	0.2
world trade (%)	Exp.	0.2	0.2	0.2	0.2	0.2	0.2	0.2	0.2	0.2	0.2	0.2	0.2	0.2	0.2	0.2

Graph 1: Annual growth rates of exports, 1999–2013
(In percentage by year)

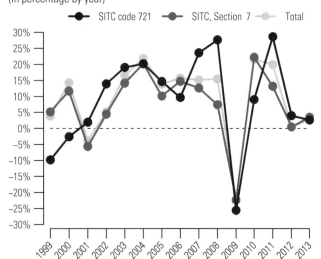

Table 2: Top exporting countries or areas in 2013

Country or area	Value (million US$)	Avg. Growth (%) 09-13	Growth (%) 12-13	World share %	Cum.
World	39538.0	10.6	2.6	100.0	
Germany	7252.7	11.9	3.6	18.3	18.3
USA	6119.7	11.3	-8.7	15.5	33.8
Italy	3063.9	7.9	5.5	7.7	41.6
China	2497.1	12.7	2.8	6.3	47.9
Netherlands	2471.4	10.5	5.4	6.3	54.1
Belgium	2020.3	8.0	13.6	5.1	59.2
France	1961.6	5.8	3.0	5.0	64.2
Canada	1652.2	9.0	5.9	4.2	68.4
Poland	1068.9	20.2	24.4	2.7	71.1
Austria	841.6	6.4	6.9	2.1	73.2
United Kingdom	813.7	6.4	6.8	2.1	75.3
Brazil	792.6	18.1	5.5	2.0	77.3
Denmark	778.6	1.7	-1.7	2.0	79.3
Sweden	704.1	15.3	6.1	1.8	81.0
Hungary	594.5	7.6	4.1	1.5	82.5

Graph 2: Trade Balance by MDG regions 2013
(Bln US$)

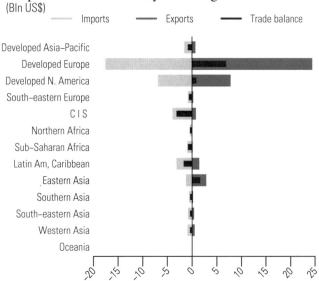

Table 3: Top importing countries or areas in 2013

Country or area	Value (million US$)	Avg. Growth (%) 09-13	Growth (%) 12-13	World share %	Cum.
World	38959.2	10.7	1.6	100.0	
USA	4060.9	13.7	12.5	10.4	10.4
France	3177.3	8.1	12.3	8.2	18.6
Germany	2993.3	10.2	5.6	7.7	26.3
Canada	2823.9	12.9	5.0	7.2	33.5
Russian Federation	2206.3	25.4	-8.5	5.7	39.2
United Kingdom	1458.3	2.6	0.0	3.7	42.9
Belgium	1246.1	7.5	25.3	3.2	46.1
Netherlands	1125.7	8.6	-3.5	2.9	49.0
Poland	888.1	12.7	10.6	2.3	51.3
Australia	831.5	2.8	-26.2	2.1	53.4
China	802.5	18.7	-8.7	2.1	55.5
Ukraine	743.7	33.5	-6.7	1.9	57.4
Austria	729.5	4.9	-1.7	1.9	59.3
Italy	651.0	5.7	3.0	1.7	60.9
Sweden	650.9	7.6	-3.3	1.7	62.6

In 2013, the value (in current US$) of exports of "tractors (other than those of headings 744.14 and 744.15)" (SITC group 722) decreased by 2.3 percent (compared to 10.1 percent average growth rate from 2009-2013) to reach 23.8 bln US$ (see table 2), while imports increased by 2.4 percent to reach 23.3 bln US$ (see table 3). Exports of this commodity accounted for 0.4 percent of world exports of SITC section 7, and 0.1 percent of total world merchandise exports (see table 1). Germany, USA and Italy were the top exporters in 2013 (see table 2). They accounted for 20.2, 14.5 and 9.7 percent of world exports, respectively. USA, France and Canada were the top destinations, with respectively 14.9, 9.9 and 7.4 percent of world imports (see table 3).

The top 15 countries/areas accounted for 88.5 and 64.6 percent of total world exports and imports, respectively (see tables 2 and 3). In 2013, Germany was the country/area with the highest value of net exports (+3.4 bln US$), followed by Italy (+1.7 bln US$). By MDG regions (see graph 2), the largest surpluses in this product group were recorded by Developed Europe (+2.6 bln US$), Southern Asia (+711.5 mln US$) and Developed Asia-Pacific (+702.2 mln US$). The largest trade deficits were recorded by Developed North America (-1.4 bln US$), Sub-Saharan Africa (-992.1 mln US$) and Northern Africa (-423.4 mln US$).

Table 1: Imports (Imp.) and exports (Exp.), 1999-2013, in current US$

		1999	2000	2001	2002	2003	2004	2005	2006	2007	2008	2009	2010	2011	2012	2013
Values in Bln US$	Imp.	7.7	7.6	7.4	8.6	10.4	13.4	15.0	16.0	17.8	22.2	15.6	16.5	21.0	22.8	23.3
	Exp.	8.2	7.8	7.4	8.7	10.2	13.0	14.2	15.6	19.1	24.1	16.2	17.1	22.7	24.4	23.8
As a percentage of SITC section (%)	Imp.	0.3	0.3	0.3	0.3	0.4	0.4	0.4	0.4	0.4	0.4	0.4	0.3	0.4	0.4	0.4
	Exp.	0.3	0.3	0.3	0.3	0.3	0.4	0.4	0.3	0.4	0.4	0.4	0.3	0.4	0.4	0.4
As a percentage of world trade (%)	Imp.	0.1	0.1	0.1	0.1	0.1	0.1	0.1	0.1	0.1	0.1	0.1	0.1	0.1	0.1	0.1
	Exp.	0.1	0.1	0.1	0.1	0.1	0.1	0.1	0.1	0.1	0.2	0.1	0.1	0.1	0.1	0.1

Graph 1: Annual growth rates of exports, 1999–2013

(In percentage by year)

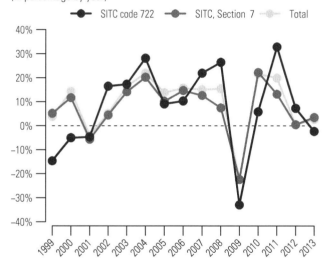

Graph 2: Trade Balance by MDG regions 2013

(Bln US$)

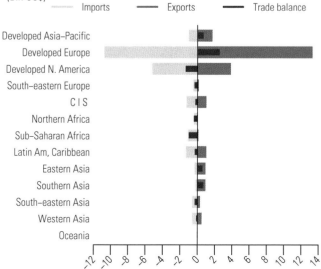

Table 2: Top exporting countries or areas in 2013

Country or area	Value (million US$)	Avg. Growth (%) 09-13	Growth (%) 12-13	World share %	Cum.
World	23793.4	10.1	-2.3	100.0	
Germany	4817.5	10.8	23.3	20.2	20.2
USA	3445.0	6.4	-28.1	14.5	34.7
Italy	2308.3	7.7	6.9	9.7	44.4
Japan	1695.7	6.7	-16.1	7.1	51.6
United Kingdom	1657.6	8.1	-1.4	7.0	58.5
France	1609.1	11.2	2.4	6.8	65.3
Austria	924.0	8.5	5.4	3.9	69.2
Belarus	877.8	11.7	-16.1	3.7	72.9
India	858.0	34.0	8.6	3.6	76.5
Brazil	520.0	3.8	2.4	2.2	78.6
China	497.2	15.9	4.9	2.1	80.7
Belgium	494.4	11.5	4.6	2.1	82.8
Mexico	475.7	32.9	19.8	2.0	84.8
Finland	461.2	2.8	-1.7	1.9	86.8
Rep. of Korea	426.9	17.5	-7.0	1.8	88.5

Table 3: Top importing countries or areas in 2013

Country or area	Value (million US$)	Avg. Growth (%) 09-13	Growth (%) 12-13	World share %	Cum.
World	23318.8	10.5	2.4	100.0	
USA	3466.5	14.8	0.8	14.9	14.9
France	2313.0	12.4	21.4	9.9	24.8
Canada	1723.8	13.0	5.3	7.4	32.2
Germany	1461.4	10.0	6.7	6.3	38.4
United Kingdom	911.4	-0.3	-10.1	3.9	42.4
Belgium	827.4	14.0	18.5	3.5	45.9
Poland	696.0	13.3	-0.8	3.0	48.9
Australia	568.8	-1.0	-25.1	2.4	51.3
Italy	564.9	4.5	5.9	2.4	53.7
Netherlands	458.9	10.6	1.3	2.0	55.7
Spain	453.1	2.3	19.5	1.9	57.7
Ukraine	426.5	49.4	12.0	1.8	59.5
Russian Federation	409.0	48.3	-15.9	1.8	61.2
Austria	401.1	6.4	-0.1	1.7	63.0
South Africa	392.0	14.3	-5.3	1.7	64.6

723 Civil engineering and contractors' plant and equipment; parts thereof

In 2013, the value (in current US$) of exports of "civil engineering and contractors' plant and equipment; parts thereof" (SITC group 723) decreased by 9.3 percent (compared to 10.1 percent average growth rate from 2009-2013) to reach 113.1 bln US$ (see table 2), while imports decreased by 12.0 percent to reach 110.1 bln US$ (see table 3). Exports of this commodity accounted for 1.9 percent of world exports of SITC section 7, and 0.6 percent of total world merchandise exports (see table 1). USA, China and Japan were the top exporters in 2013 (see table 2). They accounted for 17.4, 11.3 and 9.4 percent of world exports, respectively. USA, Canada and Russian Federation were the top destinations, with respectively 10.2, 5.1 and 4.9 percent of world imports (see table 3).

The top 15 countries/areas accounted for 80.7 and 54.0 percent of total world exports and imports, respectively (see tables 2 and 3). In 2013, Japan was the country/area with the highest value of net exports (+9.1 bln US$), followed by China (+9.1 bln US$). By MDG regions (see graph 2), the largest surpluses in this product group were recorded by Developed Europe (+16.0 bln US$), Eastern Asia (+13.1 bln US$) and Developed Asia-Pacific (+6.2 bln US$). The largest trade deficits were recorded by Sub-Saharan Africa (-8.2 bln US$), Latin America and the Caribbean (-8.1 bln US$) and Commonwealth of Independent States (-7.1 bln US$).

Table 1: Imports (Imp.) and exports (Exp.), 1999-2013, in current US$

		1999	2000	2001	2002	2003	2004	2005	2006	2007	2008	2009	2010	2011	2012	2013
Values in Bln US$	Imp.	29.1	29.6	30.8	33.7	40.6	52.2	65.8	81.7	103.3	117.5	73.5	89.9	118.6	125.2	110.1
	Exp.	31.0	32.6	34.0	36.3	43.7	56.0	69.5	84.6	108.5	125.3	77.0	95.8	123.8	124.7	113.1
As a percentage of SITC section (%)	Imp.	1.2	1.1	1.2	1.3	1.4	1.5	1.7	1.8	2.1	2.2	1.7	1.7	2.0	2.1	1.8
	Exp.	1.3	1.2	1.4	1.4	1.5	1.6	1.8	1.9	2.2	2.3	1.8	1.9	2.1	2.1	1.9
As a percentage of world trade (%)	Imp.	0.5	0.5	0.5	0.5	0.5	0.6	0.6	0.7	0.7	0.7	0.6	0.6	0.7	0.7	0.6
	Exp.	0.6	0.5	0.6	0.6	0.6	0.6	0.7	0.7	0.8	0.8	0.6	0.6	0.7	0.7	0.6

Graph 1: Annual growth rates of exports, 1999-2013
(In percentage by year)

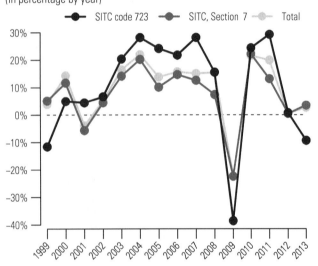

Legend: ● SITC code 723 ● SITC, Section 7 ● Total

Graph 2: Trade Balance by MDG regions 2013
(Bln US$)

Legend: Imports — Exports — Trade balance

Developed Asia–Pacific
Developed Europe
Developed N. America
South–eastern Europe
C I S
Northern Africa
Sub–Saharan Africa
Latin Am, Caribbean
Eastern Asia
Southern Asia
South–eastern Asia
Western Asia
Oceania

Table 2: Top exporting countries or areas in 2013

Country or area	Value (million US$)	Avg. Growth (%) 09-13	Growth (%) 12-13	World share %	Cum.
World	113 080.2	10.1	-9.3	100.0	
USA	19 648.4	4.7	-13.9	17.4	17.4
China	12 765.6	22.1	-5.8	11.3	28.7
Japan	10 654.9	12.9	-25.3	9.4	38.1
Germany	8 838.4	6.5	-7.6	7.8	45.9
Rep. of Korea	6 065.6	20.2	-13.7	5.4	51.3
Singapore	5 988.6	3.1	-1.2	5.3	56.6
United Kingdom	4 489.9	8.4	-6.9	4.0	60.5
Belgium	4 125.6	14.8	-4.2	3.6	64.2
Netherlands	3 891.6	9.3	-0.8	3.4	67.6
Italy	3 385.3	4.8	-2.3	3.0	70.6
France	3 358.2	5.2	-15.9	3.0	73.6
Sweden	2 167.0	14.1	-11.6	1.9	75.5
Spain	2 028.2	43.1	110.5	1.8	77.3
United Arab Emirates	*1 966.4*	21.6	21.7	1.7	79.0
Brazil	1 927.5	27.9	-19.2	1.7	80.7

Table 3: Top importing countries or areas in 2013

Country or area	Value (million US$)	Avg. Growth (%) 09-13	Growth (%) 12-13	World share %	Cum.
World	110 089.0	10.6	-12.0	100.0	
USA	11 266.8	23.0	-18.7	10.2	10.2
Canada	5 630.0	12.5	-18.5	5.1	15.3
Russian Federation	5 443.3	31.8	-15.6	4.9	20.3
Singapore	5 035.3	-0.6	-17.5	4.6	24.9
Germany	3 923.3	11.4	-7.2	3.6	28.4
China	3 653.7	-3.6	-19.4	3.3	31.7
Australia	3 339.4	13.1	-52.7	3.0	34.8
France	3 297.4	14.8	-6.2	3.0	37.8
Saudi Arabia	2 996.4	17.8	-8.1	2.7	40.5
Belgium	2 732.2	15.5	-9.3	2.5	43.0
United Kingdom	2 651.1	13.2	2.0	2.4	45.4
Netherlands	2 628.9	16.4	0.7	2.4	47.8
United Arab Emirates	*2 434.4*	4.3	11.4	2.2	50.0
Indonesia	2 297.6	10.5	-41.0	2.1	52.1
Mexico	2 170.5	2.6	-7.5	2.0	54.0

Source: UN Comtrade and UN Service Trade

In 2013, the value (in current US$) of exports of "textile and leather machinery and parts thereof, nes" (SITC group 724) increased by 8.1 percent (compared to 12.4 percent average growth rate from 2009-2013) to reach 30.8 bln US$ (see table 2), while imports increased by 6.5 percent to reach 32.4 bln US$ (see table 3). Exports of this commodity accounted for 0.5 percent of world exports of SITC section 7, and 0.2 percent of total world merchandise exports (see table 1). China, Germany and Japan were the top exporters in 2013 (see table 2). They accounted for 18.2, 16.1 and 10.1 percent of world exports, respectively. China, USA and Turkey were the top destinations, with respectively 14.2, 11.9 and 6.8 percent of world imports (see table 3).

The top 15 countries/areas accounted for 88.3 and 66.8 percent of total world exports and imports, respectively (see tables 2 and 3). In 2013, Germany was the country/area with the highest value of net exports (+4.0 bln US$), followed by Japan (+2.3 bln US$). By MDG regions (see graph 2), the largest surpluses in this product group were recorded by Developed Europe (+7.4 bln US$), Eastern Asia (+3.7 bln US$) and Developed Asia-Pacific (+2.1 bln US$). The largest trade deficits were recorded by Southern Asia (-3.5 bln US$), Developed North America (-3.0 bln US$) and Western Asia (-2.3 bln US$).

Table 1: Imports (Imp.) and exports (Exp.), 1999-2013, in current US$

		1999	2000	2001	2002	2003	2004	2005	2006	2007	2008	2009	2010	2011	2012	2013
Values in Bln US$	Imp.	18.2	20.3	19.1	21.1	23.6	25.2	25.9	27.0	30.7	29.4	20.8	27.9	33.4	30.4	32.4
	Exp.	18.1	19.6	18.5	19.7	23.0	24.5	24.8	26.9	29.8	27.3	19.3	26.7	31.5	28.5	30.8
As a percentage of SITC section (%)	Imp.	0.8	0.8	0.8	0.8	0.8	0.7	0.7	0.6	0.6	0.5	0.5	0.5	0.6	0.5	0.5
	Exp.	0.8	0.7	0.7	0.8	0.8	0.7	0.6	0.6	0.6	0.5	0.5	0.5	0.5	0.5	0.5
As a percentage of world trade (%)	Imp.	0.3	0.3	0.3	0.3	0.3	0.3	0.2	0.2	0.2	0.2	0.2	0.2	0.2	0.2	0.2
	Exp.	0.3	0.3	0.3	0.3	0.3	0.3	0.2	0.2	0.2	0.2	0.2	0.2	0.2	0.2	0.2

Graph 1: Annual growth rates of exports, 1999–2013
(In percentage by year)

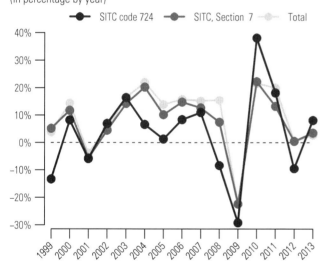

Table 2: Top exporting countries or areas in 2013

Country or area	Value (million US$)	Avg. Growth (%) 09-13	Growth (%) 12-13	World share %	Cum.
World	30 806.3	12.4	8.1	100.0	
China	5 618.2	23.4	20.3	18.2	18.2
Germany	4 968.1	11.1	1.8	16.1	34.4
Japan	3 120.6	18.1	6.6	10.1	44.5
Italy	2 914.5	8.6	3.5	9.5	54.0
Rep. of Korea	2 590.4	7.9	-4.3	8.4	62.4
USA	1 418.3	3.7	-1.4	4.6	67.0
Other Asia, nes	1 117.4	12.3	4.4	3.6	70.6
Switzerland	973.2	9.3	7.9	3.2	73.8
France	879.4	14.9	16.1	2.9	76.6
Mexico	768.7	20.0	-9.1	2.5	79.1
China, Hong Kong SAR	735.7	0.7	21.1	2.4	81.5
Singapore	667.9	20.4	23.9	2.2	83.7
Czech Rep.	504.7	11.4	8.8	1.6	85.3
Thailand	464.9	8.1	3.4	1.5	86.8
India	464.4	34.7	40.0	1.5	88.3

Graph 2: Trade Balance by MDG regions 2013
(Bln US$)

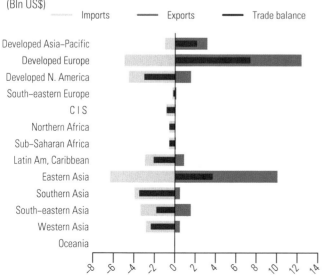

Table 3: Top importing countries or areas in 2013

Country or area	Value (million US$)	Avg. Growth (%) 09-13	Growth (%) 12-13	World share %	Cum.
World	32 379.0	11.7	6.5	100.0	
China	4 582.3	12.5	-0.3	14.2	14.2
USA	3 855.5	8.2	11.3	11.9	26.1
Turkey	2 211.2	44.6	16.1	6.8	32.9
India	2 180.6	13.9	11.8	6.7	39.6
Germany	988.7	8.4	7.2	3.1	42.7
Indonesia	973.8	30.1	-4.7	3.0	45.7
Viet Nam	925.9	16.5	33.8	2.9	48.5
China, Hong Kong SAR	840.5	3.9	15.2	2.6	51.1
Japan	832.0	11.9	15.0	2.6	53.7
Mexico	799.5	14.0	9.7	2.5	56.2
Bangladesh	799.2	9.7	-1.6	2.5	58.6
Brazil	720.8	6.3	-10.1	2.2	60.9
Canada	709.5	2.5	5.3	2.2	63.1
Italy	689.7	7.8	10.7	2.1	65.2
Singapore	512.3	18.6	7.0	1.6	66.8

725 Paper and paper manufacture machinery, and parts thereof

In 2013, the value (in current US$) of exports of "paper and paper manufacture machinery, and parts thereof" (SITC group 725) decreased by 1.0 percent (compared to 4.5 percent average growth rate from 2009-2013) to reach 11.0 bln US$ (see table 2), while imports decreased by 5.4 percent to reach 10.0 bln US$ (see table 3). Exports of this commodity accounted for 0.2 percent of world exports of SITC section 7, and 0.1 percent of total world merchandise exports (see table 1). Germany, Italy and China were the top exporters in 2013 (see table 2). They accounted for 19.4, 13.6 and 10.4 percent of world exports, respectively. USA, China and Germany were the top destinations, with respectively 9.4, 9.4 and 6.6 percent of world imports (see table 3).

The top 15 countries/areas accounted for 88.6 and 61.3 percent of total world exports and imports, respectively (see tables 2 and 3). In 2013, Germany was the country/area with the highest value of net exports (+1.5 bln US$), followed by Italy (+1.2 bln US$). By MDG regions (see graph 2), the largest surpluses in this product group were recorded by Developed Europe (+4.5 bln US$) and Eastern Asia (+411.2 mln US$). The largest trade deficits were recorded by Latin America and the Caribbean (-1.1 bln US$), South-eastern Asia (-906.3 mln US$) and Western Asia (-441.2 mln US$).

Table 1: Imports (Imp.) and exports (Exp.), 1999-2013, in current US$

		1999	2000	2001	2002	2003	2004	2005	2006	2007	2008	2009	2010	2011	2012	2013
Values in Bln US$	Imp.	6.6	6.5	6.6	6.1	7.6	8.3	9.1	9.1	11.4	12.3	9.2	9.4	11.0	10.6	10.0
	Exp.	6.6	6.9	6.7	6.6	7.7	8.7	9.3	10.0	11.8	12.1	9.2	10.1	11.5	11.1	11.0
As a percentage of SITC section (%)	Imp.	0.3	0.2	0.3	0.2	0.3	0.2	0.2	0.2	0.2	0.2	0.2	0.2	0.2	0.2	0.2
	Exp.	0.3	0.3	0.3	0.3	0.3	0.2	0.2	0.2	0.2	0.2	0.2	0.2	0.2	0.2	0.2
As a percentage of world trade (%)	Imp.	0.1	0.1	0.1	0.1	0.1	0.1	0.1	0.1	0.1	0.1	0.1	0.1	0.1	0.1	0.1
	Exp.	0.1	0.1	0.1	0.1	0.1	0.1	0.1	0.1	0.1	0.1	0.1	0.1	0.1	0.1	0.1

Graph 1: Annual growth rates of exports, 1999–2013
(In percentage by year)

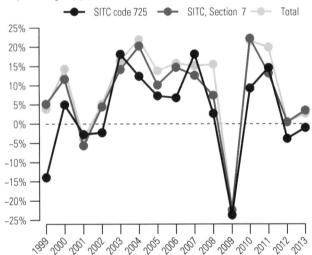

— SITC code 725   — SITC, Section 7   — Total

Table 2: Top exporting countries or areas in 2013

Country or area	Value (million US$)	Avg. Growth (%) 09-13	Growth (%) 12-13	World share %	Cum.
World.....................	10 987.7	4.5	-1.0	100.0	
Germany.................	2 132.1	-1.9	0.3	19.4	19.4
Italy.......................	1 497.9	5.8	2.8	13.6	33.0
China.....................	1 138.8	26.6	29.8	10.4	43.4
Finland...................	784.3	-4.9	-12.7	7.1	50.5
USA.......................	694.2	5.0	-5.0	6.3	56.9
France....................	587.0	6.1	13.1	5.3	62.2
Switzerland.............	538.0	3.5	6.6	4.9	67.1
Sweden..................	491.7	5.0	-26.5	4.5	71.6
Other Asia, nes........	331.9	15.6	1.6	3.0	74.6
Austria...................	315.4	-8.8	-28.8	2.9	77.5
Japan.....................	303.7	8.2	-27.0	2.8	80.2
Spain.....................	261.9	5.3	5.7	2.4	82.6
United Kingdom........	244.3	5.6	24.7	2.2	84.8
Netherlands.............	208.9	8.9	21.5	1.9	86.7
Denmark.................	206.2	35.0	253.3	1.9	88.6

Graph 2: Trade Balance by MDG regions 2013
(Bln US$)

— Imports   — Exports   — Trade balance

Developed Asia–Pacific
Developed Europe
Developed N. America
South–eastern Europe
CIS
Northern Africa
Sub–Saharan Africa
Latin Am, Caribbean
Eastern Asia
Southern Asia
South–eastern Asia
Western Asia
Oceania

-4 -3 -2 -1 0 1 2 3 4 5 6 7 8

Table 3: Top importing countries or areas in 2013

Country or area	Value (million US$)	Avg. Growth (%) 09-13	Growth (%) 12-13	World share %	Cum.
World.....................	10 033.7	2.2	-5.4	100.0	
USA.......................	947.0	4.4	-21.7	9.4	9.4
China.....................	944.3	-5.8	-23.0	9.4	18.8
Germany.................	664.2	-1.8	8.7	6.6	25.5
Indonesia...............	533.4	19.7	-11.5	5.3	30.8
France....................	421.1	4.3	8.6	4.2	35.0
Brazil.....................	392.7	9.1	22.6	3.9	38.9
Russian Federation...	326.1	3.1	0.3	3.2	42.1
Mexico...................	290.6	16.7	24.2	2.9	45.0
Turkey....................	255.3	18.1	11.5	2.5	47.6
Italy.......................	252.8	-2.8	0.8	2.5	50.1
United Kingdom........	244.9	5.2	8.7	2.4	52.5
Canada...................	242.2	2.9	-6.1	2.4	55.0
Poland....................	234.2	11.7	48.8	2.3	57.3
Sweden..................	206.7	7.7	26.8	2.1	59.4
India......................	199.4	-4.7	-34.0	2.0	61.3

In 2013, the value (in current US$) of exports of "printing and bookbinding machinery and parts thereof" (SITC group 726) decreased by 1.0 percent (compared to 2.8 percent average growth rate from 2009-2013) to reach 14.7 bln US$ (see table 2), while imports decreased by 2.3 percent to reach 14.6 bln US$ (see table 3). Exports of this commodity accounted for 0.2 percent of world exports of SITC section 7, and 0.1 percent of total world merchandise exports (see table 1). Germany, Japan and USA were the top exporters in 2013 (see table 2). They accounted for 27.7, 6.9 and 6.5 percent of world exports, respectively. China, USA and Germany were the top destinations, with respectively 10.4, 7.5 and 5.9 percent of world imports (see table 3).

The top 15 countries/areas accounted for 83.3 and 57.5 percent of total world exports and imports, respectively (see tables 2 and 3). In 2013, Germany was the country/area with the highest value of net exports (+3.2 bln US$), followed by Japan (+731.5 mln US$). By MDG regions (see graph 2), the largest surpluses in this product group were recorded by Developed Europe (+4.8 bln US$), Developed Asia-Pacific (+553.6 mln US$) and Western Asia (+28.9 mln US$). The largest trade deficits were recorded by Eastern Asia (-1.2 bln US$), Latin America and the Caribbean (-1.2 bln US$) and South-eastern Asia (-922.8 mln US$).

Table 1: Imports (Imp.) and exports (Exp.), 1999-2013, in current US$

		1999	2000	2001	2002	2003	2004	2005	2006	2007	2008	2009	2010	2011	2012	2013
Values in Bln US$	Imp.	13.8	13.9	13.8	13.0	14.0	16.5	18.4	20.0	19.5	19.2	13.7	15.3	16.3	14.9	14.6
	Exp.	14.3	14.3	14.3	13.2	14.0	16.4	18.5	20.4	19.3	19.9	13.2	14.8	15.8	14.8	14.7
As a percentage of	Imp.	0.6	0.5	0.6	0.5	0.5	0.5	0.5	0.4	0.4	0.4	0.3	0.3	0.3	0.3	0.2
SITC section (%)	Exp.	0.6	0.5	0.6	0.5	0.5	0.5	0.5	0.5	0.4	0.4	0.3	0.3	0.3	0.3	0.2
As a percentage of	Imp.	0.2	0.2	0.2	0.2	0.2	0.2	0.2	0.2	0.1	0.1	0.1	0.1	0.1	0.1	0.1
world trade (%)	Exp.	0.3	0.2	0.2	0.2	0.2	0.2	0.2	0.2	0.1	0.1	0.1	0.1	0.1	0.1	0.1

Graph 1: Annual growth rates of exports, 1999–2013
(In percentage by year)

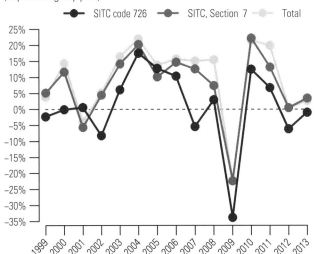

Table 2: Top exporting countries or areas in 2013

Country or area	Value (million US$)	Avg. Growth (%) 09-13	Growth (%) 12-13	World share %	Cum.
World	14697.2	2.8	-1.0	100.0	
Germany	4078.1	-0.9	-6.1	27.7	27.7
Japan	1016.8	1.1	3.4	6.9	34.7
USA	948.0	-2.6	-9.6	6.5	41.1
Italy	904.2	10.6	9.1	6.2	47.3
Israel	814.2	33.7	13.3	5.5	52.8
Switzerland	718.8	-2.1	-9.2	4.9	57.7
Belgium	682.5	2.5	8.0	4.6	62.3
United Kingdom	621.4	8.0	-3.7	4.2	66.6
China	535.1	11.6	1.4	3.6	70.2
France	410.8	-5.8	-16.5	2.8	73.0
Netherlands	392.1	-7.6	-5.9	2.7	75.7
China, Hong Kong SAR	308.9	3.1	-13.4	2.1	77.8
Austria	296.5	-2.9	-5.7	2.0	79.8
Other Asia, nes	275.5	10.1	-4.4	1.9	81.7
Philippines	245.6	260.8	294.9	1.7	83.3

Graph 2: Trade Balance by MDG regions 2013
(Bln US$)

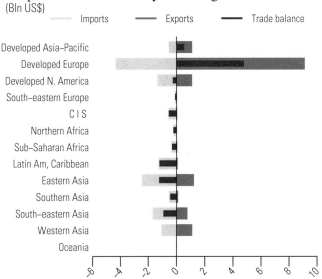

Table 3: Top importing countries or areas in 2013

Country or area	Value (million US$)	Avg. Growth (%) 09-13	Growth (%) 12-13	World share %	Cum.
World	14605.0	1.6	-2.3	100.0	
China	1521.2	8.2	-6.9	10.4	10.4
USA	1088.5	2.1	1.2	7.5	17.9
Germany	860.1	-1.4	-10.4	5.9	23.8
Indonesia	716.6	7.4	-15.0	4.9	28.7
Belgium	533.6	-3.9	-2.0	3.7	32.3
China, Hong Kong SAR	503.9	2.6	3.7	3.4	35.8
France	422.8	-5.9	-20.6	2.9	38.7
United Arab Emirates	417.2	3.1	11.4	2.9	41.5
Brazil	370.1	-4.7	-19.9	2.5	44.1
United Kingdom	363.9	-1.2	-13.0	2.5	46.5
Russian Federation	363.4	15.2	16.5	2.5	49.0
Mexico	326.5	8.2	34.3	2.2	51.3
Italy	309.0	-8.7	-3.9	2.1	53.4
Malaysia	297.8	7.8	-10.0	2.0	55.4
India	297.1	2.4	-22.1	2.0	57.5

727 Food- processing machines (excluding domestic); parts thereof

In 2013, the value (in current US$) of exports of "food- processing machines (excluding domestic); parts thereof" (SITC group 727) increased by 7.3 percent (compared to 9.9 percent average growth rate from 2009-2013) to reach 16.2 bln US$ (see table 2), while imports increased by 3.9 percent to reach 15.4 bln US$ (see table 3). Exports of this commodity accounted for 0.3 percent of world exports of SITC section 7, and 0.1 percent of total world merchandise exports (see table 1). Germany, Italy and Netherlands were the top exporters in 2013 (see table 2). They accounted for 17.1, 13.9 and 11.1 percent of world exports, respectively. USA, Russian Federation and Germany were the top destinations, with respectively 8.1, 6.5 and 3.4 percent of world imports (see table 3).

The top 15 countries/areas accounted for 83.0 and 49.5 percent of total world exports and imports, respectively (see tables 2 and 3). In 2013, Germany was the country/area with the highest value of net exports (+2.2 bln US$), followed by Italy (+2.0 bln US$). By MDG regions (see graph 2), the largest surpluses in this product group were recorded by Developed Europe (+7.0 bln US$), Eastern Asia (+462.5 mln US$) and Developed Asia-Pacific (+1.2 mln US$). The largest trade deficits were recorded by Latin America and the Caribbean (-1.5 bln US$), Commonwealth of Independent States (-1.4 bln US$) and Sub-Saharan Africa (-1.1 bln US$).

Table 1: Imports (Imp.) and exports (Exp.), 1999-2013, in current US$

		1999	2000	2001	2002	2003	2004	2005	2006	2007	2008	2009	2010	2011	2012	2013
Values in Bln US$	Imp.	5.8	5.5	5.6	5.9	6.9	8.1	8.9	9.7	11.6	12.6	10.7	11.5	14.5	14.8	15.4
	Exp.	5.8	5.6	5.6	6.2	7.3	8.6	9.3	10.5	12.7	14.2	11.1	12.0	15.0	15.1	16.2
As a percentage of SITC section (%)	Imp.	0.2	0.2	0.2	0.2	0.2	0.2	0.2	0.2	0.2	0.2	0.3	0.2	0.2	0.2	0.3
	Exp.	0.2	0.2	0.2	0.2	0.2	0.2	0.2	0.2	0.3	0.3	0.3	0.2	0.3	0.3	0.3
As a percentage of world trade (%)	Imp.	0.1	0.1	0.1	0.1	0.1	0.1	0.1	0.1	0.1	0.1	0.1	0.1	0.1	0.1	0.1
	Exp.	0.1	0.1	0.1	0.1	0.1	0.1	0.1	0.1	0.1	0.1	0.1	0.1	0.1	0.1	0.1

Graph 1: Annual growth rates of exports, 1999–2013
(In percentage by year)

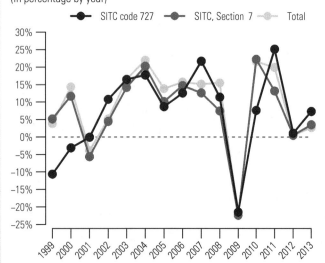

Table 2: Top exporting countries or areas in 2013

Country or area	Value (million US$)	Avg. Growth (%) 09-13	Growth (%) 12-13	World share %	Cum.
World	16 233.8	9.9	7.3	100.0	
Germany	2 774.3	6.3	7.5	17.1	17.1
Italy	2 260.0	8.6	6.0	13.9	31.0
Netherlands	1 809.3	10.7	4.0	11.1	42.2
USA	1 066.0	8.5	0.6	6.6	48.7
China	1 047.2	21.5	20.8	6.5	55.2
Switzerland	754.8	5.5	6.9	4.6	59.8
Denmark	656.8	9.7	3.4	4.0	63.9
France	608.4	1.9	-0.4	3.7	67.6
Spain	448.8	13.9	30.8	2.8	70.4
Belgium	389.7	7.1	15.7	2.4	72.8
Austria	388.2	10.3	26.4	2.4	75.2
United Kingdom	346.2	7.3	2.1	2.1	77.3
Turkey	325.6	11.8	5.5	2.0	79.3
Japan	316.5	14.3	-10.0	1.9	81.3
Malaysia	278.0	19.4	3.3	1.7	83.0

Graph 2: Trade Balance by MDG regions 2013
(Bln US$)

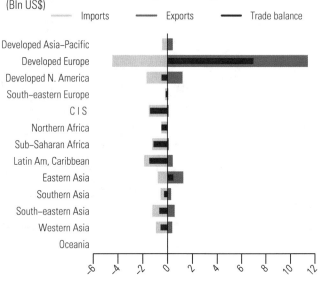

Table 3: Top importing countries or areas in 2013

Country or area	Value (million US$)	Avg. Growth (%) 09-13	Growth (%) 12-13	World share %	Cum.
World	15 415.2	9.6	3.9	100.0	
USA	1 245.8	14.8	18.5	8.1	8.1
Russian Federation	1 006.3	24.0	0.3	6.5	14.6
Germany	527.2	4.3	2.6	3.4	18.0
Indonesia	522.5	29.6	-10.0	3.4	21.4
China	492.0	18.1	3.4	3.2	24.6
Venezuela	474.4	15.6	-0.3	3.1	27.7
France	446.6	1.6	-5.5	2.9	30.6
United Kingdom	445.0	7.7	4.6	2.9	33.5
Canada	443.9	8.9	40.7	2.9	36.4
Netherlands	431.3	18.3	-0.4	2.8	39.1
Mexico	358.4	11.5	32.8	2.3	41.5
Turkey	345.0	23.6	8.5	2.2	43.7
Spain	301.6	-1.8	31.4	2.0	45.7
Brazil	295.4	16.7	7.8	1.9	47.6
Saudi Arabia	288.5	14.5	63.3	1.9	49.5

Other machinery, equipment, for specialized industries; parts nes 728

In 2013, the value (in current US$) of exports of "other machinery, equipment, for specialized industries; parts nes" (SITC group 728) decreased by 0.9 percent (compared to 10.9 percent average growth rate from 2009-2013) to reach 171.6 bln US$ (see table 2), while imports decreased by 0.7 percent to reach 169.7 bln US$ (see table 3). Exports of this commodity accounted for 2.8 percent of world exports of SITC section 7, and 0.9 percent of total world merchandise exports (see table 1). Germany, Japan and USA were the top exporters in 2013 (see table 2). They accounted for 14.9, 14.0 and 12.1 percent of world exports, respectively. China, USA and Other Asia, nes were the top destinations, with respectively 13.5, 10.4 and 8.1 percent of world imports (see table 3).

The top 15 countries/areas accounted for 85.1 and 66.2 percent of total world exports and imports, respectively (see tables 2 and 3). In 2013, Japan was the country/area with the highest value of net exports (+19.6 bln US$), followed by Germany (+17.9 bln US$). By MDG regions (see graph 2), the largest surpluses in this product group were recorded by Developed Europe (+40.8 bln US$), Developed Asia-Pacific (+18.3 bln US$) and Developed North America (+2.8 bln US$). The largest trade deficits were recorded by Eastern Asia (-21.6 bln US$), Latin America and the Caribbean (-9.5 bln US$) and Commonwealth of Independent States (-7.8 bln US$).

Table 1: Imports (Imp.) and exports (Exp.), 1999-2013, in current US$

		1999	2000	2001	2002	2003	2004	2005	2006	2007	2008	2009	2010	2011	2012	2013
Values in Bln US$	Imp.	61.9	72.3	63.1	62.1	73.0	95.5	99.7	110.2	141.8	153.6	115.8	159.6	191.6	170.9	169.7
	Exp.	61.8	74.3	63.0	61.5	73.4	94.2	97.9	110.6	147.9	160.7	113.2	159.7	190.0	173.2	171.6
As a percentage of	Imp.	2.6	2.8	2.5	2.4	2.5	2.7	2.5	2.5	2.8	2.9	2.7	3.1	3.2	2.9	2.8
SITC section (%)	Exp.	2.6	2.8	2.6	2.4	2.5	2.7	2.5	2.5	2.9	3.0	2.7	3.1	3.3	3.0	2.8
As a percentage of	Imp.	1.1	1.1	1.0	0.9	1.0	1.0	0.9	0.9	1.0	0.9	0.9	1.0	1.1	0.9	0.9
world trade (%)	Exp.	1.1	1.2	1.0	1.0	1.0	1.0	0.9	0.9	1.1	1.0	0.9	1.1	1.1	1.0	0.9

Graph 1: Annual growth rates of exports, 1999–2013
(In percentage by year)

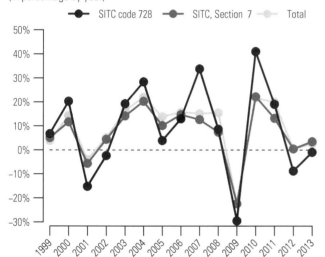

Table 2: Top exporting countries or areas in 2013

Country or area	Value (million US$)	Avg. Growth (%) 09-13	Growth (%) 12-13	World share %	Cum.
World	171 593.1	10.9	-0.9	100.0	
Germany	25 578.2	6.9	2.4	14.9	14.9
Japan	23 985.9	10.5	-19.3	14.0	28.9
USA	20 734.0	11.4	2.5	12.1	41.0
Italy	12 260.5	4.3	1.9	7.1	48.1
China	12 235.2	20.1	10.4	7.1	55.2
Netherlands	9 569.9	21.1	12.1	5.6	60.8
Rep. of Korea	9 363.6	22.1	20.8	5.5	66.3
Singapore	7 014.7	30.2	-11.1	4.1	70.4
Other Asia, nes	4 672.0	13.7	2.5	2.7	73.1
Austria	4 203.1	8.6	-1.6	2.4	75.5
United Kingdom	3 794.3	8.6	0.2	2.2	77.7
Switzerland	3 480.8	0.6	-5.1	2.0	79.8
France	3 414.5	4.4	-0.5	2.0	81.8
Canada	2 934.4	5.1	-3.5	1.7	83.5
China, Hong Kong SAR	2 700.0	24.7	-7.5	1.6	85.1

Graph 2: Trade Balance by MDG regions 2013
(Bln US$)

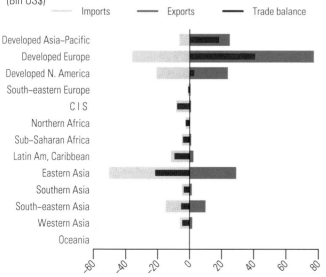

Table 3: Top importing countries or areas in 2013

Country or area	Value (million US$)	Avg. Growth (%) 09-13	Growth (%) 12-13	World share %	Cum.
World	169 738.5	10.0	-0.7	100.0	
China	22 997.8	11.8	0.3	13.5	13.5
USA	17 654.3	14.6	-4.3	10.4	23.9
Other Asia, nes	13 801.5	14.7	13.8	8.1	32.1
Rep. of Korea	11 209.4	8.1	-12.1	6.6	38.7
Germany	7 691.4	7.4	0.0	4.5	43.2
Russian Federation	6 422.0	18.2	11.8	3.8	47.0
Singapore	4 717.2	11.5	-6.6	2.8	49.8
Mexico	4 488.9	15.3	12.0	2.6	52.4
Japan	4 411.1	9.6	6.0	2.6	55.0
France	3 507.9	2.4	-0.8	2.1	57.1
Netherlands	3 462.8	20.3	7.6	2.0	59.1
Canada	3 216.3	10.3	-2.2	1.9	61.0
Brazil	3 008.1	16.4	5.9	1.8	62.8
India	2 999.7	0.9	-14.3	1.8	64.6
Malaysia	2 716.2	10.5	-4.2	1.6	66.2

731 Machine tools working by removing metal or other material

In 2013, the value (in current US$) of exports of "machine tools working by removing metal or other material" (SITC group 731) decreased by 12.4 percent (compared to 14.1 percent average growth rate from 2009-2013) to reach 36.2 bln US$ (see table 2), while imports decreased by 13.7 percent to reach 35.6 bln US$ (see table 3). Exports of this commodity accounted for 0.6 percent of world exports of SITC section 7, and 0.2 percent of total world merchandise exports (see table 1). Germany, Japan and Other Asia, nes were the top exporters in 2013 (see table 2). They accounted for 22.5, 21.7 and 7.9 percent of world exports, respectively. China, USA and Germany were the top destinations, with respectively 22.3, 12.8 and 7.1 percent of world imports (see table 3).

The top 15 countries/areas accounted for 92.3 and 73.6 percent of total world exports and imports, respectively (see tables 2 and 3). In 2013, Japan was the country/area with the highest value of net exports (+7.2 bln US$), followed by Germany (+5.6 bln US$). By MDG regions (see graph 2), the largest surpluses in this product group were recorded by Developed Europe (+8.5 bln US$) and Developed Asia-Pacific (+7.0 bln US$). The largest trade deficits were recorded by Eastern Asia (-3.4 bln US$), Developed North America (-2.8 bln US$) and South-eastern Asia (-2.2 bln US$).

Table 1: Imports (Imp.) and exports (Exp.), 1999-2013, in current US$

		1999	2000	2001	2002	2003	2004	2005	2006	2007	2008	2009	2010	2011	2012	2013
Values in Bln US$	Imp.	16.8	19.0	18.2	16.0	18.1	24.0	27.4	32.0	33.6	37.0	21.2	26.3	38.1	41.3	35.6
	Exp.	16.7	18.6	17.6	15.9	18.1	23.7	27.3	32.1	32.7	36.9	21.4	26.9	38.3	41.3	36.2
As a percentage of SITC section (%)	Imp.	0.7	0.7	0.7	0.6	0.6	0.7	0.7	0.7	0.7	0.7	0.5	0.5	0.6	0.7	0.6
	Exp.	0.7	0.7	0.7	0.6	0.6	0.7	0.7	0.7	0.7	0.7	0.5	0.5	0.7	0.7	0.6
As a percentage of world trade (%)	Imp.	0.3	0.3	0.3	0.2	0.2	0.3	0.3	0.3	0.2	0.2	0.2	0.2	0.2	0.2	0.2
	Exp.	0.3	0.3	0.3	0.2	0.2	0.3	0.3	0.3	0.2	0.2	0.2	0.2	0.2	0.2	0.2

Graph 1: Annual growth rates of exports, 1999–2013
(In percentage by year)

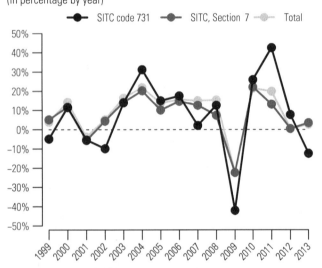

Graph 2: Trade Balance by MDG regions 2013
(Bln US$)

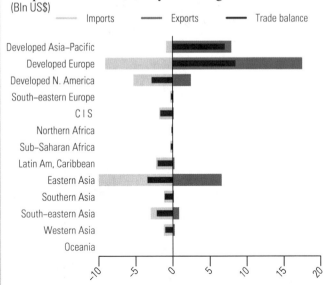

Table 2: Top exporting countries or areas in 2013

Country or area	Value (million US$)	Avg. Growth (%) 09-13	Growth (%) 12-13	World share %	World share % Cum.
World	36 173.4	14.1	-12.4	100.0	
Germany	8 140.9	11.2	2.5	22.5	22.5
Japan	7 856.1	22.9	-33.7	21.7	44.2
Other Asia, nes	2 857.3	21.2	-19.6	7.9	52.1
Italy	2 502.8	7.2	-4.1	6.9	59.0
USA	2 335.9	15.0	0.5	6.5	65.5
Switzerland	2 288.1	11.5	-6.2	6.3	71.8
China	1 883.4	18.5	1.3	5.2	77.0
Rep. of Korea	1 581.7	16.4	-12.4	4.4	81.4
Belgium	733.1	14.3	8.3	2.0	83.4
Spain	699.2	6.7	12.0	1.9	85.4
Czech Rep.	679.9	6.3	-3.0	1.9	87.2
United Kingdom	606.1	11.8	3.4	1.7	88.9
Austria	457.6	3.6	3.2	1.3	90.2
Singapore	404.5	17.4	-25.9	1.1	91.3
France	364.1	4.0	-9.2	1.0	92.3

Table 3: Top importing countries or areas in 2013

Country or area	Value (million US$)	Avg. Growth (%) 09-13	Growth (%) 12-13	World share %	World share % Cum.
World	35 604.4	13.8	-13.7	100.0	
China	7 953.3	14.9	-28.8	22.3	22.3
USA	4 540.9	23.9	-12.8	12.8	35.1
Germany	2 514.8	7.9	-4.2	7.1	42.2
Russian Federation	1 317.9	17.7	5.6	3.7	45.9
Rep. of Korea	1 241.7	11.3	4.8	3.5	49.3
Mexico	1 205.7	22.8	-1.9	3.4	52.7
Thailand	1 179.1	28.1	-42.4	3.3	56.0
India	1 034.6	10.7	-29.2	2.9	58.9
Italy	828.3	3.9	12.8	2.3	61.3
Turkey	789.7	26.9	-6.1	2.2	63.5
Belgium	762.0	11.0	11.6	2.1	65.6
Canada	753.1	18.6	-6.0	2.1	67.7
France	720.8	4.3	-3.8	2.0	69.8
United Kingdom	682.9	13.6	0.6	1.9	71.7
Indonesia	676.4	37.1	16.1	1.9	73.6

In 2013, the value (in current US$) of exports of "machine tools for working metal, sintered metal carbides or cermets" (SITC group 733) decreased by 3.2 percent (compared to 9.7 percent average growth rate from 2009-2013) to reach 13.2 bln US$ (see table 2), while imports decreased by 6.9 percent to reach 13.1 bln US$ (see table 3). Exports of this commodity accounted for 0.2 percent of world exports of SITC section 7, and 0.1 percent of total world merchandise exports (see table 1). Germany, Italy and Japan were the top exporters in 2013 (see table 2). They accounted for 17.8, 13.2 and 13.1 percent of world exports, respectively. China, USA and Thailand were the top destinations, with respectively 16.2, 8.5 and 6.2 percent of world imports (see table 3).

The top 15 countries/areas accounted for 87.9 and 69.2 percent of total world exports and imports, respectively (see tables 2 and 3). In 2013, Germany was the country/area with the highest value of net exports (+1.9 bln US$), followed by Italy (+1.6 bln US$). By MDG regions (see graph 2), the largest surpluses in this product group were recorded by Developed Europe (+4.6 bln US$) and Developed Asia-Pacific (+1.5 bln US$). The largest trade deficits were recorded by South-eastern Asia (-1.7 bln US$), Latin America and the Caribbean (-1.5 bln US$) and Commonwealth of Independent States (-808.2 mln US$).

Table 1: Imports (Imp.) and exports (Exp.), 1999-2013, in current US$

		1999	2000	2001	2002	2003	2004	2005	2006	2007	2008	2009	2010	2011	2012	2013
Values in Bln US$	Imp.	6.3	6.6	6.3	5.9	6.8	8.3	9.7	10.8	12.4	13.8	9.5	10.1	13.4	14.0	13.1
	Exp.	6.2	6.5	6.1	5.7	6.6	7.9	9.0	10.2	12.3	13.4	9.1	9.8	13.1	13.6	13.2
As a percentage of SITC section (%)	Imp.	0.3	0.3	0.3	0.2	0.2	0.2	0.2	0.2	0.2	0.3	0.2	0.2	0.2	0.2	0.2
	Exp.	0.3	0.2	0.2	0.2	0.2	0.2	0.2	0.2	0.2	0.2	0.2	0.2	0.2	0.2	0.2
As a percentage of world trade (%)	Imp.	0.1	0.1	0.1	0.1	0.1	0.1	0.1	0.1	0.1	0.1	0.1	0.1	0.1	0.1	0.1
	Exp.	0.1	0.1	0.1	0.1	0.1	0.1	0.1	0.1	0.1	0.1	0.1	0.1	0.1	0.1	0.1

Graph 1: Annual growth rates of exports, 1999–2013
(In percentage by year)

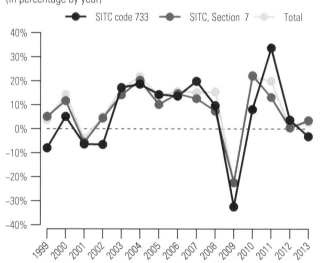

Table 2: Top exporting countries or areas in 2013

Country or area	Value (million US$)	Avg. Growth (%) 09-13	Growth (%) 12-13	World share %	Cum.
World	13 159.9	9.7	-3.2	100.0	
Germany	2 348.2	6.5	-6.3	17.8	17.8
Italy	1 731.5	3.8	-4.6	13.2	31.0
Japan	1 727.3	17.3	-14.4	13.1	44.1
China	975.2	20.8	10.5	7.4	51.5
USA	887.0	8.3	-8.3	6.7	58.3
Rep. of Korea	673.6	17.8	-8.6	5.1	63.4
Other Asia, nes	672.2	12.5	-1.1	5.1	68.5
Spain	448.2	14.8	17.5	3.4	71.9
Austria	445.9	15.7	16.0	3.4	75.3
Switzerland	436.4	5.4	5.7	3.3	78.6
Turkey	322.7	9.3	1.4	2.5	81.1
France	284.5	5.5	-0.3	2.2	83.2
Belgium	277.9	1.3	21.2	2.1	85.3
United Kingdom	191.6	5.3	-10.1	1.5	86.8
Sweden	147.8	11.9	-0.6	1.1	87.9

Graph 2: Trade Balance by MDG regions 2013
(Bln US$)

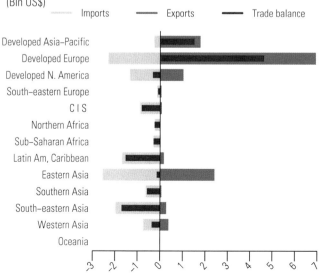

Table 3: Top importing countries or areas in 2013

Country or area	Value (million US$)	Avg. Growth (%) 09-13	Growth (%) 12-13	World share %	Cum.
World	13 067.8	8.2	-6.9	100.0	
China	2 112.7	12.1	-15.1	16.2	16.2
USA	1 113.9	18.5	5.6	8.5	24.7
Thailand	813.9	29.8	-17.1	6.2	30.9
Mexico	768.3	18.7	39.2	5.9	36.8
Russian Federation	626.2	12.8	-2.7	4.8	41.6
Brazil	607.9	9.6	25.5	4.7	46.2
Indonesia	556.2	41.0	19.8	4.3	50.5
India	528.5	0.9	-37.7	4.0	54.5
Germany	439.0	5.0	-12.9	3.4	57.9
Turkey	314.1	13.1	-12.2	2.4	60.3
Rep. of Korea	264.6	-5.0	-8.5	2.0	62.3
Viet Nam	255.0	5.8	-26.2	2.0	64.3
Canada	228.3	8.9	3.3	1.7	66.0
France	213.5	-1.0	-0.3	1.6	67.7
Saudi Arabia	207.2	0.9	13.3	1.6	69.2

735 Parts, nes, accessories suitable for use with machines falling within 731&733

In 2013, the value (in current US$) of exports of "parts, nes, accessories suitable for use with machines falling within 731&733" (SITC group 735) decreased by 6.0 percent (compared to 10.9 percent average growth rate from 2009-2013) to reach 15.7 bln US$ (see table 2), while imports decreased by 5.9 percent to reach 15.6 bln US$ (see table 3). Exports of this commodity accounted for 0.3 percent of world exports of SITC section 7, and 0.1 percent of total world merchandise exports (see table 1). Germany, USA and Japan were the top exporters in 2013 (see table 2). They accounted for 20.1, 11.4 and 9.5 percent of world exports, respectively. USA, China and Germany were the top destinations, with respectively 13.2, 10.5 and 9.8 percent of world imports (see table 3).

The top 15 countries/areas accounted for 84.4 and 70.3 percent of total world exports and imports, respectively (see tables 2 and 3). In 2013, Germany was the country/area with the highest value of net exports (+1.6 bln US$), followed by Japan (+892.8 mln US$). By MDG regions (see graph 2), the largest surpluses in this product group were recorded by Developed Europe (+2.4 bln US$) and Developed Asia-Pacific (+830.7 mln US$). The largest trade deficits were recorded by Latin America and the Caribbean (-785.6 mln US$), South-eastern Asia (-458.0 mln US$) and Developed North America (-396.7 mln US$).

Table 1: Imports (Imp.) and exports (Exp.), 1999-2013, in current US$

		1999	2000	2001	2002	2003	2004	2005	2006	2007	2008	2009	2010	2011	2012	2013
Values in Bln US$	Imp.	7.0	7.6	7.3	6.7	8.1	9.9	11.0	12.4	13.5	15.6	9.6	12.3	16.6	16.6	15.6
	Exp.	7.5	8.3	7.5	7.3	8.6	10.6	11.8	13.2	13.7	16.4	10.4	13.0	16.9	16.7	15.7
As a percentage of SITC section (%)	Imp.	0.3	0.3	0.3	0.3	0.3	0.3	0.3	0.3	0.3	0.3	0.2	0.2	0.3	0.3	0.3
	Exp.	0.3	0.3	0.3	0.3	0.3	0.3	0.3	0.3	0.3	0.3	0.2	0.3	0.3	0.3	0.3
As a percentage of world trade (%)	Imp.	0.1	0.1	0.1	0.1	0.1	0.1	0.1	0.1	0.1	0.1	0.1	0.1	0.1	0.1	0.1
	Exp.	0.1	0.1	0.1	0.1	0.1	0.1	0.1	0.1	0.1	0.1	0.1	0.1	0.1	0.1	0.1

Graph 1: Annual growth rates of exports, 1999–2013
(In percentage by year)

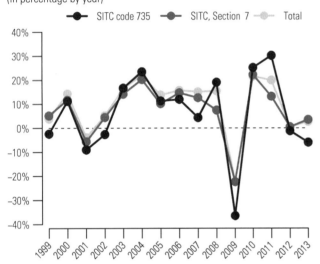

— SITC code 735   — SITC, Section 7   — Total

Table 2: Top exporting countries or areas in 2013

Country or area	Value (million US$)	Avg. Growth (%) 09-13	Growth (%) 12-13	World share %	Cum.
World................................	15711.6	10.9	-6.0	100.0	
Germany.............................	3156.5	12.0	-1.2	20.1	20.1
USA..................................	1790.7	9.3	-0.4	11.4	31.5
Japan...............................	1488.5	15.7	-29.5	9.5	41.0
Italy................................	1044.9	8.6	-2.6	6.7	47.6
Switzerland........................	1023.9	9.4	-6.5	6.5	54.1
China...............................	768.6	14.2	-16.2	4.9	59.0
Other Asia, nes....................	687.7	20.1	-8.9	4.4	63.4
Netherlands........................	541.2	14.4	-3.4	3.4	66.8
France..............................	464.0	-3.5	-17.6	3.0	69.8
Rep. of Korea......................	443.7	16.2	3.6	2.8	72.6
Belgium.............................	415.2	13.6	6.3	2.6	75.3
Sweden..............................	402.8	13.6	-3.8	2.6	77.8
United Kingdom.....................	374.0	7.4	-4.5	2.4	80.2
Spain...............................	336.0	6.9	19.1	2.1	82.3
Austria.............................	326.0	5.6	-4.8	2.1	84.4

Graph 2: Trade Balance by MDG regions 2013
(Bln US$)

— Imports   — Exports   — Trade balance

Developed Asia–Pacific
Developed Europe
Developed N. America
South–eastern Europe
CIS
Northern Africa
Sub–Saharan Africa
Latin Am, Caribbean
Eastern Asia
Southern Asia
South–eastern Asia
Western Asia
Oceania

-8 -6 -4 -2 0 2 4 6 8 10

Table 3: Top importing countries or areas in 2013

Country or area	Value (million US$)	Avg. Growth (%) 09-13	Growth (%) 12-13	World share %	Cum.
World................................	15626.6	12.9	-5.9	100.0	
USA..................................	2062.4	19.5	-2.3	13.2	13.2
China...............................	1642.6	14.5	-17.3	10.5	23.7
Germany.............................	1525.6	10.9	-1.6	9.8	33.5
France..............................	644.0	8.0	-6.6	4.1	37.6
Japan...............................	595.7	13.7	-26.3	3.8	41.4
Switzerland........................	561.4	8.8	-3.6	3.6	45.0
Netherlands........................	541.5	17.2	-0.6	3.5	48.5
Mexico..............................	526.7	16.5	1.6	3.4	51.8
Italy................................	503.2	6.9	1.5	3.2	55.1
United Kingdom.....................	470.1	8.4	-5.4	3.0	58.1
India...............................	415.8	14.1	2.1	2.7	60.7
Belgium.............................	400.5	12.9	14.6	2.6	63.3
Rep. of Korea......................	380.8	11.5	-3.7	2.4	65.7
Canada..............................	361.6	8.8	-9.8	2.3	68.0
Austria.............................	346.3	6.5	-3.5	2.2	70.3

Metalworking machinery and parts thereof, nes 737

In 2013, the value (in current US$) of exports of "metalworking machinery and parts thereof, nes" (SITC group 737) increased by 0.4 percent (compared to 3.8 percent average growth rate from 2009-2013) to reach 21.7 bln US$ (see table 2), while imports decreased by 5.4 percent to reach 21.3 bln US$ (see table 3). Exports of this commodity accounted for 0.4 percent of world exports of SITC section 7, and 0.1 percent of total world merchandise exports (see table 1). Germany, China and Japan were the top exporters in 2013 (see table 2). They accounted for 16.6, 15.2 and 10.0 percent of world exports, respectively. USA, China and Mexico were the top destinations, with respectively 11.5, 9.7 and 4.9 percent of world imports (see table 3).

The top 15 countries/areas accounted for 83.9 and 61.5 percent of total world exports and imports, respectively (see tables 2 and 3). In 2013, Germany was the country/area with the highest value of net exports (+2.6 bln US$), followed by Japan (+1.9 bln US$). By MDG regions (see graph 2), the largest surpluses in this product group were recorded by Developed Europe (+5.7 bln US$), Developed Asia-Pacific (+1.7 bln US$) and Eastern Asia (+938.4 mln US$). The largest trade deficits were recorded by Latin America and the Caribbean (-2.0 bln US$), South-eastern Asia (-1.4 bln US$) and Western Asia (-1.1 bln US$).

Table 1: Imports (Imp.) and exports (Exp.), 1999-2013, in current US$

		1999	2000	2001	2002	2003	2004	2005	2006	2007	2008	2009	2010	2011	2012	2013
Values in Bln US$	Imp.	10.2	10.1	9.1	9.3	11.0	13.9	15.7	18.5	20.3	23.4	19.5	19.7	22.4	22.6	21.3
	Exp.	9.4	9.8	9.0	9.0	10.8	14.0	15.9	19.0	20.8	24.4	18.7	19.7	22.1	21.6	21.7
As a percentage of SITC section (%)	Imp.	0.4	0.4	0.4	0.4	0.4	0.4	0.4	0.4	0.4	0.4	0.5	0.4	0.4	0.4	0.3
	Exp.	0.4	0.4	0.4	0.3	0.4	0.4	0.4	0.4	0.4	0.5	0.4	0.4	0.4	0.4	0.4
As a percentage of world trade (%)	Imp.	0.2	0.2	0.1	0.1	0.1	0.1	0.1	0.2	0.1	0.1	0.2	0.1	0.1	0.1	0.1
	Exp.	0.2	0.2	0.1	0.1	0.1	0.2	0.2	0.2	0.2	0.2	0.2	0.1	0.1	0.1	0.1

Graph 1: Annual growth rates of exports, 1999–2013
(In percentage by year)

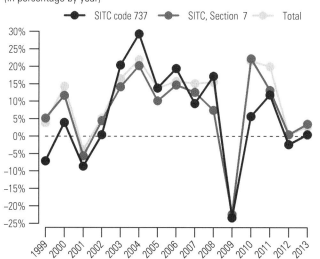

Graph 2: Trade Balance by MDG regions 2013
(Bln US$)

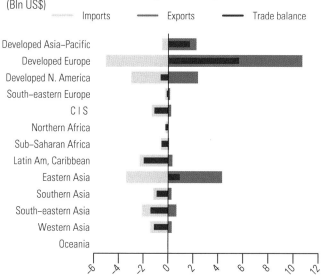

Table 2: Top exporting countries or areas in 2013

Country or area	Value (million US$)	Avg. Growth (%) 09-13	Growth (%) 12-13	World share %	Cum.
World	21 655.9	3.8	0.4	100.0	
Germany	3 591.9	1.4	10.9	16.6	16.6
China	3 283.2	7.1	1.1	15.2	31.7
Japan	2 173.1	5.2	-19.0	10.0	41.8
Italy	2 150.2	-5.4	4.4	9.9	51.7
USA	1 966.3	6.0	-5.6	9.1	60.8
Switzerland	754.3	7.6	2.6	3.5	64.3
Rep. of Korea	664.2	12.4	13.1	3.1	67.3
Austria	600.4	1.8	-2.4	2.8	70.1
France	537.8	-1.8	-5.3	2.5	72.6
Sweden	513.6	4.6	-5.6	2.4	75.0
Netherlands	455.2	16.4	10.4	2.1	77.1
United Kingdom	423.1	-1.6	-2.5	2.0	79.0
Canada	412.0	15.2	8.0	1.9	80.9
Belgium	347.9	8.1	-1.4	1.6	82.5
Thailand	287.5	41.0	157.9	1.3	83.9

Table 3: Top importing countries or areas in 2013

Country or area	Value (million US$)	Avg. Growth (%) 09-13	Growth (%) 12-13	World share %	Cum.
World	21 336.9	2.3	-5.4	100.0	
USA	2 448.7	11.2	8.8	11.5	11.5
China	2 066.0	-4.6	-18.6	9.7	21.2
Mexico	1 041.1	23.2	18.4	4.9	26.0
Russian Federation	1 020.4	-5.3	-10.0	4.8	30.8
Germany	942.7	4.0	-2.5	4.4	35.2
India	874.0	-3.9	-31.4	4.1	39.3
Brazil	649.0	22.2	-37.9	3.0	42.4
Rep. of Korea	635.0	-7.4	-13.3	3.0	45.4
Thailand	557.8	9.8	-5.3	2.6	48.0
Canada	542.8	16.7	7.0	2.5	50.5
Indonesia	498.1	32.6	23.4	2.3	52.8
Turkey	482.6	-6.6	13.8	2.3	55.1
Malaysia	478.2	16.0	13.9	2.2	57.3
Netherlands	457.6	19.9	28.2	2.1	59.5
United Arab Emirates	*436.8*	-1.0	11.4	2.0	61.5

741 Heating and cooling equipment and parts thereof, nes

In 2013, the value (in current US$) of exports of "heating and cooling equipment and parts thereof, nes" (SITC group 741) increased by 3.6 percent (compared to 6.8 percent average growth rate from 2009-2013) to reach 114.9 bln US$ (see table 2), while imports increased by 4.4 percent to reach 117.5 bln US$ (see table 3). Exports of this commodity accounted for 1.9 percent of world exports of SITC section 7, and 0.6 percent of total world merchandise exports (see table 1). China, Germany and USA were the top exporters in 2013 (see table 2). They accounted for 18.1, 10.7 and 9.4 percent of world exports, respectively. USA, Germany and China were the top destinations, with respectively 11.1, 5.7 and 5.4 percent of world imports (see table 3).

The top 15 countries/areas accounted for 79.0 and 56.3 percent of total world exports and imports, respectively (see tables 2 and 3). In 2013, China was the country/area with the highest value of net exports (+14.5 bln US$), followed by Italy (+7.0 bln US$). By MDG regions (see graph 2), the largest surpluses in this product group were recorded by Developed Europe (+17.1 bln US$), Eastern Asia (+16.4 bln US$) and South-eastern Asia (+421.3 mln US$). The largest trade deficits were recorded by Western Asia (-8.5 bln US$), Commonwealth of Independent States (-6.6 bln US$) and Latin America and the Caribbean (-5.4 bln US$).

Table 1: Imports (Imp.) and exports (Exp.), 1999-2013, in current US$

		1999	2000	2001	2002	2003	2004	2005	2006	2007	2008	2009	2010	2011	2012	2013
Values in Bln US$	Imp.	41.6	42.3	42.1	43.1	51.2	63.9	70.9	80.6	98.2	111.8	89.9	96.1	112.9	112.5	117.5
	Exp.	39.2	41.3	41.1	42.8	50.5	63.0	68.5	80.3	99.1	112.4	88.2	94.6	111.1	110.9	114.9
As a percentage of	Imp.	1.8	1.6	1.7	1.7	1.7	1.8	1.8	1.8	2.0	2.1	2.1	1.8	1.9	1.9	1.9
SITC section (%)	Exp.	1.7	1.6	1.7	1.7	1.7	1.8	1.8	1.8	2.0	2.1	2.1	1.8	1.9	1.9	1.9
As a percentage of	Imp.	0.7	0.6	0.7	0.7	0.7	0.7	0.7	0.7	0.7	0.7	0.7	0.6	0.6	0.6	0.6
world trade (%)	Exp.	0.7	0.6	0.7	0.7	0.7	0.7	0.7	0.7	0.7	0.7	0.7	0.6	0.6	0.6	0.6

Graph 1: Annual growth rates of exports, 1999–2013
(In percentage by year)

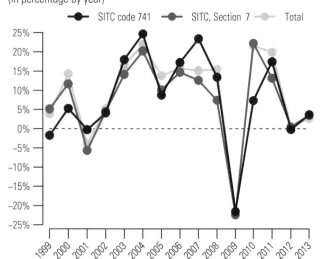

Table 2: Top exporting countries or areas in 2013

Country or area	Value (million US$)	Avg. Growth (%) 09-13	Growth (%) 12-13	World share %	Cum.
World	114920.3	6.8	3.6	100.0	
China	20826.3	14.4	3.3	18.1	18.1
Germany	12321.3	2.6	3.5	10.7	28.8
USA	10783.6	8.4	1.9	9.4	38.2
Italy	9803.4	2.5	7.6	8.5	46.8
Thailand	5117.9	14.7	10.2	4.5	51.2
Japan	4678.5	-1.3	-12.6	4.1	55.3
Rep. of Korea	4613.8	8.5	-5.0	4.0	59.3
Mexico	4297.7	13.8	8.9	3.7	63.0
France	4122.4	1.5	7.0	3.6	66.6
Czech Rep.	3054.9	9.8	10.9	2.7	69.3
Belgium	2639.5	1.6	22.4	2.3	71.6
Netherlands	2398.3	9.0	8.2	2.1	73.7
Sweden	2195.3	2.4	3.4	1.9	75.6
Austria	2005.1	0.9	11.3	1.7	77.3
United Kingdom	1978.6	1.2	3.3	1.7	79.0

Graph 2: Trade Balance by MDG regions 2013
(Bln US$)

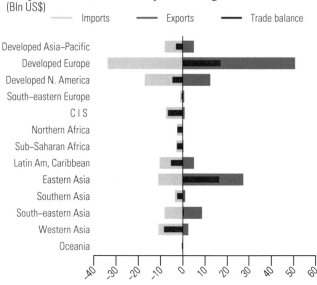

Table 3: Top importing countries or areas in 2013

Country or area	Value (million US$)	Avg. Growth (%) 09-13	Growth (%) 12-13	World share %	Cum.
World	117476.0	6.9	4.4	100.0	
USA	13029.3	9.8	4.8	11.1	11.1
Germany	6647.3	6.0	4.5	5.7	16.7
China	6312.3	1.6	-8.4	5.4	22.1
Russian Federation	5159.9	16.8	1.6	4.4	26.5
Japan	4581.4	8.9	-0.6	3.9	30.4
Canada	3993.7	10.7	5.6	3.4	33.8
France	3622.2	-0.1	5.1	3.1	36.9
Mexico	3254.9	14.6	15.7	2.8	39.7
Australia	3162.6	16.7	34.8	2.7	42.4
Saudi Arabia	2962.6	11.7	-1.1	2.5	44.9
United Arab Emirates	2949.0	8.8	11.4	2.5	47.4
United Kingdom	2860.2	5.4	9.4	2.4	49.8
Italy	2780.9	3.3	7.2	2.4	52.2
Brazil	2598.3	18.8	37.9	2.2	54.4
Belgium	2254.6	3.3	22.1	1.9	56.3

Pumps for liquids; liquid elevators; parts for such pumps and liquid elevators 742

In 2013, the value (in current US$) of exports of "pumps for liquids; liquid elevators; parts for such pumps and liquid elevators" (SITC group 742) increased by 4.5 percent (compared to 10.2 percent average growth rate from 2009-2013) to reach 64.0 bln US$ (see table 2), while imports increased by 3.9 percent to reach 67.3 bln US$ (see table 3). Exports of this commodity accounted for 1.1 percent of world exports of SITC section 7, and 0.3 percent of total world merchandise exports (see table 1). Germany, USA and China were the top exporters in 2013 (see table 2). They accounted for 17.9, 15.2 and 10.0 percent of world exports, respectively. USA, Germany and China were the top destinations, with respectively 15.0, 6.9 and 6.6 percent of world imports (see table 3).

The top 15 countries/areas accounted for 81.5 and 60.6 percent of total world exports and imports, respectively (see tables 2 and 3). In 2013, Germany was the country/area with the highest value of net exports (+6.8 bln US$), followed by Japan (+3.1 bln US$). By MDG regions (see graph 2), the largest surpluses in this product group were recorded by Developed Europe (+10.9 bln US$), Developed Asia-Pacific (+2.3 bln US$) and Eastern Asia (+1.3 bln US$). The largest trade deficits were recorded by Western Asia (-4.0 bln US$), Latin America and the Caribbean (-3.5 bln US$) and Commonwealth of Independent States (-2.6 bln US$).

Table 1: Imports (Imp.) and exports (Exp.), 1999-2013, in current US$

		1999	2000	2001	2002	2003	2004	2005	2006	2007	2008	2009	2010	2011	2012	2013
Values in Bln US$	Imp.	19.9	20.1	20.5	21.9	26.1	30.7	34.2	38.5	48.2	55.3	44.9	53.8	65.0	64.8	67.3
	Exp.	19.1	19.5	19.7	21.1	25.6	31.2	33.8	38.0	47.0	54.3	43.3	51.1	60.9	61.3	64.0
As a percentage of SITC section (%)	Imp.	0.9	0.8	0.8	0.8	0.9	0.9	0.9	0.9	1.0	1.0	1.1	1.0	1.1	1.1	1.1
	Exp.	0.8	0.7	0.8	0.8	0.9	0.9	0.9	0.9	0.9	1.0	1.0	1.0	1.0	1.1	1.1
As a percentage of world trade (%)	Imp.	0.3	0.3	0.3	0.3	0.3	0.3	0.3	0.3	0.3	0.4	0.4	0.4	0.4	0.4	0.4
	Exp.	0.3	0.3	0.3	0.3	0.3	0.3	0.3	0.3	0.3	0.3	0.3	0.3	0.3	0.3	0.3

Graph 1: Annual growth rates of exports, 1999–2013
(In percentage by year)

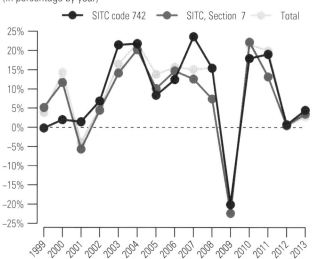

Table 2: Top exporting countries or areas in 2013

Country or area	Value (million US$)	Avg. Growth (%) 09-13	Growth (%) 12-13	World share %	Cum.
World	64 012.8	10.2	4.5	100.0	
Germany	11 479.9	8.4	6.6	17.9	17.9
USA	9 739.5	15.3	3.6	15.2	33.1
China	6 423.2	22.0	10.6	10.0	43.2
Italy	4 387.7	5.2	7.1	6.9	50.0
Japan	4 290.6	5.3	-10.7	6.7	56.7
France	2 587.4	1.7	7.3	4.0	60.8
United Kingdom	2 515.8	11.2	3.0	3.9	64.7
Czech Rep.	1 786.4	15.5	8.3	2.8	67.5
Mexico	1 650.6	15.6	7.0	2.6	70.1
Netherlands	1 542.9	2.4	16.3	2.4	72.5
Canada	1 507.8	12.6	-12.2	2.4	74.8
Rep. of Korea	1 243.5	14.0	-6.5	1.9	76.8
Denmark	1 083.7	3.7	-0.9	1.7	78.5
Belgium	995.0	9.3	17.9	1.6	80.0
Sweden	931.5	4.3	3.4	1.5	81.5

Graph 2: Trade Balance by MDG regions 2013
(Bln US$)

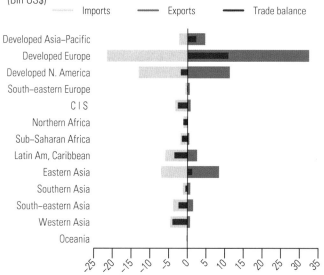

Table 3: Top importing countries or areas in 2013

Country or area	Value (million US$)	Avg. Growth (%) 09-13	Growth (%) 12-13	World share %	Cum.
World	67 292.0	10.7	3.9	100.0	
USA	10 093.8	17.7	-0.1	15.0	15.0
Germany	4 650.1	10.1	2.4	6.9	21.9
China	4 446.8	8.4	7.1	6.6	28.5
Canada	2 988.4	13.1	-8.7	4.4	33.0
France	2 561.5	4.9	3.5	3.8	36.8
Russian Federation	2 260.7	22.8	11.4	3.4	40.1
United Kingdom	2 188.6	5.2	-0.8	3.3	43.4
Mexico	2 109.0	17.7	-1.4	3.1	46.5
Rep. of Korea	1 866.3	4.8	1.0	2.8	49.3
Italy	1 494.4	2.7	3.1	2.2	51.5
Saudi Arabia	1 398.9	13.1	17.1	2.1	53.6
Belgium	1 222.2	7.1	16.6	1.8	55.4
Japan	1 217.3	7.5	-1.5	1.8	57.2
Brazil	1 162.1	17.3	11.9	1.7	58.9
Netherlands	1 121.6	9.3	2.7	1.7	60.6

743 Pumps (other than liquid), air or other gas compressors and fans, etc; parts

In 2013, the value (in current US$) of exports of "pumps (other than liquid), air or other gas compressors and fans, etc; parts" (SITC group 743) increased by 6.3 percent (compared to 10.1 percent average growth rate from 2009-2013) to reach 130.7 bln US$ (see table 2), while imports increased by 6.4 percent to reach 133.3 bln US$ (see table 3). Exports of this commodity accounted for 2.2 percent of world exports of SITC section 7, and 0.7 percent of total world merchandise exports (see table 1). Germany, USA and China were the top exporters in 2013 (see table 2). They accounted for 16.6, 12.9 and 12.4 percent of world exports, respectively. USA, China and Germany were the top destinations, with respectively 12.5, 7.5 and 7.4 percent of world imports (see table 3).

The top 15 countries/areas accounted for 79.6 and 60.9 percent of total world exports and imports, respectively (see tables 2 and 3). In 2013, Germany was the country/area with the highest value of net exports (+11.8 bln US$), followed by China (+6.2 bln US$). By MDG regions (see graph 2), the largest surpluses in this product group were recorded by Developed Europe (+18.4 bln US$), Eastern Asia (+6.1 bln US$) and Developed Asia-Pacific (+1.0 bln US$). The largest trade deficits were recorded by Western Asia (-6.7 bln US$), Latin America and the Caribbean (-6.4 bln US$) and Commonwealth of Independent States (-5.6 bln US$).

Table 1: Imports (Imp.) and exports (Exp.), 1999-2013, in current US$

		1999	2000	2001	2002	2003	2004	2005	2006	2007	2008	2009	2010	2011	2012	2013
Values in Bln US$	Imp.	40.2	42.8	45.4	47.2	54.3	66.0	72.3	82.8	98.2	109.4	92.7	107.8	126.1	125.3	133.3
	Exp.	38.4	41.4	43.0	44.5	53.0	65.1	69.4	79.9	96.5	107.1	88.8	105.4	123.6	122.9	130.7
As a percentage of SITC section (%)	Imp.	1.7	1.6	1.8	1.8	1.8	1.9	1.8	1.9	2.0	2.0	2.2	2.1	2.1	2.1	2.2
	Exp.	1.6	1.6	1.7	1.7	1.8	1.8	1.8	1.8	1.9	2.0	2.1	2.1	2.1	2.1	2.2
As a percentage of world trade (%)	Imp.	0.7	0.7	0.7	0.7	0.7	0.7	0.7	0.7	0.7	0.7	0.7	0.7	0.7	0.7	0.7
	Exp.	0.7	0.7	0.7	0.7	0.7	0.7	0.7	0.7	0.7	0.7	0.7	0.7	0.7	0.7	0.7

Graph 1: Annual growth rates of exports, 1999–2013
(In percentage by year)

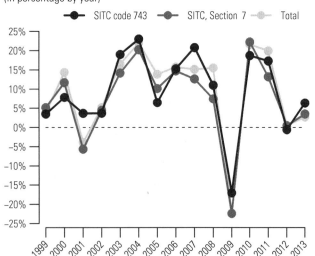

Graph 2: Trade Balance by MDG regions 2013
(Bln US$)

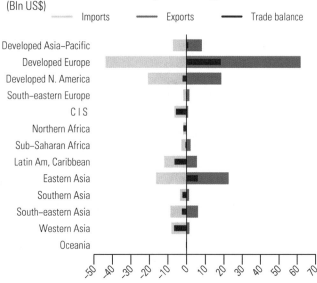

Table 2: Top exporting countries or areas in 2013

Country or area	Value (million US$)	Avg. Growth (%) 09-13	Growth (%) 12-13	World share %	Cum.
World.....................................	130 673.7	10.1	6.3	100.0	
Germany................................	21 686.0	8.7	7.1	16.6	16.6
USA.......................................	16 809.7	10.0	5.5	12.9	29.5
China....................................	16 265.7	18.9	14.2	12.4	41.9
Japan....................................	7 945.3	5.2	-10.9	6.1	48.0
Italy......................................	7 089.3	2.8	3.2	5.4	53.4
France...................................	5 358.1	3.9	1.7	4.1	57.5
Belgium.................................	4 788.5	15.6	11.3	3.7	61.2
Mexico..................................	4 232.7	18.1	8.3	3.2	64.4
United Kingdom.....................	4 016.5	7.9	6.9	3.1	67.5
Rep. of Korea........................	3 813.8	23.9	18.7	2.9	70.4
Netherlands...........................	3 143.5	11.0	10.1	2.4	72.8
Thailand................................	2 431.9	14.9	9.3	1.9	74.7
Switzerland............................	2 302.2	6.5	16.9	1.8	76.4
South Africa...........................	2 138.0	6.1	-5.9	1.6	78.1
Czech Rep.............................	2 000.2	17.0	8.2	1.5	79.6

Table 3: Top importing countries or areas in 2013

Country or area	Value (million US$)	Avg. Growth (%) 09-13	Growth (%) 12-13	World share %	Cum.
World.....................................	133 298.9	9.5	6.4	100.0	
USA.......................................	16 678.7	12.5	3.5	12.5	12.5
China....................................	10 058.2	8.6	9.5	7.5	20.1
Germany................................	9 907.0	11.8	11.8	7.4	27.5
Mexico..................................	5 151.3	15.7	0.9	3.9	31.4
France...................................	4 737.4	6.8	1.3	3.6	34.9
Russian Federation.................	4 534.8	21.1	12.5	3.4	38.3
Canada..................................	4 036.0	8.3	3.1	3.0	41.3
Japan....................................	3 917.7	10.1	-4.9	2.9	44.3
United Kingdom.....................	3 843.4	10.4	13.9	2.9	47.2
Rep. of Korea........................	3 668.4	10.2	14.6	2.8	49.9
Italy......................................	3 393.8	5.1	4.6	2.5	52.5
Australia................................	3 062.0	1.4	22.3	2.3	54.8
Belgium.................................	3 042.3	7.1	14.3	2.3	57.0
Thailand................................	2 546.7	17.5	3.9	1.9	58.9
Netherlands...........................	2 540.4	12.1	7.5	1.9	60.9

In 2013, the value (in current US$) of exports of "mechanical handling equipment and parts thereof, nes" (SITC group 744) increased by 4.1 percent (compared to 8.4 percent average growth rate from 2009-2013) to reach 86.6 bln US$ (see table 2), while imports increased by 4.7 percent to reach 87.0 bln US$ (see table 3). Exports of this commodity accounted for 1.4 percent of world exports of SITC section 7, and 0.5 percent of total world merchandise exports (see table 1). Germany, China and USA were the top exporters in 2013 (see table 2). They accounted for 15.3, 15.2 and 10.3 percent of world exports, respectively. USA, China and Germany were the top destinations, with respectively 11.9, 5.2 and 5.1 percent of world imports (see table 3).

The top 15 countries/areas accounted for 82.0 and 58.2 percent of total world exports and imports, respectively (see tables 2 and 3). In 2013, Germany was the country/area with the highest value of net exports (+8.8 bln US$), followed by China (+8.7 bln US$). By MDG regions (see graph 2), the largest surpluses in this product group were recorded by Developed Europe (+19.3 bln US$), Eastern Asia (+8.5 bln US$) and Developed Asia-Pacific (+1.3 bln US$). The largest trade deficits were recorded by Latin America and the Caribbean (-6.8 bln US$), Western Asia (-5.3 bln US$) and South-eastern Asia (-5.0 bln US$).

Table 1: Imports (Imp.) and exports (Exp.), 1999-2013, in current US$

		1999	2000	2001	2002	2003	2004	2005	2006	2007	2008	2009	2010	2011	2012	2013
Values in Bln US$	Imp.	28.4	28.9	28.9	28.6	33.6	42.0	51.3	60.8	74.2	87.0	60.3	62.9	78.6	83.1	87.0
	Exp.	28.9	29.6	29.8	30.1	34.9	44.3	52.1	62.3	77.4	91.8	62.8	65.3	80.5	83.2	86.6
As a percentage of	Imp.	1.2	1.1	1.2	1.1	1.1	1.2	1.3	1.4	1.5	1.6	1.4	1.2	1.3	1.4	1.4
SITC section (%)	Exp.	1.2	1.1	1.2	1.2	1.2	1.3	1.3	1.4	1.5	1.7	1.5	1.3	1.4	1.4	1.4
As a percentage of	Imp.	0.5	0.4	0.5	0.4	0.4	0.4	0.5	0.5	0.5	0.5	0.5	0.4	0.4	0.5	0.5
world trade (%)	Exp.	0.5	0.5	0.5	0.5	0.5	0.5	0.5	0.5	0.6	0.6	0.5	0.4	0.4	0.5	0.5

Graph 1: Annual growth rates of exports, 1999–2013
(In percentage by year)

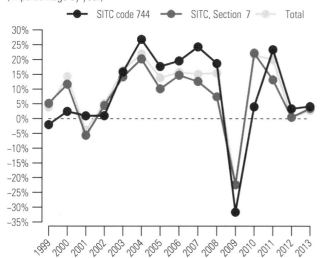

Table 2: Top exporting countries or areas in 2013

Country or area	Value (million US$)	Avg. Growth (%) 09-13	Growth (%) 12-13	World share %	Cum.
World	86 612.3	8.4	4.1	100.0	
Germany	13 279.0	6.1	1.6	15.3	15.3
China	13 173.9	12.5	13.4	15.2	30.5
USA	8 957.6	8.5	-1.0	10.3	40.9
Italy	6 211.5	10.2	10.3	7.2	48.1
Japan	4 663.0	5.2	-6.4	5.4	53.4
France	3 684.9	3.8	1.3	4.3	57.7
Netherlands	3 315.6	10.5	4.6	3.8	61.5
United Kingdom	2 810.0	7.7	2.3	3.2	64.8
Sweden	2 567.8	5.5	-2.6	3.0	67.7
Spain	2 426.5	9.9	11.6	2.8	70.5
Canada	2 410.3	8.2	-0.3	2.8	73.3
Rep. of Korea	2 408.5	13.6	11.3	2.8	76.1
Austria	2 190.3	4.0	-8.1	2.5	78.6
Belgium	1 765.4	6.1	12.1	2.0	80.7
Singapore	1 157.5	1.7	-2.1	1.3	82.0

Graph 2: Trade Balance by MDG regions 2013
(Bln US$)

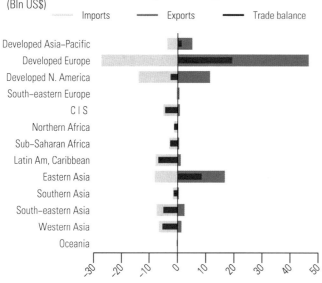

Table 3: Top importing countries or areas in 2013

Country or area	Value (million US$)	Avg. Growth (%) 09-13	Growth (%) 12-13	World share %	Cum.
World	86 956.5	9.6	4.7	100.0	
USA	10 328.2	14.5	5.3	11.9	11.9
China	4 507.7	9.1	-2.2	5.2	17.1
Germany	4 458.8	8.2	0.4	5.1	22.2
France	3 640.8	5.6	4.8	4.2	26.4
Canada	3 567.2	19.5	3.6	4.1	30.5
Russian Federation	3 563.7	19.0	-0.8	4.1	34.6
United Kingdom	2 845.6	7.8	7.2	3.3	37.8
Australia	2 486.9	16.8	-5.4	2.9	40.7
Netherlands	2 457.8	10.9	1.6	2.8	43.5
Rep. of Korea	2 312.0	6.0	25.4	2.7	46.2
Saudi Arabia	2 264.5	14.3	17.1	2.6	48.8
Singapore	2 251.3	10.6	10.6	2.6	51.4
Brazil	2 076.9	20.2	3.4	2.4	53.8
Belgium	1 994.9	5.7	2.0	2.3	56.1
Mexico	1 835.5	14.8	6.5	2.1	58.2

745 Non-electrical machinery, tools and mechanical apparatus, parts thereof, nes

In 2013, the value (in current US$) of exports of "non-electrical machinery, tools and mechanical apparatus, parts thereof, nes" (SITC group 745) increased by 6.0 percent (compared to 8.9 percent average growth rate from 2009-2013) to reach 60.1 bln US$ (see table 2), while imports increased by 5.4 percent to reach 59.8 bln US$ (see table 3). Exports of this commodity accounted for 1.0 percent of world exports of SITC section 7, and 0.3 percent of total world merchandise exports (see table 1). Germany, Italy and China were the top exporters in 2013 (see table 2). They accounted for 20.5, 15.4 and 12.5 percent of world exports, respectively. USA, China and Germany were the top destinations, with respectively 12.7, 7.5 and 5.3 percent of world imports (see table 3).

The top 15 countries/areas accounted for 84.2 and 59.0 percent of total world exports and imports, respectively (see tables 2 and 3). In 2013, Germany was the country/area with the highest value of net exports (+9.1 bln US$), followed by Italy (+7.9 bln US$). By MDG regions (see graph 2), the largest surpluses in this product group were recorded by Developed Europe (+15.6 bln US$) and Eastern Asia (+4.2 bln US$). The largest trade deficits were recorded by Latin America and the Caribbean (-4.6 bln US$), Commonwealth of Independent States (-3.3 bln US$) and Developed North America (-2.6 bln US$).

Table 1: Imports (Imp.) and exports (Exp.), 1999-2013, in current US$

		1999	2000	2001	2002	2003	2004	2005	2006	2007	2008	2009	2010	2011	2012	2013
Values in Bln US$	Imp.	22.6	22.7	22.9	24.9	29.4	35.0	38.1	42.3	47.4	52.3	41.7	47.4	57.0	56.7	59.8
	Exp.	23.0	23.1	23.4	25.8	30.0	36.9	39.5	44.0	50.6	55.9	42.7	47.4	56.2	56.7	60.1
As a percentage of SITC section (%)	Imp.	1.0	0.9	0.9	1.0	1.0	1.0	1.0	0.9	0.9	1.0	1.0	0.9	1.0	1.0	1.0
	Exp.	1.0	0.9	0.9	1.0	1.0	1.0	1.0	1.0	1.0	1.0	1.0	0.9	1.0	1.0	1.0
As a percentage of world trade (%)	Imp.	0.4	0.3	0.4	0.4	0.4	0.4	0.4	0.3	0.3	0.3	0.3	0.3	0.3	0.3	0.3
	Exp.	0.4	0.4	0.4	0.4	0.4	0.4	0.4	0.4	0.4	0.4	0.3	0.3	0.3	0.3	0.3

Graph 1: Annual growth rates of exports, 1999–2013
(In percentage by year)

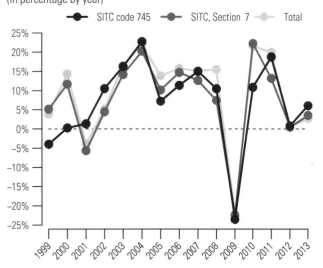

Graph 2: Trade Balance by MDG regions 2013
(Bln US$)

Table 2: Top exporting countries or areas in 2013

Country or area	Value (million US$)	Avg. Growth (%) 09-13	Growth (%) 12-13	World share %	Cum.
World	60070.5	8.9	6.0	100.0	
Germany	12311.5	5.9	6.2	20.5	20.5
Italy	9246.7	8.4	8.9	15.4	35.9
China	7495.5	17.1	9.7	12.5	48.4
USA	5887.4	6.6	-1.4	9.8	58.2
Japan	1997.3	9.0	-8.2	3.3	61.5
Netherlands	1755.0	9.8	7.6	2.9	64.4
France	1661.5	8.0	0.1	2.8	67.2
Switzerland	1538.2	6.2	-2.3	2.6	69.7
Sweden	1515.1	9.3	0.4	2.5	72.3
United Kingdom	1433.8	7.1	9.1	2.4	74.6
Belgium	1315.6	12.1	13.7	2.2	76.8
Other Asia, nes	1288.8	14.7	5.8	2.1	79.0
Spain	1222.4	11.1	6.1	2.0	81.0
China, Hong Kong SAR	996.8	22.9	14.2	1.7	82.7
Austria	914.6	13.2	27.6	1.5	84.2

Table 3: Top importing countries or areas in 2013

Country or area	Value (million US$)	Avg. Growth (%) 09-13	Growth (%) 12-13	World share %	Cum.
World	59766.5	9.4	5.4	100.0	
USA	7569.9	10.0	3.7	12.7	12.7
China	4459.4	18.3	0.5	7.5	20.1
Germany	3194.2	5.9	0.6	5.3	25.5
France	2838.9	4.8	7.1	4.7	30.2
Russian Federation	2405.2	17.3	5.5	4.0	34.2
United Kingdom	1983.1	7.2	19.4	3.3	37.6
Mexico	1860.4	11.7	14.6	3.1	40.7
Canada	1786.6	6.4	-2.4	3.0	43.7
Belgium	1540.1	8.1	9.6	2.6	46.2
Brazil	1434.6	18.1	7.5	2.4	48.6
Italy	1335.3	2.2	1.5	2.2	50.9
Netherlands	1313.8	12.8	14.5	2.2	53.1
Japan	1293.5	11.3	-3.4	2.2	55.2
Australia	1182.4	9.1	2.7	2.0	57.2
Spain	1084.8	-0.6	-0.1	1.8	59.0

In 2013, the value (in current US$) of exports of "ball or roller bearings" (SITC group 746) increased by 0.4 percent (compared to 10.5 percent average growth rate from 2009-2013) to reach 32.8 bln US$ (see table 2), while imports decreased by 1.5 percent to reach 33.1 bln US$ (see table 3). Exports of this commodity accounted for 0.5 percent of world exports of SITC section 7, and 0.2 percent of total world merchandise exports (see table 1). Germany, China and Japan were the top exporters in 2013 (see table 2). They accounted for 15.7, 13.6 and 13.3 percent of world exports, respectively. Germany, China and USA were the top destinations, with respectively 13.2, 10.0 and 9.0 percent of world imports (see table 3).

The top 15 countries/areas accounted for 83.4 and 68.2 percent of total world exports and imports, respectively (see tables 2 and 3). In 2013, Japan was the country/area with the highest value of net exports (+3.7 bln US$), followed by China (+1.2 bln US$). By MDG regions (see graph 2), the largest surpluses in this product group were recorded by Developed Asia-Pacific (+3.5 bln US$), Developed Europe (+1.8 bln US$) and Eastern Asia (+542.7 mln US$). The largest trade deficits were recorded by Latin America and the Caribbean (-2.2 bln US$), Developed North America (-1.3 bln US$) and South-eastern Asia (-800.0 mln US$).

Table 1: Imports (Imp.) and exports (Exp.), 1999-2013, in current US$

		1999	2000	2001	2002	2003	2004	2005	2006	2007	2008	2009	2010	2011	2012	2013
Values in Bln US$	Imp.	12.2	13.2	12.6	13.0	15.5	18.5	20.8	22.9	26.8	31.6	23.6	30.3	36.2	33.6	33.1
	Exp.	11.5	12.5	12.0	12.5	14.8	17.7	19.7	21.9	26.0	30.9	22.0	29.4	35.6	32.6	32.8
As a percentage of SITC section (%)	Imp.	0.5	0.5	0.5	0.5	0.5	0.5	0.5	0.5	0.5	0.6	0.6	0.6	0.6	0.6	0.5
	Exp.	0.5	0.5	0.5	0.5	0.5	0.5	0.5	0.5	0.5	0.6	0.5	0.6	0.6	0.6	0.5
As a percentage of world trade (%)	Imp.	0.2	0.2	0.2	0.2	0.2	0.2	0.2	0.2	0.2	0.2	0.2	0.2	0.2	0.2	0.2
	Exp.	0.2	0.2	0.2	0.2	0.2	0.2	0.2	0.2	0.2	0.2	0.2	0.2	0.2	0.2	0.2

Graph 1: Annual growth rates of exports, 1999–2013
(In percentage by year)

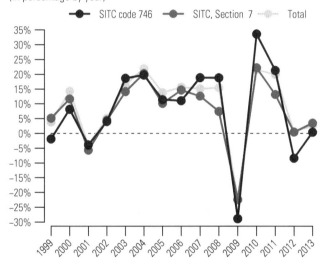

Table 2: Top exporting countries or areas in 2013

Country or area	Value (million US$)	Avg. Growth (%) 09-13	Growth (%) 12-13	World share %	Cum.
World	32 776.0	10.5	0.4	100.0	
Germany	5 140.1	6.6	3.6	15.7	15.7
China	4 463.7	23.2	6.1	13.6	29.3
Japan	4 362.3	11.0	-14.3	13.3	42.6
USA	2 258.7	11.3	-0.8	6.9	49.5
France	1 990.0	3.9	3.8	6.1	55.6
Italy	1 444.4	6.9	3.7	4.4	60.0
Singapore	1 381.9	3.8	-5.3	4.2	64.2
Belgium	1 015.9	13.6	11.8	3.1	67.3
Sweden	876.1	4.5	0.2	2.7	70.0
Slovakia	831.3	15.3	9.0	2.5	72.5
Netherlands	784.6	9.2	3.3	2.4	74.9
Austria	733.9	11.8	11.0	2.2	77.1
Romania	692.9	7.5	-2.5	2.1	79.3
United Kingdom	692.1	8.5	-3.0	2.1	81.4
Rep. of Korea	655.4	20.5	16.5	2.0	83.4

Graph 2: Trade Balance by MDG regions 2013
(Bln US$)

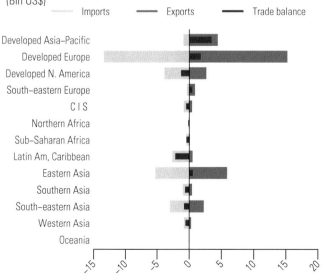

Table 3: Top importing countries or areas in 2013

Country or area	Value (million US$)	Avg. Growth (%) 09-13	Growth (%) 12-13	World share %	Cum.
World	33 075.1	8.8	-1.5	100.0	
Germany	4 362.0	11.5	5.5	13.2	13.2
China	3 295.1	4.2	-2.5	10.0	23.2
USA	2 964.6	17.2	-7.1	9.0	32.1
France	1 594.6	7.6	4.9	4.8	36.9
Italy	1 249.4	7.2	4.6	3.8	40.7
Singapore	1 166.8	3.8	-13.1	3.5	44.2
Belgium	1 138.2	8.7	12.6	3.4	47.7
Mexico	1 051.1	18.0	-0.9	3.2	50.9
Rep. of Korea	1 033.0	10.6	-3.2	3.1	54.0
Canada	927.2	9.0	-8.4	2.8	56.8
Brazil	850.2	11.2	5.3	2.6	59.4
India	820.0	9.7	-13.0	2.5	61.8
Thailand	729.1	15.1	-10.2	2.2	64.0
Netherlands	703.4	8.7	-0.3	2.1	66.2
United Kingdom	674.8	8.5	2.8	2.0	68.2

747 Taps, cocks, valves, etc; pressure-reducing, thermostatically control valves

In 2013, the value (in current US$) of exports of "taps, cocks, valves, etc; pressure-reducing, thermostatically control valves" (SITC group 747) increased by 7.1 percent (compared to 10.9 percent average growth rate from 2009-2013) to reach 86.1 bln US$ (see table 2), while imports increased by 6.1 percent to reach 89.6 bln US$ (see table 3). Exports of this commodity accounted for 1.4 percent of world exports of SITC section 7, and 0.5 percent of total world merchandise exports (see table 1). China, Germany and USA were the top exporters in 2013 (see table 2). They accounted for 16.1, 14.1 and 13.6 percent of world exports, respectively. USA, China and Germany were the top destinations, with respectively 15.8, 8.8 and 6.4 percent of world imports (see table 3).

The top 15 countries/areas accounted for 81.6 and 63.2 percent of total world exports and imports, respectively (see tables 2 and 3). In 2013, Italy was the country/area with the highest value of net exports (+6.8 bln US$), followed by Germany (+6.4 bln US$). By MDG regions (see graph 2), the largest surpluses in this product group were recorded by Developed Europe (+13.4 bln US$), Eastern Asia (+5.5 bln US$) and Developed Asia-Pacific (+1.1 bln US$). The largest trade deficits were recorded by Western Asia (-5.4 bln US$), Developed North America (-4.6 bln US$) and Latin America and the Caribbean (-3.7 bln US$).

Table 1: Imports (Imp.) and exports (Exp.), 1999-2013, in current US$

		1999	2000	2001	2002	2003	2004	2005	2006	2007	2008	2009	2010	2011	2012	2013
Values in Bln US$	Imp.	24.0	25.1	25.5	27.8	32.8	39.4	44.0	52.6	64.0	72.5	59.5	68.6	80.7	84.4	89.6
	Exp.	22.2	23.0	23.4	25.4	29.9	36.4	40.8	50.0	62.3	70.7	56.9	65.2	77.0	80.4	86.1
As a percentage of	Imp.	1.0	1.0	1.0	1.1	1.1	1.1	1.1	1.2	1.3	1.3	1.4	1.3	1.4	1.4	1.5
SITC section (%)	Exp.	0.9	0.9	0.9	1.0	1.0	1.0	1.0	1.1	1.2	1.3	1.4	1.3	1.3	1.4	1.4
As a percentage of	Imp.	0.4	0.4	0.4	0.4	0.4	0.4	0.4	0.4	0.5	0.4	0.5	0.4	0.4	0.5	0.5
world trade (%)	Exp.	0.4	0.4	0.4	0.4	0.4	0.4	0.4	0.4	0.5	0.4	0.5	0.4	0.4	0.4	0.5

Graph 1: Annual growth rates of exports, 1999–2013
(In percentage by year)

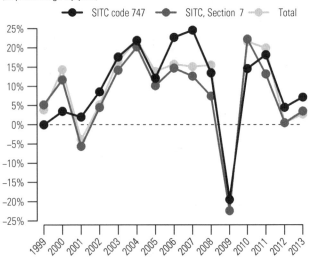

Table 2: Top exporting countries or areas in 2013

Country or area	Value (million US$)	Avg. Growth (%) 09-13	Growth (%) 12-13	World share %	Cum.
World	86 144.8	10.9	7.1	100.0	
China	13 903.8	16.5	6.2	16.1	16.1
Germany	12 155.1	8.6	8.1	14.1	30.3
USA	11 699.8	15.7	12.7	13.6	43.8
Italy	8 815.1	5.2	7.1	10.2	54.1
Japan	4 512.6	11.2	-9.1	5.2	59.3
United Kingdom	3 632.9	11.2	-0.9	4.2	63.5
France	3 093.5	5.1	7.1	3.6	67.1
Mexico	2 076.4	10.7	6.3	2.4	69.5
Rep. of Korea	1 880.5	14.1	-7.6	2.2	71.7
Switzerland	1 468.1	8.6	4.4	1.7	73.4
Spain	1 461.6	4.1	8.9	1.7	75.1
Czech Rep.	1 454.6	18.9	10.2	1.7	76.8
Denmark	1 407.5	9.9	4.2	1.6	78.4
Canada	1 378.0	7.4	3.6	1.6	80.0
Netherlands	1 325.0	3.9	14.3	1.5	81.6

Graph 2: Trade Balance by MDG regions 2013
(Bln US$)

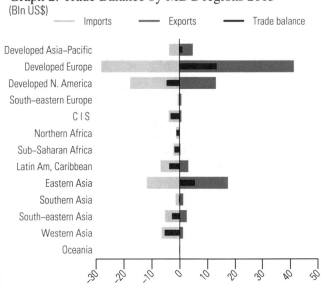

Table 3: Top importing countries or areas in 2013

Country or area	Value (million US$)	Avg. Growth (%) 09-13	Growth (%) 12-13	World share %	Cum.
World	89 581.1	10.8	6.1	100.0	
USA	14 129.3	16.0	4.9	15.8	15.8
China	7 920.3	11.8	9.9	8.8	24.6
Germany	5 746.8	8.2	4.8	6.4	31.0
Canada	3 564.6	11.5	-2.3	4.0	35.0
United Kingdom	3 552.4	9.5	12.7	4.0	39.0
France	3 141.3	5.4	5.1	3.5	42.5
Mexico	2 835.2	14.7	1.5	3.2	45.6
Rep. of Korea	2 685.2	15.8	19.7	3.0	48.6
Russian Federation	2 315.6	20.5	-22.5	2.6	51.2
Japan	2 068.2	10.7	-6.9	2.3	53.5
Saudi Arabia	2 060.9	16.0	24.4	2.3	55.8
Italy	2 034.9	5.4	2.1	2.3	58.1
Singapore	1 547.8	8.0	14.1	1.7	59.8
United Arab Emirates	1 514.0	8.5	11.4	1.7	61.5
Netherlands	1 501.4	8.1	13.3	1.7	63.2

In 2013, the value (in current US$) of exports of "transmission shafts (camshafts, crankshafts) and cranks; parts thereof" (SITC group 748) increased by 2.0 percent (compared to 11.2 percent average growth rate from 2009-2013) to reach 56.0 bln US$ (see table 2), while imports increased by 0.2 percent to reach 57.4 bln US$ (see table 3). Exports of this commodity accounted for 0.9 percent of world exports of SITC section 7, and 0.3 percent of total world merchandise exports (see table 1). Germany, China and Japan were the top exporters in 2013 (see table 2). They accounted for 22.3, 11.5 and 10.9 percent of world exports, respectively. USA, China and Germany were the top destinations, with respectively 14.3, 9.5 and 8.9 percent of world imports (see table 3).

The top 15 countries/areas accounted for 82.7 and 67.5 percent of total world exports and imports, respectively (see tables 2 and 3). In 2013, Germany was the country/area with the highest value of net exports (+7.4 bln US$), followed by Japan (+4.4 bln US$). By MDG regions (see graph 2), the largest surpluses in this product group were recorded by Developed Europe (+8.3 bln US$), Developed Asia-Pacific (+3.8 bln US$) and Eastern Asia (+1.3 bln US$). The largest trade deficits were recorded by Latin America and the Caribbean (-4.7 bln US$), Developed North America (-3.5 bln US$) and South-eastern Asia (-2.3 bln US$).

Table 1: Imports (Imp.) and exports (Exp.), 1999-2013, in current US$

		1999	2000	2001	2002	2003	2004	2005	2006	2007	2008	2009	2010	2011	2012	2013
Values in Bln US$	Imp.	17.0	17.5	17.7	19.0	22.2	27.4	31.1	35.1	43.0	51.3	38.7	46.9	57.9	57.3	57.4
	Exp.	15.4	16.2	16.3	17.6	20.7	25.4	29.6	33.5	40.4	48.3	36.7	44.4	54.8	54.9	56.0
As a percentage of SITC section (%)	Imp.	0.7	0.7	0.7	0.7	0.8	0.8	0.8	0.8	0.9	1.0	0.9	0.9	1.0	1.0	0.9
	Exp.	0.7	0.6	0.7	0.7	0.7	0.7	0.8	0.8	0.8	0.9	0.9	0.9	0.9	0.9	0.9
As a percentage of world trade (%)	Imp.	0.3	0.3	0.3	0.3	0.3	0.3	0.3	0.3	0.3	0.3	0.3	0.3	0.3	0.3	0.3
	Exp.	0.3	0.3	0.3	0.3	0.3	0.3	0.3	0.3	0.3	0.3	0.3	0.3	0.3	0.3	0.3

Graph 1: Annual growth rates of exports, 1999–2013

(In percentage by year)

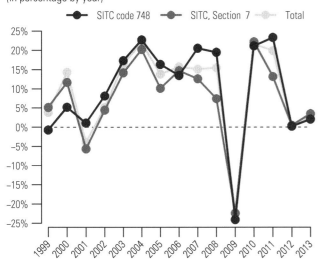

Table 2: Top exporting countries or areas in 2013

Country or area	Value (million US$)	Avg. Growth (%) 09-13	Growth (%) 12-13	World share %	Cum.
World	56 040.8	11.2	2.0	100.0	
Germany	12 499.8	6.7	1.9	22.3	22.3
China	6 444.0	24.2	5.8	11.5	33.8
Japan	6 095.8	9.9	-12.0	10.9	44.7
USA	5 655.4	15.8	2.5	10.1	54.8
Italy	3 475.3	9.2	4.7	6.2	61.0
France	2 084.3	5.6	4.3	3.7	64.7
Belgium	1 661.6	-0.3	2.1	3.0	67.7
Canada	1 245.2	11.8	2.9	2.2	69.9
United Kingdom	1 177.0	9.7	5.0	2.1	72.0
Rep. of Korea	1 119.7	14.5	-3.2	2.0	74.0
Spain	1 106.4	10.9	-0.4	2.0	76.0
Other Asia, nes	1 098.3	27.1	2.4	2.0	77.9
Slovakia	1 009.9	20.4	-2.3	1.8	79.7
Mexico	861.5	13.7	-2.3	1.5	81.3
Austria	837.8	6.7	1.4	1.5	82.7

Graph 2: Trade Balance by MDG regions 2013

(Bln US$)

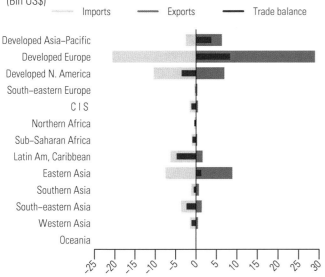

Table 3: Top importing countries or areas in 2013

Country or area	Value (million US$)	Avg. Growth (%) 09-13	Growth (%) 12-13	World share %	Cum.
World	57 393.7	10.4	0.2	100.0	
USA	8 187.5	14.2	-5.7	14.3	14.3
China	5 480.4	8.5	0.7	9.5	23.8
Germany	5 102.2	12.2	1.4	8.9	32.7
Mexico	2 683.5	21.6	5.9	4.7	37.4
Canada	2 225.2	9.9	-5.1	3.9	41.3
France	2 049.2	8.6	1.1	3.6	44.8
Brazil	1 917.4	17.9	14.0	3.3	48.2
United Kingdom	1 824.8	13.1	10.7	3.2	51.3
Japan	1 717.2	10.9	-6.9	3.0	54.3
Italy	1 568.7	6.6	3.7	2.7	57.1
Rep. of Korea	1 427.0	7.2	-8.4	2.5	59.6
Thailand	1 204.8	24.3	-2.8	2.1	61.7
Belgium	1 154.1	4.5	9.4	2.0	63.7
Hungary	1 103.2	10.0	7.5	1.9	65.6
Austria	1 080.9	9.2	-0.7	1.9	67.5

749 Non-electric parts and accessories of machinery, nes

In 2013, the value (in current US$) of exports of "non-electric parts and accessories of machinery, nes" (SITC group 749) increased by 5.5 percent (compared to 9.5 percent average growth rate from 2009-2013) to reach 33.0 bln US$ (see table 2), while imports increased by 5.9 percent to reach 31.4 bln US$ (see table 3). Exports of this commodity accounted for 0.5 percent of world exports of SITC section 7, and 0.2 percent of total world merchandise exports (see table 1). China, Germany and Japan were the top exporters in 2013 (see table 2). They accounted for 15.0, 12.5 and 9.4 percent of world exports, respectively. China, USA and Germany were the top destinations, with respectively 10.4, 9.5 and 6.5 percent of world imports (see table 3).

The top 15 countries/areas accounted for 79.9 and 60.2 percent of total world exports and imports, respectively (see tables 2 and 3). In 2013, Germany was the country/area with the highest value of net exports (+2.1 bln US$), followed by Japan (+2.0 bln US$). By MDG regions (see graph 2), the largest surpluses in this product group were recorded by Developed Europe (+4.7 bln US$), Eastern Asia (+3.7 bln US$) and Developed Asia-Pacific (+1.8 bln US$). The largest trade deficits were recorded by Latin America and the Caribbean (-2.6 bln US$), South-eastern Asia (-2.0 bln US$) and Western Asia (-1.1 bln US$).

Table 1: Imports (Imp.) and exports (Exp.), 1999-2013, in current US$

		1999	2000	2001	2002	2003	2004	2005	2006	2007	2008	2009	2010	2011	2012	2013
Values in Bln US$	Imp.	13.5	13.9	13.7	14.3	16.1	19.0	20.6	22.2	23.9	26.6	22.9	24.8	28.8	29.6	31.4
	Exp.	14.9	15.6	15.3	16.0	18.2	21.1	21.9	24.3	25.8	28.5	23.0	25.5	30.3	31.3	33.0
As a percentage of SITC section (%)	Imp.	0.6	0.5	0.5	0.6	0.5	0.5	0.5	0.5	0.5	0.5	0.5	0.5	0.5	0.5	0.5
	Exp.	0.6	0.6	0.6	0.6	0.6	0.6	0.6	0.5	0.5	0.5	0.5	0.5	0.5	0.5	0.5
As a percentage of world trade (%)	Imp.	0.2	0.2	0.2	0.2	0.2	0.2	0.2	0.2	0.2	0.2	0.2	0.2	0.2	0.2	0.2
	Exp.	0.3	0.2	0.3	0.2	0.2	0.2	0.2	0.2	0.2	0.2	0.2	0.2	0.2	0.2	0.2

Graph 1: Annual growth rates of exports, 1999–2013
(In percentage by year)

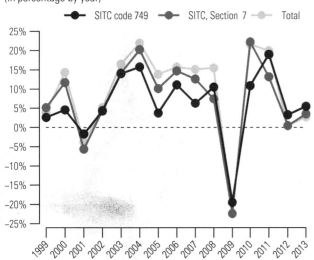

Legend: ● SITC code 749 ● SITC, Section 7 ○ Total

Table 2: Top exporting countries or areas in 2013

Country or area	Value (million US$)	Avg. Growth (%) 09-13	Growth (%) 12-13	World share %	Cum.
World	32 987.8	9.5	5.5	100.0	
China	4 956.8	15.2	11.8	15.0	15.0
Germany	4 110.3	6.5	6.2	12.5	27.5
Japan	3 110.6	6.4	-13.4	9.4	36.9
USA	2 592.4	9.5	4.2	7.9	44.8
Rep. of Korea	2 093.6	18.3	7.1	6.3	51.1
Italy	1 957.3	5.9	3.7	5.9	57.1
France	1 071.9	5.0	2.5	3.2	60.3
Canada	1 024.2	10.8	18.0	3.1	63.4
Other Asia, nes	934.1	9.1	-2.4	2.8	66.2
United Kingdom	925.9	9.6	13.7	2.8	69.0
Singapore	803.5	-0.5	-7.5	2.4	71.5
Portugal	774.0	11.7	12.4	2.3	73.8
Austria	703.0	9.1	3.6	2.1	76.0
China, Hong Kong SAR	659.5	7.9	-6.0	2.0	78.0
Mexico	647.6	22.3	10.2	2.0	79.9

Graph 2: Trade Balance by MDG regions 2013
(Bln US$)

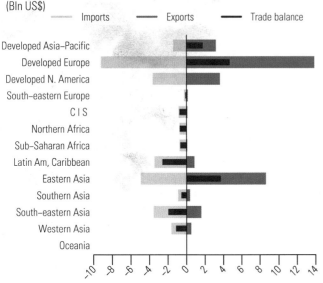

Legend: Imports Exports Trade balance

Developed Asia–Pacific
Developed Europe
Developed N. America
South–eastern Europe
CIS
Northern Africa
Sub–Saharan Africa
Latin Am, Caribbean
Eastern Asia
Southern Asia
South–eastern Asia
Western Asia
Oceania

Table 3: Top importing countries or areas in 2013

Country or area	Value (million US$)	Avg. Growth (%) 09-13	Growth (%) 12-13	World share %	Cum.
World	31 382.7	8.1	5.9	100.0	
China	3 263.6	7.1	6.9	10.4	10.4
USA	2 975.3	15.5	8.1	9.5	19.9
Germany	2 025.2	10.3	12.0	6.5	26.3
Mexico	1 926.6	8.4	2.0	6.1	32.5
Japan	1 152.8	9.1	-3.1	3.7	36.1
Thailand	1 015.4	18.5	-12.0	3.2	39.4
France	918.9	5.3	-0.5	2.9	42.3
Italy	839.4	7.3	5.5	2.7	45.0
Rep. of Korea	768.7	-2.5	5.9	2.4	47.4
United Kingdom	745.6	7.4	2.0	2.4	49.8
Indonesia	684.6	21.8	18.8	2.2	52.0
Canada	662.3	6.4	-7.7	2.1	54.1
Malaysia	649.7	9.7	7.0	2.1	56.2
India	643.5	13.7	-2.1	2.1	58.2
China, Hong Kong SAR	630.9	5.2	1.4	2.0	60.2

In 2013, the value (in current US$) of exports of "office machines" (SITC group 751) decreased by 3.3 percent (compared to 4.9 percent average growth rate from 2009-2013) to reach 50.2 bln US$ (see table 2), while imports decreased by 1.7 percent to reach 49.1 bln US$ (see table 3). Exports of this commodity accounted for 0.8 percent of world exports of SITC section 7, and 0.3 percent of total world merchandise exports (see table 1). China, Netherlands and Germany were the top exporters in 2013 (see table 2). They accounted for 39.1, 8.5 and 8.4 percent of world exports, respectively. USA, Germany and Netherlands were the top destinations, with respectively 18.1, 9.7 and 7.5 percent of world imports (see table 3).

The top 15 countries/areas accounted for 90.7 and 73.7 percent of total world exports and imports, respectively (see tables 2 and 3). In 2013, China was the country/area with the highest value of net exports (+16.9 bln US$), followed by Viet Nam (+2.1 bln US$). By MDG regions (see graph 2), the largest surpluses in this product group were recorded by Eastern Asia (+17.4 bln US$) and South-eastern Asia (+4.7 bln US$). The largest trade deficits were recorded by Developed North America (-7.2 bln US$), Developed Europe (-4.4 bln US$) and Developed Asia-Pacific (-2.5 bln US$).

Table 1: Imports (Imp.) and exports (Exp.), 1999-2013, in current US$

		1999	2000	2001	2002	2003	2004	2005	2006	2007	2008	2009	2010	2011	2012	2013
Values in Bln US$	Imp.	14.3	13.9	13.0	12.3	14.1	16.2	17.3	19.6	47.1	52.4	41.4	49.7	50.5	49.9	49.1
	Exp.	14.2	14.5	13.6	11.6	11.7	12.8	15.2	18.3	44.2	49.4	41.4	50.1	51.1	52.0	50.2
As a percentage of SITC section (%)	Imp.	0.6	0.5	0.5	0.5	0.5	0.5	0.4	0.4	0.9	1.0	1.0	1.0	0.9	0.8	0.8
	Exp.	0.6	0.6	0.6	0.4	0.4	0.4	0.4	0.4	0.9	0.9	1.0	1.0	0.9	0.9	0.8
As a percentage of world trade (%)	Imp.	0.3	0.2	0.2	0.2	0.2	0.2	0.2	0.2	0.3	0.3	0.3	0.3	0.3	0.3	0.3
	Exp.	0.3	0.2	0.2	0.2	0.2	0.1	0.1	0.2	0.3	0.3	0.3	0.3	0.3	0.3	0.3

Graph 1: Annual growth rates of exports, 1999–2013
(In percentage by year)

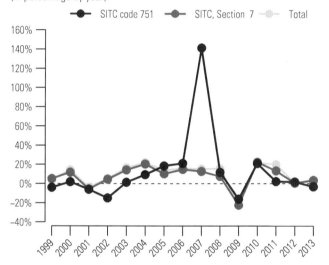

Table 2: Top exporting countries or areas in 2013

Country or area	Value (million US$)	Avg. Growth (%) 09-13	Growth (%) 12-13	World share %	Cum.
World	50 225.2	4.9	-3.3	100.0	
China	19 659.0	10.1	-2.4	39.1	39.1
Netherlands	4 287.3	-5.2	5.3	8.5	47.7
Germany	4 215.0	7.2	-5.8	8.4	56.1
USA	2 488.7	-1.0	-5.4	5.0	61.0
Viet Nam	2 308.0	17.5	7.8	4.6	65.6
China, Hong Kong SAR	2 221.0	9.1	-13.0	4.4	70.0
Thailand	1 631.9	10.9	9.0	3.2	73.3
Japan	1 472.5	-7.6	-18.6	2.9	76.2
Singapore	1 280.0	-5.8	-21.6	2.5	78.8
Indonesia	1 231.8	85.2	-22.9	2.5	81.2
Rep. of Korea	1 170.4	9.1	-7.5	2.3	83.6
Malaysia	982.4	-11.5	-6.7	2.0	85.5
Belgium	917.5	-1.2	14.1	1.8	87.3
France	892.6	-9.0	-6.1	1.8	89.1
United Kingdom	797.1	44.5	-1.0	1.6	90.7

Graph 2: Trade Balance by MDG regions 2013
(Bln US$)

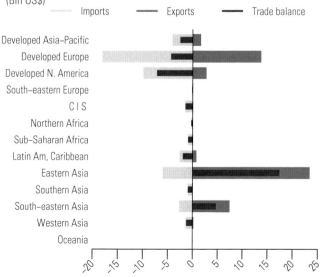

Table 3: Top importing countries or areas in 2013

Country or area	Value (million US$)	Avg. Growth (%) 09-13	Growth (%) 12-13	World share %	Cum.
World	49 052.5	4.3	-1.7	100.0	
USA	8 896.8	0.0	-1.5	18.1	18.1
Germany	4 762.5	7.2	2.0	9.7	27.8
Netherlands	3 658.6	-0.2	6.1	7.5	35.3
Japan	3 140.0	5.8	-13.4	6.4	41.7
China	2 794.0	10.7	-11.2	5.7	47.4
China, Hong Kong SAR	2 278.4	10.2	-10.5	4.6	52.0
France	1 963.8	-2.5	5.7	4.0	56.1
United Kingdom	1 699.5	43.5	0.8	3.5	59.5
Russian Federation	1 208.1	14.3	-5.0	2.5	62.0
Singapore	1 175.0	0.9	-16.2	2.4	64.4
Italy	1 031.6	-4.3	-2.0	2.1	66.5
Canada	1 026.7	2.8	1.6	2.1	68.6
Mexico	871.5	2.0	1.7	1.8	70.3
Australia	847.2	2.4	-9.2	1.7	72.1
Belgium	814.1	1.9	24.5	1.7	73.7

752 Automatic data processing machines and units thereof

"Automatic data processing machines and units thereof" (SITC group 752) is amongst the top exported commodities in 2013 with 1.9 percent of total exports (see table 1). For the first time since 2009, export of this commodity recorded negative growth rate. The value (in current US$) of exports of this commodity decreased by 2.4 percent (compared to 7.7 percent average growth rate from 2009-2013) to reach 351.6 bln US$ (see table 2), while imports decreased by 2.6 percent to reach 360.9 bln US$ (see table 3). Exports of this commodity accounted for 5.8 percent of world exports of SITC section 7 (see table 1). China, USA and Mexico were the top exporters in 2013 (see table 2). They accounted for 47.4, 7.8 and 5.0 percent of world exports, respectively. USA, China and China, Hong Kong SAR were the top destinations, with respectively 24.0, 8.1 and 6.4 percent of world imports (see table 3).

The top 15 countries/areas accounted for 90.5 and 75.0 percent of total world exports and imports, respectively (see tables 2 and 3). In 2013, China was the country/area with the highest value of net exports (+137.4 bln US$), followed by Mexico (+8.3 bln US$). By MDG regions (see graph 2), the largest surpluses in this product group were recorded by Eastern Asia (+131.1 bln US$) and South-eastern Asia (+20.9 bln US$). The largest trade deficits were recorded by Developed North America (-67.3 bln US$) and Developed Europe (-44.9 bln US$).

Table 1: Imports (Imp.) and exports (Exp.), 1999-2013, in current US$

		1999	2000	2001	2002	2003	2004	2005	2006	2007	2008	2009	2010	2011	2012	2013
Values in Bln US$	Imp.	197.8	221.7	201.3	202.6	225.3	264.6	287.3	307.5	293.7	301.7	259.2	321.2	357.9	370.4	360.9
	Exp.	180.2	199.3	184.1	182.0	209.4	249.4	271.4	298.9	302.9	304.5	261.6	319.7	345.3	360.2	351.6
As a percentage of SITC section (%)	Imp.	8.5	8.4	8.1	7.9	7.6	7.4	7.3	6.9	5.9	5.6	6.1	6.1	6.1	6.2	5.9
	Exp.	7.7	7.6	7.5	7.1	7.1	7.0	7.0	6.7	6.0	5.6	6.2	6.2	5.9	6.2	5.8
As a percentage of world trade (%)	Imp.	3.5	3.4	3.2	3.1	2.9	2.8	2.7	2.5	2.1	1.9	2.1	2.1	2.0	2.0	1.9
	Exp.	3.2	3.1	3.0	2.8	2.8	2.7	2.6	2.5	2.2	1.9	2.1	2.1	1.9	2.0	1.9

Graph 1: Annual growth rates of exports, 1999–2013
(In percentage by year)

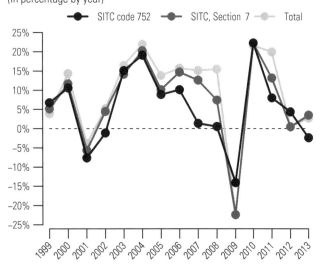

Graph 2: Trade Balance by MDG regions 2013
(Bln US$)

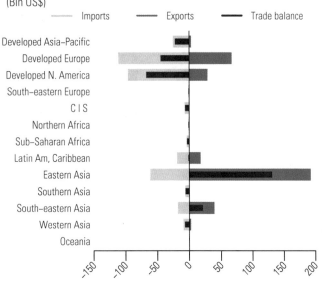

Table 2: Top exporting countries or areas in 2013

Country or area	Value (million US$)	Avg. Growth (%) 09-13	Growth (%) 12-13	World share %	Cum.
World..................................	351 614.4	7.7	-2.4	100.0	
China..................................	166 589.7	10.5	-1.6	47.4	47.4
USA....................................	27 378.1	6.7	-5.1	7.8	55.2
Mexico................................	17 511.4	20.3	-6.3	5.0	60.1
China, Hong Kong SAR.........	17 411.6	14.2	-10.7	5.0	65.1
Netherlands.........................	17 354.0	4.2	0.9	4.9	70.0
Thailand..............................	12 221.3	2.0	-11.2	3.5	73.5
Germany..............................	11 385.8	-0.9	-2.3	3.2	76.7
Singapore............................	9 932.5	6.2	3.0	2.8	79.6
Czech Rep............................	9 383.4	9.9	-10.5	2.7	82.2
Malaysia..............................	9 148.0	-2.6	-8.3	2.6	84.8
Rep. of Korea.......................	4 861.4	1.6	-8.1	1.4	86.2
United Kingdom....................	4 162.6	-0.7	5.4	1.2	87.4
Philippines...........................	3 890.2	-9.3	-1.4	1.1	88.5
Other Asia, nes....................	3 541.1	10.7	-8.1	1.0	89.5
Viet Nam..............................	3 500.8	145.6	121.4	1.0	90.5

Table 3: Top importing countries or areas in 2013

Country or area	Value (million US$)	Avg. Growth (%) 09-13	Growth (%) 12-13	World share %	Cum.
World..................................	360 854.8	8.6	-2.6	100.0	
USA....................................	86 691.0	10.3	-3.0	24.0	24.0
China..................................	29 212.2	6.5	-16.8	8.1	32.1
China, Hong Kong SAR.........	22 957.3	19.5	-0.5	6.4	38.5
Netherlands.........................	19 810.5	9.4	1.9	5.5	44.0
Germany..............................	19 057.9	2.2	-2.7	5.3	49.3
Japan..................................	17 311.4	9.4	-2.6	4.8	54.0
United Kingdom....................	15 031.2	2.7	1.2	4.2	58.2
France.................................	10 594.8	3.2	2.6	2.9	61.2
Canada...............................	9 399.3	7.5	-3.0	2.6	63.8
Mexico................................	9 255.1	12.8	3.3	2.6	66.3
Australia..............................	7 008.8	9.8	-5.0	1.9	68.3
Singapore............................	6 831.9	10.1	-6.2	1.9	70.2
Italy....................................	5 977.2	3.4	-2.3	1.7	71.8
Czech Rep............................	5 839.4	10.6	-13.5	1.6	73.4
Rep. of Korea.......................	5 600.7	9.4	-0.7	1.6	75.0

Parts and accessories (not covers, carrying cases, etc) for machines of 751-752 759

In 2013, the value (in current US$) of exports of "parts and accessories (not covers, carrying cases, etc) for machines of 751-752" (SITC group 759) decreased by 0.4 percent (compared to 1.5 percent average growth rate from 2009-2013) to reach 185.9 bln US$ (see table 2), while imports decreased by 2.0 percent to reach 187.9 bln US$ (see table 3). Exports of this commodity accounted for 3.1 percent of world exports of SITC section 7, and 1.0 percent of total world merchandise exports (see table 1). China, China, Hong Kong SAR and USA were the top exporters in 2013 (see table 2). They accounted for 20.2, 18.3 and 10.6 percent of world exports, respectively. USA, China, Hong Kong SAR and China were the top destinations, with respectively 14.5, 14.3 and 13.4 percent of world imports (see table 3).

The top 15 countries/areas accounted for 91.6 and 79.7 percent of total world exports and imports, respectively (see tables 2 and 3). In 2013, China was the country/area with the highest value of net exports (+12.4 bln US$), followed by Japan (+7.4 bln US$). By MDG regions (see graph 2), the largest surpluses in this product group were recorded by Eastern Asia (+25.6 bln US$), Developed Asia-Pacific (+6.4 bln US$) and South-eastern Asia (+5.6 bln US$). The largest trade deficits were recorded by Developed Europe (-13.8 bln US$), Latin America and the Caribbean (-10.4 bln US$) and Developed North America (-9.2 bln US$).

Table 1: Imports (Imp.) and exports (Exp.), 1999-2013, in current US$

		1999	2000	2001	2002	2003	2004	2005	2006	2007	2008	2009	2010	2011	2012	2013
Values in Bln US$	Imp.	135.2	156.0	142.0	139.8	156.6	182.1	199.8	221.2	220.1	217.9	179.5	212.9	199.6	191.7	187.9
	Exp.	136.7	166.2	148.7	149.2	162.2	182.9	201.6	222.1	217.1	212.7	175.0	202.9	195.9	186.6	185.9
As a percentage of SITC section (%)	Imp.	5.8	5.9	5.7	5.4	5.3	5.1	5.1	5.0	4.4	4.1	4.2	4.1	3.4	3.2	3.1
	Exp.	5.8	6.3	6.0	5.8	5.5	5.2	5.2	5.0	4.3	3.9	4.2	4.0	3.4	3.2	3.1
As a percentage of world trade (%)	Imp.	2.4	2.4	2.3	2.1	2.0	1.9	1.9	1.8	1.6	1.3	1.4	1.4	1.1	1.1	1.0
	Exp.	2.5	2.6	2.4	2.3	2.2	2.0	1.9	1.8	1.6	1.3	1.4	1.3	1.1	1.0	1.0

Graph 1: Annual growth rates of exports, 1999–2013
(In percentage by year)

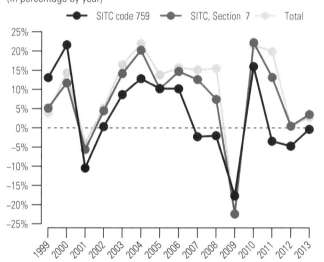

Graph 2: Trade Balance by MDG regions 2013
(Bln US$)

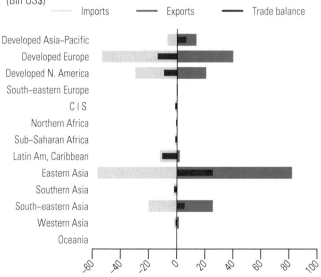

Table 2: Top exporting countries or areas in 2013

Country or area	Value (million US$)	Avg. Growth (%) 09-13	Growth (%) 12-13	World share %	Cum.
World	185876.7	1.5	-0.4	100.0	
China	37549.1	4.0	-2.4	20.2	20.2
China, Hong Kong SAR	34041.3	12.7	0.8	18.3	38.5
USA	19735.1	5.5	1.4	10.6	49.1
Netherlands	14915.6	0.7	-2.9	8.0	57.2
Japan	12829.7	-0.7	-6.5	6.9	64.1
Singapore	12821.9	-4.5	-14.5	6.9	71.0
Germany	8767.5	-5.5	1.2	4.7	75.7
Other Asia, nes	5746.6	-1.4	6.3	3.1	78.8
Malaysia	5689.5	-12.3	-5.4	3.1	81.8
Rep. of Korea	4799.3	-4.6	21.0	2.6	84.4
Thailand	4187.5	6.6	11.6	2.3	86.7
United Kingdom	2632.9	-7.3	12.8	1.4	88.1
Czech Rep.	2367.8	7.7	0.6	1.3	89.4
Belgium	2111.1	-3.5	-0.1	1.1	90.5
Philippines	2004.0	-4.4	27.2	1.1	91.6

Table 3: Top importing countries or areas in 2013

Country or area	Value (million US$)	Avg. Growth (%) 09-13	Growth (%) 12-13	World share %	Cum.
World	187864.5	1.1	-2.0	100.0	
USA	27272.5	-2.0	3.4	14.5	14.5
China, Hong Kong SAR	26923.9	8.0	-2.8	14.3	28.8
China	25170.9	8.1	-2.2	13.4	42.2
Netherlands	13591.7	0.9	-6.0	7.2	49.5
Germany	10844.4	-2.3	2.0	5.8	55.3
Singapore	7873.1	-3.1	-10.5	4.2	59.4
Mexico	6797.8	9.9	-2.3	3.6	63.1
Japan	5398.8	-0.3	-5.6	2.9	65.9
United Kingdom	4970.7	2.9	-1.9	2.6	68.6
Malaysia	4045.0	-11.3	-7.4	2.2	70.7
France	3943.6	-1.1	-3.1	2.1	72.8
Thailand	3779.2	-4.0	-13.8	2.0	74.8
Czech Rep.	3445.3	-0.3	-5.7	1.8	76.7
Brazil	3015.3	12.8	-5.6	1.6	78.3
Rep. of Korea	2723.3	-0.2	-0.1	1.4	79.7

761 Television receivers

In 2013, the value (in current US$) of exports of "television receivers" (SITC group 761) decreased by 4.8 percent (compared to -0.3 percent average growth rate from 2009-2013) to reach 83.6 bln US$ (see table 2), while imports decreased by 7.9 percent to reach 79.5 bln US$ (see table 3). Exports of this commodity accounted for 1.4 percent of world exports of SITC section 7, and 0.4 percent of total world merchandise exports (see table 1). China, Mexico and Slovakia were the top exporters in 2013 (see table 2). They accounted for 26.1, 19.8 and 8.3 percent of world exports, respectively. USA, Germany and United Kingdom were the top destinations, with respectively 30.0, 7.2 and 4.9 percent of world imports (see table 3).

The top 15 countries/areas accounted for 87.3 and 70.0 percent of total world exports and imports, respectively (see tables 2 and 3). In 2013, China was the country/area with the highest value of net exports (+21.6 bln US$), followed by Mexico (+14.1 bln US$). By MDG regions (see graph 2), the largest surpluses in this product group were recorded by Eastern Asia (+23.2 bln US$), Latin America and the Caribbean (+10.4 bln US$) and South-eastern Asia (+4.8 bln US$). The largest trade deficits were recorded by Developed North America (-22.4 bln US$), Developed Europe (-3.8 bln US$) and Developed Asia-Pacific (-3.2 bln US$).

Table 1: Imports (Imp.) and exports (Exp.), 1999-2013, in current US$

		1999	2000	2001	2002	2003	2004	2005	2006	2007	2008	2009	2010	2011	2012	2013
Values in Bln US$	Imp.	22.1	26.1	27.8	31.6	36.1	49.2	59.6	78.4	91.0	101.3	84.0	101.4	92.7	86.3	79.5
	Exp.	23.4	29.1	28.8	32.5	37.6	49.0	57.5	77.7	89.1	96.9	84.7	100.3	94.8	87.8	83.6
As a percentage of SITC section (%)	Imp.	0.9	1.0	1.1	1.2	1.2	1.4	1.5	1.8	1.8	1.9	2.0	1.9	1.6	1.4	1.3
	Exp.	1.0	1.1	1.2	1.3	1.3	1.4	1.5	1.7	1.8	1.8	2.0	2.0	1.6	1.5	1.4
As a percentage of world trade (%)	Imp.	0.4	0.4	0.4	0.5	0.5	0.5	0.6	0.6	0.6	0.6	0.7	0.7	0.5	0.5	0.4
	Exp.	0.4	0.5	0.5	0.5	0.5	0.5	0.6	0.6	0.6	0.6	0.7	0.7	0.5	0.5	0.4

Graph 1: Annual growth rates of exports, 1999–2013
(In percentage by year)

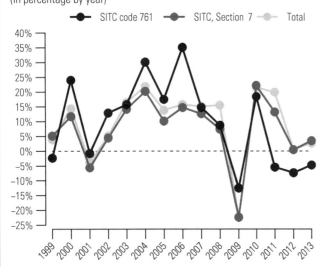

Graph 2: Trade Balance by MDG regions 2013
(Bln US$)

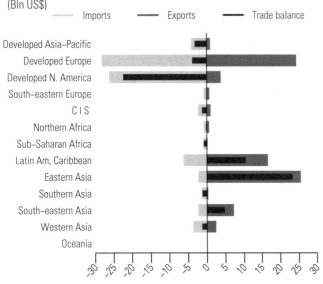

Table 2: Top exporting countries or areas in 2013

Country or area	Value (million US$)	Avg. Growth (%) 09-13	Growth (%) 12-13	World share %	Cum.
World	83597.4	-0.3	-4.8	100.0	
China	21785.3	7.4	-0.1	26.1	26.1
Mexico	16578.8	-1.9	-5.3	19.8	45.9
Slovakia	6897.8	-3.0	7.1	8.3	54.1
Poland	4710.2	-8.2	-3.0	5.6	59.8
Malaysia	3714.1	11.4	-0.5	4.4	64.2
USA	3342.8	4.5	-12.9	4.0	68.2
Hungary	3125.2	-12.2	-18.1	3.7	72.0
Rep. of Korea	2109.1	5.3	17.3	2.5	74.5
Germany	2094.0	-0.6	-8.7	2.5	77.0
Czech Rep	1753.5	-9.8	-25.9	2.1	79.1
Turkey	1706.6	-0.5	-21.2	2.0	81.1
Netherlands	1598.4	-19.1	-12.7	1.9	83.0
Thailand	1545.7	4.4	-14.0	1.8	84.9
Indonesia	1065.7	35.2	-13.8	1.3	86.2
Japan	916.7	-1.2	-14.5	1.1	87.3

Table 3: Top importing countries or areas in 2013

Country or area	Value (million US$)	Avg. Growth (%) 09-13	Growth (%) 12-13	World share %	Cum.
World	79492.2	-1.4	-7.9	100.0	
USA	23880.4	-5.0	-12.4	30.0	30.0
Germany	5720.0	-5.1	-13.6	7.2	37.2
United Kingdom	3881.6	88.8	-4.6	4.9	42.1
France	3059.5	-9.5	-1.0	3.8	46.0
Japan	2478.5	0.1	-10.6	3.1	49.1
Mexico	2450.4	16.4	5.5	3.1	52.2
Canada	2253.7	-3.1	-14.3	2.8	55.0
Netherlands	2143.9	-14.7	-10.0	2.7	57.7
Italy	1703.8	-15.6	-16.1	2.1	59.8
Poland	1491.7	8.3	32.0	1.9	61.7
Spain	1437.7	-12.7	-5.4	1.8	63.5
Australia	1421.0	-10.1	-9.5	1.8	65.3
India	1317.0	22.9	8.3	1.7	67.0
Sweden	1185.1	-6.2	-7.7	1.5	68.5
Russian Federation	1181.9	7.0	-7.4	1.5	70.0

In 2013, the value (in current US$) of exports of "radio-broadcast receivers" (SITC group 762) decreased by 3.1 percent (compared to 5.2 percent average growth rate from 2009-2013) to reach 16.1 bln US$ (see table 2), while imports decreased by 7.8 percent to reach 16.7 bln US$ (see table 3). Exports of this commodity accounted for 0.3 percent of world exports of SITC section 7, and 0.1 percent of total world merchandise exports (see table 1). China, Mexico and USA were the top exporters in 2013 (see table 2). They accounted for 27.7, 9.1 and 8.9 percent of world exports, respectively. USA, Germany and Japan were the top destinations, with respectively 29.4, 8.4 and 5.8 percent of world imports (see table 3).

The top 15 countries/areas accounted for 89.9 and 77.2 percent of total world exports and imports, respectively (see tables 2 and 3). In 2013, China was the country/area with the highest value of net exports (+4.2 bln US$), followed by Thailand (+1.1 bln US$). By MDG regions (see graph 2), the largest surpluses in this product group were recorded by Eastern Asia (+4.7 bln US$), South-eastern Asia (+2.4 bln US$) and Northern Africa (+13.5 mln US$). The largest trade deficits were recorded by Developed North America (-4.4 bln US$), Developed Asia-Pacific (-1.1 bln US$) and Developed Europe (-1.1 bln US$).

Table 1: Imports (Imp.) and exports (Exp.), 1999-2013, in current US$

		1999	2000	2001	2002	2003	2004	2005	2006	2007	2008	2009	2010	2011	2012	2013
Values in Bln US$	Imp.	20.2	22.7	20.8	21.2	20.5	21.3	21.5	21.5	21.7	18.9	14.5	17.7	18.5	18.2	16.7
	Exp.	17.3	19.4	16.9	16.9	16.7	17.9	18.7	18.9	19.5	18.1	13.2	16.0	16.6	16.6	16.1
As a percentage of SITC section (%)	Imp.	0.9	0.9	0.8	0.8	0.7	0.6	0.5	0.5	0.4	0.4	0.3	0.3	0.3	0.3	0.3
	Exp.	0.7	0.7	0.7	0.7	0.6	0.5	0.5	0.4	0.4	0.3	0.3	0.3	0.3	0.3	0.3
As a percentage of world trade (%)	Imp.	0.4	0.3	0.3	0.3	0.3	0.2	0.2	0.2	0.2	0.1	0.1	0.1	0.1	0.1	0.1
	Exp.	0.3	0.3	0.3	0.3	0.2	0.2	0.2	0.2	0.1	0.1	0.1	0.1	0.1	0.1	0.1

Graph 1: Annual growth rates of exports, 1999–2013
(In percentage by year)

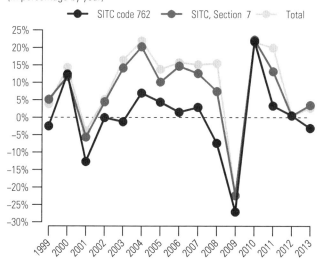

Table 2: Top exporting countries or areas in 2013

Country or area	Value (million US$)	Avg. Growth (%) 09-13	Growth (%) 12-13	World share %	Cum.
World	16 135.5	5.2	-3.1	100.0	
China	4 466.8	10.0	-6.6	27.7	27.7
Mexico	1 465.5	20.2	29.7	9.1	36.8
USA	1 431.7	15.9	-1.7	8.9	45.6
Malaysia	1 179.0	-5.8	-17.5	7.3	52.9
Thailand	1 177.8	19.5	7.9	7.3	60.2
Czech Rep.	876.4	16.9	35.4	5.4	65.7
China, Hong Kong SAR	703.8	-7.2	-30.3	4.4	70.0
Portugal	694.8	-6.5	-29.8	4.3	74.3
Germany	648.5	3.9	-7.5	4.0	78.4
Belgium	512.6	4.6	7.2	3.2	81.5
Rep. of Korea	455.4	56.9	47.9	2.8	84.4
Indonesia	239.0	-8.9	-16.9	1.5	85.8
Hungary	235.2	-5.6	-13.4	1.5	87.3
Japan	225.7	10.5	-1.3	1.4	88.7
France	194.5	-3.2	-17.0	1.2	89.9

Graph 2: Trade Balance by MDG regions 2013
(Bln US$)

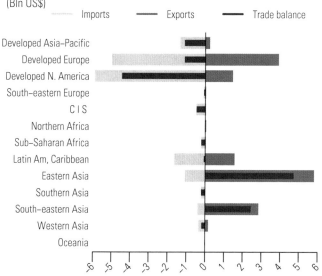

Table 3: Top importing countries or areas in 2013

Country or area	Value (million US$)	Avg. Growth (%) 09-13	Growth (%) 12-13	World share %	Cum.
World	16 732.4	3.6	-7.8	100.0	
USA	4 925.0	11.2	-6.2	29.4	29.4
Germany	1 409.0	5.3	-0.1	8.4	37.9
Japan	973.9	2.4	-11.2	5.8	43.7
Canada	969.1	10.1	-10.4	5.8	49.5
United Kingdom	658.3	-7.1	-7.5	3.9	53.4
Belgium	634.7	6.4	-4.4	3.8	57.2
China, Hong Kong SAR	537.4	-5.8	-28.9	3.2	60.4
Mexico	468.9	12.3	-10.3	2.8	63.2
France	453.9	-7.0	-6.9	2.7	65.9
Russian Federation	441.5	10.3	-19.2	2.6	68.6
Brazil	369.4	26.6	16.5	2.2	70.8
Australia	317.0	-0.9	-17.6	1.9	72.7
China	266.6	10.4	23.0	1.6	74.3
Spain	249.3	-6.7	1.3	1.5	75.7
Sweden	239.1	12.6	-0.7	1.4	77.2

763 Sound recorders or reproducers; television image and sound recorders

In 2013, the value (in current US$) of exports of "sound recorders or reproducers; television image and sound recorders" (SITC group 763) decreased by 6.8 percent (compared to -1.4 percent average growth rate from 2009-2013) to reach 55.3 bln US$ (see table 2), while imports decreased by 7.4 percent to reach 60.3 bln US$ (see table 3). Exports of this commodity accounted for 0.9 percent of world exports of SITC section 7, and 0.3 percent of total world merchandise exports (see table 1). China, Japan and China, Hong Kong SAR were the top exporters in 2013 (see table 2). They accounted for 40.0, 10.9 and 7.1 percent of world exports, respectively. China, USA and China, Hong Kong SAR were the top destinations, with respectively 22.3, 14.5 and 8.6 percent of world imports (see table 3).

The top 15 countries/areas accounted for 91.2 and 79.0 percent of total world exports and imports, respectively (see tables 2 and 3). In 2013, China was the country/area with the highest value of net exports (+8.7 bln US$), followed by Japan (+2.8 bln US$). By MDG regions (see graph 2), the largest surpluses in this product group were recorded by Eastern Asia (+8.9 bln US$), South-eastern Asia (+2.2 bln US$) and Developed Asia-Pacific (+1.9 bln US$). The largest trade deficits were recorded by Developed North America (-7.2 bln US$), Developed Europe (-4.9 bln US$) and Latin America and the Caribbean (-2.1 bln US$).

Table 1: Imports (Imp.) and exports (Exp.), 1999-2013, in current US$

		1999	2000	2001	2002	2003	2004	2005	2006	2007	2008	2009	2010	2011	2012	2013
Values in Bln US$	Imp.	24.2	30.0	30.4	36.6	46.9	61.6	67.7	67.9	68.3	70.9	57.0	68.0	67.7	65.0	60.3
	Exp.	23.2	27.6	27.1	32.7	42.9	56.5	62.4	62.4	64.3	67.1	58.5	63.1	61.5	59.4	55.3
As a percentage of SITC section (%)	Imp.	1.0	1.1	1.2	1.4	1.6	1.7	1.7	1.5	1.4	1.3	1.3	1.3	1.1	1.1	1.0
	Exp.	1.0	1.1	1.1	1.3	1.5	1.6	1.6	1.4	1.3	1.2	1.4	1.2	1.1	1.0	0.9
As a percentage of world trade (%)	Imp.	0.4	0.5	0.5	0.6	0.6	0.7	0.6	0.6	0.5	0.4	0.5	0.4	0.4	0.4	0.3
	Exp.	0.4	0.4	0.4	0.5	0.6	0.6	0.6	0.5	0.5	0.4	0.5	0.4	0.3	0.3	0.3

Graph 1: Annual growth rates of exports, 1999–2013
(In percentage by year)

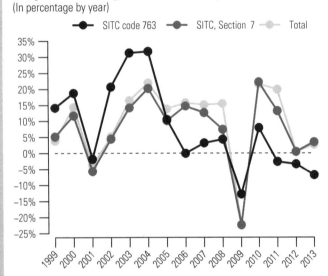

Table 2: Top exporting countries or areas in 2013

Country or area	Value (million US$)	Avg. Growth (%) 09-13	Growth (%) 12-13	World share %	World share % Cum.
World	55 317.9	-1.4	-6.8	100.0	
China	22 106.1	0.7	10.6	40.0	40.0
Japan	6 053.4	-10.1	-36.7	10.9	50.9
China, Hong Kong SAR	3 902.3	-9.6	-20.0	7.1	58.0
Netherlands	3 360.9	6.1	-10.5	6.1	64.0
USA	2 465.2	-0.1	-9.0	4.5	68.5
Thailand	2 200.6	14.9	-7.2	4.0	72.5
Germany	2 188.4	-1.3	-7.6	4.0	76.4
Other Asia, nes	2 059.5	36.2	5.9	3.7	80.1
Singapore	1 121.0	5.8	-5.3	2.0	82.2
Indonesia	1 012.0	-14.8	-7.4	1.8	84.0
Malaysia	991.8	-8.5	-26.6	1.8	85.8
Rep. of Korea	914.7	-1.8	-12.4	1.7	87.5
United Kingdom	815.2	41.4	-5.9	1.5	88.9
Slovakia	730.1	-8.7	-13.6	1.3	90.2
Canada	518.3	10.0	7.7	0.9	91.2

Graph 2: Trade Balance by MDG regions 2013
(Bln US$)

Imports   Exports   Trade balance

Developed Asia–Pacific
Developed Europe
Developed N. America
South–eastern Europe
CIS
Northern Africa
Sub–Saharan Africa
Latin Am, Caribbean
Eastern Asia
Southern Asia
South–eastern Asia
Western Asia
Oceania

Table 3: Top importing countries or areas in 2013

Country or area	Value (million US$)	Avg. Growth (%) 09-13	Growth (%) 12-13	World share %	World share % Cum.
World	60 256.6	1.4	-7.4	100.0	
China	13 454.0	40.5	33.3	22.3	22.3
USA	8 742.6	-7.1	-14.7	14.5	36.8
China, Hong Kong SAR	5 168.9	-4.9	-14.7	8.6	45.4
Japan	3 239.1	0.5	-6.5	5.4	50.8
Germany	3 155.5	-7.0	-15.8	5.2	56.0
Netherlands	3 028.1	2.1	-18.1	5.0	61.1
United Kingdom	1 695.0	9.6	-22.9	2.8	63.9
France	1 580.6	-7.2	-15.8	2.6	66.5
Canada	1 396.2	-4.7	-12.2	2.3	68.8
Russian Federation	1 287.3	7.6	-29.8	2.1	70.9
Singapore	1 256.4	0.1	-16.1	2.1	73.0
Mexico	1 042.1	1.4	-7.8	1.7	74.8
Viet Nam	915.4	71.9	25.9	1.5	76.3
Australia	893.7	-8.4	-24.5	1.5	77.8
Other Asia, nes	752.7	10.3	-4.9	1.2	79.0

Source: UN Comtrade and UN Service Trade

Telecommunications equipment, nes, and parts, nes, and accessories of 76 764

"Telecommunications equipment, nes, and parts, nes, and accessories of 76" (SITC group 764) is the fifth largest exported commodity in 2013, with 3.1 percent of total exports (see table 1). The value (in current US$) of exports of this commodity increased by 9.7 percent (compared to 11.2 percent average growth rate from 2009-2013) to reach 578.2 bln US$ (see table 2), while imports increased by 7.5 percent to reach 635.8 bln US$ (see table 3). Exports of this commodity accounted for 9.6 percent of world exports of SITC section 7 (see table 1). China, China, Hong Kong SAR and USA were the top exporters in 2013 (see table 2). They accounted for 35.4, 14.6 and 7.3 percent of world exports, respectively. Together, China and China, Hong Kong SAR accounted for nearly half of world exports of this product group in 2013, as was the case last year. USA, China, Hong Kong SAR and China were the top destinations, with respectively 16.8, 12.4 and 9.4 percent of world imports (see table 3).

The top 15 countries/areas accounted for 88.2 and 71.3 percent of total world exports and imports, respectively (see tables 2 and 3). In 2013, China was the country/area with the highest value of net exports (+144.5 bln US$), followed by Rep. of Korea (+26.9 bln US$). By MDG regions (see graph 2), the largest surplus in this product group was recorded by Eastern Asia (+182.2 bln US$). The largest trade deficits were recorded by Developed North America (-72.8 bln US$) and Developed Europe (-55.0 bln US$).

Table 1: Imports (Imp.) and exports (Exp.), 1999-2013, in current US$

		1999	2000	2001	2002	2003	2004	2005	2006	2007	2008	2009	2010	2011	2012	2013
Values in Bln US$	Imp.	169.1	222.5	205.0	193.2	219.1	287.2	342.1	408.0	425.5	472.1	397.0	495.1	561.6	591.4	635.8
	Exp.	171.8	224.2	207.0	207.7	230.2	296.4	352.5	425.1	417.9	451.3	378.2	446.6	510.6	527.2	578.2
As a percentage of	Imp.	7.2	8.5	8.2	7.5	7.4	8.1	8.7	9.2	8.5	8.8	9.3	9.5	9.5	9.9	10.3
SITC section (%)	Exp.	7.3	8.6	8.4	8.1	7.8	8.4	9.0	9.5	8.3	8.3	9.0	8.7	8.8	9.0	9.6
As a percentage of	Imp.	3.0	3.4	3.3	2.9	2.9	3.1	3.2	3.4	3.0	2.9	3.2	3.2	3.1	3.2	3.4
world trade (%)	Exp.	3.1	3.5	3.4	3.2	3.1	3.3	3.4	3.5	3.0	2.8	3.0	3.0	2.8	2.9	3.1

Graph 1: Annual growth rates of exports, 1999–2013
(In percentage by year)

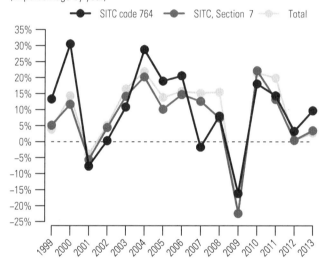

Graph 2: Trade Balance by MDG regions 2013
(Bln US$)

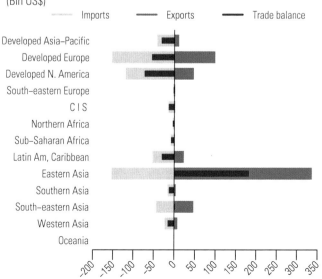

Table 2: Top exporting countries or areas in 2013

Country or area	Value (million US$)	Avg. Growth (%) 09-13	Growth (%) 12-13	World share %	Cum.
World..................................	578230.5	11.2	9.7	100.0	
China..................................	204458.7	17.3	11.8	35.4	35.4
China, Hong Kong SAR........	84144.6	16.8	14.3	14.6	49.9
USA....................................	42477.5	9.8	6.3	7.3	57.3
Rep. of Korea.....................	34944.2	-0.9	19.3	6.0	63.3
Viet Nam............................	23069.0	114.2	62.8	4.0	67.3
Mexico...............................	21831.3	4.8	6.3	3.8	71.1
Germany............................	18972.0	9.5	3.4	3.3	74.3
Netherlands........................	16465.5	5.6	6.8	2.8	77.2
Other Asia, nes...................	12623.6	12.4	-4.5	2.2	79.4
Singapore..........................	10894.6	7.3	0.7	1.9	81.3
Japan.................................	9744.3	-7.8	-13.9	1.7	82.9
United Kingdom..................	8682.7	44.0	6.4	1.5	84.4
France................................	7521.8	4.5	-1.8	1.3	85.7
Sweden..............................	7209.2	0.7	-2.1	1.2	87.0
Hungary.............................	7058.2	-10.4	-13.5	1.2	88.2

Table 3: Top importing countries or areas in 2013

Country or area	Value (million US$)	Avg. Growth (%) 09-13	Growth (%) 12-13	World share %	Cum.
World..................................	635769.9	12.5	7.5	100.0	
USA....................................	106909.8	10.2	7.7	16.8	16.8
China, Hong Kong SAR........	78990.8	19.5	9.6	12.4	29.2
China..................................	59989.7	18.7	15.1	9.4	38.7
Japan.................................	32919.9	19.1	-1.7	5.2	43.9
Mexico...............................	26820.4	6.0	5.6	4.2	48.1
Germany............................	26332.5	10.6	3.7	4.1	52.2
United Kingdom..................	20573.8	58.2	8.9	3.2	55.5
Netherlands........................	19536.6	8.8	11.6	3.1	58.5
France................................	13721.0	5.9	5.9	2.2	60.7
India..................................	12666.6	4.7	11.3	2.0	62.7
Canada...............................	12430.2	11.2	-0.6	2.0	64.6
Singapore..........................	11369.4	6.5	-5.2	1.8	66.4
Russian Federation..............	11142.3	18.8	-1.4	1.8	68.2
Viet Nam............................	10105.6	34.4	56.6	1.6	69.8
Brazil.................................	9478.2	20.0	14.9	1.5	71.3

771 Electric power machinery, and parts thereof

In 2013, the value (in current US$) of exports of "electric power machinery, and parts thereof" (SITC group 771) increased by 5.7 percent (compared to 9.5 percent average growth rate from 2009-2013) to reach 97.9 bln US$ (see table 2), while imports increased by 4.8 percent to reach 97.8 bln US$ (see table 3). Exports of this commodity accounted for 1.6 percent of world exports of SITC section 7, and 0.5 percent of total world merchandise exports (see table 1). China, China, Hong Kong SAR and Germany were the top exporters in 2013 (see table 2). They accounted for 28.9, 11.2 and 8.9 percent of world exports, respectively. China, USA and China, Hong Kong SAR were the top destinations, with respectively 16.0, 13.8 and 9.8 percent of world imports (see table 3).

The top 15 countries/areas accounted for 79.5 and 70.2 percent of total world exports and imports, respectively (see tables 2 and 3). In 2013, China was the country/area with the highest value of net exports (+12.7 bln US$), followed by Germany (+3.0 bln US$). By MDG regions (see graph 2), the largest surpluses in this product group were recorded by Eastern Asia (+14.2 bln US$), Developed Europe (+5.3 bln US$) and South-eastern Asia (+613.9 mln US$). The largest trade deficits were recorded by Developed North America (-8.3 bln US$), Latin America and the Caribbean (-3.1 bln US$) and Western Asia (-2.4 bln US$).

Table 1: Imports (Imp.) and exports (Exp.), 1999-2013, in current US$

		1999	2000	2001	2002	2003	2004	2005	2006	2007	2008	2009	2010	2011	2012	2013
Values in Bln US$	Imp.	33.7	39.8	35.9	34.5	38.1	45.0	49.8	58.5	70.9	80.0	69.4	88.3	96.3	93.3	97.8
	Exp.	31.3	37.1	33.9	31.8	35.5	41.8	45.7	55.8	69.1	79.6	68.2	85.6	92.7	92.6	97.9
As a percentage of	Imp.	1.4	1.5	1.4	1.3	1.3	1.3	1.3	1.3	1.4	1.5	1.6	1.7	1.6	1.6	1.6
SITC section (%)	Exp.	1.3	1.4	1.4	1.2	1.2	1.2	1.2	1.2	1.4	1.5	1.6	1.7	1.6	1.6	1.6
As a percentage of	Imp.	0.6	0.6	0.6	0.5	0.5	0.5	0.5	0.5	0.5	0.5	0.6	0.6	0.5	0.5	0.5
world trade (%)	Exp.	0.6	0.6	0.6	0.5	0.5	0.5	0.4	0.5	0.5	0.5	0.5	0.6	0.5	0.5	0.5

Graph 1: Annual growth rates of exports, 1999–2013
(In percentage by year)

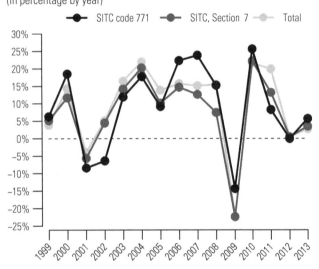

- SITC code 771
- SITC, Section 7
- Total

Graph 2: Trade Balance by MDG regions 2013
(Bln US$)

Imports — Exports — Trade balance

Developed Asia–Pacific
Developed Europe
Developed N. America
South–eastern Europe
C I S
Northern Africa
Sub–Saharan Africa
Latin Am, Caribbean
Eastern Asia
Southern Asia
South–eastern Asia
Western Asia
Oceania

Table 2: Top exporting countries or areas in 2013

Country or area	Value (million US$)	Avg. Growth (%) 09-13	Growth (%) 12-13	World share %	Cum.
World	97 853.9	9.5	5.7	100.0	
China	28 279.2	17.8	19.3	28.9	28.9
China, Hong Kong SAR	10 928.1	12.5	4.4	11.2	40.1
Germany	8 727.6	5.7	-1.5	8.9	49.0
USA	6 181.3	10.9	7.9	6.3	55.3
Japan	4 011.3	8.9	1.0	4.1	59.4
Mexico	2 684.4	7.5	0.8	2.7	62.1
Italy	2 456.4	2.4	-1.4	2.5	64.7
Rep. of Korea	2 398.8	-0.8	-14.0	2.5	67.1
Netherlands	2 369.9	13.4	3.7	2.4	69.5
Philippines	1 904.6	19.0	2.5	1.9	71.5
France	1 774.2	-0.5	-3.8	1.8	73.3
Austria	1 628.6	-1.0	-3.8	1.7	75.0
Other Asia, nes.	1 570.8	6.8	-3.5	1.6	76.6
Singapore	1 458.5	2.0	2.7	1.5	78.0
Thailand	1 426.7	13.3	0.1	1.5	79.5

Table 3: Top importing countries or areas in 2013

Country or area	Value (million US$)	Avg. Growth (%) 09-13	Growth (%) 12-13	World share %	Cum.
World	97 793.6	8.9	4.8	100.0	
China	15 621.3	15.9	28.0	16.0	16.0
USA	13 495.2	8.2	3.2	13.8	29.8
China, Hong Kong SAR	9 589.9	13.2	5.3	9.8	39.6
Germany	5 758.8	6.4	-3.0	5.9	45.5
Japan	3 420.9	10.0	1.8	3.5	49.0
Mexico	3 189.4	10.1	7.9	3.3	52.2
Rep. of Korea	2 437.9	7.6	2.3	2.5	54.7
France	2 285.4	6.9	1.5	2.3	57.1
United Kingdom	2 095.9	7.9	3.7	2.1	59.2
Netherlands	2 087.8	14.0	9.6	2.1	61.3
Canada	2 049.2	7.3	3.8	2.1	63.4
Russian Federation	1 859.5	17.8	-12.8	1.9	65.3
Singapore	1 775.4	8.7	1.5	1.8	67.1
Italy	1 550.7	3.3	-9.9	1.6	68.7
India	1 450.6	8.9	7.0	1.5	70.2

Electrical apparatus for switching, protecting or connecting electrical circuits 772

"Electrical apparatus for switching, protecting or connecting electrical circuits" (SITC group 772) is amongst the top exported commodities in 2013, with 1.3 percent of total exports (see table 1). The value (in current US$) of exports of this commodity increased by 4.9 percent (compared to 11.4 percent average growth rate from 2009-2013) to reach 248.8 bln US$ (see table 2), while imports increased by 4.3 percent to reach 253.6 bln US$ (see table 3). Exports of this commodity accounted for 4.1 percent of world exports of SITC section 7 (see table 1). China, Germany and USA were the top exporters in 2013 (see table 2), with USA moving up from fifth largest exporter in 2012 to third largest exporter. These importers accounted for 14.7, 13.1 and 8.7 percent of world exports, respectively. China, USA and China, Hong Kong SAR were the top destinations, with respectively 15.3, 10.2 and 8.0 percent of world imports (see table 3).

The top 15 countries/areas accounted for 81.3 and 68.6 percent of total world exports and imports, respectively (see tables 2 and 3). In 2013, Germany was the country/area with the highest value of net exports (+15.4 bln US$). By MDG regions (see graph 2), the largest surpluses in this product group were recorded by Developed Europe (+20.1 bln US$), Developed Asia-Pacific (+10.2 bln US$) and Eastern Asia (+5.9 bln US$). The largest trade deficit was recorded by Latin America and the Caribbean (-11.0 bln US$).

Table 1: Imports (Imp.) and exports (Exp.), 1999-2013, in current US$

		1999	2000	2001	2002	2003	2004	2005	2006	2007	2008	2009	2010	2011	2012	2013
Values in Bln US$	Imp.	80.8	95.8	88.7	88.8	103.3	127.1	141.9	165.1	189.2	203.4	165.6	208.6	237.7	243.2	253.6
	Exp.	81.8	96.3	86.9	89.2	104.3	128.2	142.4	164.2	185.9	200.1	161.7	204.7	231.9	237.1	248.8
As a percentage of SITC section (%)	Imp.	3.5	3.6	3.6	3.4	3.5	3.6	3.6	3.7	3.8	3.8	3.9	4.0	4.0	4.1	4.1
	Exp.	3.5	3.7	3.5	3.5	3.5	3.6	3.7	3.7	3.7	3.7	3.9	4.0	4.0	4.1	4.1
As a percentage of world trade (%)	Imp.	1.4	1.5	1.4	1.4	1.4	1.4	1.3	1.4	1.3	1.2	1.3	1.4	1.3	1.3	1.4
	Exp.	1.5	1.5	1.4	1.4	1.4	1.4	1.4	1.4	1.3	1.3	1.3	1.4	1.3	1.3	1.3

Graph 1: Annual growth rates of exports, 1999–2013
(In percentage by year)

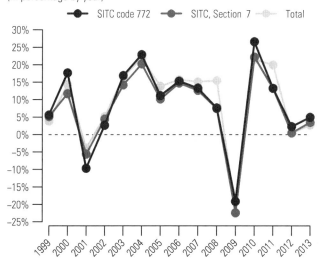

Graph 2: Trade Balance by MDG regions 2013
(Bln US$)

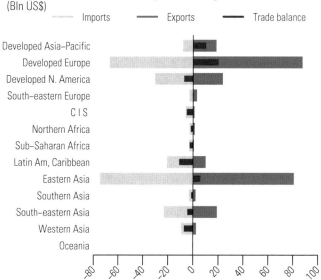

Table 2: Top exporting countries or areas in 2013

Country or area	Value (million US$)	Avg. Growth (%) 09-13	Growth (%) 12-13	World share %	Cum.
World..................	248835.5	11.4	4.9	100.0	
China..................	36534.5	16.4	4.5	14.7	14.7
Germany.............	32624.4	9.1	7.0	13.1	27.8
USA....................	21710.3	11.2	6.7	8.7	36.5
China, Hong Kong SAR........	21142.1	12.1	2.0	8.5	45.0
Japan..................	17711.5	5.7	-13.1	7.1	52.1
Rep. of Korea........	14090.3	31.2	27.8	5.7	57.8
France.................	9511.8	3.6	4.0	3.8	61.6
Other Asia, nes........	8904.6	9.7	-1.5	3.6	65.2
Mexico.................	8432.5	14.5	9.6	3.4	68.6
Singapore.............	6530.7	9.5	-5.4	2.6	71.2
Italy....................	5708.2	5.8	11.0	2.3	73.5
Malaysia...............	5579.3	14.2	-5.0	2.2	75.7
Czech Rep.............	4955.8	15.0	14.9	2.0	77.7
Switzerland............	4462.1	4.7	2.5	1.8	79.5
United Kingdom.......	4402.9	7.6	3.7	1.8	81.3

Table 3: Top importing countries or areas in 2013

Country or area	Value (million US$)	Avg. Growth (%) 09-13	Growth (%) 12-13	World share %	Cum.
World..................	253558.5	11.2	4.3	100.0	
China..................	38888.4	9.7	0.9	15.3	15.3
USA....................	25767.7	15.4	7.1	10.2	25.5
China, Hong Kong SAR........	20368.1	13.4	-3.3	8.0	33.5
Germany.............	17254.8	13.2	8.4	6.8	40.3
Mexico.................	12889.2	15.7	11.9	5.1	45.4
Rep. of Korea........	11587.2	19.6	13.5	4.6	50.0
France.................	6932.4	8.1	6.4	2.7	52.7
Japan..................	6102.3	8.0	-1.8	2.4	55.1
Thailand...............	5477.9	11.2	-2.7	2.2	57.3
Singapore.............	5451.7	9.5	2.6	2.2	59.4
United Kingdom.......	5243.4	7.3	8.5	2.1	61.5
Malaysia...............	4963.1	5.9	-6.5	2.0	63.5
Canada................	4822.9	9.4	-1.5	1.9	65.4
Italy....................	4402.2	6.4	5.7	1.7	67.1
Russian Federation..............	3854.7	19.8	-17.4	1.5	68.6

773 Equipment for distributing electricity, nes

In 2013, the value (in current US$) of exports of "equipment for distributing electricity, nes" (SITC group 773) increased by 6.4 percent (compared to 13.1 percent average growth rate from 2009-2013) to reach 120.1 bln US$ (see table 2), while imports increased by 5.1 percent to reach 119.2 bln US$ (see table 3). Exports of this commodity accounted for 2.0 percent of world exports of SITC section 7, and 0.6 percent of total world merchandise exports (see table 1). China, USA and Mexico were the top exporters in 2013 (see table 2). They accounted for 17.0, 8.6 and 8.5 percent of world exports, respectively. USA, Germany and China were the top destinations, with respectively 15.0, 8.5 and 5.8 percent of world imports (see table 3).

The top 15 countries/areas accounted for 70.2 and 64.1 percent of total world exports and imports, respectively (see tables 2 and 3). In 2013, China was the country/area with the highest value of net exports (+13.5 bln US$), followed by Mexico (+4.4 bln US$). By MDG regions (see graph 2), the largest surpluses in this product group were recorded by Eastern Asia (+14.8 bln US$), Latin America and the Caribbean (+2.2 bln US$) and Northern Africa (+2.1 bln US$). The largest trade deficits were recorded by Developed North America (-10.7 bln US$), Developed Asia-Pacific (-4.9 bln US$) and Western Asia (-2.3 bln US$).

Table 1: Imports (Imp.) and exports (Exp.), 1999-2013, in current US$

		1999	2000	2001	2002	2003	2004	2005	2006	2007	2008	2009	2010	2011	2012	2013
Values in Bln US$	Imp.	39.9	43.9	43.6	42.6	47.2	55.5	62.5	77.8	92.2	101.4	73.7	94.6	113.6	113.5	119.2
	Exp.	37.9	43.1	41.5	39.9	44.7	54.1	61.3	77.3	91.6	101.6	73.3	93.0	111.0	112.8	120.1
As a percentage of SITC section (%)	Imp.	1.7	1.7	1.8	1.7	1.6	1.6	1.6	1.7	1.8	1.9	1.7	1.8	1.9	1.9	1.9
	Exp.	1.6	1.6	1.7	1.5	1.5	1.5	1.6	1.7	1.8	1.9	1.7	1.8	1.9	1.9	2.0
As a percentage of world trade (%)	Imp.	0.7	0.7	0.7	0.6	0.6	0.6	0.6	0.6	0.7	0.6	0.6	0.6	0.6	0.6	0.6
	Exp.	0.7	0.7	0.7	0.6	0.6	0.6	0.6	0.6	0.7	0.6	0.6	0.6	0.6	0.6	0.6

Graph 1: Annual growth rates of exports, 1999–2013
(In percentage by year)

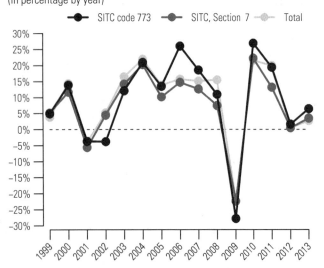

- ●— SITC code 773
- ●— SITC, Section 7
- ●— Total

Table 2: Top exporting countries or areas in 2013

Country or area	Value (million US$)	Avg. Growth (%) 09-13	Growth (%) 12-13	World share %	Cum.
World	120055.1	13.1	6.4	100.0	
China	20450.2	20.2	11.2	17.0	17.0
USA	10377.9	13.7	3.5	8.6	25.7
Mexico	10238.8	19.1	14.7	8.5	34.2
Germany	8837.0	9.0	6.0	7.4	41.6
China, Hong Kong SAR	4028.9	20.2	4.6	3.4	44.9
Rep. of Korea	3719.1	9.8	-2.1	3.1	48.0
Romania	3632.3	12.5	12.6	3.0	51.0
Italy	3585.4	8.6	5.1	3.0	54.0
Japan	3053.9	1.5	-7.3	2.5	56.6
Czech Rep	3029.3	14.5	4.2	2.5	59.1
Poland	2890.6	10.0	15.6	2.4	61.5
Spain	2774.7	16.8	13.7	2.3	63.8
Turkey	2551.8	15.5	4.9	2.1	65.9
Viet Nam	2547.5	29.8	16.7	2.1	68.1
France	2535.6	2.0	-3.3	2.1	70.2

Graph 2: Trade Balance by MDG regions 2013
(Bln US$)

- Imports
- Exports
- Trade balance

Developed Asia–Pacific
Developed Europe
Developed N. America
South–eastern Europe
C I S
Northern Africa
Sub–Saharan Africa
Latin Am, Caribbean
Eastern Asia
Southern Asia
South–eastern Asia
Western Asia
Oceania

-40 -30 -20 -10 0 10 20 30 40

Table 3: Top importing countries or areas in 2013

Country or area	Value (million US$)	Avg. Growth (%) 09-13	Growth (%) 12-13	World share %	Cum.
World	119229.8	12.8	5.1	100.0	
USA	17832.4	17.8	5.7	15.0	15.0
Germany	10158.0	9.4	2.5	8.5	23.5
China	6974.9	12.3	9.4	5.8	29.3
Japan	6549.1	13.3	-2.0	5.5	34.8
Mexico	5841.4	15.9	15.3	4.9	39.7
United Kingdom	4320.2	21.7	11.8	3.6	43.3
Canada	4004.1	14.6	-1.4	3.4	46.7
China, Hong Kong SAR	3883.6	20.7	7.4	3.3	50.0
France	3834.1	6.9	-1.8	3.2	53.2
Rep. of Korea	2669.8	15.1	2.7	2.2	55.4
Spain	2383.1	6.7	23.1	2.0	57.4
Czech Rep	2342.8	18.1	4.7	2.0	59.4
Romania	1866.3	13.8	18.1	1.6	60.9
Hungary	1859.2	4.6	11.6	1.6	62.5
Italy	1856.2	9.3	9.3	1.6	64.1

Source: UN Comtrade and UN Service Trade

In 2013, the value (in current US$) of exports of "electro-medical and radiological equipment" (SITC group 774) decreased by 1.4 percent (compared to 5.3 percent average growth rate from 2009-2013) to reach 42.1 bln US$ (see table 2), while imports decreased by 3.1 percent to reach 41.8 bln US$ (see table 3). Exports of this commodity accounted for 0.7 percent of world exports of SITC section 7, and 0.2 percent of total world merchandise exports (see table 1). USA, Germany and Netherlands were the top exporters in 2013 (see table 2). They accounted for 22.7, 20.3 and 8.3 percent of world exports, respectively. USA, China and Germany were the top destinations, with respectively 19.6, 12.9 and 6.8 percent of world imports (see table 3).

The top 15 countries/areas accounted for 89.8 and 73.5 percent of total world exports and imports, respectively (see tables 2 and 3). In 2013, Germany was the country/area with the highest value of net exports (+5.7 bln US$), followed by USA (+1.4 bln US$). By MDG regions (see graph 2), the largest surpluses in this product group were recorded by Developed Europe (+7.8 bln US$), Developed North America (+921.1 mln US$) and Developed Asia-Pacific (+291.2 mln US$). The largest trade deficits were recorded by Eastern Asia (-2.3 bln US$), Commonwealth of Independent States (-1.7 bln US$) and Latin America and the Caribbean (-1.7 bln US$).

Table 1: Imports (Imp.) and exports (Exp.), 1999-2013, in current US$

		1999	2000	2001	2002	2003	2004	2005	2006	2007	2008	2009	2010	2011	2012	2013
Values in Bln US$	Imp.	13.1	13.8	15.6	17.0	19.2	22.1	25.1	28.9	32.3	35.5	33.4	37.0	41.2	43.2	41.8
	Exp.	14.1	14.7	15.7	17.2	20.2	23.1	25.9	29.4	33.7	36.9	34.2	37.9	41.8	42.7	42.1
As a percentage of	Imp.	0.6	0.5	0.6	0.7	0.6	0.6	0.6	0.6	0.6	0.7	0.8	0.7	0.7	0.7	0.7
SITC section (%)	Exp.	0.6	0.6	0.6	0.7	0.7	0.7	0.7	0.7	0.7	0.7	0.8	0.7	0.7	0.7	0.7
As a percentage of	Imp.	0.2	0.2	0.2	0.3	0.3	0.2	0.2	0.2	0.2	0.2	0.3	0.2	0.2	0.2	0.2
world trade (%)	Exp.	0.3	0.2	0.3	0.3	0.3	0.3	0.2	0.2	0.2	0.2	0.3	0.3	0.2	0.2	0.2

Graph 1: Annual growth rates of exports, 1999–2013
(In percentage by year)

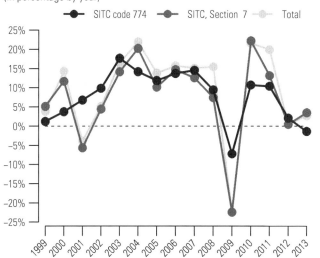

— SITC code 774 — SITC, Section 7 — Total

Table 2: Top exporting countries or areas in 2013

Country or area	Value (million US$)	Avg. Growth (%) 09-13	Growth (%) 12-13	World share %	Cum.
World	42 104.1	5.3	-1.4	100.0	
USA	9 575.1	2.9	-3.9	22.7	22.7
Germany	8 526.1	4.3	-1.9	20.3	43.0
Netherlands	3 497.8	0.2	-17.7	8.3	51.3
Japan	3 492.2	3.7	-4.0	8.3	59.6
China	2 894.1	17.7	8.7	6.9	66.5
France	1 970.3	2.6	-6.7	4.7	71.1
United Kingdom	1 934.7	8.1	12.8	4.6	75.7
Rep. of Korea	1 104.7	17.7	9.0	2.6	78.4
Singapore	910.6	27.1	41.3	2.2	80.5
Israel	816.3	-0.3	-4.9	1.9	82.5
Italy	698.5	5.8	-1.1	1.7	84.1
Finland	624.8	8.9	9.8	1.5	85.6
Mexico	588.3	19.2	8.9	1.4	87.0
China, Hong Kong SAR	583.3	14.6	12.0	1.4	88.4
Switzerland	578.0	5.9	-1.8	1.4	89.8

Graph 2: Trade Balance by MDG regions 2013
(Bln US$)

Imports — Exports — Trade balance

Developed Asia–Pacific
Developed Europe
Developed N. America
South–eastern Europe
C I S
Northern Africa
Sub–Saharan Africa
Latin Am, Caribbean
Eastern Asia
Southern Asia
South–eastern Asia
Western Asia
Oceania

-15 -10 -5 0 5 10 15 20 25

Table 3: Top importing countries or areas in 2013

Country or area	Value (million US$)	Avg. Growth (%) 09-13	Growth (%) 12-13	World share %	Cum.
World	41 841.7	5.8	-3.1	100.0	
USA	8 212.4	6.4	-1.0	19.6	19.6
China	5 378.3	19.2	7.3	12.9	32.5
Germany	2 861.8	2.0	-1.7	6.8	39.3
Japan	2 589.4	8.8	-8.6	6.2	45.5
Netherlands	2 301.1	1.0	-3.5	5.5	51.0
France	1 667.9	3.2	1.0	4.0	55.0
United Kingdom	1 300.5	3.9	8.2	3.1	58.1
Russian Federation	1 262.3	-2.1	-47.4	3.0	61.1
Canada	902.4	2.8	-6.3	2.2	63.3
Brazil	797.6	10.4	9.6	1.9	65.2
Rep. of Korea	764.8	6.9	-5.8	1.8	67.0
Italy	760.5	-4.6	-7.9	1.8	68.8
India	724.9	7.9	-6.0	1.7	70.6
Australia	647.6	6.8	-10.0	1.5	72.1
Singapore	591.2	3.1	-8.0	1.4	73.5

775 Household-type electrical and non-electrical equipment, nes

In 2013, the value (in current US$) of exports of "household-type electrical and non-electrical equipment, nes" (SITC group 775) increased by 6.2 percent (compared to 8.1 percent average growth rate from 2009-2013) to reach 100.9 bln US$ (see table 2), while imports increased by 4.1 percent to reach 101.8 bln US$ (see table 3). Exports of this commodity accounted for 1.7 percent of world exports of SITC section 7, and 0.5 percent of total world merchandise exports (see table 1). China, Germany and Italy were the top exporters in 2013 (see table 2). They accounted for 35.2, 9.3 and 4.8 percent of world exports, respectively. USA, Germany and Japan were the top destinations, with respectively 17.2, 8.1 and 5.7 percent of world imports (see table 3).

The top 15 countries/areas accounted for 83.1 and 67.0 percent of total world exports and imports, respectively (see tables 2 and 3). In 2013, China was the country/area with the highest value of net exports (+34.1 bln US$), followed by Mexico (+3.9 bln US$). By MDG regions (see graph 2), the largest surpluses in this product group were recorded by Eastern Asia (+36.0 bln US$), South-eastern Asia (+3.5 bln US$) and Latin America and the Caribbean (+504.7 mln US$). The largest trade deficits were recorded by Developed North America (-16.8 bln US$), Developed Asia-Pacific (-7.6 bln US$) and Developed Europe (-6.8 bln US$).

Table 1: Imports (Imp.) and exports (Exp.), 1999-2013, in current US$

		1999	2000	2001	2002	2003	2004	2005	2006	2007	2008	2009	2010	2011	2012	2013
Values in Bln US$	Imp.	34.4	36.8	38.1	42.1	49.4	57.7	64.3	71.7	82.1	88.0	76.2	87.9	96.6	97.8	101.8
	Exp.	35.0	36.3	37.4	41.7	48.8	58.2	63.8	71.1	81.2	86.0	73.9	84.8	94.2	95.0	100.9
As a percentage of SITC section (%)	Imp.	1.5	1.4	1.5	1.6	1.7	1.6	1.6	1.6	1.6	1.6	1.8	1.7	1.6	1.6	1.7
	Exp.	1.5	1.4	1.5	1.6	1.7	1.6	1.6	1.6	1.6	1.6	1.8	1.7	1.6	1.6	1.7
As a percentage of world trade (%)	Imp.	0.6	0.6	0.6	0.6	0.6	0.6	0.6	0.6	0.6	0.5	0.6	0.6	0.5	0.5	0.5
	Exp.	0.6	0.6	0.6	0.6	0.7	0.6	0.6	0.6	0.6	0.5	0.6	0.6	0.5	0.5	0.5

Graph 1: Annual growth rates of exports, 1999–2013
(In percentage by year)

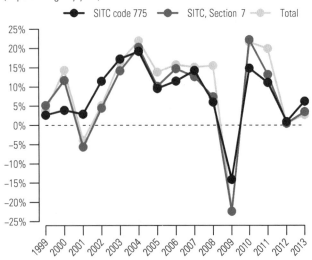

Table 2: Top exporting countries or areas in 2013

Country or area	Value (million US$)	Avg. Growth (%) 09-13	Growth (%) 12-13	World share %	Cum.
World	100 912.4	8.1	6.2	100.0	
China	35 548.1	14.5	9.7	35.2	35.2
Germany	9 398.1	2.1	5.5	9.3	44.5
Italy	4 835.2	-2.4	3.1	4.8	49.3
Poland	4 810.9	11.4	16.4	4.8	54.1
Mexico	4 803.1	5.4	3.3	4.8	58.9
Turkey	3 847.4	9.4	2.6	3.8	62.7
USA	3 563.0	5.0	3.1	3.5	66.2
Rep. of Korea	3 522.8	5.0	-1.0	3.5	69.7
Thailand	3 265.1	8.4	0.8	3.2	72.9
China, Hong Kong SAR	2 111.3	1.1	-11.0	2.1	75.0
France	2 027.7	0.6	4.4	2.0	77.0
Netherlands	1 581.8	10.7	13.9	1.6	78.6
Spain	1 530.8	11.8	5.8	1.5	80.1
Hungary	1 502.5	4.8	-2.5	1.5	81.6
Sweden	1 463.5	5.1	3.8	1.5	83.1

Graph 2: Trade Balance by MDG regions 2013
(Bln US$)

Imports — Exports — Trade balance

Developed Asia–Pacific
Developed Europe
Developed N. America
South–eastern Europe
CIS
Northern Africa
Sub–Saharan Africa
Latin Am, Caribbean
Eastern Asia
Southern Asia
South–eastern Asia
Western Asia
Oceania

Table 3: Top importing countries or areas in 2013

Country or area	Value (million US$)	Avg. Growth (%) 09-13	Growth (%) 12-13	World share %	Cum.
World	101 779.9	7.5	4.1	100.0	
USA	17 509.9	8.6	5.7	17.2	17.2
Germany	8 280.4	7.2	6.5	8.1	25.3
Japan	5 830.1	8.7	-3.3	5.7	31.1
France	5 592.3	2.4	0.4	5.5	36.6
United Kingdom	5 483.8	6.8	11.2	5.4	41.9
Russian Federation	4 524.7	19.2	-1.6	4.4	46.4
Canada	3 305.2	7.8	2.9	3.2	49.6
Italy	2 937.6	2.2	8.4	2.9	52.5
Netherlands	2 398.4	3.8	9.8	2.4	54.9
Australia	2 370.1	9.5	0.7	2.3	57.2
Belgium	2 251.0	5.7	13.3	2.2	59.4
China, Hong Kong SAR	2 169.2	4.7	-5.3	2.1	61.6
Spain	2 046.8	-1.0	8.5	2.0	63.6
Sweden	1 765.2	2.7	3.7	1.7	65.3
Poland	1 699.1	6.5	15.8	1.7	67.0

"Thermionic, microcircuits, transistors, valves, cathodes, diodes, etc" (SITC group 776) is the fourth largest exported commodity in 2013, with 3.3 percent of total exports (see table 1). The value (in current US$) of exports of this commodity increased by 11.1 percent (compared to 11.2 percent average growth rate from 2009-2013) to reach 613.4 bln US$ (see table 2), while imports increased by 9.7 percent to reach 721.0 bln US$ (see table 3). Exports of this commodity accounted for 10.2 percent of world exports of SITC section 7 (see table 1). For the second straight year, China was the top exporter in 2013, followed by Singapore and China, Hong Kong SAR, each accounting for 19.1, 14.7 and 12.7 percent of world exports, respectively. China, Singapore and China, Hong Kong SAR were the top exporters in 2013 (see table 2). They accounted for 19.1, 14.7 and 12.7 percent of world exports, respectively. China, China, Hong Kong SAR and Singapore were the top destinations, with respectively 36.3, 13.1 and 8.9 percent of world imports (see table 3). Together, China and China, Hong Kong SAR accounted for almost half of world imports of this product group.

The top 15 countries/areas accounted for 95.5 and 92.0 percent of total world exports and imports, respectively (see tables 2 and 3). In 2013, Other Asia, nes was the country/area with the highest value of net exports (+36.6 bln US$). By MDG regions (see graph 2), the largest surplus in this product group was recorded by South-eastern Asia (+20.9 bln US$). The largest trade deficit was recorded by Eastern Asia (-105.4 bln US$).

Table 1: Imports (Imp.) and exports (Exp.), 1999-2013, in current US$

		1999	2000	2001	2002	2003	2004	2005	2006	2007	2008	2009	2010	2011	2012	2013
Values in Bln US$	Imp.	242.4	328.0	262.5	278.5	321.8	398.4	430.0	490.5	522.7	529.9	465.8	633.9	654.6	657.3	721.0
	Exp.	241.2	310.1	238.7	253.4	291.2	347.5	365.5	424.2	453.6	449.4	401.1	535.5	551.4	552.2	613.4
As a percentage of	Imp.	10.4	12.5	10.5	10.8	10.9	11.2	10.9	11.0	10.5	9.8	10.9	12.1	11.1	11.0	11.7
SITC section (%)	Exp.	10.3	11.8	9.7	9.8	9.9	9.8	9.4	9.5	9.0	8.3	9.6	10.4	9.5	9.5	10.2
As a percentage of	Imp.	4.3	5.0	4.2	4.2	4.2	4.3	4.1	4.0	3.7	3.3	3.7	4.2	3.6	3.6	3.9
world trade (%)	Exp.	4.3	4.9	3.9	3.9	3.9	3.8	3.5	3.5	3.3	2.8	3.2	3.6	3.0	3.0	3.3

Graph 1: Annual growth rates of exports, 1999–2013
(In percentage by year)

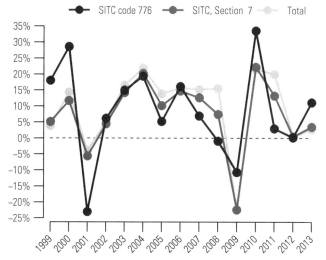

Table 2: Top exporting countries or areas in 2013

Country or area	Value (million US$)	Avg. Growth (%) 09-13	Growth (%) 12-13	World share %	Cum.
World	613 368.8	11.2	11.1	100.0	
China	117 046.5	30.5	42.2	19.1	19.1
Singapore	90 372.3	10.0	10.3	14.7	33.8
China, Hong Kong SAR	77 864.0	10.7	12.7	12.7	46.5
Other Asia, nes	70 954.3	12.9	7.2	11.6	58.1
Rep. of Korea	52 774.0	18.2	12.6	8.6	66.7
USA	41 856.8	2.5	0.7	6.8	73.5
Japan	36 403.6	-0.2	-13.0	5.9	79.4
Malaysia	35 467.3	7.6	7.3	5.8	85.2
Germany	18 609.9	5.3	3.1	3.0	88.3
Philippines	13 636.6	5.4	10.8	2.2	90.5
France	9 746.0	10.7	1.8	1.6	92.1
Thailand	8 146.3	2.5	6.3	1.3	93.4
Netherlands	5 554.6	1.5	-3.6	0.9	94.3
Israel	4 286.9	4.0	45.1	0.7	95.0
United Kingdom	3 163.7	18.2	-7.7	0.5	95.5

Graph 2: Trade Balance by MDG regions 2013
(Bln US$)

Imports — Exports — Trade balance

Developed Asia–Pacific
Developed Europe
Developed N. America
South–eastern Europe
CIS
Northern Africa
Sub–Saharan Africa
Latin Am, Caribbean
Eastern Asia
Southern Asia
South–eastern Asia
Western Asia
Oceania

-500 -400 -300 -200 -100 0 100 200 300 400

Table 3: Top importing countries or areas in 2013

Country or area	Value (million US$)	Avg. Growth (%) 09-13	Growth (%) 12-13	World share %	Cum.
World	721 048.5	11.5	9.7	100.0	
China	262 027.9	17.6	19.1	36.3	36.3
China, Hong Kong SAR	94 677.5	10.8	13.7	13.1	49.5
Singapore	64 326.0	11.3	9.7	8.9	58.4
USA	39 009.5	15.5	1.1	5.4	63.8
Other Asia, nes	34 319.5	6.3	-0.5	4.8	68.6
Rep. of Korea	33 007.5	6.8	8.6	4.6	73.1
Malaysia	30 525.1	8.1	5.0	4.2	77.4
Japan	25 068.6	7.4	12.4	3.5	80.8
Germany	18 751.5	-1.8	-8.9	2.6	83.4
Mexico	16 320.8	14.5	13.9	2.3	85.7
Viet Nam	10 956.0	76.2	37.6	1.5	87.2
Thailand	10 881.3	4.8	0.6	1.5	88.7
Philippines	10 824.9	2.3	-1.1	1.5	90.2
France	7 343.8	6.0	-5.9	1.0	91.3
Brazil	5 434.4	11.9	10.0	0.8	92.0

778 Electrical machinery and apparatus, nes

"Electrical machinery and apparatus, nes" (SITC group 778) is amongst the top exported commodities in 2013, with 1.3 percent of total exports (see table 1). The value (in current US$) of exports of this commodity increased by 6.1 percent (compared to 11.1 percent average growth rate from 2009-2013) to reach 239.3 bln US$ (see table 2), while imports increased by 4.1 percent to reach 227.3 bln US$ (see table 3). Exports of this commodity accounted for 4.0 percent of world exports of SITC section 7 (see table 1). China was again the top exporter in 2013, with more than double the amount of the second largest exporter, Germany, and then followed by Japan (see table 2). These three exporters accounted for 22.0, 8.8 and 8.6 percent of world exports, respectively, together accounting for nearly 40 percent of world exports. USA, China and Germany were the top destinations, with respectively 14.0, 11.9 and 7.8 percent of world imports (see table 3).

The top 15 countries/areas accounted for 81.4 and 68.1 percent of total world exports and imports, respectively (see tables 2 and 3). In 2013, China was the country/area with the highest value of net exports (+25.7 bln US$), followed by Japan (+13.6 bln US$). By MDG regions (see graph 2), the largest surpluses in this product group were recorded by Eastern Asia (+42.2 bln US$) and Developed Asia-Pacific (+11.2 bln US$). The largest trade deficits were recorded by Developed North America (-17.9 bln US$) and Latin America and the Caribbean (-7.3 bln US$).

Table 1: Imports (Imp.) and exports (Exp.), 1999-2013, in current US$

		1999	2000	2001	2002	2003	2004	2005	2006	2007	2008	2009	2010	2011	2012	2013
Values in Bln US$	Imp.	88.1	106.6	94.6	96.8	113.5	140.4	149.3	163.6	177.4	193.3	158.9	197.0	223.9	218.4	227.3
	Exp.	87.6	103.1	89.4	94.1	108.8	135.4	147.5	166.7	179.4	194.9	157.3	198.1	224.3	225.6	239.3
As a percentage of	Imp.	3.8	4.1	3.8	3.8	3.9	3.9	3.8	3.7	3.6	3.6	3.7	3.8	3.8	3.7	3.7
SITC section (%)	Exp.	3.7	3.9	3.6	3.6	3.7	3.8	3.8	3.7	3.6	3.6	3.7	3.9	3.9	3.9	4.0
As a percentage of	Imp.	1.5	1.6	1.5	1.5	1.5	1.5	1.4	1.3	1.3	1.2	1.3	1.3	1.2	1.2	1.2
world trade (%)	Exp.	1.6	1.6	1.5	1.5	1.5	1.5	1.4	1.4	1.3	1.2	1.3	1.3	1.2	1.2	1.3

Graph 1: Annual growth rates of exports, 1999–2013
(In percentage by year)

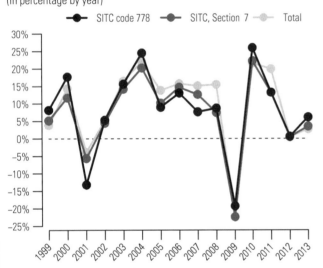

Legend: SITC code 778 — SITC, Section 7 — Total

Table 2: Top exporting countries or areas in 2013

Country or area	Value (million US$)	Avg. Growth (%) 09-13	Growth (%) 12-13	World share %	World share % Cum.
World	239 340.6	11.1	6.1	100.0	
China	52 650.4	17.3	12.9	22.0	22.0
Germany	21 165.8	8.8	7.9	8.8	30.8
Japan	20 665.6	5.3	-9.6	8.6	39.5
Rep. of Korea	19 131.7	27.3	15.7	8.0	47.5
USA	17 721.0	10.6	3.5	7.4	54.9
China, Hong Kong SAR	12 190.8	11.9	7.1	5.1	60.0
Mexico	8 321.8	10.8	5.8	3.5	63.4
Other Asia, nes	8 321.3	-1.6	9.0	3.5	66.9
Singapore	6 300.6	9.8	-5.7	2.6	69.6
France	6 190.3	2.7	3.5	2.6	72.1
United Kingdom	4 762.8	10.4	3.1	2.0	74.1
Netherlands	4 622.1	7.5	1.1	1.9	76.1
Belgium	4 555.6	4.2	9.5	1.9	78.0
Czech Rep.	4 343.4	14.2	9.4	1.8	79.8
Italy	3 964.8	4.2	8.3	1.7	81.4

Graph 2: Trade Balance by MDG regions 2013
(Bln US$)

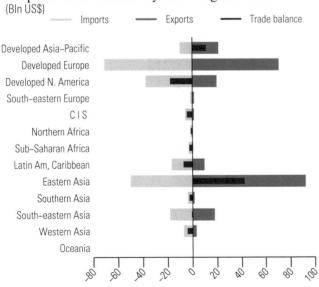

Legend: Imports — Exports — Trade balance

Regions (top to bottom): Developed Asia–Pacific, Developed Europe, Developed N. America, South–eastern Europe, CIS, Northern Africa, Sub–Saharan Africa, Latin Am, Caribbean, Eastern Asia, Southern Asia, South–eastern Asia, Western Asia, Oceania

Table 3: Top importing countries or areas in 2013

Country or area	Value (million US$)	Avg. Growth (%) 09-13	Growth (%) 12-13	World share %	World share % Cum.
World	227 260.5	9.4	4.1	100.0	
USA	31 710.2	12.7	4.8	14.0	14.0
China	26 947.3	9.4	8.9	11.9	25.8
Germany	17 811.7	10.4	8.3	7.8	33.6
China, Hong Kong SAR	11 722.2	8.8	3.0	5.2	38.8
Mexico	8 617.3	13.7	8.4	3.8	42.6
France	8 033.9	7.0	8.6	3.5	46.1
Rep. of Korea	7 685.6	4.2	11.0	3.4	49.5
United Kingdom	7 180.4	11.1	9.5	3.2	52.7
Japan	7 074.4	9.7	-7.4	3.1	55.8
Canada	5 857.1	11.6	4.1	2.6	58.4
Thailand	4 667.6	14.4	-10.9	2.1	60.4
Singapore	4 598.7	7.7	-5.4	2.0	62.4
Netherlands	4 562.9	8.7	4.4	2.0	64.4
Italy	4 214.1	3.2	5.5	1.9	66.3
Russian Federation	4 108.8	24.3	-2.3	1.8	68.1

Source: UN Comtrade and UN Service Trade
2013 International Trade Statistics Yearbook, Vol. II

"Cars, other motor vehicles principally designed for the transports of persons" (SITC group 781) is the third top exported commodity in 2013, with 3.6 percent of total exports (see table 1). The value (in current US$) of exports of this commodity increased by 4.3 percent (compared to 11.5 percent average growth rate from 2009-2013) to reach 677.9 bln US$ (see table 2), while imports increased by 4.3 percent to reach 671.6 bln US$ (see table 3). Exports of this commodity accounted for 11.2 percent of world exports of SITC section 7 (see table 1). Germany, Japan and USA were the top exporters in 2013 (see table 2). They accounted for 21.9, 13.5 and 8.4 percent of world exports, respectively. While still the second largest exporter, Japan's exports decreased by 5.9 percent in 2013. USA was again the top destination, accounting for nearly one-fourth of world imports, followed by China and Germany. These three importers accounted for respectively 23.2, 7.1 and 6.1 percent of world imports (see table 3).

The top 15 countries/areas accounted for 87.3 and 72.1 percent of total world exports and imports, respectively (see tables 2 and 3). In 2013, Germany was the country/area with the highest value of net exports (+107.7 bln US$), followed by Japan (+81.1 bln US$). By MDG regions (see graph 2), the largest surpluses in this product group were recorded by Developed Europe (+99.6 bln US$) and Developed Asia-Pacific (+62.3 bln US$). The largest trade deficit was recorded by Developed North America (-79.7 bln US$).

Table 1: Imports (Imp.) and exports (Exp.), 1999-2013, in current US$

		1999	2000	2001	2002	2003	2004	2005	2006	2007	2008	2009	2010	2011	2012	2013
Values in Bln US$	Imp.	295.3	310.2	317.8	346.5	396.3	462.6	483.7	539.7	622.9	629.8	444.6	552.8	636.3	643.9	671.7
	Exp.	293.7	303.9	309.1	344.4	393.9	455.8	487.1	537.6	623.4	636.7	438.6	559.1	640.3	649.8	677.9
As a percentage of SITC section (%)	Imp.	12.6	11.8	12.8	13.4	13.4	13.0	12.3	12.1	12.5	11.7	10.4	10.6	10.8	10.8	10.9
	Exp.	12.5	11.6	12.5	13.4	13.4	12.9	12.5	12.0	12.4	11.8	10.5	10.9	11.0	11.1	11.2
As a percentage of world trade (%)	Imp.	5.2	4.7	5.0	5.3	5.2	5.0	4.6	4.4	4.4	3.9	3.5	3.6	3.5	3.5	3.6
	Exp.	5.3	4.8	5.1	5.4	5.3	5.0	4.7	4.5	4.5	4.0	3.5	3.7	3.5	3.6	3.6

Graph 1: Annual growth rates of exports, 1999–2013
(In percentage by year)

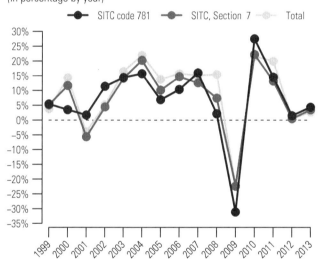

Graph 2: Trade Balance by MDG regions 2013
(Bln US$)

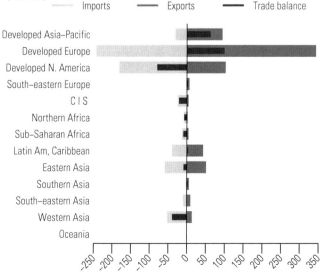

Table 2: Top exporting countries or areas in 2013

Country or area	Value (million US$)	Avg. Growth (%) 09-13	Growth (%) 12-13	World share %	Cum.
World	677 917.4	11.5	4.3	100.0	
Germany	148 651.1	9.8	1.6	21.9	21.9
Japan	91 688.8	10.2	-5.9	13.5	35.5
USA	57 132.2	19.1	4.8	8.4	43.9
Canada	45 230.4	18.0	-3.6	6.7	50.6
Rep. of Korea	44 283.4	18.6	4.5	6.5	57.1
United Kingdom	38 228.3	19.8	12.5	5.6	62.7
Mexico	32 389.4	21.0	11.0	4.8	67.5
Belgium	32 124.8	7.8	17.1	4.7	72.2
Spain	29 175.6	2.8	16.1	4.3	76.5
France	18 658.1	-1.6	-7.5	2.8	79.3
Czech Rep.	15 324.0	9.7	0.8	2.3	81.6
Slovakia	14 446.9	17.4	9.3	2.1	83.7
Italy	10 021.1	6.0	8.7	1.5	85.2
Hungary	7 399.1	17.1	45.3	1.1	86.3
Poland	6 900.9	-8.1	1.7	1.0	87.3

Table 3: Top importing countries or areas in 2013

Country or area	Value (million US$)	Avg. Growth (%) 09-13	Growth (%) 12-13	World share %	Cum.
World	671 650.4	10.9	4.3	100.0	
USA	155 689.4	17.3	4.0	23.2	23.2
China	47 465.8	34.8	4.3	7.1	30.2
Germany	40 913.6	1.2	1.8	6.1	36.3
United Kingdom	38 762.8	8.4	12.3	5.8	42.1
France	31 336.2	0.7	3.4	4.7	46.8
Belgium	30 013.1	7.0	17.6	4.5	51.2
Canada	26 337.9	11.5	1.6	3.9	55.2
Italy	20 206.7	-9.2	-0.4	3.0	58.2
Australia	17 646.8	17.5	0.7	2.6	60.8
Russian Federation	16 996.9	18.9	-16.0	2.5	63.3
Saudi Arabia	16 089.8	18.1	0.6	2.4	65.7
Spain	11 325.3	-3.2	12.4	1.7	67.4
Netherlands	11 015.3	6.8	-1.6	1.6	69.1
Japan	10 608.7	23.3	-2.6	1.6	70.6
Switzerland	10 184.2	9.1	-7.5	1.5	72.1

782 Motor vehicles for the transport of goods; special-purpose motor vehicles

In 2013, the value (in current US$) of exports of "motor vehicles for the transport of goods; special-purpose motor vehicles" (SITC group 782) decreased by 0.4 percent (compared to 14.4 percent average growth rate from 2009-2013) to reach 137.0 bln US$ (see table 2), while imports decreased by 0.2 percent to reach 137.4 bln US$ (see table 3). Exports of this commodity accounted for 2.3 percent of world exports of SITC section 7, and 0.7 percent of total world merchandise exports (see table 1). USA, Mexico and Germany were the top exporters in 2013 (see table 2). They accounted for 13.2, 12.9 and 11.0 percent of world exports, respectively. USA, Canada and United Kingdom were the top destinations, with respectively 14.0, 10.5 and 4.6 percent of world imports (see table 3).

The top 15 countries/areas accounted for 83.0 and 62.1 percent of total world exports and imports, respectively (see tables 2 and 3). In 2013, Mexico was the country/area with the highest value of net exports (+15.2 bln US$), followed by Thailand (+10.2 bln US$). By MDG regions (see graph 2), the largest surpluses in this product group were recorded by Developed Europe (+10.0 bln US$), Latin America and the Caribbean (+8.0 bln US$) and South-eastern Asia (+6.7 bln US$). The largest trade deficits were recorded by Developed North America (-14.3 bln US$), Western Asia (-5.2 bln US$) and Sub-Saharan Africa (-4.9 bln US$).

Table 1: Imports (Imp.) and exports (Exp.), 1999-2013, in current US$

		1999	2000	2001	2002	2003	2004	2005	2006	2007	2008	2009	2010	2011	2012	2013
Values in Bln US$	Imp.	56.4	59.3	59.0	63.8	71.5	83.5	94.2	106.9	132.7	138.7	84.3	109.2	130.1	137.7	137.4
	Exp.	53.4	56.9	56.3	60.2	68.2	80.2	89.9	103.4	128.1	134.2	79.9	105.3	128.4	137.5	137.0
As a percentage of SITC section (%)	Imp.	2.4	2.3	2.4	2.5	2.4	2.3	2.4	2.4	2.7	2.6	2.0	2.1	2.2	2.3	2.2
	Exp.	2.3	2.2	2.3	2.3	2.3	2.3	2.3	2.3	2.5	2.5	1.9	2.1	2.2	2.4	2.3
As a percentage of world trade (%)	Imp.	1.0	0.9	0.9	1.0	0.9	0.9	0.9	0.9	0.9	0.9	0.7	0.7	0.7	0.8	0.7
	Exp.	1.0	0.9	0.9	0.9	0.9	0.9	0.9	0.9	0.9	0.8	0.6	0.7	0.7	0.8	0.7

Graph 1: Annual growth rates of exports, 1999–2013
(In percentage by year)

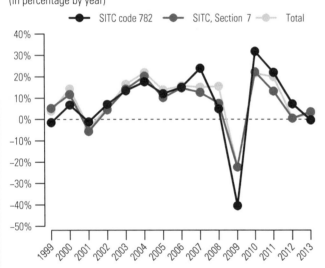

- SITC code 782
- SITC, Section 7
- Total

Graph 2: Trade Balance by MDG regions 2013
(Bln US$)

----- Imports   —— Exports   —— Trade balance

Developed Asia–Pacific
Developed Europe
Developed N. America
South–eastern Europe
CIS
Northern Africa
Sub–Saharan Africa
Latin Am, Caribbean
Eastern Asia
Southern Asia
South–eastern Asia
Western Asia
Oceania

Table 2: Top exporting countries or areas in 2013

Country or area	Value (million US$)	Avg. Growth (%) 09-13	Growth (%) 12-13	World share %	Cum.
World	137047.4	14.4	-0.4	100.0	
USA	18145.2	11.5	-7.6	13.2	13.2
Mexico	17613.9	28.1	18.6	12.9	26.1
Germany	15099.2	9.8	1.0	11.0	37.1
Thailand	10613.0	31.4	0.6	7.7	44.9
Japan	10385.1	11.1	-19.4	7.6	52.4
Italy	5869.4	10.0	5.0	4.3	56.7
China	5743.8	18.2	-10.9	4.2	60.9
Spain	5545.5	9.6	13.4	4.0	65.0
France	4953.9	8.0	16.0	3.6	68.6
Argentina	4124.1	29.3	7.4	3.0	71.6
Turkey	3999.9	13.2	11.9	2.9	74.5
Netherlands	3172.6	12.3	13.9	2.3	76.8
South Africa	3040.5	35.9	-2.3	2.2	79.0
Belgium	2819.5	10.3	8.1	2.1	81.1
Rep. of Korea	2642.2	7.9	-3.2	1.9	83.0

Table 3: Top importing countries or areas in 2013

Country or area	Value (million US$)	Avg. Growth (%) 09-13	Growth (%) 12-13	World share %	Cum.
World	137404.9	13.0	-0.2	100.0	
USA	19276.8	22.6	13.3	14.0	14.0
Canada	14429.4	15.6	2.4	10.5	24.5
United Kingdom	6252.1	18.2	16.0	4.6	29.1
Australia	6202.7	15.7	-30.0	4.5	33.6
France	6098.1	8.1	25.8	4.4	38.0
Germany	5975.2	8.9	1.7	4.3	42.4
Saudi Arabia	4207.4	13.2	11.4	3.1	45.4
Belgium	3632.3	7.1	11.1	2.6	48.1
Brazil	3579.8	22.3	8.8	2.6	50.7
Russian Federation	3468.5	41.2	-21.3	2.5	53.2
Chile	2768.8	26.6	-13.1	2.0	55.2
Algeria	2582.3	8.9	0.1	1.9	57.1
Netherlands	2564.2	9.4	-4.9	1.9	59.0
Mexico	2377.5	3.6	-0.2	1.7	60.7
Italy	1940.7	-9.6	0.0	1.4	62.1

In 2013, the value (in current US$) of exports of "road motor vehicles, nes" (SITC group 783) increased by 1.9 percent (compared to 16.7 percent average growth rate from 2009-2013) to reach 46.5 bln US$ (see table 2), while imports increased by 3.9 percent to reach 42.2 bln US$ (see table 3). Exports of this commodity accounted for 0.8 percent of world exports of SITC section 7, and 0.2 percent of total world merchandise exports (see table 1). Germany, Mexico and Netherlands were the top exporters in 2013 (see table 2). They accounted for 15.3, 11.1 and 11.1 percent of world exports, respectively. USA, Canada and France were the top destinations, with respectively 13.6, 6.5 and 5.5 percent of world imports (see table 3).

The top 15 countries/areas accounted for 90.5 and 56.7 percent of total world exports and imports, respectively (see tables 2 and 3). In 2013, Germany was the country/area with the highest value of net exports (+4.8 bln US$), followed by Mexico (+4.7 bln US$). By MDG regions (see graph 2), the largest surpluses in this product group were recorded by Developed Europe (+10.3 bln US$), Eastern Asia (+3.4 bln US$) and Developed Asia-Pacific (+3.1 bln US$). The largest trade deficits were recorded by Developed North America (-4.7 bln US$), Sub-Saharan Africa (-2.2 bln US$) and Commonwealth of Independent States (-2.1 bln US$).

Table 1: Imports (Imp.) and exports (Exp.), 1999-2013, in current US$

		1999	2000	2001	2002	2003	2004	2005	2006	2007	2008	2009	2010	2011	2012	2013
Values in Bln US$	Imp.	16.5	15.3	13.7	14.8	17.6	23.4	25.8	30.9	39.0	44.9	25.4	30.3	42.2	40.6	42.2
	Exp.	17.8	16.3	14.8	16.6	20.9	27.7	30.2	34.2	41.5	49.9	25.1	32.7	46.3	45.7	46.5
As a percentage of SITC section (%)	Imp.	0.7	0.6	0.5	0.6	0.6	0.7	0.7	0.7	0.8	0.8	0.6	0.6	0.7	0.7	0.7
	Exp.	0.8	0.6	0.6	0.6	0.7	0.8	0.8	0.8	0.8	0.9	0.6	0.6	0.8	0.8	0.8
As a percentage of world trade (%)	Imp.	0.3	0.2	0.2	0.2	0.2	0.3	0.2	0.3	0.3	0.3	0.2	0.2	0.2	0.2	0.2
	Exp.	0.3	0.3	0.2	0.3	0.3	0.3	0.3	0.3	0.3	0.3	0.2	0.2	0.3	0.3	0.2

Graph 1: Annual growth rates of exports, 1999–2013
(In percentage by year)

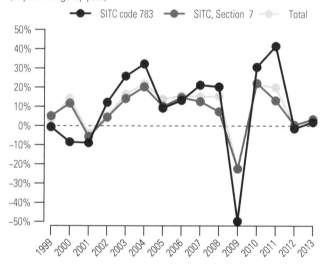

Table 2: Top exporting countries or areas in 2013

Country or area	Value (million US$)	Avg. Growth (%) 09-13	Growth (%) 12-13	World share %	Cum.
World	46 549.5	16.7	1.9	100.0	
Germany	7 124.3	16.6	5.9	15.3	15.3
Mexico	5 168.0	22.5	-9.5	11.1	26.4
Netherlands	5 155.0	26.1	13.5	11.1	37.5
USA	3 389.4	19.6	-15.8	7.3	44.8
Japan	3 386.2	12.0	-8.8	7.3	52.0
Belgium	3 284.9	24.9	8.4	7.1	59.1
China	2 967.0	30.0	0.6	6.4	65.5
Sweden	2 085.1	28.4	25.5	4.5	69.9
France	1 883.6	10.1	-7.9	4.0	74.0
Spain	1 730.2	47.3	112.9	3.7	77.7
Poland	1 698.1	2.9	9.1	3.6	81.4
Rep. of Korea	1 228.3	11.3	-22.4	2.6	84.0
Turkey	1 182.8	1.6	7.6	2.5	86.5
Brazil	1 107.1	28.1	6.6	2.4	88.9
Czech Rep.	730.0	4.2	20.7	1.6	90.5

Graph 2: Trade Balance by MDG regions 2013
(Bln US$)

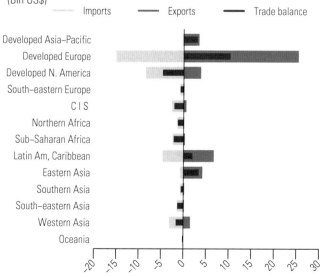

Table 3: Top importing countries or areas in 2013

Country or area	Value (million US$)	Avg. Growth (%) 09-13	Growth (%) 12-13	World share %	Cum.
World	42 173.1	13.6	3.9	100.0	
USA	5 755.4	18.0	9.8	13.6	13.6
Canada	2 724.0	21.3	-12.2	6.5	20.1
France	2 327.2	7.1	25.0	5.5	25.6
Germany	2 302.3	20.5	33.6	5.5	31.1
Russian Federation	1 624.8	47.3	-38.5	3.9	34.9
Poland	1 361.3	34.8	21.6	3.2	38.2
Belgium	1 094.9	12.3	13.6	2.6	40.8
Italy	1 064.1	8.6	23.1	2.5	43.3
United Kingdom	1 062.4	23.4	55.6	2.5	45.8
Chile	1 013.8	27.9	6.7	2.4	48.2
Saudi Arabia	748.3	13.7	-3.4	1.8	50.0
Spain	725.6	31.9	13.5	1.7	51.7
Peru	724.4	30.5	-1.2	1.7	53.4
Netherlands	718.4	2.9	1.5	1.7	55.1
Algeria	667.7	-0.8	9.5	1.6	56.7

784 Parts and accessories of the motor vehicles of 722, 781, 782 and 783

"Parts and accessories of the motor vehicles of 722, 781, 782 and 783" (SITC group 784) is amongst the top exported commodities in 2013 with 2.0 percent of total exports (see table 1). The value (in current US$) of exports of this commodity increased by 4.9 percent (compared to 13.4 percent average growth rate from 2009-2013) to reach 377.0 bln US$ (see table 2), while imports increased by 6.0 percent to reach 373.6 bln US$ (see table 3). Exports of this commodity accounted for 6.2 percent of world exports of SITC section 7 (see table 1). Germany, USA and Japan were the top exporters in 2013 (see table 2). They accounted for 15.3, 11.6 and 9.8 percent of world exports, respectively. USA, Germany and China were the top destinations, with respectively 16.0, 9.9 and 6.5 percent of world imports (see table 3).

The top 15 countries/areas accounted for 81.4 and 73.7 percent of total world exports and imports, respectively (see tables 2 and 3). In 2013, Japan was the country/area with the highest value of net exports (+29.7 bln US$), followed by Germany (+20.8 bln US$). Export from Japan dropped by 11.3 percent, while most of the other top exporters recorded relatively strong growth rates. By MDG regions (see graph 2), the largest surpluses in this product group were recorded by Developed Asia-Pacific (+27.5 bln US$), Eastern Asia (+23.5 bln US$) and Developed Europe (+21.1 bln US$). The largest trade deficit was recorded by Developed North America (-27.2 bln US$).

Table 1: Imports (Imp.) and exports (Exp.), 1999-2013, in current US$

		1999	2000	2001	2002	2003	2004	2005	2006	2007	2008	2009	2010	2011	2012	2013
Values in Bln US$	Imp.	138.4	145.0	140.8	156.3	182.7	216.0	231.2	255.4	293.7	305.7	223.4	292.4	347.2	352.4	373.6
	Exp.	134.1	142.8	137.6	152.8	179.5	214.3	234.4	258.3	295.4	309.8	227.8	301.3	354.8	359.5	377.0
As a percentage of SITC section (%)	Imp.	5.9	5.5	5.7	6.1	6.2	6.1	5.9	5.7	5.9	5.7	5.2	5.6	5.9	5.9	6.1
	Exp.	5.7	5.5	5.6	5.9	6.1	6.1	6.0	5.8	5.9	5.7	5.4	5.9	6.1	6.2	6.2
As a percentage of world trade (%)	Imp.	2.4	2.2	2.2	2.4	2.4	2.3	2.2	2.1	2.1	1.9	1.8	1.9	1.9	1.9	2.0
	Exp.	2.4	2.2	2.3	2.4	2.4	2.4	2.3	2.2	2.1	1.9	1.8	2.0	2.0	2.0	2.0

Graph 1: Annual growth rates of exports, 1999–2013
(In percentage by year)

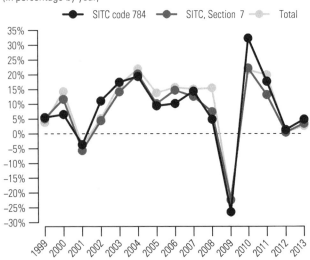

Graph 2: Trade Balance by MDG regions 2013
(Bln US$)

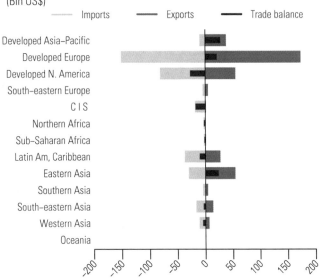

Table 2: Top exporting countries or areas in 2013

Country or area	Value (million US$)	Avg. Growth (%) 09-13	Growth (%) 12-13	World share %	Cum.
World	377 041.2	13.4	4.9	100.0	
Germany	57 709.2	14.3	8.5	15.3	15.3
USA	43 580.9	16.0	2.6	11.6	26.9
Japan	36 861.5	9.9	-11.3	9.8	36.6
China	25 763.5	21.8	13.0	6.8	43.5
Rep. of Korea	23 927.0	21.4	5.2	6.3	49.8
Mexico	20 622.1	22.0	7.6	5.5	55.3
France	17 730.5	3.9	2.9	4.7	60.0
Italy	15 285.0	9.6	8.6	4.1	64.0
Czech Rep	11 743.8	11.3	12.3	3.1	67.2
Spain	11 097.0	4.5	6.4	2.9	70.1
Canada	10 724.8	13.2	2.6	2.8	72.9
Poland	9 972.3	10.0	14.4	2.6	75.6
Belgium	8 163.5	9.0	18.9	2.2	77.8
Sweden	7 125.5	16.5	8.6	1.9	79.6
United Kingdom	6 610.8	10.8	-2.1	1.8	81.4

Table 3: Top importing countries or areas in 2013

Country or area	Value (million US$)	Avg. Growth (%) 09-13	Growth (%) 12-13	World share %	Cum.
World	373 628.6	13.7	6.0	100.0	
USA	59 793.5	18.3	1.1	16.0	16.0
Germany	36 951.8	12.4	9.1	9.9	25.9
China	24 324.1	18.2	10.3	6.5	32.4
Canada	21 704.4	13.2	0.2	5.8	38.2
Mexico	20 806.0	17.4	0.2	5.6	43.8
Spain	17 424.7	6.3	16.5	4.7	48.4
United Kingdom	16 122.6	14.1	4.9	4.3	52.8
Russian Federation	15 632.7	43.2	6.2	4.2	56.9
France	13 286.2	4.0	3.1	3.6	60.5
Belgium	10 894.0	7.7	12.3	2.9	63.4
Brazil	8 403.3	22.9	21.3	2.2	65.7
Thailand	8 101.2	27.0	-6.3	2.2	67.8
Czech Rep	7 483.7	11.3	2.2	2.0	69.8
Slovakia	7 313.1	17.8	6.4	2.0	71.8
Japan	7 150.6	15.9	2.9	1.9	73.7

In 2013, the value (in current US$) of exports of "motorcycles and cycles motorized and non-motorized; invalid carriages" (SITC group 785) increased by 2.3 percent (compared to 8.6 percent average growth rate from 2009-2013) to reach 49.0 bln US$ (see table 2), while imports increased by 0.6 percent to reach 44.9 bln US$ (see table 3). Exports of this commodity accounted for 0.8 percent of world exports of SITC section 7, and 0.3 percent of total world merchandise exports (see table 1). China, Japan and Other Asia, nes were the top exporters in 2013 (see table 2). They accounted for 29.9, 9.1 and 8.4 percent of world exports, respectively. USA, Germany and France were the top destinations, with respectively 12.0, 8.1 and 5.2 percent of world imports (see table 3).

The top 15 countries/areas accounted for 87.5 and 62.0 percent of total world exports and imports, respectively (see tables 2 and 3). In 2013, China was the country/area with the highest value of net exports (+14.0 bln US$), followed by Other Asia, nes (+3.0 bln US$). By MDG regions (see graph 2), the largest surpluses in this product group were recorded by Eastern Asia (+16.4 bln US$), South-eastern Asia (+1.7 bln US$) and Southern Asia (+1.1 bln US$). The largest trade deficits were recorded by Developed Europe (-4.8 bln US$), Developed North America (-3.8 bln US$) and Latin America and the Caribbean (-3.3 bln US$).

Table 1: Imports (Imp.) and exports (Exp.), 1999-2013, in current US$

		1999	2000	2001	2002	2003	2004	2005	2006	2007	2008	2009	2010	2011	2012	2013
Values in Bln US$	Imp.	18.9	20.9	20.2	21.0	24.7	29.0	32.1	34.7	41.1	45.5	35.2	38.5	44.1	44.7	44.9
	Exp.	19.4	21.4	19.9	21.1	25.0	29.7	32.5	35.5	40.5	46.6	35.2	40.0	46.7	47.9	49.0
As a percentage of	Imp.	0.8	0.8	0.8	0.8	0.8	0.8	0.8	0.8	0.8	0.8	0.8	0.7	0.7	0.7	0.7
SITC section (%)	Exp.	0.8	0.8	0.8	0.8	0.8	0.8	0.8	0.8	0.8	0.9	0.8	0.8	0.8	0.8	0.8
As a percentage of	Imp.	0.3	0.3	0.3	0.3	0.3	0.3	0.3	0.3	0.3	0.3	0.3	0.3	0.2	0.2	0.2
world trade (%)	Exp.	0.3	0.3	0.3	0.3	0.3	0.3	0.3	0.3	0.3	0.3	0.3	0.3	0.3	0.3	0.3

Graph 1: Annual growth rates of exports, 1999–2013
(In percentage by year)

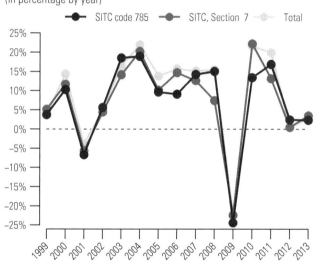

Graph 2: Trade Balance by MDG regions 2013
(Bln US$)

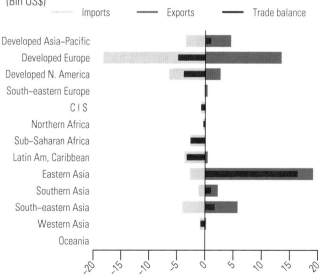

Table 2: Top exporting countries or areas in 2013

Country or area	Value (million US$)	Avg. Growth (%) 09-13	Growth (%) 12-13	World share %	Cum.
World	48 966.6	8.6	2.3	100.0	
China	14 640.8	15.5	7.2	29.9	29.9
Japan	4 433.1	-1.3	-12.6	9.1	39.0
Other Asia, nes	4 116.0	4.9	-13.5	8.4	47.4
Italy	2 833.4	-0.1	-5.7	5.8	53.1
Germany	2 745.6	7.5	9.3	5.6	58.8
USA	2 375.4	5.6	3.9	4.9	63.6
Thailand	2 239.0	16.2	18.0	4.6	68.2
India	2 088.2	28.3	21.1	4.3	72.4
Netherlands	1 597.1	3.1	5.2	3.3	75.7
Belgium	1 263.5	-0.7	13.8	2.6	78.3
Singapore	1 249.2	21.6	4.8	2.6	80.8
Austria	1 018.8	11.1	14.0	2.1	82.9
United Kingdom	770.4	9.7	17.3	1.6	84.5
France	764.0	-3.2	4.3	1.6	86.0
Indonesia	705.9	26.8	-11.3	1.4	87.5

Table 3: Top importing countries or areas in 2013

Country or area	Value (million US$)	Avg. Growth (%) 09-13	Growth (%) 12-13	World share %	Cum.
World	44 936.3	6.3	0.6	100.0	
USA	5 410.2	5.5	-4.7	12.0	12.0
Germany	3 643.1	4.1	0.5	8.1	20.1
France	2 314.8	-3.1	2.9	5.2	25.3
Japan	2 268.9	6.5	-2.1	5.0	30.3
Netherlands	2 011.2	3.9	3.6	4.5	34.8
United Kingdom	1 850.4	-0.4	6.4	4.1	38.9
Belgium	1 632.2	8.2	6.4	3.6	42.6
Italy	1 589.7	-6.1	-8.2	3.5	46.1
Nigeria	1 137.0	25.4	22.9	2.5	48.6
Other Asia, nes	1 094.7	7.1	-11.9	2.4	51.1
Canada	1 075.7	2.9	3.4	2.4	53.5
Australia	1 060.5	5.7	0.4	2.4	55.8
Singapore	961.7	19.5	-2.7	2.1	58.0
Spain	957.0	-6.4	-7.9	2.1	60.1
Indonesia	873.1	14.3	-2.5	1.9	62.0

786 Trailers, semi-trailers; other vehicles, not mechanically propelled

In 2013, the value (in current US$) of exports of "trailers, semi-trailers; other vehicles, not mechanically propelled" (SITC group 786) increased by 1.5 percent (compared to 18.1 percent average growth rate from 2009-2013) to reach 33.8 bln US$ (see table 2), while imports increased by 5.4 percent to reach 26.9 bln US$ (see table 3). Exports of this commodity accounted for 0.6 percent of world exports of SITC section 7, and 0.2 percent of total world merchandise exports (see table 1). China, Germany and USA were the top exporters in 2013 (see table 2). They accounted for 32.7, 16.7 and 13.3 percent of world exports, respectively. Canada, USA and Germany were the top destinations, with respectively 12.0, 10.1 and 8.4 percent of world imports (see table 3).

The top 15 countries/areas accounted for 86.0 and 64.1 percent of total world exports and imports, respectively (see tables 2 and 3). In 2013, China was the country/area with the highest value of net exports (+10.9 bln US$), followed by Germany (+3.4 bln US$). By MDG regions (see graph 2), the largest surpluses in this product group were recorded by Eastern Asia (+10.8 bln US$) and Developed Europe (+2.5 bln US$). The largest trade deficits were recorded by Commonwealth of Independent States (-1.6 bln US$), Developed Asia-Pacific (-1.1 bln US$) and Developed North America (-996.0 mln US$).

Table 1: Imports (Imp.) and exports (Exp.), 1999-2013, in current US$

		1999	2000	2001	2002	2003	2004	2005	2006	2007	2008	2009	2010	2011	2012	2013
Values in Bln US$	Imp.	8.3	9.3	8.3	8.9	11.0	14.3	16.9	20.6	26.6	28.3	15.5	18.6	25.1	25.5	26.9
	Exp.	10.3	11.1	10.4	11.2	14.9	20.0	23.2	26.7	34.9	37.1	17.4	25.6	36.4	33.3	33.8
As a percentage of SITC section (%)	Imp.	0.4	0.4	0.3	0.3	0.4	0.4	0.4	0.5	0.5	0.5	0.4	0.4	0.4	0.4	0.4
	Exp.	0.4	0.4	0.4	0.4	0.5	0.6	0.6	0.6	0.7	0.7	0.4	0.5	0.6	0.6	0.6
As a percentage of world trade (%)	Imp.	0.1	0.1	0.1	0.1	0.1	0.2	0.2	0.2	0.2	0.2	0.1	0.1	0.1	0.1	0.1
	Exp.	0.2	0.2	0.2	0.2	0.2	0.2	0.2	0.2	0.3	0.2	0.1	0.2	0.2	0.2	0.2

Graph 1: Annual growth rates of exports, 1999–2013
(In percentage by year)

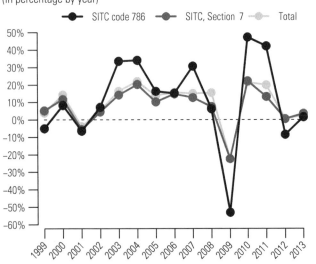

Legend: SITC code 786 — SITC, Section 7 — Total

Graph 2: Trade Balance by MDG regions 2013
(Bln US$)

Legend: Imports — Exports — Trade balance

Regions: Developed Asia–Pacific, Developed Europe, Developed N. America, South–eastern Europe, CIS, Northern Africa, Sub–Saharan Africa, Latin Am, Caribbean, Eastern Asia, Southern Asia, South–eastern Asia, Western Asia, Oceania

Table 2: Top exporting countries or areas in 2013

Country or area	Value (million US$)	Avg. Growth (%) 09-13	Growth (%) 12-13	World share %	Cum.
World	33 780.7	18.1	1.5	100.0	
China	11 030.1	33.4	-2.7	32.7	32.7
Germany	5 645.8	15.0	3.2	16.7	49.4
USA	4 508.9	22.1	10.2	13.3	62.7
Netherlands	1 180.9	11.6	12.4	3.5	66.2
Poland	918.2	18.6	4.8	2.7	68.9
France	829.4	1.1	0.7	2.5	71.4
Mexico	780.2	36.6	-10.0	2.3	73.7
Belgium	742.8	3.7	12.4	2.2	75.9
Italy	669.6	8.3	5.8	2.0	77.9
United Kingdom	582.9	5.6	19.5	1.7	79.6
Hungary	553.6	21.3	8.1	1.6	81.2
Austria	483.7	10.2	-1.7	1.4	82.7
Canada	418.3	15.0	-5.3	1.2	83.9
Czech Rep.	363.6	14.2	1.8	1.1	85.0
Denmark	346.2	3.9	-12.8	1.0	86.0

Table 3: Top importing countries or areas in 2013

Country or area	Value (million US$)	Avg. Growth (%) 09-13	Growth (%) 12-13	World share %	Cum.
World	26 853.6	14.8	5.4	100.0	
Canada	3 217.1	21.7	5.9	12.0	12.0
USA	2 702.3	21.1	-1.2	10.1	22.0
Germany	2 246.1	13.6	4.6	8.4	30.4
Russian Federation	1 282.0	35.2	-12.0	4.8	35.2
France	1 156.3	3.5	1.8	4.3	39.5
Netherlands	1 042.9	17.4	13.6	3.9	43.4
United Kingdom	837.6	9.4	9.9	3.1	46.5
Australia	788.5	22.6	7.1	2.9	49.4
Belgium	711.8	3.5	8.1	2.7	52.1
Poland	631.8	27.2	16.6	2.4	54.4
Mexico	561.9	23.3	11.1	2.1	56.5
Norway	541.0	11.8	7.2	2.0	58.5
Austria	540.0	9.6	7.3	2.0	60.5
Denmark	492.5	8.1	-11.7	1.8	62.4
Italy	459.5	5.2	26.7	1.7	64.1

In 2013, the value (in current US$) of exports of "railway vehicles (including hovertrains) and associated equipment" (SITC group 791) decreased by 11.1 percent (compared to 7.9 percent average growth rate from 2009-2013) to reach 29.6 bln US$ (see table 2), while imports decreased by 11.6 percent to reach 28.1 bln US$ (see table 3). Exports of this commodity accounted for 0.5 percent of world exports of SITC section 7, and 0.2 percent of total world merchandise exports (see table 1). Germany, USA and China were the top exporters in 2013 (see table 2). They accounted for 15.0, 11.8 and 10.5 percent of world exports, respectively. Russian Federation, Germany and Australia were the top destinations, with respectively 10.4, 9.7 and 5.1 percent of world imports (see table 3).

The top 15 countries/areas accounted for 88.6 and 63.4 percent of total world exports and imports, respectively (see tables 2 and 3). In 2013, USA was the country/area with the highest value of net exports (+2.2 bln US$), followed by China (+2.1 bln US$). By MDG regions (see graph 2), the largest surpluses in this product group were recorded by Developed Europe (+3.4 bln US$), Eastern Asia (+1.7 bln US$) and Developed North America (+1.5 bln US$). The largest trade deficits were recorded by Commonwealth of Independent States (-1.6 bln US$), Developed Asia-Pacific (-849.8 mln US$) and South-eastern Asia (-722.5 mln US$).

Table 1: Imports (Imp.) and exports (Exp.), 1999-2013, in current US$

		1999	2000	2001	2002	2003	2004	2005	2006	2007	2008	2009	2010	2011	2012	2013
Values in Bln US$	Imp.	9.0	8.1	8.7	8.3	11.5	14.3	15.2	16.5	19.1	24.4	21.3	23.3	28.1	31.7	28.1
	Exp.	8.9	8.3	8.8	9.2	12.5	15.8	16.3	18.4	21.6	26.2	21.8	24.5	28.9	33.2	29.6
As a percentage of SITC section (%)	Imp.	0.4	0.3	0.4	0.3	0.4	0.4	0.4	0.4	0.4	0.5	0.5	0.4	0.5	0.5	0.5
	Exp.	0.4	0.3	0.4	0.4	0.4	0.4	0.4	0.4	0.4	0.5	0.5	0.5	0.5	0.6	0.5
As a percentage of world trade (%)	Imp.	0.2	0.1	0.1	0.1	0.2	0.2	0.1	0.1	0.1	0.2	0.2	0.2	0.2	0.2	0.2
	Exp.	0.2	0.1	0.1	0.1	0.2	0.2	0.2	0.2	0.2	0.2	0.2	0.2	0.2	0.2	0.2

Graph 1: Annual growth rates of exports, 1999–2013
(In percentage by year)

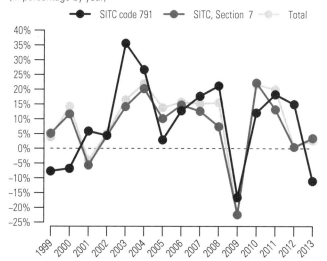

Table 2: Top exporting countries or areas in 2013

Country or area	Value (million US$)	Avg. Growth (%) 09-13	Growth (%) 12-13	World share %	Cum.
World	29 555.9	7.9	-11.1	100.0	
Germany	4 425.9	-0.9	-5.7	15.0	15.0
USA	3 479.7	13.6	-0.9	11.8	26.7
China	3 114.2	35.2	-30.2	10.5	37.3
Mexico	2 539.0	44.7	17.6	8.6	45.9
Ukraine	2 460.4	33.6	-40.0	8.3	54.2
Austria	2 070.1	1.6	26.9	7.0	61.2
Spain	1 371.3	6.4	-16.5	4.6	65.8
Switzerland	1 238.0	5.8	18.1	4.2	70.0
France	1 149.3	0.6	-0.5	3.9	73.9
Poland	874.7	15.3	27.7	3.0	76.9
Czech Rep.	869.7	0.6	-15.5	2.9	79.8
Russian Federation	819.4	17.6	-44.0	2.8	82.6
Japan	768.2	-6.6	3.9	2.6	85.2
Italy	636.9	-14.8	-34.4	2.2	87.3
Rep. of Korea	384.4	6.0	-50.9	1.3	88.6

Graph 2: Trade Balance by MDG regions 2013
(Bln US$)

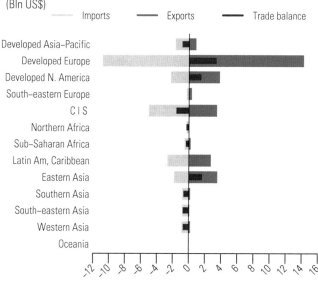

Table 3: Top importing countries or areas in 2013

Country or area	Value (million US$)	Avg. Growth (%) 09-13	Growth (%) 12-13	World share %	Cum.
World	28 074.8	7.1	-11.6	100.0	
Russian Federation	2 931.1	32.6	-10.9	10.4	10.4
Germany	2 712.7	10.8	52.9	9.7	20.1
Australia	1 424.8	20.2	10.2	5.1	25.2
USA	1 268.9	4.8	-20.1	4.5	29.7
Kazakhstan	1 193.7	22.8	-49.2	4.3	33.9
Mexico	1 084.2	45.0	-1.3	3.9	37.8
Belgium	1 016.8	34.7	-9.7	3.6	41.4
Canada	1 012.6	8.5	-13.4	3.6	45.0
China	984.0	-11.0	-15.8	3.5	48.5
Italy	888.3	6.8	12.2	3.2	51.7
Austria	868.7	-0.6	6.3	3.1	54.8
France	752.8	5.4	-5.4	2.7	57.5
Turkey	576.3	-6.1	6.4	2.1	59.5
Brazil	545.1	21.7	-22.3	1.9	61.5
Sweden	529.7	26.5	-38.9	1.9	63.4

792 Aircraft and associated equipment; spacecraft and their launch vehicles; parts

In 2013, the value (in current US$) of exports of "aircraft and associated equipment; spacecraft and their launch vehicles; parts" (SITC group 792) increased by 7.8 percent (compared to 9.7 percent average growth rate from 2009-2013) to reach 185.0 bln US$ (see table 2), while imports increased by 8.8 percent to reach 207.6 bln US$ (see table 3). Exports of this commodity accounted for 3.1 percent of world exports of SITC section 7, and 1.0 percent of total world merchandise exports (see table 1). France, Germany and Canada were the top exporters in 2013 (see table 2). They accounted for 30.5, 23.7 and 5.7 percent of world exports, respectively. USA, which accounted for 36.5 percent of world exports in 2008, has experienced a decline in their share, accounting for only 5.3 percent of export in 2013. France, USA and Germany were the top destinations, with respectively 14.2, 14.1 and 12.8 percent of world imports (see table 3).

The top 15 countries/areas accounted for 88.0 and 78.3 percent of total world exports and imports, respectively (see tables 2 and 3). In 2013, France was the country/area with the highest value of net exports (+26.9 bln US$), followed by Germany (+17.3 bln US$). By MDG regions (see graph 2), the largest surpluses in this product group were recorded by Developed Europe (+49.8 bln US$) and Southern Asia (+1.1 bln US$). The largest trade deficit was recorded by Eastern Asia (-25.5 bln US$).

Table 1: Imports (Imp.) and exports (Exp.), 1999-2013, in current US$

		1999	2000	2001	2002	2003	2004	2005	2006	2007	2008	2009	2010	2011	2012	2013
Values in Bln US$	Imp.	90.8	83.3	88.5	83.8	87.9	104.6	110.6	132.2	144.2	171.1	151.3	157.1	174.0	190.8	207.6
	Exp.	110.5	100.6	108.5	109.7	108.3	120.7	128.9	162.6	184.1	197.4	127.6	137.2	154.6	171.6	185.0
As a percentage of SITC section (%)	Imp.	3.9	3.2	3.6	3.3	3.0	2.9	2.8	3.0	2.9	3.2	3.5	3.0	2.9	3.2	3.4
	Exp.	4.7	3.8	4.4	4.3	3.7	3.4	3.3	3.6	3.7	3.6	3.0	2.7	2.7	2.9	3.1
As a percentage of world trade (%)	Imp.	1.6	1.3	1.4	1.3	1.1	1.1	1.0	1.1	1.0	1.1	1.2	1.0	1.0	1.0	1.1
	Exp.	2.0	1.6	1.8	1.7	1.4	1.3	1.2	1.4	1.3	1.2	1.0	0.9	0.9	0.9	1.0

Graph 1: Annual growth rates of exports, 1999–2013
(In percentage by year)

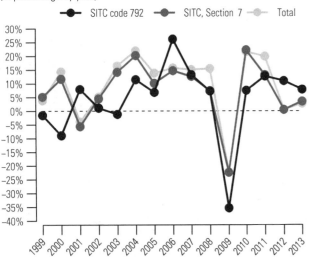

● SITC code 792　● SITC, Section 7　● Total

Table 2: Top exporting countries or areas in 2013

Country or area	Value (million US$)	Avg. Growth (%) 09-13	Growth (%) 12-13	World share %	Cum.
World	185 007.4	9.7	7.8	100.0	
France	56 423.2	13.1	3.6	30.5	30.5
Germany	43 815.5	8.2	1.6	23.7	54.2
Canada	10 468.8	2.3	2.0	5.7	59.8
USA	9 760.5	4.5	-3.2	5.3	65.1
Spain	6 906.9	19.5	54.4	3.7	68.8
Singapore	6 578.1	13.1	9.9	3.6	72.4
Italy	5 936.7	6.1	4.5	3.2	75.6
Japan	4 372.5	14.6	11.2	2.4	78.0
Brazil	4 368.5	1.0	-16.3	2.4	80.3
India	4 151.3	39.7	133.8	2.2	82.6
Austria	2 085.5	34.8	47.0	1.1	83.7
Switzerland	2 082.8	-1.6	2.7	1.1	84.8
Israel	1 976.8	3.0	16.8	1.1	85.9
Netherlands	1 959.9	13.8	9.5	1.1	87.0
China	1 931.7	19.8	24.5	1.0	88.0

Graph 2: Trade Balance by MDG regions 2013
(Bln US$)

Imports　Exports　Trade balance

Developed Asia–Pacific
Developed Europe
Developed N. America
South–eastern Europe
C I S
Northern Africa
Sub–Saharan Africa
Latin Am, Caribbean
Eastern Asia
Southern Asia
South–eastern Asia
Western Asia
Oceania

-80 -60 -40 -20 0 20 40 60 80 100 120 140

Table 3: Top importing countries or areas in 2013

Country or area	Value (million US$)	Avg. Growth (%) 09-13	Growth (%) 12-13	World share %	Cum.
World	207 606.5	8.2	8.8	100.0	
France	29 516.9	16.2	-5.1	14.2	14.2
USA	29 267.9	12.2	20.4	14.1	28.3
Germany	26 551.3	1.5	16.3	12.8	41.1
China	23 180.7	21.8	31.6	11.2	52.3
United Arab Emirates	8 378.9	12.8	11.4	4.0	56.3
Japan	7 040.7	9.7	-3.1	3.4	59.7
Canada	6 550.8	4.9	16.2	3.2	62.9
Singapore	5 721.2	-7.5	3.0	2.8	65.6
Malaysia	5 390.3	34.9	26.7	2.6	68.2
Thailand	4 691.0	53.5	94.4	2.3	70.5
Russian Federation	4 462.9	...	28.0	2.1	72.6
Spain	3 088.0	5.3	56.3	1.5	74.1
Rep. of Korea	2 904.0	18.5	-2.6	1.4	75.5
Brazil	2 869.6	6.7	-0.8	1.4	76.9
China, Hong Kong SAR	2 838.9	34.6	20.0	1.4	78.3

In 2013, the value (in current US$) of exports of "ships, boats (including hovercraft) and floating structures" (SITC group 793) decreased by 6.6 percent (compared to 0.1 percent average growth rate from 2009-2013) to reach 145.6 bln US$ (see table 2), while imports increased by 4.6 percent to reach 72.5 bln US$ (see table 3). Exports of this commodity accounted for 2.4 percent of world exports of SITC section 7, and 0.8 percent of total world merchandise exports (see table 1). Rep. of Korea, China and Japan were the top exporters in 2013 (see table 2). They accounted for 24.6, 19.7 and 10.6 percent of world exports, respectively. India, Congo and Germany were the top destinations, with respectively 9.7, 7.5 and 6.2 percent of world imports (see table 3).

The top 15 countries/areas accounted for 82.6 and 60.8 percent of total world exports and imports, respectively (see tables 2 and 3). In 2013, Rep. of Korea was the country/area with the highest value of net exports (+34.2 bln US$), followed by China (+26.6 bln US$). By MDG regions (see graph 2), the largest surpluses in this product group were recorded by Eastern Asia (+60.9 bln US$), Developed Asia-Pacific (+13.9 bln US$) and Latin America and the Caribbean (+6.2 bln US$). The largest trade deficits were recorded by Sub-Saharan Africa (-5.9 bln US$), Southern Asia (-5.4 bln US$) and Commonwealth of Independent States (-549.7 mln US$).

Table 1: Imports (Imp.) and exports (Exp.), 1999-2013, in current US$

		1999	2000	2001	2002	2003	2004	2005	2006	2007	2008	2009	2010	2011	2012	2013
Values in Bln US$	Imp.	18.8	19.4	19.4	21.4	30.3	36.1	43.5	52.8	51.4	71.2	63.1	76.7	74.7	69.3	72.5
	Exp.	40.3	40.0	43.8	46.4	53.0	62.8	69.4	86.9	106.0	142.8	145.1	171.4	188.5	156.0	145.6
As a percentage of SITC section (%)	Imp.	0.8	0.7	0.8	0.8	1.0	1.0	1.1	1.2	1.0	1.3	1.5	1.5	1.3	1.2	1.2
	Exp.	1.7	1.5	1.8	1.8	1.8	1.8	1.8	1.9	2.1	2.6	3.5	3.3	3.2	2.7	2.4
As a percentage of world trade (%)	Imp.	0.3	0.3	0.3	0.3	0.4	0.4	0.4	0.4	0.4	0.4	0.5	0.5	0.4	0.4	0.4
	Exp.	0.7	0.6	0.7	0.7	0.7	0.7	0.7	0.7	0.8	0.9	1.2	1.1	1.0	0.9	0.8

Graph 1: Annual growth rates of exports, 1999–2013
(In percentage by year)

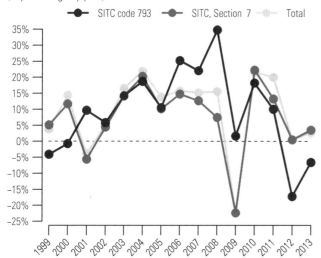

Table 2: Top exporting countries or areas in 2013

Country or area	Value (million US$)	Avg. Growth (%) 09-13	Growth (%) 12-13	World share %	Cum.
World	145 604.7	0.1	-6.6	100.0	
Rep. of Korea	35 869.8	-4.1	-5.2	24.6	24.6
China	28 681.2	0.3	-26.1	19.7	44.3
Japan	15 383.8	-8.8	-30.8	10.6	54.9
Brazil	7 933.7	185.9	412.2	5.4	60.3
Poland	5 444.9	12.3	36.4	3.7	64.1
Germany	4 573.8	10.3	-10.3	3.1	67.2
India	3 597.5	-1.1	-12.8	2.5	69.7
Italy	3 048.1	-14.2	-5.9	2.1	71.8
USA	2 673.1	7.0	-24.3	1.8	73.6
Singapore	2 488.5	1.3	-24.1	1.7	75.3
France	2 374.5	2.9	22.9	1.6	77.0
Congo	2 261.2	3.7	77.0	1.6	78.5
Saudi Arabia	2 239.9	6.4	45.0	1.5	80.1
United Arab Emirates	*1 930.9*	38.0	21.7	1.3	81.4
Netherlands	1 740.1	-7.4	-18.8	1.2	82.6

Graph 2: Trade Balance by MDG regions 2013
(Bln US$)

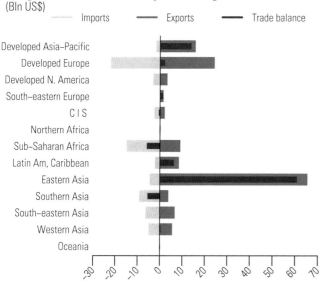

Table 3: Top importing countries or areas in 2013

Country or area	Value (million US$)	Avg. Growth (%) 09-13	Growth (%) 12-13	World share %	Cum.
World	72 473.2	3.5	4.6	100.0	
India	7 004.9	23.4	13.7	9.7	9.7
Congo	5 419.7	18.0	20.7	7.5	17.1
Germany	4 461.1	-9.3	-25.8	6.2	23.3
Poland	4 446.4	17.8	38.8	6.1	29.4
Thailand	2 762.5	37.2	4.3	3.8	33.2
Norway	2 727.0	-4.3	20.7	3.8	37.0
Côte d'Ivoire	2 701.7	376.5	573.1	3.7	40.7
Russian Federation	2 113.5	11.8	51.7	2.9	43.7
China	2 034.9	-4.8	14.1	2.8	46.5
Saudi Arabia	1 946.3	16.0	15.9	2.7	49.1
USA	1 854.0	9.5	-2.1	2.6	51.7
Denmark	1 713.0	-14.2	220.0	2.4	54.1
Rep. of Korea	1 693.7	-12.0	-33.4	2.3	56.4
Greece	1 615.1	-25.8	-36.1	2.2	58.6
Italy	1 554.8	-10.1	-40.1	2.1	60.8

Miscellaneous manufactured articles

(SITC Section 8)

811 Prefabricated buildings

In 2013, the value (in current US$) of exports of "prefabricated buildings" (SITC group 811) increased by 13.6 percent (compared to 11.6 percent average growth rate from 2009-2013) to reach 10.2 bln US$ (see table 2), while imports decreased by 2.6 percent to reach 8.3 bln US$ (see table 3). Exports of this commodity accounted for 0.5 percent of world exports of SITC section 8, and 0.1 percent of total world merchandise exports (see table 1). China, USA and Singapore were the top exporters in 2013 (see table 2). They accounted for 16.4, 11.4 and 10.0 percent of world exports, respectively. Canada, Norway and Venezuela were the top destinations, with respectively 8.3, 6.4 and 5.9 percent of world imports (see table 3).

The top 15 countries/areas accounted for 74.1 and 56.7 percent of total world exports and imports, respectively (see tables 2 and 3). In 2013, China was the country/area with the highest value of net exports (+1.6 bln US$), followed by USA (+924.9 mln US$). By MDG regions (see graph 2), the largest surpluses in this product group were recorded by Developed Europe (+1.6 bln US$), Eastern Asia (+1.6 bln US$) and South-eastern Asia (+910.6 mln US$). The largest trade deficits were recorded by Latin America and the Caribbean (-1.1 bln US$), Sub-Saharan Africa (-648.5 mln US$) and Commonwealth of Independent States (-447.7 mln US$).

Table 1: Imports (Imp.) and exports (Exp.), 1999-2013, in current US$

		1999	2000	2001	2002	2003	2004	2005	2006	2007	2008	2009	2010	2011	2012	2013
Values in Bln US$	Imp.	2.6	2.5	2.7	2.7	3.2	4.0	4.6	5.5	6.7	7.8	5.6	6.1	7.5	8.5	8.3
	Exp.	3.0	2.8	2.8	3.1	3.8	4.7	5.4	6.3	8.0	9.4	6.6	7.3	8.6	9.0	10.2
As a percentage of	Imp.	0.3	0.3	0.3	0.3	0.3	0.4	0.4	0.4	0.4	0.5	0.4	0.4	0.4	0.5	0.4
SITC section (%)	Exp.	0.4	0.4	0.4	0.4	0.4	0.4	0.5	0.5	0.5	0.6	0.5	0.4	0.5	0.5	0.5
As a percentage of	Imp.	0.0	0.0	0.0	0.0	0.0	0.0	0.0	0.0	0.0	0.0	0.0	0.0	0.0	0.0	0.0
world trade (%)	Exp.	0.1	0.0	0.0	0.0	0.1	0.1	0.1	0.1	0.1	0.1	0.1	0.0	0.0	0.0	0.1

Graph 1: Annual growth rates of exports, 1999–2013
(In percentage by year)

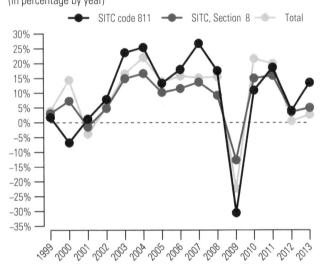

Legend: SITC code 811 · SITC, Section 8 · Total

Table 2: Top exporting countries or areas in 2013

Country or area	Value (million US$)	Avg. Growth (%) 09-13	Growth (%) 12-13	World share %	Cum.
World....................	10 186.0	11.6	13.6	100.0	
China....................	1 673.3	11.9	2.8	16.4	16.4
USA.....................	1 160.2	16.2	6.5	11.4	27.8
Singapore.............	1 021.1	142.7	2772.5	10.0	37.8
Germany...............	527.9	7.1	-11.3	5.2	43.0
Netherlands..........	501.6	20.5	24.0	4.9	47.9
Italy.....................	332.1	-2.4	32.8	3.3	51.2
Czech Rep............	325.1	4.8	8.3	3.2	54.4
Turkey..................	297.9	11.0	8.2	2.9	57.3
Estonia.................	290.3	21.8	12.5	2.9	60.2
Sweden................	272.4	6.9	3.8	2.7	62.9
Spain...................	265.2	6.5	35.4	2.6	65.5
Belgium................	249.9	-7.1	6.2	2.5	67.9
France..................	227.9	4.6	-9.8	2.2	70.1
Canada.................	201.8	-0.8	-9.1	2.0	72.1
Finland.................	200.9	-1.0	3.5	2.0	74.1

Graph 2: Trade Balance by MDG regions 2013
(Bln US$)

Legend: Imports · Exports · Trade balance

Developed Asia–Pacific
Developed Europe
Developed N. America
South–eastern Europe
CIS
Northern Africa
Sub-Saharan Africa
Latin Am, Caribbean
Eastern Asia
Southern Asia
South–eastern Asia
Western Asia
Oceania

-3 -2 -1 0 1 2 3 4 5

Table 3: Top importing countries or areas in 2013

Country or area	Value (million US$)	Avg. Growth (%) 09-13	Growth (%) 12-13	World share %	Cum.
World....................	8 282.1	10.2	-2.6	100.0	
Canada.................	684.6	19.6	-0.9	8.3	8.3
Norway.................	532.8	22.8	22.4	6.4	14.7
Venezuela.............	485.6	45.6	-41.6	5.9	20.6
Germany...............	475.5	7.4	2.9	5.7	26.3
Switzerland...........	343.9	11.3	13.4	4.2	30.5
Russian Federation...	326.6	18.7	13.3	3.9	34.4
Australia...............	306.7	41.8	-27.8	3.7	38.1
France..................	293.4	-2.8	-11.3	3.5	41.6
USA.....................	235.3	1.1	-7.0	2.8	44.5
United Kingdom......	186.0	-6.2	24.8	2.2	46.7
Mexico.................	182.3	5.9	-18.1	2.2	48.9
Singapore.............	176.2	24.8	-13.1	2.1	51.1
Nigeria.................	166.6	68.2	147.2	2.0	53.1
Brazil...................	155.1	63.9	167.0	1.9	54.9
Saudi Arabia..........	147.1	14.4	49.2	1.8	56.7

In 2013, the value (in current US$) of exports of "sanitary, plumbing and heating fixtures and fittings, nes" (SITC group 812) increased by 12.3 percent (compared to 6.1 percent average growth rate from 2009-2013) to reach 16.6 bln US$ (see table 2), while imports increased by 3.9 percent to reach 16.0 bln US$ (see table 3). Exports of this commodity accounted for 0.8 percent of world exports of SITC section 8, and 0.1 percent of total world merchandise exports (see table 1). Germany, China and Italy were the top exporters in 2013 (see table 2). They accounted for 14.8, 14.1 and 10.1 percent of world exports, respectively. Germany, USA and United Kingdom were the top destinations, with respectively 10.9, 9.9 and 9.6 percent of world imports (see table 3).

The top 15 countries/areas accounted for 81.8 and 71.8 percent of total world exports and imports, respectively (see tables 2 and 3). In 2013, China was the country/area with the highest value of net exports (+2.0 bln US$), followed by Italy (+1.0 bln US$). By MDG regions (see graph 2), the largest surpluses in this product group were recorded by Eastern Asia (+2.0 bln US$), Developed Europe (+923.1 mln US$) and Western Asia (+479.1 mln US$). The largest trade deficits were recorded by Developed North America (-1.5 bln US$), Commonwealth of Independent States (-1.1 bln US$) and Developed Asia-Pacific (-270.6 mln US$).

Table 1: Imports (Imp.) and exports (Exp.), 1999-2013, in current US$

		1999	2000	2001	2002	2003	2004	2005	2006	2007	2008	2009	2010	2011	2012	2013
Values in Bln US$	Imp.	5.9	5.6	5.7	6.6	8.4	10.2	11.3	13.3	14.8	16.2	13.3	14.1	15.8	15.4	16.0
	Exp.	6.0	6.2	5.8	6.6	8.5	10.2	11.3	13.6	15.0	16.3	13.1	13.6	15.2	14.7	16.6
As a percentage of	Imp.	0.8	0.7	0.7	0.8	0.9	0.9	0.9	1.0	1.0	1.0	0.9	0.9	0.9	0.8	0.8
SITC section (%)	Exp.	0.8	0.8	0.8	0.8	0.9	0.9	1.0	1.0	1.0	1.0	0.9	0.8	0.8	0.7	0.8
As a percentage of	Imp.	0.1	0.1	0.1	0.1	0.1	0.1	0.1	0.1	0.1	0.1	0.1	0.1	0.1	0.1	0.1
world trade (%)	Exp.	0.1	0.1	0.1	0.1	0.1	0.1	0.1	0.1	0.1	0.1	0.1	0.1	0.1	0.1	0.1

Graph 1: Annual growth rates of exports, 1999–2013
(In percentage by year)

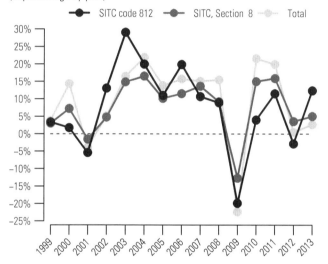

Table 2: Top exporting countries or areas in 2013

Country or area	Value (million US$)	Avg. Growth (%) 09-13	Growth (%) 12-13	World share %	Cum.
World	16 562.6	6.1	12.3	100.0	
Germany	2 459.3	1.6	1.0	14.8	14.8
China	2 336.1	29.4	86.4	14.1	29.0
Italy	1 672.4	1.0	2.2	10.1	39.1
Turkey	1 039.8	9.0	4.7	6.3	45.3
Austria	800.1	9.4	21.5	4.8	50.2
Slovakia	710.5	6.7	11.2	4.3	54.4
France	686.0	-1.0	2.3	4.1	58.6
Poland	674.6	6.1	15.1	4.1	62.7
Netherlands	660.6	0.5	3.0	4.0	66.7
USA	599.9	2.1	6.4	3.6	70.3
Mexico	543.8	9.5	18.2	3.3	73.6
Belgium	503.3	1.8	13.7	3.0	76.6
Czech Rep.	437.2	5.1	-2.1	2.6	79.2
United Kingdom	218.2	0.3	11.8	1.3	80.6
Spain	199.7	-0.4	12.1	1.2	81.8

Graph 2: Trade Balance by MDG regions 2013
(Bln US$)

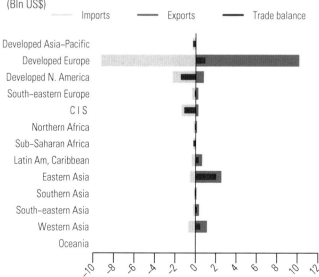

Table 3: Top importing countries or areas in 2013

Country or area	Value (million US$)	Avg. Growth (%) 09-13	Growth (%) 12-13	World share %	Cum.
World	16 021.3	4.8	3.9	100.0	
Germany	1 752.4	4.8	7.3	10.9	10.9
USA	1 582.5	7.6	11.1	9.9	20.8
United Kingdom	1 532.9	1.9	12.3	9.6	30.4
France	1 173.1	2.2	1.9	7.3	37.7
Russian Federation	899.1	24.9	7.6	5.6	43.3
Canada	678.5	4.2	2.9	4.2	47.6
Italy	653.4	-0.2	1.0	4.1	51.6
Belgium	651.7	3.3	5.0	4.1	55.7
Netherlands	548.1	0.3	-1.2	3.4	59.1
Spain	403.5	-8.0	-0.9	2.5	61.6
Austria	395.7	4.7	4.8	2.5	64.1
Poland	387.3	3.7	11.6	2.4	66.5
China	306.9	22.4	25.8	1.9	68.4
Switzerland	296.8	4.5	7.0	1.9	70.3
Turkey	242.9	7.9	-8.3	1.5	71.8

813 Lighting fixtures and fittings, nes

In 2013, the value (in current US$) of exports of "lighting fixtures and fittings, nes" (SITC group 813) increased by 16.1 percent (compared to 19.7 percent average growth rate from 2009-2013) to reach 48.4 bln US$ (see table 2), while imports increased by 9.3 percent to reach 39.2 bln US$ (see table 3). Exports of this commodity accounted for 2.3 percent of world exports of SITC section 8, and 0.3 percent of total world merchandise exports (see table 1). China, Germany and Italy were the top exporters in 2013 (see table 2). They accounted for 54.0, 6.8 and 4.1 percent of world exports, respectively. USA, Germany and France were the top destinations, with respectively 23.4, 8.2 and 4.6 percent of world imports (see table 3).

The top 15 countries/areas accounted for 88.8 and 67.3 percent of total world exports and imports, respectively (see tables 2 and 3). In 2013, China was the country/area with the highest value of net exports (+25.6 bln US$), followed by Italy (+1.2 bln US$). By MDG regions (see graph 2), Eastern Asia (+26.8 bln US$) was the only region that recorded a surplus in this product group. The largest trade deficits were recorded by Developed North America (-8.4 bln US$), Developed Europe (-2.4 bln US$) and Developed Asia-Pacific (-2.1 bln US$).

Table 1: Imports (Imp.) and exports (Exp.), 1999-2013, in current US$

		1999	2000	2001	2002	2003	2004	2005	2006	2007	2008	2009	2010	2011	2012	2013
Values in Bln US$	Imp.	13.9	14.9	14.5	15.5	17.6	20.3	22.3	24.4	27.9	29.6	25.0	29.9	33.6	35.9	39.2
	Exp.	11.9	12.5	12.5	13.4	15.3	17.2	19.1	21.1	24.9	28.5	23.6	27.8	34.1	41.7	48.4
As a percentage of SITC section (%)	Imp.	1.8	1.8	1.8	1.8	1.8	1.8	1.8	1.8	1.8	1.8	1.7	1.8	1.8	1.9	2.1
	Exp.	1.6	1.6	1.6	1.7	1.7	1.6	1.6	1.6	1.7	1.7	1.7	1.7	1.8	2.1	2.3
As a percentage of world trade (%)	Imp.	0.2	0.2	0.2	0.2	0.2	0.2	0.2	0.2	0.2	0.2	0.2	0.2	0.2	0.2	0.2
	Exp.	0.2	0.2	0.2	0.2	0.2	0.2	0.2	0.2	0.2	0.2	0.2	0.2	0.2	0.2	0.3

Graph 1: Annual growth rates of exports, 1999–2013
(In percentage by year)

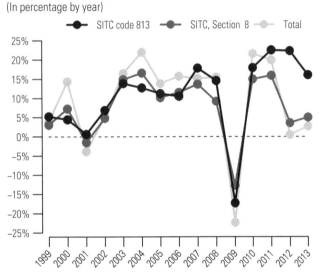

Legend: SITC code 813 — SITC, Section 8 — Total

Table 2: Top exporting countries or areas in 2013

Country or area	Value (million US$)	Avg. Growth (%) 09-13	Growth (%) 12-13	World share %	Cum.
World	48 360.6	19.7	16.1	100.0	
China	26 098.4	33.3	23.9	54.0	54.0
Germany	3 296.0	7.0	6.4	6.8	60.8
Italy	1 996.7	3.4	7.3	4.1	64.9
USA	1 901.1	11.7	3.6	3.9	68.8
Mexico	1 491.1	14.5	11.0	3.1	71.9
Rep. of Korea	1 125.9	78.0	27.6	2.3	74.3
Austria	989.1	8.6	20.9	2.0	76.3
Netherlands	983.1	17.4	19.0	2.0	78.3
France	940.9	4.0	0.4	1.9	80.3
China, Hong Kong SAR	923.7	8.1	13.1	1.9	82.2
Belgium	766.3	-0.3	13.9	1.6	83.8
United Kingdom	689.5	5.4	3.2	1.4	85.2
Spain	688.1	7.1	9.0	1.4	86.6
Canada	529.2	10.1	2.7	1.1	87.7
Poland	510.1	12.6	22.9	1.1	88.8

Graph 2: Trade Balance by MDG regions 2013
(Bln US$)

Legend: Imports — Exports — Trade balance

Developed Asia–Pacific
Developed Europe
Developed N. America
South–eastern Europe
C I S
Northern Africa
Sub–Saharan Africa
Latin Am, Caribbean
Eastern Asia
Southern Asia
South–eastern Asia
Western Asia
Oceania

Table 3: Top importing countries or areas in 2013

Country or area	Value (million US$)	Avg. Growth (%) 09-13	Growth (%) 12-13	World share %	Cum.
World	39 246.5	12.0	9.3	100.0	
USA	9 186.6	16.0	12.4	23.4	23.4
Germany	3 211.4	12.2	9.8	8.2	31.6
France	1 787.2	5.8	1.9	4.6	36.1
United Kingdom	1 755.9	8.7	15.6	4.5	40.6
Canada	1 585.5	12.0	4.9	4.0	44.7
Japan	1 260.7	22.4	-4.5	3.2	47.9
Netherlands	1 169.7	14.4	11.3	3.0	50.9
Belgium	959.6	6.8	18.3	2.4	53.3
Australia	899.3	19.1	11.2	2.3	55.6
Italy	844.2	6.2	6.4	2.2	57.7
Austria	840.7	7.6	10.8	2.1	59.9
Russian Federation	795.2	28.0	-8.8	2.0	61.9
Switzerland	755.5	10.2	11.2	1.9	63.8
China, Hong Kong SAR	702.8	9.9	7.6	1.8	65.6
Sweden	648.8	10.5	9.0	1.7	67.3

Source: UN Comtrade and UN Service Trade

2013 International Trade Statistics Yearbook, Vol. II

In 2013, the value (in current US$) of exports of "furniture and parts thereof; stuffed furnishings" (SITC group 821) increased by 6.2 percent (compared to 10.2 percent average growth rate from 2009-2013) to reach 165.9 bln US$ (see table 2), while imports increased by 4.6 percent to reach 152.1 bln US$ (see table 3). Exports of this commodity accounted for 8.0 percent of world exports of SITC section 8, and 0.9 percent of total world merchandise exports (see table 1). China, Germany and Italy were the top exporters in 2013 (see table 2). They accounted for 35.8, 7.4 and 6.9 percent of world exports, respectively. USA, Germany and France were the top destinations, with respectively 27.1, 9.1 and 5.2 percent of world imports (see table 3).

The top 15 countries/areas accounted for 79.6 and 73.4 percent of total world exports and imports, respectively (see tables 2 and 3). In 2013, China was the country/area with the highest value of net exports (+57.1 bln US$), followed by Italy (+9.1 bln US$). By MDG regions (see graph 2), the largest surpluses in this product group were recorded by Eastern Asia (+56.6 bln US$), South-eastern Asia (+7.1 bln US$) and South-eastern Europe (+2.4 bln US$). The largest trade deficits were recorded by Developed North America (-36.5 bln US$), Developed Asia-Pacific (-9.2 bln US$) and Commonwealth of Independent States (-3.5 bln US$).

Table 1: Imports (Imp.) and exports (Exp.), 1999-2013, in current US$

		1999	2000	2001	2002	2003	2004	2005	2006	2007	2008	2009	2010	2011	2012	2013
Values in Bln US$	Imp.	58.6	63.4	63.7	70.1	82.5	97.2	107.0	117.6	135.1	140.6	113.4	130.5	143.4	145.4	152.1
	Exp.	57.1	61.4	60.8	65.4	76.1	89.8	97.5	108.3	127.0	136.4	112.5	129.1	145.9	156.3	165.9
As a percentage of	Imp.	7.8	7.8	7.8	8.2	8.5	8.6	8.6	8.6	8.8	8.4	7.9	8.0	7.8	7.9	8.0
SITC section (%)	Exp.	7.9	7.9	8.0	8.2	8.3	8.4	8.3	8.2	8.5	8.3	7.9	7.9	7.7	7.9	8.0
As a percentage of	Imp.	1.0	1.0	1.0	1.1	1.1	1.0	1.0	1.0	1.0	0.9	0.9	0.9	0.8	0.8	0.8
world trade (%)	Exp.	1.0	1.0	1.0	1.0	1.0	1.0	0.9	0.9	0.9	0.9	0.9	0.9	0.8	0.9	0.9

Graph 1: Annual growth rates of exports, 1999–2013

(In percentage by year)

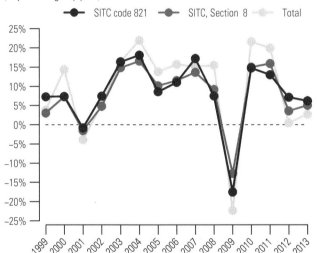

Table 2: Top exporting countries or areas in 2013

Country or area	Value (million US$)	Avg. Growth (%) 09-13	Growth (%) 12-13	World share %	Cum.
World	165 938.8	10.2	6.2	100.0	
China	59 488.2	18.6	5.9	35.8	35.8
Germany	12 356.0	4.5	2.0	7.4	43.3
Italy	11 434.5	2.3	6.1	6.9	50.2
Poland	9 730.6	8.3	13.5	5.9	56.1
USA	7 549.6	12.0	5.3	4.5	60.6
Mexico	6 471.8	19.6	11.5	3.9	64.5
Viet Nam	4 032.2	13.6	10.8	2.4	66.9
Canada	3 828.8	7.4	-0.4	2.3	69.2
Czech Rep.	2 972.2	10.9	19.4	1.8	71.0
France	2 854.3	-2.6	6.0	1.7	72.7
Malaysia	2 408.9	2.0	-9.7	1.5	74.2
Sweden	2 354.8	3.1	-2.2	1.4	75.6
United Kingdom	2 217.8	9.6	7.8	1.3	77.0
Turkey	2 185.1	16.6	17.1	1.3	78.3
Denmark	2 175.5	0.1	-1.8	1.3	79.6

Graph 2: Trade Balance by MDG regions 2013

(Bln US$)

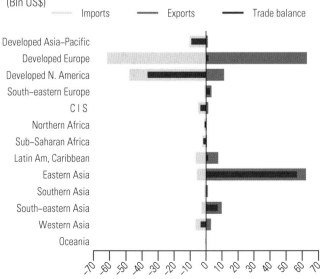

Table 3: Top importing countries or areas in 2013

Country or area	Value (million US$)	Avg. Growth (%) 09-13	Growth (%) 12-13	World share %	Cum.
World	152 120.5	7.6	4.6	100.0	
USA	41 218.2	11.5	6.7	27.1	27.1
Germany	13 819.0	5.0	4.6	9.1	36.2
France	7 863.7	0.6	-6.6	5.2	41.3
United Kingdom	7 779.2	2.6	5.0	5.1	46.5
Japan	6 819.8	8.6	-1.3	4.5	50.9
Canada	6 621.9	8.5	-0.8	4.4	55.3
Belgium	3 770.9	4.3	21.4	2.5	57.8
Switzerland	3 547.7	5.9	5.9	2.3	60.1
Russian Federation	3 462.9	23.5	7.4	2.3	62.4
Netherlands	3 408.3	2.6	-1.7	2.2	64.6
Australia	3 064.3	10.1	1.9	2.0	66.6
Mexico	2 708.7	21.9	16.2	1.8	68.4
Spain	2 597.5	-2.9	3.5	1.7	70.1
Austria	2 584.6	1.6	1.9	1.7	71.8
China	2 424.5	18.6	9.5	1.6	73.4

831 Travel goods, handbags, etc, of leather, plastics, textile, others

In 2013, the value (in current US$) of exports of "travel goods, handbags, etc, of leather, plastics, textile, others" (SITC group 831) increased by 8.7 percent (compared to 16.3 percent average growth rate from 2009-2013) to reach 60.7 bln US$ (see table 2), while imports increased by 3.8 percent to reach 57.2 bln US$ (see table 3). Exports of this commodity accounted for 2.9 percent of world exports of SITC section 8, and 0.3 percent of total world merchandise exports (see table 1). China, Italy and France were the top exporters in 2013 (see table 2). They accounted for 45.8, 11.2 and 9.6 percent of world exports, respectively. USA, Japan and China, Hong Kong SAR were the top destinations, with respectively 19.4, 9.3 and 9.2 percent of world imports (see table 3).

The top 15 countries/areas accounted for 93.9 and 76.2 percent of total world exports and imports, respectively (see tables 2 and 3). In 2013, China was the country/area with the highest value of net exports (+26.3 bln US$), followed by Italy (+4.3 bln US$). By MDG regions (see graph 2), the largest surpluses in this product group were recorded by Eastern Asia (+24.4 bln US$), Southern Asia (+991.0 mln US$) and South-eastern Asia (+867.7 mln US$). The largest trade deficits were recorded by Developed North America (-11.0 bln US$), Developed Asia-Pacific (-6.4 bln US$) and Latin America and the Caribbean (-1.9 bln US$).

Table 1: Imports (Imp.) and exports (Exp.), 1999-2013, in current US$

		1999	2000	2001	2002	2003	2004	2005	2006	2007	2008	2009	2010	2011	2012	2013
Values in Bln US$	Imp.	18.5	19.7	19.6	19.8	22.1	26.2	29.3	32.8	38.7	43.0	37.2	43.8	52.8	55.1	57.2
	Exp.	15.3	16.5	16.3	16.0	17.8	21.3	23.8	27.1	32.4	37.7	33.2	40.8	53.2	55.9	60.7
As a percentage of SITC section (%)	Imp.	2.5	2.4	2.4	2.3	2.3	2.3	2.4	2.4	2.5	2.6	2.6	2.7	2.9	3.0	3.0
	Exp.	2.1	2.1	2.1	2.0	1.9	2.0	2.0	2.1	2.2	2.3	2.3	2.5	2.8	2.8	2.9
As a percentage of world trade (%)	Imp.	0.3	0.3	0.3	0.3	0.3	0.3	0.3	0.3	0.3	0.3	0.3	0.3	0.3	0.3	0.3
	Exp.	0.3	0.3	0.3	0.2	0.2	0.2	0.2	0.2	0.2	0.2	0.3	0.3	0.3	0.3	0.3

Graph 1: Annual growth rates of exports, 1999–2013
(In percentage by year)

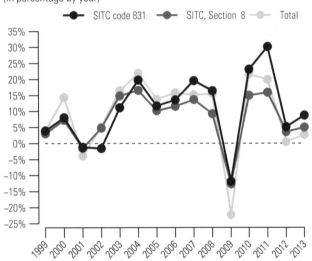

Legend: SITC code 831 — SITC, Section 8 — Total

Table 2: Top exporting countries or areas in 2013

Country or area	Value (million US$)	Avg. Growth (%) 09-13	Growth (%) 12-13	World share %	Cum.
World	60 747.4	16.3	8.7	100.0	
China	27 841.2	21.2	9.1	45.8	45.8
Italy	6 821.7	19.8	14.1	11.2	57.1
France	5 842.0	13.0	2.3	9.6	66.7
China, Hong Kong SAR	5 591.5	3.2	-8.3	9.2	75.9
Viet Nam	1 687.3	29.8	29.8	2.8	78.7
Germany	1 427.0	9.2	8.7	2.3	81.0
Belgium	1 314.4	6.2	16.2	2.2	83.2
India	1 216.6	16.1	21.4	2.0	85.2
USA	1 164.6	10.3	6.9	1.9	87.1
Netherlands	963.4	21.2	16.6	1.6	88.7
United Kingdom	808.5	13.8	4.7	1.3	90.0
Spain	799.7	11.6	17.7	1.3	91.3
Rep. of Korea	610.5	77.5	77.6	1.0	92.3
Singapore	532.0	14.3	18.4	0.9	93.2
Czech Rep.	394.2	30.0	34.1	0.6	93.9

Graph 2: Trade Balance by MDG regions 2013
(Bln US$)

Legend: Imports — Exports — Trade balance

Developed Asia–Pacific
Developed Europe
Developed N. America
South–eastern Europe
C I S
Northern Africa
Sub–Saharan Africa
Latin Am, Caribbean
Eastern Asia
Southern Asia
South–eastern Asia
Western Asia
Oceania

-20 -15 -10 -5 0 5 10 15 20 25 30 35

Table 3: Top importing countries or areas in 2013

Country or area	Value (million US$)	Avg. Growth (%) 09-13	Growth (%) 12-13	World share %	Cum.
World	57 188.3	11.4	3.8	100.0	
USA	11 079.2	13.0	5.5	19.4	19.4
Japan	5 319.5	5.4	-7.4	9.3	28.7
China, Hong Kong SAR	5 234.7	7.9	-2.9	9.2	37.8
France	3 425.4	11.4	-2.4	6.0	43.8
Germany	3 030.4	10.8	11.4	5.3	49.1
United Kingdom	2 905.1	6.7	4.7	5.1	54.2
Italy	2 477.5	5.7	-0.7	4.3	58.5
Rep. of Korea	1 831.5	21.5	5.8	3.2	61.7
China	1 564.7	28.7	4.1	2.7	64.5
Canada	1 249.8	12.2	8.1	2.2	66.7
Spain	1 227.3	3.8	0.0	2.1	68.8
Netherlands	1 102.1	17.9	16.5	1.9	70.7
Belgium	1 085.3	8.9	12.2	1.9	72.6
Singapore	1 039.1	19.0	13.4	1.8	74.4
Australia	1 022.5	13.4	6.7	1.8	76.2

Men's or boys' outerwear, of textile fabrics, not knitted or crocheted 841

In 2013, the value (in current US$) of exports of "men's or boys' outerwear, of textile fabrics, not knitted or crocheted" (SITC group 841) increased by 6.5 percent (compared to 7.1 percent average growth rate from 2009-2013) to reach 73.3 bln US$ (see table 2), while imports increased by 4.3 percent to reach 70.0 bln US$ (see table 3). Exports of this commodity accounted for 3.5 percent of world exports of SITC section 8, and 0.4 percent of total world merchandise exports (see table 1). China, Bangladesh and Italy were the top exporters in 2013 (see table 2). They accounted for 29.3, 9.8 and 5.8 percent of world exports, respectively. USA, Germany and Japan were the top destinations, with respectively 21.1, 10.2 and 8.1 percent of world imports (see table 3).

The top 15 countries/areas accounted for 80.2 and 77.2 percent of total world exports and imports, respectively (see tables 2 and 3). In 2013, China was the country/area with the highest value of net exports (+20.1 bln US$), followed by Bangladesh (+7.2 bln US$). By MDG regions (see graph 2), the largest surpluses in this product group were recorded by Eastern Asia (+18.5 bln US$), Southern Asia (+10.9 bln US$) and South-eastern Asia (+5.9 bln US$). The largest trade deficits were recorded by Developed North America (-15.4 bln US$), Developed Europe (-11.4 bln US$) and Developed Asia-Pacific (-6.7 bln US$).

Table 1: Imports (Imp.) and exports (Exp.), 1999-2013, in current US$

		1999	2000	2001	2002	2003	2004	2005	2006	2007	2008	2009	2010	2011	2012	2013
Values in Bln US$	Imp.	39.4	41.3	40.2	39.7	44.1	48.5	51.5	54.8	59.5	63.5	54.9	58.9	70.8	67.1	70.0
	Exp.	39.7	41.7	39.5	40.5	45.4	49.5	53.4	56.6	60.6	65.1	55.6	59.7	72.0	68.9	73.3
As a percentage of SITC section (%)	Imp.	5.2	5.1	5.0	4.7	4.5	4.3	4.2	4.0	3.9	3.8	3.8	3.6	3.8	3.6	3.7
	Exp.	5.5	5.4	5.2	5.1	4.9	4.6	4.5	4.3	4.0	4.0	3.9	3.6	3.8	3.5	3.5
As a percentage of world trade (%)	Imp.	0.7	0.6	0.6	0.6	0.6	0.5	0.5	0.4	0.4	0.4	0.4	0.4	0.4	0.4	0.4
	Exp.	0.7	0.7	0.6	0.6	0.6	0.5	0.5	0.5	0.4	0.4	0.4	0.4	0.4	0.4	0.4

Graph 1: Annual growth rates of exports, 1999–2013
(In percentage by year)

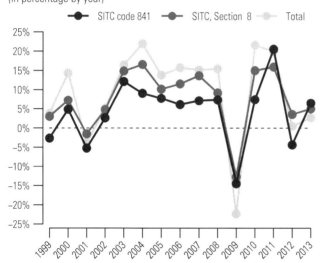

Graph 2: Trade Balance by MDG regions 2013
(Bln US$)

Imports — Exports — Trade balance

Developed Asia–Pacific
Developed Europe
Developed N. America
South–eastern Europe
CIS
Northern Africa
Sub-Saharan Africa
Latin Am, Caribbean
Eastern Asia
Southern Asia
South–eastern Asia
Western Asia
Oceania

Table 2: Top exporting countries or areas in 2013

Country or area	Value (million US$)	Avg. Growth (%) 09-13	Growth (%) 12-13	World share %	Cum.
World	73316.6	7.1	6.5	100.0	
China	21489.5	8.8	7.3	29.3	29.3
Bangladesh	7172.8	15.7	7.6	9.8	39.1
Italy	4270.5	3.3	7.1	5.8	44.9
Germany	4023.7	3.8	2.5	5.5	50.4
Viet Nam	3843.0	19.3	16.2	5.2	55.6
China, Hong Kong SAR	2715.5	1.2	-4.1	3.7	59.4
India	2315.3	10.0	17.0	3.2	62.5
Turkey	2175.6	6.0	2.2	3.0	65.5
Mexico	1914.3	3.6	-1.9	2.6	68.1
Netherlands	1738.8	8.9	10.3	2.4	70.5
Indonesia	1671.5	9.0	3.5	2.3	72.7
Spain	1616.2	13.7	22.1	2.2	74.9
Belgium	1488.8	1.8	24.2	2.0	77.0
United Kingdom	1289.5	13.2	11.7	1.8	78.7
Pakistan	1054.7	7.6	6.0	1.4	80.2

Table 3: Top importing countries or areas in 2013

Country or area	Value (million US$)	Avg. Growth (%) 09-13	Growth (%) 12-13	World share %	Cum.
World	69952.7	6.2	4.3	100.0	
USA	14767.1	6.7	3.1	21.1	21.1
Germany	7101.4	5.3	5.4	10.2	31.3
Japan	5667.0	8.5	-2.0	8.1	39.4
United Kingdom	4162.1	-0.2	4.0	5.9	45.3
France	3550.4	1.7	3.2	5.1	50.4
Italy	3068.7	0.5	-1.1	4.4	54.8
Spain	2532.6	5.6	6.2	3.6	58.4
China, Hong Kong SAR	2220.5	5.2	0.1	3.2	61.6
Netherlands	2004.9	5.6	3.9	2.9	64.4
Rep. of Korea	1906.8	27.0	23.1	2.7	67.2
Belgium	1573.9	0.9	16.6	2.2	69.4
Canada	1524.3	7.4	5.7	2.2	71.6
Russian Federation	1438.9	21.7	16.4	2.1	73.6
China	1421.0	34.3	16.8	2.0	75.7
Switzerland	1055.6	0.9	0.1	1.5	77.2

842 Women's or girls' outerwear, of textile fabrics, not knitted or crocheted

In 2013, the value (in current US$) of exports of "women's or girls' outerwear, of textile fabrics, not knitted or crocheted" (SITC group 842) increased by 9.2 percent (compared to 6.1 percent average growth rate from 2009-2013) to reach 86.1 bln US$ (see table 2), while imports increased by 4.0 percent to reach 84.2 bln US$ (see table 3). Exports of this commodity accounted for 4.2 percent of world exports of SITC section 8, and 0.5 percent of total world merchandise exports (see table 1). China, Italy and China, Hong Kong SAR were the top exporters in 2013 (see table 2). They accounted for 34.1, 6.4 and 5.3 percent of world exports, respectively. USA, Germany and Japan were the top destinations, with respectively 19.3, 9.0 and 8.5 percent of world imports (see table 3).

The top 15 countries/areas accounted for 82.9 and 77.1 percent of total world exports and imports, respectively (see tables 2 and 3). In 2013, China was the country/area with the highest value of net exports (+28.2 bln US$), followed by India (+4.2 bln US$). By MDG regions (see graph 2), the largest surpluses in this product group were recorded by Eastern Asia (+27.2 bln US$), Southern Asia (+8.4 bln US$) and South-eastern Asia (+5.3 bln US$). The largest trade deficits were recorded by Developed North America (-17.1 bln US$), Developed Europe (-13.0 bln US$) and Developed Asia-Pacific (-8.7 bln US$).

Table 1: Imports (Imp.) and exports (Exp.), 1999-2013, in current US$

		1999	2000	2001	2002	2003	2004	2005	2006	2007	2008	2009	2010	2011	2012	2013
Values in Bln US$	Imp.	43.1	46.1	47.4	50.2	57.0	63.8	69.5	74.3	79.7	82.1	72.0	75.8	85.4	81.0	84.2
	Exp.	40.4	43.0	43.1	47.0	52.6	59.5	65.0	69.8	75.5	78.9	68.0	72.3	82.4	78.9	86.1
As a percentage of SITC section (%)	Imp.	5.7	5.7	5.8	5.9	5.9	5.7	5.6	5.4	5.2	4.9	5.0	4.6	4.6	4.4	4.4
	Exp.	5.6	5.5	5.6	5.9	5.7	5.5	5.5	5.3	5.0	4.8	4.8	4.4	4.3	4.0	4.2
As a percentage of world trade (%)	Imp.	0.8	0.7	0.8	0.8	0.7	0.7	0.7	0.6	0.6	0.5	0.6	0.5	0.5	0.4	0.5
	Exp.	0.7	0.7	0.7	0.7	0.7	0.7	0.6	0.6	0.5	0.5	0.5	0.5	0.5	0.4	0.5

Graph 1: Annual growth rates of exports, 1999–2013
(In percentage by year)

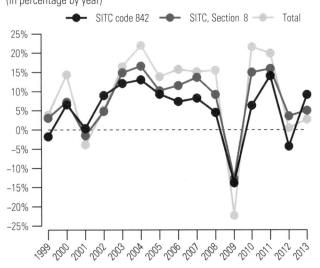

Legend: SITC code 842 — SITC, Section 8 — Total

Table 2: Top exporting countries or areas in 2013

Country or area	Value (million US$)	Avg. Growth (%) 09-13	Growth (%) 12-13	World share %	Cum.
World....................	86 128.7	6.1	9.2	100.0	
China....................	29 392.8	9.4	13.9	34.1	34.1
Italy....................	5 535.2	4.1	6.3	6.4	40.6
China, Hong Kong SAR........	4 588.9	-3.1	-3.5	5.3	45.9
India....................	4 243.1	5.2	14.5	4.9	50.8
Germany....................	3 928.1	-0.1	-0.9	4.6	55.4
Viet Nam....................	3 768.0	17.5	20.4	4.4	59.7
Spain....................	3 660.0	13.8	20.1	4.2	64.0
Turkey....................	3 227.5	8.1	6.2	3.7	67.7
Bangladesh....................	*2 786.3*	15.0	7.6	3.2	71.0
France....................	2 200.4	0.3	12.0	2.6	73.5
United Kingdom....................	2 113.7	12.5	17.5	2.5	76.0
Netherlands....................	1 652.9	11.9	10.4	1.9	77.9
Indonesia....................	1 560.6	2.4	5.4	1.8	79.7
Morocco....................	1 375.8	2.1	6.2	1.6	81.3
Belgium....................	1 362.0	-3.2	14.3	1.6	82.9

Graph 2: Trade Balance by MDG regions 2013
(Bln US$)

Legend: Imports — Exports — Trade balance

Developed Asia–Pacific
Developed Europe
Developed N. America
South–eastern Europe
C I S
Northern Africa
Sub–Saharan Africa
Latin Am, Caribbean
Eastern Asia
Southern Asia
South–eastern Asia
Western Asia
Oceania

(axis: -40 -30 -20 -10 0 10 20 30 40)

Table 3: Top importing countries or areas in 2013

Country or area	Value (million US$)	Avg. Growth (%) 09-13	Growth (%) 12-13	World share %	Cum.
World....................	84 231.6	4.0	4.0	100.0	
USA....................	16 225.6	2.4	2.6	19.3	19.3
Germany....................	7 613.8	3.2	6.5	9.0	28.3
Japan....................	7 147.6	7.1	-0.8	8.5	36.8
United Kingdom....................	5 886.1	-2.0	1.5	7.0	43.8
France....................	4 919.1	0.6	6.1	5.8	49.6
Spain....................	4 020.8	5.8	12.5	4.8	54.4
China, Hong Kong SAR........	3 477.7	0.6	1.2	4.1	58.5
Italy....................	2 885.2	-0.7	-0.5	3.4	61.9
Netherlands....................	2 232.4	5.2	3.2	2.7	64.6
Russian Federation....................	2 131.5	16.2	-3.1	2.5	67.1
Rep. of Korea....................	1 966.0	19.2	24.6	2.3	69.5
Canada....................	1 847.4	4.8	3.5	2.2	71.7
Belgium....................	1 796.6	-2.4	13.4	2.1	73.8
Australia....................	1 445.5	12.0	2.1	1.7	75.5
Switzerland....................	1 331.6	1.9	3.5	1.6	77.1

Men's or boys' outerwear, of textile fabrics, knitted or crocheted 843

In 2013, the value (in current US$) of exports of "men's or boys' outerwear, of textile fabrics, knitted or crocheted" (SITC group 843) increased by 12.0 percent (compared to 12.9 percent average growth rate from 2009-2013) to reach 34.6 bln US$ (see table 2), while imports increased by 6.2 percent to reach 22.1 bln US$ (see table 3). Exports of this commodity accounted for 1.7 percent of world exports of SITC section 8, and 0.2 percent of total world merchandise exports (see table 1). China, Bangladesh and Viet Nam were the top exporters in 2013 (see table 2). They accounted for 49.0, 4.4 and 4.0 percent of world exports, respectively. USA, Japan and United Kingdom were the top destinations, with respectively 26.7, 7.6 and 7.0 percent of world imports (see table 3).

The top 15 countries/areas accounted for 84.8 and 77.1 percent of total world exports and imports, respectively (see tables 2 and 3). In 2013, China was the country/area with the highest value of net exports (+16.7 bln US$), followed by Bangladesh (+1.5 bln US$). By MDG regions (see graph 2), the largest surpluses in this product group were recorded by Eastern Asia (+16.5 bln US$), Southern Asia (+4.1 bln US$) and South-eastern Asia (+3.6 bln US$). The largest trade deficits were recorded by Developed North America (-6.2 bln US$), Developed Europe (-3.7 bln US$) and Developed Asia-Pacific (-2.0 bln US$).

Table 1: Imports (Imp.) and exports (Exp.), 1999-2013, in current US$

		1999	2000	2001	2002	2003	2004	2005	2006	2007	2008	2009	2010	2011	2012	2013
Values in Bln US$	Imp.	9.8	10.1	9.8	10.0	11.1	12.0	13.1	14.7	16.7	18.1	16.3	18.5	21.9	20.8	22.1
	Exp.	10.2	10.4	10.3	11.0	12.8	14.2	15.1	18.2	24.0	24.5	21.3	24.5	30.0	30.9	34.6
As a percentage of SITC section (%)	Imp.	1.3	1.2	1.2	1.2	1.1	1.1	1.1	1.1	1.1	1.1	1.1	1.1	1.2	1.1	1.2
	Exp.	1.4	1.3	1.3	1.4	1.4	1.3	1.3	1.4	1.6	1.5	1.5	1.5	1.6	1.6	1.7
As a percentage of world trade (%)	Imp.	0.2	0.2	0.2	0.2	0.1	0.1	0.1	0.1	0.1	0.1	0.1	0.1	0.1	0.1	0.1
	Exp.	0.2	0.2	0.2	0.2	0.2	0.2	0.1	0.2	0.2	0.2	0.2	0.2	0.2	0.2	0.2

Graph 1: Annual growth rates of exports, 1999–2013
(In percentage by year)

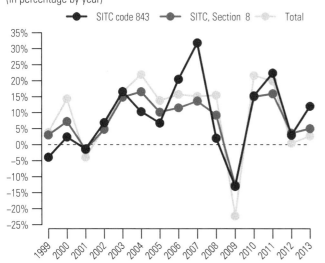

Table 2: Top exporting countries or areas in 2013

Country or area	Value (million US$)	Avg. Growth (%) 09-13	Growth (%) 12-13	World share %	Cum.
World	34558.6	12.9	12.0	100.0	
China	16921.5	18.1	14.1	49.0	49.0
Bangladesh	*1519.7*	15.7	7.6	4.4	53.4
Viet Nam	1382.7	20.9	19.8	4.0	57.4
India	1371.6	8.3	24.0	4.0	61.3
China, Hong Kong SAR	1110.6	0.8	-1.4	3.2	64.5
Cambodia	1106.3	18.6	12.2	3.2	67.7
Pakistan	923.3	5.6	2.1	2.7	70.4
Belgium	819.3	16.6	50.4	2.4	72.8
Italy	786.9	10.7	6.1	2.3	75.1
Turkey	745.2	9.0	19.5	2.2	77.2
Germany	645.7	9.5	5.6	1.9	79.1
Indonesia	594.2	11.9	9.6	1.7	80.8
Netherlands	577.5	16.4	25.0	1.7	82.5
Thailand	414.9	-1.4	-6.6	1.2	83.7
N. Mariana Isds	*373.7*	3.0	3.0	1.1	84.8

Graph 2: Trade Balance by MDG regions 2013
(Bln US$)

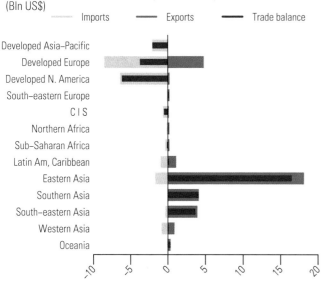

Table 3: Top importing countries or areas in 2013

Country or area	Value (million US$)	Avg. Growth (%) 09-13	Growth (%) 12-13	World share %	Cum.
World	22052.0	7.9	6.2	100.0	
USA	5892.4	6.5	5.0	26.7	26.7
Japan	1672.7	9.4	0.0	7.6	34.3
United Kingdom	1541.3	6.2	5.3	7.0	41.3
Germany	1404.2	8.1	10.4	6.4	47.7
France	1045.2	5.6	6.5	4.7	52.4
China, Hong Kong SAR	911.1	2.1	-1.1	4.1	56.5
Italy	902.5	1.8	-2.2	4.1	60.6
Spain	657.7	1.2	4.6	3.0	63.6
Belgium	570.8	9.6	16.7	2.6	66.2
Netherlands	567.2	8.0	4.6	2.6	68.8
Canada	518.7	8.5	6.2	2.4	71.1
Russian Federation	376.1	35.0	19.5	1.7	72.8
Australia	331.7	13.8	12.1	1.5	74.3
Rep. of Korea	315.9	26.0	20.3	1.4	75.8
Brazil	285.1	34.8	4.0	1.3	77.1

844 Women's or girls' outerwear, of textile fabrics, knitted or crocheted

In 2013, the value (in current US$) of exports of "women's or girls' outerwear, of textile fabrics, knitted or crocheted" (SITC group 844) increased by 11.8 percent (compared to 14.0 percent average growth rate from 2009-2013) to reach 65.0 bln US$ (see table 2), while imports increased by 6.3 percent to reach 43.6 bln US$ (see table 3). Exports of this commodity accounted for 3.1 percent of world exports of SITC section 8, and 0.3 percent of total world merchandise exports (see table 1). China, China, Hong Kong SAR and Viet Nam were the top exporters in 2013 (see table 2). They accounted for 53.3, 3.6 and 3.4 percent of world exports, respectively. USA, Germany and Japan were the top destinations, with respectively 24.5, 9.0 and 8.9 percent of world imports (see table 3).

The top 15 countries/areas accounted for 83.8 and 79.5 percent of total world exports and imports, respectively (see tables 2 and 3). In 2013, China was the country/area with the highest value of net exports (+34.3 bln US$), followed by Viet Nam (+2.2 bln US$). By MDG regions (see graph 2), the largest surpluses in this product group were recorded by Eastern Asia (+34.5 bln US$), South-eastern Asia (+5.5 bln US$) and Southern Asia (+3.7 bln US$). The largest trade deficits were recorded by Developed North America (-11.1 bln US$), Developed Europe (-8.1 bln US$) and Developed Asia-Pacific (-4.6 bln US$).

Table 1: Imports (Imp.) and exports (Exp.), 1999-2013, in current US$

		1999	2000	2001	2002	2003	2004	2005	2006	2007	2008	2009	2010	2011	2012	2013
Values in Bln US$	Imp.	16.7	17.1	17.0	18.2	20.8	23.0	24.2	27.1	32.4	34.9	32.8	37.3	41.9	41.0	43.6
	Exp.	17.7	17.5	17.0	19.1	23.1	25.9	26.5	32.1	41.7	41.7	38.4	45.0	53.2	58.1	65.0
As a percentage of SITC section (%)	Imp.	2.2	2.1	2.1	2.1	2.1	2.0	2.0	2.0	2.1	2.1	2.3	2.3	2.3	2.2	2.3
	Exp.	2.4	2.3	2.2	2.4	2.5	2.4	2.2	2.4	2.8	2.5	2.7	2.7	2.8	3.0	3.1
As a percentage of world trade (%)	Imp.	0.3	0.3	0.3	0.3	0.3	0.2	0.2	0.2	0.2	0.2	0.3	0.2	0.2	0.2	0.2
	Exp.	0.3	0.3	0.3	0.3	0.3	0.3	0.3	0.3	0.3	0.3	0.3	0.3	0.3	0.3	0.3

Graph 1: Annual growth rates of exports, 1999–2013
(In percentage by year)

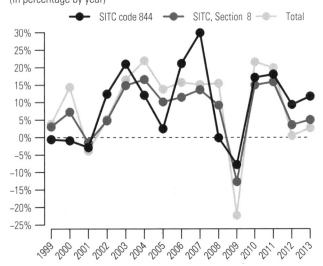

Table 2: Top exporting countries or areas in 2013

Country or area	Value (million US$)	Avg. Growth (%) 09-13	Growth (%) 12-13	World share %	Cum.
World..................................	64 980.8	14.0	11.8	100.0	
China..................................	34 630.4	24.0	14.2	53.3	53.3
China, Hong Kong SAR.........	2 348.0	-1.9	-0.6	3.6	56.9
Viet Nam.............................	2 227.8	19.6	14.7	3.4	60.3
Turkey................................	2 068.0	5.1	4.4	3.2	63.5
Germany..............................	2 011.2	7.1	7.3	3.1	66.6
Cambodia............................	1 665.5	16.8	13.7	2.6	69.2
India...................................	1 442.8	1.2	24.3	2.2	71.4
Italy....................................	1 310.5	8.2	5.1	2.0	73.4
Indonesia............................	1 054.0	7.8	6.1	1.6	75.0
Bangladesh..........................	*1 034.1*	16.7	7.6	1.6	76.6
Sri Lanka.............................	992.1	11.9	23.6	1.5	78.2
France.................................	967.0	3.2	3.3	1.5	79.6
Spain..................................	965.2	1.0	14.7	1.5	81.1
United Kingdom....................	895.9	15.5	29.7	1.4	82.5
Belgium...............................	813.0	4.1	26.3	1.3	83.8

Graph 2: Trade Balance by MDG regions 2013
(Bln US$)

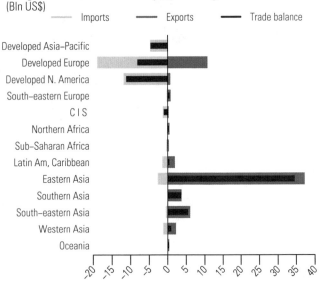

Table 3: Top importing countries or areas in 2013

Country or area	Value (million US$)	Avg. Growth (%) 09-13	Growth (%) 12-13	World share %	Cum.
World..................................	43 598.2	7.4	6.3	100.0	
USA....................................	10 685.1	8.6	6.1	24.5	24.5
Germany..............................	3 915.4	6.3	10.1	9.0	33.5
Japan..................................	3 890.3	7.1	0.2	8.9	42.4
United Kingdom....................	3 040.2	5.7	7.7	7.0	49.4
France.................................	2 355.7	4.8	7.7	5.4	54.8
China, Hong Kong SAR.........	1 786.0	0.1	2.2	4.1	58.9
Spain..................................	1 453.6	3.7	11.8	3.3	62.2
Italy....................................	1 393.7	3.2	0.8	3.2	65.4
Canada...............................	1 161.6	10.7	12.1	2.7	68.1
Netherlands.........................	1 137.7	9.1	6.7	2.6	70.7
Russian Federation...............	1 018.4	30.6	-22.1	2.3	73.0
Belgium...............................	898.7	3.1	15.3	2.1	75.1
Australia..............................	681.2	13.6	3.0	1.6	76.6
Austria................................	648.4	5.9	8.6	1.5	78.1
Switzerland..........................	580.7	6.2	4.5	1.3	79.5

Articles of apparel, of textile fabrics, whether or not knitted or crocheted, nes 845

In 2013, the value (in current US$) of exports of "articles of apparel, of textile fabrics, whether or not knitted or crocheted, nes" (SITC group 845) increased by 8.2 percent (compared to 7.2 percent average growth rate from 2009-2013) to reach 146.6 bln US$ (see table 2), while imports increased by 6.0 percent to reach 137.9 bln US$ (see table 3). Exports of this commodity accounted for 7.1 percent of world exports of SITC section 8, and 0.8 percent of total world merchandise exports (see table 1). China, China, Hong Kong SAR and Bangladesh were the top exporters in 2013 (see table 2). They accounted for 33.4, 6.5 and 6.0 percent of world exports, respectively. USA, Germany and Japan were the top destinations, with respectively 22.7, 8.9 and 7.9 percent of world imports (see table 3).

The top 15 countries/areas accounted for 80.4 and 78.2 percent of total world exports and imports, respectively (see tables 2 and 3). In 2013, China was the country/area with the highest value of net exports (+47.7 bln US$), followed by Bangladesh (+8.7 bln US$). By MDG regions (see graph 2), the largest surpluses in this product group were recorded by Eastern Asia (+48.5 bln US$), Southern Asia (+15.6 bln US$) and South-eastern Asia (+9.9 bln US$). The largest trade deficits were recorded by Developed North America (-32.4 bln US$), Developed Europe (-22.6 bln US$) and Developed Asia-Pacific (-13.0 bln US$).

Table 1: Imports (Imp.) and exports (Exp.), 1999-2013, in current US$

		1999	2000	2001	2002	2003	2004	2005	2006	2007	2008	2009	2010	2011	2012	2013
Values in Bln US$	Imp.	63.8	70.2	72.1	73.9	82.8	93.3	99.7	108.2	117.3	125.8	114.3	122.8	139.3	130.1	137.9
	Exp.	57.2	62.5	62.4	65.2	74.6	84.7	93.0	108.0	119.9	126.5	110.9	121.5	140.0	135.4	146.6
As a percentage of SITC section (%)	Imp.	8.5	8.6	8.9	8.7	8.5	8.3	8.1	7.9	7.6	7.6	8.0	7.5	7.5	7.1	7.2
	Exp.	7.9	8.1	8.2	8.1	8.1	7.9	7.9	8.2	8.0	7.7	7.8	7.4	7.4	6.9	7.1
As a percentage of world trade (%)	Imp.	1.1	1.1	1.1	1.1	1.1	1.0	0.9	0.9	0.8	0.8	0.9	0.8	0.8	0.7	0.7
	Exp.	1.0	1.0	1.0	1.0	1.0	0.9	0.9	0.9	0.9	0.8	0.9	0.8	0.8	0.7	0.8

Graph 1: Annual growth rates of exports, 1999–2013
(In percentage by year)

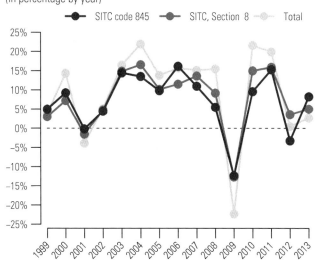

Graph 2: Trade Balance by MDG regions 2013
(Bln US$)

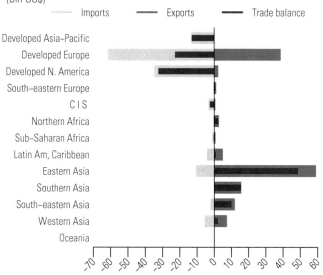

Table 2: Top exporting countries or areas in 2013

Country or area	Value (million US$)	Avg. Growth (%) 09-13	Growth (%) 12-13	World share %	Cum.
World	146587.7	7.2	8.2	100.0	
China	48988.7	10.0	9.0	33.4	33.4
China, Hong Kong SAR	9480.8	-1.1	-2.2	6.5	39.9
Bangladesh	8732.1	13.6	7.6	6.0	45.8
Italy	6988.7	4.5	7.2	4.8	50.6
Germany	5857.1	3.6	5.2	4.0	54.6
Turkey	5475.4	8.5	9.5	3.7	58.3
Viet Nam	5217.5	19.0	20.9	3.6	61.9
India	5174.5	13.8	29.2	3.5	65.4
France	4740.3	2.8	6.4	3.2	68.7
Spain	4118.1	10.3	20.8	2.8	71.5
Belgium	3525.5	1.0	10.6	2.4	73.9
Netherlands	2871.7	7.3	9.9	2.0	75.8
United Kingdom	2381.1	8.3	20.4	1.6	77.5
Indonesia	2259.1	6.7	-2.5	1.5	79.0
Cambodia	1995.1	20.5	22.4	1.4	80.4

Table 3: Top importing countries or areas in 2013

Country or area	Value (million US$)	Avg. Growth (%) 09-13	Growth (%) 12-13	World share %	Cum.
World	137910.6	4.8	6.0	100.0	
USA	31362.3	5.7	3.7	22.7	22.7
Germany	12207.7	3.9	9.2	8.9	31.6
Japan	10852.7	5.9	-0.9	7.9	39.5
United Kingdom	8718.6	-1.2	5.6	6.3	45.8
France	8314.4	2.3	4.9	6.0	51.8
China, Hong Kong SAR	6489.3	0.0	0.8	4.7	56.5
Italy	5576.0	-0.6	0.2	4.0	60.6
Spain	5004.9	0.7	5.8	3.6	64.2
Belgium	3651.2	1.2	12.4	2.6	66.8
Netherlands	3580.1	5.9	7.5	2.6	69.4
Canada	3370.4	7.1	6.7	2.4	71.9
Russian Federation	2387.6	23.3	4.2	1.7	73.6
Rep. of Korea	2229.6	22.2	18.1	1.6	75.2
Austria	2052.6	4.0	8.6	1.5	76.7
Australia	1988.8	10.4	4.9	1.4	78.2

846 Clothing accessories, of textile fabrics, whether or not knitted or crocheted

In 2013, the value (in current US$) of exports of "clothing accessories, of textile fabrics, whether or not knitted or crocheted" (SITC group 846) increased by 8.7 percent (compared to 10.1 percent average growth rate from 2009-2013) to reach 31.2 bln US$ (see table 2), while imports increased by 5.9 percent to reach 27.4 bln US$ (see table 3). Exports of this commodity accounted for 1.5 percent of world exports of SITC section 8, and 0.2 percent of total world merchandise exports (see table 1). China, Italy and Turkey were the top exporters in 2013 (see table 2). They accounted for 43.7, 8.3 and 4.1 percent of world exports, respectively. USA, Japan and Germany were the top destinations, with respectively 17.8, 9.3 and 8.4 percent of world imports (see table 3).

The top 15 countries/areas accounted for 82.4 and 70.1 percent of total world exports and imports, respectively (see tables 2 and 3). In 2013, China was the country/area with the highest value of net exports (+13.3 bln US$), followed by Italy (+1.6 bln US$). By MDG regions (see graph 2), the largest surpluses in this product group were recorded by Eastern Asia (+14.1 bln US$), Southern Asia (+1.4 bln US$) and Western Asia (+450.7 mln US$). The largest trade deficits were recorded by Developed North America (-4.7 bln US$), Developed Europe (-2.9 bln US$) and Developed Asia-Pacific (-2.8 bln US$).

Table 1: Imports (Imp.) and exports (Exp.), 1999-2013, in current US$

		1999	2000	2001	2002	2003	2004	2005	2006	2007	2008	2009	2010	2011	2012	2013
Values in Bln US$	Imp.	12.1	12.5	12.3	12.6	14.2	16.2	17.0	17.7	19.3	22.0	19.4	23.3	27.3	25.9	27.4
	Exp.	12.3	12.9	12.5	12.9	14.5	16.3	17.5	18.6	20.2	23.7	21.2	24.5	29.1	28.7	31.2
As a percentage of SITC section (%)	Imp.	1.6	1.5	1.5	1.5	1.5	1.4	1.4	1.3	1.3	1.3	1.4	1.4	1.5	1.4	1.4
	Exp.	1.7	1.7	1.6	1.6	1.6	1.5	1.5	1.4	1.3	1.4	1.5	1.5	1.5	1.5	1.5
As a percentage of world trade (%)	Imp.	0.2	0.2	0.2	0.2	0.2	0.2	0.2	0.1	0.1	0.1	0.2	0.2	0.2	0.1	0.1
	Exp.	0.2	0.2	0.2	0.2	0.2	0.2	0.2	0.2	0.1	0.1	0.2	0.2	0.2	0.2	0.2

Graph 1: Annual growth rates of exports, 1999–2013
(In percentage by year)

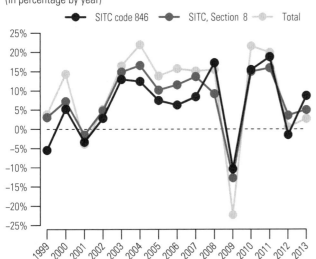

Table 2: Top exporting countries or areas in 2013

Country or area	Value (million US$)	Avg. Growth (%) 09-13	Growth (%) 12-13	World share %	World share % Cum.
World	31 164.2	10.1	8.7	100.0	
China	13 621.7	15.0	10.6	43.7	43.7
Italy	2 592.2	2.0	3.8	8.3	52.0
Turkey	1 270.0	7.2	16.2	4.1	56.1
Germany	1 230.1	4.3	5.0	3.9	60.0
India	1 155.2	9.2	22.9	3.7	63.8
Rep. of Korea	966.5	14.9	15.1	3.1	66.9
France	810.5	5.5	8.2	2.6	69.5
USA	694.7	3.7	-6.0	2.2	71.7
Belgium	669.9	5.1	19.0	2.1	73.8
Netherlands	571.9	9.5	11.6	1.8	75.7
China, Hong Kong SAR	473.4	0.8	-7.1	1.5	77.2
Pakistan	471.7	7.2	10.1	1.5	78.7
United Kingdom	467.2	11.1	2.3	1.5	80.2
Spain	384.1	8.2	-4.9	1.2	81.4
Viet Nam	306.5	26.1	32.8	1.0	82.4

Graph 2: Trade Balance by MDG regions 2013
(Bln US$)

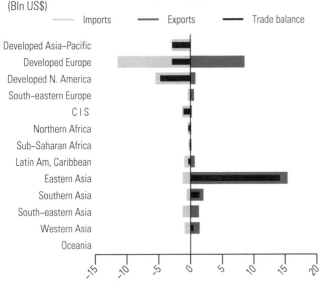

Table 3: Top importing countries or areas in 2013

Country or area	Value (million US$)	Avg. Growth (%) 09-13	Growth (%) 12-13	World share %	World share % Cum.
World	27 381.0	8.9	5.9	100.0	
USA	4 876.8	10.8	6.0	17.8	17.8
Japan	2 553.0	9.5	0.7	9.3	27.1
Germany	2 287.2	7.1	5.9	8.4	35.5
United Kingdom	1 675.0	26.8	18.6	6.1	41.6
France	1 571.0	5.0	11.3	5.7	47.3
Italy	959.9	2.1	-0.9	3.5	50.8
Russian Federation	838.8	24.5	-1.1	3.1	53.9
Netherlands	657.7	6.8	13.1	2.4	56.3
Belgium	639.3	5.4	19.7	2.3	58.6
Spain	635.1	0.9	1.4	2.3	61.0
Canada	632.6	7.9	7.6	2.3	63.3
Singapore	541.0	30.3	13.9	2.0	65.3
Bangladesh	*497.6*	1.2	-1.6	1.8	67.1
China, Hong Kong SAR	448.8	2.6	1.0	1.6	68.7
Austria	391.4	6.4	5.4	1.4	70.1

Articles of apparel, and clothing accessories not textile fabrics; headgear 848

In 2013, the value (in current US$) of exports of "articles of apparel, and clothing accessories not textile fabrics; headgear" (SITC group 848) increased by 6.4 percent (compared to 11.6 percent average growth rate from 2009-2013) to reach 32.3 bln US$ (see table 2), while imports increased by 0.9 percent to reach 29.2 bln US$ (see table 3). Exports of this commodity accounted for 1.6 percent of world exports of SITC section 8, and 0.2 percent of total world merchandise exports (see table 1). China, Malaysia and Italy were the top exporters in 2013 (see table 2). They accounted for 38.4, 10.7 and 7.0 percent of world exports, respectively. USA, Germany and Japan were the top destinations, with respectively 24.7, 7.6 and 6.3 percent of world imports (see table 3).

The top 15 countries/areas accounted for 86.3 and 73.6 percent of total world exports and imports, respectively (see tables 2 and 3). In 2013, China was the country/area with the highest value of net exports (+11.9 bln US$), followed by Malaysia (+3.3 bln US$). By MDG regions (see graph 2), the largest surpluses in this product group were recorded by Eastern Asia (+11.8 bln US$), South-eastern Asia (+4.7 bln US$) and Southern Asia (+1.9 bln US$). The largest trade deficits were recorded by Developed North America (-7.1 bln US$), Developed Europe (-2.8 bln US$) and Developed Asia-Pacific (-2.2 bln US$).

Table 1: Imports (Imp.) and exports (Exp.), 1999-2013, in current US$

		1999	2000	2001	2002	2003	2004	2005	2006	2007	2008	2009	2010	2011	2012	2013
Values in Bln US$	Imp.	12.6	14.7	15.4	15.3	16.3	17.9	19.4	20.8	22.2	24.6	21.8	25.1	29.2	29.0	29.2
	Exp.	11.8	13.7	14.2	14.5	17.0	19.0	21.1	20.7	21.5	23.3	20.8	24.7	29.7	30.3	32.3
As a percentage of	Imp.	1.7	1.8	1.9	1.8	1.7	1.6	1.6	1.5	1.4	1.5	1.5	1.5	1.6	1.6	1.5
SITC section (%)	Exp.	1.6	1.8	1.9	1.8	1.8	1.8	1.8	1.6	1.4	1.4	1.5	1.5	1.6	1.5	1.6
As a percentage of	Imp.	0.2	0.2	0.2	0.2	0.2	0.2	0.2	0.2	0.2	0.2	0.2	0.2	0.2	0.2	0.2
world trade (%)	Exp.	0.2	0.2	0.2	0.2	0.2	0.2	0.2	0.2	0.2	0.1	0.2	0.2	0.2	0.2	0.2

Graph 1: Annual growth rates of exports, 1999–2013
(In percentage by year)

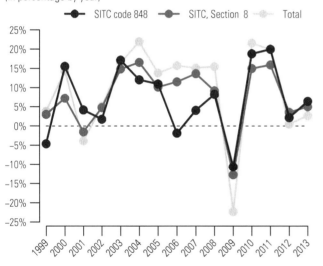

Table 2: Top exporting countries or areas in 2013

Country or area	Value (million US$)	Avg. Growth (%) 09-13	Growth (%) 12-13	World share %	Cum.
World	32 255.5	11.6	6.4	100.0	
China	12 390.3	16.2	9.2	38.4	38.4
Malaysia	3 442.1	13.2	-1.4	10.7	49.1
Italy	2 244.7	12.0	13.6	7.0	56.0
Germany	1 288.0	7.0	7.6	4.0	60.0
China, Hong Kong SAR	1 204.4	4.0	-6.8	3.7	63.8
Thailand	1 193.1	12.7	-7.7	3.7	67.5
India	1 140.3	13.3	21.8	3.5	71.0
France	1 028.8	9.1	12.4	3.2	74.2
USA	785.7	3.7	-2.2	2.4	76.6
Netherlands	617.3	14.8	9.6	1.9	78.5
Belgium	593.0	7.0	10.5	1.8	80.4
Pakistan	588.7	5.8	14.7	1.8	82.2
United Kingdom	479.6	8.9	22.7	1.5	83.7
Turkey	434.2	6.8	2.0	1.3	85.0
Viet Nam	402.9	17.6	10.7	1.2	86.3

Graph 2: Trade Balance by MDG regions 2013
(Bln US$)

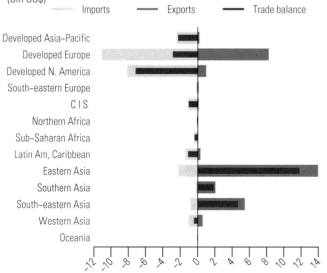

Table 3: Top importing countries or areas in 2013

Country or area	Value (million US$)	Avg. Growth (%) 09-13	Growth (%) 12-13	World share %	Cum.
World	29 215.7	7.6	0.9	100.0	
USA	7 219.5	8.2	-0.7	24.7	24.7
Germany	2 216.8	5.8	5.7	7.6	32.3
Japan	1 848.4	5.7	-3.0	6.3	38.6
France	1 633.9	6.2	5.7	5.6	44.2
United Kingdom	1 367.0	3.9	5.5	4.7	48.9
China, Hong Kong SAR	1 114.3	8.6	-1.5	3.8	52.7
Italy	1 022.5	2.9	2.9	3.5	56.2
Canada	893.7	6.3	2.8	3.1	59.3
Russian Federation	823.0	19.7	-21.5	2.8	62.1
Spain	664.2	0.5	3.6	2.3	64.4
Netherlands	648.9	6.2	-2.2	2.2	66.6
Belgium	602.8	2.8	9.2	2.1	68.6
China	518.5	28.4	0.8	1.8	70.4
Australia	491.7	9.4	-1.0	1.7	72.1
Switzerland	445.6	3.9	10.2	1.5	73.6

851 Footwear

In 2013, the value (in current US$) of exports of "footwear" (SITC group 851) increased by 9.5 percent (compared to 11.6 percent average growth rate from 2009-2013) to reach 126.5 bln US$ (see table 2), while imports increased by 6.1 percent to reach 120.7 bln US$ (see table 3). Exports of this commodity accounted for 6.1 percent of world exports of SITC section 8, and 0.7 percent of total world merchandise exports (see table 1). China, Italy and Viet Nam were the top exporters in 2013 (see table 2). They accounted for 40.1, 9.3 and 6.9 percent of world exports, respectively. USA, Germany and France were the top destinations, with respectively 21.4, 7.6 and 5.8 percent of world imports (see table 3).

The top 15 countries/areas accounted for 86.4 and 72.8 percent of total world exports and imports, respectively (see tables 2 and 3). In 2013, China was the country/area with the highest value of net exports (+48.8 bln US$), followed by Viet Nam (+8.3 bln US$). By MDG regions (see graph 2), the largest surpluses in this product group were recorded by Eastern Asia (+46.8 bln US$), South-eastern Asia (+11.9 bln US$) and Southern Asia (+2.6 bln US$). The largest trade deficits were recorded by Developed North America (-26.5 bln US$), Developed Europe (-9.0 bln US$) and Developed Asia-Pacific (-7.6 bln US$).

Table 1: Imports (Imp.) and exports (Exp.), 1999-2013, in current US$

		1999	2000	2001	2002	2003	2004	2005	2006	2007	2008	2009	2010	2011	2012	2013
Values in Bln US$	Imp.	50.0	51.4	53.0	55.0	60.4	66.7	73.7	80.7	88.6	96.7	86.8	100.8	114.9	113.7	120.7
	Exp.	45.4	46.6	47.2	48.6	54.1	60.4	66.6	73.4	82.6	91.7	81.6	96.1	113.6	115.5	126.5
As a percentage of	Imp.	6.6	6.3	6.5	6.5	6.2	5.9	6.0	5.9	5.8	5.8	6.0	6.1	6.2	6.2	6.3
SITC section (%)	Exp.	6.3	6.0	6.2	6.1	5.9	5.6	5.6	5.6	5.5	5.6	5.7	5.9	6.0	5.9	6.1
As a percentage of	Imp.	0.9	0.8	0.8	0.8	0.8	0.7	0.7	0.7	0.6	0.6	0.7	0.7	0.6	0.6	0.7
world trade (%)	Exp.	0.8	0.7	0.8	0.8	0.7	0.7	0.6	0.6	0.6	0.6	0.7	0.6	0.6	0.6	0.7

Graph 1: Annual growth rates of exports, 1999–2013
(In percentage by year)

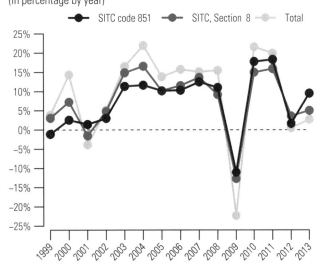

— SITC code 851   — SITC, Section 8   — Total

Table 2: Top exporting countries or areas in 2013

Country or area	Value (million US$)	Avg. Growth (%) 09-13	Growth (%) 12-13	World share %	Cum.
World	126 467.1	11.6	9.5	100.0	
China	50 761.3	16.0	8.4	40.1	40.1
Italy	11 714.4	6.6	8.8	9.3	49.4
Viet Nam	8 721.9	20.4	16.1	6.9	56.3
Belgium	5 130.5	9.9	19.1	4.1	60.4
Germany	4 984.7	9.6	13.5	3.9	64.3
China, Hong Kong SAR	4 688.8	-0.4	-9.5	3.7	68.0
Indonesia	3 860.4	22.1	9.5	3.1	71.1
Netherlands	3 416.2	10.8	12.0	2.7	73.8
Spain	3 148.9	4.8	13.6	2.5	76.2
France	2 828.0	10.4	7.3	2.2	78.5
India	2 608.2	15.2	33.2	2.1	80.5
Portugal	2 362.5	10.1	11.7	1.9	82.4
United Kingdom	1 899.8	13.7	19.1	1.5	83.9
Romania	1 701.5	5.8	8.4	1.3	85.3
USA	1 383.7	10.0	4.0	1.1	86.4

Graph 2: Trade Balance by MDG regions 2013
(Bln US$)

— Imports   — Exports   — Trade balance

Developed Asia–Pacific
Developed Europe
Developed N. America
South–eastern Europe
CIS
Northern Africa
Sub–Saharan Africa
Latin Am, Caribbean
Eastern Asia
Southern Asia
South–eastern Asia
Western Asia
Oceania

Table 3: Top importing countries or areas in 2013

Country or area	Value (million US$)	Avg. Growth (%) 09-13	Growth (%) 12-13	World share %	Cum.
World	120 657.2	8.6	6.1	100.0	
USA	25 789.0	9.0	3.7	21.4	21.4
Germany	9 222.4	9.3	10.7	7.6	29.0
France	7 012.7	5.9	8.9	5.8	34.8
United Kingdom	6 427.6	4.5	5.7	5.3	40.2
Italy	6 032.9	3.8	4.4	5.0	45.2
Japan	5 937.9	7.9	0.6	4.9	50.1
China, Hong Kong SAR	4 612.5	2.4	-4.8	3.8	53.9
Russian Federation	4 577.8	19.2	7.4	3.8	57.7
Netherlands	3 789.1	10.6	12.4	3.1	60.8
Belgium	3 513.0	6.8	14.5	2.9	63.7
Spain	2 865.2	2.8	4.0	2.4	66.1
Canada	2 304.6	8.0	4.1	1.9	68.0
Rep. of Korea	2 029.8	21.8	11.5	1.7	69.7
China	1 955.3	22.1	9.5	1.6	71.3
Austria	1 745.8	7.0	17.8	1.4	72.8

In 2013, the value (in current US$) of exports of "optical instruments and apparatus, nes" (SITC group 871) decreased by 3.1 percent (compared to 9.9 percent average growth rate from 2009-2013) to reach 105.7 bln US$ (see table 2), while imports increased by 0.3 percent to reach 87.6 bln US$ (see table 3). Exports of this commodity accounted for 5.1 percent of world exports of SITC section 8, and 0.6 percent of total world merchandise exports (see table 1). China, Rep. of Korea and Other Asia, nes were the top exporters in 2013 (see table 2). They accounted for 37.0, 24.0 and 15.0 percent of world exports, respectively. China, China, Hong Kong SAR and USA were the top destinations, with respectively 64.1, 7.5 and 3.9 percent of world imports (see table 3).

The top 15 countries/areas accounted for 97.7 and 94.4 percent of total world exports and imports, respectively (see tables 2 and 3). In 2013, Rep. of Korea was the country/area with the highest value of net exports (+22.1 bln US$), followed by Other Asia, nes (+14.1 bln US$). By MDG regions (see graph 2), the largest surpluses in this product group were recorded by Eastern Asia (+17.2 bln US$), Developed Asia-Pacific (+5.5 bln US$) and Developed North America (+172.6 mln US$). The largest trade deficits were recorded by Latin America and the Caribbean (-3.4 bln US$), Southern Asia (-514.6 mln US$) and South-eastern Asia (-426.6 mln US$).

Table 1: Imports (Imp.) and exports (Exp.), 1999-2013, in current US$

		1999	2000	2001	2002	2003	2004	2005	2006	2007	2008	2009	2010	2011	2012	2013
Values in Bln US$	Imp.	9.9	13.5	12.3	13.8	25.3	39.9	49.8	63.1	75.8	80.6	62.0	80.2	85.6	87.4	87.6
	Exp.	12.6	14.6	12.3	12.5	20.2	32.6	44.7	57.3	71.8	81.5	72.3	97.3	102.8	109.0	105.7
As a percentage of SITC section (%)	Imp.	1.3	1.7	1.5	1.6	2.6	3.5	4.0	4.6	4.9	4.8	4.3	4.9	4.6	4.7	4.6
	Exp.	1.7	1.9	1.6	1.6	2.2	3.0	3.8	4.3	4.8	5.0	5.1	5.9	5.4	5.5	5.1
As a percentage of world trade (%)	Imp.	0.2	0.2	0.2	0.2	0.3	0.4	0.5	0.5	0.5	0.5	0.5	0.5	0.5	0.5	0.5
	Exp.	0.2	0.2	0.2	0.2	0.3	0.4	0.4	0.5	0.5	0.5	0.6	0.6	0.6	0.6	0.6

Graph 1: Annual growth rates of exports, 1999–2013
(In percentage by year)

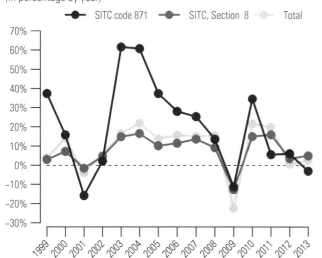

● SITC code 871   ● SITC, Section 8   ○ Total

Table 2: Top exporting countries or areas in 2013

Country or area	Value (million US$)	Avg. Growth (%) 09-13	Growth (%) 12-13	World share %	Cum.
World	105 689.5	9.9	-3.1	100.0	
China	39 132.4	17.3	-0.3	37.0	37.0
Rep. of Korea	25 351.9	2.0	-8.0	24.0	61.0
Other Asia, nes	15 830.4	7.2	-5.6	15.0	76.0
Japan	7 426.0	13.4	-16.2	7.0	83.0
China, Hong Kong SAR	4 609.3	15.6	14.5	4.4	87.4
USA	3 436.2	4.7	5.8	3.3	90.6
Germany	3 287.6	11.9	3.7	3.1	93.7
United Kingdom	779.9	12.2	9.5	0.7	94.5
Canada	615.0	7.8	-3.6	0.6	95.1
Singapore	537.9	7.7	3.6	0.5	95.6
Netherlands	491.1	7.0	11.7	0.5	96.0
Thailand	469.5	26.7	19.7	0.4	96.5
Czech Rep.	460.0	23.2	0.4	0.4	96.9
Mexico	422.4	46.9	37.6	0.4	97.3
France	415.3	5.1	-0.5	0.4	97.7

Graph 2: Trade Balance by MDG regions 2013
(Bln US$)

Imports   Exports   Trade balance

Developed Asia–Pacific
Developed Europe
Developed N. America
South–eastern Europe
CIS
Northern Africa
Sub–Saharan Africa
Latin Am, Caribbean
Eastern Asia
Southern Asia
South–eastern Asia
Western Asia
Oceania

Table 3: Top importing countries or areas in 2013

Country or area	Value (million US$)	Avg. Growth (%) 09-13	Growth (%) 12-13	World share %	Cum.
World	87 646.9	9.1	0.3	100.0	
China	56 199.1	9.8	-0.7	64.1	64.1
China, Hong Kong SAR	6 604.6	16.0	23.2	7.5	71.7
USA	3 406.5	7.1	-0.3	3.9	75.5
Mexico	3 276.5	7.6	1.3	3.7	79.3
Rep. of Korea	3 209.5	15.2	-14.8	3.7	82.9
Slovakia	1 885.7	28.9	-3.8	2.2	85.1
Japan	1 765.8	0.9	-14.2	2.0	87.1
Other Asia, nes	1 703.4	8.4	27.2	1.9	89.1
Germany	1 191.6	6.8	-10.9	1.4	90.4
Malaysia	837.9	22.1	15.0	1.0	91.4
United Kingdom	628.1	1.9	13.0	0.7	92.1
Singapore	551.7	3.0	-1.6	0.6	92.7
India	526.6	-2.5	8.3	0.6	93.3
Netherlands	513.2	18.0	9.8	0.6	93.9
Canada	471.9	-1.5	11.9	0.5	94.4

872 Instruments and appliances, nes, for medical and veterinary sciences

In 2013, the value (in current US$) of exports of "instruments and appliances, nes, for medical and veterinary sciences" (SITC group 872) increased by 7.5 percent (compared to 8.0 percent average growth rate from 2009-2013) to reach 98.8 bln US$ (see table 2), while imports increased by 6.8 percent to reach 98.9 bln US$ (see table 3). Exports of this commodity accounted for 4.8 percent of world exports of SITC section 8, and 0.5 percent of total world merchandise exports (see table 1). USA, Germany and Netherlands were the top exporters in 2013 (see table 2). They accounted for 22.5, 12.5 and 7.2 percent of world exports, respectively. USA, Germany and Belgium were the top destinations, with respectively 17.3, 8.1 and 6.1 percent of world imports (see table 3).

The top 15 countries/areas accounted for 83.8 and 71.8 percent of total world exports and imports, respectively (see tables 2 and 3). In 2013, USA was the country/area with the highest value of net exports (+5.0 bln US$), followed by Germany (+4.3 bln US$). By MDG regions (see graph 2), the largest surpluses in this product group were recorded by Developed Europe (+5.0 bln US$), Developed North America (+2.8 bln US$) and Latin America and the Caribbean (+1.4 bln US$). The largest trade deficits were recorded by Developed Asia-Pacific (-3.9 bln US$), Commonwealth of Independent States (-3.3 bln US$) and Western Asia (-2.0 bln US$).

Table 1: Imports (Imp.) and exports (Exp.), 1999-2013, in current US$

		1999	2000	2001	2002	2003	2004	2005	2006	2007	2008	2009	2010	2011	2012	2013
Values in Bln US$	Imp.	25.9	27.5	30.2	32.9	39.2	47.4	54.6	59.7	66.8	76.5	73.8	80.1	89.2	92.6	98.9
	Exp.	25.5	26.5	29.8	32.5	39.8	46.5	53.2	56.6	63.8	74.9	72.5	78.8	88.2	91.8	98.8
As a percentage of SITC section (%)	Imp.	3.4	3.4	3.7	3.9	4.0	4.2	4.4	4.4	4.3	4.6	5.1	4.9	4.8	5.0	5.2
	Exp.	3.5	3.4	3.9	4.1	4.3	4.3	4.5	4.3	4.3	4.6	5.1	4.8	4.6	4.7	4.8
As a percentage of world trade (%)	Imp.	0.5	0.4	0.5	0.5	0.5	0.5	0.5	0.5	0.5	0.6	0.5	0.5	0.5	0.5	0.5
	Exp.	0.5	0.4	0.5	0.5	0.5	0.5	0.5	0.5	0.5	0.6	0.5	0.5	0.5	0.5	0.5

Graph 1: Annual growth rates of exports, 1999–2013

(In percentage by year)

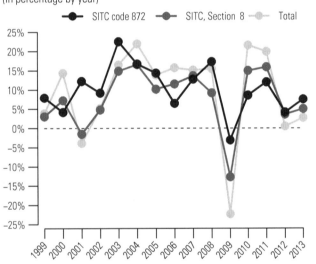

Legend: SITC code 872 — SITC, Section 8 — Total

Table 2: Top exporting countries or areas in 2013

Country or area	Value (million US$)	Avg. Growth (%) 09-13	Growth (%) 12-13	World share %	Cum.
World	98 754.7	8.0	7.5	100.0	
USA	22 188.6	6.9	3.4	22.5	22.5
Germany	12 327.5	7.3	10.3	12.5	35.0
Netherlands	7 150.9	11.7	4.5	7.2	42.2
Belgium	6 299.8	9.6	16.9	6.4	48.6
China	6 140.2	14.6	12.3	6.2	54.8
Mexico	5 350.2	7.4	9.7	5.4	60.2
Ireland	3 868.2	3.6	4.5	3.9	64.1
Singapore	3 519.8	24.2	15.1	3.6	67.7
France	3 331.1	1.3	9.6	3.4	71.1
Switzerland	3 158.3	10.3	10.0	3.2	74.3
Japan	2 728.6	5.0	-3.5	2.8	77.0
United Kingdom	2 385.7	2.9	6.4	2.4	79.4
Italy	2 094.2	2.5	9.8	2.1	81.6
Costa Rica	1 121.0	21.3	13.5	1.1	82.7
Sweden	1 043.7	-0.1	-0.2	1.1	83.8

Graph 2: Trade Balance by MDG regions 2013

(Bln US$)

Legend: Imports — Exports — Trade balance

Developed Asia–Pacific
Developed Europe
Developed N. America
South–eastern Europe
C I S
Northern Africa
Sub–Saharan Africa
Latin Am, Caribbean
Eastern Asia
Southern Asia
South–eastern Asia
Western Asia
Oceania

-50 -40 -30 -20 -10 0 10 20 30 40 50

Table 3: Top importing countries or areas in 2013

Country or area	Value (million US$)	Avg. Growth (%) 09-13	Growth (%) 12-13	World share %	Cum.
World	98 938.3	7.6	6.8	100.0	
USA	17 163.8	7.9	5.9	17.3	17.3
Germany	8 011.4	7.9	11.1	8.1	25.4
Belgium	6 008.0	8.1	18.6	6.1	31.5
Netherlands	5 618.2	7.4	7.2	5.7	37.2
Japan	5 604.4	7.7	-6.9	5.7	42.9
France	4 642.8	4.5	7.1	4.7	47.6
China	3 791.5	22.0	14.1	3.8	51.4
United Kingdom	3 658.8	-2.7	5.1	3.7	55.1
Italy	2 957.9	0.5	8.3	3.0	58.1
Canada	2 858.7	6.7	0.2	2.9	61.0
Russian Federation	2 407.8	17.9	-13.2	2.4	63.4
Singapore	2 166.9	26.8	27.2	2.2	65.6
Mexico	2 143.1	7.7	10.6	2.2	67.8
Australia	2 029.2	8.7	0.2	2.1	69.8
Spain	1 974.3	0.4	11.3	2.0	71.8

In 2013, the value (in current US$) of exports of "meters and counters, nes." (SITC group 873) increased by 4.0 percent (compared to 12.2 percent average growth rate from 2009-2013) to reach 13.2 bln US$ (see table 2), while imports increased by 5.2 percent to reach 13.7 bln US$ (see table 3). Exports of this commodity accounted for 0.6 percent of world exports of SITC section 8, and 0.1 percent of total world merchandise exports (see table 1). China, Germany and Mexico were the top exporters in 2013 (see table 2). They accounted for 15.4, 12.8 and 11.3 percent of world exports, respectively. USA, Germany and Mexico were the top destinations, with respectively 19.2, 9.0 and 4.8 percent of world imports (see table 3).

The top 15 countries/areas accounted for 76.9 and 68.2 percent of total world exports and imports, respectively (see tables 2 and 3). In 2013, China was the country/area with the highest value of net exports (+1.4 bln US$), followed by Mexico (+833.7 mln US$). By MDG regions (see graph 2), the largest surpluses in this product group were recorded by Eastern Asia (+1.4 bln US$), Developed Europe (+551.7 mln US$) and Latin America and the Caribbean (+490.0 mln US$). The largest trade deficits were recorded by Developed North America (-2.0 bln US$), Commonwealth of Independent States (-332.0 mln US$) and Sub-Saharan Africa (-256.9 mln US$).

Table 1: Imports (Imp.) and exports (Exp.), 1999-2013, in current US$

		1999	2000	2001	2002	2003	2004	2005	2006	2007	2008	2009	2010	2011	2012	2013
Values in Bln US$	Imp.	4.4	4.6	4.6	5.0	6.0	6.8	7.2	7.7	9.1	9.9	8.5	10.1	12.1	13.0	13.7
	Exp.	3.9	4.1	4.2	4.7	5.4	6.2	6.6	7.1	8.6	9.7	8.3	10.1	12.1	12.7	13.2
As a percentage of SITC section (%)	Imp.	0.6	0.6	0.6	0.6	0.6	0.6	0.6	0.6	0.6	0.6	0.6	0.6	0.7	0.7	0.7
	Exp.	0.5	0.5	0.6	0.6	0.6	0.6	0.6	0.5	0.6	0.6	0.6	0.6	0.6	0.6	0.6
As a percentage of world trade (%)	Imp.	0.1	0.1	0.1	0.1	0.1	0.1	0.1	0.1	0.1	0.1	0.1	0.1	0.1	0.1	0.1
	Exp.	0.1	0.1	0.1	0.1	0.1	0.1	0.1	0.1	0.1	0.1	0.1	0.1	0.1	0.1	0.1

Graph 1: Annual growth rates of exports, 1999–2013
(In percentage by year)

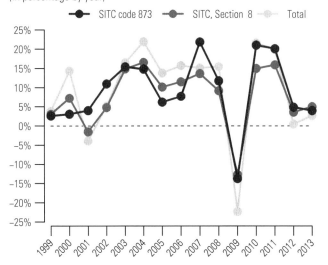

Table 2: Top exporting countries or areas in 2013

Country or area	Value (million US$)	Avg. Growth (%) 09-13	Growth (%) 12-13	World share %	World share % Cum.
World	13 192.1	12.2	4.0	100.0	
China	2 032.0	21.7	5.8	15.4	15.4
Germany	1 691.0	8.5	3.6	12.8	28.2
Mexico	1 496.7	15.5	19.6	11.3	39.6
USA	1 214.7	12.4	-3.3	9.2	48.8
France	566.7	4.5	0.5	4.3	53.1
Japan	478.6	7.0	-16.1	3.6	56.7
Italy	423.9	10.6	6.9	3.2	59.9
United Kingdom	420.4	12.2	9.1	3.2	63.1
Hungary	383.2	-0.3	-26.7	2.9	66.0
China, Hong Kong SAR	357.4	10.6	5.2	2.7	68.7
Slovakia	238.2	7.3	6.3	1.8	70.5
Poland	222.3	20.7	5.8	1.7	72.2
Czech Rep.	214.5	9.7	7.5	1.6	73.8
Spain	203.5	7.9	17.7	1.5	75.4
Thailand	199.1	13.7	-1.7	1.5	76.9

Graph 2: Trade Balance by MDG regions 2013
(Bln US$)

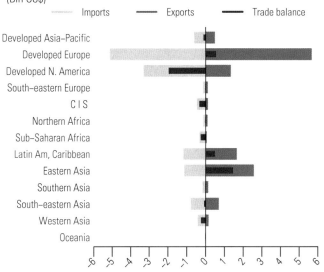

Table 3: Top importing countries or areas in 2013

Country or area	Value (million US$)	Avg. Growth (%) 09-13	Growth (%) 12-13	World share %	World share % Cum.
World	13 713.9	12.8	5.2	100.0	
USA	2 635.1	14.7	7.6	19.2	19.2
Germany	1 241.0	13.7	8.5	9.0	28.3
Mexico	663.1	25.4	34.1	4.8	33.1
Canada	660.2	13.5	-6.5	4.8	37.9
China	648.8	24.4	8.6	4.7	42.6
United Kingdom	584.7	15.2	10.1	4.3	46.9
France	571.8	5.6	3.3	4.2	51.1
Japan	393.3	11.2	-2.3	2.9	53.9
Spain	318.4	10.2	3.6	2.3	56.3
Netherlands	315.0	21.4	4.6	2.3	58.6
China, Hong Kong SAR	295.5	14.9	38.4	2.2	60.7
Belgium	295.4	7.9	8.5	2.2	62.9
Italy	273.1	3.6	-0.5	2.0	64.9
Poland	229.9	11.9	14.1	1.7	66.5
Thailand	227.7	22.1	-9.0	1.7	68.2

874 Measuring, checking, analyzing and controlling instruments, apparatus nes

"Measuring, checking, analyzing and controlling instruments, apparatus nes" (SITC group 874) is amongst the top exported commodities in 2013 with 1.0 percent of total exports (see table 1). The value (in current US$) of exports of this commodity increased by 1.5 percent (compared to 10.9 percent average growth rate from 2009-2013) to reach 187.5 bln US$ (see table 2), while imports increased by 1.6 percent to reach 190.5 bln US$ (see table 3). Exports of this commodity accounted for 9.1 percent of world exports of SITC section 8 (see table 1). USA, Germany and Japan were the top exporters in 2013 (see table 2). They accounted for 18.1, 17.0 and 9.1 percent of world exports, respectively. China, USA and Germany were the top destinations, with respectively 14.3, 13.1 and 7.4 percent of world imports (see table 3). Imports to China grew on average by 16.8 percent per year from 2009-2013, but in 2013 Chinese import recorded a slower growth of 1.4 percent.

The top 15 countries/areas accounted for 82.8 and 69.7 percent of total world exports and imports, respectively (see tables 2 and 3). In 2013, Germany was the country/area with the highest value of net exports (+17.9 bln US$), followed by Japan (+9.4 bln US$). By MDG regions (see graph 2), the largest surpluses in this product group were recorded by Developed Europe (+27.9 bln US$), Developed Asia-Pacific (+7.3 bln US$) and Developed North America (+6.8 bln US$). The largest trade deficit was recorded by Eastern Asia (-20.9 bln US$).

Table 1: Imports (Imp.) and exports (Exp.), 1999-2013, in current US$

		1999	2000	2001	2002	2003	2004	2005	2006	2007	2008	2009	2010	2011	2012	2013
Values in Bln US$	Imp.	66.2	77.0	75.0	74.8	86.0	106.2	112.5	127.6	142.7	152.3	125.7	155.1	181.7	187.5	190.5
	Exp.	63.7	72.9	72.1	72.8	83.2	103.4	110.8	125.9	140.3	149.5	123.8	153.2	178.9	184.6	187.5
As a percentage of	Imp.	8.8	9.5	9.2	8.8	8.9	9.4	9.1	9.4	9.3	9.2	8.8	9.5	9.8	10.2	10.0
SITC section (%)	Exp.	8.8	9.4	9.4	9.1	9.0	9.6	9.4	9.6	9.4	9.1	8.7	9.3	9.4	9.4	9.1
As a percentage of	Imp.	1.2	1.2	1.2	1.1	1.1	1.1	1.1	1.0	1.0	0.9	1.0	1.0	1.0	1.0	1.0
world trade (%)	Exp.	1.1	1.1	1.2	1.1	1.1	1.1	1.1	1.0	1.0	0.9	1.0	1.0	1.0	1.0	1.0

Graph 1: Annual growth rates of exports, 1999–2013
(In percentage by year)

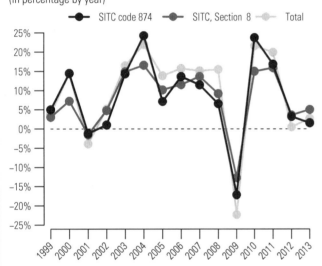

Table 2: Top exporting countries or areas in 2013

Country or area	Value (million US$)	Avg. Growth (%) 09-13	Growth (%) 12-13	World share %	Cum.
World	187 486.7	10.9	1.5	100.0	
USA	33 941.0	8.8	0.3	18.1	18.1
Germany	31 931.9	10.4	5.3	17.0	35.1
Japan	16 996.6	11.7	-13.0	9.1	44.2
China	12 522.9	18.8	4.2	6.7	50.9
United Kingdom	10 200.5	8.1	5.9	5.4	56.3
France	7 577.1	6.7	6.6	4.0	60.4
Singapore	7 199.5	18.5	5.0	3.8	64.2
China, Hong Kong SAR	5 076.5	12.3	-6.6	2.7	66.9
Netherlands	4 804.7	9.0	7.2	2.6	69.5
Switzerland	4 789.3	6.0	1.2	2.6	72.0
Italy	4 226.7	7.4	5.3	2.3	74.3
Malaysia	4 163.7	18.6	-22.0	2.2	76.5
Mexico	4 037.7	13.8	5.5	2.2	78.7
Rep. of Korea	3 947.4	28.6	14.5	2.1	80.8
Canada	3 809.4	5.9	2.5	2.0	82.8

Graph 2: Trade Balance by MDG regions 2013
(Bln US$)

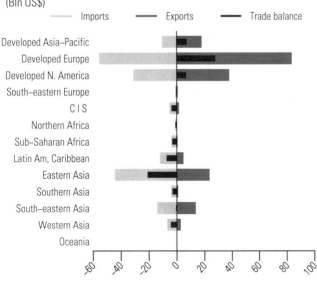

Table 3: Top importing countries or areas in 2013

Country or area	Value (million US$)	Avg. Growth (%) 09-13	Growth (%) 12-13	World share %	Cum.
World	190 481.2	11.0	1.6	100.0	
China	27 214.5	16.8	1.4	14.3	14.3
USA	24 942.0	12.2	1.8	13.1	27.4
Germany	14 060.9	7.2	0.6	7.4	34.8
United Kingdom	7 739.0	8.9	7.2	4.1	38.8
Japan	7 572.6	10.1	-2.0	4.0	42.8
Rep. of Korea	7 364.0	13.1	-8.4	3.9	46.7
France	6 043.3	5.1	1.9	3.2	49.8
Canada	6 039.3	9.3	-3.6	3.2	53.0
Singapore	5 563.4	12.5	3.8	2.9	55.9
Other Asia, nes	5 332.8	15.7	2.5	2.8	58.7
Mexico	4 802.2	11.5	5.0	2.5	61.3
China, Hong Kong SAR	4 464.0	12.0	-6.5	2.3	63.6
Netherlands	4 053.7	9.1	4.6	2.1	65.7
Italy	3 766.5	2.8	-1.7	2.0	67.7
Russian Federation	3 714.7	26.0	-2.9	2.0	69.7

In 2013, the value (in current US$) of exports of "photographic apparatus and equipments, nes" (SITC group 881) decreased by 4.5 percent (compared to 3.8 percent average growth rate from 2009-2013) to reach 7.4 bln US$ (see table 2), while imports decreased by 7.3 percent to reach 5.6 bln US$ (see table 3). Exports of this commodity accounted for 0.4 percent of world exports of SITC section 8, and less than 0.1 percent of total world merchandise exports (see table 1). Viet Nam, China and USA were the top exporters in 2013 (see table 2). They accounted for 20.5, 13.5 and 9.7 percent of world exports, respectively. China, USA and China, Hong Kong SAR were the top destinations, with respectively 10.5, 10.3 and 9.4 percent of world imports (see table 3).

The top 15 countries/areas accounted for 87.1 and 70.4 percent of total world exports and imports, respectively (see tables 2 and 3). In 2013, Viet Nam was the country/area with the highest value of net exports (+1.1 bln US$), followed by China (+411.6 mln US$). By MDG regions (see graph 2), the largest surpluses in this product group were recorded by South-eastern Asia (+1.9 bln US$), Eastern Asia (+316.3 mln US$) and Developed North America (+107.6 mln US$). The largest trade deficits were recorded by Latin America and the Caribbean (-242.0 mln US$), Western Asia (-101.6 mln US$) and Southern Asia (-87.4 mln US$).

Table 1: Imports (Imp.) and exports (Exp.), 1999-2013, in current US$

		1999	2000	2001	2002	2003	2004	2005	2006	2007	2008	2009	2010	2011	2012	2013
Values in Bln US$	Imp.	15.1	18.1	15.5	14.8	15.4	17.9	16.1	16.1	10.2	8.8	5.1	5.9	6.0	6.0	5.6
	Exp.	15.1	19.0	16.1	15.5	15.8	18.6	16.9	17.4	8.5	8.0	6.4	6.3	6.7	7.7	7.4
As a percentage of SITC section (%)	Imp.	2.0	2.2	1.9	1.7	1.6	1.6	1.3	1.2	0.7	0.5	0.4	0.4	0.3	0.3	0.3
	Exp.	2.1	2.4	2.1	1.9	1.7	1.7	1.4	1.3	0.6	0.5	0.4	0.4	0.4	0.4	0.4
As a percentage of world trade (%)	Imp.	0.3	0.3	0.2	0.2	0.2	0.2	0.2	0.1	0.1	0.1	0.0	0.0	0.0	0.0	0.0
	Exp.	0.3	0.3	0.3	0.2	0.2	0.2	0.2	0.1	0.1	0.1	0.1	0.0	0.0	0.0	0.0

Graph 1: Annual growth rates of exports, 1999–2013
(In percentage by year)

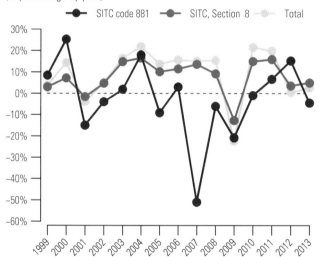

Graph 2: Trade Balance by MDG regions 2013
(Bln US$)

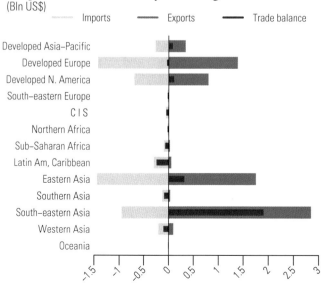

Table 2: Top exporting countries or areas in 2013

Country or area	Value (million US$)	Avg. Growth (%) 09-13	Growth (%) 12-13	World share %	Cum.
World	7 386.4	3.8	-4.5	100.0	
Viet Nam	1 511.6	38.8	-6.3	20.5	20.5
China	997.6	14.8	9.2	13.5	34.0
USA	717.4	-2.6	-13.5	9.7	43.7
China, Hong Kong SAR	457.8	-4.8	-7.9	6.2	49.9
Singapore	378.9	2.7	7.5	5.1	55.0
Philippines	378.9	-14.2	-32.7	5.1	60.1
Germany	337.2	-4.3	-0.6	4.6	64.7
Japan	294.1	-7.9	-2.6	4.0	68.7
Thailand	286.6	22.2	4.4	3.9	72.6
Malaysia	277.3	-2.2	-23.3	3.8	76.3
Other Asia, nes	212.5	1.6	52.5	2.9	79.2
Italy	178.7	0.7	-8.0	2.4	81.6
United Kingdom	161.5	-0.6	13.9	2.2	83.8
Netherlands	148.5	0.5	-0.1	2.0	85.8
Switzerland	96.7	9.4	-1.8	1.3	87.1

Table 3: Top importing countries or areas in 2013

Country or area	Value (million US$)	Avg. Growth (%) 09-13	Growth (%) 12-13	World share %	Cum.
World	5 602.8	2.3	-7.3	100.0	
China	586.0	12.2	-4.4	10.5	10.5
USA	579.0	-0.1	-2.5	10.3	20.8
China, Hong Kong SAR	528.3	5.0	3.8	9.4	30.2
Viet Nam	375.0	43.7	0.2	6.7	36.9
Germany	355.8	8.9	-11.1	6.4	43.3
Singapore	241.4	2.3	-8.4	4.3	47.6
Rep. of Korea	233.7	23.7	-3.3	4.2	51.7
United Kingdom	177.6	3.6	12.5	3.2	54.9
Japan	164.4	-6.8	-2.1	2.9	57.8
France	154.5	-11.7	-4.1	2.8	60.6
Netherlands	148.1	-2.0	-12.8	2.6	63.3
Canada	114.2	-0.8	-10.4	2.0	65.3
Thailand	106.4	8.6	-42.9	1.9	67.2
Malaysia	91.6	-16.4	-51.3	1.6	68.8
Mexico	91.0	8.3	-9.5	1.6	70.4

882 Photographic and cinematographic supplies

In 2013, the value (in current US$) of exports of "photographic and cinematographic supplies" (SITC group 882) decreased by 3.3 percent (compared to 1.3 percent average growth rate from 2009-2013) to reach 16.9 bln US$ (see table 2), while imports decreased by 2.6 percent to reach 16.7 bln US$ (see table 3). Exports of this commodity accounted for 0.8 percent of world exports of SITC section 8, and 0.1 percent of total world merchandise exports (see table 1). Japan, USA and Netherlands were the top exporters in 2013 (see table 2). They accounted for 26.7, 15.1 and 9.4 percent of world exports, respectively. China, USA and Other Asia, nes were the top destinations, with respectively 13.9, 9.6 and 8.4 percent of world imports (see table 3).

The top 15 countries/areas accounted for 94.5 and 73.1 percent of total world exports and imports, respectively (see tables 2 and 3). In 2013, Japan was the country/area with the highest value of net exports (+4.2 bln US$), followed by USA (+950.4 mln US$). By MDG regions (see graph 2), the largest surpluses in this product group were recorded by Developed Asia-Pacific (+4.0 bln US$), Developed Europe (+1.3 bln US$) and Developed North America (+853.9 mln US$). The largest trade deficits were recorded by Eastern Asia (-2.8 bln US$), Latin America and the Caribbean (-919.3 mln US$) and South-eastern Asia (-532.6 mln US$).

Table 1: Imports (Imp.) and exports (Exp.), 1999-2013, in current US$

		1999	2000	2001	2002	2003	2004	2005	2006	2007	2008	2009	2010	2011	2012	2013
Values in Bln US$	Imp.	18.0	18.8	16.6	17.2	18.2	19.6	19.5	19.4	19.7	19.2	16.4	17.0	18.0	17.1	16.7
	Exp.	17.3	18.5	16.3	16.9	18.8	19.8	19.2	19.0	18.7	18.4	16.0	17.1	18.2	17.4	16.9
As a percentage of SITC section (%)	Imp.	2.4	2.3	2.0	2.0	1.9	1.7	1.6	1.4	1.3	1.2	1.1	1.0	1.0	0.9	0.9
	Exp.	2.4	2.4	2.1	2.1	2.0	1.8	1.6	1.4	1.2	1.1	1.1	1.0	1.0	0.9	0.8
As a percentage of world trade (%)	Imp.	0.3	0.3	0.3	0.3	0.2	0.2	0.2	0.2	0.1	0.1	0.1	0.1	0.1	0.1	0.1
	Exp.	0.3	0.3	0.3	0.3	0.3	0.2	0.2	0.2	0.1	0.1	0.1	0.1	0.1	0.1	0.1

Graph 1: Annual growth rates of exports, 1999–2013
(In percentage by year)

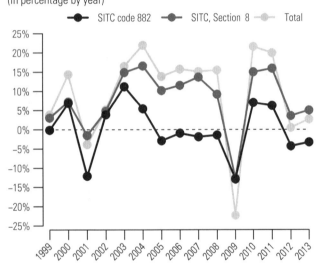

Graph 2: Trade Balance by MDG regions 2013
(Bln US$)

Table 2: Top exporting countries or areas in 2013

Country or area	Value (million US$)	Avg. Growth (%) 09-13	Growth (%) 12-13	World share %	Cum.
World	16 855.3	1.3	-3.3	100.0	
Japan	4 504.4	3.7	-5.8	26.7	26.7
USA	2 549.4	-1.7	0.0	15.1	41.8
Netherlands	1 583.7	7.3	1.4	9.4	51.2
Germany	1 523.1	1.0	3.4	9.0	60.3
Belgium	1 423.5	-1.2	-17.6	8.4	68.7
China	1 217.6	10.9	0.6	7.2	76.0
United Kingdom	805.8	-0.7	4.6	4.8	80.7
France	471.2	-13.1	-14.7	2.8	83.5
Rep. of Korea	465.0	16.4	1.0	2.8	86.3
Other Asia, nes	425.2	10.9	4.3	2.5	88.8
China, Hong Kong SAR	257.6	-4.9	-9.3	1.5	90.3
Mexico	195.6	-7.0	1.4	1.2	91.5
Singapore	181.1	-13.2	-12.3	1.1	92.6
Italy	170.2	-2.2	-14.8	1.0	93.6
Malaysia	156.3	10.9	12.3	0.9	94.5

Table 3: Top importing countries or areas in 2013

Country or area	Value (million US$)	Avg. Growth (%) 09-13	Growth (%) 12-13	World share %	Cum.
World	16 665.1	0.4	-2.6	100.0	
China	2 319.2	11.5	2.0	13.9	13.9
USA	1 599.0	6.7	-0.4	9.6	23.5
Other Asia, nes	1 402.5	5.8	-2.7	8.4	31.9
Rep. of Korea	1 078.6	6.6	-7.7	6.5	38.4
Germany	1 058.3	2.5	3.6	6.4	44.7
Netherlands	739.6	10.0	-0.4	4.4	49.2
United Kingdom	719.3	-3.3	7.4	4.3	53.5
France	541.4	-11.4	-7.6	3.2	56.8
Belgium	510.7	-6.2	-3.9	3.1	59.8
Mexico	485.8	-0.3	2.6	2.9	62.7
Italy	403.2	-11.5	-10.0	2.4	65.2
Singapore	391.9	-7.0	-7.3	2.4	67.5
China, Hong Kong SAR	372.9	-3.1	-2.0	2.2	69.7
Japan	301.2	-4.1	-20.3	1.8	71.5
India	259.7	-1.7	-17.2	1.6	73.1

Source: UN Comtrade and UN Service Trade

In 2013, the value (in current US$) of exports of "cinematographic film, exposed and developed" (SITC group 883) decreased by 51.0 percent (compared to -42.6 percent average growth rate from 2009-2013) to reach 80.1 mln US$ (see table 2), while imports decreased by 41.7 percent to reach 94.0 mln US$ (see table 3). Exports of this commodity accounted for less than 0.1 percent of world exports of SITC section 8, and less than 0.1 percent of total world merchandise exports (see table 1). United Kingdom, Mexico and USA were the top exporters in 2013 (see table 2). They accounted for 18.1, 15.4 and 14.0 percent of world exports, respectively. Spain, Malaysia and United Arab Emirates were the top destinations, with respectively 18.4, 10.7 and 10.0 percent of world imports (see table 3).

The top 15 countries/areas accounted for 92.8 and 76.3 percent of total world exports and imports, respectively (see tables 2 and 3). In 2013, United Kingdom was the country/area with the highest value of net exports (+13.8 mln US$), followed by India (+10.5 mln US$). By MDG regions (see graph 2), the largest surpluses in this product group were recorded by Southern Asia (+9.5 mln US$), Developed North America (+7.8 mln US$) and Latin America and the Caribbean (+1.4 mln US$). The largest trade deficits were recorded by Western Asia (-10.6 mln US$), Developed Europe (-7.1 mln US$) and South-eastern Asia (-6.5 mln US$).

Table 1: Imports (Imp.) and exports (Exp.), 1999-2013, in current US$

		1999	2000	2001	2002	2003	2004	2005	2006	2007	2008	2009	2010	2011	2012	2013
Values in Mln US$	Imp.	343.5	361.1	447.4	428.4	535.5	604.0	660.8	700.8	708.7	706.4	721.7	611.4	504.5	161.2	94.0
	Exp.	431.3	369.6	369.8	472.2	573.1	665.4	668.6	737.8	819.1	795.7	737.5	637.4	495.3	163.7	80.1
As a percentage of	Imp.	0.0	0.0	0.1	0.1	0.1	0.1	0.1	0.1	0.0	0.0	0.1	0.0	0.0	0.0	0.0
SITC section (%)	Exp.	0.1	0.0	0.0	0.1	0.1	0.1	0.1	0.1	0.1	0.0	0.1	0.0	0.0	0.0	0.0
As a percentage of	Imp.	0.0	0.0	0.0	0.0	0.0	0.0	0.0	0.0	0.0	0.0	0.0	0.0	0.0	0.0	0.0
world trade (%)	Exp.	0.0	0.0	0.0	0.0	0.0	0.0	0.0	0.0	0.0	0.0	0.0	0.0	0.0	0.0	0.0

Graph 1: Annual growth rates of exports, 1999–2013
(In percentage by year)

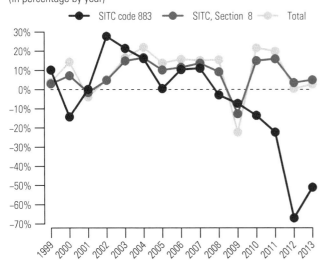

Table 2: Top exporting countries or areas in 2013

Country or area	Value (million US$)	Avg. Growth (%) 09-13	Growth (%) 12-13	World share %	Cum.
World	80.1	-42.6	-51.0	100.0	
United Kingdom	14.5	-22.7	51.5	18.1	18.1
Mexico	12.4	-2.4	0.3	15.4	33.6
USA	11.2	-29.4	-55.9	14.0	47.6
India	11.2	-10.2	-33.1	14.0	61.5
Thailand	9.1	-21.1	-68.2	11.3	72.9
Argentina	3.9	-12.0	-19.1	4.9	77.8
Italy	2.2	-65.9	-89.9	2.7	80.5
Nicaragua	1.6	301.6	0.6	2.0	82.5
United Arab Emirates	1.5	1.1	21.7	1.8	84.4
France	1.4	-41.4	-69.1	1.8	86.1
Germany	1.2	-43.0	-41.9	1.5	87.7
China, Hong Kong SAR	1.2	-30.7	-56.7	1.5	89.1
Spain	1.0	-50.0	-87.1	1.3	90.4
Jordan	1.0	260.3	27435.9	1.2	91.7
Canada	0.9	-77.4	-94.0	1.1	92.8

Graph 2: Trade Balance by MDG regions 2013
(Mln US$)

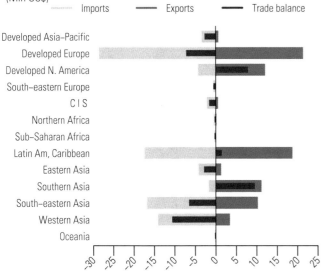

Table 3: Top importing countries or areas in 2013

Country or area	Value (million US$)	Avg. Growth (%) 09-13	Growth (%) 12-13	World share %	Cum.
World	94.0	-39.9	-41.7	100.0	
Spain	17.3	28.8	494.9	18.4	18.4
Malaysia	10.1	26.7	69.2	10.7	29.1
United Arab Emirates	9.4	-0.4	11.4	10.0	39.0
Chile	5.4	4.0	-0.8	5.7	44.7
Thailand	4.0	-14.5	-34.8	4.2	49.0
Turkey	3.4	-19.1	-30.8	3.6	52.6
Mexico	3.3	-20.3	-62.3	3.5	56.1
Australia	3.1	-26.5	-44.7	3.3	59.4
Austria	2.9	-27.5	-73.1	3.1	62.4
USA	2.7	-70.1	-84.2	2.9	65.3
Venezuela	2.6	-10.5	-25.2	2.8	68.1
China	2.6	-47.2	-47.4	2.8	70.9
Italy	1.9	-3.8	96.7	2.0	72.9
Philippines	1.7	-14.0	-38.5	1.8	74.7
Belarus	1.5	-8.4	8.9	1.6	76.3

884 Optical goods, nes

In 2013, the value (in current US$) of exports of "optical goods, nes" (SITC group 884) increased by 1.9 percent (compared to 10.0 percent average growth rate from 2009-2013) to reach 58.4 bln US$ (see table 2), while imports increased by 1.1 percent to reach 56.8 bln US$ (see table 3). Exports of this commodity accounted for 2.8 percent of world exports of SITC section 8, and 0.3 percent of total world merchandise exports (see table 1). China, Japan and China, Hong Kong SAR were the top exporters in 2013 (see table 2). They accounted for 17.6, 14.8 and 7.6 percent of world exports, respectively. China, USA and China, Hong Kong SAR were the top destinations, with respectively 20.6, 11.2 and 7.5 percent of world imports (see table 3).

The top 15 countries/areas accounted for 91.0 and 80.7 percent of total world exports and imports, respectively (see tables 2 and 3). In 2013, Japan was the country/area with the highest value of net exports (+5.0 bln US$), followed by Italy (+2.3 bln US$). By MDG regions (see graph 2), the largest surpluses in this product group were recorded by Developed Asia-Pacific (+4.3 bln US$), South-eastern Asia (+1.8 bln US$) and Eastern Asia (+1.1 bln US$). The largest trade deficits were recorded by Developed North America (-3.1 bln US$), Latin America and the Caribbean (-1.1 bln US$) and Western Asia (-1.0 bln US$).

Table 1: Imports (Imp.) and exports (Exp.), 1999-2013, in current US$

		1999	2000	2001	2002	2003	2004	2005	2006	2007	2008	2009	2010	2011	2012	2013
Values in Bln US$	Imp.	14.2	18.0	18.2	16.5	20.0	25.0	28.9	34.1	39.6	44.3	40.2	50.2	54.6	56.1	56.8
	Exp.	14.7	19.4	19.5	17.8	21.0	26.7	30.8	35.2	40.4	43.5	40.0	50.3	55.2	57.3	58.4
As a percentage of SITC section (%)	Imp.	1.9	2.2	2.2	1.9	2.1	2.2	2.3	2.5	2.6	2.7	2.8	3.1	3.0	3.0	3.0
	Exp.	2.0	2.5	2.6	2.2	2.3	2.5	2.6	2.7	2.7	2.7	2.8	3.1	2.9	2.9	2.8
As a percentage of world trade (%)	Imp.	0.2	0.3	0.3	0.3	0.3	0.3	0.3	0.3	0.3	0.3	0.3	0.3	0.3	0.3	0.3
	Exp.	0.3	0.3	0.3	0.3	0.3	0.3	0.3	0.3	0.3	0.3	0.3	0.3	0.3	0.3	0.3

Graph 1: Annual growth rates of exports, 1999–2013
(In percentage by year)

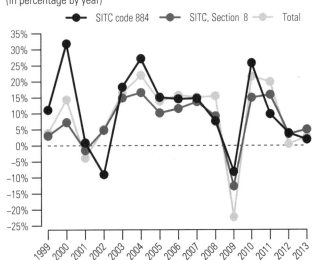

Graph 2: Trade Balance by MDG regions 2013
(Bln US$)

Table 2: Top exporting countries or areas in 2013

Country or area	Value (million US$)	Avg. Growth (%) 09-13	Growth (%) 12-13	World share %	Cum.
World..................................	58 400.2	10.0	1.9	100.0	
China..................................	10 296.6	18.8	6.0	17.6	17.6
Japan.................................	8 619.0	5.0	-12.3	14.8	32.4
China, Hong Kong SAR.........	4 418.2	9.2	1.7	7.6	40.0
Germany..............................	4 288.7	11.4	10.9	7.3	47.3
Rep. of Korea.......................	4 277.7	8.6	-2.9	7.3	54.6
USA....................................	4 135.3	5.4	-2.9	7.1	61.7
Italy....................................	3 832.3	8.9	9.7	6.6	68.3
Other Asia, nes....................	3 518.1	16.5	1.8	6.0	74.3
Thailand..............................	1 841.7	7.2	4.5	3.2	77.4
United Kingdom....................	1 670.2	7.7	13.6	2.9	80.3
Netherlands.........................	1 668.8	17.5	6.2	2.9	83.2
Singapore............................	1 518.4	20.2	21.2	2.6	85.8
Ireland................................	1 377.4	2.5	-2.2	2.4	88.1
France.................................	1 010.4	3.6	3.0	1.7	89.9
Philippines...........................	674.9	44.7	35.7	1.2	91.0

Table 3: Top importing countries or areas in 2013

Country or area	Value (million US$)	Avg. Growth (%) 09-13	Growth (%) 12-13	World share %	Cum.
World..................................	56 760.0	9.0	1.1	100.0	
China..................................	11 669.8	10.1	1.9	20.6	20.6
USA....................................	6 372.6	8.4	2.6	11.2	31.8
China, Hong Kong SAR.........	4 237.3	13.5	-0.4	7.5	39.3
Rep. of Korea.......................	3 662.0	15.1	-4.6	6.5	45.7
Japan.................................	3 643.3	7.2	-14.7	6.4	52.1
Germany..............................	2 886.5	6.9	2.1	5.1	57.2
Netherlands.........................	2 539.0	18.1	23.5	4.5	61.7
France.................................	2 084.2	7.5	6.3	3.7	65.4
Other Asia, nes....................	1 772.6	2.8	-9.8	3.1	68.5
United Kingdom....................	1 694.6	5.0	5.1	3.0	71.5
Italy....................................	1 541.9	6.8	7.5	2.7	74.2
Singapore............................	1 062.0	8.5	2.5	1.9	76.0
Canada...............................	1 040.5	7.1	-0.1	1.8	77.9
Thailand..............................	864.2	16.3	-6.9	1.5	79.4
Australia..............................	708.6	11.2	-0.4	1.2	80.7

Watches and clocks 885

In 2013, the value (in current US$) of exports of "watches and clocks" (SITC group 885) increased by 4.9 percent (compared to 16.9 percent average growth rate from 2009-2013) to reach 54.5 bln US$ (see table 2), while imports increased by 3.4 percent to reach 51.2 bln US$ (see table 3). Exports of this commodity accounted for 2.6 percent of world exports of SITC section 8, and 0.3 percent of total world merchandise exports (see table 1). Switzerland, China, Hong Kong SAR and China were the top exporters in 2013 (see table 2). They accounted for 43.2, 18.2 and 10.2 percent of world exports, respectively. China, Hong Kong SAR, USA and China were the top destinations, with respectively 20.4, 10.2 and 7.6 percent of world imports (see table 3).

The top 15 countries/areas accounted for 95.9 and 80.9 percent of total world exports and imports, respectively (see tables 2 and 3). In 2013, Switzerland was the country/area with the highest value of net exports (+19.8 bln US$), followed by China (+1.7 bln US$). By MDG regions (see graph 2), the largest surplus in this product group was recorded solely by Developed Europe (+16.1 bln US$). The largest trade deficits were recorded by Developed North America (-4.4 bln US$), Developed Asia-Pacific (-2.3 bln US$) and Western Asia (-2.2 bln US$).

Table 1: Imports (Imp.) and exports (Exp.), 1999-2013, in current US$

		1999	2000	2001	2002	2003	2004	2005	2006	2007	2008	2009	2010	2011	2012	2013
Values in Bln US$	Imp.	19.5	19.8	18.9	19.6	21.5	24.4	25.5	27.1	31.5	35.5	28.9	36.0	46.5	49.5	51.2
	Exp.	19.6	19.9	18.8	19.4	21.3	24.3	25.3	27.3	31.4	35.9	29.2	36.8	47.9	52.0	54.5
As a percentage of	Imp.	2.6	2.4	2.3	2.3	2.2	2.2	2.1	2.0	2.0	2.1	2.0	2.2	2.5	2.7	2.7
SITC section (%)	Exp.	2.7	2.6	2.5	2.4	2.3	2.3	2.1	2.1	2.1	2.2	2.0	2.2	2.5	2.6	2.6
As a percentage of	Imp.	0.3	0.3	0.3	0.3	0.3	0.3	0.2	0.2	0.2	0.2	0.2	0.2	0.3	0.3	0.3
world trade (%)	Exp.	0.4	0.3	0.3	0.3	0.3	0.3	0.2	0.2	0.2	0.2	0.2	0.2	0.3	0.3	0.3

Graph 1: Annual growth rates of exports, 1999–2013
(In percentage by year)

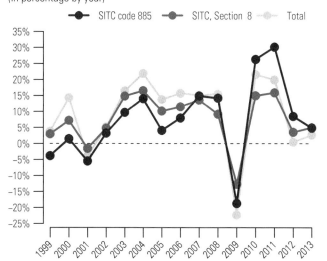

Graph 2: Trade Balance by MDG regions 2013
(Bln US$)

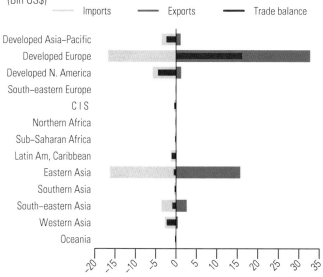

Table 2: Top exporting countries or areas in 2013

Country or area	Value (million US$)	Avg. Growth (%) 09-13	Growth (%) 12-13	World share %	Cum.
World	54 546.7	16.9	4.9	100.0	
Switzerland	23 554.6	17.9	3.1	43.2	43.2
China, Hong Kong SAR	9 934.9	15.2	3.6	18.2	61.4
China	5 568.4	22.8	10.0	10.2	71.6
France	2 395.9	16.9	10.6	4.4	76.0
Germany	2 335.2	16.6	14.5	4.3	80.3
Italy	1 773.6	20.7	5.0	3.3	83.5
Singapore	1 708.4	13.4	2.7	3.1	86.7
USA	1 231.3	12.1	-1.7	2.3	88.9
Japan	1 079.8	9.6	-19.4	2.0	90.9
United Kingdom	799.5	23.1	24.6	1.5	92.4
Thailand	543.2	10.5	17.7	1.0	93.4
Spain	430.5	11.3	9.7	0.8	94.1
Austria	362.5	10.9	4.4	0.7	94.8
Netherlands	307.8	19.6	14.6	0.6	95.4
United Arab Emirates	*289.0*	21.5	21.7	0.5	95.9

Table 3: Top importing countries or areas in 2013

Country or area	Value (million US$)	Avg. Growth (%) 09-13	Growth (%) 12-13	World share %	Cum.
World	51 212.5	15.4	3.4	100.0	
China, Hong Kong SAR	10 427.0	19.8	-0.6	20.4	20.4
USA	5 236.8	13.5	6.4	10.2	30.6
China	3 903.2	25.5	-5.9	7.6	38.2
Switzerland	3 756.4	16.4	4.8	7.3	45.5
France	3 060.7	14.8	7.0	6.0	51.5
Japan	2 936.3	12.0	-3.7	5.7	57.3
Germany	2 805.4	17.0	5.4	5.5	62.7
Singapore	1 958.4	13.5	-0.5	3.8	66.6
Italy	1 730.2	7.5	4.4	3.4	69.9
United Kingdom	1 716.0	10.7	11.4	3.4	73.3
United Arab Emirates	*953.8*	17.0	11.4	1.9	75.1
Spain	848.0	5.5	5.0	1.7	76.8
China, Macao SAR	*739.3*	30.5	12.9	1.4	78.2
Thailand	733.1	17.9	17.3	1.4	79.7
Malaysia	628.9	9.8	2.2	1.2	80.9

891 Arms and ammunition

In 2013, the value (in current US$) of exports of "arms and ammunition" (SITC group 891) increased by 10.6 percent (compared to 3.9 percent average growth rate from 2009-2013) to reach 13.0 bln US$ (see table 2), while imports increased by 7.6 percent to reach 11.2 bln US$ (see table 3). Exports of this commodity accounted for 0.6 percent of world exports of SITC section 8, and 0.1 percent of total world merchandise exports (see table 1). USA, Italy and Canada were the top exporters in 2013 (see table 2). They accounted for 44.0, 5.9 and 5.7 percent of world exports, respectively. USA, Canada and Australia were the top destinations, with respectively 38.7, 9.3 and 4.0 percent of world imports (see table 3).

The top 15 countries/areas accounted for 85.0 and 78.3 percent of total world exports and imports, respectively (see tables 2 and 3). In 2013, USA was the country/area with the highest value of net exports (+1.4 bln US$), followed by Italy (+637.9 mln US$). By MDG regions (see graph 2), the largest surpluses in this product group were recorded by Developed Europe (+1.4 bln US$), Developed North America (+1.0 bln US$) and Eastern Asia (+299.2 mln US$). The largest trade deficits were recorded by South-eastern Asia (-717.1 mln US$), Developed Asia-Pacific (-322.4 mln US$) and Western Asia (-165.8 mln US$).

Table 1: Imports (Imp.) and exports (Exp.), 1999-2013, in current US$

		1999	2000	2001	2002	2003	2004	2005	2006	2007	2008	2009	2010	2011	2012	2013
Values in Bln US$	Imp.	4.5	3.8	3.8	4.8	6.0	7.5	7.2	7.9	9.0	10.7	11.2	10.9	11.0	10.4	11.2
	Exp.	6.3	5.3	4.8	5.8	6.2	7.5	7.3	8.2	9.6	10.5	11.1	11.9	11.2	11.7	13.0
As a percentage of SITC section (%)	Imp.	0.6	0.5	0.5	0.6	0.6	0.7	0.6	0.6	0.6	0.6	0.8	0.7	0.6	0.6	0.6
	Exp.	0.9	0.7	0.6	0.7	0.7	0.7	0.6	0.6	0.6	0.6	0.8	0.7	0.6	0.6	0.6
As a percentage of world trade (%)	Imp.	0.1	0.1	0.1	0.1	0.1	0.1	0.1	0.1	0.1	0.1	0.1	0.1	0.1	0.1	0.1
	Exp.	0.1	0.1	0.1	0.1	0.1	0.1	0.1	0.1	0.1	0.1	0.1	0.1	0.1	0.1	0.1

Graph 1: Annual growth rates of exports, 1999–2013
(In percentage by year)

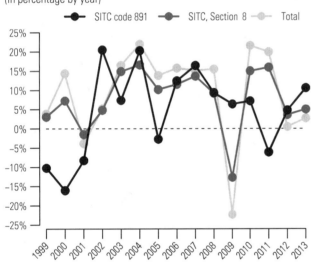

Legend: ● SITC code 891 ● SITC, Section 8 ○ Total

Graph 2: Trade Balance by MDG regions 2013
(Bln US$)

Legend: Imports, Exports, Trade balance

Developed Asia–Pacific
Developed Europe
Developed N. America
South–eastern Europe
CIS
Northern Africa
Sub–Saharan Africa
Latin Am, Caribbean
Eastern Asia
Southern Asia
South–eastern Asia
Western Asia
Oceania

Table 2: Top exporting countries or areas in 2013

Country or area	Value (million US$)	Avg. Growth (%) 09-13	Growth (%) 12-13	World share %	Cum.
World	12 953.6	3.9	10.6	100.0	
USA	5701.1	6.4	14.3	44.0	44.0
Italy	758.3	4.6	25.0	5.9	49.9
Canada	733.3	-6.0	-38.1	5.7	55.5
Germany	673.8	7.3	17.0	5.2	60.7
Rep. of Korea	472.6	18.6	21.7	3.6	64.4
Norway	357.0	-7.9	-17.4	2.8	67.1
Brazil	349.2	1.1	12.9	2.7	69.8
Finland	326.3	26.0	141.8	2.5	72.3
Czech Rep	298.8	11.6	21.9	2.3	74.7
Turkey	274.1	23.8	52.8	2.1	76.8
Spain	235.2	-0.7	52.9	1.8	78.6
Russian Federation	230.3	54.5	-23.7	1.8	80.4
Japan	228.2	-4.5	121.7	1.8	82.1
South Africa	209.0	...	-28.9	1.6	83.7
China	159.2	25.8	14.8	1.2	85.0

Table 3: Top importing countries or areas in 2013

Country or area	Value (million US$)	Avg. Growth (%) 09-13	Growth (%) 12-13	World share %	Cum.
World	11 216.6	0.1	7.6	100.0	
USA	4337.7	1.1	9.0	38.7	38.7
Canada	1047.6	10.1	28.9	9.3	48.0
Australia	450.3	1.4	-4.3	4.0	52.0
Indonesia	364.5	43.1	125.8	3.2	55.3
Rep. of Korea	348.1	4.7	9.2	3.1	58.4
Norway	327.0	1.8	3.6	2.9	61.3
Thailand	295.2	7.3	-5.3	2.6	63.9
Germany	266.8	10.1	6.2	2.4	66.3
United Arab Emirates	246.6	27.9	11.4	2.2	68.5
France	223.2	6.1	11.3	2.0	70.5
Netherlands	217.7	103.7	3.7	1.9	72.4
United Kingdom	177.6	-11.1	-15.9	1.6	74.0
Russian Federation	172.4	41.5	51.9	1.5	75.6
Japan	168.7	-6.2	22.4	1.5	77.1
Poland	141.8	-1.2	-21.8	1.3	78.3

In 2013, the value (in current US$) of exports of "printed matter" (SITC group 892) increased by 5.6 percent (compared to 2.1 percent average growth rate from 2009-2013) to reach 51.8 bln US$ (see table 2), while imports increased by 5.0 percent to reach 49.2 bln US$ (see table 3). Exports of this commodity accounted for 2.5 percent of world exports of SITC section 8, and 0.3 percent of total world merchandise exports (see table 1). USA, Germany and Singapore were the top exporters in 2013 (see table 2). They accounted for 11.9, 11.2 and 8.9 percent of world exports, respectively. USA, Canada and United Kingdom were the top destinations, with respectively 9.6, 6.4 and 5.7 percent of world imports (see table 3).

The top 15 countries/areas accounted for 80.2 and 61.5 percent of total world exports and imports, respectively (see tables 2 and 3). In 2013, Singapore was the country/area with the highest value of net exports (+4.0 bln US$), followed by Germany (+3.4 bln US$). By MDG regions (see graph 2), the largest surpluses in this product group were recorded by Developed Europe (+4.9 bln US$), South-eastern Asia (+4.4 bln US$) and Eastern Asia (+3.0 bln US$). The largest trade deficits were recorded by Latin America and the Caribbean (-1.9 bln US$), Commonwealth of Independent States (-1.9 bln US$) and Developed Asia-Pacific (-1.6 bln US$).

Table 1: Imports (Imp.) and exports (Exp.), 1999-2013, in current US$

		1999	2000	2001	2002	2003	2004	2005	2006	2007	2008	2009	2010	2011	2012	2013
Values in Bln US$	Imp.	27.3	27.6	27.8	29.1	32.8	36.9	39.6	42.1	48.2	50.9	44.5	45.8	49.9	46.8	49.2
	Exp.	26.7	27.1	27.5	28.7	32.6	36.8	39.7	42.2	48.6	52.8	47.6	49.8	54.8	49.0	51.8
As a percentage of SITC section (%)	Imp.	3.6	3.4	3.4	3.4	3.4	3.3	3.2	3.1	3.1	3.1	3.1	2.8	2.7	2.5	2.6
	Exp.	3.7	3.5	3.6	3.6	3.5	3.4	3.4	3.2	3.2	3.2	3.3	3.0	2.9	2.5	2.5
As a percentage of world trade (%)	Imp.	0.5	0.4	0.4	0.4	0.4	0.4	0.4	0.3	0.3	0.3	0.4	0.3	0.3	0.3	0.3
	Exp.	0.5	0.4	0.5	0.4	0.4	0.4	0.4	0.4	0.4	0.3	0.4	0.3	0.3	0.3	0.3

Graph 1: Annual growth rates of exports, 1999–2013
(In percentage by year)

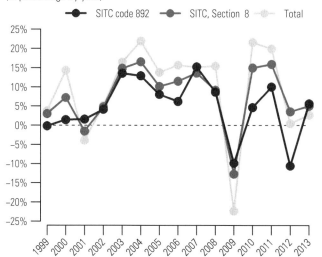

Table 2: Top exporting countries or areas in 2013

Country or area	Value (million US$)	Avg. Growth (%) 09-13	Growth (%) 12-13	World share %	Cum.
World	51 759.1	2.1	5.6	100.0	
USA	6 173.8	1.1	-1.5	11.9	11.9
Germany	5 776.3	-1.7	4.2	11.2	23.1
Singapore	4 599.2	45.5	86.4	8.9	32.0
United Kingdom	4 410.0	1.8	-0.4	8.5	40.5
China	4 317.4	12.2	7.0	8.3	48.8
China, Hong Kong SAR	2 408.6	3.1	4.9	4.7	53.5
Cambodia	2 261.5	3.1	-1.0	4.4	57.9
France	2 227.5	-0.9	2.3	4.3	62.2
Netherlands	1 892.7	6.1	4.9	3.7	65.8
Italy	1 850.2	-0.4	-1.6	3.6	69.4
Belgium	1 569.7	0.0	0.6	3.0	72.4
Spain	1 040.2	-0.8	6.5	2.0	74.4
Canada	1 029.3	-2.5	-7.9	2.0	76.4
Czech Rep.	1 020.3	-4.0	-3.8	2.0	78.4
Poland	953.8	7.8	16.0	1.8	80.2

Graph 2: Trade Balance by MDG regions 2013
(Bln US$)

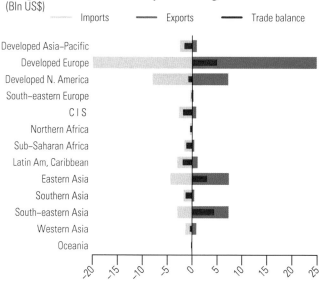

Table 3: Top importing countries or areas in 2013

Country or area	Value (million US$)	Avg. Growth (%) 09-13	Growth (%) 12-13	World share %	Cum.
World	49 152.4	2.5	5.0	100.0	
USA	4 729.4	1.7	-1.4	9.6	9.6
Canada	3 156.0	0.1	-3.1	6.4	16.0
United Kingdom	2 811.7	0.3	-4.8	5.7	21.8
France	2 657.0	-2.0	-3.6	5.4	27.2
Germany	2 372.5	-3.4	-3.0	4.8	32.0
China	2 171.8	13.0	19.3	4.4	36.4
Switzerland	1 945.3	1.1	-0.1	4.0	40.4
China, Hong Kong SAR	1 651.0	3.9	0.6	3.4	43.7
Belgium	1 501.6	1.8	5.5	3.1	46.8
Netherlands	1 374.6	4.3	1.3	2.8	49.6
Kazakhstan	1 278.4	76.5	183.4	2.6	52.2
Japan	1 259.2	5.7	0.5	2.6	54.7
Austria	1 227.3	-0.4	1.8	2.5	57.2
Mexico	1 061.0	4.2	0.9	2.2	59.4
Cambodia	1 039.7	114.8	1727.4	2.1	61.5

893 Articles, nes, of plastics

In 2013, the value (in current US$) of exports of "articles, nes, of plastics" (SITC group 893) increased by 7.2 percent (compared to 11.3 percent average growth rate from 2009-2013) to reach 152.7 bln US$ (see table 2), while imports increased by 6.7 percent to reach 144.9 bln US$ (see table 3). Exports of this commodity accounted for 7.4 percent of world exports of SITC section 8, and 0.8 percent of total world merchandise exports (see table 1). China, Germany and USA were the top exporters in 2013 (see table 2). They accounted for 23.1, 11.1 and 8.4 percent of world exports, respectively. USA, Germany and France were the top destinations, with respectively 14.8, 7.5 and 5.6 percent of world imports (see table 3).

The top 15 countries/areas accounted for 73.7 and 63.4 percent of total world exports and imports, respectively (see tables 2 and 3). In 2013, China was the country/area with the highest value of net exports (+30.8 bln US$), followed by Germany (+6.0 bln US$). By MDG regions (see graph 2), the largest surpluses in this product group were recorded by Eastern Asia (+34.9 bln US$), Developed Europe (+3.0 bln US$) and Southern Asia (+422.4 mln US$). The largest trade deficits were recorded by Developed North America (-10.5 bln US$), Latin America and the Caribbean (-6.8 bln US$) and Developed Asia-Pacific (-5.7 bln US$).

Table 1: Imports (Imp.) and exports (Exp.), 1999-2013, in current US$

		1999	2000	2001	2002	2003	2004	2005	2006	2007	2008	2009	2010	2011	2012	2013
Values in Bln US$	Imp.	50.7	54.2	54.3	59.5	68.4	79.0	87.7	97.6	110.4	120.6	103.0	119.5	134.5	135.8	144.9
	Exp.	49.7	53.9	53.9	57.5	66.1	77.0	85.7	95.3	107.8	116.3	99.4	115.0	133.7	142.4	152.7
As a percentage of SITC section (%)	Imp.	6.7	6.7	6.7	7.0	7.1	7.0	7.1	7.2	7.2	7.2	7.2	7.3	7.3	7.4	7.6
	Exp.	6.9	6.9	7.0	7.2	7.2	7.2	7.2	7.2	7.2	7.1	7.0	7.0	7.0	7.2	7.4
As a percentage of world trade (%)	Imp.	0.9	0.8	0.9	0.9	0.9	0.8	0.8	0.8	0.8	0.7	0.8	0.8	0.7	0.7	0.8
	Exp.	0.9	0.8	0.9	0.9	0.9	0.8	0.8	0.8	0.8	0.7	0.8	0.8	0.7	0.8	0.8

Graph 1: Annual growth rates of exports, 1999–2013
(In percentage by year)

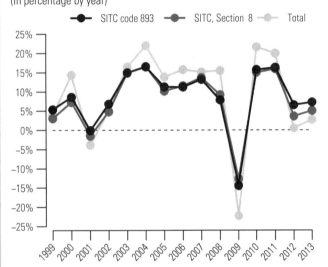

Table 2: Top exporting countries or areas in 2013

Country or area	Value (million US$)	Avg. Growth (%) 09-13	Growth (%) 12-13	World share %	Cum.
World	152703.2	11.3	7.2	100.0	
China	35299.3	25.1	11.8	23.1	23.1
Germany	16885.8	6.7	7.9	11.1	34.2
USA	12886.7	9.5	4.5	8.4	42.6
France	5938.6	3.6	7.3	3.9	46.5
Italy	5892.6	5.4	6.7	3.9	50.4
Netherlands	4503.6	12.0	14.2	2.9	53.3
Belgium	4432.6	4.1	14.5	2.9	56.2
Poland	4234.5	14.1	19.5	2.8	59.0
Mexico	3640.3	15.4	13.2	2.4	61.4
United Kingdom	3550.1	7.0	11.2	2.3	63.7
Canada	3415.5	3.7	-0.6	2.2	65.9
Other Asia, nes	3267.1	9.4	-0.5	2.1	68.1
China, Hong Kong SAR	3200.7	7.6	4.7	2.1	70.2
Rep. of Korea	2820.7	15.7	6.3	1.8	72.0
Japan	2589.2	6.8	-12.8	1.7	73.7

Graph 2: Trade Balance by MDG regions 2013
(Bln US$)

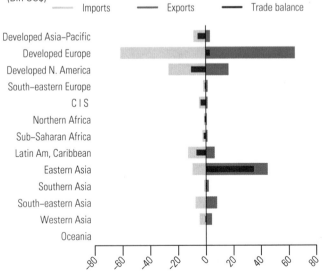

Table 3: Top importing countries or areas in 2013

Country or area	Value (million US$)	Avg. Growth (%) 09-13	Growth (%) 12-13	World share %	Cum.
World	144874.6	8.9	6.7	100.0	
USA	21373.5	9.9	5.3	14.8	14.8
Germany	10935.8	7.9	7.5	7.5	22.3
France	8045.7	5.1	5.4	5.6	27.9
Mexico	6395.4	11.4	4.7	4.4	32.3
United Kingdom	6186.7	5.5	9.0	4.3	36.5
Japan	5972.1	8.6	-2.1	4.1	40.7
Canada	5356.6	8.5	3.2	3.7	44.4
Netherlands	4554.5	10.2	14.2	3.1	47.5
China	4514.4	9.8	0.4	3.1	50.6
Belgium	4191.3	3.9	12.3	2.9	53.5
Italy	3386.3	7.2	11.4	2.3	55.8
Russian Federation	2975.0	18.6	5.0	2.1	57.9
Poland	2828.7	8.1	16.3	2.0	59.9
Spain	2640.6	-0.9	11.6	1.8	61.7
China, Hong Kong SAR	2547.1	7.8	8.9	1.8	63.4

In 2013, the value (in current US$) of exports of "baby carriages, toys, games and sporting goods" (SITC group 894) decreased by 0.6 percent (compared to 2.2 percent average growth rate from 2009-2013) to reach 92.1 bln US$ (see table 2), while imports decreased by 2.0 percent to reach 107.3 bln US$ (see table 3). Exports of this commodity accounted for 4.5 percent of world exports of SITC section 8, and 0.5 percent of total world merchandise exports (see table 1). China, China, Hong Kong SAR and USA were the top exporters in 2013 (see table 2). They accounted for 41.8, 10.7 and 7.4 percent of world exports, respectively. USA, China, Hong Kong SAR and Japan were the top destinations, with respectively 27.1, 7.8 and 6.1 percent of world imports (see table 3).

The top 15 countries/areas accounted for 87.1 and 76.7 percent of total world exports and imports, respectively (see tables 2 and 3). In 2013, China was the country/area with the highest value of net exports (+37.2 bln US$), followed by Other Asia, nes (+1.7 bln US$). By MDG regions (see graph 2), the largest surpluses in this product group were recorded by Eastern Asia (+39.0 bln US$) and South-eastern Asia (+1.4 bln US$). The largest trade deficits were recorded by Developed North America (-25.5 bln US$), Developed Europe (-12.2 bln US$) and Developed Asia-Pacific (-7.0 bln US$).

Table 1: Imports (Imp.) and exports (Exp.), 1999-2013, in current US$

		1999	2000	2001	2002	2003	2004	2005	2006	2007	2008	2009	2010	2011	2012	2013
Values in Bln US$	Imp.	55.7	60.2	59.0	62.6	67.4	74.0	83.9	91.7	111.6	128.0	107.6	113.1	115.6	109.5	107.3
	Exp.	46.2	48.1	45.4	49.1	52.2	57.0	64.5	71.4	86.3	101.2	84.4	87.3	95.4	92.7	92.1
As a percentage of	Imp.	7.4	7.4	7.3	7.4	6.9	6.6	6.8	6.7	7.3	7.7	7.5	6.9	6.3	5.9	5.6
SITC section (%)	Exp.	6.4	6.2	5.9	6.1	5.7	5.3	5.5	5.4	5.8	6.2	5.9	5.3	5.0	4.7	4.5
As a percentage of	Imp.	1.0	0.9	0.9	1.0	0.9	0.8	0.8	0.8	0.8	0.8	0.9	0.7	0.6	0.6	0.6
world trade (%)	Exp.	0.8	0.8	0.7	0.8	0.7	0.6	0.6	0.6	0.6	0.6	0.7	0.6	0.5	0.5	0.5

Graph 1: Annual growth rates of exports, 1999–2013
(In percentage by year)

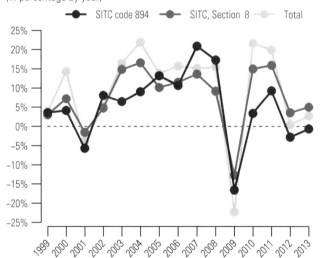

Table 2: Top exporting countries or areas in 2013

Country or area	Value (million US$)	Avg. Growth (%) 09-13	Growth (%) 12-13	World share %	Cum.
World	92 111.9	2.2	-0.6	100.0	
China	38 528.1	8.1	1.3	41.8	41.8
China, Hong Kong SAR	9 823.3	-7.7	-15.9	10.7	52.5
USA	6 785.1	-0.8	-4.3	7.4	59.9
Germany	4 399.8	-12.5	-11.2	4.8	64.6
Czech Rep.	3 016.1	17.9	13.0	3.3	67.9
Netherlands	2 442.8	-8.1	15.8	2.7	70.6
Other Asia, nes	2 147.1	8.5	-2.3	2.3	72.9
Japan	1 961.1	-5.0	-7.1	2.1	75.0
United Kingdom	1 946.3	10.0	6.4	2.1	77.1
Italy	1 856.4	3.5	4.3	2.0	79.1
Belgium	1 815.2	2.4	12.3	2.0	81.1
France	1 679.4	1.2	2.9	1.8	82.9
Austria	1 367.7	0.3	1.2	1.5	84.4
Mexico	1 341.4	-5.4	3.9	1.5	85.9
Canada	1 161.4	2.0	9.7	1.3	87.1

Graph 2: Trade Balance by MDG regions 2013
(Bln US$)

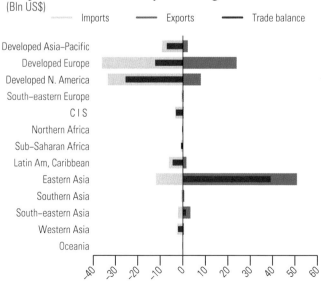

Table 3: Top importing countries or areas in 2013

Country or area	Value (million US$)	Avg. Growth (%) 09-13	Growth (%) 12-13	World share %	Cum.
World	107 276.8	-0.1	-2.0	100.0	
USA	29 060.3	0.1	-1.0	27.1	27.1
China, Hong Kong SAR	8 321.2	-8.5	-14.3	7.8	34.8
Japan	6 520.9	1.8	-11.0	6.1	40.9
Germany	6 070.7	-8.8	-5.5	5.7	46.6
United Kingdom	5 899.6	2.2	3.3	5.5	52.1
France	4 677.7	-0.1	-0.2	4.4	56.4
Canada	4 321.9	0.8	0.5	4.0	60.5
Russian Federation	2 608.3	26.3	3.0	2.4	62.9
Italy	2 421.5	-4.0	-9.1	2.3	65.2
Australia	2 343.0	1.2	-2.1	2.2	67.3
Netherlands	2 307.0	-12.4	3.4	2.2	69.5
Belgium	2 139.4	2.1	9.1	2.0	71.5
Spain	2 045.1	-3.4	1.6	1.9	73.4
Mexico	2 028.4	-3.4	5.6	1.9	75.3
Rep. of Korea	1 483.7	6.6	4.3	1.4	76.7

895 Office and stationery supplies, nes

In 2013, the value (in current US$) of exports of "office and stationery supplies, nes" (SITC group 895) increased by 7.1 percent (compared to 11.2 percent average growth rate from 2009-2013) to reach 17.9 bln US$ (see table 2), while imports increased by 4.8 percent to reach 17.7 bln US$ (see table 3). Exports of this commodity accounted for 0.9 percent of world exports of SITC section 8, and 0.1 percent of total world merchandise exports (see table 1). China, Germany and Netherlands were the top exporters in 2013 (see table 2). They accounted for 20.0, 18.3 and 7.5 percent of world exports, respectively. Germany, USA and France were the top destinations, with respectively 16.3, 11.0 and 8.3 percent of world imports (see table 3).

The top 15 countries/areas accounted for 84.6 and 69.2 percent of total world exports and imports, respectively (see tables 2 and 3). In 2013, China was the country/area with the highest value of net exports (+3.1 bln US$), followed by Japan (+791.1 mln US$). By MDG regions (see graph 2), the largest surpluses in this product group were recorded by Eastern Asia (+3.1 bln US$), Developed Asia-Pacific (+585.7 mln US$) and South-eastern Asia (+75.3 mln US$). The largest trade deficits were recorded by Developed North America (-1.6 bln US$), Western Asia (-713.6 mln US$) and Latin America and the Caribbean (-627.7 mln US$).

Table 1: Imports (Imp.) and exports (Exp.), 1999-2013, in current US$

		1999	2000	2001	2002	2003	2004	2005	2006	2007	2008	2009	2010	2011	2012	2013
Values in Bln US$	Imp.	8.5	9.1	8.7	9.1	9.7	11.1	11.7	12.6	14.1	14.7	13.2	15.6	16.9	16.9	17.7
	Exp.	8.0	8.3	7.4	7.9	8.9	9.9	10.5	11.6	12.9	13.6	11.7	14.0	16.4	16.8	17.9
As a percentage of	Imp.	1.1	1.1	1.1	1.1	1.0	1.0	0.9	0.9	0.9	0.9	0.9	1.0	0.9	0.9	0.9
SITC section (%)	Exp.	1.1	1.1	1.0	1.0	1.0	0.9	0.9	0.9	0.9	0.8	0.8	0.9	0.9	0.9	0.9
As a percentage of	Imp.	0.1	0.1	0.1	0.1	0.1	0.1	0.1	0.1	0.1	0.1	0.1	0.1	0.1	0.1	0.1
world trade (%)	Exp.	0.1	0.1	0.1	0.1	0.1	0.1	0.1	0.1	0.1	0.1	0.1	0.1	0.1	0.1	0.1

Graph 1: Annual growth rates of exports, 1999–2013
(In percentage by year)

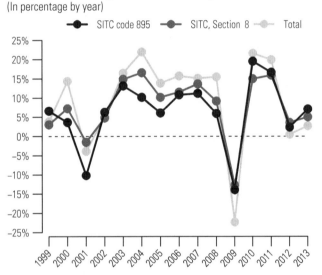

- SITC code 895
- SITC, Section 8
- Total

Graph 2: Trade Balance by MDG regions 2013
(Bln US$)

- Imports
- Exports
- Trade balance

Developed Asia–Pacific
Developed Europe
Developed N. America
South–eastern Europe
C I S
Northern Africa
Sub–Saharan Africa
Latin Am, Caribbean
Eastern Asia
Southern Asia
South–eastern Asia
Western Asia
Oceania

Table 2: Top exporting countries or areas in 2013

Country or area	Value (million US$)	Avg. Growth (%) 09-13	Growth (%) 12-13	World share %	Cum.
World	17 940.5	11.2	7.1	100.0	
China	3 594.9	12.1	3.8	20.0	20.0
Germany	3 284.3	24.6	15.6	18.3	38.3
Netherlands	1 352.9	6.9	8.8	7.5	45.9
Japan	1 168.8	0.5	-14.2	6.5	52.4
France	1 086.8	10.8	13.6	6.1	58.5
Czech Rep.	1 058.1	61.1	13.9	5.9	64.4
United Kingdom	824.9	3.9	16.6	4.6	69.0
USA	649.1	1.4	1.9	3.6	72.6
Ireland	360.4	47.2	68.1	2.0	74.6
Mexico	346.0	6.5	-7.8	1.9	76.5
Belgium	312.5	13.2	22.3	1.7	78.3
China, Hong Kong SAR	300.4	3.2	1.0	1.7	79.9
Singapore	292.4	5.8	6.4	1.6	81.6
India	281.0	18.3	13.9	1.6	83.1
Italy	265.3	0.4	5.4	1.5	84.6

Table 3: Top importing countries or areas in 2013

Country or area	Value (million US$)	Avg. Growth (%) 09-13	Growth (%) 12-13	World share %	Cum.
World	17 744.8	7.6	4.8	100.0	
Germany	2 896.6	29.0	16.6	16.3	16.3
USA	1 943.5	6.5	0.7	11.0	27.3
France	1 466.2	0.3	16.3	8.3	35.5
Netherlands	1 086.5	5.8	10.7	6.1	41.7
United Kingdom	1 000.3	3.5	7.9	5.6	47.3
Italy	539.0	2.4	1.9	3.0	50.3
China	455.6	7.5	-4.0	2.6	52.9
Spain	439.8	-5.8	-14.3	2.5	55.4
Mexico	412.2	6.0	-1.4	2.3	57.7
China, Hong Kong SAR	378.7	5.2	-0.4	2.1	59.8
Japan	377.8	7.1	-1.6	2.1	62.0
Belgium	359.3	6.5	7.3	2.0	64.0
Czech Rep.	322.3	26.0	13.7	1.8	65.8
Canada	304.4	3.9	0.3	1.7	67.5
United Arab Emirates	303.0	11.4	11.4	1.7	69.2

Works of art, collectors' pieces and antiques 896

In 2013, the value (in current US$) of exports of "works of art, collectors' pieces and antiques" (SITC group 896) increased by 4.8 percent (compared to 12.5 percent average growth rate from 2009-2013) to reach 24.4 bln US$ (see table 2), while imports increased by 3.8 percent to reach 23.8 bln US$ (see table 3). Exports of this commodity accounted for 1.2 percent of world exports of SITC section 8, and 0.1 percent of total world merchandise exports (see table 1). USA, United Kingdom and France were the top exporters in 2013 (see table 2). They accounted for 31.5, 28.2 and 8.7 percent of world exports, respectively. USA, United Kingdom and Switzerland were the top destinations, with respectively 38.1, 24.2 and 9.6 percent of world imports (see table 3).

The top 15 countries/areas accounted for 95.1 and 94.7 percent of total world exports and imports, respectively (see tables 2 and 3). In 2013, France was the country/area with the highest value of net exports (+1.5 bln US$), followed by United Kingdom (+1.1 bln US$). By MDG regions (see graph 2), the largest surpluses in this product group were recorded by Developed Europe (+2.7 bln US$), Southern Asia (+237.7 mln US$) and Sub-Saharan Africa (+76.9 mln US$). The largest trade deficits were recorded by Developed North America (-1.3 bln US$), Eastern Asia (-710.8 mln US$) and Western Asia (-137.1 mln US$).

Table 1: Imports (Imp.) and exports (Exp.), 1999-2013, in current US$

		1999	2000	2001	2002	2003	2004	2005	2006	2007	2008	2009	2010	2011	2012	2013
Values in Bln US$	Imp.	10.1	11.8	11.7	11.6	10.4	12.9	14.3	16.5	23.6	20.9	13.8	17.6	22.2	22.9	23.8
	Exp.	7.8	10.1	10.2	9.8	11.2	12.7	14.7	17.1	20.8	21.2	15.3	17.6	20.2	23.3	24.4
As a percentage of SITC section (%)	Imp.	1.3	1.4	1.4	1.4	1.1	1.1	1.2	1.2	1.5	1.3	1.0	1.1	1.2	1.2	1.2
	Exp.	1.1	1.3	1.3	1.2	1.2	1.2	1.2	1.3	1.4	1.3	1.1	1.1	1.1	1.2	1.2
As a percentage of world trade (%)	Imp.	0.2	0.2	0.2	0.2	0.1	0.1	0.1	0.1	0.2	0.1	0.1	0.1	0.1	0.1	0.1
	Exp.	0.1	0.2	0.2	0.2	0.1	0.1	0.1	0.1	0.2	0.1	0.1	0.1	0.1	0.1	0.1

Graph 1: Annual growth rates of exports, 1999–2013
(In percentage by year)

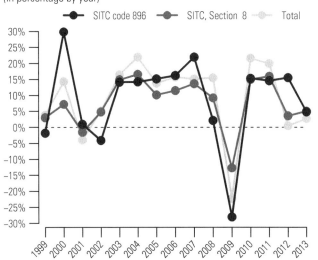

Table 2: Top exporting countries or areas in 2013

Country or area	Value (million US$)	Avg. Growth (%) 09-13	Growth (%) 12-13	World share %	Cum.
World	24431.8	12.5	4.8	100.0	
USA	7685.3	4.3	3.4	31.5	31.5
United Kingdom	6901.8	19.4	-7.7	28.2	59.7
France	2113.7	15.5	13.8	8.7	68.4
Switzerland	1840.2	14.8	18.3	7.5	75.9
China	1041.0	113.1	94.8	4.3	80.1
Germany	898.0	8.3	-22.8	3.7	83.8
Italy	561.4	42.3	39.4	2.3	86.1
China, Hong Kong SAR	523.4	23.2	10.0	2.1	88.3
Austria	321.1	24.8	153.5	1.3	89.6
Canada	288.4	0.1	40.6	1.2	90.8
India	281.0	8.2	15.0	1.1	91.9
Japan	265.4	24.0	54.9	1.1	93.0
Singapore	217.1	19.0	42.3	0.9	93.9
Rep. of Korea	173.5	-12.1	40.8	0.7	94.6
Spain	129.0	-12.0	17.8	0.5	95.1

Graph 2: Trade Balance by MDG regions 2013
(Bln US$)

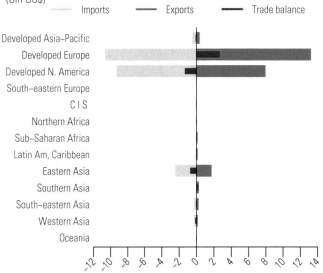

Table 3: Top importing countries or areas in 2013

Country or area	Value (million US$)	Avg. Growth (%) 09-13	Growth (%) 12-13	World share %	Cum.
World	23771.8	14.6	3.8	100.0	
USA	9060.4	15.7	16.1	38.1	38.1
United Kingdom	5757.4	12.4	-26.6	24.2	62.3
Switzerland	2273.2	15.4	30.4	9.6	71.9
China, Hong Kong SAR	1479.2	28.5	19.0	6.2	78.1
Germany	772.6	19.1	4.2	3.2	81.4
China	770.8	190.9	776.4	3.2	84.6
France	620.3	3.0	1.2	2.6	87.2
Netherlands	328.7	11.9	96.7	1.4	88.6
Japan	284.7	0.5	19.2	1.2	89.8
Singapore	255.6	22.7	35.2	1.1	90.9
Canada	232.8	7.2	-2.8	1.0	91.9
Austria	208.1	9.3	25.8	0.9	92.7
Belgium	184.3	6.2	23.5	0.8	93.5
Australia	150.2	14.9	10.5	0.6	94.1
Rep. of Korea	144.2	-9.4	-13.0	0.6	94.7

897 Gold, silverware, jewellery and articles of precious materials, nes

In 2013, the value (in current US$) of exports of "gold, silverware, jewellery and articles of precious materials, nes" (SITC group 897) increased by 0.6 percent (compared to 20.5 percent average growth rate from 2009-2013) to reach 139.1 bln US$ (see table 2), while imports decreased by 0.9 percent to reach 82.2 bln US$ (see table 3). Exports of this commodity accounted for 6.7 percent of world exports of SITC section 8, and 0.7 percent of total world merchandise exports (see table 1). China, India and USA were the top exporters in 2013 (see table 2). They accounted for 32.5, 7.9 and 7.8 percent of world exports, respectively. China, Hong Kong SAR, USA and Switzerland were the top destinations, with respectively 16.2, 13.9 and 11.2 percent of world imports (see table 3).

The top 15 countries/areas accounted for 92.5 and 82.1 percent of total world exports and imports, respectively (see tables 2 and 3). In 2013, China was the country/area with the highest value of net exports (+43.6 bln US$), followed by India (+10.1 bln US$). By MDG regions (see graph 2), the largest surpluses in this product group were recorded by Eastern Asia (+37.2 bln US$), Southern Asia (+10.9 bln US$) and Developed Europe (+6.1 bln US$). The largest trade deficits were recorded by Developed North America (-1.6 bln US$), Developed Asia-Pacific (-1.2 bln US$) and Northern Africa (-1.2 bln US$).

Table 1: Imports (Imp.) and exports (Exp.), 1999-2013, in current US$

		1999	2000	2001	2002	2003	2004	2005	2006	2007	2008	2009	2010	2011	2012	2013
Values in Bln US$	Imp.	17.6	19.9	20.3	23.3	26.5	31.7	36.7	42.3	49.4	53.4	48.8	62.0	74.7	82.9	82.2
	Exp.	21.2	22.4	23.3	25.8	28.8	35.9	41.0	48.7	58.2	65.2	65.9	77.8	112.5	138.3	139.1
As a percentage of SITC section (%)	Imp.	2.3	2.4	2.5	2.7	2.7	2.8	3.0	3.1	3.2	3.2	3.4	3.8	4.0	4.5	4.3
	Exp.	2.9	2.9	3.0	3.2	3.1	3.3	3.5	3.7	3.9	4.0	4.6	4.7	5.9	7.0	6.7
As a percentage of world trade (%)	Imp.	0.3	0.3	0.3	0.4	0.3	0.3	0.3	0.3	0.4	0.3	0.4	0.4	0.4	0.5	0.4
	Exp.	0.4	0.4	0.4	0.4	0.4	0.4	0.4	0.4	0.4	0.4	0.5	0.5	0.6	0.8	0.7

Graph 1: Annual growth rates of exports, 1999–2013
(In percentage by year)

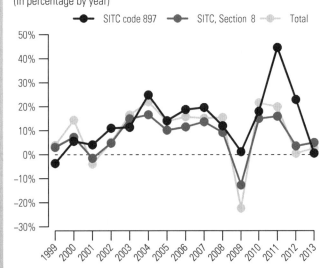

Graph 2: Trade Balance by MDG regions 2013
(Bln US$)

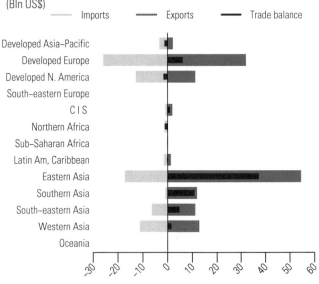

Table 2: Top exporting countries or areas in 2013

Country or area	Value (million US$)	Avg. Growth (%) 09-13	Growth (%) 12-13	World share %	Cum.
World	139 067.4	20.5	0.6	100.0	
China	45 152.2	84.7	10.6	32.5	32.5
India	11 043.8	-5.1	-44.1	7.9	40.4
USA	10 872.8	14.6	17.3	7.8	48.2
Switzerland	9 533.4	18.0	6.0	6.9	55.1
China, Hong Kong SAR	8 542.7	16.5	5.4	6.1	61.2
United Arab Emirates	7 917.3	26.8	21.7	5.7	66.9
Italy	7 504.9	12.0	11.6	5.4	72.3
United Kingdom	4 961.3	6.8	-16.3	3.6	75.9
France	4 572.8	23.5	18.6	3.3	79.2
Thailand	4 115.0	10.7	-1.4	3.0	82.1
Singapore	4 105.1	25.1	20.7	3.0	85.1
Turkey	3 442.6	30.8	27.5	2.5	87.6
Germany	2 578.4	13.8	12.9	1.9	89.4
Malaysia	2 456.8	11.7	6.5	1.8	91.2
Russian Federation	1 864.1	468.2	41.9	1.3	92.5

Table 3: Top importing countries or areas in 2013

Country or area	Value (million US$)	Avg. Growth (%) 09-13	Growth (%) 12-13	World share %	Cum.
World	82 163.3	13.9	-0.9	100.0	
China, Hong Kong SAR	13 347.3	31.7	3.0	16.2	16.2
USA	11 453.2	6.6	7.2	13.9	30.2
Switzerland	9 236.6	11.1	-3.8	11.2	41.4
United Arab Emirates	7 510.2	8.6	11.4	9.1	50.6
United Kingdom	4 564.4	5.1	-1.2	5.6	56.1
Singapore	4 443.1	24.0	-2.9	5.4	61.5
France	4 342.4	21.2	18.1	5.3	66.8
Germany	2 338.6	11.0	-2.7	2.8	69.7
Japan	2 112.3	8.4	-7.2	2.6	72.2
Italy	1 673.1	12.5	-7.4	2.0	74.3
China	1 518.7	27.9	19.5	1.8	76.1
Canada	1 380.8	12.1	3.9	1.7	77.8
China, Macao SAR	1 298.4	41.7	12.9	1.6	79.4
Malaysia	1 166.5	35.3	-21.7	1.4	80.8
Australia	1 095.9	8.0	5.4	1.3	82.1

Musical instruments, parts/accessories; records, tapes and similar recordings 898

In 2013, the value (in current US$) of exports of "musical instruments, parts/accessories; records, tapes and similar recordings" (SITC group 898) decreased by 10.7 percent (compared to -1.0 percent average growth rate from 2009-2013) to reach 50.2 bln US$ (see table 2), while imports decreased by 3.6 percent to reach 57.2 bln US$ (see table 3). Exports of this commodity accounted for 2.4 percent of world exports of SITC section 8, and 0.3 percent of total world merchandise exports (see table 1). China, Germany and USA were the top exporters in 2013 (see table 2). They accounted for 12.8, 10.9 and 10.4 percent of world exports, respectively. USA, China and China, Hong Kong SAR were the top destinations, with respectively 10.5, 9.2 and 8.6 percent of world imports (see table 3).

The top 15 countries/areas accounted for 87.5 and 71.6 percent of total world exports and imports, respectively (see tables 2 and 3). In 2013, Other Asia, nes was the country/area with the highest value of net exports (+3.6 bln US$), followed by Singapore (+2.6 bln US$). By MDG regions (see graph 2), the largest surpluses in this product group were recorded by Eastern Asia (+2.9 bln US$) and South-eastern Asia (+2.0 bln US$). The largest trade deficits were recorded by Developed Europe (-2.5 bln US$), Developed North America (-2.4 bln US$) and Latin America and the Caribbean (-1.9 bln US$).

Table 1: Imports (Imp.) and exports (Exp.), 1999-2013, in current US$

		1999	2000	2001	2002	2003	2004	2005	2006	2007	2008	2009	2010	2011	2012	2013
Values in Bln US$	Imp.	33.9	34.1	32.9	34.4	39.1	45.6	51.8	54.9	59.9	65.5	55.2	61.4	65.7	59.3	57.2
	Exp.	34.4	34.3	33.1	33.7	39.2	44.4	50.6	53.3	59.1	62.8	52.2	57.6	60.6	56.2	50.2
As a percentage of SITC section (%)	Imp.	4.5	4.2	4.1	4.0	4.0	4.0	4.2	4.0	3.9	3.9	3.8	3.7	3.6	3.2	3.0
	Exp.	4.8	4.4	4.3	4.2	4.3	4.1	4.3	4.0	3.9	3.8	3.7	3.5	3.2	2.9	2.4
As a percentage of world trade (%)	Imp.	0.6	0.5	0.5	0.5	0.5	0.5	0.5	0.5	0.4	0.4	0.4	0.4	0.4	0.3	0.3
	Exp.	0.6	0.5	0.5	0.5	0.5	0.5	0.5	0.4	0.4	0.4	0.4	0.4	0.3	0.3	0.3

Graph 1: Annual growth rates of exports, 1999–2013
(In percentage by year)

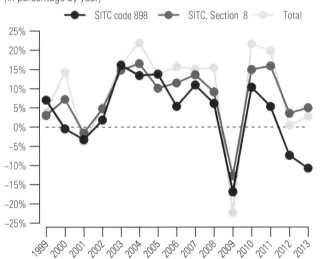

Table 2: Top exporting countries or areas in 2013

Country or area	Value (million US$)	Avg. Growth (%) 09-13	Growth (%) 12-13	World share %	Cum.
World................................	50150.8	-1.0	-10.7	100.0	
China................................	6413.9	-1.9	-15.3	12.8	12.8
Germany..........................	5464.4	-4.8	-7.5	10.9	23.7
USA.................................	5220.7	0.0	-4.0	10.4	34.1
Other Asia, nes................	5099.1	5.3	-13.3	10.2	44.3
Singapore........................	4153.3	1.8	-24.0	8.3	52.5
China, Hong Kong SAR.........	3291.8	3.1	-13.3	6.6	59.1
Netherlands.....................	2754.4	4.0	3.6	5.5	64.6
Japan..............................	2741.5	-8.8	-15.6	5.5	70.1
United Kingdom................	1665.1	118.9	0.7	3.3	73.4
Austria............................	1335.1	-2.9	-0.1	2.7	76.0
France.............................	1278.1	-1.3	-3.1	2.5	78.6
Malaysia..........................	1259.4	-3.2	-9.2	2.5	81.1
Czech Rep........................	1106.0	-4.5	-6.3	2.2	83.3
Rep. of Korea...................	1067.7	-6.5	-11.1	2.1	85.4
Ireland............................	1016.8	-10.9	-10.1	2.0	87.5

Graph 2: Trade Balance by MDG regions 2013
(Bln US$)

Table 3: Top importing countries or areas in 2013

Country or area	Value (million US$)	Avg. Growth (%) 09-13	Growth (%) 12-13	World share %	Cum.
World................................	57207.7	0.9	-3.6	100.0	
USA.................................	6001.3	4.9	6.6	10.5	10.5
China................................	5236.1	1.1	-19.6	9.2	19.6
China, Hong Kong SAR.........	4944.5	5.5	-5.1	8.6	28.3
Germany..........................	4375.4	-0.1	2.0	7.6	35.9
United Kingdom................	2741.4	70.7	2.5	4.8	40.7
Japan..............................	2374.7	-2.0	-19.6	4.2	44.9
France.............................	2357.2	-0.3	5.0	4.1	49.0
Netherlands.....................	2120.4	2.6	-12.7	3.7	52.7
Canada............................	1947.7	-0.6	-2.3	3.4	56.1
Thailand..........................	1923.7	-0.3	1.2	3.4	59.5
Russian Federation..............	1559.9	43.7	117.6	2.7	62.2
Singapore........................	1504.9	12.5	3.6	2.6	64.8
Other Asia, nes................	1487.0	2.4	-18.6	2.6	67.4
Rep. of Korea...................	1282.4	-6.7	-12.8	2.2	69.7
Italy................................	1128.0	-8.3	-5.3	2.0	71.6

899 Miscellaneous manufactured articles, nes

In 2013, the value (in current US$) of exports of "miscellaneous manufactured articles, nes" (SITC group 899) increased by 6.5 percent (compared to 8.5 percent average growth rate from 2009-2013) to reach 88.4 bln US$ (see table 2), while imports increased by 5.4 percent to reach 85.5 bln US$ (see table 3). Exports of this commodity accounted for 4.3 percent of world exports of SITC section 8, and 0.5 percent of total world merchandise exports (see table 1). China, USA and Germany were the top exporters in 2013 (see table 2). They accounted for 23.8, 12.7 and 7.7 percent of world exports, respectively. USA, Germany and Netherlands were the top destinations, with respectively 18.7, 8.1 and 6.9 percent of world imports (see table 3).

The top 15 countries/areas accounted for 86.2 and 72.9 percent of total world exports and imports, respectively (see tables 2 and 3). In 2013, China was the country/area with the highest value of net exports (+17.7 bln US$), followed by Switzerland (+4.5 bln US$). By MDG regions (see graph 2), the largest surpluses in this product group were recorded by Eastern Asia (+18.1 bln US$), Developed Europe (+4.0 bln US$) and South-eastern Asia (+718.9 mln US$). The largest trade deficits were recorded by Developed North America (-6.5 bln US$), Developed Asia-Pacific (-5.5 bln US$) and Western Asia (-1.9 bln US$).

Table 1: Imports (Imp.) and exports (Exp.), 1999-2013, in current US$

		1999	2000	2001	2002	2003	2004	2005	2006	2007	2008	2009	2010	2011	2012	2013
Values in Bln US$	Imp.	24.9	26.0	27.7	30.5	37.0	43.0	46.9	51.2	58.2	66.6	64.2	71.8	80.6	81.1	85.5
	Exp.	22.9	24.3	25.1	27.2	33.3	40.0	44.5	49.7	56.5	65.9	63.8	72.9	80.4	83.0	88.4
As a percentage of SITC section (%)	Imp.	3.3	3.2	3.4	3.6	3.8	3.8	3.8	3.8	3.8	4.0	4.5	4.4	4.4	4.4	4.5
	Exp.	3.2	3.1	3.3	3.4	3.6	3.7	3.8	3.8	3.8	4.0	4.5	4.4	4.2	4.2	4.3
As a percentage of world trade (%)	Imp.	0.4	0.4	0.4	0.5	0.5	0.5	0.4	0.4	0.4	0.4	0.5	0.5	0.4	0.4	0.5
	Exp.	0.4	0.4	0.4	0.4	0.4	0.4	0.4	0.4	0.4	0.4	0.5	0.5	0.4	0.5	0.5

Graph 1: Annual growth rates of exports, 1999–2013
(In percentage by year)

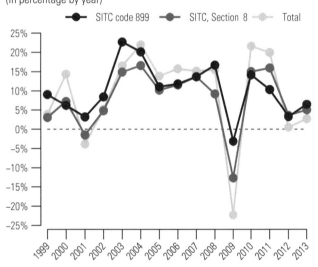

— SITC code 899   — SITC, Section 8   — Total

Graph 2: Trade Balance by MDG regions 2013
(Bln US$)

— Imports   — Exports   — Trade balance

Developed Asia–Pacific
Developed Europe
Developed N. America
South–eastern Europe
CIS
Northern Africa
Sub–Saharan Africa
Latin Am, Caribbean
Eastern Asia
Southern Asia
South–eastern Asia
Western Asia
Oceania

Table 2: Top exporting countries or areas in 2013

Country or area	Value (million US$)	Avg. Growth (%) 09-13	Growth (%) 12-13	World share %	Cum.
World	88 357.5	8.5	6.5	100.0	
China	21 043.1	15.9	5.4	23.8	23.8
USA	11 225.0	5.2	5.3	12.7	36.5
Germany	6 768.5	8.2	8.6	7.7	44.2
Netherlands	6 748.9	17.7	17.0	7.6	51.8
Switzerland	6 624.8	2.6	4.5	7.5	59.3
Ireland	5 010.1	4.5	4.1	5.7	65.0
Belgium	4 171.8	15.0	18.4	4.7	69.7
France	4 143.3	-2.2	1.8	4.7	74.4
China, Hong Kong SAR	2 042.2	1.2	-8.4	2.3	76.7
Italy	1 800.8	6.1	4.3	2.0	78.7
United Kingdom	1 659.0	-2.7	7.1	1.9	80.6
Singapore	1 343.5	17.4	23.2	1.5	82.1
Denmark	1 198.8	1.1	-3.9	1.4	83.5
Sweden	1 192.0	0.1	-19.4	1.3	84.9
Mexico	1 151.3	6.4	3.1	1.3	86.2

Table 3: Top importing countries or areas in 2013

Country or area	Value (million US$)	Avg. Growth (%) 09-13	Growth (%) 12-13	World share %	Cum.
World	85 485.1	7.4	5.4	100.0	
USA	15 991.7	7.8	5.3	18.7	18.7
Germany	6 936.1	8.8	10.9	8.1	26.8
Netherlands	5 915.5	12.4	4.0	6.9	33.7
France	5 241.8	0.9	0.9	6.1	39.9
Japan	4 915.1	7.0	-7.5	5.7	45.6
United Kingdom	3 455.6	4.9	13.9	4.0	49.7
China	3 308.7	19.2	13.6	3.9	53.5
Belgium	3 270.2	10.4	20.4	3.8	57.4
Italy	2 648.5	1.5	6.9	3.1	60.5
Canada	2 162.0	7.6	3.8	2.5	63.0
Switzerland	2 100.6	2.6	11.2	2.5	65.4
Australia	1 883.5	11.0	6.2	2.2	67.6
Spain	1 714.0	2.1	-2.0	2.0	69.7
China, Hong Kong SAR	1 459.3	1.7	-15.9	1.7	71.4
Russian Federation	1 324.7	19.0	10.2	1.5	72.9

Commodities and transactions not classified elsewhere in the SITC

(SITC Section 9)

961 Coin (other than gold coin), not being legal tender

In 2013, the value (in current US$) of exports of "coin (other than gold coin), not being legal tender" (SITC group 961) increased by 2.3 percent (compared to -6.1 percent average growth rate from 2009-2013) to reach 343.0 mln US$ (see table 2), while imports decreased by 1.9 percent to reach 645.2 mln US$ (see table 3). Exports of this commodity accounted for less than 0.1 percent of world exports of SITC section 9, and less than 0.1 percent of total world merchandise exports (see table 1). USA, Germany and Canada were the top exporters in 2013 (see table 2). They accounted for 14.8, 13.6 and 11.0 percent of world exports, respectively. Germany, Singapore and USA were the top destinations, with respectively 61.8, 5.8 and 5.5 percent of world imports (see table 3).

The top 15 countries/areas accounted for 91.7 and 91.6 percent of total world exports and imports, respectively (see tables 2 and 3). In 2013, Canada was the country/area with the highest value of net exports (+23.3 mln US$), followed by Slovakia (+19.1 mln US$). By MDG regions (see graph 2), the largest surpluses in this product group were recorded by Developed North America (+30.3 mln US$), Latin America and the Caribbean (+10.4 mln US$) and Commonwealth of Independent States (+5.2 mln US$). The largest trade deficits were recorded by Developed Europe (-264.0 mln US$), South-eastern Asia (-39.6 mln US$) and Eastern Asia (-18.1 mln US$).

Table 1: Imports (Imp.) and exports (Exp.), 1999-2013, in current US$

		1999	2000	2001	2002	2003	2004	2005	2006	2007	2008	2009	2010	2011	2012	2013
Values in Mln US$	Imp.	81.1	708.3	99.9	93.4	119.4	112.6	106.3	104.2	148.4	189.4	442.0	554.3	923.8	657.5	645.2
	Exp.	68.3	716.7	90.3	105.8	155.6	217.4	186.7	233.7	333.2	361.2	442.0	576.3	409.4	335.4	343.0
As a percentage of SITC section (%)	Imp.	0.0	0.3	0.0	0.0	0.0	0.0	0.0	0.0	0.0	0.0	0.1	0.1	0.1	0.1	0.1
	Exp.	0.0	0.3	0.0	0.0	0.0	0.1	0.0	0.1	0.1	0.0	0.1	0.1	0.0	0.0	0.0
As a percentage of world trade (%)	Imp.	0.0	0.0	0.0	0.0	0.0	0.0	0.0	0.0	0.0	0.0	0.0	0.0	0.0	0.0	0.0
	Exp.	0.0	0.0	0.0	0.0	0.0	0.0	0.0	0.0	0.0	0.0	0.0	0.0	0.0	0.0	0.0

Graph 1: Annual growth rates of exports, 1999–2013
(In percentage by year)

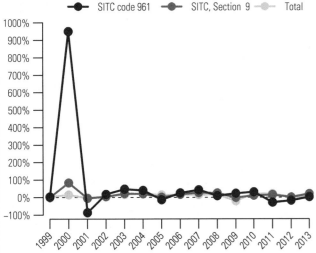

Table 2: Top exporting countries or areas in 2013

Country or area	Value (million US$)	Avg. Growth (%) 09-13	Growth (%) 12-13	World share %	Cum.
World	343.0	-6.1	2.3	100.0	
USA	50.8	17.9	-35.7	14.8	14.8
Germany	46.5	21.4	-9.9	13.6	28.4
Canada	37.9	-9.0	46.1	11.0	39.4
United Kingdom	29.2	-29.9	46.0	8.5	47.9
Slovakia	26.8	2.9	108.5	7.8	55.7
France	23.9	-1.4	-34.0	7.0	62.7
Finland	19.6	-13.6	-25.0	5.7	68.4
Netherlands	17.3	29.6	340.3	5.1	73.5
Spain	14.8	88.1	76.4	4.3	77.8
Mexico	10.5	-3.8	166.8	3.1	80.9
Poland	9.1	-1.9	27.3	2.7	83.5
Czech Rep.	8.9	39.7	1909.8	2.6	86.1
Russian Federation	7.5	...	574.3	2.2	88.3
Austria	5.9	17.7	1.7	1.7	90.0
Italy	5.8	22.8	0.5	1.7	91.7

Graph 2: Trade Balance by MDG regions 2013
(Mln US$)

Legend: Imports, Exports, Trade balance

Developed Asia–Pacific
Developed Europe
Developed N. America
South–eastern Europe
CIS
Sub–Saharan Africa
Latin Am, Caribbean
Eastern Asia
Southern Asia
South–eastern Asia
Western Asia
Oceania

Table 3: Top importing countries or areas in 2013

Country or area	Value (million US$)	Avg. Growth (%) 09-13	Growth (%) 12-13	World share %	Cum.
World	645.2	9.9	-1.9	100.0	
Germany	398.5	23.8	-5.2	61.8	61.8
Singapore	37.2	62.2	81.5	5.8	67.5
USA	35.5	-11.7	-13.5	5.5	73.0
France	21.6	146.5	49.9	3.4	76.4
Other Asia, nes	16.3	156.8	72.7	2.5	78.9
Canada	14.5	83.2	-30.9	2.3	81.2
Netherlands	11.4	-34.2	-6.8	1.8	82.9
United Kingdom	10.3	22.9	-38.3	1.6	84.5
Czech Rep.	9.9	191.0	291.2	1.5	86.1
Slovakia	7.6	277.1	296.5	1.2	87.2
Australia	7.1	77.1	15.2	1.1	88.4
Angola	6.9	...	992.2	1.1	89.4
Saint Pierre and Miquelon	6.6	...		1.0	90.4
Indonesia	3.9	77.7	>	0.6	91.1
Austria	3.6	10.4	17.7	0.6	91.6

"Gold, non-monetary (excluding gold ores and concentrates)" (SITC group 971) is amongst the top exported commodities in 2013 with 1.9 percent of total exports (see table 1). The value (in current US$) of exports of this commodity increased by 21.2 percent (compared to 30.0 percent average growth rate from 2009-2013) to reach 352.7 bln US$ (see table 2), while imports increased by 23.6 percent to reach 288.4 bln US$ (see table 3). Exports of this commodity accounted for 32.5 percent of world exports of SITC section 9 (see table 1). Export from United Kingdom, in particular to Switzerland, increased by 1822.1 percent in 2013, making United Kingdom the top exporter, followed by China, Hong Kong SAR and USA (see table 2). They accounted for 22.7, 21.6 and 9.5 percent of world exports, respectively. China, Hong Kong SAR, India and United Arab Emirates were the top destinations, with respectively 33.9, 13.1 and 11.1 percent of world imports (see table 3).

The top 15 countries/areas accounted for 85.2 and 93.6 percent of total world exports and imports, respectively (see tables 2 and 3). In 2013, United Kingdom was the country/area with the highest value of net exports (+64.8 bln US$), followed by USA (+17.6 bln US$). By MDG regions (see graph 2), the largest surpluses in this product group were recorded by Developed Europe (+71.3 bln US$), Latin America and the Caribbean (+25.3 bln US$) and Developed North America (+23.9 bln US$). The largest trade deficit was recorded by Southern Asia (-36.1 bln US$).

Table 1: Imports (Imp.) and exports (Exp.), 1999-2013, in current US$

		1999	2000	2001	2002	2003	2004	2005	2006	2007	2008	2009	2010	2011	2012	2013
Values in Bln US$	Imp.	26.3	27.4	30.1	32.1	39.6	49.0	49.4	61.4	74.1	109.8	97.7	139.9	213.8	233.4	288.4
	Exp.	21.1	23.1	24.0	24.3	34.0	40.3	38.9	61.9	73.4	107.7	123.5	155.2	239.8	291.1	352.7
As a percentage of SITC section (%)	Imp.	15.8	9.9	12.6	13.6	14.0	13.9	14.6	13.7	11.9	14.2	15.8	21.6	28.7	28.2	34.3
	Exp.	14.3	8.5	9.3	9.1	10.4	10.3	10.0	13.5	12.6	14.9	17.4	19.8	26.8	32.2	32.5
As a percentage of world trade (%)	Imp.	0.5	0.4	0.5	0.5	0.5	0.5	0.5	0.5	0.5	0.7	0.8	0.9	1.2	1.3	1.6
	Exp.	0.4	0.4	0.4	0.4	0.5	0.4	0.4	0.5	0.5	0.7	1.0	1.0	1.3	1.6	1.9

Graph 1: Annual growth rates of exports, 1999–2013
(In percentage by year)

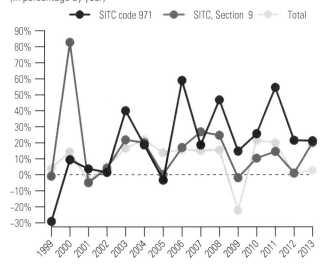

Graph 2: Trade Balance by MDG regions 2013
(Bln US$)

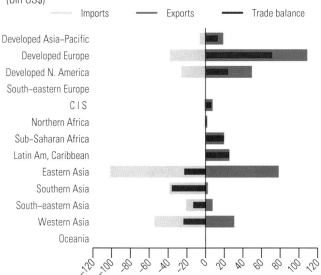

Table 2: Top exporting countries or areas in 2013

Country or area	Value (million US$)	Avg. Growth (%) 09-13	Growth (%) 12-13	World share %	Cum.
World	352 747.0	30.0	21.2	100.0	
United Kingdom	80 229.9	142.4	1822.1	22.7	22.7
China, Hong Kong SAR	76 229.3	62.6	52.1	21.6	44.4
USA	33 534.8	24.5	-7.7	9.5	53.9
United Arab Emirates	26 527.1	23.3	21.7	7.5	61.4
Canada	16 346.9	20.9	0.9	4.6	66.0
Australia	13 404.8	3.2	-16.6	3.8	69.8
Peru	8 028.4	4.4	-17.0	2.3	72.1
Germany	7 464.6	25.7	-21.6	2.1	74.2
South Africa	6 813.1	141.5	-23.2	1.9	76.1
Italy	6 351.6	20.7	-39.6	1.8	77.9
Mexico	5 919.2	9.9	-27.2	1.7	79.6
Russian Federation	5 574.6	...	8.7	1.6	81.2
Ghana	5 385.5	16.3	-24.1	1.5	82.7
Japan	5 257.4	4.1	-25.2	1.5	84.2
Switzerland	3 457.8	74.3	12.1	1.0	85.2

Table 3: Top importing countries or areas in 2013

Country or area	Value (million US$)	Avg. Growth (%) 09-13	Growth (%) 12-13	World share %	Cum.
World	288 423.1	31.1	23.6	100.0	
China, Hong Kong SAR	97 860.5	111.2	99.3	33.9	33.9
India	37 718.9	12.7	-28.3	13.1	47.0
United Arab Emirates	32 153.5	21.4	11.4	11.1	58.2
USA	15 946.1	16.3	-10.8	5.5	63.7
United Kingdom	15 466.9	91.0	164.0	5.4	69.0
Turkey	15 129.2	74.5	98.0	5.2	74.3
Thailand	14 981.6	41.0	39.5	5.2	79.5
Canada	10 033.1	14.0	-9.8	3.5	83.0
Germany	7 529.0	14.3	-4.6	2.6	85.6
Italy	5 800.0	12.8	-25.1	2.0	87.6
Australia	4 626.8	-10.7	-23.5	1.6	89.2
Saudi Arabia	4 472.7	61.6	97.7	1.6	90.7
Malaysia	3 594.4	17.7	22.7	1.2	92.0
Austria	2 558.1	-2.2	-7.0	0.9	92.9
Other Asia, nes	2 126.4	6.1	-1.6	0.7	93.6

2013
International Trade
Statistics Yearbook

Volume II
Trade by Product

Part 3 – Service Trade Profiles

- Transportation (EBOPS code 205)

- Travel (EBOPS code 236)

- Communications services (EBOPS code 245)

- Construction services (EBOPS code 249)

- Insurance services (EBOPS code 253)

- Financial services (EBOPS code 260)

- Computer and information services (EBOPS code 262)

- Royalties and license fees (EBOPS code 266)

- Other business services (EBOPS code 268)

- Personal, cultural and recreational services (EBOPS code 287)

- Government services, n.i.e. (EBOPS code 291)

Transportation (EBOPS 2002 code 205)

In 2012, "transportation" (EBOPS 2002 code 205) was the third largest exported service category, accounting for 19.0 percent of total world services exports (see table 1). The value (in current US$) of exports of this service category increased by 1.1 percent (compared to -0.1 percent average growth rate from 2008-2012) to reach 846.3 bln US$ (see table 2), while imports increased by 2.8 percent to reach 1071.1 bln US$ (see table 3). USA, Germany and France were the top exporters in 2012 (see table 2). They accounted for 9.8, 6.8 and 5.3 percent of world exports, respectively. USA, China and Germany were the top importers, with respectively 8.4, 8.0 and 6.3 percent of world imports (see table 3).

The top 15 countries/areas accounted for 65.7 and 59.9 percent of total world exports and imports, respectively (see tables 2 and 3). In 2012, Rep. of Korea was the country/area with the highest value of net exports (+10.6 bln US$), followed by Denmark (+9.7 bln US$). By MDG regions (see graph 2), the largest surpluses in this product group were recorded by Developed Europe (+40.3 bln US$), Commonwealth of Independent States (+10.0 bln US$) and South-eastern Europe (+1.7 bln US$). The largest trade deficits were recorded by Western Asia (-72.2 bln US$), South-eastern Asia (-43.6 bln US$) and Eastern Asia (-37.6 bln US$).

Table 1: Imports (Imp.) and exports (Exp.), 2000-2012, in current US$

		2000	2001	2002	2003	2004	2005	2006	2007	2008	2009	2010	2011	2012
Values in Bln US$	Imp.	389.7	381.3	392.1	451.4	561.9	645.6	713.7	839.9	970.5	763.8	896.7	1041.9	1071.1
	Exp.	319.7	314.1	337.9	383.5	480.5	547.1	608.8	728.4	849.5	659.7	764.4	837.3	846.3
As a percentage of world trade (%)	Imp.	26.5	25.6	24.3	24.4	25.6	26.4	26.3	26.1	26.5	22.9	24.7	25.7	25.7
	Exp.	21.6	21.2	20.8	20.3	21.1	21.5	21.2	21.0	21.8	18.6	19.7	19.2	19.0

Graph 1: Annual growth rates of exports, 2000–2012
(In percentage by year)

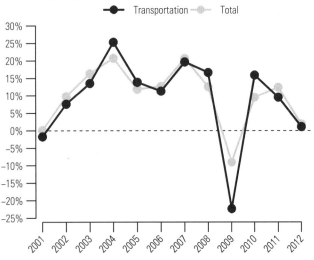

Graph 2: Trade Balance by MDG regions 2012
(Bln US$)

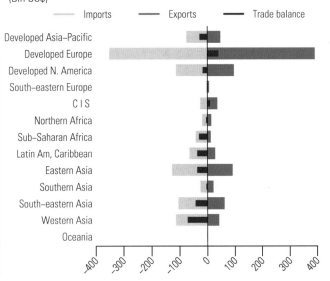

Table 2: Top exporting countries or areas in 2012

Country or area	Value (million US$)	Avg. Growth (%) 08-12	Growth (%) 11-12	World share %	Cum.
World	846297.8	-0.1	1.1	100.0	
USA	82826.0	2.6	4.1	9.8	9.8
Germany	57906.0	-2.2	-5.6	6.8	16.6
France	45236.5	2.8	-2.9	5.3	22.0
Singapore	43294.6	4.5	3.3	5.1	27.1
Rep. of Korea	40700.7	-2.4	10.2	4.8	31.9
Japan	40164.9	-3.8	4.8	4.7	36.6
Denmark	40045.4	-3.8	-0.7	4.7	41.4
China	38912.2	0.3	9.4	4.6	46.0
United Kingdom	34866.3	-3.0	-2.4	4.1	50.1
Netherlands	29350.3	-1.4	-1.9	3.5	53.6
Belgium	26112.8	-2.4	-0.8	3.1	56.6
Spain	23276.4	-1.5	-2.7	2.8	59.4
Russian Federation	19016.5	6.1	10.4	2.2	61.6
India	17481.7	10.9	-1.1	2.1	63.7
Norway	17178.7	-4.6	-1.4	2.0	65.7

Table 3: Top importing countries or areas in 2012

Country or area	Value (million US$)	Avg. Growth (%) 08-12	Growth (%) 11-12	World share %	Cum.
World	1071117.0	2.5	2.8	100.0	
USA	89657.0	0.5	5.0	8.4	8.4
China	85861.6	14.3	6.7	8.0	16.4
Germany	67870.9	-1.9	-3.0	6.3	22.7
Japan	55353.8	0.6	11.9	5.2	27.9
United Arab Emirates	47702.6	72.0	13.7	4.5	32.3
France	45737.9	2.1	-8.7	4.3	36.6
Singapore	35783.6	4.6	12.2	3.3	40.0
United Kingdom	33247.1	-1.5	0.5	3.1	43.1
Denmark	30312.9	-2.6	-1.2	2.8	45.9
Rep. of Korea	30146.3	-4.8	2.1	2.8	48.7
Thailand	28793.5	5.8	7.8	2.7	51.4
Italy	24434.3	-4.7	-10.2	2.3	53.7
Canada	22965.6	3.0	-0.3	2.1	55.8
Spain	22373.9	-4.2	-5.9	2.1	57.9
Belgium	21437.6	-1.7	-0.8	2.0	59.9

In 2012, "travel" (EBOPS 2002 code 236) was the second largest exported service category, accounting for 23.8 percent of total world services exports (see table 1). The value (in current US$) of exports of this service increased by 3.1 percent (compared to 3.2 percent average growth rate from 2008-2012) to reach 1059.3 bln US$ (see table 2), while imports increased by 5.2 percent to reach 951.6 bln US$ (see table 3). USA was the top exporter in 2012, accounting for 15.2 percent of world exports alone (see table 2). Spain and France were the second and third largest exporters, accounting for 5.3 and 5.1 percent of world exports, respectively. China, USA and Germany were the top importers, with respectively 10.7, 9.7 and 8.8 percent of world imports (see table 3).

The top 15 countries/areas accounted for 61.1 and 66.7 percent of total world exports and imports, respectively (see tables 2 and 3). In 2012, USA was the country/area with the highest value of net exports (+68.8 bln US$). By MDG regions (see graph 2), the largest surpluses in this product group were recorded by Developed North America (+51.4 bln US$), South-eastern Asia (+36.6 bln US$) and Developed Europe (+23.3 bln US$). The largest trade deficits were recorded by Commonwealth of Independent States (-31.4 bln US$), Eastern Asia (-14.3 bln US$) and Developed Asia-Pacific (-6.1 bln US$).

Table 1: Imports (Imp.) and exports (Exp.), 2000-2012, in current US$

		2000	2001	2002	2003	2004	2005	2006	2007	2008	2009	2010	2011	2012
Values in Bln US$	Imp.	413.3	405.9	439.9	494.4	580.5	636.7	675.3	772.9	833.8	759.9	821.1	904.6	951.6
	Exp.	456.1	445.0	472.6	533.6	635.5	690.4	744.8	854.3	935.5	849.6	917.8	1 027.0	1 059.3
As a percentage of world trade (%)	Imp.	28.1	27.2	27.3	26.7	26.4	26.1	24.8	24.0	22.8	22.8	22.6	22.3	22.9
	Exp.	30.9	30.1	29.1	28.3	27.9	27.1	25.9	24.6	24.0	23.9	23.6	23.5	23.8

Graph 1: Annual growth rates of exports, 2000–2012
(In percentage by year)

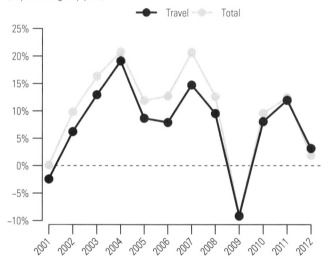

Graph 2: Trade Balance by MDG regions 2012
(Bln US$)

Table 2: Top exporting countries or areas in 2012

Country or area	Value (million US$)	Avg. Growth (%) 08-12	Growth (%) 11-12	World share %	Cum.
World	1 059 335.3	3.2	3.1	100.0	
USA	160 732.6	3.6	8.8	15.2	15.2
Spain	55 936.6	-2.5	-6.6	5.3	20.5
France	53 577.9	-1.3	-2.0	5.1	25.5
China	50 028.0	5.2	3.2	4.7	30.2
China, Macao SAR	43 886.4	26.9	14.1	4.1	34.4
Italy	41 206.3	-2.5	-4.0	3.9	38.3
Germany	38 134.4	-1.0	-1.8	3.6	41.9
United Kingdom	36 613.4	0.4	4.4	3.5	45.3
Thailand	33 785.2	16.8	24.2	3.2	48.5
Australia	31 731.2	6.4	1.3	3.0	51.5
Turkey	25 653.0	2.4	2.4	2.4	53.9
Malaysia	19 695.3	6.5	0.5	1.9	55.8
Singapore	18 938.9	15.5	4.7	1.8	57.6
Austria	18 903.9	-3.2	-4.7	1.8	59.4
India	17 971.8	11.0	1.5	1.7	61.1

Table 3: Top importing countries or areas in 2012

Country or area	Value (million US$)	Avg. Growth (%) 08-12	Growth (%) 11-12	World share %	Cum.
World	951 561.7	3.4	5.2	100.0	
China	101 976.6	29.6	40.5	10.7	10.7
USA	91 918.1	1.3	6.6	9.7	20.4
Germany	83 482.8	-2.0	-2.6	8.8	29.1
United Kingdom	51 473.3	-6.9	0.9	5.4	34.6
Russian Federation	42 797.7	15.8	30.1	4.5	39.1
France	39 084.3	-1.1	-12.8	4.1	43.2
Canada	35 058.5	6.9	5.2	3.7	46.8
Australia	27 968.5	15.2	2.5	2.9	49.8
Japan	27 883.2	0.0	2.5	2.9	52.7
Italy	26 366.2	-3.7	-7.9	2.8	55.5
Singapore	23 649.7	9.7	10.0	2.5	58.0
Brazil	22 232.9	19.3	4.6	2.3	60.3
Belgium	20 198.4	0.7	-1.5	2.1	62.4
Netherlands	20 192.0	-1.9	-1.6	2.1	64.6
Rep. of Korea	20 101.1	1.3	0.8	2.1	66.7

Communications services (EBOPS 2002 code 245)

In 2012, the value (in current US$) of exports of "communications services" (EBOPS 2002 code 245) increased by 5.2 percent (compared to 3.1 percent average growth rate from 2008-2012) to reach 107.0 bln US$ (see table 2), while imports increased by 2.7 percent to reach 88.2 bln US$ (see table 3). Exports of this service accounted for 2.4 percent of total world services exports (see table 1). USA, Germany and United Kingdom were the top exporters in 2012 (see table 2). They accounted for 13.5, 11.2 and 8.9 percent of world exports, respectively. Germany, USA and United Kingdom were the top importers, with respectively 13.1, 9.6 and 8.0 percent of world imports (see table 3).

The top 15 countries/areas accounted for 71.9 and 70.6 percent of total world exports and imports, respectively (see tables 2 and 3). In 2012, USA was the country/area with the highest value of net exports (+5.9 bln US$). By MDG regions (see graph 2), the largest surpluses in this product group were recorded by Developed North America (+6.7 bln US$), Developed Europe (+6.5 bln US$) and Northern Africa (+1.9 bln US$). The largest trade deficits were recorded by Eastern Asia (-722.4 mln US$), Commonwealth of Independent States (-588.2 mln US$) and Oceania (-68.7 mln US$).

Table 1: Imports (Imp.) and exports (Exp.), 2000-2012, in current US$

		2000	2001	2002	2003	2004	2005	2006	2007	2008	2009	2010	2011	2012
Values in Bln US$	Imp.	28.1	29.9	31.8	36.7	44.3	48.1	59.7	68.0	79.0	77.9	80.9	85.8	88.2
	Exp.	27.9	29.2	30.7	37.5	47.9	55.1	68.8	80.4	94.8	89.4	91.5	101.7	107.0
As a percentage of world trade (%)	Imp.	1.9	2.0	2.0	2.0	2.0	2.0	2.2	2.1	2.2	2.3	2.2	2.1	2.1
	Exp.	1.9	2.0	1.9	2.0	2.1	2.2	2.4	2.3	2.4	2.5	2.4	2.3	2.4

Graph 1: Annual growth rates of exports, 2000–2012
(In percentage by year)

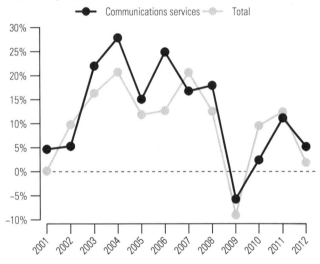

Table 2: Top exporting countries or areas in 2012

Country or area	Value (million US$)	Avg. Growth (%) 08-12	Growth (%) 11-12	World share %	Cum.
World	106 992.1	3.1	5.2	100.0	
USA	14 398.0	8.7	10.1	13.5	13.5
Germany	11 979.2	23.3	108.1	11.2	24.7
United Kingdom	9 490.6	3.7	12.6	8.9	33.5
France	7 293.7	12.8	-8.7	6.8	40.3
Italy	5 688.5	-2.2	-15.8	5.3	45.7
Netherlands	5 127.6	3.1	-13.7	4.8	50.5
Belgium	4 715.1	4.4	-6.1	4.4	54.9
Kuwait	3 445.4	-13.2	-4.4	3.2	58.1
Canada	3 337.7	3.2	5.0	3.1	61.2
Luxembourg	2 560.6	-2.6	-0.4	2.4	63.6
Spain	2 114.3	-1.3	-8.1	2.0	65.6
China	1 793.4	3.4	3.9	1.7	67.2
Sweden	1 773.4	-5.1	-18.4	1.7	68.9
India	1 647 4	-9.7	-1.4	1.5	70.4
Russian Federation	1 550.0	0.9	5.2	1.4	71.9

Graph 2: Trade Balance by MDG regions 2012
(Bln US$)

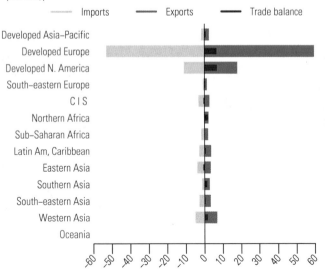

Table 3: Top importing countries or areas in 2012

Country or area	Value (million US$)	Avg. Growth (%) 08-12	Growth (%) 11-12	World share %	Cum.
World	88 177.2	2.8	2.7	100.0	
Germany	11 531.8	13.1	49.5	13.1	13.1
USA	8 449.0	0.3	3.6	9.6	22.7
United Kingdom	7 080.0	0.0	-3.5	8.0	30.7
Italy	5 604.8	-3.9	-12.7	6.4	37.0
France	4 825.6	11.3	0.8	5.5	42.5
Netherlands	4 443.4	2.9	-6.6	5.0	47.6
Belgium	3 699.5	5.2	-3.0	4.2	51.8
Spain	2 688.1	-5.3	-5.1	3.0	54.8
Canada	2 612.1	9.4	-7.6	3.0	57.8
Russian Federation	2 538.1	7.8	0.3	2.9	60.6
Sweden	2 104.8	-0.1	-13.3	2.4	63.0
Saudi Arabia	2 026.9	12.4	-22.0	2.3	65.3
China	1 647.2	2.2	38.4	1.9	67.2
Rep. of Korea	1 612.6	8.8	4.7	1.8	69.0
Ireland	1 399.9	-2.7	3.1	1.6	70.6

In 2012, the value (in current US$) of exports of "construction services" (EBOPS 2002 code 249) increased by 2.8 percent (compared to an average growth rate of less than 0.1 percent from 2008-2012) to reach 105.4 bln US$ (see table 2), while imports increased by 7.7 percent to reach 87.6 bln US$ (see table 3). Exports of this service accounted for 2.4 percent of total world services exports (see table 1). Rep. of Korea, China and Japan were the top exporters in 2012 (see table 2). They accounted for 20.8, 11.6 and 11.0 percent of world exports, respectively. Germany, Japan and Russian Federation were the top importers, with respectively 9.0, 8.9 and 8.7 percent of world imports (see table 3).

The top 15 countries/areas accounted for 83.4 and 69.3 percent of total world exports and imports, respectively (see tables 2 and 3). In 2012, Rep. of Korea was the country/area with the highest value of net exports (+16.8 bln US$), followed by China (+8.6 bln US$). By MDG regions (see graph 2), the largest surpluses in this product group were recorded by Eastern Asia (+24.7 bln US$), Developed Europe (+10.2 bln US$) and Developed Asia-Pacific (+3.8 bln US$). The largest trade deficits were recorded by Sub-Saharan Africa (-8.8 bln US$), Commonwealth of Independent States (-5.8 bln US$) and Western Asia (-3.7 bln US$).

Table 1: Imports (Imp.) and exports (Exp.), 2000-2012, in current US$

		2000	2001	2002	2003	2004	2005	2006	2007	2008	2009	2010	2011	2012
Values in Bln US$	Imp.	21.4	24.1	27.0	30.2	40.7	47.7	58.0	76.1	90.4	85.0	75.4	81.3	87.6
	Exp.	27.1	28.2	32.5	35.3	44.1	53.8	65.2	81.1	105.3	101.2	95.0	102.5	105.4
As a percentage of world trade (%)	Imp.	1.5	1.6	1.7	1.6	1.9	2.0	2.1	2.4	2.5	2.6	2.1	2.0	2.1
	Exp.	1.8	1.9	2.0	1.9	1.9	2.1	2.3	2.3	2.7	2.9	2.4	2.3	2.4

Graph 1: Annual growth rates of exports, 2000–2012
(In percentage by year)

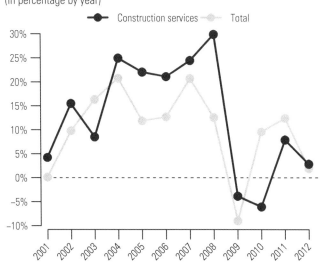

Table 2: Top exporting countries or areas in 2012

Country or area	Value (million US$)	Avg. Growth (%) 08-12	Growth (%) 11-12	World share %	Cum.
World....................	105 362.5	0.0	2.8	100.0	
Rep. of Korea..........	21 904.9	12.5	41.5	20.8	20.8
China......................	12 245.9	4.3	-16.8	11.6	32.4
Japan......................	11 585.1	-4.1	5.8	11.0	43.4
Germany..................	10 503.5	-10.1	-17.4	10.0	53.4
Spain......................	4 984.3	-2.0	13.3	4.7	58.1
France....................	4 745.9	-8.0	-20.9	4.5	62.6
Russian Federation....	4 728.7	0.4	7.3	4.5	67.1
USA........................	3 335.0	-3.7	2.7	3.2	70.3
Netherlands.............	3 001.3	-2.0	10.6	2.8	73.1
Belgium..................	2 414.1	0.9	-15.5	2.3	75.4
United Kingdom........	2 383.7	1.0	-1.7	2.3	77.7
Singapore................	1 605.5	10.3	4.0	1.5	79.2
Poland....................	1 582.4	-4.4	-1.8	1.5	80.7
Finland...................	1 461.9	2.6	90.1	1.4	82.1
Turkey....................	1 371.0	4.6	10.1	1.3	83.4

Graph 2: Trade Balance by MDG regions 2012
(Bln US$)

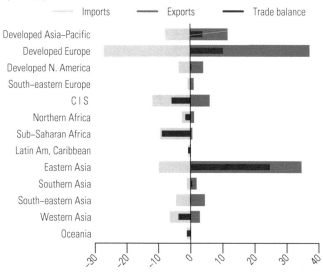

Table 3: Top importing countries or areas in 2012

Country or area	Value (million US$)	Avg. Growth (%) 08-12	Growth (%) 11-12	World share %	Cum.
World....................	87 572.1	-0.8	7.7	100.0	
Germany..................	7 913.3	-8.7	-0.7	9.0	9.0
Japan......................	7 755.3	-9.0	0.7	8.9	17.9
Russian Federation....	7 594.2	-3.7	35.6	8.7	26.6
Angola....................	6 229.9	5.6	-21.5	7.1	33.7
Rep. of Korea..........	5 153.0	18.6	35.8	5.9	39.6
China......................	3 618.7	-4.6	-2.9	4.1	43.7
USA........................	3 276.0	-1.3	10.5	3.7	47.4
Kazakhstan..............	2 755.4	-3.6	45.1	3.1	50.6
Saudi Arabia............	2 728.8	-11.7	5.8	3.1	53.7
Netherlands.............	2 515.2	9.3	15.4	2.9	56.6
France....................	2 397.4	-1.8	-23.2	2.7	59.3
Kuwait....................	2 378.0	20.8	63.2	2.7	62.0
United Kingdom........	2 304.7	3.4	22.0	2.6	64.7
Malaysia.................	2 046.9	9.5	51.6	2.3	67.0
Algeria...................	2 037.4	-6.5	2.5	2.3	69.3

Insurance services (EBOPS 2002 code 253)

In 2012, the value (in current US$) of exports of "insurance services" (EBOPS 2002 code 253) decreased by 1.0 percent (compared to 6.6 percent average growth rate from 2008-2012) to reach 102.4 bln US$ (see table 2), while imports increased by 0.4 percent to reach 170.1 bln US$ (see table 3). Exports of this service accounted for 2.3 percent of total world services exports (see table 1). United Kingdom, USA and Ireland were the top exporters in 2012 (see table 2). They accounted for 23.3, 15.7 and 11.2 percent of world exports, respectively. USA, China and Ireland were the top importers, with respectively 30.9, 12.1 and 4.7 percent of world imports (see table 3).

The top 15 countries/areas accounted for 85.7 and 74.8 percent of total world exports and imports, respectively (see tables 2 and 3). In 2012, United Kingdom was the country/area with the highest value of net exports (+18.3 bln US$), followed by Switzerland and Liechtenstein (+4.8 bln US$). By MDG regions (see graph 2), the largest surpluses in this product group were recorded by Developed Europe (+27.9 bln US$) and Southern Asia (+573.5 mln US$). The largest trade deficits were recorded by Developed North America (-40.3 bln US$), Eastern Asia (-18.4 bln US$) and Developed Asia-Pacific (-8.5 bln US$).

Table 1: Imports (Imp.) and exports (Exp.), 2000-2012, in current US$

		2000	2001	2002	2003	2004	2005	2006	2007	2008	2009	2010	2011	2012
Values in Bln US$	Imp.	35.2	46.5	59.5	75.4	84.9	88.1	109.4	129.4	153.4	156.6	164.5	169.5	170.1
	Exp.	24.0	27.0	40.9	51.7	51.4	44.3	57.8	71.6	79.4	94.7	94.2	103.5	102.4
As a percentage of world trade (%)	Imp.	2.4	3.1	3.7	4.1	3.9	3.6	4.0	4.0	4.2	4.7	4.5	4.2	4.1
	Exp.	1.6	1.8	2.5	2.7	2.3	1.7	2.0	2.1	2.0	2.7	2.4	2.4	2.3

Graph 1: Annual growth rates of exports, 2000–2012
(In percentage by year)

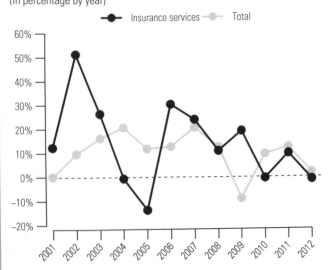

Graph 2: Trade Balance by MDG regions 2012
(Bln US$)

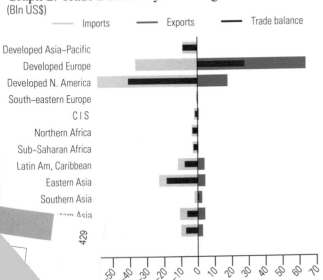

Table 2: Top exporting countries or areas in 2012

Country or area	Value (million US$)	Avg. Growth (%) 08-12	Growth (%) 11-12	World share %	Cum.
World	102 406.4	6.6	-1.0	100.0	
United Kingdom	23 818.1	23.4	-6.1	23.3	23.3
USA	16 067.0	4.6	7.4	15.7	38.9
Ireland	11 453.4	-1.0	2.3	11.2	50.1
Switzerland	5 873.5	-0.3	2.1	5.7	55.9
Germany	5 620.0	5.2	-8.3	5.5	61.4
China	3 329.2	24.6	10.3	3.3	64.6
Luxembourg	3 265.7	0.8	0.9	3.2	67.8
Singapore	3 253.1	12.8	11.1	3.2	71.0
France	3 196.9	40.2	-22.2	3.1	74.1
Italy	2 939.1	-6.4	25.1	2.9	77.0
India	2 257.0	9.7	-12.7	2.2	79.2
Mexico	2 014.9	0.1	-10.9	2.0	81.1
Canada	1 879.5	13.4	-14.4	1.8	83.0
Spain	1 607.9	3.2	14.5	1.6	84.5
Belgium	1 158.2	-2.1	-5.0	1.1	85.7

Table 3: Top importing countries or areas in 2012

Country or area	Value (million US$)	Avg. Growth (%) 08-12	Growth (%) 11-12	World share %	Cum.
World	170 122.6	2.6	0.4	100.0	
USA	52 564.0	-2.8	-5.8	30.9	30.9
China	20 600.1	12.8	4.4	12.1	43.0
Ireland	8 047.0	-3.3	-3.3	4.7	47.7
Japan	7 382.6	9.6	8.5	4.3	52.1
Canada	5 654.6	15.4	20.1	3.3	55.4
United Kingdom	5 533.6	28.4	19.1	3.3	58.7
Singapore	4 571.1	13.4	0.6	2.7	61.3
Italy	3 863.3	-9.6	1.3	2.3	63.6
Mexico	3 848.2	8.9	-5.8	2.3	65.9
Germany	3 609.6	-3.9	-20.7	2.1	68.0
Thailand	3 071.7	9.8	11.6	1.8	69.8
Iraq	2 402.0	14.3	24.1	1.4	71.2
Saudi Arabia	2 300.4	6.0	18.0	1.4	72.6
Spain	1 902.6	-3.4	-8.9	1.1	73.7
Luxembourg	1 861.7	-0.2	2.2	1.1	74.8

In 2012, the value (in current US$) of exports of "financial services" (EBOPS 2002 code 260) decreased by 2.8 percent (compared to 0.8 percent average growth rate from 2008-2012) to reach 292.8 bln US$ (see table 2), while imports decreased by 4.6 percent to reach 127.0 bln US$ (see table 3). Exports of this service accounted for 6.6 percent of total world services exports (see table 1). USA, United Kingdom and Luxembourg were the top exporters in 2012 (see table 2). They accounted for 26.1, 20.2 and 13.7 percent of world exports, respectively. Luxembourg, USA and United Kingdom were the top importers, with respectively 16.2, 13.3 and 8.3 percent of world imports (see table 3).

The top 15 countries/areas accounted for 91.1 and 78.4 percent of total world exports and imports, respectively (see tables 2 and 3). In 2012, USA was the country/area with the highest value of net exports (+59.5 bln US$), followed by United Kingdom (+48.4 bln US$). By MDG regions (see graph 2), the largest surpluses in this product group were recorded by Developed Europe (+93.7 bln US$), Developed North America (+60.2 bln US$) and South-eastern Asia (+12.8 bln US$). The largest trade deficits were recorded by Commonwealth of Independent States (-2.2 bln US$), Western Asia (-2.2 bln US$) and Latin America and the Caribbean (-463.1 mln US$).

Table 1: Imports (Imp.) and exports (Exp.), 2000-2012, in current US$

		2000	2001	2002	2003	2004	2005	2006	2007	2008	2009	2010	2011	2012
Values in Bln US$	Imp.	44.4	42.4	43.2	49.2	63.2	76.7	99.7	118.6	119.8	102.4	115.5	133.2	127.0
	Exp.	85.6	81.8	89.1	108.6	139.5	166.6	209.9	282.0	283.4	249.1	265.5	301.2	292.8
As a percentage of world trade (%)	Imp.	3.0	2.8	2.7	2.7	2.9	3.1	3.7	3.7	3.3	3.1	3.2	3.3	3.1
	Exp.	5.8	5.5	5.5	5.8	6.1	6.5	7.3	8.1	7.3	7.0	6.8	6.9	6.6

Graph 1: Annual growth rates of exports, 2000–2012
(In percentage by year)

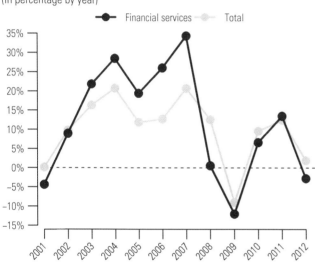

Table 2: Top exporting countries or areas in 2012

Country or area	Value (million US$)	Avg. Growth (%) 08-12	Growth (%) 11-12	World share %	Cum.
World	292 819.4	0.8	-2.8	100.0	
USA	76 418.0	4.9	-2.3	26.1	26.1
United Kingdom	59 032.0	-4.9	-5.4	20.2	46.3
Luxembourg	40 055.1	-0.8	-2.9	13.7	59.9
Singapore	16 496.6	10.4	8.7	5.6	65.6
Switzerland	16 075.2	-4.4	-5.5	5.5	71.1
Germany	14 343.1	1.4	-4.5	4.9	76.0
Ireland	9 092.0	-1.5	-0.8	3.1	79.1
France	6 507.0	35.0	-12.3	2.2	81.3
India	5 351.2	5.7	-14.4	1.8	83.1
Japan	4 644.3	-3.9	13.0	1.6	84.7
Canada	4 590.7	9.4	6.8	1.6	86.3
Spain	4 414.9	-6.0	-15.3	1.5	87.8
Belgium	3 830.7	2.0	7.6	1.3	89.1
Rep. of Korea	3 192.0	-4.2	-5.8	1.1	90.2
Italy	2 762.1	-2.2	6.5	0.9	91.1

Graph 2: Trade Balance by MDG regions 2012
(Bln US$)

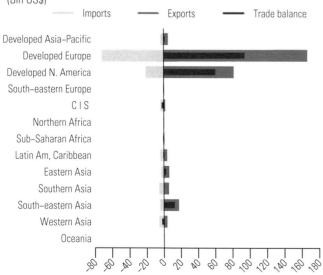

Table 3: Top importing countries or areas in 2012

Country or area	Value (million US$)	Avg. Growth (%) 08-12	Growth (%) 11-12	World share %	Cum.
World	127 029.5	1.5	-4.6	100.0	
Luxembourg	20 618.4	0.5	-3.5	16.2	16.2
USA	16 952.0	-0.4	-3.5	13.3	29.6
United Kingdom	10 604.3	-6.7	-13.5	8.3	37.9
Germany	7 792.4	0.0	-18.9	6.1	44.1
Ireland	5 923.4	-2.4	-9.5	4.7	48.7
Spain	5 400.7	0.6	7.1	4.3	53.0
India	5 343.0	10.8	-35.6	4.2	57.2
Italy	5 087.2	7.5	-3.1	4.0	61.2
France	4 509.4	23.9	-0.7	3.5	64.7
Canada	4 020.3	0.4	-4.2	3.2	67.9
Japan	3 224.2	-5.1	-3.6	2.5	70.4
Singapore	3 135.1	5.6	3.3	2.5	72.9
Russian Federation	2 774.6	7.5	14.2	2.2	75.1
Belgium	2 185.3	-4.9	-0.2	1.7	76.8
Norway	2 050.7	15.9	9.3	1.6	78.4

Computer and information services (EBOPS 2002 code 262)

In 2012, the value (in current US$) of exports of "computer and information services" (EBOPS 2002 code 262) increased by 5.4 percent (compared to 7.1 percent average growth rate from 2008-2012) to reach 269.7 bln US$ (see table 2), while imports increased by 4.8 percent to reach 128.7 bln US$ (see table 3). Exports of this service accounted for 6.1 percent of total world services exports (see table 1). India, Ireland and Germany were the top exporters in 2012 (see table 2). They accounted for 24.3, 17.0 and 7.5 percent of world exports, respectively. USA, Germany and France were the top importers, with respectively 19.9, 13.4 and 6.4 percent of world imports (see table 3).

The top 15 countries/areas accounted for 86.2 and 78.4 percent of total world exports and imports, respectively (see tables 2 and 3). In 2012, India was the country/area with the highest value of net exports (+63.0 bln US$), followed by Ireland (+45.4 bln US$). By MDG regions (see graph 2), the largest surpluses in this product group were recorded by Developed Europe (+69.4 bln US$), Southern Asia (+63.6 bln US$) and Eastern Asia (+10.5 bln US$). The largest trade deficits were recorded by Developed North America (-4.2 bln US$), Developed Asia-Pacific (-3.4 bln US$) and Latin America and the Caribbean (-1.4 bln US$).

Table 1: Imports (Imp.) and exports (Exp.), 2000-2012, in current US$

		2000	2001	2002	2003	2004	2005	2006	2007	2008	2009	2010	2011	2012
Values in Bln US$	Imp.	26.4	29.9	33.2	37.8	48.3	56.7	69.3	84.5	100.2	99.8	106.9	122.9	128.7
	Exp.	31.3	44.8	52.2	68.7	92.4	104.5	130.9	163.7	204.9	199.0	223.8	255.8	269.7
As a percentage of world trade (%)	Imp.	1.8	2.0	2.1	2.0	2.2	2.3	2.6	2.6	2.7	3.0	2.9	3.0	3.1
	Exp.	2.1	3.0	3.2	3.6	4.1	4.1	4.6	4.7	5.3	5.6	5.8	5.9	6.1

Graph 1: Annual growth rates of exports, 2000–2012
(In percentage by year)

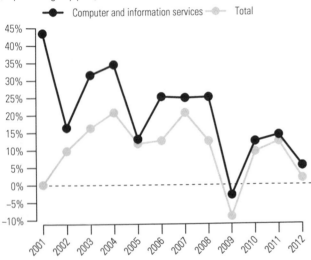

Graph 2: Trade Balance by MDG regions 2012
(Bln US$)

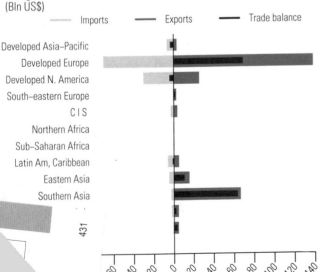

Table 2: Top exporting countries or areas in 2012

Country or area	Value (million US$)	Avg. Growth (%) 08-12	Growth (%) 11-12	World share %	Cum.
World............................	269 669.9	7.1	5.4	100.0	
India..............................	65 558.8	7.5	8.5	24.3	24.3
Ireland..........................	45 866.4	7.0	5.0	17.0	41.3
Germany........................	20 308.9	7.0	4.3	7.5	48.9
USA...............................	17 340.0	7.2	3.0	6.4	55.3
United Kingdom..............	14 926.2	2.6	6.1	5.5	60.8
China............................	14 453.5	23.3	18.6	5.4	66.2
Canada..........................	8 230.7	9.3	2.5	3.1	69.2
Sweden..........................	8 037.5	0.7	-7.5	3.0	72.2
Spain.............................	6 502.2	1.4	-6.8	2.4	74.6
Netherlands....................	6 499.2	-0.9	3.1	2.4	77.0
France...........................	6 251.2	35.8	-10.3	2.3	79.3
Finland..........................	5 832.3	-8.4	-13.4	2.2	81.5
Belgium.........................	5 316.7	10.1	8.6	2.0	83.5
Israel.............................	4 311.3	6.6	14.9	1.6	85.1
Austria...........................	3 132.7	9.7	20.6	1.2	86.2

Table 3: Top importing countries or areas in 2012

Country or area	Value (million US$)	Avg. Growth (%) 08-12	Growth (%) 11-12	World share %	Cum.
World............................	128 740.3	6.5	4.8	100.0	
USA...............................	25 657.0	11.0	5.4	19.9	19.9
Germany........................	17 265.0	5.8	3.6	13.4	33.3
France...........................	8 296.3	38.6	3.6	6.4	39.8
United Kingdom..............	6 822.6	1.5	5.1	5.3	45.1
Netherlands....................	5 364.0	-2.0	1.7	4.2	49.3
Italy..............................	4 569.9	0.4	1.2	3.5	52.8
Japan............................	4 495.6	3.2	6.6	3.5	56.3
Brazil............................	4 446.5	12.4	10.2	3.5	59.7
Belgium.........................	4 109.6	9.4	10.5	3.2	62.9
Canada..........................	4 088.3	11.6	14.3	3.2	66.1
Sweden..........................	3 873.6	4.1	14.3	3.0	69.1
China............................	3 843.2	5.0	0.0	3.0	72.1
Spain.............................	2 983.8	1.2	-7.6	2.3	74.4
Russian Federation..........	2 650.8	16.8	9.0	2.1	76.5
India..............................	2 518.0	-9.7	35.6	2.0	78.4

431

Royalties and license fees (EBOPS 2002 code 266)

In 2012, the value (in current US$) of exports of "royalties and license fees" (EBOPS 2002 code 266) increased by 1.0 percent (compared to 6.3 percent average growth rate from 2008-2012) to reach 292.5 bln US$ (see table 2), while imports increased by 4.4 percent to reach 303.8 bln US$ (see table 3). Exports of this service accounted for 6.6 percent of total world services exports (see table 1). USA was the top exporter in 2012, alone accounting for 42.5 percent of world exports, followed by Japan and Netherlands, each accounting for 10.9 and 10.6 percent, respectively (see table 2). Ireland, USA and Switzerland were the top importers, with respectively 13.9, 13.1 and 7.9 percent of world imports (see table 3).

The top 15 countries/areas accounted for 95.0 and 83.4 percent of total world exports and imports, respectively (see tables 2 and 3). In 2012, USA was the country/area with the highest value of net exports (+84.3 bln US$), followed by Japan (+12.0 bln US$). By MDG regions (see graph 2), the largest surpluses in this product group were recorded by Developed North America (+77.4 bln US$) and Developed Asia-Pacific (+8.0 bln US$). The largest trade deficits were recorded by Eastern Asia (-25.4 bln US$), Developed Europe (-25.2 bln US$) and South-eastern Asia (-24.5 bln US$).

Table 1: Imports (Imp.) and exports (Exp.), 2000-2012, in current US$

		2000	2001	2002	2003	2004	2005	2006	2007	2008	2009	2010	2011	2012
Values in Bln US$	Imp.	74.6	76.0	84.1	101.8	137.6	149.4	164.2	187.2	233.8	245.3	264.4	291.0	303.8
	Exp.	83.4	81.0	88.4	104.3	138.2	156.2	174.4	203.5	229.5	235.3	254.7	289.6	292.5
As a percentage of world trade (%)	Imp.	5.1	5.1	5.2	5.5	6.3	6.1	6.0	5.8	6.4	7.4	7.3	7.2	7.3
	Exp.	5.6	5.5	5.4	5.5	6.1	6.1	6.1	5.9	5.9	6.6	6.5	6.6	6.6

Graph 1: Annual growth rates of exports, 2000–2012
(In percentage by year)

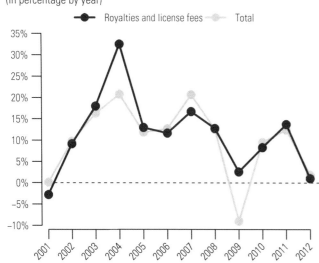

Table 2: Top exporting countries or areas in 2012

Country or area	Value (million US$)	Avg. Growth (%) 08-12	Growth (%) 11-12	World share %	Cum.
World	292 490.3	6.3	1.0	100.0	
USA	124 182.0	5.0	2.9	42.5	42.5
Japan	31 889.6	5.6	9.7	10.9	53.4
Netherlands	30 866.8	11.8	-0.1	10.6	63.9
Switzerland	20 459.4	15.8	4.1	7.0	70.9
Germany	13 848.2	5.9	-6.5	4.7	75.6
United Kingdom	12 626.2	-3.7	-10.3	4.3	80.0
France	12 386.7	2.7	-23.2	4.2	84.2
Sweden	6 728.8	9.5	6.8	2.3	86.5
Ireland	4 997.9	35.3	-0.2	1.7	88.2
Italy	4 065.7	0.5	2.3	1.4	89.6
Canada	3 994.2	-0.7	19.4	1.4	91.0
Rep. of Korea	3 435.5	9.6	-20.8	1.2	92.1
Finland	3 310.7	22.4	2.8	1.1	93.3
Belgium	2 658.3	15.2	4.6	0.9	94.2
Denmark	2 403.6	-3.4	-3.1	0.8	95.0

Graph 2: Trade Balance by MDG regions 2012
(Bln US$)

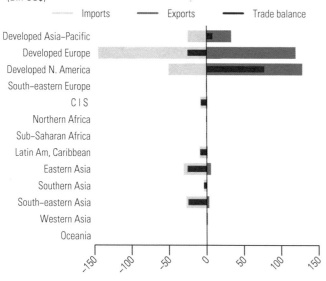

Table 3: Top importing countries or areas in 2012

Country or area	Value (million US$)	Avg. Growth (%) 08-12	Growth (%) 11-12	World share %	Cum.
World	303 845.6	6.8	4.4	100.0	
Ireland	42 105.2	4.3	3.2	13.9	13.9
USA	39 889.0	7.7	14.7	13.1	27.0
Switzerland	23 977.5	23.3	8.2	7.9	34.9
Netherlands	22 243.7	11.5	2.4	7.3	42.2
Japan	19 896.7	2.1	3.9	6.5	48.7
Singapore	19 854.3	10.1	4.1	6.5	55.3
China	17 749.0	14.5	20.7	5.8	61.1
Germany	12 190.0	-1.5	-7.4	4.0	65.1
Canada	10 854.8	5.0	4.3	3.6	68.7
France	9 575.4	15.0	-13.1	3.2	71.9
United Kingdom	8 408.5	-5.6	-20.1	2.8	74.6
Rep. of Korea	8 386.9	10.4	15.0	2.8	77.4
Russian Federation	7 629.3	13.5	30.9	2.5	79.9
Italy	6 050.7	-6.2	-13.5	2.0	81.9
Other Asia, nes	4 549.0	10.8	-21.4	1.5	83.4

Other business services (EBOPS 2002 code 268)

In 2012, "other business services" (EBOPS 2002 code 268) was the largest exported service category, accounting for 24.2 percent of total world services exports (see table 1). The value (in current US$) of exports of this service category increased by 1.9 percent (compared to 5.2 percent average growth rate from 2008-2012) to reach 1076.2 bln US$ (see table 2), while imports increased by 0.6 percent to reach 961.1 bln US$ (see table 3). USA, Germany and United Kingdom were the top exporters in 2012 (see table 2). They accounted for 12.5, 8.5 and 8.3 percent of world exports, respectively. USA, Germany and France were the top importers, with respectively 9.1, 8.4 and 5.6 percent of world imports (see table 3).

The top 15 countries/areas accounted for 72.5 and 69.6 percent of total world exports and imports, respectively (see tables 2 and 3). In 2012, USA was the country/area with the highest value of net exports (+46.6 bln US$), followed by United Kingdom (+40.2 bln US$). By MDG regions (see graph 2), the largest surpluses in this product group were recorded by Developed Europe (+114.0 bln US$), Developed North America (+53.6 bln US$) and Eastern Asia (+11.7 bln US$). The largest trade deficits were recorded by Sub-Saharan Africa (-19.5 bln US$), Latin America and the Caribbean (-10.8 bln US$) and Developed Asia-Pacific (-10.5 bln US$).

Table 1: Imports (Imp.) and exports (Exp.), 2000-2012, in current US$

		2000	2001	2002	2003	2004	2005	2006	2007	2008	2009	2010	2011	2012
Values in Bln US$	Imp.	278.3	300.6	332.6	383.9	453.4	493.3	583.3	706.3	811.2	778.3	821.9	955.0	961.1
	Exp.	274.8	290.8	326.5	391.1	469.2	541.7	638.3	784.2	879.6	842.4	917.0	1056.5	1076.2
As a percentage of world trade (%)	Imp.	18.9	20.2	20.6	20.7	20.7	20.2	21.5	22.0	22.2	23.4	22.6	23.5	23.1
	Exp.	18.6	19.7	20.1	20.7	20.6	21.2	22.2	22.6	22.5	23.7	23.6	24.2	24.2

Graph 1: Annual growth rates of exports, 2000–2012
(In percentage by year)

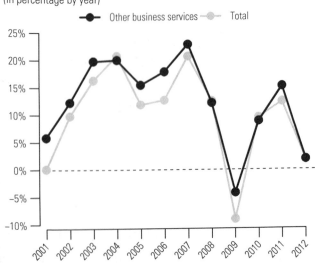

Legend: ● Other business services ─ Total

Graph 2: Trade Balance by MDG regions 2012
(Bln US$)

Legend: Imports — Exports — Trade balance

Developed Asia-Pacific, Developed Europe, Developed N. America, South-eastern Europe, CIS, Northern Africa, Sub-Saharan Africa, Latin Am, Caribbean, Eastern Asia, Southern Asia, ... Asia

(axis: -400 -300 -200 -100 0 100 200 300 400 500 600)

433

Table 2: Top exporting countries or areas in 2012

Country or area	Value (million US$)	Avg. Growth (%) 08-12	Growth (%) 11-12	World share %	Cum.
World.....................	1076243.3	5.2	1.9	100.0	
USA........................	134225.4	8.1	9.4	12.5	12.5
Germany..................	91969.4	3.3	-1.6	8.5	21.0
United Kingdom...........	89235.1	2.6	-0.9	8.3	29.3
France.....................	71327.5	16.9	-10.3	6.6	35.9
China.......................	66622.5	9.5	-1.8	6.2	42.1
Netherlands...............	39617.2	-1.4	-7.0	3.7	45.8
Belgium....................	38487.9	6.2	10.5	3.6	49.4
Japan......................	37519.2	-2.2	-17.3	3.5	52.9
Spain......................	34561.1	1.1	-1.7	3.2	56.1
Ireland....................	33334.5	3.2	2.6	3.1	59.2
Italy.......................	29960.0	-0.2	0.6	2.8	62.0
Sweden....................	28967.0	1.9	3.9	2.7	64.7
India......................	28842.0	11.2	20.5	2.7	67.3
Canada....................	28272.9	4.7	8.1	2.6	70.0
Singapore.................	26889.2	9.7	15.0	2.5	72.5

Table 3: Top importing countries or areas in 2012

Country or area	Value (million US$)	Avg. Growth (%) 08-12	Growth (%) 11-12	World share %	Cum.
World.....................	961060.7	4.3	0.6	100.0	
USA........................	87620.9	7.7	3.3	9.1	9.1
Germany..................	80629.1	4.4	2.5	8.4	17.5
France.....................	53576.6	10.4	-7.9	5.6	23.1
United Kingdom...........	49037.4	0.9	5.3	5.1	28.2
Japan......................	46549.0	3.6	1.4	4.8	33.0
Ireland....................	45700.6	1.2	-6.0	4.8	37.8
China.......................	42353.6	2.3	-13.9	4.4	42.2
Netherlands...............	39849.0	1.6	-3.5	4.1	46.3
Rep. of Korea.............	38132.2	8.8	10.0	4.0	50.3
India......................	35277.6	14.8	15.3	3.7	54.0
Spain......................	33761.5	-1.5	-1.3	3.5	57.5
Belgium....................	30890.8	5.4	12.9	3.2	60.7
Singapore.................	30072.6	7.7	11.0	3.1	63.8
Brazil......................	28345.6	20.2	11.7	2.9	66.8
Italy.......................	27426.7	-6.7	-8.4	2.9	69.6

Personal, cultural, and recreational services (EBOPS 2002 code 287)

In 2012, the value (in current US$) of exports of "personal, cultural, and recreational services" (EBOPS 2002 code 287) increased by 5.1 percent (compared to 8.9 percent average growth rate from 2008-2012) to reach 36.7 bln US$ (see table 2), while imports increased by 2.9 percent to reach 43.4 bln US$ (see table 3). Exports of this service accounted for 0.8 percent of total world services exports (see table 1). United Kingdom, France and Luxembourg were the top exporters in 2012 (see table 2). They accounted for 14.6, 13.6 and 9.2 percent of world exports, respectively. France, Venezuela and Canada were the top importers, with respectively 10.4, 8.6 and 6.0 percent of world imports (see table 3).

The top 15 countries/areas accounted for 76.9 and 66.2 percent of total world exports and imports, respectively (see tables 2 and 3). In 2012, United Kingdom was the country/area with the highest value of net exports (+4.7 bln US$), followed by Luxembourg (+1.3 bln US$). By MDG regions (see graph 2), the largest surpluses in this product group were recorded by Developed Europe (+1.8 bln US$), Developed North America (+215.3 mln US$) and Southern Asia (+214.0 mln US$). The largest trade deficits were recorded by Latin America and the Caribbean (-5.2 bln US$), Developed Asia-Pacific (-1.3 bln US$) and Commonwealth of Independent States (-718.5 mln US$).

Table 1: Imports (Imp.) and exports (Exp.), 2000-2012, in current US$

		2000	2001	2002	2003	2004	2005	2006	2007	2008	2009	2010	2011	2012
Values in Bln US$	Imp.	16.9	16.6	15.5	17.4	23.6	24.9	29.4	31.9	34.1	30.0	33.7	42.2	43.4
	Exp.	12.3	10.5	12.4	13.8	18.8	20.2	21.7	24.3	26.1	24.7	29.9	34.9	36.7
As a percentage of world trade (%)	Imp.	1.1	1.1	1.0	0.9	1.1	1.0	1.1	1.0	0.9	0.9	0.9	1.0	1.0
	Exp.	0.8	0.7	0.8	0.7	0.8	0.8	0.8	0.7	0.7	0.7	0.8	0.8	0.8

Graph 1: Annual growth rates of exports, 2000–2012
(In percentage by year)

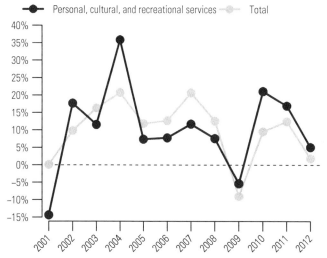

Table 2: Top exporting countries or areas in 2012

Country or area	Value (million US$)	Avg. Growth (%) 08-12	Growth (%) 11-12	World share %	Cum.
World................................	36716.3	8.9	5.1	100.0	
United Kingdom....................	5378.7	6.4	4.4	14.6	14.6
France...............................	4983.7	22.4	-0.7	13.6	28.2
Luxembourg........................	3359.8	39.5	6.3	9.2	37.4
Canada..............................	2900.4	4.8	18.8	7.9	45.3
Spain................................	2276.2	6.5	4.8	6.2	51.5
Hungary.............................	1389.5	8.7	-8.3	3.8	55.3
Rep. of Korea......................	1252.6	24.1	34.8	3.4	58.7
Turkey...............................	1216.0	-0.2	-4.0	3.3	62.0
Germany............................	939.7	-3.8	-11.8	2.6	64.5
Australia............................	909.1	8.5	3.1	2.5	67.0
Belgium.............................	776.4	7.7	-1.5	2.1	69.1
India.................................	766.7	2.0	121.8	2.1	71.2
USA..................................	760.0	0.4	-7.8	2.1	73.3
Netherlands........................	721.5	-1.2	-8.8	2.0	75.3
New Zealand.......................	586.6	12.2	36.2	1.6	76.9

Graph 2: Trade Balance by MDG regions 2012
(Bln US$)

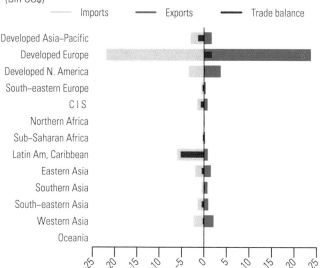

Table 3: Top importing countries or areas in 2012

Country or area	Value (million US$)	Avg. Growth (%) 08-12	Growth (%) 11-12	World share %	Cum.
World................................	43394.9	6.2	2.9	100.0	
France...............................	4508.1	5.4	2.6	10.4	10.4
Venezuela..........................	3747.0	45.3	2.6	8.6	19.0
Canada..............................	2617.1	4.5	13.8	6.0	25.1
Germany............................	2532.4	-3.7	-10.9	5.8	30.9
Luxembourg........................	2098.9	26.7	-14.0	4.8	35.7
Spain................................	1910.3	-7.6	-8.3	4.4	40.1
Australia............................	1689.8	8.5	2.5	3.9	44.0
Norway..............................	1572.8	23.3	0.8	3.6	47.6
Qatar................................	1398.4	...	-2.1	3.2	50.9
Japan................................	1198.9	-0.4	22.7	2.8	53.6
Rep. of Korea......................	1167.1	7.0	14.0	2.7	56.3
Russian Federation...............	1117.2	7.5	5.5	2.6	58.9
Austria..............................	1063.1	2.8	5.9	2.4	61.3
Poland...............................	1056.6	34.3	-2.2	2.4	63.8
Brazil................................	1034.0	4.4	-7.8	2.4	66.2

Government services, n.i.e. (EBOPS 2002 code 291)

In 2012, the value (in current US$) of exports of "government services, n.i.e." (EBOPS 2002 code 291) decreased by 0.7 percent (compared to 2.0 percent average growth rate from 2008-2012) to reach 72.6 bln US$ (see table 2), while imports decreased by 7.8 percent to reach 102.3 bln US$ (see table 3). Exports of this service accounted for 1.6 percent of total world services exports (see table 1). USA, Germany and United Kingdom were the top exporters in 2012 (see table 2). They accounted for 29.2, 6.9 and 4.8 percent of world exports, respectively. USA, Saudi Arabia and United Kingdom were the top importers, with respectively 27.2, 23.0 and 6.1 percent of world imports (see table 3).

The top 15 countries/areas accounted for 70.8 and 78.2 percent of total world exports and imports, respectively (see tables 2 and 3). In 2012, Germany was the country/area with the highest value of net exports (+3.9 bln US$), followed by Pakistan (+2.5 bln US$). By MDG regions (see graph 2), the largest surpluses in this product group were recorded by Developed Europe (+8.3 bln US$), Southern Asia (+3.3 bln US$) and Developed Asia-Pacific (+1.2 bln US$). The largest trade deficits were recorded by Western Asia (-25.2 bln US$), Developed North America (-6.4 bln US$) and Latin America and the Caribbean (-6.2 bln US$).

Table 1: Imports (Imp.) and exports (Exp.), 2000-2012, in current US$

		2000	2001	2002	2003	2004	2005	2006	2007	2008	2009	2010	2011	2012
Values in Bln US$	Imp.	52.9	52.1	59.5	67.3	73.1	78.1	89.8	94.4	107.1	111.1	113.0	111.0	102.3
	Exp.	26.4	27.5	32.6	41.3	47.8	54.0	61.0	66.5	66.9	64.7	65.6	73.1	72.6
As a percentage of world trade (%)	Imp.	3.6	3.5	3.7	3.6	3.3	3.2	3.3	2.9	2.9	3.3	3.1	2.7	2.5
	Exp.	1.8	1.9	2.0	2.2	2.1	2.1	2.1	1.9	1.7	1.8	1.7	1.7	1.6

Graph 1: Annual growth rates of exports, 2000–2012
(In percentage by year)

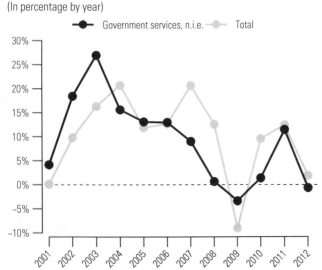

Graph 2: Trade Balance by MDG regions 2012
(Bln US$)

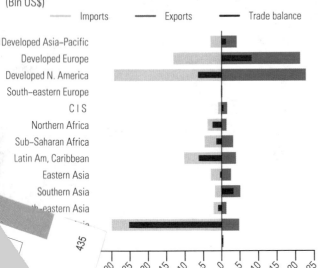

Table 2: Top exporting countries or areas in 2012

Country or area	Value (million US$)	Avg. Growth (%) 08-12	Growth (%) 11-12	World share %	Cum.
World	72 579.6	2.0	-0.7	100.0	
USA	21 208.0	6.1	-0.1	29.2	29.2
Germany	5 015.9	-0.5	-4.7	6.9	36.1
United Kingdom	3 492.6	-3.4	-2.9	4.8	40.9
Pakistan	3 377.0	18.2	104.9	4.7	45.6
Japan	3 101.0	7.6	4.9	4.3	49.9
Netherlands	2 359.8	-4.7	-10.3	3.3	53.1
Belgium	2 059.3	-1.2	-1.6	2.8	56.0
Switzerland	1 939.4	2.5	-5.9	2.7	58.6
Brazil	1 742.4	1.7	-1.8	2.4	61.0
Canada	1 532.2	-0.6	-3.2	2.1	63.1
Italy	1 283.8	-7.7	-0.3	1.8	64.9
Rep. of Korea	1 234.9	0.6	3.4	1.7	66.6
Qatar	1 070.9	-1.7	-40.9	1.5	68.1
Bangladesh	991.0	-2.5	4.5	1.4	69.5
China	990.0	10.4	31.5	1.4	70.8

Table 3: Top importing countries or areas in 2012

Country or area	Value (million US$)	Avg. Growth (%) 08-12	Growth (%) 11-12	World share %	Cum.
World	102 290.9	-1.1	-7.8	100.0	
USA	27 861.0	-0.9	-11.0	27.2	27.2
Saudi Arabia	23 518.1	-2.2	2.0	23.0	50.2
United Kingdom	6 211.2	-3.5	-3.7	6.1	56.3
Mexico	3 947.3	63.2	-7.6	3.9	60.2
Brazil	3 156.3	3.6	-0.3	3.1	63.2
Italy	2 073.4	-2.3	2.9	2.0	65.3
Japan	1 873.0	-2.8	1.1	1.8	67.1
Qatar	1 779.9	84.3	35.0	1.7	68.8
Turkey	1 717.0	8.5	9.8	1.7	70.5
Morocco	1 599.4	10.5	-8.7	1.6	72.1
Nigeria	1 541.4	-4.0	-27.2	1.5	73.6
Canada	1 315.1	7.8	-0.1	1.3	74.9
Kuwait	1 171.2	-9.5	-23.2	1.1	76.0
Rep. of Korea	1 120.8	4.6	-1.4	1.1	77.1
Venezuela	1 088.0	25.2	65.1	1.1	78.2

435